CW00402188

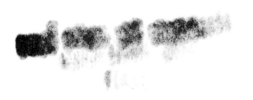

THE COMMON LAW LIBRARY

GOFF & JONES

THE LAW OF UNJUST ENRICHMENT

OTHER VOLUMES IN THE COMMON LAW LIBRARY

THE COMMON LAW LIBRARY

GOFF & JONES

THE LAW
OF
UNJUST ENRICHMENT

Eighth Edition

edited by

Charles Mitchell
*Professor of Law, University College
London*

and

Paul Mitchell
*Professor of Law, University College
London*

and

Stephen Watterson
*Senior Lecturer in Law, London School of
Economics*

SWEET & MAXWELL

THOMSON REUTERS

First Edition .... 1966, by Robert Goff and Gareth Jones
Second Edition ... 1978, by Sir Robert Goff and Gareth Jones
Third Edition ...... 1986, by Lord Goff of Chieveley and Gareth Jones
Fourth Edition .... 1993, by Gareth Jones
Fifth Edition .... 1998, by Gareth Jones
Sixth Edition ...... 2002, by Gareth Jones
Seventh Edition .. 2007, by Gareth Jones

Published in 2011 by Sweet & Maxwell
100 Avenue Road, London NW3 3PF
part of Thomson Reuters (Professional) UK Limited
(Registered in England & Wales, Company No 1679046.
Registered Office and address for service:
Aldgate House, 33 Aldgate High Street, London EC3N 1DL)

Computerset by Interactive Sciences Ltd, Gloucester
Printed and bound by CPI Group (UK) Ltd, Croydon, CR0 4YY

For further information on our products and services,
visit www.sweetandmaxwell.co.uk

No natural forests were destroyed to make this product;
only farmed timber was used and replanted

A CIP catalogue record for
this book is available
from the British Library

ISBN–978 1847039101

PREFACE

When Robert Goff and Gareth Jones wrote the first edition of this book, published in 1966, the law of unjust enrichment was virtually unknown in England.
In the ensuing decades it came to be recognised that unjust enrichment is one of
the central sources of rights and obligations in English private law. The successive editions of this book were hugely influential in this development. So, too,
were Robert Goff's seminal decisions on the subject during his exceptionally
distinguished judicial career, and many other scholarly works by Gareth Jones,
written in the course of his equally illustrious career as an academic at Cambridge University. Their learning and their intellectual creativity set an inspiring
standard. There are few books of which it can be said that they changed the legal
landscape, but this is one of them.

Recent cases at the highest appellate level have now conclusively established
that unjust enrichment is a distinct source of rights and obligations in English
private law, ranking alongside contract and tort. In this edition we have acted on
these authorities to focus the book's discussion more tightly on the topic with
which it has always been centrally concerned: the law of unjust enrichment. To
this end we have removed the discussion of gain-based remedies for wrongdoing
which has appeared in previous editions. Our intention is that this material should
appear in updated form in a second volume, to be published at a later date. These
changes are explained in Chapter 1. They have necessitated some rearrangement
of the material in this book, and they are signalled by a change of title, from *The
Law of Restitution* to *The Law of Unjust Enrichment*.

In addition to this reorganisation of the text, we have undertaken some
substantial updating to reflect the many important cases and scholarly works that
have appeared since the last edition. Cases of particular significance include
Deutsche Morgan Grenfell Group Plc v IRC (2007) (on mistake, the recovery of
money paid as tax that is not due, and limitation of actions); *Abou-Rahmah v
Abacha* (2007) (on change of position); *Halpern v Halpern* (2008) (on the
requirement that a claimant must make counter-restitution of benefits received
from a defendant); *Charter Plc v City Index Ltd* (2008) (on contribution and
knowing receipt); *Sempra Metals Ltd v IRC* (2008) (on enrichment by the use
value of money and the award of compound interest); *Cobbe v Yeoman's Row
Management Ltd* (2008) (on enrichment by the performance of services and
failure of basis); *Monro v HMRC* (2009) (on statute as a justifying ground and the
recovery of money paid as tax that is not due); *Serious Fraud Office v Lexi
Holdings Plc* (2009) (on tracing); *Chief Constable of Greater Manchester v
Wigan Athletic AFC Ltd* (2009) (on enrichment by the performance of services
and free acceptance); *Test Claimants in the F.I.I. Group Litigation v HMRC*
(2010) (on the requirement that a defendant's enrichment must have been gained
at the claimant's expense, the recovery of money paid as tax that is not due,
limitation of actions, and statute as a justifying ground); *Haugesund Kommune v*

Depfa A.C.S. Bank (2010) (on claims to recover benefits under void contracts on the ground of failure of basis); *Gibb v Maidstone and Tunbridge Wells NHS Trust* (2010) (on enrichment by the release of an obligation); *Benedetti v Sawiris* (2010) (on free acceptance and enrichment by the performance of services); *R. (Child Poverty Action Group) v Secretary of State for Work and Pensions* (2011) (on the recovery of ultra vires payments by a public authority and statute as a justifying ground); *Royal Bank of Scotland Plc v Chandra* (2011) (on undue influence); and *Costello v MacDonald* (2011) (on contract as a justifying ground).

The past five years have also seen the publication of some outstanding scholarly works and we have sought to incorporate the insights of their authors into the discussion as far as has been possible. There have been many articles, acknowledged in the text at appropriate places; longer works of particular note are James Edelman and Elise Bant, *Unjust Enrichment in Australia* (2006); Michael Rush, *The Defence of Passing On* (2006); David Fox, *Property Rights in Money* (2008); Dominic O'Sullivan, Steven Elliott and Rafal Zakrzewski, *The Law of Rescission* (2008); Elise Bant, *The Change of Position Defence* (2009); Tariq Baloch, *Unjust Enrichment and Contract* (2009); Birke Häcker, *Consequences of Impaired Consent Transfers* (2009); and Rebecca Williams, *Unjust Enrichment and Public Law* (2010). We have also learnt much from new editions of three fine books: Keith Mason, John Carter, and Greg Tolhurst, *Mason & Carter's Restitution Law in Australia*, 2nd edn (2008); Andrew Burrows, *The Law of Restitution*, 3rd edn (2010); and Peter Maddaugh and John McCamus, *The Law of Restitution*, looseleaf edn (2011).

Charles Mitchell exercised a general editorial oversight over the whole of this edition, and responsibility for particular chapters was distributed in the following way: Charles Mitchell—chapters 1–2, 4–5, 6 (with Stephen Watterson), 7, 10–11 (with Paul Mitchell), 18–38, and 40; Paul Mitchell—chapters 3 (with Stephen Watterson), 10–11 (with Charles Mitchell), and 12–17; and Stephen Watterson —chapters 3 (with Paul Mitchell), 6 (with Charles Mitchell), 8–9, and 39.

We are grateful to Greg Smith and Michelle Afford at Sweet & Maxwell for their calm professionalism and hard work on the project.

We are grateful to Gareth Jones for trusting us to take the book forward into this new edition. It has been a privilege to travel down the path which he and Robert Goff have laid down, and onwards into new territory.

Above all, we are grateful to our families for their encouragement and support, and in particular to Charlotte Mitchell, Susan Chan, and Amy Goymour.

Charles Mitchell
Paul Mitchell
Stephen Watterson

CONTENTS

PART 7—REMEDIES

TABLE OF CASES

.

TABLE OF STATUTES

TABLE OF STATUTORY INSTRUMENTS

TABLE OF NON-UK STATUTES

Part One
INTRODUCTION

CHAPTER 1

INTRODUCTION

1. UNJUST ENRICHMENT AND RESTITUTION

The modern English law of unjust enrichment has developed as the law of **1-01** restitution, following the decision taken by Robert Goff and Gareth Jones in 1966 to publish the first edition of this book with the title *The Law of Restitution*. In making this choice they followed the decision taken by the American Law Institute, whose *Restatement of the Law of Restitution* had appeared in 1937.[1] When their book was first published, the subject was virtually unknown in England, but it has since come to be recognised that unjust enrichment is one of the main sources of rights and obligations in English private law. The successive editions of Goff and Jones' book have been highly influential in this development,[2] and their choice of title has been emulated by many other writers,[3] although a preference for "unjust enrichment" over "restitution" can be observed in more recent works.[4]

---

[1] American Law Institute, *Restatement of the Law of Restitution* (St. Paul, Minn.: ALI, 1937). The Reporters were Austin Scott and Warren Seavey. The reasons for their preference for "restitution" over "unjust enrichment" are discussed in A. Kull, "James Barr Ames and the Early Modern History of Unjust Enrichment" (2005) 25 O.J.L.S. 297, who concludes, at 319, that the ALI were, "afraid of using a name [*sc.* "unjust enrichment"] that might mean too much" and settled on, "a name that meant too little, requiring definition by fiat as a term of art." Andrew Kull was the reporter for the ALI's most recent *Restatement* in this area: American Law Institute, *Restatement of the Law (Third), Restitution and Unjust Enrichment* (St Paul, Minn.: American Law Institute Publishers, 2011). It is to be hoped that the appearance of the *Restatement, Third* stimulates American legal scholars to pay greater attention to the subject, which they have neglected in recent years, as noted in J. Langbein, "The Later History of Restitution" in W.R. Cornish et al. (eds), *Restitution: Past, Present and Future* (Oxford: Hart, 1998), 57 and C. Saiman, "Restitution in America: Why the U.S. Refuses to Join the Global Restitution Party" (2008) 28 O.J.L.S. 99.

[2] As, of course, have the works of other scholars, as acknowledged by Lord Goff in *Kleinwort Benson Ltd v Lincoln CC* [1999] 2 A.C. 349 at 373. See too *Jones v Commerzbank AG* [2003] EWCA Civ 1663 at [31]; *Deutsche Morgan Grenfell Group Plc v IRC* [2006] UKHL 49; [2007] 1 A.C. 558 at [38] and [151]; *Benedetti v Sawiris* [2010] EWCA Civ 1427 at [53]. The modern history of academic work in this area is sketched out in F. Rose, "The Evolution of the Species" in A. Burrows and Lord Rodger (eds), *Mapping the Law* (Oxford: OUP, 2006), 13.

[3] e.g. P. Birks, *Introduction to the Law of Restitution*, revised edn (Oxford: Clarendon Press, 1989); F.D. Rose (ed.), *Restitution and the Conflict of Laws* (Oxford: Mansfield Press, 1995); F.D. Rose (ed.), *Restitution and Banking Law* (Oxford: Mansfield Press, 1998); P. Birks and F.D. Rose (eds), *Restitution and Equity* (Oxford: Mansfield Press, 2000); P. Jaffey, *The Nature and Scope of Restitution* (Oxford: Hart, 2000); F.D. Rose (ed.), *Restitution and Insolvency* (London: LLP, 2000); A. Jones, *Restitution and European Community Law* (London: LLP, 2000); S. Hedley, *A Critical Introduction to Restitution* (London: Butterworths, 2001); S. Hedley and M. Halliwell (eds), *The Law of Restitution* (London: Butterworths, 2002); A. Tettenborn, *The Law of Restitution*, 3rd edn (London: Cavendish, 2002); G. Virgo, *The Principles of the Law of Restitution*, 2nd edn (Oxford: OUP, 2006); A. Burrows, *The Law of Restitution*, 3rd edn (Oxford: OUP, 2010).

[4] e.g. P. Birks, *Unjust Enrichment*, 2nd edn (Oxford: OUP, 2005); T. Baloch, *Unjust Enrichment and Contract* (Oxford: Hart, 2009); R. Williams, *Unjust Enrichment and Public Law* (Oxford: Hart, 2010). And cf. J. Edelman and E. Bant, *Unjust Enrichment in Australia* (Melbourne: OUP, 2006).

1–02   The difference between these terms is the difference between event and response.[5] Unjust enrichment at another party's expense is an event to which the law responds by giving claimants different rights in different situations. A right to restitution is one possible response to the event of unjust enrichment. When one person is unjustly enriched at the expense of another, that other may acquire a right to restitution of that enrichment—a right that that enrichment be returned to him.

1–03   If the only possible response to unjust enrichment were restitution, and if unjust enrichment were the only event capable of generating a right to restitution, then little would turn on the question whether books were written on "the law of unjust enrichment" or "the law of restitution", since these could only be concerned with one subject, addressed either from an event-based or from a response-based perspective. However, that is not the case. Responses to unjust enrichment other than restitution are possible, for example prophylactic remedies, which prevent unjust enrichment from arising rather than reversing it after it has happened.[5a] Moreover, a right to restitution may arise from events other than unjust enrichment. Most notably, restitution is a possible response to acquisitive wrongs. Suppose, for example, that a defendant commits the tort of conversion by selling a claimant's asset to a third party. His conversion of the asset gives rise to more than one remedial right. Founding on the tort, the claimant can claim either compensation of his own loss or restitution of the sale proceeds that constitute the defendant's gain. This restitutionary right arises from the wrong, not from unjust enrichment.[6]

1–04   Restitution as a response to wrongdoing is therefore a different topic from restitution as a response to unjust enrichment. It concerns such questions as when gain-based remedies should be awarded for breach of contract, tort, and equitable wrongdoing, whether there is more than one measure of gain-based relief for the victims of wrongs, and how gain-based remedies for wrongs are quantified.

---

[5] P. Birks, "A Letter to America: The New Restatement of Restitution" (2003) 3 *Global Jurist Frontiers* 1, p.20. Cf. R. Jackson, "The Restatement of Restitution" (1930) 10 Miss. L.J. 95, pp.95–96. For Birks' event-based classification of private law, see, e.g. P. Birks, "Introduction", in P. Birks (ed.), *English Private Law* (Oxford: OUP, 2000), xxxv–xliii. Sceptical views of this classificatory approach are taken in G. Samuel, "*English Private Law*: Old and New Thinking in the Taxonomy Debate" (2004) 24 O.J.L.S. 335; S. Hedley, "Rival Taxonomies Within the Law of Obligations: Is There a Problem?" in S. Degeling and J. Edelman (eds), *Equity in Commercial Law* (Sydney: Lawbook Co., 2004), 77; J. Dietrich, "What is 'Lawyering'? The Challenge of Taxonomy" (2006) 65 C.L.J. 549; and C. Webb, "What Is Unjust Enrichment?" (2009) 29 O.J.L.S. 215.

[5a] See paras 36–28——36–37.

[6] *United Australia Ltd v Barclays Bank Ltd* [1941] A.C. 1. See too L. Smith, "The Province of the Law of Restitution" (1992) 71 Can. Bar Rev. 672; P. Birks, "Misnomer", in Cornish et al., *Restitution: Past, Present and Future*, 1; Birks, *Unjust Enrichment*, pp.11–16, accepted in *Sempra Metals Ltd v IRC* [2007] UKHL 34; [2008] 1 A.C. 561 at [231]. For a different view, attributing the award of gain-based relief against wrongdoers to the direct enforcement of the victim's (quasi-)proprietary rights, see D. Friedmann, "Restitution of Benefits Obtained Through the Appropriation of Property or the Commission of a Wrong" (1980) 80 Columbia L.R. 504; J. Beatson, "The Nature of Waiver of Tort", in J. Beatson, *The Use and Abuse of Unjust Enrichment* (Oxford: OUP, 1991), 206; D. Friedmann, "Restitution for Wrongs: The Basis of Liability" in Cornish et al., *Restitution: Past, Present and Future*, 133; T. Krebs, "The Fallacy of 'Restitution for Wrongs'" in Burrows and Rodger (eds), *Mapping the Law*, 379.

Discussion of these matters can be found in books on remedies[7] and many books on restitution, including the first seven editions of the present work.[8]

In this eighth edition, however, we have decided to excise all discussion of **1–05** restitution for wrongdoing, and to focus our attention exclusively on the subject with which this work has always been centrally concerned, namely the law of unjust enrichment and the remedies that it generates. This narrowing of focus is signalled by a change of title to *The Law of Unjust Enrichment*. It reflects the fact that the highest courts have now conclusively recognised that unjust enrichment is a distinct source of rights and obligations in English private law that ranks alongside contract and civil wrongs in importance and accordingly calls for discrete stand-alone treatment.[9]

2. Unjust Enrichment as a Legal Concept

Most mature systems of law have found it necessary to provide, outside of the **1–06** law of contract and civil wrongs, for the restoration of benefits on the grounds of unjust enrichment.[10] By comparison with civil law systems, however, English law has been slow to recognise unjust enrichment as a discrete source of rights and obligations.[11] Many of the rules collected in this book were previously thought to form part of the law of "quasi-contract", and were shakily conceptualised as a part of the law of contract, or else were treated as isolated

---

[7] e.g. J. Edelman, *Gain-Based Damages* (Oxford: Hart, 2002); A. Burrows, *Remedies for Torts and Breach of Contract*, 3rd edn (Oxford: OUP, 2004), Ch.17; D. Harris, D. Campbell, and R. Halson, *Remedies in Contract and Tort*, 2nd edn (Cambridge: CUP, 2002), Ch.17; H. McGregor, *McGregor on Damages*, 18th edn (London: Sweet & Maxwell, 2009), Ch.12.

[8] Most recently, see G. Jones, *Goff & Jones: The Law of Restitution*, 7th edn (London: Sweet & Maxwell, 2006), Chs 32–38. See too Virgo, *The Principles of the Law of Restitution*, Chs 15–18; Burrows, *The Law of Restitution*, Chs 23–27.

[9] e.g. *Lipkin Gorman v Karpnale Ltd* [1991] 2 A.C. 548 at 578; *Woolwich Equitable Building Society v IRC* [1993] A.C. 70 at 154 and 196–197; *Westdeutsche Landesbank Girozentrale v Islington LBC* [1996] A.C. 669 at 710; *Kleinwort Benson Ltd v Glasgow CC (No.2)* [1999] 1 A.C. 153 at 167 and 186; *Banque Financière de la Cité v Parc (Battersea) Ltd* [1999] 1 A.C. 221 at 227 and 234; *Cressman v Coys of Kensington (Sales) Ltd* [2004] EWCA Civ 47; [2004] 1 W.L.R. 2775 at [22]; *Niru Battery Manufacturing Co v Milestone Trading Ltd (No.2)* [2004] EWCA Civ 487; [2004] 1 All E.R. (Comm.) 289 at [28] and [41]; *Deutsche Morgan Grenfell* [2006] UKHL 49; [2007] 1 A.C. 558 at [21]; *Benedetti* [2010] EWCA Civ 1427 at [2]. All prefigured by *Fibrosa Spolka Akcyjna v Fairbairn Lawson Combe Barbour Ltd* [1943] A.C. 32 at 61.

[10] *Fibrosa Spolka* [1943] A.C. 32 at 61, per Lord Wright.

[11] A historical account of the English law of unjust enrichment is given in *Goff & Jones: The Law of Restitution*, 7th edn, paras 1–02—1–11. See too R. M. Jackson, *The History of Quasi-Contract in English Law* (Cambridge: CUP, 1936); G.E. Palmer, "History of Restitution in Anglo-American Law", Vol.X *International Encyclopaedia of Comparative Law* (Tübingen: Mohr Siebeck, 1989); J.H. Baker, "The History of Quasi-Contract in English Law", in Cornish et al., *Restitution: Past, Present and Future* 37; J.H. Baker, "The Use of Assumpsit for Restitutionary Money Claims 1600–1800", D.J. Ibbetson, "Unjust Enrichment in England before 1600", and G. Jones, "The Role of Equity in the English Law of Restitution", in E.J.H. Schrage (ed.), *Unjust Enrichment: The Comparative Legal History of the Law of Restitution*, 2nd edn (Berlin: Dunkler & Humblot, 1999), 31, 121, and 149; D.J. Ibbetson, *A Historical Introduction to the Law of Obligations* (Oxford: OUP, 1999), Ch.14; C. Mitchell and P. Mitchell (eds), *Landmark Cases in the Law of Restitution* (Oxford: Hart, 2006); M. Lobban, "Restitutionary Remedies" in W.R. Cornish et al., *The Oxford History of the Laws of England, vol.XII: Private Law, 1820–1914* (Oxford: OUP, 2010), 563.

incidents of equitable doctrine. The theory that all "quasi-contractual" claims rested on an implied contract between the parties was most notably articulated in *Sinclair v Brougham*,[12] but it was decisively rejected in *Westdeutsche Landesbank Girozentrale v Islington LBC*,[13] and the implied contract theory is now unequivocally "a ghost of the past".[14] Nor is it any longer, "appropriate . . . to draw a distinction between law and equity" by holding that rights in unjust enrichment belong to separate legal categories governed by substantially different principles by reason of their jurisdictional origin,[15] and in appropriate cases extending equity's auxiliary jurisdiction to make good the inadequacy of a common law remedy may well be a, "permissible step in the progress which [the courts have] made towards developing . . . a coherent law of restitution."[16]

1-07   It has been said that unjust enrichment is a vague principle of justice of no practical value.[17] However, the search for principle should not be confused with the definition of concepts. Unjust enrichment is not a high-level notion lacking in substantive content, "an indefinable idea in the same way that justice is an indefinable idea."[18] Instead, as Deane J. held in the High Court of Australia, unjust enrichment is a[19]:

> "unifying legal concept, which explains why the law recognises, in a variety of distinct categories of case, an obligation on the part of the defendant to make fair and just restitution for a benefit derived at the expense of a plaintiff and which assists in the determination, by the ordinary processes of legal reasoning, of the question whether the law should, in justice, recognise such an obligation in a new or developing category of case."

---

[12] *Sinclair v Brougham* [1914] A.C. 398, discussed in E. O'Dell, "*Sinclair v Brougham*" in C. Mitchell and P. Mitchell, *Landmark Cases in the Law of Restitution*, 213.

[13] *Westdeutsche Landesbank Girozentrale v Islington LBC* [1996] A.C. 669 at 710, per Lord Browne-Wilkinson. See too *Pavey & Matthews Pty Ltd v Paul* (1987) 162 C.L.R. 221; *Sempra* [2008] A.C. 561 at [112]–[113], per Lord Nicholls.

[14] *Cleveland Bridge UK Ltd v Multiplex Constructions (UK) Ltd* [2010] EWCA Civ 139 at [121], approving a statement to this effect in *Goff & Jones: The Law of Restitution*, 7th edn, para.1–11, citing *United Australia Ltd* [1941] A.C. 1, at 28–29, per Lord Atkin. On the need to distinguish between claims in contract and unjust enrichment, see also Lord Hoffmann's comments in *Banque Financière* [1999] 1 A.C. 221 at 232–233; for further discussion of this point, see paras 3–02—3–09.

[15] *Nelson v Larholt* [1948] 1 K.B. 339 at 343. See too *Baltic Shipping Co v Dillon (The Mikhail Lermentov)* (1993) 176 C.L.R. 344 at 376; *Burke v L.F.O.T. Pty Ltd* [2002] HCA 17; (2002) 209 C.L.R. 282 at [38]. More recent decisions of the High Court of Australia have insisted that doctrines such as contribution and subrogation cannot form part of the law of unjust enrichment to the extent that they arise in equity: *Friend v Brooker* [2009] HCA 21; (2009) 239 C.L.R. 129; *Bofinger v Kingsway Group Ltd* [2009] HCA 44; (2009) 239 C.L.R. 269. This reasoning sets up a false opposition between unjust enrichment and equity, and does not represent English law: see the authorities cited at paras 19–03, fn.4, 39–08, fn.8 and 39–12, fn.15.

[16] *Sempra* [2008] 1 A.C. 561 at [185], per Lord Walker. See too Lord Hope's remarks at [46].

[17] "To ask what course would be *ex aequo et bono* to both sides never was a very precise guide": *Baylis v Bishop of London* [1913] 1 Ch. 127 at 140, per Hamilton L.J. See too *Holt v Markham* [1923] 1 K.B. 504 at 513, per Scrutton L.J.

[18] G. Palmer, *The Law of Restitution* (Boston, Mass: Little, Brown, & Co, 1978), p.5.

[19] *Pavey* (1987) 162 C.L.R. 221 at 256–257; quoted with approval in *David Securities Pty Ltd v Commonwealth Bank of Australia* (1992) 275 C.L.R. 353 at 379.

Whatever may be the underlying moral justifications for the award of restitu-   **1-08**
tion in all these cases,[20] the "unjust" element in "unjust enrichment" is simply
a "generalisation of all the factors which the law recognises as calling for
restitution".[21] In other words, unjust enrichment is not an abstract moral principle to which the courts must refer when deciding cases[22]; it is an organising
concept that groups decided authorities on the basis that they share a set of
common features, namely that in all of them the defendant has been enriched by
the receipt of a benefit that is gained at the claimant's expense in circumstances
that the law deems to be unjust. The reasons why the courts have held a
defendant's enrichment to be unjust vary from one set of cases to another, and in
this respect the law of unjust enrichment more closely resembles the law of torts
(recognising a variety of reasons why a defendant must compensate a claimant
for harm) than it does the law of contract (embodying the single principle that
expectations engendered by binding promises must be fulfilled).[23]

3. THE INGREDIENTS OF A CLAIM IN UNJUST ENRICHMENT

(a) Overview

The courts have held that a claimant must demonstrate three things in order to   **1-09**
make out a cause of action in unjust enrichment: that the defendant has been

---

[20] A disputed topic on which there is a large and growing literature: e.g. K. Barker, "Unjust Enrichment: Containing the Beast" (1995) 15 O.J.L.S. 457; L. Smith, "Restitution: The Heart of Corrective Justice" (2001) 79 Texas L.R. 1927; K. Barker, "Understanding the Unjust Enrichment Principle in Private Law" and D. Klimchuk, "Unjust Enrichment and Corrective Justice" in J. Neyers et al. (eds), *Understanding Unjust Enrichment* (Oxford: Hart, 2004) 79 and 111; H. Dagan, *The Law and Ethics of Restitution* (Cambridge: CUP, 2004), reviewed in K. Barker, "Theorising Unjust Enrichment Law: Being Realist(ic)?" (2006) 26 O.J.L.S. 609; E.J. Weinrib, "The Normative Struc-ture of Unjust Enrichment" and K. Barker, "Responsibility for Gain: Unjust Factors or Absence of Basis", in C. Rickett and R. Grantham (eds), *Structure and Justification in Private Law* (Oxford: Hart, 2008), 21 and 47; J.M. Nadler, "What Right Does Unjust Enrichment Law Protect?" (2008) 28 O.J.L.S. 245; R. Grantham and C. Rickett, "A Normative Account of Defences to Restitutionary Liability" (2008) 67 C.L.J. 92; R. Chambers et al. (eds), *Philosophical Foundations of the Law of Unjust Enrichment* (Oxford: OUP, 2009), reviewed in A. Simester, "Correcting Unjust Enrichments" (2010) 30 O.J.L.S. 579; Z. Sinel, "Through Thick and Thin: The Place of Corrective Justice in Unjust Enrichment" (2011) 31 O.J.L.S. 551.
[21] *Wasada Pty Ltd v State Rail Authority of New South Wales (No.2)* [2003] NSWSC 987 at [16], per Campbell J., quoting K. Mason and J. Carter, *Restitution Law in Australia* (Sydney: Butterworths, 1995), 59–60.
[22] As asserted by members of the High Court of Australia in a series of recent decisions which have lost sight of Deane J.'s meaning in *Pavey* (1987) 162 C.L.R. 221 at 256–257, mischaracterised unjust enrichment as an abstract principle of justice, and condemned reference to this supposed principle as impermissible "top-down reasoning": *Roxborough v Rothmans of Pall Mall Australia Ltd* [2001] HCA 68; (2001) 208 C.L.R. 516 at [70]–[74]; *Farah Constructions Pty Ltd v Say-Dee Pty Ltd* [2007] HCA 22; (2007) 230 C.L.R. 89 at [151]; *Lumbers v W. Cook Builders Pty Ltd (In Liquidation)* [2008] HCA 27; (2008) 232 C.L.R. 635 at [83]–[85]; *Bofinger* (2009) 239 C.L.R. 269 at [86]–[91]. For critical comment, see K. Mason, "What Is Wrong with Top-Down Legal Reasoning?" (2004) 78 *Australian Law Journal* 574; K. Mason, "Do Top-Down and Bottom-Up Reasoning Ever Meet?" and A. Burrows, "The Australian Law of Restitution: Has the High Court Lost Its Way?" in E. Bant and M. Harding (eds), *Exploring Private Law* (Cambridge: CUP, 2010), 19 and 67.
[23] S. Smith, "Unjust Enrichment: Nearer to Tort than Contract" in Chambers et al. (eds), *Philosoph-ical Foundations of the Law of Unjust Enrichment*, 181, pp.202–206.

enriched, that this enrichment was gained at the claimant's expense, and that the defendant's enrichment at the claimant's expense was unjust.[24] If these three requirements are all satisfied, then the further question arises, whether there are any defences to the claim, and if there are not, then the court must decide what remedy should be awarded. However, there is an additional consideration that the court must also bear in mind, namely that some overriding legal principle justify the defendant's enrichment and thereby nullify the claimant's right to restitution.

1–10   This book is organised in line with this analytical structure. Part 2 discusses the circumstances in which the law may deem a defendant's enrichment at the claimant's expense to be justified notwithstanding the presence of a factor that would ordinarily mean that it was unjust. Part 3 considers the principles governing the identification and quantification of a defendant's enrichment. Part 4 examines the tests used to determine whether a defendant's enrichment has been gained at the claimant's expense. Part 5 looks at the reasons why a defendant's enrichment at the claimant's expense might be unjust. Part 6 concerns defences to claims in unjust enrichment, and Part 7 concerns the remedies that can be awarded to successful claimants. We will make some preliminary comments here about each of these matters.

(b) *Justifying Grounds*

1–11   Many civilian and mixed law systems have a law of unjustified enrichment, under which a claimant will be entitled to restitution if he can show that a defendant was enriched at his expense and that there was no legal ground for the defendant's enrichment. Under these systems a defendant can escape restitutionary liability by showing that there was a legal ground for his enrichment, for example because the claimant was required to benefit the defendant by statute or by contract. The reason why there is no liability in these circumstances is that the defendant's enrichment is not unjustified and so the claimant has no prima facie right to restitution.

1–12   The English law of unjust enrichment frequently produces the same results as the law of civilian and mixed law systems, but it works in a different way. Under English law, a claimant will be entitled to restitution if he can show that a defendant was enriched at his expense, and that the circumstances are such that the law regards this enrichment as unjust. For example, a claimant will have a prima facie right to restitution where he has transferred a benefit to a defendant by mistake, under duress, or on a basis that fails. Nevertheless, the defendant can escape liability if another legal rule entitles him to keep the benefit, and this rule overrides the rule generated by the law of unjust enrichment which entitles the claimant to restitution. For example, a claimant may have paid money to a defendant by mistake, but even so, the payment may be irrecoverable if the

---

[24] *Portman Building Society v Hamlyn Taylor Neck (A Firm)* [1998] 4 All E.R. 202 at 206; *Banque Financière* [1999] A.C. 221 at 227; *R. (Rowe) v Vale of White Horse DC* [2003] EWHC 388 (Admin); [2003] 1 Lloyd's Rep. 418 at [11]; *Cressman* [2004] EWCA Civ 47; [2004] 1 W.L.R. 2775 at [22]; *Chief Constable of Greater Manchester v Wigan Athletic AFC Ltd* [2008] EWCA Civ 1449; [2009] 1 W.L.R. 1580 at [38], [54] and [62]. See too *Shanghai Tongji Science and Technology Industrial Co Ltd v Casil Clearing Ltd* [2004] HKCFA 21; (2004) 7 H.K.C.F.A.R. 79 at [67].

claimant was required to pay the money by a statute or by a contract previously entered by the parties. Although the claimant would otherwise have a claim in unjust enrichment, the defendant's enrichment is justified by the statute or contract. In Chs 2 and 3 we discuss sources of entitlement that can operate as justifying grounds, looking in turn at statutes, judgments and court orders, natural obligations, and contracts.

(c) *Enrichment*

As a matter of history English law gave claimants different types of action to **1–13** recover the value of different types of benefit. Money fell to the action for money had and received.[25] Actions for quantum meruit and quantum valebat awards dealt with services and goods. Actions for money paid to the defendant's use lay where the defendant was benefited through the claimant's payment to a third party, for example to discharge the defendant's liability to a creditor.[26]

More than 150 years have elapsed since the abolition of the forms of action, **1–14** and the law of unjust enrichment now rests on a single set of common principles. The important issue is no longer whether particular types of benefit have been transferred, but whether the defendant has been enriched by receiving value from the claimant. Not everyone agrees that it is possible to have one law for all enrichment received, in whatever form.[27] However, we consider that there is a single set of rules governing the identification and quantification of benefit, by application of which the courts can pay due regard to a defendant's freedom to make his own spending choices without debarring claims in respect of particular types of benefit,[28] and without insisting that different types of claim should govern the recovery of different types of benefit. These rules are set out in Chs 4 and 5.

---

[25] The courts resisted attempts to use this action to recover the value of other benefits. See e.g. *Nightingal v Devisme* (1770) 5 Burr. 2589 at 2592; 98 E.R. 361 at 363, where Lord Mansfield would not allow an action for money had and received to recover the value of stock because the action would not lie "where no money has been received". In *Spratt v Hobhouse* (1827) 4 Bing. 173 at 178; 130 E.R. 734 at 737, Best C.J. stated that "if a party gives another what may be readily turned into money, it may be treated as such in an action for money had and received". But he was referring only to financial instruments that were treated by the parties as equivalent to money, such as country banknotes or bank drafts, as in, e.g. *Pickard v Bankes* (1810) 13 East. 20; 104 E.R. 273. See too *Ehrensberger v Anderson* (1848) 3 Ex. 148 at 156; 154 E.R. 793 at 796–797 (action lay for foreign currency); but note *Depcke v Munn* (1828) 3 Carr. & P. 112; 172 E.R. 347 (action did not extend to the use value of money, i.e. interest).

[26] The latter counts all required the plaintiff to recite that the benefit was conferred at the defendant's request, and where an actual request was made and the benefit conferred, the claim was clearly contractual. However the law would infer the making of a request in some circumstances that would now be regarded as giving rise to liability in unjust enrichment. For example, an action for money paid to the defendant's use would lie where the plaintiff was compelled to pay the defendant's debt as "the compulsion [was] evidence of the request": *Osborne v Rogers* (1669) 1 Wms. Saund. 264 at 265n.; 85 E.R. 318 at 320. See too *Exall v Partridge* (1799) 8 T.R. 308; 101 E.R. 1405; *Pownal v Ferrand* (1827) 6 B. & C. 439 at 443–444; 108 E.R. 513 at 515; *Moule v Garrett* (1872) L.R. 7 Ex. 101 at 104.

[27] e.g. P. Watts, "Restitution: A Property Principle and a Services Principle" [1995] R.L.R. 30.

[28] e.g. claims to recover mistaken improvements to land, considered at para.9–04.

(d) *At the Claimant's Expense*

1-15 This deceptively simple term signifies that the claimant must have suffered a loss that was sufficiently closely linked with the defendant's gain for the law to hold that there was a transfer of value between the parties. This rule reflects the principle that the law of unjust enrichment is not concerned with the disgorgement of gains by defendants, nor with compensation for losses sustained by claimants, but with the reversal of transfers of value between claimants and defendants.[29]

1-16   Whether a transfer has taken place is not a question of fact but a question of combined fact and law; that is, it turns on the application of legal tests to the facts of the case. Unfortunately, what these legal tests are is currently uncertain. There is a danger that if too narrow a view is taken then claimants will inappropriately be denied a remedy; conversely, if too wide a view is taken then too many claimants will be enabled to recover, and the law will become too difficult to manage as the number of interlinked claims exponentially increases in multi-party cases. However, problems of the latter kind should not be exaggerated, for the law has other mechanisms in place that will prevent many of the bad effects that would otherwise flow from the adoption of a broad test: for example, rules requiring proof of an unjust factor, rules relieving defendants from liability where they are bona fide purchasers or have changed their position, rules disallowing claims in unjust enrichment where the defendant's enrichment is justified by a contract, and rules against double liability and double recovery, Hence in Ch.6 we advocate the adoption of a broad causal test to determine whether a transfer of value has taken place.

1-17   Where a claimant seeks a personal remedy, he only needs to satisfy this test, but where he seeks a proprietary remedy, he must also show either that he previously owned the property in which he now claims an interest, or else that the defendant acquired this property in exchange for property that was previously owned by the claimant, or else that this property was formerly the subject matter of an interest that was discharged with property that was previously owned by the claimant.[30] This is a stringent requirement that serves as a control mechanism to prevent proprietary restitutionary remedies from becoming too freely available. To satisfy this requirement, claimants must have recourse to the rules of following and tracing. These are rules of evidence that determine when property is treated for legal purposes as having passed from one party to another (following), and when property is treated for legal purposes as having been exchanged for other property, so that the new property represents the product of the old property (tracing). These rules are examined in Ch.7.

---

[29] *Commissioner of State Revenue (Victoria) v Royal Insurance Australia Ltd* (1994) 182 C.L.R. 51 at 75; affirmed *Roxborough v Rothmans of Pall Mall Australia Ltd* [2001] HCA 68; (2001) 208 C.L.R. 516 at [26]; *Gribbon v Lutton* [2001] EWCA Civ 1956; [2002] Q.B. 902 at [60]; *Pacific National Investments Ltd v City of Victoria* [2004] SCC 75; [2004] 3 S.C.R. 575 at [25] and [34]; *Kingstreet Investments Ltd v New Brunswick (Department of Finance)* [2007] SCC 1; [2007] 1 S.C.R. 3 at [32].

[30] See the cases cited at para.7–39, fn.87.

(e) *Grounds for Restitution*

(i) *The English "Unjust Factors" Approach Contrasted with the Civilian "Absence of Basis" Approach*

The law must say when an enrichment at another's expense is an unjust enrich- **1–18** ment. As we have noted already,[31] civilian and mixed legal systems commonly approach this question by asking whether there is a legal ground for the transfer from claimant to defendant: if not, then the defendant's enrichment is unjustified and restitution will follow. English law approaches the task differently, by identifying specific grounds for restitution, sometimes referred to as "unjust factors" because they are legally recognised factors that make the defendant's enrichment unjust.[32] For example, in a case of mistaken payment, the payment is the enrichment of the defendant at the claimant's expense, and the mistake is the ground for restitution or unjust factor.

It has been contended by some legal writers that English law would do better **1–19** to adopt the "absence of basis" model of civilian and mixed legal systems, among other reasons because it achieves a tighter conceptual unity by grounding recovery on a single juristic principle.[33] Peter Birks additionally took the view that as a matter of authority English law has already been committed to the civilian approach by certain cases concerned with the recovery of payments under void but fully executed interest rate swap contracts.[34]

We doubt that English law would work more efficiently, or produce fairer **1–20** outcomes, if it adopted the "absence of basis" approach. On the contrary, it seems likely to us that such a change would produce confusion and uncertainty,[35] especially if the courts were to adopt Birks' "limited reconciliation" of the two approaches by treating unjust factors as reasons why, higher up, there is no legal ground for the defendant's acquisition.[36] Experience suggests that the courts fare

---

[31] See para.1–11.

[32] *Banque Financière* [1999] 1 A.C. 221 at 227, per Lord Steyn: "Restitutionary liability is triggered by a range of unjust factors or grounds of restitution". For the use of "unjust factor" terminology, see too *Kleinwort Benson Ltd v Lincoln CC* [1999] 2 A.C. 349 at 363, 386, 395 and 405; *Foskett v McKeown* [2001] 1 A.C. 102 at 127; *Wigan Athletic* [2008] EWCA Civ 1449; [2009] 1 W.L.R. 1580 at [50] and [67]; *Haugesund Kommune v Depfa ACS Bank* [2009] EWHC 2227 (Comm); [2010] Lloyd's Rep. P.N. 21 at [142].

[33] S. Meier, "Unjust Factors and Legal Grounds" in D. Johnston and R. Zimmermann (eds), *Unjustified Enrichment: Key Issues in Comparative Perspective* (Cambridge: CUP, 2002) 37; Birks, *Unjust Enrichment*, Ch.5; R. Stevens, "Is There a Law of Unjust Enrichment?" in J. Edelman and S. Degeling (eds), *Unjust Enrichment in Commercial Law* (Sydney: Thomson, 2008), 11.

[34] Birks, *Unjust Enrichment*, pp.108–113, invoking *Kleinwort Benson Ltd v Sandwell BC*, reported with the first instance decision in *Westdeutsche Landesbank Girozentrale v Islington LBC* [1994] 4 All E.R. 890; and *Guinness Mahon Plc v Kensington & Chelsea RLBC* [1999] Q.B. 215.

[35] The structural differences between English law and German law, which takes an "absence of basis" approach, are emphasised in T. Krebs, *Restitution at the Crossroads: A Comparative Study* (London: Cavendish Press, 2001), but are played down in S. Meier, "No Basis: A Comparative View" and G. Dannemann, "Unjust Enrichment as Absence of Basis: Can English Law Cope?", in Burrows and Rodger, *Mapping the Law*, 343 and 363. Cf. H. Scott, "Restitution of Extra-Contractual Transfers: Limits of the Absence of Legal Ground Analysis" [2006] R.L.R. 93.

[36] Birks, *Unjust Enrichment*, p.116; developed in T. Baloch, "The Unjust Enrichment Pyramid" (2007) 123 L.Q.R. 636; and Baloch, *Unjust Enrichment and Contract*, Ch.3, but criticised in A. Burrows, "Absence of Basis: The New Birksian Scheme', in Burrows and Rodger, *Mapping the Law*, 33; revisited in Burrows, *The Law of Restitution*, pp.95–116. Lord Walker saw attractions in Birks' approach in *Deutsche Morgan Grenfell* [2006] UKHL 49; [2007] 1 A.C. 558 at [158].

badly when asked to operate several tests at the same time, particularly when the relationship between these tests is imperfectly understood.[37]

1–21   Moreover we disagree with Birks that English law has already made the switch to "absence of basis" reasoning. This claim rested on a tendentious reading of the case law that ignored alternative explanations of the swaps cases,[38] and glossed over some key authorities, in particular *Woolwich Equitable Building Society v IRC*, where Lord Goff declined to find for the claimant on the basis that there was no legal ground for the defendant's enrichment, because although English law "might have developed so as to recognize a *condictio indebiti*—an action for the recovery of money on the ground that it was not due . . . it did not do so".[39] A negative answer to the question whether English law takes this approach has also been given in *Deutsche Morgan Grenfell Plc v IRC*, where Lord Walker thought that this would "represent a distinct departure from established doctrine",[40] and where Lord Hoffmann held that[41]:

> "[A]t any rate for the moment, . . . unlike civilian systems, English law has no general principle that to retain money paid without any legal basis (such as debt, gift, compromise, etc.) is unjust enrichment . . . In England, the claimant has to prove that the circumstances in which the payment was made come within one of the categories which the law recognizes as sufficient to make retention by the recipient unjust."

1–22   In line with these judicial statements, the discussion of grounds for restitution in Chs 8–26 proceeds on the basis that claimants in unjust enrichment must demonstrate a positive reason for restitution. These chapters are concerned with the following topics: lack of consent and want of authority; mistake; duress; undue influence; failure of basis; necessity; secondary liability; ultra vires

---

[37] Cf. *Customs & Excise Commissioners v Barclays Bank Plc* [2005] EWCA 1555; [2005] 1 W.L.R. 2082, only partially redeemed on appeal: [2006] UKHL 28; [2007] 1 A.C. 181 (concerning negligence liability for pure economic loss). The Canadian law of unjustified enrichment requires the courts to consider whether there was a legal ground for the defendant's enrichment and whether restitution would be contrary to the parties' reasonable expectations or public policy: e.g. *Garland v Consumers' Gas Co* [2004] SCC 25; [2004] 1 S.C.R. 629; *Kerr v Baranow* [2011] SCC 10; [2011] 1 S.C.R. 269 at [40] and [120]–[121]. However, positive grounds for recovery have been identified as the reason for restitution in some recent cases, e.g. *BMP Global Distribution Ltd v Bank of Nova Scotia* [2009] SCC 15; [2009] 1 S.C.R. 504 at [52]. This may bear out the assertion in the leading practitioners' text that the "absence of basis" approach is confined to new "cases where it [is] necessary . . . to go beyond the existing law or the existing categories of recovery": P. Maddaugh and J. McCamus, *The Law of Restitution*, looseleaf edn (Aurora, Ont.: Canada Law Book Co., August 2010 issue), para.3:200. But for the view that this bifurcated approach would, if correct, render the law conceptually incoherent, see M. McInnes, *"Garland's Unitary Test of Unjust Enrichment: A Reply to Professor McCamus"* (2011) 38 *Advocates' Quarterly* 16.

[38] In line with *Kleinwort Benson* [1999] 2 A.C. 349, the same result could have been produced by allowing recovery on the ground of mistake of law. As discussed at para.9–79, however, the mistake recognised in *Kleinwort Benson* was a fictional "deemed mistake", and so a surer ground for recovery may be found in failure of basis (see paras 13–20—13–25) or in the policy considerations underlying the rule of law which rendered the parties' swaps contracts void (see paras 23–30—23–31).

[39] *Woolwich Equitable Building Society v IRC* [1993] A.C. 70 at 172. The *Woolwich* case is discussed further at paras 22–13—22–21.

[40] *Deutsche Morgan Grenfell* [2006] UKHL 49; [2007] 1 A.C. 558 at [155].

[41] *Deutsche Morgan Grenfell* [2006] UKHL 49 at [21]; followed in *Marine Trade SA v Pioneer Freight Futures Co Ltd BVI* [2009] EWHC 2656 (Comm); [2010] 1 Lloyd's Rep. 631 at [62]–[65]. See too *Kleinwort Benson* [1999] 2 A.C. 349 at 405; *Sempra* [2007] UKHL 34; [2008] 1 A.C. 561 at [23]–[25]; *Test Claimants in the F.I.I. Group Litigation v IRC* [2010] EWCA Civ 103; [2010] S.T.C. 1251 at [156].

receipts and payments by public bodies; legal incapacity; illegality; and money paid pursuant to a judgment that is later reversed. The first four of these all concern situations where the claimant's intention to benefit the defendant is absent or vitiated; the next concerns the situation where the parties have a common understanding, objectively assessed, that the defendant's enrichment is conditional on the happening of an event that does not occur; and the last six concern situations where restitution is awarded in order to accomplish various policy objectives that do not turn on the parties' intentions.

(ii) *Recognising New Grounds for Recovery*

A claimant must be able to point to a ground of recovery that is established by   **1–23** past authority, or at least is justifiable by a process of principled analogical reasoning from past authority. "As yet there is in English law no *general rule* giving the plaintiff a right of recovery from a defendant who has been unjustly enriched at the plaintiff's expense",[42] and the courts' jurisdiction to order restitution on the ground of unjust enrichment is subject "to the binding authority of previous decisions": they do not have "a discretionary power to order repayment whenever it seems . . . just and equitable to do so".[43] Claims in unjust enrichment must be pleaded by bringing them "within or close to some established category or factual recovery situation".[44] However, "the categories of unjust enrichment are not closed",[45] and *Woolwich*[46] shows that the courts may sometimes take a bold approach to the recognition of new grounds of recovery.

The limits of the courts' power to do this were considered by Laws L.J. in   **1–24** *Gibb v Maidstone and Tunbridge Wells NHS Trust*.[47] He said that the categories of unjust enrichment claims "cannot be closed, for if they were this branch of the law would be condemned to ossify for no apparent reason; and nothing could be further from the common law's incremental method." On the other hand, he applauded the authorities' "reluctance to assert first principles", attributing this to "the justified fear of the palm tree", and adding that "if the principle of unjust enrichment does no more than to invite one judge after another, case by case, to declare that this or that enrichment is inherently just or unjust, it is not much of a principle." He concluded that "clear reasoning" that provides "clear analogues with other cases" is "required for the elaboration of any extension of unjust enrichment".

---

[42] *Woolwich* [1993] A.C. 70 at 196–197, per Lord Browne-Wilkinson.

[43] *Kleinwort Benson Ltd v Birmingham CC* [1996] 4 All ER 733 at 737 per Evans L.J.

[44] *Uren v First National Home Finance Ltd* [2005] EWHC 2529 (Ch.) at [16]–[18] per Mann J. See too *Wasada Pty Ltd v State Rail Authority of New South Wales (No.2)* [2003] NSWSC 987 at [16].

[45] *C.T.N. Cash & Carry Ltd v Gallaher Ltd* [1994] 4 All E.R. 714 at 720 per Nicholls V.C.

[46] *Woolwich* [1993] A.C. 70. See especially Lord Goff's comments at 172, though contrast Lord Browne-Wilkinson's remarks at 197. Support for a bold approach can also be derived from *Westdeutsche* [1996] A.C. 669 at 691 and 722; and *Kleinwort Benson* [1999] A.C. 221 at 372 and 393.

[47] *Gibb v Maidstone and Tunbridge Wells NHS Trust* [2010] EWCA Civ 678; [2010] I.R.L.R. 786 at [26]–[27]. See too *Ledger-Beadell v Peach* [2006] EWHC 2940 (Ch); [2007] 2 F.L.R. 210 at [263].

(f) *Defences*

1–25   As the English law of unjust enrichment has evolved over the last few decades, existing grounds for recovery have been liberalised and new grounds for recovery have been recognised. One reason why the courts have felt able to develop the law in this way is that they have also recognised the change of position defence, and have developed other defences, with a view to striking a more nuanced balance between the claimant's interest in restitution and the defendant's interest in security of receipt.[48] These developments are tracked in Chs 27 to 35, where we examine the defences of change of position, ministerial receipt, bona fide purchase, estoppel, counter-restitution impossible, passing on, limitation, legal incapacity and illegality.

(g) *Remedies*

1–26   As discussed in Ch.36, some remedies for unjust enrichment are preventative: their function is to prevent a defendant from becoming unjustly enriched at a claimant's expense. Remedies of this kind are comparatively rare for the obvious reason that a claimant who knows that a defendant is about to be unjustly enriched at his expense can usually take steps to avoid this outcome without obtaining a court order, most obviously by choosing not to transfer a benefit to him.

1–27   Most remedies for unjust enrichment are restitutionary. Compensatory remedies for wrongdoing are sometimes described as restitutionary, meaning that they are awarded in order to restore the claimant to the whole position that he would have occupied if the wrong had not been committed.[49] That is not the sense in which the term "restitutionary" is used in this book: rather, we use the term to describe remedies whose effect is to reverse transfers of value between claimants and defendants.

1–28   In most cases, claims are made for personal restitutionary remedies, i.e. for an order that the defendant account for and pay over a sum of money that represents the value of his unjust enrichment at the claimant's expense. These are discussed in Ch.37. In some cases, however, claims are made for proprietary restitutionary remedies, i.e. for an order that restitution should be effected by the realization of a right in an asset held by the defendant, whether the very asset which carried the enrichment to him or an asset which is the traceable substitute of the original asset. In Chs 37–40 we consider the circumstances in which a claimant in unjust enrichment is entitled to some kind of proprietary interest in assets owned by the defendant, and then discuss the different kinds of proprietary interest that claimants may obtain.

---

[48] Cf. *Lipkin Gorman (A Firm) v Karpnale Ltd* [1991] 2 A.C. 548 at 581 per Lord Goff: recognition of the change of position defence "will enable a more generous approach to be taken to the recognition of the right to restitution, in the knowledge that the defence is, in appropriate cases, available."

[49] For example, the Chancery courts have long used the term "restitution" to denote a particular type of compensatory liability owed by defaulting trustees and fiduciaries: *Nocton v Lord Ashburton* [1914] A.C. 932 at 952; *Re Dawson* [1966] 2 N.S.W.R. 211 at 215; endorsed in *Bartlett v Barclays Bank Trust Co Ltd (No.2)* [1980] Ch. 515 at 543; and in *Target Holdings Ltd v Redferns (A Firm)* [1996] A.C. 421 at 434; *Swindle v Harrison* [1997] 4 All E.R. 705 at 715–717.

4. PLEADING CLAIMS IN UNJUST ENRICHMENT

A 150 years after the abolition of the forms of action, it would be desirable for **1–29**
claimants to abandon the old language of the forms of action when pleading
claims in unjust enrichment. The old language of "money had and received",
"money paid to the plaintiff's use", "*quantum meruit*", and "*quantum valebant*"
conceals as much as it reveals about the nature of a claim. This is particularly true
of the last two, for these actions straddled the boundaries of what we now call
contract and unjust enrichment, so that the "mere framing of a claim as a
quantum meruit [or *quantum valebant*] . . . does not assist in classifying the
claim".[50] Claims to enforce a contractual obligation to pay the reasonable value
of services or goods are different from claims in unjust enrichment for restitution
of their value,[51] and litigants should make it clear which type of claim they are
bringing.

When pleading claims in unjust enrichment, all that is required is for a **1–30**
claimant to state the nature of the claim and the facts on which he relies, and that
can be done without mentioning the old forms of action.[52] When the pleadings
clearly state that the claim lies in contract, or unjust enrichment, or both in the
alternative, this will clarify the issues for the parties and make it easier for the
court to determine whether the ingredients of the claim have been established; it
will also make it easier to decide whether there are any defences, for example
because a rule of public policy debars claims of one sort but not the other.[53]

Consistently with what has been said in the previous part about the necessary **1–31**
ingredients of claims in unjust enrichment, it should made be clear in a statement
of claim what facts are being relied upon to establish that the defendant was
enriched,[54] that his enrichment was gained at the claimant's expense, and that his
enrichment is unjust. The courts have stressed in connection with this last
requirement that it will not do for claimants to plead generalised claims in unjust
enrichment, nor is it acceptable to assert that the circumstances make the

---

[50] *British Steel Corp v Cleveland Bridge Engineering Ltd* [1984] 1 All E.R. 504 at 509 per Robert
Goff J. See too *Brenner v First Artists' Management Pty Ltd* [1993] 2 V.R. 221 at 256 (Victoria Sup
Ct); *Rawlinson v Westbrook*, unreported, CA, December 8, 1994 per Staughton L.J.; *Hewitt v Alex
Sayer Project Services* Unreported CA, January 15, 1996 per Schiemann L.J. Contract and unjust
enrichment are the *only* reasons why a quantum meruit award might be made, and so it is incoherent
to discuss "*quantum meruit* claims" as though they derived from some other source of entitlement,
as in e.g. *Rover International Ltd v Cannon Film Sales Ltd* [1989] 1 W.L.R. 912 at 926–928 (CA);
Countrywide Communications Ltd v I.C.L. Pathway Ltd [2000] C.L.C. 324 at 338 and following; and
cf. *Yeoman's Row Management Ltd v Cobbe* [2008] UKHL 55, [2008] 1 W.L.R. 1752 at [3]–[4] and
[40]–[44].
[51] *Zavodnyik v Alex Constructions Pty Ltd* [2005] NSWCA 438 at [31] per Mason P.: "alternative and
inconsistent causes of action". Cf. *Gott v Commonwealth of Australia* [2000] TASSC 86 at [15]–[18]:
pleading that work was done pursuant to an "implied promise" is insufficient to found claim in unjust
enrichment. But cf. *Coleman v Seaborne Pty Ltd* [2007] NSWCA 60 at [39]–[41]: where the facts
might support either a claim in unjust enrichment or a contractual claim, "a pleading alleging a
quantum meruit will be sufficient to cover both types of claim"; *Adamson v Williams* [2001] QCA
38 at [2]–[4] is to like effect.
[52] For the contents of the claim form see CPR r.16.2. For the contents of the particulars of claim see
CPR r.16.4.
[53] As in e.g. *Mohamed v Alaga & Co (A Firm)* [2000] 1 W.L.R. 1815 (CA). Cf. *A.L. Barnes Ltd v
Time Talk (UK) Ltd* [2003] EWCA Civ 402; [2003] B.L.R. 331.
[54] On the topic of pleading enrichment, see para.4–59.

defendant's enrichment unfair in a broad sense, or in accordance with the claimant's own idiosyncratic notions of unfairness: specific reasons anchored in the case law must be given to justify the assertion that the defendant's enrichment is unjust.[55]

1-32   There does not currently appear to be any rule of English law that prevents a claimant from relying on one established ground for restitution at common law in preference to another,[56] but claimants should be alive to the fact that in situations where they are given a restitutionary right by a statutory regime they may be prevented from relying instead on a common law right to restitution.[57]

1-33   Given that "pleadings [should not be used] as a means of firing 'warning shots' to the other side",[58] it would seem to be unnecessary and undesirable for a claimant to assert the absence of any justifying ground in his statement of claim, but this is obviously something that he must address if the defendant asserts that his enrichment was justified by reason of a statute, judgment, contract, etc.

1-34   A claimant must specify the remedy which he seeks.[59] Most commonly, that will be the personal restitutionary remedy of an order for the payment of a sum of money which will have the effect of reversing the defendant's unjust enrichment.[60] Where a claimant seeks a proprietary restitutionary remedy such as a declaration that the defendant holds property on trust for the claimant, or that property is impressed with a lien to secure the defendant's restitutionary obligation, the claimant must specify which property forms the subject-matter of the claim, and explain how the rules of tracing and following enable him to identify this as property that he formerly owned, or as property that was obtained in exchange for such property.

1-35   In a number of recent cases concerned with the recovery of money paid as tax that was not due, group litigation orders have made to enable collective claims in unjust enrichment to be brought against HMRC.[61] Practical problems can arise

---

[55] *Uren* [2005] EWHC 2529 (Ch) at [16]; citing *Woolwich* [1993] A.C. 70 at 196–197; and *South Tyneside Metropolitan BC v Svenska International Plc* [1995] 1 All E.R. 545 at 556–557. See too *Pavey* (1987) 162 C.L.R. 221 at 256; *Shell Co of Australia Ltd v Esso Australia Ltd* [1987] V.R. 317 at 342 and 345–346; *Marriott Industries Pty Ltd v Mercantile Credits Ltd* (1990) 55 S.A.S.R. 228 at 237–238; *Lactos Fresh Pty Ltd v Finishing Services Ltd (No.2)* [2006] FCA 748 at [111]; *Coshott v Lenin* [2007] NSWCA 153 at [8]–[11].

[56] Cf. *Kleinwort Benson* [1999] 2 A.C. 349 at 387 (no rule forcing a claimant to rely on mistake rather than failure of basis or vice versa); *Deutsche Morgan Grenfell* [2006] UKHL 49; [2007] 1 A.C. 558 (no rule forcing a claimant to rely on the rule in *Woolwich* [1993] A.C. 70 rather than mistake of law).

[57] See paras 2–13—2–20.

[58] *K./S. Lincoln v C.B. Richard Ellis Hotels Ltd* [2009] EWHC 2344 (TCC); [2010] P.N.L.R. 5 at [11].

[59] See CPR r.16.2(b).

[60] *Portman Building Society v Hamlyn Taylor Neck (A Firm)* [1998] 4 All E.R. 202 at 205; *Navier v Leicester* [2002] EWHC 2596 (Ch) at [21].

[61] *Deutsche Morgan Grenfell* [2006] UKHL 49; [2007] 1 A.C. 558; *Boake Allen Ltd v HMRC* [2006] EWCA Civ 25; [2006] S.T.C. 606; affirmed on a different point [2007] UKHL 25; [2007] 1 W.L.R. 1386; *Sempra* [2007] UKHL 34; [2008] 1 A.C. 561; *F.I.I.* [2010] EWCA Civ 103; [2010] S.T.C. 1251; *F.J. Chalke Ltd v HMRC* [2010] EWCA Civ 313; [2010] S.T.C. 1640; *Test Claimants in the Thin Cap Group Litigation v HMRC* [2011] EWCA Civ 127; [2011] S.T.C. 738; *John Wilkins (Motor Engineers) Ltd v HMRC* [2011] EWCA Civ 429; [2011] S.T.C. 1371.

where collective claims in unjust enrichment are made that depend on the assertion that each claimant's intention to benefit the defendant was vitiated in some way, since the court may then have to investigate the motives and actions of each claimant in turn.[62]

---

[62] For general discussion of the practical problems that can arise out of the making of GLOs in this area, see S. Degeling and J. Seymour, "Collective Claims for Unjust Enrichment" (2010) 29 C.J.Q. 449.

Part Two
JUSTIFYING GROUNDS

CHAPTER 2

JUSTIFYING GROUNDS: STATUTES, JUDGMENTS, AND NATURAL OBLIGATIONS

1. INTRODUCTION

English law provides that a claimant will be entitled to restitution if he can show **2–01** that a defendant was enriched at his expense, and that the circumstances are such that the law regards this enrichment as unjust. For example, a claimant will have a prima facie right to restitution where he has transferred a benefit to a defendant by mistake, under duress, or for a basis that fails. Nevertheless, the defendant can escape liability if another legal rule entitles him to keep the benefit, and this rule overrides the rule generated by the law of unjust enrichment which holds that the defendant should make restitution. For example, a claimant may have paid money to a defendant by mistake, but the payment may be irrecoverable if the claimant was required to pay by statute or by contract. Although the claimant has a prima facie claim in unjust enrichment, the defendant's enrichment is justified by the statute or contract, with the result that the claimant's right to restitution is nullified.[1]

In a study of this topic, Charles Rickett and Ross Grantham have argued that **2–02** the law of unjust enrichment "is not a primary regulator of rights and duties" in English private law because its scope and operation "are necessarily constrained by the scope and operation of the other core doctrines", and its function is "either to supplement these primary doctrines or [to work] in the interstitial spaces between the primary doctrines".[2] They contend that the law of unjust enrichment is "subsidiary" to other "primary" sources of private law rules such as the law of contract, and that it follows from the "subsidiary" nature of the law of unjust enrichment that recognition of unjust enrichment as a source of rights within English private law will not create undesirable "overlaps with, and even take-overs of, areas which belong to other core doctrines of the private common law", because "subsidiarity is a key to 'containing the beast'".[3]

These observations seem to have caught the attention of Sedley L.J., who **2–03** expressed the view in *Niru Battery Manufacturing Co v Milestone Trading Ltd (No.1)* that the law of unjust enrichment is a means of adjusting the relationships between parties "whose rights are not met by some stronger doctrine of law" and

---

[1] *Kleinwort Benson Ltd v Lincoln CC* [1999] 2 A.C. 349 at 407–408, per Lord Hope, followed in *Test Claimants in the F.I.I. Litigation v HMRC* [2010] EWCA Civ 103; [2010] S.T.C. 1251 at [181], per Arden L.J.
[2] R. Grantham and C. Rickett, "On the Subsidiarity of Unjust Enrichment" (2000) 117 L.Q.R. 273, pp.273–274.
[3] Grantham and Rickett, "On the Subsidiarity of Unjust Enrichment", at p.299, referring to K. Barker, "Unjust Enrichment: Containing the Beast" (1995) 15 O.J.L.S. 457.

that the courts award restitution is a means of solving "residual" problems.[4] Moreover, it is clearly true that the operation of the English law of unjust enrichment is affected by the operation of other legal doctrines, and that the effect of these doctrines can be to nullify rights generated for a claimant by the law of unjust enrichment. Nevertheless, we do not believe that it is helpful to characterise the relationship between the law of unjust enrichment and other sources of rights and obligations in private law as one of "subsidiarity" and "primacy".

2–04   One problem is that this terminology is unstable. Lawyers from common law systems, lawyers from civilian and mixed legal systems, and comparative lawyers have all used the language of "subsidiarity" to express a number of different ideas about the reasons why a claimant might be debarred from relying on rights generated by one part of the law because his relationship with the defendant is also affected by rules emanating from another part of the law.[5] Another problem is that the language of "subsidiarity" suggests that English law maintains a hierarchy of rights under which rights generated by the law of unjust enrichment are invariably placed at the bottom.[6] Although English law does frequently subordinate rights in unjust enrichment to rights generated by other sources, it does not always do so, and we share Stephen Waddams' view that the relationship between mutually interdependent bodies of law such as contract and unjust enrichment is more complex and more subtle than is suggested by the concept of a hierarchy of rights.[7] For these reasons we consider that the language of subsidiarity is best avoided when analysing the interplay between the law of

---

[4] *Niru Battery Manufacturing Co v Milestone Trading Ltd (No.1)* [2003] EWCA Civ 1446; [2004] Q.B. 985 at [192].

[5] See e.g. B. Nicholas, "Unjust Enrichment and Subsidiarity" in F. Santoro Passarelli and M. Lupoi (eds), *Scintillae Iuris: Studi in Memoria di Gino Gorla* (Milan: A. Giuftre, 1994), 2037; B Nicholas, "Modern Developments in the French Law of Unjustified Enrichment", in P.W.L. Russell (ed.), *Unjustified Enrichment: A Comparative Study of the Law of Restitution* (Amsterdam: Vrije Universiteit, 1996), 77, pp.87–95; L. Smith, "Property, Subsidiarity, and Unjust Enrichment" in D. Johnston and R. Zimmermann (eds), *Unjustified Enrichment: Key Issues in Comparative Perspective* (Cambridge: CUP, 2002), 588; J. Beatson and E.J.H. Schrage (eds), *Cases, Materials and Text on Unjustified Enrichment* (Oxford: Hart Publishing, 2003), Ch.7; G.E. van Maanen, "Subsidiarity of the Action for Unjustified Enrichment—French Law and Dutch Law: Different Solutions for the Same Problem" (2006) 14 E.R.P.L 409; N.R. Whitty, "*Transco plc v Glasgow City Council*: Developing Enrichment Law after *Shilliday*" (2006) 10 Edinburgh Law Rev. 113, pp.122–132; D. Visser, "Unjustified Enrichment" in J.M. Smits (ed.), *Elgar Encyclopedia of Comparative Law* (Cheltenham: Edward Elgar, 2006), 767, pp.771–772.

[6] Grantham and Rickett, "On the Subsidiarity of Unjust Enrichment" is a case in point. At pp.273–274, they rightly state that "the extent or strength of the subsidiarity of unjust enrichment will depend upon the proper construction of the primary doctrine, and in particular whether in denying the plaintiff a claim the primary doctrine continues, by negative implication, to regulate the relationship"; but this qualification is lost from view as their argument proceeds.

[7] S. Waddams, "Contract and Unjust Enrichment: Competing Categories, or Complementary Concepts?" in C. Rickett and R. Grantham (eds), *Structure and Justification in Private Law* (Oxford: Hart, 2008), 167. Stephen Smith, in his article on "Concurrent Liability in Contract and Unjust Enrichment: the Fundamental Breach Requirement" (1999) 115 L.Q.R. 245, takes an even stronger position and claims that, in principle, the relationship between contract and unjust enrichment should be "the same as the relationship between contract and tort, namely there would be 'general' concurrent liability in each case." However, he concedes that there are formidable difficulties to the acceptance of this view, not the least being that the House of Lords (now the Supreme Court) would have to accept that a claim in unjust enrichment would lie even though the breach of contract is not so fundamental as to enable the claimant to elect to terminate the contract.

unjust enrichment and other sources of rights that might generate overriding justifications for the defendant's enrichment at the claimant's expense.

In this chapter and the next, we discuss several reasons why the courts might 2–05 hold that a defendant's enrichment is justified notwithstanding the claimant's prima facie right to restitution. In this chapter, we look at statutes, judgments and court orders, and natural obligations; in the next chapter we look at contracts.

Obviously, where a defendant relies on a statute or judgment or contract as a 2–06 factor justifying his enrichment, the claimant may be able to defeat this argument if he can show some reason why the justifying ground invoked by the defendant should be disregarded. If it simply does not arise on the facts of the case then it will not affect the claimant's restitutionary right. It may also be that the claimant can attack the underlying validity of the justifying ground, for example by showing that the statute is ultra vires,[8] or by persuading an appellate court to overturn the judgment, or by showing that the contract is void for illegality. If a claimant seeks to avoid a contract by making an argument based on vitiated consent, for example by arguing mistake, duress or undue influence, then it should not be assumed that the rules governing the question when a contract can be set aside on these grounds are the same as the rules governing the question whether a benefit can be recovered on similar grounds in the law of unjust enrichment. However, detailed consideration of the rules governing the avoidance of contracts lies beyond the scope of the present work, and specialist texts should be consulted on this topic.[9]

2. STATUTES

There are different ways in which a statute might affect rights that would 2–07 otherwise arise in the law of unjust enrichment. First, the statute might require the claimant to benefit the defendant, so that the defendant's enrichment is directly justified by the legislation. Secondly, the statute might expressly or impliedly extinguish a claimant's rights in unjust enrichment. Thirdly, a claim in unjust enrichment might be disallowed in order to avoid stultifying the policy underlying a statute that forbids parties to enter transactions of a certain type.

(a) *Statute Requires the Claimant to Benefit the Defendant*

Where a statute requires a claimant to transfer a benefit to a defendant the courts 2–08 can usually be expected to hold that the defendant's enrichment is justified by the statute, so that no claim in unjust enrichment will lie to recover the benefit, even if the claimant can show that he made a mistake, or transferred the benefit for some other reason that would normally lead the courts to hold that the defendant's enrichment was unjust. To give a common example, taxpayers often overlook opportunities to arrange their affairs in a more tax-efficient way, and so

---

[8] For discussion of the different methods by which a claimant might attack a statute that apparently justifies the defendant's enrichment, see M. Chowdry and C. Mitchell, "Tax Legislation as a Justifying Factor" [2005] R.L.R. 1, pp.13–18.
[9] e.g. H. Beale (ed.), *Chitty on Contracts*, 30th edn (London: Sweet & Maxwell, 2008), Chs 5–7.

they are legally obliged to pay more tax than they would have had to pay if they had arranged their affairs in a more tax-efficient way. Assuming that a taxpayer in this situation could show that he would have rearranged his affairs to reduce his tax liability if he had known that he could do this, he would still be unable to recover his mistaken overpayment, because the relevant tax statute justifies the tax authorities' enrichment at his expense: they are entitled to receive tax calculated in accordance with the relevant statutory rules by reference to the taxpayer's affairs as they actually are, and not as they might have been if the taxpayer had arranged his affairs differently.[10]

2–09　　In *Deutsche Morgan Grenfell Plc v IRC*[11] a majority of the House of Lords did not apply this principle. This was a test claim under a group litigation order made to manage claims that were brought against the Revenue following *Metall-gesellschaft Ltd v IRC* and *Hoechst AG v IRC*.[12] There the European Court of Justice held that the Income and Corporation Taxes Act 1988 s.247 infringed the EC Treaty. This section enabled UK resident corporate groups to postpone the time at which they paid corporation tax, but withheld this advantage from corporate groups with subsidiaries resident in the UK and parent companies resident elsewhere in the EU. Such groups had to pay tax sooner than their wholly UK-resident competitors: they had to pay advance corporation tax (ACT) while the others could make a "group income election" and pay mainstream corporation tax (MCT) at a later date. The ECJ held that this disparity of treatment was contrary to EU law, and directed the UK courts to provide disadvantaged groups with "an effective legal remedy in order to obtain reimbursement or reparation of the financial loss which they [had] sustained and from which the [tax] authorities [had] benefited".[13]

2–10　　The issue in *Deutsche Morgan Grenfell* was whether the claimant could bring an action in unjust enrichment against the Revenue founded on its "retrospective mistake of law",[14] or whether it could only rely on the principle established in *Woolwich Equitable BS v IRC*,[15] a point that was understood to have consequences for the limitation period that would govern the claim.[16] For reasons that are discussed elsewhere,[17] the House of Lords held that the claimant could rely on retrospective mistake of law, and also held that on the facts the claimant was entitled to restitution on this ground. However, the latter finding of fact is hard to understand when one considers the structure of the statutory regime under which ACT was payable. The Income and Corporation Taxes Act 1988 imposed a liability to pay ACT from which corporate groups could escape by making a group income election. If a group made an election then it could wait and pay MCT later on, but if it did not, then ACT was payable. In *Metallgesellschaft* the ECJ held that the option to make an election should not have been withheld from

---

[10] A point made by counsel at first instance in *F.I.I.* [2008] EWHC 2893 (Ch); [2009] S.T.C. 254 at [257].

[11] *Deutsche Morgan Grenfell Plc v IRC* [2006] UKHL 49; [2007] 1 A.C. 558.

[12] *Metallgesellschaft Ltd v IRC* (Joined cases C–397/98 and C–410/98) [2001] All E.R. (E.C.) 496.

[13] *Metallgesellschaft* (Joined case C–397/98 and C–410/98) [2001] All E.R. (E.C.) 496 at [97].

[14] A ground of recovery established by *Kleinwort Benson Ltd v Lincoln CC* [1999] 2 A.C. 349; discussed at paras 9–71—9–94.

[15] *Woolwich Equitable BS v IRC* [1993] A.C. 70; discussed at paras 22–13—22–31.

[16] For the limitation aspect of the case, see paras 33–32—33–34.

[17] See paras 22–29—22–31.

corporate groups such as the claimant, but this finding did not affect the validity of the basic liability established by s.247, which stated that the tax was due unless an election was made. Since the claimant had in fact made no election, the ACT was therefore due under the statute when it was paid, suggesting that recovery should have been denied notwithstanding DMG's retrospective mistake, because the Revenue had been legally entitled to receive it.

At first instance, Park J. sought to overcome this problem by holding both that **2–11** the claimant would have made an election and that the Revenue would have allowed it to do so, had the rule laid down in *Metallgesellschaft* been known to both of them at the time when the payments were made.[18] The Court of Appeal did not need to address this point, because they thought that the claimant could not rely on mistake as a ground of recovery, but in obiter dicta Jonathan Parker L.J. held that if the claimant had been allowed to claim for mistake of law, then it would have succeeded because the "relevant statutory regime was contrary to Article 52" so that it "gave rise to no obligation to pay".[19] In the House of Lords, Lord Hope agreed with the whole of Park J.'s analysis.[20] Lord Hoffmann and Lord Walker both rejected his characterisation of the claimant's mistake, and preferred Jonathan Parker L.J.'s view that the claimant had been mistaken in thinking that the tax was due—but like Park J. and Lord Hope, they also needed to rewrite the facts of the case to make their analysis work, asserting that "D.M.G. would undoubtedly have used" the election provisions in the statute if it had appreciated that it was entitled to do so.[21] Lord Brown agreed with all three of them,[22] while Lord Scott dissented, holding that DMG's mistake had been "that they did not realize that they could successfully challenge the failure of the ACT tax regime to allow them ... to make a group income election", but holding that even if this mistake had caused the claimant to pay, recovery should still be denied because "in the events that actually happened DMG paid the ACT that was due" under the statute.[23] In our view, Lord Scott's characterisation of the claimant's mistake missed the point of retrospective mistake as a ground for recovery, but even so he was correct to hold that recovery should have been denied on the basis that the Revenue's enrichment was justified by the statute.

The House of Lords' decision in *Deutsche Morgan Grenfell* can be **2–12** contrasted with the Court of Appeal's decision in *Test Claimants in the F.I.I. Group Litigation v IRC*.[24] The assumed facts of the latter case were that a claimant had used tax reliefs to reduce its liability to pay tax that had been unlawfully levied in breach of EU law. The question arose whether a claim would lie for the value of these reliefs, on the assumed basis that the claimant would have used them to reduce other, lawful, tax liabilities if it had not already used them to reduce its unlawful tax liabilities. The court held that no such claim would lie, for two reasons. One was that HMRC's gain would have been too remote a consequence of the claimant's loss to be recoverable. This is discussed

---

[18] *Deutsche Morgan Grenfell* [2004] EWHC 2387 (Ch); [2004] S.T.C. 1178 at [25].

[19] *Deutsche Morgan Grenfell* [2005] EWCA Civ 389; [2006] Q.B. 37 at [231].

[20] *Deutsche Morgan Grenfell* [2006] UKHL 49; [2007] 1 A.C. 558 at [62].

[21] *Deutsche Morgan Grenfell* [2006] UKHL 49; [2006] 1 A.C. 558 at [32], per Lord Hoffmann. Cf. Lord Walker's comment at [143]: "the fact that there was a procedural requirement for a GIE does not alter the substance of its mistake".

[22] *Deutsche Morgan Grenfell* [2006] UKHL 49; [2006] 1 A.C. 558 at [161].

[23] *Deutsche Morgan Grenfell* [2006] UKHL 49; [2006] 1 A.C. 558 at [89].

[24] *F.I.I.* [2010] EWCA Civ 103; [2010] S.T.C. 1251.

elsewhere.[25] The other was that HMRC could not have been unjustly enriched by a payment made to discharge a lawful tax liability because ex hypothesi this payment must have been due under the relevant statute.[26] This finding is hard to reconcile with the House of Lords' decision in *Deutsche Morgan Grenfell*.[27]

(b) *Statute Removes the Claimant's Common Law Rights*

2–13   A statute may expressly prohibit common law claims in unjust enrichment, and give claimants no other rights, in which case they will be left without a remedy. For example, a claimant's common law rights may be extinguished by a limitation statute.[28]

2–14   A statute may also expressly remove a claimant's common law rights and give him a set of statutory rights in their place, in which case he will obviously need to know whether the statute applies to his case, as this will determine which of two possible sets of rights he has. An example is provided by the Civil Liability (Contribution) Act 1978 s.7(3), which states that rights conferred by the statute supersede any rights which the claimant would otherwise have at common law. There is a practical reason why it matters whether a claimant's contribution rights arise at common law or under the statute, namely that different limitation rules apply to the two types of claim: the Limitation Act 1980 s.2 provides that a claimant has only two years within which to claim under the 1978 Act, rather than the six years that he would otherwise have at common law. Unfortunately, however, the courts have not always clearly understood the test to determine whether or not a claim falls within the scope of the legislation. This is discussed in Ch.19.[29]

2–15   A statute may also preclude common law rights in unjust enrichment by implication. Whether a statute has this effect is a question of interpretation. In cases where claimants have common law rights, but are also given statutory rights, the courts have tended to hold that Parliament's intention must have been to extinguish the claimant's common law rights in order to replace them with a different (and possibly narrower) set of statutory rights. In Sir John Dyson S.C.J.'s words, "If the two remedies cover precisely the same ground and are inconsistent with each other, then the common law remedy will almost certainly have been excluded by necessary implication."[30] However the courts have found

---

[25] See para.6–09.

[26] *F.I.I.* [2010] EWCA Civ 103; [2010] S.T.C. 1251 at [179]–[184], esp. [181].

[27] Cf. A. Burrows, *The Law of Restitution*, 3rd edn (Oxford: OUP, 2010), p.91, argues that "as a matter of policy the injustice of the *ultra vires* exaction [in *Deutsche Morgan Grenfell*] outweighed the point that, technically, the Revenue was legally entitled to the tax." But why was this not also true of the *F.I.I.* case (which he describes with approval on p.89)?

[28] See Ch.33. For another example, see *Butler v Broadhead* [1975] Ch. 97, interpreting s.264 of the Companies Act 1948 and the Companies (Winding Up) Rules 1949 (SI 1949/330) reg.106, made under the Companies Act 1948 s.273(e).

[29] See paras 19–22—19–34.

[30] *R. (Child Poverty Action Group) v Secretary of State for Work and Pensions* [2010] UKSC 54; [2011] 2 A.C. 15 at [33], adding that "A good example of this is *Marcic v Thames Water Utilities Ltd* [2003] UKHL 66; [2004] 2 A.C. 42, where a sewerage undertaker was subject to an elaborate scheme of statutory regulation which included an independent regulator with powers of enforcement whose decisions were subject to judicial review. The statutory scheme provided a procedure for making complaints to the regulator. The House of Lords held that a cause of action in nuisance would be inconsistent with the statutory scheme. It would run counter to the intention of Parliament."

it harder to interpret Parliament's intention in cases where claimants have common law rights, some of which arise in situations where they also have statutory rights, but some of which arise in situations where they do not: in such cases, it can be hard to decide whether Parliament intended to extinguish all of the claimants' common law rights, or only those which overlap with their statutory rights.

A case of the first kind is *Monro v HMRC*,[31] where the Court of Appeal held **2–16** that Parliament intended to exclude common law recovery in unjust enrichment in cases where the Taxes Management Act 1970 s.33 applies; this section gives taxpayers a statutory right to relief where they have overpaid income tax, corporation tax or capital gains tax.[32] However, the court also held that Parliament cannot have intended to deprive taxpayers of their wider common law rights where European law requires them to be given an effective remedy.[33] A similar conclusion was also drawn by the Court of Appeal in *F.I.I.*,[34] but there the court invoked the *Marleasing* principle[35] to read a restriction on claimants' rights under s.33 as "subject to the limitation that it applies only if and to the extent that the United Kingdom can consistently with its Treaty obligations impose such a restriction".

Cases of the second kind include *Woolwich*,[36] and *Deutsche Morgan Gren-* **2–17** *fell.*[37] In both of these the House of Lords held that it did not follow from the fact that claimants have a right of recovery under the Taxes Management Act 1970 s.33 in some situations that Parliament intended to exclude common law recovery in other situations where the section does not apply.[38] However, these decisions may be contrasted with the Supreme Court's decision in *R. (Child Poverty Action Group) v Secretary of State for Work and Pensions*,[39] which concerned the question whether the Department for Work and Pensions has a common law claim in unjust enrichment where it mistakenly makes an ultra vires payment in circumstances which do not fall within the scope of the Social Security Administration Act 1992 s.71. This section gives the Department a statutory right to recover ultra vires payments, but only those made pursuant to a misrepresentation or failure to disclose a material fact.

Drawing an analogy with *Deutsche Morgan Grenfell*, the trial judge held that **2–18** the section does not preclude recovery in cases where the section does not

---

[31] *Monro v HMRC* [2008] EWCA Civ 306; [2009] Ch. 69; affirming Morritt C.'s decision at first instance: [2007] EWHC 114 (Ch); [2007] S.T.C. 1182.

[32] For further discussion of this section see paras 22–04—22–10.

[33] *Monro* [2009] Ch. 69 at [34].

[34] *F.I.I.* [2010] EWCA Civ 103; [2010] S.T.C. 1251 at [261].

[35] Named for *Marleasing v La Comercial Internacional de Alimentación* (C–106/89) [1990] E.C.R. I–4135.

[36] *Woolwich* [1993] A.C. 70 at 169 and 199–200.

[37] *Deutsche Morgan Grenfell* [2006] UKHL 49; [2007] 1 A.C. 558 at [19], [55] and [135].

[38] Section 33 did not apply on the facts of *Woolwich* because there is no payment made pursuant to a relevant "assessment" if money is paid under ultra vires legislation: [1993] A.C. 70 at 169 and 199–200; and did not apply on the facts of *Deutsche Morgan Grenfell* because there is no payment under an "assessment" where money is paid under legislation that is contrary to European law: [2006] UKHL 49; [2007] 1 A.C. 558 at [19], [54] and [135].

[39] *R. (Child Poverty Action Group) v Secretary of State for Work and Pensions* [2009] EWHC 341 (Admin); [2009] 3 All E.R. 633; reversed [2009] EWCA Civ 1058; [2010] 1 W.L.R. 1886; affirmed [2010] UKSC 54; [2011] 2 A.C. 15.

apply,[40] but the appellate courts disagreed. In the Court of Appeal, Sedley L.J. held that s.71 "was introduced into an established statutory scheme which had always been understood to be exhaustive of the rights, obligations and remedies of both the individual and the state."[41] And in the Supreme Court, Lord Brown thought it:

> "inconceivable that Parliament would have contemplated leaving the suggested common law restitutionary route to the recovery of overpayments available to the Secretary of State to be pursued by way of ordinary court proceedings alongside the carefully prescribed scheme of recovery set out in the statute".[42]

The existence of two schemes would create serious practical problems, e.g. co-ordinating the parallel recovery proceedings that might then be brought against recipients,[43] and the likelihood that Parliament intended such an outcome was also diminished by the fact that there was no common law right of recovery at the time when the 1992 Act was enacted.[44] Lord Brown took this to follow from the fact that the only possible ground for recovery at common law must have been mistake, and yet the Secretary of State could never have made any mistaken overpayment pursuant to an award in 1992 because there was then a division of functions between the adjudication of awards and their payment, responsibility for the former being allocated to adjudication officers and responsibility for the latter to the Secretary of State, who had a statutory duty to pay whatever amount was awarded.[45]

2-19   This assumed—probably incorrectly—that the Secretary of State could not have recovered an overpayment on the ground that he mistakenly believed the award to have been correctly calculated.[46] It also overlooked the possibility that even at the time when responsibility for awards and payments was divided, a common law claim to recover an overpayment could probably have been made pursuant to the principle in *Auckland Harbour Board v R*.[47] Even if they had accepted that a common law recovery right had existed in 1992, however, Lord Brown and Sir John Dyson S.C.J. would still have held that Parliament intended to prevent the Secretary of State from relying on it, either in cases falling within the scope of s.71 or in cases falling outside it. Ultimately this was an issue of statutory construction, and in Sir John's view the question whether common law rights are impliedly excluded by a statute that gives claimants a different set of rights turns not on "whether there are *any* differences between the common law remedy and the statutory scheme" but on "whether the differences are so substantial that they demonstrate that Parliament could not have intended the

---

[40] *CPAG* [2009] 3 All E.R. 633 at [30]. Cf. *R. v Secretary of State for the Environment Ex p. London Borough of Camden* (1995) 28 H.L.R. 31, where Schiemann J. made a similar finding in relation to the Local Government and Housing Act 1989 s.86.
[41] *CPAG* [2010] 1 W.L.R. 1886 at [33].
[42] *CPAG* [2011] 2 A.C. 15 at [14].
[43] *CPAG* [2011] 2 A.C. 15 at [14]. See too Sir John Dyson S.C.J.'s comments at [35].
[44] *CPAG* [2011] 2 A.C. 15 at [13].
[45] *CPAG* [2011] 2 A.C. 15 at [13]. See too Sir John Dyson S.C.J.'s comments at [20]–[25].
[46] *CPAG* [2011] 2 A.C. 15 at [21] where Sir John Dyson S.C.J. thought it "doubtful" that such an argument would have succeeded but does not explain why. Possibly his reason was that the mistake of law bar was not abolished until *Kleinwort Benson* [1999] 2 A.C. 349, but cases can be imagined where the Secretary of State might have made a mistake of fact.
[47] See paras 23–24—23–34.

common law remedy to survive the introduction of the statutory scheme".[48] The court:

> "should not be too ready to find that a common law remedy has been displaced by a statutory one, not least because it is always open to Parliament to make the position clear by stating explicitly whether the statute is intended to be exhaustive",[49]

On the facts of *CPAG*, however, this was the correct conclusion.

Reviewing this area in *Legal Services Commission v Henthorn*,[50] His Honour **2–20** Judge Anthony Thornton QC, sitting as a High Court judge, concluded that in cases where a claimant has both common law and statutory rights, "these are the operable principles that should be applied in order to determine whether a parallel claim [in common law] survives or co-exists with the statutory one"[51]:

> "(1) The question as to whether the statutory remedy is exclusive or is complementary to other remedies is to be answered by the provisions of the statutory provisions giving rise to the statutory remedy.
>
> (2) Where no clear answer is provided by the statutory provisions, they must be analysed in their statutory context to determine whether it is the intention of the legislature or the implied and necessary meaning of the provisions that they are to provide an exclusive remedy.
>
> (3) In ascertaining the meaning to be given to, and the implication to be derived from, the legislation, attention should be given to any preceding legislation which the current legislation has replaced or amended in providing the statutory remedy; to the statutory code in its entirety in which the remedy finds a place; to any obvious problems or difficulties that would arise if both types of remedy exist together and to whether there are situations in which the abolition of a common law remedy as a result of the introduction of the statutory remedy would be left without a remedy which would be available if the common law remedy remained."

(c) *Stultification of Statutory Policy*

The courts may refuse to allow a claim in unjust enrichment where this would **2–21** lead to the enforcement of a transaction that a statute deems to be unenforceable. To decide whether a claim should be allowed, the courts must identify the policy

---

[48] *CPAG* [2011] 2 A.C. 15 at [34].

[49] *CPAG* [2011] 2 A.C. 15 at [34], adding that "The mere fact that there are some differences between the common law and the statutory positions is unlikely to be sufficient unless they are substantial. The fact that the House of Lords was divided in *HMRC v Total Network S.L.* [2008] UKHL 19; [2008] A.C. 1174 shows how difficult it may sometimes be to decide on which side of the line a case falls. The question is whether, looked at as a whole, a common law remedy would be incompatible with the statutory scheme and therefore could not have been intended to co-exist with it."

[50] *Legal Services Commission v Henthorn* [2011] EWHC 258 (QB).

[51] *Henthorn* [2011] EWHC 258 (QB) at [72], citing *Woolwich* [1993] A.C. 70; *Marcic* [2003] UKHL 66; [2004] 2 A.C. 42; *Autologic Holdings Plc v IRC* [2005] UKHL 54; [2006] 1 A.C. 118; *HMRC v Total Network S.L.* [2008] UKHL 19; [2008] 1 A.C. 1174; *CPAG* [2009] EWCA Civ 1058; [2010] 1 W.L.R. 1886; affirmed [2010] UKSC 54; [2011] 2 A.C. 15. Applying his tests to the facts of *Henthorn* the judge concluded that common law rights in unjust enrichment were precluded by the relevant statute.

of the statute and then decide whether this would be stultified if restitution were awarded.[52]

2–22   For example, in *R. Leslie Ltd v Sheill*,[53] the Court of Appeal dismissed a claim in unjust enrichment to recover money lent by an adult to an infant, reasoning that if the claim had been allowed, then the infant would have been indirectly compelled to perform his primary obligation under a contract of loan which the Infants Relief Act 1874 had declared to be void. Again, in *Boissevain v Weil*[54] the House of Lords held that money lent to a British subject, contrary to the Defence (Finance) Regulations 1939, could not be recovered via a claim in unjust enrichment. Lord Radcliffe concluded that[55]:

> "If reg. 2 did extend to this transaction it forbade the very act of borrowing, not merely the contractual promise to repay. The act itself being forbidden, I do not think that it can be a source of civil rights in the courts of this country. It is very well to say that the respondent ought not in conscience to retain this money and that that consideration is enough to found an action for money had and received. But there are two answers to this. Firstly, when the transaction by which the money has reached the respondent is actually an offence by our laws, the matter passes beyond the field in which the requirements of the individual conscience are the determining consideration. Secondly, . . . if this claim based on unjust enrichment were a valid one, the court would be enforcing on the respondent just the exchange and just the liability, without her promise, which the Defence Regulation has said that she is not to undertake by her promise. A court that extended a remedy in such circumstances would merit rather to be blamed for stultifying the law than to be applauded for extending it. I would borrow the words which Lord Sumner used in *Sinclair v Brougham*: 'the law cannot *de jure* impute promises to repay, whether for money had and received or otherwise, which, if made *de facto*, it would inexorably avoid.' His principle is surely right whether the action for money had and received does or does not depend on an imputed promise to pay."

2–23   These decisions were fairly clear-cut examples of the principle that a restitutionary claim will not lie if its recognition would stultify the particular statutory provision. But at times the courts have tended too readily to deny a restitutionary claim on this ground. Such a case was *Sinclair v Brougham*,[56] which concerned the winding up of a building society that had undertaken ultra vires banking business. The House of Lords held that claimants who had deposited money with the building society under ultra vires contracts of deposit could not recover their money in a personal action either at law or in equity, because allowing their claim would have circumvented the "doctrine of ultra vires as established in the jurisprudence of this country".[57] The court's decision in relation to the actions for money had and received was later overruled by a majority of the House of

---

[52] For additional discussion of this topic, see Chs 24 and 34–35.
[53] *R. Leslie Ltd v Sheill* [1914] 3 K.B. 607.
[54] *Boissevain v Weil* [1950] A.C. 327; cf. *Re H.P.C. Productions Ltd* [1962] Ch. 466.
[55] *Boissevain* [1950] A.C. 327 at 341. See also *Kasumu v Baba-Egbe* [1956] A.C. 539 at 549.
[56] *Sinclair v Brougham* [1914] A.C. 398.
[57] *Sinclair* [1914] A.C. 398 at 414 per Viscount Haldane L.C.

Lords in *Westdeutsche Landesbank Girozentrale v Islington LBC*,[58] for reasons that we discuss elsewhere.[59] In brief, these were that the ultra vires rule had been designed to protect the members of the building society, and its intra vires depositors, from expenditure of their money on purposes to which they had not consented; but this policy did not justify their enrichment at the expense of ultra vires depositors who had paid money to the building society, rather than receiving it.

The principle that statutory policy may preclude a restitutionary claim enables **2–24** the recipient to retain a benefit which in other circumstances he would be bound to restore. It should, therefore, only be applied where the particular manifestation of policy is quite clear. Consequently, a court may be faithful to the statutory provisions, declare an agreement to be illegal, and yet hold that the restitutionary claim, being independent, might succeed at the trial. One such case is *Mohamed v Alaga & Co*.[60] The claimant was a professional translator of the Somali language who introduced Somali asylum seekers to the defendant firm of solicitors. In turn, the defendant promised to share fees received from the Legal Aid Board in respect of those clients. Lightman J. and the Court of Appeal both held that rules made under the Solicitors Act 1974 rendered this agreement illegal and unenforceable. Lightman J., adopting Lord Radcliffe's reasoning in *Boissevain*,[61] held that the restitutionary claim must also fail; in substance it was a claim for a reasonable sum in consideration for the introduction of clients and similarly prohibited. However, the Court of Appeal reinstated the claim in unjust enrichment. The "preferable view . . . is that the plaintiff is not seeking to recover any part of the consideration payable under the unlawful contract, but simply a reasonable reward for professional services rendered",[62] "such as interpreting and translating actually performed by the claimant for the solicitors' clients."[63]

A similar principle emerges from *Close v Wilson*,[64] where the claimant **2–25** advanced £20,000 to the defendant for the purpose of betting the money on horse races and accounting to him for the proceeds. The defendant refused to pay him anything, and the Court of Appeal held that the parties' agreement was void under the Gaming Act 1892 s.1. However, it formed part of the claimant's case that the defendant had not actually used all the money to place bets, and had used

---

[58] *Westdeutsche Landesbank Girozentrale v Islington LBC* [1996] A.C. 669 at 709–710 and 713–714, per Lord Browne-Wilkinson, at 718, per Lord Slynn, and at 738, per Lord Lloyd. A different view was taken at 688–689, per Lord Goff, and at 721, per Lord Woolf. For a careful analysis of their Lordships' reasoning, see *Haugesund Kommune v Depfa ACS Bank* [2010] EWCA Civ 579; [2011] 1 All E.R. 190 at [65]–[80], per Aikens L.J., who concluded, at [87], that "the majority of the House of Lords in [*Westdeutsche*] did depart from the decision in *Sinclair v Brougham* that a lender under a borrowing contract that is void because *ultra vires* the borrower, cannot recover the sum lent in a restitutionary claim at law."

[59] See paras 34–32—34–34.

[60] *Mohamed v Alaga & Co* [1998] 2 All E.R. 720; reversed in part [2000] 1 W.L.R. 1815 (CA). Cf. *Awwad v Geraghty & Co* [2001] Q.B. 570 (CA); *Westlaw Services Ltd v Boddy* [2010] EWCA Civ 929; [2011] P.N.L.R. 4; *Langsam v Beachcroft LLP* [2011] EWHC 1451 (Ch) at [252]–[253].

[61] *Boissevain* [1950] A.C. 327; above, para.2–22.

[62] *Alaga & Co* [2000] 1 W.L.R. 1815 at 1825 per Lord Bingham C.J.

[63] *Alaga & Co* [2000] 1 W.L.R. 1815 at 1827 per Robert Walker L.J.

[64] *Close v Wilson* [2011] EWCA Civ 5.

some of it for his own purposes instead. With regard to this part of the claim, Toulson L.J. held that[65]:

> "If part of [the money] was used by Mr. Wilson for his own purposes, Mr. Close would . . . be entitled to recover that sum under ordinary principles of restitution. It would be simply a case in which Mr. Wilson had used money outside the scope of the agreement under which it had been provided. The unenforceable nature of the agreement itself would be no bar to Mr. Close's restitutionary claim if the money was used for a purpose extraneous to the agreement. Mr. Close's claim would not amount to enforcement of the agreement. It would be for the recovery of money put by Mr. Wilson to his own use."

2–26   Another illustration of the court analysing a statutory provision to determine whether a restitutionary claim should succeed is the decision of the Supreme Court of Canada in *Deglman v Guaranty Trust Co of Canada*.[66] The claimant entered an oral agreement with his aunt under which she promised to leave him her house in her will and he promised to perform various personal services (running errands, taking her out on trips, etc). He performed the services but she did not leave him the house in her will, and the court held that their contract was unenforceable because it was not evidenced in writing as required by the Ontario Statute of Frauds 1950. Nevertheless he was entitled to recover the value of his services from her estate because the statute did "not touch the principle of restitution against what would otherwise be an unjust enrichment of the defendant at the expense of the plaintiff."[67]

2–27   Likewise in *Pavey & Matthews Pty Ltd v Paul*,[68] the High Court of Australia had to consider whether a New South Wales statute, under which a building contract was not enforceable by the builder against the other party to the contract unless the contract was "in writing signed by each of the parties or his agent in that behalf, and sufficiently describes the building work the subject of the contract," barred a restitutionary claim, in circumstances where the builder had completed the building in accordance with the terms of the oral contract. A majority of the court held that it did not, and granted the builder reasonable remuneration, which was, fortuitously, the sum which the defendant had orally promised to pay for the work requested by him. The intent of the legislature had to be gleaned from the bare language of the statute. This had been enacted so as to ensure that the other party could not be forced to comply with the terms of the contact, and it did embrace the situation where the other party requested and accepted the building work. The builder was not deprived of his common law right to recover fair and reasonable remuneration for work done and accepted, for the statute was not intended to penalise the builder beyond making the agreement unenforceable by him. The majority gave a further reason for their decision, namely, that dismissal of the builder's claims would be so draconian a result that it is difficult to suppose that the legislature intended it.[69]

---

[65] *Close* [2011] EWCA Civ 5 at [31].
[66] *Deglman v Guaranty Trust Co of Canada* [1954] 3 D.L.R. 785.
[67] *Deglman* [1954] 3 D.L.R. 785 at 788.
[68] *Pavey & Matthews Pty Ltd v Paul* (1987) 162 C.L.R. 221.
[69] For a fuller discussion of the reasons given by the High Court see D.J. Ibbetson, "Implied Contracts and Restitution" (1988) 8 O.J.L.S. 312.

On occasion the English courts have also been moved by such considerations. **2–28**
For example, in *Congresbury Motors Ltd v Anglo-Belge Finance Co Ltd*,[70] the
defendant had lent the claimant money to buy certain property. On the claimant's
instructions the defendant handed the money over to the vendor who conveyed
the title to the claimant. Contemporaneously a legal mortgage was executed in
the defendant's favour. Both the loan and the mortgage were declared to be
unenforceable under the Moneylenders Act 1927 s.6, since no proper memorandum had been executed. Nevertheless the Court of Appeal allowed the defendant's counterclaim, and held that it should be subrogated to the vendor's lien for
unpaid purchase money. The defendant was not attempting to enforce a contract
of repayment for money lent and the statute only required formalities for such a
contract. Nor was it decisive that the defendant must have known that the
contract of repayment was unenforceable. Nor did its acceptance of the invalid
legal mortgage mean that the valid lien had been waived, abandoned or superseded.[71]

The court considered that the facts were similar to those in *Thurstan v* **2–29**
Nottingham Permanent Benefit Building Society.[72] There the defendant had lent
money to the plaintiff, who was then an infant. On the infant's instructions part
of the loan was applied to the purchase of land; the vendor conveyed the land to
the infant and a legal mortgage was contemporaneously executed in the defendant's favour. Both the loan and the security were void under the Infants Relief
Act 1874. The claimant brought an action against the defendant, seeking a
declaration that the mortgage was void and claiming delivery of title deeds and
possession of the property. Both the Court of Appeal and the House of Lords
rejected the claim. The defendant should be subrogated to the vendor's lien for
unpaid purchase money. This did not conflict "with the legislation or its policy",[73] although the claim was without "ethical merits".[74]

However, in *Orakpo v Manson Investments Ltd*[75] the prospect of the defen- **2–30**
dant's unjust enrichment did not persuade the House of Lords to allow the
restitutionary claim. The court overruled *Congresbury Motors* and held that it
was improper to allow subrogation if the result was to enable the moneylender
"to escape from the consequences of his breach of the statute".[76] The Court of
Appeal, in the latter case, had paid "too little attention . . . to a consideration of
the construction of section 6 of the Act of 1927."[77] Its terms were manifestly
different from those of the Infants Relief Act 1874. The Moneylenders Act
rendered the loan unenforceable; the Infants Relief Act made the loan void. In
one case, the lender had a valid security; in the other, he had none. *Thurstan* was,

---

[70] *Congresbury Motors Ltd v Anglo-Belge Finance Co Ltd* [1971] Ch. 81. Cf. *Bradford Advance Co v Ayers* [1924] W.N. 152 (money advanced under a bill of sale void under Bills of Sale Act 1882 recoverable).
[71] *Congresbury Motors* [1971] Ch. 81, per curiam.
[72] *Thurstan v Nottingham Permanent Benefit Building Society* [1902] 1 Ch. 1 (CA); [1903] A.C. 6 (HL).
[73] *Congresbury Motors* [1971] Ch. 81 at 93, per curiam, commenting on *Thurstan*.
[74] *Congresbury Motors* [1971] Ch. 81 at 90, per curiam.
[75] *Orakpo v Manson Investments Ltd* [1978] A.C. 95. Cf. *Menaka v Lum Kum Chaum* [1977] 1 W.L.R. 267 (PC).
[76] *Orakpo* [1978] A.C. 95 at 111 per Lord Salmon.
[77] *Orakpo* [1978] A.C. 95 at 118 per Lord Keith of Kinkel.

therefore, "decided correctly".[78] But there can be no doubt that the policy of the Infants Relief Act is stronger than that of s.6 of the Moneylenders Act 1927; and it is for that reason that the lender "obtains nothing"[79] for his loan to an infant. Yet, as the law now stands, he can be subrogated to an unpaid vendor's lien while a moneylender who falls foul of s.6 cannot. This is a strange result.[80]

2–31   In *Boissevain*[81] the claimant sued on a contract of loan. But the principle which Lord Radcliffe formulated cannot be so limited. In *Dimond*[82] the facts were similar to those in *Orakpo*. A consumer credit agreement was improperly executed. Dimond's car was damaged in an accident caused by Lovell's negligence. Whilst her car was being repaired Dimond hired a replacement vehicle from a company which allowed Dimond credit on the hire charges until her claim for damages against Lovell was concluded. Under the agreement between Dimond and the company, the company was given the right to pursue claims, in her name. The House of Lords held that the company had provided Dimond with credit and that the agreement was a consumer credit agreement which had not been properly executed. Consequently it was unenforceable against Dimond. Since the agreement was unenforceable, Dimond had suffered no loss through obtaining the replacement vehicle. According to Lord Hoffmann, the company's subrogated claim against Lovell failed because "Parliament intended that ... subject to the enforcement powers of the court, the debtor should not have to pay. This meant that Parliament contemplated that he might be enriched". And in these circumstances it was not "open to the court to say that this consequence is unjust and should be reversed by a remedy at common law".[83]

3. JUDGMENTS AND COURT ORDERS

2–32   A court may order the unsuccessful party to a suit to pay money or transfer property to the successful party. In these circumstances the recipient's enrichment is justified by the court order, and so there is generally no prospect of the unsuccessful party recovering the benefit for as long as the order subsists. Thus, in *Marriot v Hampton*[84] the claimant paid for goods bought from the defendant, and the defendant then brought an action for payment of the price, alleging that he had not been paid. The claimant could not find the receipt he had been given following the first payment, and was ordered by the court to pay again. He then found the receipt and brought an action for money had and received to recover the second payment. The claimant was non-suited, Lord Kenyon C.J. stating that[85]:

---

[78] *Orakpo* [1978] A.C. 95 at 114–115 per Lord Edmund-Davies.
[79] *Orakpo* [1978] A.C. 95 at 110 per Lord Salmon.
[80] *Orakpo* [1978] A.C. 95 at 114 per Lord Edmund-Davies.
[81] *Boissevain* [1950] A.C. 327.
[82] *Dimond v Lovell* [2002] 1 A.C. 384; followed in *Wilson v First County Trust Ltd (No.2)* [2003] UKHL 40; [2004] 1 A.C. 816.
[83] *Dimond* [2002] 1 A.C. 384 at 398.
[84] *Marriot v Hampton* (1797) 7 T.R. 269; 101 E.R. 969; 2 Esp. 546; 170 E.R. 450. See too *Knibbs v Hall* (1794) 1 Esp. 84; 170 E.R. 287; *Brown v M'Kinally* (1795) 1 Esp. 279; 170 E.R. 356.
[85] *Marriot* (1797) 7 T.R. 269 at 269; 101 E.R. 969 at 969.

"If this action could be maintained I know not what cause of action could ever be at rest. After a recovery by process of law there must be an end of litigation, otherwise there would be no security for any person."

In the course of reaching his decision, Lord Kenyon distinguished *Moses v* **2–33** *Macferlan*.[86] There Moses endorsed four promissory notes to Macferlan for 30 shillings each. The parties agreed that Moses would not be liable for the payment of the notes, but in breach of this agreement Macferlan sued Moses on the notes in the Court of Conscience. In his defence, Moses tried to rely on the agreement, but the court held that it lacked the power to consider evidence of this and ordered Moses to pay. Moses paid the four notes and brought an action for money had and received in King's Bench where Lord Mansfield C.J. ordered restitution. In his Lordship's view:

"[T]he ground of this action [was] not, 'that the judgment was wrong' but, 'that, (for a reason which the now plaintiff could not avail himself of against that judgment,) the defendant ought not in justice to keep the money."[87]

But in *Marriot* Lord Kenyon held that this principle did not apply, ruling that[88]:

"[T]he plaintiff [in *Moses*] had been allowed to recover back money adjudged to the defendant in the Court of Conscience, not on the footing of the merits, but that from the nature of the jurisdiction of the Court below, the plaintiff could not avail himself of a legal defence: but in this case the present plaintiff, at the time the former action was brought, must have been possessed of that instrument upon which he now grounded his claims, and on which, had he relied, the present defendant could not have recovered against him."

In other cases the view was expressed that the decision in *Moses* was simply **2–34** wrong, suggesting that claims would never lie to recover money paid pursuant to a subsisting court order, whatever the reason why the claimant had failed to persuade the court in the original action to find in his favour.[89] In *Duke de Cadaval v Collins*,[90] however, the court departed from *Marriot* for another reason, namely that a distinction had to be drawn between judgments obtained in good faith and judgments obtained by fraud. The facts were that the claimant was arrested by the defendant on the false basis that he owed him money. He paid £500 to secure his release and then successfully recovered his payment in an action for money had and received. For Lord Denman C.J., the question was "is

---

[86] *Moses v Macferlan* (1760) 2 Burr. 1005; 97 E.R. 676.
[87] *Moses* at 2 Burr. 1009; 97 E.R. 680.
[88] *Marriot* (1797) 2 Esp. 546 at 548; 170 E.R. 450 at 451.
[89] *Phillips v Hunter* (1795) 2 H. Bl. 402 at 416; 126 E.R. 618 at 626 per Eyre C.J.: "Shall the same judgment create a duty for the recoveror, upon which he may have debt, and a duty against him, upon which an action for money had and received will lie? This goes beyond my comprehension. I believe that judgment did not satisfy Westminster Hall at the time; I never could subscribe to it; it seemed to me to unsettle foundations." In *Brisbane v Dacres* (1813) 5 Taunt. 143 at 160; 128 E.R. 641 at 649, Heath J. referred to these comments with approval although Lord Mansfield was sitting with him on the bench.
[90] *Duke de Cadaval v Collins* (1836) 4 Ad. & El. 858; 111 E.R. 1006.

it still the plaintiff's money? How is it shewn not to be so?", and he gave this answer[91]:

> "Why, by striving to give effect to a fraud. That is the finding of the jury: the arrest was fraudulent; and the money was parted with under the arrest, to get rid of the pressure. This case differs from all which have been cited as being otherwise decided: in none of those was the *bona fides* negatived, not even in *Marriott v Hampton* ... for, in default of evidence to the contrary, the party there might have believed the debt to be due. But here the jury find that the defendant did know that he had no claim."

2–35   Revisiting these cases three years later in *Wilson v Ray*, Lord Denman drew the same distinction[92]:

> "[The] principle established in *Marriott v Hampton* ... [is] that what a party recovers from another by legal process, without fraud, the loser shall never recover back by virtue of any facts which could have availed him in the former proceeding. Money so recovered was ... received to the use of the successful party by authority of law. If any error was committed in the former proceeding, still the plaintiff is estopped from proving it after failing to do so at that time. If this were otherwise, the rights of parties could never be finally settled by the most solemn proceeding; and verdicts and judgments might be rendered nugatory by evidence which, if produced at the proper season, might have received a complete answer. The *Duke de Cadaval's case* was not intended to be, nor is it, inconsistent with this doctrine. It turned on fraud and extortion practised by an abuse of *ex parte* legal process by one who knew that he had no right to the money he obtained."

2–36   The general rule, therefore, is that money paid pursuant to a court order is irrecoverable for as long as the order subsists, but there is an exception to this principle in cases where the order has been obtained by fraud[93]—a situation, it may be noted, in which the claimant may alternatively be entitled to recover compensatory damages for the tort of malicious abuse of process.[94]

2–37   The general rule has been extended to the situation where money is paid following the issue of proceedings which do not proceed to judgment,[95] and it applies to orders issued by a foreign court as well by the English courts. For example, in *Clydesdale Bank Ltd v Schröder & Co*[96] the claimants were mortgagees of a ship that was arrested in Chile when the defendants successfully brought proceedings before the Chilean court to assert a lien over the vessel in respect of money lent to the owners and master. To secure the release of the ship

---

[91] *Duke de Cadaval* at 4 Ad & El. 864–865; 111 E.R. 1010.

[92] *Wilson v Ray* (1839) 10 Ad. & El. 82 at 88–89; 113 E.R. 32 at 35–36.

[93] See too *Pitt v Coomes* (1835) 2 Ad. & El. 459; 111 E.R. 178; *De Medina v Grove* (1846) 10 Q.B. 152 at 171; 116 E.R. 59 at 68; *Ward & Co v Wallis* [1900] 1 K.B. 675.

[94] *Grainger v Hill* (1838) 4 Bing. N.C. 212; 132 E.R. 769; *Varawa v Howard Smith Co Ltd* (1911) 13 C.L.R. 35; *Metall und Rohstoff AG v Donaldson Lufkin & Jenrette Inc* [1990] 1 Q.B. 391 at 467–473 (CA).

[95] *Hamlet v Richardson* (1833) 9 Bing. 644; 131 E.R. 756; *Maskell v Horner* [1915] 3 K.B. 106 at 121–122; *Henderson v Folkestone Waterworks Co* (1885) 1 T.L.R. 329; *William Whiteley Ltd v R.* (1909) 101 L.T. 741; *Sargood Brothers v Commonwealth of Australia* (1910) 11 C.L.R. 258 at 301; *Woolwich* [1993] A.C. 70 at 165. In *Moore v Vestry of Fulham* [1895] 1 Q.B. 399 at 401–402, Lord Halsbury said that "when a person has had an opportunity of defending an action if he chose, but has thought proper to pay the money claimed by the action, the law will not allow him to try in a second action what he might have set up in the defence to the original action."

[96] *Clydesdale Bank Ltd v Schroder & Co* [1913] 2 K.B. 1.

the claimants paid the amount due under protest, and then sued to recover their payment in the English court. Their claim was rejected by Bray J., who stated that[97]:

> "It is quite clear on the authorities that if an action is brought in the English courts against a person and he pays the claim, he cannot afterwards recover the money back although he may have said that he only paid under protest and that he reserved all his rights. If he desires to prove that he is not liable to pay the money, he must defend the action which has been brought for the very purpose of deciding whether the money is payable or not. He cannot by paying under protest reserve his right to raise the question of his liability in some subsequent proceedings. . . . [There] is no difference in principle for this purpose between proceedings in a foreign court and proceedings in this country. . . . If a person is given an opportunity of contesting a claim in a court of law, whether in this country or abroad, and if instead of doing so he pays the claim under protest, he cannot afterwards recover back the money. In both cases the money has been paid under compulsion of law."

The rule that money paid pursuant to a court order is generally irrecoverable   **2–38** in an action for unjust enrichment applies even if there are good reasons for thinking that the court has made a mistake. The court has jurisdiction to decide wrongly as well as rightly,[98] and if it makes a mistake, then the mistake is conclusive between the parties unless and until it is corrected by an appellate court.[99] The unsuccessful party can appeal from the court's order, and if the appeal is successful then he will be entitled to recover the benefit that he transferred to the recipient.[100] But "once the time for appealing has elapsed, the respondent who was successful in the court below is entitled to regard the judgment in his favour as being final".[101]

This suggests that the judgment will continue to operate as a justifying factor   **2–39** as between the parties to the case even if it is later overruled in a separate case. However, in these circumstances the unsuccessful party might conceivably argue that he should be entitled to recover his money on the ground that it was paid under a "retrospective mistake of law" of the kind that was recognised by the House of Lords in *Kleinwort Benson v Lincoln CC*.[102] Disallowing recovery would mean that the unsuccessful party was treated differently from other payors who were not parties to the litigation, but who also paid money to a recipient in the belief that they were legally required to do so under the rule established by the case in which the claimant was ordered to pay. However, we consider that the principle of finality in litigation is sufficiently important to override this consideration. Support for this conclusion can be drawn from parts of Croom-Johnson J.'s judgment in *Sawyer v Window Brace Ltd*,[103] although that case was decided at a time when the bar against recovery on the ground of mistake of law was in place.[104]

---

[97] *Schroder* [1913] 2 K.B. 1 at 5.
[98] *Philips v Bury* (1694) Skin. 447 at 485; 90 E.R. 198 at 216.
[99] *Meyers v Casey* (1913) 17 C.L.R. 90 at 115.
[100] See Ch.26.
[101] *Norwich & Peterborough Building Society v Steed* [1991] 1 W.L.R. 449 at 454.
[102] *Kleinwort Benson v Lincoln CC* [1999] 2 A.C. 349, discussed at paras 9–71—9–94.
[103] *Sawyer v Window Brace Ltd* [1943] K.B. 32 at 35–36.
[104] See para.9–71.

2–40   Finally, note that the basic rule against recovery does not apply in cases where money is paid under a void judgment, for example because the court had no jurisdiction,[105] or because the correct procedure was not followed.[106]

4. NATURAL OBLIGATIONS

2–41   In *Moses*[107] Lord Mansfield said that an action for money had and received would not lie:

> "for money paid by the plaintiff, which is claimed of him as payable in point of honour and honesty, although it could not have been recovered from him by any course of law; as in payment of a debt barred by the Statute of Limitations, or contracted during his infancy, or to the extent of principal and legal interest on an usurious contract, or, for money fairly lost at play; because in all these cases, the defendant may retain it with a safe conscience, though by positive law he was barred from recovering."

This rule was applied in other 18th century cases. For example, in *Munt v Stokes*,[108] the plaintiff executors repaid a sum borrowed by the deceased during his lifetime, but then sued to recover their payment on the ground that the loan was void. Lord Kenyon C.J. denied recovery because the plaintiffs:

> "were bound both in honour and conscience to refund the money which the defendants had advanced, though the original contract were contrary to a positive law; for this is not a penalty, but money which the defendants had actually advanced; and the original contract was not *malum in se*, but *malum prohibitum.*"[109]

2–42   These cases stood as authority for the proposition that a defendant's enrichment might be justified, and restitution might therefore be precluded, where the claimant owed him a natural obligation, i.e. a legally unenforceable obligation that was binding on his conscience. This proposition effectively ceased to form part of the courts' thinking at the start of the 19th century following Lord Ellenborough's decision in *Bilbie v Lumley*[110] that payments made under a mistake of law should be irrecoverable. Payments made pursuant to a natural obligation could very often be characterised as payments made in the mistaken belief that the natural obligation was legally enforceable, in which case the mistake of law bar could explain why they were irrecoverable and there was no work left to do for the idea of natural obligations as a justifying ground. Following the abolition of the mistake of law bar in *Kleinwort Benson*,[111]

---

[105] *Newdigate v Davy* (1701) 1 Ld. Raym. 742; 91 E.R. 1397.
[106] *Farrow v Mayes* (1852) 18 Q.B. 516; 118 E.R. 195; *Gowan v Wright* (1886) 18 Q.B.D. 209; *Re Smith* (1888) 20 Q.B.D. 321.
[107] *Moses* (1760) 2 Burr. 1005 at 1012; 97 E.R. 677 at 681–682.
[108] *Munt v Stokes* (1792) 4 T.R. 561; 100 E.R. 1176. See too *Farmer v Arundel* (1772) 2 W. Bl. 824 at 825–826; 96 E.R. 485 at 486; *Bize v Dickason* (1786) 1 T.R. 285 at 286–287; 99 E.R. 1097 at 1098.
[109] *Munt* at 4 T.R. 563–564; 100 E.R. 1179.
[110] *Bilbie v Lumley* (1802) 2 East. 469; 102 E.R. 448.
[111] *Kleinwort Benson* [1999] 2 A.C. 349; see paras 9–71—9–94.

however, defendants may start once more to argue that recovery should be denied on the ground that the claimant acted pursuant to a natural obligation.

A recent example is provided by an Australian case, *Re Magarey Farlam* **2–43** *Lawyers Trust Accounts (No.3)*,[112] where the partners in a solicitors' firm refunded money to eight clients that had been stolen by an employee, mistakenly believing that this was the only money he had stolen. When they found out that in fact he had also stolen much larger sums, they could not recover their payments to the clients on the ground of mistake because the money had been "due in point of honour and conscience"[113]—although the judge went on to give several other reasons why no claim would lie, including that the partners had not paid the clients pursuant to a recoverable mistake, and (still more tellingly) that the clients were in fact legally entitled to be paid.

In the event that the English courts begin once again to recognise natural **2–44** obligations as a justifying ground, the question obviously arises which natural obligations should have this effect. Duncan Sheehan has suggested that a natural obligation should be treated as a justifying ground where the claimant has performed a promise that is legally unenforceable by reason of a rule that does not impugn the claimant's act in itself, and that exists to protect the claimant.[114] This would take in several of the situations identified by Lord Mansfield in *Moses*—payments made pursuant to gambling contracts, usurious contracts and contracts entered by minors—although none of these remains a good illustration of the principle, following changes in the law over the last 250 years.[115] More-over, as Sheehan recognises, his test does not take in another situation identified by Lord Mansfield, namely payments made pursuant to an obligation that has been extinguished by the passage of time. Unlike the others, this type of obligation is not void from the outset, but is initially valid, and only becomes unenforceable on the expiry of the relevant period. Furthermore, the effect of a lapsed limitation period is generally procedural rather than substantive under English law: the obligation continues to exist although it can no longer be sued upon.[116] However, we do not believe that it follows from this that "natural obligations" can never be a justifying ground distinct from contract.[117] Other

---

[112] *Re Magarey Farlam Lawyers Trust Accounts (No.3)* [2007] SASC 9; (2007) 96 S.A.S.R. 337. In Australia the mistake of law bar was abolished by *David Securities Pty Ltd v Commonwealth Bank of Australia* (1992) 175 C.L.R. 353.

[113] *Re Magarey* [2007] SASC 9; (2007) 96 S.A.S.R. 337 at [166].

[114] D. Sheehan, "Natural Obligations in English Law" [2004] L.M.C.L.Q. 170, p.185. See too M. McInnes, "Natural Obligations and Unjust Enrichment" in E. Bant and M. Harding (eds), *Exploring Private Law* (Cambridge: CUP, 2010), 175, pp.184–185.

[115] The repeal of the Usury Laws was achieved through a series of legislative measures culminating in the Usury Laws Repeal Act 1854. Gambling contracts are now legally enforceable under the Gambling Act 2005 s.335. Contracts with minors are discussed at paras 24–13—24–19.

[116] *Huber v Steiner* (1835) 2 Bing. N.C. 202; 132 E.R. 80; *Leroux v Brown* (1852) 12 C.B. 801; 138 E.R. 1119; *Phillips v Eyre* (1870) L.R. 6 Q.B. 1 at 29; *Black-Clawson International Ltd v Papier-werke Waldhof-Aschaffenberg AG* [1975] A.C. 591 at 630. The Limitation Act 1980 generally bars action on a claimant's subsisting rights, and these are extinguished only by a few sections: ss.3(2), 17, and 25(3).

[117] As contended in G. Virgo, "Demolishing the Pyramid: The Presence of Basis and Risk-Taking in the Law of Unjust Enrichment" in A. Robertson and H.W. Tang (eds), *The Goals of Private Law* (Oxford: Hart, 2009), 477, pp.498–500.

situations may yet be identified in which it is desirable to debar restitution because the claimant has performed a promise, pursuant to a general policy that people should honour their promises even if these are not supported by consideration or are otherwise legally unenforceable.[118]

---

[118] Cf. T. Krebs, *Restitution at the Crossroads: A Comparative Study* (London: Cavendish Publishing, 2001), pp.268–269. And consider the underlying facts of *Larner v LCC* [1949] 2 K.B. 683.

CHAPTER 3

JUSTIFYING GROUNDS: CONTRACTS

1. INTRODUCTION

A claim in unjust enrichment may be entirely excluded, deferred, or limited, by **3–01** the existence of a contract. The parties to the contract might be the same as the parties to the potential unjust enrichment action, or the contract might have been made between one (or both) of them and a third party.[1] What effect the contract will have on the unjust enrichment claim will depend on the terms of the contract, and also on whether it was legally enforceable, whether it is still in existence, and, if it is been terminated, how that termination came about.[2] The most common situation in which the existence of a contract has influenced liability in unjust enrichment is where the contract is between the parties to the unjust enrichment action, the contract has been breached, and the unjust enrichment claim is made on the ground that the basis for the transfer of a benefit under the contract has failed.[3] Much of this chapter is concerned with analysing cases of this kind. However, there is no reason to doubt that the principles developed in relation to failure of basis apply generally, whatever unjust factor is being relied upon. As will be seen, the extent to which the existence of a contract does (or should) affect claims in unjust enrichment ultimately turns on the wider question of the relationship between liability in contract and liability in unjust enrichment. The relationship has been, and continues to be, a problematic one.

2. UNJUST ENRICHMENT, QUASI-CONTRACT, AND CONTRACT

(a) *Quasi contract*

A clear analysis of the relationship between liability in contract and liability in **3–02** unjust enrichment was particularly difficult whilst the assumption persisted that liability in unjust enrichment was quasi-contractual. It followed from this assumption that express contractual liability should take precedence. Thus, no liability in unjust enrichment could exist unless the express contract had been rescinded ab initio.[4] Similarly, it was held that no liability in unjust enrichment

---

[1] For discussion of the effect of a contract between one of the parties to the unjust enrichment claim and a third party, see below para.3–58 and following.

[2] Where the contract has been frustrated, a special statutory scheme has replaced liability in unjust enrichment: see Ch.15.

[3] Failure of basis is discussed in Chs 12–14.

[4] *Chandler v Webster* [1904] 1 K.B. 493. See further, paras 3–17—3–18; also P. Birks and C. Mitchell, "Unjust Enrichment" in A. Burrows (ed), *English Private Law*, 2nd edn (Oxford: OUP, 2007), para.18.93.

was possible if express contractual liability could not have arisen on the same facts.[5] Fortunately this misunderstanding about the nature of liability in unjust enrichment has now been eliminated, but its prevalence, particularly during the 19th and early 20th centuries, means that judicial pronouncements on the issue from that period must be treated with caution.[6]

(b) *Loans of Money*

3–03   The influence of the quasi-contractual analysis was particularly powerful when applied to contracts for loans of money. Thus, in *Sinclair v Brougham (Sinclair)*[7] the House of Lords had to decide whether depositors could recover in full the sums they had deposited in bank accounts at the Birkbeck Building Society. The banking business was beyond the Society's statutory powers, and one ground on which the depositors claimed to be entitled to recovery was that, as a result of the banking business being ultra vires, the basis for making those deposits had failed. Their claim on this basis was dismissed, it being said that since an express promise by the Society to repay the funds held in the bank accounts would have been void, no such promise could be implied in quasi-contract.

3–04   Despite subsequent clarification of the nature of liability in unjust enrichment,[8] the conclusion of the House of Lords in *Sinclair*[9] was to prove surprisingly tenacious. In *Westdeutsche Landesbank Girozentrale v Islington LBC*,[10] Hobhouse J. held that the general principle of liability in unjust enrichment where the basis for a transfer has failed was:

> "[S]ubject to the requirement that the courts should not grant a remedy which amounts to the direct or indirect enforcement of a contract which the law requires to be treated as ineffective".[11]

This would be the case, he indicated, where the void contract purported to create a creditor and debtor relationship.[12] On the facts of the case, the contract was not a loan, and so the exception did not apply. In the Court of Appeal, Leggatt L.J. expressly endorsed Hobhouse J.'s analysis[13]; Dillon L.J. made no objection to it, and Kennedy L.J. agreed with both appellate judgments.[14] The appeal to the House of Lords was on grounds that did not concern the claim in unjust

---

[5] *Sinclair v Brougham* [1914] A.C. 398.
[6] The beginnings of a new approach in the mid-20th century can be seen by a comparison of P. Winfield, *The Law of Quasi-Contracts* (London: Sweet & Maxwell, 1952) with the first edition of this work: R. Goff and G. Jones, *The Law of Restitution* (London: Sweet & Maxwell, 1966). Winfield's division of the subject into categories including "pseudo-quasi-contracts", "pure quasi-contracts" and "doubtful quasi-contracts" (at p.26) indicates the analytical difficulties inherent in the quasi-contractual idea.
[7] *Sinclair v Brougham* [1914] A.C. 398.
[8] e.g. Lord Wright's speech in *Fibrosa Spolka Akcyjna v Fairbairn Lawson Combe Barbour Ltd* [1943] A.C. 32.
[9] *Sinclair* [1914] A.C. 398.
[10] *Westdeutsche Landesbank Girozentrale v Islington LBC* [1994] 4 All E.R. 890.
[11] *Westdeutsche* [1994] 4 All E.R. 890 at 929.
[12] *Westdeutsche* [1994] 4 All E.R. 890 at 930.
[13] *Westdeutsche* [1994] 4 All E.R. 890 at 967.
[14] *Westdeutsche* [1994] 4 All E.R. 890 at 971.

enrichment for failure of basis of the transfer.[15] Their Lordships, however, made some observations on the decision in *Sinclair* so far as it related to the claim for recovery on the ground of failure of basis. Lord Browne-Wilkinson described the reasoning used in *Sinclair* as "no longer sound", since it was now recognised that that "the common law restitutionary claim is based not on implied contract but on unjust enrichment".[16] The depositors in *Sinclair*, he continued, "should have had a personal claim to recover the moneys at law based on a total failure of consideration".[17] Lord Slynn and Lord Lloyd agreed with him. Lord Goff, by contrast, held that the decision in *Sinclair* should be seen as "a response to that problem in the case of ultra vires borrowing contracts", and that it should not be departed from since it might be supported on the ground of "public policy". In Lord Goff's view, giving a remedy where the ineffective contract had purported to create a relationship of creditor and debtor would not indirectly enforce that void contract:

> "[F]or such an action would be unaffected by any of the contractual terms governing the borrowing, and moreover would be subject (where appropriate) to any available restitutionary defences".[18]

Lord Woolf agreed with Lord Goff.

The position has now been further clarified by the Court of Appeal's decision **3–05** in *Haugesund Kommune v Depfa ACS Bank*.[19] There, on facts concerning loan contracts, it was held that the majority of the House of Lords in *Westdeutsche* had departed from the decision in *Sinclair*. A claim in unjust enrichment on the ground of failure of basis was, therefore, available.[20] The Court of Appeal agreed with Lord Goff that such a claim would not indirectly enforce a void contract, and also acknowledged that a claim might be defeated if recovery were found to be inconsistent with the policy of the statute rendering the parties' contract void. On the facts of the case, however, the statute governing the powers of the local authority in question neither expressly nor implicitly barred recovery.[21]

The Court of Appeal's approach in *Haugesund* has much to commend it. **3–06** Technically, it could have disregarded the House of Lords' remarks in the *Westdeutsche* case since they were unnecessary for the decision of the appeal, but, instead, the Court of Appeal seized the opportunity to clarify the law. The approach it took allows claims for unjust enrichment in respect of ineffective loan contracts to be dealt with under the same general principles as claims arising in respect of other types of ineffective contract. The main argument against that approach was based on the now discredited theory of quasi-contract. However, two points will require further clarification.

---

[15] *Westdeutsche* (HL) [1996] A.C. 669.
[16] *Westdeutsche* (HL) [1996] A.C. 669 at 710, noting statements to the same effect by the High Court of Australia in *Pavey & Matthews Pty Ltd v Paul* (1987) 162 C.L.R. 221 at 227 and 255. For discussion of the *Pavey* court's repudiation of implied contract as the basis of claims in unjust enrichment, see D.J. Ibbetson, "Implied Contracts and Restitution" (1988) 8 O.J.L.S. 312.
[17] *Westdeutsche* (HL) [1996] A.C. 669 at 710.
[18] *Westdeutsche* (HL) [1996] A.C. 669 at 688–689.
[19] *Haugesund Kommune v Depfa ACS Bank* [2010] EWCA Civ 579; [2011] 1 All E.R. 190.
[20] *Haugesund* [2010] EWCA Civ 579; [2011] 1 All E.R. 190 at [87].
[21] *Haugesund* [2010] EWCA Civ 579; [2011] 1 All E.R. 190 at [102]. The statute was the Norwegian Local Government Act 1992.

3-07 CHAPTER 3——JUSTIFYING GROUNDS: CONTRACTS

3–07   First, the Court of Appeal drew on Lord Goff's suggestion that a claim in unjust enrichment would not indirectly enforce the ineffective contract, because it "would be unaffected by any of the contractual terms governing the borrowing". Lord Goff was undoubtedly correct, to the extent that terms providing for a particular rate or type of interest would not be given effect in an unjust enrichment claim for the return of the principal sum. The rate and type of interest awarded would be a matter for the court, applying the relevant legal principles. However, as a matter of general principle, contractual terms relating to the possibility that the loan might be ultra vires should be given effect—otherwise the claim in unjust enrichment could be used for the illegitimate purpose of subverting the parties' allocation of risk.[22] Giving effect to such terms would not indirectly enforce the ineffective contract; rather, it would be an accurate reflection of the basis on which the loan was made.

3–08   Second, whilst the Court of Appeal's approach allows unjust enrichment claims relating to all ineffective contracts to be dealt with in a uniform way, the focus of analysis in ineffective loan cases will now turn to public policy. The extent to which statutory provisions may justify what would otherwise be unjust enrichments is discussed elsewhere,[23] but two brief comments can be made. As the Court of Appeal's analysis made clear, the role of public policy in unjust enrichment is underdeveloped, indeed, it is uncertain whether it even applies outside the statutory context.[24] Within the statutory context, the principle applies where allowing a claim would "circumvent legislation whose object and effect is to bar such a recovery".[25] If the statute expressly prohibits recovery, the principle is relatively simple to apply.[26] However, if the statute is silent, silence cannot be taken to signify that unjust enrichment claims are permitted. For instance, if at the time of enacting the statute it was not thought that a claim in unjust enrichment would lie, then it would not be surprising for the statute to make no reference to such claims. In such cases it will be difficult to say whether the object of the statute was to bar recovery, or merely to be consistent with whatever common law principles happened to be prevailing from time to time.

3–09   Before leaving this general topic, it should finally be noted that in *Sempra Metals Ltd v IRC*,[27] the House of Lords departed from the *Westdeutsche* case to hold that a common law claim lies in unjust enrichment to recover compound interest as the user value of money received by the defendant. In a line of earlier cases culminating in *Johnson v R.*,[28] the courts had previously set themselves against awarding compound interest on claims for money had and received, because they had understood these to be "quasi-contractual" and thus to be essentially contractual, so that they were caught by the rule in *London, Chatham and Dover Railway Co v South Eastern Railway Co*,[29] that formerly debarred the

---

[22] See para.3–15 and following.
[23] See paras 2–07—2–31.
[24] *Haugesund* [2010] EWCA Civ 579; [2011] 1 All E.R. 190 at [96].
[25] *Haugesund* [2010] EWCA Civ 579; [2011] 1 All E.R. 190 at [96].
[26] e.g. *Orphanos v Queen Mary College* [1985] 1 A.C. 761.
[27] *Sempra Metals Ltd v IRC* [2007] UKHL 34; [2008] A.C. 561; discussed at paras 5–05—5–14.
[28] *Johnson v R.* [1904] A.C. 817. See too *Walker v Constable* (1798) 1 Bos. & Pul. 306; 126 E.R. 919; *De Havilland v Bowerbank* (1807) 1 Camp. 50 at 52; 170 E.R. 872 at 874; *De Bernales v Fuller* (1810) 2 Camp. 426; 170 E.R. 1206; *Depcke v Munn* (1828) 3 Car. & P. 112; 172 E.R. 347; *Fruhling v Schroeder* (1835) 2 Bing. N.C. 77 at 79–80; 132 E.R. 31 at 33.
[29] *London, Chatham and Dover Railway Co v South Eastern Railway Co* [1893] A.C. 429.

award of compound interest in the form of damages for non-payment of a contractual debt. Reviewing these authorities, Lord Nicholls held that it is now "accepted law that a claim for restitutionary relief is not founded on a fictitious implied contract or 'quasi-contract'", and that this was "a false and misleading characterisation of the nature of claims for restitution as a remedy for unjust enrichment."[30] Now that the law of unjust enrichment had been "released from the shackles of implied contract and, hence, the restraints of the *London, Chatham and Dover Railway* case", it was possible to hold that the courts can make awards of compound interest "in the exercise of [their] common law restitutionary jurisdiction" where they are "necessary to achieve full restitution and, hence, a just result."[31]

3. CONTRACT AND UNJUST ENRICHMENT

(a) *Overview*

The current understanding of the relationship between contractual liability and unjust enrichment liability starts from the position that unjust enrichment is an independent category of obligations. However, it also acknowledges that, in certain circumstances, the principles of contractual liability require that the claim in unjust enrichment should be restricted. The circumstances where contractual principles have this effect are discussed below.[32] However, before turning to that detailed discussion, it is necessary to consider one relatively recent decision, where a more limited role for unjust enrichment liability appears to be suggested. **3–10**

In *Taylor v Motability Finance Ltd*[33] the claimant had been employed by the **3–11** defendant as its finance director, and was alleging that he had been wrongfully dismissed. Whilst in post, he had made great efforts to secure a highly beneficial settlement of an insurance claim, which had resulted in the company receiving a payment in excess of £80 million. He was paid the maximum amount possible under the defendant's bonus scheme. The claimant now claimed for 0.5 per cent of the £80 million, as representing the value of his services in obtaining the settlement, and argued that this was an entitlement which arose outside of his contract of employment. Cooke J. gave summary judgment against the claimant on this aspect of his claim, stating that[34]:

> "In the context of contract and restitution, it is clear that the parties, in agreeing a contract, intend that to apply and there is no room for restitution at all where there is full contractual performance by one party and, even on the Claimant's own case part performance by the other. Not only is it true to say that, historically, restitution has emerged as a remedy where there is no contract or no effective contract, but there is no room for a remedy outside the terms of the contract where what is done amounts to a

---

[30] *Sempra* [2007] UKHL 34; [2008] A.C. 561 at [107].
[31] *Sempra* [2007] UKHL 34; [2008] A.C. 561 at [112]–[113].
[32] See para.3–13 and following.
[33] *Taylor v Motability Finance Ltd* [2004] EWHC 2619 (Comm).
[34] *Taylor* [2004] EWHC 2619 (Comm) at [23].

breach of it where ordinary contractual remedies can apply and payment of damages is the secondary liability for which the contract provides."

3–12   The very broad terms of the reasoning quoted above are not supported by authority. The suggestion, in the final sentence quoted, that where there is a breach of contract, there is "no room" for a remedy other than damages, is incorrect—there are many authorities in which, following a breach of contract, a remedy in unjust enrichment has been given.[35] It is also incorrect to assert that an intention to exclude all remedies in unjust enrichment can be imputed to contracting parties. Certainly the parties might expressly exclude or limit remedies in unjust enrichment, or the terms of their contract may lead to the conclusion that a remedy in unjust enrichment has been displaced[36]; but those possibilities depend on the facts of the individual case, and cannot be automatically presumed. Finally, the point about the historical development of unjust enrichment in situations where there was no contract or no effective contract has worrying echoes of the quasi-contract fallacy. The fact that, under the influence of that fallacy, remedies in unjust enrichment were previously confined to such situations is hardly an argument for continuing those restrictions now that the quasi-contract fallacy has been exploded. In short, the current relationship between unjust enrichment and contractual liability is far more subtle and nuanced than Cooke J. was prepared to allow. As a matter of authority, *Taylor* can be supported on a narrower basis, which is hinted at later in the judgment,[37] namely, that if the claimant had been allowed to claim in unjust enrichment, it would have subverted the contractual allocation of risk. The claimant having performed services which were given a financial value in his contract of employment (through salary and the bonus scheme), it would have been inappropriate for the law of unjust enrichment to allow him to reopen the question of the value of those services.[38]

(b) Subsisting Contract

(i) Current Law

3–13   Where there is a contract between the parties relating to the benefit transferred, no claim in unjust enrichment will generally lie whilst the contract is subsisting.[39] Thus, in *Kwei Tek Chao v British Traders and Shippers Ltd*[40] the buyer of goods was unable to recover the price paid on the ground of failure of consideration

---

[35] e.g. *Rowland v Divall* [1923] 2 K.B. 500; *Warman v Southern Counties Car Finance Corp Ltd* [1949] 2 K.B. 576; *Butterworth v Kingsway Motors Ltd* [1954] 1 W.L.R. 1286; *Barber v NWS Bank Plc* [1996] 1 W.L.R. 641.

[36] See para.3–28 and following.

[37] *Taylor* [2004] EWHC 2619 (Comm) at [25].

[38] See further, para.3–40 and following.

[39] *Weston v Downes* (1778) 1 Doug. 23; 99 E.R. 19; *Towers v Barrett* (1786) 1 T.R. 133; 99 E.R. 1014; *Hulle v Heightman* (1802) 2 East. 145; 102 E.R. 324; *De Bernardy v Harding* (1853) 8 Exch. 822, 155 E.R. 1586; *Kwei Tek Chao v British Traders and Shippers Ltd* [1954] 2 Q.B. 459. For a critique of the rule see A. Tettenborn, "Subsisting Contracts and Failure of Consideration—A Little Scepticism" [2002] R.L.R. 1; for a proposal that the rule should be abolished see S. Smith, "Concurrent Liability in Contract and Unjust Enrichment: The Fundamental Breach Requirement" (1999) 115 L.Q.R. 245.

[40] *Kwei Tek Chao v British Traders and Shippers Ltd* [1954] 2 Q.B. 459.

because he had accepted the goods and affirmed the contract. Once the contract has come to an end for a reason other than frustration,[41] a claim in unjust enrichment may be available provided that the requirements for liability in unjust enrichment are satisfied.

(ii) *Historical Explanations for Subsisting Contract Rule*

Historically, two explanations were often given for the principle that a claim in unjust enrichment was not available if the contract remained open. The first was that the claim in unjust enrichment should not be overused. As Lord Mansfield C.J. remarked, "I am a great friend to the action for money had and received; and therefore I am not for stretching, lest I should endanger it".[42] The concern about overuse was particularly relevant in the late 18th century, when the full scope of the action was beginning to be explored,[43] and its lack of formal requirements made it an attractive alternative to a claim for breach of contract (where the contract had to be accurately pleaded). Today the action for money had and received is too well-established to be put at risk of extinction through overuse, and the pleading arguments do not apply.   **3–14**

The second explanation often used was that a remedy in unjust enrichment was a kind of implied contractual remedy, and, as such, could not be permitted where it differed from the remedy under an express contract. For instance, in *Steven v Bromley & Son* Scrutton L.J. observed that: **3–15**

> "It is a commonplace of the law that there can be no implied contract as to matters covered by an express contract until the express contract is displaced."[44]

Since it is now recognised that liability in unjust enrichment cannot be explained by reference to an implied contract, this kind of reasoning can no longer be supported. However, today the general principle is justifiable on a different basis, which emphasises the parties' own allocations of risk and valuations, as expressed in the contract.

(iii) *Contractual Allocation of Risk*

The general principle that no claim in unjust enrichment is permitted where a contract governing the benefit in question is still in force between the parties is today justifiable on the basis that the law should give effect to the parties' own allocations of risk and valuations, as expressed in the contract, and should not permit the law of unjust enrichment to be used to overturn those allocations or   **3–16**

---

[41] Law Reform (Frustrated Contracts) Act 1943 regulates the consequences of frustration. See Ch.15.

[42] *Weston v Downes* (1778) 1 Doug 23; 99 E.R. 19. See also *Longchamp v Kenny* (1779) 1 Doug. 137; 99 E.R. 91.

[43] *Moses v Macferlan* (1760) 2 Burr. 1005; 97 E.R. 676, considered in W. Swain, "*Moses v Macferlan* (1760)" in C. Mitchell and P. Mitchell (eds), *Landmark Cases in the Law of Restitution* (Oxford: Hart, 2006), p.19.

[44] *Steven v Bramley & Son* [1919] 2 K.B. 722 at 727. For further examples see *Stoomvaart Maatschappij Nederlandsche Lloyd v General Mercantile Co Ltd (The Olanda)* [1919] 2 K.B. 728n. at 730, per Lord Dunedin: "As regards *quantum meruit* where there are two parties who are under contract *quantum meruit* must be a new contract, and in order to have a new contract you must get rid of the old contract"; *Re Richmond Gate Property Co Ltd* [1965] 1 W.L.R. 335.

valuations.[45] The point can be illustrated by reference to *Re Richmond Gate Property Co Ltd*,[46] where the claimant had been employed by the company as its managing director. The company's articles provided that the managing director's remuneration was to be "such amount as the directors shall determine", but the company went into voluntary liquidation before any amount had been fixed. The claimant claimed £400 as the value of enriching services which, at the company's request, he had conferred on it. His claim failed. Plowman J. clearly regarded a claim in unjust enrichment as an inferior type of contractual claim, stating that:

> "Since there is an express contract with the company in regard to the payment of remuneration it seems to me that any question of *quantum meruit* is automatically excluded."[47]

Whilst that language would not be appropriate today (for reasons given above), the result can be supported in terms of risk allocation. The claimant took the risk of the directors fixing his remuneration at whatever level they chose, which might be above or below the market rate, and which included the risk that they might not fix it at all. If the claimant had been allowed to claim in unjust enrichment, that contractually allocated risk would have been subverted.

3–17   **(iv) The scope of the contractual allocation of risk**   If the underlying explanation for the principle that there is no claim in unjust enrichment where the contract is still subsisting, is that the contractual allocation of risk must be respected, an important consequence follows: claims in unjust enrichment should be permitted, even where a contract is still subsisting, if those claims do not undermine the contractual risks. For instance, a claim in unjust enrichment might yield a lower award than a claim for damages for breach of a subsisting contract, but might be preferred for procedural or evidential reasons. In principle, such a claim should be allowed.[48]

(iv) *Subsisting Contract: Earlier Authorities*

3–18   It is important to note that before the House of Lords' decision in *Fibrosa Spolka Akcynja v Fairbairn Lawson Combe Barbour Ltd*,[49] it was thought that no claim in unjust enrichment could lie unless the contract had been rescinded ab initio.[50] In other words, before 1942 it was necessary for the parties to be put back into the position they had occupied before the contract was entered into. This view no longer prevails; indeed, it has been recognised that where a contract is discharged for breach, the discharge operates only prospectively, leaving rights already

---

[45] E. McKendrick, "The Battle of Forms and the Law of Restitution" (1988) 8 O.J.L.S. 197, 202 and following; J. Beatson, "Restitution and Contract: Non-Cumul?" (2000) 1 *Theoretical Inquiries in Law* 83; Birks and Mitchell, "Unjust Enrichment" in Burrows (ed), *English Private Law*, para.18–93.
[46] *Re Richmond Gate Property Co Ltd* [1965] 1 W.L.R. 335.
[47] *Re Richmond Gate* [1965] 1 W.L.R. 335 at 337.
[48] Beatson, "Restitution and Contract: Non–Cumul?" at 93–94.
[49] *Fibrosa Spolka Akcyjna v Fairbairn Lawson Combe Barbour Ltd* [1943] A.C. 32.
[50] *Chandler v Webster* [1904] 1 K.B. 493; *Mussen v Van Diemen's Land Co* [1938] 1 Ch. 253. The rule can be traced back at least as far as *Dutch v Warren* (1721) 1 Str. 406; 93 E.R. 598, reported more fully by Mansfield C.J. in *Moses* (1760) 2 Burr. 1005 at 1010–1012; 97 E.R. 676 at 681.

accrued under the contract undisturbed.[51] The result is that unjust enrichment remedies are available in a wider variety of situations than was previously the case; it is also necessary to approach cases decided before 1942 with particular caution, because the courts were often concerned with the—now irrelevant —question of whether the parties could be put back to their original positions.

One such case, which was given some prominence in earlier editions of this **3–19** work, is *Hunt v Silk*.[52] There the parties agreed that in consideration of the claimant paying £10 to the defendant, the defendant would grant a lease of a house to the claimant within 10 days, and also effect certain repairs to the property. The claimant paid, and took possession immediately, but the repairs were never completed, and no lease was granted. Some days after the 10-day period had elapsed, the claimant left the house, and sought to recover back his earlier payment. His claim failed, because he had been in possession after the 10-day period expired, and this "intermediate occupation" (as it was described[53]) was not capable of being rescinded. If the same facts arose today, the courts would be likely to focus on whether the basis for the claimant's payment had failed—for instance, was the payment made, at least partly, in exchange for the initial period of 10 days occupation? There might also be issues to consider in relation to a possible affirmation of the contract by the claimant when he stayed on beyond the initial 10-day period. However, the decision in *Hunt v Silk* itself is concerned with requirements that are now obsolete.[54]

(v) *Availability of Unjust Enrichment Claim where Contract Subsisting?*

As explained above, where a contract is still subsisting, it is generally thought **3–20** that no remedy in respect of matters governed by the contract is available in unjust enrichment. However, in *Miles v Wakefield MDC*,[55] dicta of Lord Bright-man[56] and Lord Templeman[57] indicated that where an employee's industrial action took the form of offering partial performance, and the employer accepted that performance, the employee would be entitled to sue for the value of the services given. On the facts of the case, the claimant's employers had indicated that they refused to accept such services, so the point did not require decision; Lord Brandon and Lord Oliver reserved their opinion, and Lord Bridge indicated that he found it "difficult to understand the basis"[58] on which remuneration for

---

[51] *Johnson v Agnew* [1980] A.C. 367, discussed in C. Mitchell, "*Johnson v Agnew* (1979)" in Mitchell and Mitchell (eds), *Landmark Cases in the Law of Contract* (Oxford: Hart, 2008), at 351.

[52] *Hunt v Silk* (1804) 5 East 449; 102 E.R. 1142. See G. Jones, *Goff & Jones: The Law of Restitution*, 7th edn (London: Sweet & Maxwell, 2006), para.20–013.

[53] *Hunt v Silk* at 4 East 452; 102 E.R. 1145, per Lord Ellenborough C.J., and at 4 East 453; 102 E.R. 1145, per Lawrence J.

[54] For further analysis of *Hunt v Silk* see P. Mitchell, "Artificiality in Failure of Consideration" (2010) 29 *University of Queensland Law Journal* 191, at 193–196.

[55] *Miles v Wakefield MDC* [1987] 1 A.C. 539.

[56] *Miles v Wakefield* [1987] 1 A.C. 539 at 552–553.

[57] *Miles v Wakefield* [1987] 1 A.C. 539 at 561.

[58] *Miles v Wakefield* [1987] 1 A.C. 539 at 552.

services could be claimed. In Lord Bridge's view, recovery of the value of the services:

> "would presuppose that the original contract of employment had in some way been superseded by a new agreement by which the employee undertook to work as requested by the employer for remuneration in a reasonable sum",

which, he thought, was "contrary to the realities of the situation".

3–21   It may be possible to reconcile Lord Brightman and Lord Templeman's view with the general principle that a subsisting contract prevents a claim in unjust enrichment from arising by interpreting their remarks narrowly, so as to limit them to situations where the work offered differs significantly from the work required by the contract of employment. In such a situation it might be legitimately said that no exisiting contract governed the parties' relationship.[59] However, it must be doubtful whether Lord Brightman and Lord Templeman had such a narrow situation in mind: on the facts of the case they were considering, a superintendent registrar had peformed all of his duties except for conducting marriage ceremonies on Saturday mornings, and had been willing to attend his office on Saturday mornings to carry out other tasks. Had these services been accepted by his employer, it is difficult to see how the employee could be said to have been performing significantly different duties to those required by his contract of employment.

3–22   On the other hand, it is unlikely that Lord Brightman and Lord Templeman intended, with little discussion, to effect a major change in the relationship between the law of contract and the law of unjust enrichment, by relegating the existence of a contract governing the situation to a mere matter of "background" in the unjust enrichment claim.[60] The context of their dicta may well explain their true significance: the case concerned a long-running campaign of industrial action, and it may be that Lord Brightman and Lord Templeman had in mind a situation where parties affected by such a campaign had, temporarily, come to an informal understanding that would cause less damage to the employer's business than a strike, whilst being consistent with the employee's industrial action. In such circumstances, services would be offered and accepted on a different basis to the basis expressed in the contract, until the trade dispute was settled; once the dispute was settled, the ordinary contract of employment would resume. It would not, in such circumstances, be necessary to find, as Lord Bridge thought, that the original contract has been "superseded", merely that it had been temporarily suspended. The true significance of the dicta may be to highlight that deciding whether a subsisting contract governs the situation or not requires subtle and careful analysis. By contrast, where it is clear that the contract of employment continues to govern the relationship between the parties, it has been held that the dicta of Lord Brightman and Lord Templeman have no application.[61]

---

[59] G. Mead, "Restitution within Contract?" (1991) 11 L.S. 172.

[60] Cf. P. Sales, "Contract and Restitution in the Employment Relationship: No Work, No Pay" (1988) 8 O.J.L.S. 301, at 307: "there is no reason in principle why the existence of the contract of employment in the background should preclude the operation of the usual rules allowing recovery in restitution".

[61] *Spackman v London Metropolitan University* [2007] I.R.L.R. 744 at [56] (County Ct).

(c) *Where the Contract Has Been Discharged by Performance*

(i) *The General Rule*

Where a contract has been discharged by performance, there is generally no **3–23** remedy in unjust enrichment in respect of benefits transferred under that contract. Thus, in *Stoomvaart Maatschappij Nederlandsche Lloyd v General Mercantile Company Ltd (The Olanda)*[62] a charterparty provided for the ship to receive a full cargo of wheat, maize, rye or linseed or rape seed. Any wheat, maize or rye was to be paid for at 32s per ton; linseed and rape seed were to be paid for at 33s per ton. The charterparty provided that the cargo must be not more than 50 per cent linseed, but the cargo shipped in fact consisted of significantly more than 50 per cent of that product. The charterer paid for the quantity of linseed carried at 33s per ton. The shipowners, however, sought to recover in unjust enrichment, calculating the value of the benefit they had conferred by reference to the prevailing rate of freight for linseed (which was significantly higher than 33s per ton). The House of Lords rejected their claim, holding that both parties intended that the excess linseed should be carried at the price per ton specified in the charterparty. Whilst it might be questioned whether the owners really did have that intention (if they did, then the term requiring no more than 50 per cent linseed seems rather pointless), the decision provides an excellent illustration of why, in general, no claim in unjust enrichment can be brought in respect of contracts discharged by performance. Had the claim been allowed, it would have effectively allowed the owners to recover a higher price than the one by which they had agreed to be bound. The obvious explanation for the disparity between the agreed rate and the market rate was that the market had risen after the contract had been made. The owners had taken the risk of that rise, just as the charterers had taken the risk of a fall in the market. In other words, allowing the owners to recover at the prevailing market rate would have enabled them to avoid the consequences of a risk that they had agreed to bear.

A similar approach can be seen in *Taylor*.[63] There the claimant had worked as **3–24** the defendant's finance director until being dismissed. Whilst in post he had succeeded in bringing about the settlement of a £80 million insurance claim, as a result of which he received the maximum possible award under the company's bonus scheme. Following his dismissal, he sought to recover in unjust enrich-ment for the services he had given to obtain the settlement, valuing those services at £400,000. His claim was rejected, with Cooke J. commenting that:

> "[I]f it were otherwise, not only would the claimant be able to recover more than his contractual entitlement in respect of bonus, but he could also seek to establish that he was underpaid in terms of salary, despite his agreement thereto."[64]

As this reasoning highlights, when a price for services is agreed by contract in advance, the provider takes the risk of the services proving more valuable than expected, and the recipient of the services takes the risk of them being less

---

[62] *Stoomvaart Maatschappij Nederlandsche Lloyd v General Mercantile Co Ltd (The Olanda)* [1919] 2 K.B. 728n.
[63] *Taylor* [2004] EWHC 2619 (Comm).
[64] *Taylor* [2004] EWHC 2619 (Comm) at [25].

valuable. It is important that the law of unjust enrichment does not provide a means of subverting that allocation of risk.

(ii) *Exception to the General Rule*

3–25   In exceptional circumstances, it may be possible to show that the contract price was understood not to represent a definitive allocation of risk. Thus, in *Easat Antennas Ltd v Racal Defence Electronics Ltd*[65] the defendants were interested in tendering for a Ministry of Defence contract, and had approached the claimants to provide the antenna element that would be necessary for such a tender. The parties agreed that if the tender was successful, the defendants would place the sub-contract for the antennas required with the claimants, at a price "based upon Easat's quotation subject to demonstration that the prices are fair and reasonable".[66] The parties also agreed, separately, that a model of the proposed equipment should be produced, which could be shown to the Ministry. Under this separate agreement, the defendants were to pay half of the cost of the materials used in making the model, with the claimants bearing the remainder of the cost of the materials and all of the manufacturing costs. The model was duly made, and the defendants paid their agreed share. The defendants' tender succeeded, but they placed the sub-contract for antennas with one of the claimant's competitors. Hart J. held that the agreement to place the sub-contract with the claimants was void for uncertainty,[67] and that the claimants were entitled to recover the costs they had incurred on the project under a quantum meruit. The judge also held that the claimants were entitled to recover the costs of work done on the model, despite the fact that those were costs which it had agreed to absorb, and the contract had not been rescinded. "It was the common understanding", he said, "that the claimant would recover these [extra costs] from the sub-contract promised".[68] In this rather unusual situation it seems appropriate to permit a claim in unjust enrichment, because the contract has taken place in a context where it was understood that payment for the contractual services was not limited to the price specified in the agreement. There was, therefore, no undermining of the allocation of risk.

3–26   The decision of the High Court of Australia in *Roxborough v Rothmans of Pall Mall Australia*[69] has directly challenged the orthodoxy that no claim in unjust enrichment can arise in respect of a contract discharged by performance. There in a contract for the sale of cigarettes by a wholesaler to a retailer, the price had included a sum representing a tax liability to which the parties expected the recipient would be subject. The tax was subsequently held to be unconstitutional, but the wholesaler refused to return the payment. The High Court of Australia held that repayment should be made, despite the fact that the wholesaler had performed the valid contract in full. The decision has divided English commentators, with the point of dispute being whether the remedy in unjust enrichment undermines the contractual allocation of risk. Those who have criticised the

---

[65] *Easat Antennas Ltd v Racal Defence Electronics Ltd* Unreported Ch. D., June 21, 2000.
[66] *Easat Antennas* Unreported Ch. D., June 21, 2000 at [11].
[67] *Easat Antennas* Unreported Ch. D., June 21, 2000 at [43]–[44].
[68] *Easat Antennas* Unreported Ch. D., June 21, 2000 at [73].
[69] *Roxborough v Rothmans of Pall Mall Australia* [2001] HCA 68; (2001) 208 C.L.R. 516.

decision argue that the contract allocated the risk of the tax becoming unconstitutional to the retailer, because it made no provision for the payment to be returned.[70] On the other hand, it has been argued that because the amount paid for tax was fixed from the outset, and was not the product of any negotiation between the parties, it was no subversion of the contract to allow that sum to be recovered in unjust enrichment.[71] On balance, the former view is more convincing. Whilst it is quite true that the parties had not negotiated about the sum payable in respect of the licence fee, and the unjust enrichment remedy coincided with the value that the parties had agreed, the fact remains that, by requiring its repayment in the absence of any contractual term, the court reallocated the risk to the wholesaler.

(d) Exclusion of Unjust Enrichment Claim by Contract

A contract may expressly exclude or limit a claim for unjust enrichment. Any **3–27** such exclusion must satisfy three requirements before it will be given effect. First, it must be incorporated into the contract. Second, it must, on proper construction, apply to the claim being brought.[72] Third, it must not fall foul of the Unfair Contract Terms Act 1977, or the Unfair Terms in Consumer Contracts Regulations 1999.[73] A detailed account of these requirements can be found in specialist works on the law of contract.[74] It should be noted that, under the Regulations, a list of examples of presumptively unfair terms is given in Sch.2. That list includes terms:

> "[I]nappropriately excluding or limiting the legal rights of the consumer *vis-à-vis* the seller or supplier or another party in the event of total or partial non-performance or inadequate performance by the seller or supplier of any of the contractual obligations."[75]

An attempt to exclude a consumer's claim in unjust enrichment where the price has been paid in advance, but no counter-performance has been received, clearly falls within this description. It must, therefore, be doubtful whether such a term could be enforceable.

---

[70] J. Beatson and G. Virgo, "Contract, Unjust Enrichment and Unconscionability" (2002) 118 L.Q.R. 352, pp.355–356.

[71] P Birks, "Failure of Consideration and its Place on the Map" (2002) 2 O.U.C.L.J. 1, p.5.

[72] In *Dhanani v Crasnianski* [2011] EWHC 926 (Comm) at [126] it was said that "clear words" would be needed to exclude a claim in unjust enrichment.

[73] Cf. *Swotbooks.com Ltd v Royal Bank of Scotland Plc* [2011] EWHC 2025 (QB) at [55], where the judge found that there were provisions in the contract "which would, on their face, prevent the claimant recovering from the [defendant]"; however the defendant elected not to rely on the provisions at trial when the claimant pleaded that they did not meet the requirement of reasonableness under s.3 of the Unfair Contract Terms Act 1977, and the defendant could not "elect not to rely on contract terms and then simply assert that recovery by the claimant which would be prohibited by those terms would be unjust."

[74] H. Beale (ed.), *Chitty on Contracts*, 30th edn (London: Sweet & Maxwell, 2008), Chs 14–15.

[75] Unfair Terms in Consumer Contracts Regulations 1999 (SI 1999/2083) Sch.2 para.1(b).

(e) Displacement of Unjust Enrichment Claim by Contractual Provisions

(i) The General Rule

3–28   If the parties to a contract have made express or implied provision for the return of payments where the basis for those payments has failed, the contractual remedy excludes a remedy in unjust enrichment.[76] In *Pan Ocean Shipping Co Ltd v Creditcorp Ltd (The Trident Beauty)*[77] the time charterer of a vessel had paid an instalment of hire in advance (as required by the charterparty) to the defendants, to whom the right to receive the hire had been assigned by the disponent owners as part of a financing arrangement. The vessel was off-hire for the entire period, and the claimants sought to recover their payment from the defendants. The charter provided for the disponent owners to repay any overpaid hire immediately, and Lord Goff (with whom Lord Lowry agreed) commented that, since there was a contractual regime which legislated for the overpaid hire:

> "[T]he law of restitution has no part to play in the matter; the existence of the agreed regime renders the imposition by the law of a remedy in restitution both unnecessary and inappropriate."[78]

Lord Woolf (with whom Lord Slynn and Lord Keith agreed) preferred to emphasise that the assignee was never intended to be under an obligation to supply the vessel, and could not, therefore, be made liable to return a payment when the vessel was not supplied. His speech is perhaps best interpreted as meaning that the basis of the payment to the assignee was understood by both the charterer and assignee to be unconditional (with any recourse lying against the disponent owners). Whilst, on the facts of the case, the unjust enrichment remedy against the disponent owners was identical to the express contractual remedy against them, and could therefore be said to be "unnecessary", other situations can easily be imagined where contractual rights to recover benefits are limited, or, indeed, nonexistent. These situations raise the question as to what Lord Goff meant by his comment that a remedy in unjust enrichment would be "inappropriate". The most likely interpretation is that he was referring to the potential for a remedy in unjust enrichment to undermine the parties' contractual allocation of risk. If so, Lord Goff's reasoning would extend beyond express or implied contractual provisions for the return of benefits, to situations where it can be inferred from the parties' agreement that no claim in unjust enrichment should be available.

(ii) Implicit Displacement of Unjust Enrichment by Entire Obligations

3–29   The terms of the contract between the parties will frequently provide for payment to be due only once specified conditions are satisfied. Where the conditions for payment are not satisfied, a party who has done work, or incurred expense in some other way in a failed attempt to complete the contractual performance, is

---

[76] On the importance of construing the contract terms, see G. McMeel, "Unjust Enrichment, Discharge for Breach, and the Primacy of Contract" in A. Burrows and Lord Rodger (eds), *Mapping the Law* (Oxford: OUP, 2006), 223.

[77] *Pan Ocean Shipping Co Ltd v Creditcorp Ltd (The Trident Beauty)* [1994] 1 W.L.R. 161.

[78] *The Trident Beauty* [1994] 1 W.L.R. 161 at 164.

not permitted to have recourse to a claim in unjust enrichment for the value of that work or expense. For instance, in *Cutter v Powell*[79] the captain of a ship promised to pay the claimant's husband 30 guineas if he would serve as second mate on a voyage from Kingston, Jamaica to Liverpool, which typically took two months. The mate served on board the ship, but died three weeks before it reached its destination. There was evidence before the court that the standard wages for a second mate were £4 per month. The mate's widow's claim for her husband's work and labour (which we would now recognise as a claim in unjust enrichment) was disallowed, the Court of King's Bench giving particular emphasis to the wording of the contract, and the fact that the total promised for completion of the voyage was so much larger than the standard wage. In effect the mate was seen as having promised to receive either 30 guineas or nothing; his widow was not entitled to "desert the agreement"[80] by having recourse to a claim in unjust enrichment.[81] Alternatively, it could be said that the contractual terms defined the basis on which the services were provided: only if the condition of payment was satisfied, but the defendant failed to pay, could it be said that the basis of the transaction had failed.[82]

Similarly, in *Sumpter v Hedges*[83] the claimant contracted to build two houses   **3–30** and some stables on the defendant's land for £565. After completing part of the work, he abandoned the project, and the defendant completed the buildings himself. The Court of Appeal held that no claim could lie for the value of the work completed by the claimant. Although the Court of Appeal's reasoning is typical of its time in focusing on whether a new contract to pay for the partially complete buildings could be inferred from the facts, the result of the case would not be different if modern principles of unjust enrichment were applied.[84] Leaving aside the issue of enrichment,[85] the builder's claim does not satisfy the requirements for liability. Either it could be said that the provisions for payment are "a species of contracting out" of liability in unjust enrichment,[86] or, the basis on which he did the work was that he was to be paid once it was finished, and that basis has not been met.[87]

---

[79] *Cutter v Powell* (1795) 6 T.R. 320; 101 E.R. 573. See further J. Barton, "Contract and *Quantum Meruit*: The Antecedents of *Cutter v Powell*" (1987) 8 J.L.H. 48.

[80] *Cutter v Powell* at 6 T.R. 325, 101 E.R. 577, per Ashhurst J.

[81] The facts of *Cutter v Powell* would be dealt with today under the Law Reform (Frustrated Contracts) Act 1943, discussed in Ch.15. On the ability of the parties to exclude the legislation by contract see s.2(3), discussed at paras 15–51—15–57.

[82] R. Stevens and B. McFarlane, "In Defence of *Sumpter v Hedges*" (2002) 118 L.Q.R. 569, 576–577.

[83] *Sumpter v Hedges* [1898] 1 Q.B. 673. See also *Munro v Butt* (1858) 8 E. & B. 738; 120 E.R. 275.

[84] *Cleveland Bridge UK Ltd v Multiplex Constructions (UK) Ltd* [2010] EWCA Civ 139 at [135]–[138], per May L.J.

[85] See para.4–32, fn.73.

[86] *Cleveland Bridge* [2010] EWCA Civ 139 at [133], per May L.J., summarising the successful submissions of counsel. Express language seems not to be needed in order to exclude claims in unjust enrichment: McMeel, "Unjust Enrichment, Discharge for Breach and the Primacy of Contract" in Burrows and Rodger, *Mapping the Law*, pp.236–237.

[87] Stevens and McFarlane, "In Defence of *Sumpter v Hedges*", whose argument that no unjust factor can be identified is confirmed by *Cleveland Bridge* [2010] EWCA Civ 139 at [127], where the only unjust factor that counsel could identify was that "the value of the benefit conferred is out of all proportion to the loss . . . suffered". This is not a recognised ground for recovery.

3–31   **Late completion of contractual performance**   By contrast, where the contract provides for work to be completed by a specified time, and the work is completed late, it seems that a claim for unjust enrichment is available. In *Burn v Miller*[88] a landlord agreed with his tenant, that the tenant would build a tap-room within two months of the date of the agreement, pursuant to a plan to be agreed between the parties; at the end of the tenant's lease, the landlord would pay the value of the new room. No plan was agreed, but the tenant built a tap-room, which he took four months to complete. At some point after the end of the second month, the landlord encouraged the tenant to continue with work on a room above the tap-room. On these facts, the court held that the tenant was entitled to recover the value of the work done, observing that:

> "[T]here are many contracts made with relation to time, upon which, although the works are not finished when the time is expired, the work and labour or other beneficial matter may nevertheless be recovered for."[89]

It may be possible to regard this statement as a dictum, since the tap-room as built did not conform to any agreed plan,[90] and it may also be possible to interpret the landlord's encouragement to the tenant as redefining the basis of the arrangement.[91] The Court of Common Pleas, however, clearly regarded the point about late performance as a general principle.

3–32   If the court's view is accepted, then the different treatment of incomplete and late performance is not easy to explain, as it could be said, in both situations, that the sole basis on which the defendant agreed to pay for the work was set out in the contract.[92] However, the distinction may be explained by analogy with the rules governing the enforceability of express exclusion clauses.[93] Where the claimant has received what he bargained for under the contract, albeit later than expected, it would not generally be reasonable to regard the contractual provisions as to time of performance as having implicitly displaced any remedy in unjust enrichment. Of course, if it is shown that the contractual performance was so time-sensitive that late performance is of little or no value, it may then be reasonable to regard the contractual provisions as to time of performance as having implicitly displaced an unjust enrichment claim in respect of late performance. Where work has been done under a contract imposing conditions as to both time and complete performance before payment is due, and the work is both late and incomplete, no claim in unjust enrichment is available.[94]

3–33   **Deviation in a contract for carriage by sea**   Where, under a contract for carriage by sea, the ship has deviated from the agreed route, any deviation

---

[88] *Burn v Miller* (1813) 4 Taunt. 745; 128 E.R. 523.
[89] *Burn v Miller* at 4 Taunt. 748; 128 E.R. 526.
[90] The decision on the facts might have to be explained as a case of free acceptance. See Ch.17.
[91] See the cautious approach to this case taken by Barton, "Contract and *Quantum Meruit*: The Antecedents of *Cutter v Powell*", p.59.
[92] Cf. *British Steel Corp v Cleveland Bridge Engineering Co Ltd* [1984] 1 All E.R. 504, discussed at paras 16–04—16–05, where non-contractual specifications as to time of delivery were not held to be part of the basis for payment.
[93] See above, para.3–27.
[94] *Munro v Butt* (1858) 8 E. & B. 738; 120 E.R. 275.

amounts to a repudiatory breach of contract,[95] which may be accepted by the innocent party. The contractual obligation to pay freight is usually conditional on the successful completion of the contracted voyage.[96] Since the contracted voyage has not been performed, the contractual right to freight has not been earned, and the question arises whether there is liability in unjust enrichment. If the voyage is only partly completed, there would appear, applying the general principles set out above, to be no liability in unjust enrichment. Where, however, the voyage has been completed before the charterer becomes aware of the deviation, the charterer is still entitled to terminate the contract for a repudiatory breach, and—since the voyage was not as specified in the contract—the contractual right to freight has not been earned. Whether the shipowner may bring a claim in unjust enrichment for the value of the benefit conferred on the charterer is not absolutely clear. However, in *Hain Steamship Co Ltd v Tate & Lyle Ltd*[97] the House of Lords tentatively endorsed the view that a claim would be available. As Lord Wright M.R. commented, the contrary view would have "startling consequences", as it would mean that, if there had been even a very minor deviation, a charterer would be entitled to receive the benefits of a successful voyage without being liable to pay.[98]

(f) *Whether a Benefit Falls within the Contract*

Since contractual provisions governing payment for a benefit will implicitly displace a claim for unjust enrichment in respect of that benefit, careful analysis may be needed in order to ascertain whether the benefit in question falls within the contract. For instance, in *Harrison v James*[99] the claimant had agreed to take the defendant's son as an apprentice on the following terms. There would be an initial trial period of one month; if at the conclusion of that month both parties were satisfied, the son was to become the claimant's apprentice for four years, with the defendant paying £40 on execution of the indenture of apprenticeship, and £20 in each of the following three years. The son went to work in the defendant's shop in August 1859, and remained there until December 1860. No indenture was ever executed. The defendant's claim for the value of board and lodging he had provided during this period was rejected, with Pollock C.B. commenting that "the parties meant nothing more than the extension of the month's trial."[100] Since it had been agreed that no payment should be made for the month's trial, it followed that none could be demanded for the extended trial period either. The decision is best interpreted as an example of contractual terms being varied by conduct so as to displace any possible claim in unjust enrichment.

3–34

---

[95] *Joseph Thorley Ltd v Orchis Steamship Co Ltd* [1907] 1 K.B. 660; *Hain Steamship Co Ltd v Tate & Lyle Ltd* [1936] 2 All E.R. 597.

[96] e.g. *Hopper v Burness* (1876) 1 C.P.D. 137.

[97] *Hain Steamship Co Ltd v Tate & Lyle Ltd* [1936] 2 All E.R. 597.

[98] *Hain Steamship* [1936] 2 All E.R. 597 at 612. See further Stevens and McFarlane, "In Defence of *Sumpter v Hedges*", pp.592–594 (arguing that the obligation not to deviate should not be seen as a condition precedent to the right to claim the contract freight).

[99] *Harrison v James* (1862) 7 H. & N. 804; 158 E.R. 693.

[100] *Harrison v James* at 7 H. & N. 808; 158 E.R. 695. See also per Wilde B. at 7 H. & N. 809; 158 E.R. 696.

4. Breach of Contract and Unjust Enrichment

3–35　　The fact that a party has committed a breach of contract does not deprive him of the right to claim in unjust enrichment. This holds true even where the claimant has committed a repudiatory breach, which has led to the contract being terminated.[101] For instance, in *Palmer v Temple*[102] a part payment was made under an agreement to grant a lease. The payer subsequently repudiated the agreement, and successfully recovered the payment. Lord Denman C.J. explained the decision in terms that made clear that it rested on failure of basis, saying that:

> "[T]he very idea of payment falls to the ground when both [parties] have treated the bargain as at an end; and from that moment the vender holds the money advanced to the use of the purchaser."[103]

3–36　　Similarly, in *Dies v British and International Mining and Finance Corp Ltd* (*Dies*)[104] the claimant had contracted to purchase rifles and ammunition for £270,000, of which £100,000 was paid in advance. He subsequently refused to take delivery of any of the goods or to make further payment. The sellers accepted the breach, thereby putting an end to the contract. Stable J. held that the buyer could recover the advance payment (subject to any damages for breach of contract), and rejected the argument that the buyer's breach ruled out a claim in unjust enrichment. In his view, because the contract had not identified the part payment as being an earnest, or deposit, the payment fell under the "general rule . . . that the law confers on the purchaser the right to recover his money".[105] The obvious foundation of such a right was that the basis for making the advance payment had failed, but Stable J., rather confusingly, went on to assert that:

> "[T]he foundation of the right . . . is not a total failure of consideration. There was no failure of consideration, total or partial. It was not the consideration that failed but the party to the contract."[106]

No foundation for the right was identified, other than that it was a "principle of law".[107]

3–37　　This analysis was unfortunate, since it seems to have been based on a confusion between "consideration" in the contractual sense, and "consideration"

---

[101] *Palmer v Temple* (1839) 9 Ad. & E. 508; 112 E.R. 1304; *Mayson v Clouet* [1924] A.C. 980; *Dies v British and International Mining and Finance Corp Ltd* [1939] 1 K.B. 724; *Hyundai Shipbuilding & Heavy Industries Co Ltd v Pournaras* [1978] 2 Lloyd's Rep. 502 at 507–508; *Hyundai Heavy Industries Co Ltd v Papadopoulos* [1980] 1 W.L.R 1129; *Rover International Ltd v Cannon Film Sales Ltd* [1989] 1 W.L.R 912 at 928–932, per Kerr L.J., and 935–937, per Dillon L.J. See too P. Birks, "Restitution after Ineffective Contracts: Issues for the 1990s" (1990) 2 J.C.L. 227, at p.233. And cf. *Cuff v Brown* (1818) 5 Price 297 at 302; 146 E.R. 613, 616 ("not fair" for party in breach to recover); *Warman v Southern Counties Car Finance Corp Ltd* [1949] 2 K.B. 576 at 582 (citing no authority).
[102] *Palmer v Temple* (1839) 9 Ad. & E. 508; 112 E.R. 1304.
[103] *Palmer v Temple* at 9 Ad. & E. 520–521; 112 E.R. 1310. For discussion of why the payment in question was not a deposit, despite being described as such in the contract, see para.14–05.
[104] *Dies v British and International Mining and Finance Corp Ltd* [1939] 1 K.B. 724.
[105] *Dies* [1939] 1 K.B. 724 at 743.
[106] *Dies* [1939] 1 K.B. 724 at 744.
[107] *Dies* [1939] 1 K.B. 724 at 744.

in the unjust enrichment sense[108]: for the purposes of the law of unjust enrichment, it *was* a failure of consideration for the claimant to pay money in advance and receive no counter-performance. That failure of consideration (or failure of basis) provides the foundation for the right to recover the payment. It was also unfortunate that, despite being referred to the decision in *Palmer v Temple*, and setting out the judgment in its entirety,[109] Stable J. referred to that decision only for assistance in ascertaining whether the payment in question was a deposit or a part payment. He did not draw on what Denman C.J. had said about the basis of liability for returning that payment. Part of the explanation for the difficulty that Stable J. experienced may lie in underlying ideas about unjust enrichment that were prevalent at the time of his decision, in particular that a claim in unjust enrichment could not arise unless any governing contract had been rescinded ab initio.[110] That assumption would soon be corrected,[111] but it may have hindered Stable J. in his attempts to articulate the basis of his decision.[112] Once the confusion created by the misleading terminology is removed, the decision in *Dies* can be seen as an orthodox application of the failure of basis principle.[113]

Although the decision in *Dies* was doubted by the Court of Appeal in *Hyundai* **3–38** *Shipbuilding & Heavy Industries Co Ltd v Pournaras*,[114] it was distinguished, without being overruled, by the House of Lords in *Hyundai Heavy Industries Co Ltd v Papadopoulos*.[115] Unfortunately there was no clarification in that later case that *Dies* should be seen as resting on failure of basis.[116] However, in *Rover International Ltd v Cannon Film Sales Ltd*,[117] the Court of Appeal applied the decision in *Dies* to a claim for unjust enrichment by a party whose repudiatory breach had brought the contract to an end. The statement of Dillon L.J. that the crucial question was whether the claimant in unjust enrichment "had received any of the consideration"[118] under the agreement is particularly helpful in showing that failure of consideration (or failure of basis, as we would prefer to express it), is the ground for recovery.

The availability of a claim in unjust enrichment to a party in breach of contract **3–39** depends, as it does for claims by the innocent party, on the contract having been terminated.[119] Since the power to terminate for breach lies with the innocent party, it follows that the innocent party has the ability to suppress a claim for unjust enrichment by his contracting partner: if the innocent party continues to

---

[108] See para.12–10 and following.

[109] *Dies* [1939] 1 K.B. 724 at 740–742.

[110] See above, para.3–18.

[111] *Fibrosa Spolka* [1943] A.C. 32.

[112] J. Beatson, "Discharge for Breach: The Position of Instalments, Deposits and Other Payments Before Completion" (1981) 97 L.Q.R. 389, p.403, fn.86.

[113] See also the criticism of the language used in *Dies* by Birks, "Restitution After Ineffective Contracts: Issues for the 1990s", p.234.

[114] *Hyundai Shipbuilding & Heavy Industries Co Ltd v Pournaras* [1978] 2 Lloyd's Rep. 502 at 507–508, per Roskill L.J.

[115] *Hyundai Shipbuilding & Heavy Industries Co Ltd v Papadopoulos* [1980] 1 W.L.R. 1129.

[116] Beatson, "Discharge for Breach: The Position of Instalments, Deposits and Other Payments Before Completion", pp.401–405.

[117] *Rover International Ltd v Cannon Film Sales Ltd* [1989] 1 W.L.R. 912, noted by J. Beatson, "Restitutionary Remedies for Void and Ineffective Contracts" and Birks, "Restitution After Ineffective Contracts: Issues for the 1990s".

[118] *Rover International* [1989] 1 W.L.R. 912 at 936.

[119] See para.3–13 and following.

affirm the contract, and press for performance, the contract continues in exis- tence, and the precondition for a claim in unjust enrichment does not arise. Andrew Tettenborn has highlighted that this rule has the potential to create injustice where a buyer under an instalment contract finds himself unable to raise the funds needed to complete the purchase, since, by continuing to affirm the contract, the seller could prevent him recovering back his payments.[120] One possible solution to this potential injustice would be for the courts to draw on the principles that prevent a contracting party from insisting on rendering unwanted performance so as to satisfy the conditions for payment under the contract.[121] Unwanted affirmation of a contract seems to have similar underlying policy features.[122] Thus, if it was "wholly unreasonable" for the innocent party to continue to affirm the contract, the court could hold that the contract had been terminated, thereby permitting a claim in unjust enrichment for instalments paid. However, it should be noted that, if the court did intervene in this way, it would be going beyond the principles governing situations where a party insists on rendering unwanted performance. Under those principles, the innocent party is not forced to accept the other party's breach; he is merely prevented from claiming for debt rather than claiming in damages.[123]

5. CONTRACTUAL VALUATION OF BENEFITS CONFERRED

3–40 Where a claim for unjust enrichment arises out of a contractual arrangement, the price agreed for the benefit to be transferred will often be useful evidence of the value of the benefit.[124] However, whether the contractual terms regarding pay- ment can have a further role, in fixing the amount of recovery in unjust enrich- ment is far more controversial. It is necessary to distinguish between void and valid contracts, and between attempts to limit the claim in three different ways. First, to the full contract price, second to a pro-rated contract price, and third, to the contractual payment that would have been earned on the facts of the case.

(a) *Void Contracts*

3–41 In *Rover International*[125] the defendant's predecessor, EMI, agreed to a joint venture with an Italian film distributor for the dubbing and distribution of

---

[120] Tettenborn, "Subsisting Contracts and a Failure of Consideration—A Little Scepticism", pp.2–3.

[121] *White and Carter (Councils) Ltd v McGregor* [1962] A.C. 413 at 431, per Lord Reid; *Clea Shipping Corp v Bulk Oil International Ltd (The Alaskan Trader)* [1984] 1 All E.R. 129.

[122] McMeel "Unjust Enrichment, Discharge for Breach and the Primacy of Contract" in Burrows and Rodger, *Mapping the Law*, pp.237–238.

[123] *The Alaskan Trader* [1984] 1 All E.R. 129 at 137. P. Birks, *An Introduction to the Law of Restitution*, revised edn (Oxford: OUP, 1989), p.236, fn.48, seems to be expressed too broadly when it states that "the innocent party cannot keep the contract open unless he has a 'legitimate interest' in doing so."

[124] *Renard Constructions (ME) Pty Ltd v Minister for Public Works* (1992) 26 N.S.W.L.R. 234 at 278; *Sopov v Kane Constructions Pty Ltd (No.2)* [2009] VSCA 141; (2009) 257 A.L.R. 182 at [24]–[30].

[125] *Rover International* [1989] 1 W.L.R. 912, noted by J. Beatson, "Restitutionary Remedies for Void and Ineffective Contracts", P. Birks, "Restitution After Ineffective Contracts: Issues for the 1990s".

seventeen films belonging to EMI. The parties agreed that a new company, Rover, should be created to carry out the dubbing and distribution work and to make payments due to EMI. The contractual arrangements were made between EMI and this new company. Rover was to bear the initial costs of dubbing and distribution, recouping them out of the gross receipts from distributing the films. Once those expenses had been recouped, the gross receipts were to be shared with EMI. EMI was to determine release dates. Unfortunately, at the date of the agreement, Rover had not yet been incorporated, with the result that the intended contract was void. Before the parties realised that the agreement was void, various steps were taken to perform it, including the distribution by Rover of one film in advance of the date approved for distribution by the defendants. EMI terminated the agreement for this breach, and also sought to rely on the fact that the contract was void. Rover sought to recover the repayment of advances it had paid to EMI after it had been incorporated, and also to recover for its dubbing and distribution expenses.

The defendants argued that recovery should be subject to a "ceiling" of: **3–42**

"[T]he maximum which Rover could have recovered under the agreement if this had been valid, bearing in mind . . . that it would in any event have been lawfully terminated by Cannon".[126]

On the facts, this would have been a very small amount, as very little had been earned in gross receipts at the date that the agreement was terminated. The Court of Appeal rejected the imposition of such a ceiling. Kerr L.J. gave both pragmatic and principled reasons. The pragmatic reasons were that it was unfair for the defendant to rely on the invalidity of the agreement and simultaneously try to limit the claimant's claim to what would have been recovered if it had been valid. The reason of principle was that the contract and unjust enrichment claims should be kept separate.[127] Dillon L.J. agreed, stating that the ceiling argument involved "a confusion of ideas",[128] it being irrelevant what the contractual position would have been if the agreement had been valid. Nicholls L.J. agreed with both judgments.

It is important to note two features of the situation in the *Rover International* **3–43** case, which limit its application. First, that the agreement was void. Although some of the language used by the judges, particularly Kerr L.J., might suggest that a similar approach would apply to valid contracts,[129] different considerations apply.[130] Second, that the ceiling argued for was not what the claimants could have expected to receive following full performance of the contract, but was limited to what the provisions of the agreement would have allowed the claimants to earn up to the date that they breached the supposed contract. Where the proposed limit is either the total price that would have been paid under the contract, or a portion of that price pro-rated to the quantity of work carried out,

---

[126] *Rover International* [1989] 1 W.L.R. 912 at 923.
[127] *Rover International* [1989] 1 W.L.R. 912 at 927.
[128] *Rover International* [1989] 1 W.L.R. 912 at 936.
[129] J. Beatson, "Restitutionary Remedies for Void and Ineffective Contracts", p.181.
[130] See para.3–44 and following.

a different analysis is required, although that is not to say that a limit will be imposed in all situations.[131]

(b) *Valid Contracts Where the Proposed Ceiling is the Damages Award for Breach of Contract*

3–44   Where a valid contract is terminated for breach, a party to the contract who brings an action in unjust enrichment will not have his claim limited to the amount that he can prove he would have recovered had he brought an action for damages for breach of contract. The leading case is *Lodder v Slowey*,[132] in which the Privy Council approved a quantum meruit award made by the Court of Appeal of New Zealand,[133] in circumstances where the claimant had offered no evidence that, had he been allowed to complete performance, he would have made a profit.

3–45   Although the reasoning used by the Court of Appeal of New Zealand might be open to question today, since it seems to assume that a contract terminated for breach is rescinded ab initio,[134] the result in the case can clearly be supported on general principles. The law of unjust enrichment is independent of the law of contract, and there is no reason why the different bases on which liability arises should yield the same outcome. Unlike the situation when damages for breach of contract might be formulated in terms of expectation or reliance loss,[135] there is no compelling policy reason why a claimant in such circumstances should not be able to avail himself of the law of unjust enrichment in order to escape from a bad bargain.

(c) *Valid Contracts Where the Proposed Ceiling is the Total Contract Price*

(i) *Commonwealth Authorities*

3–46   There is no English authority on whether the full contract price serves as a limit on recovery in unjust enrichment where a valid contract has been terminated for breach. In Australia, where the issue has been considered in several cases,[136] a consensus has emerged that the award in an action for unjust enrichment should not be limited by the full contract price. Thus, in *Renard Constructions (ME) Pty Ltd v Minister for Public Works*[137] the New South Wales Court of Appeal held that an attempt to limit liability in unjust enrichment to the contract price would be contrary to authority, citing *Lodder v Slowey*,[138] *Boomer*

---

[131] See paras 3–51—3–56.
[132] *Lodder v Slowey* [1904] A.C. 442.
[133] (1901) 20 N.Z.L.R. 321.
[134] See in particular Williams J.'s comments at 358. See too E. McKendrick, "The Battle of Forms and the Law of Restitution" (1988) 8 O.J.L.S. 197, 206 fn.43.
[135] *C&P Haulage Ltd v Middleton* [1983] 1 W.L.R. 1461; *CCC Films (London) Ltd v Impact Quadrant Films Ltd* [1985] 1 Q.B. 16.
[136] *Renard Constructions* (1992) 26 N.S.W.L.R. 234; *Iezzi Constructions Pty Ltd v Watkins Pacific (Qld) Pty Ltd* [1995] 2 Qd R. 350; *Sopov* [2009] VSCA 141; (2009) 257 A.L.R. 182.
[137] *Renard Constructions* (1992) 26 N.S.W.L.R. 234.
[138] *Lodder v Slowey* [1904] A.C. 442.

v Muir,[139] *Re Montgomery's Estate*,[140] and *United States v Zara Contracting Co.*[141] The nature of the remedies for breach of contract and for quantum meruit were different, and it followed, therefore, that it was quite likely that the awards made in respect of each would also be different. There was nothing "anomalous" about the award being higher on a quantum meruit than the total contract price, because there was no rule of law that the contractually agreed remuneration was the greatest possible remuneration available.[142]

The analysis in *Renard Constructions* has proved highly influential in Aus-   **3-47**
tralia,[143] but a cautious approach must be taken to its claims to be supported by authority. *Lodder v Slowey*,[144] as explained above, concerned an attempt to limit recovery in unjust enrichment to the amount recoverable in an action for damages for breach of contract; it was not concerned with an attempt to limit damages to the total contract price. *Boomer v Muir*[145] and *Zara Contracting*[146] both concerned attempts to limit recovery in unjust enrichment to a pro-rated part of the contract price. As we shall see, limitation to a pro-rated part of the contract price involves very different considerations to attempts to limit recovery to the full contract price.[147] It is true that in *Re Montgomery's Estate*[148] a claim was allowed in unjust enrichment which exceeded the total contract price agreed for the services. However, that case was a very unusual one, in which a client had exercised her right to discharge her attorney for no good reason, and to employ a different one. The court described the client as having "voluntarily canceled"[149] the contract, and saw no reason why the attorney should be bound by its terms. However, the court also held that, where a contract is terminated involuntarily, for instance by reason of the death or disability of the attorney, the contract price would impose a limit.[150] *Re Montgomery's Estate*, therefore, stands for a more complicated proposition about the relationship between the contract price and claims in unjust enrichment than its treatment in *Renard Constructions* would suggest.

A further reason for caution in assessing the analysis in *Renard Constructions*   **3-48**
is that, as Meagher J.A. acknowledged, in several of the authorities on which he relied, courts based their reasoning on the assumption that once a contract had been terminated for breach, it was rescinded ab initio. Thus, for instance, in *Boomer v Muir*, it was said that "A rescinded contract ceases to exist for all purposes".[151] As a matter of current English law, this assumption is incorrect.[152] Although Meagher J.A. stated that the American courts' reasoning "still remains

---

[139] *Boomer v Muir* 24 P. 2d 570 (1933).
[140] *Re Montgomery's Estate* 6 N.E. 2d 40 (1936).
[141] *United States v Zara Contracting Co* 146 F. 2d 606 (1944).
[142] *Renard Constructions* (1992) 26 N.S.W.L.R. 234 at 276–278, per Meagher J.A.
[143] See paras 3–49—3–50.
[144] *Lodder v Slowey* [1904] A.C. 442.
[145] *Boomer v Muir* 24 P. 2d 570 (1933).
[146] *Zara Contracting* 146 F. 2d 606 (1944).
[147] See paras 3–55—3–56.
[148] *Re Montgomery's Estate* 6 N.E. 2d 40 (1936).
[149] *Re Montgomery's Estate* 6 N.E. 2d 40 (1936) at 41.
[150] *Re Montgomery's Estate* 6 N.E. 2d 40 (1936) at 41. See also the dissenting judgment of Lehman J. at 42.
[151] *Boomer v Muir* 24 P. 2d 570 at 577 (1933).
[152] *Johnson v Agnew* [1980] A.C. 367.

unimpaired" despite their position on rescission,[153] the assumption that rescission for breach operates ab initio was an absolutely fundamental part of the courts' analysis, and must cast considerable doubt on its potential application in England today.

3-49   The Court of Appeal of Queensland applied the reasoning from *Renard Constructions* in *Iezzi Constructions Pty Ltd v Watkins Pacific (Qld) Pty Ltd*.[154] There, a contract between a subcontractor and main contractor stated that the subcontractor was only to be paid once the main contractor had "already actually received" payment from the proprietor in respect of the subcontractor's work. The subcontractor had completed a very large amount of work, and had received some payment, but the proprietor then went into liquidation and the main contractor refused to make any further payments to the subcontractor. A majority of the court held that the term in the subcontract applied only to progress payments, but the court went on to hold, unanimously, that, had the term applied to final payment for the work, it would not have affected a quantum meruit claim. Significantly, the court saw the question in terms of whether the parties intended that the term was to continue to govern their relationship after termination of the contract.[155] Concluding that there was no such intention, the court indicated that it would be inappropriate to give effect to the term indirectly, by introducing a limitation to the quantum meruit claim. As can be seen from the facts of the decision, it was not concerned with an attempt to recover an amount in unjust enrichment that exceeded the contract price. Rather, the case concerned an attempt to limit recovery by reference to contractual terms governing how the price was to be paid.

3-50   The most recent consideration of the issue, by the Court of Appeal of Victoria in *Sopov v Kane Constructions Pty Ltd (No.2)*,[156] reluctantly endorsed the approach taken in these two earlier cases. The Court took the view that a quantum meruit claim should not be available as an alternative to damages for breach of contract, and that the decision in *Lodder v Slowey* was based on the misunderstanding that termination for breach had the effect of rescinding the contract ab initio. However, the current position was so well entrenched that only the High Court of Australia could alter it.[157] The court also rejected the approach that had been taken by the trial judge, Warren C.J., where she had held that remedies in unjust enrichment should not be permitted to subvert the contractual bargain. In the Court of Appeal's view, the remedy in unjust enrichment was only possible because of the "fiction of the contract's having ceased to exist ab initio"[158]; it therefore followed that, if there was a claim, it could not be limited by the contract price.

(ii) *General Principle*

3-51   As the brief survey of authorities above demonstrates, the cases show a variety of conflicting approaches to the issue. Since the point remains open in England,

---

[153] *Renard Constructions* (1992) 26 N.S.W.L.R. 234 at 277, per Meagher J.A.
[154] *Iezzi Constructions Pty Ltd v Watkins Pacific (Qld) Pty Ltd* [1995] 2 Qd R. 350.
[155] See particularly *Iezzi Constructions* [1995] 2 Qd R. 350 at 361, per McPherson J.A.
[156] *Sopov v Kane Constructions Pty Ltd (No.2)* [2009] VSCA 141; (2009) 257 A.L.R. 182.
[157] *Sopov* [2009] VSCA 141; (2009) 257 A.L.R. 182 at [12].
[158] *Sopov* [2009] VSCA 141; (2009) 257 A.L.R. 182 at [21].

an approach based on general principle would seem to be the most convincing solution. Three fundamental points must inform this solution. First, the law of unjust enrichment is independent of the law of contract, and is not, therefore, automatically constrained by contractual provisions.[159] Second, the claim in unjust enrichment following termination for breach of contract is brought on the ground of failure of basis. Unfortunately none of the recent Australian cases identified which unjust factor was involved, referring to the claim as being in quantum meruit. Third, it is recognised that the law of unjust enrichment should not undermine the parties' allocations of risk.[160] This proposition does not reflect inappropriate deference to the law of contract; rather, it flows from the fact that the claim in unjust enrichment is grounded on failure of basis, and the (contractual) dealings between the parties indicate the basis on which the benefit was to be retained by the recipient.

Sometimes the point that the law of unjust enrichment should respect the **3–52** parties' allocation of risk is expressed in terms of the exclusion of remedies in unjust enrichment.[161] Thus, if the parties have agreed that, should the contract fail, any claim in unjust enrichment should be limited to the contract price, the parties' contractual agreement is respected.[162] It may well be possible to go further, and, similarly to the approach in relation to part performance of entire contractual obligations,[163] to regard the contractual stipulation regarding price as implicitly excluding a different valuation from being put on the benefit conferred in a claim in unjust enrichment.[164]

Alternatively, and more straightforwardly, the analysis can be undertaken by **3–53** express reference to the general principle that the law of unjust enrichment should respect the contracting parties' allocation of risk. As explained above, this is not indirectly to enforce the terms of a contract that has been terminated; rather, it is a reflection of the fact that the ground of recovery is failure of basis, and the parties have agreed what the basis of the transfer is to be. The contract price implicitly allocates certain risks to the supplier of the goods or services, such as the risk that the market value of the goods or services will increase before performance, and the risk that the goods or services prove to be more costly to supply than the supplier had anticipated. Allowing a supplier bringing an action in unjust enrichment to recover more than the contract price for any goods or services supplied under the contract would clearly reallocate those risks to the purchaser. In our view, this approach, which was essentially the approach adopted by Warren C.J. in *Sopov*, is the most convincing as a matter of principle.

---

[159] G. Palmer, "The Contract Price as a Limit on Restitution for Defendant's Breach" (1959) 20 Ohio State L.J. 264, 274–275; K. Barker, "Unjust Enrichment: Containing the Beast" (1995) 15 O.J.L.S. 457, pp.460–462; P. Birks "Failure of Consideration" in F. Rose (ed.), *Consensus Ad Idem* (London: Sweet & Maxwell, 1996), 179, p.188, fn.29.

[160] See above, para.3–16.

[161] See above, para.3–30.

[162] Barker, "Unjust Enrichment: Containing the Beast", 462. See also, in the context of the Law Reform (Frustrated Contracts) Act 1943 s.1(3), the example given in *BP Exploration Co (Libya) Ltd v Hunt (No.2)* [1979] 1 W.L.R. 783 at 806, of a poor householder agreeing with a builder for work to be done at a price below the market rate: Robert Goff J. held that liability would be limited to the contract price.

[163] See above, paras 3–29—3–30.

[164] Cf. *Iezzi Constructions* [1995] 2 Qd R. 350 at 361, per MacPherson J.A.

In a case like *Iezzi Constructions*,[165] for instance, if the contract term had applied to final payments, a careful analysis of the basis on which the benefit of the work was to be retained by the main contractor would have indicated that the risk of the proprietor's default was to be borne by the subcontractor. In other words, when the main contractor refused to pay because the proprietor had gone into liquidation, there was no failure of the agreed basis on which the benefit of the subcontractor's work was to be retained by the main contractor.

(iii) *Allocation of Risk in Void Contracts*

3–54   The above analysis applies most obviously to the allocation of risk effected by valid contracts that are subsequently terminated. Whether the same analysis should be applied to void contracts is a more difficult question. On the one hand it could be said that the agreement, being void, has failed effectively to allocate any risks. On the other hand, the terms of the ineffective contract show the basis on which benefits were to be conferred, part of which includes the price that the defendant was prepared to pay for the benefits that were conferred on him. The point is finely balanced, but it would seem that the underlying principle of failure of basis—which has never required the basis to be expressed in terms of a contractual obligation[166]—points to the use of the parties' agreement, even though it could never have been given effect under the law of contract.

(iv) *Prorated Contract Price*

3–55   Although, as explained above, the total contract price should act as a limit on recovery in an action in unjust enrichment, it does not follow, where only part performance has been rendered by the defendant, that recovery in unjust enrichment is limited to a divisible or prorated part of the price. Whilst it is legitimate to infer from the contract that the claimant has agreed to accept no more than the agreed price for the goods or services in question, he has not agreed to accept no more than a proportionate part of the price for a proportionate part of the performance. In particular, as George Palmer has pointed out, it is likely that the price per unit in a contract is strongly influenced by the volume of units contracted for.[167] It may well also be the case, particularly in construction contracts, that, although the price is expressed in equal instalments, some parts of the work are more onerous than others. If the claimant has carried out the more demanding parts of the contract, a claim in unjust enrichment that was limited to the extent of the contractual payments due would not adequately reflect the benefit that had been conferred on the defendant.[168]

3–56   Thus, in *Boomer v Muir*,[169] the defendant had subcontracted the construction of a dam to the claimant on terms that the claimant was to be paid according to

---

[165] *Iezzi Constructions* [1995] 2 Qd R. 350. The facts of the case are given above at para.3–49.

[166] See paras 12–12—12–13.

[167] See generally Palmer, "The Contract Price as a Limit on Restitution for Defendant's Breach", particularly at p.276.

[168] *Zara Contracting* 146 F. 2d 606 (1944). See also *Taylor v Laird* (1856) 25 L.J. Ex. 329 at 331, per Pollock C.B., highlighting that the value of work done each month by an agricultural labourer fluctuates depending on the time of year. Cf. *Lodder v Slowey* (1901) 20 N.Z.L.R. 321; [1904] A.C. 442, where the claim in unjust enrichment was calculated using the contractual rates (see (1901) 20 N.Z.L.R. 321 at 356).

[169] *Boomer v Muir* 24 P. 2d 570 (1933).

a schedule of unit prices. The defendant breached the contract by failing to perform his obligation to supply materials as rapidly as they were needed. The claimant terminated the contract, leaving the job incomplete. The claimant then recovered the value of the work he had done, which was assessed as far in excess of the price as calculated by reference to the contract schedule. Although some of the court's broader assertions are difficult to support, the result can be supported on the narrower ground, expressed by the court, that "the payments are received as satisfaction only on condition that the entire contract be performed according to its own terms". In other words, the basis of the transfer of benefit was solely that the completed dam would be paid for at the contract prices; it did not follow that, where the dam was only partly completed, only the price as calculated by reference to the contract schedule should be payable.

(v) *Possible Relevance of Breach*

A more complex approach, supported by some United States jurisdictions and by Ewan McKendrick, is to impose the contract price as a ceiling where services have been performed under a contract valid at the time of performance, unless the claim is being brought against a party who has breached the contract.[170] McKendrick argues that the exception for claims brought against the party in breach is to reflect the fact that: **3–57**

> "[B]y breaking the contract, [the defendant] had demonstrated that he was not prepared to comply with the terms of the contract so he could not confine the innocent party to the terms of that contract".

This approach, however, is not without difficulty. Not all breaches demonstrate that a party is "not prepared to comply" with the terms of the contract; even repudiatory breaches may easily be the result of oversight, or simply a failed attempt to comply with the contractual terms.[171] Indeed, a repudiatory breach may be a response to a mistaken belief that the other party has committed a breach entitling the other to terminate.[172] It would be necessary, therefore, to distinguish between different kinds of breaches and also to inquire into the defendant's motive for breaching. At a broader level, it is not clear that an exception for claims against a party in breach would be consistent with the wider scheme of liability for unjust enrichment on the ground of failure of basis. As explained above, a party in breach of contract may bring an action in unjust enrichment[173]—such a party is not denied the right to claim despite the fact that, by breaching the contract, he has shown himself unwilling to comply with the basis of the transaction.

---

[170] E. McKendrick, "The Battle of Forms and the Law of Restitution", 205–206.
[171] e.g. *Arcos Ltd v EA Ronaasen & Son* [1933] A.C. 470; *Bunge Corp v Tradax Export SA* [1981] 1 W.L.R. 711.
[172] e.g. *Woodar Investment Development Ltd v Wimpey Construction UK Ltd* [1980] 1 W.L.R. 277; Palmer, "Contract Price as a Limit on Restitution for Defendant's Breach", p.268.
[173] See para.3–35 and following.

6. Contract and Unjust Enrichment in Multi-Party Cases

(a) *Overview*

3-58 The foregoing discussion has concerned the impact of contractual dealings between the parties in cases where there are only two parties, the claimant and the defendant. A similar, but more complex, set of considerations also arises in multi-party cases. There are many possible permutations. For example, a defendant, D, may be enriched at the expense of a claimant, C, through the intermediation of a third party, X, and D may be entitled to receive the benefit under a contract between C and D. Or a defendant, D, may be directly enriched by a claimant, C, and D may be entitled to receive the benefit under a contract that C and/or D has entered with a third party, X. Or it may be that a claimant, C, was obliged to enrich a defendant, D, under a contract between C and a third party, X, to which contract D may or may not have been a party. Or it may be that a defendant, D, was entitled to receive a benefit from a claimant, C, under a contract between D and a third party, X, to which C may or may not have been a party.

3-59 Recent cases make it clear that a contract between C and X, and a contract between D and X, may have just as significant an impact on C's claim in unjust enrichment against D as a contract between C and D.[174] However, the circumstances in which such contracts will debar or limit the claim, and the reasons why they should have this effect, are under-examined in the cases and the literature. This section briefly surveys the field, examining in turn: contracts between C and D, contracts between C and X, and contracts between D and X. The easiest cases are those in which there is only one contract between all three parties; less easy are those in which there is one contract between two parties and not the third; also difficult are those in which there are several contracts between different parties whose terms may or may not interlock. Moreover, it seems that when disentangling complex three-party cases of this kind, the courts must be alive to the whole of the parties' dealings with one another, so that a decision by the parties that two of them *should not* contract with one another may have just as great significance as a decision that two of them *should* form a contract, to the court's assessment of the way in which they have chosen to configure their legal relations.[175]

(b) *Contract between the Claimant and a Defendant*

3-60 There are many three-party cases, where D is enriched at C's expense through the intermediation of a third party, X, and where D's claim may be barred by a contract between C and D which provides that D is entitled to the benefit. Although these cases involve three parties, the fact that C and D have contracted directly with one another means that the impact of the contract on the claim can

---

[174] *The Trident Beauty* [1994] 1 W.L.R. 161 (HL) at 166; *Lumbers v W. Cook Builders Pty Ltd (In Liquidation)* [2008] HCA 27; (2008) 232 C.L.R. 635; *Yew Sang Hong Ltd v Hong Kong Housing Authority* [2008] HKCA 109; *Costello v MacDonald* [2011] EWCA Civ 930.
[175] *Costello* [2011] EWCA Civ 930 at [21], per Etherton L.J.

and should be resolved in accordance with the principles which have already been discussed in this chapter.

To give a common example, suppose that C has a contractual obligation to pay **3–61** money or provide services to D, and that C decides to perform this obligation by paying X to make the payment or provide the services on C's behalf. In one sense, this is a three-party case, since D's enrichment is immediately gained at X's expense, and remotely gained at C's expense. Nevertheless, if C brings a claim in unjust enrichment against D, to recover the value of the benefit received from C via X, then an answer to D's claim can often be found by applying the principles governing two-party cases. If the contract between C and D provided that D was entitled to the benefit, then the claim will often be debarred in line with the principles discussed earlier in this chapter; and if D's entitlement was contingent upon counter-performance of his own contractual obligations, which he breaches, then this problem, too, will be resolved in line with the considerations that have already been discussed above.

(c) *Contract between a Claimant and a Third Party*

Although they do not exhaust the circumstances in which C's contract with a **3–62** third party, X, may potentially bear on his claim, a recurring fact pattern in the cases is that D receives a benefit as a result of C's performance of a contract with X.

Where D is also a party to this contract between C and X, then the effect of this **3–63** contract on a claim in unjust enrichment by C against D can, again, be determined in accordance with the principles governing two-party cases, discussed above.

Rather more common are cases where D is not a party to the contract between **3–64** C and X. Typical fact situations are as follows: (1) a building subcontractor, C, undertakes construction work, pursuant to a subcontract with a main contractor, X, which benefits a developer, D[176]; (2) a garage, C, is employed by an insurance company, X, to repair a car belonging to a policyholder, D, which was damaged on the happening of an insured event[177]; (3) a contractor, C, is engaged by a tenant, X, to repair or improve premises leased by X from a landlord, D[178]; (4) a bank, C, effects a funds transfer to the account of a third party, D, pursuant to the instructions of X, an account-holding customer.[179]

In each of these cases, C acts pursuant to a contract with X when he confers **3–65** a benefit on D. If D is not also a party to this contract, then what significance does it have for C's claim in unjust enrichment against D? And in cases where X might also be able to bring a claim in unjust enrichment against D, what is the impact of this contract on X's claim? The cases suggest that there are several reasons why a contract between C and X may lead to the denial of a claim by either party, although D is not party to this contract.

---

[176] e.g. *Yew Sang Hong Ltd* [2008] HKCA 109.
[177] e.g. *Brown and Davis Ltd v Galbraith* [1972] 1 W.L.R. 977 (CA).
[178] Cf. e.g. *Ayott Bros Construction v Finney* 680 A. 2d 330 (1996).
[179] e.g. *Lloyds Bank Plc v Independent Insurance Co Ltd* [2000] Q.B. 110 (CA).

(i) *No Absolute Rule against Leapfrogging*

3–66 Some academic accounts suggest that there is a rule against "leapfrogging", such that C, who confers a benefit on D under a valid contract between C and X, may never "leapfrog" his immediate counterparty, X, and bring a claim in unjust enrichment against D.[180] However, no case clearly establishes that there is any such broad-brush rule, and the better view is that there are rather several overlapping considerations, arising out of the contract between C and X, which will often lead the courts to deny C's claim, but will not invariably do so.

(ii) *Considerations that May Bar or Limit C's Claim*

3–67 In the leading English authority of *Costello v MacDonald*,[181] the claimant builders did work on land owned by the defendants. There was no contract between them, because for tax reasons which they had explained to the claimants, the defendants had wished pay for the work through a company of which they were the sole shareholders and directors. The builders had previously done work for the company, and were content to proceed in the same way on this occasion. A dispute then arose about the standard of the works, and following the company's refusal to pay some £65,000 in respect of invoices for work done under the contract and for additional work done outside the terms of the contract, the builders won judgment in the County Court against the defendants for the outstanding amount, on the basis that they had been unjustly enriched at the builders' expense.

3–68 The Court of Appeal overturned this decision. Etherton L.J. accepted that "in terms of causation" the defendants had been enriched at the claimants' expense,[182] but held that recovery would undermine the parties' choices with regard to the way in which they had arranged their affairs, including their decision that the claimant builders should contract with the company and their decision that they should not contract with the defendants. In two important passages of his judgment, Etherton L.J. said[183]:

> "The obligation to pay for the [claimants'] services, and so the risk of non-payment, was contractually confined to [the company]. If a claim was permitted directly against [the defendants], it would shatter that contractual containment. It would also alter the usual consequences of [the company's] insolvency, which was one of the risks assumed by the [claimants] in contracting with [the company], since a direct claim against [the defendants] would improve the [claimants'] position over [the company's] other unsecured creditors. . . .
> I am clear . . . that the unjust enrichment claim against [the defendants] must fail because it would undermine the contractual arrangements between the parties, that is to say the contract between the [claimants] and [the company] and the absence of any contract between the [claimants] and [the defendants]. The general rule should be to uphold contractual arrangements by which parties have defined and allocated and, to

---

[180] P. Birks, *Unjust Enrichment*, 2nd edn (Oxford: OUP, 2005), pp.87–88 and 89–98; see too P. Birks, "'At the Expense of the Claimant': Direct and Indirect Enrichment in English Law" in D. Johnston and R. Zimmermann (eds), *Unjustified Enrichment: Key Issues in Comparative Perspective* (Cambridge: CUP, 2002).

[181] *Costello v MacDonald* [2011] EWCA Civ 930.

[182] *Costello* [2011] EWCA Civ 930 at [20].

[183] *Costello* [2011] EWCA Civ 930 at [21] and [23].

that extent, restricted their mutual obligations, and, in so doing, have similarly allocated and circumscribed the consequences of non-performance. That general rule reflects a sound legal policy, which acknowledges the parties' autonomy to configure the legal relations between them and provides certainty, and so limits disputes and litigation."

Unpacking Etherton L.J.'s judgment, against the background of the wider case law, there were three overlapping objections to C's claim.   **3–69**

No contradiction of a valid contract between C and X   One concern was   **3–70**
that C should not generally be permitted to recover from D where this would be inconsistent with the terms of C's contract with X. In practice, the question whether this bar should apply depends on the legal validity of C and X's contract, and the proper construction of its terms. In construing the terms of C's contract with X, it is always necessary to take into account the wider history of the dealings between all three parties, which might lead to the conclusion that C and X were indeed contracting on the basis that C would not sue D.

Illegitimately relieving C of voluntarily assumed risks   A second and   **3–71**
overlapping concern was that C should not be afforded a claim in unjust enrichment against D, if this would illegitimately relieve C of risks that he assumed when transacting with X. As Etherton L.J. put it in *Costello*, it would be wrong for recovery in unjust enrichment to "undermine . . . the way in which the parties chose to allocate the risks involved in the transaction".[184]

So, in particular, where C contracts with X, to confer a benefit on D, in return   **3–72**
for payment from X, the proper conclusion in all the circumstances *may* be that C has assumed the risk that X may default and become insolvent, and that the terms of this bargain may not be favourable to him. Where this is the case, as in *Costello* itself, the courts may well be reluctant to allow C to escape from the materialisation of these risks by claiming in unjust enrichment against D. In the absence of special facts, the courts are likely to say: (i) that C must look only to his counterparty, X, for payment; (ii) that if X wrongfully fails to pay C, then C should not be entitled to sue D in unjust enrichment, so as to turn D into the de facto guarantor of the performance of X's contractual obligations[185]; (iii) that if C's bargain with X turns out to be "bad", then C should not be entitled to escape this risk by seeking greater remuneration from D in unjust enrichment[186]; and (iv) that if X lawfully refuses to pay to C in accordance with the terms of his contract with C, then C should not be entitled to circumvent this obstacle, by suing D in unjust enrichment.

Note that a difficult question inevitably arises as to what facts might displace   **3–73**
this objection. For example, could C avoid it by proving that his decision to contract with X, and/or his decision to benefit D pursuant to the contract, was materially impaired, for example by some causative mistake? Consider *Lloyds*

---

[184] *Costello* [2011] EWCA Civ 930 at [21]. See similarly, in a different context, *The Trident Beauty* [1994] 1 W.L.R. 161 at 166: "[I]t is always recognised that serious difficulties arise if the law seeks to expand the law of restitution to redistribute risks for which provision has been made under an applicable contract".
[185] As in *Costello* [2011] EWCA Civ 930.
[186] A concern apparent from *Costello* [2011] EWCA Civ 930 at [31].

Bank Plc v Independent Insurance Co Ltd,[187] where the claimant bank effected a funds transfer in favour of the defendant pursuant to its customer's instructions, in the mistaken belief that the payment was covered by a sufficient credit balance to the customer's account—a mistake which negated the suggestion that the bank consciously assumed any credit risk vis-à-vis its customer. Alternatively, could C avoid this objection by proving conduct on D's part, which disables D from arguing that C should bear the relevant risk? Consider a case where D encourages C to confer the benefit in the belief, for which D is responsible, that C could look to D to pay him, if C's counter-party, X, should fail to do so.[188]

3–74   Note too that that the objection to allowing C to avoid a risk which he assumed when transacting with X will be particularly strong, where this also would upset the basis on which D himself dealt with X, a fortiori if C himself accepted the basis on which D and X contracted.[189] To quote from a recent case in the Hong Kong Court of Appeal[190]:

> "Where parties have expressly or impliedly allocated risks among themselves through a network of back-to-back or interlinking agreements, the law of restitution will not without compelling reason interfere with that allocation. It is unwise to tinker with the parties' allocation because a revision of risks as between (say) A and B may bring about adverse consequences as between (say) B and C or others in the contractual network. Attempting to do justice between A and B alone may lead to injustice being done as between B and C."

3–75   **Undermining the insolvency regime**   A final policy-based concern identified in *Costello*, and in other cases, is that allowing C to claim in unjust enrichment against D, the third-party beneficiary of his contract with X, may sometimes illegitimately undermine the law of insolvency's rules governing the distribution of an insolvent's assets, and in particular, the basic *pari passu* priority rule.[191] To quote again from the Hong Kong Court of Appeal[192]:

> "[T]he law of restitution will not normally cut across long-established statutory regimes regulating creditors' rights against insolvent debtors. Otherwise, the law of restitution may undermine the *pari passu* principle whereby unsecured creditors share rateably in the assets of an insolvent debtor. To allow a creditor a restitutionary remedy in the interests of 'doing justice' in a specific case would only lead to that creditor jumping the queue of unsecured creditors and so bring about injustice in everyone else's case."

3–76   The worry here is that in the event of X's insolvency, allowing C an alternative claim in unjust enrichment against D, may enable C to recover from D in

---

[187] *Lloyds Bank Plc v Independent Insurance Co Ltd* [2000] Q.B. 110 (CA). The claim failed on the ground that the defendant creditor had received the payment in good faith in discharge of the customer's debt.

[188] e.g. *Mike Glynn & Co v Hy-Brasil Restaurants Inc* 914 N.E. 2d. 103 (2009) (unpaid sub-contractor encouraged to continue work by employer's representations regarding payment).

[189] See para.3–86.

[190] *Yew Sang Hong Ltd* [2008] HKCA 109 at [12].

[191] Cf. the different and broader objection, that it would be wrong for the law of unjust enrichment to afford preferential treatment to one category of disappointed unsecured contractual creditor, by affording him alternative recourse, on his counterparty's default and insolvency, in the form of an unjust enrichment claim against D.

[192] *Yew Sang Hong Ltd* [2008] HKCA 109 at [13].

preference to, and to the prejudice of, X's other unsecured creditors. This problem principally arises when X has some form of unsatisfied claim against D, which might be adversely affected by C's own claim against D. Consider a case where X main contractor contracts with C subcontractor, for C to undertake construction work for the benefit of D employer, for which D had himself agreed to pay X under the main contract, and where neither X nor C is paid before X becomes insolvent. X's right to be paid by D is an asset belonging to his insolvent estate. If the law were to hold that, with a view to avoiding double liability, X's right against D would abate to the extent that C recovered from D, then there is a worry that C may thereby recover in full, to the prejudice of X's other unsecured creditors: but for C's direct claim against D, the fruits of X's right against D would be available to be shared *pari passu* between all of X's unsecured creditors, including C.[193]

(d) *Contract between a Defendant and a Third Party*

(i) *Introduction*

If D receives a benefit at C's expense to which D is entitled by a contract between   **3–77** D and a third party, X, then can D rely on this contract as a bar to C's claim in unjust enrichment? Where C is himself a party to the contract between X and D, then C's ability to bring a claim in unjust enrichment can be resolved in accordance with the principles governing two-party cases. Where, more often, C is *not* a party to this contract, a different analysis may be required. From D's perspective, allowing C to recover will be objectionable if it would upset the allocation of risk and benefit between D and X which is embodied in their contract, and which may be inconsistent with D's owing a liability to pay anyone else for the benefit. However, C might answer that since he was not party to the contract between X and D, D should not be entitled to rely on this contract to bar C's claim.

Consider *Brown and Davis Ltd v Galbraith*.[194] The defendant insured's car   **3–78** was damaged, and his insurer arranged for the car to be repaired by the claimant garage at its expense. Before the garage was paid, the insurer became insolvent. The garage sought payment for its work from the defendant, but the Court of Appeal held that he was not liable. The insurance contract no doubt provided that, in return for the insured's paying the premiums, the insurer would shoulder the cost of making good the insured damage. This contractual allocation of risk and benefit between insurer and insured would inevitably have been undermined if the insured could have been forced to pay the repairer, in the event that the insurer failed to do so: why did the insured pay the premiums, if not to avoid having to bear this cost himself? On the facts of *Galbraith*, the garage knew that it was being employed by an insurer that had been paid premiums by the insured owner of the car, and so it might be said that the garage had impliedly agreed to do the work on the basis that the insurer, and the insurer alone, would be liable

---

[193] *Yew Sang Hong Ltd* [2008] HKCA 109 at [30]–[32]. See too *Green Quarries Inc v Raasch* 676 S.W. 2d. 261 (1984). And cf. *Costello* [2011] EWCA Civ 930 at [21], where the insolvency point is less carefully explained.
[194] *Brown and Davis Ltd v Galbraith* [1972] 1 W.L.R. 997 (CA).

to pay for it. In other cases, however, the facts will not support such an interpretation of the basis on which the claimant transfers a benefit to the defendant. The justification for denying the claimant's claim on the basis of the defendant's contract may then seem less compelling.

(b) *Other Bars and Defences to the Claim*

3–79   The English courts have not yet developed a clear framework and set of principles for dealing with the issues raised by such cases. One reason may be that the claim may fail as a result of the operation of a defence or bar that is more limited in scope than the broad principle with which this chapter is concerned—that contracts can operate as a justifying ground debarring claims in unjust enrichment.

3–80   For example, if a defendant benefits by receiving a sum of money from a claimant that is paid to discharge a debt owed to the defendant by a third party, the English courts have sometimes allowed him a defence of "good consideration".[195] Again, if a defendant is paid money by a third party, X, who has stolen it from a claimant, and the defendant is entitled to the money under a contract he has entered with X, then the defendant might rely on his status as a bona fide purchaser of the money, to defeat an action in unjust enrichment by the claimant.[196] Again, in some cases the defendant may be able to raise the change of position defence, pleading as the relevant change of circumstances his performance of his contract with the third party, or perhaps even his mere assumption of contractual liability to the third party.[197]

(iii) *A General Bar that Protects the Integrity of D's Contractual Relations?*

3–81   As already explained, C may well be prevented from claiming in unjust enrichment against D, if this would be inconsistent either with *C's* contract with D, or with *C's* contract with X, a third party. A difficult question for the future is whether the courts should also recognise a general bar which would enable D to resist a claim in unjust enrichment by C, if allowing the claim would upset the contractual allocation of risk and reward reflected in a contract between D and a third party, X.

3–82   Our tentative view, which seems broadly consistent with the authorities, is as follows: (i) that the courts might deny C a claim in unjust enrichment against D, who was enriched pursuant to a valid contract with X, insofar as D shows that C's claim would be inconsistent with, and upset, the contractual allocation of risk and reward; (ii) that the argument for this outcome is particularly compelling when C can be said to have accepted the basis on which D contracted with X; (iii) that the argument for this outcome is less compelling when C cannot be said to have accepted the basis on which D contracted with X, with the result the courts should at least be more willing to identify a compelling countervailing reason why C's claim should be allowed.

---

[195] e.g. *Lloyds Bank v Independent Insurance* [2000] Q.B. 110 (CA), applying dicta of Robert Goff J. in *Barclays Bank v W.J. Simms Son & Cooke (Southern) Ltd* [1980] Q.B. 677. At paras 29–15—29–22, it is doubted that the defence of "good consideration" has work to do within the law of unjust enrichment that cannot be performed by other principles.

[196] Cf. *Lipkin Gorman v Karpnale Ltd* [1991] 2 A.C. 548, discussed at paras 29–09—29–13.

[197] See Ch.27 for general discussion.

Upsetting a valid contractual allocation of risk between X and D   Taking   **3–83**
this approach, the threshold question will always be (i) whether D received the
benefit for which C seeks restitution pursuant to a valid contract with X,[198] and
if so, (ii) whether it would be substantially inconsistent with the allocation of
risk/benefit in this contract, if C could sue D in unjust enrichment. Often, it will
be. Nevertheless, the correct answer will depend on the proper construction of the
terms of the contract between D and X. The onus should probably be on D, to
show that he contracted for the benefit with X, and that this contract is inconsistent with C's prima facie claim.

In some cases, it will be obvious that there is no conceivable inconsistency. To   **3–84**
give a routine example, C may procure an inter-bank funds transfer from his
account, to the credit of D customer's account with X bank. Here, D benefits at
C's expense, via X's performance of its banking contract with D. If C's payment
occurs in circumstances which reveal a ground for restitution, such as a restitution-grounding mistake, there is no reason to think that the banking contract
between X and D would be upset by C's bringing a claim in unjust enrichment,
to recover the sums received by D through X.

In other cases, the correct answer will require a much closer analysis of the   **3–85**
parties' contractual relations. This can be illustrated by comparing *Galbraith*,[199]
which has already been discussed, with *Gray's Truck Centre Ltd v Olaf L.
Johnson Ltd*.[200] As in *Galbraith*, the claimant garage there repaired the defendant's vehicle under a contract with a third party, which became insolvent before
the garage was paid. However, the contract between the defendant and the third
party was materially different. The garage had not been willing to extend credit
to the defendant, and had only agreed to repair its vehicle under a contract with
the third party truck dealer, which the garage considered more creditworthy.
Significantly, the third party was not the defendant's insurer, and very probably
had agreed to commission the work on the defendant's behalf only on the basis
that it would be reimbursed by the defendant for the costs of paying the garage
for this work. On these facts, allowing the garage to bring a claim in unjust
enrichment directly against the defendant would probably not have upset the
allocation of risk and benefit in the defendant's agreement with the third party,
since it was always intended that the defendant would ultimately pay for the
repairs.

C's acceptance of the basis of D's contract with X   Where C's claim will   **3–86**
upset D's contract with X, the case for denying C's claim will be most compelling where C can be shown to have accepted the basis of D's contract, expressly
or by implication. It will not always be easy to identify when this has occurred,
where C is not himself party to the contract. Nevertheless, the decision in
Galbraith is explicable in such terms, and so are others. These include cases

---

[198] This formulation is intended to confine any bar to cases where the benefit for which restitution is
sought is acquired under the contract on which D relies. Cf. a case where D has a contract with X to
perform certain services (e.g. clean his windows periodically), and where a stranger, C, happens to
render the same services to D. The benefit D receives from C cannot be regarded as the benefit that
D has contracted to receive from X, and D should not be able to appeal to this contract, to bar C's
claim.
[199] *Galbraith* [1972] 1 W.L.R. 997; discussed at para.3–78.
[200] *Gray's Truck Centre Ltd v Olaf L. Johnson Ltd* Unreported CA, January 25, 1990.

involving networks of interlinked contracts, as in complex construction projects, where it can be assumed that each party to one of these contracts contracted on the basis that his own rights and obligations, as well as those of other parties to contracts in the network, were to be governed by the contracts to which they were directly a party.[201]

3–87   There will inevitably be many cases in which it is not realistic to say that C accepted the basis of D's contract with X, and where the case for denying C's claim, on the basis that it would upset D's contract, will be correspondingly less compelling. Take a case where C carries out repair work to premises under a contract with X, who occupies them. Unknown to C, X is a tenant of the premises, and the lease between X and his landlord, D, places an obligation on the tenant to undertake the repair work, at the tenant's cost. If X were to fail to pay C, could D landlord resist a claim in unjust enrichment by C on the basis that this claim would upset the contractual allocation of risk and reward in the lease?

3–88   A rule that D can *never* argue that C's claim would upset his contract with X, unless C has accepted the basis of this contract, may be too strong. A middle way, which might better reconcile the competing interests of C and D, is to say that where C has *not* accepted the basis of D's contract, D's claim to have his contract with X respected is relatively weaker. So, while the courts should not automatically ignore D's contract, they should be more willing to identify countervailing reasons why this is appropriate.

3–89   **Special grounds for disregarding D's contract with X**   Where C's claim would upset D's contract with X, the question arises whether there is a compelling countervailing reason why the law might disregard this concern, and allow C's claim. Past cases offer little clear guidance in resolving this question. Future courts will need to explore the possible significance of several factors.

3–90   First, it seems that the courts may certainly disregard D's contract with X, where C's claim against D rests on D's receipt of an asset to which C retains some legal or equitable beneficial title. Property law's title-clearing rules do not afford a good title, free of pre-existing third-party interests, to every person who acquires an asset through an exchange transaction with another. On the one hand, a bona fide purchaser of money is afforded such protection, through a wide common law exception to the *nemo dat* principle which underpins money's role as a universal medium of exchange. On the other hand, in relation to other assets, property law's title-clearing rules are more patchy, with the result that there are sometimes cases in which D has obtained a non-money asset under a contract with X, in good faith, and even for some executed consideration, but (i) where no *nemo dat* exception is available to afford D a clear title, free of C's prior title; and (ii) where D is therefore exposed to liability to C, based on the title which C retains. In this limited subset of cases, the law necessarily prioritises the preservation and protection/vindication of C's pre-existing proprietary rights, over the protection of D's contractual relations with X.

3–91   Secondly, an important question will arise as to whether D's entitlement to have his contract with X respected should depend on (i) the nature of the counter-

---

[201] The objection to allowing claims in unjust enrichment between non-contracting parties in such a case is particularly clearly put in *Yew Sang Hong Ltd* [2008] HKCA 109 at [12]; see para.3.74.

performance that D was to provide to X, in exchange for the benefit for which C seeks restitution; and (ii) the extent to which this counter-performance has actually been provided. The better view in principle is that, assuming a genuine contract between X and D, involving a bilateral exchange between them, the availability of the bar should not depend on a favourable inquiry into the equality or adequacy of the exchange. But more difficult is whether any bar should be equally available to D, whether (i) D has fully provided the agreed counter-performance to X; (ii) D has not fully provided the agreed counter-performance to X, but is willing and able to do so, in accordance with the terms of his contract with X; (iii) D has lawfully refused to provide the agreed counter-performance to X, in accordance with the terms of the contract with X (which may subsist or be terminated); or (iv) D has wrongfully, in breach of contract, failed to provide the agreed counter-performance to X.

Thirdly, an important question will also arise as to the impact of D's conduct   **3–92** on his right to have his contract with X respected: that is, whether D's conduct may disable him from claiming, vis-à-vis C, that the court should disallow C's claim because it would upset D's relations with X? It seems doubtful that this complex question can be reduced to a simple inquiry into whether D was in "good faith"—a formula which begs a series of further questions, into what "good faith" means in this context, and what aspects of D's conduct will be encompassed by the inquiry. In shaping the boundaries of any bar based on D's contract with X, the courts might need to consider the materiality or otherwise of, inter alia: (i) D's conduct towards X, which resulted in X's contracting with D (e.g. misrepresentations by D); (ii) D's non-performance and wrongful repudiation of his contract with X; (iii) D's conduct towards C (e.g. misrepresentations by D, which led C to confer the benefit); (iv) D's responsibility for the circumstances that generate C's claim (e.g. where D's non-performance of his obligations to X means that X does not perform his obligations to C).

Part Three
ENRICHMENT

CHAPTER 4

ENRICHMENT: GENERAL PRINCIPLES

1. INTRODUCTION

The law of unjust enrichment is concerned with transfers of value between **4-01**
claimants and defendants, and a claim in unjust enrichment is "not a claim for
compensation for loss, but for recovery of a benefit unjustly gained [by a
defendant] ... at the expense of the claimant".[1] The question whether the
defendant has been enriched is therefore "centre stage".[2] It is not enough for a
claimant to show that he has suffered a loss,[3] since "a person cannot be unjustly
enriched if he has not been enriched at all ... and the fact that a payment may
have been made, e.g. by mistake, is not by itself sufficient to justify a restitutionary remedy".[4] The claimant must also show that the defendant has made a
corresponding gain,[5] and proving the defendant's enrichment is therefore "not
merely material to success, but the whole essence of the action".[6]

This chapter gives an account of the general principles governing the identi- **4-02**
fication and quantification of value for the purposes of making claims in unjust
enrichment. The next chapter explains how these principles apply to different
types of benefit: money, land and goods, services and discharged obligations.

---

[1] *Boake Allen Ltd v HMRC* [2006] EWCA Civ 25; [2006] S.T.C. 606 at [175]. See too Lord Wright,
"Restatement of the Law of Restitution" in *Legal Essays and Addresses* (Cambridge: CUP, 1939), 34,
p.36; *Commissioner of State Revenue (Victoria) v Royal Insurance Australia Ltd* (1994) 182 C.L.R.
51 at 75; reaffirmed *Roxborough v Rothmans of Pall Mall Australia Ltd* [2001] HCA 68; (2001) 208
C.L.R. 516 at [26]; *Gribbon v Lutton* [2001] EWCA Civ 1956; [2002] Q.B. 902 at [60]; *Pacific
National Investments Ltd v City of Victoria* [2004] SCC 75; [2004] 3 S.C.R. 575 at [25] and [34];
Kingstreet Investments Ltd v New Brunswick (Department of Finance) [2007] SCC 1; [2007] 1 S.C.R.
3 at [32].
[2] *Gibb v Maidstone and Tunbridge Wells NHS Trust* [2010] EWCA Civ 678; [2010] I.R.L.R. 786 at
[32].
[3] As in e.g. *Sorrell v Finch* [1977] A.C. 728 (no liability where payment was made to third party who
was not defendant's agent); *Regional Municipality of Peel v Ontario* [1992] 3 S.C.R. 762 (no liability
where defendant was under no obligation to bear costs of housing delinquents paid for by claimant);
Regalian Plc v London Docklands Development Corp. [1995] 1 W.L.R. 212 (no liability for work that
did not benefit defendant). See too *Haugesund Kommune v Depfa ACS Bank* [2010] EWHC 227
(Comm); [2010] 1 All E.R. (Comm.) 1109 at [18] per Tomlinson J.: "a restitutionary claim is not one
for damages for loss suffered." For discussion of the question whether a claim in unjust enrichment
can nevertheless be characterised as a claim for "damage" for the purposes of the Civil Liability
(Contribution) Act 1978, see para.19–30.
[4] *Portman Building Society v Hamlyn Taylor Neck (A Firm)* [1998] 4 All ER 202 at 206 per Millett
L.J.
[5] For discussion of the requirement that the defendant's enrichment must have been gained at the
claimant's expense, see Ch.6, and note the argument made at paras 6–63—6–74, that recovery should
be capped at the lesser amount of the defendant's gain and the claimant's loss.
[6] *Deutsche Morgan Grenfell Plc v IRC* [2005] EWCA Civ 78; [2006] Ch. 243 at [294] per Buxton
L.J. See too *Sempra Metals Ltd v IRC* [2007] UKHL 34; [2008] A.C. 561 at [28]; *Benedetti v Sawiris*
[2010] EWCA Civ 1427 at [142].

2. MONETARY VALUE

(a) *Value Must Be Financially Quantifiable*

4–03   Benefits are only capable of generating claims in unjust enrichment if they have monetary value.[7] The law pays no attention to the cultural, religious, intellectual or emotional value of a benefit, unless they affect its financial value. So, for example, a claim might lie for the monetary value of services, such as psychiatric counselling, which make the defendant happier.[8] But the reason why such services are relevantly valuable is not because of their effect on the defendant's emotional well-being, but because they can be bought and sold on the market. The affection and companionship of family members also make people happier, but these cannot be bought and sold, and the law does not recognise claims for benefits of this kind.[9]

(b) *Exchange Value and Use Value*

4–04   When assessing the monetary value of property, the courts frequently look at the property's exchange value, i.e. the amount for which the right to own the property can be bought and sold. However, this is not the only method of quantifying monetary value, and other methods can also be appropriate. Most notably, the courts sometimes assess the use value of property, i.e. the amount for which the right to use the property can be bought and sold. In *Sempra Metals Ltd v IRC*,[10] for example, the claimant mistakenly paid money as tax sooner than was legally required. By the date of proceedings, no claim lay to recover the exchange (face) value of the money, since by then the tax had become payable. However the House of Lords held that a claim would lie to recover the use value of the money during the period of prematurity, i.e. between the date of payment and the date when the tax was legally due.

4–05   The court's analysis in *Sempra* suggests that a claimant who has paid money to a defendant can combine a claim for its exchange (face) value with a claim for its use value. A claimant who mistakenly pays a defendant £10,000 and then claims after one year can recover £10,000 and also the defendant's saved

---

[7] *Peter v Beblow* [1993] 1 S.C.R. 980 at 990 per McLachlin J.: the law takes a "straightforward economic approach" to the assessment of value. This was reaffirmed in *Garland v Consumers Gas Co* [2004] SCC 25; [2004] 1 S.C.R. 629 at [31], and in *Pacific National Investments* [2004] SCC 75; [2004] 3 S.C.R. 575 at [15].

[8] See e.g. *Brenner v First Artists' Management Pty Ltd* [1993] 2 V.R. 221 at 265 (Victoria Sup Ct) (benefits conferred by manager include lifting spirits of despondent pop artist).

[9] *Single v Macharski Estate* [1996] 3 W.W.R. 23 (Manitoba CA); *Barnaby v Petersen Estate* (1996) 15 E.T.R. (2d) 138 (British Columbia Sup Ct); *Stanhope v Stanhope Estate* (1998) 166 Sask. R. 293 (Saskatchewan QB); affirmed [2001] SKCA 80. See too *Walsh v Singh* [2009] EWHC 3219 (Ch); [2010] 1 F.L.R. 1658 at [66]: quantifying the contributions made by the parties to a domestic relationship is "a highly undesirable process which the court can rarely undertake satisfactorily". The contrary view has been taken in some other Canadian cases, e.g. *Clarkson v McCrossen Estate* (1995) 122 D.L.R. (4th) 239 (British Columbia CA), followed in *Proulx v Daniels* [2001] BCSC 441; *Schogl v Blazicevic* [2005] BCCA 575; (2005) 21 E.T.R. (3d) 32; *Moyes v Ollerich Estate* [2005] BCCA 518; (2005) 21 E.T.R. (3d) 40; *Gould v Royal Trust Corp of Canada* [2009] BCSC 1528. However these cases are out of line with the authorities cited in fn.7.

[10] *Sempra Metals Ltd v IRC* [2007] UKHL 34; [2008] A.C. 561; discussed further at paras 5–05—5–14.

borrowing cost, which is likely to be the market interest rate on a £10,000 loan for one year. In principle, however, claims for exchange value and use value cannot be combined where the defendant has received a non-money benefit such as goods, and where the exchange value of the goods subsumes their use value. In other words, where the ownership of goods is priced to reflect the fact that they have a use value, the claimant cannot recover both the exchange value and the use value because this would comprise double recovery.

3. PROTECTION OF THE DEFENDANT'S AUTONOMY

(a) *Subjectivity of Value*

People have different means and spending priorities, and they value benefits **4–06** differently according to their personal tastes. Consequently, as Lord Nicholls said in *Sempra*, "a benefit is not always worth its market value to a particular defendant", and "when it is not it may be unjust to treat the defendant as having received a benefit possessing the value it has to others."[11] The common law "places a premium on the right to choose how to spend one's money",[12] and this right might be unfairly compromised if a defendant were forced to make restitution of the market value of a benefit which he would only have bought for himself at a lower price, or which he would not have bought at all.[13] To avoid this, the court may therefore assess the value of the benefit by reference to the defendant's personal value system rather than the market. This is sometimes described as allowing the defendant to "subjectively devalue" the benefit.[14]

For example, in *Sempra*,[15] the House of Lords recognised that the government **4–07** can borrow money more cheaply than commercial entities, and held that the

---

[11] *Sempra* [2007] UKHL 34; [2008] A.C. 561 at [119]. See too *Cressman v Coys of Kensington (Sales) Ltd* [2004] EWCA 133; [2004] 1 W.L.R. 2774 at [28] per Mance L.J.: "The law's general concern is with benefit to the particular defendant".

[12] *Peel v Ontario* [1992] 3 S.C.R. 762 at [25] per McLachlin J. See too *Magical Waters Fountains Ltd v City of Sarnia* (1990) 74 O.R. (2d) 682 at 691 per Gautreau J. (Ontario Sup Ct); reversed on another point (1992) 91 D.L.R. (4th) 760 (Ontario CA): the defendant can say "it's not your job to make my choices".

[13] *Sharwood & Co v Municipal Financial Corp* (2001) 142 O.A.C. 350 (Ontario CA) at [26] per Laskin J.A.: "The receipt of services may not be a benefit because the defendant may not have wanted the services or may not have wanted them if it had to pay for them." Cf. M McInnes, "Enrichment Revisited", in J. Neyers et al (eds), *Understanding Unjust Enrichment* (Oxford: Hart, 2005), 165, p.175: a defendant should not have to pay full market price for a benefit if "he did not freely assume financial responsibility for his gain".

[14] e.g. *Cressman* [2004] EWCA Civ 47; [2004] 1 W.L.R. 2775 at [28]; *Sempra* [2007] UKHL 34; [2008] A.C. 561 at [119]. The source of this terminology is P. Birks, *An Introduction to the Law of Restitution* (Oxford: Clarendon Press, 1985), p.109.

[15] *Sempra* [2007] UKHL 34; [2008] A.C. 561, discusssed further at paras 5–05—5–14. See also *Ministry of Defence v Ashman* (1993) 25 H.L.R. 513 (CA) (which was a claim for restitution of the profits of wrongdoing), considered in *Shi v Jiangsu Native Produce Import & Export Corp* [2009] EWCA Civ 1582 at [18]–[28] (also a claim for the profits of wrongdoing). And cf. *Carriage Way Property Owners Association v Western National Bank of Cicero*, 487 N.E. 2d 974 (Illinois App Ct, 1985) (maintenance of residential development's common areas worth less to owners of apartments on short leases than to long-term home owners); the approach taken here is preferable to that taken in *Cassels v Body Corporate No.86975* (2007) 8 N.Z. Conveyancing and Property Reports 740 (N.Z. High Ct) (maintenance of apartment block's common areas worth the same to owners of subdivided and unsubdivided apartments).

value of saved borrowing costs to the government is therefore less than the amount which commercial entities must pay to borrow money. Again, in *J.S. Bloor Ltd v Pavillion Developments Ltd*,[16] the parties agreed that the defendant would build a road that was later mistakenly built by the claimant. The judge accepted that the defendant had gained some advantages from this, but held that these were outweighed by the disadvantages to the defendant of the road having been built in the particular way that the claimant had built it. Hence enrichment was not established.

4–08   When a defendant wishes to argue that a benefit is worth less to him than its market value, does the burden of proof lie on the claimant or the defendant? In other words, must the claimant prove that the defendant valued the benefit at the market rate; or is there a presumption to this effect, which the defendant can rebut by proving that he would only have bought the benefit at a lower price, or that he would not have bought it at all? This issue divided the court in the *Sempra* case. The minority held that the claimant must prove the "actual benefit" obtained by the defendant,[17] by which they meant that the claimant can only recover to the extent that he can prove the value which the defendant attributed to the benefit. However the majority held that the claimant merely has to prove that the benefit has an objective market value, and the onus then switches to the defendant to prove that a lower subjective valuation is a more appropriate measure of his enrichment.[18] This is discussed further elsewhere.[19]

4–09   A defendant is unlikely to persuade a court that he attached a low value to a benefit simply by relying on self-serving testimony that he has a (previously unexpressed) personal value system that attributes a low value to such benefits, particularly if this testimony is not borne out by his previous conduct.[20] If a defendant can produce stronger evidence of his personal spending preferences, however, then we believe that he should be able to rely on this evidence, consistently with the view expressed in the foregoing authorities that the law is concerned to protect his freedom to make his own spending choices.

4–10   Against this, there is Etherton L.J.'s obiter dictum in *Benedetti v Sawiris*, that a defendant's personal outlook (e.g. his "generous or parsimonious personality") is irrelevant, and, indeed, that the subjective value of a benefit to a particular defendant is irrelevant, and that the only matters on which a defendant can rely are "conditions increasing or decreasing the objective value of the benefit to any reasonable person in the same (unusual) position".[21] These "conditions" seem to

---

[16] *J.S. Bloor Ltd v Pavillion Developments Ltd* [2008] EWHC 724 (TCC); [2008] 2 E.G.L.R. 85.
[17] *Sempra* [2007] UKHL 34; [2008] A.C. 561 [231] (Lord Mance). See too Lord Scott's comments at [147].
[18] *Sempra* [2007] UKHL 34; [2008] A.C. 561 at [48] (Lord Hope), [116]–[117] (Lord Nicholls), and [186] (Lord Walker).
[19] At paras 5–07—5–10.
[20] An argument of this kind was given short shrift in *Cressman* [2004] EWCA Civ 47; [2004] 1 W.L.R. 2775.
[21] *Benedetti v Sawiris* [2010] EWCA Civ 1427 at [145]. This comment was obiter because on the facts there was no evidence of the defendant's subjective preferences that could have led the court to form an objective valuation: see para.4–51. Although their work was not cited, Etherton L.J. seems to have adopted the approach towards valuation that is taken in J. Edelman and E. Bant, *Unjust Enrichment in Australia* (Melbourne: OUP, 2006), p.108, and in J. Edelman, "The Meaning of Loss and Enrichment" in R. Chambers et al. (eds), *Philosophical Foundations of the Law of Unjust Enrichment* (Oxford: OUP, 2009), 211, esp. pp.235–239. A critical view of this approach is taken in A. Burrows, *The Law of Restitution*, 3rd edn (Oxford: OUP, 2010), pp.44–45.

include matters such as buying power in a market, so that a defendant who can invariably negotiate a better price for a product than any other buyer will be allowed to say that this price reflects the "objective" value of the product to him, or, in effect, that there is one market for him and another for everyone else. We would agree that a defendant in this position should not have to make restitution of the higher value that would be attributed to the benefit if it had been received by another defendant. In our view, however, the underlying reason for this would still be that the law wishes to protect the defendant's freedom of choice, since a defendant who is able to pay a low price for a product will invariably choose not to pay a higher price. By insisting that the law always requires defendants to repay the objective value of benefits (and asserting that there is a meaningful difference between "subjective value" and "objective value to a person in an unusual position") Etherton L.J. denies that the law is concerned to protect a defendant's freedom of choice, and in our view this is both undesirable in principle and contrary to the cases cited in the previous paragraphs.

If a defendant can rely on evidence of his personal characteristics and circum- **4–11** stances to show that his enrichment is worth less to him than the market value, then can a claimant make the reverse argument, i.e. can he lead evidence of the defendant's characteristics and circumstances to show that the defendant's enrichment is worth more to him than the market value? In *Benedetti*,[22] Etherton L.J. observed there is no English authority for the proposition that claimants can do this, and in *Benedetti* itself the Court of Appeal denied that there was evidence establishing that the defendant attached a higher value to the claimant's services than their market value. During settlement negotiations the defendant had offered to pay the claimant a fee that was higher than the market value of the claimant's services, but the claimant had rejected this offer and the Court of Appeal held that the offer was not reliable evidence of the value attributed to the services by the defendant.[23] However, if one accepts that "subjective devaluation" arguments can be made by defendants, then it might also be argued that fairness between the parties requires valuation arguments based on the personal characteristics of defendants to cut both ways.[24] It should be borne in mind, however, that allowing a claimant to recover more than the market value of a benefit may require a court to depart from the rule that should arguably govern restitutionary awards, that a claimant should not be entitled to recover more than the amount of his loss where this is less than the amount of the defendant's gain. This is discussed further elsewhere.[25]

(b) *Money and Saved Expenditure*

In some circumstances, there is no danger that a defendant's freedom to make his **4–12** own spending choices will be compromised by ordering him to repay the market value of a benefit. The most obvious example is where the defendant receives

---

[22] *Benedetti* [2010] EWCA Civ 1427 at [145].
[23] *Benedetti* [2010] EWCA Civ 1427 at [74]–[89], [144]–[162], and [172].
[24] A Burrows, "Free Acceptance and the Law of Restitution" (1988) 104 L.Q.R. 576, pp.587, fn.47, 589, fn.62, and 590, fn.68; M Garner, "The Role of Subjective Benefit in the Law of Unjust Enrichment" (1990) 10 O.J.L.S. 42, p.43.
[25] See paras 6–63—6–74.

money. Money is a universal means of exchange and defendants invariably desire things that money can buy. Hence they are invariably benefited by the receipt of money, and its face value is a reliable measure of their enrichment at the time when they receive it.[26]

4–13   For the same reason, the courts have refused to let defendants make the argument from freedom of choice where they have realised the market value of a benefit in money by the time of the action, and also where their legal obligations have been discharged, so that they can use the funds that would have been needed to meet these liabilities for other purposes. Moving outwards from these core examples, market value has also been attributed to realisable as well as realised benefits, and to savings of factually as well as legally necessary expenditure.

(i) Realised and Realisable Benefits

4–14   If a defendant sells property which the claimant has improved or repaired, then he cannot deny that he is enriched to the extent that he has benefited from the sale proceeds. This explains *Greenwood v Bennett*,[27] where a car was stolen and wrecked by the thief in an accident. The thief sold the car to an innocent purchaser, who repaired it. The car was then repossessed and sold by the owner pursuant to an order of the county court. The Court of Appeal held that this order should have been made conditional upon the owner's paying the market value of the repairs, in Lord Denning M.R.'s view because he would otherwise be unjustly enriched.

4–15   The amount recoverable in *Greenwood* was the market value of the work, and not the increase in the car's market value which resulted from the work. Hence the case shows that the market value of services can be realised by selling the end-product of the services. However this is not the only way of showing that a defendant has been enriched by the market value of services, and a claimant may wish to rely on other arguments where the end-product of his services has a lower market value than the services themselves, and again where his services do not lead to the creation or improvement of an asset which can be sold.[28]

4–16   Should the courts value a benefit at the market rate where the defendant has not realised its market value by the time of the claim, but can readily do so whenever he wishes? This was considered in *Cressman v Ceys of Kensington (Sales) Ltd*,[29] where the defendant acquired the right to a personalised car number-plate through an administrative error. The defendant argued that he had not been enriched, but this was rejected, primarily because his refusal to return the right,

---

[26] *BP Exploration Co (Ltd) v Hunt (No.2)* [1979] 1 W.L.R. 783 at 799; *Garland v Consumers Gas Co* [2004] SCC 25; [2004] 1 S.C.R. 629 at [36]. The use value of money presents greater difficulties, because different people can borrow at different rates: see para.5–05 and following.
[27] *Greenwood v Bennett* [1973] Q.B. 195. See too *Munro v Willmott* [1949] 1 K.B. 295 (repairs to car later sold at auction); *Olchowy v McKay* [1996] 1 W.W.R. 36 (Saskatchewan QB) at [18]–[19] (defendant enriched when he harvests canola crop seeded on his land, although enrichment not unjust); *McKeown v Cavalier Yachts Pty Ltd* (1998) 13 N.S.W.L.R. 303 (New South Wales Sup Ct) (improvements to yacht); *Conrad v Feldbar Construction Co Ltd* (2004) 70 O.R. (3d) 298 (Ontario Sup Ct) (defendant enriched when he sells land on which road has been built); *Cox v Young* (2005) 6 N.Z. Conveyancing and Property Reports 761 (NZ High Ct) (improvements to motel).
[28] See paras 5–21—5–26.
[29] *Cressman v Ceys of Kensington (Sales) Ltd* [2004] EWCA 133; [2004] 1 W.L.R. 2774 at [33]–[36] and [40].

in circumstances where it would have been easy to do so, proved that he regarded the right as valuable.[30] However, Mance L.J. also reviewed three possible approaches to the question whether market value should be ascribed to realisable as well as realised benefits. He rejected the view that realised benefits alone should be treated in this way,[31] and also the view that market value should only be ascribed to realisable benefits when it is reasonably certain that the defendant intends to realise them at a future date.[32] The problem with both approaches was that they might encourage tactical stances and manoeuvring by defendants: they might be incentivised to wait until after trial to realise the benefit and to disguise their true intentions in the meantime. Hence Mance L.J. concluded that the preferable approach was for the court to order or assume a sale of readily realisable benefits at market value, whatever the defendant's actual intentions.[33]

On the facts of *Cressman*, the right to the plate was clearly distinct from the   **4-17** defendant's other property, and a market for the right clearly existed. However not every asset can be so easily sold, nor can every asset be so easily disentangled from a defendant's other property, and in some cases it would cause a defendant unfair hardship if he were forced to sell assets to which a claimant has added value. Suppose, for example, that the claimant repairs or improves unique chattels with sentimental value to the defendant, or land which the defendant occupies as his home. Rather than forcing the defendant to sell the property in such cases, it might be fairer to charge it with a lien, entitling the claimant to a share of the proceeds only if the property is sold.[34]

(ii) *Saving of Necessary Expenditure*

The courts have often held that a defendant is enriched when his debt or other   **4-18** legal obligation is discharged, and that the measure of his enrichment is the value of the discharged liability.[35] Because the defendant has been relieved of a legally necessary expense, he can now spend his money on whatever else he chooses.

A defendant will also be held to have been enriched by the receipt of market   **4-19** value when he is relieved from the burden of paying for goods and services

---

[30] Cf. *Read v Rann* (1830) 10 B. & C. 438 at 441; 109 E.R. 513 at 514; *Weatherby v Banham* (1832) 5 C. & P. 228; 172 E.R. 950.

[31] As argued in Birks, *An Introduction to the Law of Unjust Enrichment*, pp.121–124.

[32] As argued in A. Burrows, *The Law of Restitution*, 2nd edn (London: Butterworths, 2004), p.19. German law appears to have a similar rule: T. Krebs, "Unrequested Benefits in German Law" in Neyers, *Understanding Unjust Enrichment*, 247, pp.259–260.

[33] As argued in the 6th edition of this work: G. Jones, *Goff & Jones: The Law of Restitution*, 6th edn (London: Sweet & Maxwell, 2002), para.1.023, which was also approved in *Procter & Gamble Philippine Manufacturing Corp v Peter Cremer GmbH (The Manila)* [1988] 3 All E.R. 843 at 855; *Marston Construction Co Ltd v Kigass Ltd* (1989) 46 B.L.R. 109 at 125–126.

[34] Cf. *Re Gareau Estate* (1995) 9 E.T.R. (2d) 95 (Ontario Sup Ct), discussed at para.27–16.

[35] e.g. *Filby v Mortgage Express (No.2) Ltd* [2004] EWCA Civ 759 at [62] per May L.J.: "the defendant is enriched if his financial position is materially improved . . . as here where the defendant is relieved of a financial burden". See too *Moule v Garrett* (1872) L.R. 7 Ex. 101 at 104; *Brook's Wharf and Bull Wharf Ltd v Goodman Bros* [1937] 1 K.B. 534 at 544 (CA); *Regional Municipality of Peel v Canada* [1992] 3 S.C.R. 762 at 790; *Aetna Insurance Co v Canadian Surety Co* (1994) 114 D.L.R. (4th) 577 at 628 (Alberta CA); *AMP Workers' Compensation Services (NSW) Ltd v QBE Insurance Ltd* [2001] NSWCA 267; (2001) 53 N.S.W.L.R. 35 at 40; *Amertek Inc v Canadian Commercial Corp* (2003) 229 D.L.R. (4th) 419 at [472]; *Littlewoods Retail Ltd v HMRC* [2010] EWHC 1071 (Ch); [2010] S.T.C. 2072 at [121].

which it was factually necessary for him to acquire. When deciding whether an expense was factually necessary, the courts take a broad and commonsensical view, and do not insist, for example, that the expense must have related to the bare essentials of life.[36] It is enough that the expense was one that the defendant would have borne if the claimant had not relieved him of the need to do so.[37] So, in *Craven-Ellis v Canons Ltd*,[38] the defendant company would have bought the services of another managing director if the claimant had not served in this capacity; in *China Pacific SA v Food Corp of India (The Winson)*,[39] cargo owners were enriched when salvors of the cargo incurred storage charges while awaiting instructions as to what should be done with it; and in *R. (Rowe) v Vale of White Horse DC*,[40] the defendant would have had to pay someone else for sewerage services if the claimant had not supplied them.

4–20   These cases may be contrasted with *Amin v Amin*[41] where a woman worked for her father's business for 19 years without payment. She acted in the hope and expectation of reward, but would have worked for nothing if asked to do so, or would have accepted low pay if this had been all that he could have afforded.[42] After her father's death she claimed the value of her services, which she argued was the market rate that would otherwise have been paid to a third party for the work. Warren J. held that this was not an appropriate yardstick by which to measure the value of her services. She had not shown that the business would

---

[36] Birks, *An Introduction to the Law of Restitution*, p.120: the courts can disregard "unrealistic or fanciful possibilities of [the defendant's] doing without [the benefit]".

[37] Birks, *An Introduction to the Law of Restitution*, p.122, adding that such a liberal test can be supported by analogy with cases on the liability of minors to pay for necessaries; these indicate that goods and services are necessary not only when they support life but also when they maintain the defendant according to his circumstances of life: *Peters v Fleming* (1840) 6 M. & W. 42; 151 E.R. 314; *Chapple v Cooper* (1844) 13 M. & W. 252; 153 E.R. 105; *Ryder v Wombwell* (1868) L.R. 4 Exch. 32; Sale of Goods Act 1979 s.3(3).

[38] *Craven-Ellis v Canons Ltd* [1936] 2 K.B. 403. Further examples are: *Great Northern Railway Co v Swaffield* (1874) L.R. 9 Ex. 132 (stabling fees); *Re Rhodes* (1889) 44 Ch. D. 94 especially at 105 (CA) (costs of keeping mentally incapable relative in an asylum; no liability because payment made as a gift); *Upton-on-Severn RDC v Powell* [1942] 1 All E.R. 220 (fire rescue services); *Monks v Poynice Pty Ltd* (1987) 11 A.C.L.R. 637 (NSW Sup Ct) (receiver's services); *Re Berkeley Applegate (Investment Consultants) Ltd* [1989] Ch. 32 especially at 50 (liquidator's services); *Countrywide Communications Ltd v ICL Pathway Ltd* [2000] C.L.C. 324 at 351 (public relations services); *Gidney v Feuerstein* (1995) 101 Man. R. (2d) 197 (Manitoba QB) (repairs to canoe), reversed on a different point (1995) 107 Man. R. (2d) 208 (Manitoba CA); *Guildford BC v Hein* [2005] EWCA Civ 979 (kenneling fees); *H&I Enterprises (Vankleek) Ltd v Amco Express Inc* (2006) 40 M.V.R. (5th) 99 (Ontario Sup Ct) (highway accident recovery services).

[39] *China Pacific SA v Food Corp of India (The Winson)* [1982] A.C. 939, distinguished in *E.N.E. 1 Kos Ltd v Petroleo Brasileiro SA (The Kos)* [2010] EWCA Civ 772; [2010] 2 Lloyd's Rep. 409, where the court held at [31] that the defendant charterers had received a benefit by being saved the expense of looking after their cargo for two and a half days, but also held that their enrichment was not unjust.

[40] *R. (Rowe) v Vale of White Horse DC* [2003] EWHC 388 (Admin); [2003] 1 Lloyd's Rep. 418. Cf. *Clarke v Guardians of the Cuckfield Union* (1852) 21 L.J. (QB) 349 (water closets); *Nicholson v Guardians of the Bradfield Union* (1866) L.R. 1 Q.B. 620 (coal); *Lawford v Billericay RDC* [1903] 1 K.B. 772 (CA) (sewers). In all of these cases, corporations were ordered to pay for necessaries although their contracts with their suppliers were not under seal.

[41] *Amin v Amin* [2009] EWHC 3356 (Ch); further proceedings [2010] EWHC 528 (Ch). See too *Oddguys Holdings Ltd v S.C.Y. Chow Enterprises Co* [2010] BCCA 176; (2010) 5 B.C.L.R. (5th) 229 (landowner not benefited by neighbour's reconstruction of party wall after fire when it chose not to rebuild on plot).

[42] *Amin* [2009] EWHC 3356 (Ch) at [393]–[395].

inevitably have employed a third party if she had not done the work, and in these circumstances "[if] a particular employer acting fairly and reasonably [can] obtain the services of a particular person for less than [the] market rate, there is no reason . . . to grant a remedy of 'full' restitution."[43]

Just as a defendant is enriched in a three-party case when a claimant discharges his legal liability to a third party, so too is a defendant enriched in a two-party case where a claimant releases him from a liability owed to a claimant. Thus the Court of Appeal held in *Gibb v Maidstone and Tunbridge Wells NHS Trust*[44] that in principle a claim in unjust enrichment would lie to recover the value of a legal right foregone in a void compromise agreement, Laws L.J. stating that there is no difference between "a benefit consisting in money paid and a benefit consisting in a claim foregone".[45] This case may be contrasted with *Test Claimants in the F.I.I. Group Litigation v HMRC*[46] where the claimants used tax reliefs to reduce their liability to pay tax that had allegedly been levied in breach of EU law. The question arose whether a claim would lie for the value of these reliefs, on the basis that the claimants would otherwise have used them to reduce their liability to pay lawful tax. The Court of Appeal held not, because HMRC's gain was too remote a consequence of the claimants' use of the reliefs,[47] and in any case the money paid must ex hypothesi have been due under the relevant tax statute.[48] These findings are both discussed elsewhere.[49] *Gibb* may also be contrasted with *Hudson v HM Treasury*,[50] where the claimant servicemen failed to persuade the court that the Treasury had been enriched at their expense because their gross pay had been set at a lower level than it would have been had they not been members of a non-contributory pension scheme.

4–21

(iii) *Pre-emptive Liabilities*

It sometimes happens that the law can choose whether to make a claimant or a defendant liable to a third party, and that its choice falls upon the claimant, with the result that the defendant never becomes liable, even though it is the defendant rather than the claimant upon whom the burden of paying the third party should ultimately rest. In cases of this kind, the claimant should be able to say that his payment has relieved the defendant of a burden even though the defendant never owed a legal liability which was discharged by the claimant.

4–22

---

[43] *Amin* [2010] EWHC 528 (Ch) at [11].

[44] *Gibb v Maidstone and Tunbridge Wells NHS Trust* [2010] EWCA Civ 678; [2010] I.R.L.R. 786 at [24]–[37].

[45] *Gibb* [2010] EWCA Civ 678 at [30]. Cf. *Insurance Corp of British Columbia v Pohl's Bakery & Pastry Ltd* [2006] BCCA 51, where the claimant mistakenly undercharged the defendant for insurance coverage and was entitled to recover the difference between the premium actually paid and the premium that should have been paid.

[46] *Test Claimants in the F.I.I. Group Litigation v HMRC* [2010] EWCA Civ 103; [2010] S.T.C. 1251.

[47] *F.I.I.* [2010] EWCA Civ 103; [2010] S.T.C. 1251 at [179]–[184].

[48] *F.I.I.* [2010] EWCA Civ 103; [2010] S.T.C. 1251 at [181].

[49] See paras 2–10—2–12 and 6–07—6–09.

[50] *Hudson v HM Treasury* [2003] EWCA Civ 1612.

4–23   *Receiver for Metropolitan Police District v Croydon Corp*[51] was like this. The claimant police authority was under a statutory obligation to pay wages to its officers while they were incapacitated by injuries received in the course of duty. The claimant therefore paid wages to an officer who was injured at work through the defendant's negligence. The officer recovered damages from the defendant which were reduced to take the wages into account, and the authority sued the defendant to recover the amount of the wages on the ground that it had effectively discharged a portion of the defendant's liability. At first instance, Slade J. found for the police authority, holding that if the officer had not been paid the wages then the damages payable by the defendant would inevitably have been increased by a corresponding amount.[52]

4–24   Unfortunately this decision was reversed on appeal. The Court of Appeal reasoned that the police authority had been under a statutory duty regardless of whether a third party was also liable for the officer's injuries, that the defendant had therefore been liable only for the amount of damages which had been awarded after the authority's payment had been taken into account and, hence, that its payment had not discharged any liability owed by the defendant. This analysis begs the question of why the authority's payment should have been disregarded when the officer's damages were assessed, and as the Law Commission points out in its report on collateral benefits, "the payment under legal compulsion of a deductible collateral benefit does in reality benefit the tortfeasor by discharging his or her liability to the victim".[53]

4–25   Another case like this is *A.M.P. Workers Compensation Services (NSW) Ltd v Q.B.E. Insurance Ltd.*[54] An employer held a third party motor insurance policy with Q.B.E. in respect of one of its vehicles and a workers' compensation policy with A.M.P. One of its employees negligently injured another of its employees while driving the vehicle and while both employees were acting in the course of their employment. The injured employee sued the negligent employee, but he did not seek to join the employer to his action even though it would have been vicariously liable in tort for his injuries. The proceedings were settled, and Q.B.E. satisfied the judgment debt as the motor policy covered the employee as

---

[51] *Receiver for Metropolitan Police District v Croydon Corp* [1957] 2 Q.B. 154; affirming *Monmouthshire CC v Smith* [1956] 1 W.L.R. 1132; impliedly overruling *Receiver for the Metropolitan Police District v Tatum* [1948] 2 K.B. 68, and reversing Slade J.'s decision at first instance, which is reported at [1956] 1 W.L.R. 1113. See too *Re Nott and Cardiff Corp* [1918] 2 K.B. 146 (CA), reversed on another point sub. nom. *Brodie v Cardiff Corp* [1919] A.C. 337 (HL); *Condev Project Planning Ltd v Kramer Auto Sales Ltd* [1982] 2 W.W.R. 445 (Alberta Q.B.).
[52] *Croydon Corp* [1956] 1 W.L.R. 1113 at 1130–1131.
[53] Law Commission, *Damages for Personal Injury: Medical, Nursing, and Other Expenses; Collateral Benefits* (1999), Law Com. No.262 para.12.28. See too Law Commission, *Damages for Personal Injuries: Collateral Benefits* (1997), LCCP No.147, paras 5.4–5.6. See too Sachs J.'s comments in *Land Hessen v Gray* Unreported QBD, July 31, 1998.
[54] *A.M.P. Workers Compensation Services (NSW) Ltd v Q.B.E. Insurance Ltd* (2001) 53 N.S.W.L.R. 35 (NSWCA), followed in *WorkCover Qld v Suncorp Metway Insurance Ltd* [2005] QCA 155 at [46]–[50]; *Limit (No.3) Ltd v A.C.E. Insurance Ltd* [2009] NSWSC 514 at [259]–[303]; *Zurich Australian Insurance Ltd v G.I.O. General Ltd* [2011] NSWCA 47. See too *Jefferys v Gurr* (1831) 2 B. & Ad. 833 at 844; 109 E.R. 1352 at 1356 per Taunton J., rejecting the defendants' argument that they had owed the creditor no liability because the claimant had been "the defendant on the record" in the creditor's proceedings. These cases all differ from *Fuji Xerox Finance Ltd v Elizabeth Taylor Graphics Ltd* [2009] NZHC 167 at [27], where the basis on which the defendant was alleged to be liable to the creditor was factually inconsistent with the basis on which the claimant was allegedly liable.

the driver of the vehicle. Q.B.E. then sought contribution from A.M.P., which refused to pay on the grounds that the workers' compensation policy did not cover the negligent employee who had been sued, and that the employer who would have been covered by this policy had not been sued by the innocent employee, with the result that it had never been entitled to claim under the policy. Hence Q.B.E.'s payment had not discharged A.M.P. from liability, because A.M.P. had never been liable. This argument was rejected on the robust grounds that the employer had owed a "liability in tort to pay damages contemporaneously with the accrual to [the injured employee] of a cause of action", that the A.M.P. policy covered the risk of the employer's liability, and that "the payment by Q.B.E. extinguished the employer's liability", and with it A.M.P.'s "contingent liability . . . to indemnify the employer".[55]

Even if the courts accept that a claim should lie where the claimant's payment **4-26** has effectively pre-empted the defendant's exposure to liability, this principle would not apply unless the defendant's liability would *inevitably* have arisen but for the claimant's payment. This is illustrated by *Peel v Ontario*.[56] The claimant municipality was ordered to pay for the support of juveniles in foster homes and charitable institutions, pursuant to the courts' jurisdiction under a Canadian statute, the Juvenile Delinquents Act 1970. The municipality paid under protest, but it later established that the legislation was ultra vires, and sought to recover the value of its payments from the provincial and federal governments. The claim failed because the municipality could not establish that the defendants had been enriched by its payments. To show this, it would have had to prove that the defendants would inevitably have been liable to pay the costs but for the claimant's payments, and this was something which it could not do. In McLachlin J.'s words, it was:

> "neither inevitable nor likely . . . that in the absence of a scheme which required payment by the municipality the federal or provincial government would have made such payments; an entirely different scheme could have been adopted, for example."[57]

(c) *Requested and Freely Accepted Benefits*

A defendant cannot complain of interference with his freedom of choice where **4-27** he has freely exercised a choice to accept a benefit which he knows has not been offered gratuitously, or at less than the market price. The clearest example is where the defendant expressly requests a benefit. Here the parties are likely to have a contract, in which case the contract will govern their relationship, and the claimant will not be allowed to claim in unjust enrichment if this would subvert the contractual allocation of risk. But a claim in unjust enrichment may lie where the parties have a contract which is terminated for breach, or where their

---

[55] *A.M.P. Workers* (2001) 53 N.S.W.L.R. 35 at 39 per Handley J.A.; quoting *Australian Iron & Steel Pty Ltd v Government Insurance Office of New South Wales* [1978] 2 N.S.W.L.R. 59 at 62 per Glass J.A. (NSWCA).
[56] *Peel v Ontario* [1992] 3 S.C.R. 762; distinguished in *Skibinski v Community Living British Columbia* [2010] BCSC 1500; (2010) 13 B.C.L.R. (5th) 271 at [146]–[176] (where the defendant was under an obligation to pay for the care of a mentally disabled woman cared for the claimant).
[57] *Peel v Ontario* [1992] 3 S.C.R. 762 at 798.

agreement is frustrated or legally unenforceable, or where they have been negotiating towards a contract without settling the terms prior to the claimant's performance.

4–28   For example, in *Pavey & Matthews Ltd v Paul*,[58] the defendant was held to have been enriched by building work which she had requested, and which the claimant had completed, before the defendant refused to pay on the ground that their agreement was unenforceable for want of writing. In *Vedatech Corp v Crystal Decisions (UK) Ltd*,[59] the defendant software company asked the claimant to do consulting work leading to the introduction of its products into the Japanese market. The parties never agreed the terms on which this work would be done, but a claim lay in unjust enrichment to recover its value, to be quantified on a commission basis since this was consistent with the parties' general expectations. In *Pacific National Investments Ltd v City of Victoria*,[60] the claimant developer improved the defendant municipality's land under an agreement that was partially ultra vires. The defendant argued that the improvements were a burden rather than a benefit because it was now required to pay for annual upkeep. The court rejected this, and held that the improvements constituted an enrichment because the defendant had asked for them.

4–29   More controversial is the question whether a market valuation should be used where a defendant has not requested a benefit, but has failed to take a reasonable opportunity to reject it, in circumstances where a reasonable person would have known that the claimant expected to be paid at the market price. In the first and subsequent editions of this work, it was argued that defendants who behave in this way are enriched because they have "freely accepted" the relevant benefit at the market price,[61] and this terminology has now passed into general judicial usage.[62] Free acceptance has been criticised as a test for enrichment because the defendant's behaviour may simply reflect indifference to the benefit being rendered, suggesting that market value should be ascribed to the benefit only where the defendant's conduct shows that he has actively sought it out, although he now refuses to pay for it.[63] Nevertheless, the Australian, Canadian and New Zealand courts have all held that when a defendant does not take a reasonable opportunity

---

[58] *Pavey & Matthews Ltd v Paul* (1987) 167 C.L.R. 221. See too *Dimond v Lovell* [2002] 1 A.C. 384 at 397–398, where Lord Hoffmann accepted that the defendant was enriched but dismissed the claim for reasons of statutory policy.

[59] *Vedatech Corp v Crystal Decisions (UK) Ltd* [2002] EWHC 818 (Ch). See too *William Lacey (Hounslow) Ltd v Davis* [1957] 1 W.L.R. 932.

[60] *Pacific National Investments Ltd v City of Victoria* [2004] SCC 75; [2004] 3 S.C.R. 575. Cf. *Darmanin v Cowan* [2010] NSWSC 1118 at [266]–[267] (no enrichment where claimant builds house on defendants' land with their permission, but which they do not want, and the costs of demolishing which they must bear when he leaves).

[61] R. Goff and G. Jones, *The Law of Restitution*, 1st edn (London: Sweet & Maxwell, 1966), pp. 30–31. See too Birks, *An Introduction to the Law of Restitution*, p.265: "A free acceptance occurs where a recipient knows that a benefit is being offered to him non-gratuitously and where he, having the opportunity to reject, elects to accept."

[62] *Bridgewater v Griffiths* [2000] 1 W.L.R. 524 at 532; *Rowe* [2003] EWHC 388 (Admin); [2003] 1 Lloyd's Rep. 418 at [12]; *Cressman* [2004] EWCA Civ 47; [2004] 1 W.L.R. 2775 at [27]–[32]; *J.S. Bloor* [2008] EWHC 724 (TCC); [2008] 2 E.G.L.R. 85 at [50]; *Chief Constable of Greater Manchester v Wigan Athletic AFC Ltd* [2008] EWCA Civ 1449; [2009] 1 W.L.R. 1580 at [47]–[48]; *Benedetti* [2010] EWCA Civ 1427 at [105]–[106] and [118]–[120].

[63] A. Burrows, "Free Acceptance and the Law of Restitution" (1988) 104 L.Q.R. 576; Burrows, *The Law of Restitution*, pp.57–58.

to reject a benefit, this constitutes unconscientious behaviour that precludes him from denying that he values the benefit at the market rate because he has "freely accepted" it,[64] and there are signs that the English courts are now moving in the same direction.

In *Rowe*,[65] it was common ground that "free acceptance" can establish **4-30** enrichment, but Lightman J. held that it was not made out on the facts because the defendant had reasonably believed that the claimant's services had already been paid for. In *Cressman*[66] Mance L.J. held that the defendant's enrichment could have been established using a free acceptance test, but that this was established in any case because the defendant had consciously chosen not to return a readily returnable benefit. In *Chief Constable of Greater Manchester Police v Wigan Athletic AFC*,[67] Mann J. held that the defendant football club was enriched when it freely accepted special police services provided by the claimant police authority. The defendant had agreed to pay for a certain level of services, but had disputed the police authority's contention that additional services were needed. Nevertheless it freely accepted the additional services that were provided rather than cancel its home matches which would have been its only alternative because the police authority could otherwise have refused to issue a safety certificate for the matches. This decision was overturned by a majority of the Court of Appeal, which held that there had been no free acceptance on the facts: because the club had been unable to reject the additional services without also rejecting the services that it had requested, it could not be said to have freely accepted them.[68] This reasoning is suspect because a defendant in this position is free not to take any of the services, albeit that he would prefer to take some without the rest. Although the majority disagreed with this interpretation of the facts, Maurice Kay L.J. held in his dissenting judgment that enrichment could also have been established on the basis that the additional officers were a factually necessary expense for the club, because the home matches could not have been played without them.[69]

---

[64] Commonwealth cases where "free acceptance" reasoning has expressly been used to establish enrichment are: *Van den Berg v Giles* [1979] 2 N.Z.L.R. 111 at 120–121 (NZ High Ct); *Brenner* [1993] 2 V.R. 221 at 259–260 (Victoria Sup Ct); *Angelopoulos v Sabatino* [1995] SASC 5536; (1995) 65 S.A.S.R. 1 at [49]–[51]; *Andrew Shelton & Co Pty Ltd v Alpha Healthcare Ltd* [2002] VSC 248 at [128]; *W. Cook Builders Pty Ltd (In Liquidation) v Lumbers* [2007] SASC 20; (2007) 96 S.A.S.R. 406 at [77]–[85] (Full Ct of Sup Ct of South Australia); reversed on a different point [2008] HCA 27; (2008) 232 C.L.R. 635. In many family property cases starting with *Pettkus v Becker* [1980] 2 S.C.R. 834, the Canadian courts have assumed that the defendant was enriched and then used "free acceptance" to explain why his enrichment was unjust, but "free acceptance" also explains the finding of enrichment: M. McInnes, "Enrichment Revisited" in Neyers, *Understanding Unjust Enrichment*, 165, pp.180–183.
[65] *Rowe* [2003] EWHC 388 (Admin); [2003] 1 Lloyd's Rep. 418. Earlier English cases which might also be explained in terms of "free acceptance" are: *Lamb v Bunce* (1815) 4 M. & S. 275; 105 E.R. 836; *Weatherby v Banham* (1832) 5 C. & P. 228; 172 E.R. 950; *Paynter v Williams* (1833) 1 Cr. & M. 810; 149 E.R. 626; *Alexander v Vane* (1836) 1 M. & W. 511; 150 E.R. 537.
[66] *Cressman* [2004] EWCA 133; [2004] 1 W.L.R. 2774 at [28]–[32]. For the facts see para.4–16. And cf. *Rumsey v North Eastern Railway Co* (1863) 14 C.B. (N.S.) 641 at 650; 143 E.R. 596 at 600 (carriage of plaintiff's baggage on railway procured by deception).
[67] *Chief Constable of Greater Manchester Police v Wigan Athletic AFC* [2007] EWHC 3095 (Ch); [2007] Po. L.R. 246; reversed [2008] EWCA Civ 1449; [2009] 1 W.L.R. 1590.
[68] *Wigan Athletic* [2009] 1 W.L.R. 1590 at [47].
[69] See para 4–19.

4–31   The *Wigan Athletic* case was distinguished by Patten J. in *Benedetti*,[70] which concerned a claim for the value of services by a financial consultant who had promoted and facilitated a takeover deal. The defendants included some companies which had received the benefit of the claimant's work, knowing that he expected to be paid, which "were not in the position of subsequent purchasers of an asset with no connection to what had gone before" and which "were not required to enter into the acquisition". Their decision to do so, "although necessary for the completion of the transaction, had a sufficient degree of freedom" to make it possible to say that they had freely accepted the claimant's work. On appeal, this finding was reversed. Arden L.J. held that the defendants could not have freely accepted the services because they had never had the opportunity to reject them and still proceed with the deal.[71] She took this to follow from the *Wigan Athletic* case, but her reasoning is open to the same criticism as the reasoning in that case, and indeed the facts of *Benedetti* made it even less plausible to say that the defendants had been given no free choice. They wanted to proceed with the deal (which was financially advantageous to them), and the only reason why the deal was available to them was because the claimant had done the work of setting it up. In these circumstances why should they have been entitled to say that they would have preferred to do the deal without also taking the benefit of the claimant's work?

4–32   In *Rowe*,[72] Lightman J. gave these further examples of cases where free acceptance cannot be established on the facts[73]:

- where there is a common understanding between the claimant and the defendant that a third party shall alone be liable to pay for the services supplied[74];

- where the claimant continues to foist his services on an unwilling defendant after the defendant has insisted that, if he does so, the defendant will not pay for them[75]; and

---

[70] *Benedetti* [2009] EWHC 1330 (Ch) at [575]. See too *Proactive Sports Management Ltd v Rooney* [2010] EWHC 1807 (QB) at [742]–[762], where the defendant footballer was held to have freely accepted the services of an agent, rendered under a contract that was unenforceable as being in restraint of trade.

[71] *Benedetti* [2010] EWCA Civ 1427 at [118]–[119].

[72] *Rowe* [2003] EWHC 388 (Admin); [2003] 1 Lloyd's Rep. 418.

[73] *Rowe* [2003] EWHC 388 (Admin); [2003] 1 Lloyd's Rep. 418 at [14]. See too *Munro v Butt* (1858) 8 El. & Bl. 739; 120 E.R. 275 (no choice whether to accept work done on land); *Leigh v Dickson* (1884) 15 Q.B.D. 60 at 64 per Brett M.R., dismissing the claim because the defendant had had no "option . . . to adopt or decline the benefit"; *Sumpter v Hedges* [1898] 1 Q.B. 673 (defendant chose to take tools and materials, but had no choice whether to accept partially completed building); *Lady Manor Ltd v Fat Cat Café Bars Ltd* [2001] 2 E.G.L.R. 1 (no transaction fee for "cold-calling" estate agent); *Oliver v Lakeside Property Trust Pty Ltd* [2005] NSWSC 1040 at [88]: defendants "had no choice whether to accept or reject the plaintiffs' work at the relevant time"; *J.S. Bloor* [2008] EWHC 724 (TCC); [2008] 2 E.G.L.R. 85 especially at [47] and [50] (no choice to accept or reject benefit).

[74] Citing *Bridgewater v Griffiths* [2000] 1 W.L.R. 524 at 532.

[75] Citing *Bookmakers Afternoon Greyhound Services Ltd v Gilbert* [1994] F.S.R. 723, for discussion of which see too *Wigan Athletic* [2008] EWCA Civ 1449; [2009] 1 W.L.R. 1590 at [42]–[48]. And cf. *Damberg v Damberg* [2001] NSWCA 87; (2001) 52 N.S.W.L.R. 492 at [193].

- where an architect, having agreed a fee for specified services, renders additional services where the client when he accepted them was reasonably entitled to assume that the architect was undertaking them for no additional charge.[76]

Note that the question whether English law regards "free acceptance" as a test   **4–33**
to determine the measure of a defendant's enrichment is different from the question whether it regards "free acceptance" as a test to determine whether a defendant's enrichment is unjust. The latter question is discussed in Ch.17.

4. DATE OF ENRICHMENT

(a) *Enrichment is Tested at the Date of Receipt*

Where a claimant seeks a personal restitutionary remedy to reverse a transfer of   **4–34**
value, the questions whether the defendant was enriched, and if so, to what extent, are tested at the date of receipt.[77] Consistently with this, a cause of action to recover the value of a mistaken payment accrues at the date of receipt,[78] as does a cause of action to recover the value of money paid on a basis that immediately fails,[79] and a cause of action to recover money paid as tax which was not due.[80] Likewise, a cause of action to recover the value of a debt discharged by a claimant who was only secondarily liable to the creditor accrues at the date of payment.[81] Even where a cause of action does not accrue until later—for example, because it is founded on a failure of basis which post-dates receipt of the benefit[82]—the extent of the defendant's enrichment is still tested at the date of receipt. So an Australian judge has held that[83]:

---

[76] Citing *Gilbert v Knight* [1968] 2 All E.R. 248.

[77] Cf. *Moses v Macferlan* (1760) 2 Burr. 1005 at 1010; 97 E.R. 676 at 679 per Lord Mansfield: the defendant in an action for money had and received could be "liable no further than the money he has received".

[78] *Baker v Courage & Co* [1910] 1 K.B. 56; *Kleinwort Benson v Lincoln CC* [1999] 2 A.C. 349 at 386 and 409; *Fuller v Happy Shopper Markets Ltd* [2001] EWHC 702 (Ch); [2001] 1 W.L.R. 1681 at [12]–[18]; *Fea v Roberts* [2005] EWHC 2186 (Ch); (2005) 8 I.T.E.L.R. 231 at [61]. See too paras 33–11—33–17.

[79] *Kleinwort Benson* [1994] 4 All E.R. 972 at 978 (and note Hobhouse J.'s comment at 976 that the ground of recovery in the case was not mistake but "absence"/immediate failure of basis).

[80] *Woolwich Equitable BS v IRC* [1993] A.C. 70 at 171.

[81] *Davies v Humphreys* (1840) 6 M. & W. 153 at 168–169, 151 E.R. 361 at 367–368; *Wolmershausen v Gullick* [1893] 2 Ch. 514; *Walker v Bowry* (1924) 35 C.L.R. 48; *Hawrish v Peters* [1982] 1 S.C.R. 1083. See too CMR art.39(4); Merchant Shipping Act 1995 s.190; Limitation Act 1980 s.10. But note the problems that this rule creates in cases of double insurance, discussed at para.20–05.

[82] *David Securities Pty Ltd v Commonwealth Bank of Australia* (1992) 175 C.L.R. 353 at 389. For this reason Millett J. must have been wrong to say in *El Ajou v Dollar Land Holdings Plc* [1993] B.C.L.C. 735 at 757, that all actions for money had and received are "complete when the money is received".

[83] *Dowell v Custombuilt Homes Pty Ltd* [2004] WASCA 171 at [98] per Murray J. See too *BP Exploration Co (Libya) Ltd v Hunt (No.2)* [1979] 1 W.L.R. 783 at 836 per Robert Goff J.: "the cause of action [in unjust enrichment for a *quantum valebat* or *quantum meruit* award] arises when the goods are sold and delivered, or the services rendered, though the quantification of the recoverable sum may not be known until the court gives judgment."

> "[T]he obligation of a purchaser who accepts and retains goods under an incomplete or unenforceable contract, to make payment of a reasonable price for the benefit so obtained is based on the principles of unjust enrichment and requires the payment of the value of the benefit accepted and retained as it was at the time that the benefit was taken."

The same rule applies to services claims: the cause of action accrues when the services are rendered,[84] and the valuation has to be carried out as at the same date.[85] One consequence of this is that a defendant who asks for services cannot afterwards deny that he was enriched by the work because he has changed his mind about wanting them. For example, if a developer asks an engineer to draw up plans for a building, but then decides on a different design, he cannot deny that he was enriched by the engineer's work even though he will never use the plans: at the time when the work was done it was what he wanted.[86]

(b) *Contrary Authorities?*

4-35   Some authorities might seem to contradict the foregoing statement of the law, but on closer inspection it can be seen that they do not. First, a claimant may recover more than the value received by a defendant in cases where he wins a proprietary remedy and the property to which he is entitled has increased in value between the date of receipt and the date of judgment. However cases of this kind depend upon proof that the defendant has received a right to property or its traceable substitute,[87] and while the current value of the right may make a difference to the

---

[84] *Sydney CC v Woodward* [2000] NSWCA 201 at [94]; *Abigroup Contractors Pty Ltd v Peninsula Balmain Pty Ltd (No.2)* [2001] NSWSC 1016 at [25]–[34]; *Coshott v Lenin* [2007] NSWCA 153 at [17].

[85] *Benedetti* [2009] EWHC 1330 (Ch) at [528]; affirmed [2010] EWCA Civ 1427 at [80]; *A v B* [2009] EWHC 2859 (Ch) [68] (proposition (1)). See too *Flett v Deniliquen Publishing Co Ltd* [1964–1965] N.S.W.R. 383 at 385–386 per Herron C.J. (NSWCA): the award is "properly assessed at the normal market rate or price prevailing when the benefit was received"; *Becerra v Close Bros Corporate Finance Ltd* Unreported QBD (Comm Ct) June 25, 1999 (Thomas J.) (where the claim failed because the defendant's enrichment was not unjust); *Sharab v Salfiti* [1996] EWCA Civ 1189, where Judge L.J. did not understand that the claimant's non-contractual right to a quantum meruit award must have derived from the law of unjust enrichment, but held in connection with such awards that "the valuation of the services rendered should [not] be affected by the use to which the recipient subsequently puts them, and in particular whether that use results in a business triumph or financial disaster".

[86] *A.B.B. Engineering Construction Pty Ltd v Abigroup Contractors Pty Ltd* [2003] NSWSC 665 at [211]–[213], referring to the "three steps forward, two steps back" nature of many engineering and design projects. See too *Brewer Street Investments Ltd v Barclays Woollen Co Ltd* [1954] 1 Q.B. 428; *William Lacey* [1957] 1 W.L.R. 932. And cf. *Stinchcombe v Thomas* [1957] V.R. 509 (Victoria Sup Ct), where the defendant's estate had to pay for his housekeeper's services over the previous $5\frac{1}{2}$ years (her claims for the rest were time-barred), although senility had made him hostile and ungrateful towards her for the last two years of his life.

[87] *Boscawen v Bajwa* [1996] 1 W.L.R. 328 at 334; cf. *Serious Fraud Office v Lexi Holdings Plc (In Administration)* [2008] EWCA Crim 1443; [2009] Q.B. 376 at [49]–[50], rejecting Lord Templeman's "swollen assets" theory in *Space Investments Ltd v Canadian Imperial Bank of Commerce Trust Co (Bahamas) Ltd* [1986] 1 W.L.R. 1072 (PC) (but note that on the view controversially taken in *Foskett v McKeown* [2001] 1 A.C. 102, a beneficiary's right to claim the traceable proceeds of misdirected trust funds from a third party recipient does not arise in unjust enrichment; this is discussed at paras 8-84—8-86).

claimant for pragmatic reasons, its value at the time of receipt is irrelevant for the purposes of establishing his entitlement to proprietary restitution.[88]

Secondly, a claimant will recover more than the value received in cases where **4–36** he can recover the use value of the benefit between the date of receipt and the date of judgment, in addition to its exchange value at the time of receipt. In *Sempra*,[89] the House of Lords held that claims will lie in unjust enrichment to recover compound interest as the use value of money, over and above the exchange (face) value of the money received. But this does not mean that enrichment by value is tested at some other date than the date of receipt, since the court clearly viewed the use value of money as a distinct type of enrichment from its exchange value.[90]

Thirdly, a claimant will recover less than the value received in cases where the **4–37** defendant has a change of position defence. So, for example, Lord Templeman said in *Lipkin Gorman (A Firm) v Karpnale Ltd*[91] that a defendant who can invoke the defence because he bought an asset that has depreciated in value need pay no more than the value of the asset at the date of judgment. This does not detract from the rule that enrichment is tested at the date of receipt, either. It simply means that although the defendant was enriched by the value received, he need not repay the whole of this value because he has a partial defence to the claim—just as he need not repay it, for example, where the claim is subject to a time bar.[92] To put this in another way, the claimant does not have to show both that the defendant received the value *and that he still retains it*: he only has to show that the value was received, and subsequent disenrichments must then be proved by the defendant seeking to rely on a change of position defence. In Millett L.J.'s words, "the cause of action for money had and received is complete when the plaintiff's money is received by the defendant" and it "does not depend on the continued retention of the money by the defendant."[93]

More problematic are several cases which hold that claims for value received **4–38** are not the only claims for value recognised by the law, as claims for value surviving in the defendant's hands are also possible. However, none is particularly strong. One is *Trustee of the Property of F.C. Jones & Son (A Firm)*,[94] where the Court of Appeal held that the insolvency law doctrine of "relation

---

[88] For the argument that the receipt of rights is a separate type of enrichment from the receipt of value, see R. Chambers, "Two Types of Enrichment" in R. Chambers et al. (eds), *Philosophical Foundations of the Law of Unjust Enrichment* (Oxford: OUP, 2009), 242; and cf. B. Macfarlane, *The Structure of Property Law* (Oxford: Hart, 2008), Ch.D4.

[89] *Sempra* [2007] UKHL 34; [2008] A.C. 561.

[90] Nor was this benefit concerned with tracing the value inherent in the money received into the value inherent in another asset surviving in the defendant's hands: *Sempra* [2007] UKHL 34; [2008] A.C. 561 at [33] per Lord Hope, and at [117] per Lord Nicholls.

[91] *Lipkin Gorman v Karpnale Ltd* [1990] 2 A.C. 548 at 560.

[92] *David Securities* (1992) 175 C.L.R. 353 at 385: the availability of the defence of change of position "does not mean that the concept of unjust enrichment needs to shift the primary focus of its attention from the moment of enrichment. From the point of view of the person making the payment, what happens after he or she has mistakenly paid over the money is irrelevant, for it is at that moment that the defendant is unjustly enriched."

[93] *Portman Building Society v Hamlyn Taylor Neck (A Firm)* [1998] 4 All E.R. 202 at 207 (CA). See too *Garland v Consumers' Gas Co* [2004] SCC 25; [2004] 1 S.C.R. 629 at [37]; *Cofacredit SA v Clive Morris & Mora UK Ltd* [2006] EWHC 353 (Ch); [2007] 2 B.C.L.C. 99 at [14].

[94] *Trustee of the Property of F.C. Jones & Son (A Firm)* [1997] Ch. 159 (CA). The case is discussed further at paras 8–26—8–29.

back" generates a personal claim for the surviving value of the proceeds of money paid after an act of bankruptcy has been committed. This case is notoriously difficult to interpret, and Lord Millett, who was a member of the court, later denied in extra-judicial writings that the case had anything to do with unjust enrichment.[95]

4–39   Secondly, a line of Canadian cases concerned with cohabitational property disputes, starting with *Peter v Beblow*,[96] holds that claimants can be awarded an equitable share in property on the ground of unjust enrichment because this comprises the "surviving value" of their domestic labour. In *Kerr v Baranow*,[97] the Supreme Court of Canada also allowed a personal claim in unjust enrichment to recover the "surviving value" of the claimant's contributions to the wealth accumulated by the parties during the course of their quasi-marital "joint family venture". These authorities are unlikely to be followed by the English courts which have developed a different doctrinal vehicle through which to resolve familial property disputes, namely the common intention constructive trust.[98] Outside this context, and particularly in the context of commercial dealings, it is even less likely that the English courts will follow the Canadian cases, which take a notably loose approach to the identification of benefit, to the rule that the defendant's enrichment must have been gained at the claimant's expense, and to the question whether the claimant should be entitled to a personal or a proprietary remedy.[99]

4–40   Thirdly, there is the Court of Appeal's decision in *Cheese v Thomas*.[100] The claimant was unduly influenced by his great-nephew to buy a house with him that later declined in value. The claimant sought to recover the value of his contribution to the purchase price but the court held that the fall in value should be borne by both parties in proportion to their contributions, so that the claimant was effectively limited to recovery of the value surviving in the defendant's hands. In our view this outcome can only have been correct if the defendant was entitled to argue that he had changed his position by retaining his share of the house although its value was depreciating,[101] a debatable question because this defence may not be available in response to claims grounded on undue influence.[102]

---

[95] P. Millett, "Proprietary Restitution" in S. Degeling and J. Edelman (eds), *Equity in Commercial Law* (Sydney: Lawbook Co, 2005), 309, p.323; P. Millett, "*Jones v Jones*: Property or Unjust Enrichment?" in A. Burrows and Lord Rodger (eds), *Mapping the Law* (Oxford: OUP, 2006), 265.

[96] *Peter v Beblow* [1993] 1 S.C.R. 980.

[97] *Kerr v Baranow* [2011] SCC 10; [2011] 1 S.C.R. 269.

[98] *Stack v Dowden* [2007] UKHL 17; [2007] 2 A.C. 432; *Abbott v Abbott* [2007] UKPC 53; [2008] 1 F.L.R. 1451.

[99] For critical comment, see J. Mee, *The Property Rights of Cohabitees* (Oxford: Hart, 1999), especially pp.219–222 and 224; M. McInnes, "Reflections on the Canadian Law of Unjust Enrichment: Lessons From Abroad" (1999) 78 Can. Bar Rev. 416; M. McInnes, "The Measure of Restitution" (2002) 52 University of Toronto L.J. 163; J. McCamus, "Restitution on Dissolution of Marital or Other Intimate Relationships: Constructive Trust or *Quantum Meruit*?" in Neyers et al. (eds), *Understanding Unjust Enrichment*, 359, especially pp.372–375. See too para.6–66.

[100] *Cheese v Thomas* [1994] 1 W.L.R. 129.

[101] Cf. M. Chen-Wishart, "Loss Sharing, Undue Influence, and Manifest Disadvantage" (1994) 110 L.Q.R. 173, pp.177–178.

[102] See paras 11–25 and 27–47.

Fourthly, there is Robert Goff J.'s decision in *BP Exploration Co (Libya) Ltd*   **4–41**
v Hunt (No.2),[103] which concerned services claims under the Law Reform
(Frustrated Contracts) Act 1943 s.1(3). His Lordship held that the 1943 Act is
underpinned by the principle against unjust enrichment,[104] but he clearly did not
mean to lay down rules of general application since he also stressed the "considerable problems" created by the statutory wording.[105] Consistently with the
general rule described above, he held in relation to money claims under s.1(2)
that:

> "the money may have been paid . . . many years before the date of frustration; but the
> cause of action accrues on that date and the sum recoverable under the Act as at that
> date can be no greater than the sum actually paid".[106]

However, he laid down a different rule for services claims under s.1(3), namely
that the date for valuing the benefit received by the defendant is the date when
the contract is frustrated. He thought this to follow from s.1(3)(b), which he took
to mean that the court must have regard to the circumstances giving rise to the
frustration of the contract when quantifying the defendant's enrichment. He
reasoned that "if the effect of the frustrating event upon the value of the benefit
is to be measured, it must surely be measured upon the benefit as at the date of
frustration".[107] Consistency then required him to say that every non-money
benefit should be valued at this date for the purposes of a s.1(3) claim, although
this was inconsistent with his rule for money claims under s.1(2).

These problems could have been avoided if Robert Goff J. had construed   **4–42**
s.1(3)(b) to be relevant not to the quantification of the defendant's benefit, but to
the calculation of a "just sum" payable by the defendant under s.1(3). On this
reading, events such as the destruction of the fruits of the claimant's work might
entitle the defendant to raise a change of position defence, but would not affect
the rule that his enrichment is valued at the date of receipt—a rule which Robert
Goff J. himself would have preferred, since it would enable the courts to hold in
appropriate cases that the benefit received by the defendant was the claimant's
services, rather than their end-product.[108]

5. Significance of the Parties' Dealings Before Transfer of the Benefit

If the parties to a claim in unjust enrichment have had dealings prior to the   **4–43**
transfer which gives rise to the claim, then there are several ways in which these
may affect the identification and valuation of the defendant's enrichment.[109]
There are three main possibilities. First, the parties may have entered a contract
which still governs their relationship and the defendant's liability to pay for the
relevant benefit. Secondly, they may have entered a contract that has been

---

[103] *BP Exploration Co (Libya) Ltd v Hunt (No.2)* [1979] 1 W.L.R. 783.
[104] *BP v Hunt* [1979] 1 W.L.R. 783 at 799.
[105] *BP v Hunt* [1979] 1 W.L.R. 783 at 801.
[106] *BP v Hunt* [1979] 1 W.L.R. 783 at 800.
[107] *BP v Hunt* [1979] 1 W.L.R. 783 at 803.
[108] *BP v Hunt* [1979] 1 W.L.R. 783 at 803.
[109] For additional discussion of this topic, see paras 3–40—3–57.

terminated for breach. Thirdly, they may have been negotiating towards a contract but have failed to form a legally binding agreement, or they may have entered a contract that has been frustrated, or they may have purported to enter a contract that was void under some rule of law.

(a) Subsisting Contracts

4–44   If the parties' relationship is governed by a subsisting contract then the claimant may well be forbidden to sue in unjust enrichment to recover the value of the defendant's enrichment—something he might wish to do, for example, because the contract price is lower than the market price. It is a long-established principle that "no action can be brought for restitution while an inconsistent contractual promise subsists between the parties in relation to the subject matter of the claim".[110]

4–45   For example, in *Berkeley Community Villages Ltd v Pullen*,[111] the parties agreed that the claimant would do work to secure planning consent for the development of the defendant's farm. The contract provided for payment on a "no win, no fee" basis: the claimant would receive 10 per cent of the net returns in the event of a sale of the land with the benefit of the consent, but would receive nothing if the consent were not granted. The claimant made some progress, but before the consent was granted a third party offered to buy the land, and the claimant brought proceedings for an injunction to stop the sale. An injunction was granted, among other reasons, because the claimant would otherwise recover nothing for its work: its contractual right to payment was predicated on the granting of the consent, and "the express terms of the agreement as to remuneration [left] no scope for . . . a claim in restitution".[112]

4–46   This principle does not apply where the defendant receives a benefit that falls outside the scope of the parties' contract, as there is then no danger that recovery will subvert the parties' contractual allocation of risk.[113] In some rare cases the same can also be said of claims to recover the value of benefits which the claimant was contractually bound to provide. For example, in *Miles v Wakefield*

---

[110] *Trimis v Mina* [1999] NSWCA 140 at [54] per Mason P.; followed in *Mowlem Plc v Stena Line Ports Ltd* [2004] EWHC 2206 (TCC) at [40]. See too *Horton v Jones (No.2)* (1939) 39 S.R. (N.S.W.) 305 at 319; *Coshott v Lenin* [2007] NSWCA 153 at [10]. The history of this rule is discussed in J.W. Carter, "Discharged Contracts: Claims for Restitution" (1997) 11 J.C.L. 130, and other sources cited in C. Mitchell and C. Mitchell, "*Planché v Colburn*" in C. Mitchell and P. Mitchell (eds), *Landmark Cases in the Law of Restitution* (Oxford: Hart, 2006), 65, pp.89 and following. Note, too, that if a claimant contracts with a third party to provide services to a defendant who has contracted with the third party to receive them, then the claimant cannot sue the defendant in unjust enrichment for the value of the work: see paras 3–58—3–92.

[111] *Berkeley Community Villages Ltd v Pullen* [2007] EWHC 1330 (Ch); [2007] 3 E.G.L.R. 101.

[112] *Berkeley Community Villages* at [107] per Morgan J.

[113] As in e.g. *Astilleros Canarios SA v Cape Hatteras Shipping Co Inc (The Cape Hatteras)* [1982] 1 Lloyd's Rep. 518 at 524; *Debenham Tewson & Chinnocks Plc v Rimmington* [1989] 2 E.G.L.R. 26 at 30; *London Underground Ltd v Kenchington Ford Plc* (1998) 63 Con. L.R. 1 at 52; *Skookum Ventures Ltd v Long Hoh Enterprises Canada Ltd* [2005] BCSC 367; (2005) 3 B.L.R. (4th) 191. Note, though, that where the parties' contract expressly requires that written notice be given or other steps be taken prior to the performance of extra work, and this has not been done, a claim in unjust enrichment may be excluded: *Corpex (1977) Inc v R.* [1982] 2 S.C.R. 643.

DC,[114] Lord Brightman and Lord Templeman held that if an employee declines to perform his contractual obligations, but offers partial performance which is accepted by the employer, then the employee has no contractual right to his wages but can recover the value of his work in an action for unjust enrichment.

(b) *Terminated Contracts*

Where the parties have a contract that is terminated following a repudiatory   **4-47** breach, should the defendant's enrichment be valued by reference to the market price or the contract price? This is a difficult question, and the cases do not give a consistent answer.[115] Briefly summarised, the arguments favouring the use of a contractual valuation are, first, that it respects the defendant's freedom of choice because it requires him to pay no more than the amount which he agreed; and, secondly, that where the defendant is the party in breach, and the market price is higher than the contract price, he should not be permitted to reduce his liability by invoking the contract while simultaneously refusing to abide by its terms. Note that the first argument does not apply where the benefit is money or its close equivalent (realised benefits, etc). Arguments favouring the use of a market valuation are, first, that it takes account of the fact that the claimant may not have bargained solely for price-related benefits, but may also have expected to receive other benefits that will not materialise now that the contract has gone off, e.g. marketplace reputation, or the opportunity to bargain for further work down the line. Secondly, where the claimant is the party in breach, and the contract price is higher than the market price, he should not be allowed to increase his right by relying on the terms of the contract while refusing to abide by its terms.

(c) *No Contract*

The fear that a market valuation might subvert a contractual allocation of risk   **4-48** cannot arise in cases where the parties have never formed a contract, either because their negotiations never progressed to a binding agreement, or because their contract was rendered invalid by a rule of law, or because it was frustrated. However this does not mean that the contract terms and/or negotiations between the parties should be ignored when the court comes to identify the defendant's enrichment. On the contrary, it is well established that these matters are relevant,

---

[114] *Miles v Wakefield DC* [1987] A.C. 539 at 553 and 561, discussed in P. Sales, "Contract and Restitution in the Employment Relationship: No Work, No Pay" (1988) 8 O.J.L.S. 301, pp.307–309. See too *Roxborough v Rothmans of Pall Mall Australia Ltd* [2001] HCA 68; (2001) 108 C.L.R. 516, which raised similar issues although the parties' contract was discharged by complete performance.

[115] Authorities in point include: *Lodder v Slowey* [1904] A.C. 442 (PC); affirming (1901) 20 N.Z.L.R. 321 (NZCA); *Pavey* (1987) 167 C.L.R. 221 at 257; *Rover International Ltd v Cannon Film Sales Ltd* [1989] 1 W.L.R. 912 at 435–436 (CA); *Newton Woodhouse v Trevor Toys Ltd* Unreported CA, December 20, 1991; *Renard Constructions (ME) Pty Ltd v Minister for Public Works* (1992) 26 N.S.W.L.R. 234 at 276–278 (NSWCA); *Stephen Donald Architects Ltd v King* [2003] EWHC 1867 (TCC) at [75]–[76]; *Taylor v Motability Finance Ltd* [2004] EWHC 2619 (Comm); *Sopov v Kane Constructions Pty Ltd (No.2)* [2009] VSCA 141; (2009) 257 A.L.R. 182.

though not conclusive, evidence both of the way in which the parties conceptualised the benefit received by the defendant, and of the value which he attached to it. As Robert Walker L.J. said in *Guinness Mahon & Co v Kensington & Chelsea RLBC*[116]:

> "Where a supposed contract is void *ab initio*, or an expected contract is never concluded . . . no enforceable obligation is ever created, but the context of a supposed or expected contract is still relevant as explaining what the parties are about."

4–49   The significance of the parties' previous dealings will increase where there is no other evidence of reasonable price on which the court might draw,[117] and diminish where the benefit contemplated by the parties is of a substantially different kind to the benefit which has been conferred.[118] Also, "there is a clear difference between an ineffective agreement and one which the parties have effectively jettisoned", and if:

> "the parties ceased to regard the original contract price as an appropriate value for the services then there is no justification for the court imposing it as a measure of value unless it can be justified by other evidence as the market value of the services at the time when they were performed".[119]

Where a defendant has agreed to pay for a benefit at a particular rate he will find it hard to deny that he attached this value to the benefit. Conversely, where the claimant has fully performed his obligations, the defendant should be able to say that he values this performance at no higher rate than the rate which he agreed —although cases of part performance may be different because a prorated contract rate may undervalue work that was priced on the basis that full performance would bring additional gains such as savings from economies of scale.

4–50   In *BP v Hunt* Robert Goff J. described several ways in which the consideration agreed between the parties may be relevant evidence of the "just sum" to be awarded for non-monetary benefits under the Law Reform (Frustrated Contracts) Act 1943 s.1(3)[120]:

- First, the terms upon which the work was done may serve to indicate the full scope of the work done, and so be relevant to the sum awarded in respect of such work. For example, if I do work under a contract under which I am to receive a substantial prize if successful, and nothing if I fail, and the

---

[116] *Guinness Mahon & Co v Kensington & Chelsea RLBC* [1999] Q.B. 215 at 240 (CA). See too *Scarisbrick v Parkinson* (1869) 20 L.T. 175; *Way v Latilla* [1937] 3 All E.R. 759 at 764 and 766 (HL); *Stinchcombe v Thomas* [1957] V.R. 509 at 513 (Victoria Sup. Ct); *Jennings Construction Ltd v Q.H. & M. Birt Pty Ltd* Unreported New South Wales Sup Ct, December 16, 1988; *Rodier v Computerdial Ltd* Unreported CA, December 9, 1993; *Brenner* [1993] 2 V.R. 221 at 263 (Victoria Sup Ct); *Coleman v Seaborne Pty Ltd* [2007] NSWCA 60 at [42]; *Peet Ltd v Richmond* [2009] VSC 130 at [191]; *Benedetti* [2009] EWHC 1330 (Ch) at [528]; affirmed [2010] EWCA Civ 1427 at [63].

[117] Cf. *Flett* [1964–1965] N.S.W.R. 383 at 386 (NSWCA).

[118] Cf. *Choy Bing Wing v Hong Kong & Shanghai Hotels Ltd* [1995] HKCA 558 at [16]. Note that if the parties contract for the claimant to do work in a particular way and the claimant does it differently, he may still be able to recover the reasonable value of the work if the defendant has had a free choice whether or not to accept it, and has chosen to do so: *Steele v Tardiani* (1946) 72 C.L.R. 386.

[119] *Benedetti* [2009] EWHC 1330 (Ch); at [534]; affirmed [2010] EWCA Civ 1427 at [63]–[70].

[120] *BP v Hunt* [1979] 1 W.L.R. 783 at 805–806. Further discussion at paras 15–31——15–35.

contract is frustrated before the work is complete but not before a substantial benefit has been obtained by the defendant, the element of risk taken by the plaintiff may be held to have the effect of enhancing the amount of any sum to be awarded.

- Secondly, the contract consideration is always relevant as providing some evidence of what will be a reasonable sum to be awarded in respect of the plaintiff's work. Thus if a prospector, employed for a fee, discovers a gold mine before the contract under which he is employed is frustrated . . . at a time when his work was incomplete, the court may think it just to make an award in the nature of a reasonable fee for what he has done . . . and a rateable part of the contract fee may provide useful evidence of the level of sum to be awarded. If, however, the contract had provided that he was to receive a stake in the concession, then the just sum might be enhanced on the basis that, in all the circumstances, a reasonable sum should take account of such a factor.

- Thirdly, however, the contract consideration, or a rateable part of it, may provide a limit to the sum to be awarded. To take a fairly extreme example, a poor householder or a small businessman may obtain a contract for building work to be done to his premises at considerably less than the market price, on the basis that he cannot afford to pay more. In such a case, the court may consider it just to limit the award to a rateable part of the contract price, on the ground that it was the understanding of the parties that in no circumstances (including the circumstances of the contract being frustrated) should the plaintiff recover more than the contract price or a rateable part of it.

6. SIGNIFICANCE OF THE PARTIES' DEALINGS AFTER TRANSFER OF THE BENEFIT

In *Benedetti*[121] the claimant promoted and facilitated a takeover deal through   **4–51** which the defendant acquired a stake in an Italian telecommunications company. The parties fell out over the claimant's remuneration, as he wanted an equity stake in the target company, but the defendant was only willing to pay him a fee. At first instance, Patten J. found the market value of the claimant's services to have been €14.52 million, but he held that the defendant should pay €75.1 million, as this was the amount for which the defendant had offered to settle the claim, and this offer constituted evidence of the value that he attributed to the claimant's services. Patten J. noted the "obvious dangers in looking at negotiations between parties to a dispute" as evidence of the value attributed to a benefit by a defendant, "particularly once the threat of litigation has been made", but he held that the court should be able to receive "post-transaction evidence of the parties dealings with each other if and so far as that evidence does show the value which the paying party (albeit with the benefit of hindsight) considered that the services were worth".[122] On appeal, Arden L.J. agreed that "when the court is valuing an asset or liability as at a particular date it is entitled to have regard to

---

[121] *Benedetti* [2009] EWHC 1330 (Ch); varied on appeal [2010] EWCA Civ 1427.
[122] *Benedetti* [2009] EWHC 1330 (Ch) at [568].

evidence after that date which throws light on that value".[123] On the facts of the *Benedetti* case, however, the Court of Appeal did not accept that the defendant's settlement offer was good evidence of the value that he had attributed to the claimant's services, and the amount of the restitutionary award was therefore reduced to €14.52 million, this being the market value of these services.

7. Incidental Benefits

4-52 No claim lies in unjust enrichment to recover benefits which are "incidentally" conferred on a defendant by a claimant in the course of acting in his own interests. For example, in *Ruabon Steamship Co Ltd v London Assurance Co Ltd*,[124] a ship suffered damage for which insurers were liable to the owner. Whilst the ship was in dry dock for repairs, the owner arranged for the vessel to be surveyed by a Lloyd's surveyor, with a view to her retaining her Lloyd's classification. The insurers sought a contribution from the owner towards the costs of docking the vessel, on the basis that the owner had been saved the docking expenses which it would have incurred, if it had been obliged to have the ship surveyed on another occasion. The House of Lords rejected the claim, Lord Halsbury L.C. stating that he could not[125]:

> "understand how it can be asserted that it is part of the common law that where one person gets some advantage from the act of another a right of contribution towards the expense that arises on behalf of the person who has done it . . . [The law does not require that a contribution should be paid] where there is nothing in common between

---

[123] *Benedetti* [2010] EWCA Civ 1427 at [81]; citing *Bwllfa and Merthyr Dare Steam Collieries (1891) Ltd v Pontypridd Waterworks Co* [1903] A.C. 426. The *Bwllfa* case holds that when assessing compensation payable by a defendant the court can take evidence into account although it post-dates the claimant's loss; this principle was reaffirmed in *Golden Strait Corp v Nippon Yusen Kubishika Kaisha (The Golden Victory)* [2007] UKHL 12; [2007] 2 A.C. 353.

[124] *Ruabon Steamship Co Ltd v London Assurance Co Ltd* [1900] A.C. 6. See also *Buchanan v London & Provincial Marine Insurance Co Ltd* (1895) 1 Com. Cas 165; *The Acanthus* [1902] P. 17; *Crouan v Stanier* [1904] 1 K.B. 87; *Tanguay v Price* (1906) 37 S.C.R. 657 at 667; *Admiralty Commissioners v SS Chekiang* [1926] A.C. 637; *Sinclair Canada Oil Co v Pacific Petroleum Ltd* (1968) 67 D.L.R. (2d) 519 (Alberta CA) (affirmed on another point: (1969) 2 D.L.R. (3d) 338 (Sup Court of Canada)); *The Pythia* [1982] 2 Lloyd's Rep. 160; *Becerra v Close Bros Corporate Finance Ltd* Unreported QBD (Comm Ct), June 25, 1999 (Thomas J.); *Cockburn v G.I.O. Finance Ltd (No.2)* [2001] NSWCA 177; (2001) 51 N.S.W.L.R. 624 at 633; considered in *Burke v L.F.O.T. Pty Ltd* [2002] HCA 17; (2002) 209 C.L.R. 282 at [44]–[46]; *Neste Canada Inc v Allianz Insurance Co of Canada* [2008] ABCA 71 at [45]–[67]. Scots law has a similar principle: *Shilliday v Smith* 1998 S.C. 725 at 730–731 (Ct of Sess (IH)). American cases denying recovery of incidental benefits include: *US v Pacific Railroad Co* 120 U.S. 227 (1887); *Ulmer v Farnsworth*, 15 A. 65 (Maine Sup Ct, 1888); *Green Tree Estates Inc v Furstenburg* 124 N.W. 2d 90 (Wisconsin Sup Ct, 1963); and cases discussed in Annotation, "Unjust Enrichment of Landowner Based on Adjoining Landowner's Construction, Improvement, or Repair of Commonly Used Highway, Street or Bridge" (1994) 22 A.L.R. 5th 500. The American cases disclose some exceptions to the general principle, reflecting the courts' view that it is a hard man who reaps where he does not sow.

[125] *Ruabon Steamship* [1900] A.C. 6 at 12. See too Lord Macnaghten's comment at 15 that "there is no principle of law which requires that a person should contribute to an outlay merely because he has derived a material benefit from it".

the two persons, except that one person has taken advantage of something that another person has done, there being no conduct between them . . . "

This rule does not deny that the defendant is enriched by the receipt of **4–53** incidental benefits, but withholds restitution for other reasons. Some of the cases may be explained on the basis that the benefit received by the defendant was not one to which the claimant was exclusively entitled, so that the benefit was not received at his expense.[126] Alternative explanations are either that the claimant abandoned the benefit received by the defendant,[127] or that the defendant's enrichment is not unjust because a claimant who chooses to pursue a course of action for his own purposes that he knows must incidentally benefit the defendant, intends that outcome although it is not his primary motivation.[128]

8. JOINT AND SEVERAL ENRICHMENTS

Claims in unjust enrichment are usually brought against a single defendant who **4–54** alone has received a benefit from the claimant. However, it can happen that a benefit is received by more than one defendant—for example, where a payment is made into a joint bank account,[129] where a debt owed by several debtors is discharged,[130] or where work is done to repair or improve an asset which belongs to several owners,[131] or to secure an investment opportunity for several investors.[132] In such cases, the law generally holds that all the defendants are jointly and severally enriched, with the result that a claim for the whole amount of the

---

[126] *Edinburgh and District Tramways Co Ltd v Courtenay*, 1908 S.C. 99, discussed in C. Webb, "Property, Unjust Enrichment and Defective Transfers" in Chambers et al. (eds), *Philosophical Foundations*, 335, pp.346–351, where he also explains two tort cases on the same basis: *Bradford Corp v Pickles* [1895] A.C. 587 and *Victoria Park Racing and Recreation Grounds Co Ltd v Taylor* (1937) 58 C.L.R. 479. See too S. Meier, "No Basis: A Comparative View" in Burrows and Rodger (eds), *Mapping the Law*, 343, p.356, arguing that no liability arises for heat escaping from a flat because it "is not attributed to the owner of the flat or to the person generating it; it belongs to no one".

[127] E. Ball, "Abandonment and the Problem of Incidental Gains in the Law of Restitution of Unjust Enrichment" [2011] R.L.R. 49. Although "abandonment" is not a term of art in the law of personal property, it is not clear that the claimants' conduct and circumstances in the "incidental gains" cases align with those of parties who have been found to have abandoned property in other contexts; see A. Hudson, "Abandonment" in N. Palmer and E. McKendrick (eds), *Interests in Goods*, 2nd edn (London: LLP, 1993), 595.

[128] Cf. P. Birks, *Unjust Enrichment*, 2nd edn (Oxford: OUP, 2005), p.158, who argues that the claimant intends a gift; however, a gift is a transfer of a benefit with a positive donative intent, which is not present on the facts of the cases.

[129] *Euroactividade AG v Moeller* Unreported CA, February 1, 1995; *OEM Plc v Schneider* [2005] EWHC 1072 (Ch).

[130] *Filby* [2004] EWCA Civ 759 at [45]; *Brasher v O'Hehir* [2005] NSWSC 1194.

[131] *Cotroneo v Leslie* (1997) 43 O.T.C. 40 (Ontario Sup Ct).

[132] *Benedetti* [2009] EWHC 1330 (Ch) at [576]; subsequent proceedings [2009] EWHC 1806 (Ch). On appeal the Court of Appeal reversed Patten J.'s finding that the second and third defendants were enriched by the claimant's services, and so his further finding that they were jointly and severally liable with the first defendant fell away, but nothing in the appellate judgments casts doubt on the principle that where work enures to the benefit of several defendants they will generally be jointly and severally liable to make restitution: [2010] EWCA Civ 1427.

enrichment may lie against any or all of them. Note, though, that where a payment is made into a joint account, and money is then withdrawn by one of the account-holders without the other's knowledge, she may have a change of position defence.[133]

4-55   Where a wholly-owned company is enriched through a fraudulent scheme undertaken by its shareholder, the court may lift the corporate veil and deem the shareholder to have been enriched to the same extent as the company.[134] However, proof of fraud is required before the court will ignore the separate legal personalities of company and shareholder, and a claim will not lie against a shareholder simply because his company has received a benefit,[135] not least because there is usually no direct correlation between the value of a company's assets and the value of its shares.[136] Where a claimant provides services at a shareholder's request that enure to the benefit of the company, they may also be regarded as an enrichment received by the shareholder if it appears from the terms of the request and the parties' other dealings that they were understood to be for his benefit as well as for the company's benefit.[137]

4-56   Joint and several liabilities in unjust enrichment can also arise in cases where a benefit is received by a defendant who then passes the benefit on to a second defendant.[138] Provided that the first defendant is not entitled to raise a change of position defence, for example because he is not in good faith, and provided also that the second defendant is not a bona fide purchaser for value without notice of the benefit's provenance,[139] the claimant will be entitled to an order for restitution against both defendants, although the principle against double recovery will prevent him from enforcing judgment against both defendants in full.[140]

---

[133] *Euroactividade* Unreported CA, February 1, 1995 (where there was no evidence of the defendant's good faith); *OEM* [2005] EWHC 1072 (Ch) at [25]–[47]; *Primlake Ltd (In Liquidation) v Matthews Associates* [2006] EWHC 1227 (Ch) at [336]. A line of Australian authority starting with *National Commercial Banking Corp of Australia Ltd v Batty* (1986) 160 C.L.R. 251 may also be explicable on this basis: *Heperu Pty Ltd v Morgan Brooks Pty Ltd (No.2)* [2007] NSWSC 1438; *McNally v Harris* [2008] NSWSC 659 at [84]; *Vella v Permanent Mortgages Pty Ltd* [2008] NSWSC 505 at [638]; *S.C.E.G.S. Redlands Ltd v Barbour* [2008] NSWSC 928. For general discussion of the change of position defence, see Ch.27.

[134] *Hone v Canadian Imperial Bank of Commerce* (1989) 37 West Indies Reports 39 (PC); *Trustor AB v Smallbone (No.2)* [2001] 1 W.L.R. 1177. See too *Gencor ACP Ltd v Dalby* [2000] 2 B.C.L.C. 734 at 744; *Pulvers (A Firm) v Chan* [2007] EWHC 2406 (Ch); [2008] P.N.L.R. 9 at [379].

[135] See e.g. *O.J.S.C. Oil Co Yugraneft (In Liquidation) v Abramovich* [2008] EWHC 2613 (Comm) at [370] where there was said to be "no realistic basis" for contending that a large multinational company was a "fraud" or "sham"; *Law Society v Habitable Concepts Ltd* [2010] EWHC 1449 (Ch) at [20]–[22] where it was unproven that money withdrawn from the company's bank account was applied to the purposes of its sole shareholder; *Aerostar Maintenance International Ltd v Wilson* [2010] EWHC 2032 (Ch) at [205] where again the company was not a "sham" on the facts.

[136] R. Grantham, "Restitution and Insolvent Companies: Honing in on Shareholders" [2000] *Company, Financial and Insolvency Law Review* 26.

[137] *Killen v Horseworld Ltd* [2011] EWHC 1600 (QB).

[138] In cases of this sort the law holds that both defendants are enriched at the claimant's expense: see paras 6–35—6–51.

[139] The bona fide purchase defence is discussed in Ch.29.

[140] *Trustor AB v Smallbone (No.1)* Unreported CA, May 9, 2000 at [63]–[66], per Scott V.C. See too *Smith v Moneymart Co* (2006) 266 D.L.R. (4th) 275 (Ontario CA); *Tracy v Instaloans Financial Solution Centres (BC) Ltd* [2008] BCSC 699.

9. BENEFITS ACQUIRED IN EXCHANGE TRANSACTIONS

As we discuss in Ch.31, the law makes the counter-restitution of benefits　**4–57**
received by the claimant from the defendant a precondition for claims in unjust
enrichment. There are two ways in which this rule might be understood. It might
be a rule that claim and counter-claim must be netted off, imposed with the
pragmatic purpose of reducing multiplicity of suits. Or it might be a rule that
enrichments transferred and received in a process of exchange must be netted off,
imposed to ensure that the mutual reciprocity of the parties' performances is duly
reflected in the unwinding process that must follow failure of the basis for the
parties' exchange. English authority on this point is sparse, but in *Kleinwort
Benson Ltd v Sandwell BC*,[141] Hobhouse J. took the latter view. This suggests that
there are special rules to govern the identification and quantification of enrichment in situations where the defendant's enrichment has been gained in exchange
for an enrichment conferred on the claimant. This is discussed further in
Ch.31.[142]

10. MINISTERIAL RECEIPT

A defendant who receives assets in his capacity as an agent may immediately　**4–58**
hand them over to his principal, or simply hold them as bailee pending further
instructions, and in either case he may derive no personal benefit from the assets.
In these circumstances he may be able to escape liability in unjust enrichment on
the basis that he received the assets ministerially, and did not receive them for his
personal use and benefit. More controversially, he may also be able to make this
argument where he has used the assets for his own purposes, but where he came
under an immediate duty to account to his principal for their value at the moment
of receipt, and where the principal was liable to pay their value to the claimant
from the moment of the defendant's receipt. This is discussed further in
Ch.28.[143]

11. PLEADING ENRICHMENT

A claim in unjust enrichment "is not sufficiently pleaded unless it asserts the　**4–59**
payment [or other mode of enrichment] on which it rests".[144] Where the claim

---

[141] *Kleinwort Benson Ltd v Sandwell BC* [1994] 4 All E.R. 890.
[142] See paras 31–14—31–21.
[143] See paras 28–01—28–06.
[144] *Deutsche Morgan Grenfell* [2005] EWCA Civ 78; [2006] Ch. 243 at [294] per Buxton L.J. At
[238]–[248] and [252]–[260] Jonathan Parker and Rix L.JJ. agreed with this statement of principle,
but disagreed with Buxton L.J. about its application in the case, affirming the trial judge's conclusion
that although the pleadings had identified the payments on which the claim was based in rather
general terms, they were not so imprecise that new claims were introduced when the pleadings were
amended to describe some of the payments with more particularity. This became a dead issue on
appeal, but Lord Hoffmann and Lord Walker would have agreed with the majority of the CA: [2006]
UKHL 49; [2007] 1 A.C. 558 at [34] and [148]–[149].

rests on a money transfer, the claimant must therefore identify the relevant payments; likewise, where the claim rests on the discharge of an obligation owed by the defendant to a third party. Similarly, where a claim is made to recover the value of goods, the claimant must identify the goods and prove delivery,[145] and where a claim is made to recover the value of services, he must identify the relevant services, and also explain the basis on which they should be valued. This may not be a straightforward matter in cases where more than one approach to the valuation of services is possible,[146] and special facts may need to be pleaded to support the claimant's approach (e.g. industry levels of remuneration, hourly rate and number of hours worked[147]). Where necessary, the claimant should also state that he supplied goods or did work for the defendant and at his request, in order to meet any argument that the defendant was not enriched because he did not want the goods or services in question.[148]

---

[145] *P.G.G. Wrightson Ltd v Wai Shing Ltd* [2006] NZHC 124 at [47], per Keane J.: "Proof of delivery is . . . indispensable to [the] case in *quantum valebat*. There can be no liability for the value of goods never received."

[146] *Vedatech Corp v Crystal Decisions (UK) Ltd* Unreported Ch. D., November 7, 2001, per Hart J., stressing the need for a "sufficient pleading of the circumstances justifying the court approaching the measure of the *quantum meruit* in [the manner claimed]."

[147] *Independent Grocers' Co-operative Ltd v Noble Lowndes Superannuation Consultants Ltd* (1993) 60 S.A.S.R. 525 at 559 (Full Ct of Sup Ct of South Australia); *Yule v Little Bird Ltd* Unreported QBD, April 5, 2001 at [26]; *M.S.M. Consulting Ltd v United Republic of Tanzania* [2009] EWHC 121 (QB); (2009) 123 Con. L.R. 154 at [175] (stressing the need to check hours claimed against a time sheet); *Benourad v Compass Group Plc* [2010] EWHC 1882 (QB) at [134] (stressing that the burden lies on the claimant to adduce evidence on which the court can base its valuation of the claimant's work).

[148] *Crown House Engineering Ltd v Amec Projects Ltd* (1989) 6 Const. L.J. 141 at 150, per Slade L.J. Cf. *Granter Woodwork & Decoration Co Ltd v Hai Da Construction Ltd* [2007] HKCFI 94 at [31]: particulars should be given "as to by whom and to whom the request for work or services was made, the work or services requested and the reasonable sum to which the plaintiff is entitled."

CHAPTER 5

ENRICHMENT: TYPES OF BENEFIT

1. INTRODUCTION

The previous chapter explained the general principles governing the identifica- **5–01**
tion and quantification of value for the purposes of a claim in unjust enrichment.
This chapter explains how these principles apply to different types of benefit:
money, land and goods, services and discharged obligations.

2. MONEY

(a) *Exchange Value*

Money can be defined by reference to its various functions as a medium of **5–02**
exchange, a unit of account and a store of value.[1] For present purposes, the last
of these is the most significant and various assets can fulfil this function. Most
obviously coins and banknotes are money in this sense, but so too are the rights
of action held by a customer against a bank with which he has an account. The
customer has a right to be paid money in corporeal form, but he can also direct
the bank to make payments on his behalf to third parties, and commonly such
payments do not entail a physical transfer of notes or coins, but instead comprise
the crediting of the recipient's own account with that or another bank by an
equivalent amount.[2]

For reasons that were discussed in Ch.4,[3] claims to recover the exchange value **5–03**
of money are usually straightforward as they generally concern payments of cash
or electronic fund transfers to defendants who cannot argue that their enrichment
is worth less than the face value of the money received. However, the same
cannot be said of claims to recover the use value of money, i.e. the value of
having money at one's disposal over time, measurable as interest, and claims of
this kind are discussed in the next section.

First, though, something must be said about claims to recover the exchange **5–04**
value of money that is not paid to a defendant, but is paid to a third party at the
defendant's request. Cases of this kind can be resolved on the basis that a
defendant who requests money to be paid to another party is enriched to the same
extent as he would have been if he had received the money himself. For example,

---

[1] For helpful introductory discussions of legal and economic definitions of money, see C. Proctor
(ed.), F.A. Mann, *The Legal Aspect of Money* (Oxford: OUP, 2005), Ch.1; D. Fox, *Property Rights
in Money* (Oxford: OUP, 2008), para.1.19 and following.
[2] For discussion of interbank payment mechanisms, see Fox, *Property Rights in Money*, para.5.08 and
following, and the specialist works cited there.
[3] See para.4–12.

in *Goss v Chilcott*[4] the Privy Council held that the borrowers of money who
arranged for the funds to be paid to a third party were themselves enriched at the
expense of the original lender. However, this case may be contrasted with the
New South Wales Court of Appeal's decision in *Ford v Perpetual Trustees
Victoria Ltd*,[5] where the mentally incompetent defendant was induced by his son
to take out a mortgage loan to obtain money, most of which was paid to the son's
business. The claimant bank could not enforce the mortgage, and its claim in
unjust enrichment largely failed because the defendant was "a manipulated
intermediary with no understanding of any aspect of the overall transaction" who
had, in substance, "received no benefit from the loan".[6] In effect the case was
treated as one of ministerial receipt,[7] and it seems that the key question in cases
of this kind is whether the defendant is freely acting on his own behalf or as the
third party's agent when he causes the money to be paid to the third party.

(b) *Use Value*

5–05   The leading case on claims for the use value of money is *Sempra Metals Ltd v
IRC*.[8] This was a test claim under a group litigation order made to manage many
of the claims that were brought against the Revenue following *Metallgesellschaft
Ltd v IRC* and *Hoechst AG v IRC*.[9] There the European Court of Justice held that
the Income and Corporation Taxes Act 1988 s.247 infringed the EC Treaty. This
section enabled UK resident corporate groups to postpone the time at which they
paid corporation tax, but withheld this advantage from corporate groups with
subsidiaries resident in the UK and parent companies resident elsewhere in the
EU. Such groups had to pay tax sooner than their wholly UK resident competitors: they had to pay advance corporation tax (ACT) while the others could
make a "group income election" and pay mainstream corporation tax (MCT) at
a later date. The ECJ held that this disparity of treatment was contrary to EU law,
and directed the UK courts to provide disadvantaged groups with "an effective
legal remedy in order to obtain reimbursement or reparation of the financial loss
which they [had] sustained and from which the [tax] authorities [had] benefited".[10]

5–06   In *Sempra* the claimant company made two claims in respect of its ACT
payments: a compensatory claim based on breach of EU law and a restitutionary
claim based on unjust enrichment. The latter claim was argued on the basis that
the claimant had made a causative mistake because it would have made a group
income election had it known that it was entitled to do so, and hence would not

---

[4] *Goss v Chilcott* [1996] A.C. 788; distinguished in *Miller v Parkin* [2008] NZHC 2022 at
[36]–[41].
[5] *Ford v Perpetual Trustees Victoria Ltd* [2009] NSWCA 186; (2009) 75 N.S.W.L.R. 42.
[6] *Ford* [2009] NSWCA 186; (2009) 75 N.S.W.L.R. 42 at [127]. The defendant had to repay some
$25,000 that remained in his bank account, but was not liable for the rest of the $200,000 loan that
had gone to his son.
[7] See Ch.28.
[8] *Sempra Metals Ltd v IRC* [2007] UKHL 34; [2008] A.C. 561.
[9] *Metallgesellschaft Ltd v IRC* and *Hoechst AG v IRC* (Joined Cases C–397/98 and C–410/98) [2001]
All E.R. (E.C.) 496.
[10] *Metallgesellschaft* (Joined Cases C–397/98 and C–410/98) [2001] All E.R. (E.C.) 496 at [97].

have made any ACT payments but would have waited and paid MCT later on.[11] By the time when the action was brought, no claim could have been brought to recover the capital value of the sums paid as ACT, because by then the claimant would have had to pay the money as MCT in any case. But the claimant argued that the Revenue had been unjustly enriched by the use of the money during the period running from the date when the ACT payments were made to the date when MCT would have been payable. Hence the main issues in the case were, first, whether the common law of unjust enrichment recognised the use value of money as a recoverable benefit, and if so, how this should be measured; and, secondly, whether common law claims to recover such benefits were excluded by s.35A of the Supreme Court Act 1981 (now the Senior Courts Act 1981)?

(i) *Common Law Claims for the Use Value of Money*

To understand the House of Lords' analysis of the first question, it must be **5–07** appreciated that in the lower courts the case was argued on the basis that the restitutionary and compensatory claims were essentially identical, because the parties' respective loss and gain were the same. It was also argued on the basis that a conventional rate should be used to quantify the claimant's loss which looked not to its actual loss, but to the loss which it could be presumed to have suffered through having paid the tax prematurely. The lower courts held this to have been the rate of compound interest charged on the commercial lending market, to reflect the fact that the claimant must either have lost the opportunity to put the money on deposit (when it had a cash surplus) or have been obliged to borrow an equivalent sum (when it had a cash deficit).[12] Before the House of Lords, the point was then made that there were significant differences between the compensatory and restitutionary claims, and that the claimant's interest lay in pursuing the restitutionary claim for limitation reasons. Even so, the claimant persisted in arguing that the same conventional rate should be used to measure the Revenue's benefit. In the lower courts the Revenue had conceded that a single rate should be used to calculate the parties' gain and loss, but it was allowed to revoke this concession in the House of Lords, where it argued instead that if compound interest were awarded as restitution, then the rate should be lower than the rate charged on the commercial lending market, because the government can borrow money more cheaply than commercial entities, e.g. by issuing Treasury bills.

The majority of the court accepted that the claimant was entitled to a conven- **5–08** tional award that would reverse the benefit which the Revenue had received, and they took this benefit to be the saved cost of borrowing that the Revenue would

---

[11] This had previously been recognised as a valid ground of recovery in another case in the same series: *Deutsche Morgan Grenfell Plc v IRC* [2006] UKHL 49; [2007] 1 A.C. 558, discussed at para.9–79.
[12] Cf. *Sempra* [2005] EWCA Civ 389; [2006] Q.B. 37 at [50] per Chadwick L.J.: "if the matter is to be approached on the basis of 'one rate suits all', then (as it seems to me) there is really no alternative to adopting a borrower's rate rather than a lender's rate. To adopt a lender's rate in all cases would lead, inevitably, to under-compensation in those cases where the taxpayer was in cash deficit. To adopt a borrower's rate will (or may) lead to over-compensation where the taxpayer is in cash surplus; but that, as I understand the Revenue's position, is accepted as price worth paying for the practical advantages of a single conventional rate."

have incurred, had it borrowed an equivalent sum over the relevant period.[13] They also accepted that the Revenue could "subjectively devalue" the benefit of its saved borrowing costs down to the saved costs of governmental rather than commercial borrowing.[14] In contrast, the minority declined to hold that the Revenue had been saved *any* borrowing costs because they thought that this was a fact which should have been—and which had not been—affirmatively proved. Lord Scott held that the restitutionary claim could succeed only if "there were evidence to justify the conclusion that the Government's borrowing in the market was less . . . than it would otherwise have been"—and since there was none he held that the claim failed.[15] Similarly, but less radically, Lord Mance held that "if any claim to restitution is to be recognized . . . it must refer to any actual benefit obtained by the recipient", and so the case should be remitted to the High Court to consider what the award should be "to reflect . . . any actual benefit which the Revenue may be found to have received".[16]

5–09   Why did the majority hold that enrichment had been established? One reason is that they took the Revenue to have conceded the fact of its enrichment and to have argued only that this benefit could not be quantified. So Lord Hope stressed that the Revenue had not argued "that there was no actual benefit"; rather, its case was that:

> "because of the nature of the relationship between the Government and the Bank of England, it was impossible to measure the amount of interest earned or saved by it, or by the Government generally, on the sample A.C.T. payments".[17]

Hence, he held that:

> "the assumption that the Revenue derived some benefit from the receipt of the money prematurely has not been displaced, and . . . this justifies resort to a conventional rate of interest as the measure of the benefit."

5–10   However, it is significant that Lord Hope referred in this passage to an "assumption" that the Revenue was benefited by the use of the money. This and other passages in the majority's speeches suggest that they meant to hold that a market value will always be assigned to the use of money unless the defendant can show that it was worth less to him. For example, Lord Nicholls held that "in cases of personal restitution the value of the use of money is *prima facie* the reasonable cost of borrowing the money in question".[18] The majority's analysis therefore supports the view that non-money benefits with a market value are

---

[13] All three of their Lordships were careful to distinguish between the benefit of saved borrowing costs that formed the subject matter of the claim and the actual profits made by the defendant with the money received (that were not in issue): *Sempra* [2007] UKHL 34; [2008] A.C. 561 at [32] per Lord Nicholls, and at [117] per Lord Nicholls, and at [180] per Lord Walker.

[14] *Sempra* [2007] UKHL 34; [2008] A.C. 561 at [118]–[119] per Lord Nicholls. Cf. *Ermineskin Indian Band and Nation v Canada* [2009] SCC 9; [2009] 1 S.C.R. 222 at [184] (Canadian government not enriched by use of money held for Indian band on statutory scheme because it paid band interest at higher rate than cost of replacement funds, i.e. short-term treasury bill rate).

[15] *Sempra* [2007] UKHL 34; [2008] A.C. 561 at [147].

[16] *Sempra* [2007] UKHL 34; [2008] A.C. 561 at [231] and [241] respectively

[17] *Sempra* [2007] UKHL 34; [2008] A.C. 561 at [48]. See too Lord Walker's comments at [186].

[18] *Sempra* [2007] UKHL 34; [2008] A.C. 561 at [116]–[117].

always rebuttably presumed to be enriching.[19] It also contemplates that a lower valuation will be ascribed to the benefit if the defendant can prove that it would not have paid so much—as the Revenue was able to do. Note, though, that the Revenue's evidence related to the Government's general status as a creditor, rather than its borrowing needs at the relevant time. It therefore remains to be tested whether a defendant can subjectively devalue saved borrowing costs by arguing that he had no need to borrow, and did not generate secondary profits out of the claimant's money (e.g. by putting it on deposit), but merely spent it on consumables.

(ii) *The Supreme Court Act 1981 s.35A*

Section 35A of the Supreme Court Act 1981 (now the Senior Courts Act 1981) **5–11** empowered the courts to award simple interest on contract debts, restitutionary liabilities and damages.[20] Prior to *Sempra* the leading case on the relationship between the section and common law claims for compound interest was *Westdeutsche Landesbank Girozentrale v Islington LBC*.[21] There a bank brought a claim in unjust enrichment to recover money paid under a void interest swap transaction. By the time that the case reached the House of Lords, the defendant council had accepted that the bank had a valid claim to recover the money, and the only question was whether an award of compound interest should be made on the judgment sum. The sole basis on which the bank argued for compound interest was that the money had been held by the local authority on a resulting trust. The House of Lords unanimously rejected this. But although the point was conceded, the court also considered whether there is a power at common law or in equity to award compound interest as part of a restitutionary award. The majority held that there is not, reasoning that compound interest awards can only be made in cases of fraud or breach of trust or fiduciary duty and that otherwise a claimant is limited to simple interest under s.35A.

In their dissenting speeches, Lord Goff and Lord Woolf observed that this was **5–12** unsatisfactory because it left the court unable to order restitution of the full benefit received by the defendant.[22] Nevertheless when *Sempra* was decided in the lower courts, they assumed that *Westdeutsche* prevented them from making a compound interest award under English law, on the basis that the Revenue had been unjustly enriched by having had the use of the money paid as ACT.[23] Some doubt was then raised about this assumption in the Court of Appeal in an associated case, *Boake Allen Ltd v HMRC*, where Mummery L.J. said that *Westdeutsche* did not stop the claimant from bringing a claim in unjust enrichment to recover the use value of the money. His reason was that *Westdeutsche* concerned a claim for compound interest on the award of a capital sum, and did not decide whether a claim in unjust enrichment lies to recover compound

---

[19] See para.4–08.
[20] For discussion of the section, see paras 36–15—36–22.
[21] *Westdeutsche Landesbank Girozentrale v Islington LBC* [1996] A.C. 669.
[22] *Westdeutsche* [1996] A.C. 669 at 691 and 719–720. See too Hobhouse J.'s comments at first instance: [1994] 4 All E.R. 890 at 955.
[23] *Sempra* [2004] EWHC 2387 (Ch); [2004] S.T.C. 1178 at [24]–[27]; [2005] EWCA Civ 389; [2006] Q.B. 37 at [53].

interest as the use value of money, where no claim is made to recover its exchange value.[24] Lloyd L.J. disagreed, holding that:

> "it does not appear to me to be consistent with [*Westdeutsche*] to find a way of awarding restitution of the [use value] of money by reference to general principles of restitution."[25]

5-13   In *Sempra*, the House of Lords held that s.35A does not confer an exclusive jurisdiction on the courts to make interest awards, and that claimants can bring a common law claim in unjust enrichment to recover compound interest as restitution of the use value of money, even in cases that fall within the scope of the section.[26] Like Mummery L.J., Lord Nicholls and Lord Hope distinguished *Westdeutsche* on the basis that it was not concerned with a claim to recover compound interest as the "principal sum", but with a primary claim to recover the capital value of money and only an ancillary claim to recover compound interest.[27] In contrast, Lord Walker and Lord Mance held that this was an "anomalous" distinction, and that the majority dicta in *Westdeutsche* should not be followed.[28] In principle, this was the better view. It would be arbitrary for the law to prohibit recovery of the use value of money where its exchange value is also claimed, but to allow it where the exchange value of the money has already been repaid or is not claimed for some other reason.

5-14   In *Sempra* the claimant only sought to recover compound interest for the period between the date when ACT was paid and the date when MCT would have been payable. No claim was made for the period running from the date when MCT would have become payable to the date of judgment. However, the House of Lords' findings indicate that a claim for the later period should also have succeeded. At first instance, Park J. treated these two periods differently. In *Metallgesellschaft* the ECJ had held that an interest award relating to the first period was mandatory, because this was the "very objective" sought by the proceedings,[29] but in other cases the ECJ had also held that it was an ancillary matter for the discretion of domestic courts whether to award interest on restitutionary claims to recover charges levied in breach of EU law.[30] Park J. therefore held that EU law required him to make a compound interest award with respect to the first period, but not with respect to the second, as the claim for interest attributable to this was "truly ancillary".[31] Hence he awarded simple interest under s.35A in respect of the second period. On appeal, this aspect of Park J.'s

---

[24] *Boake Allen Ltd v HMRC* [2006] EWCA Civ 25; [2006] S.T.C. 606 at [163]–[175].

[25] *Boake Allen* at [85]–[88]. This aspect of the CA's decision was not addressed when *Boake Allen* was appealed: [2007] UKHL 25; [2007] 1 W.L.R. 1386.

[26] *Sempra* [2007] UKHL 34; [2008] A.C. 561 at [114] per Lord Nicholls.

[27] *Sempra* [2007] UKHL 34; [2008] A.C. 561 at [36] and [112].

[28] *Sempra* [2007] UKHL 34; [2008] A.C. 561 at [183]–[184] and [240].

[29] *Metallgesellschaft* (Joined Cases C–397/98 and C–410/98) [2001] All E.R. (E.C.) 496 at [87].

[30] *Société Roquette Frères v Commission* (26/74) [1976] E.C.R. 677 at [11]–[12]; *Express Dairy Foods Ltd v Intervention Board for Agricultural Produce* (130/79) [1980] E.C.R. 1887 at [16]–[17].

[31] *Sempra* [2004] EWHC 2387 (Ch); [2004] S.T.C. 1178 at [46].

decision was not challenged,[32] but Lord Nicholls and Lord Walker both indicated that they would have held the opposite if the point had been taken.[33]

3. LAND AND GOODS

(a) *Exchange Value*

In principle a claim in unjust enrichment can lie to recover the exchange value **5–15** of land or goods, but in practice few such claims are brought.[34] Cases where a right to land or goods passes from a claimant to a defendant are commonly dealt with as cases for a proprietary remedy, through actions for rescission or rectification or declaration of trust; and cases where the claimant retains title to goods which come into the possession of the defendant are generally pleaded as claims for conversion.[35]

Under the Sale of Goods Act 1979 s.30(1) a purchaser is liable to pay for **5–16** goods where he accepts them although the seller has delivered less than the quantity contracted for; and s.30(3) obliges the purchaser to pay for goods which he has accepted although the seller has delivered more than the quantity contracted for. This codifies the previous common law, with the difference that the common law allowed recovery of a reasonable sum and "not the stipulated price",[36] whereas the statute provides for recovery of the "contract rate". Where the market rate exceeds the contract rate this might be justified on the basis that the purchaser's freedom of choice would be compromised if he were forced to pay the higher market rate.

It is sometimes said that a defendant who obtains possession of assets without **5–17** obtaining ownership cannot have been enriched by receipt of their exchange value because he has no legal right to sell the property.[37] However, the better view is that possession gives the defendant a valuable right of sale which is good

---

[32] *Sempra* [2005] EWCA Civ 389; [2006] Q.B. 37 at [7]; [2007] UKHL 34; [2008] A.C. 561 at [11], [129], [156], and [227]–[228].

[33] *Sempra* [2007] UKHL 34; [2008] A.C. 561 at [129] and [156].

[34] For a recent example, see *PGG Wrightson Ltd v Wai Shing Ltd* [2006] NZHC 124, where a claim to recover the exchange value of goods failed on the facts. See too *Huyton SA v Peter Cremer GmbH & Co* [1999] 1 Lloyd's Rep. 620 at 634, where Mance J. recognised the possibility of such a claim.

[35] As in e.g. *Wilson v Robertsons (London) Ltd* [2006] EWCA Civ 1088; [2007] Consumer Credit Reports 6031 (pawned ring sold for meltdown value; loan agreement unenforceable; replacement value of ring recovered as compensatory damages). If the tort liability of innocent converters were cut back, then the availability of an unjust enrichment claim in these cases would take on much greater practical significance, as argued in A. Tettenborn, "Conversion, Tort, and Restitution" in N. Palmer and E. McKendrick (eds), *Interests in Goods*, 2nd edn (London: LLP, 1998), 825.

[36] *Shipton v Casson* (1826) 5 B. & C. 378 at 383; 108 E.R. 141 at 143 per Bayley J. See too *Oxendate v Wetherell* (1829) 9 B. & C. 386 at 387–388; 109 E.R. 143 at 144; *Steven v Bromley & Son* [1919] 2 K.B. 722 at 728 (CA).

[37] e.g. P. Birks, "Property and Unjust Enrichment: Categorical Truths" [1997] *New Zealand Law Review* 623, p.654; R. Grantham and C. Rickett, *Enrichment and Restitution in New Zealand* (Oxford: Hart, 2000), pp.61–63; W. Swadling, "Ignorance and Unjust Enrichment: The Problem of Title" (2008) 28 O.J.L.S. 627. See too para.37–08, fn.9.

against everyone except the owner or anyone with a better possessory title.[38] Hence in principle a claim for unjust enrichment by receipt of exchange value can lie in such a case.[39]

(b) *Use Value*

5-18   Where a defendant has permission to occupy the claimant's land but no binding terms are agreed about payment, a claim in unjust enrichment lies to recover the value of the defendant's use and occupation.[40] Although it is easy to confuse the two, claims of this sort differ from wrong-based claims for mesne profits, which lead to an award of damages for the tort of trespass.[41] They are not founded on wrongdoing, but on the defendant's unjust enrichment at the claimant's expense when he freely accepts the use value of the property, knowing that the claimant expects to be paid.

5-19   The use value received by the defendant is not quantified by asking what he did with the property, but by assessing the saved costs of his occupation.[42] This use value accrues day by day in the same way as the use value of money,[43] and the normal measure of the defendant's enrichment is the open market rental value

---

[38] *Armory v Delamirie* (1722) 1 Stra. 506; 93 E.R. 664; *Gollan v Nugent* (1988) 166 C.L.R. 16 at 28; *Flack v National Crime Authority* [1998] FCA 932; 156 A.L.R. 501; *Costello v Chief Constable of Derbyshire* [2001] EWCA Civ 381; [2001] 1 W.L.R. 1437.

[39] J. Edelman and E. Bant, *Unjust Enrichment in Australia* (Melbourne: OUP, 2006), pp.102–103; R. Chambers, "Two Types of Enrichment" in R. Chambers et al. (eds), *Philosophical Foundations of the Law of Unjust Enrichment* (Oxford: OUP, 2009), 242, pp.249–250. Edelman and Bant make the further point at pp.123–124 and 130–131, that although the defendant's enrichment by receipt of the right to possession is not acquired at the claimant's expense, since it does not derive from the claimant's ownership right (which remains intact), nevertheless the defendant's enrichment by receipt of value does come from the claimant, the value of whose ownership right is reduced when he loses possession.

[40] *Mayor of Thetford v Tyler* (1845) 8 Q.B. 95 at 100; 115 E.R. 810 at 812 per Lord Denman C.J.: "he who holds my premises without an express bargain agrees to pay what a jury may find the occupation to be worth". See too *Mason v Welland* (1728) Skin. 238 at 243; 90 E.R. 109 at 111; *Birch v Wright* (1786) 1 T.R. 378 at 387; 99 E.R. 1148 at 1154; *Mayor and Burgesses of Stafford v Till* (1827) 4 Bing. 75 at 77; 130 E.R. 697 at 697; *Beverley v Lincoln Gas Light and Coke Co* (1837) 6 Ad. & E. 829 at 839; 112 E.R. 318 at 322; *Churchward v Ford* (1857) 2 H. & N. 446 at 448–449; 157 E.R. 184 at 185; *Turner v York Motors Pty Ltd* (1951) 85 C.L.R. 55 at 65; *R. v Bristol CC, Ex p. Jacobs*, *The Times*, November 16, 1999; *Ovidio Carrideo Nominees v The Dog Depot Pty Ltd* [2006] VSCA 6; [2006] V. Conv. R. 54–713 at [22] and [41]; *Graves v Graves* [2007] EWCA Civ 660; [2007] 3 F.C.R. 26; *Equuscorp Pty Ltd v Acehand Pty Ltd* [2010] VSC 89. See too The Hon. Mr Justice Lewison (ed.), *Woodfall: Landlord & Tenant*, looseleaf edn (London: Sweet & Maxwell, 2008), Ch.10. And cf. *Morris v Tarrant* [1971] 2 Q.B. 143 (where a free-standing claim in unjust enrichment was rejected, but where a separately pleaded claim for the value of the defendant's use and occupation of the land was allowed, although no trespass had been committed).

[41] As in e.g. *Ministry of Defence v Ashman* (1993) 25 H.L.R. 513 (CA); *Inverugie Investments Ltd v Hackett* [1995] 1 W.L.R. 713 (PC); *Horsford v Bird* [2006] UKPC 3; [2006] 1 E.G.L.R. 75; *Jones v Merton LBC* [2008] EWCA Civ 660; [2009] 1 W.L.R. 1269.

[42] *Lewisham LBC v Masterson* (1999) 80 P. & C.R. 117 at 123 per Buxton L.J., stressing that it was nothing to the point that the defendant's occupation of the land was not fruitful to him commercially.

[43] *Slack v Sharpe* (1838) 8 Ad. & E. 366 at 373; 112 E.R. 876 at 879 per Patteson J.: "If there be no demise, and an action be brought merely for use and occupation, then the compensation due for such actual occupation accrues, like interest, de die in diem". See too *Packer v Gibbins* (1841) 1 Q.B. 421; 113 E.R. 1194.

of the property.[44] Where the parties agree another price, however, this may well be the proper measure, although their agreement is ineffective to create a binding tenancy.[45] Where the defendant has been allowed to remain in possession after expiration of a tenancy agreement, it is presumed that he continues to hold at the former rent, but this presumption can be displaced by evidence to the contrary, for example, evidence that the parties disagreed about the amount of the rent that should be payable henceforth.[46] Where the parties agree a price on the basis that the claimant will undertake repairs that he does not undertake, then a lower sum may be appropriate.[47] Where the defendant improves the property, the use value should be settled by reference to its unimproved rather than its improved state,[48] but if he has freely chosen to do this work then the amount payable for the use value of the land will not be reduced by the value of the defendant's work.[49]

The use value of goods is also a benefit that can ground a claim in unjust **5–20** enrichment. In *Dimond v Lovell*,[50] a car was provided to a driver under a hire agreement that was rendered unenforceable by the Consumer Credit Act 1974. The question arose whether the car hire company could recover the use value of the car in an action for unjust enrichment and the House of Lords held that it could not, because the policy underlying the rule which rendered the contract unenforceable also precluded restitutionary recovery. However Lord Hoffmann had no doubt that the driver had been enriched by the use of the car.[51]

4. SERVICES

(a) *Identifying the Benefit*

In some cases where the claimant has done work for the defendant the only **5–21** benefit which the defendant can have received is the provision of the services themselves, because they leave no marketable residue in the defendant's hands: once the services have been performed, nothing remains from which the defendant can derive any further benefit. One example is *R. (Rowe) v Vale of White Horse DC*,[52] where the claimant provided the defendant with sewerage services; another is *Chief Constable of Greater Manchester Police v Wigan Athletic*

---

[44] *Masterson* (1999) 80 P. & C.R. 117 (CA).
[45] *De Medina v Polson* (1815) Holt N.P. 47; 115 E.R. 157 (agreement void under Statute of Frauds but can be consulted to determine value of defendant's occupation); *Ovideo Carrideo* [2006] VSCA 6; [2006] V. Conv. R. 54–713 at [21] (rent covenant void for failure to make statutory disclosure statement but claim in unjust enrichment will lie, quantum of which to be decided by reference to lease).
[46] *Elgar v Watson* (1842) Car. & M. 494; 174 E.R. 605; *Mayor of Thetford* (1845) 8 Q.B. 95 at 100; 115 E.R. 810 at 812; *Dean and Chapter of Canterbury Cathedral v Whitbread Plc* [1995] 1 E.G.L.R. 82.
[47] *Smith v Eldridge* (1854) 15 C.B. 236; 139 E.R. 412.
[48] *McGregor v McGregor* (1884) 5 O.R. 617.
[49] *Masterson* (1999) 80 P. & C.R. 117 at 124 (CA). The reason is that the claimant is only incidentally benefited: see paras 4–52—4–53.
[50] *Dimond v Lovell* [2002] 1 A.C. 384.
[51] *Dimond* [2002] 1 A.C. 384 at 397.
[52] *R. (Rowe) v Vale of White Horse DC* [2003] EWHC 388 (Admin); [2003] 1 Lloyd's Rep. 418.

AFC,[53] where the claimant provided the defendant with specialpolicing services at football matches; a third is *Brenner v First Artists' Management Pty Ltd*,[54] where the claimant provided management services to a pop star. It is well established that "pure" services of this kind can constitute an enrichment, the value of which can be recovered in an action for unjust enrichment.

5–22   Cases where the claimant's services leave a marketable residue in the defendant's hands can be more difficult, because there is more than one way to characterise the benefit received by the defendant: it may be the services themselves, just as in the "pure" services cases, but it may also be the product of the services. An example is provided by *BP Exploration Co (Ltd) v Hunt (No.2)*.[55] The defendant was granted an oil concession in Libya. He entered a joint venture agreement with the claimant, pursuant to which the claimant explored the ground and discovered a large oilfield which it developed. The parties' contract was frustrated when the concession was expropriated and BP made a claim under the Law Reform (Frustrated Contracts) Act 1943 s.1(3). BP argued that the benefit received by Hunt (and thus the maximum amount recoverable under the statute) was the enhanced value of the concession: before its exploration work Hunt had had the right to extract oil from the ground but did not know where it was, or indeed, whether there was any oil; after BP's work, Hunt had the more valuable right to extract oil, the location of which was known, and the means of extracting which had been built. Hunt replied that the benefit he had received was BP's exploration and development work—which were worth much less.

5–23   Robert Goff J. held that the statutory wording obliged him to find for BP, because the reference in s.1(3)(b) to the effect of the frustrating event in relation to the "benefit" received could only refer to the product of the claimant's services, since a frustrating event could not affect the services themselves.[56] This was an unsatisfactory finding, since it meant that in cases where services lead to the creation of an end-product, this must always be the relevant benefit for the purposes of s.1(3), even though a more appropriate finding might sometimes be that the services themselves were the benefit.[57] Robert Goff J. gave two examples[58]: where "a prospector after some very simple prospecting discovers a large and unexpected deposit of a valuable mineral", and where a claimant redecorates a house for a defendant with bad taste with the result that its market value is reduced. On his Lordship's reading of the Act, the court could reach a fair result in the first case but not in the second, since it could reduce the amount recoverable by the prospector to the value of his services when exercising its discretion to award a "just sum", but it could not increase the amount recoverable by the

---

[53] *Chief Constable of Greater Manchester Police v Wigan Athletic AFC* [2007] EWHC 3095 (Ch); [2007] Po. L.R. 246, reversed on a different point [2008] EWCA Civ 1449; [2009] 1 W.L.R. 1590.
[54] *Brenner v First Artists' Management Pty Ltd* [1993] 2 V.R. 221 (Victoria Sup Ct). Cf. *O'Sullivan v Management Agency and Music Ltd* [1985] Q.B. 428 (CA).
[55] *BP Exploration Co (Ltd) v Hunt (No.2)* [1979] 1 W.L.R. 783; affirmed [1981] 1 W.L.R. 232 (CA); [1983] 2 A.C. 352 (HL).
[56] *BP v Hunt* [1979] 1 W.L.R. 783 at 801–802.
[57] *BP v Hunt* [1979] 1 W.L.R. 783 at 802.
[58] *BP v Hunt* [1979] 1 W.L.R. 783 at 803.

decorator to the value of his services because the upper limit to his claim would be the value of the end-product of his work.

Robert Goff J. made it clear that his discussion in *BP v Hunt* was specific to   **5–24** claims under the 1943 Act, and he did not purport to hold that the end-product should be seen as the benefit received by the defendant in every case arising in the law of unjust enrichment where the claimant's services result in an end-product. Conversely, he did not think that the services themselves should always be seen as the benefit either, although Byrne J. thought this in *Brenner*,[59] at least where the services are requested and accepted. The best approach is for the court to keep an open mind, and to take all the circumstances into account, including whether the parties themselves thought that the benefit being transferred was the services or their end-product.[60]

For example, in many construction cases where the claimant undertakes work   **5–25** at the defendant's request, the parties clearly conceptualise the benefit as the services: the benefit received from the claimant is not the building (or part of the building), but the claimant's labour. Conversely, where a claimant manufactures and delivers goods to the defendant, the parties are likely to conceptualise the benefit as the goods rather than the claimant's work in manufacturing them, with the result that the claim should not be litigated as a claim for services at all, but as a claim for the value of the goods. Consistently with this, where a claimant begins to manufacture goods, but never completes and delivers them, the defendant is probably not enriched at all, since the claimant's work in itself was probably never regarded by either party as something that would enrich the defendant. *Planché v Colburn*[61] was like this, since the defendant publisher never took delivery of the manuscript on which the claimant author had been working prior to the defendant's (wrongful) refusal to accept his book for publication. The claimant's action for a quantum meruit award succeeded, but this cannot be explained on the basis that the defendant was enriched, and if a similar case arose nowadays, the claimant would do better to seek damages for the defendant's anticipatory breach of contract.[62]

Cases where the claimant has preserved or repaired or improved the defen-   **5–26** dant's property are also controversial. In some cases besides *BP v Hunt* the courts have identified the increased market value of the property as the benefit received

---

[59] *Brenner* [1993] 2 V.R. 221 at 258 (Victoria Sup Ct).

[60] Similar enquiries have been undertaken: (i) to determine for the purposes of the sales of goods legislation whether the parties have entered a contract for the sale of goods or a contract for the provision of services involving the supply of materials: for discussion see M.G. Bridge, *The Sale of Goods* (Oxford: Clarendon Press, 1997), pp.46–49 and R. Goode, *Commercial Law*, 3rd edn (London: Butterworths, 2004), pp.197–198; (ii) to determine for the purposes of a claim in unjust enrichment whether the consideration for the defendant's enrichment has failed: e.g. *Stocznia Gdanska SA v Latvia Shipping Co* [1988] 1 W.L.R. 574 at 588 (HL); for discussion see paras 13–12—13–13.

[61] *Planché v Colburn* (1831) 8 Bing. 14; 131 E.R. 305.

[62] But cf. *Myers v Macmillan Press Ltd* Unreported QBD, March 3, 1998, discussed in para.5–33. For further discussion of *Planché*, see C. Mitchell and C. Mitchell, "*Planché v Colburn*" in C. Mitchell and P. Mitchell (eds), *Landmark Cases in the Law of Restitution* (Oxford: Hart, 2006), 65. Note that the courts had not developed a workable theory of anticipatory breach at the time when *Planché* was decided; the history of this development is discussed in P. Mitchell, "*Hochster v de la Tour*" in Mitchell and Mitchell (eds), *Landmark Cases*, 135.

by the defendant,[63] but in others they have held that the defendant is enriched only by the value of the claimant's services. For example, in *Yeoman's Row Management Ltd v Cobbe*[64] the claimant worked to obtain planning permission to develop land belonging to the claimant, and Lord Scott refused to make a restitutionary award corresponding to the enhanced value of the land, confining the claimant to the value of his work. His Lordship drew an analogy with a case where valuable silver is locked in a cupboard, the key is lost and a locksmith is employed to open the cupboard: the silver already belongs to the owner and so it cannot be regarded as a benefit which he has acquired from the locksmith. Cases in which bailees have been allowed to recover expenses and remuneration for preserving and redelivering a defendant's property in cases of necessity can be explained in a similar way.[65] So too can *Greenwood v Bennett*[66] where the claimant did work worth £226 on the defendant's car with the result that the market value of the car was increased by £325. The court awarded the lower figure, arguably because the increase in the car's value derived not only from the work but also from the car's potential for improvement, something which was attributable to the claimant.[67] Another way of putting this point in cases where the claimant has asked the defendant to repair or improve his property is that he has chosen to have the work done precisely because it will generate a profit that he can keep for himself, and it would subvert his freedom of choice if he were forced to hand any part of the profit over to the defendant.

(b) *Quantifying the Benefit*

(i) *Costs and Profits*

5-27   In *Leading Edge Events Australia Pty Ltd v Kiri Te Kanawa*,[68] the claimant concert promoter recovered its wasted expenditure on staff wages and promotional material for a proposed concert by the defendant singer, and also the costs of flying people to meet her to discuss the concert, on the basis that these were

---

[63] e.g. *Van den Berg v Giles* [1979] 2 N.Z.L.R. 111 (NZ High Ct); *Lexane Pty Ltd v Highfern Pty Ltd* [1985] 1 Qd. R. 446 at 455–456; *Fensom v Cootamundra Racecourse Reserve Trust* [2000] NSWSC 1072 at [103]; *Valley v McLeod Valley Casing Services Ltd* [2004] ABQB 302; [2005] 3 W.W.R. 153; *Taylor v Streicher* [2007] NSWSC 1006. Cf. *Pavey & Matthews Ltd v Paul* (1987) 167 C.L.R. 221 at 263, where Deane J. thought that in cases where unsolicited but subsequently accepted work is done improving property, and the market rate for the work would far exceed the enhanced value of the property, it would be unjust to value the benefit by reference only to value of the claimant's time and labour and the materials supplied. This was followed in *Hughes v Molloy* [2005] VSC 240.
[64] *Yeoman's Row Management Ltd v Cobbe* [2008] UKHL 55; [2008] 1 W.L.R. 1752 at [40]–[41]. See too *Emery v Hashimoto* [1996] 2 L.R.C. 644 at 664 (Solomon Islands CA); *Angelopoulos v Sabatino* [1995] SASC 5536; (1995) 65 S.A.S.R. 1 at [53]–[58]; *Van Lierop v Hollenbach* (2001) 15 C.C.E.L. (3d) 8 (Ontario CA); *Peet Ltd v Richmond* [2009] VSC 130. And cf. *Lee-Parker v Izzet (No.2)* [1972] 1 W.L.R. 775 (a claim for possession where no award was made for the value of the work done by the defendant because this was smaller than the value of occupying the land).
[65] *The Argos* [1873] L.R. 5 P.C. 134 at 165; *China Pacific SA v Food Corp of India (The Winson)* [1982] A.C. 939 at 961; *Guildford BC v Hein* [2005] EWCA Civ 979 at [33]; *E.N.E. 1 Kos Ltd v Petroleo Brasileiro SA Petrobras (The Kos)* [2009] EWHC 1843 (Comm); [2010] 1 Lloyd's Rep. 87 at [52]–[61] (reversed on a different point [2010] EWCA Civ 772; [2010] 2 Lloyd's Rep. 409).
[66] *Greenwood v Bennett* [1973] Q.B. 195.
[67] R. Stevens, "Three Enrichment Issues" in A. Burrows and Lord Rodger (eds), *Mapping the Law* (Oxford: OUP, 2006), 49, pp.51–54.
[68] *Leading Edge Events Australia Pty Ltd v Kiri Te Kanawa* [2007] NSWSC 228.

expenses incurred at her request. However, as Byrne J. observed in *Brenner*,[69] the valuation enquiry in restitutionary claims for the value of services is not usually "primarily directed to the cost to the plaintiff of performing the work since the law is not compensating that party for loss suffered"—although "this is not to ignore these costs for the reasonable remuneration for work must have some regard to the cost of its performance". Thus, in many cases the courts have instead awarded claimants their costs and an additional profit element, reasoning that this is a fairest approximation of the benefit received by the defendant, since this represents what he would have had to pay for the services on the market.[70]

When assessing the claimant's costs, the court will only allow what is rea-   **5–28** sonable:

> "with the assessment of reasonableness being undertaken by reference to the results produced and evidence to what it would in the ordinary course of things be necessary to outlay in order to produce those results."[71]

Deductions should be made for "time spent in repairing or repeating defective work, and for inefficient working or . . . excessive tea-breaks and the like".[72] When calculating the profit element of an award, the court should consider all the relevant circumstances, including industry pricing levels at the time when the work was done,[73] any competitive edge that the claimant might have enjoyed over his industry rivals,[74] and conversely, any indication in negotiations between the parties that the claimant was willing to accept a lower than market price.[75]

(ii) *Hourly Rates*

In *Brenner*,[76] Byrne J. observed that in many cases, "the appropriate method of   **5–29** assessing the benefit of the work is by applying an hourly rate to the time involved in performing those services", but that:

---

[69] *Brenner* [1993] 2 V.R. 221 at 263 (Victoria Sup Ct).
[70] See e.g. *O'Sullivan v Management Agency and Music Ltd* [1985] Q.B. 428 at 459, 463, and 468–469 (CA); *Dickson Elliott Lonergan Ltd v Plumbing World Ltd* [1988] 2 N.Z.L.R. 608 at 613 (NZ High Ct); *Lachhani v Destination Canada (UK) Ltd* (1996) 13 Const. L.J. 279 at 283; *Gray (Constructions) Pty Ltd v Hogan* [2000] NSWCA 26; *Four Seas Union (Holdings) Ltd v Hong Kong & Macau Scent On Engineering & Construction Ltd* [2003] HKEC 245; *A.B.B. Engineering Construction Pty Ltd v Abigroup Contractors Pty Ltd* [2003] NSWSC 665 at [195]–[198]; *E.D.R.C. Group Ltd v Brunel University* [2006] EWHC 687 (TCC); [2006] B.L.R. 255; *Sopov v Kane Constructions Pty Ltd (No.2)* [2009] VSCA 141; (2009) 257 A.L.R. 182 at [33]–[40].
[71] *Eddy Lau Constructions Pty Ltd v Transdevelopment Enterprises Pty Ltd* [2004] NSWSC 273 at [75] per Barrett J.
[72] *Serck Controls Ltd v Drake & Schull Engineering Ltd* 73 Con. L.R. 100 at [55] per Judge Hicks QC.
[73] *Goarm Engineering Ltd v Shimizu Corp* [2002] HKCFI 810 at [51].
[74] *Costain Civil Engineering Ltd v Zanen Dredging and Contracting Co Ltd* (1996) 85 B.L.R. 77 (where a dredging company already had equipment in the relevant vicinity and a workforce that could be committed to the relevant project immediately); *Happy Dynasty Ltd v Wai Kee (Zens) Construction & Transportation Co Ltd* [1998] HKCA 525 at [55] (unusual and skilled nature of work may entitle claimant to extra profit element).
[75] *Lachhani* (1996) 13 Const. L.J. 279 at 284.
[76] *Brenner* [1993] 2 V.R. 221 at 263 (Victoria Sup Ct).

"in the case where the services are of such a kind that it is difficult or impossible to assess the number of hours involved or to itemize the precise services, the court is entitled to make a global assessment".

When determining an appropriate rate, reference may be made to whatever rates are commonly accepted in the industry for a person of the claimant's standing, and/or to any previous agreement between the parties. An example is provided by *Wigan Athletic*.[77] The claimant police authority had a contract with the defendant football club to provide special police services at home fixtures. Charges were made for these services on an agreed scale. The claimant sought to renegotiate the contract to increase the amount of the services, and although the club would not agree to this Mann J. held that it was unjustly enriched when it freely accepted the increased services over the next two years. He therefore made a restitutionary award in the claimant's favour, painstakingly quantified by calculating the number of officers working on representative match days and multiplying this figure by the previously agreed rates for each officer—"individual by individual, serial by serial, horse by horse, and dog by dog".[78] This decision was reversed because the Court of Appeal did not agree that there had been free acceptance of the claimant's services,[79] but the appellate court did not criticise Mann J.'s quantification methodology.

(iii) *Commission and Royalty Payments*

5-30 In various cases the courts have quantified the value of services on a commission basis, on the ground that this is industry practice and/or reflects the parties' own understanding of how much the claimant's services are worth. For example, in *Way v Latilla*,[80] the parties agreed that the claimant should be entitled to an unspecified share of the profits of exploiting mining concessions in West Africa if he obtained these concessions for the defendant. The House of Lords therefore awarded him a percentage of these profits, although only a small one (0.5 per cent of £1 million), reasoning that the substantial effort and expense incurred by the defendant in developing the concessions made it fair for him to keep most of the

---

[77] *Wigan Athletic* [2007] EWHC 3095 (Ch); [2007] Po. L.R. 246; reversed on a different point [2008] EWCA Civ 1449; [2009] 1 W.L.R. 1590. Further cases where awards have been made on hourly basis include: *Countrywide Communications Ltd v I.C.L. Pathway Ltd* [2000] C.L.C. 324 at 352–353; *MacKenzie v Thompson* [2005] 3 N.Z.L.R. 285 at [14]–[15] (NZ High Ct) (which was unhappily decided as a case of "almost contract" rather than unjust enrichment); *H&I Enterprises (Vankleek) Ltd v Amco Express Inc* (2006) 40 M.V.R. (5th) 99 (Ontario Sup Ct); *Spencer v S. Franses Ltd* [2011] EWHC 1269 (QB) at [239]–[244]. See too *Skibinski v Community Living British Columbia* [2010] BCSC 1500; (2010) 13 B.C.L.R. (5th) 271 at [307]–[356] (monthly rate for provision of critical nursing care). And note *Rodier v Computerdial Ltd* Unreported CA, December 9, 1993, where Henry L.J. rejected the argument that a part-time consultant should necessarily be paid less than a full-time employee.

[78] *Wigan Athletic* [2008] EWCA Civ 1449 at [131].

[79] *Wigan Athletic* [2008] EWCA Civ 1449; [2009] 1 W.L.R. 1590; discussed at para.4–31.

[80] *Way v Latilla* [1937] 3 All E.R. 759 especially at 764–765 per Lord Atkin, and at 766 per Lord Wright. Besides the cases discussed in the text, see too *Graham & Baldwin v Taylor, Son & Davies* (1965) 109 Sol. Jo. 793; *Brenner* [1993] 2 V.R. 221 especially at 264 (Victoria Sup Ct); *Upjay Pty Ltd v M.J.K. Pty Ltd* [2001] SASC 62; (2001) 79 S.A.S.R. 32; *Vedatech Corp v Crystal Decisions (UK) Ltd* [2002] EWHC 818 (Ch) especially at [86]–[96]; *MacKenzie v Thompson* [2005] 3 N.Z.L.R. 285 (NZ High Ct) at [16]–[17]. And cf. *Taylor v Motability Finance Ltd* [2004] EWHC 2619 (Comm) where a claim of this kind was held to be precluded by the parties' contract.

profits. More recently, in *Andrew Shelton & Co Pty Ltd v Alpha Healthcare Ltd*,[81] the claimant company provided financial consulting services in connection with corporate mergers and acquisitions, work for which it was customarily paid on a commission basis. At the defendant's request the claimant helped to negotiate a sale and leaseback deal worth Aus $26 million, for which services it was awarded restitution of an amount equivalent to 1 per cent of the contract price. The judge settled on this rate after hearing expert evidence that rather higher rates (between 1.75 and 2.5 per cent) were customarily payable to consultants who played a more significant role than that which the claimant had undertaken.

This finding was consistent with Thomas J.'s observations in *Becerra v*   **5–31** *Close Bros Corporate Finance Ltd*,[82] that rates of remuneration in this industry "are related to ideas and success and not time spent, [and so] an approach on an hourly rate basis would plainly not be correct", yet even so "the amount of the work to be done is a significant factor in fixing a fee". Similarly, in *Benedetti* Patten J. accepted that the claimant, who had promoted and facilitated a takeover deal, should be remunerated by a percentage of the transaction price, and he did not accept that an equity share was "the standard or usual form of remuneration in the market for the tasks which [the claimant] carried out".[83] The parties had originally agreed that the claimant would receive an equity share following the acquisition, on the assumption that most of the purchase would be financed by outside investors, but that agreement had been abandoned once it had become clear that the purchase would have to be financed by the defendant and members of his family.

A problem arises where the parties have agreed to the payment of a commis-   **5–32** sion or royalty on the happening of an event that never occurs, or which only occurs some time after the claimant's services were rendered and was triggered by some more immediate cause. Clearly the claimant will recover nothing if the parties are still bound by a contract that makes payment conditional on an event that has not occurred.[84] But what if restitutionary recovery is not precluded by contract, for example, because the parties had a contract that was void or has been terminated? In such cases, the courts are faced with an exceedingly tricky task. As Byrne J. observed in *Brenner*[85]:

> "[W]hat is the sense of attempting to value the [claimant's] fruitless services performed at the request of the defendant, [if] the market or current price of those services cannot be realistically assessed otherwise than by reference to the commission which they might have earned?"

One case like this was *Myers v Macmillan Press Ltd*.[86] The parties agreed that   **5–33** the defendant would publish a book written by the claimant in exchange for

---

[81] *Andrew Shelton & Co Pty Ltd v Alpha Healthcare Ltd* [2002] VSC 248.
[82] *Becerra v Close Bros Corporate Finance Ltd* Unreported QBD (Comm Ct.), June 25, 1999.
[83] *Benedetti* [2009] EWHC 1330 (Ch) at [561]. There was no appeal from the judge's finding as to the usual market rate: [2010] EWCA Civ 1427 at [40].
[84] *Luxor (Eastbourne) Ltd v Cooper* [1941] A.C. 108 at 141.
[85] *Brenner* [1993] 2 V.R. 221 at 264 (Victoria Sup Ct). See too *Peet Ltd v Richmond* [2009] VSC 130 at [294].
[86] *Myers v Macmillan Press Ltd* Unreported QBD, March 3, 1998. A similar problem arises where a lawyer agrees to undertake work on a conditional fee basis and is then discharged by the client before the client's claim is resolved. For discussion of American case law on this topic, see G. Marshall, "*Quantum Meruit* and Conditional Fees: An Overlooked Issue" [2001] C.J.Q. 258.

royalty payments on sales of the work. After the claimant had spent some 2,400 hours working on the book the defendant breached the contract by refusing to publish it. The claimant was able to elect between damages for lost profits and restitution of the value of his work, and Neuberger J. quantified both remedies. He recognised that the exercise involved in quantifying the second remedy was unrealistic, since "as far as all the witnesses [were] aware, such a basis of remuneration has never been agreed with an author of a book such as [the work in question]." Nevertheless he proceeded to ask himself how much the parties might have agreed as a fixed hourly rate for the work done, and settled on a figure—£10 per hour—which was designed to reflect the fact that the defendant would not have agreed to a larger sum than this, knowing that it had little or no control over the hours taken by the claimant, and that the likely sales of the work would make a guaranteed sum of £24,000 "up front" seem like a reasonable deal from the claimant's point of view. This reasoning is very strained, since neither of the parties can have thought that the defendant was enriched by the claimant's work in itself: the point of their arrangement was the delivery of the manuscript, failing which the defendant cannot have been enriched. In the context of the case, however, this did not matter, since the damages award for lost royalties was significantly higher in any case.

(iv) *Equity Stakes*

5-34 If the parties' common understanding was that the claimant's services should be rewarded by the allocation of shares in a company, then the value of the shares may represent the value of the services for the purposes of a claim in unjust enrichment. For example, in *Vernon-Kell v Clinch*,[87] the claimant's work led to the reverse takeover of a company, enabling the defendants to fund the development of a project, the fruits of which took the form of shares in another company. The judge found that there had been a consensus between the parties that the claimant should participate in whatever was received from development of the project, and went on to hold that the claimant should be awarded shares in the second company rather than merely cash, reasoning that the courts are not constrained to hold that a fair reward for a claimant's services:

> "should take any particular form; it may be a fee or a participation such as a commission, or it may consist of some form of payment in kind, such as shares rather than cash, in an appropriate case."[88]

(v) *Sub-standard Performance*

5-35 On the assessment of a claim for services rendered based on a quantum meruit, can the defendant ever assert that the value of such services falls to be reduced

---

[87] *Vernon-Kell v Clinch* Unreported Ch D, September 30, 2002. See too *Benedetti* [2009] EWHC 1330 (Ch) at [247]: "there is no reason in principle not to award Mr Benedetti remuneration in the form of an equity share if that is properly to be regarded as what would constitute reasonable remuneration for the work which he did"; *A v B* [2009] EWHC 2859 (Ch) at [68]: the amount of remuneration to be awarded "may take the form of ... an equity stake in the business being developed or any other form of reward which the dealings between the parties, before, or even after, the transaction has occurred, suggest was perceived as appropriate." On the facts of the latter two cases, it was not the parties' shared understanding that the claimant should receive an equity stake as a reward for his work.

[88] *Vernon-Kell* Unreported Ch D, September 30, 2002 at [3].

because of their tardy performance, or because the unsatisfactory manner of their performance has exposed him to extra expense or claims by third parties? In *Crown House Engineering Ltd v Amec Projects Ltd*, Slade L.J. declined to investigate this question on an application for summary judgment—although he thought that if:

> "the answer . . . is an unqualified 'No, never' . . . [then] at least in some circumstances there would result an injustice of the nature which the whole law of restitution is intended to avoid."[89]

The question was revisited by His Honour Judge Hicks QC in *Serck Controls Ltd v Drake & Schull Engineering Ltd*,[90] where it was argued that the defendant should have a counterclaim for substandard performance which it could set off against its restitutionary liability. The judge held that no such counterclaim would lie, reasoning that it would have to "depend upon breach of some duty by the claimant, so the first question is as to the nature and extent of the duties owed, in the absence of express terms, when carrying out [the] work". Where there is no contract between the parties, the claimant can owe the defendant no contractual duty, for example, to adhere to a programme of work and to co-operate with other tradesmen employed by the defendant. Hence losses suffered by the defendant as a result of the claimant's failure to do these things cannot be recovered in an action by the defendant against the claimant (unless, presumably, a tort duty arises on the facts[91]).

The reasoning in *Serck* must be correct as far as it goes,[92] but it leaves the   **5–36**
problem identified in *Amec* unanswered. The answer is to be found in *Lachhani v Destination Canada (UK) Ltd*[93] and *E.R.D.C. Group Ltd v Brunel University*,[94] in both of which it was held that where a claimant does work in a way that leaves the defendant exposed to extra costs because of delays or the need for remedial work, the amount of the restitutionary award should be reduced, not because the defendant has a counterclaim for breach of duty, but because the claimant's work is simply worth less than it would be if it was carried out to a reasonable standard. Two consequences flow from this: first, the value of the claimant's services cannot be less than zero, and so no question can arise (as might have arisen on the counterclaim analysis) of the claimant owing money to the defendant; secondly, the defendant is under no duty to mitigate his loss and his net benefit "cannot be affected by whether [the claimant] was given the chance of putting the work right or an investigation as to whether it was willing to do so".[95]

---

[89] *Crown House Engineering Ltd v Amec Projects Ltd* (1989) 6 Const L.J. 141 at 152–153 (CA). At 154–155 Bingham L.J. also professed himself an agnostic.
[90] *Serck Controls Ltd v Drake & Schull Engineering Ltd* Unreported TCC, May 12, 2000.
[91] Cf. *T.T.M.I. Sarl v Statoil ASA* [2011] EWHC 1150 (Comm); [2011] 2 Lloyd's Rep. 220 at [53].
[92] Though conceivably matters might be different if the poor quality of the claimant's workmanship gave rise to a negligence claim: cf. *Barclays Bank Plc v Fairclough Building Ltd* (1995) 44 Con. L.R. 35 (CA).
[93] *Lachhani v Destination Canada (UK) Ltd* (1996) 13 Const. L.J. 279 at 284.
[94] *E.R.D.C. Group Ltd v Brunel University* [2006] EWHC 687 (TCC); [2006] B.L.R. 255 at [123]–[128]. See too *Alucraft Pty Ltd (In Liquidation) v Grocon Ltd* Unreported Victoria Sup Ct, April 22, 1994; *Roy v Lagona* [2010] VSC 250 at [341].
[95] *E.R.D.C. Group* [2006] EWHC 687 (TCC) at [128].

(vi) *Monopoly Service Providers*

5-37   In *Transpower New Zealand Ltd v Meridian Energy Ltd*,[96] the judge held that the allocation and subsidisation issues that must be addressed by a regulator when determining the fairness of future charges for regulated utility services need not be considered when retrospectively valuing services which have already been provided. In the absence of a free market, however, it is hard to see how such matters can fairly be ignored when considering such issues as the cost of performance and the pricing levels permitted by the regulator at the relevant time. An English case where similar issues might have arisen is *Wigan Athletic*,[97] where the claimant provided special police services to the defendant football club. However, the value of the claimant's services was not in dispute there, as the parties had already agreed how much they were worth and their dispute related solely to the amount of services that were needed.

5. Discharge of Obligations

(a) *The Rules on Discharge*

5-38   A defendant can be enriched by the discharge of his obligation to a creditor, whether this obligation arose in contract, tort or unjust enrichment, under a statute or for some other reason. To prove that the defendant has been enriched, the claimant must show that the creditor was paid by someone acting with the intention of discharging the liability and that this was the effect of the payment.[98]

5-39   In principle, it would have been desirable for English law to have adopted the simple rule that obligations are always discharged by payment with an intention to discharge, whether the payor is the defendant, the defendant's agent or an unauthorised intervener. Unfortunately, however, the law governing the discharge of obligations is more complex than this. Matters are relatively straightforward where the creditor is paid by the defendant himself, or by someone acting with his prior authority or later ratification. But if the creditor is paid by an unauthorised intervener, then the picture is less clear. If the unauthorised intervener was jointly or severally liable to the creditor in respect of the same obligation then his payment often discharges the defendant's liability—but not always; and if he was not legally liable to the creditor himself then his payment generally

---

[96] *Transpower New Zealand Ltd v Meridian Energy Ltd* [2001] 3 N.Z.L.R. 700 at [58]–[63] (NZ High Ct).
[97] *Wigan Athletic* [2007] EWHC 3095 (Ch); [2007] Po. L.R. 246; reversed [2008] EWCA Civ 1449; [2009] 1 W.L.R. 1590.
[98] In the great majority of cases, the defendant is liable to pay money, but it sometimes happens that he is liable to perform an irreversible and unrepeatable act; in cases of this kind, the liability is always discharged when the act is done, regardless of whether the person performing the act is the defendant, the claimant or someone else: *Gebhardt v Saunders* [1892] 2 Q.B. 452 (clearing blocked drain); *Macclesfield Corp v Great Central Railway* [1911] 2 K.B. 528 (repairing damaged bridge).

does not discharge the defendant's obligation, whether he acted voluntarily or his intention to pay was vitiated for some reason, e.g. because he made a mistake.

To understand the law in this area, it is helpful to distinguish between three **5-40** situations: (a) where the defendant himself pays the creditor; (b) where the defendant's agent pays the creditor; and (c) where an unauthorised intervener pays the creditor.

(i) *Where the Defendant Pays the Creditor*

A party can usually discharge his own obligations by paying his creditor. Hence **5-41** where a defendant owes an obligation to a creditor, and he pays the creditor with money that he has traceably received from the claimant, the obligation is almost invariably discharged and it can be said that he has been enriched at the claimant's expense. There is one exception to this rule: the defendant's obligation is not discharged if he pays the creditor with money which the creditor knows is not money to which the defendant is properly entitled. So, for example, if the claimant mistakenly pays money to the defendant, who uses the money to pay a creditor who knows of its tainted source, then the claimant can have the defendant's payment to the creditor set aside, on the ground that the creditor received the money in bad faith and so cannot be considered a bona fide purchaser.[99]

(ii) *Where the Defendant's Agent Pays the Creditor*

Just as a party can generally discharge his own liabilities by paying his creditor, **5-42** so too can his authorised agent.[100] Hence where a defendant owes an obligation to a creditor, and the defendant's agent uses the claimant's money to pay the creditor, the defendant's liability is usually discharged. This rule applies in cases where a claimant pays the creditor while acting as the defendant's agent.[101] It also applies in cases where some other party uses the claimant's money to pay the creditor while acting as the defendant's agent.[102]

Whether the payor is authorised to pay the creditor on the defendant's behalf **5-43** must be determined by reference to the parties' intentions, which "must primarily be divined from the documents they entered into, [although] it is permissible to

---

[99] *Barclays Bank Ltd v W.J. Simms & Cooke (Southern) Ltd* [1980] 677 at 695; noting *Ward & Co v Wallis* [1900] 1 Q.B. 675 at 679. See too *Martin v Morgan* (1819) 1 Brod. & B. 289, 129 E.R. 734.

[100] *Barclays Bank v Simms* [1980] Q.B. 677 at 695; *Re Emanuel (No.14) Pty Ltd (In Liquidation)* (1997) 24 A.C.S.R. 292 at 299 (Full Ct of Fed Ct of Aus); *Lloyds Bank Plc v Independent Insurance Co Ltd* [1998] EWCA Civ 1853; [2000] Q.B. 110 at 123–127; *Crantrave Ltd v Lloyds Bank Plc* [2000] EWCA Civ 127; [2000] Q.B. 917 at 924; *Treasure & Son Ltd v Dawes* [2008] EWHC 2181 (TCC). Disputes over the scope of one party's authority to pay another's debts can arise where the debtor's request that the other party should pay the creditor is expressed ambiguously, as in e.g. *Horlor v Carpenter* (1857) 3 C.B. (N.S.) 172; 140 E.R. 705; *Lloyds Bank*, (above) at 116–121.

[101] e.g. *Meux v Smith* (1843) 11 Sim. 340; 59 E.R. 931; *Pease v Jackson* (1868) L.R. 3 Ch. App. 576; *Sangster v Cochrane* (1885) 28 Ch. D. 298; *Crosbie-Hill v Sayer* [1908] 1 Ch. 132; *Ghana Commercial Bank v Chandiram* [1960] A.C. 732.

[102] e.g. *Re Byfield* [1982] Ch. 267; *Boscawen v Bajwa* [1996] 1 W.L.R. 328 (CA).

look at other evidence to consider what [their] understandings were."[103] If a payor was unauthorised, then the defendant can still ratify his payment afterwards, provided that the payor purported to act on the defendant's behalf.[104] In the event that the defendant ratifies the payment, his obligation to the creditor will be discharged.[105]

(iii) *Where an Unauthorised Intervener Pays the Creditor*

5–44   Whether a defendant's obligations can be discharged by someone other than the defendant or his agent is a more difficult question. Here the law provides that payments by an unauthorised intervener sometimes discharge another party's obligations, but that sometimes they do not. To explain this, it is helpful to group the cases according to whether the unauthorised intervener has paid the creditor by mistake, pursuant to a secondary liability or voluntarily.

5–45   **Mistake**   The courts have given inconsistent answers to the question whether a defendant's obligation is discharged by an unauthorised intervener's mistaken payment. According to one line of authority, starting with Wright J.'s decision in *B. Liggett (Liverpool) Ltd v Barclays Bank Ltd*,[106] the effect of such a payment is to discharge the defendant's liability. However, a stronger line of authority holds the opposite, starting with the Court of Appeal's decision in *Re Cleadon Trust Ltd*,[107] running through Robert Goff J.'s decision in *Barclays Bank Ltd v W.J. Simms & Cooke (Southern) Ltd*,[108] and culminating in the Court of Appeal's decision in *Crantrave Ltd v Lloyd's Bank Plc*.[109]

---

[103] *Ibrahim v Barclays Bank Plc* [2011] EWHC 1897 (Ch) at [113].

[104] Note that an undisclosed principal cannot ratify his agent's unauthorised acts: *Keighley, Maxsted & Co v Durant* [1901] A.C. 240.

[105] *Pacific & General Insurance Co Ltd v Hazell* [1997] Lloyd's Reinsurance Law Reports 65 at 79–81 per Moore-Bick J., where his Lordship also followed the rule laid down in *Walter v James* (1871) L.R. 6 Exch. 124, that the payer can rescind the payment and recover his money from the creditor at any time before the debtor ratifies his payment. See too *Brasher v O'Hehir* [2005] NSWSC 1194 at [41]; *Oakley Acquisitions Pty Ltd (In Liquidation) v Steinochr* [2005] WASCA 247; *Plaza West Pty Ltd v Simon's Earthworks (NSW) Pty Ltd* [2008] NSWSC 753 at [69]–[79]; *Re Denward Lane Pty Ltd (In Liquidation)* [2009] FCA 893 at [47].

[106] *B. Liggett Liverpool Ltd v Barclays Bank Ltd* [1928] 1 K.B. 48; followed in *Scarth v National Provincial Bank Ltd* (1930) 4 Legal Decisions Affecting Bankers 241. *Liggett* has also been followed in various overseas cases, e.g. *Shapera v Toronto-Dominion Bank* (1970) 17 D.L.R. (3d) 122 (Manitoba QB); *Royal Bank of Canada v Huber* (1971) 23 D.L.R. (3d) 209 (Saskatchewan CA); *Westpac Banking Corp v Rae* [1992] 1 N.Z.L.R. 338 (NZ High Ct); *A.E. LePage Real Estate Services Ltd v Rattray Publications Ltd* (1994) 120 D.L.R. (4th) 499 (Ontario CA); *R.C.L. Operators Ltd v National Bank of Canada* (1995) 131 D.L.R. (4th) 86 (New Brunswick CA); *Majesty Restaurant Pty Ltd (In Liquidation) v Commonwealth Bank of Australia* Unreported NSW Sup Ct (Eq Div), November 25, 1998.

[107] *Re Cleadon Trust Ltd* [1939] Ch. 286.

[108] *Barclays Bank Ltd v W.J. Simms & Cooke (Southern) Ltd* [1980] Q.B. 677 at 700; followed in various overseas cases, e.g. *K.J. Davies (1976) Ltd v Bank of New South Wales* [1981] 1 N.Z.L.R. 262 (NZ High Ct); *Bank of New South Wales v Murphett* [1983] 1 V.R. 489 (Full Ct of Sup Ct of Victoria); *Toronto-Dominion Bank v Pella/Hunt Corp* (1993) 10 O.R. (3d) 634 (Ontario High Ct).

[109] *Crantrave Ltd v Lloyd's Bank Plc* [2000] EWCA Civ 127; [2000] Q.B. 917; followed in *Swotbooks.com* [2011] EWHC 2025 (QB) at [49]–[56].

In the latter case, the defendant bank made a payment out of the claimant **5–46** company's account to the claimant's judgment creditor, in the mistaken belief that it was obliged to do so under a garnishee order which had not been made absolute. The bank argued that it was entitled to debit the claimant's account for the amount of this payment because the payment had partially discharged the claimant's debt. The court rejected this argument, and Pill L.J. stated that[110]:

> "In the absence of evidence that the bank's payment has been made on the customer's behalf or subsequently ratified by him, the payment to the creditor will not of itself discharge the company's liability to the creditor ... In the absence of authorisation or ratification of the payment, the bank must [reinstate the claimant's account] ... and recoup the sum paid, if they can, from the third party to which it was paid."

Secondary liability Where a claimant and a defendant are both legally liable **5–47** to a creditor, and the law forbids the creditor to accumulate recoveries from both of them, the law must then decide whether the claimant or the defendant is the proper person to pay the creditor, or whether they should share this burden. If the claimant pays more than his share, then the law will allow him to recover the excess from the defendant, on the basis that the defendant was "primarily", and the claimant only "secondarily" liable to pay.[111]

In cases where the claimant and the defendant are jointly, or jointly and **5–48** severally, liable to the creditor, the question whether the claimant's payment discharges the defendant's liability is straightforward. In Glanville Williams' words, "an obligation, whether joint or joint and several, has only to be performed once".[112] Hence, when the claimant pays the creditor, the defendant is generally discharged from liability.[113]

In contrast, where the parties are only severally liable to the creditor, matters **5–49** are less simple. Here the claimant's payment generally discharges the defendant's obligation, even in cases where the defendant has not requested him to do so.[114] But there are significant exceptions to this rule in the law of indemnity insurance: an insurer's payment to its insured does not discharge a third party

---

[110] *Crantrave* [2000] EWCA Civ 127 at 923. Note, though, that at 925 May L.J. adverted to the possibility that "there might conceivably be circumstances not amounting to ratification in which it would nevertheless be unconscionable to allow the customer to recover from the bank the balance of his account without deduction of a payment which the bank had made gratuitously". Further discussion of this point can be found in *Gulf International Bank BSC v Albaraka Islamic Bank BSC* [2004] EWCA Civ 416 at [25]–[37]; *Sweetman v Shepherd* [2007] EWHC 137 (QB); [2007] B.P.I.R. 455 at [142]–[147].

[111] For further discussion, see Chs 19–21.

[112] G. Williams, *Joint Obligations* (London: Butterworths, 1949), p.93, fn.2 and text.

[113] The only exception to this general rule arises under the Bills of Exchange Act 1882 s.59(2), which provides that the acceptor of a bill is not discharged from liability when the holder is paid by the drawer or indorser; s.52(4) further provides that when the bill is paid the holder must deliver it up to the party paying it who can then enforce the bill as the new holder; this party also has the right to be subrogated to the holder's securities over the acceptor's property: *Duncan, Fox & Co v North & South Wales Bank* (1880) 6 App. Cas 1.

[114] See e.g. *Exall v Partridge* (1799) 8 T.R. 308 at 311; 101 E.R. 1405 at 1406 per Lawrence J.; *The Pindaros* [1983] 2 Lloyd's Rep. 635 at 639 per Sheen J.

from various kinds of liability to the insured in respect of the insured loss, namely liabilities in tort[115] and unjust enrichment,[116] liabilities under statute,[117] and certain types of contractual liability.[118]

5–50 The reasons for these rules are historical,[119] and there is no reason in principle why the courts should not more simply hold that an indemnity insurer's payment does not extinguish the insured's rights of action against third parties. As discussed elsewhere,[120] the law currently gives the insurer a right of subrogation through which it can acquire the insured's subsisting right of action against the third party and enforce this right for its own benefit. The point of this is to prevent the two alternative outcomes that would otherwise follow: the double enrichment of the insured if he enforces the right, or the enrichment of the third party if the insured forbears from suing him. However the same effect could be achieved by holding that the third party's liability is discharged and by giving the insurer a right in unjust enrichment to sue the third party for reimbursement.

5–51 Nor do matters end there, unfortunately. Looking more closely at the situation where an insured has a contractual right against a third party, and more particularly, at the situation where the insured has a contractual right to an indemnity from a third party, we find that although most authorities hold the third party's liability to be discharged by the insurer's payment, some cases actually hold the opposite.

5–52 Thus, all are agreed that where an insured has the right to claim against two separate indemnity insurers in respect of the same loss, payment by one discharges the other,[121] assuming that the insured is fully indemnified by the first

---

[115] *Mason v Sainsbury* (1782) 3 Doug K.B. 61 at 64; 99 E.R. 538 at 540 per Lord Mansfield C.J.; *Yates v Whyte* (1838) 4 Bing. (N.C.) 272; 132 E.R. 793; *Bradburn v Great Western Railway Co* (1874) L.R. 10 Ex. 1; *King v Victoria Insurance Co Ltd* [1896] A.C. 250 (PC); *Gough v Toronto & York Radial Railway Co* (1918) 42 O.L.R. 415 at 416 (Ontario High Ct); *Parry v Cleaver* [1970] A.C. 1; *The Yasin* [1979] 2 Lloyd's Rep. 45 at 48; *Stone Vickers Ltd v Appledore Ferguson Shipbuilders Ltd* [1992] 2 Lloyd's Rep. 578; *Lord Napier and Ettrick v Hunter* [1993] A.C. 714 at 741 per Lord Goff (HL).

[116] For example, liability to pay general average contribution (on which see paras 18–40—18–49): *Dickenson v Jardine* (1868) L.R. 3 C.P. 639; *Boag v Standard Marine Insurance Co* [1937] 2 K.B. 113 at 118 (CA); *Drouot Assurances SA v Consolidated Metallurgical Industries* (C–351/96) [1999] Q.B. 497 at 505 per Advocate General Fennelly.

[117] *Mason v Sainsbury* (1782) 3 Doug. K.B. 61; 99 E.R. 538; *Clark v Inhabitants of the Hundred of Blything* (1823) 2 B. & C. 254; 107 E.R. 378; *Ballymagauran Co-operative Agricultural and Dairy Soc Ltd v County Councils of Cavan and Leitrim* [1915] 2 I.R. 85 (CA); *Ellerbeck Collieries Ltd v Cornhill Insurance Co* [1932] 1 KB 401 at 411 (CA).

[118] *Darrell v Tibbitts* (1880) 5 Q.B.D. 561 at 563 (CA) (payment by landlord's insurer does not discharge landlord's right to sue tenant on covenant to repair); *Budhia v Wellington City Corp* [1976] 1 N.Z.L.R. 766 (NZ High Ct) (payment by vendor's insurer does not extinguish his right to specific performance of contract for sale of real property).

[119] See C. Mitchell and S. Watterson, *Subrogation: Law and Practice* (Oxford: OUP, 2006), para.10.07 and following.

[120] See paras 21–01—21–06 and 21–15—21–23.

[121] *North British and Mercantile Insurance Co v London, Liverpool and Globe Insurance Co* (1877) 5 Ch. D. 569 (CA); *Sickness and Accident Assurance Association v General Accident Assurance Corp Ltd* (1892) 19 R. 977 at 980–981n. (Ct of Sess (OH)); *American Surety Co v Wrightson* (1910) 16 Com. Cas. 37 at 55; *Austin v Zurich General Accident and Liability Insurance Co Ltd* [1945] 1 K.B. 250; *Albion Insurance Co Ltd v Government Insurance Office (NSW)* (1969) 121 C.L.R. 342; *Sydney Turf Club v Crowley* (1972) 126 C.L.R. 420; *Bovis Construction Ltd v Commercial Union Assurance Co Plc* [2001] Lloyd's Rep. 416 at 418–419; *A.M.P. Workers' Compensation Services (NSW) Ltd v Q.B.E. Insurance Ltd* [2001] NSWCA 267; (2001) 53 N.S.W.L.R. 35 at 38. A similar principle applies in life insurance, where the first insurer pays the full amount of the policyholder's insurable

insurer's payment.[122] It has also been held in two Canadian cases, *Trenton Works Lavalin Inc v Panalpina Inc*[123] and *Teddington Ltd v William Finkle Machine Ltd*,[124] that an indemnity insurer's payment extinguishes its insured's rights against a third party under a performance bond. And in *Stratti v Stratti*,[125] it was held by the New South Wales Court of Appeal that an indemnity insurer's payment discharges the insured's partners from their liability to indemnify him against liabilities incurred in the course of conducting the business of the firm. The partners in this case were liable by operation of the New South Wales Partnership Act 1892 s.24(2), which corresponds to the English Partnership Act 1890 s.24(2), but the court would clearly have reached the same conclusion, had the partners' liability derived instead from a term of the partnership deed. This follows from the fact that Fitzgerald J.A. founded his decision on Jacobs J.A.'s previous statement in *Sydney Turf Club v Crowley*,[126] that an indemnity insurer's payment always discharges a third party's liability to indemnify the insured "in the strict sense", by which Jacobs J.A. meant a contractual liability.[127]

Against this line of cases, however, we must set *Beira Boating Co Ltd v Companhia de Mocambique*,[128] where Rowlatt J. assumed that an insurer's payment did not discharge the defendant's obligation to the insured under a letter of indemnity. More recently, and more importantly, there is also the House of Lords' decision in *Caledonia North Sea Ltd v British Telecommunications Plc*.[129] Caledonia owned and operated an oil platform. Following an explosion on the platform, Caledonia incurred liabilities towards injured workmen and the families of workmen who were killed. Caledonia had the right to recover an indemnity in respect of these liabilities from its liability insurer. It also had the right to recover a contractual indemnity in respect of the same liabilities from the contractors who had employed the workmen. Caledonia recovered from its liability insurer, which then sought to recover the value of its payments from the contractors via subrogated proceedings.[130] The question arose whether these proceedings had been correctly pleaded, an issue which turned on the question

5–53

---

interest in the life insured: *Hebdon v West* (1863) 3 B. & S. 579; 122 E.R. 218; *Simcock v Scottish Imperial Insurance Co* (1902) 10 S.L.T. 286 (Ct of Sess (OH)); both applying the Life Assurance Act 1774 s.3.

[122] Where the insured is not fully indemnified by the first insurer's payment, e.g. because he is under-insured, then the second insurer is not discharged from liability: *Baulderstone Hornibrook Engineering Pty Ltd v Gordian Runoff Ltd* [2008] NSWCA 243; (2008) 15 A.N.Z. Ins. Cas. 61–780 at [198]–[302].

[123] *Trenton Works Lavalin Inc v Panalpina Inc* (1994) 126 N.S.R. (2d) 287 (Nova Scotia High Ct); varied on appeal on a different point: (1995) 139 N.S.R. (2d) 46 (Nova Scotia CA).

[124] *Teddington Ltd v William Finkle Machine Ltd* Unreported Ontario Sup Ct, February 4, 2000.

[125] *Stratti v Stratti* [2000] NSWCA 258; (2000) 50 N.S.W.L.R. 324.

[126] *Sydney Turf Club* (1971) 1 N.S.W.L.R. 724 at 730 (NSWCA); affirmed on a different point (1972) 126 C.L.R. 420.

[127] *Stratti* [2000] NSWCA 258, (2000) 50 N.S.W.L.R. 324 at 331.

[128] *Beira Boating Co Ltd v Companhia de Mocambique* (1927) 29 Lloyd's List Rep. 285.

[129] *Caledonia North Sea Ltd v British Telecommunications Plc* [2002] 1 Lloyd's Rep. 553.

[130] In fact, the insurer paid the victims of the explosion and their families directly, but matters have been explained slightly differently in the text in order to emphasise that the insurer and the contractors were both liable in respect of the same loss sustained by Caledonia.

whether the contractors' obligations had been discharged by the insurer's payment.[131]

5–54   The House of Lords held that the contractors' obligations had not been discharged, reasoning that the contractors rather than the insurer should ultimately have to bear the burden of paying Caledonia, and that it followed from this that the contractors' liabilities could not have been discharged. In Lord Hoffmann's words[132]:

> "It is a general principle . . . that a person who has more than one claim to indemnity is not entitled to be paid more than once. But there are different ways of giving effect to this principle. One is to say that the person who has been paid is entitled to be subrogated to the rights against the other person liable. The other is to say that one payment discharges the liability. The authorities show that the law ordinarily adopts the first solution when the liability of the person who paid is secondary to the liability of the other party liable. It adopts the second solution when the liability of the party who paid was primary or the liabilities are equal and co-ordinate."

5–55   There are several problems with this analysis. The view that a primarily liable party's obligation "ordinarily" subsists when a secondarily liable party pays their common creditor is not borne out by the many cases in which claimants have successfully brought actions for reimbursement against defendants with whom they have shared a common liability to a creditor.[133] Nor is it consistent with cases where 100 per cent contribution awards have been made to joint tortfeasors.[134] Nor is it consistent with the Australian and Canadian authorities mentioned above,[135] where a third party's contractual liability to indemnify the insured was held to have been discharged by an indemnity insurer's payment, even though the insurer was entitled to recover his payment from the third party in full.

5–56   In principle, it is hard to see the point of the distinction drawn by Lord Hoffmann, and in practice it will make the outcome of a crucial pleading point—whether the insurer should bring a contribution claim in its own name, or a subrogated claim in the name of its insured—turn on a question of substantive law to which the insurer may not know the answer until after the claim has been decided by the court—namely, whether the insurer is entitled to shift some or all of the burden of paying the insured onto the third party. The *Caledonia* case therefore creates the practical problem for an insurer that it must commit itself before it comes to court to arguing either that it should recover the whole of its

---

[131] An insurer that acquires a subsisting right of action via subrogation must sue in the name of the insured. An insurer that sues in its own right for a contribution, or full reimbursement, from a defendant whose liability the insurer has discharged, may do so in its own name. This aspect of the case is discussed in C. Mitchell, "Claims in Unjustified Enrichment to Recover Money Paid Pursuant to a Common Liability" (2001) 5 Edin. L.R. 186.

[132] *Caledonia* [2002] 1 Lloyd's Rep. 553 at [92]. See too [12]–[13] per Lord Bingham, and [44]–[66] per Lord Mackay.

[133] See the cases cited in paras 19–16—19–21.

[134] e.g. *Nelhams v Sandells Maintenance Ltd* [1996] P.I.Q.R. 52 (CA); *The Sincerity S* [1996] 2 Lloyd's Rep. 503; *Wynniatt-Hussey v R.J. Bromley (Underwriting Agencies) Plc* [1996] Lloyd's Reinsurance L.R. 312; *Henderson v Merrett Syndicates Ltd* [1997] Lloyd's Rep. I.R. 247; *Prentice v Hereward Housing Assoc Ltd*, unreported, QBD, April 29, 1999.

[135] See para.5–52.

payment, or that it should recover some proportion of its payment up to 99.9 per cent.

Volunteers   The rule has prevailed in English law that a defendant's obliga-   **5–57** tion to a creditor is not discharged if the creditor is paid by an unauthorised intervener acting voluntarily—i.e. by an intervener whose intention to pay is not vitiated in any way, and who does not pay pursuant to a legal liability. This rule was restated by Fox L.J. in *Electricity Supply Nominees Ltd v Thorn E.M.I. Retail Ltd*[136]:

> "If a person makes a voluntary payment intending to discharge another's debt, he will only discharge the debt if he acts with that person's authority or the latter subsequently ratifies the payment. Consequently if the payor makes the payment without authority and does not obtain subsequent ratification he normally has no redress against the debtor."

(b) *Disproving Enrichment*

If money is paid to a creditor but the effect is not to discharge the defendant's   **5–58** liability to the creditor, then the defendant cannot have been enriched. Since his obligation subsists he is no better off than he was before the payment. It follows that the claimant cannot be entitled to a restitutionary remedy in this situation, although he may be entitled to acquire the creditor's subsisting rights against the defendant by subrogation, a remedy which is not designed to reverse unjust enrichment, but to prevent it from arising.[137]

However, if a defendant never owed an obligation to the recipient of the   **5–59** claimant's payment—i.e. the "creditor" never had any rights against the defend- ant—then the claimant cannot be entitled to either remedy, since he cannot have been enriched, nor is there a prospect of his becoming enriched in the future. Hence the defendant can escape liability if he can show that the creditor never had a right against him,[138] or that he would have had a defence in the event that the creditor had sued him.[139]

---

[136] *Electricity Supply Nominees Ltd v Thorn E.M.I. Retail Ltd* (1991) 63 P. & C.R. 143 at 148 (CA). See too *Grymes v Blofield* (1593) Cro. Eliz. 541; 78 E.R. 788; *M'Intyre v Miller* (1845) 13 M. & W. 725; 153 E.R. 304; *James v Isaacs* (1852) 12 C.B. 791; 138 E.R. 1115; *Re Rowe* [1904] 2 K.B. 483; *Smith v Cox* [1940] 2 K.B. 558; *Guardian Ocean Cargoes Ltd v Banco de Brasil SA* [1991] 2 Lloyd's Rep. 68 at 88; *Esso Petroleum Co Ltd v Hall Russell & Co Ltd (The Esso Bernicia)* [1989] A.C. 643, as explained in *Caledonia North Sea Ltd v London Bridge Engineering Ltd* 2000 S.L.T. 1123 at 1144–1145 (Ct of Sess (IH)).
[137] See paras 21–01—21–06 and 36–36—36–37 for further discussion.
[138] See e.g. *Bonner v Tottenham & Edmonton Permanent Investment Building Society* [1899] 1 Q.B. 161 (CA); *An Bord Bainne Co-operative Ltd v Milk Marketing Board* [1988] 1 C.M.L.R. 605; *State Bank of Victoria v Parry* (1990) 2 A.C.S.R. 15 (Sup Ct of Western Australia); *Regional Municipality of Peel v Ontario* [1992] 3 S.C.R. 762; *Wessex Regional Health Authority v John Laing Construction Ltd* (1994) 39 Con. L.R. 56; *O.L.L. Ltd v Secretary of State for Transport* [1997] 3 All E.R. 987; *Cockburn v G.I.O. Finance Ltd (No.2)* [2001] NSWCA 177; (2001) 51 N.S.W.L.R. 624.
[139] There are numerous cases in which the defendant to an insurer's subrogated claim has escaped liability by relying on a defence that would have been good against the insured in whose name the proceedings have been brought: e.g. *London Assurance Co v Johnson* (1737) West T. Hard. 266 at 269; 25 E.R. 930 at 932 (delay); *West of England Fire Insurance Co v Isaacs* [1897] 1 Q.B. 226 (settlement); *Thames & Mersey Marine Insurance Co v British and Chilian Steamship Co* [1915] 2 K.B. 244; affirmed [1916] 1 K.B. 30 (contributory negligence); *Coupar Transport (London) Ltd v*

(c) *Discharge of Secured Obligations*

5–60   Where a defendant's secured obligation to a creditor is discharged, it is not only the defendant who is benefited: the defendant's other creditors, and particularly junior charge-holders who also have rights against the relevant property, are also benefited by the extinction of the creditor's senior charge. As discussed elsewhere,[140] another type of subrogation remedy may be awarded to the claimant in these circumstances, through which the claimant is entitled to be treated as though he has acquired the creditor's extinguished charge to secure his own right of action against the defendant. This remedy responds both to the enrichment of the defendant, and to the enrichment of the defendant's other creditors[141]—or, exceptionally, to the enrichment of only one or some of them where he or they alone would otherwise be enriched at the claimant's expense.[142]

Smith's (Acton) Ltd [1959] 1 Lloyd's Rep. 369 at 380–381 (exclusion clause); *Euro-Diam Ltd v Bathurst* [1990] 1 Q.B. 1 at 38–39 (CA) (illegality).

[140] See Ch.39.

[141] *Re Warwick's ST* [1937] Ch. 561 at 569; *R. A. & J. Family Investment Corp v Orzech* (1999) 44 O.R. (3d) 385 at 391 (Ontario CA); *Hong Kong Chinese Bank Ltd v Sky Phone Ltd* [2000] HKCFI 1595; [2001] H.K.C. 50 at 53; *Eagle Star Insurance Co Ltd v Karasiewicz* [2004] EWCA Civ 940 at [4] and [11]; *National Westminster Bank Plc v Mayfair Estates Property Investments Ltd* [2007] EWHC 287 (Ch) at [24]; *Kali v Chawla Ltd* [2007] EWHC 2357 (Ch); [2008] B.P.I.R. 415 at [37] and [42]; affirmed on another point [2008] EWCA Civ 480. See too G.E. Palmer, *The Law of Restitution* (Boston, Mass.: Little, Brown & Co, 1978), pp.246–253.

[142] As in *Banque Financière de la Cité v Parc (Battersea) Ltd* [1999] 1 A.C. 221, discussed below at paras 39–41—39–51.

Part Four
AT THE CLAIMANT'S EXPENSE

Chapter 6

AT THE CLAIMANT'S EXPENSE: PERSONAL CLAIMS

1. Introduction

In Chs 4 and 5 we discuss the requirement for claims in unjust enrichment that **6–01** the defendant must have been enriched. In this chapter we consider the further requirement that the defendant's enrichment must have been gained "at the claimant's expense".[1] This deceptively simple term signifies that the claimant must have suffered a loss that was sufficiently closely linked with the defendant's gain for the law to hold that there was a transfer of value between the parties. This rule reflects the principle that the law of unjust enrichment is not concerned with the disgorgement of gains made by defendants, nor with the compensation

---

[1] Stated to be necessary in e.g. *Kleinwort Benson Ltd v Birmingham CC* [1997] Q.B. 380 at 392; *Banque Financière de la Cité SA v Parc (Battersea) Ltd* [1999] 1 A.C. 221 at 227, 234 and 239; *Cressman v Coys of Kensington (Sales) Ltd* [2004] EWCA Civ 47; [2004] 1 W.L.R. 2775 at [22]; *Niru Battery Manufacturing Co v Milestone Trading Ltd (No.2)* [2004] EWCA Civ 487; [2004] 2 All E.R. (Comm.) 289 at [38]; *Gibb v Maidstone and Tunbridge Wells NHS Trust* [2010] EWCA Civ 678; [2010] I.R.L.R. 786 at [32].

Similar language was also used in *Woolwich Equitable Building Society v IRC* [1993] A.C. 70 at 196–197; *Lipkin Gorman (A Firm) v Karpnale Ltd* [1991] 2 A.C. 548 at 572; *BP Exploration Co (Libya) Ltd v Hunt (No.2)* [1979] 1 W.L.R. 783 at 829; *Stockloser v Johnson* [1954] 1 Q.B. 476 at 492; *Fibrosa Spolka Akcyjna v Fairbairn Lawson Combe Barbour Ltd* [1943] A.C. 32 at 61, where Lord Wright spoke of the defendant having received a benefit "derived from" the claimant; and Lord Wright, "Restatement of the Law of Restitution" in *Legal Essays and Addresses* (Cambridge: CUP, 1939), 34, p.36, referring to "benefit which is enjoyed by the defendant at the cost of the plaintiff". In *Sinclair v Brougham* [1914] A.C. 398 at 415, Viscount Haldane L.C. referred to claims in Roman law "based . . . on the circumstance that the defendant has been improperly enriched at the expense of the plaintiff", but denied that English law recognised such claims because he mistook "quasi-contractual" claims for claims in contract, a view of the law that was repudiated in *Westdeutsche Landesbank Girozentrale v Islington LBC* [1996] A.C. 669 at 709–714 (as discussed at paras 3–03—3–04).

It seems that the terminology was first used in this context by the American legal historian J.B. Ames in "The History of Assumpsit" (1888) 2 Harvard L.R. 1, pp.22 and 53, p.64, referring to "the fundamental principle of justice that no one ought unjustly to enrich himself at the expense of another"; see also W.A. Keener, *Treatise on the Law of Quasi-Contracts* (New York, NY: Baker, Voorhis & Co, 1893), p.19. As noted in D.J. Ibbetson, "Unjust Enrichment and English Law" in E.J.H. Schrage (ed.), *Unjust Enrichment and the Law of Contract* (The Hague: Kluwer Law International, 2002), 45, Ames drew inspiration from Pomponius (D.12.6.14): "*Jure naturae aequum est, neminem cum alterius detrimento fieri locupletiorem*" ("it is natural justice that no-one should unjustly enrich himself to the detriment of another"). For Ames' influence on the development of American law and the American Law Institute, *Restatement of Restitution* (St. Paul, Minn.: American Law Institute, 1937) (which was reviewed by Lord Wright in the article cited above, and which fed into his comments in *Fibrosa*); see A. Kull, "James Barr Ames and the Early Modern History of Unjust Enrichment" (2005) 25 O.J.L.S. 297.

of losses sustained by claimants, but with the reversal of transfers of value between claimants and defendants.[2]

6–02   Whether a transfer has taken place is not a question of fact but a question of combined fact and law; that is, it turns on the application of legal tests to the facts of the case. Unfortunately, what these legal tests are is currently uncertain. There is generally little or no discussion of this question in simple two-party cases involving personal claims to recover the value of money paid or services rendered, because it seems to be obvious that the defendant's enrichment must have been gained "at the claimant's expense" on any sensible view of what this term means.[3] There is some discussion of the rule in more complex cases involving multiple parties, where the courts have recognised that it is unhelpful to address the problems that can arise using "loose and generalised . . . language and concepts which are not appropriate to a legal analysis of the situation".[4] Nevertheless, clear criteria have yet to emerge from the cases, and there is no consensus among scholars as to the theoretical basis of the requirement.[5]

6–03   In this chapter we discuss the requirement in the context of personal claims in unjust enrichment. In the next chapter we discuss the interplay between the requirement and the rules of following and tracing in the context of proprietary claims. The discussion in this chapter proceeds as follows. First, we advocate that a causal test should be adopted to determine whether a transfer of value between the parties has taken place. On this view, it is sufficient for a single event or transaction to have occurred, as a result of which the claimant has suffered a loss, and the defendant has made a gain. Beyond this, it may also suffice that the claimant's loss and the defendant's gain are the result of two or more causally connected events or transactions. Recent two-party cases support this view, but the picture emerging from cases involving three or more parties is much less clear. For ease of exposition we therefore take two-party and multiple-party cases separately. Finally, we consider whether English law requires a claimant to show an exact correspondence between his loss and a defendant's gain, restricting him to recovery of the highest amount that is common to the parties' respective loss and gain.

2. TRANSFERS OF VALUE: TWO-PARTY CASES

(a) *No Performance Requirement*

6–04   The German law of unjust enrichment distinguishes benefits transferred "through a performance made by another" and benefits acquired "in other ways",[6] imposing different conditions for recovery according to the mechanism by which the

---

[2] *Commissioner of State Revenue (Victoria) v Royal Insurance Australia Ltd* (1994) 182 C.L.R. 51 at 75; affirmed *Roxborough v Rothmans of Pall Mall Australia Ltd* (2001) 208 C.L.R. 516 at [26]; *Gribbon v Lutton* [2001] EWCA Civ 1956; [2002] Q.B. 902 at [60]; *Pacific National Investments Ltd v City of Victoria* [2004] 3 S.C.R. 75 at [25] and [34]; *Kingstreet Investments Ltd v New Brunswick (Department of Finance)* [2007] SCC 1; [2007] 1 S.C.R. 3 at [32].
[3] See e.g. *Cressman* [2004] EWCA Civ 47; [2004] 1 W.L.R. 2775 at [24]; *Yeoman's Row Management Ltd v Cobbe* [2008] UKHL 55; [2008] 1 W.L.R. 1752 at [40].
[4] *Uren v First National Home Finance Ltd* [2005] EWHC 2529 (Ch) at [22].
[5] *Haugesund Kommune v Depfa ACS Bank* [2011] EWCA Civ 33; [2011] P.N.L.R. 14 at [70].
[6] BGB §812.

defendant was enriched. Like German law, English law also allows claimants to recover benefits acquired by either means, but unlike German law it does not require them to bring different types of action according to the method by which the relevant benefit was transferred. Under English law a claimant can show that the defendant's enrichment was gained at his expense by showing that he took some active step in transferring a benefit to him, for example by paying him money or performing a service for him. But a claimant can also do this by showing, for example, that the defendant found and took his property without his knowledge,[7] or that he surrendered a legal right against the defendant,[8] or acquiesced in a third party using his funds to pay the defendant.[9]

(b) *Causal Links between Loss and Gain*

In a simple two-party case, must a claimant seeking a personal remedy show that   **6–05** his loss and the defendant's gain were connected by a "proprietary link", i.e. must the claimant show that he lost a property right that was gained by the defendant? Or does it suffice for the claimant to show that his loss and the defendant's gain were connected by a causal link, because an event or transaction took place that caused the claimant to suffer a loss and the defendant to make a gain? Many of the cases are equivocal on this point because they involve claims to recover the value of cash, goods or land, where the defendant has received both the right to an asset and the value of that right. However it is well established that claims in unjust enrichment lie to recover the value of services,[10] where no transfer of rights occurs, and this is also true of two-party cases where the claimant foregoes a right of action against the defendant,[11] and of three-party cases where the claimant pays off the defendant's legal obligation,[12] or relieves him of the need to pay for necessaries.[13] Since causal links are good enough in all these cases, we consider that they are also good enough in cases involving claims to recover the value of cash, goods and land.

The question then arises, what test do the courts use to decide whether there   **6–06** was a legally sufficient causal link between the claimant's loss and the defendant's gain? When answering this we must first exclude "decision causation" from the discussion. There are different reasons why a defendant's enrichment at a claimant's expense might be unjust, some of which turn on the fact that the claimant did not intend to benefit the defendant, e.g. cases of mistake, duress, and undue influence, and some of which do not, e.g. cases where a public body makes an ultra vires payment. Where vitiation of intention is in issue, questions of "decision causation" arise that do not arise in the other cases. In other words, it

---

[7] *Holiday v Sigil* (1826) 2 C. & P. 176; 172 E.R. 81; *Neate v Harding* (1851) 6 Ex. 349; 155 E.R. 577; *Moffatt v Kazana* [1969] 2 Q.B. 152.

[8] *Gibb* [2010] EWCA Civ 678; [2010] I.R.L.R. 786.

[9] *Cook v Italiano Family Fruit Co Pty Ltd (In Liquidation)* [2010] FCA 1355; (2010) 190 F.C.R. 474 at [112]: this would be "as much a 'subtraction' from the [claimant's] property . . . as a payment by the [claimant] itself".

[10] e.g. *Yeoman's Row* [2008] UKHL 55; [2008] 1 W.L.R. 1752 at [40]–[41]; and cf. *Blue Haven Enterprises Ltd v Tully* [2006] UKPC 17 at [20].

[11] e.g. *Gibb* [2010] EWCA Civ 678; [2010] I.R.L.R. 786 at [23]–[37].

[12] e.g. *Dubai Aluminium Co Ltd v Salaam* [2002] UKHL 48; [2003] 2 A.C. 366 at [72] and [76].

[13] e.g. *Sempra Metals Ltd v IRC* [2007] UKHL 34; [2008] 1 A.C. 561 at [103] and [116]–[117].

must be asked whether the mistake, etc., was a legal cause of the claimant's decision to enter a transaction with the intention of benefitting the claimant.[14] The rules governing such questions are discussed in the chapters on mistake, duress and undue influence, because they show us what kinds of mistake, etc. can ground a claim, by specifying the extent to which such vitiating factors must have affected the claimant's decision-making.[15] This is a different question from the question with which we are concerned in this chapter, and which arises in all of the cases, of whether the defendant has been enriched at the claimant's expense because there has been a transfer of value between the parties.

6–07   This question was discussed in *Test Claimants in the F.I.I. Group Litigation v HMRC*,[16] where the Court of Appeal held that: "[T]he test of causation for unjust enrichment is the 'but for' test", subject in some exceptional cases to a remoteness cap. The assumed facts of the case were that a claimant had used tax reliefs to reduce its liability to pay tax that had been unlawfully levied in breach of E.C. law. The question arose whether a claim would lie for the value of these reliefs, on the assumed basis that the claimant would have used them to reduce other, lawful, tax liabilities if it had not already used them to reduce its unlawful tax liabilities. The court held that no such claim would lie, for two reasons. First, HMRC could not have been unjustly enriched by a payment made to discharge a lawful tax liability because ex hypothesi this payment must have been due under the relevant statute.[17] Secondly, and more significantly for present purposes, even if HMRC had been enriched by the value of a claimant's foregone right to reduce its lawful tax liability, and even if this gain would not have been made but for the claimant's use of the reliefs to reduce its unlawful tax liability, HMRC's gain would not have been made at the claimant's expense because it would have been too remote a consequence of the claimant's earlier use of the reliefs to be recoverable: the link between the claimant's loss and HMRC's gain would not have been "sufficiently direct to satisfy the requirements of causation in restitution".[18]

6–08   Two features of this finding call for comment. First, the parties' submissions elided two separate issues: whether the claimant's mistake of law caused it to use the reliefs to reduce its lawful tax liability (a question going to "decision causation")[19] and whether the claimant's use of the reliefs caused the claimant to suffer a loss and HMRC to make a gain (a question going to whether HMRC's gain was acquired at the claimant's expense).[20] Unfortunately, the Court of

---

[14] E. Bant, "Causation and Scope of Liability in Unjust Enrichment" [2009] R.L.R. 60.

[15] See paras 9–15——9–31, 10–06, 10–48——10–57 and 11–23——11–24.

[16] *Test Claimants in the F.I.I. Group Litigation v HMRC* [2010] EWCA Civ 103; [2010] S.T.C. 1251 at [182].

[17] *F.I.I.* [2010] EWCA Civ 103 at [179]–[184].

[18] *F.I.I.* [2010] EWCA Civ 103 at [182].

[19] Cf. *Test Claimants in the A.C.T. Group Litigation (Class 4) v HMRC* [2010] EWHC 359 (Ch); [2010] S.T.C. 1078 at [95] and [112]–[120], another decision causation case which concerned claims made in respect of money paid as tax in the mistaken belief that the claimants could not legally defer payment of the tax until a later date. Henderson J. found that the claimants' mistake did not cause them to pay the money prematurely because they would not have exercised their right to defer payment even if they had known that they were entitled to do so. This finding was upheld on appeal: [2010] EWCA Civ 1480; [2011] S.T.C. 872 at [42]–[58].

[20] *F.I.I.* [2010] EWCA Civ 103; [2010] S.T.C. 1251 at [178]: counsel for the claimants "submitted that what should be reversed [were] the benefits to the Revenue reasonably arising from the mistake, rather than from 'the mistaken payment'".

Appeal failed to disentangle these two questions, which explains why they relied on dicta concerning decision causation when holding that a "but for" causation test should be used to determine the "at the expense of" point.[21] Nevertheless, we assume that the same "but for" test will be used to decide whether a defendant's gain has been made at a claimant's expense in cases where the state of the claimant's mind is irrelevant, e.g. where a public body makes an ultra vires payment.

Secondly, the court used a "directness" test to conclude that HMRC's gain   **6–09** was too remote for recovery, following Henderson J.'s use of similar language at first instance. However, it is hard to understand why HMRC's enrichment was only an "indirect" consequence of the claimant's decision to use the reliefs to reduce its lawful tax liability, given the decisions in *Deutsche Morgan Grenfell Plc v IRC*[22] and *Sempra Metals Ltd v IRC*,[23] in both of which the House of Lords must effectively have held that the Revenue's enrichment (by receipt of the user value of money) was a "direct" consequence of the claimants' failure to make a group income election in order to postpone the time at which they paid corporation tax. The difference in outcome between these cases demonstrates that the *F.I.I.* "directness" test for remoteness of gain in unjust enrichment will generate unpredictable outcomes, in the same way that the *Re Polemis*[24] "directness" test for remoteness of damage in tort generated unpredictable outcomes before it was rejected by the Privy Council in *Overseas Tankships (UK) Ltd v Morts Docks & Engineering Co Ltd (The Wagon Mound) (No.1).*[25] This is not to argue that a test of "reasonable foreseeability" analogous to the test for remoteness of loss introduced in *The Wagon Mound* would be a more appropriate test for remoteness of gain in unjust enrichment cases—there is no good reason to think that it would be—but simply to observe that "directness" is a conceptually unstable test for distinguishing recoverable from irrecoverable gains in the law of unjust enrichment because it is descriptively imprecise and is not underpinned by an identifiable juristic principle.

Returning to the basic "but for" causation test, it should finally be noted that   **6–10** a further qualification of this test may be needed in cases where the defendant's gain would not have accrued but for a transaction that has also left the claimant worse off, but where the defendant's gain also results from an intervening justifying cause, such as a later act by the claimant, as result of which the defendant would have been enriched anyway. This point can be illustrated by *Gibb*,[26] where the parties entered a compromise agreement under which the claimant agreed to step down from her post as chief executive of the defendant NHS trust in exchange for a payment that included £175,000 to compensate her

---

[21] *F.I.I.* [2010] EWCA Civ 103 at [182] citing *Kleinwort Benson* [1999] 2 A.C. 349 at 399; *Dextra Bank* [2001] UKPC 50; [2002] All E.R. (Comm.) 193 at [30]; *Deutsche Morgan Grenfell Plc v IRC* [2006] UKHL 49; [2007] 1 A.C. 558 at [143]. Cf. *Gibb* [2010] EWCA Civ 678; [2010] I.R.L.R. 786 at [33] where Laws L.J. similarly failed to distinguish between "decision causation" cases and "at the claimant's expense" cases.

[22] *Deutsche Morgan Grenfell Plc v IRC* [2006] UKHL 49; [2007] 1 A.C. 558.

[23] *Sempra Metals Ltd v IRC* [2007] UKHL 34; [2008] A.C. 561.

[24] Named after *Re Polemis and Furness Withy & Co Ltd* [1921] 3 K.B. 560.

[25] *Overseas Tankship (UK) Ltd v Morts Dock & Engineering Co Ltd (The Wagon Mound) (No.1)* [1961] A.C. 388. See especially Viscount Simonds' comment at 423 that a "direct consequence" test "leads to nowhere but the never-ending and insoluble problems of causation".

[26] *Gibb* [2010] EWCA Civ 678; [2010] I.R.L.R. 786.

for abandoning a claim for wrongful dismissal. The trust then refused to pay the £175,000, on the ground that the agreement was irrationally generous and therefore ultra vires. The Court of Appeal held that the agreement was not ultra vires, so that the claimant had a contractual right to the money. However the court went on to consider whether she would have had a claim in unjust enrichment, if the contract had been void as contended by the trust.

6–11   The claimant argued that in this case the trust would have been saved an inevitable expense when she agreed not to sue for wrongful dismissal, and that this enrichment would have been unjust because her intention to benefit the trust would have been qualified by the unsatisfied condition that the agreement was legally enforceable. This argument was rejected by the trial judge on the ground that the claimant had lost her ability to sue for wrongful dismissal when she had failed to issue a protective claim in the employment tribunal, although she had had the opportunity to do this after the trust had told her that it was going to challenge the validity of the contract. Applying a "but for" causation test, it followed that the defendant's enrichment had not been caused by the claimant's agreement to forgo her rights, because she would have lost these anyway through her own negligent failure to preserve them. However the Court of Appeal held that this finding of fact had not been open to the judge because the trust had not challenged the validity of the agreement until after the time for issuing a protective claim in the tribunal had elapsed, and so the claimant's failure to protect her rights had stemmed from her blameless belief that the agreement was valid. The differing attitudes taken by the trial judge and the Court of Appeal with regard to the question of fault in this case had a direct bearing on their differing findings on the intervening cause issue, Laws L.J. stressing that:

> "[T]he issue tested by causation is [often], where should responsibility lie? And in that case, of course, the assessment of causation is by no means a value-free exercise."[27]

3. TRANSFERS OF VALUE: MULTIPLE-PARTY CASES

(a) *Introduction*

6–12   The question whether a defendant's enrichment was gained at a claimant's expense becomes more complicated, and more difficult, when there are more than two parties involved in the case. To give some examples, X may pay Y, and thereby discharge a defendant's obligation to Y. Or X may pay Y, and receipt of this payment may cause Y to confer a benefit on the defendant. Or X may intend to transfer a benefit to Y, and instead transfer the benefit to the defendant. In each case, the question arises, whether the defendant is enriched at the expense of X, of Y, or of both X and Y?

---

[27] *Gibb* [2010] EWCA Civ 678; [2010] I.R.L.R. 786 at [32].

According to many legal writers, this question receives a very restricted answer.[28] They argue that the law generally limits recovery to those parties by whom a defendant has been "directly" enriched, and only exceptionally allows recovery to those parties by whom the defendant has been "indirectly" enriched —although they vary in their understanding of what "directness" means, and they all consider that their "directness" rule should be subject to various exceptions. Some writers also contend that an enrichment can only ever be gained at the expense of one party, so that a rule identifying a "direct enricher" as the source of the defendant's benefit necessarily entails that the benefit cannot also have been gained at the expense of an "indirect enricher".   **6–13**

No case clearly holds that English law has any such "direct transfer" rule,[29] and although the implementation of such a rule would be one way for the law to deal with the problems that are thrown up by cases involving multiple parties, we consider that these problems can be dealt with more transparently and more coherently in other ways. Hence, we believe that the law would do better to approach the question whether a defendant has been enriched at a claimant's expense in a three-party case, as in a two-party case, by undertaking a simple causal inquiry.[30] There is no need to qualify this test by holding that a benefit can only be gained at one party's expense, nor by holding that a defendant can only be enriched at the expense of a party who "directly" enriched him.   **6–14**

We develop this argument in the following way. Section (b) explains the underlying concerns that might shape the law's approach to identifying what does, or does not, count as a qualifying transfer of value in three-party cases. Section (c) outlines and evaluates the prevailing approach to this question in the academic literature. Section (d) describes the causal analysis that we prefer, and its implications. Section (e) gives an account of the case law that is based on this causal model.   **6–15**

(b) *Underlying Concerns*

When identifying what should count as a transfer of value, the main problem is to find a definition that is neither too narrow, nor too wide. This problem is particularly acute in cases involving three or more parties. If the definition is too narrow, then a significant number of people may be left without a remedy although they have suffered a loss that has led to an unjust gain accruing in a   **6–16**

---

[28] For a detailed appraisal of the academic literature in this area, see S. Watterson, "'Direct Transfers' in the Law of Unjust Enrichment" [2011] C.L.P. Different variants of the "direct transfer" theory are advanced by e.g. L.D. Smith, "Three-Party Restitution: A Critique of Birks's Theory of Interceptive Subtraction" (1991) 11 O.J.L.S. 481; A. Tettenborn, "Lawful Receipt—A Justifying Factor?" [1997] R.L.R. 1; L.D. Smith, "Restitution: The Heart of Corrective Justice" (2001) 79 Texas Law Rev. 2115; P. Birks, "'At the Expense of the Claimant': Direct and Indirect Enrichment in English Law", in D. Johnston and R. Zimmerman (eds), *Unjustified Enrichment: Key Issues in Comparative Perspective* (Cambridge: CUP, 2002), Ch.18; P. Birks, *Unjust Enrichment*, 2nd edn (Oxford: OUP, 2005), p.86 and following; G. Virgo, *The Principles of the Law of Restitution*, 2nd edn (Oxford: OUP, 2006), pp.105–112; B. McFarlane, "Unjust Enrichment, Property Rights, and Indirect Recipients" [2009] R.L.R. 37; A. Burrows, *The Law of Restitution*, 3rd edn (Oxford: OUP, 2010), pp.69–85.
[29] There are some loose dicta in *Re Byfield* [1982] Ch. 267 at 276, and *Uren* [2005] EWHC 2529 (Ch) at [23].
[30] See the test identified in *F.I.I.* [2010] EWCA Civ 103; [2010] S.T.C. 1251 at [182]; discussed at paras 6–07—6–09.

defendant's hands. In some cases, a claimant in this position might instead have a claim against a third party, but this might be met by a defence, or the third party might have disappeared or become insolvent.[31] Even where a claimant can recover from a third party, however, there remains the worry that the defendant may be left with his unjust gain unless he is made directly liable to the claimant, because no other person has the legal means or the will to sue him.[32] And even if there is a third party who can recover from the defendant, it might still be significantly cheaper and more efficient to allow the claimant a direct claim, rather than requiring the claimant to sue the third party and the third party to sue the defendant, a solution that in some circumstances may also cause the courts to become entangled in concerns about circuity of actions.[33]

6–17   On the other hand, if a more expansive definition is adopted, then this extension of the law's remedial capability will come at a price. First, there will be an obvious threat to transactional security, if a claimant is permitted to sue remoter parties who have benefited via a transaction with an intermediate party. Secondly, allowing a claimant to "leapfrog" his immediate counterparty, to sue a more distant recipient of benefits, may contradict the transaction he entered with this counter-party: it may enable him illegitimately to escape the risks that he ran of his counter-party's default and insolvency[34]; and on his counterparty's insolvency, it may also enable him to recover ahead of his counterparty's other unsecured creditors, inconsistently with the *pari passu* principle of insolvency law.[35] Thirdly, more expansive definitions will inevitably generate more multi-party disputes, in which a single claimant might sue two or more defendants, or one defendant might be sued by two or more claimants. This will create a number of further complications, including risks of double recovery or double liability[36]; the need to determine the appropriate distribution of the burden of liability between the multiple defendants, or the benefit of recovery between the multiple claimants; and increased time and costs, both public and private, associated with dispute settlement. Fourthly, some definitions may simply be too inclusive, identifying too many claimants as being entitled to sue a defendant, and/or too many defendants, as being enriched by a transfer of wealth from a single claimant,[37] without any rational basis being available for excluding or prioritising their entitlements or liabilities.[38] Finally, a definition may be so wide that it

---

[31] e.g. *Lloyds Bank Plc v Independent Insurance Co Ltd* [2000] Q.B. 110 (CA) (overdrawn customer); *Brown and Davis Ltd v Galbraith* [1972] 1 W.L.R. 997 (CA) (insolvent insurance company).

[32] Cf. *Reemtsma Cigarettenfabriken GmbH v Ministero delle Finanze* (C–35/05) [2008] S.T.C. 3448; *Danfoss A./S. & Sauer-Danfoss Ap.S. v Skatteministeriet* (C–94/10) [2011] EUECJ (discussed at para.6–50).

[33] Cf. *Official Custodian for Charities v Mackey (No.2)* [1985] 1 W.L.R. 1308 at 1314–1315, where Nourse J. contemplated that a concern about circuity of actions might justify affording standing to a third party; *Khan v Permayer* [2001] B.P.I.R. 95 (CA), explained in anti-circuity terms by Burrows, *The Law of Restitution*, p.84.

[34] e.g. *Galbraith* [1972] 1 W.L.R. 997 (CA); *Gray's Truck Centre Ltd v Olaf L. Johnson Ltd* Unreported CA, January 25, 1990.

[35] e.g. *Yew Sang Hong Ltd v Hong Kong Housing Authority* [2008] HKCA 109 at [13] and [30]–[32]; *Green Quarries Inc v Raasch* 676 S.W. 2d 261 (1984).

[36] e.g. *Trustor A.B. v Smallbone* Unreported CA, May 9, 2000, at [63]; *Greatworth v Sun Fook Kong Construction* [2006] HKCFI 356 at [52].

[37] As recognised by Jacob L.J. in *SmithKline Beecham Plc v Apotex Europe Ltd* [2006] EWCA Civ 658; [2007] Ch. 71 at [41]–[42]; discussed at para.6–23 below.

[38] *SmithKline* [2006] EWCA Civ 658 at [42]–[43].

generates liabilities that no plausible understanding of the law's normative underpinnings can support.[39]

(c) The "Direct Transfer" Theory

The prevailing view in the academic literature is that, as a general rule, there **6–18** must be a "direct transfer" between claimant and defendant before claims in unjust enrichment will lie.[40] Broadly speaking, this means that claims should be allowed only where there are immediate dealings between the parties—where there is a payment by the claimant to the defendant, for example—and claims should not be allowed against remote recipients of benefits, i.e. parties who have been enriched through the action of a third party who has himself dealt with the claimant in some way. To square this theory with the cases, however, these accounts are commonly refined in a number of ways. First, the concept of a "direct transfer" is extended to embrace several three-party cases, where one might have thought that the defendant had received a benefit from a third party, or that the claimant had conferred a benefit on a third party. For example, it has been said that there is a "direct transfer" where the defendant immediately receives a benefit from an agent acting for the claimant, where the claimant discharges the defendant's debt by paying his creditor, and where the claimant can establish a "proprietary connection" to the defendant's receipt, for example by showing that the defendant obtains an asset to which the claimant has title from a third party.

Secondly, most accounts also accept that there must be exceptions to the **6–19** "direct transfer" rule, permitting claims in unjust enrichment against "indirect recipients" in some cases. However, there is no consensus among legal writers as to what qualifies as an exception, and, assuming that there is an exception, what justifies its recognition. Almost all of the "exceptions" identified by some writers are treated by others as instances of "direct transfer". And in some accounts, the concepts of "direct" or "indirect" receipt are given a counter-intuitive definition; for example, Peter Birks argued that if X performs a service for D, pursuant to a contract with C, then C (who has undertaken to pay X) should be regarded as D's "direct" enricher, whilst X (who actually renders the services) should be regarded as D's "indirect" enricher.[41]

There is no doubt that the reach of claims in unjust enrichment is quite tightly **6–20** confined on the "direct transfer" theory, and that some of the problems that would flow from acceptance of a broader test are thereby avoided. Nevertheless, there are sufficient difficulties with the theory to make us think that the law should adopt a different strategy.[42]

First, the "direct transfer" theory requires a line to be drawn between qualify- **6–21** ing and non-qualifying transfers of value which is unclear and potentially

---

[39] Cf. Smith, "Restitution: The Heart of Corrective Justice", pp.2155–2174, arguing that the normative underpinnings of the law of unjust enrichment do not support liability for subtractive unjust enrichment where there is no direct nexus of transfer, where the claimant's loss and the defendant's gain are two sides of one transaction.

[40] See the works cited in fn.28.

[41] Birks, *Unjust Enrichment*, pp.87–88 and 89–93.

[42] For a full examination of these, see Watterson, "Direct Transfers in the Law of Unjust Enrichment".

unstable. "Direct transfer" has no natural or agreed meaning. It does not feature to any significant degree in judicial reasoning; it is simply an academic construct, offered as a way of rationalising a patchwork of cases.

6–22   Secondly, although there are good reasons for containing the reach of claims in unjust enrichment, the "direct transfer" rule offers a means of achieving this that is very blunt. This might be tolerable if it were the only means of containing claims in practice; but this is not the case. Concerns about the multiplicity of suits should not be exaggerated since many claimants who could use a broader test to establish that a defendant has been enriched at their expense will still have no hope of recovery because they cannot establish an unjust factor, or because the defendant has a defence. Concerns about the security of transactions can be met by giving a defence to bona fide purchasers for value,[43] and by disallowing claims in unjust enrichment which would contradict or undermine the terms of contracts entered by two or more of the parties.[44] Concerns about double recovery and double liability will not arise in cases where claimants cannot establish an unjust factor, nor in cases where defendants can establish a defence; and even where they do arise, they can be met by holding that satisfaction of one claim extinguishes another.[45] Concerns about the multiplication of ever more peripheral claimants and defendants might also be met by ruling that gains made by some parties are too remote—although we concede that a clear remoteness rule has not yet emerged from the cases, and will have to be developed if the "direct transfer" theory is rejected in favour of a wider test.

6–23   This last point can be illustrated by reference to *SmithKline Beecham Plc v Apotex Europe Ltd*.[46] An interim injunction was wrongly issued in favour of SmithKline to restrain alleged infringements of its patent by UK importers and vendors. Their Canadian suppliers, who were third parties to the proceedings, brought a claim in unjust enrichment against SmithKline, claiming that the wrongful issue of the injunction had unjustly enriched SmithKline at their expense. SmithKline had been able to sell more products and/or had sold at a higher price than if the defendants were competing in the market; the Canadian suppliers had suffered loss as a result of being unable to sell to the UK market; and on this basis, it was argued, they were entitled to recover a proportionate share of SmithKline's profits, reflective of their own lost profits. The Court of Appeal rejected this claim inter alia on the grounds that it was impossible to explain why the same claim could not be made against a large number of other parties who had also benefited as a result of the injunction, nor why the same claim could not be made by a large number of other parties who had suffered similar losses as a result of its issue, bringing with it some very real practical problems regarding the distribution of recoveries; and that the law could not, in practice, countenance this possibility.[47] According to Jacob L.J., "the court

---

[43] See Ch.29.
[44] As in e.g. *Costello v MacDonald* [2011] EWCA Civ 930; for general discussion, see paras 3–58 and following.
[45] *Trustor A.B. v Smallbone* Unreported CA, May 9, 2000, at [70]; *S.C.E.G.S. Redlands Ltd v Barbour* [2008] NSWCA 928 at [8]. See para.20–51.
[46] *SmithKline Beecham Plc v Apotex Europe Ltd* [2006] EWCA Civ 658; [2007] Ch. 71; see paras 26–13—26–16.
[47] *SmithKline* [2006] EWCA Civ 658 at [41]–[43].

cannot put the clock back so as to undo all 'winnings' and restore all 'losses' caused to all who were affected by the 'wrong' injunction".[48]

Finally, the normative basis for confining claims in unjust enrichment to the reversal of "direct transfers" is not obvious. Lionel Smith has made the case that liability for subtractive unjust enrichment is underpinned by principles of corrective justice, and that corrective justice only justifies the prevalent model of strict liability in unjust enrichment to the extent that the defendant's enrichment is simply the other side of one transaction, involving a subtraction from the claimant, to which the claimant did not consent or defectively consented, or which the law holds must be reversed for reasons of wider policy.[49] In other words, there is never any normative basis for a claim against an indirect recipient, in the absence of a "direct" nexus of transfer. We are not persuaded by this account. Theories of corrective justice are ultimately too abstract, and in any event, too disputed, to generate clear-cut answers to the sorts of concrete questions that the courts must face, when identifying the boundaries of the law of unjust enrichment.   **6–24**

(d) *An Alternative Approach: "But For" Causal Analysis*

On balance, we therefore consider that it would be more conducive to the rational development and containment of claims in unjust enrichment if the courts were to start from the bolder and simpler position, that a "but for" causal connection between D's gain and C's loss prima facie establishes a transfer of value between C and D, and thus, that D has been enriched at the expense of C. This gain and loss might be two sides of a single event or transaction, but this is not necessary. A transfer of value between C and D could also be established where C's loss and D's gain are the result of separate transactions, provided that these transactions are themselves connected by a relationship of "but for" causation. Adopting this approach, for example, in a case where C pays money to X, and X confers a benefit on D, would mean that C can establish that D is enriched at his expense, if he can prove that X would not have conferred the benefit on D, "but for" C's payment to X.   **6–25**

In advocating this approach, we do not deny that there are good reasons why the law might wish to prevent C from recovering in particular cases. Our disagreement with the prevailing view is ultimately a question of strategy.[50] Rather than insisting that a transfer of value must be "direct", we consider that the law would do better to adopt an expansive, causal approach to this initial, threshold inquiry, leaving the task of liability containment to be addressed— explicitly, and in a better focused way—by other means.   **6–26**

---

[48] *SmithKline* [2006] EWCA Civ 658 at [42].
[49] Smith, "Restitution: The Heart of Corrective Justice", pp.2141–2146 and 2155 and following.
[50] Cf. Burrows, *The Law of Restitution*, pp.71–72, who gives reasons and counter-reasons for taking a restrictive approach to the "at the expense of" requirement; we agree with the concerns he expresses, but do not agree that a restrictive approach is needed to address them.

(e) *The Causal Analysis in the Case Law*

(i) *Introduction*

6–27   In this final section, we examine the case law. Despite the prevailing view among legal scholars that claims in unjust enrichment should be confined to "direct" recipients, there are many multiple-party cases where the courts have allowed claims by a person who is a third party to a transaction between two others. Some of these are consistent with a narrow analysis, which would confine claims to cases where there is a "direct" nexus of transfer, in the form of *one* transaction, by which D gains and C suffers a subtraction from his wealth, whether or not they are both strictly parties to the transaction. However, not all of the cases can be explained in these terms, and there are some that are consistent only with our preferred analysis, according to which a "but for" causal connection is sufficient, and a transfer of value can be found even where D gains and C suffers a subtraction from his wealth as a consequence of two separate events or transactions that are themselves joined by a "but for" causal connection. In the following discussion, we distinguish four fact patterns: discharge of another's debt; contracts for the provision of services; sequential transfers; and interceptive subtractions.

(ii) *Discharge of Another's Debt*

6–28   A claim in unjust enrichment can undoubtedly lie where C discharges the obligations owed by D to another party, X. Thus, if C and D owe a common liability to pay X, then C may, by paying X, discharge D from liability. C may then be given a personal claim against D, in the form of a claim for reimbursement or contribution, to the extent that C has borne some or all of the burden of paying X that should properly have been borne by D.[51] In cases where there is no common liability,[52] C is unlikely to be able to discharge D's liability to X without his authority. However, assuming that discharge can be shown, and that a recognised ground for restitution can be identified, C can recover from D, whose debt he discharged.

6–29   These cases all clearly show that when C discharges D's debt by paying D's creditor, D's enrichment—consisting of his release from liability—is gained at C's expense. This outcome can be explained by a causal test. A transaction has occurred, consisting of the receipt and acceptance of C's payment by D's creditor in circumstances which the law deems effective to discharge D's debt, but for which C would not have suffered a loss and D would not have gained.

6–30   Some cases go even further than this, affording an unjust enrichment remedy which is designed—partly or wholly—to reverse *secondary* enrichments that accrue to third parties other than the discharged debtor, as a consequence of C's having discharged D's debt.[53] Thus, a long line of cases suggests that if C discharges a debt which D owes to another, and which is secured by a charge, then C may, via the remedy of subrogation to the paid-off creditor's extinguished

---

[51] See Ch.20.
[52] The rules governing the discharge of debts by unauthorised interveners are discussed at paras 5–44 and following.
[53] See C. Mitchell and S. Watterson, *Subrogation: Law and Practice* (Oxford: OUP, 2007), especially Chs 4 and 8.

rights, be afforded a new charge which replicates that previously held by the paid-off creditor. This remedy is afforded in order to reverse the enrichment which would otherwise accrue *both* to D, as the discharged debtor, *and* to third parties who hold subordinate ownership or security interests in the asset subject to the original charge, whose position would otherwise be materially improved as a result of its release.[54] In the leading case of *Banque Financière de la Cité SA v Parc (Battersea) Ltd*,[55] the House of Lords went even further. There, BFC, labouring under a mistake, had been responsible for paying off a first charge held by RTB over Parc's land, as a security for Parc's debts, and had thereby improved the position of OOL, another creditor of Parc which held a second charge over the same land. The House of Lords took the unprecedented step of affording BFC a subrogation remedy in a form which was *exclusively* designed to reverse the secondary enrichment that accrued to OOL, as a result of BFC's having brought about the partial discharge of Parc's debt to RTB, and of the charge that RTB held for it. It seems impossible to explain why such secondary enrichments are "at the expense of" the person who pays off the debtor's secured debt, except by means of a causal test.

(iii) *Contracts for the Provision of Services to Third Parties*

It often happens that C provides services for D, a third party, via an employee,   **6–31** agent, or other intermediary, X. In such cases, C can undoubtedly bring a claim in unjust enrichment against the third party D, on the grounds that D is enriched at C's expense, at least to the extent that the services rendered via the employee, etc. are services which fall within the ambit of those for which C is liable to pay him.

A recent case of this sort is *Chief Constable of the Greater Manchester Police*   **6–32** *v Wigan Athletic AFC Ltd*,[56] which concerned a claim for policing services rendered at football matches organised by the defendant club. The Court of Appeal denied that the club had been enriched by performance of the services, but accepted that if the club had been enriched, then its gain would have been made at the expense of the Chief Constable, and affirmed Mann J.'s finding at first instance that[57]:

"The benefit was obtained at the expense of the police, who had to pay its officers (all relevant constables and sergeants would otherwise have been on rest days, so there was

---

[54] Mitchell and Watterson, *Subrogation: Law and Practice*, para.4.09 and following. See too *Anfield (UK) Ltd v Bank of Scotland Plc* [2010] EWHC 2374 (Ch); [2011] 1 All E.R. 708 at [11]: "[i]ntermediate lenders are necessarily enriched by the discharge of a prior security".

[55] *Banque Financière de la Cité SA v Parc (Battersea) Ltd* [1999] 1 A.C. 221 (HL), discussed in Mitchell and Watterson, *Subrogation: Law and Practice*, paras 4.29–4.32, and paras 8.48–8.60, where it is explained that the limited form of the remedy granted in *Banque Financière* is exceptional.

[56] *Chief Constable of the Greater Manchester Police v Wigan Athletic AFC Ltd* [2008] EWCA Civ 1449; [2009] 1 W.L.R. 1580 at [49]. See too *BP v Hunt* [1979] 1 W.L.R. 783; affirmed [1981] 1 W.L.R. 232 (CA); affirmed [1983] 2 A.C. 352 (HL); *Ledger-Beadell v Peach* [2006] EWHC 2940 (Ch); [2007] 2 F.L.R. 210 at [265].

[57] *Wigan Athletic* [2007] EWHC 3095 (Ch) at [126].

an additional definable payment burden, and otherwise the police were providing facilities and officers who could have been deployed elsewhere)."

6–33   This might be explained in causal terms. If C contracts with X, an employee, to provide certain services, then C has "bought" X's time and labour. If X's time and labour is thereafter used, within the scope of the employment relation, to benefit a third party, then there is no artificiality in saying that this is at C's expense: X's time and labour is a valuable resource, which C has bought, and which is at C's disposal as X's employer. It is not necessary, to reach this conclusion, to assume that the services which X renders to D, as C's employee, are individually accounted for between X and C. It is sufficient that the services fall within the scope of services for which C has some general obligation to remunerate X—say, by way of general salary.

6–34   The difficult question raised by these cases is whether the employee, agent, or other intermediary who actually performs the services might *also* bring a claim in unjust enrichment against the third party. The courts are, at least, very reluctant to allow this sort of claim—a reluctance manifested in the routine denial of claims in unjust enrichment to unpaid subcontractors against an employer.[58] There is little to be gained from explaining these cases on the basis that there is no "transfer of value" between the subcontractor and the employer, so that the third party's enrichment is not at the subcontractor's expense. It is more consistent with the reasoning in the authorities, and more rational, to say that there is a qualifying transfer of value, but that even so there are other reasons why his claim must fail, for example because recovery would be inconsistent with the contracts between the parties.

(iv) Sequential Transfers

6–35   The third category of multiple-party case involves a sequential transfer of value between C and X, and X and D. The simplest form is where C confers a benefit on X, and this causes X to confer a benefit on D; but it is also possible for the transactions to take place in reverse chronological order, so that X confers a benefit on D, and this causes C to confer a benefit on X. In some cases of this kind, C has been permitted to bring a claim in unjust enrichment against D, although he is only a remote recipient from C. For the sake of exposition, we divide these cases according to whether C's gain and D's loss are connected by (1) the payment or receipt of money by an agent, (2) transactional links that satisfy the law's rules on following and tracing, and (3) the happening of other causally connected events. Some other writers would distinguish between these categories of case, and would say that a sufficient connection is established in the

---

[58] The leading English case of this sort is *Costello* [2011] EWCA Civ 930; discussed at paras 3–58 and following. See too e.g. *Turf Masters Landscaping Ltd v T.A.G. Developments Ltd* (1995) 143 N.S.R. (2d) 275; *Pacific National Exhibition v Alpine Stone Ltd* [2003] BCSC 852; *Port Coquitlam Building Supplies Ltd v Borysiak* [2003] BCSC 1471; *Concord Carriers Ltd v Alnet Holdings Ltd* (2005) 46 C.L.R. (3d) 311; *Greatworth* [2006] HKCA 460; *Yew Sang Hong* [2008] HKCA 109; *Lumbers v W. Cook Builders Pty Ltd (In Liquidation)* [2008] HCA 27; (2008) 232 C.L.R. 635; *Wah Fai Plumbing & Heating Inc v Ma* [2011] BCCA 26; (2011) 13 B.C.L.R. (5th) 231.

first and second, but that it is not established in the third. We consider that all three categories can be understood as cases in which a sufficient connection is established by the application of a "but for" causal test.

Payment or receipt of money by an agent   The cases support the view that   6–36
if X, acting as an agent for a principal, C, makes a payment to D, then C and X can each establish that D is enriched at his expense.[59] The cases also support the view that if C makes a payment to X, who receives as agent for a principal, D, then C can establish that D has been enriched at his expense. Depending on the ambit of any defence of "ministerial receipt",[60] C can also establish that X, who received as agent for D, is enriched at his expense.[61] In both types of case, the result is that C, who is the remoter source of D's gain, may bring a claim against him in unjust enrichment.

In the literature, these agency cases are widely regarded as involving an   6–37
"exception" to a "direct transfer" rule, or as consistent with the rule on the basis that receipt from or by an agent is deemed to count as a "direct receipt" from or by his principal.[62] Neither approach is particularly satisfying and other approaches are possible. In some cases, a proprietary analysis may explain the outcome: as where X pays D using C's money,[63] or where C pays money to X in circumstances that give D title to the money in X's hands.[64] In many of the agency cases, however, no proprietary link can be shown, and a better explanation of all the cases lies in a "but for" causal inquiry.[65] Whether X receives money from C as D's agent, or X pays D as C's agent, the legal incidents of the internal relationship between agent and principal allow a "but for" causal link to be readily established between the loss to C and the gain to D. Thus, where D's agent, X, receives money from C, X will owe a duty to account to his principal, D, for what he receives on D's behalf, and this liability to account enables X's receipt to be treated as D's receipt. This can be explained in causal terms: but for X's receipt from C, he would not incur a corresponding liability to D. Conversely, where C's agent, X, pays money to D, C will owe a duty to reimburse his agent, X, for his expenditure, and this reimbursement liability enables X's payment to be treated as C's payment. This can also be explained in causal terms: but for X's payment to D, he would not acquire a corresponding right against C.

---

[59] e.g. *Stevenson v Mortimer* (1778) 2 Cowp. 805 at 806; 98 E.R. 1372 at 1373 per Lord Mansfield; *Holt v Ely* (1853) 1 El. & Bl. 795; 118 E.R. 634; *Niru Battery Manufacturing Co v Milestone Trading Ltd (No.1)* [2002] EWHC 1425 (Comm); [2002] 2 All E.R. (Comm) 705 at [145].
[60] See Ch.28.
[61] e.g. *Jones v Churcher* [2009] EWHC 722 (QB); [2009] 2 Lloyd's Rep. 94 (bank *and* its customer liable for funds mistakenly transferred to the customer's account).
[62] e.g. Burrows, *The Law of Restitution*, pp.77–78, who states without further explanation, that the "relationship between [agent] and [principal] means that the two cannot be treated as if separate".
[63] e.g. a shop employee who hands over cash from the shop's till to a customer; or perfectly routine cases where an employee initiates a funds transfer from an employer's bank account.
[64] e.g. a shop employee who receives cash from a customer.
[65] Cf. *Shanghai Tongji Science & Technology Industrial Co Ltd v Casil Cleaning Ltd* [2004] HKCFA 21 at [69]–[73] (manifesting a robust causal analysis which disregards intermediate parties functioning as a conduit to effect payment).

6–38   Reasoning of this sort provides the simplest and best explanation for the availability of claims between remoter parties within bank payment systems.[66] The cases show that a claim in unjust enrichment can be brought by a customer, out of whose account a payment has purportedly been made,[67] or alternatively by his bank who made the payment.[68] Which of these is a proper claimant turns on the legal relationship between them, whether the bank acted in circumstances entitling it to charge its customer for the payment, and whether the bank has in fact reimbursed itself, usually by debiting the customer's account. Thus, if the bank has *no* right to be reimbursed by the customer for the payment it has made, usually because it acted without mandate, and has not debited the customer's account,[69] then it seems that the payment is at the expense of the bank alone; the transaction causes the customer no loss. If the bank nevertheless *wrongly* charges the customer for a payment made on his behalf, then some cases have adopted the realistic position that the customer may be a proper claimant, at least if he is unable *in practice* to have the debiting reversed.[70] The position is different if the bank is entitled to be reimbursed by its customer. Then, if the bank has been duly reimbursed, the customer can undoubtedly sue[71]; and there is some support for the view that the bank might also sue, subject to an obligation to account to the customer for its recovery.[72] If bank has not yet been reimbursed,[73] however, then it is unclear whether the customer could sue on the basis of his liability to

---

[66] For further discussion, see L.D. Smith, "Tracing and Electronic Funds Transfers" and P. Birks, "The Burden on the Bank", in F.D. Rose (ed.), *Restitution and Banking Law* (Oxford: Mansfield Press, 1998), Chs 8 and 11; C. Mitchell, "Banks, Agency and Unjust Enrichment" in J. Lowry and L. Mistelis (eds), *Commercial Law and Commercial Practice* (London: Butterworths, 2006), 109. It is widely recognised in the banking literature that the description of the bank as "agent" in this setting does not describe a relationship whereby the bank has authority to contract on its customer's behalf; rather, it is descriptive of a relationship whereby one person (the bank) acts (usually pursuant to some prior undertaking) in accordance with another's instructions, attracting the legal consequences characteristic of the internal relationship between agent and principal (in particular, an entitlement to be reimbursed or indemnified for expenses incurred and losses suffered as a result of acting on those instructions).

[67] e.g. *Lipkin Gorman* [1991] 2 A.C. 548; *Jones v Churcher* [2009] EWHC 722 (QB); [2009] 2 Lloyd's Rep. 94. See analogously, involving a letter of credit, *Niru (No.1)* [2002] EWHC 1425 (Comm); [2002] 2 All E.R. (Comm) 705.

[68] e.g. *Barclays Bank v Simms* [1980] Q.B. 677; *Australia & New Zealand Banking Group v Westpac Banking Corp* (1988) 164 C.L.R. 662.

[69] e.g. it acts on an instruction which has been duly countermanded (as in *Barclays Bank v Simms* [1980] Q.B. 677), or it mistakenly makes a second payment, which ex hypothesi was not instructed (as in *Westpac* (1988) 164 C.L.R. 662) or it honours a payment instruction which is not given by its customer or with its customer's authority (say, a forged cheque) (as in *Banque Belge* [1921] 1 K.B. 321 (CA)).

[70] See *Agip (Africa) Ltd v Jackson* [1990] Ch. 265; affirmed [1991] Ch. 547 (CA).

[71] e.g. *Lipkin Gorman* [1991] 2 A.C. 548; *Jones v Churcher* [2009] EWHC 722 (QB); [2009] 2 Lloyd's Rep. 94.

[72] *Niru (No.1)* [2002] EWHC 1425 (Comm); [2002] 2 All E.R. (Comm) 705 at [145] per Moore-Bick J. Cf. *Hilliard v Westpac Banking Corp* [2009] VSCA 211; (2009) 25 V.R. 139 at [78]–[82], stating that it does not matter, for the purpose of showing enrichment at the payee's expense, that the bank has a right to reimbursement, and has in fact exercised this right.

[73] This may be because the bank has not debited its customer's account, which is in credit; or because the bank did debit its customer but the result is to create an overdraft, which remains outstanding—as in *Lloyds Bank v Independent Insurance* [2000] Q.B. 110 (CA).

reimburse, or whether the bank could sue, despite having a right to reimbursement.[74]

Whoever is identified as the proper claimant, the cases also show that a **6–39** personal claim in unjust enrichment may lie against a remoter recipient of the sums paid. This may be the intended beneficiary of an inter-account funds transfer,[75] or the intended beneficiary's bank (subject to defences),[76] or both of them.[77] In principle, it should also be possible (subject to defences) to bring a claim against a third bank, which acted as an intermediary in the payment process. At first sight, some cases seem to be inconsistent with this, since they deny claims against the intended beneficiaries of inter-account funds transfers and their banks, on the ground that the funds became untraceable when they became "mixed" in an inter-bank clearing and settlement system.[78] However, these cases rest on a misconception. There are no problems "tracing" through the bank payment system[79]; and in any case, there will be no need to "trace" if the claimant is merely making a personal claim in unjust enrichment. Whether the claimant is the paying customer or his bank, causation-based agency reasoning is sufficient to explain why the claimant has standing to sue any of the successive recipients in the payment chain, and it does not matter how many intermediaries are employed to bring about the ultimate flow of funds from the claimant to the intended beneficiary.[80]

Transactional links between C's loss and D's gain There is a second **6–40** category of cases in which the courts have given C a claim in unjust enrichment, where C has been able to show "transactional links" between his loss and D's enrichment, by using the rules on following and tracing.[81] For example, D may have received an asset from a third party, X, which originally came from C, or an asset which represents the traceable proceeds of such an asset.[82] Alternatively, D may have benefited from X's use of C's asset or its traceable proceeds, as

---

[74] *Lloyds Bank v Independent Insurance* [2000] Q.B. 110 (CA) suggests that it might; but cf. Birks, *Unjust Enrichment*, pp.90–91, suggesting that a claim by the bank is necessarily barred.

[75] e.g. *Lloyds Bank v Independent Insurance* [2000] Q.B. 110 (CA); *Barclays Bank v Simms* [1980] Q.B. 677.

[76] e.g. *Westpac* (1988) 164 C.L.R. 662; *Customs & Excise Commissioners v National Westminster Bank Plc* [2002] EWHC 2204 (Ch); [2003] 1 All E.R. (Comm.) 327; *Jones v Churcher* [2009] EWHC 722 (QB); [2009] 2 Lloyd's Rep. 94. And cf. *Papamichael v National Westminster Bank Plc (No.2)* [2003] EWHC 164 (Comm); [2003] 1 Lloyd's Rep 341.

[77] e.g. *Jones v Churcher* [2009] EWHC 722 (QB); [2009] 2 Lloyd's Rep. 94.

[78] Cf. *Agip* [1990] Ch. 264; [1991] Ch. 547 (Ch) (where a common law personal claim against the intended beneficiary was denied on this basis); *Bank of America v Arnell* [1999] Lloyd's Rep. 399 (similar); *Bank Tejarat v Hong Kong & Shanghai Banking Corp (C.I.) Ltd* [1995] 1 Lloyd's Rep. Bank. 239 (where a common law claim for money had and received against the intended beneficiary's bank was denied on this basis).

[79] As convincingly explained by L.D. Smith, *The Law of Tracing* (Oxford: OUP, 1997), pp.249–261.

[80] Whether there is one intermediary, in the case of an in-house transfer; two, in the case of a simple inter-bank transfer; or three or more, in a case where correspondents must be used. For these different forms of transfer, see R. Cranston, *Principles of Banking Law*, 2nd edn (Oxford: OUP, 2002), pp.235–239.

[81] For discussion of which, see Ch.7.

[82] e.g. *Banque Belge* [1921] 1 K.B. 321 (CA); *Lipkin Gorman* [1991] 2 A.C. 548; *Spangaro v Corporate Investment Australia Funds Management Ltd* [2003] FCA 1025; (2003) 47 A.C.S.R. 285 at [50]; *Heperu Pty Ltd v Belle* [2009] NSWCA 252; (2009) 76 N.S.W.L.R. 230 at [127]–[153].

where money which came from C is used by X to discharge D's debt to a creditor.[83]

6–41   The significance of these cases is disputed. In Ben McFarlane's view, they provide no support for a "but for" causal analysis, because C's ability to claim against D did not rest on C's showing "transactional links" alone; C had to go further, and show some *proprietary* link to the benefit received by D, usually by showing that he could assert some form of title to the asset which D received, or which was otherwise applied to benefit D.[84] So, for example, if C pays money under a mistake to X, and X then makes a gift of this money to D, the question whether D is enriched at C's expense is made to depend on whether C's mistake was such as to cause C to retain or obtain some proprietary interest in the moneys paid to X and thereafter received by D. Indeed, on this analysis, many of the cases are not unjust enrichment authorities at all, but are rather concerned with claims that operate directly or indirectly to vindicate C's proprietary rights.

6–42   An alternative analysis of these cases, more consistent with the causal analysis that we propose, is that C can show that D was enriched at his expense by means of transactional links *alone*—these links, established in accordance with the rules of following and tracing, are on this view a proxy for a causal inquiry, establishing a sufficient causal connection between C's loss and D's gain. On this approach, where C pays cash to X, and X gives the same cash to D, C can establish that D has been enriched at C's expense provided that he can follow the cash handed to X into D's hands. C can also establish that D has been enriched at his expense if he can show that D received money from X which represents the traceable proceeds of the cash handed to X. In either case, C would not need to go further, and show that the circumstances were such that C had a proprietary interest in the money received by X and D.

6–43   Peter Birks at one time offered this as a possible explanation of the difficult decision in *Lipkin Gorman (A Firm) v Karpnale Ltd*,[85] on the basis that there might be obstacles in the way of a proprietary explanation for the solicitors' claim against the casino, based upon the casino's receipt from Cass of cash drawn from the solicitors' account. He considered that the inquiry into tracing in that case might be understood as an inquiry undertaken for the purpose of establishing a causal nexus between the debiting of the solicitors' account, and the casino's enriching receipt of the cash from Cass.[86] However, this analysis has been doubted by other writers,[87] on the grounds that in *Lipkin Gorman*, the House of Lords' reasoning (whilst difficult) was property- or title-based; that other cases that might be relied on as authority for the view that mere transactional links suffice either expressly adopted a property- or title-based analysis, or are susceptible to such analysis; and that cases that seem to rest on tracing cannot support a causal analysis, because transactional links are not the same as causal

---

[83] A fact pattern which recurs in the context of claims to be subrogated to a paid-off creditor's extinguished rights, as discussed in Mitchell and Watterson, *Subrogation: Law and Practice*, para.5.23.

[84] See e.g. McFarlane, "Unjust Enrichment, Property Rights and Indirect Recipients".

[85] *Lipkin Gorman (A Firm) v Karpnale Ltd* [1991] 2 A.C. 548. For the facts of this case, see para.8–22.

[86] Birks, "The Burden on the Bank" in Rose (ed.), *Restitution and Banking Law*, pp.230–231.

[87] e.g. Smith, "Unjust Enrichment, Property and the Structure of Trusts", pp.418–421; McFarlane, "Unjust Enrichment, Property Rights and Indirect Recipients".

links, and because the focus of tracing on identifying the value inherent in specific assets is inextricably tied to a process of establishing rights in these traceable substitutes, and so to a property- or title-based analysis.

We think that these objections have force, in so far as it is unquestionably true **6–44** that the rules of following and tracing are not causal rules, and indeed are not even concerned with the question whether a transfer of value has taken place between one party and another, since their narrower concern is with the different question whether a property right held by a defendant is the same property right that was previously held by the claimant, or else was acquired in exchange for a property right that was previously held by the claimant.[88] One consequence of this is that it may be possible to establish transactional links to an asset received by D, via tracing, even though it may be clear that D would have been abstractly enriched in any event. So, for example, if C pays cash to X, and X pays a sum of money which traceably represents this cash to D, C could establish that D was enriched at his expense on the basis of mere transactional links, even though it is clear that D would have been abstractly enriched by X even if C had never paid X—because X intended to pay D the same sum in any event. It is far from clear why the law should find a transfer of value here. If there is no proprietary connection, then one would expect the law to require at least a causal connection; and traceability alone does not conclusively establish this.

There are, however, two plausible ways of rescuing the "transactional links" **6–45** analysis. One is to say that proof of "transactional links" merely establishes a presumption or inference of "but for" causation, which D may rebut or displace. On this basis, these cases merely exemplify one situation in which a claim might be based on "but for" causal links; but they do not eliminate the possibility that a claim might be established on the basis of "but for" causal links, where no transactional links exist between C's loss and D's gain. A second, more restrictive, analysis is to say that, on pragmatic grounds, the law requires C to establish transactional links to the enrichment which D receives from X, whilst in addition insisting either that C must also prove a "but for" causal connection between his loss and D's gain,[89] or alternatively, that "transactional links" merely establish a presumption of "but for" causation that D can rebut. In other words, the law requires *both* transactional links *and* "but for" causation. This would have two advantages. On the one hand, it would avoid the unsatisfactory situation in which C could rely on transactional links alone to establish his claim against D even though it is clear that D would have been abstractly enriched even if C had not conferred the benefit on X. On the other hand, it would also, by imposing the preliminary filter of a requirement for transactional links, limit the class of

---

[88] A positive answer must be given to this question before the courts will contemplate awarding a proprietary remedy: *Foskett v McKeown* [2001] 1 A.C. 102; *Serious Fraud Office v Lexi Holdings Plc (In Administration)* [2008] EWCA Crim 1443; [2009] Q.B. 376 at [49]–[50], rejecting Lord Templeman's "swollen assets" theory in *Space Investments Ltd v Canadian Imperial Bank of Commerce Trust Co (Bahamas) Ltd* [1986] 1 W.L.R. 1072 (PC). It follows that the rules of following and tracing are more stringent than the causal test that we argue should determine whether a defendant was enriched at the claimant's expense for the purposes of making a personal claim. However, this is explicable on the basis that these rules serve as a control mechanism to prevent proprietary restitutionary remedies from becoming too freely available.

[89] Cf. Birks, *Unjust Enrichment*, pp.94–95, who seems to contemplate that if causal links alone are thought insufficient to bring a claim against a remoter recipient, then they might alternatively be thought sufficient in association with another test, for example, causation plus traceability.

defendants potentially exposed to a claim by a remoter claimant by reference to a clear set of rules and circumstances that are observable, and subject to ready proof.

6–46   In our view, the English courts have not clearly opted for any of these approaches. Although there are cases which seem to proceed on the assumption that C's claim rested on C's having title to the asset received by D, and that this proprietary link was a necessary component of C's claim,[90] there are a significant number of other cases that seem to have afforded a claimant a remedy where "transactional links" exist, without undertaking an inquiry into the existence of any proprietary link.[91] It may be that such a link could be constructed, in many of these cases, if this were thought necessary. However, the fact remains that in the relevant cases, this inquiry was not undertaken; and that some cases have specifically rejected the need for such an inquiry.[92] We consider that they were right to do so. Whilst it may be possible to show that D was enriched at C's expense by showing a proprietary link, we do not think this should be necessary. Requiring a proprietary link makes the availability of a personal claim in unjust enrichment against remoter recipients depend on the application of a very difficult and still uncertain body of law regarding the proprietary consequences of defective transfers, and the acquisition of rights to substitute assets. This seems to us to be an unnecessary distraction from the real force of C's claim in this context—that D would not have been abstractly enriched "but for" the defective transfer from C's wealth. And it seems likely to obscure the many good countervailing reasons why C's claim might need to be denied. Our one major reservation about accepting that transactional links alone may suffice is that, as already noted, such links do not conclusively establish causation: English law's tracing rules are not causal rules. In light of this, we conclude that it would be better to read the cases as supporting the view that transactional links raise a prima facie inference of "but for" causation, which may be displaced or rebutted.

6–47   **Other causally connected events**   If, as we think, "but for" causal links alone may suffice to establish a transfer of value, there is no need to place the cases discussed in the preceding subsections in separate sub-categories, since they are merely illustrations of a wider "but for" causal analysis. If that is correct, then these cases can be understood to provide authoritative support for this analysis. A number of other cases also do so.[93]

6–48   One is *Banque Financière*,[94] where BFC lent money to part-discharge a debt owed by Parc to RTB, which was secured by a first charge on Parc's land. In

---

[90] e.g. *Lipkin Gorman* [1991] 2 A.C. 548.
[91] See e.g. *Baroness Wenlock v River Dee Co (No.2)* (1887) 19 Q.B.D. 155 (CA); especially at 166 per Fry L.J.; *Butler v Rice* [1910] 2 Ch. 277; *Chetwynd v Allen* [1899] 1 Ch. 353; *Filby v Mortgage Express (No.2) Ltd* [2004] EWCA Civ 759 at [46], [52] and [62], where a proprietary link was found, but the Court of Appeal made it clear that this was not necessary; *Banque Financière* [1999] 1 A.C. 221.
[92] e.g. *Banque Financière* [1999] 1 A.C. 221; discussed below at para.6–48; *Filby* [2004] EWCA Civ 759 at [46], [52] and [62].
[93] For additional discussion of these and other cases, see C. Mitchell, "Liability Chains" in S. Degeling and J. Edelman (eds), *Unjust Enrichment in Commercial Law* (Sydney: Lawbook Co, 2008), pp.135–145.
[94] *Banque Financière* [1999] 1 A.C. 221. See too May L.J.'s obiter remarks in *Filby* [2004] EWCA Civ 759 at [46], [52] and [62]. And cf. *Shanghai Tongji Science* [2004] HKCFA 21 at [69]–[73].

order to avoid difficulties with the Swiss regulatory authorities, the loan was structured as an indirect loan via Herzig: BFC lent the money to Herzig, who lent it to Parc. The money was not repaid and BFC sought a first charge over Parc's land via subrogation, arguing that a second secured creditor, OOL, had been unjustly enriched at BFC's expense by the discharge of RTB's security, because this had increased the value of OOL's security. OOL argued that this benefit had not been gained at BFC's expense because the money used to pay the debt to RTB had come from Herzig, but Lord Steyn rejected this, stating that[95]:

> "The loan to Mr Herzig was a genuine one spurred on by the motive of avoiding Swiss regulatory requirements. But it was nevertheless no more than a formal act designed to allow the transaction to proceed. It does not alter the reality that OOL was enriched by the money advanced by BFC via Mr Herzig to Parc. To allow the interposition of Mr Herzig to alter the substance of the transaction would be pure formalism."

Another example is *Agip (Africa) Ltd v Jackson.*[96] Here, a fraudulent employee   **6-49** of Agip forged payment orders on Agip's Tunisian bank account in favour of Baker Oil, a UK-based company. Agip's bank executed the transfer as instructed, and debited the account of Agip for the payment. It seems highly likely that the bank was not entitled to do this: having paid without mandate, it would have no right to be reimbursed by Agip. Agip was nevertheless unable to get its account re-credited, with the result that, whatever the formal state of indebtedness might have been between Agip and its bank, Agip was de facto denied the benefit of the funds due to it. Both at first instance, and in the Court of Appeal, it was assumed that this de facto injury to Agip sufficed to allow Agip to bring a common law claim against the recipient of the sums paid. This result can only be satisfactorily explained on a causal basis. Agip's bank would not have debited Agip's account —rightly or wrongly—"but for" the payment it made, purportedly on Agip's behalf, pursuant to the forged payment order.

A third example is provided by a group of cases where a trader has paid money   **6-50** as VAT that is not due, and the burden of the tax has been passed on to the customer. An important recent line of authority from the European Court of Justice indicates that customers must—at least in certain circumstances—be afforded a *direct* right against the tax authority, to recover the tax wrongly paid to the authority by the trader, whose burden the customers ultimately bore. In *Reemstma Cigarettenfabriken GmbH v Ministero delle Finanze,*[97] an Italian company supplied services to a German customer, which it erroneously invoiced for sales tax which was not in fact due. Under Italian law, only the supplier could seek restitution from the tax authorities; the German customer could only seek restitution from the supplier. The German company nevertheless sought restitution from the tax authorities arguing that EU law required such a claim to be made available under domestic law.[98] The ECJ held that it was ordinarily sufficient, to satisfy inter alia EU law's requirements of effectiveness, for domestic law to give the supplier a claim for restitution against the tax authority, and

---

[95] *Banque Financière* [1999] 1 A.C. 221 at 227.
[96] *Agip (Africa) Ltd v Jackson* [1990] Ch. 265; affirmed [1991] Ch. 547 (CA).
[97] *Reemstma Cigarettenfabriken GmbH v Ministero delle Finanze* (C–35/05) [2008] S.T.C 3448.
[98] The tax was in fact directly paid by the German company to the Italian tax authorities but this was not material to the ECJ's decision.

to give the customer a claim against the supplier.[99] This would suffice to enable the customer, who had borne the burden of the overpaid tax, to obtain restitution of the sums paid.[100] But it would be otherwise, where it has "become impossible or excessively difficult" for the customer to obtain restitution in this way (for example, in the case of insolvency of the supplier). Then, the principle of effectiveness would require domestic law to afford the customer a means of obtaining restitution *directly* from the tax authority.[101] To similar effect is *Danfoss A/S & Sauer-Danfoss ApS v Skattenministeriet*,[102] which confirms that the reasoning in the *Reemstma* case applies whether the customer directly pays the tax authority (as unusually occurred in *Reemstma*) or the supplier does so (as occurred in *Danfoss*).

6-51   There are also some other cases which assume that if a trader were to recover money paid as VAT that was not due from HMRC, then the customers to whom the tax was passed on might have a claim against the supplier to the fruits of this litigation, and that it makes no difference whether the customer paid the supplier before or after he paid the tax, or whether it is possible to establish any transactional links between the money paid to the supplier and the money received by the tax authority.[103] These cases do not afford the customer a direct claim against the tax authorities, but they remain significant, to the extent the customer's claim against the *trader* depends on its ability to show a mere causal connection between the trader's payment to HMRC, and the customer's payment to the trader; it is this causal connection which establishes that the trader would be unjustly enriched at the customer's expense if he were permitted to retain the benefit of his recovery from HMRC.

(v) *"Interceptive Subtractions"*

6-52   It remains a controversial question whether the concept of "interceptive subtraction" has a part to play in the law of unjust enrichment: that is, whether C can show that D's enrichment was at C's expense, where X has conferred a benefit on D that was destined for C, and that would have accrued to C but for D's "interceptive" receipt. Peter Birks argued that in cases where it was legally or factually inevitable that C would have been enriched by X but for D's interceptive receipt then the "certainty that [C] would have obtained the wealth in question . . . genuinely indicate[s] that he became poorer by the sum in which the defendant was enriched".[104] However, the most sustained critique of Birks' argument, undertaken by Lionel Smith, exposed problems with all of the cases

---

[99] *Reemstma* (C–35/05) [2008] S.T.C. 3448 at [39].

[100] *Reemstma* (C–35/05) [2008] S.T.C. 3448 at [39].

[101] *Reemstma* (C–35/05) [2008] S.T.C. 3448 at [42].

[102] *Danfoss A/S & Sauer-Danfoss ApS v Skattenministeriet* (C–94/10) [2011] EUECJ.

[103] *Grantham Cricket Club v C&E Commissioners* [1998] B.V.C. 2272; *R. v C&E Commissioners Ex p. Building Societies Ombudsman Co Ltd* [2000] S.T.C. 892; see too VAT Act 1994 ss.80 and 80A, and the VAT Regulations 1995 (SI 1995/2518), Pt VA ("Reimbursement Arrangements"), considered in *Portsmouth City Football Club Ltd v HMRC* [2010] EWHC 75 (Ch); [2011] S.T.C. 683. The significance of these authorities is well explained in M. Chowdry, "Unjust Enrichment and Section 80(3) of the Value Added Tax Act 1994" [2004] B.T.R. 620. For additional discussion, see para.32–02 and following.

[104] P. Birks, *An Introduction to the Law of Restitution*, revised edn (Oxford: OUP, 1989), pp.133–134. Birks, *Unjust Enrichment*, pp.75–78 is more guarded, in the wake of criticisms of his earlier account, but still advocates the theory.

that he relied on, doubted his concept of "certainty", and came close to denying that C should have a claim unless D's "interception" resulted in some actual or direct subtraction from C's accrued wealth.[105]

Smith's critique rested heavily on the premise that unjust enrichment is a **6-53** "zero-sum" game, with the result that for any one subtractive unjust enrichment, there can generally only be one claimant at whose expense a defendant is enriched. On this analysis, if D "intercepts" wealth *en route* from X to C, then the law cannot hold that D is enriched at the expense of both X and C. D could only be enriched at the expense of one of them; and more often than not, it would be X, from whose accrued wealth D's gain immediately came. Unlike Smith, we see no reason why the law cannot hold that a defendant is enriched at the expense of two different people simultaneously. But clearly, if the law is prepared to accept that D can be simultaneously enriched (directly) at X's expense and (interceptively) at C's expense, then D is exposed to a risk of double liability. This risk could be readily resolved by a rule that D's liability to X and C abates to the extent that either has recovered from him. However, even then, the law would still be faced with the dilemma of resolving what might be competing claims of X (or those claiming through X) and C to the benefit received by D.[106] Before resolving this competition in C's favour, the courts would need to be satisfied that this result would not illegitimately usurp X's freedom to choose for himself how to dispose of his wealth, and would not illegitimately contradict other settled commitments of the law.

Whether this is the case will depend on the context. So, for example, if X **6-54** intends to make a gift to C, but by mistake, makes a gift to D, then, even if it is possible to say that C would have received the asset but for X's mistaken transfer to D, it might be objected that affording C a claim in unjust enrichment against D, in priority to a claim by X against D to reverse the mistaken transfer, could involve the law improperly perfecting an imperfect gift, and wrongly usurp X's continuing freedom to dispose of his wealth. If, by contrast, X contracts to transfer property to C, but by mistake, transfers it to D instead, then no such dilemma would arise, at least assuming that the law would be willing to compel X to perform his contractual obligation to C.

As we see it, the disagreement about whether "interceptive subtractions" **6-55** count is not a disagreement about whether *causation* can establish a sufficient connection between a loss to C and a gain to D. It is, instead, a disagreement about what counts as a "loss" to C. Our view is that claims in unjust enrichment should be confined to situations in which the gain to D involves a diminution to or subtraction from C's accrued wealth. A "loss" to C, and a "transfer of value" from C to D, cannot be identified merely in the fact that D's receipt has prevented wealth accruing to C, however probable that accrual may have been. The cases, viewed as a whole, are consistent with this view.

---

[105] Smith, "Three-Party Restitution: A Critique of Birk's Theory of Interceptive Subtraction". For further contributions to the debate, see M. McInnes, "The Canadian Principle of Unjust Enrichment: Comparative Insights into the Law of Restitution" (1999) 37 *Alberta Law Review* 1, pp.27–31; M. McInnes, "Interceptive Subtraction, Unjust Enrichment and Wrongs—A Reply to Professor Birks" (2003) 62 C.L.J. 697; Burrows, *The Law of Restitution*, pp.79–84.

[106] For a recent, difficult case in which the problem of competing claims formed part of the reasoning behind the court's rejection of C's claim, see *Huntley Management Ltd v Australian Olives Ltd* [2010] FCAFC 98; (2010) 79 A.C.S.R. 355, especially at [42].

6–56   The strongest support for a theory of "interceptive subtraction" comes from cases concerned with the usurpation of offices. In a line of authority starting in the late 17th century,[107] the courts held that if D had usurped an office to which C was entitled, and received from X sums to which C was entitled as of right as the lawful officeholder,[108] then C could sue D for the amounts that he had received[109] from X in an action for money had and received. A similar conclusion has been reached in cases where D received rents from X, to which C was legally entitled[110]; and where D, a self-appointed administrator or executor of a deceased, was held accountable to C, the incoming and duly appointed personal representative, for what he received as money or assets due or belonging to the deceased.[111] In our view, the preferable explanation of these cases is that the payment by X to D is effective to discharge X's liability to C—either because, exceptionally, the particular circumstances of the transfer were such that the payment by X to D was effective without more to discharge X's debt to C[112]; or, less clearly, because the law affords the creditor, C, a right to *elect* to treat the payment by X to D as an act which discharges X's debt to C. Either way, C suffers "loss" in the form of a diminution of or subtraction from C's accrued wealth—that is, C's legal rights against X.

6–57   It is not difficult to explain C's claim in these cases in terms of a causal analysis. Where X's payment to D automatically discharges C's rights against X, there is a single transaction which causes D to make a gain and C to sustain a loss. If the discharge of C's rights against X depends upon C's election, then the subtraction from C is at one further remove from the transaction between X and D in causal terms, but D's enrichment is still at C's expense, using the broader causal analysis that we favour. The greater difficulty presented by the election argument is how to explain the ground of restitution on which C can rely. It is usually assumed that in most cases of "interceptive subtraction", it is the fact that C did not know of and consent to D's enrichment that provides the reason for restitution.[113] But if that is correct, then it becomes necessary to explain why this conclusion holds good even if the subtraction from C is dependent on an election by C, and to that extent, upon C's consent.

6–58   Beyond the usurpation of office and related cases, the authorities are equivocal. A number of other cases, summarised below, afford C rights against D that

---

[107] *Arris v Stukely* (1677) 2 Mod. 260; 86 E.R. 1060; *Howard v Wood* (1688) 2 Show. K.B. 21; 89 E.R. 767; *King v Alston* (1848) 12 Q.B. 971; 116 E.R. 1134.

[108] Cf. *Lawlor v Alton* (1873) I.R. 8 C.L. 160 (no claim for a salary payable in respect of work which C did not perform); *Boyter v Dodsworth* (1796) 6 T.R. 681; 101 E.R. 770 (no claim for gratuities received by D usurper).

[109] *King v Alston* (1848) 12 Q.B. 971; 116 E.R. 1134 (claim limited to fees received; no claim for amounts that were payable but not collected by D).

[110] *Official Custodian for Charities v Mackey (No.2)* [1985] 1 W.L.R. 1308 at 1314–1315 per Nourse J; see previously *Tottenham v Bedingfield* (1572) 3 Leo. 24; 74 E.R. 517; *Arris v Stukely* (1677) 2 Mod. 260 at 262; 86 E.R. 1060 at 1063; *Lyell v Kennedy* (1889) 14 App. Cas. 437. See also *Asher v Wallis* (1707) 11 Mod. 146; 88 E.R. 956.

[111] *Jacob v Allen* (1703) 1 Salk. 27; 91 E.R. 26; *Yardley v Arnold* (1842) Car. & M. 434; 174 E.R. 577.

[112] Especially Smith, "Three-Party Restitution: A Critique of Birk's Theory of Interceptive Subtraction", pp.487 and following, where the cases are explained. Cf. *Official Custodian for Charities v Mackey (No.2)* [1985] 1 W.L.R. 1308 at 1314–1315 per Nourse J., who rests C's right against D on the avoidance of circuity of action.

[113] See Ch.8 for general discussion.

are susceptible to analysis in terms of a theory of interceptive subtraction. However, many of these are not manifestly claims in unjust enrichment and are best explained by another doctrine, whilst others can (like the usurpation of office cases) be narrowly interpreted as cases involving subtractions from C's accrued wealth.

First, there are cases where X, labouring under a mistake, has conveyed **6–59** property to D, which he had contracted to convey to C, and where D has been held to be a trustee for C of the property so conveyed.[114]

Secondly, there is an isolated dictum in one English case,[115] suggesting that if **6–60** X, who intended a gift to C, has by mistake executed a formal gift inter vivos in favour D, then, once donor X has died,[116] C, the intended donee, might be entitled to sue to have the deed of gift rectified in his favour.[117]

Thirdly, there are the cases on attornment.[118] A difficult line of old authority **6–61** suggests that if D receives a "fund" from X, to hold to the use of C, and D agrees to hold the fund, then once D "attorns" to C by communicating to C that he holds the fund for him, C could bring a claim for money had and received against D.[119] In the 19th century, unconvincing attempts were made to explain the cases by finding a contract between C and D. Today, the happiest explanation is probably that, by analogy with attornment in respect of chattels, D's act of attornment transfers legal title in the money to C; or at least an equitable title by an act equivalent to a declaration of trust. Viewed in this way, the attornment cases cannot be understood as claims in unjust enrichment based on a "true" interceptive subtraction: C's claim rests on already-vested rights, which the law has afforded C to the "fund" held by D independently of the law of unjust enrichment. But some cases go further and suggest that C has the same claim against D even where D does not hold a specific "fund", so that this proprietary analysis of "attornment" is unavailable—as in *Shamia v Joory*, where D was indebted to X, X told D to pay C, and D proceeded to "attorn" to D.[120] This seems more difficult to explain. Peter Birks suggested that D's liability to C here might be

---

[114] *Leuty v Hillas* (1858) 2 De G. & J. 110; 44 E.R. 929 (where the conveyance did not reflect the terms of the prior contract); *Craddock Bros Ltd v Hunt* [1923] 2 Ch. 136 (CA) (where the conveyance reflected the terms of the prior formal contract, but not the terms of a preceding oral agreement, and the majority considered that the contract and conveyance could be rectified); both discussed, without reference to this point, in R. Chambers, *Resulting Trusts* (Oxford: OUP, 1997), p.127.

[115] *Lister v Hodgson* (1867) L.R. 4 Eq. 30 at 34–35 per Romilly M.R.; he did not in fact specify that it was the intended donee, rather than the donor's personal representatives, who had the right to sue. Cf. *M'Mechan v Warburton* [1896] 1 I.R. 435 at 439 per Chatterton V.C.

[116] Romilly M.R. assumed that the donor, as long as he lived, should have the liberty to seek to have the mistaken gift rescinded, if he wished, and should not be compelled to perfect the gift.

[117] Cf. *Hill v van Erp* (1997) 188 C.L.R. 159 at 226–227 per Gummow J., doubting that the intended beneficiary of a will, who was disappointed when the bequest to him proved invalid, could claim in unjust enrichment against the next of kin, to whom the assets passed instead, on the basis of "interceptive subtraction".

[118] For fuller discussion, see G. Jones, *Goff & Jones: The Law of Restitution*, 7th edn (London: Sweet & Maxwell, 2006), Ch.28; also R.M. Jackson, *The History of Quasi-Contract in English Law* (Cambridge: CUP, 1937), p.99; J.D. Davies, "*Shamia v Joory*: A Forgotten Chapter in Quasi-Contract" (1959) 75 L.Q.R. 220.

[119] See especially *Griffin v Weatherby* (1868) L.R. 3 Q.B. 753 at 758–759 per Blackburn J.

[120] *Shamia v Joory* [1958] 1 Q.B. 448.

rationalised as a claim in unjust enrichment, which reverses the unjust enrich-ment of D which is interceptively at C's expense,[121] but this reasoning seems strained, and the better view is that the case is wrongly decided.

6–62   Fourthly, there is the law on secret trusts, under which D may be rendered a trustee for C, where X has by will conveyed property to D, on the basis of a prior agreement between X and D that D will hold the property bequeathed to him on trusts, not declared in the will, for C. Great difficulty has been found explaining these cases, consistently with the formality requirements of the Wills Act 1837, whether as trusts recognised despite the Act in order to prevent "fraud" by D, or as trusts which arise outside the will, to which the Act does not apply. It has been controversially suggested that these cases might be explained as trusts which arise to prevent the unjust enrichment of D legatee, which is interceptively at C's expense.[122]

4. CORRESPONDING LOSS AND GAIN

6–63   In many cases where there is a causal link between a claimant's loss and a defendant's gain, the value of the loss and gain are the same, but in some cases the loss is greater than the gain, and in others the gain is greater than the loss. The question then arises whether the claimant can recover any larger sum than the highest amount common to the parties' loss and gain? In other words, does the law identify the value transferred between the parties by calculating the extent to which the gain exactly corresponds to the loss? Or does it operate a looser conception of "transfer", requiring the claimant to show a causal link between some loss and some gain, following which he can not only recover exactly corresponding loss and gain, but can also recover compensation for loss that does not exactly correspond to the defendant's gain, and/or require the defendant to disgorge gains that do not exactly correspond to the claimant's loss?

6–64   In principle there are two reasons for thinking that claimants should have to show an exact correspondence between loss and gain.[123] The first is that in cases where the defendant has committed no wrong, and there is no contract between the parties, there is no normative justification for ordering the defendant to compensate a claimant for loss unless he has received a corresponding benefit.[124] Nor, in the absence of a contract or wrongdoing, is there a normative justification for making him disgorge a gain that does not correspond to the claimant's loss. The second (connected) reason is that it wastes scarce judicial resources to use the court system as a mechanism for reallocating the burden of a loss or the

---

[121] Birks, *Unjust Enrichment*, p.74.

[122] Birks, *An Introduction to the Law of Restitution*, pp.64–65 and 135–136.

[123] M. McInnes, "At the Plaintiff's Expense: Quantifying Restitutionary Relief" [1998] C.L.J. 472, pp.476–477. See further M. McInnes, "The Measure of Restitution" (2002) 52 University of Toronto L.J. 163; R.B. Grantham and C.E.F. Rickett, "Disgorgement for Unjust Enrichment" [2003] C.L.J. 159; P. Birks, *Unjust Enrichment*, pp.78–82; M. Rush, *The Defence of Passing On* (Oxford: Hart, 2006), Chs 5–7.

[124] For arguments to the contrary, see S.J. Stoljar, "Unjust Sacrifice" (1987) 50 M.L.R. 603; G.A. Muir, "Unjust Sacrifice and the Officious Intervener" in P.D. Finn (ed.), *Essays in Restitution* (Sydney: Lawbook Co., 1990), 297.

benefit of an enrichment between the parties when neither of them positively deserves to bear the burden or enjoy the benefit.[125]

The English courts have always insisted that the law of unjust enrichment is **6–65** not concerned with compensation for loss, and have refused to award restitution in cases where the claimant has suffered a loss but the defendant has gained nothing.[126] Again, where the defendant has been enriched, but his gain is less than the claimant's loss, the courts have capped the claimant's right of recovery at the amount of the defendant's gain. So, for example, in *Sempra*,[127] the benefit received by the Revenue was the user value of money, quantified by reference to the amount that it would have cost the government to borrow equivalent sums by issuing Treasury bonds. This was less than the claimants' loss, which was the amount that it would have cost the claimants to borrow equivalent sums as commercial borrowers,[128] and the House of Lords capped the restitutionary award at the lower figure.

Canadian law is also formally committed to the rule that a claimant must show **6–66** the defendant's gain and a "corresponding deprivation",[129] because "the law of restitution is not intended to confer windfalls [on claimants] who have suffered no loss".[130] However, this rule was rendered an empty formality by the finding in *Peter v Beblow* that "once enrichment has been found, the conclusion that the plaintiff has suffered a corresponding deprivation is virtually automatic",[131] and there are cases where the Canadian courts have allowed claimants to recover, e.g. the value of lost opportunities and personal sacrifices made in the course of performing services for the defendant, although these do not correspond to a gain in the defendant's hands.[132] These cases all concern disputes between parties who were in matrimonial or quasi-matrimonial relationships, and although the Canadian courts have couched their judgments in the language of unjust(ified) enrichment it is clear that their awards have gone beyond restitution to fulfil claimants' expectations and to compensate claimants for detriment, remedial

---

[125] *Roxborough* [2001] HCA 68; (2001) 208 C.L.R. 516 at [118]. Where a claimant has passed on a loss to a third party, it may be desirable to let the claimant recover from the defendant, provided that he is legally bound to pass the benefit back up the line to the third party. See Ch.32.

[126] e.g. *Sorrell v Finch* [1977] A.C. 728 (no liability where payment made to third party who was not defendant's agent); *Regional Municipality of Peel v Ontario* [1992] 3 S.C.R. 762 (no liability where defendant under no obligation to bear costs of housing delinquents paid for by claimant); *Regalian Plc v London Docklands Development Corp* [1995] 1 W.L.R. 212 (no liability for work that did not benefit defendant). See too *Countrywide Communications Ltd v I.C.L. Pathway Ltd* [2000] C.L.C. 324 at 349, where Nicholas Strauss QC, sitting as a deputy High Court judge, warned of the difficulties created by courts "attempting to categorise as an unjust enrichment of the defendant, for which an action in restitution is available, what is really a loss unfairly sustained by the plaintiff"; *F.I.I.* [2008] EWHC 2893 (Ch); [2009] S.T.C. 254 at [264] and [270]; affirmed [2010] EWCA Civ 103; [2010] S.T.C. 1251 at [175]–[184], where Henderson J. refused to allow recovery of what he characterised as consequential loss that did not correspond to a gain in the defendant's hands.

[127] *Sempra* [2007] UKHL 34; [2008] A.C. 561; discussed at paras 5–05—5–10.

[128] By agreement between the parties, as noted by Chadwick L.J. in the Court of Appeal: [2005] EWCA Civ 389; [2006] Q.B. 37 at [50].

[129] *Pettkus v Becker* [1980] 2 S.C.R. 834 at 848.

[130] *Air Canada v British Columbia* [1989] 1 S.C.R. 1161 at 1202.

[131] *Peter v Beblow* [1993] 1 S.C.R. 980 at 1012; applied in *Pacific National Investments* [2004] SCC 75; [2004] 3 S.C.R. 545 at [20]–[21].

[132] e.g. *Thibert v Thibert* (1992) 39 R.F.L. (3d) 376; *Clarkson v McCrossen Estate* (1995) 122 D.L.R. (4th) 239; *Schnogl v Balen Estate* (2006) 21 E.T.R. (3d) 32. For critical comment, see J. Mee, *The Property Rights of Cohabitees* (Oxford: Hart, 1999), p.214.

goals that an English court could be expected to pursue through the different doctrines of proprietary estoppel and the common intention constructive trust.[133]

6–67 The English courts' approach to cases where the amount of the defendant's gain is greater than the amount of the claimant's loss is less straightforward. There are several groups of cases that may fall into this pattern. First, there are cases where the claimant has performed a service for the defendant; secondly, there are cases where the defendant has used the claimant's asset; thirdly, there are cases where the claimant has discharged the defendant's debt to a third party; and fourthly there are cases where the claimant has passed on his loss to a third party. We will discuss all these cases in turn.

6–68 Some services leave a marketable end-product in the defendant's hands, while others do not, and in cases of the first kind the defendant's enrichment may be the value of the end-product, rather than the value of the services themselves.[134] In cases of this kind, however, the claimant can recover no more than the cost to him of providing the services, if that was less than the value of the end-product. Authority for this is *BP v Hunt*,[135] which concerned a claim under the Law Reform (Frustrated Contracts) Act 1943. Under a joint venture with Hunt, BP undertook prospecting work in the Libyan desert which increased the value of Hunt's share of an oil concession from the Libyan government. The joint venture was frustrated when the concession was expropriated, and BP claimed that it was entitled to be paid a "just sum" under s.1(3). Robert Goff J., who held that the 1943 Act embodies principles of the law of unjust enrichment,[136] also held that the enhancement in value of Hunt's share was some $85m. However he ordered Hunt to pay BP less than a quarter of this, a result that must be explained on the basis that this was the cost to BP of conferring the benefit, and that BP's claim to recover Hunt's enrichment was capped at the amount of BP's loss.

6–69 Different issues are raised by claims to recover the value of services themselves, because the value of these is essentially their market value, subject to any argument by the defendant that they were worth less to him. In cases of this kind the courts often allow recovery of the defendant's gain without worrying whether this is greater than the claimant's loss.[137] One way of explaining this is to say, like Warren J. in *Amin v Amin*, that in pure services cases "whilst a benefit must be obtained at the expense of the claimant there does not have to be a corresponding loss to the claimant in order to measure what is recoverable."[138] Another possible explanation is that the courts do require there to be a "corresponding loss", and that this requirement is satisfied when the cost to the claimant of supplying the services is the lost opportunity to sell them to the defendant for the

---

[133] R. Wells, "Testamentary Promises and Unjust Enrichment" [2007] R.L.R. 37, pp.58–62.

[134] See paras 5–21—5–26.

[135] *BP v Hunt* [1979] 1 W.L.R. 783; affirmed [1981] 1 W.L.R. 232 (CA); [1983] 2 A.C. 352 (HL).

[136] We doubt the correctness of this view; see para.15–10.

[137] See e.g. *Benedetti* [2009] EWHC 1330 (Ch) at [528]; *Proactive Sports Management Ltd v Rooney* [2010] EWHC 1807 (QB) at [747].

[138] *Amin v Amin* [2010] EWHC 528 (Ch) at [4]. See too *Benedetti* [2010] EWCA Civ 1427 at [82].

very same sum as the amount of the defendant's gain.[139] In cases where the parties have been unsuccessfully negotiating towards a contract, or have negotiated a contract that turns out to be void, this may be a realistic characterisation of the claimant's loss. However in other circumstances there may be no good reason to fix on this as the claimant's cost, rather than the lost opportunity to sell the services elsewhere for a different amount, or the lost opportunity to use the time and effort spent serving the defendant on some other activity.

It sometimes happens that a defendant uses a claimant's asset without damag- **6–70** ing it, without preventing the claimant from using it himself (e.g. because he would not have done so), and without preventing him from hiring it out to someone else (e.g. because he would not have done so).[140] In *Hambly v Trott*[141] Lord Mansfield held that in such cases a claim would lie for the value of the defendant's saved expense. This award might conceivably be viewed as restitutionary damages for trespass to goods,[142] but it is unlikely that Lord Mansfield had this in mind, and if the case authorises recovery on the ground of unjust enrichment, then the question arises whether it also holds that the whole of the defendant's gain can be recovered, even in cases where this is more than the amount of the claimant's loss?

The answer to this depends on whether one considers that the right to control **6–71** use and enjoyment of an asset has a stand-alone economic value that is lost by the claimant and gained by the defendant during the time that the asset is in the defendant's possession, regardless of whether the claimant would actually have used the asset himself or hired it out to someone else during the same period. Support for the view that loss of user value constitutes an economically quantifiable detriment in these circumstances can be drawn from tort cases awarding compensatory damages.[143] This is also consistent with the basis on which *Sempra*[144] was decided. This was a claim for the user value of money as interest, which was argued in the lower courts on the agreed basis that the claimants' loss was the cost of borrowing equivalent sums, whether or not the claimants had actually borrowed these sums after paying the defendant,[145] and that this was the same as the defendant's gain, which was the saved expense of borrowing

---

[139] In a commercial context a reasonable price will include a profit element: see para.5–27. But matters may be simpler if the claimant never intended to make a profit and simply seeks to recover the cost of paying third parties to do the work, as in e.g. *Wigan Athletic* [2007] EWHC 3095 at [126]; reversed on a different point [2008] EWCA Civ 1449; [2009] 1 W.L.R. 1590.

[140] Cf. BGH NJW 609 (7.1.1971), translated by G. Dannemann in B. Markesinis, W. Lorenz, and G. Dannemann, *The German Law of Obligations, Vol. I: The Law Of Contracts and Restitution: A Comparative Introduction* (Oxford: OUP, 1997), p.771. In this well-known German case the defendant stowed away on board the claimant's aeroplane to take a free ride to the destination.

[141] *Hambly v Trott* (1776) 1 Cowp. 371 at 375; 98 E.R. 1136 at 1138. Cf. *Sympson v Juxon* (1624) Cro. Jac. 699; 79 E.R. 607. See too M. McInnes, "*Hambly v Trott* and the Claimant's Expense: Professor Birks' Challenge" in S. Degeling and J. Edelman (eds), *Unjust Enrichment in Commercial Law* (Sydney: Lawbook Co., 2008), 105.

[142] Cf. *Att Gen v Blake* [2001] 1 A.C. 268 at 278–279, where Lord Nicholls interprets several tort cases on wrongful interference with goods on this basis, including those cited in the following footnote. In our view, however, these were concerned with compensatory rather than restitutionary damages.

[143] *The Mediana* [1900] A.C. 113 at 117; *Watson Laidlaw & Co Ltd v Pott, Cassels & Williamson* (1914) 31 R.P.C. 104 at 119–120.

[144] *Sempra* [2007] UKHL 34; [2008] A.C. 561; discussed at paras 5–05—5–10.

[145] See especially *Sempra* [2005] EWCA Civ 389; [2006] Q.B. 37 at [50].

equivalent sums, whether or not it would actually have borrowed these sums if it had not received the claimants' payments. On appeal to the House of Lords, the defendant revoked its concession that the parties' gain and loss had been the same, and successfully argued that the value of the defendant's gain had been lower than the value of the claimant's loss because the government can borrow money more cheaply than commercial entities. However, the parties' agreed starting point remained the same, and was accepted by the court, and the Australian courts have taken a similar approach to interest claims, holding that the amount recoverable is not "dependent . . . on the rate which the payer could have earned on the money if retained".[146]

6–72   Turning to the discharged debt cases, some authorities suggest that a claimant may recover no more than the amount of his payment to the defendant's creditor where this is less than the value of the discharged debt. There is Lord Scarman's statement in Parliament when introducing the bill that subsequently became the Civil Liability (Contribution) Act 1978,[147] that a claimant who settles with a creditor and then looks to a defendant for a contribution cannot "recover a higher amount . . . than that which he has agreed to pay".[148] The courts have also held that a surety's right to reimbursement against the principal debtor (and any supplementary subrogation right that he acquires) will be capped at the amount of the surety's payment which discharged the principal debt.[149] However, these authorities are inconclusive of the point as they may have concerned the surety's contractual right to an indemnity (which necessarily focuses on the claimant's loss), rather than his right in unjust enrichment to reimbursement of the defendant's gain.

6–73   Finally, we come to the cases on passing on. As we discuss in Ch.31, passing on is a defence which asserts that the claimant has lost his title to sue the defendant in unjust enrichment because the claimant has made good the loss which the defendant's enrichment inflicted on him, by passing this loss on to a third party. Passing on has been recognised as a defence to various statutory claims to recover money paid as tax that was not due, but in *Kleinwort Benson*[150] the Court of Appeal held that it was not a defence to a common law claim to recover money paid under a void interest swap contract to the defendant council, by a bank which had received payments under a hedge contract with another bank. The court held that the defence was not available for two reasons: first, because the payments received by the claimant bank under the hedge contract were not relevantly causally connected with the payments made by the claimant

---

[146] *Cornwall v Rowan (No.2)* [2005] SASC 122 at [39]. Further Australian cases to this effect are summarised in J. Edelman and E. Bant, *Unjust Enrichment in Australia* (Melbourne: OUP, 2006), p.130 fn.43.

[147] "The 1978 Act is an application of the principle that there should be restitutionary remedies for unjust enrichment": *Dubai Aluminium Co Ltd v Salaam* [2002] UKHL 48; [2003] 2 A.C. 366 at [76]. For general discussion see Chs 19 and 20.

[148] *Hansard*, HL (series 5) vol.395, col.251 (July 18, 1978). Cf. *Gnitrow Ltd v Cape Plc* [2000] 3 All E.R. 763 at 767.

[149] See especially *Butcher v Churchill* (1808) 14 Ves. Jun. 567 at 575–576; 33 E.R. 638 at 641; *Reed v Norris* (1837) 2 My. & Cr. 361 at 375–376, 40 E.R. 678 at 683; *Jamieson v Trustees of the Property of Hotel Renfrew* [1941] 4 D.L.R. 470 at 479. And cf. the insurance subrogation cases cited at paras 21–64—21–66.

[150] *Kleinwort Benson* [1997] Q.B. 380. See too *Kleinwort Benson Ltd v South Tyneside Metropolitan BC* [1994] 4 All E.R. 972 at 984–985 and 987 per Hobhouse J.

to the defendant under the swaps contract[151]; and, secondly, because claims in unjust enrichment are not subject to a general restriction that the defendant's gain must correspond to a loss in the claimant's hands.[152] The first of these reasons was essentially a finding of fact that the claimant bank had not passed on its loss to its counterparty under the hedge contract, and if that was the ground for the court's decision then its second, broader reason for denying the defence cannot have been the ratio of the case.[153]

As we discuss in Ch.32, we consider that the common law passing on cases are **6–74** unsatisfactory authorities because they are all essentially three party cases, the best resolution of which would have taken the position of all three parties into account, and not simply the position of two parties before the court. In principle the defence should not be denied in every case, and its availability should rather depend on the means by which the claimant has passed on his loss. For example, where a claimant passes on his loss by working harder at his business and generating extra profits from his customers, there is much to be said for allowing him to accumulate these profits and the fruits of his action against the defendant, and so the passing on defence should not be allowed. However, where his loss is effectively borne by a third party who is himself entitled to recover from the claimant, for example because he has paid him by mistake or under duress, there is little to be said for allowing the claimant to keep the third party's payment and the fruits of his action against the defendant. In this situation the best answer is for the defendant to repay the third party, either directly, or through the claimant; but if this is not a feasible option, for example because the third party cannot be identified, then the claimant has no better right to the benefit in the defendant's hands than the defendant, and since neither of them positively deserves it, the gain should lie where it falls.

---

[151] *Kleinwort Benson* [1997] Q.B. 380 at 399 per Morritt L.J.
[152] *Kleinwort Benson* [1997] Q.B. 380 at 394–395 per Saville L.J. The same reason was given for rejecting the defence in *Commissioner of State Revenue (Victoria) v Royal Insurance Ltd* (1994) 182 C.L.R. 51 at 75 per Mason C.J., following Windeyer J. in *Mason v New South Wales* (1959) 102 C.L.R. 108 at 146; *Roxborough* [2001] HCA 68; (2001) 208 C.L.R. 516 at [25]–[26]; *K.A.P. Motors Pty Ltd v Commissioner of Taxation* [2008] FCA 159; (2008) 168 F.C.R. 319 at [44].
[153] As noted in M. Rush, *The Defence of Passing On*, p.39.

CHAPTER 7

AT THE CLAIMANT'S EXPENSE: PROPRIETARY CLAIMS

1. INTRODUCTION

(a) *Personal and Proprietary Claims Distinguished*

Personal claims in unjust enrichment are claims for a personal restitutionary remedy, i.e. claims that the defendant should pay the claimant a sum of money corresponding to the value of a benefit that he unjustly received at the claimant's expense.[1] Proprietary claims in unjust enrichment are claims for a proprietary restitutionary remedy, i.e. claims for a declaration that the claimant has either an ownership interest or a security interest in property owned by the defendant, accompanied by whatever order is needed to enable the claimant to realize his proprietary right, such as an order for reconveyance or an order for sale and remission of proceeds.[2]

7–01

Both personal and proprietary claims are governed by the rule that the defendant's enrichment must have been gained at the claimant's expense, but the tests used to determine whether this requirement has been satisfied vary with the type of claim. Where the claimant seeks a personal remedy, he must show that there was a transfer of value between the parties, and this is tested by asking whether an event took place that caused the claimant to become worse off and the defendant to become better off. This is discussed in Ch.6. In contrast, where the claimant seeks a proprietary remedy, it is not enough for him to show that there was a transfer of value between the parties: he must also show either that he previously owned the property in which he now claims an ownership or security interest, or else that the defendant acquired this property in exchange for property that was previously owned by the claimant, or else that this property was formerly the subject matter of an interest that was discharged with property that was previously owned by the claimant.[3] This test is more stringent than the causal test used in the context of personal claims, and it serves as a control mechanism to prevent proprietary restitutionary remedies from becoming too freely available.[4]

7–02

---

[1] See Ch.36.
[2] See Chs 37–40.
[3] See paras 7–37—7–39 and the cases cited at para.7–39, fn.87.
[4] For arguments that the test currently used for proprietary claims is too stringent (which we do not find convincing), see D.A. Oesterle, "Deficiencies of the Restitutionary Right to Trace" (1983) 68 Cornell L.R. 172; S. Evans, "Rethinking Tracing and the Law of Restitution" (1999) 115 L.Q.R. 469.

(b) *The Rules of Following and Tracing*

7–03 Where the claimant transfers property to the defendant, and the defendant still has the property in its original form at the time of the claim, it should be an easy matter for the claimant to establish a sufficiently strong link between his property and the defendant's property to ground a proprietary claim. However more complex situations can arise. The claimant may transfer property to a recipient who then transfers it to a second recipient. Or he may transfer property to a recipient who mixes it with other property so that it loses its discrete identity, or who exchanges it for new property, or who mixes it with other property and then exchanges property withdrawn from the mixture for new property. In all of these cases, the claimant will need to invoke the rules of following and/or tracing. These are rules of evidence that determine when property is treated for legal purposes as having passed from one party to another (following), and when property is treated for legal purposes as having been exchanged for other property, so that the new property represents the product of the old property (tracing).

7–04 The rules of following and tracing must be distinguished from the rules of claiming, as Lord Millett held in *Foskett v McKeown*[5]:

> "[Following and tracing] are both exercises in locating assets which are or may be taken to represent an asset belonging to the plaintiffs and to which they assert ownership. The processes of following and tracing are, however, distinct. Following is the process of following the same asset as it moves from hand to hand. Tracing is the process of identifying a new asset as the substitute for the old. Where one asset is exchanged for another, a claimant can elect whether to follow the original asset into the hands of the new owner or to trace its value into the new asset in the hands of the same owner . . . Tracing is also distinct from claiming. It identifies the traceable proceeds of the claimant's property. It enables the claimant to substitute the traceable proceeds for the original asset as the subject matter of his claim. But it does not affect or establish his claim. That will depend on a number of factors including the nature of his interest in the original asset . . . [and] his claim may also be exposed to potential defences as a result of intervening transactions."

7–05 Thus, in Moore-Bick J.'s words, "the rules of following and tracing . . . [are] evidential in nature", and they are distinct from "rules which determine substantive rights":

> "[T]he former are concerned with identifying property in other hands or in another form; the latter with the rights that a claimant can assert against the property in its present form".[6]

Thus, completion of a following and tracing exercise is not enough in itself to establish a claimant's entitlement to a proprietary remedy on the ground of unjust

---

[5] *Foskett v McKeown* [2001] 1 A.C. 102 at 127–128.
[6] *Glencore International AG v Metro Trading International Ltd* [2001] 1 Lloyd's Rep. 284 at [180]. See too *Boscawen v Bajwa* [1996] 1 W.L.R. 328 at 334; *Waxman v Waxman* (2004) 7 I.T.E.L.R. 162 at [582]; *Ultraframe (UK) Ltd v Fielding* [2005] EWHC 1638 (Ch) at [1464] per Lewison J.: "the tracing exercise must be carried out first. Only then can the court consider what rights (if any) the claimant has in the assets that have been identified as being [the claimant's] property or their identifiable substitutes."

enrichment,[7] as in addition to showing that the defendant's enrichment at his expense is unjust, he may also have to satisfy further requirements, as discussed in Chs 37 to 40.

Note that a defendant who uses a claimant's property to acquire new property **7–06** without his consent is unjustly enriched at the claimant's expense, whatever the legal source of the claimant's right to the original property may have been. So, for example, a claimant may have a proprietary right in assets held by a defendant arising out of the parties' agreement (e.g. under a title retention clause), or he may make a mistaken payment to a defendant in circumstances that entitle him to a proprietary remedy in unjust enrichment, or a defendant may acquire money by committing a wrong against a claimant in circumstances that entitle the claimant to a proprietary remedy. In every case, if the defendant then uses the property to acquire new property from a third party without the claimant's consent, the defendant is thereby unjustly enriched at the claimant's expense. Whenever one party uses another party's property to acquire new property without his consent, that acquisition is obtained at the other party's expense, because the acquisitive opportunities inherent in the original property are attributed in law to its owner, and the acquisition is unjust by reason of the want of his consent. This is discussed further in Ch.7.[8]

Note, too, that in some cases the rules of following and tracing can be used to **7–07** demonstrate that the value inherent in an asset formerly owned by a claimant is now represented by the value that inheres in several other assets in the hands of several different defendants. The law therefore needs a mechanism to prevent the claimant from making proprietary claims to all of these assets, and it may be that the best way of doing this is to make the claimant's acquisition of proprietary rights contingent on the exercise of a power. This is discussed in Ch.37.[9]

(c) *Different Rules at Common Law and Equity?*

For many years it was thought that there are different tracing rules in equity and **7–08** at common law, and that the equitable rules are more favourable to claimants than the common law rules, most significantly because claimants at common law could not trace through mixtures of money in bank accounts, something which equity permits.[10] It was also thought that a claimant had to show that his property was held on trust or subject to some other fiduciary relationship before he could

---

[7] *Evans v European Bank Ltd* [2004] NSWCA 22; (2004) 61 N.S.W.L.R. 75 at [134]: "the process of identification should not be confused with a proprietorial right."

[8] See paras 8–17—8–31.

[9] See paras 37–25—37–28.

[10] *Sinclair v Brougham* [1914] A.C. 398 at 419–420; *Banque Belge pour l'Étranger v Hambrouck* [1921] 1 K.B. 321 at 328 and 330; *Re Diplock* [1948] Ch. 465 at 518; *Agip (Africa) Ltd v Jackson* [1991] Ch. 547 at 566. The point was conceded in *Lipkin Gorman (A Firm) v Karpnale Ltd* [1991] 2 A.C. 548 at 572. See too *Taylor v Plumer* (1815) 3 M. & S. 562; 105 E.R. 721, which has often been said to stand for the proposition that tracing through mixtures in bank accounts is not possible at common law, but which in fact lays down a rule about claiming; moreover, the case was ultimately decided on equitable principles, as confirmed in *Trustee of F.C. Jones & Son (A Firm) v Jones* [1997] Ch. 159 at 169.

take advantage of the equitable tracing rules with a view to tracing through mixtures in bank accounts.[11]

7–09   As Lionel Smith has explained, these findings were always suspect as a matter of authority.[12] They were inconsistent with a long line of subrogation cases in which claimants were not required to establish a fiduciary relationship before invoking the equitable tracing rules to show that their money had been used to discharge securities to which they sought to be subrogated.[13] They were inconsistent with *Marsh v Keating*,[14] where the House of Lords advised by 12 common law judges accepted that the common law could trace through a mixed bank account. Also, Viscount Haldane L.C.'s finding in *Sinclair*[15] that there can be no tracing at common law where money has been lent and placed in a bank account was founded on a misunderstanding of Thesiger L.J.'s statement in *Re Hallett's Estate*[16] that a claimant who makes an unsecured loan cannot generally make a proprietary claim against the borrower's assets to secure repayment of the loan.

7–10   These objections to the traditional view are now of subsidiary importance, however, following *Foskett*, where Lord Steyn[17] and Lord Millett[18] both said that there is now only one set of tracing rules in English law, applicable to common law and equitable claims alike. Their comments on this point were obiter, but it seems likely that they will be followed in future cases.[19] Developing the law in this way would certainly be desirable in principle. In the past, the courts have discovered fiduciary relationships between the parties to litigation, not because their relationship was of the sort that would normally attract the imposition of fiduciary duties, but because the courts have wished to let the claimant take advantage of the "equitable" tracing rules. So, for example, it has been held that a thief owes a fiduciary duty to his victim, with the result that the victim can invoke the "equitable" rules in order to trace through the thief's sale of the stolen

---

[11] *Sinclair* [1914] A.C. 398 at 421; *Re Diplock* [1948] Ch. 465 at 536–537; *Agip* [1991] Ch. 547 at 566.

[12] L.D. Smith, *The Law of Tracing* (Oxford: Clarendon Press, 1997), pp.123–130 and 168–174.

[13] e.g. *Marlow v Pitfeild* (1719) 1 P. Wms. 558; 24 E.R. 516; *Baroness Wenlock v River Dee Co* (1887) 19 Q.B.D. 15; *Orakpo v Manson Investments Ltd* [1978] A.C. 95; *Banque Financière de la Cité v Parc (Battersea) Ltd* [1999] 1 A.C. 221.

[14] *Marsh v Keating* (1834) 2 Cl. & Fin. 250; 6 E.R. 1149; discussed in J. Edelman, "*Marsh v Keating*" in C. Mitchell and P. Mitchell (eds), *Landmark Cases in the Law of Restitution* (Oxford: Hart Publishing, 2006), 97.

[15] *Sinclair* [1914] A.C. 398 at 419–421.

[16] *Re Hallett's Estate* (1880) 13 Ch.D. 696 at 723–724.

[17] *Foskett* [2001] 1 A.C. 102 at 113, adopting the approach advocated in P. Birks, "The Necessity of a Unitary Law of Tracing" in R. Cranston (ed.), *Making Commercial Law* (Oxford: OUP, 1997), 239.

[18] *Foskett* (1880) 13 Ch.D. 696 at 128–129.

[19] For dicta following *Foskett* on this point, see *Bracken Partners Ltd v Gutteridge* [2003] EWHC 1064 (Ch); [2003] 2 B.C.L.C. 84 at [121] (not relevant on appeal: [2003] EWCA Civ 1875; [2004] 1 B.C.L.C. 377, though at [29] Mantell L.J. cited Lord Millett's dicta that the tracing rules are the same at common law and in equity); *Dick v Harper* [2006] B.P.I.R. 20 at [43]; and cf. *B.M.P. Global Distribution Inc v Bank of Nova Scotia* [2009] SCC 15; [2009] 1 S.C.R. 504 at [79]–[85] where the court cited *Foskett* in the course of denying that tracing through mixtures in bank accounts is impossible at common law. But compare *Shalson v Russo* [2003] EWHC 1637 (Ch); [2005] Ch. 281 at [103]–[104]; *Cie Noga D'Importation et D'Exportation SA v Australia and New Zealand Banking Group Ltd (No.5)* [2005] EWHC 225 (Comm) at [16]; *London Allied Holdings Ltd v Lee* [2007] EWHC 2061 (Ch) at [256]–[257].

property and mixing of the proceeds in a bank account.[20] Instrumental findings of this sort debase the currency of the fiduciary concept.[21]

2. FOLLOWING

In many cases, following an asset into the hands of a defendant presents no great evidential difficulty. However, problems can arise when the asset is mixed with other assets in the defendant's hands in such a way that they lose their discrete identity.[22] Different rules are used to resolve these problems, depending on whether the asset has gone into a fungible mixture, i.e. a mixture composed of mutually interchangeable units, each of which can readily be separated from the others without causing any damage.[23]   **7–11**

(a) *Fungible Mixtures*

Suppose that a claimant's assets are mixed with other assets in such a way that no one can tell who has contributed what to the mixture, but it remains possible to divide the mixture into identical parts: suppose, for example, that a claimant's oil is mixed with other oil,[24] or that a claimant's shares are mixed with other shares.[25] Where the whole mixture is still intact, the claimant's contribution must still be somewhere in the mixture although it has lost its discrete identity, and so the rule in this case is that the claimant can identify any proportionate part of the mixture as his property.[26]   **7–12**

If part of the mixture is consumed or transferred to a third party, then the evidential problem becomes more acute. In this case no one can know whether   **7–13**

---

[20] *Black v Freedman* (1910) 12 C.L.R. 105 at 110; endorsed by Lord Templeman in *Lipkin Gorman* [1991] 2 A.C. 548 at 565–566; *Bishopsgate Investment Management Ltd v Maxwell* [1993] Ch. 1 at 70; *Westdeutsche Landesbank Girozentrale v Islington LBC* [1996] A.C. 669 at 716. But doubts are expressed in *Shalson v Russo* [2003] EWHC 1637 (Ch); [2005] Ch. 281 at [110]–[117]; and *Sinclair Investment Holdings SA v Versailles Trade Finance Ltd* [2005] EWCA Civ 722; [2006] 1 B.C.L.C. 60 at [43].

[21] Cf. *Norberg v Wynrib* (1992) 92 D.L.R. (4th) 449 at 481 per Sopinka J.: "equitable doctrines cannot be imported simply in order to improve the nature and extent of the remedy."

[22] See generally P. Birks, "Mixtures" in N. Palmer and E. McKendrick (eds), *Interests in Goods*, 2nd edn (London: LLP, 1993), 227; P. Matthews, "The Legal and Moral Limits of Common Law Tracing" in P. Birks (ed.), *Laundering and Tracing* (Oxford: Clarendon Press, 1995), 24, pp.42–47; Smith, *The Law of Tracing*, Ch.2; R.J.W. Hickey, "Dazed and Confused: Accidental Mixtures of Goods and the Theory of Acquisition of Title" (2003) 66 M.L.R. 368.

[23] *Rysaffe Trustee Co (CI) Ltd v IRC* [2002] S.T.C. 872 at [32]; *Glencore International AG v Alpina Insurance Co Ltd (No.2)* [2004] EWHC 66 (Comm); [2004] 1 All E.R. (Comm.) 858 at [16]. See too R. Campbell (ed.), J. Austin, *Lectures on Jurisprudence*, 4th edn (London: John Murray, 1879), p.807; R. Goode, "Are Intangible Assets Fungible?" in P. Birks and A. Pretto (eds), *Themes in Comparative Law* (Oxford: OUP, 2002), 97.

[24] *Indian Oil Corp v Greenstone Shipping SA* [1988] Q.B. 345; *Glencore International v Metro Trading* [2001] 1 Lloyd's Rep. 284.

[25] *Brady v Stapleton* (1952) 88 C.L.R. 322.

[26] *Lupton v White* (1808) 15 Ves. Jun. 432 at 440–441; 33 E.R. 817 at 821; *Jones v Moore* (1841) 4 Y. & C. Ex. 351; 160 E.R. 1041; *Buckley v Gross* (1863) 3 B. & S. 566; 122 E.R. 213; *McDonald v Lane* (1881) 7 S.C.R. 462; *Gill and Duffus (Liverpool) Ltd v Scruttons Ltd* [1953] 1 W.L.R. 1407; *Indian Oil* [1988] Q.B. 345 at 369–371; *Foskett* [2001] 1 A.C. 102 at 143; *Glencore International v Metro Trading* [2001] 1 Lloyd's Rep. 284 at [185].

the claimant's contribution subsists in the remainder. Two rules are used to resolve this problem. First, where the mixing is done innocently, the remainder is apportioned rateably between contributors to the mixture: e.g. if the claimant's 20,000 barrels of oil are innocently mixed with 100,000 barrels of oil belonging to others, and 30,000 barrels are consumed, then one-sixth of the 90,000 barrels remaining (i.e. 15,000 barrels) are deemed to belong to the claimant.[27]

7–14   Secondly, where the mixing is done by a bad faith defendant who knows that he is not entitled to the claimant's oil but who mixes it with his own oil anyway, a different rule applies, namely that evidential uncertainty created by wrongdoing is resolved against the wrongdoer.[28] This does not mean that the defendant is debarred from following his own contribution into the mixture, but it does mean that losses from the mixture are deemed to have come out of his portion first, because the burden of proving otherwise is placed on the defendant.[29] So, for example, if a defendant knowingly mixes 100 tons of the claimant's gravel with 100 tons of his own gravel, and 80 tons of gravel are then stolen out of the mixture, the defendant can identify 20 tons of the remaining gravel as his own, but the other 100 tons will be deemed to belong to the claimant because the defendant cannot prove that they belong to him.

7–15   These rules are designed to resolve evidential uncertainty, and they do not apply where the facts are not uncertain. So, for example, in *Re Goldcorp Exchange Ltd*,[30] customers of Walker & Hall Commodities Ltd owned gold bullion in the company's possession. Walker & Hall's business was acquired by Goldcorp Exchange Ltd, which took possession of the bullion and misappropriated it by mixing it with Goldcorp's own bullion, removing bullion from the mixed stock, and adding more bullion to the mixed stock without intending to replace the Walker & Hall bullion. When Goldcorp went into receivership, the Walker & Hall customers made proprietary claims to the surviving bullion, but the Privy Council held that they could only identify as their bullion the lowest amount of bullion in Goldcorp's possession between the accrual of the Walker & Hall customers' rights and the commencement of the receivership. On the facts it was certain that the additional surviving bullion did not belong to them.[31]

(b) *Non-Fungible Mixtures*

7–16 The process of following an asset inevitably comes to an end if the asset is destroyed. The law provides that it also comes to an end, because the asset is deemed to have been destroyed, in three situations:

---

[27] *Spence v Union Marine Insurance Co* (1868) L.R. 3 C.P. 427.

[28] This is a rule of general application in the law of evidence: *Armory v Delamirie* (1722) 1 Str. 505; 93 E.R. 664; *Lupton* (1808) 15 Ves. Jun. 432 at 439–440; 33 E.R. 817 at 821; *Infabrics Ltd v Jaytex Ltd* [1985] F.S.R. 75.

[29] *Frith v Cartland* (1865) 2 H. & M. 417 at 418; *Cook v Addison* (1869) L.R. 7 Eq. 466 at 470; *Harris v Truman* (1881) 7 Q.B.D. 340 at 358; affirmed (1882) 9 Q.B.D. 264; *Lamb v Kincaid* (1907) 38 S.C.R. 516 at 541; *Re Tilley's W.T.* [1967] Ch. 1179 at 1182; *Indian Oil* [1988] Q.B. 345 at 370–371; *Foskett* [2001] 1 A.C. 102 at 132; *Glencore International v Metro Trading* [2001] 1 Lloyd's Rep. 284 at [159] and [182]; *Sinclair Investments* [2011] EWCA Civ 347; [2011] Bus. L.R. 1126 at [138]–[141].

[30] *Re Goldcorp Exchange Ltd* [1995] 1 A.C. 74.

[31] Cf. *James Roscoe (Bolton) Ltd v Winder* [1915] 1 Ch. 62, discussed at para.7–28.

- where the asset is physically attached to another, "dominant", asset so that it would cause serious damage, or be disproportionately expensive, to separate the two: here the asset is said to "accede" to the dominant asset[32];

- where the asset is physically attached to land in such a way that it would cause serious damage, or be disproportionately expensive, to separate the two: here the asset is said to become a "fixture" on the land[33]; and

- where the asset is combined with other items to create a wholly new product, under the doctrine of "specification".[34]

At least in the case of specification, however, these rules are modified where **7-17** the mixing is knowingly performed by a wrongdoer. Here, despite the creation of the new thing, the owner of the assets which were wrongfully used to create the new asset can follow his property into the new asset. So, in *Jones v De Marchant*,[35] a husband wrongfully took 18 beaver skins belonging to his wife and used them, together with four skins of his own, to have a fur coat made up which he gave to his mistress. The wife was allowed to recover the coat, a result which can only be explained on the basis that she was permitted to follow her property into the new asset.

3. TRACING

(a) *The Nature of the Tracing Exercise*

The rules of tracing are tightly focused on the question whether an exchange of **7-18** assets has taken place so that one asset can be regarded for legal purposes as the substitute for another. Thus, in *Foskett* Lord Millett said that tracing is "the

---

[32] *Hendy Lennox (Industrial Engines) Ltd v Grahame Puttick Ltd* [1984] 1 W.L.R. 485; *McKeown v Cavalier Yachts Pty Ltd* (1988) 13 N.S.W.L.R. 303 at 311. Which of two assets accedes to the other depends on which is the "dominant" entity, a point which is decided rather impressionistically by reference to overall physical significance rather than monetary value. The doctrine of "accession" derives from the Roman doctrine of *accessio*.

[33] *Hobson v Gorringe* [1897] 1 Ch. 182; *Reynolds v Asby & Son* [1904] A.C. 406; *Melluish (Inspector of Taxes) v BMI (No.3) Ltd* [1996] A.C. 454; *Elitestone Ltd v Morris* [1997] 1 W.L.R. 687; *Chelsea Yacht & Boat Co Ltd v Pope* [2000] 1 W.L.R. 1941; *Mew v Tristmire Ltd* [2011] EWCA Civ 912. See too H.N. Bennett, "Attachment of Chattels to Land" in Palmer and McKendrick, *Interest in Goods*, 267.

[34] *International Banking Corp v Ferguson, Shaw & Sons*, 1910 S.C. 182; *Borden (UK) Ltd v Scottish Timber Products Ltd* [1981] Ch. 25. See too P. Matthews, "'Specificatio' in the Common Law" (1981) 10 Anglo-American Law Rev. 121. The doctrine derives from the Roman doctrine of *specificatio*.

[35] *Jones v De Marchant* (1916) 28 D.L.R. 561, endorsed in *Foskett* [2001] 1 A.C. 102 at 132–133. See too *Spence* (1868) L.R. 3 C.P. 427 at 437–438; *Sandeman & Sons v Tyzack and Branfoot Steamship Co Ltd* [1923] A.C. 680 at 694–695. An attempt to extend the principle to mixtures of ideas leading to the creation of a patentable product failed in *I.D.A. Ltd v University of Southampton* [2006] EWCA Civ 145; [2006] R.P.C. 21 at [40]–[42].

process of identifying a new asset as the substitute for the old"[36]; and in *O.J.S.C. Oil Co Yugraneft v Abramovich* Christopher Clarke J. said that[37]:

> "[I]n order to be able successfully to trace property it is necessary for the claimant, firstly, to identify property of his, which has been unlawfully taken from him ('a proprietary base'); secondly, that that property has been used to acquire some other new identifiable property. The new property may then have been used to acquire another identifiable asset ('a series of transactional links'). Thirdly the chain of substitutes must be unbroken."

7–19   One consequence of this tight focus on asset exchanges is that tracing is not possible where the claimant cannot show that a substitution has taken place, although he can the defendant's receipt of one asset and his acquisition of another are connected by a causal link.[38] Suppose, for example, that the claimant pays money into the defendant's bank account, and that the defendant is thereby enabled to use money from another account to buy a new asset that he would not have bought if he had not been enriched by the claimant's payment. In this case the new asset would not be regarded as the traceable product of the claimant's money because the required "nexus" between the claimant's money and the new asset is not present.[39]

7–20   The courts' insistence on exchanges of one property right for another has also led them to hold that tracing is impossible in cases where the defendant spends money received from the claimant on making alterations to property that he already owns.[40] In *Re Diplock*[41] the argument was made that tracing into the property should be allowed in such cases because the situation should be treated as though the defendant had used a mixture of his existing property and the claimant's money to acquire new property. The Court of Appeal rejected this for several reasons. However none of these stands up to scrutiny. One was that the alterations might not affect the value of the property, or might cause it to go down, and in such cases the court considered that the defendant's expenditure should be treated as a dissipation of the money.[42] Laying to one side the complicating factor of rises and falls in the property market, this reasoning leaves

---

[36] *Foskett* [2001] 1 A.C. 102 at 127. See too *Boscawen* [1996] 1 W.L.R. 328 at 334 per Millett L.J.: tracing is "the process by which the plaintiff traces what has happened to his property"; *Shalson* [2003] EWHC 1637 (Ch); [2005] Ch. 281 at [102] per Rimer J.: tracing is "the process by which a claimant seeks to show that an interest he had in an asset has become represented by an interest in a different asset"; *Sinclair Investments* [2011] EWCA Civ 347; [2011] Bus. L.R. 1126 at [138] per Lord Neuberger M.R.: "if a proprietary claim is to be made good by tracing, there must be a clear link between the claimant's funds and the asset or money into which he seeks to trace."

[37] *O.J.S.C. Oil Co Yugraneft v Abramovich* [2008] EWHC 2613 (Comm) at [349].

[38] L. Smith, "Tracing" in A. Burrows and Lord Rodger, *Mapping the Law* (Oxford: OUP, 2006), 119, pp.135–137.

[39] *Serious Fraud Office v Lexi Holdings Plc (In Administration)* [2008] EWCA Crim 1443; [2009] Q.B. 376 at [49]–[50], discussed at paras 7–37—7–39.

[40] As discussed in T. Akkouh and S. Worthington, "*Re Diplock*", in Mitchell and Mitchell (eds), *Landmark Cases in the Law of Restitution*, 285, pp.305–315. See too *Satnam Investments Ltd v Dunlop Heywood* [1993] 3 All E.R. 652 at 671 where the CA declined to hold that a development site could be the traceable product of confidential information.

[41] *Re Diplock* [1948] Ch. 465 at 545–548.

[42] See too *Re Esteem Settlement* 2002 J.L.R. 53 at 106 per Birt D.B.: where a claimant's money has been used to pay for repairs to property that do not bring about an increase in value "there can be no tracing as the funds will have been lost".

out of account the fact that real property does not hold its value even when the property market is steady. If houses are not maintained they fall into disrepair, and they fall in value. The court's conception of the value of real property was therefore too static, and to the extent that repairs to property prevent it from falling in value they should be regarded as leaving a traceable residuum in the owner's hands, and should not be treated as a dissipation of funds.

The court's second reason was that evidential problems might arise if a **7–21** defendant spent money on only one part of his property, as there would then be argument as to whether the claimant could trace into that part alone, or into the whole property. This problem could be dealt with by a court making robust findings of fact. The third reason given by the Court of Appeal was that permitting a claimant to trace through expenditure on alterations into a defendant's pre-existing property would lead to the claimant making a proprietary claim against the property, and that this would be unfair to a defendant who had acted in good faith. This problem could be dealt with by holding that good faith defendants who spend money in this way are entitled to the defence of change of position, with the result that any order for sale and remission of proceeds to the claimant could be deferred in a manner that was fair to both parties.[43]

In *Foskett*[44] the House of Lords had to decide who had the right to a death **7–22** benefit of about £1 million paid by insurers pursuant to a whole of life policy. Some of the premiums were paid with money misappropriated from the appellants by the deceased, and the respondents were the children of the deceased whom he had nominated as the policy beneficiaries. According to Lord Browne-Wilkinson[45]:

> "The question which arises in this case is whether, for tracing purposes, the payments of the fourth and fifth premiums on a policy which, up to that date, had been the sole property of the children for tracing purposes fall to be treated as analogous to the expenditure of cash on the physical property of another or as analogous to the mixture of moneys in a bank account."

A majority of the House of Lords held that the latter analogy was more appropriate and allowed the appellants to trace their money into the policy proceeds on that basis. However, Lord Browne-Wilkinson also made the obiter comment that where:

> "moneys of one person have been innocently expended on [maintaining or improving] the property of another . . . [this expenditure] normally gives rise, at the most, to a proprietary lien to recover the moneys so expended".

He also thought that *Re Diplock* merely establishes an exception to this general principle, by preventing a claimant from relying on the rules of tracing in such a case if it would be unfair to award him a proprietary interest.[46]

However, even if one accepts that a claimant who expends money on maintain- **7–23** ing or improving another person's property should be restricted to a lien to secure

---

[43] Cf. *Re Gareau Estate* (1995) 9 E.T.R. (2d) 95, discussed at paras 27–16 and 27–57.
[44] *Foskett* [2001] 1 A.C. 102. And cf. Millett L.J.'s comments in *Boscawen* [1996] 1 W.L.R. 328 at 340–341 (CA), discussed at para.27–10.
[45] *Foskett* [2001] 1 A.C. 102 at 109–110.
[46] *Foskett* [2001] 1 A.C. 102 at 109.

restitution of the value of his expenditure (and should not be allowed a proportionate ownership interest), this remedy can only be justified on the basis that the claimant can trace the value of his money into the property. Otherwise there is no link between the claimant's money and the defendant's property sufficient to justify the imposition of a lien on that property rather than any other property belonging to the defendant. Hobhouse L.J. drew the opposite conclusion in the Court of Appeal in *Foskett*, holding both that the claimants could not trace their money into the proceeds of the policy, and that they should nonetheless be entitled to a lien over the proceeds for the amount of their money.[47] But this was inconsistent with Keene L.J.'s statement of principle in *Serious Fraud Office v Lexi Holdings Plc (In Administration)*, that[48]:

> "For [an] equitable charge to attach [to assets in a defendant's hands] it must attach to assets in existence which derive from the [claimant's property]. There must be a nexus. Were it otherwise the principles of following and tracing could become otiose. On the contrary, tracing in this area is a vital process: just because it is by that process that the necessary nexus is established and the proprietary remedy, be it by way of constructive trust or equitable charge, made effectual."

7–24   It seems, then, that the situation where a claimant's money is used to repair or improve a defendant's existing property is in need of a judicial rethink, and so too is the situation where a claimant performs services for the defendant which have the same outcome. As Tim Akkouh and Sarah Worthington have written, cases of this kind are even harder to integrate into a set of tracing rules focussed on "real exchanges" because the performance of services delivers no "physical exchange".[49] Nevertheless some explanation is needed for cases in which the courts have awarded a lien over property owned by a defendant who has been unjustly enriched by a claimant performing services whose effect is to increase the property's value. An example is *Spencer v S. Franses Ltd*,[50] where an expert on antiques was awarded a lien over some embroideries to secure the owner's liability in unjust enrichment to pay for the value of research that the expert undertook to identify the embroideries. The judge held that a lien should only be awarded if the work done had increased the value of the property, but considered that this requirement was satisfied on the facts, because the effect of the work was to increase the marketability of the embroideries.[51]

(b) *Straight Substitutions*

7–25   In *Foskett*,[52] Lord Millett distinguished between cases where there is a straight substitution of one property for another, and cases of "mixed substitution", i.e.

---

[47] *Foskett* [1997] 3 All E.R. 392 at 416.
[48] *Serious Fraud Office v Lexi Holdings Plc (In Administration)* [2008] EWCA Crim 1443; [2009] Q.B. 376 at [49]–[50].
[49] Akkouh and Worthington in Mitchell and Mitchell (eds), *Landmark Cases in the Law of Restitution*, p.312.
[50] *Spencer v S. Franses Ltd* [2011] EWHC 1269 (QB).
[51] *Spencer* [2011] EWHC 1269 (QB) at [245]–[262]; considering *Hollis v Claridge* (1814) 4 Taunt. 807; 128 E.R. 549; *Steadman v Hockley* (1846) 15 M. & W. 553; 153 E.R. 969; and *Hatton v Car Maintenance Co Ltd* [1915] 1 Ch. 621.
[52] *Foskett* [2001] 1 A.C. 102 at 130.

cases where property is mixed with other property, and property is then withdrawn from the mixture and used to acquire new property. Cases of straight substitution are simple: if cash is exchanged for a car, or for a chose in action against a bank, then the car or the chose in action will be treated as the traceable product of the cash.[53]

(c) Mixed Substitutions

Cases of mixed substitution are more complicated. In these cases, the tracing 7–26 rules resemble the following rules, insofar as they provide that in cases of evidential uncertainty gains and losses to a mixture of assets must be shared rateably between innocent contributors to the mixture. They also provide that evidential uncertainty created by a bad faith defendant is resolved against him.

(i) Where a Defendant Knowingly Mixes a Claimant's Money with his Own Money

Suppose that a defendant mixes £25,000 of his own money with £25,000 7–27 received from a claimant to which the defendant knows he is not entitled and that the funds lose their separate identities as a result of the mixing. Suppose that the defendant takes £20,000 out of the mixture and loses it, and then takes a further £20,000 out of the mixture and uses it to buy a painting which triples in value. It is impossible to say whose money was lost, whose money bought the painting and whose money is left. Because the defendant acted in bad faith, the evidential problem is resolved against him,[54] by allowing the claimant to "cherry-pick" from two rules in order to reach the best result for himself.[55] The rule in *Re Hallett's Estate*[56] provides that the defendant may not say that the claimant's money was lost, and that the claimant may say that the defendant lost his own money. The rule in *Re Oatway*[57] provides that the claimant may not say that he used his own money to buy the painting, and that the beneficiaries may say that his money was used for this purpose. This produces the result that the claimant can trace his money into the painting and £5,000 of the remaining cash, the

---

[53] *Taylor v Plumer* (1815) 3 M. & S. 562; 105 E.R. 721; *Banque Belge* [1921] 1 K.B. 321; *Trustee of the Property of F.C. Jones & Son (A Firm) v Jones* [1997] Ch. 159.

[54] *Gray v Haig* (1855) 20 Beav. 219 at 226; 52 E.R. 587 at 591.

[55] *Shalson* [2003] EWHC 1637 (Ch); [2005] Ch. 281 at [144]; and *Dyson Technology Ltd & Curtis* [2010] EWHC 3289 (Ch) at [145], which are to be preferred on this point to *Turner v Jacob* [2006] EWHC 1317 (Ch); [2008] W.T.L.R. 307 at [100]–[102].

[56] *Re Hallett's Estate* (1880) 13 Ch.D. 696, especially at 727 per Jessel M.R.: "where a man does an act which may be rightfully performed . . . he is not allowed to say against the person entitled to the property or the right that he has done it wrongfully". See too *Halley v Law Society* [2002] EWHC 139 (Ch) at [160]; *Shell International Trading & Shipping Co Ltd v Tikhonov* [2010] EWHC 1399 (QB) at [43].

[57] *Re Oatway* [1903] 2 Ch. 356, especially at 360 per Joyce J.: a defendant trustee "cannot maintain that the investment which remains represents his money alone and what has been spent and can no longer be traced or recovered was money belonging to the trust". See too *Gray v Haig* (1855) 20 Beav. 219 at 226; 52 E.R. 587 at 591; *Hagan v Waterhouse* (1991) 34 N.S.W.L.R. 308 at 358; *Keefe v Law Society of New South Wales* (1998) 44 N.S.W.L.R. 451 at 461; *Heperu* [2009] NSWCA 252; (2009) 76 N.S.W.L.R. 230 at [114]; citing *Primeau v Granfield*, 184 F. 480 at 484–485 (1911) per Learned Hand J., describing the rule in *Re Oatway* as a form of "protective election".

balance being attributable to the defendant. Note that the rule in *Clayton's case*, considered below, does not apply in this situation.[58]

7-28 The rules in *Re Hallett's Estate* and *Re Oatway* are designed to resolve evidential uncertainty. Hence they have no bite in a situation that is not evidentially uncertain.[59] Suppose that a defendant mixes £50,000 of his own money and £50,000 of the claimant's money and places the mixture in an empty bank account. Suppose that he withdraws £80,000, loses it, and then adds another £30,000 of his own money, so that there is now £50,000 in the account. Here, the claimant cannot invoke the rule in *Re Hallett's Estate* to identify more than £20,000 in the account as his property because it is not evidentially uncertain that at least £30,000 of the remaining funds came from the defendant's own resources.[60] This rule, established in *James Roscoe (Bolton) Ltd v Winder*,[61] is known as "the lowest intermediate balance rule":

> "[A]bsent any payment in of money with the intention of making good earlier depredations, tracing cannot occur through a mixed account for any larger sum than is the lowest balance in the account between the time the [claimant's] money goes in, and the time the remedy is sought".[62]

7-29 Note that the claimant may be able to trace his money into later additions to the mixed fund if he can show that the defendant intended to make good the claimant's loss by replacing his missing assets.[63] Even where the defendant is a trustee for the claimant, however, the court will not presume the defendant to have had such an intention, and the onus of proving it will lie on the claimant.[64] Professor Scott has justified this result on the ground that "the real reason for

---

[58] *Re Hallett's Estate* (1880) 13 Ch. D. 696 at 728; *Heperu* [2009] NSWCA 252; (2009) 76 N.S.W.L.R. 230 at [114].

[59] Cf. *Sinclair Investments* [2010] EWHC 1614 (Ch); [2011] 1 B.C.L.C. 202 at [154].

[60] Cf. *Law Society of Upper Canada v Toronto-Dominion Bank* (1999) 169 D.L.R. (4th) 353, where the Ontario CA failed to grasp this point, as noted by L.D. Smith (2000) 33 Can. Bus. L.J. 75; this case was distinguished by the same court in *Re Graphicshoppe Ltd* (2005) 78 O.R. (3d) 401.

[61] *James Roscoe (Bolton) Ltd v Winder* [1915] 1 Ch. 62; endorsed in *Re Goldcorp* [1995] 1 A.C. 74 at 107–8; *Bishopsgate Investment* [1995] Ch. 211 at 219 and 220; *Shalson* [2003] EWHC 1637 (Ch), [2005] Ch. 281 at [143]–[144]; *Campden Hill Ltd v Chakrani* [2005] EWHC 911 (Ch) at [79]; *Turner v Jacob* [2006] EWHC 1317 (Ch); [2008] W.T.L.R. 307 at [85]. See too *Re Ontario Securities Commission and Greymac Credit Corp* (1986) 55 O.R. (2d) 673 at 677 (Ontario CA), affirmed *Greymac Trust Co v Ontario (Securities Commission)* [1988] 2 S.C.R. 172

[62] *Re French Caledonia Travel Service Pty. Ltd* (2003) 59 N.S.W.L.R. 361 at [175] per Campbell J. For application of the principle where goods are successively withdrawn and deposited in a mixed bulk, see *Glencore International v Metro Trading* [2001] 1 Lloyd's Rep. 284 at [201]–[202]; revisited in *Glencore International v Alpina* [2004] EWHC 66 (Comm); [2004] 1 All E.R. (Comm.) 858 at [14]–[20].

[63] *Westdeutsche* [1994] 4 All E.R. 890 at 939 (not considered on appeal); *Re B.A. Peters Plc (In Administration)* [2008] EWHC 2205 (Ch); [2008] B.P.I.R. 1180 at [18] and [46]–[47]; *Sinclair Investments* [2010] EWHC 1614 (Ch); [2011] 1 B.C.L.C. 202 at [152]. See too *Viscariello v Bernsteen Pty Ltd (In Liquidation)* [2004] SASC 266 at [30].

[64] *Ontario (Real Estate and Business Brokers Act, Director) v N.R.S. Mississauga Inc* (2003) 226 D.L.R. (4th) 361 at [49] (Ontario CA). See too *Brookfield Bridge Lending Fund Inc v Karl Oil and Gas Ltd* [2009] ABCA 99; [2009] 7 W.W.R. 1 at [16]: "If the trust funds were segregated, the outcome would be clearer. If the trustee misappropriated segregated funds, and then deposited non-trust funds into the segregated account, the intent must have been to replenish the trust account. But where the trust funds are commingled with other funds, the intent is not so clear. Since the trustee by definition is using the account for trust and non-trust purposes, the deposits might simply be made to enable further non-trust expenditures."

allowing the claimant to reach the balance [of the mixed fund] is that he has an equitable interest in the mingled fund which the wrongdoer cannot destroy as long as any part of the fund remains; but there is no reason for subjecting other property of the wrongdoer to the claimant's claim any more than to the claims of other creditors merely because the money happens to be put in the same place where the claimant's money formerly was, unless the wrongdoer actually intended to make restitution to the claimant."[65]

(ii) *Where Money Belonging to Equally Innocent Claimants is Mixed Together*

If money belonging to equally innocent claimants is mixed together then they **7–30** will generally have equally strong claims to a rateable share of gains, and equally weak claims to avoid taking a rateable share of losses, to the mixed fund. As Lord Millett said in *Foskett*[66]:

> "[W]here [an innocent contributor's claim] is in competition with the claims of other innocent contributors, there is no basis upon which any of the claims can be subordinated to any of the others."

Hence, gains and losses are generally shared between them in proportion to their contributions to the mixture.[67]

Until recently, there was thought to be an exception to this principle, deriving **7–31** from *Clayton's case*.[68] This concerned a dispute centring on the appropriation of payments as between a bank and its customer, but it came to be seen as authority for the rule that if a defendant places money belonging to two (or more) different claimants into the same unbroken running account,[69] any withdrawals that he makes from the account are deemed to be made in the same order as the payments in, on a "first in, first out" basis.[70] Thus, for example, if a defendant puts £10,000 from claimant A into a current bank account, and then puts in £10,000 from claimant B, and then withdraws £10,000 and loses it (or uses it to buy an asset which triples in value), then the loss (or gain) will be attributed solely to the claimant A.

---

[65] *Scott on Trusts* § 518.1. See too *Law Society of Upper Canada v Toronto Dominion Bank* (1998) 169 D.L.R. (4th) 353 at [19] per Blair J.: "[The rule] seeks to recognize that at some point in time, because of earlier misappropriations, an earlier beneficiary's money has unquestionably left the fund and therefore cannot physically still be in the fund. Accordingly, it cannot be 'traced' to any subsequent versions of the fund that have been swollen by the contributions of others, beyond the lowest intermediate balance in the fund."

[66] *Foskett* [2001] 1 A.C. 102 at 132.

[67] *Edinburgh Corp v Lord Advocate* (1879) 4 App. Cas. 823; *Re Diplock* [1948] Ch. 465 at 533, 534 and 539.

[68] *Clayton's case* (1816) 1 Mer. 529. For the history of the case see L.D. Smith, *The Law of Tracing*, pp.183–194, and *Re French Caledonia* (2003) 59 N.S.W.L.R. 361 at [20]–[172].

[69] e.g. a current bank account, a solicitor's trust account or a moneylender's account. The rule does not apply where there are distinct and separate debts: *The Mecca* [1897] A.C. 286; *Re Sherry* (1884) 25 Ch.D. 692 at 702. Nor does the rule apply to entries on the same day: it is the end-of-day balance which counts: *The Mecca* at 291.

[70] *Bank of Scotland v Christie* (1840) 8 Cl. & Fin 214; 8 E.R. 84; *Pennell v Deffell* (1853) 4 De G.M. & G. 372; 43 E.R. 551; *Brown v Adams* (1869) L.R. 4 Ch. 764; *Hancock v Smith* (1889) 41 Ch.D. 456 at 461; *Re Stenning* [1895] 2 Ch. 433; *Re Diplock* [1948] Ch. 465 at 553–554.

7–32   As between claimant A and claimant B this is an "irrational and arbitrary" result,[71] and for this reason the "first in, first out" rule has been discarded in many Commonwealth jurisdictions, in favour of a pro rata approach.[72] In *Barlow Clowes International Ltd v Vaughan*,[73] the Court of Appeal reaffirmed the general application of *Clayton's case* in English law, except where its application would be impracticable or would result in injustice between the parties. However, more recent English cases suggest that the rule will not often be applied, for the courts are now swift to find that the rule is an impracticable or unjust method of resolving disputes between the victims of shared misfortune, particularly in cases of large-scale fraud.[74]

7–33   *Barlow Clowes* concerned the liquidation of an investment company whose fraudulent managers had stolen most of the company's assets, leaving thousands of investors out of pocket. The question arose as to how the surviving assets should be distributed between the investors. The court held that the rule in *Clayton's case* should not be used to resolve this question because the investors had all intended that their money should be pooled in a single fund for investment purposes, so that it would conform with their original intentions if they all shared rateably in what remained in the pool. However, Woolf and Leggatt L.JJ.[75] also indicated that a "rolling charge" solution might be fairer than rateable sharing so that claimants should share losses and gains to the fund in proportion to their interest in the fund immediately prior to each withdrawal.

7–34   This would work as follows. Suppose that a defendant pays £2,000 from claimant A and then £4,000 from claimant B into an empty current bank account. He then withdraws £3,000 and loses it. He then pays in £3,000 from claimant C before withdrawing another £3,000 to buy shares whose value increases tenfold. He then withdraws the remaining £3,000 and loses it. Applying the "rolling charge" rule, the first loss must be borne by A and B in the ratio 1:2, and C need not bear this loss at all. Immediately after the first withdrawal the remaining £3,000 would be attributed to A and B in the ratio 1:2, and after the next deposit, the £6,000 in the account would be attributable to A, B, and C in the ratio 1:2:3. Hence, the shares should be attributed to them in the same proportion, leaving A with shares worth £5,000, B with shares worth £10,000 and C with shares worth £15,000. In contrast, the pro rata rule would attribute all gains and losses in

---

[71] *Re Walter J Schmidt & Co* 298 F. 314 (1923) at 316 per Learned Hand J.

[72] *Re Ontario Securities Commission* (1985) 30 D.L.R. (4th) 1; affirmed (1998) 52 D.L.R. (4th) 767; *Re Registered Securities Commission* [1991] 1 N.Z.L.R. 545; *Keefe* (1998) 44 N.S.W.L.R. 451; *A.S.I.C. v Enterprise Solutions 2000 Pty Ltd* [2001] QSC 82; *Re Esteem Settlement* 2002 J.L.R. 53; *Re French Caledonia Travel Service Pty Ltd* (2003) 59 N.S.W.L.R. 361; *Re International Investment Unit Trust* [2005] 1 N.Z.L.R. 270; *Re Magarey Farlam Lawyers Trust Accounts (No.3)* [2007] SASC 9; (2007) 96 S.A.S.R. 337 at [136]–[139]; *A.S.I.C. v Letten (No.7)* [2010] FCA 1231; (2010) 190 F.C.R. 59.

[73] *Barlow Clowes International Ltd v Vaughan* [1992] 4 All E.R. 22.

[74] *El Ajou v Dollar Land Holdings Plc (No.2)* [1995] 2 All E.R. 213 at 222; *Russell-Cooke Trust Co v Prentis* [2002] EWHC 2227 (Ch); [2003] 2 All E.R. 478 at 495; *Commerzbank AG v I.M.B. Morgan Plc* [2004] EWHC 2771 (Ch); [2005] Lloyd's Rep. 298 at [43]–[49]; *Re Ahmed & Co* [2006] EWHC 480 (Ch); (2006) 8 I.T.E.L.R. 779 at [131]–[138]. Note too that in *El Ajou (No.2)*, at 223–224, Robert Walker J. held that where A and B's money is mixed in an account and *Clayton's case* deems A's money (and not B's) to have been paid to D, B can still trace into the money received by D and claim against him if A makes no claim and is unlikely to do so. This finding was followed in *Campden Hill Ltd v Chakrani* [2005] EWHC 911 (Ch) at [76]–[77].

[75] *Barlow Clowes* [1992] 4 All E.R. 22 at 35 and 44.

proportion to the total contributions made by each claimant, giving a ratio of 2:4:3, and leaving A with shares worth £6,667, B with shares worth £13,333, and C with shares worth £10,000. The "first in, first out" rule, meanwhile, would produce the result that all of A's money is lost, that £1,000 of B's money is lost, that all the shares belong to B, and that all of C's money is lost.

In *Shalson v Russo*,[76] Rimer J. suggested that the rolling charge rule should **7-35** always be used to resolve cases of this kind, because the pro rata rule ignores evidence of what has actually happened to the claimants' money: thus, in the example, we know that no part of C's £3,000 can have gone into the trustee's first withdrawal, suggesting that C should not have to share this loss with A and B. Rimer J.'s position can certainly be supported by reference to *Roscoe v Winder*,[77] but in a case involving thousands of investors and hundreds of thousands of deposits and withdrawals, the expense and practical difficulties of calculation using the rolling charge rule may be prohibitive,[78] leaving the claimants with a choice between the rough justice of the pro rata rule, and the even rougher justice of "first in, first out". There are, moreover, Australian and Canadian authorities for the proposition that the rule in *Roscoe v Winder* should not be applied either, in cases involving multiple claimants where application of the rule would be excessively complex and expensive.[79]

(iii) *Where a Defendant Innocently Mixes a Claimant's Money with his Own Money*

Where a defendant innocently mixes the claimant's money with his own money, **7-36** the rules governing the situation will be the same as those which govern the case where money belonging to two innocent claimants is mixed together by the defendant[80]: gains and losses will be shared rateably, possibly subject to the rule in *Clayton's case*[81] if the court sees fit to apply it.[82]

(d) *Repudiation of the "Swollen Assets" Theory*

Space Investments Ltd v Canadian Imperial Bank of Commerce Trust Co (Baha- **7-37** *mas) Ltd*[83] concerned a bank trustee that was empowered by the trust instrument to lend trust money to itself. The bank lawfully exercised this power, and then went into liquidation. The beneficiaries were unable to trace their money into any

---

[76] *Shalson v Russo* [2005] Ch. 281 at [150].
[77] *Roscoe v Winder* [1915] 1 Ch. 62, discussed in para.7-28.
[78] In *Re Magarey Farlam (No.3)* [2007] SASC 9; (2007) 96 S.A.S.R. 337 at [141] Debelle J. held that the cost and complexity of applying the rule to the facts of the case rendered it "entirely unsuitable" as a method of resolving the issues between the parties.
[79] *Law Society of Upper Canada v Toronto Dominion Bank* (1998) 169 D.L.R. (4th) 353 at [24]–[25]; *Re Magarey Farlam (No.3)* [2007] SASC 9; (2007) 96 S.A.S.R. 337 at [140]; *A.S.I.C. v Letten (No.7)* [2010] FCA 1231; (2010) 190 F.C.R. 59 at [279].
[80] *Re Diplock* [1948] Ch. 465 at 524 and 539.
[81] *Re Diplock* [1948] Ch. 465 at 554.
[82] See paras 7-31—7-32. If the defendant pays the money into a separate account as soon as he learns of the claim, this will be regarded as effectively unmixing the fund so that the claim will then relate only to the money in the account: *Re Diplock* [1948] Ch. 465 at 551–552, dealing with the claim against the National Institute for the Deaf, reversed on an amended statement of the facts: at 559.
[83] *Space Investments Ltd v Canadian Imperial Bank of Commerce Trust Co (Bahamas) Ltd* [1986] 1 W.L.R. 1072 (PC).

particular surviving asset and so the Privy Council held that their claims ranked as unsecured debts. In obiter dicta, however, Lord Templeman contrasted the situation with the case where a trustee unlawfully dissipates trust money and the beneficiaries cannot trace their money into a particular surviving asset. Here, in his Lordship's view:

> "equity allows the beneficiaries to trace the trust money to all the assets of the bank and to recover the trust money by the exercise of an equitable charge over all the assets of the bank."[84]

7-38   In support of this conclusion he cited Jessel M.R.'s comment in *Re Hallett's Estate*,[85] that "if a man mixes trust funds with his own, the whole will be treated as trust property". However, this was to misread Jessel M.R.'s judgment, which was concerned with the case where a trustee mixes £X of trust money with £Y of his own money in a particular account and then dissipates part of the mixture. Jessel M.R. said nothing to support Lord Templeman's assertion that in such a case the whole of the trustee's assets constitutes one colossal fund which should be regarded as having been mixed with the trust money, so that if the money in the account is dissipated the beneficiaries can switch their attention to some other asset in the trustee's hands.

7-39   Moreover, Lord Templeman's analysis is inconsistent with the *Roscoe v Winder* principle discussed earlier,[86] that presumptions are made against wrong-doing defendants only where there is evidential uncertainty. In a case where it is certain that a defendant has dissipated the claimant's money out of a particular bank account, this principle prevents the claimant from arguing that some other asset in the defendant's hands should be deemed to represent the traceable proceeds of his property. Essentially for this reason, Lord Templeman's dicta were repudiated by the Court of Appeal in *Lexi Holdings*.[87]

(e) *Dissipation of Value*

7-40   Like the process of following property from hand to hand, the process of tracing the value inherent in property through mixtures and substitutions must come to an end if the asset in which the value resides is destroyed. So, if a defendant uses the claimant's money to buy a meal which he consumes, or a house which burns down, then his purchases leave no traceable residue (assuming that the house is

---

[84] *Space Investments* [1986] 1 W.L.R. 1072 (PC) at 76–77.
[85] *Re Hallett's Estate* (1880) 13 Ch. D. 696 at 719.
[86] See para.7–28.
[87] *Lexi Holdings* [2008] EWCA Crim 1443; [2009] Q.B. 376 at [49]–[50]; followed in *Re Lehman Bros (International) Europe (In Administration)* [2009] EWHC 3228 (Ch); [2010] 2 B.C.L.C. 301 at [190] and following. Lord Templeman's dicta had previously been restrictively distinguished in *Re Goldcorp* [1995] 1 A.C. 74; and *Bishopsgate Investment* [1995] Ch. 211. On the same theme, note Lewison J.'s comments in *Ultraframe (UK) Ltd v Fielding* [2005] EWHC 1638 (Ch); [2007] W.T.L.R. 835 at [1470]–[1475]; and Lord Neuberger's judgment in *Re B.A. Peters Plc (In Administration)* [2008] EWCA Civ 1604; [2009] B.P.I.R. 248; and cf. *Bell Group Ltd (In Liquidation) v Westpac Banking Corp (No.9)* [2008] WASC 239; (2008) 70 A.C.S.R. 1 at [9684]. And in the subrogation context, see *Boscawen* [1996] 1 W.L.R. 328 at 334 per Millett L.J.

uninsured): nothing is left in his hands to which the beneficiaries might assert a proprietary claim. As the Court of Appeal stated in *Re Diplock*[88]:

> "The equitable remedies [available to claimants making proprietary claims] presuppose the continued existence of the money either as a separate fund or as part of a mixed fund or as latent in property acquired by means of such a fund. If such continued existence is not established equity is . . . helpless."

Of course, if a defendant uses the claimant's money (or its traceable product) **7–41** to buy property from a third party, then the claimant may follow the money (or its traceable product) into the third party's hands. However there will be no point in the claimant undertaking this exercise if the third party is a bona fide purchaser for value without notice of the claimant's rights, as he will then have a defence to any claim in unjust enrichment that the claimant might hope to bring.[89]

(f) *Payment of Debts*

The rule that the tracing process comes to an end when the value being traced is **7–42** dissipated generally applies in the case where a defendant uses the claimant's money to pay off a debt, for example, by paying the money into an overdrawn bank account.[90] However, there are two exceptions to this principle. First, if the debt was secured by a charge over the defendant's property then Equity can treat the debt and the charge, by a legal fiction, as though they were not extinguished by the payment, thereby enabling the beneficiaries to trace the value inherent in their money into the value inherent in the creditor's fictionally subsisting chose in action against the defendant.[91] As discussed in Ch.39, the point of this is that the beneficiaries can acquire the fictionally subsisting security via subrogation and enforce it for their own benefit.

Secondly, and more doubtfully, it may be that if a defendant borrows money **7–43** and uses it to buy an asset, and subsequently uses the claimant's money to repay his creditor, then the claimant can trace "backwards" through the loan transaction into the asset and identify the value inherent in the asset as the proceeds of

---

[88] *Re Diplock* [1948] Ch. 465 at 521.
[89] *Brady v Stapleton* (1952) 88 C.L.R. 322; *Agip* [1990] Ch. 265 at 290; *Foskett* [2001] 1 A.C. 102 at 128; *Sinclair Investments* [2011] EWCA Civ 347; [2011] W.T.L.R. 1043 at [38]; *i Trade Finance Inc v Bank of Montreal* [2011] SCC 26; [2011] S.C.R. 360. For discussion of the bona fide purchase defence, see Ch.29.
[90] *Northern Counties of England Fire Insurance Co v Whipp* (1884) 26 Ch.D. 482 at 495–496; *Thomson v Clydesdale Bank Ltd* [1893] A.C. 282; *Bishopsgate Investment* [1995] Ch. 211; *Re Global Finance Group Pty Ltd (In Liquidation)* [2002] WASC 63; (2002) 26 W.A.R. 385 at [129]; *Re B.A. Peters Plc (In Administration)* [2008] EWHC 2205 (Ch); [2008] B.P.I.R. 1180; affirmed [2008] EWCA Civ 1604; [2009] B.P.I.R. 248; *Williams v Peters* [2009] QCA 180; (2009) 72 A.C.S.R. 365 at [31]–[37]. Where a defendant has several accounts with the same bank, the asset into which a deposit can be traced is the net balance due from the bank on *all* the accounts, and not only the account against which the deposit is credited: *Cooper v P.R.G. Powerhouse Ltd* [2008] EWHC 498 (Ch); [2008] 2 All E.R. (Comm.) 964 at [32].
[91] *Boscawen* [1996] 1 W.L.R. 328 at 340; rejecting *Re Diplock* [1948] Ch. 465 at 549–550; *Primlake Ltd (In Liquidation) v Matthews Assocs* [2006] EWHC 1227 (Ch); [2007] 1 B.C.L.C. 666 at [340].

the value inherent in the claimant's money.[92] There is some measure of support for this idea in the case law,[93] but it is not particularly strong,[94] and unless some limit is placed on the idea, backwards tracing has the potential to undermine other tracing rules, and in particular the *Roscoe v Winder* principle that presumptions should be made only in cases of evidential uncertainty. Suppose, for example, that a defendant makes a series of withdrawals out of an overdrawn bank account to buy a number of different assets, that he makes a series of deposits into the account during the same period without ever bringing it into credit, but that he finally uses the claimant's money to clear the overdraft. It would seem to be edging the law back towards the discredited *Space Investments* swollen assets theory if the claimant were able to backwards trace into all or any of the assets bought with money withdrawn from the account.

7–44   To avoid this outcome, Scott V.C. suggested in *Foskett* that it should only be possible to "trace backwards" through a wrongdoing trustee's payment of a debt into the asset purchased with the borrowed money if it could be shown that it was the trustee's intention at the time of borrowing the money that he would later wrongfully use the trust money to repay his creditor.[95] However, this may be hard to prove, particularly in cases like *Foskett* itself, where the wrongdoing trustee was dead by the time of the action.

---

[92] L.D. Smith, "Tracing into the Payment of a Debt" [1995] C.L.J. 290, especially 292–295, expanded in Smith, *The Law of Tracing*, pp.146–152.

[93] Smith's analysis has the support of Dillon L.J. in *Bishopsgate Investment* [1995] Ch. 211 at 216–217 (but was disapproved by Leggatt L.J. at 221 and 222). It was also adopted by Hobhouse J. in *Westdeutsche* [1994] 4 All E.R. 890 at 939–940 (approved by CA without comment); by Scott V.C. in *Foskett* [1998] Ch. 265 at 283–284 (though Hobhouse L.J. disagreed at 289; the issue was not considered on appeal to HL); by Rimer J. in *Shalson* [2003] EWHC 1637 (Ch); [2005] Ch. 281 at [144] (obiter); and (in effect) by David Richards QC, sitting as a deputy High Court judge in *Law Society v Haider* [2003] EWHC 2486 (Ch) at [40]–[41]. See too *Re Global Finance* (2002) 26 W.A.R. 385 at [133].

[94] M. Conaglen, "Difficulties with Tracing Backwards" (2011) 127 L.Q.R. 432.

[95] *Foskett* [1998] Ch. 265 at 283–284 (not considered on appeal to the HL).

Part Five
GROUNDS FOR RESTITUTION

Chapter 8

LACK OF CONSENT AND WANT OF AUTHORITY

1. Introduction

It often happens that a defendant, D, obtains an enrichment by immediate transfer   **8–01**
from a claimant, C, in circumstances where C did not consent to the enrichment.
It is also common for a defendant, D, to obtain an enrichment from a claimant,
C, more remotely, as a result of the actions of a third party, X, which were neither
authorised nor consented to by C. Cases of this kind span a large spectrum. They
include cases of simple theft, where D steals directly from C, or where X steals
from C and then transfers the stolen asset to D. They also include a different
category of cases, exemplified by misapplications of trust assets by trustees,
where X holds or controls assets subject to duties and powers to deal with the
assets for the benefit of another, and where D is enriched as a result of X's
unauthorised dealings with the assets.

In our view, a claim in unjust enrichment may be available in all of these cases,   **8–02**
which can be explained in terms of two distinct, though overlapping, grounds for
recovery. Where D is directly enriched at C's expense without the intermediation
of any third party—as where D simply steals from C—C's "lack of consent" is
a sufficient description of the operative ground. However, in more complex cases
where D is immediately enriched by X, but more remotely by C, the position may
be different. Where X holds assets subject to duties and powers to deal with them
for C's benefit, and acts within his authority, C will have no remedy. But where
X acts outside his authority, his "want of authority" will itself constitute a
sufficient ground for recovery by C.

In the literature, taking a lead from Peter Birks, the ground of restitution that   **8–03**
explains why a claim in unjust enrichment should be afforded in these cases has
commonly been attributed to C's "ignorance" of D's enrichment at his expense.[1]
However, this description creates a number of difficulties, and it should be
avoided. C's lack of consent, and/or X's want of authority to affect C's position,
can do the necessary explanatory work. First, to talk of C's "ignorance" as
grounding a claim in unjust enrichment risks eliding two different situations. One
is where C intended to confer a benefit on D, but where he would not have acted

---

[1] See e.g. P. Birks, *An Introduction to the Law of Restitution*, revised edn (Oxford: OUP, 1989),
pp.140–146; A.S. Burrows, *The Law of Restitution*, 3rd edn (Oxford: OUP, 2010) Ch.16; J. Edelman
and E. Bant, *Unjust Enrichment in Australia* (Melbourne: OUP, 2006), pp.271 and following.
Compare R. Chambers and J. Penner, "Ignorance" in S. Degeling and J. Edelman (eds), *Unjust
Enrichment in Commercial Law* (Sydney: Lawbook Co, 2008), Ch.13. Some commentators have
argued that many of these cases do not lie within the law of unjust enrichment at all, a view which
we do not share: e.g. W.J. Swadling, "Ignorance and Unjust Enrichment: The Problem of Title"
(2008) 28 O.J.L.S. 627; G. Virgo, *The Principles of the Law of Restitution*, 2nd edn (Oxford: OUP,
2006), pp.11–17 and Ch.7; R. Grantham and C. Rickett, *Enrichment and Restitution in New Zealand*
(Oxford: Hart, 2000), Ch.12.

as he did but for his ignorance of some material fact. If a claim is available in these cases, then it is because C acted on the basis of a restitution-grounding "mistake"; discussion of these cases therefore belongs in Ch.9.[2] The other situation, which properly falls within this chapter, is where D obtains some benefit from C, and where C is ignorant of this event, and had no intention that it should occur. Secondly, C's "ignorance" cannot explain all the cases where the unjustness of D's enrichment at C's expense ultimately stems from the fact that it has occurred without C's consent—for example, where C is aware of some taking from him, but is powerless to prevent it. Thirdly, identifying the ground for restitution as C's "ignorance" creates particular difficulties where corporate assets are misapplied by a company director; for if the courts hold that the company's "mind" should be identified with that of the director, then it is hard to say that the company is "ignorant" of the misapplication.[3] No such difficulty arises if the focus is on whether the director had authority to act as he did. Finally, in important categories of case, basing the availability of a restitutionary remedy on C's "ignorance" of the transaction through which D was benefited will fail to capture the real reason for his claim. This is so where X holds or controls assets for the benefit of a principal, and disposes of those assets outside his authority. Here what justifies a restitutionary remedy against the third party is not the principal's "ignorance" of the transaction; it is that X acted outside the authority conferred on him.

8–04　This chapter is organised as follows. Part 2 considers the two-party cases where D is immediately enriched at C's expense, and where the ground for C's claim in unjust enrichment is C's lack of consent for D's enrichment. Parts C and D then examine three-party cases, where D is immediately enriched by X, but remotely enriched by C, and the ground for recovery is either C's lack of consent or X's want of authority. The primary concern, and the subject matter of Part 3, is whether C has a claim against D. However, in three-party cases where X holds or controls assets for the benefit of C, and transfers these assets to D in an unauthorised transaction, the question arises whether X might himself bring a claim in unjust enrichment against D, relying on his own want of authority. This question is addressed in Part 4. Part 5 concludes by briefly examining the equitable personal liability for "knowing receipt". The purpose of this discussion is to clarify that this is not a personal liability imposed to reverse unjust enrichment, and to counter the arguments of some legal writers that it should be understood in this way.

2. TWO-PARTY CASES

(a) *Introduction*

8–05　Although such claims are not often brought in practice, a claim in unjust enrichment may be available on the ground of C's lack of consent in a simple two-party case, where D receives a benefit immediately from C and C did not

---

[2] See especially paras 9–32—9–42.
[3] Cf. the discussion of *Re Hampshire Land Co* [1896] 2 Ch. 743 in *Stone Rolls Ltd v Moore Stephens (A Firm)* [2009] UKHL 39; [2009] 1 A.C. 1391.

consent to the transfer. D may benefit in this way wholly without C's knowledge —for example, because D found some item lost by C, or D stole from C; or it may be that C was simply powerless to prevent D's acts. Provided that D has been enriched, and that this enrichment was at C's expense, C's lack of consent is a sufficient explanation for C's having a claim in unjust enrichment.

This part examines the main categories of two-party cases that can be explained in these terms, starting with cases involving personal claims, before turning to cases where the law arguably affords C some form of proprietary right in relation to an asset in D's hands, as a mechanism for reversing his unjust enrichment. The availability of an unjust enrichment claim can often be obscured in the cases because C often has another cause of action on the same facts—often for a tort or some form of equitable wrong—rendering it unnecessary for C to plead his claim in unjust enrichment. **8–06**

(b) *Personal Claims*

(i) *Unauthorised Receipt of C's Asset*

There are a number of common law cases where, without C's consent, D obtained a tangible money asset—coins, notes—to which C held legal title, where D could not claim to have obtained a good legal title as a bona fide purchaser,[4] and where D was held liable for the sum of money received.[5] For example, in *Holiday v Sigil*,[6] the jury was directed that if the claimant could prove that he had lost a £500 banknote, and that the defendant had found it, he was entitled to recover its value from the defendant in an action for money had and received. In *Neate v Harding*,[7] two defendants, a parish overseer and constable, were held jointly liable for £163, being the amount of cash belonging to the claimant which one of them had found during a search at the claimant's mother's house, and then paid into their joint bank acount. More recently, in *Moffatt v Kazana*,[8] the same result followed where the defendant, the purchaser of a bungalow from the claimant, had discovered a tin containing a large number of bank-notes concealed there by the claimant, and had paid the notes into his bank account, wrongly believing that he had become owner. In principle, the **8–07**

---

[4] For discussion of the bona fide purchase defence, see Ch.29.

[5] Some authors reject the suggestion that the restitutionary remedy awarded in these cases is awarded to reverse D's unjust enrichment, on the basis that if C retains legal title to the money in D's hands, it is not possible to say that D has been "enriched" by the asset's capital value at C's expense, and that properly understood, the remedies awarded in these cases were a response to a tort committed by D, or simply awarded to vindicate C's legal title. See e.g. Swadling, "Ignorance and Unjust Enrichment: The Problem of Title"; Grantham and Rickett, *Enrichment and Restitution in New Zealand*, Ch.12. See further para.8–34 and following.

[6] *Holiday v Sigil* (1826) 2 C. & P. 176; 172 E.R. 81.

[7] *Neate v Harding* (1851) 6 Exch. 349; 155 E.R. 577.

[8] *Moffatt v Kazana* [1969] 2 Q.B. 152. The tin was actually discovered by workmen, who took it to the police, who then returned the tin to the defendant. To this extent, the case looks like a three-party case; however, the reasoning would have been the same even without those intermediate transactions. See further para.8–39.

same result should follow where the defendant is enriched by receiving some other, non-money asset of which the claimant is legal owner.[9]

(ii) *Unauthorised Use of C's Asset*

8–08   Where D temporarily deprives C of possession of an asset to which C has legal title, without C's consent, then C may have a personal claim in unjust enrichment against D for the use value of the asset. In many cases, a claim may lie to recover restitutionary damages for a wrong committed by D, for example, D's trespass to C's land, or D's trespass to or conversion of C's goods. However, a personal claim in unjust enrichment might in principle lie in the same circumstances, based on D's unauthorised use of C's asset, without it being necessary to prove a wrong committed by D.

8–09   Some support for this proposition can found in a classic dictum of Lord Mansfield in *Hambly v Trott*.[10] In the course of discussing actions that survive the death of a tortfeasor, Lord Mansfield expressed the view that an action in tort would be extinguished by the *actio personalis* rule, but that another action could still be brought[11]:

> "[I]f a man take a horse from another, and bring him back again; an action for trespass will not lie against his executor, though it would against him; but an action for the use and hire of the horse will lie against the executor."

More recent recognition of the same sort of claim can be found in the Australian case of *Torpey Vander Have Pty Ltd v Mass Constructions Pty Ltd*,[12] where a purchaser of land from a company in liquidation developed land in accordance with plans which architects had previously prepared for the company. A majority of the court held that the purchaser had a licence to use the architects' plans in this way, but on the assumption that this was not the case, all of the court considered that the purchasers would be liable to the architects, on the basis that they would then have been unjustly enriched at the architects' expense.

(iii) *Unauthorised Substitution of C's Asset*

8–10   Where D receives an asset to which C retains legal title, and D subsequently transfers the asset to a third party without C's consent, C may have a personal claim in unjust enrichment against D for the value of the unauthorised substitute which D receives from the third party in exchange.[13] This is supported by an old

---

[9] Cf. *Huyton SA v Peter Cremer GmbH & Co* [1999] 1 Lloyd's Rep. 620, where the defendant had possession of the claimant's wheat, although title did not pass, and Mance J. suggested at 634 that if the defendant did not return the wheat then the claimant might have a "restitutionary right or a right in damages".

[10] *Hambly v Trott* (1776) 1 Cowp. 371 at 375; 98 E.R. 1136 at 1138. See too, by analogy, the case of *Foster v Stewart* (1814) 3 M. & S. 191; 105 E.R. 582, where Lord Mansfield's words were relied on to support the conclusion that a claim might be brought for the value of the services of the claimant's apprentice, whom the defendant had enticed to work for him. See further para.8–49.

[11] *Hambly* (1776) 1 Cowp. 371 at 375; 98 E.R. 1136 at 1138.

[12] *Torpey Vander Have Pty Ltd v Mass Constructions Pty Ltd* [2002] NSWCA 263; see Edelman and Bant, *Unjust Enrichment in Australia*, p.274.

[13] This remedial option will be appealing if the value of the unauthorised substitute exceeds the value of the asset first received by the defendant. See paras 8–17 and following and 8–83 and following on the nature and basis of the proprietary rights which the law affords in cases of unauthorised substitutions.

line of cases in which D was held liable for the amount of the money proceeds of the disposal of C's asset in an action for money had and received.[14] An example is *Oughton v Seppings*,[15] where a sheriff's officer mistakenly seized and sold Oughton's pony under a writ of execution for another party's debts, and was held liable to Oughton for the proceeds in an action for money had and received. Many of these cases, historically said to involve "waiver of the tort" committed by D, might now be explained as cases awarding a gain-based money award for a wrong—usually the tort of conversion, committed when D disposes of C's goods without C's consent.[16] But the cases may also be explained on the basis that where D disposes of C's asset to a third party without C's authority, and receives a substitute asset in exchange, D is unjustly enriched at C's expense by the value of the unauthorised substitute which he receives from the third party.[17]

An unjust enrichment explanation of these cases presents several difficulties. However, all of these reflect concerns about whether it might be said that D has been enriched by the value of the substitute at C's expense, and none cast doubt on the viability of C's lack of consent as the restitution-justifying ground. **8–11**

First, it might be thought that holding D liable for the value of the asset which he receives from X, in exchange for C's asset, is inconsistent with the basic proposition that for a personal claim in unjust enrichment, D's enrichment is measured at the time of its receipt—which suggests that D's liability should be for the original asset's value at the time of his original receipt.[18] However, the answer may be that C's claim is a new cause of action, based upon D's subsequent unjust enrichment at C's expense, which occurs when D uses C's asset without his consent to acquire a new asset. Consistently with basic principle, the prima facie measure of C's personal claim would be the value of the unauthorised substitute at the time of its receipt by D. **8–12**

Secondly, it might be thought that D is enriched at X's expense, and not C's expense, given that the substitute asset came from X and not from C.[19] However, this objection rests on a narrow view of the "at the expense of" requirement, which we do not think is correct.[20] In these cases, C can show that D was enriched at his expense by showing that the new asset which D received was acquired in exchange for C's original asset, whether or not C retains title to the original asset in the third party's hands.[21] **8–13**

---

[14] e.g. *Lamine v Dorrell* (1701) 2 Ld. Raym. 1216; 92 E.R. 303; *Oughton v Seppings* (1830) 1 B. & Ad. 241; 109 E.R. 776; *King v Leith* (1787) 2 T.R. 141; 100 E.R. 77; *Parker v Norton* (1796) 6 T.R. 695; 101 E.R. 777. And see *United Australia Ltd v Barclays Bank Ltd* [1941] A.C. 1.

[15] *Oughton v Seppings* (1830) 1 B. & Ad. 241; 109 E.R. 776.

[16] See for examination of gain-based damages awards of this type, J. Edelman, *Gain-Based Damages* (Oxford: Hart, 2002), Ch.4.

[17] This analysis is consistent with our preferred explanation for the proprietary rights that the law affords claimants to the unauthorised substitutes for their assets, at least where the substitution is carried out by someone other than a trustee or fiduciary: see paras 8–83 and following, and 8–17 and following.

[18] See paras 4–34—4–42.

[19] Cf. L.D. Smith, "Unjust Enrichment, Property and the Structure of Trusts" (2000) 116 L.Q.R. 412, pp.424–425; L.D. Smith, "Restitution: The Heart of Corrective Justice" (2001) 79 *Texas Law Review* 2115, pp.2157–2159.

[20] See para.6–12 and following.

[21] This follows from the wider causal analysis explained in Ch.6.

8–14   Thirdly, C might recover a sum in excess of his loss if he is able to recover the value of the substitute asset from D. It is a controversial issue, discussed in Ch.6, whether the law should cap the amount of restitutionary recovery at the amount of a claimant's loss, where this is less than the amount of the defendant's gain.[22] Assuming that the law does insist on such a correspondence, however, a sufficient correspondence might still be found between C's loss and D's enrichment, to the extent that the substitute asset represents the exchange product of an asset to which the law is prepared to afford C title. If correct, then the same process of reasoning might suggest that C could make a similar personal claim to the value of a subsequent unauthorised substitute for the original unauthorised substitute for his asset, which D receives under some subsequent transaction, and to which the law would afford C title. However, this is a conclusion for which there is, at present, scant authority.[23]

(c) Proprietary Claims

(i) Rights to the Original Asset

8–15   In general, where D obtains an asset to which C holds legal title, without C's consent, then C will usually retain a superior legal title, and can enforce this title by whatever means the law affords. The law of unjust enrichment has no role to play in explaining this: the survival of C's legal title is a result of the law of property's rules regarding transfers of title. There are, however, cases which suggest that in some such situations—and more particularly, in cases of theft—C might acquire new rights, insofar as equity might render D a trustee of the original asset for C. This is so notwithstanding that the victim of the theft, C, retains the superior legal and beneficial title, and D, the thief, acquires at best an inferior possessory title.[24] In *Westdeutsche Landesbank Girozentrale v Islington LBC*,[25] Lord Browne-Wilkinson proposed, obiter, that a thief who stole a bag of coins would hold the money on constructive trust for the victim[26]:

---

[22] See paras 6–63—6–74.

[23] Cf. *Trustee of the Property of F.C. Jones & Sons (A Firm) v Jones* [1997] Ch. 159 (CA), discussed at para.8–26 and following. Whether this alternative rationalisation is available may become important, in the event of subsequent unauthorised substitutions by D. Even if the law may afford C some form of legal right to the unauthorised substitute for his asset, immediately on the substitution, these rights do not allow D to be characterised retrospectively as a wrongdoer: *Lipkin Gorman (A Firm) v Karpnale Ltd* [1991] 2 A.C. 548 at 573 per Lord Goff. That is, whilst he may commit conversion of C's *original* asset, when he transfers it to a third party, he does not commit conversion of any tangible substitute asset, at least pending an election by C to claim legal title to the asset, in lieu of his original asset. It follows that if D is to be liable for the value of a substitute for C's asset, it cannot easily be explained as a remedy for wrongdoing, and will need to be explained on some other basis, e.g. as a remedy for unjust enrichment.

[24] An earlier case is *Black v S. Freedman & Co* (1910) 12 C.L.R. 105 at 110 per O'Connor J. This has been consistently followed in Australia: e.g. *Creake v James Moore & Sons Pty Ltd* (1912) 15 C.L.R. 426; *Australian Postal Corp v Lutak* (1991) 21 N.S.W.L.R. 584; *Evans v European Bank Ltd* [2004] NSWCA 82; (2004) I.T.E.L.R. 19. See too J. Tarrant, "The Theft Principle in Private Law" (2006) 80 A.L.J. 531; D. Fox, *Property Rights in Money* (Oxford: OUP, 2008), paras 4.92 and following.

[25] *Westdeutsche Landesbank Girozentrale v Islington LBC* [1996] A.C. 669.

[26] *Westdeutsche* [1996] A.C. 669 at 715–716 per Lord Browne-Wilkinson.

"I agree that stolen moneys are traceable in equity. But the proprietary interest which equity is enforcing in such circumstances arises under a constructive trust, not a resulting trust. Although it is difficult to find clear authority for the proposition, when property is obtained by fraud, equity imposes a constructive trust on the fraudulent recipient: the property is recoverable and traceable in equity."

This trust creates some conceptual difficulties,[27] and may be an unnecessary **8–16** strategem devised to enable the victim of the theft to trace into and assert an equitable title to a traceable substitute for the stolen property.[28] However that may be, the important point here is that the law of unjust enrichment probably has no role in explaining any trust which is imposed over the original stolen asset. It is, as Lord Browne-Wilkinson explained it, a constructive trust imposed as a response to D's wrongdoing—the dishonest appropriation of the thief's property to himself.[29] The trust is not generated by the victim's lack of consent, since a person who innocently acquires another's asset, for example as a good faith finder, is not a trustee in accordance with Lord Browne-Wilkinson's dictum. The position may be otherwise, however, as regards an unauthorised substitute for C's asset—as we explain in the next section.

(ii) *Rights to an Unauthorised Substitute Asset*

Even if the law of unjust enrichment has no role to play in explaining any rights **8–17** that C may have in his original asset, where D has obtained it from him without his consent, the position may be otherwise in relation to a new asset, which D acquires from a third party in exchange for C's original asset, via an unauthorised transaction with a third party. In this case, and regardless of whether D acquired C's original asset innocently, the courts are prepared to afford C some form of property right to the asset which is the unauthorised substitute for the asset to which he formerly had title. The exact nature of these rights is examined elsewhere.[30] For present purposes, their significance is that they provide another —albeit disputed—illustration of the law affording rights as a response to unjust enrichment, where the ground of restitution can be understood to be C's lack of consent or D's want of authority.

Equitable rights Beginning with the position in equity, there is a long **8–18** history of the courts holding that where D holds title to assets as trustee,[31] or otherwise occupies a fiduciary position vis-à-vis another's assets,[32] and he sells or invests these assets in an unauthorised transaction, the beneficiary or principal can elect to assert equitable title to any substitute which D receives in

---

[27] See esp. *Shalson v Russo* [2003] EWHC 1637 (Ch); [2005] Ch. 281 at [110] and following, where conceptual difficulties are raised which are convincingly addressed in Fox, *Property Rights in Money*, paras 4.103–4.106.
[28] At least in the English cases, it has been offered as a way of getting round the problem that equity's more generous tracing rules have been historically limited—erroneously—to cases where some form of initial fiduciary relationship can be shown. See paras 7–08—7–10.
[29] Similarly, Fox, *Property Rights in Money*, paras 4–96—4–97. Cf. R. Chambers, "Trust and Theft" in E. Bant and M. Harding (eds), *Exploring Private Law* (Cambridge: CUP, 2010), Ch.10.
[30] See Ch.38.
[31] e.g. *Foskett v McKeown* [2001] 1 A.C. 102.
[32] e.g. *Re Hallett's Estate* (1879) 13 Ch.D. 696 (CA). See too *Re Diplock* [1948] Ch. 465 (CA).

exchange.[33] In principle, the same should also be true where D merely has possession of an asset of which C is legal owner—as where D steals C's goods, and then sells them.[34] To achieve this result it should be unnecessary for C to characterise D as a "trustee" or "fiduciary",[35] as the unauthorised substitution of C's asset should be enough without more to enable C to assert an equitable title to the substitute asset, identified in accordance with the tracing rules.

8–19   The basis on which these rights arise is disputed. As we explain further when discussing three-party cases, the rights that C may acquire to an unauthorised substitute in the hands of an *express trustee* may be adequately explained without reference to the law of unjust enrichment.[36] The same may also be true of a person who has voluntarily assumed a fiduciary position vis-à-vis the assets otherwise than as trustee.[37] However, where D owes no fiduciary duties in connection with the relevant assets, the preferable view is that the equitable title which C may assert to the unauthorised substitute arises under a trust that is imposed to reverse D's unjust enrichment. In other words, and consistently with the personal claim which C appears have to the value of the unauthorised substitute,[38] C's new equitable title can be explained as a restitutionary response to D's unjust enrichment, on the ground of C's lack of consent. As Robert Chambers has explained, there is a close parallel between these cases, and the purchase money resulting trust which arises where C funds the acquisition of an asset in D's name.[39]

8–20   **Legal rights**   A clear picture of the rights which the law may afford to unauthorised traceable substitutes is complicated by the difficult assumption underlying a number of cases, that where C has *legal* title to an asset, the common law may allow him to assert some form of *legal* right to an unauthorised substitute,[40] whether this consists of the money proceeds[41] or its specific product.[42] It is strongly arguable that these cases rest on a misreading of the early

---

[33] See further para.8–79 and following.

[34] But cf. *Trustee of Jones v Jones* [1997] Ch. 159 (CA) at 164 and following, where Millett L.J. assumes the contrary.

[35] In *Westdeutsche* [1996] A.C. 669 at 715–716, Lord Browne-Wilkinson assumed it was necessary to characterise a thief as a trustee, in order to bring equity's tracing rules into play. In *Foskett* [2001] 1 A.C. 102 at 113 and 128–129, Lord Steyn and Lord Millett rejected the view that the tracing rules are different at common law and in equity; see paras 7–08—7–10.

[36] See paras 8–88—8–90.

[37] See para.8–90.

[38] See paras 8–91—8–93.

[39] R. Chambers, "Tracing and Unjust Enrichment" in J. Neyers et al, *Understanding Unjust Enrichment* (Oxford: Hart, 2004), pp.293 and following. Note that it is highly controversial whether resulting trusts respond to unjust enrichment, a point that is discussed in Ch.38.

[40] Well discussed in L.D. Smith, *The Law of Tracing* (Oxford: OUP, 1997), pp.320 and following; D. Fox, "Common Law Claims to Substituted Assets" [1999] R.L.R. 55; Fox, *Property Rights in Money*, paras 5.96–5.106.

[41] See the cases discussed in Fox, "Common Law Claims to Substituted Assets", pp.62 and following, including *Marsh v Keating* (1834) 1 Bing. N.C. 198; 131 E.R. 1094 and *Lipkin Gorman* [1991] 2 A.C. 548.

[42] See the cases discussed in Fox, "Common Law Claims to Substituted Assets", pp.57 and following, including *Taylor v Plumer* (1815) 3 M. & S. 562; 105 E.R. 721; as interpreted in *Lipkin Gorman* [1991] 2 A.C. 548 at 573 per Lord Goff; and in *Trustee of Jones v Jones* [1997] Ch. 159 (CA).

common law decision of *Taylor v Plumer*,[43] and that the law would be made significantly simpler and more coherent if the courts were to hold instead that the only title that may be generated to an unauthorised substitute is an equitable title arising under a trust.[44] However, this is not currently the law.

In the past, the possibility that C has some sort of *legal* title to an unauthorised **8–21** substitute for an asset to which he originally held legal title has been most significant in three-party cases, where C has sought to bring a common law personal claim in unjust enrichment against D who was remotely enriched at his expense—i.e. where without C's consent, X transfers an asset to D, and this asset represents an unauthorised substitute for an asset to which C held legal title.[45]

The key modern illustration is *Lipkin Gorman (A Firm) v Karpnale Ltd*,[46] **8–22** where Cass, a partner in the claimant firm of solicitors, withdrew cash from the partnership's client account, and then spent this cash gambling at the defendant casino. The House of Lords held that the firm could prima facie recover the sum received by the casino, reduced to the extent of the casino's change of position. Lord Goff, who gave the leading speech, explained that this was a case in which the casino had immediately received the money from Cass, and not from the claimant, and that in order to show that the casino had been unjustly enriched at the firm's expense, it would "at least, as a general rule" therefore be necessary to show that Cass had paid the casino with money to which the firm had legal title.[47] This precondition raised an immediate difficulty: authority established that Cass became legal owner of the cash withdrawn from the bank.[48] Lord Goff nevertheless thought there was an answer. In his view, authority established that the claimant firm could elect to assert some form of legal title to the cash in Cass's hands, on the basis that the cash represented the traceable substitute for the chose in action of which they were legal owner—i.e. the debt owed to the firm by its bank, as represented by the credit balance to the firm's bank account —and that this cash could be followed, first into Cass's hands, and then into the hands of the casino.[49]

For reasons that we explain in more detail in Ch.6, this proprietary analysis **8–23** was unnecessary.[50] The finding that the firm had some form of title to the cash paid to the casino was not needed to establish the firm's claim in unjust enrichment. The injustice of the casino's enrichment was sufficiently established by showing that the casino was enriched by Cass at the firm's expense without the firm's consent or authority. It was also possible to find that the casino was enriched by Cass at the firm's expense as a result of its receipt of the cash from

---

[43] *Taylor v Plumer* (1815) 3 M. & S. 562; 105 E.R. 721; on which see L.D. Smith, "The Stockbroker and the Solicitor-General: the Story Behind *Taylor v Plumer*" (1994) 15 J.L.H. 1; L.D. Smith, "Tracing in *Taylor v Plumer*: Equity in the Court of King's Bench" [1995] L.M.C.L.Q. 240.

[44] D. Smith, "Simplifying Claims to Traceable Proceeds" (2009) 125 L.Q.R. 338.

[45] *Taylor v Plumer* (1815) 3 M. & S. 562; 105 E.R. 721, as interpreted in *Lipkin Gorman* [1991] 2 A.C. 548 at 573 per Lord Goff, and in *Trustee of Jones v Jones* [1997] Ch. 159 (CA).

[46] *Lipkin Gorman (A Firm) v Karpnale Ltd* [1991] 2 A.C. 548.

[47] *Lipkin Gorman* [1991] 2 A.C. 548 at 572 per Lord Goff.

[48] *Union Bank of Australia Ltd v McClintock* [1922] 1 A.C. 240 (PC); *Commercial Banking Co of Sydney Ltd v Mann* [1961] A.C. 1 (PC); accepted by Lord Goff in *Lipkin Gorman* [1991] 2 A.C. 548 at 573.

[49] *Lipkin Gorman* [1991] 2 A.C. 548 at 573–574 per Lord Goff; relying on *Taylor v Plumer* (1815) 3 M. & S. 562; 105 E.R. 721; and *Marsh v Keating* (1834) 1 Bing. N.C. 198; 131 E.R. 1094.

[50] See para.6–12 and following.

Cass, using a "but for" causal analysis and without recourse to proprietary reasoning.

8–24   Leaving those caveats to one side, what is the nature and significance of the legal right which *Lipkin Gorman* suggests might exist in a traceable substitute? The first point is that on Lord Goff's analysis, it is not full legal ownership. At best, it is some form of inchoate legal right. Authority established that Cass became legal owner of the cash paid to him by the bank, and instead of its chose in action against the bank, the firm acquired the ability to assert some form of lesser legal title to this cash. Furthermore, even though the firm had not elected to assert its title before the cash came into the casino's hands, Lord Goff apparently considered that this provided a sufficient basis for saying that the casino's receipt of the cash represented an unjust enrichment at its expense, at least for the purpose of generating an immediate personal claim against the casino for the money so received.[51]

8–25   The second point is that in *Lipkin Gorman* itself, the firm's inchoate legal title to the cash paid to the casino had a limited significance: it provided a basis for finding that the casino came under a personal liability to the firm for the sum of money received, notwithstanding that the cash was received from a third party, Cass.[52] There is no indication in the case that the legal title which the firm had or might acquire would have larger consequences than this—for example, that it might result in an order requiring the recipient to transfer the substitute asset to the firm *in specie*, or to the extent that the asset or a traceable product remained in its hands, that the recipient should pay its present value. However, in *Trustee of Jones v Jones*, the Court of Appeal took a bolder view.

8–26   In *Trustee of the Property of F.C. Jones (A Firm) v Jones*,[53] Mrs Jones had received a sum of money drawn from a partnership's account, at a time when the partnership was bankrupt and its assets were retrospectively deemed to be vested at law in the trustee in bankruptcy. Mrs Jones used the money to make a profitable investment in potato futures and subsequently paid the proceeds of these investments to her account at Raphael's Bank. The trustee in bankruptcy brought proceedings, claiming that it was entitled to the balance of the account, as the traceable proceeds of the moneys originally taken from the partnership. The bank interpleaded, and the dispute was between the trustee in bankruptcy and Mrs Jones. The Court of Appeal held that the trustee in bankruptcy was entitled to succeed in its claim, thereby recovering the fruits of Mrs Jones's exceptionally profitable investment. The basis on which the Court of Appeal apparently proceeded was that the trustee in bankruptcy, and not Mrs Jones, was the legal owner of the money first received by Mrs Jones, and of every substitute asset into which the money was traceable in accordance with the common law's tracing rules—including the final asset, which consisted of the debt that

---

[51] The viability of this analysis is disputed. Cf. Smith, *The Law of Tracing*, pp.320 and following; and Fox, *Property Rights in Money*, paras 5.96–5.106 and 9.19 and following, where the title which is acquired by the claimant is explained as a legal title, secondary to the defendant's legal title, which is initially inchoate, but becomes a vested secondary title when the claimant elects to assert title to the substitute.

[52] See Smith, *The Law of Tracing*, pp.332 and following, exploring the possibility that *Lipkin Gorman* might stand as authority for the common law's affording a person some limited form of property right to an unauthorised traceable substitute, the only consequence of which would be to generate a restitutionary liability on the part of a subsequent recipient.

[53] *Trustee of the Property of F.C. Jones (A Firm) v Jones* [1997] Ch. 159 (CA).

Raphael's Bank incurred to Mrs Jones, when the proceeds of the investments were credited to her account with the bank.

Three features of this difficult decision require comment. First, the Court of **8–27** Appeal's analysis of the trustee in bankruptcy's proprietary position was at least surprising. Millett L.J.'s explicit assumption was that the trustee in bankruptcy automatically became legal owner of every unauthorised substitute asset, as identified in accordance with the common law's rules of tracing. This is unsustainable.[54] Its correctness can be tested by asking what the position might have been as regards the final asset in the chain of substitutions—the chose in action, represented by the credit balance to Mrs Jones's account with Raphael's Bank. Mrs Jones was indisputably the legal owner of this right: such a right is the product of the bank's undertaking to repay its customer, and the undertaking it gives is to *its customer*, and not to anyone else. The trustee in bankruptcy could not have sued in its own name to enforce the bank's debt: it was owed to Mrs Jones. It follows that even if it was right to say that the trustee in bankruptcy had some form of proprietary right to the chose, which in turn afforded it a better right than Mrs Jones to the fruits paid into court, it was not the case that the trustee in bankruptcy had legal title and Mrs Jones had none. Mrs Jones was the legal owner of the chose, and any right the trustee in bankruptcy held must have been some form of secondary right *to* Mrs Jones's right, which was either (1) some form of novel secondary inchoate *legal* title to the chose in action of which Mrs Jones remained legal owner[55]; or (as Millett L.J. denied, but which seems to be the best view in principle) (2) an equitable right, arising under a trust.[56]

Secondly, a question arises as to the basis of the proprietary rights which **8–28** *Trustee of Jones v Jones* (and *Lipkin Gorman*) suggest the law affords to the traceable substitute. On one view, which Lord Millett shares, the generation of these rights has nothing to do with the law of unjust enrichment.[57] It is simply the result of a policy decision of the law of property, concerning the ambit of protection afforded to legal and equitable titles. However, the better view is that at least in cases such as *Trustee of Jones v Jones*, where an unauthorised substitution is made by a stranger who is not an express trustee and who has not otherwise voluntarily assumed a fiduciary position vis-à-vis these assets, these rights—whether legal or (preferably) equitable—arise to reverse the unjust enrichment of the defendant at the expense of the owner, on the ground of his lack of consent.[58]

Thirdly, from the perspective of the law of unjust enrichment, a doubt also **8–29** arises concerning the measure of the claim recognised in *Trustee of Jones v Jones*. If viewed as a personal claim founded on unjust enrichment, the decision looks exceptional to the extent that the measure of the claim was not the value

---

[54] A view convincingly criticised in Fox, *Property Rights in Money*, paras 5.96–5.106. See also the doubts expressed in *Uzinterimpex J.S.C. v Standard Bank plc* [2008] EWCA Civ 819; [2008] 2 Lloyd's Rep. 456 at [34]–[35].

[55] See Fox, *Property Rights in Money*, paras 5.96–5.106.

[56] Cf. *Uzinterimpex* [2008] EWCA Civ 819; [2008] 2 Lloyd's Rep. 456. And see Smith, "Simplifying Claims to Traceable Proceeds".

[57] Lord Millett, "Proprietary Restitution" in S. Degeling and J. Edelman (eds), *Equity in Commercial Law* (Sydney: Lawbook Co, 2005), Ch.12; Lord Millett, "*Jones v Jones*: Property or Unjust Enrichment?" in A. Burrows and Lord Rodger (eds), *Mapping the Law* (Oxford: OUP, 2006), Ch.14.

[58] See paras 8–18—8–19, 8–91—8–93.

received by Mrs Jones—represented by the original money, or the value of the subsequent traceable substitute for the original money at the subsequent time of its receipt. It was a claim for the higher *present* value of the traceable substitute: a claim for the value traceably surviving. It is not clear whether a personal claim in unjust enrichment can be properly made on this basis.[59] Hence the better answer seems to be—as Millett L.J. has insisted—that the remedy the court afforded was not *itself* a personal claim in unjust enrichment. It was simply a remedy which enforced the title which the Court of Appeal held that the trustee in bankruptcy had acquired to Mrs Jones's chose in action against Raphael's Bank (and the proceeds paid into court), as a result of the chain of unauthorised substitutions. The Court of Appeal's decision is difficult primarily because of its premise that the trustee in bankruptcy was legal owner of this asset. If the Court of Appeal had taken the alternative course of saying that the trustee in bankruptcy's entitlement to each unauthorised substitute in Mrs Jones's hands was an *equitable title*, arising under an imposed trust, then the relief afforded might be explained in orthodox terms. Relying on this equitable title, the trustee in bankruptcy might in the ordinary way seek to have this equitable title enforced, by means of a court order confirming the defendant's status as trustee, and ordering the defendant to transfer the asset *in specie* or pay its present monetary value as appropriate.

8-30   **Summary** To sum up, the law would in future be simpler and more coherent if the courts were to accept the following propositions. First, whilst an unauthorised substitution by D may afford C a proprietary right to the unauthorised traceable substitute, the only title that C will acquire is an equitable title. This proposition would involve some re-working of the reasoning in *Lipkin Gorman* and *Trustee of Jones v Jones*; nevertheless, it has the merits of avoiding the conceptual difficulties that are raised by any attempt to explain C's right as a legal right. Secondly, C may acquire such a right, by virtue of the unauthorised substitution, whether he was legal owner of the asset, whose value was used to acquire the new asset without his consent, or merely the equitable owner. Thirdly, although unjust enrichment is not a necessary explanation for the generation of this right where D, who effects the substitution, is an express trustee or other fiduciary, it is the preferable explanation in other cases—including *Trustee of Jones v Jones* itself. And where unjust enrichment is the explanation, the operative ground can readily be understood as C's lack of consent or D's want of authority regarding the substitution.

8-31   This re-conceptualisation of the proprietary rights afforded to unauthorised substitutes would inevitably have knock-on consequences for the courts' explanation of cases—discussed in Part 3—which have imposed a strict personal liability on remoter recipients, who are enriched by receiving from a third party a traceable substitute for an asset of which C was legal owner, without C's consent. The availability of such a claim could no longer be justified, as *Lipkin Gorman* assumes, on the basis that C has legal title to the substitute. There are, however, two answers to this. The first is that C might show that a remoter recipient is enriched at his expense, for the purpose of making a personal claim in unjust enrichment, by proving "but for" causal links between the subtraction

---

[59] See paras 8-69—8-72.

from C and the gain to D. Inquiry into C's title may therefore not be necessary for the success of his claim. The second is that C might in any event show that D has been unjustly enriched at his expense because without C's consent or authority, D has received an asset to which C can assert equitable title. As explained in Part 3 below, the better view is that English courts should in future hold that recipients of misapplied trust assets can owe a strict personal liability in unjust enrichment to trust beneficiaries.

3. THREE-PARTY CASES: CLAIMS BY C

(a) *Introduction*

In practice, most decided cases that are susceptible to explanation in terms of   **8–32** lack of consent or want of authority are three-party cases: where D immediately receives a benefit from X, but this benefit is acquired more remotely at C's expense. This section examines the authorities that fit this pattern, and how C's lack of consent or X's want of authority are viable explanations for the law to afford a remedy against D on the ground of unjust enrichment.

We begin by exploring cases which appear to afford a personal claim to reverse   **8–33** a defendant's enrichment on the ground of C's lack of consent or X's want of authority. We start with the common law authorities, before turning to consider what support there is for a parallel liability in the equity cases. We then consider various situations in which the law gives a proprietary remedy—usually equitable in origin—which can plausibly be understood to be designed to reverse the unjust enrichment of the defendant, on the same grounds.

(b) *Personal Claims*

(i) *The Significance of C Having Title to an Asset in D's Hands*

In most of the cases discussed in this section, D, a remoter recipient, has been   **8–34** held personally liable to C for the value of an asset which he has received from X, where this asset is (1) an asset to which C retained title, or (2) an unauthorised traceable substitute for such an asset, to which the law affords C some form of title. Furthermore, insofar as the courts have offered any explicit justification for C's claim, they have tended to focus on the fact that D has received an asset to which C has title.[60] C's lack of consent, or X's want of authority to affect C's position, is rarely offered as the reason for D's liability.[61] This has led some writers to suggest that, properly understood, these cases do not involve claims in unjust enrichment at all, and must be regarded as awarding restitutionary remedies on some other basis—for example, the "vindication" of C's property rights

---

[60] *Clarke v Shee & Johnson* (1774) 1 Cowp. 197; 98 E.R. 1047; see para.8–34; *Lipkin Gorman* [1991] 2 A.C. 548; see paras 8–22, 8–43.
[61] Cf. *Nelson v Larholt* [1948] 1 Ch. 339 at 342 per Denning J.; *Criterion Properties Plc v Stratford UK Properties LLC* [2004] UKHL 28; [2004] 1 W.L.R. 1846 at [3]–[4] per Lord Nicholls.

to the asset which D received or retained.[62] We do not accept this. In our view, these cases can be explained as involving personal claims in unjust enrichment. This is consistent with the leading decision of *Lipkin Gorman*,[63] where the House of Lords explicitly rationalised the defendant casino's personal liability to the claimant firm as based on the casino's unjust enrichment at the firm's expense.[64]

8–35   Assuming that these cases do involve personal claims in unjust enrichment, what exactly is the significance of C's ability to assert title to the asset which D receives and may retain in his hands? In our view, any title which C might have had to the asset has no more than a contingent relevance to his personal claim in unjust enrichment, and there is no need for C to prove that he had title.[65] The reason why D's enrichment is unjust does not turn on C's having title, but on C's lack of consent to D's enrichment at his expense, and/or D's want of authority to enrich D at C's expense. And although one way for C to prove that D was enriched at his expense is to show that D received an asset to which C had title, it is not the only way, since C can also establish this by proving "but for" causal links between X's actions, on the one hand, and C's loss and D's gain, on the other.[66]

8–36   Consider *Lipkin Gorman*,[67] where Cass, a fraudulent partner of a firm of solicitors, took cash from the firm's client account and gambled it away at the defendant casino. The House of Lords' decision that the casino was liable for the value of the cash was explicitly stated to rest on the firm's ability to assert some form of legal title to the cash which the casino received. If, as their Lordships assumed, the firm did have title to the cash, then this title provided one route to concluding that the casino was enriched at the firm's expense when the cash was paid to the casino. Nevertheless, this was not essential to the firm's claim, since it could also have proved that Cass would not have paid the cash to the casino but for his unauthorised withdrawals from the firm's account, i.e. it could have proved "but for" causal links.[68] Likewise, the injustice of the casino's enrichment at the firm's expense could have been established by showing that the firm did not consent to or authorise Cass's withdrawal of the cash from the client account, and his transfer of the cash to the casino.

---

[62] e.g. R. Grantham and C. Rickett, "Property and Unjust Enrichment: Categorical Truths or Unnecessary Complexity" [1997] N.Z.L. Rev. 668 especially 684–685; Grantham and Rickett, *Enrichment and Restitution in New Zealand*, Ch.12; Virgo, *The Principles of the Law of Restitution*, pp.11–17.

[63] *Lipkin Gorman* [1991] 2 A.C. 548.

[64] *Lipkin Gorman* [1991] 2 A.C. 548 at 558 per Lord Bridge, at 559, 560, 564 and 566 per Lord Templeman, and at 572, 577 and 578 per Lord Goff.

[65] Nor is it fatal to the claimant's claim that the defendant has been unjustly enriched at his expense by the asset's value, that the claimant retains title to the asset or its traceable proceeds still in the defendant's hands: Burrows, *The Law of Restitution*, pp.195 and following, R. Stevens, "Three Enrichment Issues" in Burrows and Rodger, *Mapping the Law*, pp.62 and following, which we find more persuasive than the contrary position taken in Swadling, "Ignorance and Unjust Enrichment: The Problem of Title".

[66] See para.6–12 and following.

[67] *Lipkin Gorman* [1991] 2 A.C. 548. See too the discussion at para.8–21 and following.

[68] See too P. Birks, "The Burden on the Bank" in F.D. Rose (ed.), *Restitution and Banking Law* (Oxford: Mansfield Press, 1998), pp.230 and following; P. Birks, "'At the Expense of the Claimant': Direct and Indirect Enrichment in English Law" in D. Johnston and R. Zimmerman (eds), *Unjustified Enrichment: Key Issues in Comparative Perspective* (Cambridge: CUP, 2002), p.519.

(ii) *Personal Claims at Common Law for Value Remotely Received*

There are many common law cases where D has immediately received a benefit **8–37**
from X, but more remotely received the benefit from C, and C has been given a
personal claim against D which can be explained as responding to C's lack of
consent or X's want of authority. Consistently with the general character of
personal claims in unjust enrichment, D's prima facie liability is strict—it does
not depend on C's proving fault on D's part—and is measured by the value
received.

Historically, all or almost all cases of this type have involved D's receiving a **8–38**
tangible money asset—coins or notes—to which C had legal title. At one time,
the protection for C's title to such tangible money assets lay primarily in the law
of tort.[69] However, at least by the late 18th century, it came to be accepted that
C might alternatively bring a restitutionary claim against a remoter recipient of
his money, without relying on an allegation of a wrong by D, and without proving
fault on D's part, via an action for money had and received.[70] This action was
afforded where C had previously been dispossessed of the money without his
consent—as where X had stolen C's money and then handed it to D,[71] or where
X found money which C had lost and then handed it to D.[72] But it was equally
available where X had possession of C's money as bailee with C's consent,[73] or
where X was a servant of C with custody of C's money with C's consent,[74] and
where X subsequently handed it to D without C's authority.

So, for example, in *Clarke v Shee & Johnson*,[75] the claimant's clerk had **8–39**
received cash and negotiable notes from the claimant's customers, and paid some
of the cash and notes to the defendant, in exchange for tickets in an illegal lottery.
On the assumption that the claimant was legal owner of the cash and notes
received by the defendant from the clerk, and that the defendant could not invoke
the plea of bona fide purchase, the court held that the claimant could bring a
personal claim for the sum received. In *Moffatt v Kazana*,[76] the defendant had
purchased a bungalow from the claimant, and a workman discovered a tin
containing a large number of bank notes which the claimant had concealed in the
property some years later and had then forgotten about. The workman handed the
tin to the police, who thereafter returned it to the defendant, who in turn paid the
bank notes into his bank account in the honest belief that he was owner. In
proceedings subsequently brought by the claimant's executors, Wrangham J.
gave judgment for the sum of cash which the defendant had received, on being
satisfied that title to the tin and its contents had not passed to the defendant with

---

[69] *Clarke v Shee* (1774) 1 Cowp. 197; 98 E.R. 1041.
[70] For a useful account of the development of the law, see D. Fox, "Legal Title as a Ground of
Restitutionary Liability" [2000] R.L.R. 465.
[71] Cf. *Clarke v Shee* (1774) 1 Cowp. 197; 98 E.R. 1041.
[72] As in e.g. *Moffatt v Kazana* [1969] 2 Q.B. 152.
[73] As in e.g. *Calland v Loyd* (1841) 6 M. & W. 26; 151 E.R. 307.
[74] As in e.g. *Clarke v Shee* (1774) 1 Cowp. 197; 98 E.R. 1041; *Corking v Jarrard* (1897) 1 Camp.
37; 170 E.R. 867.
[75] *Clarke v Shee & Johnson* (1774) 1 Cowp. 197; 98 E.R. 1041. Similarly, *Corking v Jarrard* (1897)
1 Camp. 37; 170 E.R. 867 (servant entrusted with his employer's money pays the money to the
defendant in connection with an illegal lottery). See further *Lipkin Gorman* [1991] 2 A.C. 548 at 572
per Lord Goff, where *Clarke v Shee* was relied upon to support the relief awarded.
[76] *Moffatt v Kazana* [1969] 2 Q.B. 152.

the conveyance of the bungalow. Again, in *Calland v Loyd*,[77] the claimant had handed £73 to his wife to take care of. Without the claimant's knowledge, his wife took a £50 note—part of the £73—and paid it to the defendant bank, for an account in the name of her infant son. When the claimant subsequently discovered the deposit of the £50 note, the claimant successfully brought an action against the defendant bank, to recover the sum of money thus deposited, which it could not claim to have received as a bona fide purchaser.[78]

8–40   In these cases, where C retained his original legal title to the cash received by D from X, some authors have argued that D's liability has nothing to do with the law of unjust enrichment; that C's subsisting title may prevent the conclusion that D is "enriched" at C's expense; and that D's liability for the value received is a restitutionary liability for a wrong (usually, the tort of conversion), or is awarded to vindicate C's legal title.[79] In our view, C's subsisting title does not prevent a finding that D is unjustly enriched at C's expense.[80] In any event, these cases are very much the exception. In parallel cases today, D will not receive any money asset that C ever previously owned, and to which C can have retained his original legal title. Most monetary wealth is represented by credit balances to accounts held with financial institutions, and the majority of monetary transactions are conducted via the medium of inter-account transfers. In these cases, this simple title-based objection is of comparatively limited significance.

8–41   There are other cases which indicate that a similar personal claim in unjust enrichment will lie against a recipient, where without C's consent or other lawful authority, X disposes of some non-money asset of which C was legal owner, and the money proceeds of this disposition are subsequently traceably received by D.[81] An early example is *Kitchen v Campbell*,[82] where a sheriff seized and sold a judgment debtor's goods in execution of a judgment debt, and paid the money proceeds of the execution to the judgment creditor, without notice of a prior act of bankruptcy committed by the debtor. The court assumed that the assignees in bankruptcy, in whom property in the debtor's goods was deemed to be vested from the time of the act of bankruptcy, could bring a common law claim for money had and received against the creditor for the sum received.[83] To similar

---

[77] *Calland v Loyd* (1840) 6 M. & W. 26; 151 E.R. 307.
[78] Cf. *Reid v Rigby & Co* [1894] 2 Q.B. 40, where, without authority, D's manager borrowed £20 from C via fraudulent misrepresentations, for the purpose of replacing funds that he had previously stolen, and these moneys were paid into D's account and later used by the manager to pay D's employees.
[79] e.g. Swadling, "Ignorance and Unjust Enrichment: The Problem of Title"; Grantham and Rickett, *Enrichment and Restitution in New Zealand*, Ch.12. See paras 8–34—8–36.
[80] See para.8–35, fn.65.
[81] e.g. *Kitchen v Campbell* (1772) 3 Wils. K.B. 304; 95 E.R. 1069; *Allanson v Atkinson* (1813) 1 M. & S. 583; 105 E.R. 218; *Marsh v Keating* (1834) 1 Bing. N.C. 198; 131 E.R. 1094. See too *Abbotts v Barry* (1820) 2 Brod. & B. 369; 129 E.R. 1009, where X acquired goods from C by fraud, to which D was party, sold them, and in discharge of a debt of X to D, endorsed to D the bill of exchange given by the buyer in payment.
[82] *Kitchen v Campbell* (1772) 3 Wils. K.B. 304; 95 E.R. 1069.
[83] *Kitchen v Campbell* (1772) at 3 Wils. K.B. 304 at 307–308; 95 E.R. 1069 at 1070–1071. On the facts, the claim failed because of an issue estoppel arising as a result of prior proceedings brought for trover against the sheriff and the creditor, which were taken to have determined that the assignee in bankruptcy had no title to the goods. But in *Allanson v Atkinson* (1813) 1 M. & S. 583; 105 E.R. 218, a similar claim succeeded against a creditor, where the bankrupt debtor's goods had been pledged for the purpose of securing his release from custody, the money proceeds were received by the sheriff, and an equivalent sum was paid by the sheriff to the creditor.

effect is *Marsh v Keating*,[84] where a partner of a banking firm fraudulently sold Bank of England stock of which the claimant was legal owner, pursuant to a forged power of attorney, and the proceeds of the sale were paid into a bank account in the firm's name, before being dissipated by the fraudulent partner. The House of Lords held that the claimant could elect to forgo any rights she might have in the stock sold, and bring a claim for money had and received against the other partners, who were unaware of the frauds, for the money proceeds which they had thereby received.

The same possibility is demonstrated by other cases, where C's bank account **8–42** has been drawn on by a third party without C's authority, and D is shown to have received the money proceeds, whether in the form of cash or a credit to his own bank account.[85] If C cannot have his account re-credited, then the cases show that he may bring a common law claim for the value which D thereby receives at C's expense. For example, in the leading case of *Lipkin Gorman*,[86] Cass, a partner of the claimant firm of solicitors and signatory on the firm's client account, fraudulently withdrew cash without authority, which he then spent gambling at the defendant casino. Relying on a number of leading common law authorities, the House of Lords held that the casino, which was unable to invoke the defence of bona fide purchase, was unjustly enriched at the expense of the claimant firm when (however innocently) it had received the cash from Cass, which represented the traceable proceeds of the firm's credit balance. The casino was prima facie liable for the sum received, subject to the defence of change of position.

A similar result might have followed in *Agip (Africa) Ltd v Jackson*,[87] where **8–43** a fraudulent employee of the claimant Tunisian company was able, via forged payment instructions, to procure a funds transfer from the claimant's Tunisian bank account, to an account held by another company with a UK bank; from there, the funds were transferred to accounts held by the defendant firm of accountants, before being dissipated by transfers to third parties. The claimant company, whose account had been debited for the payment by its bank and was never re-credited, brought proceedings against the defendant accountants on various bases, one of which was a common law personal claim for money had and received. Millett J., in a judgment affirmed by the Court of Appeal, explained that liability for money had and received was strict, and complete at the time of the defendants' receipt of the money. The ground for the claim, reflecting the pleadings, was said to be mistake—the claimant's bank had honoured the payment instructions under a mistake that they were duly authorised, and the claimant could rely on this mistake of the bank as its agent. However, a better description is that the claimant did not consent to or authorise the transfer from its account; it was, in substance, a simple case of theft. The claim failed principally on the doubtful basis that the common law's tracing rules did not allow the funds received by the defendant firm to be identified with the debiting

---

[84] *Marsh v Keating* (1834) 1 Bing. N.C. 198; 131 E.R. 1094.
[85] e.g. *Nelson v Larholt* [1948] 1 K.B. 339 (Denning J.); *Agip (Africa) Ltd v Jackson* [1990] Ch. 265; [1991] Ch. 547 (CA); *Lipkin Gorman* [1991] 2 A.C. 548.
[86] *Lipkin Gorman* [1991] 2 A.C. 548; see paras 8–22 and following and 8–36.
[87] *Agip (Africa) Ltd v Jackson* [1990] Ch. 265; [1991] Ch. 547 (CA).

from the claimant's account, because of intermediate mixing in inter-bank clearing and settlement systems.[88]

8-44   In none of these cases is C's lack of consent or X's want of authority expressly identified as the ground for recovery. Indeed, to the extent that any rationalisation appears from leading cases, the language suggests that the reason for the claim is that the claimant had title to the asset D received. Nevertheless, the courts' title-based reasoning is not inconsistent with an explanation based upon C's lack of consent or X's want of authority, and this was precisely the language used by Denning J. in *Nelson v Larholt*.[89] There an executor fraudulently drew cheques on the estate's account in favour of a turf accountant, who received the proceeds into his own account. In proceedings brought by the beneficiaries and a co-executor, Denning J. boldly proposed "one uniform principle", existing to protect a person's rights to money, in all of its various forms, tangible or intangible, according to which the legal or beneficial owner of money, paid away "without his authority", could recover the amount from any person into whose hands the money could be traced unless and until it was received by a person in good faith, for value and without notice of the "want of authority".[90] Denning J.'s suggestion was novel, to the extent that it suggests that a recipient of misapplied trust funds might be strictly liable to the trust beneficiary.[91] However, for present purposes, the significance of the case is that the recipient's strict restitutionary liability, which Denning J. thought should be recognised, was grounded on the intermediate party's "want of authority".

8-45   To this case can now be added some important dicta of Lord Nicholls in *Criterion Properties Plc v Stratford UK Properties Ltd*.[92] This case concerned the question whether a company was bound by a poison pill agreement which its directors had entered on its behalf with a third party. The House of Lords held that insufficient information was available to decide this question, and that until it was decided it could not be determined whether the company was entitled to any remedy in unjust enrichment against a recipient of benefits paid under the agreement. Nevertheless, Lord Nicholls made some comments on this issue in an important passage where he stated that a recipient of assets from a company paid in an unauthorised transaction owes a strict personal liability in unjust enrichment, on the ground of "want of authority". The recipient's liability is not limited—as assumed by some earlier cases—to a liability for "knowing receipt". To quote from his Lordship's speech[93]:

> "If a company (A) enters into an agreement with B under which B acquires benefits from A, A's ability to recover these benefits from B depends essentially on whether the

---

[88] This was followed in *Bank Tejarat v Hong Kong & Shanghai Banking Corp (CI) Ltd* [1995] 1 Lloyd's Rep. 239 and *Bank of America v Arnell* [1999] Lloyd's Rep. Bank. 399. However, these cases all rest on the false premises that tracing is needed in cases of interbank transfer, and that tracing through mixtures in bank accounts is impossible at common law. For critical comment, see Smith, *The Law of Tracing*, pp.249–261; and see too paras 7–08—7–10.

[89] *Nelson v Larholt* [1948] 1 K.B. 339.

[90] *Nelson v Larholt* [1948] 1 K.B. 339 at 342.

[91] See paras 8–50 and following, and 8–58 and following.

[92] *Criterion Properties Plc v Stratford UK Properties Ltd* [2004] UKHL 28; [2004] 1 W.L.R. 1846.

[93] *Criterion* [2004] UKHL 28; [2004] 1 W.L.R. 1846 at [4]; see also at [3].

agreement is binding on A. If the directors of A were acting for an improper purpose when they entered into the agreement, A's ability to have the agreement set aside depends upon the application of familiar principles of agency and company law. If, applying these principles, the agreement is found to be valid and is therefore not set aside, questions of 'knowing receipt' by B do not arise. So far as B is concerned there can be no question of A's assets having been misapplied. B acquired the assets from A, the legal and beneficial owner of the assets, under a valid agreement made between him and A. If, however, the agreement is set aside, B will be accountable for any benefits he may have received from A under the agreement. A will have a proprietary claim, if B still has the assets. Additionally, and irrespective of whether B still has the assets in question, A will have a personal claim against B for unjust enrichment, subject always to a defence of change of position. B's personal accountability will not be dependent upon proof of fault or 'unconscionable' conduct on his part. B's accountability, in this regard, will be 'strict'."

Looking more generally, there are other cases where D appears to have been **8-46** more remotely enriched at C's expense, without C's consent, but without receiving any asset which belonged to C or any traceable substiute for C's asset. In these cases, any personal claim C might have to recover the value of D's benefit obviously cannot be explained as vindicating any title C which might retain or be afforded to any asset which D receives or retains. However, it can be explained as a claim in unjust enrichment, based on either C's lack of consent or X's want of authority.

So, for example, in a line of authority starting in the late 17th century,[94] the **8-47** common law courts held that if D had usurped an office to which C was entitled, and received from X sums to which C was entitled as of right as the lawful office-holder,[95] C could sue D for the amounts he received[96] from X in an action for money had and received. A similar conclusion has been reached in cases where D received rents from X, to which C was legally entitled[97]; and where D, a self-appointed administrator or executor of a deceased, has been held accountable to C, the incoming and duly appointed personal representative, for what he received as money or assets due or belonging to the deceased.[98] The best explanation of these cases is that D was enriched at C's expense, notwithstanding that the money paid to D came from X, because the payment by X to D was effective to discharge X's liability to pay C.[99] When it is asked what ground for restitution

---

[94] *Arris v Stukely* (1677) 2 Mod. 260; 86 E.R. 1060; *Howard v Wood* (1688) 2 Show. K.B. 21; 89 E.R. 767; *King v Alston* (1848) 12 Q.B. 971; 116 E.R. 1134.

[95] Cf. *Lawlor v Alton* (1873) I.R. 8 C.L. 160 (no claim for a salary payable in respect of work which C did not perform); *Boyter v Dodsworth* (1796) 6 T.R. 681; 101 E.R. 770 (no claim for gratuities received by D usurper).

[96] *King* (1848) 12 Q.B. 971; 116 E.R. 1134 (claim limited to fees received; no claim to amounts that were payable but not collected by D).

[97] *Official Custodian for Charities v Mackey (No.2)* [1985] 1 W.L.R. 1308 at 1314–1315 per Nourse J.; see previously, *Tottenham v Bedingfield* (1572) 3 Leo. 24; 74 E.R. 517; *Arris* (1677) 2 Mod. 260 at 262; 86 E.R. 1060 at 1063; *Lyell v Kennedy* (1889) 14 App. Cas. 437. See also *Asher v Wallis* (1707) 11 Mod. 146; 88 E.R. 956.

[98] *Jacob v Allen* (1703) 1 Salk. 27; 91 E.R. 26; *Yardley v Arnold* (1842) Car. & M. 434; 174 E.R. 577.

[99] See paras 6–56—6–57.

can support this claim, the only satisfactory answer is that C did not consent to D's enrichment.[100]

8–48   A second example is where X procures a payment to D's creditor, via funds obtained from C without his consent, in circumstances which are effective to discharge D's debt. In principle, C should be able to bring a personal claim in unjust enrichment against D, for the value of the debt discharged, on the basis that C did not consent to this enrichment at his expense.[101] A personal claim of this sort would be a simple parallel of the relief afforded in a long line of equitable authorities, described below, which hold that where C's moneys are used without C's consent to pay D's secured creditor, C is entitled to the equitable remedy of subrogation to the secured creditor's extinguished rights, for the purpose of reversing the unjust enrichment that would otherwise accrue to D and other parties, as a result of the discharge of D's debt.[102]

8–49   A third example might be found in the early case of *Foster v Stewart*,[103] where the claimant successfully sued the defendant for the value of services rendered by a ship's apprentice, whom the defendant had persuaded to work onboard his ship after he had deserted the claimant's service. Although the court recognised that the claim might have been brought for what was then recognised as the tort of seduction, it also considered that the claimant might alternatively "waive" the tort and bring a claim against the defendant for the value of the apprentice's services. This might, again, be explained as a personal claim in unjust enrichment, where the defendant was enriched by the value of the apprentice's services, at the expense of the claimant, who was contractually entitled to them, without the claimant's consent.

(iii) *Personal Claims in Equity for Value Remotely Received*

8–50   Whatever may be the position at common law, it is far more controversial whether equity imposes a parallel liability—and in particular, whether equity holds a recipient of misapplied trust assets subject to a strict personal liability in unjust enrichment on the ground of want of authority. The orthodox view is that it does not, and there are many who will defend this orthodox view as correct in principle. However, there are also several lines of authority which—in varying degrees—cast doubt on this orthodox view. And although the question is finely balanced, we consider that in principle, there are good reasons for the courts to impose a strict personal liability on the recipients of misapplied trust assets.

8–51   **The Re Diplock personal claim**   A small but important group of cases suggests that the courts are not opposed to imposing strict personal liability on the recipients of misapplied assets in which claimants have an equitable interest.

---

[100] See too Burrows, *The Law of Restitution* p.431 (explaining this in terms of the claimant's "ignorance"); Virgo, *The Principles of the Law of Restitution*, pp.133–134 (ditto).

[101] Cf. *Reid v Rigby & Co* [1894] 2 Q.B. 40 (where moneys fraudulently borrowed by D's manager from C, to replace funds that he had previously stolen, were paid to D's account and then withdrawn by the manager to pay D's workmen).

[102] e.g. *Primlake Ltd (In Liquidation) v Matthews Associates* [2006] EWHC 1227 (Ch); [2007] 1 B.C.L.C. 666 at [337]–[340]; see para.8–75 and following.

[103] *Foster v Stewart* (1814) 3 M. & S. 191; 105 E.R. 582. And see to *Lightly v Cluston* (1808) 1 Taunt. 112; 127 E.R. 774.

These concern what has become known as the "*Re Diplock* personal claim".[104] They show that where moneys forming part of a deceased's estate are distributed by personal representatives to someone who is not entitled to them, then the recipient of these moneys comes under a strict restitutionary liability, enforceable at the suit of the persons to whom they should have been paid, whether as creditors of the deceased, will beneficiaries or next-of-kin entitled under the rules of intestate succession.

In *Re Diplock*,[105] executors had distributed money representing the residue of   **8–52** the deceased's estate to a number of charities, pursuant to the provision of a will which was later held to be invalid.[106] The next-of-kin, to whom the moneys should accordingly have been distributed, brought a combination of personal and proprietary claims against the recipient charities. The Court of Appeal held that the charities did not have knowledge or notice that the moneys were improperly paid sufficient to render them personally liable to account as constructive trustees[107]—or in modern terminology, to fix them with an equitable personal liability for knowing receipt.[108] Nevertheless, the Court of Appeal went on to hold, drawing on a line of authority going back to the late 17th century dealing with the administration of estates,[109] that the next-of-kin had a direct claim in equity against the recipient charities, rendering them personally liable to repay the capital amount of the moneys they had received (though not interest), on the basis of their having received moneys to which they were not entitled, though subject to the proviso that the next-of-kin should have first exhausted their claims against the executors. The House of Lords unanimously affirmed this decision on appeal.[110]

Neither the Court of Appeal nor the House of Lords identified this personal   **8–53** liability as a liability in unjust enrichment. Nevertheless, looking back at this line of authority through the lens of the modern law, there are good grounds for thinking that it can be analysed in such terms. As the court described it, the recipient's liability was a strict personal liability, generated immediately on his receipt,[111] for the sum he had received. It arose simply by virtue of his having received a share of the deceased's estate to which he was not entitled,[112] whether

---

[104] The leading authority is *Re Diplock* [1948] Ch. 465 (CA); affirmed [1951] A.C. 251, relying on a line of equitable authority stretching back to the 17th century: *Noel v Robinson* (1682) 1 Vern. 90; 23 E.R. 334; *Newman v Barton* (1690) 2 Vern. 205; 23 E.R. 733; *Anon.* (1718) 1 P. Wms. 495; 24 E.R. 487; *Orr v Kaines* (1750) 2 Ves. Sen. 194; 28 E.R. 125; *Walcott v Hall* (1788) 2 Bro. C.C. 305; 29 E.R. 167; *Gillespie v Alexander* (1827) 3 Russ. 130; 38 E.R. 525; *Greig v Somerville* (1830) 1 Russ. & My. 338; 39 E.R. 131; *David v Frowd* (1833) 1 My. & K. 200; 39 E.R. 657; *Sawyer v Birchmore* (1836) 1 Keen. 391; 48 E.R. 357; *Thomas v Griffith* (1860) 2 Giff. 504; 66 E.R. 211; *Fenwicke v Clarke* (1862) 4 De G. F. & J. 240; 45 E.R. 1176; *Peterson v Peterson* (1866) L.R. 3 Eq. 111; *Mohan v Broughton* [1900] P. 56; *Re Rivers* [1920] 1 Ch. 320. The history is surveyed in S.J. Whittaker, "An Historical Perspective to the 'Special Equitable Action' in *Re Diplock*" (1983) 4 J.L.H. 3. A modern view is given in T. Akkouh and S. Worthington, "*Re Diplock* (1948)" in C. Mitchell and P. Mitchell (eds.), *Landmark Cases in the Law of Restitution* (Oxford: Hart, 2006), Ch.11.
[105] *Re Diplock* [1948] Ch. 465 (CA); affirmed [1951] A.C. 231.
[106] *Chichester Diocesan Fund and Board of Finance (Inc) v Simpson* [1944] A.C. 341.
[107] *Re Diplock* [1948] Ch. 465 (CA) at 477–479.
[108] See paras 8–123—8–130.
[109] See the cases cited in fn.104.
[110] *Re Diplock* [1951] A.C. 251 at 265.
[111] *Re Diplock* [1948] Ch. 465 (CA) at 504–505 per Lord Greene M.R.
[112] *Re Diplock* [1948] Ch. 465 at 503 per Lord Greene M.R.

or not he had notice that the assets might have been improperly distributed,[113] and regardless of whether he was a complete stranger without any entitlement to share in the deceased's estate or a person who had received more than his proper entitlement.[114] The liability was owed to those to whom the sums should have been paid—whether as creditors, or as beneficiaries under the will, or as next-of-kin.[115] So described, it might seem that—in all but name—the claim is an example of a strict liability personal claim in unjust enrichment, of equitable origin, based upon the personal representatives' want of authority.[116]

8-54   Some features of the *Re Diplock* claim are not easy to square with this rationalisation. First, it was held by Lord Simonds on appeal in the case that the change of position defence is not available to the recipient of money paid by personal representatives in an unauthorised transaction.[117] In our view this is regrettable for reasons that we discuss in Ch.27.[118] Secondly, it was said by Lord Greene M.R. that the *Re Diplock* claim does not bear interest.[119] No explanation was given for this, and there is no reason today why the *Re Diplock* claim should not bear interest in the same way as any other personal restitutionary claim. Thirdly, it was said that the recipient's liability is subject to the condition that the claimant must first exhaust his remedies against the personal representatives who were responsible for the improper distribution[120]; and is limited to such amounts

---

[113] *Re Diplock* [1948] Ch. 465 at 503 per Lord Greene M.R.
[114] *Re Diplock* [1948] Ch. 465 at 502–503 per Lord Greene M.R. See also [1951] A.C. 251 at 269 per Lord Simmonds.
[115] *Re Diplock* [1948] Ch. 465 (CA) at 502 per Lord Greene M.R., finding that the claim was available "equally" to an "unpaid or underpaid creditor, legatee, or next-of-kin". See e.g. *Gillespie v Alexander* (1827) 3 Russ. 130; 38 E.R. 525 (creditor); *Re Rivers* [1920] 1 Ch. 320 (legatee); *David v Frowd* (1833) 1 My. & K. 200; 39 E.R. 657 (next-of-kin). Similarly [1951] A.C. 251 at 266, 268 per Lord Simmonds.
[116] It might be said that the personal representatives' "want of authority" looks like a difficult explanation, to the extent that the cases show that a *Re Diplock* claim can be brought even though—and indeed, because—no claim is available against the personal representative responsible for the misapplication, because the distribution has occurred pursuant to a court order. However, the answer to this is that the court's order affords the personal representative an immunity from *personal* liability for the improper distribution—as recognised in e.g. *David v Frowd* (1833) 1 My. & K. 200; 39 E.R. 657; *Thomas v Griffith* (1860) 2 Giff. 504; 66 E.R. 211; *Re Diplock* [1948] Ch. 465 (CA) at 503 per Lord Greene M.R. It does not render the distribution a "proper" distribution for all purposes, so as to afford a third party recipient a corresponding immunity from liability. The same result follows where, say, a trustee is granted relief under the Trustee Act 1925 s.61, for a misapplication of trust assets in breach of trust; this will afford the trustee a personal immunity, but it does not render the trustee's act "authorised" for the purpose of affecting the rights of—and claims that may be brought against—third party recipients.
[117] *Re Diplock* [1951] A.C. 251 at 276.
[118] See para.27-46.
[119] *Re Diplock* [1948] Ch. 465 at 506–507; relying on *Gittins v Steele* (1818) 1 Swans. 199; 36 E.R. 356. *Gittins* was distinguished in *Re West* [1909] 2 Ch. 180 (specific legacy of shares; income payable), and this aspect of *Re Diplock* was discussed critically in *Westdeutsche* [1996] A.C. 669 at 694 per Lord Goff, 728–730 per Lord Woolf; and in *Sempra Metals Ltd v IRC* [2007] UKHL 34; [2008] 1 A.C. 561 at [176] per Lord Walker, where it was said to be an "anomaly" that a personal restitutionary claim to recover a mistakenly paid legacy appears not to have carried interest when a proprietary claim might.
[120] *Re Diplock* [1948] Ch. 465 at 503–504 per Lord Greene M.R.; relying on *Orr v Kaines* (1750) 2 Ves. Sen. 194; 28 E.R. 125, whilst acknowledging it to be the only direct authority; assumed in *Butler v Broadhead* [1975] Ch. 97 at 107–108; applied in *Re J. Leslie Engineers Co Ltd (In Liquidation)* [1976] 1 W.L.R. 292 at 299 300.

as cannot be recovered from the personal representatives.[121] This requirement lacks any obvious parallel in the law of unjust enrichment, and also seems deeply problematic.[122]

In other cases where a breach of duty by X results in D's being unjustly **8–55** enriched at C's expense, the courts afford C a free choice of whether to seek compensation from X or restitution from D.[123] Futhermore, when it comes to deciding how the burden of their common liability should be re-distributed between X and D in proceedings for contribution or reimbursement, many cases hold that it should fall on D who made the gain, rather than X who merely committed a breach of duty, however dishonestly.[124] Translated to the *Re Diplock* cases, this would mean that the claimant should have a free choice between suing the personal representative and the recipient, and that as between the personal representative who is guilty of the misapplication and the recipient who gained by the improper distribution, the burden of liability should fall on the recipient. However, the limitation insisted on in *Re Diplock* is to opposite effect: the personal representative must be sued first, and the recipient who gains bears only the residual burden. Once the *Re Diplock* claim is situated within the general law of unjust enrichment, this looks unjustified, since it results in an improper distribution of the burden of liability, and should be discarded.

Lionel Smith at one time sought to defend the exhaustion of remedies require- **8–56** ment as a necessary step in establishing that the recipient's enrichment was "at the expense of the claimant".[125] His essential premise was that in a *Re Diplock* case, where personal representatives pay the wrong people, they remain liable to pay those truly entitled. On this assumption, the latter suffer no immediate loss as a result of the improper distribution, and the recipient is only enriched at their expense if and to the extent that they are unable to recover from the personal representatives. We are not convinced by this. Smith's argument involves some controversial premises about what it means to say that an enrichment is "at the claimant's expense".[126] In any event, even if it cannot be said that claimants

---

[121] *Re Diplock* [1948] Ch. 465 at 503–504.

[122] Cf. Lord Nicholls, "Knowing Receipt: The Need for a New Landmark" in W.R. Cornish et al. (eds), *Restitution: Past, Present and Future* (Oxford: Hart, 1998), p.241, recommending that the requirement should be abolished.

[123] This is implicit in the cases cited in fn.124 below.

[124] See e.g. *K. v P.* [1993] Ch. 140 at 149; *Dubai Aluminium Co Ltd v Salaam* [2002] UKHL 48; [2003] 2 A.C. 366; *Niru Battery Manufacturing Co v Milestone Trading Ltd (No.2)* [2004] EWCA Civ 487; [2004] 2 All E.R. (Comm.) 289; *Cressman v Coys of Kensington (Sales) Ltd* [2004] EWCA Civ 47; [2004] 1 W.L.R. 2774 at [48].

[125] See L.D. Smith, "Three-Party Restitution—A Critique of Birks's Theory of Interceptive Subtraction" (1991) 11 O.J.L.S. 481 esp. 487 and following. Smith has since taken a different line, arguing that his original explanation proves to much: Smith, "Unjust Enrichment, Property and the Structure of Trusts", pp.437 and following. He now explains the *Re Diplock* claim as a sui generis policy-based claim, justified by the policy of vindicating the distribution rules of the regime of testate or intestate succession; and on this view, the cause of action against the recipient is primarily vested in the personal representative, but the next-of-kin, etc. are afforded derivative standing to pursue the recipient, on proof that a claim against the personal representative is insufficient. This is a surprising rationalisation for the exhaustion of remedies requirement, given that the founding premise of the decision in *Re Diplock* was that the personal representatives had no cause of action against the recipients (as a result of the bar which then existed to recovery for mistake of law), and that the *Re Diplock* claim was understood to be a direct claim, enforceable by the next-of-kin, etc in their own right.

[126] See for general discussion of this component, Chs 6 and 7 above.

invoking the *Re Diplock* claim individually have any right to the assets forming the deceased's estate, the personal representatives do hold the assets in question subject to fiduciary duties, and their acts do deplete the pool of assets available for distribution to the claimants. So even if the personal representatives come under a personal liability to restore the misapplied funds, it can still be said that there has been a "subtraction" from the claimants which is sufficient to justify their having standing to sue the recipient for repayment of the money to the personal representatives so that it can be properly distributed.

8–57 This last point has a general significance for three-party cases where C brings a claim against D in respect of assets transferred by X in an unauthorised transaction. In many older cases, the *Re Diplock* claim took a simple form, involving an individual claimant seeking an order that the recipient pay him the sums which he had received. However, *Re Diplock* itself shows that the courts may be prepared to accept that claims can be brought via a "representative" form of standing, justifying a different remedy. The next-of-kin bringing the proceedings, who formed a sub-set of the larger group, were in substance, if not technically, suing in a representative capacity. The order they sought against the recipient charities was not an order for payment to them individually, but an order that they repay the sums to the judicial trustee, who would thereafter have responsibility for the proper distribution of the proceeds amongst the next-of-kin. Although this seems to have been a novel way of proceeding, it was not suggested that it was incorrect, and that the only order that could be sought and made would be an order to pay the particular claimants the amount to which they were individually entitled.[127] This seems correct. It parallels the treatment of claims by beneficiaries against trustees or third parties, where trust assets are misapplied. More often than not, the beneficiary will be proceeding in a representative or quasi-representative capacity for a remedial order that requires the trustee or third party to restore the lost assets or value to the trust fund, so that it can be duly administered for the benefit of all beneficiaries.

8–58 **Further authority for a strict personal restitutionary liability** Authoritative support for the imposition of strict restitutionary liability, other than the *Re Diplock* liability, is hard to find. Indeed, the dominant assumption is that, outside of the *Re Diplock* line of cases, the only personal liability that a recipient of misapplied assets can incur is a fault-based equitable liability for "knowing receipt"—at least in the sphere of misapplied trust assets. On examination, however, there are some important lines of authority and analogies that can be drawn which at least raise doubts about the status of this historic orthodoxy.

8–59 First, there are numerous cases where X owes fiduciary duties in respect of assets that are legally owned by C, where X disposes of these assets to D in an unauthorised transaction, and where D has been subjected to a strict personal liability.[128] This is a perfectly routine situation, exemplified by the unauthorised disposal of corporate assets by a director. Over the last few decades, a clear

---

[127] See *Re Diplock* [1948] Ch. 465 (CA) at 506 per Lord Greene M.R.; see too [1951] A.C. 231 at 277 per Lord Simmonds.
[128] e.g. *Lipkin Gorman* [1991] 2 A.C. 548 (partner); *Agip* [1990] Ch. 265; [1991] Ch. 547 (CA) (company employee); *Primlake* [2006] EWHC 1227 (Ch); [2007] 1 B.C.L.C. 666 (company director).

appreciation of the full range of remedies available to a company in this situation may have been obscured by an assumption that the recipient's only personal liability is a fault-based liability for "knowing receipt".[129] However, this is a misconception. If an agent acting for a company misapplies assets of which the company is legal owner, then the recipient will owe a strict personal liability to the company, on a ground that can be understood as "want of authority". This should be seen as an uncontroversial example of the strict liability recognised in *Lipkin Gorman*,[130] and this was also the essential thrust of the important dicta of Lord Nicholls in *Criterion*,[131] that have already been quoted.[132]

Secondly, if a trustee transfers trust assets to a third party under a mistake, then **8–60** it is uncontroversial[133] that the *trustee* could bring a simple common law personal claim in unjust enrichment, based on this mistake, in which the recipient's liability would be strict.[134] Historically, the availability of this sort of action was restricted because of the common law's starting-point that a claim could only be based on a mistake of fact, and not on a mistake of law—thereby potentially excluding those cases where a trustee makes a mistake as to the extent of his authority.[135] However, now that the mistake of law bar has been abrogated,[136] there is no obstacle to a trustee bringing a claim of this type where he transfers trust assets to a third party under such a mistake. Of course, this is not a cause of action vested in the trust's beneficiaries (even if it is a cause of action which the trustee might, in accordance with his duties to get in and recover the trust assets, be required to pursue for their benefit). Nevertheless, the reality is that an innocent recipient would be subject to a strict personal liability in unjust enrichment for his receipt of misapplied trust assets; that the benefit of the recovery in the action would accrue to the beneficiaries; and that in certain circumstances, the beneficiaries themselves might be able to bring the proceedings—sometimes in

---

[129] For cases where recipients have been sued, where they have received corporate assets that have been misapplied by a company director or by an employee, see e.g. *Belmont Finance Corp Ltd v Williams Furniture Ltd (No.2)* [1980] 1 All E.R. 393; *Baden, Delvaux v Société Générale pour Favoriser le Développement du Commerce et de l'Industrie en France SA* [1993] 1 W.L.R. 509n; *Rolled Steel Products (Holdings) Ltd v British Steel Corp* [1986] Ch. 246; *Precision Dippings Ltd v Precision Dippings Marketing Ltd* [1986] Ch. 447; *Agip* [1990] Ch. 265; [1991] Ch. 547 (CA); *Heinl v Jyske Bank (Gibraltar) Ltd* [1999] Lloyd's Rep. Bank. 511; *CMS Dolphin Ltd v Simonet* [2001] 2 B.C.L.C. 704; *Primlake* [2006] EWHC 1227 (Ch); [2007] 1 B.C.L.C. 666.

[130] *Lipkin Gorman* [1991] 2 A.C. 548.

[131] *Criterion* [2004] UKHL 28; [2004] 1 W.L.R. 1846 at [4].

[132] See para.8–45.

[133] See the assumptions reflected in e.g. *Re Robinson* [1911] 1 Ch. 502 at 507–508 per Warrington J; *Re Mason* [1928] Ch. 385 at 291–292 per Romer J.; [1929] Ch. 1 (CA); *Re Blake* [1932] 1 Ch. 54; *Re Diplock* [1948] Ch. 465 (CA) at 498–502 per Lord Greene M.R.; [1951] A.C. 251 at 273 and following per Lord Simmonds.

[134] For general discussion of standing to sue third parties, otherwise than in respect of a breach of trust, see J. Mowbray et al., *Lewin on Trusts*, 18th edn (London: Sweet and Maxwell, 2008), paras 43.01–43.05.

[135] In *Re Diplock* [1948] Ch. 465 (CA); [1951] A.C. 251, it was assumed that the personal representatives might bring a common law restitutionary claim, but that on the facts, where the personal representatives had paid the sums under a mistake as to the validity of the governing provisions of the testator's will, this mistake was a mistake of law, which could not be restitution-grounding.

[136] See para.9–71 and following.

the name of the trustees,[137] and more exceptionally by a derivative action in the beneficiaries' own name but on behalf of the trust.[138]

8–61   Thirdly, there are some older common law decisions in which a recipient has been held liable where moneys have been received by X from C on the express understanding that they are only to be used for some specific purpose, where contrary to his authority X has paid the moneys to D, and where D was held liable for the sum received in an action for money had and received. The arrangement in question looks, to modern eyes, very much like a *Quistclose* trust,[139] of which C could be regarded as the beneficiary pending the due application of the moneys by X. A case in point is *Litt v Martindale*,[140] where the claimant had remitted a letter of credit for £2,010 to a broker at Liverpool, payable to the broker or to his order, solely for the purpose of purchasing a £2,000 bond for him. The broker owed debts of £1,940 to the defendant, and for the purpose of obtaining satisfaction for his debts, persuaded the broker to indorse the letter of credit to him and received its proceeds, despite knowing that the proceeds were not properly at the broker's disposal. The court had no difficulty concluding that the claimant, on discovering the true facts, was entitled to recover the sum received by the defendant, which the court regarded as the claimant's moneys, in an action for money had and received.

8–62   Fourthly, there are some cases where the English courts have contemplated that a recipient of misapplied trust assets may owe a strict personal liability in unjust enrichment, sometimes by way of expansion of the *Re Diplock* personal claim,[141] and sometimes on an independent basis[142]; or at least that properly understood, English law should develop in this direction. Writing extra-judicially, Lord Nicholls,[143] Lord Millett[144] and Lord Walker[145] have each, at various times, advocated this position. It is also a step which has been taken by the Jersey courts,[146] and was at one time mooted by state-level courts in Australia,[147] prior

---

[137] Mowbray, *Lewin on Trusts*, paras 43.03–43.04.

[138] Mowbray, *Lewin on Trusts*, para.43.05.

[139] Named for *Barclays Bank Ltd v Quistclose Investments Ltd* [1970] A.C. 567; the modern understanding of such arrangements follows Lord Millett's analysis in *Twinsectra Ltd v Yardley* [2002] UKHL 12; [2002] 2 A.C. 164.

[140] *Litt v Martindale* (1856) 18 C.B. 314; 139 E.R. 1390.

[141] e.g. *Baker Ltd v Medway Building & Supplies Ltd* [1958] 2 All E.R. 532 (Dankwerts J.); [1958] 3 All E.R. 540 (CA); *Re Leslie Engineers* [1976] 1 W.L.R. 292 (Oliver J.); and see too *Butler v Broadhead* [1975] Ch. 97.

[142] e.g. *Nelson v Larholt* [1948] 1 K.B. 339 per Denning J.; *Twinsectra* [2002] UKHL 12; [2002] 2 A.C. 164 at 1105 per Lord Millett; *Dubai Aluminium* [2002] UKHL 48; [2003] 2 A.C. 366 at [87] per Lord Millett.

[143] Nicholls, "Knowing Receipt: The Need for a New Landmark" in Cornish et al., *Restitution: Past, Present and Future*.

[144] Millett, "Proprietary Restitution" in Degeling and Edelman, *Equity in Commercial Law*, pp.311–312. See also *Twinsectra* [2002] UKHL 12; [2002] 2 A.C. 164 at 194 per Lord Millett; *Dubai Aluminium* [2002] UKHL 48; [2002] 2 A.C. 366 at [87] per Lord Millett.

[145] Lord Walker, "Dishonesty and Unconscionable Conduct in Commercial Life—Some Reflections on Accessory Liability and Knowing Receipt" (2005) 27 *Sydney Law Review* 187, p.202; Lord Walker, "Fraud, Fault and Fiduciary Liability" (2006) 10 *Jersey Law Review* 139, para.[31].

[146] *Re Esteem Settlement*, 2002 J.L.R. 53 at [148]–[161].

[147] *Koorootang Nominees Pty Ltd v Australian & New Zealand Banking Group Ltd* [1998] 3 V.R. 16 at 78 and following, especially 105 per Hansen J.; *Say-Dee Pty Ltd v Farah Constructions Pty Ltd* [2005] NSWCA 309 at [207] and following.

to the High Court of Australia's decision in *Farah Constructions Pty Ltd v Say-Dee Pty Ltd*.[148]

The position in principle   What is the correct answer in principle? As the   **8–63** better view is that the law does protect a *legal* owner of assets from unauthorised dealings with his assets by subjecting a recipient to a strict (common law) personal liability in unjust enrichment, the dispute boils down to whether equitable "owners" should receive a lesser degree of protection—being able to bring a claim against a recipient of misapplied trust assets only via a claim for "knowing receipt"?[149] We ultimately take the view that, notwithstanding the conceptual differences that may exist between legal and equitable "ownership", there is no satisfactory justification for this distinction. The English courts should take the step of holding that trust beneficiaries can bring a strict liability personal claim in unjust enrichment against third party recipients, who are enriched by receiving misapplied trust assets, on the ground of the trustees' want of authority.

It is not obvious why the legal ownership of natural or legal persons is   **8–64** protected via a strict liability regime, but the equitable title of beneficiaries is not, given (1) that vast quantities of wealth are held on trust; (2) that the law affords such protection to persons, such as those entitled to a deceased's estate, who are similarly placed; and (3) that the law affords other remedies to trust beneficiaries against third party recipients, whose existence does not depend on proof of fault on the recipient's part (for example, the remedy of subrogation to a debt paid off via misapplied trust funds and an equitable proprietary claim to the unauthorised proceeds of misapplied trust funds in the third party's hands).[150] Several arguments might be made to the contrary; but on examination, none of them seem adequate to justify the courts continuing to deny equivalent protection to trust beneficiaries.

One objection sometimes raised is that strict liability would impact too harshly   **8–65** on recipients, given that equitable interests are often hidden from view. This is far from clear. Strict liability is the norm in the law of unjust enrichment, with the result that in many routine cases, it will be impossible for a recipient to know of the circumstances that establish a ground of restitution against him (for example, a mistaken assumption by the claimant). The apparent harshness of this strict personal liability for innocent recipients is nevertheless substantially counterbalanced by defences, in particular, the defences of change of position and bona fide purchase. It is not clear why these defences are not adequate, or if not adequate in their current form, could not be adjusted in a manner which would enable them to operate adequately (e.g. by distributing the onus of proof in a manner that is favourable to defendants). Indeed, as a *trustee* can bring a common law personal claim in unjust enrichment against an innocent third party

---

[148] *Farah Constructions Pty Ltd v Say-Dee Pty Ltd* [2007] HCA 22; (2007) 230 C.L.R. 89 at [148]–[158]. The Supreme Court of Canada has taken the step of treating liability for "knowing receipt" as a fault-based liability in unjust enrichment, a view which regrettably confuses liability in unjust enrichment and the historically distinct equitable liability for knowing receipt: *Gold v Rosenberg* [1997] 3 S.C.R. 767; *Citadel General Assurance Co v Lloyds Bank Canada* [1997] 3 S.C.R. 805. See para.8–123 and following.

[149] Academic works addressing this question are cited at fn.275.

[150] See para.8–75 and following.

recipient where trust assets are paid away under a mistake,[151] it would seem that innocent third party recipients of misapplied trust assets are already more vulnerable than is sometimes assumed—albeit ordinarily in proceedings brought by or in the name of trustees—when trust assets have been honestly misapplied.

8–66   A second possible objection is that to afford trust beneficiaries a direct claim in unjust enrichment against a third party recipient would be "unorthodox": the historic orthodoxy is that beneficiaries can only sue their trustees.[152] The answer to this is that the law has long afforded trust beneficiaries a direct claim against such recipients—albeit via the device of holding recipients personally liable to account as constructive trustees on the basis of their "knowing receipt".[153] It may be true that the language of accountability as a constructive trustee was a device used to reconcile this sort of claim with the historic assumption that beneficiaries could only sue their trustees. However, the fact remains that this is in substance a direct claim, which the beneficiaries are afforded in their own right.

8–67   A third possible objection is that to afford trust beneficiaries a direct claim in unjust enrichment would "collapse" the trust, and would be incompatible with the derivative nature of the equitable title of trust beneficiaries. The answer to this is that it rests on a false premise concerning the remedial implications of holding recipients of misapplied trust assets liable in unjust enrichment to the trust's beneficiaries. As in many routine cases where proceedings are brought in respect of a breach of trust—whether against the trustees themselves, or against third parties—the claim being brought by the beneficiary would in substance be a representative claim, seeking a remedy that would operate to restore lost assets or lost value to the trust. In the ordinary case of a claim for "knowing receipt", beneficiaries bringing the claim against a third party recipient will seek an order requiring the knowing recipient to account to the trust for the value of the assets which have passed through his hands. In the same way, if the law was to hold recipients of misapplied trust assets strictly liable in unjust enrichment, then in the ordinary course, the basis of the beneficiaries' claim would be that the defendant was enriched at the expense of the trust beneficiaries collectively, and the remedy being sought would, in the ordinary course, be an order requiring the defendant to make restitution of the value received to the trust, so that the trust estate could be reconstituted and duly administered in accordance with the trust's terms, for their benefit and for the benefit of other beneficiaries. This way of proceeding would neither "collapse" the trust, nor ignore the derivative status of the beneficiaries' rights. Individual beneficiaries would not obtain an order requiring the defendant to make restitution to them individually, regardless of the quality and quantum of their entitlements as trust beneficiaries.

8–68   It is important to emphasise that in advocating the recognition of a strict liability personal claim in unjust enrichment against recipient of misapplied trust assets, we do not intend to cast doubt on the continued existence of the long-standing equitable personal liability for "knowing receipt". As explained below, this liability is not a liability in unjust enrichment, and it has different remedial consequences.[154]

---

[151] See para.8–83 and following.
[152] L.D. Smith, "Constructive Trusts and Constructive Trustees" (1999) 58 C.L.J. 294.
[153] See para.8–123 and following.
[154] See para.8–123 and following.

(iv) *Personal Claims for Value Surviving in a Remoter Recipient's Hands*

The cases discussed in Part 3 support the view that in three-party cases, just as **8–69** in two-party cases, a defendant who is merely a remoter recipient will owe a strict personal restitutionary liability for the value received where D is immediately enriched by X, but more remotely at C's expense, and this enrichment is unjust because of C's lack of consent or X's want of authority. Thus if, as in *Lipkin Gorman*,[155] X fraudulently draws cash from C's account, and hands this cash to D, the cases suggest that C will have a personal claim in unjust enrichment against D for the sum received, without having to prove fault on D's part.

An important question nevertheless arises whether C might be able to seek a **8–70** different measure of personal claim against D in these cases. The starting-point of the law of unjust enrichment, as explained in Ch.4, is that for the purposes of a personal claim, the defendant's "enrichment" is measured at the time of its receipt.[156] However, where D receives an asset from X, in circumstances which entitle C to assert some continuing title to the asset, or to an asset which represents its subsequent unauthorised product,[157] might C rely on his continuing rights to the asset surviving in D's hands, and seek to have D's "enrichment" measured on an alternative basis: on the basis of the value of the surviving asset in D's hands, whether at the time C makes D aware of his claim, or when the court is asked to grant a remedy? This would involve C making a personal claim based on what is sometimes described as the "value traceably surviving".

The law undoubtedly allows C to make a claim of this nature independently of **8–71** the law of unjust enrichment. If, for example, D retains possession of C's chattel without C's consent, then C can obtain an award of damages, in lieu of delivery up of the goods *in specie*, reflecting the chattel's present value.[158] So too, if D trustee holds an asset on bare trust for C, then C may call upon the trustee to transfer the asset to him, and should the trustee fail to do so, C may hold the trustee personally liable for its present value, whether by way of substitutive performance of the trustee's primary obligation to transfer the asset *in specie*, or as a measure of compensation for his breach of trust. Again, if D receives an asset from trustees, which has been transferred by the trustees outside their powers and in breach of trust, then once D acquires knowledge of the breach, D will be fixed with an obligation to restore the assets to the trust, to the extent that the assets traceably survive in his hands, and an equitable personal liability to account for their present value—the so-called equitable liability for "knowing receipt".[159]

It is a more difficult question whether C can make a claim for the value **8–72** traceably surviving via a personal claim *in unjust enrichment*. There are certainly a handful of cases in which this measure of award has been given—notably, *Banque Belge pour l'Etranger v Hambrouck*,[160] and more recently, in *Heperu Pty Ltd v Belle*.[161] Less clear is whether, properly understood, this remedy should be

---

[155] *Lipkin Gorman* [1991] 2 A.C. 548.
[156] See paras 4–34—4–42.
[157] See para.8–83 and following.
[158] See Torts (Interference with Goods) Act 1977 s.3.
[159] See para.8–123 and following.
[160] *Banque Belge pour l'Etranger v Hambrouck* [1921] 1 K.B. 321 (CA).
[161] *Heperu Pty Ltd v Belle* [2009] NSWCA 252.

understood to be a personal claim in unjust enrichment. It might be said that where D retains an asset to which C can claim title, then D is enriched by its present value at C's expense; and that it is not implausible to say that this enrichment is unjust on the ground of C's lack of consent. However, the better answer may be that this rationalisation for D's liability is unnecessarily duplicative. It can be explained as a remedy which enforces C's continuing title—legal or more often equitable—to the asset that survives in D's hands, by means of a substitutive money award.

(c) Proprietary Claims

(i) Introduction

8–73   In the three-party cases examined in Part 3, where D is remotely enriched at C's expense through a transaction with X, a third party, C will often be afforded some form of proprietary entitlement to some asset which is identifiable in D's hands. In some of these cases, the law of unjust enrichment has no role in explaining the availability of the claim. C will be relying on a right which he held before the relevant unauthorised transactions involving the asset, and which subsists despite them. For example, if X steals a car of which C is legal owner, then C—who did not consent to transfer his title to the car to X—will retain his original title to the car in X's hands. If X in turn transfers the car to D, C's original and superior title subsists and remains enforceable against D, unless D can claim to have obtained the car in circumstances that establish an exception to the principle *nemo dat quod non habet*. In this case, the title on which C will rely vis-à-vis D is his original title, which survives despite the non-consensual taking by X and the further unauthorised transfer from X to D. The law of unjust enrichment has no role in explaining this outcome. It is a result of rules that form part of the law of property and are essential to the security of property rights, which dictate that such rights should not ordinarily be transferred to another (or otherwise lost) without some consensual act by the right-holder.

8–74   However, there are other cases where any right which C obtains to the asset in D's hands must be understood as a *new* right, which the law affords him in the circumstances—most often, because it is a right to an asset which is different from any asset to which C had title before the unauthorised transactions. Where this is so, the source of this right must be explained. In many, though not all cases, the right can be understood to be a proprietary mechanism for reversing D's unjust enrichment at C's expense; and the ground of restitution that explains the injustice of D's enrichment is, depending on the circumstances, either C's lack of consent or X's want of authority. The following sections examine several categories of case where this is arguably the case. Fuller examination of the form of the rights created in each case is postponed to subsequent chapters.[162]

(ii) Subrogation Where Debts Are Paid with Misapplied Assets

8–75   Many recent cases hold that if assets have been misappropriated, and traceably used to pay secured debts owed to a third party, then the party entitled to the

---

[162] See Chs 37–40.

misappropriated assets may be entitled to the equitable remedy of subrogation to the paid-off creditor's extinguished security interest and associated rights,[163] as a remedy to reverse the unjust enrichment that would otherwise accrue to the discharged debtor(s) and other parties with subordinate interests in the property subject to the security interest.[164]

The cases show that this remedy is widely available. Thus, it has been recognised where debts are discharged using trust moneys that are transferred by an express trustee in breach of trust,[165] where company assets are transferred by a director without authority and in breach of fiduciary duty[166]; where partnership assets are misapplied in breach of fiduciary duty by a partner[167]; where assets from a deceased's estate were wrongly transferred by a personal representative[168]; and where assets were simply stolen from their owner, by an employee or stranger.[169] In some of these cases, subrogation has been awarded against the party who was responsible for the initial misapplication, and who used the assets to discharge his own debts. However, it is also very clear that the remedy is not limited in this way, and that it is equally available against an innocent third party, who benefits by having his debts discharged as a result of *another's* application of the misappropriated assets. In other words, subrogation is available in these cases on a strict liability basis—i.e. without proof of fault of the defendant against whom the remedy is sought.[170]

8–76

---

[163] *Primlake* [2006] EWHC 1227 (Ch); [2007] 1 B.C.L.C. 666 at [337]–[340], and [2009] EWHC 2774 (Ch); also *Bishopsgate Investment Management Ltd (In Liquidation) v Homan* [1995] Ch. 211 (CA) at 221 per Leggatt L.J.; *Boscawen v Bajwa* [1996] 1 W.L.R. 328 (CA); *Scotlife Home Loans (No.2) Ltd v Melinek* (1999) 78 P. & C.R. 389 (CA) at 398. See too *Whitehand v Jenkins* (Victoria Sup Ct, February 6, 1987); *Gertsch v Atsas* [1999] NSWSC 898; (1999) 10 B.P.R. 18,431 at [19]–[20]; *National Australia Bank Ltd v Rusu* [2001] NSWSC 32 at [51]; *Raulfs v Fishy Bite* [2008] NSWSC 1195 at [25]; *Cook v Italiano Family Fruit Co Ltd (In Liquidation)* [2010] FCA 1355; (2010) 190 F.C.R. 474 at [81] and following; *McCullough v Marsden* (1919) 45 D.L.R. 645 at 646–647 (Alberta CA) (subsequent proceedings: *McCullough v Elliott* (1922) 62 D.L.R. 257). See further C. Mitchell and S. Watterson, *Subrogation: Law and Practice* (Oxford: OUP, 2007), paras 6.38 and following.

[164] See *Banque Financière de la Cité v Parc (Battersea) Ltd* [1999] 1 A.C. 221, and more particularly, for recognition of this in the context of cases of the present nature, see esp. *Primlake* [2006] EWHC 1227 (Ch); [2007] 1 B.C.L.C. 666 at [337]–[340], and [2009] EWHC 2774 (Ch); *Gertsch v Atsas* [1999] NSWSC 898; (1999) 10 B.P.R. 18,431; also *Boscawen v Bajwa* [1996] 1 W.L.R. 328 (CA). See further Ch.39 below, where this is explained.

[165] *Bishopsgate Investment* [1995] Ch. 211 (CA) at 221 per Leggatt L.J.; *Scotlife* (1999) 78 P. & C.R. 389 (CA) at 398; *Cook v Italiano* [2010] FCA 1355; (2010) 190 F.C.R. 474 at [81] and following; *McCullough v Marsden* (1919) 45 D.L.R. 645 at 646–647 (Alberta CA) (subsequent proceedings: *McCullough v Elliott* (1922) 62 D.L.R. 257). And see too *Boscawen* [1996] 1 W.L.R. 328 (CA).

[166] Especially *Primlake* [2006] EWHC 1227 (Ch); [2007] 1 B.C.L.C. 666 at [337]–[340], and [2009] EWHC 2774 (Ch).

[167] *Raulfs* [2008] NSWSC 1195 at [25].

[168] *Gertsch* [1999] NSWSC 898; (1999) 10 B.P.R. 18,431 at [19]–[20]; contrast the earlier decision in *Re Diplock* [1948] Ch. 465 (CA), criticised in *Boscawen* [1996] 1 W.L.R. 328 (CA) at 340–341, and considered further in *Cook v Italiano* [2010] FCA 1355; (2010) 190 F.C.R. 474 at [81] and following.

[169] *National Australia Bank* [2001] NSWSC 32; see also *Ex p. Salting* (1883) 25 Ch.D. 148 (CA).

[170] e.g. *McCullough v Marsden* (1919) 45 D.L.R. 645 (Alberta CA) and *McCullough v Elliott* (1922) 62 D.L.R. 257 (Alberta CA); *Scotlife* (1999) 78 P. & C.R. 389 (CA) at 398; *Primlake* [2006] EWHC 1227 (Ch); [2007] 1 W.L.R. 2489 at [337]–[340]; *Gertsch* [1999] NSWSC 898; (1999) 10 B.P.R. 18,431 (where it was the defendant who innocently used the moneys in this way); *National Australia Bank* [2001] NSWSC 32. See further Mitchell and Watterson, *Subrogation: Law and Practice*, paras 6.38 and following.

8–77   For example, in *Scotlife Home Loans (No.2) Ltd v Melinek*,[171] where a solicitor had, in breach of trust, traceably used moneys from his partnership's client account to pay off a charge over his matrimonial home, Scott V.-C. considered that any clients whose moneys had been so used would be entitled to be subrogated to the charge paid off, not only vis-à-vis the fraudulent solicitor, but also vis-à-vis his innocent wife.[172] In *Primlake Ltd v Matthews Associates*,[173] where a de facto director of a company had, without authority and in breach of his fiduciary duty, procured substantial transfers of company funds for his own benefit, Lawrence Collins J. held that, to the extent that these funds were traceably used to discharge a charge over property co-owned by the fraudulent director and his innocent wife, the company was entitled to be subrogated to the paid-off charge vis-à-vis both parties. In *Gertsch v Atsas*,[174] where the innocent recipient of a legacy under a forged will had traceably used a large part of the legacy to discharge a charge over her land, Foster J.A. held that the sole beneficiary and administrator of the deceased's intestate estate would be prima facie entitled to be subrogated to the paid-off charge. And in *National Australia Bank Ltd v Rusu*,[175] where moneys stolen from a bank by an employee were traceably used by her de facto partner, knowing of their wrongful origins, to discharge a charge over his parents' land which secured debts for which he and his parents were all liable, the bank was only denied the remedy of subrogation vis-à-vis the parents on the basis that they were able to establish a defence.

8–78   These cases are highly significant. First, they provide a clear example of an equitable remedy being afforded, without proof of fault or wrongdoing, against a person who benefits as a result of a misapplication of another's assets. Secondly, this remedy has been explicitly rationalised by the courts as a remedy to reverse unjust enrichment,[176] with the result inter alia that its availability is subject to defences that are characteristically available to claims of this nature.[177] Thirdly, although the language of "lack of consent" or "want of authority" has not been used to explain why the remedy is afforded, the results of the cases can be explained in such terms. Indeed, in the important recent case of *Primlake*,[178] Lawrence Collins J. considered that subrogation was available against both defendants on the simple basis that they were "unjustly enriched by the *unlawful* use of [the company's] funds to repay their loan and redeem their charge".[179] As Mrs Matthews had not participated in the misapplication of the claimant company's funds by Mr Matthews, its de facto director, it is apparent that it was

---

[171] *Scotlife Home Loans (No.2) Ltd v Melinek* (1999) 78 P. & C.R. 389 (CA).

[172] *Scotlife* (1999) 78 P. & C.R. 389 (CA) at 398.

[173] *Primlake Ltd v Matthews Associates* [2006] EWHC 1227 (Ch); [2007] 1 B.C.L.C. 666 at [340]; and see subsequently [2009] EWHC 2774 (Ch).

[174] *Gertsch* [1999] NSWSC 898; (1999) 10 B.P.R. 18,431 at [99]–[100], discussed in Mitchell and Watterson, *Subrogation: Law and Practice*, paras 7.76–7.77.

[175] *National Australia Bank Ltd v Rusu* [2001] NSWSC 32 at [44]–[45], [51], as explained in Mitchell and Watterson, *Subrogation: Law and Practice*, paras 7.100–7.101.

[176] See further below Ch.39, and fn.164 above, where this is explained.

[177] e.g. change of position (as in *Gertsch* [1999] NSWSC 898; (1999) 10 B.P.R. 18,431; and recognised in *Boscawen* [1996] 1 W.L.R. 328 (CA) at 340–341); *Anfield (UK) Ltd v Bank of Scotland Plc* [2010] EWHC 2374 (Ch); [2011] All E.R. 708 at [31]). For discussion, see Mitchell and Watterson, *Subrogation: Law and Practice*, Ch.7.

[178] *Primlake* [2006] EWHC 1227 (Ch); [2007] 1 W.L.R. 2489.

[179] *Primlake* [2006] EWHC 1227 (Ch); [2007] 1 W.L.R. 2489 at [340].

sufficient that the defendants had benefited by the *unauthorised*—in Lawrence Collins J.'s words "unlawful"—use of the claimant company's funds. Finally, it is uncontroversial that this remedy is available where the assets which are traceably used to discharge the relevant debts are *trust* assets, which have been misapplied in breach of trust by a trustee.[180] In this way, the subrogation cases provide further support for the view that it would be appropriate for the courts finally to take the step of affording trust beneficiaries a personal claim in unjust enrichment, on a strict liability basis, against a recipient of misapplied trust assets. Unless this step is taken, the law is left with what appears to be an anomaly. As the law currently stands, a party who receives misapplied trust assets is only under a personal liability for their value if he can be held liable as a "knowing recipient".[181] In contrast, if he—or another—applies the trust assets in discharge of his debts, he will be immediately liable to the remedy of subrogation, as a remedy to reverse his unjust enrichment, without proof of fault.

(iii) *Equitable Proprietary Rights to Misapplied Assets*

It is well-established that where trust assets are transferred by a trustee to a third **8–79** party in breach of trust, a beneficiary of the trust can bring an equitable proprietary claim against the recipient, which the court may enforce by an order requiring the asset to be restored in specie (usually to the trust). The same applies in cases where fiduciary assets are disposed of without authority and in breach of duty by someone who cannot necessarily be regarded as a trustee—as in *Re Diplock* or in cases involving misapplications of corporate assets. In some, though not all of these cases, this equitable property claim might plausibly be analysed as a proprietary mechanism for reversing the unjust enrichment of the recipient, on the ground of the want of authority of the transferor.

The cases which seem least susceptible to this rationalisation are where the **8–80** assets are originally held on trust. Where trust assets are disposed of without authority, an unauthorised transfer will be ineffective to overreach the beneficiaries' interests. However, it cannot be said that the recipient holds the assets on the same trusts—subject to the same obligations and with the same powers and authorities—as the original trustee. Manifestly, he does not. To the extent that the recipient has any obligation at all, it is simply an obligation to restore the assets to the trust *in specie*—an imposed obligation, different from that of the original trustee, which results in the routine description of the recipient as holding on a constructive trust. It is a controversial question how this obligation, and the associated trust, should be explained. Whilst it may be tempting to say that it is a new obligation, which the law generates in order to reverse the recipient's unjust enrichment, the better answer is that it is simply a mechanism through which the law directly protects the beneficiaries' subsisting equitable rights to the assets which have come into the recipient's hands. The recipient's liability shares none of the features that one might expect to see in an obligation borne of unjust enrichment—including, inter alia, its vulnerability to a plea of "change of position".

---

[180] See the cases cited in fn.165.
[181] See para.8–123 and following.

8–81   Matters begin to look slightly different, however, where the assets which the recipient receives were not previously held on trust—as where corporate assets are transferred to a third party, as a consequence of unauthorised dealings by an agent for the company, and by a transaction which is not binding on the company. There may be cases of this sort where legal title passes but where, as a result of the circumstances in which the assets are disposed of, the transaction is void (or voidable) in equity (for example, because it involves a disposition for improper purposes, or "self-dealing" by a company director), and where the company can assert an equitable title to the assets in the recipient's hands. If so, this will be a new title, which arises as a result of the circumstances in which the company's assets have been transferred, and reflects an obligation on the recipient to reconvey the asset transferred *in specie* to the company. The recipient is rendered a trustee to this extent, under a trust which is either constructive or resulting, and which is plausibly explained as a proprietary mechanism for reversing what would otherwise be an unjust enrichment of the recipient at the company's expense. If this analysis is indeed correct, then the ground of restitution looks like "want of authority".

8–82   Some recent support for this analysis might be found in the analysis of Lord Nicholls in *Criterion*.[182] As previously explained, he took the view that a recipient of corporate assets pursuant to a transaction which was unauthorised and not binding on the company in accordance with the law of agency would owe a strict personal liability in unjust enrichment for the value of the assets received; he would also be subject to a "proprietary claim". Lord Nicholls did not elaborate the nature of this "proprietary claim", but it seems very likely that he envisaged a claim arising under some form of resulting or constructive trust.

(iv) *Equitable Proprietary Rights to Unauthorised Substitutes*

8–83   It is well-established that the law allows trust beneficiaries to assert equitable rights to assets which represent the unauthorised substitutes for the original trust assets, identified in accordance with the law's tracing rules,[183] in the hands of the trustee or a third party. An equivalent right has also been recognised in cases concerning assets misapplied by other fiduciaries.[184] As explained above, the better view is that the same consequence should also follow even where the unauthorised substitution is made by someone who does not occupy either of these positions—e.g. a mere thief.[185] It can be argued that, in at least some situations, these rights arise to reverse unjust enrichment, and that the ground of restitution is "lack of consent" or "want of authority". This is, however, a controversial proposition which is fiercely disputed,[186] and the leading authority

---

[182] *Criterion* [2004] UKHL 28; [2004] 1 W.L.R. 1846 at [4]. See para.8–45.
[183] See Ch.7.
[184] e.g. *Re Hallett's Estate* (1879) 13 Ch.D. 696 (CA); *Re Diplock* [1948] Ch. 465 (CA); *Agip* [1990] Ch. 265.
[185] See para.8–18.
[186] The literature is voluminous. Besides the works cited in the following footnotes, see A.S. Burrows, "Proprietary Restitution: Unmasking Unjust Enrichment" (2001) 117 L.Q.R. 417; P. Birks, *Unjust Enrichment*, 2nd edn (Oxford: OUP, 2005), pp.34 and following; Edelman and Bant, *Unjust Enrichment in Australia*, pp.136 and following; Burrows, *The Law of Restitution*, pp.169–171.

of *Foskett v McKeown*[187] stands against it. There are nevertheless some difficulties with the majority's reasoning in that case, and it should not necessarily be regarded as the last word on the topic.

In *Foskett*,[188] a trustee, acting fraudulently and in breach of trust, used £20,440 **8–84** of trust moneys to pay two annual premiums of a life insurance policy previously taken out in his name. He subsequently appointed the benefit of the policy to trustees for the benefit of his children, and on his death two years later, £1 million was paid by the insurers pursuant to the policy to the trustees. The beneficiaries of the trust from which the £20,440 was misappropriated thereupon brought proceedings against the policy trustees and the children, claiming a proportionate beneficial interest in the policy proceeds in the policy trustees' hands. A majority of the House of Lords upheld their claim, holding that where a trustee, acting in breach of trust, uses trust assets to acquire other assets, the beneficiary of the trust (or if more than one, all of the beneficiaries if of full age and sui juris) can opt to assert a beneficial entitlement to the new asset, proportionate to the contribution which the trust assets made to the cost of the new asset's acquisition; otherwise, they are entitled in the alternative to an equitable lien over the new assets to secure the trustee's personal liability to make good the loss to the trust fund. Furthermore, these claims to the traceable proceeds could be maintained not only against the trustee who committed the breach of trust, but also against anyone, such as the policy trustees and the children in *Foskett*, who obtained title from him otherwise than as a bona fide purchaser for value without notice of the breach.

The immediate importance of *Foskett* lies in the explanation which a majority **8–85** of their Lordships offered for the beneficiaries' entitlement to assert an equitable title to the unauthorised traceable product of the original trust assets. The majority were emphatic that these rights were *not* afforded to reverse unjust enrichment. As Lord Millett put it, the transmission of a claimant's property rights "from one asset to its traceable proceeds is part of our law of property, not of the law of unjust enrichment".[189] The law of unjust enrichment had no part in explaining why these rights arose; and for the same reason, the rights so acquired were not susceptible to defences (in particular, change of position) characteristic of claims in unjust enrichment.[190] In the majority's view, the claim being asserted by the trust beneficiaries was simply a claim to vindicate their continuing proprietary interest in the trust assets and their traceable proceeds; unjust enrichment did not come into it.[191]

The majority's analysis in *Foskett* presents a number of difficulties. First, **8–86** although they spoke of the beneficiaries having a continuing beneficial interest in the original trust assets and their traceable proceeds, this cannot be literally true. A property right is a right to a specific thing, which cannot be detached from the

---

[187] *Foskett v McKeown* [2001] 1 A.C. 102.
[188] *Foskett* [2001] 1 A.C. 102.
[189] *Foskett* [2001] 1 A.C. 102 at 127 per Lord Millett.
[190] *Foskett* [2001] 1 A.C. 102 at 129 per Lord Millett.
[191] *Foskett* [2001] 1 A.C. 102 at 127, 129 per Lord Millett, 108, 110 per Lord Browne-Wilkinson, 115 per Lord Hoffmann. See too Millett, "Proprietary Restitution" in Degeling and Edelman, *Equity in Commercial Law*, pp.315–316.

thing to which it relates and reattach to some new thing.[192] Insofar as the rights asserted are to a new asset which represents the unauthorised traceable proceeds of original trust assets, the right being asserted is manifestly not the same right, but rather, a new right, whose existence must be explained. Secondly, to the extent that any explanation for these rights emerges from the majority's speeches, it is that these rights are awarded to vindicate the beneficiaries' proprietary rights in the original trust assets[193]; or as Lord Millett has since put it extra-judicially, the right to claim an unauthorised substitute "is a right given [to the beneficiaries] by the law of property", as an "incident of their property rights in the original asset".[194] However, this is not self-evidently correct, since there is nothing inherent in the concept of ownership which dictates that the owner of an asset must also own its unauthorised substitute. If an owner is afforded such rights, it is a contingent choice which our system has made, which must itself be justified.[195] Thirdly, in insisting that a beneficiary's rights to unauthorised substitutes are "part of our law of property, not of the law of unjust enrichment",[196] the majority in *Foskett* is in danger of committing the categorical error that the law of property and the law of unjust enrichment cannot be in issue in a single claim. A property right is a type of right; whilst unjust enrichment is a source of rights, personal or proprietary.[197] The fact that trust beneficiaries are afforded rights to traceable proceeds in another's hands does not, without more, dictate that these rights can never be designed to reverse the unjust enrichment of that person. Fourthly, the majority in *Foskett* lumped together all cases of unauthorised substitutions, analysing the rights of beneficiaries to substitutes in the hands of an express trustee in the same way as their rights to substitutes in the hands of others (such as third-party recipients). However, their positions are manifestly different. Although it may be possible satisfactorily to explain the rights of trust beneficiaries to unauthorised substitutes in the hands of *express* trustees without recourse to the law of unjust enrichment, this is far less obviously true of persons who have never occupied that position.

8–87   Clear understanding of the circumstances in which unjust enrichment may (or may not) have a role in explaining claims to traceable substitutes requires close attention to be paid to the circumstances in which the substitution has occurred. Several different situations need to be distinguished.

8–88   The first and simplest situation involves an authorised substitution by an express trustee: where an *express* trustee, acting within his powers of sale and

---

[192] See P. Birks, "Property, Unjust Enrichment and Tracing" (2001) 54 C.L.P. 231, pp.244–245; Chambers, "Tracing and Unjust Enrichment" in Neyers et al, *Understanding Unjust Enrichment*, pp.273–274.

[193] *Foskett* [2001] 1 A.C. 102 at 129 per Lord Millett; also at 110 per Lord Browne-Wilkinson, and 115 per Lord Hoffmann.

[194] Millett, "Proprietary Restitution" in Degeling and Edelman, *Equity in Commercial Law*, p.315. One perceived corollary of this is that wrongfully substituted assets "continue to be held on the same trusts" as the original trust assets (whether express, resulting or constructive): at pp.315–316; a view which is consistent with the reasoning of Lord Browne-Wilkinson in *Foskett* [2001] 1 A.C. 102 at 108.

[195] See more fully, Chambers, "Tracing and Unjust Enrichment" in Neyers et al, *Understanding Unjust Enrichment*; this is dramatically demonstrated by the fact that many civilian jurisdictions do not recognise rights to traceable products.

[196] *Foskett* [2001] 1 A.C. 102 at 127 per Lord Millett.

[197] See further below Chs 37–40.

investment, sells trust assets or acquires other assets using trust funds. There is undoubtedly no need to invoke the law of unjust enrichment here. The beneficiaries' rights to the original assets are overreached by the authorised transaction, and the new assets received by the trustees in exchange are automatically subject to the same trusts as the original assets, by a process which the beneficiaries cannot subsequently challenge. The rights which the beneficiaries thereby acquire to the substitute assets are in their nature new rights, for reasons already given, but they do not arise to reverse unjust enrichment. They arise as a consequence of the settlor's intention (agreed to by the trustee) to afford the beneficiaries rights to the original trust assets and their proceeds, as mediated by the trustee's authorised exercise of his powers of sale and investment.

More difficulty arises in a second situation, which was the situation in issue in **8–89** *Foskett*, involving an unauthorised substitution of trust assets by an express trustee. Where an express trustee transfers trust assets in breach of trust, and outside the powers of sale and investment conferred on him, then—as a consequence of this unauthorised substitution—the beneficiaries immediately acquire at least inchoate rights to the traceable substitute in the hands of the trustee, reflecting the option which the law affords them of adopting the substitute as a trust asset, or if this should not occur, of asserting a lien over the substitute, for the purpose of securing the trustee's personal liability to restore the trust estate. Subsequent unauthorised substitutes for the original unauthorised substitute in the trustee's hands are governed by the same principles.

In this second situation, where ex hypothesi the settlor did not consent to the **8–90** unauthorised transaction, there is more room for argument that the source of the beneficiaries' rights is unjust enrichment. However, even here, and consistently with the premises of the majority of the House of Lords in *Foskett*, unjust enrichment is not a necessary explanation. If the trustee purported to acquire the new assets *for the beneficiaries*, and the beneficiaries, if of full age and sui juris, together elect retrospectively to claim the substitute as a trust asset, then the source of the beneficiaries' rights to the substitute might be said to be the settlor's intention, agreed to by the trustees, to create such rights in the beneficiaries' favour, albeit in a different form from that which the settlor originally intended, by a process which can be regarded as an ad hoc variation of the original express trust. If, alternatively, the trustee purported to acquire the new assets *for his own benefit*, then any trust imposed upon the unauthorised substitute is explicable in the same terms as the trust which is imposed on any unauthorised profit which a trustee or other fiduciary makes from his position, consistently with the duties which the trustee voluntarily assumed when he took office. This latter explanation is also available where the substitution is made by a person who, whilst not strictly a trustee, voluntarily assumed a fiduciary position (and associated duties) vis-à-vis the assets which he disposed of without authority.

Most difficulty arises in a third situation, involving an unauthorised substitu- **8–91** tion by a third party who has not assumed the position of express trustee, and who has not otherwise voluntarily assumed a fiduciary position (and associated duties) vis-à-vis the assets. It is well-established that a third party who receives title to trust assets from trustees under an unauthorised transaction, and in circumstances that do not operate to give him a clear title,[198] will take that title

---

[198] e.g. under the land registration rules or because he is a bona fide purchaser.

subject to the prior interests of the trust's beneficiaries, and can be ordered to restore the assets to the trustees in specie, so that the trust fund can be reconstituted and administered for the benefit of the beneficiaries. It is also well-established that if this third party, acting without authority, in turn transfers these assets to another and receives other assets in exchange, the trust's beneficiaries can likewise opt to assert an equitable title to the unauthorised substitutes (and further unauthorised substitutes) in the third party's hands.

8–92   In *Foskett*,[199] Lord Millett seemed to assume that the beneficiaries' rights had the same source in the third situation as in the second, involving an unauthorised substitution by an express trustee. However, *Foskett* was in substance an example of the second situation, and not the third, and there are material differences between the position of a third party and that of an express trustee, which mean that they cannot necessarily be analysed identically. There are several possible explanations. One is that the unauthorised substitution *itself* constitutes an equitable wrong, to which the law responds by fastening a constructive trust on its proceeds. However, whilst this rationale might work if a third party has previously become fixed with custodial obligations as a knowing recipient of misapplied trust assets,[200] it cannot provide a universal explanation, because it does not explain why the same entitlement arises even if the third party recipient is innocent of wrongdoing, because he exchanged the original assets *prior* to his acquiring knowledge that they were transferred to him in breach of trust, and so before these custodial obligations arose. A second possibility is that these rights are simply the way in which the law has opted, on policy grounds, robustly to protect the rights of trust beneficiaries in cases of non-wrongful interference with their rights.[201] A third possibility is that unjust enrichment can and should be recognised as the explanation, on a ground that can be understood to be lack of consent or want of authority.[202]

8–93   The unjust enrichment explanation should be preferred. Adopting this explanation, the rights which the trust beneficiary acquires to the unauthorised substitute in the third-party's hands are generated to reverse unjust enrichment on the following basis. When the third party acquires the new asset in exchange for the original asset, the new asset is acquired at the beneficiary's expense, to the extent that that the value inherent in the original asset is used to acquire the new asset. It is, in effect, as if the beneficiary paid all or part of the cost of the third party's acquisition of the new asset. This enrichment is "unjust" because ex hypothesi it occurs without the beneficiary's consent. As Chambers has put it[203]:

---

[199] *Foskett* [2001] 1 A.C. 102 at 130.

[200] See para.8–123 and following.

[201] Although expressed in different language, this is effectively the approach preferred by L.D. Smith, "Unravelling Proprietary Restitution" (2004) 40 *Canadian Business Law Journal* 317; R. Grantham and C. Rickett, "Property Rights as a Legally Significant Event" (2003) 62 C.L.J. 717; C. Rickett, "Old and New in the Law of Tracing" in Degeling and Edelman, *Equity in Commercial Law*, Ch.6; G. Virgo, "Restitution Through the Looking Glass" in J. Getzler (ed.), *Rationalizing Property, Equity and Trusts—Essays in Honour of Edward Burn* (London: LexisNexis Butterworths, 2003).

[202] See especially Birks, "Property, Unjust Enrichment and Tracing"; Burrows, *The Law of Restitution*, pp.169–171; Chambers, "Tracing and Unjust Enrichment" in Neyers et al, *Understanding Unjust Enrichment*, pp.294–296 (observing that the equitable rights that arise can be regarded as functionally equivalent to purchase-money resulting trusts).

[203] Chambers, "Tracing and Unjust Enrichment" in Neyers et al, *Understanding Unjust Enrichment*, p.294.

"[The defendant] acquired the new asset at the claimant's expense because the defendant used the value of the claimant's right to the initial asset to pay for the new asset. Essentially, the claimant paid all or part of the purchase price for the new asset. If the new asset is exchanged for another asset, the process repeats. The second new asset was purchased for the defendant by the claimant, who paid for it by involuntarily exchanging her or his rights to the first new asset. So long as the claimant's value remains identifiable under the tracing rules, this may occur over and over again ... "

(v) *Void and Voidable Exercise of Powers over Another Person's Assets*

A trustee or other fiduciary will routinely hold powers to dispose of the assets to   **8–94** which he holds title or otherwise controls.[204] In the purported exercise of these powers, the fiduciary may confer a benefit on a third party—most often in the form of transferring or creating rights to the fiduciary assets. The law has evolved a number of different techniques for controlling the exercise of powers of this sort. In some cases, the exercise will be void, as where it falls outside the scope of the power, properly construed[205]; or it is not exercised in good faith[206]; or it is exercised for improper purposes,[207] a ground that includes those cases conventionally understood to involve "fraud on a power".[208] In other cases, the exercise may be within the terms of the power, but occur in circumstances which render it voidable. As Lloyd L.J. recently explained it in *Pitt v Holt*[209]:

"if an exercise by trustees of a discretionary power is within the terms of the power, but the trustees have in some way breached their duties in respect of that exercise, then (unless it is a case of a fraud on the power) the trustees' act is not void but it may be voidable at the instance of a beneficiary who is adversely affected. The interest of a beneficiary in the trust property continues until it is brought to an end by an act of the trustees done in accordance with the terms of the trust (or the general law). This is an incident of the beneficiary's right to have the trust duly administered in accordance with the provisions of the trust instrument and the general law[.]"

A key example is where the exercise infringes the rule in *Re Hastings-Bass*, as recently re-formulated by the Court of Appeal in *Pitt v Holt*,[210] because it is

---

[204] On powers, see McGee (gen. ed.), *Snell's Equity*, 32nd edn (London: Sweet & Maxwell, 2010), Chs 10 and 11; R. Nolan, "Controlling Fiduciary Power" [2009] C.L.J. 293. Similar principles should apply to the extent that a person holds a power otherwise in a fiduciary capacity—an exercise by such a person is subject to fewer limitations, but will still be subject to requirements inter alia that the power be exercised within its terms, in good faith, and for proper purposes.

[205] McGhee, *Snell's Equity* para.10.018; *Pitt v Holt* [2011] EWCA Civ 197; [2011] 3 W.L.R. 19 at [39]–[67] and [96], where the decisions in *Re Abrahams* [1911] 1 Ch. 108 and *Re Hastings Bass (Deceased)* [1975] Ch. 25 were thought to raise a question whether an exercise of a power of advancement was void because it was outside its scope.

[206] McGhee, *Snell's Equity*, para.10.119.

[207] McGhee, *Snell's Equity*, paras 10.020–10.027.

[208] As classically described by Lord Parker in *Vatcher v Paull* [1915] A.C. 372 (PC) at 378. Fraud on a power was held to render an exercise of a power void in *Cloutte v Storey* [1911] 1 Ch. 18 (CA), a view which was accepted as the law, albeit with some obvious reservations, by Lloyd L.J. in *Pitt v Holt* [2011] EWCA Civ 197; [2011] 3 W.L.R. 19 at [97]–[98].

[209] *Pitt v Holt* [2011] EWCA Civ 197; [2011] 3 W.L.R. 19 at [99].

[210] *Pitt v Holt* [2011] EWCA Civ 197; [2011] 3 W.L.R. 19. The Court of Appeal settled a long-running debate about whether the exercise of a power contrary to the rule in *Re Hastings-Bass* renders the exercise void or voidable: e.g. *Abacus Trust (Isle of Man) Ltd v Barr* [2003] EWHC 114 (Ch); [2003] Ch. 409; *Gallaher Ltd v Gallaher Pensions Ltd* [2005] EWHC 42 (Ch); *Futter v Futter* [2010] EWHC 449 (Ch); [2010] S.T.C. 982 at [34].

vitiated by the fiduciary's failure, in breach of duty, to take into account relevant considerations or by his having, in breach of duty, taken into account irrelevant considerations.[211]

8–95   Where a third party receives a benefit pursuant to the exercise of a power which is either void or voidable for the reasons indicated above, then the law might in principle afford a remedy against the third party to the person otherwise entitled to the assets disposed of, for the purpose of reversing his unjust enrichment on the ground of want of authority.[212] Nevertheless, this possibility has yet to be explicitly acknowledged in the cases. Both the ground of restitution, and the circumstances in which the relief available is appropriately regarded as restitutionary, will be controversial.

8–96   Starting with the ground of restitution, "want of authority" is undoubtedly a viable explanation if the exercise of the power is void, since the rule which renders the exercise void involves a limitation on the fiduciary's capacity or authority validly to act. However, want of authority will inevitably be a more problematic explanation if the exercise of the power is merely voidable—which *Pitt v Holt* now holds is the result of an exercise which infringes the rule in *Re Hastings Bass*. One view is that the rule in *Re Hastings Bass* is not about the limits of a fiduciary's powers at all,[213] with the consequence that infringement of the rule can never justify a restitutionary claim based on want of authority. Ex hypothesi the exercise would be within the terms of the power, albeit in breach of duty. An opposing view is that any fiduciary power is subject to the implied limitation that it is exercised consistently with the rule in *Re Hastings Bass*,[214] bringing the perceived consequence—which *Pitt v Holt* rejects—that any exercise which infringes the rule should be void. An intermediate position, which avoids sterile debates about whether a particular rule regulating the exercise of a power does or does not go to the limits of the power, is to accept that the rule in *Re Hastings Bass* does involve a limit on a fiduciary's capacity or authority validly to transact, taking "validly" to mean "without susceptibility to being impugned". On this view, irrespective of whether a particular rule regulating the exercise of a fiduciary's power renders its exercise "void" or "voidable", the rule limits the fiduciary's capacity or authority validly to act, and "want of authority" can provide an explanation for a restitutionary remedy vis-à-vis a third party who benefits as a result of the exercise.

8–97   It is a difficult question whether any of the remedial consequences that follow from an invalid exercise of a power by a fiduciary are appropriately viewed as designed to reverse the unjust enrichment of any person who benefits from its exercise.

---

[211] See *Pitt v Holt* [2011] EWCA Civ 197; [2011] 3 W.L.R. 19 at [102] and following, where Lloyd L.J. sought to elaborate the duties of trustees, in relation to their dispositive discretionary powers.

[212] In a third category of case, the exercise of the power is neither void nor voidable, but merely a breach of a duty—most obviously, a duty of care and skill—which the law casts on the power-holder, which generates personal liabilities for him without impugning the validity of the power's exercise, and any resulting transaction: see McGhee, *Snell's Equity*, para.10.038. There is no room for a claim to be brought in unjust enrichment, on the ground of "want of authority", against the third party in this case.

[213] See especially McGhee, *Snell's Equity*, para.10.33; Nolan, "Controlling Fiduciary Power", pp.294 and 306 and following.

[214] See especially D. Hayton et al., *Underhill & Hayton—Law of Trusts and Trustees*, 18th edn (London: LexisNexis, 2010), para.57.22.

Where the exercise of a power is void, it is prima facie a nullity. If the exercise **8–98** merely purported to alter the distribution of equitable entitlement in assets held by the fiduciary—as in the case of, for example, a void exercise of a power of appointment—then the exercise will have no effect in altering the distribution of equitable entitlement to the fiduciary asset. As in the case of an ineffective transfer of *legal* title, the law of unjust enrichment has no part in explaining this outcome. Matters become slightly more complicated where the fiduciary is so placed that he is able to transfer legal title to the fiduciary assets to a third party, even though this is pursuant to the exercise of a power which is void in equity. This would be true of a trustee, who has capacity to transfer legal title as an incident of his legal ownership of the trust assets. Such a disposition will not overreach the equitable entitlements of the beneficiaries, who will be able to assert an equitable title to the assets transferred to the third party (and any traceable substitutes). To the extent that the beneficiaries rely only on their continuing equitable title to the original asset transferred, which is not over-reached by the disposition, then it might be said that the law of unjust enrichment has no role to play.[215] However, the position may well be otherwise to the extent that they claim rights to a traceable substitute for their original asset in the third party's hands, for reasons already explained: these rights may be best explained as arising to reverse the unjust enrichment of the third party, when the asset to which the beneficiaries have equitable title is substituted without their consent.[216]

If the exercise of the power is voidable and not void then, in principle, similar **8–99** proprietary consequences should follow to those already described, deferred to the point in time when the exercise is effectively avoided. In this situation, a better case might be made that the beneficiaries' entitlement to seek avoidance of the disposition can be explained as a proprietary restitutionary remedy, designed to reverse the recipient's unjust enrichment, which is based on the power-holder's want of authority.

The important distinction just drawn between the effects of an invalid exercise **8–100** of a power is well-illustrated by *Cloutte v Storey*.[217] A power of appointment was purportedly exercised over a trust fund, but in fraud of the power; and the beneficiaries entitled in default of appointment alleged that they were still entitled to the trust fund as against the purported appointee's assignee. The beneficiaries won. The appointment was void, and gave the purported appointee no equitable title to the fund. However, the Court of Appeal also recognised that if legal title to trust assets had been transferred to the purported appointee by the trustees, the transfer of legal title would have been effective. Although this transaction would not overreach the beneficiaries' prior equitable title, a subsequent assignee of the legal title might then have a chance of taking a clear title from the appointee by recourse to the plea of bona fide purchase.

Turning to personal claims, there is currently little authority—at least outside **8–101** of the sphere of the administration of a deceased's estate—for the view that a third party who receives a benefit pursuant to the invalid exercise of a power by a fiduciary is strictly liable in unjust enrichment on the ground of want of

---

[215] See paras 8–79—8–90.
[216] See paras 8–83 and following, and in particular, 8–82 and following.
[217] *Cloutte v Storey* [1911] 1 Ch. 18 (CA).

authority. The prevailing view is no doubt that the recipient is only subject to personal liability as a knowing recipient, or otherwise, if they have dishonestly assisted the fiduciary's breach of duty. However, the cases are not completely consistent in this respect,[218] and for reasons already explained, it would be preferable if the courts were to recognise that a recipient of a benefit pursuant to an invalid exercise of a power might owe a strict personal restitutionary liability in unjust enrichment on the ground of want of authority to the trust's beneficiaries or to the fiduciary's principal.[219]

(vi) *Voidable Transactions by Self-Dealing Fiduciaries*[220]

8-102   Suppose that one person, acting as agent, arranges a sale of assets belonging to his principal to himself and his wife, or to a company of which he is sole shareholder; or that two trustees jointly sell trust assets to one of them. This sort of transaction—involving what is sometimes described as "self-dealing" by a fiduciary, who stands on both sides of the relevant transaction—is likely to trigger restitutionary consequences. At least some of these consequences may be susceptible to rationalisation as remedies afforded to reverse unjust enrichment, based on the fiduciary's want of authority.

8-103   The distinguishing obligation of a fiduciary is the duty of loyalty,[221] a key facet of which is that a fiduciary is prohibited from acting in a situation where there is risk of a conflict between the fiduciary's duty and his personal interest.[222] One specific corollary of this prohibition is the "self-dealing" rule, which renders a sale of trust property to the trustee, from himself alone or from co-trustees,[223] "voidable by any beneficiary *ex debito justitiae*, however fair the transaction".[224] The same rule extends to transactions other than sales[225]; and to fiduciaries other than trustees, who deal in circumstances where the fiduciary is on both sides of the transaction.[226] A fiduciary is only absolved from the prima facie consequences of these rules, and the transaction unimpugnable, to the extent that he

---

[218] See para.8–50 and following.

[219] See para.8–63 and following.

[220] The facts of these cases vary widely, and are not susceptible to neat classification as either "two-party" or "three-party" cases; however, since they involve a fiduciary dealing with assets which he holds or controls for another, in transactions that may involve other parties, it seems appropriate to discuss all of these cases at this point.

[221] *Bristol & West Building Society v Mothew* [1998] Ch. 1 at 18. For a full discussion, see M. Conaglen, *Fiduciary Loyalty: Protecting the Due Performance of Non-Fiduciary Duties* (Oxford: Hart, 2010).

[222] For company directors, see now Companies Act 2006 s.175.

[223] e.g. *Re Harvey (Deceased)* (1888) 58 L.T. 449; *Wright v Morgan* [1926] A.C. 788 (PC).

[224] *Tito v Waddell (No.2)* [1977] Ch. 106 at 241. In narrower circumstances, the transaction by the trustee or other fiduciary may be wholly void, as a result of distinct rules (1) requiring two parties to a contract or other transaction and (2) requiring a "genuine transaction", as explained by Conaglen, *Fiduciary Loyalty*, pp.76–79.

[225] e.g. the grant of a lease, as in *Ex p. Hughes* (1802) 6 Ves. Jr. 617 at 622; 31 E.R 1223 at 1226; *Att Gen v Earl of Clarendon* (1810) 17 Ves. Jr. 491 at 500; 34 E.R. 190 at 194; or the vesting of property in a partnership of which a trustee is a member or a company of which he is managing director, as in *Re Thompson's Settlement* [1986] Ch. 99.

[226] e.g. the purchase by a company of property from a firm in which a director of the company was a partner, as in *Aberdeen Railway Co v Blaikie Bros* (1854) 1 Macq. 461; [1943–60] All E.R. Rep. 249; or the purchase by an agent of his principal's property where the agent arranges the transaction on both sides, as in *De Bussche v Alt* (1878) 8 Ch.D. 286; *Charter v Trevelyan* (1844) 11 Cl. & Fin. 714; 9 E.R. 1273.

has proper authorisation[227] from the person who created his fiduciary position,[228] or the fully-informed consent of his principal,[229] or the transaction had court sanction.[230]

The proper characterisation of the remedies available in cases involving self-dealing fiduciaries is disputed. In *Tito v Waddell (No.2)*,[231] Megarry V.C. apparently took the view that equity's self-dealing rules—and its related fair-dealing rules—subjected fiduciaries to "disabilities", rather than "duties" whose breach constituted a wrong.[232] However, this was doubted in *Gwembe Valley Development Co Ltd v Koshy (No.3)*,[233] where the distinction between disabilities and duties in this context was described as an "unnecessary complication".[234] In fact, the better view is that both analyses are valid.[235] A fiduciary who acts in a situation where his duty and his interest conflict *may* breach a duty which he owes, and therefore commit a wrong which exposes him to remedies characteristic of wrong-based claims—in particular, a compensatory remedy for losses suffered by the principal.[236] However, it is also possible to say, without contradiction, that the self-dealing rules import disabilities, including limits on the fiduciary's transactional capacity, which bring remedial consequences which do not need to be explained as generated by a wrong committed by the fiduciary —such as a right in the principal to rescind a self-dealing transaction. **8–104**

To the extent that the self-dealing rules create a *disability*, it is arguable that a self-dealing transaction can generate remedial consequences that might be explained as arising to reverse unjust enrichment. Richard Nolan put an argument along these lines in a perceptive article written over a decade ago.[237] The defendant against whom relief is sought in respect of a self-dealing transaction, whether the self-dealing fiduciary and/or a third party, will generally have benefited at the expense of the principal. To this extent, a restitutionary remedy may be available to recover benefits received as a result of such transactions on a ground which can be understood to be the fiduciary's "want of authority" and/ or his principal's "lack of consent". In effect, the fiduciary relationship brings with it a presumptive limitation on a fiduciary's capacity or authority effectively **8–105**

---

[227] See generally, e.g. McGhee, *Snell's Equity*, paras 7.014 and following; Conaglen, *Fiduciary Loyalty*, pp.204 and following.

[228] e.g. the trust instrument, as in *Re Beatty (Deceased)* [1990] 1 W.L.R. 1503 at 1506; *Edge v Pensions Ombudsman* [2000] Ch. 602 (CA) at 621–622.

[229] e.g. *Boardman v Phipps* [1967] 2 A.C. 46 at 109; *Re Haslam & Hier-Evans* [1902] 1 Ch. 765 at 769–770; *New Zealand Netherlands Society ("Oranje") Inc v Kuys* [1973] 1 W.L.R. 1126 at 1132.

[230] e.g. *Campbell v Walker* (1800) 5 Ves. 678 at 688; 31 E.R. 801 at 802; *Farmer v Dean* (1863) 32 Beav. 327; 55 E.R. 128; *Holder v Holder* [1968] 1 Ch. 353 at 398, 402.

[231] *Tito v Waddell (No.2)* [1977] Ch. 106.

[232] *Tito v Waddell (No.2)* [1977] Ch. 106 at 248.

[233] *Gwembe Valley Development Co Ltd v Koshy (No.3)* [2003] EWCA Civ 1048; [2004] 1 B.C.L.C. 131.

[234] *Gwembe Valley* [2003] EWCA Civ 1048; [2004] 1 B.C.L.C. 131 at [108].

[235] Cf. McGhee, *Snell's Equity*, para.7.051; Nolan, "Conflicts of Interest, Unjust Enrichment and Wrongdoing" in Cornish et al, *Restitution: Past, Present and Future*, which distinguishes between fiduciary conflict rules that might be understood as based on unjust enrichment, and others that might be understood to be based on wroingdoing.

[236] *Gwembe Valley* [2003] EWCA Civ 1048; [2004] 1 B.C.L.C 131 at [108].

[237] Nolan, "Conflicts of Interest, Unjust Enrichment and Wrongdoing" in Cornish et al., *Restitution—Past, Present and Future*, especially p.92, where he argued that claims based on the self-dealing rules "conform closely to the paradigm of an action in unjust enrichment".

to commit his principal's assets in self-dealing transactions, in which the fiduciary is involved on both sides. This in turn brings about the consequence that benefits received as a result of such transactions, and at the expense of the principal, are prima facie recoverable for want of authority. Consistently with this explanation, a self-dealing transaction is only unimpugnable if it is shown that the principal gave his prior consent to the transaction or subsequently affirmed it, after full disclosure of all material circumstances by the fiduciary—a high-hurdle explicable on policy grounds.

8–106   If the self-dealing rules are indeed properly viewed in these terms, then some important remedial consequences may prima facie follow where a self-dealing transaction occurs. Starting with *proprietary* claims, a self-dealing transaction, including an actual disposition of the fiduciary asset, is prima facie voidable, thereby enabling the principal to recover the asset in specie from its immediate recipient. In addition, if the fiduciary asset is transferred to a third party, then it seems that the principal might, on avoiding the self-dealing transaction, assert an equitable title to any unauthorised traceable substitute in the immediate recipient's hands.[238] The principal's right to set aside the transfer and recover the asset or its substitute could be viewed as a proprietary restitutionary remedy, designed to reverse the unjust enrichment of the recipient at the principal's expense, based on the fiduciary's want of authority. It might be argued that if it is the fiduciary himself against whom this relief is sought, then his unjust enrichment is a redundant explanation—the fiduciary's obligation to re-transfer the asset or its unauthorised traceable substitute in specie could be explained by the duties which the fiduciary voluntarily assumed when taking office. However, the unjust enrichment explanation may be a better explanation in other cases, where the immediate recipient under the self-dealing transaction is at least nominally a third party.[239] Where the fiduciary asset or its traceable substitute has been transferred by its immediate recipient to some other person, then the principal would seem to have the further option, on avoiding the self-dealing transaction, of asserting an equitable title to the asset in the third party's hands, subject to defences. As earlier explained in relation to invalid exercises of powers by fiduciaries, the principal's equitable entitlement to the asset in the third party's hands might be best regarded as arising to reverse this third party's unjust enrichment, on the ground of the fiduciary's want of authority.

8–107   More difficult is the question of the *personal* claims potentially available against the immediate recipient of the assets under the self-dealing transaction and/or remoter recipients. The fiduciary's accountability for any benefit received as a result of the self-dealing transaction can be readily explained, without recourse to the law of unjust enrichment, by the duties which he voluntarily assumed when taking office. However, to the extent that a personal claim is being brought against some other person—as where the fiduciary brings about a transfer of fiduciary assets to a company in which he is interested—then this explanation is unavailable. There are reasons for thinking that any recipients under a self-dealing transaction should be strictly liable in unjust enrichment on

---

[238] See para.8–53 and following.
[239] For a recent case in which the restoration of the asset transferred under a self-dealing transaction was explained as a remedy for unjust enrichment, see *Catley v Waipa Corp* [2010] NZHC 128 at [47]–[49].

the ground of the fiduciary's want of authority, although this is not easy to maintain as a matter of authority because of the prevailing view—criticised above—that recipients of misapplied fiduciary assets (including misapplied trust assets) are generally personally liable only for "knowing receipt" or for their dishonest assistance in another's breach of fiduciary duty.[240]

4. THREE-PARTY CASES: CLAIMS BY X, THE INTERMEDIARY

(a) *Introduction*

D may benefit as a result of a misapplication by X of assets to which one or more **8–108** others are entitled—most obviously, because X holds title as trustee, or because X has control over assets to which another has title and in relation to which X owes fiduciary duties. Might X, having misapplied these assets, bring a claim in unjust enrichment against D, relying on his want of authority to dispose of the assets which he holds or controls? This question can be tested by asking what happens if a trustee transfers trust assets outside his powers. Could he bring a personal claim in unjust enrichment against a recipient of these assets, or against a person who otherwise benefits from their application?

(b) *Misapplications of Trust Assets by Trustees*

In principle, there seems no reason why X trustee could not successfully bring a **8–109** claim in unjust enrichment in his capacity as office-holder, with a view to recovering the assets or their value for the benefit of the trust. Insofar as X has transferred away funds or other assets that he held as trustee, then any enrichment accruing to the defendant recipient can be regarded as at the expense of X trustee, for the purpose of supporting a claim by X in his capacity as trustee, to the extent that it represents a depletion of the trust assets which X holds. And since X is suing in his capacity as office-holder, the question whether X suffers any *personal* loss, and to what extent he does so, should be immaterial. This is supported by cases which assume that where a trustee, or a person occupying a similar position, inter alia pays money under a mistake, then he might bring a personal claim in unjust enrichment against the recipient based on the mistake.[241]

More difficulty arises from the suggestion that the ground for restitution on **8–110** which the trustee might rely is his *want of authority* to dispose of the trust assets. Whether a claim can be made on this basis, and the conditions on which it can be made, may depend on whether trust beneficiaries can bring a similar claim. That is, whether a third party recipient can be strictly liable in unjust enrichment for having received assets from a trustee, when acting outside his authority, ought to be answered in the same way, whether proceedings are brought by a beneficiary *or by a trustee.*

---

[240] See para.8–123 and following.
[241] See the cases cited at fn.133.

8–111   If, contrary to the arguments offered in Part 3, the English courts remain committed to the view that a trust beneficiary can only hold a recipient of misapplied trust assets personally liable on the ground of "knowing receipt", then this is inconsistent with the law affording the beneficiary, or the trustee, a strict liability personal claim in unjust enrichment against the third party recipient based on the ground of want of authority. Ex hypothesi, if a third party will only be fixed with personal liability where the third party had some degree of knowledge that the trustee had exceeded his authority, then this must be the case whether the claim to have the transfer from the trust made good is brought by the beneficiary or by his trustee. For if, as some argue,[242] there are good reasons for confining a third party recipient's personal liability to beneficiaries to a fault-based liability for knowing receipt, then these reasons almost certainly support the denial of *any* strict liability in unjust enrichment, based on "want of authority" alone, whether to the beneficiaries or to the trustees. It would be incoherent for the law to disallow a claim by the beneficiaries, but allow a claim by the trustees—indirectly undermining the innocent third party's immunity.

8–112   The position would be otherwise if, as advocated in Part 3, the English courts were finally to hold that trust beneficiaries might bring a strict liability personal claim in unjust enrichment against third party recipients of misapplied assets, based on the ground of want of authority. A good argument could then be made that the trustees might also be afforded standing to bring a similar claim, for the benefit of the trust, on proof that they, or former trustees whom they replaced, or their continuing co-trustees, had transferred trust funds or assets without authority.

8–113   Several lines of authority can be cited in support of this suggestion. First, it is well-established that trustees—including new trustees—have standing, concurrently with the trust's beneficiaries, to bring proceedings against former or continuing co-trustees to seek restoration of the trust assets or other relief for breach of trust on the beneficiaries' behalf,[243] even if the claimant trustees were themselves guilty of the breach.[244] Indeed, a trustee who fails to bring such proceedings runs the risk of committing a breach of trust.[245] A trustee's "paramount obligation" is "recovering, securing, and duly applying the trust fund",[246]

---

[242] See para.8–63.

[243] e.g. *Re Forest of Dean Coal Mining Co* (1878) 10 Ch.D. 450; *Re Cross* (1881) 20 Ch.D. 109 (CA) at 120; *Space Investments Ltd v Canadian Imperial Bank of Commerce Trust Co (Bahamas) Ltd* [1986] 1 W.L.R. 1072 (PC) at 1074; *Young v Murphy* [1996] 1 V.R. 279 (Vict. CA) at 281–283 (where the point is particularly fully reviewed); *Morlea Professional Services Ltd v Richard Walter Pty Ltd (In Liquidation)* [1999] FCA 1820; (1999) 96 F.C.R. 217 at [51]; *Re Cemcon* [2009] FCA 696 at [20]. To the extent that they are merely seeking to recover the trust assets or otherwise obtain relief for a breach, it seems that they can bring these proceedings without joining the beneficiaries, on the basis that the trustee generally sufficiently represents the beneficiaries' interests: e.g. *Franco v Franco* (1796) 3 Ves. Jr. 75 at 77; 30 E.R. 902; *May v Selby* (1842) 1 Y. & C.C.C. 235 at 238; (1842) 62 E.R. 869 at 871; *Re Cross* (1881) 20 Ch.D. 109 (CA) at 120; *Young v Murphy* [1996] 1 V.R. 279 at 283–284; *Morlea* [1999] FCA 1820; (1999) 96 F.C.R. 217 at [51]. Cf. *Butler v Butler* (1877) 7 Ch.D. 116 (CA) at 120.

[244] e.g. *Baynard v Woolley* (1855) 20 Beav. 583 at 585; 52 E.R. 729 at 730 ("[T]he books are full of cases" of trustees suing co-trustees); *Butler v Butler* (1877) 7 Ch.D. 116 at 120–121 per Baggallay L.J., at 121 per Thesiger L.J.; *Young v Murphy* [1996] 1 V.R. 279 at 283; *Morlea* [1999] FCA 1820; (1999) 6 F.C.R. 217 at [51].

[245] *Young v Murphy* [1996] 1 V.R. 279 at 281–282.

[246] *Re Brogden* (1888) 38 Ch.D. 546 at 571.

and this entails not only that he must get in the trust assets, but also that if he or any other trustee misapplies trust assets, then he must bring proceedings to recover the assets or otherwise obtain relief on the beneficiaries' behalf.[247]

Secondly, the courts have also held that where trust assets have been mis-   **8–114** applied, express trustees (including new trustees) have standing to bring proceedings against *third parties*, inter alia to recover the assets or their traceable proceeds in specie,[248] or to hold the third parties personally liable as knowing recipients of misapplied trust assets,[249] even if the claimant trustees were themselves responsible for the breach of trust,[250] once again as a corollary of the trustees' duty to get in the trust estate. The same reasoning has also been further extended to support equivalent proceedings by a person who has become liable to account as a constructive trustee as a consequence of his knowing receipt of misapplied trust assets.[251] If such a knowing recipient afterwards misapplies the assets, by transferring them to a third party without authority, recent cases have held that this party may itself bring proceedings against the third party inter alia for knowing receipt, on the basis inter alia that he owes the same duty as an express trustee to get in the trust estate.[252] This second category of cases provides a particularly strong analogy for affording a trustee standing to sue a third party in unjust enrichment on the ground of want of authority. For whilst the liability of a third party recipient for knowing receipt is not a liability in unjust enrichment,[253] if the law were to hold that third party recipients of misapplied trust assets are subject to a strict liability personal claim in unjust enrichment by the beneficiaries, then it would seem that—by analogy—a trustee should similarly be able to bring such a claim. Indeed, a claim by the trustee, who by virtue of his office represents all the beneficiaries, would generally seem to be more appropriate than a claim brought by one or more individual beneficiaries.

Thirdly, in a long line of authority, the courts have been prepared, in proceed-   **8–115** ings *brought by trustees*, to declare the trustees' own exercises of a dispositive

---

[247] *Re Forest of Dean* (1879) 10 Ch.D. 450 at 453–454; *Young v Murphy* [1996] 1 V.R. 279 at 281–282; *Morlea* [1999] FCA 1820; (1999) 96 F.C.R. 217 at [57]; *Evans v European Bank Ltd* [2004] NSWCA 82; (2004) 7 I.T.E.L.R. 19 at [116]. There is no distinction between claims to recover the trust assets *in specie* and claims to monetary compensation for losses caused to the trust: see *Young* [1996] 1 V.R. 279 at 284. And a trustee will also have standing to sue another trustee, for an order that he account for fees or other profits that it obtains, without authority and in breach of its fiduciary duties, from third parties: e.g. *Williams v Barton* [1927] 2 Ch. 9.
[248] e.g. *Case v James* (1861) 3 De G. F. & J. 256 at 270; 45 E.R. 876 at 883 per Turner L.J.; *Carson v Sloane* (1884) 13 L.R. Ir. 139 at 147 (cited with approval in *Young v Murphy* [1996] 1 V.R. 279 at 282).
[249] *Morlea* [1999] FCA 1820; (1999) 96 F.C.R. 217 at [51], [57] (where the express trustee's standing is understood to be a "representative" form of standing, derivative of the beneficiaries' action); similarly, *Evans* [2004] NSWCA 82; (2004) 7 I.T.E.L.R. 19 at [116]. Cf. too *Kizquari Pty Ltd v Prestoo Pty Ltd* (1993) 10 A.C.S.R. 606 (corporate trustee of unit trust paid excessive salaries to employees who were also unit-holders; it should recover back the sums, and if not otherwise recoverable, do so by adjusting the future distributions due to the employees).
[250] e.g. *Morlea* [1999] FCA 1820; (1999) 96 F.C.R. 217 at [51].
[251] *Evans* [2004] NSWCA 82; (2004) 7 I.T.E.L.R. 19 at [116] (where the claimant itself was not actually liable as a knowing recipient of misapplied trust assets, but was liable on the basis of its having received funds stolen from credit-card holders).
[252] *Evans* [2004] NSWCA 82; (2004) 7 I.T.E.L.R. 19 at [116]; also *Bracken Partners Ltd v Gutteridge* [2003] EWCA Civ 1875; [2004] 1 B.C.L.C. 374 (to similar effect, though rationalised with a less clarity).
[253] See para.8–123 and following.

power to be void (because exercised ultra vires)[254] or voidable (for example, under the rule in *Re Hastings-Bass*).[255]

8–116   Some authorities may seem, at first sight, to be inconsistent with these suggestions. Thus, in *Re Diplock*,[256] already discussed,[257] it was apparently assumed that a common law restitutionary claim by the executors, who had paid substantial sums by way of legacies under invalid provisions of a will, would be a claim for mistake of law and would fail on that basis.[258] This might appear inconsistent with the proposition that the executors might have brought a claim in unjust enrichment based on the ground of "want of authority" alone. However, the better answer is that the prevailing assumption in *Re Diplock* should be attributed to the strength of the common law bar to restitution for mistake of law at that time; that the law has since moved on[259]; and that by analogy to the law's treatment of trustees, executors should be permitted to proceed on the basis of their want of authority.

8–117   Less easy to dismiss are recent dicta of Lloyd L.J. in *Pitt v Holt*,[260] in the context of a comprehensive re-examination of the rule in *Re Hastings-Bass*. Lloyd L.J.'s conclusion was that the rule only rendered voidable an exercise of a dispositive power by trustees, by reason of their failure to take into account relevant considerations (or of their having taken into account irrelevant considerations), if in acting as they did, the trustees could be said to have breached one of their duties as trustees.[261] He then went on to suggest that in future, proceedings to challenge the exercise of a dispositive power on the basis of the rule in *Re Hastings-Bass* should almost always be brought by a beneficiary, and not by the trustees[262]:

> "One practical consequence, if I am right, is that if in future it is desired to challenge an exercise by trustees of a discretionary power on this basis, it will be necessary for one or more beneficiaries to grasp the nettle of alleging and proving a breach of fiduciary duty on the part of the trustees. Only rarely would it be appropriate for the trustees to take the initiative in the proceedings; it might be so if (as in the Abacus case) they need to seek directions from the court if a beneficiary alleges breach of trust but does not bring his own proceedings. Presumably proceedings by a beneficiary would generally need to be brought by a C.P.R. Pt 7 claim form, since it should not be assumed that there will not be a substantial dispute of fact that needs to be resolved, and statements of case will be needed in order to set out the allegation of breach of trust and the answer to that case."

---

[254] e.g. *Re Abrahams Will Trusts* [1969] 1 Ch. 463; *Re Hastings-Bass* [1975] Ch. 25 (as interpreted in *Pitt v Holt* [2011] EWCA Civ 197; [2011] 3 W.L.R. 19).

[255] e.g. *Green v Cobham* [2002] S.T.C. 820; *Abacus Trust Co (IOM) Ltd v NSPCC* [2001] S.T.C. 1344; *Abacus Trust Co (IOM) Ltd v Barr* [2003] EWHC 114 (Ch); [2003] Ch. 409; *Burrell v Burrell* [2005] EWHC 245 (Ch); [2005] S.T.C. 569; *Sieff v Fox* [2005] EWHC 1312 (Ch); [2005] 1 W.L.R. 3811.

[256] *Re Diplock* [1948] Ch. 465 (CA); [1951] A.C. 251.

[257] See paras 8–51—8–57.

[258] *Re Diplock* [1948] Ch. 465 (CA) at 479–481.

[259] See *Kleinwort Benson v Lincoln CC* [1999] 2 A.C. 349 (abolishing the mistake of law bar); discussed at para.9–71 and following.

[260] *Pitt v Holt* [2011] EWCA Civ 197; [2011] 3 W.L.R. 19.

[261] *Pitt v Holt* [2011] EWCA Civ 197; [2011] 3 W.L.R. 19 at [126] and following.

[262] *Pitt v Holt* [2011] EWCA Civ 197; [2011] 3 W.L.R. 19 at [130].

Lloyd L.J.'s view would entail a significant alteration to established practice, **8–118** where it was common for trustees to challenge their own decisions on the basis of the rule in *Re Hastings-Bass*.[263] He did not elaborate the reasons for his view. Possibly he had in mind the dilemma which a trustee might face if he was required to incriminate himself, and run the risk of exposing himself to possible liability to the beneficiaries, by pleading his own breach of trust. However, this concern—whilst understandable—has not deterred courts in other cases finding that trustees can (or indeed must) bring proceedings on behalf of the beneficiaries, even where they must plead their own misconduct as a necessary element of the claim.[264] Viewed in this broader context, Lloyd L.J.'s suggestion in *Pitt v Holt* therefore are both novel and difficult to sustain.

As the claims being brought here are claims brought by a trustee officeholder, **8–119** pursuant to his duties as officeholder, it should follow that (1) the standing of a particular trustee to sue should be broadly co-extensive with his status as trustee (so that if he resigns as trustee, or the trust terminates, then in the ordinary course, this standing, which is a corollary of his duty to recover the trust assets so that the trust can be reconstituted and administered, may fall away)[265]; and (2) that standing should be available on a similar basis to anyone who subsequently comes to occupy the office.[266]

(c) *Misapplications by Persons Other than Trustees*

In principle, the law applying to trustees might be applied—by analogical **8–120** extension—to at least some other categories of intermediary, who are fixed with duties and invested with limited powers of disposition over assets for the benefit of others. It could certainly be expected that similar principles might be applied to executors or administrators of a deceased's estate, who have similar duties to get in and duly distribute the estate, irrespective of the extent to which these persons are properly regarded as "trustees". It is less obvious that they might be applied more broadly to other parties who occupy a fiduciary relationship in respect of another's assets—as in the case of company directors and a company, or agents and principals more generally.

In principle, there are two major constraints on the availability of a claim to **8–121** persons occupying these positions. One consideration is the plausibility of saying that a defendant's enrichment was at the relevant claimant's expense. This seems easy where, as in the case of a personal representative, the claimant held title to the assets which are the subject of the unauthorised disposition to the third party. However, it seems more difficult in the case of a company director acting for a company, where the title is vested in the company and the assets are (at best) under the control of the company's director(s) and other human agents.

A second consideration is whether it is necessary or appropriate to recognise **8–122** a concurrent cause of action, in the name of the relevant claimant. This is clear in the case of a trustee, because of his ongoing responsibilities to get in (and recover) the trust assets and administer those assets for the benefit of the trust's

---

[263] See the cases cited in fn.255.
[264] See the cases cited in fn.243.
[265] Cf. *Morlea* [1999] FCA 1820; (1999) 96 F.C.R. 217 at [61]–[66].
[266] As recognised in e.g. *Young v Murphy* [1996] 1 V.R. 279.

beneficiaries. The same is plausible in the case of an executor and an administrator of an estate in the course of administration. But in a simple case where assets owned absolutely by a natural or legal person have been misapplied by an intermediary, there is no obvious reason for extending a cause of action to someone other than the absolute owner.

5. LIABILITY FOR KNOWING RECEIPT

8–123   Where trust assets are misapplied by trustees in breach of trust, a recipient of the misapplied assets or their traceable proceeds may incur an equitable personal liability to the trust's beneficiaries[267] for "knowing receipt".[268] A recipient will do so if he received the misapplied assets or their traceable proceeds[269] beneficially,[270] in circumstances where he cannot claim to take free of the beneficiaries' interests,[271] and if he knows that the assets have been transferred to him in breach of trust at the time he receives the assets, or if not, then at some later time whilst he still holds the assets or their traceable proceeds. As currently defined, "knowledge" refers here to a state of mind that includes but is not limited to dishonesty, which is "such as to make it unconscionable for [the recipient] to retain the benefit of the receipt".[272] An equivalent liability will also be incurred where assets belonging to a principal but under the control of some other fiduciary are misapplied in breach of the duties which this fiduciary owes to his principal.[273]

8–124   So described, the equitable personal liability for knowing receipt clearly depends on proof of some measure of fault. However, as already explained,[274] it

---

[267] Trustees can also bring an action for knowing receipt in a representative capacity, as discussed in *Morlea* [1999] FCA 1820; (1999) 96 F.C.R. 217; and in rare cases, a knowing recipient may also bring an action in knowing receipt against a knowing recipient from him, pursuant to his duty to get in the property so that the trust fund can be reconstituted: see *Bracken Partners* [2003] EWCA Civ 1875; [2004] 1 B.C.L.C. 377; *Evans* [2004] NSWCA 82; (2004) 7 I.T.E.L.R. 19.

[268] For a full account, see e.g. *Underhill and Hayton*, paras 98.11–98.36.

[269] e.g. *El Ajou v Dollar Land Holdings Plc* [1994] 2 All E.R. 685 at 700 per Hoffmann L.J.

[270] i.e. in a non-ministerial capacity: *Barnes v Addy* (1874) 9 Ch. App. 244 at 254–255; *Adams v Bank of New South Wales* [1984] 1 N.S.W.L.R. 285 at 290–292; *Westpac Banking Corp v Savin* [1985] 2 N.Z.L.R. 41 at 69; *Agip* [1990] Ch. 265 at 291–292; *Cukurooa Celik Enduustrisi AS v Hill Taylor Dickinson (A Firm)* Unreported QBD (Comm Ct.) June 7, 1996; *Trustor A.B. v Smallbone (No.2)* [2001] 3 All E.R. 987 at 994; *Twinsectra v Yardley* [2002] UKHL 12; [2002] 2 A.C. 164 at [106].

[271] e.g. as a bona fide purchaser of the legal title.

[272] *Bank of Credit and Commerce International (Overseas) Ltd v Akindele* [2001] Ch. 437 (CA) at 455 per Nourse L.J., eschewing the over-subtle distinctions drawn between types or degrees of knowledge in earlier cases, based on the five-fold classification articulated by Peter Gibson J. in *Baden* [1993] 1 W.L.R. 509n. at 575–587. Although criticised because of its lack of clarity, the *BCCI* test has been reaffirmed by the Court of Appeal on several occasions: *Criterion* [2002] EWCA Civ 1883; [2003] 1 W.L.R. 2108 at [20]–[39] (not reviewed on appeal [2004] UKHL 28; [2004] 1 W.L.R. 1846); *Charter Plc v City Index Ltd* [2007] EWCA Civ 1382; [2008] Ch. 313; *Uzinterimpex* [2008] EWCA Civ 819; [2008] 2 Lloyd's Rep. 456.

[273] e.g. a company director, who owes fiduciary duties in relation to his handling of company property to the company, his principal, or an employee: as in *Belmont Finance (No.2)* [1980] 1 All E.R. 393; *Baden* [1993] 1 W.L.R. 509n.; *Rolled Steel Products* [1986] Ch. 246; *Precision Dippings* [1986] Ch. 447; *Agip* [1991] Ch. 547; *Heinl v Jyske Bank* [1999] Lloyd's Rep. Bank. 511; *CMS Dolphin Ltd v Simonet* [2001] 2 B.C.L.C. 704; *Primlake* [2006] EWHC 1227 (Ch); [2007] 1 B.C.L.C. 666.

[274] See paras 8–50 and following (and in particular 8–63 and following).

is an important and controversial question whether recipients of assets transferred by a trustee in breach of trust should owe a *strict* personal liability in unjust enrichment directly to the trust's beneficiaries.[275] Some advocates of this development have supported this suggestion on the basis that, properly understood, the liability for knowing receipt *is* a liability for unjust enrichment, to which a fault element has been inappropriately attached.[276] However, in our view, this rests on a misconception. Properly understood, and for the reasons which follow, the equitable liability for knowing receipt is *not* a liability in unjust enrichment. Accordingly, whilst a good case can be made that the law *should* in future subject recipients of misapplied trust assets to a strict personal liability in unjust enrichment,[277] the appropriate medium for this legal development is the recognition of a new *concurrent* strict personal liability in unjust enrichment, alongside the existing fault-based personal liability for knowing receipt.[278]

Historically, it has been said that a knowing recipient of misapplied trust assets **8–125** comes under a personal liability "to account as a constructive trustee" for the assets he received.[279] Over the last two decades or so, it has nevertheless become fashionable to say that this language adds nothing to our understanding of the liability of knowing recipients, and indeed obscures the liability's true nature.[280] We disagree. Properly understood, there is nothing intolerably fictional or misleading about saying that a knowing recipient is personally liable to account as a constructive trustee. Liability for knowing receipt is a distinctive, custodial

---

[275] Supportive: e.g. P. Birks, "Misdirected Funds: Restitution from the Recipient" [1989] L.M.C.L.Q. 296; P. Birks, "Receipt" in P. Birks and A. Pretto (eds), *Breach of Trust* (Oxford: Hart, 2002), Ch.7, pp.228 and following; Burrows, *The Law of Restitution*, pp.424 and following; Chambers and Penner, "Ignorance" in Degeling and Edelman, *Unjust Enrichment in Commercial Law*; *Twinsectra* [2002] UKHL 12; [2002] 2 A.C. 164 at [105] per Lord Millett; *Dubai Aluminium* [2003] UKHL 48; [2003] 2 A.C. 366 at [87] per Lord Millett; Nicholls, "Knowing Receipt: The Need for a New Landmark" in Cornish et al, *Restitution: Past, Present and Future*; Walker, "Dishonesty and Unconscionable Conduct in Commercial Life", p.202; Millett, "Proprietary Restitution" in Degeling and Edelman, *Equity in Commercial Law*, pp.311–312. Opposed: Smith, "Unjust Enrichment, Property and the Structure of Trusts", critically examined in M. Bryan, "The Liability of the Recipient: Restitution at Common Law or Wrongdoing in Equity?" in Degeling and Edelman (eds), *Equity in Commercial Law*, Ch.13.

[276] See especially Birks, "Misdirected Funds: Restitution from the Recipient". He subsequently came round for the different view, that the law should recognise concurrent heads of fault-based liability for knowing receipt and strict liability in unjust enrichment: see e.g. Birks, "Receipt" in Birks and Pretto, *Breach of Trust*. Cf. the position in Canada, where the courts have effectively held that knowing receipt is a (fault-based) liability in unjust enrichment: *Gold v Rosenberg* [1997] 3 S.C.R. 767; *Citadel* [1997] 3 S.C.R. 805.

[277] See the discussion at para.8–63 and following.

[278] As contemplated by Nicholls, "Knowing Receipt: The Need for a New Landmark" in Cornish et al, *Restitution: Past, Present and Future*; Birks, "Receipt" in Birks and Pretto, *Breach of Trust*; Walker, "Dishonesty and Unconscionable Conduct in Commercial Life", p.202; Walker, "Fraud, Fault and Fiduciary Liability", para.[31]. This step was taken by the Jersey courts in *Re Esteem Settlement*, 2002 J.L.R. 53 at [148]–[161], but rejected by the High Court of Australia in *Farah Constructions* [2007] HCA 22; (2007) 230 C.L.R. 89 at [148]–[158].

[279] See for fuller discussion, C. Mitchell and S. Watterson, "Remedies for Knowing Receipt", in C. Mitchell (ed.), *Constructive and Resulting Trusts* (Oxford: Hart, 2010), Ch.4, pp.128–131.

[280] A recurring theme in the work of Peter Birks: see e.g. Birks, *An Introduction to the Law of Restitution*, pp.80–82; P. Birks, "Persistent Problems in Misdirected Money: A Quintet" [1993] L.M.C.L.Q. 218, 236. Similar views are expressed by, inter alia, C. Rickett, "The Classification of Trusts" (1999) 18 N.Z.U.L.R. 305, 321–324; Burrows, *The Law of Restitution*, p.429. Birks' analysis seems to have exercised a strong influence on the thinking of some members of the judiciary: see e.g. *Paragon Finance Plc v D.B. Thakerar & Co* [1999] 1 All E.R. 400 (CA) at 409 per Millett L.J.

liability, which closely resembles the liability of express trustees to account for the trust property with which they are charged. When the courts say that a knowing recipient is "personally liable to account as a constructive trustee", they mean exactly what they say. As a result of the circumstances in which knowing recipients acquire title to the misapplied property, equity fixes them with custodial duties which are of the same nature as some of those voluntarily assumed by express trustees. Furthermore, the accounting mechanisms through which a knowing recipient can be made liable for the performance of their duties, or their breach, are the same as those through which trust beneficiaries can take action against express trustees.

8–126   The core custodial duty of a knowing recipient is a restorative duty[281]: a duty immediately to restore the misapplied assets, usually to the trustees, so that the trust can be reconstituted and administered for the benefit of the beneficiaries,[282] and not to deal with the assets in any other way. In certain circumstances, a knowing recipient may also incur further custodial duties, over and above this core restorative duty[283]—in particular, a duty to preserve and/or invest the assets, including a duty to take steps to recover them if they are lost[284]—but it is usually only the restorative duty that is of practical significance.

8–127   The remedies available to a beneficiary against a knowing recipient for the performance or non-performance of his core restorative duty are the same as those available against an ordinary express trustee.[285] Where the assets remain in his hands, then he can be ordered to restore the assets *in specie*: a measure of specific performance of his restorative duty. Where the assets have been disposed of, and the knowing recipient cannot show that the disposal was authorised, then by analogy to the law's treatment of express trustees, the account will be falsified. Two remedial consequences may then follow, mirroring the treatment of express trustees. First, without alleging any breach of trust,[286] the beneficiary may obtain an order that obliges the knowing recipient, in lieu of restoring the assets *in specie*, to pay the current monetary value of the assets, or where the assets comprise money, the capital sum plus interest: i.e. an order for substitutive performance of the knowing recipient's restorative duty. Secondly, and alternatively, the beneficiary might opt to allege a breach of trust, and seek instead an order requiring the knowing recipient to pay compensation for the losses caused to the trust by the breach.

8–128   Once the nature of a knowing recipient's duties and his associated liabilities are properly perceived, then it becomes easier to see why it might have been

---

[281] See for fuller analysis, Mitchell and Watterson, "Remedies for Knowing Receipt" in Mitchell, *Constructive Trusts*, pp.132 and following. Cf. *Re Holmes* [2004] EWHC 2020 (Admin); [2005] 1 W.L.R. 1857 at [22]; *Darkingjung Pty Ltd v Darkingjung Local Aboriginal Land Council* [2006] NSWSC 1217 at [47].

[282] If the trust is a bare trust, rather than a more complex continuing trust, the duty might be discharged by restoring the assets to the bare trust beneficiary instead.

[283] See generally Mitchell and Watterson, "Remedies for Knowing Receipt" in Mitchell, *Constructive Trusts*, pp.138 and following.

[284] *Evans* [2004] NSWCA 82; (2004) 7 I.T.E.L.R. 19, discussed in Mitchell and Watterson, "Remedies for Knowing Receipt" in Mitchell, *Constructive Trusts*, pp.138–139. See too *Bracken Partners*; [2003] EWCA Civ 1875; [2004] 1 B.C.L.C. 377.

[285] For a full account, see e.g. Mitchell and Watterson, "Remedies for Knowing Receipt" in Mitchell, *Constructive Trusts*, pp.120–127, 135–138.

[286] See *Green v Weatherill* [1929] 2 Ch. 213 at 222–223.

tempting for some—as we see it, wrongly—to re-characterise liability for knowing receipt as a liability in unjust enrichment. One possible source of confusion is the description of knowing receipt as a "receipt-based" liability, a description that dates from Millett J.'s decision in *Agip*.[287] This description is tolerable, insofar as it correctly identifies that receipt of misapplied trust assets is a necessary ingredient of liability, and therefore distinguishes liability for knowing receipt from the liability of a person who is liable for having dishonestly participated in another's breach of trust. Unfortunately, the terminology "receipt-based" has sometimes been used in a different sense, reflecting an assumption that liability for knowing receipt rests on proof that the recipient was unjustly enriched.[288] This is a dangerous error. As the law now stands, the reason why the defendant must have received trust assets before he can be liable[289] is not that the defendant must have been unjustly enriched, but that liability for knowing receipt depends on the defendant owing custodial duties as a trustee of assets which he has actually received. If the only reason why it mattered that the defendant had received title to trust assets was to establish that he had been enriched, then liability for knowing receipt could be expected to arise in a far wider range of cases—as where the defendant has never received any assets, but has been enriched as a result of assets being used in some other way, as in the discharge of his debts. However, the courts have expressly denied that "receipt" has this extended meaning.[290]

A second possible source for confusion arises from a latent ambiguity in the term "restitution". This word has now passed into common usage as a term to describe the gain-based remedy awarded to claimants in unjust enrichment. However, in breach of trust cases, it has frequently been used—and is still sometimes used—as a synonym for restoration of the trust estate as a compensatory device, either by returning the trust property in specie or by paying its current value—whether or not this value has ever been received by the defendant.[291] A final, related source of confusion arises because a knowing recipient is liable to perform or render substitutive performance of his primary restorative duty, without it being necessary to allege a *breach* of any duty on his part. A claim in unjust enrichment also generates a primary "restitutionary" liability, which entails performance of a primary duty to pay the value of benefits received by the defendant, rather than performance of a secondary duty to pay money trig-

8-129

---

[287] *Agip* [1990] Ch. 265 at 291–292 per Millett J.

[288] *Twinsectra* [2002] 2 A.C. 264 at [105] per Lord Millett; *Dubai Aluminium* [2002] UKHL 48; [2003] 2 A.C. 366 at [87]–[111] per Lord Millett. See too *Citadel* [1997] 3 S.C.R. 805 at [46] (followed in *Gold v Rosenberg* [1997] 3 S.C.R. 767 at [41]), borrowing this terminology from the article by Lord Millett, "Tracing the Proceeds of Fraud" (1991) 107 L.Q.R. 71.

[289] e.g. *Satnam Investments Ltd v Dunlop Heywood & Co Ltd* [1999] 1 B.C.L.C. 385 (CA) at 404; *Goose v Wilson Sandford & Co (A Firm)* [2001] Lloyd's Rep. P.N. 189 (CA) at [88]; *Trustor A.B. v Smallbone (No.2)* [2001] 1 W.L.R. 1177 at [18]–[19] per Morritt V.C.; *O.J.S.C. Oil Co Yugraneft (In Liquidation) v Abramovich* [2008] EWHC 2613 (Comm) at [372].

[290] *Quince v Varga* [2008] QCA 376; (2008) 11 I.T.L.E.R. 939 at [48]–[53]; *O.J.S.C. Oil* [2008] EWHC 2613 (Comm) at [365]; *Commonwealth Oil & Gas Co Ltd v Baxter* [2009] CSIH 75; 2010 S.C. 156; and cf. *St. Vincent de Paul Society Qld v Ozcare Ltd* [2009] QCA 335.

[291] e.g. *Gray v Johnston* (1868) L.R. 3 H.L. 1 at 14; *Ex p. Adamson* (1878) 8 Ch.D. 807 at 819; *Nocton v Lord Ashburton* [1914] A.C. 932 at 952; *Bartlett v Barclays Bank Trust Co Ltd (No.2)* [1980] Ch. 515 at 543; *Target Holdings Ltd v Redferns* [1996] A.C. 421 at 436; *Att Gen v Trustees of the British Museum* [2005] EWHC 1089 (Ch); [2005] Ch. 397 at [20].

gered by breach of a primary duty.[292] However, as already explained, a liability to make restitution of an unjust enrichment is crucially different from a liability to effect restoration of misapplied trust property.

8–130   Whilst they may often appear to coincide, a simple illustration shows that the measure of a knowing recipient's liability can sometimes be very different from the measure of the personal liability he might owe if he were personally liable in unjust enrichment. Suppose, for example, that a defendant receives and then sells shares which later increase in value and spends the cash proceeds on a holiday. Assuming that any change of position defence were disallowed, any liability he might owe in unjust enrichment would be limited to the value of the shares at the time of receipt, or (possibly) the value that he received when he disposed of them,[293] plus interest. If the defendant were liable as a knowing recipient, however, then he would be chargeable with the current value of the shares. An example is *Re Rothko*,[294] an American case where executors of the renowned painter, Mark Rothko, had improperly transferred a large number of his paintings to third parties, who subsequently disposed of them. The value of Rothko's works then appreciated greatly, and in proceedings by the beneficiaries of his estate, the New York Court of Appeals held that the third parties were liable for the current market value of the paintings.

---

[292] S. Smith, "Unjust Enrichment: Nearer to Tort than Contract" in R. Chambers et al. (eds), *Philosophical Foundations of the Law of Unjust Enrichment* (Oxford: OUP, 2009), Ch.7.
[293] See paras 4–34—4–42, for discussion of whether liability in unjust enrichment is confined to the value received.
[294] *Re Rothko* 43 N.Y. 2d 305; 372 N.E. 2d 291 (1977).

CHAPTER 9

MISTAKE

1. INTRODUCTION

Fundamental developments in the law over the last 30 years allow the law **9–01** governing the operation of mistake as a ground for restitution to be presented more simply than has previously been the case. First and foremost amongst these developments has been a fundamental liberalisation of the ambit of restitution-grounding mistakes. Stage-by-stage, previous limitations have been abandoned, with the result that the law's starting-point is now that any causative mistake of fact or law, spontaneous or induced, can qualify.[1] The much-criticised rule against recovery for mistakes of law has been abandoned,[2] and the courts have eschewed any requirement for the mistake to be a "liability mistake",[3] a "fundamental" mistake,[4] or a mistake of any other particular type.[5] This simple picture is not completely unqualified. A mistaken party is likely to confront higher hurdles, set by the law of contract, if the benefit in respect of which restitution is sought is conferred pursuant to a contract.[6] Some recent cases clearly signal that the same may also be true of mistaken gifts.[7] And it remains a controversial question how far the courts do or should set higher hurdles where the claimant seeks a proprietary remedy.[8] Nevertheless, if the claimant is only bringing a personal claim, for the value of a benefit that was not conferred under a contract, nor as a gift, the authorities now overwhelmingly indicate that the liberal test of causative mistake governs the case.

The second important development concerns the types of benefit for which **9–02** restitution may be sought on the ground of mistake. Historically, the overwhelming majority of claims brought on the ground of mistake have been personal claims for money received by the defendant. Comparatively few cases have recognised that the value of non-money benefits can be recovered on this ground. In part, this reluctance can be attributed to a failure to recognise the law of unjust enrichment for what it is—a single body of law governing claims to recover enrichments of every type.[9] Now that this has been recognised by the courts, former inhibitions should fall away. If defendant was enriched at the claimant's expense as a result of an operative mistake, then a restitutionary remedy should be available to recover the value of this enrichment, regardless of

---

[1] See para.9–67 and following.
[2] See para.9–71 and following.
[3] See para.9–95 and following.
[4] See para.9–97 and following.
[5] See para.9–95 and following.
[6] See paras 9–68—9–69.
[7] See paras 9–101—9–106, 9–110.
[8] See para.9–111 and Ch.37.
[9] See paras 1–13—1–14, and Chs 4 and 5.

whether the benefit received by the defendant is the face value of money[10] the use value of money,[11] the capital value or the use value of some other type of asset,[12] the receipt of services,[13] or the discharge of an obligation which the defendant owed to another party.[14]

9–03 So, for example, in *Sempra Metals Ltd v IRC*,[15] the House of Lords awarded a restitutionary remedy, in the form of an award of interest, reflecting the use value of money paid by mistake. In *Cressmann v Coys of Kensington (Sales) Ltd*[16] where the right to a personalised car number-plate was transferred to a car's purchaser by mistake, the Court of Appeal awarded a restitutionary remedy reflecting the value of this right. And in *Craven-Ellis v Canons Ltd*[17] a restitutionary remedy was awarded to the acting managing director of a the company, reflecting the value of the services that he had mistakenly rendered to company, pursuant to a void contract.

9–04 In previous editions of this work, discussion of mistake as a ground for restitution was divided into different chapters, according to the type of benefit conferred.[18] The present edition takes a different approach, of examining in a single chapter the types of mistake that may support a claim in unjust enrichment. To maintain the former divided treatment would run the risk of perpetuating the idea that the old authorities and the distinctions they entail remain good law —even though, when viewed through the lens of the modern law, it seems doubtful that a future court would reach the same conclusion. For example, it has previously been suggested that greater difficulties arise in connection with claims for the value of services which take the form of mistaken improvements to land,

---

[10] Whether in cash, or more often today, in the form of a credit to a bank account: e.g. *Barclays Bank Ltd v W.J. Simms, Sons and Cooke (Southern) Ltd* [1980] Q.B. 677; *Lloyds Bank Plc v Independent Insurance Co Ltd* [2000] Q.B. 110 (CA); *Jones v Churcher* [2009] EWHC 722 (QB); [2009] 2 Lloyd's Rep. 94.

[11] *Sempra Metals Ltd v IRC* [2007] UKHL 34; [2008] 1 A.C. 561.

[12] *Cressman v Coys of Kensington (Sales) Ltd* [2004] EWCA 47; [2004] 1 W.L.R. 2775. See also cases awarding a *proprietary* restitutionary remedy, as where a trust is imposed on an asset received by the defendant as a result of a mistake (e.g. *Chase Manhattan Bank NA v Israel-British Bank (London) Ltd* [1981] Ch. 105), where a transfer of title to an asset can be rescinded for an induced mistake at law or in equity (e.g. *Car & Universal Finance Co Ltd v Caldwell* [1965] 1 Q.B. 525), or where a voluntary settlement or transfer of an asset can be rescinded in equity for spontaneous mistake (e.g. *Re Griffiths* [2008] EWHC 118 (Ch); [2009] Ch. 162).

[13] *Craven-Ellis v Canons Ltd* [1936] 2 K.B. 403 (CA); *Rover International Ltd v Cannon Film Sales Ltd (No.3)* [1989] 1 W.L.R. 912 (CA) especially at 926–927 per Kerr L.J. (film distribution services mistakenly provided under a void contract); *Greenwood v Bennett* [1973] Q.B. 195 (CA) (improvements to car rendered under a mistake as to ownership). Cf. *R. (Rowe) v Vale of White Horse DC* [2003] EWHC 388 (Admin); [2003] 1 Lloyd's Rep. 418 (sewerage services: no mistake on facts).

[14] *B. Liggett (Liverpool) Ltd v Barclays Bank Ltd* [1928] 1 K.B. 48 (discharge of a monetary obligation by mistake); *County of Carleton v City of Ottawa* (1965) 52 D.L.R. (2d) 220 (discharge of a statutory obligation to provide assistance to an indigent mistakenly believed to be within municipal boundaries). See also cases where the remedy of subrogation to a paid-off creditor's extinguished security interest is awarded on the ground of mistake, to reverse the enrichment of the discharged debtor and his other creditors: e.g. *Banque Financière de la Cité v Parc (Battersea) Ltd* [1999] 1 A.C. 221 at 227 and 234; *Filby v Mortgage Express (No.2) Ltd* [2004] EWCA Civ 759; C. Mitchell and S. Watterson, *Subrogation: Law and Practice* (Oxford, OUP, 2007) Ch.6D; see further Ch.39.

[15] *Sempra Metals Ltd v IRC* [2007] UKHL 34; [2008] 1 A.C. 561; see further paras 5–05—5–14.

[16] *Cressman v Coys of Kensington (Sales) Ltd* [2004] EWCA 47; [2004] 1 W.L.R. 2775.

[17] *Craven-Ellis v Canons Ltd* [1936] 2 K.B. 403 (CA).

[18] G. Jones, *Goff & Jones: The Law of Restitution*, 7th edn (London: Sweet & Maxwell, 2006), Chs 4–9.

and that a restitutionary remedy will only be available under, or at least consistently with, the law of proprietary estoppel—with the result that something more than a merely causative mistake is needed, amounting to unconscionable conduct on the part of the defendant.[19] Once these cases are set in the context of the wider law of mistake, however, this argument seems doubtful.[20]

This chapter approaches the subject matter in the following way. It first **9–05** examines what counts as a "mistake" for the purpose of the law of unjust enrichment (Part 2), before turning to the requirement that the claimant's mistake must have caused him to confer a benefit on the defendant, and the possibility that some transactions may be "too remote" from the operative mistake to count (Part 3). It then examines the under-explored question of *whose* mistake counts where benefits are conferred via employees or agents (Part 4), before turning to examine at more length the type or quality of mistakes that can ground restitution (Part 5), the relevance of fault on the defendant's side (Part 6), and disqualifying circumstances, including fault on the claimant's side, that might bar a claim (Part 7). The form of the restitutionary remedy available where benefits are conferred as a result of a mistake—and the question whether, and in what form, a *proprietary* restitutionary remedy may be available—are discussed in later chapters.[21]

2. THE NATURE OF A MISTAKE

(a) *Introduction*

What counts as a "mistake" for the purposes of the law of restitution? At its core, **9–06** a mistake involves an incorrect belief or assumption about a past or present state of affairs. But is a misprediction a qualifying mistake? Can a claimant make a mistake if he has doubts as to the matter about which he claims to be mistaken? Can a state of ignorance qualify? And how are automated transactions to be analysed?

(b) *Mispredictions*

It is clearly established that a "misprediction", consisting of a present belief or **9–07** assumption about a future state of affairs which is subsequently falsfied, is not an operative mistake for the purposes of the law of unjust enrichment, even when it

---

[19] *Goff & Jones: The Law of Restitution*, paras 6–002 and following; *Blue Haven Enterprises Ltd v Tully* [2006] UKPC 17 at [20]; *J.S. Bloor Ltd v Pavillion Developments Ltd* [2008] EWHC 724 at [48].
[20] The commingling of the law of unjust enrichment and the law on proprietary estoppel which is reflected in the authorities cited in fn.19 is powerfully criticised by T. Wu, "An Unjust Enrichment Claim for the Mistaken Improver of Land" [2011] Conv. 8.
[21] See Chs 37–40.

causes one person to confer a benefit on another; nor does a misprediction constitute a ground for restitution in its own right.[22]

9–08   This restriction has been rationalised on two related grounds.[23] First, a misprediction is different from a mistake: the decision-making process of a person who makes a misprediction is not impaired in the same sense as the decision-making process of a person who acts on an incorrect belief or assumption about some past or present state of affairs. It was not informed by data which were incorrect when acted on: there was no incorrect perception of the reality when the mispredictor acted; he merely made a speculation about the future, which turned out to be wrong. As Peter Birks put it in a passage quoted with approval in *Dextra Bank & Trust Co Ltd v Bank of Jamaica*[24]:

> "restitution for mistake rests on the fact that the plaintiff's judgement was vitiated in the matter of the transfer of wealth to the defendant. A mistake as to the future, a misprediction, does not show that the plaintiff's judgement was vitiated, only that as things turned out it was incorrectly exercised".[25]

Secondly, and reinforcing this, a mispredictor can generally be viewed as a conscious risk-taker, who assumed the risk of his speculation proving to be incorrect. The future is, in most cases at least, not merely inherently uncertain, but also known to be such:

> "[A] prediction is an exercise of judgement. To act on the basis of a prediction is to accept the risk of disappointment. If you then complain of having been mistaken you are merely asking to be relieved of a risk knowingly run".[26]

9–09   The distinction between mistakes and mispredictions was accepted by the Privy Council in *Dextra Bank*,[27] where Dextra had paid US$2.99 million to BOJ

---

[22] *Kleinwort Benson Ltd v Lincoln CC* [1999] 2 A.C. 349 at 399 per Lord Hoffmann, and 409 per Lord Hope; *Fashion Gossip Ltd v Esprit Telecoms UK Ltd*, unreported, CA, July 27, 2000; *Dextra Bank & Trust Co Ltd v Bank of Jamaica* [2001] UKPC 50; [2002] 1 All E.R. (Comm.) 193; *Re Griffiths* [2008] EWHC 118 (Ch); [2009] Ch. 162; *Cadorange Pty Ltd (In Liquidation) v Wua Holdings Pty Ltd* (1990) 20 N.S.W.L.R. 26 at 32; *Sunstar Fruit Pty Ltd v Cosmo* [1995] 2 Qd R. 214 at 225–227; *Hookway v Racing Victoria Ltd* [2005] VSCA 310; (2005) 13 V.R. 444 at [61]–[62]; *Re Magarey Farlam Lawyers Trust Accounts (No.3)* [2007] SASC 9; (2006) 96 S.A.S.R. 337 at 387; *Lahoud v Lahoud* [2010] NSWSC 1297 at [179]–[180]; *A.S.B. Securities Ltd v Geurts* [2005] 1 N.Z.L.R. 484 at [44]; *Takahashi v Cheng Zhen Chu* [2008] HKCFI 781 at [102] and following; *Dex Asia Ltd v D.B.S. Bank (Hong Kong)* [2009] HKCFI 560 at [111] and [114]. For academic discussion, see especially the influential account of P. Birks, *An Introduction to the Law of Restitution*, revised edn, (Oxford: OUP, 1989), pp.147–148; and the illuminating analysis of W. Seah, "Mispredictions, Mistake and the Law of Unjust Enrichment" [2007] R.L.R. 93.

[23] Birks, *An Introduction to the Law of Restitution*, pp.147–148; Seah, "Mispredictions, Mistake and the Law of Unjust Enrichment", p.95, and following.

[24] *Dextra Bank & Trust Co Ltd v Bank of Jamaica* [2001] UKPC 50; [2002] 1 All E.R. (Comm.) 193 (PC) at [29].

[25] Birks, *An Introduction to the Law of Restitution*, pp.147–148.

[26] Birks, *An Introduction to the Law of Restitution*, pp.147–148.

[27] *Dextra Bank* [2001] UKPC 50; [2002] 1 All E.R. (Comm.) 193 (PC). The distinction has long been implicit in the law governing relief for misrepresentations—that is, induced mistakes—where the general rule is that a misrepresentation must involve a false statement of past or existing fact, and that a representation as to the future is not sufficient without more (e.g. *Strachan & Henshaw Ltd v Stein Industrie (UK) Ltd* (1997) 87 B.L.R. 52 (CA); *The Seaflower* [2000] 2 Lloyd's Rep. 37 at 42). This means, for example, that a statement as to a person's future conduct will not as such ground relief as a misrepresentation if he merely fails to do what he said he would; but the position changes if he can

pursuant to a cheque which Dextra had drawn up in favour of BOJ, and delivered to BOJ via intermediaries. As a result of third parties' frauds, Dextra believed it was making a loan to BOJ, whereas BOJ believed it was receiving US dollars in exchange for an equivalent sum of Jamaican dollars. Dextra subsequently sought to recover the US$2.999 million from BOJ on the ground of mistake of fact, alleging a mistaken belief that the money was being paid by way of a loan to BOJ, or that BOJ had previously made an in-principle agreement to take a loan. The Privy Council rejected Dextra's claim, holding that Dextra's payment had been caused by a misprediction, and that a misprediction could not ground recovery for mistake of fact.[28] Dextra's mistaken belief that the money was being paid as a loan was not a mistake as to any past or existing fact, but a misprediction as to "the nature of the transaction which would come into existence when [Dextra's] cheque was delivered to [BOJ]", itself the consequence of a misprediction as to whether Dextra's agent would obey its specific instructions not to deliver the cheque to BOJ except in return for a promissory note evidencing the loan and its terms.[29] And, whilst Dextra's mistaken belief that BOJ had previously agreed to take a loan was a mistake of fact, it did not cause Dextra's payment. It had led to the instructions which Dextra gave its agent; but the Privy Council held that it was Dextra's misprediction that its agent would comply with these instructions and that a loan would result, not Dextra's earlier mistaken belief, that had caused Dextra's payment.[30]

The same distinction was recently accepted in relation to the equitable jurisdiction to set aside voluntary transactions entered into under a mistake. In *Re Griffiths*,[31] the deceased made three transfers of assets in 2003 and 2004, with a view to mitigating future inheritance tax liabilities. In fact, though, all three transfers became chargeable for IHT purposes as a result of the deceased's premature death from cancer, and the deceased's executors applied to have the transfers set aside for mistake. Without referring to *Dextra Bank* or other common law decisions, Lewison J. held that an "operative mistake" must be a mistake "which existed at the time when the transaction was entered into"; "mere falsification of expectations entertained at the date of the transaction is not . . . enough".[32] There was an obvious difficulty finding an operative mistake in this sense on the facts. The deceased had made no mistake as to the legal nature and effect of the transactions he had entered into, the applicable tax law or the tax consequences of the transactions. Indeed, on the face of it, he had just made a misprediction that he would live for more than seven years; this was not, without more, enough.[33] Lewison J. ultimately held that a distinction should be drawn between the 2003 and 2004 transactions. Relief *was* available in relation to the 2004 transaction, which was entered into after the deceased had developed lung cancer. Ignorant of this fact, the deceased had made a mistake of existing

9–10

---

be found to have made a statement, which is false, as to his present state of mind (e.g. *Edgington v Fitzmaurice* (1885) 29 Ch.D. 459 (CA)).

[28] *Dextra Bank* [2001] UKPC 50; [2002] 1 All E.R. (Comm.) 193 (PC) at [29]–[30],

[29] *Dextra Bank* [2001] UKPC 50; [2002] 1 All E.R. (Comm.) 193 (PC) at [29].

[30] *Dextra Bank* [2001] UKPC 50; [2002] 1 All E.R. (Comm.) 193 (PC) at [30].

[31] *Re Griffiths* [2008] EWHC 118 (Ch); [2009] Ch. 162.

[32] *Re Griffiths* [2008] EWHC 118 (Ch); [2009] Ch. 162 at [23] and [24].

[33] *Re Griffiths* [2008] EWHC 118 (Ch); [2009] Ch. 162 at [23]. Lewison J. thought that it followed that if the deceased had been a healthy young man, who had died in a road accident one week after the transactions had been entered into, there could have been no relief for mistake.

fact as to the then state of his health; and but for this mistake, he would not have entered into the transaction. "Had he known in . . . 2004 that he was suffering from lung cancer he would also have known that his chance of surviving for three years, let alone for seven years, was remote".[34] However, relief was not available in relation to the 2003 transactions, which had been entered into before the deceased had developed lung cancer. Either he had made no mistake as to the existing state of his health at all, and had merely made a prediction, which proved wrong, as to his likely life-span.[35] Or any mistake that he might have made as to the existing state of his health—in particular, that his life expectancy had already been reduced by drugs he had been taking for rheumatoid arthritis—was not shown to have been causative.[36]

9–11   As these decisions show, the mistake-misprediction distinction is not always easy to draw, and can result in some uncomfortably fine distinctions. The decision in *Dextra Bank*,[37] where the claim failed on the basis that the facts disclosed only a misprediction, can be contrasted with *R.E. Jones Ltd v Waring & Gillow Ltd*,[38] where on similar facts, the House of Lords allowed recovery on the basis of a mistake of fact. Likewise, as a "mistake" requires a belief about some past or existing state of affairs which is incorrect when acted upon,[39] the availability of relief for mistake can turn on the precise time when circumstances change, and the claimant's belief is falsified. *Re Griffiths* illustrates this. So does *Re Farepak Food & Gifts Ltd (In Administration)*.[40] There, a company received moneys from its customers in connection with its Christmas savings scheme, and continued to do so after it had decided to cease trading. Mann J. saw that the availability of restitutionary relief for mistake, via a constructive trust of the moneys received, would turn on whether the customers had made the relevant payments after the company had made the decision to cease trading, or only before—in the latter case, they would not have been mistaken as to the company's trading status.

9–12   Note, however, that the barrier to recovery created by the exclusion of mispredictions from the ambit of restitution-grounding "mistakes" is not as extensive as it might first appear. Whilst a misprediction cannot *itself* ground restitution, it does not follow that a claimant who has made a misprediction cannot recover at all, since there may be some ground of recovery on which the claimant can rely despite his misprediction. Hence it can be said that a misprediction is a "non-qualifier" rather than a "disqualifier".[41] Most obviously, restitution may be available to a mispredicting claimant on the ground of failure of basis.[42] However, there will also be cases where a claimant makes *both* a

---

[34] *Re Griffiths* [2008] EWHC 118 (Ch); [2009] Ch. 162 at [30].
[35] *Re Griffiths* [2008] EWHC 118 (Ch); [2009] Ch. 162 at [28].
[36] *Re Griffiths* [2008] EWHC 118 (Ch); [2009] Ch. 162 at [28].
[37] *Dextra Bank* [2001] UKPC 50; [2002] 1 All E.R. (Comm.) 193 (PC).
[38] *R.E. Jones Ltd v Waring & Gillow Ltd* [1926] A.C. 670.
[39] But note the courts' acceptance of "retrospective" mistakes of law, discussed at para.9–73 and following.
[40] *Re Farepak Food & Gifts Ltd (In Administration)* [2006] EWHC 3272 (Ch), [2008] B.C.C. 22.
[41] Seah, "Mispredictions, Mistake and the Law of Unjust Enrichment", p.112, rightly observes that a mispredictor is only disqualified from relief to the extent that he relies on facts that reveal him to be nothing more than unimpaired risk-taker.
[42] See Chs 12–14.

causative misprediction *and* a causative mistake, and where the causative mistake will justify restitution, notwithstanding the misprediction.

The question whether, where mispredictions and mistakes coincide, the claim-   **9–13** ant should be disqualified from recovery by the misprediction, is difficult and under-examined.[43] The correct answer seems likely to depend on the relationship between the mistake and the associated misprediction, and the relationship that each bears to the claimant's decision to act. A claimant will certainly need to show that his mistake was causative, usually in a "but for" sense.[44] Assuming that he can do this, then the answer probably depends on whether the nature of the risk-taking reflected in the claimant's misprediction and the misprediction's causative significance so overwhelms the element of impairment reflected in the mistake made by the claimant and its causative significance as to require the claimant to be denied relief.

A common situation of this sort is where the claimant acts as a result of a belief   **9–14** about the future, which is itself the result of an exercise of judgement which is impaired by a mistake as to some past or existing fact. A number of cases implicitly confirm that, at least in many cases of this sort, the claimant can recover on the ground of the underlying mistake.[45] *Re Griffiths,*[46] discussed above, is one example. Another is *Kerrison v Glyn, Mills, Currie & Co,*[47] where a rolling credit arrangement was arranged between a bank and a mining company, under which the bank would advance money to the mining company, by honouring cheques drawn by the company's manager. The claimant, who was the owner of the company, would in turn be obliged to pay the bank whatever amounts the bank told him they had advanced to the company. In the event, the claimant paid the defendant bank sums for the account of the lending bank before he had been notified of advances by the lending bank, and in anticipation of liabilities which the claimant had reason to think would probably soon accrue. However, unknown to the claimant, when the sums were paid to the defendant, the lending bank had committed an act of bankruptcy and the relevant liabilities never arose. The claimant successfully recovered the payments on the basis of a mistake of fact. In one sense the sums were paid because of what could be regarded as a misprediction: a belief, which was falsified, that the claimant would in future come under a liability to the lending bank to repay the sums advanced. Nevertheless, the House of Lords held that the claimant was entitled to restitution, and this can be explained on the basis that the claimant made a mistake of fact, which itself caused or contributed to the misprediction: the incorrect belief that the lending bank, at the time of the payment, was a solvent commercial entity

---

[43] But see Seah, "Mispredictions, Mistake and the Law of Unjust Enrichment".
[44] See para.9–49 and following. Cf. *Dextra Bank* [2001] UKPC 50; [2002] 1 All E.R. (Comm.) 193 (PC) at [29]–[30], where the prior mistake that there was an agreement for a loan *may* have been a "but for" cause, but the Privy Council in effect found that the prior mistake was too remote from the ultimate payment. See para.9–09
[45] See too E.A. Farnsworth, *Alleviating Mistakes* (Oxford: OUP, 2004), pp.56–57, supporting relief for mistake in these cases; and Seah, "Mispredictions, Mistake and the Law of Unjust Enrichment", p.114 and following.
[46] *Re Griffiths* [2008] EWHC 118 (Ch); [2009] Ch. 162.
[47] *Kerrison v Glyn, Mills, Currie & Co* (1911) 81 L.J.K.B. 465 (HL).

capable of honouring the mining company's cheques up to the sum which the claimant had in anticipation sent the lending bank for its advances.[48]

(c) *Doubts*

(i) *Introduction*

9–15　What is the significance of a claimant's conscious appreciation that the facts or law may not be as he believes them to be? Is a state of doubt inconsistent with the claimant's holding and acting on a mistaken belief, and/or will a state of doubt otherwise prevent a claimant from bringing a claim for mistake?[49]

9–16　　In principle, there are several ways in which doubt might be factored into an inquiry whether a claimant should obtain relief based on mistake, which the authorities have not adequately disentangled. Doubts may prevent a positive answer to the threshold inquiry whether the claimant made a "mistake", or the distinct threshold inquiry whether the claimant's mistake "caused" him to benefit the defendant. Beyond this, the existence of doubts may bear on the distinct inquiries into whether the claimant should be refused relief for mistake because he "assumed the risk" of error, or because, in acting as he did, the claimant did not respond "reasonably" to his doubts. Only the first of these possibilities strictly concerns the nature of a "mistake" in the law of unjust enrichment.[50] However, in view of the uncertain state of the case law, and in the hope of facilitating clear analysis and understanding of doubt's impact on a mistake-based claim, all four issues are surveyed here in turn.

(ii) *Did the Claimant Make a "Mistake"?*

9–17　In a number of recent cases, it has been assumed that a claimant who has doubts about the facts or law cannot obtain relief for mistake because his doubts mean that he cannot show that he was mistaken. In a dictum in *Kleinwort Benson Ltd v Lincoln CC*[51] Lord Hope suggested that a "state of doubt is different from that of a mistake".[52] To similar effect is the recent Queensland decision in *Queensland Alumina Ltd v Alinta D.Q.P. Pty Ltd*,[53] where the claimant contracting party

---

[48] Cf. *Dextra Bank* [2001] UKPC 50; [2002] 1 All E.R. (Comm.) 193 (PC), discussed at para.9–09, where the Privy Council arguably overlooked that what was identified as a misprediction as to whether the fraudulent intermediary would follow his instructions was itself the result of what could be characterised as a mistake about the intermediary's trustworthiness, but for which Dextra would not have transmitted the money to BOJ as it did.

[49] Besides the academic works cited in the following footnotes, further discussion of these questions can be found in T. Krebs, *Restitution at the Crossroads* (London: Cavendish, 2001), pp.37–39; A.S. Burrows, *The Law of Restitution* 3rd edn (Oxford: OUP, 2010) pp.209–212.

[50] See paras 9–17—9–21.

[51] *Kleinwort Benson v Lincoln CC* [1999] 2 A.C. 349.

[52] *Kleinwort Benson* [1999] 2 A.C. 349 at 410 per Lord Hope. Lord Hope's dictum was relied on with approval in *Nurdin & Peacock Plc v D.B. Ramsden & Co Ltd* [1999] 1 W.L.R. 1249 at 1270; *Mallusk Cold Storage Ltd v Department of Finance* [2003] NIQB 58; *Brennan v Bolt Burdon* [2004] EWCA Civ 1017; [2005] Q.B. 303 (CA); *Deutsche Morgan Grenfell Group Plc v IRC* [2005] EWCA Civ 78; [2006] Ch. 243 at [262] per Rix L.J., [279]–[284] per Buxton L.J. See too *Deutsche Morgan Grenfell Group Plc v IRC* [2006] UKHL 49; [2007] 1 A.C. 558 at [164]–[176] per Lord Brown; and *Queensland Alumina Ltd v Alinta D.Q.P. Pty Ltd* [2006] QSC 391; [2007] QCA 387; *Re Ng Shiu Fan* [2008] HKCFI 613 at [77] (cf. [2009] HKCA 584).

[53] *Queensland Alumina Ltd v Alinta D.Q.P. Pty Ltd* [2006] QSC 391; [2007] QCA 387.

was denied restitution of sums allegedly overpaid on the basis of a mistake as to the contract's effect, after the claimant's in-house counsel had given (correct) preliminary advice that there were inconsistencies in the contractual documentation, and that properly construed, the contract might impose a cap on the sums payable. From that point onwards, the claimant did not labour under an (incorrect) "positive belief" as to the validity of the relevant contract provisions, nor was it in a state of "sheer ignorance".[54] And subsequent payments made notwithstanding the claimant's belief that the relevant contract provisions "might be invalid" were not caused by a mistaken belief as to the claimant's legal position.[55]

At first sight, Lord Hope's dictum might be taken to suggest that *any* doubt **9–18** will prevent a finding that the claimant was mistaken. However, more recent authorities suggest that this is too strong, and that a state of doubt is not invariably inconsistent with a finding that the claimant was mistaken. In *Deutsche Morgan Grenfell Group Plc v IRC*,[56] it was argued before the House of Lords that a payment of advanced corporation tax (ACT) made in 1996 was not made under a mistake of law, because it was made after the taxpayer had become aware of a legal challenge to the legality of the UK's ACT regime under EU law (which was ultimately successful), which denied the taxpayer the right to avoid ACT liability by making a group income election.[57] It was argued that the ACT payment was therefore made in a state of doubt and, as Lord Hope had said in *Kleinwort Benson*, a state of doubt was not a mistake. This argument met with a very qualified response.[58] Lord Hope said that his earlier statements were "capable of further refinement", and that the difficult question was "what degree of doubt is compatible with a mistake claim".[59] Lord Hoffmann went further, suggesting that Lord Hope cannot have meant that a state of doubt was "actually inconsistent with making a mistake",[60] that the real question is whether the payer "took the risk that he might be wrong", and that the fact that the payer had doubts about his liability was not conclusive of this question.[61]

If doubts do not inevitably prevent a finding that a claimant was mistaken, the **9–19** difficult question, which *Deutsche Morgan Grenfell* does not resolve, is what

---

[54] *Queensland Alumina* [2007] QCA 387 at [72].

[55] *Queensland Alumina* [2007] QCA 387 at [72].

[56] *Deutsche Morgan Grenfell Group Plc v IRC* [2006] UKHL 49; [2007] 1 A.C. 558. See too *Stiassney v CIR* [2010] NZHC 1935 at [118]–[119].

[57] *Deutsche Morgan Grenfell* [2006] UKHL 49; [2007] 1 A.C. 558 at [24].

[58] Cf. per Lord Brown, *Deutsche Morgan Grenfell* [2006] UKHL 49; [2007] 1 A.C. 558 at [164]–[176], suggesting that a person would cease to act under a mistake of law once he came to realise that he had a "worthwhile claim" that he should not have to pay, and that on the facts, this realisation existed when the claimants became aware of a "serious legal challenge" to the UK's ACT regime. A blanket rule of this type seems inappropriately restrictive approach, forcing claimants in this position to bring proceedings, if they are to be protected from the risk of paying and then finding the sums paid irrecoverable because of the absence of a qualifying "mistake".

[59] *Deutsche Morgan Grenfell* [2006] UKHL 49; [2007] 1 A.C. 558 at [65].

[60] *Deutsche Morgan Grenfell* [2006] UKHL 49; [2007] 1 A.C. 558 at [26]. He gave the example of a quiz contestant, who had doubts about the answer he was giving, but if he gave the wrong answer, made a "mistake": *Deutsche Morgan Grenfell* at [26]. There is an ambiguity here between a mistake, understood to mean simply "an error", and a mistake, understood as an incorrect belief, which causes one to act. Arguably Lord Hoffmann is eliding the second crucial sense with the first. Cf. Lord Brown's disagreement with Lord Hoffmann's example: *Deutsche Morgan Grenfell* at [175] per Lord Brown.

[61] *Deutsche Morgan Grenfell* [2006] UKHL 49; [2007] 1 A.C. 558 at [27].

degree of doubt about the facts or law is incompatible with this conclusion. The view which has found favour in the literature, and in the most recent authority to address this point, requires the claimant's belief to surmount a balance of probabilities threshold. That is, the test of whether the claimant was mistaken *despite* his doubts is whether the claimant believed that it was more probable than not that the facts or law were otherwise than they in fact were. If the claimant believed that it was more probable than not that the facts or law were as they in fact were, he is not relevantly mistaken.

9–20   In *Marine Trade SA v Pioneer Freight Futures Co Ltd BVI*,[62] restitution was sought of sums paid between parties to a series of freight derivative contracts. Pioneer had paid US$5 million under protest which would have been owing to Pioneer, if Pioneer had a right under the master agreement between them, to set-off sums which Pioneer itself owed under the contracts. When it paid, Marine Trade believed that Pioneer did not have such a right, because it believed that Pioneer was affected by an event of default which would have prevented Marine Trade's liability, which Pioneer was claiming to set-off, from accruing. Marine Trade nevertheless paid the sum to avoid the risk that Pioneer might prematurely terminate the relationship between them, resulting in a substantial liability for Marine Trade which it could not afford. Marine Trade then sought restitution on the basis that it had paid in the mistaken belief that there was a "real and substantial chance" that Pioneer was not affected by an event of default and that the US$5 million was due. On these facts, the question arose as to how far a state of doubt precludes a finding of causative mistake.[63] After a full review of the leading authorities, Flaux J. concluded that he could not go further than saying that there might be cases where a payer could still be said to be labouring under a mistake as to his liability to pay, even if he had doubts, if he paid concluding that it was "more likely than not" that he was liable to pay.[64] At the same time, a payer could not be said to have made such a mistake, where he paid thinking that it was "more likely than not" that he was not liable to make the payment.[65] Marine Trade's claim failed on this ground.

9–21   The approach adopted in the *Marine Trade* decision should be preferred to a second and broader approach, which asks simply whether the claimant would have acted as he did, had he known the true facts or the true state of the law for certain. This alternative approach seems unacceptably wide. First, it would deem a claimant to be "mistaken" despite a very high degree of doubt. Only those

---

[62] *Marine Trade SA v Pioneer Freight Futures Co Ltd BVI* [2009] EWHC 2656 (Comm); [2010] 1 Lloyd's Rep. 631.

[63] *Marine Trade* [2009] EWHC 2656 (Comm); [2010] 1 Lloyd's Rep. 631 at [67]–[75]. Three views were put to Flaux J.: that the law did not require the claimant to demonstrate that he believed he was liable to pay, despite his doubts, and that in principle, there was no maximum amount of doubts (the claimant's argument); that any substantial degree of doubt is inconsistent with a mistake (the defendant's primary argument); and that a claimant could not establish payment under a mistake if he paid thinking that the payment was "probably not due" (the defendant's secondary argument): *Marine Trade* at [68].

[64] *Marine Trade* [2009] EWHC 2656 (Comm); [2010] 1 Lloyd's Rep. 631 at [76], taking this to be the view of E. McKendrick, "Mistake of Law—Time for a Change?" in W.J. Swadling (ed.), *The Limits of Restitutionary Claims: A Comparative Analysis* (London: BIICL, 1997), pp.231–232, to which Lord Hope had referred in *Deutsche Morgan Grenfell* [2006] UKHL 49; [2007] 1 A.C. 558.

[65] *Marine Trade* [2009] EWHC 2656 (Comm); [2010] 1 Lloyd's Rep. 631 at [77].

claimants who intended to benefit the defendant irrespective of the true facts would be excluded, whilst a claimant would be deemed to have been mistaken even when he acted in the belief that there was only a small possibility that certain facts existed, and therefore when he consciously took a risk, against the perceived odds, that the facts existed. Secondly, this approach goes too far beyond the core meaning of a "mistake": an intention vitiated by an incorrect belief about some past or existing state of affairs. If a claimant believes that it is merely possible that certain facts exist, and that it is probable that they do not exist, it is difficult to say that the claimant holds any "belief" that the facts exist; or at least, that if they do not exist, that the belief he holds is incorrect. Thirdly, the courts could not adopt this expansive approach without some other limit on the ambit of recovery, designed to exclude those claimants who in some sense unacceptably run the risk of error.

(iii) *Did the Claimant's Mistake "Cause" the Benefit to be Conferred?*

The cases show that a claimant who proceeds in a state of unresolved doubt about **9–22** the facts or law may often be denied relief in any event, because he cannot prove that any belief he may have held *caused* him to benefit the defendant.[66] Relief for a spontaneous mistake depends upon proof of "but for" causation: that the claimant would not have acted as he did, but for his mistake.[67] The greater the claimant's doubts, the less likely it is that this hurdle will be satisfied, simply because it is more likely that there will be other reasons which caused him to act, and would have caused him to act in the same way irrespective of his belief.[68] The *Marine Trade* case illustrates this point. An alternative ground for the failure of Marine Trade's claim to recover the sums paid to Pioneer was that it could not show that the alleged mistake was a "but for" cause of its payment.[69] Marine Trade had paid, despite believing that it was probably not liable to pay, in order to avoid the risk of Pioneer designating an early termination of their relationship, and a crippling liability which it could not afford.[70]

Statements can sometimes be found in the case law to the effect that the **9–23** claimant will be denied relief if he intended the defendant to benefit in all events, irrespective of the truth or falsity of the fact or law about which he was allegedly

---

[66] See e.g. *Marine Trade* [2009] EWHC 2656 (Comm); [2010] 1 Lloyd's Rep. 631; *Queensland Alumina* [2006] QSC 391; [2007] QCA 387; *Re Magarey Farlam* [2007] SASC 9; [2006] 96 S.A.S.R. 337 at [175] (expressed in the language of "voluntary payment"); *Mok Kwong Yue v Ding Leng Kong* [2008] SGHC 65 at [44]–[46]; *Re Ng Shiu Fan* [2008] HKCFI 613 at [79]–[80]. And see Lord Hope in *Deutsche Morgan Grenfell* [2006] UKHL 49; [2007] 1 A.C. 558 at [65], where he went so far as to say that the question might "essentially [be] one of causation . . . [w]hat was the effect of the mistake on the payer?".

[67] See para.9–50.

[68] Cf. if a looser test of "contributory cause" applies as explained in para.9–50.

[69] *Marine Trade* [2009] EWHC 2656 (Comm); [2010] 1 Lloyd's Rep. 631 at [78]; citing *Barclays Bank Ltd v W.J. Simms, Son & Cooke (Southern) Ltd* [1980] Q.B. 677.

[70] *Marine Trade* [2009] EWHC 2656 (Comm); [2010] 1 Lloyd's Rep. 631 at [80]. Cf. the doubtful assumption of Henderson J. in *F.J. Chalke Ltd v Revenue and Customs Comissioners* [2009] EWHC 952 (Ch); [2009] S.T.C. 2027 at [137]–[138], that payments of VAT were still made as a result of a mistake of law, even after the taxpayer knew that they were levied contrary to EU law.

mistaken.[71] In *Barclays Bank v Simms Plc v W.J. Simms, Son & Cooke (Southern) Ltd*,[72] Robert Goff J. articulated this as a separate obstacle to recovery for a causative mistake. However, this seems unnecessary. It would be better to say simply that such a claimant fails because the circumstances reveal that the mistake did not cause him to act.

(iv) *Did the Claimant Respond Reasonably to His State of Doubt?*

9–24   It has sometimes also been said that a claim will fail where the claimant deliberately or consciously waived inquiry into the true facts.[73] There is some difficulty understanding what these statements may mean. On one view, "waiver of inquiry" might simply be evidence that the claimant intended the defendant to benefit in any event, irrespective of the true facts, and thus that the claimant's decision to act was not impaired by any causative mistake. If references to "waiver of inquiry" are intended to mean more than this, however, then the objection might in future be better expressed as a requirement that, in order to recover, the claimant must have responded "reasonably" to the doubts he harboured. This has several advantages over the language of "waiver of inquiry". First, it makes explicit the key underlying question: whether the claimant, when acting despite his doubts, has unreasonably assumed the risk of error. Secondly, it enables the courts to articulate openly the standards of conduct by reference to which the claimant is to be judged. Thirdly, it offers a more flexible standard, which is sensitive to the circumstances in which the claimant has acted: for example, the strength of the claimant's doubts; whether opportunities were reasonably available to ascertain the true facts; whether these opportunities were taken; and if taken, their impact on the state of the claimant's mind. In many cases, the reasonable course of action might be to inquire further into the facts, and/or to seek advice before acting, for the purpose of resolving the doubts, and then only act insofar as the doubts are reasonably resolved. Finally, it potentially strikes a better balance between the interests of the claimant and the defendant than an approach (which some have favoured) which denies the claimant restitution, in the interest of upholding the security of a defendant's receipt, wherever the claimant had doubts.[74]

---

[71] Especially *Kelly v Solari* (1841) 9 M. & W. 54 at 59; 152 E.R. 24 at 26 per Parke B.; *Barclays Bank v Simms* [1980] Q.B. 677 at 695 per Robert Goff J.; cf. *Scottish Equitable Plc v Derby* [2001] EWCA Civ 369; [2001] 3 All E.R. 818 at [19]–[25].

[72] *Barclays Bank Ltd v W.J. Simms, Son & Cooke (Southern) Ltd* [1980] Q.B. 677 at 695, per Robert Goff J.

[73] See especially *Scottish Equitable* [2001] EWCA Civ 369; [2001] 3 All E.R. 818 at [19]–[25] ("deliberate waiver of inquiry"); *Kelly v Solari* (1841) 9 M. & W. 54 at 58; 152 E.R. 24 at 26 per Lord Abinger C.B. (the claimant "might by investigation learn the state of facts more accurately, [but] he declines to do so, and chooses to pay the money notwithstanding"), cf. (1841) 9 M. & W. 54 at 59; 152 E.R. 24 at 26 per Parke B., agreeing (money is "intentionally paid, without reference to the truth or falsehood of the fact, the plaintiff meaning to waive all inquiry into it, and that the person receiving shall have the money at all events, whether the fact be true or false").

[74] Cf. S. Arrowsmith, "Mistake and the Role of Submission to an Honest Claim" in A.S. Burrows (ed.), *Essays on the Law of Restitution* (Oxford: OUP, 1991), Ch.2; G. Virgo, *The Principles of the Law of Restitution*, 2nd edn (Oxford: OUP, 2006), pp.162 and following.

Two recent cases can be contrasted. In *Re Magarey Farlam Lawyers Trust* **9–25**
Accountants (No.3),[75] solicitors were denied restitution for mistake where they
had made good lost client funds resulting from an employee's misconduct,
believing that these represented the full extent of the defaults, but without
waiting for the outcome of a pending inquiry which revealed, shortly afterwards,
that a substantially greater number of clients were affected. Although expressed
in different terms, including the language of "assumption of risk", the failure of
their claim can be readily explained on the basis that, in the circumstances, they
had failed to respond reasonably to their state of doubt. A different conclusion
was reached in *Haugesund Kommune v Depfa ACS Bank*,[76] where the bank had
advanced substantial sums to a Norwegian local authority, pursuant to a novel
financial transaction that turned out to be ultra vires the authority's powers and
void under Norwegian law. The bank was conscious of this danger before it
entered the agreement, and it only entered the agreement after obtaining an
unqualified, positive legal opinion from an expert in Norwegian law, which
resolved its concerns.

To deny restitution to a claimant who, in acting as he did, "unreasonably" **9–26**
responded to his doubts, might at first sight seem inconsistent with the long-
standing view that a claimant will not be denied recovery for mistake merely
because he is negligent.[77] However, this is not the case. The cases which hold
that a claimant's negligence is irrelevant to his claim based on his mistake are
cases where the claimant was *unaware* of the risk that his belief or assumption
might be incorrect. These cases do not directly address the question of how a
claimant should respond to a state of doubt—that is, how a claimant should be
expected to behave where he is *aware* of the risk that his belief or assumption
might be incorrect. A "reasonable response" requirement would only apply in
the latter cases, and would not capture those who are unconscious of a risk of
error, however unreasonably. And in any event, a "reasonable response" requirement is not necessarily the same as a negligence standard. As in *Scottish
Equitable Plc v Derby*,[78] a claimant who, in good faith, carries out an investigation of the facts which is in fact inadequate, but which resolves his doubts, may
have responded "reasonably", even though his investigation might be described
as negligent.

---

[75] *Re Magarey Farlam Lawyers Trust Accountants (No.3)* [2007] SASC 9; [2006] 96 S.A.S.R. 337,
especially at [173]; also at [174]–[175].
[76] *Haugesund Kommune v Depfa ACS Bank* [2009] EWHC 2227 (Comm); [2010] Lloyd's Rep. P.N.
21.
[77] *Kelly v Solari* (1841) 9 M. & W. 54; 152 E.R. 24; *Imperial Bank of Canada v Bank of Hamilton*
[1903] A.C. 49 (PC) at 56; *R.E. Jones v Waring* [1926] A.C. 670 at 688–689; *Anglo-Scottish Beet
Sugar Corp Ltd v Spalding UDC* [1937] 2 K.B. 607; *Saronic Shipping Co v Huron Liberian Co*
[1979] 1 Lloyd's Rep. 341 at 363; [1980] 2 Lloyd's Rep. 26 (CA); *Barclays Bank v Simms* [1980]
Q.B. 677 at 686–687; *Banque Financière* [1999] 1 A.C. 221 at 227, 235, 242–243; *Kleinwort Benson*
[1999] 2 A.C. 349 at 399; *Scottish Equitable* [2000] 3 All E.R. 793 at 799–800 per Harrison J.; [2001]
EWCA Civ 368; [2001] 3 All E.R. 818; *Dextra Bank* [2001] UKPC 50; [2002] 1 All E.R. (Comm.)
193 at [45]. Cf. T. Wu, "The Role of Negligence and Non-Financial Detriment in the Law of Unjust
Enrichment" [2006] R.L.R. 55. See further para.9–119.
[78] *Scottish Equitable Plc v Derby* [2001] EWCA Civ 369; [2001] 3 All E.R. 818.

(v) *Did the Claimant "Assume the Risk" of Error?*

9–27   Some recent cases have suggested that the claimant's claim for mistake may fail on the independent ground that he in some sense assumed the risk of error.[79] This was, notably, Lord Hoffmann's view in *Deutsche Morgan Grenfell*,[80] where, after suggesting that doubt was not inconsistent with making a mistake, he proposed that the real question was whether the payer "took the risk that he might be wrong", and that the fact that the payer had doubts was not conclusive of this question.[81] Several later cases use similar language.[82]

9–28   It is at least doubtful that "assumption of risk" should be elevated to the status of an independent bar in this way. First, it is difficult to give this idea clear content. In principle, risk-taking might be assessed subjectively or objectively.[83] A subjective test, which would look to whether the claimant *consciously* took a risk, is likely to be too wide, or if narrower, then redundant. On the one hand, there is a sense in which any claimant who acts despite unresolved doubts, and without making explicit that he is only acting conditionally on certain factual or legal assumptions being correct, consciously runs the risk that he may be wrong; yet the dicta in *Deutsche Morgan Grenfell* indicate that doubts will not necessarily prevent a claim. On the other hand, if the concept of conscious risk-taking is intended to be narrower than this, embracing only those claimants who intend to act irrespective of the true facts, then an independent bar seems unnecessary, because relief can be denied on the conventional basis that the alleged mistake did not cause the claimant to act. In any event, it is clear that in *Deutsche Morgan*

---

[79] *Westdeutsche Landesbank Girozentrale v Islington LBC* [1994] 4 All E.R. 890 at 933–934; *Kleinwort Benson* [1999] 2 A.C. 349 at 413 per Lord Hope (citing Hobhouse J.'s dicta; "the precise limits of [the defence] have still to be clarified"); *Deutsche Morgan Grenfell* [2006] UKHL 49; [2007] 1 A.C. 558 at [26] and following per Lord Hoffmann; *Haugesund* [2009] EWHC 2227 (Comm); [2010] Lloyd's Rep. P.N. 21 at [143] and following (citing *Deutsche Morgan Grenfell*). Cf. *Re Magarey* [2007] SASC 9; (2006) 96 S.A.S.R. 337 at [172] (citing dicta in *Kelly v Solari* (1841) 9 M. & W. 54; 152 E.R. 24, and in *Barclays Bank v Simms* [1980] Q.B. 677 at 695 per Robert Goff J.); *Leighton Contractors Pty Ltd v Public Transport Authority of Western Australia (No.6)* [2008] WASC 193 at [335]–[343] (citing *Deutsche Morgan Grenfell*); *Hilliard v Westpac Banking Corp* [2009] VSCA 211; (2009) 2 V.R. 139 at [67] and following; *Mok Kwong Yue* [2008] SGHC 65 at [44]–[46] (citing earlier editions of *Goff and Jones*); *Re Ng Shiu Fan* [2008] HKCFI 613 at [77] (citing *Deutsche Morgan Grenfell*). Cf. the difficult and much-criticised language of "voluntary payment" used in Australian authorities: *David Securities Pty. Ltd v Commonwealth Bank of Australia* (1992) 175 C.L.R. 353; *Hookway v Racing Victoria Ltd* [2005] VCSA 310; (2005) 13 V.R. 444 at [22] and following; *Queensland Alumina* [2007] QCA 387 at [70]–[72]; *Re Magarey Farlam (No.3)* [2007] SASC 9; (2006) 96 S.A.S.R. 337 at [175]; *Lahoud v Lahoud* [2010] NSWSC 1297 at [179].

[80] *Deutsche Morgan Grenfell* [2006] UKHL 49; [2007] 1 A.C. 558.

[81] *Deutsche Morgan Grenfell* [2006] UKHL 49; [2007] 1 A.C. 558 at [26] and [27]. Cf. *Kleinwort Benson* [1999] 2 A.C. 349 at 401 per Lord Hoffmann (where he talks of "acceptance of risk"). Cf. J. Edelman and E. Bant, *Unjust Enrichment in Australia* (Melbourne: OUP, 2006), p.169, asserting that a person who takes a risk that a fact might not be true is not mistaken "at least in a legal sense", and explaining *Brennan v Bolt Burdon* [2005] Q.B. 303 (CA) in these terms. For a risk-taking analysis, see also Farnsworth, *Alleviating Mistakes*, pp.38 and following, 153 and following (preferring a rationale turning on the allocation of the risk of conscious ignorance, to a "no mistake" analysis).

[82] See the cases in fn.79.

[83] Cf. argument in *Haugesund* [2009] EWHC 2227 (Comm); [2010] Lloyd's Rep. P.N. 21 at [143] and following, where opposing counsel offered subjective and objective interpretations of the assumption of risk idea.

Grenfell, Lord Hoffmann envisaged an alternative, *objective* approach to risk-taking:

> "the question of whether a party should be treated as having taken the risk depend[s] upon the objective circumstances surrounding the payment as they could reasonably have been known to both parties, including of course the extent to which the law was known to be in doubt".[84]

Unfortunately, this alternative formulation seems little clearer.

Secondly, there is a danger that the language of assumption of risk functions **9–29** as a conclusory label only. The claimant will be *deemed* to assume the risk of error, and therefore denied restitution for mistake,[85] without it being made clear why this conclusion follows. There is also a corresponding danger that the language of assumption of risk will obscure what is ultimately a normative question, which is best posed directly: i.e. how should a claimant respond to a state of doubt, and in what circumstances should a claimant, who acts despite doubts, be left to bear the risk of error?

Thirdly, it is difficult to identify what work an independent assumption of risk **9–30** principle can usefully do in this context, which is not already done by some other principle. A person who acts despite unresolved doubts may often be denied restitution in any event because he is not mistaken, because any mistake does not cause him to act, or, because in acting as he did, he responded unreasonably to his doubts.[86] Otherwise, his claim may fail on the basis that he has accepted the risk of error under some form of settlement or compromise.[87]

(vi) *Summary*

Taking all of the foregoing together, an appropriate way forward may be the **9–31** following. First, the concept of a "mistake" requires, as a threshold matter, that a claimant believed that it was more likely than not that the true facts or the true state of the law were *otherwise* than they in fact were. Secondly, this belief must cause the claimant to confer the benefit on the defendant, in the required sense. Thirdly, even if a causative mistake can be shown, a claimant may sometimes be denied relief on the basis that he responded unreasonably to his doubts, and so unreasonably ran the risk of error. Fourthly, beyond this, a claimant who had doubts may be denied relief on the distinct grounds that he has compromised or settled with the defendant, or on the basis that he is estopped from pleading his mistake. There is no need for any independent "assumption of risk" bar in this

---

[84] *Deutsche Morgan Grenfell* [2006] UKHL 49; [2007] 1 A.C. 558 at [27].
[85] See e.g. *Deutsche Morgan Grenfell* [2006] UKHL 49; [2007] 1 A.C. 558 at [27] per Lord Hoffmann, using the language of whether the person should be *treated* as having taken the risk; see too at [65] per Lord Hope, proposing that the reasons for a payer paying despite his doubts will have a part to play in resolving whether the payer, who would not have paid had he known the true facts or law at the time of payment, "*should bear the risk*" or can recover for mistake.
[86] See paras 9–17—9–21, 9–22—9–23, 9–24—9–26.
[87] Cf. *Deutsche Morgan Grenfell* [2006] UKHL 49; [2007] 1 A.C. 558 at [26]–[27], drawing an analogy with the approach of the courts when deciding whether a common mistake should render a contract void, where there is a preliminary inquiry into whether the contract allocates the risk to one or other party.

context, and the language of assumption of risk is a redundant way of expressing the conclusion that a claimant's claim must fail on one or more of the foregoing grounds.

(d) *Ignorance*

(i) *Introduction*

9–32 Can a state of "ignorance" constitute an operative mistake for the purposes of the law of unjust enrichment?[88] A claimant may intentionally confer a benefit on another, without consciously adverting to some past or present state of affairs, and therefore without holding any belief in relation to it; yet it might be possible to say that the claimant would not have acted as he did, had he known about the state of affairs of which he is ignorant. Will this do? Clear analysis of this question, and of what is at stake, requires three different situations to be distinguished. It also requires all three situations—where the claimant *intentionally* conferred a benefit on the defendant—to be distinguished from the very different sort of situation which is discussed in Ch.8. This is where the defendant obtained a benefit from the claimant, immediately or more remotely, where the claimant was unaware of this happening, and where he therefore had no intention whatsoever that it should occur—as where the defendant simply stole from the claimant, without the claimant's knowledge. In cases such as these, it is the claimant's "lack of consent" which explains the award of a restitutionary remedy.[89]

(ii) *Incorrect Conscious Beliefs*

9–33 The first situation requiring discussion is where, owing to his ignorance of some fact or facts, the claimant held an incorrect conscious belief which caused him to act. Although this might be described as a case of "ignorance", it is actually a routine and uncontroversial example of an incorrect consciously-held belief—of what might be called an "active mistake". As the Victorian Court of Appeal recently expressed it in *Hookway v Racing Victoria Ltd*,[90] mistake certainly "comprehends . . . a mistaken belief *arising from* inadvertence to or ignorance of a specific fact or legal requirement".[91]

---

[88] Cf. T. Wu, "Restitution for Mistaken Gifts" (2004) 20 J.C.L. 1, pp.5–9; D Sheehan, "What is a Mistake?" (2000) L.S. 538, pp.541–545; Seah, "Mispredictions, Mistake and The Law of Unjust Enrichment", pp.96–98; Virgo, *The Principles of the Law of Restitution*, pp.139–140, 145–146; Burrows, *The Law of Restitution*, p.216; Farnsworth, *Alleviating Mistakes*, Chs 2 and 3.

[89] Borderline cases may be susceptible to alternative analyses—as where the claimant intentionally transferred a collection of items to the defendant, which included certain items of which the claimant was unaware, and which he had no intention to transfer to the defendant. Restitution might plausibly be based on the claimant's mistake as to the subject matter being transferred or alternatively, on the claimant's lack of consent to the transfer of the unexpected subject matter.

[90] *Hookway v Racing Victoria Ltd* [2005] VSCA 310; (2005) 13 V.R. 444.

[91] *Hookway* [2005] VSCA 310; (2005) 13 V.R. 444 at [21] (emphasis added).

An illustration is *David Securities Pty Ltd v Commonwealth Bank of Aus-* **9–34**
tralia,[92] where the claimant borrower made loan repayments to the defendant
bank that included an additional amount which it believed was payable under a
withholding tax gross-up clause in the loan contract. In fact, that additional sum
was not payable, as a result of a statutory provision, of which the claimant was
unaware, which rendered the clause void. The High Court of Australia held that
the borrower might recover the sum paid on the ground of a mistake of law. The
majority held that a mistake "not only signifies a positive belief in the existence
of something which does not exist", but also may include "sheer ignorance of
something relevant to the transaction in hand".[93] This seems, at first sight, to be
an unambiguous statement that ignorance may be enough. However, the decision
is susceptible to the narrower reading that the facts disclosed an incorrect
conscious belief. The borrower paid in the conscious belief that it was legally
liable to make the payment, which was incorrect because of an invalidating
statutory provision, of which the borrower was ignorant.

(iii) *Incorrect Tacit Assumptions*

The second situation is where the claimant acted on the basis of a tacit assump- **9–35**
tion about some fact which was falsified by some other fact of which he was
ignorant; or on the basis of an incorrect tacit assumption about a fact. This might
be described as a "tacit mistake", to denote the fact that it rests on an incorrect
tacit assumption, rather than an incorrect conscious belief. It seems that this will
also do.

A recent illustration may be *Re Griffiths*,[94] where the deceased had made **9–36**
transfers of certain assets with the aim of mitigating future IHT liabilities, and
this aim was frustrated by the deceased's premature death from cancer. Lewison
J. held that the transfer executed after he had developed cancer could be set aside
under equity's jurisdiction to set aside voluntary transactions on the ground of
mistake. As the judge put it, the transfer was executed by the deceased in a state
of ignorance as to that existing condition, and it would not have been executed
but for that "mistake"; "[h]ad he known in . . . 2004 that he was suffering from
lung cancer he would also have known that his chance of surviving for three
years, let alone for seven years, was remote".[95] Despite the judge's use of the
language of "ignorance", the facts arguably disclose at least a tacit mistake. The

---

[92] *David Securities Pty Ltd v Commonwealth Bank of Australia* (1992) 175 C.L.R. 353; similarly,
Mercantile Mutual Health Ltd v Commissioner of Stamp Duties (Qd) [2002] QCA 256; [2003] 2 Qd.
R. 515 (belief that tax was payable was incorrect because of change in tax law, of which the payer
was ignorant); cf. *J. & S. Holdings v N.R.M.A. Insurance Ltd* [1982] FCA 78; (1982) 41 A.L.R. 539
(similar, but pre-dated abolition of the mistake of law bar). For other cases susceptible to rationalisation in similar terms, see *University of Canterbury v Att Gen* [1995] 1 N.Z.L.R. 78; *Hookway* [2005]
VSCA 310; (2005) 13 V.R. 444 at [61]–[62] (belief that decision of race-horse stewards was final was
incorrect because of the existence of a right of appeal, of which the payer was ignorant); *Hilliard*
[2009] VSCA 211; (2009) 25 V.R. 139 at [75]–[76]; *Pitt v Holt* [2011] EWCA Civ 197; [2011] 3
W.L.R. 19 at [216], [224] (belief that the transaction had no adverse tax consequences was incorrect
because of inheritance tax rules, of which the claimant was ignorant).
[93] *David Securities* (1992) 175 C.L.R. 353 at [369] (also at [379]), cited with approval in *Kleinwort
Benson* [1999] 2 A.C. 349 at 410 per Lord Hope.
[94] *Re Griffiths* [2008] EWHC 118 (Ch); [2009] Ch. 162; discussed at para.9–10.
[95] *Re Griffiths* [2008] EWHC 118 (Ch); [2009] Ch. 162 at [30].

deceased acted on the basis of an incorrect tacit assumption that his state of health was such that he was likely to live for at least seven more years.

(iv) *True Cases of Mere Causative Ignorance*

9–37   The third and final situation is where the claimant made neither an active nor a tacit mistake and simply acted in a state of mere causative ignorance. He would not have acted as he did had he known of some fact of which he was ignorant; but when he acted, he held no belief or assumption about that fact, conscious or tacit.

9–38   True cases of mere causative ignorance seem likely to be exceptional. A possible illustration arises in the decision at first instance in *Pitt v Holt*,[96] where Mrs Pitt, acting on behalf of her husband, had executed a settlement of sums paid pursuant to a personal injury claim by Mr Pitt. Unknown to Mrs Pitt, the settlement attracted very substantial inheritance tax charges, which could have been easily avoided. At first instance, Robert Englehart Q.C. held that the settlement could not be set aside in equity for mistake, inter alia, on the basis that there was "in reality", no "mistake".[97] Had someone told Mrs Pitt that substantial sums of IHT would have been payable, she would not have entered into the settlement.[98] However, the truth of the matter was that Mrs Pitt had given no thought to the IHT position, and having given no thought to it, she made no "real mistake" about it. As the judge put it:

> "It is not as if Mrs Pitt ever wrongly thought, for whatever reason, that inheritance tax would not be payable. She simply never thought about it at all. . . . [I]f someone does not apply his mind to a point at all, it is difficult to say that there has been some real mistake about the point".[99]

On appeal, the Court of Appeal took a different view, finding what was, in effect, an incorrect conscious belief, or active mistake.[100] Mrs Pitt had been advised that there were no adverse tax implications arising from what was proposed. Her resulting general belief that there were no tax consequences was false, because of the IHT position. She had therefore made a mistake, even though neither she, nor any other relevant person, had ever applied their minds to the question whether, and if so how, IHT might affect the transaction.[101]

9–39   As they stand, the authorities do not conclusively determine whether restitution is available in this third type of case—where the claimant's claim rests on mere causative ignorance of some fact. There are dicta that a "mistake" includes

---

[96] *Pitt v Holt* [2010] EWHC 45 (Ch); [2010] 1 W.L.R. 1199.

[97] *Pitt v Holt* [2010] EWHC 45 (Ch); [2010] 1 W.L.R. 1199 at [50].

[98] *Pitt v Holt* [2010] EWHC 45 (Ch); [2010] 1 W.L.R. 1199 at [50].

[99] *Pitt v Holt* [2010] EWHC 45 (Ch); [2010] 1 W.L.R. 1199 at [50].

[100] *Pitt v Holt* [2011] EWCA Civ 197; [2011] 3 W.L.R. 19. It is clear from the way in which Robert Englehart Q.C. distinguished the earlier decision in *Lady Hood of Avalon v Mackinnon* [1909] 1 Ch. 476, that he did not regard this as a case where Mrs Pitt held a belief, conscious or tacit, which was falsified by the fact of which she was ignorant: see [2010] EWHC 45 (Ch); [2010] 1 W.L.R. 1199 at [50].

[101] *Pitt v Holt* [2010] EWHC 45 (Ch); [2010] 1 W.L.R. 1199 at [216], [224].

"ignorance",[102] and some decisions can be explained in the same terms. However, these cases are inconclusive to the extent that they are susceptible to re-analysis as cases where the claimant made an active or a tacit mistake: i.e. he acted on the basis of a conscious belief or tacit assumption about some past or existing state of affairs, which was falsified by another fact of which he was ignorant.[103] Conversely, there are few cases that unequivocally decide that mere causative ignorance is insufficient.[104] The only recent decision which appears expressly to have rejected a claim to relief for "mistake" on the basis that it involved a state of mere causative ignorance is *Pitt v Holt*.[105] But the general significance of this decision is unclear. It was directly concerned with the ambit of equity's jurisdiction to set aside voluntary transactions for mistake which, as presently understood, is substantially narrower than the general common law rules governing the availability of a personal claim to restitution for mistake[106]; the Court of Appeal's decision on this point was strictly obiter, because the claim failed in any event on the basis that any mistake was not of the right quality[107]; and neither court in *Pitt v Holt* appeared to have had the benefit of extended argument on this point, based on past authority and academic commentary.

From the perspective of principle, the question whether mere causative igno-   **9–40** rance can ground a claim to restitution is finely balanced. Opponents will say that mere causative ignorance is by definition not a mistake, and that recovery on the ground of ignorance cannot be justified on that basis. First, a mistake involves a flawed perception of reality: an incorrect belief or assumption about a past or existing state of affairs.[108] A person who holds no belief or assumption about a fact is not "mistaken" without more; he is only mistaken if his ignorance of the fact falsifies a belief or assumption that he actually holds. Secondly, in the real world, in which decisions are made in a state of "bounded rationality", ignorance of a fact cannot be converted into a positive belief that the fact does not exist. Real-world actors do not attempt to weigh up every possible consideration before they act, and do not entertain beliefs or assumptions about every possible factor that may inform their decisions. Thirdly, a person who makes decisions in a state

---

[102] See especially *Kleinwort Benson* [1999] 2 A.C. 349 at 410 per Lord Hope. See too inter alia *David Securities* (1992) 175 C.L.R. 353 at 369, 374; *Newitt v Leitch* (1997) 6 Tas. R. 396 at 408; *Mercantile Mutual* [2002] QCA 356; [2003] 2 Qd. R. 515; *Hookway* [2005] VSCA 310; (2005) 13 V.R. 444 at [21]; *Queensland Alumina* [2006] QSC 391; [2007] QCA 387; *Hilliard* [2009] VSCA 211; [2009] 25 V.R. 139 at [75]–[76]; *University of Canterbury* [1995] 1 N.Z.L.R 78; *Mok Wong Yue* [2008] SGHC 65. Cf. *South Australian Cold Stores Ltd v Electricity Trust of South Australia* (1957) 98 C.L.R. 65 at 74–75. Cf. *Pitt v Holt* [2010] EWHC 45 (Ch); [2010] 1 W.L.R. 1199; [2011] EWCA Civ 197; [2011] 3 W.L.R. 19.

[103] See the cases cited in fn.92.

[104] Cf. dicta that mistake includes a mistaken belief which arises from ignorance of some fact or legal requirement (e.g. *Hookway* [2005] VSCA 310; (2005) 13 V.R. 444 at [21]; *Hilliard* [2009] VSCA 211; (2009) 25 V.R. 139 at [75]–[76]), which do not in terms rule out the possibility of mere causative ignorance sufficing.

[105] *Pitt v Holt* [2010] EWHC 45 (Ch); [2010] 1 W.L.R. 1199 at [50]. See too the Court of Appeal, which might be taken implicitly to endorse the first instance judge's assumption that mere ignorance is not enough, as it apparently found it necessary to identify an incorrect consciously-held belief: see [2011] EWCA Civ 197; [2011] 3 W.L.R. 19 at [216], [214].

[106] See para.9–104 and following.

[107] See further para.9–105.

[108] For judicial dicta to this effect, see e.g. *Pitt v Holt* [2010] EWHC 45 (Ch); [2010] 1 W.L.R. 1199 at [50]; and *South Australia Cold Stores* (1957) 98 C.L.R. 65 at 74–75; and from other contexts, e.g. *Roles v Pascall & Sons* [1911] 1 K.B. 982 (CA) at 985–986, 986, 987.

of bounded rationality may be deemed to be a "risk-taker", who should be refused relief because he runs the risk that there may be facts which are material to his decision, but of which he is unaware. Fourthly, the causal connection, where a person acts in a state of ignorance about some fact, is different and arguably weaker. Even if he would have acted differently had he known of the fact, his ignorance does not actually induce or influence his decision, in the same sense as where he acts on the basis of an incorrect consciously-held belief.[109] Fifthly, allowing relief for mere causative ignorance could open the floodgates to a large number of potentially dubious claims. As actors of bounded rationality, we routinely act without bringing all potentially material factors to bear on our decisions, and it is often possible to argue that, had we done so, we would or might have acted differently. There is also a related worry about claims being brought by those who merely change their mind: those who, after acting, can point to some fact of which they were ignorant, and are able to mount a plausible argument that had they known of it, they would have acted differently.

9–41   Answers are available to all of these objections. First, it is not obvious why a claimant, who confers a benefit on another, and who would not have done so but for his ignorance of some fact, is not deserving of relief. Secondly, a priori definitions of what counts as a mistake cannot conclude the question whether mere causative ignorance should be sufficient to justify restitution, and whether, for the purposes of the law of unjust enrichment, the conferral of a benefit on another in a state of ignorance should be treated as an operative mistake. A state of mere causative ignorance may well be different from a mistake, defined as an incorrect belief or assumption, but it does not inevitably follow that a person who acts in such a state is undeserving of relief. Thirdly, a person who acts in a state of bounded rationality cannot be automatically dismissed as a "risk-taker" as regards facts of which he is unaware. Adopting a subjective approach to risk-taking, this would not be a proper conclusion unless he consciously adverted to the possibility that there were other facts which he had not weighed, and where, despite suspecting that such facts existed, he proceeded to act without further inquiry. However, such cases, which involve some degree of *conscious* ignorance on the claimant's part, can be adequately dealt with without denying that mere causative ignorance can ever ground restitution: for example, by refusing relief on the basis that the claimant unreasonably responded to his state of doubt.[110] This would still leave some genuine cases of mere causative ignorance, where the claimant was not conscious of the possible existence of other facts which might be material to him. Fourthly, in practice, it seems unlikely that allowing restitution for mere causative ignorance will greatly extend the law's boundaries or open the floodgates to large numbers of dubious claims.[111] True cases of mere

---

[109] Wu, "Restitution for Mistaken Gifts", p.9; one might say that he is caused to act by a set of beliefs and assumptions which do not include beliefs and assumptions about the fact and are not falsified by his ignorance of that fact.

[110] See para.9–24 and following.

[111] Allowing relief for mere causative ignorance will not mean that relief will become available to those who merely change their minds. A claimant would only succeed if he could persuade the court that if the fact of which he was ignorant was present in his mind at the time he acted, he would *not* have acted as he did. There is an important difference in principle between this case, and a case where the claimant would have acted as he did *even if* the fact of which he was ignorant had been present in his mind when he acted. An example would be where the claimant is ignorant of a donee's religion, and where, when he made the gift, this fact was not significant to him; it only became significant subsequently, because of some later religious conversion.

causative ignorance are likely to be rare. In any event, the normal burden of proof will be an important filter. Indeed, in practice, a claimant will find it difficult to convince a court that his ignorance was causative without identifying a conscious belief or tacit assumption which induced him to act, and which was falsfied by the fact of which he was ignorant. In other words, in the absence of satisfactory proof of an active or tacit mistake, a claimant may be unlikely to succeed. Fifthly, denying relief for mere causative ignorance produces a boundary line which may be difficult to draw in practice, and which is susceptible to judicial manipulation, according to whether it is felt that relief should be afforded—with the courts finding or declining to find incorrect conscious beliefs or tacit assumptions according to the court's perception of the merits of the claim.[112]

On balance, the arguments in favour of recognising mere causative ignorance **9–42** as a ground for restitution seem stronger. Even if mere causative ignorance is different from a causative mistake in its core sense—i.e. an incorrect belief about some past or existing state of affairs which causes a person to act—it seems sufficiently deserving of relief to warrant recognition by the law.

(e) Automated Processes and Mistake

In the modern world, benefits are commonly conferred by one person on another **9–43** through an automated—now generally computerised—process. These processes may result in the conferral of a benefit on another "in error", which it may be possible to say was not intended, but where it can nevertheless be difficult to say that the conferral of the benefit was caused by a mistake in its core sense, if this means an incorrect belief or assumption about some past or existing state of affairs, held by the claimant or some human agent acting for him.[113]

In these cases, the benefit is immediately conferred via an automated process, **9–44** and not via a human agent whose decision-making process can have been relevantly vitiated in this way. For example, a computer may malfunction, resulting in an employee being paid several times his proper salary.[114] Or a fraudulent third party may be able to procure a payment from a bank, without practising any deception on any human intermediary, because the bank's computer systems automatically execute payment instructions which pass the bank's electronic verification procedure.[115] Neither employer nor bank would have intended the payment to be made in either case, and as the recipient had no entitlement to receive the moneys, it is inconceivable that the law would allow the recipient to retain the moneys. However, is the ground for recovery "mistake", or is it something else? There is surprisingly little authority which squarely addresses this problem.

The cases suggest that the ground of mistake—certainly if extended to include **9–45** a state of causative ignorance—can often be forced to do the necessary work. For,

---

[112] Compare the different readings of the facts at first instance and in the Court of Appeal in *Pitt v Holt* [2010] EWHC 45 (Ch); [2010] 1 W.L.R. 1199; [2011] EWCA Civ 197; [2011] 3 W.L.R. 19.
[113] See paras 9–06, 9–07, 9–54 and following.
[114] Cf. *Barclays Bank v Simms* [1980] Q.B. 677 at 697 per Robert Goff J., giving the example of a substantial charity which uses a computer for the purpose of distributing small benefactions. The computer runs mad and pays one beneficiary the same gift one hundred times over.
[115] Cf. *Re Holmes* [2004] EWHC 2020 (Admin); [2005] 1 W.L.R. 1857 (DC).

even if the benefit is *immediately* conferred via an automated process, it may not have been conferred but for some act or omission of the claimant or his agent, which is affected by some relevant mistake. This mistake may mean that the automated process is set in motion, when it would not otherwise have been; and/ or not halted, when it would otherwise have been. For example, a clerk in a company's finance department may by mistake enter a new part-time employee into the company's computer system as a full-time employee, with the consequence that, until this error is noticed and rectified, the employee receives a full-time monthly salary via the company's automated payment system. Here, the company might seek restitution based on the clerk's initial mistake of fact, which is responsible for setting the automated payment system in motion. Alternatively, it might seek restitution based upon its continuing ignorance of the initial error, which results in an ongoing failure to stop the over-payment(s) from being made.[116] Viewing the facts in this way, a person who uses an automated process is similarly placed to a person who uses a human agent. A principal who gives instructions to a human agent to confer a benefit on another, under a "mistake", might recover on this basis.[117] So too, a principal who, under a "mistake", omits to revoke or modify earlier instructions.[118]

9–46   These cases may seem uncontroversial, to the extent that the over-payments could be attributed to a mistaken act or omission on the part of the claimant or some human agent, which had the result that an automated payment process was initiated (when it would not otherwise have been) or not halted (when it might otherwise have been).[119] However, it is not clear that all cases can—without artificiality—be dealt with in this way. For example, if a computer spontaneously malfunctions without warning, and this results in an over-payment, there is no difficulty saying that this payment was not intended, but there is more difficulty saying that the payment was invariably *caused* by a mistaken act or omission of the claimant. So too, if a fraudster procures an automated bank payment, via misuse of a customer's on-line banking security details.

9–47   These cases will always present difficulty within an unjust factors model of the law of unjust enrichment. One answer, which will sometimes do, is to accept that a state of causative ignorance can qualify as a restitution-grounding mistake. That is, it is enough that the payment would not have been made but for the ignorance of the claimant, or some person acting for him, of some material fact—for example, that the rent payable under a lease had reverted to some earlier, lower rate.[120]

---

[116] For illustrations, see *Avon CC v Howlett* [1983] 1 W.L.R. 605 (CA) at 619–620 per Slade L.J. (overpaid sick pay: as a result of a mistake, a pay clerk fails to give instruction to reduce sick pay); and *Nurdin & Peacock Plc v D.B. Ramsden & Co Ltd* [1999] 1 W.L.R. 1249 (overpaid rent: as a result of a mistake as to the fact that a lease provided for rent to revert to an earlier, lower rate from year six in the absence of a rent review, no instructions were given by the tenant company's secretary to its accounts department to reduce the amount paid).

[117] e.g. where a customer, acting under a causative mistake, instructs his bank to make a payment (*Customs & Excise Commissioners v National Westminster Bank Plc* [2002] EWHC 2204 (Ch); [2003] 1 All E.R. (Comm.) 327).

[118] e.g. where a customer, acting under a causative mistake, fails to revoke a standing order given to his bank.

[119] See the analysis in *Goff and Jones: The Law of Restitution*, para.4.001.

[120] As in *Nurdin & Peacock* [1999] 1 W.L.R. 1249.

A second answer may be more simply found in the separate ground for **9–48** restitution, explained in Ch.8, which is described there as the claimant's "lack of consent": the defendant received a benefit, wholly without the claimant's consent, and which was therefore not intended for him.[121] This ground is sufficient to explain what Robert Goff J. regarded as a clear case for relief in *Barclays Bank v Simms*[122]: "[a] substantial charity uses a computer for the purpose of distributing small benefactions. The computer runs mad, and pays one beneficiary the same gift one hundred times over". Robert Goff J. apparently considered that this payment could be recoverable as a payment made under a mistake. However, this analysis presents the obvious difficulty, that the agent of the payment is a computer and, on the facts given, it is not easy to attribute the payment to any causative mistake of the claimant, or of any human agent. It is, quite simply, an unintended payment. In light of this, it seems impossible to say in all cases of this type that the claimant can recover on the basis of a causative mistake, unless the courts are prepared to say that a *computer* has an "intention" for this purpose, which is vitiated,[123] and that this "intention" can be attributed to the claimant, in the same way as the intention of a human agent of a principal may be. The simplest answer is that this is unnecessary, because the ground of "lack of consent" can do the work; it is not invariably necessary to hunt for a mistake.[124]

3. CAUSATION

There must be a causal relationship between the claimant's mistake and his act **9–49** (or omission), which results in the conferral of a benefit on the defendant. This requires the claimant's mistaken belief or assumption to influence the claimant's decision to act (or not act) in this way. In what sense must this be so? In other words, what is the law's approach to decision-causation?[125] In principle, there are several different approaches that could be adopted to this question. The courts

---

[121] Cf. earlier editions of this work, which did not recognise such a separate ground and sought to bring these cases within an expansive concept of "mistake": *Goff and Jones: The Law of Restitution*, para.4.001.

[122] *Barclays Bank v Simms* [1980] Q.B. 677 at 697.

[123] Cf. the historic assumption within the criminal law, that a person who obtains a benefit, by some dishonest practice on a machine, without the intervention of a human mind, cannot be guilty of a deception offence: "[t]o deceive is . . . to induce a man to believe that a thing is true which is false, and which the person practising the deceit knows or believes to be false": *Re London & Globe Finance Co Ltd* [1903] 1 Ch. 728 at 732. See e.g. D. Ormerod and D.H. Williams, *Smith's Law of Theft*, 9th edn (Oxford: OUP, 2007), paras 3.64 and following; *Re Holmes* [2004] EWHC 2020 Admin; [2005] 1 W.L.R. 1857 (DC). Cf. now the Fraud Act 2006 s.2(5).

[124] See too Birks, *An Introduction to the Law of Restitution*, p.142, recognising that the pressure to expand the concept of "mistake" is reduced once it is recognised that other grounds of restitution can do the required work in these cases; Birks relied on the ground of "ignorance", which we prefer to cast in wider terms, as either "lack of consent" or "want of authority": see Ch.8.

[125] For analysis, see especially Birks, *An Introduction to the Law of Restitution*, pp.156–158; Wu, "Restitution for Mistaken Gifts"; Farnsworth, *Alleviating Mistakes*, pp.93–101; G. Virgo, "Causation and Remoteness in the Law of Unjust Enrichment" in J. Edelman and S. Degeling, *Unjust Enrichment in Commercial Law* (Sydney: Lawbook Co, 2008), 147; E. Bant, "Causation and Scope of Liability in Unjust Enrichment" [2009] R.L.R. 60; Burrows, *The Law of Restitution*, pp.91–95, and p.209.

may require the mistake have been a "contributory cause" (such that it is enough that it influenced the claimant's decision making process, whether or not the claimant would have acted in the same way but for his mistake), a "but for" cause (such that the claimant would not have acted as he did "but for" his mistake), or even more narrowly, a "fundamental" or "dominant" cause or the "sole" cause.

9–50　　　Looking to the cases, no single test of causation seems to apply. The English authorities, both common law[126] and equitable,[127] overwhelmingly indicate that "but for" causation is necessary where the claimant's mistake is spontaneous, whether the mistake is of fact or law. In contrast, a looser "contributory cause" test may apply where the mistake was induced by a misrepresentation for which the defendant was responsible.[128] On this approach, it is enough that the claimant's mistaken belief or assumption played *a* part in the claimant's decision-making process, and it is not fatal that the claimant would have acted in the same way in any event.

9–51　　　Elise Bant has recently argued that this conventional approach is misguided, and that in principle a looser "contributory cause" or "a factor" test is appropriate in all cases, whether the mistake is spontaneous or induced.[129] In her view, the "but for" causal test fails in routine cases of over-determination, where there are two or more sufficient causes. It also raises forensic questions that are often difficult to resolve, compelling difficult inquiries into the considerations that

---

[126] e.g. *Barclays Bank v Simms* [1980] Q.B. 677 at 695; *Banque Financière* [1999] 1 A.C. 221 at 227, 234; *Nurdin & Peacock* [1999] 1 W.L.R. 1249 at 1270 and following; *Independent Insurance* [2000] Q.B. 110 (CA) at 115–116; *Dextra Bank* [2001] UKPC 50; [2002] 1 All E.R. (Comm.) 193 at [28] and following; *Customs & Excise Commissioners* [2002] EWHC 2204 (Ch); [2003] 1 All E.R. (Comm.) 327 at [2]; *Papamichael v National Westminster Bank Plc* [2003] EWHC 164 (Comm); [2003] 1 Lloyd's Rep. 341 at [196]; *Deutsche Morgan Grenfell* [2006] UKHL 49; [2007] 1 A.C. 558 at [59]–[60] per Lord Hope, [84]–[87] per Lord Scott, [143] per Lord Walker; *Jones v Churcher* [2009] EWHC 722 (QB); [2009] 2 Lloyd's Rep. 94 at [47]; *Marine Trade* [2009] EWHC 2656 (Comm.); [2010] 1 Lloyd's Rep. 631 at [65], [78]–[81]; *Test Claimants in the F.I.I. Group Litigation v IRC* [2008] EWHC 2893 (Ch); [2009] S.T.C. 254 at [264]; [2010] EWCA Civ 103; [2010] S.T.C. 1251 at [182]; *Test Claimants in the Thin Cap Group Litigation v HMRC* [2009] EWHC 2908 (Ch); [2010] S.T.C. 301 at [234]; *Chalke* [2009] EWHC 952 (Ch); [2009] S.T.C. 2027 at [158]; *Deutsche Bank AG v Vik* [2010] EWHC 551 (Comm) at [3].

[127] e.g. cases considering equity's jurisdiction to set aside voluntary settlements, discussed at para.9–103: *Re Griffiths* [2008] EWHC 118 (Ch); [2009] Ch. 162 at [24], [28]–[30]; *Fender v National Westminster Bank Plc* [2008] EWHC 2242 (Ch); [2008] 3 E.G.L.R. 80 at [25]; *Bhatt v Bhatt* [2009] EWHC 734 (Ch); [2009] S.T.C. 1540 at [27]–[28]; cf. *Pitt v Holt* [2010] EWHC 45 (Ch); [2010] 1 W.L.R. 1199; [2011] EWCA Civ 197; [2011] 3 W.L.R. 19. See too *Clarkson v Barclays Private Bank & Trust (Isle of Man) Ltd* [2007] W.T.L.R. 1703; *McBurney v McBurney, Re Betsam Trust* [2009] W.T.L.R. 1489; *Re A Trust, B v C* [2009] JRC 447; [2011] W.T.L.R. 745; *Re First Conferences Ltd 2003 Employee Benefit Trust* [2010] JRC 055A; *Re Lochmore Trust* [2010] JRC 068; *Re Representation of R, Re S Trust* [2011] JRC 117. The disagreement in the authorities is not in relation to whether "but for" causation is needed, but as to whether there is a further requirement for the mistake to be "serious" or of some other specific type or quality: see para.9–102 and following.

[128] See, by analogy, the courts' approach to the recission of contracts induced by misrepresentation. In that context, the "a cause" approach apparently applies to fraudulent misrepresentations: *Edgington* (1885) 29 Ch.D. 459 (CA) (not a rescission case); *Standard Chartered Bank v Pakistan National Shipping Corp (No.2)* [2003] 1 A.C. 959 at 967. The position for non-fraudulent misrepresentations seems to be less clear: see D. O'Sullivan, S. Elliott and R. Zakrzekski, *The Law of Rescission* (Oxford: OUP, 2007), paras 4.93–4.94.

[129] Bant, "Causation and Scope of Liability in Unjust Enrichment" , pp.66–69 and following. Cf. Farnsworth, *Alleviating Mistakes*, pp.94–101.

weighed in the claimant's mind and their relative significance: "the undeniable truth [is] that to identify and assess the relative importance of the factors, considerations or reasons that together prompt a person's decision to act is often impossible".[130] These arguments are powerful, but it seems doubtful that English courts can or should follow Bant's recommendations. First, all recent English authority is against it.[131] Secondly, it could not be adopted without disruptive knock-on consequences for other settled aspects of English law; it would be likely to require other novel restrictions on the claimant's claim and/or expanded defences.[132] Thirdly, the defendant's role in inducing the claimant's mistaken belief or assumption does seem to be a good reason for distinguishing induced mistakes from spontaneous mistakes. Finally, it is difficult to see why a claimant who is spontaneously mistaken, and who would have acted in the same way in any event, has a strong claim to recover. The forensic difficulties identified are susceptible to resolution by other means—for example, via processes of inference/proof.

Accepting that a "but for" causative mistake is generally a necessary require-**9–52** ment, do the courts ever require more, imposing a stricter test of decision-causation, such that the mistake must be the "dominant", "fundamental" or "sole cause" of a claimant's decision to act (or not act)? Most recent authority appears to be against this: a "but for" causative mistake of fact or law is sufficient to ground restitution for mistake.[133] However, a higher threshold will apply in practice where the benefit is mistakenly conferred pursuant to a contract,[134] or otherwise for value[135]; and less clearly, in the case of mistaken gifts.[136] In both cases, the courts may require the mistake to be not merely causative but also, in some sense, "fundamental" or "serious". The better view is that these additional requirements do not import a stricter approach to decision-causation, with all of the forensic difficulties which this may entail. They instead invite a distinct inquiry into the quality or nature of the mistake.[137] For this

---

[130] Bant, "Causation and Scope of Liability in Unjust Enrichment", pp.67–69. See too Birks, *An Introduction to the Law of Restitution*, p.157: "The problem arises because mental processes cannot be weighed and measured. Will-power has no voltage".

[131] See the cases cited in fn.126. Bant concedes this: pp.69–70.

[132] For example, distinguishing types of mistake, imposing requirements of defendant fault, disqualifying the claimant based on his fault, and/or using defences to confine liability.

[133] See the cases cited in fn.126.

[134] If a common mistake, then it must be "fundamental" (especially *Bell v Lever Bros Ltd* [1932] A.C. 161; *Great Peace Shipping Ltd v Tsavliris Salvage (International) Ltd* [2002] EWCA Civ 1407; [2005] Q.B. 679); or if a unilteral mistake, then it must usually be a mistake as to the contract's terms known to the other party (e.g. *Hartog v Colin & Shields* [1939] 3 All E.R. 566); see paras 9–68—9–69.

[135] See *Smithson v Hamilton* [2007] EWHC 2900 (Ch); [2008] 1 W.L.R. 1453.

[136] See as regards the common law and gifts: *Deutsche Morgan Grenfell* [2006] UKHL 49; [2007] 1 A.C. 558 at [87] per Lord Scott; Wu, "Restitution for Mistaken Gifts". And as regards equity's jurisdiction to set aside voluntary settlements, see especially *Pitt v Holt* [2010] EWHC 45 (Ch); [2010] 1 W.L.R. 1199; [2011] EWCA Civ 197; [2011] 3 W.L.R. 19. See further paras 9–101 and following, and 9–110.

[137] Cf. the equity cases, where the tendency is to treat the causation requirement as distinct from the requirement that the mistake be "serious" etc: see e.g. the analysis in *Re Griffiths* [2008] EWHC 118 (Ch); [2009] Ch. 162; and Jersey cases, such as *Re A Trust* [2009] JRC 447; [2011] W.T.L.R. 745; *Re Lochmore Trust* [2010] JRC 068; *Re S Trust* [2011] JRC 117.

reason, they are examined in Part 5 below, in the context of a discussion of what type or quality of mistake is restitution-grounding.[138]

9–53 It is important finally to note that in some recent cases involving claims to recover benefits received on the ground of mistake, the English courts have been willing to declare certain benefits which the defendant received as a result of the claimant's mistake as "too remote" to be the subject matter of a claim.[139] As explained in Ch.6, these decisions elide the issue of "decision-causation" for the purposes of claims based on mistake, with the distinct question whether, in these cases, the defendant's gain was at the claimant's expense. Discussion of these cases, and of the remoteness criteria they invoke, can be found there.[140]

4. WHOSE MISTAKE?

(a) *Introduction*

9–54 In a straightforward case, the claimant will rely on his own mistake to support a claim to restitution for a benefit conferred by him on another. However, in many routine cases, the actual facts will be more complicated: the benefit will have been conferred through one or more others acting *on behalf of* the claimant. The operation of the law governing recovery for mistaken payments in such cases, and in particular, in the context of decision-making within organisations, is under-explored.

(b) *The Possibility of Relying on the Mistake of the Activating Agent*

9–55 If a principal/employer's moneys are paid away by an agent/employee, acting on its behalf, then the principal/employer can undoubtedly seek restitution based on the mistake of this agent (the "activating agent"). Thus, in *Barclays Bank v Simms*,[141] where Barclays had honoured a countermanded cheque, because an employee had overlooked a countermand instruction from its customer, Barclays was able to seek restitution from the payee, based on its employee's mistake. Similarly, in *Jones v Churcher*,[142] where an employee had mistakenly drawn up and issued funds transfer instructions in favour of the wrong beneficiary, her employer was able to seek restitution from the payee and its bank, based on the employee's mistake.

9–56 The same principle appears to apply where a third party, operating outside the claimant's organisation, pays its own moneys on behalf of the claimant and at the claimant's expense—as where, for example, a bank by mistake honours payment

---

[138] See para.9–67 and following.
[139] *F.I.I.* [2008] EWHC 2893 (Ch); [2009] STC 254; [2010] EWCA Civ 103; [2010] S.T.C. 1251. See also *Thin Cap Group Litigation* [2009] EWHC 2908 (Ch); [2010] S.T.C. 301.
[140] See paras 6–05—6–09.
[141] *Barclays Bank v Simms* [1980] Q.B. 677. See too e.g. *Anglo-Scottish Sugar* [1937] 2 K.B. 607; *Turvey v Dentons (1923) Ltd* [1953] 1 Q.B. 218; *Royal Muncipality of Storthoaks v Mobil Oil Canada Ltd* [1976] 2 S.C.R. 147; *Simos v National Bank of Australia* (1976) 10 A.C.T.R. 4.
[142] *Jones v Churcher* [2009] EWHC 722 (QB).

instructions drawn on a customer's account (for which it charges the customer),[143] or pays out pursuant to a letter of credit opened by an applicant (for which it charges the applicant).[144] In either case, there is authority that the customer/applicant can bring a claim based on the mistake of the bank as its paying agent. For example, in *Niru Battery Manufacturing Co v Milestone Trading Ltd (No.1)*,[145] where Bank Sepah paid out pursuant to a letter of credit which Niru had opened for the purpose of discharging its payment obligations under a contract of sale, Moore-Bick J. held that Niru might claim restitution of the moneys so paid on the ground of the mistake made by Bank Sepah that the documents presented to it were valid documents. Similarly, in *Agip (Africa) Ltd v Jackson*,[146] where a Tunisian bank had honoured a forged payment order drawn on Agip's account, it was held that Agip could establish a claim to restitution of the moneys relying on the mistake made by the bank that the order had been duly authorised by its customer. In this case, the objection was specifically raised that Agip could not rely on its bank's mistake: to ground restitution, the mistake had to be the mistake of the claimant or its lawfully authorised agent; and the bank, when it mistakenly honoured forged payment instructions drawn on Agip's account in the mistaken belief that it was duly authorised by Agip to pay, was not acting as the lawfully authorised agent. However, both Millett J. and the Court of Appeal rejected this argument, apparently regarding it as sufficient that the bank had general authority to effect payment on Agip's instructions, as its customer, and had paid in good faith, purportedly on Agip's behalf.

(c) *The Relevance of the State of Mind of the Principal or Other Agents*

Accepting that an activating agent acted as a result of some mistaken belief, of what relevance might it be that another agent/employee, or even the principal/employer, knew the facts, as to which the activating agent was allegedly mistaken? **9–57**

Starting with the principal, it is implicit in the cases, most of which involve mistaken payments, that to establish a prima facie claim, the principal only needs to show that the activating agent acted on a mistaken belief. It is not necessary to inquire into the *principal's* state of mind and prove that the agent's mistaken belief was shared by him. Nevertheless, it does not follow from this that the state of mind of the principal is wholly irrelevant: it might sometimes be material to the establishment of a defence or bar to the principal's claim. In particular, if it can be shown that the principal was aware of the true facts, and had consciously omitted to intervene and stop its agent from making a payment, then the principal might be denied restitution because he intended that the payment be made in all events, irrespective of the truth or falsity of the relevant facts.[147] This would bar a claim by the principal based on his own allegedly mistaken belief; and it seems **9–58**

---

[143] e.g. *Agip (Africa) Ltd v Jackson* [1990] Ch. 265; [1991] Ch. 547 (CA).

[144] e.g. *Niru Battery Manufacturing Co v Milestone Trading Ltd (No.1)* [2002] EWHC 1425 (Comm); [2002] 2 All E.R. (Comm) 705.

[145] *Niru Battery Manufacturing Co v Milestone Trading Ltd (No.1)* [2002] EWHC 1425 (Comm); [2002] 2 All E.R. (Comm.) 705.

[146] *Agip (Africa) Ltd v Jackson* [1990] Ch. 265; [1991] Ch. 547 (CA).

[147] See further paras 9–22—9–23.

that it should also prevent the principal bringing a claim based on his agent's mistake. An argument of this sort might have been advanced in *Niru (No.1)*. There, the defendant argued that, during the month that intervened between presentation of the documents for payment to Bank Sepah and payment by Bank Sepah under the letter of credit, Niru had become aware that the goods had not been dispatched and that the bill of lading was false, but had decided—for other reasons—to permit Bank Sepah to make payment. In the event, Moore-Bick J. rejected that interpretation of the facts, concluding that both Bank Sepah and Niru had mistakenly believed that the goods had been dispatched and that the bill of lading was valid.[148]

9-59   Turning to the position of other agents, it has sometimes been argued that a principal (including a company) should be denied restitution based upon its agent's mistake, because *another* agent knew the true facts, about which the activating agent was mistaken. A leading decision is *Anglo-Scottish Beet Sugar Co Ltd v Spalding UDC*,[149] where the claimant company had overpaid for water supplied to its factory by Spalding UDC. These overpayments were made pursuant to instructions of the factory's manager, who was unaware of a new agreement which had been entered into by the company with Spalding UDC, providing for a reduced minimum quarterly payment. The existence and terms of this agreement were known to the company's managing director, who had negotiated it, and it was argued that this knowledge prevented the company from claiming restitution for mistake. It was said that the knowledge of its servants and agents was its knowledge, and that it followed that the company could not be heard to say that the payments were made in ignorance of any relevant fact. Atkinson J. did not think that the authorities went so far. In his view, the fact that another agent of the company knew the true facts about which the activating agent was mistaken—in this case, the existence of the new agreement—was irrelevant at least as long as the agent having that knowledge was not aware that another agent was acting on the mistake.[150]

9-60   A very similar conclusion was reached in *Turvey v Dentons (1923) Ltd*.[151] Rent was overpaid by a company because the company's assistant secretary and its accountant, acting on the assistant secretary's instructions, had mistakenly believed that the company's lease was for 10 (and not 99) years, with the result that deductions for tax were not made which the company would have been permitted to make if the lease was for 99 years. The company's secretary, who was in charge of the company's property deals, knew the length of the lease —that is, he knew of the true facts, about which the assistant secretary and accountant were mistaken. However, Pilcher J. did not think this was decisive, finding that the *Anglo-Scottish Sugar* case established a principle that "where . . . payments are made under a bona fide mistake of fact by an authorized agent of [a] company, the fact that some other agent of the company may have had full knowledge of all of the facts does not disentitle the company to recover the

---

[148] *Niru (No.1)* [2002] EWHC 1425 (Comm); [2002] 2 All E.R. (Comm.) 705 at [46]–[47]. This argument in fact seems to have been more centrally directed at establishing that Niru had not *relied* on any misrepresentation as to the veracity or authenticity of the documents.

[149] *Anglo Scottish Beet Sugar Co Ltd v Spalding UDC* [1937] 2 K.B. 607.

[150] *Anglo Scottish Sugar* [1937] 2 K.B. 607 at 617 and following, and in particular at 627.

[151] *Turvey v Dentons (1923) Ltd* [1953] 1 Q.B. 218.

money so paid, provided that the agent with the full knowledge does not know that the payments are being made on an erroneous basis".[152]

The principle which Pilcher J. derived from Atkinson J.'s very tentative statements is not obviously correct. Although it seems easy to accept that a claim based on an activating agent's mistake should not fail merely because another agent knows the true facts, it is less obvious why relief should be *automatically* denied where another agent knows the true facts, and that another agent will or may pay under a mistaken belief, but fails to take steps to ensure that that agent is informed of the truth before he acts. This would in effect penalise the principal for a failure of internal communication within his organisation—an outcome which sits uneasily alongside the long-established principle that a claimant's own negligent failure to discover the truth will not prevent recovery on the ground of mistake.[153] It might instead be more consistent with the general law governing restitutionary claims for mistake to say that another agent's knowledge is only material if this knowledge, coupled with a failure to intervene to prevent the payment, enables it to be said that it was intended that the payment should be made in all events, regardless of the true facts.[154] If it is not the *principal* who actually has this knowledge—and thus, an unvitiated intention to benefit the defendant—but another agent acting for the principal, then this finding would seem to depend on it being permissible to attribute that other agent's intention to the principal for this purpose. And that should probably depend on that agent having some superior responsibility for the decision-making process in question.[155] **9–61**

(d) *Complex Decision Making*

In practice, the decision to enter into a transaction within an organisation may be the product of a sequence of decisions that are ultimately acted on when payment is effected. Consider the recent case of *Haugesund*,[156] where a financial transaction with a local authority was agreed by the Bank's Credit Committee, but its execution was ultimately conditional on a positive decision on the part of the Legal Department of the Bank that the transaction would be legally effective. In principle, it seems that it should ordinarily be sufficient, to establish a prima facie claim, to show that one of the necessary decisions in the decision-making process was made under a mistake, and that "but for" that mistake, the transaction would not have been entered into. Thus, in *Haugesund*, it seems to have been sufficient to show that the Head of the Legal Department had approved the transaction, in **9–62**

---

[152] *Turvey* [1953] 1 Q.B. 218. See too *Royal Municipality of Storthoaks* [1976] 2 S.C.R. 147; *Platemaster Pty Ltd v M. & T. Investment Pty Ltd* [1973] V.R. 93; *Simos* (1976) 10 A.C.T.R. 4; *Westpac Banking Corp v A.T.L. Pty Ltd* [1985] 2 Qd. R. 577.
[153] See further para.9–119 and following.
[154] See further paras 9–22—9–23.
[155] Cf. the analogous questions arising in connection with whether, and on what basis, a state of mind can be attributed to a *company* for the purpose of fixing it with *liability*—where the question also arises as to which particular individual's knowledge and thought processes should be attributed to the company. On this see esp. *Meridian Global Funds Management Asia Ltd v Securities Commission* [1995] 2 A.C. 500 (PC).
[156] *Haugesund* [2009] EWHC 2227 (Comm); [2010] Lloyd's Rep. P.N. 21; affirmed [2010] EWCA Civ 579; [2011] 1 All E.R. 190.

the mistaken belief that the Norwegian local authority could lawfully enter into it.

9–63   It is a difficult question whether this starting-point always holds good. Two cases can be contrasted. One is where, on the basis of a mistaken belief, A1 instructs or authorises A2 to make a payment. If A2, despite knowing of the true facts, proceeds to make a payment, does A2's knowledge disentitle the principal from relying on the causative mistake of A1? The payment would not have been made but for the mistake of A1. The answer here must depend on whether the intervention of a conscious agent would be deemed to "break" the chain of causation; and it is not obvious that it should. Another case is where A1, knowing of the true facts, instructs or authorises A2 to make a payment. A2 may not advert to the true facts, and merely obey instructions, in which case there is no possible basis for recovery for mistake. But A2 may sometimes proceed on the basis of a mistaken belief, and if this can be shown to be causative, the question arises as to whether the payment can be recovered. A solution might be found in the relative positions of A1 and A2 in the decision-making process. As indicated above, it is arguable that a claim will be barred by the unvitiated intention of an agent who has some superior responsibility for the decision making process, and who initiated the transaction, aware of the true facts.

9–64   A similar problem might arise in relation to decisions jointly made on behalf of a principal, where one agent knows the true facts and the another does not. In *Platemaster Pty Ltd v M. & T. Investments Pty Ltd*,[157] two company employees, its manager and its purchasing officer, acting with the authority of the managing director, had drawn a cheque in favour of Platemaster, in satisfaction of an invoice for services rendered by Platemaster in reconditioning a piece of machinery. The company subsequently sought restitution of the sums paid, based on the evidence of the purchasing officer that he had signed the cheque believing that the reconditioned machine belonged to the company, and that he would not have signed, without further inquiry, if he had known that the machine belonged to another firm run by the managing director's two daughters. The company alleged, based on this evidence, that the payment had been made under a mistake of fact as to the business on whose behalf the work was done. Gower J. rejected the claim. Relying on the *Anglo-Scottish Sugar* case and *Turvey*, he said that it might be that the purchasing officer's mistake in signing the cheque could be attributed to the company if it could be established that the other paying officer, the other signatory, and the authorising officer, the managing director, did not know the true position and the basis on which the payment was being made. However, there had been no attempt to establish that that was the position, and the onus was on the company to establish this.

9–65   Gower J.'s approach, reflecting the reasoning in the English cases relied on, seems a rather roundabout way of addressing the question. It might have been better to begin by asking whether the purchasing officer's mistake was causative of the payment; the claim might have failed on the basis that the payment would have been made in any event. Even if that question were answered affirmatively, because the purchasing officer could and would have prevented the payment being made, had he appreciated the true facts, it would be necessary to determine the significance of the states of mind of the other parties to the decision.

---

[157] *Platemaster Pty Ltd v M. & T. Investments Pty Ltd* [1973] V.R. 93.

Applying the approach suggested above, if these other actors who were party to the decision-making process knew of the true facts, and intended the payment to be made in all events, and certainly if one or both of these other actors also had some superior responsibility for authorising the payment on behalf of the company, then their unvitiated intention could be properly attributed to the company, barring any claim based on the purchasing officer's mistake.

The decision in *Platemaster* raises a wider question whether, where a benefit   **9–66** is conferred as a result of a joint decision—as in the case of a disposition of jointly held property—it is sufficient to show a relevant mistake on behalf of *one* party, or whether it is necessary to show that *both* proceeded under a relevant mistake. In the recent decision in *Re Griffiths*,[158] Lewison J. considered that a jointly granted lease could only have been set aside for mistake under equity's jurisdiction if it were shown that *both* of the joint grantors made a mistake.[159] It is not clear that this represents a rule of general application, within the law of unjust enrichment. The "joint intent" is the result of a coincidence of *two* states of mind. In principle, and in the absence of any special transactional issues, one might expect the law to say that restitution can be sought on the basis that *one* necessary consent is vitiated.

5. THE QUALITY OF THE MISTAKE

(a) *Introduction*

A long-standing question in the law of unjust enrichment has been whether   **9–67** restitution is available for any causative mistake, or whether the law confines the availability of relief more narrowly than this, by insisting that the mistake must be of a certain degree of seriousness and/or of one or more specific types. In the absence of any governing contract,[160] the clear trend in recent authorities has been to expand the ambit of restitution-grounding mistakes to the point where any causative mistake of fact or law will prima facie ground a common law personal claim to restitution.[161] However, it is not entirely clear whether this position will hold. There is a counter-trend in some recent cases, which suggests that—at least in the sphere of mistaken gifts—restitution may be more tightly

---

[158] *Re Griffiths* [2008] EWHC 118 (Ch); [2009] Ch. 162.
[159] *Re Griffiths* [2008] EWHC 118 (Ch); [2009] Ch. 162 at [29].
[160] See paras 9–68—9–69.
[161] e.g. *Barclays Bank v Simms* [1980] Q.B. 677; *Banque Financière* [1999] 1 A.C. 221 at 227, 234; *Nurdin & Peacock* [1999] 1 W.L.R. 1249 at 1270 and following; *Lloyds Bank v Independent Insurance* [2000] Q.B. 110 (CA) at 115–116; *Dextra Bank* [2001] UKPC 50; [2002] 1 All E.R. (Comm.) 193 at [28] and following; *Customs & Excise Commissioners* [2002] EWHC 2204 (Ch); [2003] 1 All E.R. (Comm.) 327 at [2]; *Papamichael* [2003] EWHC 164 (Comm); [2003] 1 Lloyd's Rep. 341 at [196]; *Deutsche Morgan Grenfell* [2006] UKHL 49 at [59]–[60] per Lord Hope [84]–[87] per Lord Scott, [143] per Lord Walker; *Jones v Churcher* [2009] EWHC 722 (QB); [2009] 2 Lloyd's Rep. 94 at [47]; *Marine Trade* [2009] EWHC 2656 (Comm); [2010] 1 Lloyd's Rep. 631 at [65], [78]–[81]; *F.I.I.* [2008] EWHC 2893 (Ch); [2009] S.T.C. 254 at [264]; [2010] EWCA Civ 103, [2010] S.T.C. 1251 at [182]; *Thin Cap Group Litigation* [2009] EWHC 2908 (Ch); [2010] S.T.C. 301 at [234]; *Deutsche Bank v Vik* [2010] EWHC 551 (Comm) at [3].

confined. In *Deutsche Morgan Grenfell*,[162] Lord Scott registered strong reservations about the law's allowing a common law claim for restitution of a gift on the basis of proof of a merely causative, spontaneous mistake, implying that a "serious" mistake is needed.[163] To similar effect are some recent cases considering the ambit of equity's jurisdiction to set aside voluntary transactions, which have eschewed attempts to liberalise the jurisdiction along the same lines as the common law, and re-emphasised historic requirements for a "serious" mistake.[164]

(b) *Where a Contract Provides a Justifying Ground*

9–68 Where a benefit is mistakenly conferred by one party on another pursuant to a contract, a claim in unjust enrichment will commonly fail even if the mistake would support a claim in the absence of that contractual nexus. The contract between them prima facie serves as a justifying ground, barring the claim, to the extent that it governs the defendant's receipt and retention of the benefit.[165] For the claim to succeed, the claimant will generally need to show that the contract is invalid, being either non-existent, void or voidable. This is not a matter for the law of unjust enrichment, but the law of contract.[166]

9–69 If the claimant, who is mistaken, wishes to call into question the contract's validity on the basis of his mistake, he will often face greater hurdles than are set by the law of unjust enrichment: a contract is not rendered void or voidable by any causative mistake. There is a very important divide between induced and uninduced mistakes. An induced mistake will readily render a contract voidable, if induced by a misrepresentation, whether fraudulent[167] or non-fraudulent,[168] by the other contracting party, his agent or a third party to his knowledge.[169] So too, if induced by the other party's non-disclosure, in circumstances where the law exceptionally requires pre-contractual disclosure.[170] In contrast, a common mistaken assumption only renders the contract void at law if the risk of error is not

---

[162] *Deutsche Morgan Grenfell* [2006] UKHL 49; [2007] 1 A.C. 558.

[163] *Deutsche Morgan Grenfell* [2006] UKHL 49; [2007] 1 A.C. 558 at [84]–[87] per Lord Scott.

[164] Especially *Pitt v Holt* [2010] EWHC 45 (Ch); [2010] 1 W.L.R. 1199; [2011] EWCA Civ 197; [2011] 3 W.L.R. 19. Compare *Re Griffiths* [2008] EWHC 118 (Ch); [2009] Ch. 162 at [24] and following; *Fender* [2008] EWHC 2232 (Ch); [2008] 3 E.G.L.R. 80 at [25]; *Bhatt v Bhatt* [2009] EWHC 734 (Ch); [2009] S.T.C. 1540 at [27]–[28]. See too *Clarkson* [2007] W.T.L.R. 1703; *Re Betsam Trust* [2009] W.T.L.R. 1489; *Re A Trust* [2009] JRC 447; [2011] W.T.L.R. 745; *Re First Conferences* [2010] JRC 055A; *Re Lochmore Trust* [2010] JRC 068; *Re S Trust* [2011] JRC 117. See further para.9–101 and following.

[165] See Ch.3.

[166] For a full description, see leading works on the law of contract: e.g. H.G. Beale (gen. ed.), *Chitty on Contracts*, 30th edn (London: Sweet and Maxwell, 2008) vol.1, Chs 5 and 6. See too O'Sullivan, Elliott and Zakrzewski, *The Law of Rescission*, especially Chs 4 and 5; and J. Cartwright, *Misrepresentation, Mistake and Non-Disclosure*, 2nd edn (London: Sweet and Maxwell, 2006), Ch.7.

[167] At law or in equity: *Peek v Gurney* (1871) L.R. 13 Eq. 79 (CA); *Newbigging v Adam* (1886) 34 Ch.D. 582 (CA) at 592.

[168] Historically, generally in equity only: see *Redgrave v Hurd* (1881) 20 Ch.D. 1 (CA) at 12.

[169] e.g. *Bainbrigge v Browne* (1881) 18 Ch.D. 188 at 197; *Barclays Bank v O'Brien* [1994] 1 A.C. 180 at 197; *Credit Lyonnais Bank Nederland N.V. v Burch* [1997] 1 All E.R. 144 (CA) at 152; *Royal Bank of Scotland plc v Etridge (No.2)* [2002] 2 A.C. 773 at [40]. On third party misrepresentations generally, see O'Sullivan, Elliott and Zakrzewski, *The Law of Restitution*, Ch.9.

[170] On which see *Chitty*, paras 6–142 and following; O'Sullivan, Elliott and Zakrzewski, *The Law of Restitution* Ch.5.

allocated by the contract, and the mistake is "fundamental"[171]; and an uninduced unilateral mistake similarly generates relief only in very limited circumstances.[172]

(c) *Spontaneous or Induced*

The law of unjust enrichment will relieve a mistake, whether spontaneous (uninduced) or induced. Nevertheless, the distinction between the two remains significant for the following reasons. First, a more generous test of decision-causation applies in relation to at least some types of induced mistake: "contributory cause" or "a cause" causation, rather than "but for" causation.[173] Secondly, to the extent that the courts sometimes insist that a mistake must be not merely causative, but also in some sense fundamental or serious—as may be the case in relation to gift transactions[174]—this additional threshold will not apply if the mistake is induced.[175] Thirdly, the law of contract will more readily relieve a contracting party who enters into a contract under an induced mistake, via its rules on rescission for misrepresentation.[176] This is of obvious importance where a mistaken claimant seeks restitution for a benefit conferred pursuant to a contract, as it means that any obstacle to his claim, based upon that contract, is more easily cast aside.

9–70

(d) *Fact or Law*

(i) *The Abrogation of the Historic Mistake of Law "Bar"*

The English law of unjust enrichment will now relieve a mistake, whether of fact or of law; and, it would seem, on the same basis. English law was not always so clear. Beginning in the early 19th century, it came to be said that the courts would not generally grant relief for a mistake of law.[177] Always of doubtful pedigree, the so-called mistake of law "bar" came to look increasingly anomalous over subsequent decades. The "bar" become encrusted with a miscellaneous series of

9–71

---

[171] Especially *Bell v Lever Bros Ltd* [1932] A.C. 161; *Great Peace Shipping Ltd v Tsavliris Salvage (International) Ltd* [2002] EWCA Civ 1407; [2003] Q.B. 679. The *Great Peace* case clarifies that there is no separate, and potentially wider equitable doctrine of common mistake: cf. *Solle v Butcher* [1950] 1 K.B. 671 (CA).

[172] e.g. a mistake as to the contract's terms, known to the other party, as in *Hartog v Colin & Shields* [1939] 3 All E.R. 566.

[173] See paras 9–49—9–50.

[174] See paras 9–101 and following, and 9–110.

[175] See paras 9–102, 9–104.

[176] See para.9–69.

[177] Usually traced to *Bilbie v Lumley* (1802) 2 East. 469; 102 E.R. 448; subsequently, *Brisbane v Dacres* (1813) 5 Taunt 143; 128 E.R. 641; *Henderson v Folkestone Waterworks Co* (1885) 1 T.L.R. 329; *William Whiteley Ltd v R.* (1909) 101 L.T. 741; *Re Hatch* [1919] 1 Ch. 351; *Holt v Markham* [1923] 1 K.B. 504; *National Pari-Mutuel Association Ltd v R.* (1930) 47 T.L.R. 110; *Dixon v Monkland Canal Co* (1931) 5 W. & S. 445 (HL); *Sawyer & Vincent v Window Brace Ltd* [1943] 1 K.B. 32; *Avon CC v Howlett* [1983] 1 W.L.R. 605 (CA). Cf. pre-*Bilbie v Lumley* authorities: e.g. *Framson v Delamere* (1594) Cro. Eliz. 458; 78 E.R. 711; *Hewer v Bartholomew* (1596) Cro. Eliz. 885; 78 E.R. 855; *Bonnel v Foulke* (1657) 2 Sid. 4; 82 E.R. 1224; *Landsdown v Landsdown* (1730) Mos. 364; 25 E.R. 441; *Pusey v Desbouvrie* (1734) 2 P. Wms. 315; 24 E.R. 1081; *Farmer v Arundel* (1772) 2 Wm. Bl. 824; 96 E.R. 485; *Bize v Dickason* (1786) 1 T.R. 285; 99 E.R. 1097.

exceptions, commonly of uncertain scope, which threatened to overwhelm the general rule[178]; some types of mistake of law were treated as mistakes of fact,[179] and the uncertainty of the fact/law distinction left it vulnerable to manipulation in individual cases, according to the perceived merits or otherwise of the claim. Even more compellingly, it came to be recognised that the force of a claimant's prima facie claim did not depend upon the classification of the mistake: his intention to benefit the defendant was equally vitiated, and a defendant's enrichment was equally "unjust", whether the mistake was of fact or law.[180] Modern developments in the law of unjust enrichment also meant that the various concerns that might have led earlier courts to impose the "bar" could be more sensitively and coherently addressed by allowing recovery for mistakes of law, leaving the task of liability-containment to one or more well-targeted defences.[181] For all of these reasons, and in the wake of the abolition of the bar by the highest courts[182] or legislatures[183] of other major common law jurisdictions, as well as a report of the Law Commission recommending its removal,[184] the mistake of law "bar" was finally abrogated by a majority of the House of Lords in 1998, in its landmark decision in *Kleinwort Benson*.[185]

9–72 In the *Kleinwort Benson* case, Kleinwort Benson sought restitution of sums which it had paid pursuant to swaps transactions with local authorities. When these transactions were entered into, it was widely assumed that such transactions were valid. However, in 1992, after the relevant swap transactions had been fully executed, *Hazell v Hammersmith and Fulham LBC*[186] decided that these transactions were ultra vires the local authorities, and therefore void. Kleinwort Benson therefore sought restitution of its net payments on the basis that they had been paid under a mistake of law. A majority of the Lords held that the rule precluding recovery for a mistake of law should no longer form part of English law, and that

---

[178] In particular: (1) payments mistakenly made to an officer of the court (e.g. *Ex p. James* (1874) L.R. 9 Ch. App. 609; *Re Carnac, Ex p. Simmonds* (1885) 16 Q.B.D. 308; *Re Byfield* [1982] Ch. 267); (2) payments mistakenly by a court (*Re Birkbeck Permanent Benefit Building Society* [1915] 1 Ch. 91 at 93); (3) overpayments mistakenly made by trustees to their beneficiaries (*Dibbs v Goren* (1849) 11 Beav. 483; 50 E.R. 904; *Re Musgrave* [1916] 2 Ch. 417; *Williams v Allen (No.2)* (1863) 32 Beav. 650; 55 E.R. 255; (4) disbursements of public money without statutory authority (*Auckland Harbour Board v R.* [1924] A.C. 318 (PC)); (5) where rescission was sought in equity of a voluntary settlement or other voluntary transaction (e.g. *Gibbon v Mitchell* [1990] 1 W.L.R. 1304); (6) where the payer was not *in pari delicto* with the payee (e.g. *Kiriri Cotton Co Ltd v Dewani* [1960] A.C. 192 (PC)). For fuller discussion of these exceptions, which are now of mainly historical interest, see *Goff and Jones: The Law of Restitution* paras 5–011 and following.

[179] In particular: (1) mistakes as to private right (e.g. *Cooper v Phibbs* (1867) L.R. 2 H.L. 149 at 170; *Solle v Butcher* [1950] 1 K.B. 671 (CA)); (2) mistakes as to foreign law (*Lazard Bros & Co v Midland Bank Ltd* [1933] A.C. 289).

[180] See especially *Kleinwort Benson* [1999] 2 A.C. 349 at 372 per Lord Goff.

[181] *Kleinwort Benson* [1999] 2 A.C. 349 at 373 per Lord Goff.

[182] *Air Canada v British Columbia* (1989) 59 D.L.R. (4d.) 161 (Canada); *David Securities* (1992) 175 C.L.R. 353 (Australia); *Willis Faber Enthoven (Pty) Ltd v Receiver of Revenue*, 1992 (4) S.A. 202 (A.) (South Africa); *Morgan Guaranty Trust Co of New York v Lothian Regional Council*, 1995 S.C. 151 (Scotland).

[183] Judicature Act 1908 s.94A (as inserted by Judicature Amendment Act 1958 s.2) (New Zealand); Property Law Act 1969 ss.124, 125 (Western Australia).

[184] Law Commission, *Restitution: Mistake of Law and Ultra Vires Public Authority Receipts and Payments* (HMSO, 1994) Law Com. No.227, Cm.2731.

[185] *Kleinwort Benson* [1999] 2 A.C. 348.

[186] *Hazell v Hammersmith and Fulham LBC* [1992] 2 A.C. 1.

assuming that the claimant could establish that it had paid the money under a mistake of law, it was entitled to succeed, and to take advantage of the more generous limitation period applicable to an action for relief from the consequences of a "mistake".[187]

(ii) *Identifying Mistakes of Law: Judicial Development of the Law*

An important point that divided the majority from the minority in *Kleinwort* **9–73** *Benson* concerned whether, and on what assumptions, a person might act on the basis of a "mistake of law". In many routine cases, there may be no doubt that the claimant has acted on the basis of a mistake of law—as where, for example, the claimant merely overlooks a legislative provision which renders void his contractual liability to pay the defendant.[188] However, there are also other cases where the process of identifying a mistake of law is more complicated because of the difficulty of saying what the law is or was at any particular point of time, and/or because of the capacity of the law to develop over time, often with retrospective application.[189]

This problem arises most acutely in cases involving judicial development of **9–74** the law—whether in the form of judicial development of the common law or judicial interpretations of legislation. If a person pays money, believing or assuming that the law is X, but a court subsequently declares the law to be otherwise, has he paid under a "mistake of law"? This problem can arise in number of key forms. In some cases, a later decision may overrule an earlier decision which declared the law to be X. In other cases, although no decision may have previously declared the law to be X, the prevailing view amongst the legal community may have been that X represented the best understanding of the law. In yet other cases there may have been no clear consensus.

Overruling an earlier decision If a person confers a benefit on another on **9–75** the basis of the law as declared in a court decision, and this decision is subsequently overruled by the decision of a higher court, can he claim to have paid under a "mistake of law" as a consequence of the second judgment?

On one view, and taking the concept of a "mistake" in its core sense, he does **9–76** not make a mistake. To say that a person paid money under a mistake of law assumes that he acted on a belief about the law which was incorrect *at the time he paid*. He must have misperceived the true state of the law *at that time*. The

---

[187] See Ch.33 on limitation of actions.
[188] As in *David Securities* (1992) 175 C.L.R. 353.
[189] Much academic ink has been spilt, in an attempt to unpick these questions: L.D. Smith, "Restitution for Mistake of Law" [1999] R.L.R. 148; J. Finnis, "The Fairy Tale's Moral" (1999) 115 L.Q.R. 170; S. Meier and R. Zimmermann, "Judicial Development of the Law, *Error Iuris*, and the Law of Unjustified Enrichment—a View from Germany" (1999) 115 L.Q.R. 556; Sheehan, "What is a Mistake?"; P. Birks, "Mistakes of Law" [2000] C.L.P. 205; J. Beatson, "Unlawful Statutes and Mistake of Law: Is there a Smile on the Face of Schrödinger's Cat?" in A.S. Burrows and Lord Rodger (eds), *Mapping the Law* (Oxford: OUP, 2006), Ch.9; M. Bhandari and C. Mitchell, "Lessons of the *Metallgesellschaft* Litigation" [2008] R.L.R. 1 at pp.8–10; A. Nair, "Mistakes of Law and Legal Reasoning: Interpreting *Kleinwort Benson Ltd v Lincoln City Council*" in R. Chambers, C. Mitchell and J. Penner (eds), *Philosophical Foundations of the Law of Unjust Enrichment* (Oxford: OUP, 2009). And see Burrows, *The Law of Restitution*, pp.221 and following; Virgo, *The Principles of the Law of Restitution*, pp.165 and following.

question whether he has made a "mistake" thus depends on the proper character-isation of what occurred, when the subsequent court overruled the earlier deci-sion, and declared the law to be Y. If the proper analysis was that the payer correctly perceived the law—that the law at the time he acted, and as established by the earlier decision, was X, but the law was changed by subsequent judicial decision—then it might seem to follow that the payer makes no "mistake". The inherent retrospectivity of judicial decisions about the law means that this development of the law will have retrospective effect. Nevertheless, it cannot, on this view, change the fact that when the payer acted, he correctly perceived the law *as then applicable*. Put differently, he held no mistaken belief about the law *at that time*; and the retrospective change in the law cannot falsify his earlier perception, so as to render him "retrospectively" mistaken.[190]

9–77 This was in effect the view of the minority in *Kleinwort Benson*.[191] Lord Browne-Wilkinson considered that a person who has made a payment on an understanding of the law which was correct according to the law as it stood at the date of payment does not make the payment under a mistake of law where the law is subsequently changed.[192] As he saw it[193]:

> "[T]he . . . question is whether the fact that the later overruling decision operates retrospectively so far as the substantive law is concerned also requires it to be assumed (contrary to the facts) that *at the date of each payment* the plaintiff made a mistake as to what the law then was. In my judgment it does not. . . . He was not mistaken at the date of payment. He paid on the basis that the then binding . . . decision stated the law, which it did: the fact that the law was later retrospectively changed cannot alter retrospectively the state of the payer's mind at the time of payment."

Lord Lloyd was of the same view.[194]

9–78 The second and more robust view is to say that a person makes a "mistake" provided only that he acted on the basis of an understanding of the law which is different from the law as later declared to be applicable to his prior transaction. Adopting this view, a person can sometimes be, in effect, "retrospectively" mistaken—he will make a restitution-grounding "mistake" even where he *correctly* perceived the law at the time he acted, and so acted on a belief which was correct at the time, because the law is subsequently changed by judicial decision, albeit with retrospective effect. It is not necessary, on this approach, to undertake any inquiry into whether his understanding of the law actually represented the law at the time he acted, and/or into whether the later decision has "changed" the law or simply "clarified" or "declared" the law, as it was at the time. If the claimant believed the applicable law was X, and it is subsequently held to be

---

[190] *Kleinwort Benson* [1999] 2 A.C. 349 at 358–562, especially at 359 per Lord Browne-Wilkinson, and at 394 per Lord Lloyd; see too Birks, "Mistakes of Law"; Meier and Zimmermann, "Judicial Development of the Law, *Error Juris*, and the Law of Unjustified Enrichment—A View from Germany"; J. Beatson, "Unlawful Statutes and Mistakes of Law: Is there a Smile on the Face of Schrödinger's Cat?" in Burrows and Rodger, *Mapping the Law*; Bhandari and Mitchell , "Lessons of the *Metallgesellschaft* Litigation", pp.8–10.
[191] *Kleinwort Benson* [1999] 2 A.C. 349.
[192] *Kleinwort Benson* [1999] 2 A.C. 349 at 359; and more generally at 358–362.
[193] *Kleinwort Benson* [1999] 2 A.C. 349 at 359.
[194] *Kleinwort Benson* [1999] 2 A.C. 349 at 394. He also supported his conclusion with the pragmatic argument that courts should not be deterred from in changing the law, by concerns about unsettling prior transactions as a result of the retrospectivity of their decisions, at 395.

otherwise, he has made a mistake. This was, in substance, the majority's view in *Kleinwort Benson*.[195]

Although controversial, the majority's robust view has gone unchallenged in later cases.[196] In an important passage in *Deutsche Morgan Grenfell*,[197] Lord Hoffmann revisited this issue in the wake of academic criticisms of the majority's reasoning. As he saw it, the point in issue in *Kleinwort Benson* had been whether a person whose understanding of the law is falsified by a subsequent decision of the courts "should, for the purposes of the law of unjust enrichment, *be treated as having made a mistake*".[198] And the answer the majority had given was that it should be so treated, based upon "practical considerations of fairness". The effect of the later judgment was that, "contrary to his opinion at the time, the money was not owing"; it was therefore fair that he should recover it. Lord Hoffmann recognised that this involved an artificial extension to the concept of a mistake—or, in substance, the law's *deeming* the payer to have made a mistake, because the law was *deemed* to be different at the relevant date. However, he considered that this was justified by "practical considerations of fairness", to compensate for the lack of the equivalent of a more general *condictio indebiti*.[199]
9–79

A later decision declares the law to be contrary to a "settled understanding" There will be cases where the claimant acted on the basis that the law was X, where no decision had previously declared the law to be X, but where there was nevertheless a general consensus of legal opinion that X was the law. If a later case in fact declares the law to be otherwise, has the claimant acted on the basis of a mistake of law?
9–80

Kleinwort Benson potentially presented facts of this nature. There was no judicial decision, prior to the litigation in *Hazell*,[200] holding that local authorities had capacity to enter into the swap transactions. It was nevertheless assumed by those participating in these transactions that the local authorities had such capacity. Before the House of Lords in *Kleinwort Benson*, the defendant local authorities argued that if, despite the absence of any decision settling the point, there was a "settled view" that the local authorities had capacity, and a later judicial decision had held otherwise, there could be no recovery for mistake of law.
9–81

A majority of the House of Lords rejected this argument. A person who acted on the basis of a settled understanding of the law, which was subsequently declared to be incorrect, *did* make a mistake of law.[201] This conclusion followed inexorably from the majority's artificially-extended understanding of the nature of a mistake, according to which a restitution-grounding mistake of law can be established merely by showing that when the claimant acted he believed the law
9–82

---

[195] See *Kleinwort Benson* [1999] 2 A.C. 349 at 379–381 per Lord Goff, at 398–400 per Lord Hoffmann, and at 409–412 per Lord Hope.
[196] Cf. *Brennan v Bolt Burdon* [2004] EWCA Civ 1017; [2005] Q.B. 303 (CA), especially per Bodey J.
[197] *Deutsche Morgan Grenfell* [2006] UKHL 49; [2007] 1 A.C. 558 at [23].
[198] *Deutsche Morgan Grenfell* [2006] UKHL 49; [2007] 1 A.C. 558 at [23].
[199] *Deutsche Morgan Grenfell* [2006] UKHL 49; [2007] 1 A.C. 558 at [23].
[200] *Hazell* [1992] 2 A.C. 1.
[201] *Kleinwort Benson* [1999] 2 A.C. 349 at 379–380 per Lord Goff, at 398–401 per Lord Hoffman, and at 409–412 per Lord Hope.

to be X, and that a decision has subsequently declared the applicable law to be otherwise. Adopting this approach, it would be enough in *Kleinwort Benson* to find that the bank acted in the belief that the local authorities had capacity to enter the swap tranactions, and that the House of Lords had later declared that they did not.[202] Lord Lloyd and Lord Browne-Wilkinson dissented on the basis that a person who acted on the basis of a settled understanding of the law was not mistaken as to the law, because, as Lord Lloyd put it, "that was the law at the time of payment".[203]

9–83   The majority in *Kleinwort Benson* also rejected the related argument that there should in any event be a bar to restitution for mistake of law, where the claimant had acted on the basis of a "settled view of the law" which was subsequently overturned. A similar bar is found in Commonwealth statutes that have abolished the mistake of law bar[204]; and it was recommended in the report of the Law Commission that recommended its abolition in England.[205] The majority did not accept the major premise of the Law Commission's recommendation: that a person who acts in accordance with a settled view of the law is not "mistaken".[206] It followed that if restitution was to be denied where the claimant had acted on a settled view of the law, it had to be because such a bar was independently justified on policy grounds—most obviously, to preserve the security of past transactions on the basis that where the law was thought to have been settled, it was more likely that many transactions would be entered into in reliance upon it.[207] The majority ultimately declined to take this step. It could only be appropriately taken by the legislature[208]; there were other defences, such as change of position, that could do the desired work of protecting the security of past transactions[209]; it was very difficult to define the ambit of the defence, and in particular, what constituted a settled view of the law[210]; and the proposed defence would have the counter-intuitive effect of denying restitution where a claimant's "mistake" was most likely to be excusable.[211]

---

[202] *Kleinwort Benson* [1999] 2 A.C. 349 at 379–381 per Lord Goff, at 400–401 per Lord Hoffmann, and at 409–412 per Lord Hope.
[203] *Kleinwort Benson* [1999] 2 A.C. 349 at 396–397 per Lord Lloyd; cf. at 362–364 per Lord Browne-Wilkinson, who reaches a similar conclusion, but is less emphatic that a settled understanding represents the law.
[204] New Zealand Judicature Act 1908 s.94A(2); Western Australian Law Act 1969 s.124(2).
[205] Law Commission, *Restitution: Mistake of Law and Ultra Vires Public Authority Receipts and Payments*, paras 5.1–5.13 (and draft bill, cl.3). See too the "prevailing practice" defence available under s.33(2A), Taxes Management Act 1970 (on which see para.22–08, fn.23). Cf. the changing views of the Scottish Law Commission: *Recovery of Benefits Conferred under Error of Law* (HMSO, 1993), D.P. No.95, Vol 1, paras 2.108–2.124; *Judicial Abolition of the Error of Law Rule and its Aftermath* (HMSO, 1996), D.P. No.99 para.3–51; *Unjustified Enrichment, Error of Law and Public Authority Receipts and Disbursements* (TSO, 1999), Law Com. No.169, paras 2.47–2.49.
[206] Law Commission, *Restitution: Mistake of Law and Ultra Vires Public Authority Receipts*, para.5.3. See *Kleinwort Benson* [1999] 2 A.C. 349 at 379–381, 382 per Lord Goff, at 398–401 per Lord Hoffmann; see too, by implication, at 409–412 per Lord Hope.
[207] See especially *Kleinwort Benson* [1999] 2 A.C. 349 at 401 per Lord Hoffmann.
[208] *Kleinwort Benson* [1999] 2 A.C. 349 at 401 per Lord Hoffmann, at 415 per Lord Hope. See too *Deutsche Morgan Grenfell* [2006] UKHL 49; [2007] 1 A.C. 558 at [145] per Lord Walker; see in the Court of Appeal [2005] EWCA Civ 78; [2006] Ch. 243 at [237] per Jonathan Parker L.J.
[209] *Kleinwort Benson* [1999] 2 A.C. 349 at 382 per Lord Goff.
[210] *Kleinwort Benson* [1999] 2 A.C. 349 at 383 per Lord Goff, and at 414–415 per Lord Hope.
[211] *Kleinwort Benson* [1999] 2 A.C. 349 at 414–415 per Lord Hope.

A later decision declares the law, where it was previously in **9–84** **doubt** There will be other cases where, at the time the claimant acted, the law was genuinely unclear. These are true "hard cases", where there is no decision on point, and where the appropriate answer is disputed amongst the legal community. In this situation, a person who is *conscious* that the law is disputed, and who nevertheless proceeds in a state of unresolved doubt, may well be denied restitution for mistake of law on the basis that his doubts mean that he is not truly mistaken as to the law, that any "mistake" was not causative of his decision to act, or that in acting as he did, he unreasonably responded to his state of doubt.[212] But what if he was not conscious that the law was disputed when he acted and he honestly believed the law to be X? The majority's robust approach in *Kleinwort Benson*[213] again seems inexorably to produce the conclusion that he also makes a restitution-grounding mistake of law here. If he acts in the belief, however unreasonably formed, that the law is X, and if a later decision determines the applicable law to be otherwise, then he makes a mistake of law.

Prospective judicial development of the law A different conclusion would **9–85** be reached if an English court, when bringing about a development in the law—most obviously, when overruling an earlier decision—was exceptionally to declare that its decision on the law had only *prospective* effect.[214] A person who had acted on the basis of the law declared in the earlier decision would not act as a result of any mistake of law, on any analysis. When he acted, he correctly perceived that the law applying to him was the law as declared in the earlier decision. He therefore made no mistake at that time; but neither can he become "retrospectively" mistaken as a result of the decision's subsequent overruling (as the majority in the *Kleinwort Benson* case allowed, where the law is judicially developed with *retrospective* effect).[215] The prospective operation of the overruling means that the law applicable to his previous dealings remains unchanged. It remains the law as declared in the earlier decision, and as he perceived it to be.

(iii) *Identifying Mistakes of Law: Legislative Changes*

Fewer problems arise from legislative changes in the law. Most have prospective **9–86** effect only. A person who, prior to the legislative change, acted on the basis of the law as then in force, makes no mistake of law. He made no mistake when he acted: the belief he held at that time, as to the law then applying to his dealings, was correct. But neither can he become "retrospectively" mistaken[216] as a result

---

[212] See para.9–15 and following.
[213] *Kleinwort Benson* [1999] 2 A.C. 349 at 379–381 per Lord Goff, at 398–401 per Lord Hoffmann, and at 409–412 per Lord Hope.
[214] See especially *Re Spectrum Plus Ltd (In Liquidation)* [2005] UKHL 41; [2005] 2 A.C. 680 at [2]–[43] per Lord Nicholls, at [45] per Lord Steyn, at [71]–[74] per Lord Hope, at [121]–[127] per Lord Scott, at [161] per Lord Walker, at [162] per Baroness Hale, at [165] per Lord Brown, where their Lordships considered at length the question whether the House of Lords could ever exercise a power to only "prospectively" overrule an earlier decision, and left open whether there might be cases in future where, exceptionally, this would be appropriate.
[215] See paras 9–75—9–79.
[216] See para.9–78.

of the subsequent prospective legislative change. The legislation, being prospective in operation only, does not change the law that applies to his previous dealings, which remains the law as he perceived it to be.

9–87   Where legislative changes exceptionally have retrospective effect, matters are less clear. This issue arose for decision by the High Court of Australia in *Commissioner of State Revenue v Royal Insurance Australia Ltd*,[217] where an insurance company sought to recover overpaid stamp duty levied on insurance premiums. Some of these premiums had been legally due when paid, but legislation had subsequently and retrospectively granted an exemption, deeming the duty not to have been due. The High Court of Australia divided on the question whether these premiums were paid under a "mistake". A majority held not.[218] The insurance company was liable to pay the premiums, *when they were paid*, with the result that it had not paid under any mistaken belief as to its liability; and, by implication, the respective legislative change could not retrospectively "create" a restitution-grounding mistake. Mason C.J. thought otherwise: the retrospective operation of the exempting legislation "enable[d] one to say that, in the light of the law as it was enacted with retrospective effect . . . the [earlier] payments of duty were made under a mistake as to the legal liability to pay them".[219]

9–88   English authority is inconclusive. In *Kleinwort Benson*,[220] where the question did not immediately arise, the court divided along similar lines. The minority judges, Lord Browne-Wilkinson and Lord Lloyd, could find no mistake[221]; but neither could some of the majority. Thus, Lord Goff, despite finding that there could be a "mistake" where the law was developed judicially, suggested that retrospective legislative change stood on a different footing, both because "it has the effect that as from the date of the legislation a new legal provision will apply retrospectively in place of that previously applicable", and therefore that "retrospective legislative change in the law does not necessarily have the effect that a previous payment was, as a result of the change in the law, made under a mistake of law at the time of payment"[222]; and because of the possibility of drafting the legislation to prevent unjust consequences for prior transactions.[223] Lord Hoffmann took an opposing and more robust view. He expressly agreed with Mason C.J.'s opinion in the *Royal Insurance Australia* case[224] that a person who acted in accordance with the law as it was at the time, but which a statute subsequently requires to be deemed to have been different, should be *"deemed* to have made a mistake"; whilst recognising that in practice, the recoverability of benefits

---

[217] *Commissioner of State Revenue v Royal Insurance Australia Ltd* (1994) 126 A.L.R. 1. Cf. *Commonwealth v S.C.I. Operations Pty Ltd* (1998) 192 C.L.R. 285 at 322–323.
[218] *Royal Insurance Australia* (1994) 126 A.L.R. 1 at 26–27 per Brennan J., (with whom Toohey and McHugh J.J. agreed); see too at 35 per Dawson J. The majority held, in any event, that there was a *statutory* liability to refund; this was the only way in which the amendment could be given the retrospective effect intended: at 27 per Brennan J.
[219] *Royal Insurance Australia* (1994) 126 A.L.R. 1 at 9 per Mason C.J.
[220] *Kleinwort Benson* [1999] 2 A.C. 349.
[221] *Kleinwort Benson* [1999] 2 A.C. 349 at 359, 361–362 per Lord Browne-Wilkinson, and at 394, 395 per Lord Lloyd.
[222] *Kleinwort Benson* [1999] 2 A.C. 349 at 381 per Lord Goff. See too at 410 per Lord Hope.
[223] *Kleinwort Benson* [1999] 2 A.C. 349 at 381 per Lord Goff.
[224] *Royal Insurance Australia* (1994) 126 A.L.R. 1 at 9 per Mason C.J.

conferred on the basis of the previous law would usually turn on the construction of the statute.[225]

(iv) *Confining Restitution for Mistake of Law?*

The decision in *Kleinwort Benson* prompts several further questions, as to the **9–89** ambit of recovery for mistake of law.

First, what type or quality of mistake of law can be restitution-grounding? The **9–90** answer to this, which is implicit in the majority's reasoning and assumed in later decisions, is that a mistake of law will ground restitution to the same extent as a mistake of fact. A causative mistake of fact is prima facie sufficient; so too, post-*Kleinwort Benson*, a causative mistake of law.[226]

Secondly, do claims based upon a mistake of law attract any special defences **9–91** or bars? In *Kleinwort Benson* a central premise of the majority's reasoning in support of removal of the mistake of law bar was that there was no principled reason for distinguishing claims based on mistakes of law from claims based on mistakes of fact: a mistaken claimant's intention to benefit the defendant was equally vitiated, and the defendant's enrichment was equally unjust. Rather than denying restitution for mistake of law *in limine*, the better strategy was to contain liability by means of one or more well-targeted defences.[227] Accepting this, did the removal of the bar require the introduction of one or more mistake of law-specific defences, on policy grounds?

The majority in *Kleinwort Benson* proceeded with caution. First, they recog- **9–92** nised that established defences already went far in addressing cases in which recovery might lead to injustice—including change of position, estoppel, com-promise, and submission to an honest claim.[228] Secondly, they specifically declined invitations to introduce a novel and very extensive defence of "honest receipt"[229]; or a rule denying restitution for mistake of law to a person who had acted on the basis of a settled view of the law which was subsequently over-turned.[230] Thirdly, like the minority, they saw that problems might arise as a result of s.32(1)(c) of the Limitation Act 1980, which postpones the accrual of a cause of action based on mistake until the mistake is discovered or is reasonably discoverable, and their view that a person might be "retrospectively" mistaken when the law applicable to an earlier transaction is subsequently declared to be otherwise that he believed it to be. However, they considered that this was a problem for the legislature to resolve.[231]

---

[225] *Kleinwort Benson* [1999] 2 A.C. 349 at 400 per Lord Hoffmann, contemplating that the statute might inter alia expressly provide for the refund of money declared not to be due, or impliedly do so; and that the absence of an express provision for repayment might show a parliamentary intention that transactions entered into under the previous law should not be disturbed.

[226] See para.9–99 and following.

[227] *Kleinwort Benson* [1999] 2 A.C. 349 at 373, 382 per Lord Goff, and at 412–415 per Lord Hope.

[228] *Kleinwort Benson* [1999] 2 A.C. 349 at 382 per Lord Goff, and at 412–414 per Lord Hope.

[229] As suggested by Brennan J. in *David Securities* (1992) 175 C.L.R. 353 at 399; see *Kleinwort Benson* [1999] 2 A.C. 349 at 384–385 per Lord Goff, and at 413–414 per Lord Hope.

[230] *Kleinwort Benson* [1999] 2 A.C. 349 at 381–383 per Lord Goff, at 401 per Lord Hoffmann, and at 414–415 per Lord Hope. See further paras 9–80—9–83.

[231] *Kleinwort Benson* [1999] 2 A.C. 349 at 389 per Lord Goff, and at 401 per Lord Hoffmann, and at 417–418 per Lord Hope.

9–93   There are no signs in post-*Kleinwort Benson* decisions of any strong judicial inclination to develop any further mistake of law-specific defences or bars. What activity there has been in cutting back the decision's prima facie implications has been legislative—in particular, by the disapplication of the postponement provisions in s.32(1)(c) of the Limitation Act 1980, to address the risk of a flood of claims to recover tax payments which are discovered, potentially many years later, to have been wrongly paid.[232]

9–94   Finally, is the ground of mistake of law generally available? For a time, it was thought not, to the extent that it was thought that unlawfully levied tax payments might only be recoverable via a *Woolwich*-based claim, and could not be recovered via a common law claim for mistake of law. The House of Lords then held otherwise in *Deutsche Morgan Grenfell*.[233] Following that decision, it is clear that mistake of law is a general ground of restitution, no less than mistake of fact. However, it of course remains possible that, as is common in the tax and benefits settings, a statutory regime exists for the recovery of over-payments which is understood to be exhaustive and to exclude a concurrent common law restitutionary claim.[234]

(e) *Merely Causative or Something More?*

(i) *The Emergence of a General Test of Causative Mistake at Common Law*

9–95   As long as the mistake of law "bar" prevailed, English law's starting-point was inevitably that a personal claim to restitution, usually for money paid, was only available on the ground of mistake of *fact*. However, it was also long thought that the availability of relief for mistake, at least where spontaneous, was more restricted than this. Not every spontaneous mistake of fact that caused a payment to be made or some other benefit to be conferred, would ground relief: only a *liability* mistake of fact would do. As Bramwell B. expressed it in *Aiken v Short*,[235] in an influential passage that was frequently cited:

> "In order to entitle a person to recover back money paid under a mistake of fact, the mistake must be as to a fact which, if true, would make the person liable to pay the money; not where, if true, it would merely make it desirable that he should pay the money".[236]

9–96   Over the course of the 20th century, it became increasingly difficult to accept that Bramwell B.'s dictum provided an exhaustive description of restitution-

---

[232] See esp. Finance Act 2004 s.320; Finance Act 2007 s.107.

[233] *Deutsche Morgan Grenfell* [2006] UKHL 49; [2007] 1 A.C. 558; overruling [2005] EWCA Civ 78; [2006] Ch. 243. See paras 22–25——22–29.

[234] See esp. Taxes Management Act 1970 s.33 (considered in *Monro v HMRC* [2008] EWCA Civ 306; [2009] Ch. 69); VAT Act 1994 ss.78 and 80 (considered in *Chalke* [2009] EWHC 952 (Ch); [2009] S.T.C. 2027 at [57]–[75]); *Littlewoods Retail Ltd v HMRC* [2010] EWHC 1071 (Ch); [2011] S.T.C. 2072 at [45]–[62]; Social Security Administration Act 1992 s.71 (considered in *Child Poverty Action Group v Secretary of State for Work and Pensions* [2010] UKSC 54; [2011] 2 A.C. 15). See paras 2–15——2–19.

[235] *Aiken v Short* (1856) 1 H. & N. 210, 156 E.R. 1180.

[236] *Aiken v Short* (1856) 1 H. & N. 210 at 215; 156 E.R. 1180 at 1182; similarly, *Kelly v Solari* (1854) 9 M. & W. 54 at 58; 152 E.R. 24 at 26 per Parke B.; *Deutsche Bank v Beriro & Co* (1895) 1 Com. Cas. 255 at 259 per Lindley L.J.; *Re Bodega Co* [1904] 1 Ch. 276.

grounding mistakes of fact, either in principle or as a matter of authority. There were undoubtedly many older cases where the courts allowed claimants to recover money paid consistently with this restriction,[237] as exemplified by *Kelly v Solari*,[238] where insurers had paid sums to the executrix of an assured pursuant to an insurance policy on his life, shortly after his death, forgetting that the premiums had not been paid, and that the policy had therefore lapsed. At the same time, there were also other cases, some of the very highest authority, where the outcome could not be explained in those terms. In some, a requirement for a "liability mistake" could only survive by stretching that idea beyond mistakes of fact which lead the claimant to believe that he has a present legal liability to the recipient, to embrace those that lead him to believe that he will *in future* incur a legal liability[239]; that he is legally liable to a *third party*[240]; or that he will have merely a *moral* obligation.[241] But other cases could not be explained even in these extended terms. There were, in particular, dicta to the effect that even gifted money might sometimes be recoverable on the ground of mistake—an assumption which is wholly inconsistent with any universal requirement for a mistake as to liability, to the donee or otherwise.[242]

One route to reconciling these various decisions would have been for the **9–97** courts to forgo any attempt to identify any particular types of restitution-grounding mistake, in favour of an overarching requirement for a *"fundamental"* mistake—perhaps mirroring the criterion that governs whether a contract is void for common mistake, or whether a mistake prevents the passing of title to property.[243] On this view, a liability mistake of fact would be one important

---

[237] e.g. *Buller v Harrison* (1777) 2 Cowp. 565; 98 E.R. 1243; *De Hahn v Hartley* (1786) 1 T.R. 343; 99 E.R. 1130; *Anderson v Pitcher* (1800) 2 Bos. & P. 164; 126 E.R. 1216; *Jones v Ryde* (1814) 5 Taunt. 488; 128 E.R. 779; *Bruce v Bruce* (1814) 5 Taunt. 495; 128 E.R. 782; *Wilkinson v Johnson* (1824) 3 B. & C. 428; 107 E.R. 792; *Milnes v Duncan* (1827) 6 B. & C. 671; 108 E.R. 598; *Dupen v Keeling* (1829) 4 C. & P. 107; 172 E.R. 626; *Newsome v Graham* (1829) 10 B. & C. 234; 109 E.R. 437; *Kelly v Solari* (1841) 9 M. & W. 54; 152 E.R. 24; *Standish v Ross* (1849) 3 Ex. 527; 154 E.R. 954; *Barber v Brown* (1856) 1 C.B. N.S. 121; 140 E.R. 50; *Townsend v Crowdy* (1860) 8 C.B. N.S. 477; 141 E.R. 1251; *Newall v Tomlinson* (1871) L.R. 6 C.P. 405; *Durrant v Ecclesiastical Commissioners for England and Wales* (1880) 6 Q.B.D. 234; *Leeds & County Bank Ltd v Walker* (1883) 11 Q.B.D. 84; *King v Stewart* (1892) 66 L.T. 339; *Imperial Bank of Canada Ltd v Bank of Hamilton* [1903] A.C. 49; *Re Bodega Co* [1904] 1 Ch. 276; *Continental Caoutchouc & Gutta Percha Co v Kleinwort Sons & Co* (1904) 90 L.T. 474; *Meadows v Grand Junction Waterworks Co* (1905) 69 J.P. 255; *Kleinwort, Sons & Co v Dunlop Rubber Co* (1907) 97 L.T. 263 (HL); *Kerrison* (1911) 81 L.J.K.B. 465 (HL); *Baylis v Bishop of London* [1913] 1 Ch. 127; *Scottish Metropolitan Assurance Co Ltd v P. Samuel & Co* [1923] 1 K.B. 348; *R.E. Jones v Waring* [1926] A.C. 670; *Anglo-Scottish Sugar* [1937] 2 K.B. 607; *Norwich Union Fire Society Ltd v Wm. H. Price Ltd* [1934] A.C. 455 (PC); *Weld-Blundell v Synott* [1940] 2 K.B. 107; *Larner v LCC* [1949] 2 K.B. 683; *Turvey* [1953] 1 Q.B. 218.

[238] *Kelly v Solari* (1841) 9 M. & W. 54; 154 E.R. 24.

[239] *Kerrison* (1911) 81 L.J.K.B. 465 (HL), a difficult rationalisation, because it involves a misprediction. See paras 9–07 and following, and 9–14.

[240] See e.g. *Colonial Bank v Exchange Bank of Yarmouth, Nova Scotia* (1885) 11 App. Cas. 84 (PC); *Kleinwort v Dunlop Rubber* (1907) 97 L.T. 263 (HL); *R.E. Jones v Waring* [1926] A.C. 670.

[241] *Larner v LCC* [1949] 2 K.B. 683.

[242] See *Morgan v Ashcroft* [1938] 1 K.B. 49 (CA) at 74 per Scott L.J.; and also the equity cases, on the setting aside of voluntary transactions, discussed at para.9–101 and following.

[243] A development contemplated, with reservations, in Birks, *An Introduction to the Law of Restitution*, pp.153–159.

example of a "fundamental mistake", but would not exhaust the category. There are hints of this view in some earlier cases.[244]

9–98 The modern English law of unjust enrichment has taken a different course. In 1980, in the landmark decision in *Barclays Bank v Simms*,[245] Robert Goff J. undertook a comprehensive review of earlier authorities, and concluded that the law, properly understood, was that money paid was prima facie recoverable provided only that it was paid under a causative mistake of fact. Recovery was not restricted to one or more sub-categories of causative mistake of fact, whether "liability" mistakes or otherwise; nor to a sub-category of fundamental mistakes. As Robert Goff J. put it: "if a person pays money to another under a mistake of fact, he is prima facie entitled to recover it".[246] Although only a first instance decision, Robert Goff J.'s decision in *Barclays Bank v Simms* has proved highly influential, and a long line of later English cases has accepted its premises, expressly or by implication.[247] In light of them, it must now be regarded as settled that a causative mistake of fact without more will prima facie support a personal claim in unjust enrichment.

9–99 A question which *Barclays Bank v Simms* could not and did not settle was what types of mistake of *law* might be restitution-grounding: it was almost another 20 years before the mistake of law bar was finally abrogated by the House of Lords in *Kleinwort Benson*.[248] The majority in the *Kleinwort Benson* case did not unequivocally define the ambit of restitution-grounding mistakes of law; nevertheless, the general thrust of their reasoning strongly suggests that they must have intended that mistakes of law should in future be treated in the same way as mistakes of fact. That must in turn mean that a causative mistake of law, just as a causative mistake of fact, is prima facie sufficient to support a personal claim in unjust enrichment. Any other view, involving a narrower test for

---

[244] Cf. *Norwich Union v Price* [1934] A.C. 455 (PC) at 461–462, 463; *Morgan v Ashcroft* [1938] 1 K.B. 49 at 64–67 per Sir Wilfred Greene M.R., and at 77 per Scott L.J. See too the approach of the Court of Appeal in the long-neglected decision—now resurrected—on equity's jurisdiction to set aside voluntary transactions: *Ogilvie v Littleboy* (1897) 13 T.L.R. 399 (CA); approved on appeal sub nom *Ogilvie v Allen* (1899) 15 T.L.R. 294 (HL). See para.9–101 and following.

[245] *Barclays Bank v Simms* [1980] Q.B. 677. See also especially *David Securities* (1992) 175 C.L.R. 353 at 376–378 (rejecting a fundamentality restriction).

[246] *Barclays Bank v Simms* [1980] Q.B. 677 at 695.

[247] See especially *Rover International Ltd v Cannon Film Sales Ltd* [1989] 1 W.L.R. 912 (CA) at 933; *Banque Financière* [1999] 1 A.C. 221 at 227, 234; *Nurdin & Peacock* [1999] 1 W.L.R. 1249 at 1270 and following; *Lloyds Bank v Independent Insurance* [2000] Q.B. 110 (CA) at 115–116; *Dextra Bank* [2001] UKPC 50; [2002] 1 All E.R. (Comm.) 193 at [28] and following; *Customs & Excise Commissioners* [2002] EWHC 2204 (Ch); [2003] 1 All E.R. (Comm.) 327 at [2]; *Papamichael* [2003] EWHC 164 (Comm); [2003] 1 Lloyd's Rep. 341 at [196]; *Deutsche Morgan Grenfell* [2006] UKHL 49; [2007] 1 A.C. 558 at [59]–[60] per Lord Hope, at [84]–[87] per Lord Scott, at [143]–[144] per Lord Walker; *Jones v Churcher* [2009] EWHC 722 (QB); [2009] 2 Lloyd's Rep. 94 at [47]; *Marine Trade* [2009] EWHC 2656 (Comm); [2010] 1 Lloyd's Rep. 631 at [65], [78]–[81]; *Chalke* [2009] EWHC 952 (Ch); [2009] S.T.C. 2027 at [138]; *F.I.I.* [2008] EWHC 2893 (Ch); [2009] S.T.C. 254 at [264]; [2010] EWCA Civ 103, [2010] S.T.C. 1251 at [182]; *Thin Cap Group Litigation* [2009] EWHC 2908 (Ch); [2010] S.T.C. 301 at [234]; *Deutsche Bank v Vik* [2010] EWHC 551 (Comm) at [3].

[248] *Kleinwort Benson* [1999] 2 A.C. 349. See subsequently esp. *Nurdin & Peacock* [1999] 1 W.L.R. 1249 at 1270 and following; *Deutsche Morgan Grenfell* [2006] UKHL 49; [2007] 1 A.C. 558; *Marine Trade* [2009] EWHC 2656 (Comm); [2010] 1 Lloyd's Rep. 631 at [65], [78]–[81]; *F.I.I.* [2008] EWHC 2893 (Ch); [2009] S.T.C. 254 at [264]; [2010] EWCA Civ 103; [2010] S.T.C. 1251 at [182]; *Thin Cap Group Litigation* [2009] EWHC 2908 (Ch); [2010] S.T.C. 301 at [234].

qualifying mistakes of law, would perpetuate the distinction between mistakes of fact and law. And this would be wholly contrary to key premises of the majority's decision that the mistake of law "bar" had to be removed: that the line between fact and law is difficult to draw; and that the effect on the payer is the same, whether the mistake is of fact or law, with the result that a person is no less unjustly enriched where he receives money as a result of a mistake of law than where he receives it under a mistake of fact.[249]

An attempt was made to argue otherwise in the first decision after *Kleinwort*   **9–100**
Benson to consider the scope of restitution-grounding mistakes of law. In *Nurdin & Peacock Plc v D.B. Ramsden & Co Ltd*,[250] a commercial tenant had sought restitution of overpaid rent. Some of these overpayments were made believing that they were probably *not* due, but also in the belief that they could be recovered back if subsequent proceedings confirmed that they were not due. Later proceedings confirmed that the rent had indeed been overpaid, but the landlord nevertheless resisted the tenant's claim, arguing that even if the tenant *had* made a mistake of law, it was not as to its liability to *pay* the rent, but as to its right to recover the payment back; and that only a liability mistake would do.[251] Neuberger J. disagreed, concluding that the causative mistake test propounded by Robert Goff J. in *Barclays Bank v Simms*[252] should apply equally to cases where money was paid under a mistake of law.[253] As he saw it,

"[f]or the issue of recoverability to turn up on a nice analysis as to the precise nature of the mistake [would] be almost as undesirable as it is for recoverability to turn upon whether the mistake made by the payer was one of fact or law".[254]

There was no principled reason for insisting on a narrower test for mistakes of law[255]; and it would be contrary to authority to do so, given Lord Goff's reasoning in *Kleinwort Benson* that the same principles applied to mistakes of law as to mistakes of fact.[256] Subsequent decisions confirm Neuberger J.'s conclusions: i.e. a test of causative mistake now applies, without further limitation, irrespective of whether the mistake is fact *or* law.[257]

---

[249] See para.9–71.
[250] *Nurdin & Peacock Plc v D.B. Ramsden & Co Ltd* [1999] 1 W.L.R. 1249.
[251] *Nurdin & Peacock* [1999] 1 W.L.R. 1249 at 1270–1271.
[252] *Barclays Bank v Simms* [1980] Q.B. 677 at 691.
[253] *Nurdin & Peacock* [1999] 1 W.L.R. 1249 at 1273. The particular mistake pleaded—a mistake of law as to the recoverability of the overpayments—presented a logical condundrum: if the law afforded relief for this mistake, there would be no mistake; but if relief was denied on that basis, there would be a mistake, demanding of relief; but if relief were awarded, there would be no mistake, and so on, *ad infinitum*. Neuberger J. thought that this circle could and should be broken.
[254] *Nurdin & Peacock* [1999] 1 W.L.R. 1249 at 1272.
[255] *Nurdin & Peacock* [1999] 1 W.L.R. 1249 at 1273.
[256] *Nurdin & Peacock* [1999] 1 W.L.R. 1249 at 1273.
[257] See especially *Deutsche Morgan Grenfell* [2006] UKHL 49; [2007] 1 A.C. 558 at [59]–[60] per Lord Hoffmann, at [143] per Lord Walker (cf. at [84]–[87] per Lord Scott) (whose only reservations appear to relate to gifts); *Marine Trade* [2009] EWHC 2656 (Comm); [2010] 1 Lloyd's Rep. 631 at [65], [78]–[81]; *F.I.I.* [2008] EWHC 2893 (Ch); [2009] S.T.C. 254 at [264]; [2010] EWCA Civ 103; [2010] S.T.C. 1251 at [182]; *Thin Cap Group Litigation* [2009] EWHC 2908 (Ch); [2010] S.T.C. 301 at [234]. Where, after *Kleinwort Benson* [1999] 2 AC 349, the courts are prepared to "deem" the claimant retrospectively to have been mistaken, where the applicable law is subsequently declared to be otherwise than he believed it to be, then it seems the requirement that the claimant's "mistake" have been "causative" may not be satisfied without a further layer of "deeming": see the note by R. Chambers (2006) 6 O.U.C.L.J. 227, pp.230 and following.

(ii) *Equity's Jurisdiction to Set Aside Voluntary Transactions: A Narrower Approach*

9–101 The simple picture which emerges from recent common law authorities concerning personal claims to recover the value of benefits conferred under a mistake may need some modification in light of recent decisions examining the ambit of the long-standing equitable jurisdiction to set aside voluntary transactions on the ground of mistake.

9–102 For some time, the most influential formulation of the ambit of equity's jurisdiction was to be found in Millett J.'s 1990 judgment in *Gibbon v Mitchell*.[258] After a review of a number of earlier authorities, Millett J. concluded that equity could set aside a voluntary transaction for a spontaneous mistake of fact or law, as long as the mistake was as to "the effect of the transaction itself and not merely as to its consequences, or the advantages to be obtained from it."[259] Subsequent decisions, all at first instance, assumed that this represented the law—whilst sometimes voicing reservations about the difficulty of drawing the distinction between effects and consequences[260]—until Lloyd L.J.'s 2005 decision in *Sieff v Fox*,[261] where counsel's more extensive researches brought to light the long-forgotten decision in *Ogilvie v Littleboy*,[262] in which Lindley L.J. had expressed the ambit of equity's jurisdiction in more general terms. Responding to the bold suggestion that in equity, the onus lay on the *donee* to prove that the donor knew what he was doing, and had made no mistake as to the effect of the transaction he was entering, Lindley L.J. said that in the absence of what he described as "circumstances of suspicion"[263]:

> "[A] donor can only obtain back property which he has given away by showing that he was under some mistake of so serious a character as to render it unjust on the part of the donee to retain the property given to him."

9–103 In *Sieff v Fox*[264] itself, it was not necessary for Lloyd L.J. to resolve the relationship between the *Gibbon* approach and the decision in *Ogilvie v Littleboy*. However, in the wake of that case, three competing lines of first instance authority began to emerge. In one line of cases, the *Gibbon v Mitchell* approach was assumed to remain authoritative, and to offer an exhaustive description of the types of mistake that would justify relief.[265] In a second line of cases, *Ogilvie v Littleboy* was used as a basis for rejecting the *Gibbon v Mitchell* approach in

---

[258] *Gibbon v Mitchell* [1990] 1 W.L.R. 1304.

[259] *Gibbon v Mitchell* [1990] 1 W.L.R. 1304 at 1309.

[260] See especially *Dent v Dent* [1996] 1 W.L.R. 683 at 693; *A.M.P. (UK) plc v Barker* [2001] O.P.L.R. 197 at [70]; *Anker-Peterson v Christiansen* [2002] W.T.L.R. 313; *Gallaher Ltd v Gallaher Pensions Ltd* [2005] EWHC 42 (Ch); [2005] O.P.L.R. 57; *Wolff v Wolff* [2004] EWHC 2110 (Ch); [2004] S.T.C. 1633; *Sieff v Fox* [2005] EWHC 1312 (Ch); [2005] 1 W.L.R. 3811. Cf. *Re D.S.L. Remuneration Trust* [2009] W.T.L.R. 373 (English law); *J.P. v Atlas Trading Co (Jersey) Ltd* [2009] W.T.L.R. 873 (Jersey law); *G.L. Nautilus Trustees Ltd* [2010] W.T.L.R. 497 (English law).

[261] *Sieff v Fox* [2005] EWHC 1312 (Ch); [2005] 1 W.L.R. 3811.

[262] *Ogilvie v Littleboy* (1897) 13 T.L.R. 399 (CA), approved on appeal sub nom *Ogilvie v Allen* (1899) 15 T.L.R. 294 (HL).

[263] *Ogilvie v Littleboy* (1897) 13 T.L.R. 399 (CA) at 400. As described, these were "fraud", "undue influence", a "fiduciary relation between donor and donee", and a "mistake induced by those who derive any benefit by it": at 400.

[264] *Sieff v Fox* [2005] EWHC 1312 (Ch); [2005] 1 W.L.R. 3811.

[265] *Pitt v Holt* [2010] EWHC 45 (Ch); [2010] 1 W.L.R. 11.

favour of a wider test of "serious causative mistake"—necessitating an inquiry into whether the mistake was both causative *and* "serious" in the *Ogilvie v Littleboy* sense, but without requiring that the mistake must otherwise be of some particular type. This was Lewison J.'s view in *Re Griffiths*[266]; but the same approach is also adopted by the Jersey courts.[267] A third line of cases went even further, favouring a simple "causative mistake" test which parallels the common law's prevailing approach. This bold step was first taken in the Isle of Man decision of *Clarkson v Barclays Private Bank & Trust (Isle of Man) Ltd*,[268] where the court held that the authorities supported a "serious mistake" test, but drawing an explicit analogy to the common law authorities, the court then interpreted this to mean that the mistake had to be merely "causative", in the "but for" sense: "the best measure as to whether the mistake was so serious as to render it unjust for the volunteer donee to retain the moneys is if the payment would not have been made 'but for' the mistake".[269] A similar view was taken in *Fender v National Westminster Bank*,[270] where the judge held that relief could be granted in accordance with *Gibbon v Mitchell* if necessary, but was nevertheless inclined to accept counsel's argument, that in future, equity should follow the common law's more liberal approach, of asking simply whether there was a causative mistake of fact or law.[271]

The leading decision on equity's jurisdiction to set aside voluntary transactions   **9–104** is now the decision of the Court of Appeal in *Pitt v Holt*.[272] After a full review of case law stretching back to *Ogilvie v Littleboy*, the Court of Appeal emphatically rejected a causative mistake test, in favour of a stricter, hybrid approach.[273] This approach has two distinguishing features. First, and consistently with Millett J.'s approach in *Gibbon v Mitchell*,[274] the mistake must be of one of two specified types. Without purporting to offer any hard-and-fast rule (admitting of no

---

[266] *Re Griffiths* [2008] EWHC 118 (Ch); [2009] Ch. 162 at [24]–[25]; *Bhatt v Bhatt* [2009] EWHC 734 (Ch); [2009] S.T.C. 1540 at [27]–[28], where Lewison J.'s approach in *Re Griffiths* was endorsed. Cf. *Fender* [2008] EWHC 2242 (Ch); [2008] 3 E.G.L.R. 80 at [25], where Lewison J. was taken to adopt a "causative mistake" test.

[267] *Re A Trust* [2009] JRC 447; [2011] W.T.L.R. 745; *Re First Conferences* [2010] JRC 055A; *Re Lochmore Trust* [2010] JRC 068; *Re S Trust* [2011] JRC 117. See too earlier decisions in which the conflict was noted, but not reserved, as the *Gibbon v Mitchell* test was met: *Re D.S.L. Remuneration Trust* [2009] W.T.L.R. 373 (English law); *J.P. v Atlas Trading* [2009] W.T.L.R. 873; *G.L. Nautilus Trustee* [2010] W.T.L.R. 497 (English law). See too *Re Bestam Trust* [2009] W.T.L.R. 1489 (adopting the *Ogilvie v Littleboy* formulation following *Re Griffiths*), and *Clarkson* [2007] W.T.L.R. 1703.

[268] *Clarkson v Barclays Private Bank & Trust (Isle of Man) Ltd* [2007] W.T.L.R. 1703. Cf. too *Re Bestam Trust* [2009] W.T.L.R. 1489.

[269] *Clarkson* [2007] W.T.L.R. 1703 at [41], criticised in *Pitt v Holt* [2011] EWCA Civ 197; [2011] 3 W.L.R. 19 at [207]–[209].

[270] *Fender v National Westminister Bank* [2008] EWHC 2242 (Ch); [2008] 3 E.G.L.R. 80.

[271] *Fender* [2008] EWHC 2242 (Ch); [2008] 3 E.G.L.R. 80 at [21], [22], [25], arguing that: (1) equity historically had a *wider* jurisdiction to relieve from the consequences of a mistake, and it would be "very strange" if it would now be more circumscribed than the common law's approach; (2) the effects/consequences distinction had been the subject of much adverse comment; (3) Lewison J. in *Re Griffiths* [2008] EWHC 118 (Ch); [2009] Ch. 162 had adopted a causative mistake test.

[272] *Pitt v Holt* [2011] EWCA Civ 197; [2011] 3 W.L.R. 19, upholding the first instance decision ([2010] EWHC 45 (Ch); [2010] 1 W.L.R. 1199) on different grounds. At the time of writing an appeal to the Supreme Court is pending.

[273] *Pitt v Holt* [2011] EWCA Civ 197; [2011] 3 W.L.R. 19 at [203] and following, and especially at [210].

[274] *Gibbon v Mitchell* [1990] 1 W.L.R. 1304.

exceptions) Lloyd L.J. held that in the absence of some "additional vitiating factor", such as misrepresentation or concealment, the mistake would have to be as to "the legal effect of the disposition" rather than its consequences,[275] or as to "an existing fact which is basic to the transaction".[276] It is not enough that the transaction gives rise to unforeseen fiscal liabilities: this is a "consequence", not an "effect", and is not sufficient to bring the equitable jurisdiction into play. Secondly, the mistake must be a sufficiently serious mistake, in the sense identified in *Ogilvie v Littleboy*,[277] and approved by the House of Lords[278]: i.e. the mistake had to be of "so serious a nature as to render it unjust on the part of the donee to retain the property given to him".[279] Lloyd L.J. thought that this set a "very high test as to the gravity of the mistake", resting upon the need to protect the recipient's possession and enjoyment from too ready an ability of the donor to recall his gift.[280]

9–105 The decision on the facts in *Pitt v Holt* shows the strictness of this approach. Acting as the court-appointed receiver for her incapacitated husband, Mrs Pitt had executed a settlement of a lump sum and annuity to which her husband was entitled in settlement of a personal injuries claim. She subsequently sought to have this settlement set aside when it turned out to have unanticipated, immediate inheritance tax consequences. Lloyd L.J. found that Mrs Pitt had entered the transaction under a mistaken belief that the transaction had no adverse tax effects, even though no-one had in fact turned their mind specifically to IHT[281]; and that the mistake satisfied the *Ogilvie v Littleboy* test of gravity, given that the unanticipated tax liabilities would significantly deplete the assets available to meet Mr Pitt's needs for the rest of his life.[282] The claim to have the transaction set aside nevertheless failed because the mistake was as to the consequences of the transaction and *not* as to its legal effect.[283] The mistake was as to the tax treatment of the transaction, and for this purpose, this was a "consequence" and not an "effect".[284]

9–106 It is very regrettable that the Court of Appeal in *Pitt v Holt* chose to maintain the distinction between mistakes as to the "effects" of a transaction, and mistakes as to its "consequences". The rationale of this distinction is unclear, and it is difficult to apply in practice. If, as the Court of Appeal thought, a more restrictive

---

[275] *Pitt v Holt* [2011] EWCA Civ 197; [2011] 3 W.L.R. 19 at [203]–[205], [210]; explaining in these terms the decisions in *Gibbon v Mitchell* [1990] 1 W.L.R. 1304; *Ellis v Ellis* (1909) 26 T.L.R. 166; *Re Walton's Settlement* [1922] 2 Ch. 509; *Anker-Peterson v Christensen* [2002] W.T.L.R. 313; *Meadows v Meadows* (1863) 16 Beav. 401; 51 E.R. 833; *Walker v Armstrong* (1858) 8 De G. M. & G. 531; 44 E.R. 495; *Wolff v Wolff* [2004] EWHC 2110 (Ch); [2004] S.T.C. 1633; disapproving of *Phillipson v Kerry* (1863) 32 Beav. 628; 55 E.R. 247.
[276] *Pitt v Holt* [2011] EWCA Civ 197; [2011] 3 W.L.R. 19 at [203], [206], [210]; explaining in these terms the decisions in *Lady Hood v Mackinnon* [1909] 1 Ch. 476; *Re Griffiths* [2008] EWHC 118 (Ch); [2009] Ch. 162; *University of Canterbury v Att Gen* [1995] 1 N.Z.L.R. 78.
[277] *Ogilvie v Littleboy* (1897) 13 T.L.R. 399 (CA) at 400.
[278] *Sub nom Ogilvie v Allen* (1899) 15 T.L.R. 294 (HL).
[279] *Pitt v Holt* [2011] EWCA Civ 197; [2011] 3 W.L.R. 19 at [203], [210].
[280] *Pitt v Holt* [2011] EWCA Civ 197; [2011] 3 W.L.R. 19 at [203].
[281] *Pitt v Holt* [2011] EWCA Civ 197; [2011] 3 W.L.R. 19 at [216], [219].
[282] *Pitt v Holt* [2011] EWCA Civ 197; [2011] 3 W.L.R. 19 at [214]–[215], [219].
[283] *Pitt v Holt* [2011] EWCA Civ 197; [2011] 3 W.L.R. 19 at [217], [219]. It is not explained why it could not be said that the mistaken assumption about tax treatment was not a mistaken assumption as to a fact "basic" to the transaction.
[284] *Pitt v Holt* [2011] EWCA Civ 197; [2011] 3 W.L.R. 19 at [218], [219].

approach must be maintained to identifying qualifying mistakes in the context of the equitable jurisdiction to set aside voluntary transactions, then it would have been better if the court had followed the lead of recent Jersey courts,[285] and of Lewison J. in *Re Griffiths*.[286] This involves saying that to justify the setting aside of a voluntary transaction, there must be a mistake which is both causative *and* "serious" in the *Ogilivie v Littleboy* sense, but that otherwise the type or kind of mistake is not important.

(iii) *Future Developments Regarding the Ambit of Qualifying Mistakes*

For the time being, *Pitt v Holt* must be regarded as the final word on the ambit **9–107** of equity's jurisdiction to set aside voluntary transactions.[287] Unfortunately, its wider implications remain unclear. It confirms that there remains a substantial contrast between this jurisdiction and the common law's prevailing approach to restitution for spontaneous mistakes, without reconciling the two.[288] Whereas the common law has unequivocally moved towards the position that a personal claim in unjust enrichment is available for any causative mistake of fact or law, and has eschewed both the need for the mistake to be "fundamental" or "serious" in any stricter sense, and attempts to confine relief to particular types of mistake,[289] *Pitt v Holt* confirms a counter-trend in relation to the equitable jurisdiction. A spontaneous causative mistake of fact or law is not by itself sufficient for relief: it must also be a mistake which is sufficiently serious, and be either a mistake as to the legal effect of the transaction or as to an assumption which is basic to it. The question arises whether, and if so, on what basis, these competing approaches can in future reconciled. There are several possible directions the law might take.

First, future courts might generalise the liberal test of causative mistake, **9–108** bringing the ambit of equity's jurisdiction to set aside voluntary transactions into line with the common law's liberal approach to personal claims in unjust enrichment. Some pre-*Pitt v Holt* decisions certainly supported this step.[290] However, in light of the Court of Appeal's emphatic insistence in *Pitt v Holt* on a narrower test, it seems that this development could now only be brought about by the Supreme Court.

Secondly, future courts might generalise a narrower test of serious or funda- **9–109** mental mistake. In other words, *Pitt v Holt* might be taken to signal the start of a more general retreat away from recent liberalisations of the ambit of restitution-grounding mistakes, culminating in the wholesale rejection of the proposition that a spontaneous causative mistake is enough, and the introduction of a general requirement that a spontaneous mistake must be "serious" or "fundamental". This development would involve a dramatic departure from the principled position reflected in a long line of recent authorities that a causative mistake is

---

[285] See especially *Re S Trust* [2011] JRC 117, where the decision in *Pitt v Holt* is subjected to sustained and persuasive criticism; see earlier, *Re A Trust* [2009] JRC 447; [2011] W.T.L.R. 745; *Re First Conferences* [2010] JRC 055A; *Re Lochmore Trust* [2010] JRC 068.
[286] *Re Griffiths* [2008] EWHC 118 (Ch); [2009] Ch. 162 at [24]–[25].
[287] At the time of writing an appeal to the Supreme Court is pending.
[288] Lloyd L.J. saw that there were differences, but expressly declined to discuss the ambit of common law unjust enrichment claims: *Pitt v Holt* [2011] EWCA Civ 197; [2011] 3 W.L.R. 19 at [166].
[289] See para.9–95 and following.
[290] *Clarkson* [2007] W.T.L.R. 1703; *Fender* [2008] EWHC 2242 (Ch); [2008] 3 E.G.L.R. 80.

generally a sufficient impairment to render a defendant's enrichment prima facie unjust, and that the work of containing liability is better done via bars or defences. On that ground alone, it seems inconceivable that the law will develop in this way. If the restrictive approach reflected in *Pitt* is to survive, it must be on some more limited basis.

9-110   Thirdly, and more plausibly, future courts might insist that *gift transactions as a class* require special treatment, such that a spontaneous causative mistake is insufficient without more to justify restitution of the subject matter of a gift, whether in specie or via a personal claim. To ground any form of restitutionary remedy in respect of a gift, a spontaneous mistake would need to be in some sense "serious" or "fundamental". This would involve much less disruption to prevailing assumptions. A key premise of the Court of Appeal's decision in *Pitt* is that gifts should be less easily reversed. There are also hints of a similar view in some common law decisions. Historically, the prevailing view that only liability mistakes of fact were restitution-grounding effectively ruled out *in limine* a personal claim to restitution for a mistaken gift, leaving donors to look to equity's jurisdiction.[291] With the progressive liberalisation of the common law's approach, it has become possible to contemplate these claims being made, in accordance with the prevailing causative mistake test. No English case yet finally decides the point either way.[292] One earlier case sometimes cited is *Morgan v Ashcroft*,[293] where Scott L.J. was prepared obiter to contemplate restitution for mistaken gifts, provided that the mistake was as to some aspect "fundamental" to the transaction.[294] However, these dicta are inconclusive, because they pre-date the modern liberalisation of the law: Scott L.J. was in one sense offering an expansive view of the law as then understood, rather than suggesting that restitution for mistake should be more narrowly confined in relation to gift transactions.[295] Less easy to dismiss are recent dicta of Lord Scott in *Deutsche Morgan Grenfell*,[296] where his Lordship doubted that a causative mistake of fact or law should not be sufficient, without more, to enable the gift to be set aside.[297] The argument of principle for this position is not clear. Were the courts to ever accept that gifts as a category require special treatment, one way of articulating the point would be to say that receipt as a gift prima facie provides a "justifying ground" for the donee's enrichment (just as a contract does); that to obtain restitution, it is necessary to show that the gift is "invalid"; and that the category of mistakes that render a gift "invalid" is more narrowly conceived (just as the category of mistakes that invalidate a contract is more

---

[291] See paras 9–95—9–96.
[292] Cf. *David Securities* (1992) 175 C.L.R. 353 at 392–393 (dicta, inconclusively envisaging restitution for gifts on the basis of causative mistake); *University of Canterbury v Att Gen* [1995] 1 N.Z.L.R. 78 at 85–86 (decision inconclusive as between a test of causative mistake, and a higher threshold of seriousness); *Re Magarey* [2007] SASC 9; (2006) S.A.S.R. 337 at [170] (dicta, envisaging restitution for gifts, but expressing the availability in narrower terms than causative mistake); cf. *Clarkson* [2007] W.T.L.R. 1703 (decision applying the common law causative mistake test).
[293] *Morgan v Ashcroft* [1938] 1 K.B. 49 (CA).
[294] *Morgan v Ashcroft* [1938] 1 K.B. 49 (CA) at 74 per Scott L.J. Cf. at 66, per Sir Wilfred Greene M.R.
[295] Cf. *Clarkson* [2007] W.T.L.R. 1703 at [28]–[29], rejecting the argument based on *Morgan v Ashcroft* [1938] 1 K.B. 49 (CA), that a fundamental mistake was needed.
[296] *Deutsche Morgan Grenfell* [2006] UKHL 49; [2007] 1 A.C. 558.
[297] *Deutsche Morgan Grenfell* [2006] UKHL 49; [2007] 1 A.C. 558 at [87].

narrowly conceived).[298] However, this is a rather civilian way of putting the point, which may not be consistent with English law.

Fourthly, more narrowly, the *Pitt v Holt* approach might in future be taken to **9–111** embody a peculiarly restrictive approach to the availability of *proprietary relief* for spontaneous mistakes. The equitable jurisdiction to set aside voluntary transactions paradigmatically brings proprietary consequences: the claimant seeks to recover the subject matter of the voluntary settlement or outright gift *in specie*.[299] To this extent, the relief sought differs from that sought in the common law decisions, which deal with the availability of a personal claim to restitution of the value received by the defendant. Seen in this way, the restrictive *Pitt v Holt* approach is not necessarily inconsistent with the common law's wider approach: they define the ambit of restitution-grounding mistakes for different purposes. However, this rationalisation in turn raises a different and difficult question: whether the availability of proprietary relief, of whatever nature, to a person who is spontaneously mistaken should generally be conditional on the mistake meeting a higher threshold, along the lines imposed in *Pitt v Holt*.[300]

Finally, even more narrowly, the *Pitt v Holt* approach might in future be taken **9–112** to embody a peculiarly restrictive approach, warranted on pragmatic grounds, to the setting aside of *settlements* (i.e. trusts) for spontaneous mistake. A simple outright transfer seems likely to present fewer restitutionary complications than the setting aside of a complex settlement, where beneficial entitlement may be dispersed, in complex ways, between multiple beneficiaries. It would not be nonsense for the courts to set higher hurdles in the way of the reversal of the latter—insisting that the setting aside of a settlement depends on stricter criteria, along the lines identified in *Pitt v Holt*. On this view, a simple outright gift of money might still generate a personal claim to restitution based on a spontaneous causative mistake; but a settlement could not be set aside without proof of a more serious mistake.

6. FAULT OF THE DEFENDANT

Recovery on the ground of mistake is not fault-based. A claimant who proves a **9–113** qualifying mistake, and whose claim is not barred by the presence of some disqualifying circumstance, has a prima facie claim. It is not necessary for a claimant, in order to have a prima facie claim, to establish fault, of any nature, on the part of the defendant. Nevertheless, for several reasons—not all of which are not unique to mistake cases—fault on the part of the defendant may have an indirect bearing on whether the claimant succeeds.

First, where the claimant's mistake has been induced by a misrepresentation of **9–114** the defendant or his agent, the claimant will face fewer hurdles. In particular, a

---

[298] Cf. Meier and Zimmermann, "Judicial Development of the Law, *Error Juris*, and the Law of Unjust Enrichment"; O'Sullivan, Elliott and Zakrzewski, *The Law of Rescission*, Ch.24 and in particular at paras 29.27–29.30.

[299] See especially *Pitt v Holt* [2011] EWCA Civ 197; [2011] 3 W.L.R. 19 at [166], indicating that the claimant had to proceed via the equitable jurisdiction because it was seeking "proprietary relief by setting aside the transaction".

[300] See further, on proprietary relief, Chs 37–40.

less demanding test of causation may apply in cases of induced mistakes,[301] and there is no question of the courts insisting that the mistake be "fundamental" or "serious".[302]

9-115 Secondly, fault may be indirectly relevant because of its bearing on whether the claimant can challenge a contract that prima facie governs the defendant's receipt of the benefit. So, in particular, a contract induced by a misrepresentation by the defendant or his agent, or of which the defendant had notice, is readily avoided, whether fraudulent or non-fraudulent. In contrast, a contract is only exceptionally vitiated by an uninduced mistake, whether common or unilateral.[303]

9-116 Thirdly, fault will be indirectly relevant to the availability of one or more defences—with proof of fault, or of its absence, bearing on the availability of, inter alia, the pleas of change of position,[304] payment over by an agent,[305] and bona fide purchase.[306]

9-117 Finally, on one view of the law, fault may be relevant to the form of the restitutionary remedy, and in particular, whether a proprietary restitutionary remedy is available—commonly in the form of a trust imposed by the law. In *Westdeutsche Landesbank Girozentrale v Islington LBC*,[307] Lord Browne-Wilkinson insisted that the law would not automatically render the spontaneously mistaken recipient of money or some other asset an immediate trustee for the person from whom the money or other asset came; that a trust will not arise until the recipient's conscience is affected; but that a constructive trust might be imposed at least from the time when the recipient became *aware* of the mistake.[308] This is a controversial analysis, which is open to doubt. It is examined in Ch.37.

7. DISQUALIFYING CIRCUMSTANCES

9-118 Are there any circumstances in which a claimant, who can establish that he made a qualifying mistake, and that the mistake caused him to confer a benefit on the defendant, will nevertheless be denied restitution, otherwise than because of the

---

[301] See para.9–51.
[302] See paras 9–70, 9–102 and 9–104.
[303] See paras 9–68—9–69.
[304] See Ch.27.
[305] See Ch.28.
[306] See Ch.29.
[307] *Westdeutsche Landesbank Girozentrale v Islington LBC* [1996] A.C. 669.
[308] *Westdeutsche* [1996] A.C. 669 at 705–706, 707–709, 714–715, explaining *Chase Manhattan Bank NA v Israel-British Bank (London) Ltd* [1981] Ch. 105; followed in, inter alia, *Papamichael* [2003] EWHC 164 (Comm); [2003] 1 Lloyd's Rep. 341 at [221]–[231]; *Getronics Holdings EMEA BV v Logistic & Transport Consulting Co* Unreported April 30, 2004; *Commerzbank AG v I.M.B. Morgan Plc* [2004] EWHC 2771 (Ch); [2005] 2 All E.R. (Comm.) 56 at [36]; *Re Farepak Food* [2006] EWHC 3272 (Ch); [2008] B.C.C. 22 at [37] and following; *Jones v Churcher* [2009] EWHC 722 (QB); [2009] 2 Lloyd's Rep. 94 at [98]–[99]; *Deutsche Bank v Vik* [2010] EWHC 551 (Comm) at [4]; *Fitzalan-Howard v Hibbert* [2009] EWHC 2855 (QB); [2010] P.N.L.R. 11 at [49]; *Bank of Ireland v Pexxnet Ltd* [2010] EWHC 1872 (Comm) at [55]–[57].

availability of a general defence to a claim in unjust enrichment or some justifying ground? In particular, to what extent is the claimant's "fault" significant for the availability of relief?

It is a long-standing assumption within the law of unjust enrichment that a **9–119** claimant will not be denied restitution for mistake merely because he was "negligent".[309] On this basis, as long as that the claimant can show that he acted because of a mistaken belief as to some past or existing state of affairs, he will not be denied relief because that belief was the consequence of (for example) his having carelessly forgotten or overlooked the true facts,[310] or his having carelessly made no inquiry or only an inadequate inquiry, despite adequate means of knowledge being available.[311]

Crucially, the authorities for this proposition all assume a claimant who was **9–120** *unconscious* of the risk of error: a claimant who acted on the basis of an incorrect belief, without any conscious appreciation that their belief might be wrong, or that there might be material circumstances of which they were ignorant (whether because they never knew of the circumstances, had forgotten them, or simply failed to call them to mind).[312] They do not go so far as to establish that a person who has doubts about the true circumstances, or who is consciously ignorant of the true circumstances, can invariably recover on the ground of mistake. Often he cannot do so, because his doubts are so extensive that he cannot claim to have been mistaken[313]; because he cannot claim to have been caused to act by any mistaken belief[314]; and/or because, in acting as he did, he unreasonably responded to his state of doubt and so unreasonably ran the risk of error.[315]

It is sometimes said, more generally, that a claimant should also be denied **9–121** relief for mistake on the ground of his having "assumed the risk" of error.[316] However, as we explain elsewhere,[317] we doubt that this should be regarded as an independent bar to recovery. The same is true, a fortiori, of statements, more common in the past, that a claimant will be denied relief where he has conferred

---

[309] *Kelly v Solari* (1841) 9 M. & W. 54; 152 E.R. 24; *Imperial Bank of Canada v Bank of Hamilton* [1903] A.C. 49 (PC) at 56; *R.E. Jones v Waring* [1926] A.C. 670 at 688–689; *Anglo-Scottish Sugar* [1937] 2 K.B. 607; *Saronic Shipping* [1979] 1 Lloyd's Rep. 341 at 363; [1980] 2 Lloyd's Rep 26 (CA); *Barclays Bank v Simms* [1980] Q.B. 677 at 686–687; *Banque Financière* [1999] 1 A.C. 221 at 227, 235, 242–243; *Kleinwort Benson* [1999] 2 A.C. 349 at 399; *Scottish Equitable* [2000] 3 All E.R. 793 at 799–800 per Harrison J.; [2001] EWCA Civ 369; [2001] 3 All E.R. 818; *Dextra Bank* [2001] UKPC 50; [2002] 1 All E.R. (Comm.) 193 at [45]. Cf. Wu, "The Role of Negligence and Non-Financial Detriment in the Law of Unjust Enrichment". Cf. too *Anfield (UK) Ltd v Bank of Scotland Plc* [2010] EWHC 2374 (Ch); [2011] 1 All E.R. 708 at [29] and following (which may be better analysed as involving a claim grounded on failure of basis).
[310] See e.g. *Kelly v Solari* (1841) 9 M. & W. 54; 152 E.R. 24; *Barclays Bank v Simms* [1980] Q.B. 677 at 686–687.
[311] See e.g. *Scottish Equitable* [2000] 3 All ER 793 at 799–800 per Harrison J; [2001] EWCA Civ 368; [2001] 3 All ER 818 at [19]–[25].
[312] Cf. e.g. *Kelly v Solari* (1841) 9 M. & W. 54; 152 E.R. 24; *Lady Hood v Mackinnon* [1909] 1 Ch. 476.
[313] See para.9–17 and following.
[314] See para.9–22.
[315] See para.9–24.
[316] See para.9–27.
[317] See para.9–28.

a benefit "voluntarily" on another.[318] This language seems even more dangerously opaque and should be forgotten. In this context, it merely re-states, redundantly and at the risk of confusion, the conclusion that the claimant was not caused to act by any restitution-grounding mistake (or any other restitution-triggering ground), or sometimes, that his claim should fail on some other established ground.

---

[318] This language rarely features in modern English cases (though *cf. Westdeutsche* [1994] 4 All ER 890 at 933–934; *Haugesund* [2009] EWHC 2227 (Comm); [2010] Lloyd's Rep. P.N. 21 at [143] and following). It remains more prominent in Australian cases: see esp. *David Securities* (1992) 175 C.L.R. 353 (majority), cf. per Brennan J.; *Hookway* [2005] VSCA 310; (2005) 13 V.R. 444 at [22] and following (where the language of "voluntary payment" was examined at length); *Queensland Alumina* [2007] QCA 387 at [70]–[72]; *Re Magarey Farlam (No.3)* [2007] SASC 9; (2006) 96 S.A.S.R. 337 at [175]; *Lahoud v Lahoud* [2010] NSWSC 1297 at [179].

CHAPTER 10

DURESS

1. INTRODUCTION

If a claimant confers a benefit on a defendant under duress then a claim will lie **10–01** in unjust enrichment to recover it, whether the benefit is money, services, or goods. Contracts are voidable for duress at the instance of the coerced party,[1] but until the contract has been avoided, any benefits transferred thereto are transferred under a binding contract and cannot be recovered in unjust enrichment.[2] In exceptional circumstances, duress can render a document void if it is so extreme that the coerced party can establish that "it is not his" document, *non est factum*.[3]

This chapter looks in turn at the established categories of duress. Part 2 **10–02** discusses actual or threatened violence to the person, Part 3 the improper application of legal process, Part 4 duress of goods, Part 5 the refusal by those in public or quasi-public position to fulfil their duty and Part 6 economic duress, i.e. threats to break a contract or to exert some other economic pressure on the claimant. However, duress is not restricted to these categories.[4] Any pressure which the law "does not regard as legitimate" amounts to duress[5]; for the common law:

---

[1] *Pao On v Lau Yiu Long* [1980] A.C. 614 at 634 and 636 per Lord Scarman; *Universe Tankships Inc of Monrovia v I.T.W.F. (The Universe Sentinel)* [1983] 1 A.C. 366 at 383 per Lord Diplock, and at 400 per Lord Scarman; *Dimskal Shipping Co SA v I.T.W.F. (The Evia Luck)* [1992] 2 A.C. 152 at 168 per Lord Goff. The contract may be affirmed after the duress has been removed: *North Ocean Shipping Co Ltd v Hyundai Construction Co Ltd (The Atlantic Baron)* [1979] Q.B. 705. It is an open question how far the principles governing fraudulent misrepresentation apply where the contract is sought to be rescinded for duress. In *Barton v Armstrong* [1976] A.C. 104, where there was duress to the person, the Privy Council suggested that their analogy should determine whether a transaction, which has been induced by duress, can be rescinded (including the rule in *Car and Universal Finance Co v Caldwell* [1965] Q.B. 525); in *Halpern v Halpern (No.2)* [2007] EWCA 291; [2008] Q.B. 195 at [55]–[75], Carnwath L.J. denied that there is any rule excluding the requirement that a claimant must make counter-restitution as a condition for rescission on the ground of duress.

[2] *The Evia Luck* [1992] 2 A.C. 152 at 165 per Lord Goff; *Enimont Overseas AG v Jugotanker Zadar (The Olib)* [1991] 2 Lloyd's Rep. 108 at 118 per Webster J.; *I.F.R. Ltd v Federal Trade SpA* Unreported QBD (Comm. Ct), September 19, 2001 per Colman J., quoted in the text to fn.19. These authorities lay to the rest the argument advanced in D. Lanham, "Duress and Void Contracts" (1966) 29 M.L.R. 615, that duress always renders a contract void rather than voidable. For discussion of contract as a justifying ground, see Ch.3.

[3] For discussion, see D. Friedmann, "The Objective Principle and Mistake and Involuntariness in Contract and Restitution" (2003) 119 L.Q.R. 68, pp.81–82.

[4] e.g. *Smith v Cuff* (1817) 6 M. & S. 160; *Kendall v Wood* (1871) L.R. 6 Ex. 243; see also *Smith v Bromley* (1760) 2 Doug. 696n; *Borrelli v Ting* [2010] UKPC 21; [2010] Bus. L.R. 1718.

[5] *Barton v Armstrong* [1976] A.C. 104 at 121 per Lord Wilberforce and Lord Simon, dissenting. Their Lordships' dissent was on the application of these principles to the facts of the case; cf. Lord Cross's discussion at 118.

"under the influence of equity, has developed from the old common law conception of duress—threat to life and limb—and it has arrived at the modern generalisation expressed by Holmes J.—'subjected to an improper motive for action'."[6]

10–03   Illegitimate pressure includes, but is not limited to, any illegal act, such as a criminal act; for example, harassing a debtor.[7] It also embraces a tortious act.[8] In some circumstances, it may be duress to refuse to pay a debt or to carry out a contractual obligation owed to the claimant. Indeed, it may be wrongful to threaten to do what one is entitled to do. For example, it may be duress[9] to threaten to "do an act, which is not unlawful, but which is calculated seriously to injure another".[10] In many cases such a threat will be made to obtain a benefit to which the person who made the threat is not entitled. It may also amount in law to duress if a benefit to which a person is entitled has been obtained by an improper threat (for example, if a creditor gains payment of a debt by threatening to tell the debtor's wife of the debtor's adulterous relationship).[11] It is possible that a threat may amount to duress if the court concludes that a person's threat to exercise power over another was unconscionable or immoral.[12] But it is not always easy to tell when a threat will be characterised as one which a person is

---

[6] *Barton v Armstrong* [1976] A.C. 104 at 121 per Lord Wilberforce and Lord Simon, dissenting. The quotation from Holmes J., which was also cited by the majority (see Lord Cross at 118), is from *Fairbanks v Snow*, 13 N.E. 568 at 598 (1887). Holmes J. was then a Justice of the Supreme Judicial Court of Massachusetts.

[7] It is a criminal offence if a person, with the object of coercing another "to pay money claimed from the other as a debt due under a contract, . . . harasses the other with demands for payment, which, in respect of their frequency or the manner or occasion of making any such demand, or of any threat of publicity by which any demand is accompanied, are calculated to subject him or members of his family or household to alarm, distress or humiliation": Administration of Justice Act 1970 s.40(1), interpreted in *Norweb Plc v Dixon* [1995] 1 W.L.R. 636. The courts might hold that such conduct, though criminal, is *not* illegitimate pressure sufficient to ground a restitutionary claim. Cf. *Chapman v Honig* [1963] 2 Q.B. 502 (no action for damages lies for contempt of court).

[8] It has been said that such examples as fall outside the established categories can be classified as waiver of tort: see P.H. Winfield, *The Law of Quasi-Contracts* (London: Sweet & Maxwell, 1952), pp.97–98. But the governing precedent, *Morgan v Palmer* (1824) 2 B. & C. 729; 107 E.R. 554, was not a case of waiver of tort and in many cases no tort had been committed: see e.g. *Steele v Williams* (1853) 8 Ex. 625; 155 E.R. 1502, discussed at para.10–31. Moreover, intimidation is only tortious if it is a threat to do an act which is itself illegal: *Rookes v Barnard* [1964] A.C. 1129. In *Marshall Shipping Co v Board of Trade* [1923] 2 K.B. 243 and *Brocklebank Ltd v R.* [1925] K.B. 52, the Court of Appeal regarded extortion *colore officii* as a tort; but it is hard to see what tort had been committed. Moreover, blackmail, which is a crime, may not be a tort; see para.10–86. Note, too, that economic duress is not a tort per se: see fn.130.

[9] *The Universe Sentinel* [1983] 1 A.C. 366 at 388 and 401 per Lord Scarman (dissenting on a different point).

[10] *Thorne v Motor Trade Association* [1937] A.C. 797 at 822–823, per Lord Wright (speaking of blackmail).

[11] This may be an academic question. The debtor may succeed on his claim in unjust enrichment but the creditor, who made the improper threat, will still have a counter-claim for the debt; cf. *Wilbur v Blanchard*, 126 P. 1069 (1912). The position would formerly have been different if the debt had been a gaming debt, as in *Norreys v Zeffert* [1939] 2 All E.R. 187, but see now the Gambling Act 2005 ss.334 and 335.

[12] Cf. *Lloyds Bank Ltd v Bundy* [1975] 1 Q.B. 326 at 339 per Lord Denning M.R. Contrast *National Westminster Bank v Morgan* [1985] A.C. 686.

not entitled to make,[13] and while many situations of duress involve threats, there is no requirement that a threat must have been made.[14]

Most of the old cases have concerned either duress of goods or duress **10–04** exercised by a person in a public or quasi-public position. But, in more recent times, English courts have been confronted with the analogous claim that the defendant gained a benefit by exerting improper economic pressure on the claimant, and so they have had to draw distinctions between legitimate and illegitimate commercial pressure. As the law now stands, such an enquiry is essential because English courts will not generally set aside a bargain and order restitution of benefits conferred thereunder simply because its terms appear to be unconscionable, although terms which appear to be unconscionable may go some way in persuading a court to conclude that a person has obtained those terms by illegitimate pressure.[15]

It has been said that duress must amount to "a coercion of will so as to vitiate **10–05** consent."[16] But, as Justice Holmes said in *Union Pacific RR v Public Service Commission*[17]:

> "It always is for the interest of a party under duress to choose the lesser of two evils. But the fact that a choice was made according to interest does not exclude duress. It is the characteristic of duress properly so called."

We agree with Professor Palmer's conclusion that:

> "[T]he test that a party's will must be overcome is not useful except as it expresses an indispensable element of causation: in order to obtain relief the coercion must have caused a party to do something he otherwise would not have done."[18]

---

[13] *Thorne* [1937] A.C. 797 at 807 per Lord Atkin: a threat to put the claimant on the "stop list" was proper if it was "for some legitimate purpose other than the mere acquisition of money"; *Norreys* [1939] 2 All E.R. 187 at 189–190 per Atkinson J.: a threat to report a gaming debtor to Tattersalls was one which the creditor was entitled to make, but threats to tell members of a social club or a trade protection association were not legitimate. See too J. Beatson, "Duress, Restitution, and Contractual Negotiation", in J. Beatson, *The Use and Abuse of Unjust Enrichment* (Oxford: Clarendon Press, 1991), 95, pp.129–134; and cf. P. Birks, *An Introduction to the Law of Restitution* (Oxford: Clarendon Press, 1985), pp.177–179.

[14] *Borrelli* [2010] UKPC 21; [2010] Bus. L.R. 1718.

[15] *Bundy* [1975] 1 Q.B. 326 at 339 per Lord Denning M.R. But cf. *Crédit Lyonnais Nederland NV v Burch* [1997] 1 All E.R. 144. Unconscionable bargains are discussed at paras 11–57—11–68.

[16] *Occidental Worldwide Investment Corp v Skibs A/S Avanti (The Siboen and The Sibotre)* [1976] 1 Lloyd's Rep. 293 at 336 per Kerr J. See too *Pao On* [1980] A.C. 614 at 635–636 per Lord Scarman; *Syros Shipping Co SA v Elaghill Trading Co (The Proodos C)* [1981] 3 All E.R. 189 at 192 per Lloyd J.; *The Universe Sentinel* [1983] 1 A.C. 366 at 383 per Lord Diplock, and at 400 per Lord Scarman; *B. & S. Contracts and Design Ltd v Victor Green Publications Ltd* [1984] I.C.R. 419; *Hennessy v Craigmyle & Co Ltd* [1986] I.C.R. 461 at 468 per Donaldson M.R.; *Jones v Morgan* [2001] EWCA Civ 995; [2001] Lloyd's Rep. Bank. 323 at [43] per Chadwick L.J.

[17] *Union Pacific RR v Public Service Commission* 248 U.S. 67 at 70 (1918). See also *The Evia Luck* [1992] 2 A.C. 152 at 166 per Lord Goff; *Crescendo Management Pty Ltd v Westpac Banking Corp* (1988) 19 N.S.W.L.R. 40 at 45–456 per McHugh J.A. See too P.S. Atiyah, "Economic Duress and the Overborne Will" (1982) 98 L.Q.R. 197; Beatson, "Duress, Restitution and Contractual Negotiation" in Beatson, *The Use and Abuse of Unjust Enrichment*, pp.113–117.

[18] G.E. Palmer, *The Law of Restitution* (Boston, Mass: Little Brown & Co 1978), vol.II, p.247. See also K.N. Llewellyn, "What Price Contract? An Essay in Perspective" (1931) 40 Yale L.J. 704, p.728; M. H. Ogilvie, "Commercial Duress, Inequality of Bargaining Power and Threatened Breach of Contract" (1980) 26 McGill L.J. 289.

We also note Colman J.'s statement in *I.F.R. Ltd v Federal Trade SpA*, that[19]:

> "Although ... the authorities do contain references to the coercion of the innocent party's will so as to vitiate his consent, the weight of authority binding in this court is to the effect that economic duress leads to the contract being voidable and not void *ab initio*. If the references to consent being vitiated are to be understood as being to the absence of an intention to contract, they are, in my view, wrong in principle."

This is consistent with Lord Diplock's previous finding in *Universe Tankships Inc of Monrovia v I.T.W.F. (The Universe Sentinel)* that[20]:

> "The rationale [of duress] is that [the claimant's] apparent consent was induced by pressure exercised upon him by [the defendant] which the law does not regard as legitimate, with the consequence that the consent is treated in law as *revocable* unless approbated either expressly or by implication after the illegitimate pressure has ceased to operate on his mind."

2. ACTUAL OR THREATENED VIOLENCE TO THE PERSON

10–06 It has long been settled[21] that actual or threatened violence to the person[22] constitutes duress. Although the violence must generally be directed against the claimant[23] it is also sufficient if it is directed against his wife, child or other near relative.[24] Any deed, contract or transaction entered into under duress of this kind is voidable by the person coerced.[25] It is said that it is enough to demonstrate duress to the person that the threats were only *a* reason, as distinct from *the* predominant reason, for the claimant entering into the transaction. He "is entitled to relief even though he might well have entered into the contract if [the defendant] had uttered no threats to induce him to do so."[26] The onus is then on the person making the threat to demonstrate that the threat "contributed nothing"

---

[19] *I.F.R. Ltd v Federal Trade SpA* Unreported QBD (Comm Ct), September 19, 2001.

[20] *Universe Tankships Inc of Monrovia v I.T.W.F. (The Universe Sentinel)* [1983] 1 A.C. 366 at 384 (emphasis added).

[21] For ancient authority, see Bracton, f. 16b; Sir F. Pollock and F.W. Maitland, *The History of English Law Before the Time of Edward I*, 2nd edn (Cambridge: CUP, 1898) vol.II, pp.535–536, and cases from Bracton's *Notebook* there cited; Y.B. 21 Edw. 4, f. 13, pls, 4 and 22; *Thoroughgood's Case* (1584) 2 Co at f. 9b; 2 Co Inst. 483; 1 Roll. Abr. 688; 1 Bl. Comm. 131.

[22] *Scott v Sebright* (1886) 12 P.D. 21; *Hussein v Hussein* [1938] P. 159. Such duress includes false imprisonment: see *The Earl of Northumberland's Case* (1583) 4 Leon. 91. Contrast *R v Att Gen for England and Wales* [2003] UKPC 22; [2003] E.M.L.R. 24 (threat to return member of SAS to his unit was lawful and demand that he would be returned unless he signed a confidentiality contract was not unreasonable).

[23] Cf. *Huscombe v Standing* (1607) Cro. Jac. 187; 79 E.R. 163 (duress against a principal debtor is no defence to a surety); 1 Roll. Abr. 687, pl. 7.

[24] The categories may be wider: *Williams v Bayley* (1866) L.R. 1 H.L. 200; *Kaufman v Gerson* [1904] 1 K.B. 591; *Royal Boskalis Westminster NV v Mountain* [1999] Q.B. 674.

[25] *Thoroughgood's Case* 2 Co Inst. 483; *Scott* (1886) 12 P.D. 21; *The Evia Luck* [1992] 2 A.C. 152 at 165 per Lord Goff; *The Olib* [1991] 2 Lloyd's Rep. 108 at 118 per Webster J.

[26] *Barton v Armstrong* [1976] A.C. 104 at 119 per Lord Cross. Cf. *The Universe Sentinel* [1983] 1 A.C. 366 at 387 per Lord Diplock, and at 391 per Lord Cross; *The Evia Luck* [1992] 2 A.C. 152 at 165 per Lord Goff (economic pressure).

to that other's decision to enter into the contract.[27] Presumably there is also a right to recover money paid under such duress, but there is no direct authority on the point. This is hardly surprising. Duress to the person will normally constitute both a crime and a tort, in which case the claimant will have other remedies for the recovery of his money.[28] But, in principle, a claim in unjust enrichment should lie.

3. IMPROPER APPLICATION OF LEGAL PROCESS

The proper use of legal process does not constitute duress. Everyone is free to **10–07** invoke the aid of the law in a proper case; and where a settlement is made or a payment exacted under such pressure as the law allows and provides, there is no reason for the law to interfere to upset the transaction. Thus it is well settled that to threaten or to institute a civil action in good faith does not constitute duress.[29] Money paid cannot be recovered, and a settlement cannot be set aside, on that ground. This appears to be the case even though the civil action may result in the imprisonment of the defendant, as in the case of imprisonment for debt. Nor probably did a threat or commencement of bankruptcy proceedings, made in good faith, amount to duress; nor even, in a proper case, a bona fide threat or commencement of criminal prosecution.[30] The same rule applies to lawful arrest, imprisonment,[31] or threat of imprisonment.[32] In each of these cases the law's aid is invoked to bring pressure to bear on a person; but provided that the proceedings are regular, lawfully invoked in good faith, and not abused, it cannot be said that duress has been exercised on the person against whom they have been brought.

Where, however, pressure has been brought to bear by the improper applica- **10–08** tion of legal process, this will amount to duress. A transaction induced by this means will be set aside, and money paid under such duress can be recovered.[33] A clear example is where there is some irregularity of procedure. Thus, where a person is arrested on an irregular warrant, not only may he have a right of action

---

[27] *Barton v Armstrong* [1976] A.C. 104 at 119 per Lord Cross.

[28] The injured person may have his property refunded to him in the course of criminal proceedings, for under the Powers of Criminal Courts (Sentencing) Act 2000 s.148, the court may make an order for the restoration of the stolen property if the offender is convicted. Even where the wrongdoer is not convicted, courts of summary jurisdiction have power to restore to the rightful owner property which has come into the hands of the police "in connection with any criminal charge": see Police (Property) Act 1897 s.1. The injured party may also, if he considers it worth his while, sue in conversion and seek either a compensatory or a restitutionary remedy.

[29] *Hamlet v Richardson* (1833) 9 Bing. 644; 131 E.R. 756; *Powell v Hoyland* (1851) 6 Exch. 67 at 71; 155 E.R. 456 at 459 per Parke B.; *William Whiteley Ltd v R.* (1910) 101 L.T. 741 at 745 per Walton J. Cf. *Moore v Vestry of Fulham* [1895] 1 Q.B. 399; *Self v Hove Commissioners* [1895] 1 Q.B. 685 at 690 per Wright J.; *Sawyer & Vincent v Window Brace Ltd* [1943] K.B. 32.

[30] See below, para.10–11; *Ward v Lloyd* (1843) 6 Man. & G. 785; 134 E.R. 1109; *Flower v Sadler* (1883) 10 Q.B.D. 572; *Fisher & Co v Apollinaris Co* (1875) L.R. 10 Ch. 297. See also *Goodall v Lowndes* (1844) 6 Q.B. 464; 115 E.R. 173.

[31] *Anon.* (1662) 1 Lev. 68; 83 E.R. 301; *Smith v Monteith* (1884) 13 M. & W. 427; 153 E.R. 178.

[32] *Biffin v Bignell* (1862) 7 H. & N. 877; 158 E.R. 725, though in that case there was not even a threat of imprisonment, only a warning.

[33] *Newdigate v Davy* (1692) 1 Ld Raym. 742; 91 E.R. 1397.

in tort against the judicial officer responsible,[34] but he may also recover money paid to obtain his release, even though the money is lawfully due.[35] But where the payment has been made not to those responsible for the irregular arrest but to a third party, no action is available against the former for recovery of money, for the good reason that they have not received it. So, in *O'Connor v Isaacs*,[36] the defendant magistrates made an order in good faith that the claimant should pay his wife maintenance. This order was on its face bad for want of jurisdiction. The claimant fell into arrears with the payments, and consequently was imprisoned on three occasions. When he learnt that the order was bad, he brought an action against the magistrates, claiming damages for false imprisonment and for acts done by the defendants while sitting as magistrates. Diplock J., whose judgment was affirmed by the Court of Appeal, held that the claimant's action of trespass was in the circumstances barred by the Limitation Act 1939 s.21, and that no action lay against the magistrates in respect of the money which he had paid, for the money had not been paid to them but to their collecting officer to the use of the wife.[37]

10–09   Again, an agreement entered into under pressure of wrongful arrest will not be enforced,[38] and money paid under such pressure is recoverable.[39] Similarly, the institution of proceedings in bad faith without reasonable and probable cause amounts to duress,[40] and although there is a general rule that money paid pursuant to a court order is irrecoverable for as long as the order subsists, there is an exception to this principle in cases where the order has been obtained by fraud.[41] In *Duke de Cadaval v Collins*,[42] the duke was arrested for £10,000 by Collins, although Collins knew that he had no legal claim on him. The duke paid £500 to obtain his release, and the writ was later set aside. It was held that he could recover the money in an action for money had and received, for "the arrest was fraudulent; and the money was parted with under the arrest, to get rid of the pressure".[43]

10–10   It has also been held that if a person takes advantage of legal proceedings to apply pressure on the defendant in a matter unconnected with the subject matter of the process, then money paid under such pressure by the defendant to the proceedings so brought is recoverable, for there has been an abuse of legal process.[44]

---

[34] *Clark v Woods* (1848) 2 Exch. 395; 154 E.R. 545; cf. *O'Connor v Issacs* [1956] 2 Q.B. 288.

[35] *Clark* (1848) 2 Exch. 395; 154 E.R. 545: see also *Pitt v Coomes* (1835) 2 A. & E. 459; 111 E.R. 178.

[36] *O'Connor v Isaacs* [1956] 2 Q.B. 288.

[37] The claimant could not sue his wife because of an undertaking he had given to the Divisional Court: see [1956] 2 Q.B. 288 at 292 and 312–313 per Diplock J. cf. *R. v Barnet Magistrates' Court Ex p. Cantor* [1999] 1 W.L.R. 334 at 342–324 per Garland J., where *O'Conner* was not cited.

[38] *Bromley v Norton* (1872) 27 L.T. 478; semble; see also *Pitt v Coomes* (1835) Ad. & El. 459; 111 E.R. 178 and *Cumming v Ince* (1847) 11 Q.B. 112; 116 E.R. 418.

[39] *De Mesnil v Dakin* (1867) L.R. 3 Q.B. 18 at 23–24 per Cockburn C.J.; and see *Oughton v Seppings* (1830) 1 B. & Ad. 241; 109 E.R. 776.

[40] Or, semble, a *mala fide* threat to institute proceedings: see *Scott* (1866) 12 P.D. 21.

[41] See paras 2–32—2–40.

[42] *Duke de Cadaval v Collins* (1836) 4 Ad. & El. 858; 111 E.R. 1006.

[43] *Duke de Cadaval* at 4 Ad. & El. 864; 111 E.R. 1010 per Lord Denman C.J.

[44] *Unwin v Leaper* (1840) 1 Man. & G. 747; 133 E.R. 533 approved in *Goodall v Lowndes* (1844) 6 Q.B. 464 at 467; 115 E.R. 173 at 176 per Lord Denman C.J. Cf. *Land Securities Plc v Fladgate Fielder (A Firm)* [2009] EWCA Civ 1402; [2010] Ch. 467 (no recovery of economic loss as damages for tort of abuse of process).

A similar problem arises if a person promises to confer, or does confer, a **10–11** benefit on another because of a threat that, if he does not do so, either he or a third party will be criminally prosecuted. The general principle is that any agreement to compromise criminal proceedings is illegal and any benefits conferred thereunder may be recoverable either because the coerced party is not *in pari delicto*[45] or because he acted under duress. Money paid in consequence of the threat is recoverable at law; and agreements, bills, or securities may be cancelled in equity.[46] At one time English law distinguished between felonies and misdemeanors. Felonies could never be compounded. Whether misdemeanors could be compounded was more uncertain, for there was a suggestion in *Fisher & Co v Apollinaris Co*[47] that, where a person had a choice between a civil and a criminal remedy, he could enter into a compromise. But the better view was that misdemeanours of a public nature could not be stifled even though a civil remedy was available.[48] The Criminal Law Act 1967 s.1(2), now provides that:

> "[O]n all matters on which a distinction has previously been made between felony and misdemeanour . . . the law and practice in relation to all offences cognisable under the law of England and Wales . . . shall be the law and practice applicable at the commencement of this Act in relation to misdemeanour."

It would appear, therefore, that the only criminal proceedings which can now be compromised are proceedings relating to what before 1967 were described as non-public misdemeanours, namely, assault, criminal libel and the infringement of trade marks.[49]

It is most unlikely[50] that s.5 of the Criminal Law Act 1967 changed the law **10–12** and validated some compromises which were previously illegal. This section provides that the compounding of an offence is itself an offence where a person:

> "accepts or agrees to accept for not disclosing . . . information [to secure the prosecution or conviction of an offender] any consideration other than the making good of loss or injury caused by the offence, or the making of reasonable compensation for that loss or injury."

But there is nothing in the section to suggest that an agreement not to prosecute, in consideration of a promise to make reasonable compensation, is necessarily binding. Indeed, if such an agreement were to be upheld, criminal proceedings of

---

[45] *Davies v London and Provincial Marine Insurance Co* (1878) 8 Ch. D. 469 at 477 per Fry L.J.
[46] A leading case is *Williams* (1866) L.R. 1 H.L. 200; see para.10–15. See also *Kaufman v Gerson* [1904] 1 K.B. 591; *Mutual Finance Ltd v John Wetton & Sons Ltd* [1937] 2 K.B. 389; and P. Birks and N.Y. Chin, "On the Nature of Undue Influence", in J. Beatson and D. Friedmann (eds), *Good Faith and Fault in Contract Law* (Oxford: OUP, 1995), 57, pp.63–67.
[47] *Fisher & Co v Apollinaris Co* (1875) L.R. 10 Ch. App. 297 at 302 per James L.J., and at 303 per Mellish L.J.
[48] *Keir v Leeman* (1846) 9 Q.B. 371 at 394–395; 115 E.R. 1315 at 1324–1325 per Tindal C.J.; *Clubb v Hutson* (1865) 18 C.B. (N.S.) 414; 144 E.R. 506; *Windhill Local Board of Health v Vint* (1890) 45 Ch. D. 351.
[49] *Keir* (1846) 9 Q.B. 371 at 395; 115 E.R. 1315 at 1324–1325 per Tindal C.J. (assault); *Jones v Merionethshire Permanent BS* [1892] 1 Ch. 173 at 184 per Bowen L.J.; *Fisher* (1875) 10 Ch. App. 297 at 303 per Mellish L.J. (libel); *Fisher* (1875) 10 Ch. App. 297 (trade marks).
[50] R.A. Buckley, "Contracts to Stifle Prosecutions" (1974) 3 Anglo-American L.R. 472; A.H. Hudson, "Contractual Compromises of Criminal Liability" (1980) 43 M.L.R. 532.

a serious nature could be compromised. This would be a most undesirable result which the legislature surely could not have intended to effect by implication.

10–13   It is a distinct but related question whether an agreement induced by threats of criminal prosecution can be set aside for duress. A threat to prosecute may constitute duress if it enables a person to gain a benefit through an improper application of legal process. However, in practice the two questions, whether an agreement to stifle prosecution is illegal, and whether it is voidable for duress, shade into one another.[51] In most cases where the courts have held the agreement to be illegal, they have also held there was duress.[52] The coerced party may then recover the benefits transferred under the agreement; he is not *in pari delicto*[53] and the benefit has been conferred in consequence of a wrongful threat.

10–14   Exceptionally the agreement not to prosecute may be legal but still voidable for duress.[54] Generally, however, if the court finds that there was a lawful compromise, it will also conclude that it was not entered into under duress. In *Flower v Sadler*[55] it was alleged[56] that the claimants had threatened to prosecute their rent collector, Maynard, for embezzlement. Subsequently, Maynard indorsed to the claimants bills of exchange drawn on and accepted by the defendant. The claimants sued on the bills and recovered. The Court of Appeal found that the claimants' threats to prosecute Maynard did not mean that they had agreed not to prosecute him if he made good the defalcation. "A creditor may use strong expressions and even threats . . . strong language is not conclusive evidence of an agreement to compound a felony or stifle a prosecution."[57] Brett and Cotton L.JJ. were also prepared to hold that:

> "because a debt was due from Maynard . . . there is nothing illegal in a creditor endeavouring to obtain payment of his debt . . . even though there may have been a threat by the creditor of criminal proceedings".[58]

10–15   The fine line between the honest compromise and the improper threat is essentially one of fact. A threat to prosecute may often be coupled with an implied promise that there will be no prosecution if money is paid to the person making the threat. The threat may be made to a debtor, such as Maynard in *Flower*, or to a third party, such as the debtor's relative or friend. In the latter case the court may be more ready to find that there was an agreement which was illegal and voidable for duress. Such a case was *Williams v Bayley*[59] where the

---

[51] *Fisher* (1875) 10 Ch. App. 297 at 303 per Mellish L.J. See also *Smith* (1844) 13 M. & W. 427; 153 E.R. 178. Cf. *Société des Hotels Réunis v Hawker* (1913) 29 T.L.R. 578 at 579 per Scrutton J.

[52] *Williams* (1866) L.R. 1 H.L. 200; *Société des Hotels Réunis* (1913) 29 T.L.R. 578; cf. *Kesarmal s/o Letchman Das v NKV Valliappa Chettiar s/o Nagappa Chettiar* [1954] 1 W.L.R. 380 at 385, per curiam (L.M.D. de Silva).

[53] *Davies* (1878) 8 Ch. D. 469 at 477 per Fry J., following *Williams v Bayley* (1866) L.R. 1 H.L. 200.

[54] *Kaufman* [1904] 1 K.B. 591 (where the agreement not to prosecute was valid by French law).

[55] *Flower v Sadler* (1882) 10 Q.B.D. 572; see also *Re Mapleback* (1874) 4 Ch.D. 150.

[56] There was some doubt whether there was in fact such a threat: see Brett L.J.'s comments at 575.

[57] *Flower* (1882) 10 Q.B.D. 572 at 573 per Lord Coleridge C.J.

[58] *Flower* (1882) 10 Q.B.D. 572 at 575 per Brett L.J.; see also at 576 per Cotton L.J., following *Ward v Lloyd* (1843) 6 M. & G. 785; 134 E.R. 1109. See too *Mutual Finance* [1937] 2 K.B. 389 at 396 per Porter J.

[59] *Williams v Bayley* (1866) L.R. 1 H.L. 200.

claimant had assigned securities to the defendant in consequence of a threat that, if he did not do so, his son would be prosecuted for forgery. The House of Lords held that the securities should be delivered up and cancelled. As Porter J. said in the later case of *Mutual Finance v John Wetton & Sons Ltd,*[60] no direct threat is necessary, no promise need be given to abstain from prosecution:

> "It is enough if the undertaking were given owing to a desire to prevent a prosecution and that desire were known to those to whom the undertaking was given. In such a case one may imply . . . a term in the contract that no prosecution should take place."[61]

Consequently, a compromise will be upheld only if it is evident that a person **10–16** is settling a civil claim against another and that the settlement has not been reached by any express or implied promise that, if there is no settlement, the matter will be reported to the police or that the threatened person or some third person will be prosecuted.

4. DURESS OF GOODS

(a) *Recovery of Money*

"The extension of duress into the field of economic pressure began in the **10–17** eighteenth century. The situation which inspired the development involved a relatively simple and clear-cut type of oppression—the wrongful seizure or detention of personal property."[62] It was soon established that money paid under duress of goods could be recovered in an action at law provided the claimant could show that he owned,[63] or was entitled to possession of,[64] the goods. In the leading case of *Astley v Reynolds,*[65] the claimant pawned plate to the defendant for £20. At the end of three years he went to redeem it, but the defendant insisted on £10 interest. The claimant tendered £4 knowing that to be more than the legal interest allowed, but the defendant refused to take it; so later the claimant paid the £10 and recovered his plate. The Court of King's Bench held that he was entitled to recover the surplus over and above the legal rate of interest in an action for money had and received. The court said[66]:

> "This is a payment by compulsion; the plaintiff might have such an immediate want of his goods, that an action of trover would not do his business: where the rule *volenti non fit injuria* is applied, it must be where the party had his freedom of exercising his will,

---

[60] *Mutual Finance v John Wetton & Sons Ltd* [1937] 2 K.B. 389.

[61] *Mutual Finance* [1937] 2 K.B. 389 at 395, citing *Jones v Merionethshire P.B.B.S.* [1892] 1 Ch. 173.

[62] J. Dawson, "Economic Duress: An Essay in Perspective," (1947) 45 *Michigan Law Review* 253, p.255.

[63] An equitable proprietary interest was enough: see *Close v Phipps* (1844) 7 Man. & G. 586; 135 E.R. 236; *Frazer v Pendlebury* (1861) 31 L.J.C.P. 1 at 2 per Erle C.J.

[64] *Fell v Whittaker* (1871) L.R. 7 Q.B. 120; see para.10–24.

[65] *Astley v Reynolds* (1731) 2 Str. 915; 93 E.R. 939.

[66] *Astley* at 2 Str. 916; 93 E.R. 940.

which this man had not: we must take it he paid the money relying on his legal remedy to get it back again."[67]

10–18　　No distinction is drawn in this context between actual seizure and threatened seizure; each amounts to duress of goods.[68] So, money paid to prevent a threatened, wrongful sale of goods is also recoverable as paid under duress.[69]

10–19　　These principles have been applied to goods, insurance policies[70] and deeds.[71] Money paid to prevent a wrongful sale by a mortgagee, with power of sale, may also be recovered in this way[72]; a similar principle has also been applied in two appeals from India concerned with wrongful seizure of real property.[73] Many of the cases are concerned with claims to liens. For example, in *Somes v British Empire Shipping Co*,[74] the defendants held the claimants' ship under a lien for money due for repairs to the ship, and then wrongfully claimed to add a charge for the occupation of their graving dock by the ship during the period of time while they so held it. The claimants paid this extra sum under protest simply to recover possession of the ship. The House of Lords held that they were entitled to recover their money.[75]

(b) *Setting Aside Contracts*

10–20　　Although it is well established that money paid under duress of goods is recoverable, in all the books a curious distinction was at one time drawn between contracts and money payments; for it was stated that the rule of common law is that for duress to render a contract voidable it must be duress to the person and

---

[67] See also *Ashmole v Wainwright* (1842) 2 Q.B. 837; 114 E.R. 325; *Irving v Wilson* (1791) 4 T.R. 485; 100 E.R. 1132; *D. Owen & Co v Cronk* [1895] 1 Q.B. 265 at 271 per Lord Esher M.R.

[68] *Snowdon v Davis* (1808) 1 Taun. 359; 127 E.R. 872; *Maskell v Horner* [1915] 3 K.B. 106 at 120 per Lord Reading C.J.

[69] *Valpy v Manley* (1845) 1 C.B. 594 at 602; 135 E.R. 673 at 678 per Tindal C.J.

[70] *Shaw v Woodcock* (1827) 7 B. & C. 73; 108 E.R. 652.

[71] *Pratt v Vizard* (1833) 5 B. & Ad. 808; 110 E.R. 989; *Smith v Sleap* (1844) 12 M. & W. 585; 152 E.R. 1332; *Wakefield v Newbon* (1844) 6 Q.B. 276; 115 E.R. 107; *Oates v Hudson* (1851) 6 Ex. 346; 155 E.R. 576; *Gibbon v Gibbon* (1853) 13 C.B. 205; 138 E.R. 1176; *Fraser v Pendlebury* (1861) 31 L.J.C.P. 1. See also *Re Llewellin* [1891] 3 Ch. 145. By this means money paid under duress of land can be recovered.

[72] *Close v Phipps* (1844) 7 Man. & G. 586; 135 E.R. 236. In *The Atlantic Baron* [1979] Q.B. 705 at 716–717, counsel and Mocatta J. thought that, on the facts of *Close v Phipps*, the duress was a threatened breach of contract. But the court treated the threat as akin to duress of goods: "the plaintiff was obliged either to pay it or suffer her estate to be sold".

[73] *Dooli Chand v Ram Kishen Singh* (1881) L.R. 8 Ind. App. 93; *Kanhaya Lal v National Bank of India* (1913) 29 T.L.R. 314.

[74] *Somes v British Empire Shipping Co* (1860) 8 H.L.C. 338; 11 E.R. 459. The court held that the defendants, who were lienors, were not entitled to claim the expenses incurred in maintaining the value of goods as security for the owners' indebtedness: see *China-Pacific SA v Food Corp of India (The Winson)* [1982] A.C. 939 at 962–963 per Lord Diplock.

[75] In *Huth v Lamport* (1886) 16 Q.B.D. 735 the Court of Appeal left open the question whether the ship-owners, who had a lien on the cargo to secure payment of general average, could refuse the cargo owner's offer of reasonable security. If the ship's master "requires security he cannot impose unreasonable terms": at 738 per Lindley L.J.

not duress of goods. The authority cited for this proposition was *Skeate v Beale*.[76] The claimant distrained for arrears of rent, and the defendant agreed that if the claimant would withdraw the distress he would pay the arrears demanded. The distress was withdrawn, but the defendant only paid a smaller part of the agreed sum. The claimant sued for the outstanding amount; the defendant pleaded that the seizure was unlawful and that he had only entered into the agreement to prevent the claimant carrying out his threat to sell the goods. The Court of King's Bench held, however, that the agreement could not be set aside because duress of goods was no ground for rescinding an agreement, and that the full sum was therefore payable.

There is little to be said for so dogmatic a rule, which was based largely on **10–21** ancient precedent[77] and decided in disregard of some authority to the contrary.[78] Since money paid under duress of goods may be recovered, there is an apparent conflict between *Astley* and *Skeate*: if A demands a sum of money from B under duress of goods, and B pays the money, then he can recover it; yet if B makes a promise to pay a sum of money under similar duress from A, then provided that there is some consideration for the promise, B is bound to pay the money.

It is very difficult to support a distinction of this kind, since there must have **10–22** been a *scintilla temporis* when A must have agreed to pay before making the payment.[79] In *Skeate* Lord Denman C.J. justified the rule on the ground that, whereas duress to the person is "a constraining force," "the fear that goods may be taken or injured does not deprive anyone of his free agency who possesses that ordinary degree of firmness which the law requires all to exert".[80] But this requirement of bravery has surely now been abandoned.[81] In fact, the rule in *Skeate* is in direct conflict with the modern view of duress, namely, that where a transaction has been entered into as a result of illegitimate pressure, consent has not been freely given and the transaction is voidable.[82] The test whether consent has been freely given is subjective, not objective; and this is as true of duress of goods as it is of duress to the person. As Kerr J. said in *Occidental Worldwide*

---

[76] *Skeate v Beale* (1841) 11 Ad. & E. 983; 113 E.R. 688. See also *Sumner v Ferryman* (1708) 11 Mod. 201; 88 E.R. 989 (where the bond was a civil bond); *Atlee v Backhouse* (1838) 3 M. & W. 633 at 650; 150 E.R. 1298 at 1306 per Parke B.; *Liverpool Marine Credit v Hunter* (1868) 3 Ch. App. 479 at 487–488 per Lord Chelmsford L.C.; *Willoughby v Backhouse* (1824) 3 B. & C. 821; 107 E.R. 587.

[77] *Thoroughgood's case* 2 Co Inst. 483; E.G. Atherly (ed.), W. Sheppard, *The Touchstone of Common Assurances*, 8th edn (London: Brooke, 1826), p.61; 1 Bl. Comm. 131. The reason stated for the distinction is that, in the case of threatened distress of goods, should the threat be carried out, a man may have satisfaction by recovering damages; but no suitable atonement can be made for loss of life or limb. This reasoning was, however, rejected in *Astley* (1731) 2 Str. 915; 93 E.R. 939, where it was pointed out that the man might have such immediate want of his goods that the remedy of trover would be insufficient. *Sumner v Ferryman* (1708) 11 Mod. 201; 88 E.R. 989 was cited to the court in *Astley* and apparently disregarded.

[78] See 1 Roll.Abr. 687; Vin.Abr., Duress (B) 3; Bacon, *Maxims, Regula* 18.

[79] Beatson, *The Use and Abuse of Unjust Enrichment*, p.107.

[80] *Skeate* (1841) 11 Ad. & E. 983 at 990; 113 E.R. 688 at 691; cf. *Wakefield* (1844) 6 Q.B. 276 at 280–281; 115 E.R. 107 at 109 per Lord Denman C.J.

[81] *Scott* (1886) 12 P.D. 21 at 24 per Butt J.

[82] *Astley* (1731) 2 Str. 915 at 916; 93 E.R. 939 at 940 per curiam; *Scott* (1886) 12 P.D. 21 at 24 per Butt J.; *Kaufman* [1903] 2 K.B. 114 at 119 per Wright J.; [1904] 1 K.B. 691 at 697 per Collins M.R.; *Barton v Armstrong* [1976] A.C. 104 at 118 and 121; and see para.10–05.

Investment Corp v Skibs A/S Avanti (The Siboen and The Sibotre),[83] "the true question is ultimately whether or not an agreement in question is to be regarded as having been concluded voluntarily."[84] *Skeate* is no longer good law.[85] An agreement induced by duress of goods is voidable at the instance of the coerced party, so that any money paid thereunder will be recoverable in an action for unjust enrichment.

10–23   A further ground of the decision in *Skeate* was that, on the case as pleaded, there was consideration for the defendant's promise, in that the defendant had been benefited by the withdrawal of distress. Yet on the facts it appears that the distress might well have been excessive and, therefore, unlawful. A promise to pay money to obtain the release of goods unlawfully detained is likely to be unsupported by consideration and so unenforceable.[86] Agreements of this kind will often, therefore, be unenforceable for want of consideration.[87] However, for reasons already stated, such an agreement should, in our view, be voidable even where there is consideration for that agreement.[88]

(c) *Exceptional Cases*

10–24   Usually the duress has been exercised on goods which belong to the claimant. But this was not the case in *Fell v Whittaker*.[89] A tenant allowed his rent to fall into arrears by £9. The landlord distrained for £18 and costs, and seized goods worth £100 which were vested in a trustee on trust for the tenant's wife. The rent actually due was tendered but refused, and before the distress was withdrawn the tenant was forced to give an undertaking to pay the full £18, and he paid part of that sum. It was held that he should succeed in an action for excessive distress and on the money counts, though he was neither the legal nor equitable owner of the goods seized; it was sufficient that he had the possession and enjoyment of them. On the other hand, where money has been paid by B under duress of A's goods, A is not entitled to recover that money in an action for money had and

---

[83] *Occidental Worldwide Investment Corp v Skibs A/S Avanti (The Siboen and The Sibotre)* [1976] 1 Lloyd's Rep. 293. cf. *Fell v Whitaker* [1871] L.R. 7 Q.B. 120; *Tamvaco v Simpson* (1866) L.R. 1 C.P. 363.

[84] *The Siboen and The Sibotre* [1976] 1 Lloyd's Rep 293 at 335; citing *Kaufman* [1904] 1 K.B. 591 and *D&C Builders Ltd v Rees* [1966] 2 Q.B. 617.

[85] *The Evia Luck* [1992] 2 A.C. 152 at 165 per Lord Goff; *The Atlantic Baron* [1979] Q.B. 705 at 717–719 per Mocatta J.; *Pao On* [1980] A.C. 614. See also *Hills v Street* (1828) 5 Bing. 37; 130 E.R. 973 and *Vantage Navigation Corp v Suhail and Saud Bahwan Building Materials Inc (The Alev)* [1989] 1 Lloyd's Rep. 138.

[86] *Longridge v Dorville* (1821) 5 B. & Ald. 117; 106 E.R. 1136; *Callisher v Bischoffsheim* (1870) L.R. 5 Q.B. 449; *Re Blythe* (1881) 17 Ch. D. 480. If there is consideration, then there is probably a compromise of a disputed claim. It is significant that in *Wakefield* (1844) 6 Q.B. 276 at 280–281; 115 E.R. 107 at 110 Lord Denman C.J. hinted that *Skeate* was a case "where the parties had come to a voluntary settlement of their concerns"; and that in *Valpy* (1845) 1 C.B. 594 at 605; 135 E.R. 673 at 679, Cresswell J. said that *Atlee v Backhouse* (1838) 3 M. & W. 633; 150 E.R. 1298 was a case "where money paid for the settlement of a doubtful claim was held not to be recoverable back".

[87] See para.10–71.

[88] See para.10–22.

[89] *Fell v Whittaker* (1871) L.R. 7 Q.B. 120; cf. *Scarfe v Hallifax* (1840) 7 M. & W. 288; 151 E.R. 775.

received since it was not his money which was paid over,[90] unless the money has been paid on A's behalf under an agreement of loan.[91]

5. MONEY PAID TO OBTAIN THE PERFORMANCE OF A PUBLIC DUTY: DEMANDS *COLORE OFFICII*[92]

Where money has been paid to a public officer to obtain performance by him of   **10–25**
a duty which he is bound to carry out for nothing or for less than the sum paid, such money or, where some money is due, the excess is recoverable in the language of the old pleaders as money had and received. For the duty is a "public duty imposed by law; and for the execution of that he had no right of any payment".[93] It is:

> "not necessary to show that the defendant acted in bad faith. . . . Nevertheless the phrase [*colore officii*] bears an imputation of imposition by a person in authority upon another person ignorant of his rights."[94]

(a) *The Implications of Woolwich Equitable Building Society v IRC*

The *colore officii* line of cases discussed here figures prominently in the submis-   **10–26**
sions of counsel and the speeches of members of the House of Lords in *Woolwich Equitable Building Society v IRC*[95] There the House of Lords held that the claimant could recover payments, with interest, made in pursuance of an ultra vires demand, resting the claimant's right of recovery either on the principle contained in the Bill of Rights 1689 art.4, that there shall be no taxation without Parliament, or possibly on the wider public law principle that public authorities are constrained by the rule of law. The House considered that the Revenue had not exercised any illegitimate pressure:

> "since the possibility of distraint by the revenue was very remote, the concept of compulsion would have to be stretched to the utmost to embrace the circumstances of such a case as this."[96]

By way of contrast, in the *colore officii* cases the claimant's success depended   **10–27**
upon him proving duress; the mere fact that the person making the demand held some official position did not elevate that demand into a coercive demand. As Windeyer J. said, in *Mason v State of New South Wales*[97]:

---

[90] *Scarfe* (1840) 7 M. & W. 288; 151 E.R. 775.
[91] *Fraser* (1861) 31 L.J.C.P. 1, following *Close v Phipps* (1844) 7 M. & G. 586; 135 E.R. 236.
[92] For the history of this subject, see *Mason v State of New South Wales* (1959) 102 C.L.R. 108 at 139–142 per Windeyer J.
[93] *Morgan v Palmer* (1842) 2 B. & C. 729 at 737; 107 E.R. 554 at 558 per Littledale J.
[94] *Mason v State of New South Wales* (1959) 102 C.L.R. 108 at 141 per Windeyer J. See also *Julian v Mayor of Auckland* [1927] N.Z.L.R. 453 at 458 per Skerrett C.J.; cited in *Waikato Regional Airport Ltd v Att Gen of New Zealand* [2003] UKPC 50; [2004] 3 N.Z.L.R. 1 at [47].
[95] *Woolwich Equitable Building Society v IRC* [1993] A.C. 70; discussed at paras 22–13—22–21.
[96] *Woolwich* [1993] A.C. 70 at 173 per Lord Goff.
[97] *Mason v State of New South Wales* (1959) 102 C.L.R. 108 at 140; followed in *Woolwich* [1993] A.C. 70 at 162 per Lord Keith and at 189–191 per Lord Jauncey. Their Lordships were dissenting, but they were, in these passages, explaining the *colore officii* cases.

"[E]xtortion by colour of office occurs when a public officer demands and is paid money he is not entitled to, or more than he is entitled to, for the performance of his public duty."

Whether the *colore officii* cases are now subsumed within the principle established by the *Woolwich* case, is open to question. In some of the *colore officii* cases the public officer was entitled to make a demand but was not entitled to the particular fee which he demanded; in others he was not entitled to make the demand. Before *Woolwich* it was assumed that the two situations were indistinguishable. In *Mason*, the High Court of Australia held that the claimants were entitled to recover payments which had been made to enable them to carry on their trade as inter-state carriers. The statute under which the defendants had purported to act was ultra vires. The majority of the court found that the payments had been made in consequence of the defendants' wrongful, if implicit, threat to exercise their statutory powers, which included the seizure of vehicles. It was not sufficient to ground recovery that the demand was ultra vires. Menzies J.[98] appears to have thought that there was a demand *colore officii*. But Windeyer J.[99] held that there was no such demand, but nonetheless, the demand was wrongful.

10–28   In *Woolwich* Lord Browne-Wilkinson considered that[100]:

"[A]s a matter of principle the *colore officii* cases are merely examples of a wider principle, *viz.* that where the parties are on an unequal footing so that money is paid by way of tax or other impost in pursuance of a demand by some public officer, these moneys are recoverable since the citizen is, in practice, unable to resist the payment save at the risk of breaking the law or exposing himself to penalties or other disadvantages."

Lord Slynn was more cautious. In his view, "although . . . the facts do not fit easily into the existing category of duress or of claims *colore officii*, they shade into them".[101] The other Law Lords in *Woolwich* did not suggest that the *colore officii* cases are "merely examples" of the *Woolwich* principle. Lords Keith and Jauncey, who dissented, adopted the reasoning of the majority of the High Court of Australia in *Mason*, and Lord Goff did not question it.

10–29   It follows that the *colore officii* line of cases may retain their independent existence, and so we have retained our discussion of them here. We recognise that a claimant who has paid money pursuant to an ultra vires demand by a public officer may well be able to rely on the *Woolwich* principle, and that strong arguments support the view that claims falling within the scope of the *Woolwich* rule should be litigated as such. However the House of Lords' decision in *Deutsche Morgan Grenfell Plc v IRC*[102] makes it clear that claimants are entitled

---

[98] *Mason* (1959) 102 C.L.R. 108 at 132–133; cf. the *dicta* at 123–124 per Fullagar J., and at 129–30 per Taylor J.
[99] *Mason* (1959) 102 C.L.R. 108 at 140–142. Contrast *Bell Bros Pty Ltd v Serpentine-Jarrahdale Shire* (1969) 121 C.L.R. 137.
[100] *Woolwich* [1993] A.C. 70 at 198. Cf. *Atchison, Topeka and Santa Fe Rly Co v O'Connor*, 223 U.S. 280 at 285–286 (1911) per Holmes J.; and *Mason* (1959) 102 C.L.R. 108 at 116–117 per Dixon C.J., and at 126 and 129 per Kitto J.
[101] *Woolwich* [1993] A.C. 70 at 108.
[102] *Deutsche Morgan Grenfell Plc v IRC* [2006] UKHL 49; [2007] 1 A.C. 558.

to rely on some other ground than the *Woolwich* principle if they wish to do so.[103]

There are several possible differences between the principles disclosed by the **10–30** *colore officii* cases and the *Woolwich* principle. First, in the *colore officii* cases illegitimate pressure was exerted by a public officer, who had to make a demand for payment in return for the performance of a duty which he was bound to perform for nothing or for less than the sum paid; and such exaction was for his own benefit. Secondly, some of the officers who have been compelled to make restitution can only be described, with generosity, as *public* officers, for example, arbitrators and umpires as well as common carriers. It is debatable whether their position is akin to that of the Revenue or some other public authority. Thirdly, the claimant may have received from the public officer part of the consideration for which he had bargained. In such a case his payment cannot be said to have been made "without consideration", yet in *Woolwich* Lord Browne-Wilkinson identified this as a reason for allowing the claim.[104] However, it may be that this no longer constitutes a limit to the *Woolwich* principle, following the Privy Council's decision in *Waikato Regional Airport Ltd v Att-Gen of New Zealand*.[105] Under the New Zealand Biosecurity Act 1993, certain airports could not operate international flights without border control services provided by the government. The cost of these was partly met from central government funding, and the balance was recovered from regional but not from metropolitan airports, under a policy which the regional airports successfully challenged in public law proceedings. Allowing recovery of the charges, Lord Nicholls and Lord Walker held that it did not matter that the airports had received services in exchange for their money, because these had been of no commercial benefit to them.

(b) *The Colore Officii Cases*

A leading decision is *Piggott's Case*.[106] The steward of a manor made an **10–31** extravagant charge for providing some deeds and court rolls at a trial. It was held that the person charged could recover his money, because he could not do without the deeds and so the money was paid "through necessity and the urgency of the case".[107] Similarly, in *Steele v Williams*[108] it was held that an action for money had and received would lie against a parish clerk who had illegally charged the claimant for taking extracts from the parish register. Parke B. said[109]:

---

[103] See paras 22–25—22–31.
[104] *Woolwich* [1993] A.C. 70 at 197; and cf. *R. v Tower Hamlets London BC Ex p. Chetnik Developments Ltd* [1988] A.C. 858.
[105] *Waikato Regional Airport Ltd v Att Gen of New Zealand* [2003] UKPC 50; [2004] 3 N.Z.L.R. 1; discussed at para.22–17.
[106] Cited in *Cartwright v Rowley* (1799) 2 Esp. 723; 170 E.R. 509.
[107] *Piggott's Case* (1799) 2 Esp. 723 at 724; 170 E.R. 509 at 510 (Lord Kenyon's post hoc comment).
[108] *Steele v Williams* (1853) 8 Ex. 625; 155 E.R. 1502 (a strong case, since the claimant was not required to pay until after he made the abstract, although he knew of the fees before he began). Cf. F.C. Woodward, *The Law of Quasi-Contracts* (Boston, Mass: Little, Brown and Co, 1912), pp.351–352; P. Birks, "Restitution from Public Authorities" [1980] C.L.P. 191, pp.200–205.
[109] *Steele* at 8 Ex. 630; 155 E.R. 1505.

"I think that, upon the true constriction of the evidence, the payment in this case was not voluntary, because, in effect, the defendant told the claimant's clerk, that if he did not pay for certificates when he wanted to make extracts, he could not be permitted to search."

There are many other cases.[110]

10–32   In the past it has been usual to speak of such payments as being demanded *colore officii*. The right of recovery has, however, been extended to include all cases where the defendant is in a quasi-public or monopolistic position and demands a money payment, to which he is not entitled, for the fulfilment of a duty owed by him. It is irrelevant that no protest was made or question raised at the time of payment by the claimant. The principal cases can be classified as follows.

10–33   (1) If a public officer takes advantage of his official situation to exact money for the fulfilment of his duty, such exaction being for his own benefit rather than for the public funds, he is not making the charge *colore officii*, and yet the money is recoverable. This is the case even though, for example, the public officer had a discretion to refuse the grant of a licence and thought he was entitled to demand payment for a licence. So, in *Morgan v Palmer*[111] money was paid to a mayor for the renewal of a licence, the mayor mistakenly believing that he had a right to exact such a fee for his own benefit. It was held that the licensee was entitled to recover the money, though the charge was not made *colore officii*.[112] Moreover, it is not every charge wrongfully exacted by a public officer, or other such person, which can be recovered in this way. The charge must have been paid by the

---

[110] *Empson v Bathurst* (1620) Hutton 52; 123 E.R. 1095 (excessive fees paid to sheriff); *Irving v Wilson* (1791) 4 T.R. 485; 100 E.R. 1132 (carts seized by a revenue collector); *Jons v Perchard* (1796) 2 Esp. 507; 170 E.R. 436 (excessive fees paid to sheriff's bailiff when giving bail); *Lovell v Simpson* (1800) 3 Esp. 153; 170 E.R. 570 (excessive charge paid to sheriff's officer on arrest); *Parsons v Blandy* (1810) Wight. 22; 145 E.R. 1160 (payment of extra toll); *Longdill v Jones* (1816) 1 Stark. 345; 171 E.R. 492 (retention of money by sheriff after executing *fi. fa.* at claimant's suit); *Umphelby v M'lean* (1817) 1 B. & Ald. 42; 106 E.R. 16 (excessive charge by collector of taxes on a distress of claimant's property); *Dew v Parsons* (1819) 2 B. & Ald. 562; 106 E.R. 471 (payment of excessive fee to sheriff); *Morgan* (1824) 2 B. & C. 729; 107 E.R. 554 (illegal fee paid to mayor for renewal of licence); *Traherne v Gardner* (1856) 5 E. & B. 913; 119 E.R. 721 (steward of copyhold court refused to admit except on payment of fines and fees which were not due); *Hooper v Exeter Corp* (1887) 56 L.J.Q.B. 457 (recovery of harbour dues on limestone); *Martin v Tomkinson* [1893] 2 Q.B. 121 (claimant entitled to recover from returning officer, out of his deposit, half the amount of the officer's charges which had been disallowed at the instance of the other candidate); *Queen of the River Steamship Co v Conservators of the River Thames* (1899) 15 T.L.R. 474 (recovery of tolls on a ship); *Malkin v R.* [1906] 2 K.B. 886 (suppliant entitled to recover in petition of right money, paid under protest to the IRC, which he was not liable to pay and which was demanded in circumstances in which he was compelled to pay it); *Eadie v Township of Brantford* (1967) 63 D.L.R. (2d) 561 (taxpayers entitled to recover excessive levies); cf. *Campbell v Hall* (1774) 1 Cowp. 204; 98 E.R. 1045. See also *Anon.* (1697) Comb. 446 at 447; 90 E.R. 582 at 584 per Holt C.J.; *Lewis v Hammond* (1818) 2 B. & Ald. 206; 106 E.R. 342; *R&W Paul Ltd v Wheat Commission* [1937] A.C. 139; *George (Porky) Jacobs Enterprises Ltd v City of Regina* (1964) 47 W.W.R. 305; *Eadie v Township of Brantford* [1967] S.C.R. 573; *Bell Bros Pty Ltd v Shire of Serpentine-Jarrahdale* (1969) 44 A.L.J.R. 26. In some cases actions failed because the claimant failed to give the required notice to a public officer before commencing his action: see *Waterhouse v Keen* (1825) 4 B. & C. 200; 107 E.R. 1033; *Selmes v Judge* (1871) L.R. 6 Q.B. 724.

[111] *Morgan v Palmer* (1824) 2 B. & C. 729; 107 E.R. 554. See also *Steele* (1853) 8 Ex. 625; 155 E.R. 1502; *Hooper* (1887) 56 L.J.Q.B. 457. But cf. *Bell Bros* (1969) 44 A.J.L.R. 26 at 29 per Kitto J.

[112] If the payment was a bribe, the payer cannot recover; for he has not been compelled to pay the money to get what he is entitled to have.

claimant to obtain performance of the public officer's duty which he wrongfully refused to perform.[113]

(2) It has been held that, where an arbitrator or umpire fixes his own fee in a **10–34** case where he has no jurisdiction to do so,[114] or where he charges an exorbitant fee,[115] a party who pays the fee in order to take up the award is entitled to recover the money paid. In such cases, the party taking up the award has been prevented by a person in a quasi-public position from obtaining something to which he was entitled without paying the money demanded of him. Nowadays, by the Arbitration Act 1996 s.56, a simpler and less expensive procedure is available to the party imposed on in this way. Under this section the High Court can, on application, order that the arbitrator or umpire shall "deliver the award on the payment into court by the applicant of the fees demanded, or such lesser amount as the court may specify".

(3) There is a group of cases where the person or body who makes an **10–35** excessive demand is in a monopolistic position and where the claimant pays because he is not able to obtain the services or goods elsewhere. For that reason the common law imposed upon the common carrier an obligation:

> "to accept and carry all goods delivered to him for carriage according to his profession (unless he had some reasonable excuse for not doing so) on being paid a *reasonable* compensation for so doing; and if the carrier refused to accept such goods, an action lay against him for so refusing; and if the customer, in order to induce the carrier to perform his duty, paid, under protest, a larger sum than was reasonable, he might recover back the surplus beyond which the carrier was entitled to receive",[116]

in an action for money had and received as being money extorted from him.

A further illustration of an excessive demand by a monopolistic supplier is **10–36** *South of Scotland Electricity Board v British Oxygen Co Ltd (No.2).*[117] The respondents were supplied with electricity at high voltage by the appellants. Electricity at high voltage was less costly to supply than electricity at low voltage, and the respondents paid for their electricity according to tariffs under which they were charged less than low voltage consumers. In this action the respondents sought to attack the tariffs on the grounds of "undue discrimination" against high voltage consumers in the position of the respondents, in that the tariffs did not fairly differentiate between high and low voltage consumers. Such discrimination was, they alleged, contrary to statute.[118] They also claimed repayment of the overcharges made because of "undue discrimination", The House of Lords, affirming the decision of the Second Division of the Court of Session, held

---

[113] *Morgan* (1842) 2 B. & C. 729 at 737; 107 E.R. 554 at 558.

[114] *Re Coombs and Freshfield and Fernley* (1850) 4 Ex. 839 at 841; 154 E.R. 1456 at 1458.

[115] *Fernley v Branson* (1851) 20 L.J.Q.B. 178; *Barnes v Hayward* (1857) 1 H. & N. 742 at 743; 156 E.R. 1400 at 1400 per Pollock C.B.; *Barnes v Braithwaite* (1857) 2 H. & N. 569; 157 E.R. 234; *Roberts v Eberhardt* (1858) 28 L.J.C.P. 74 at 75 per Watson B. See also *Canadian Northern Railway Co v Ousley* [1918] 2 W.W.R. 1005.

[116] *Great Western Railway Co v Sutton* (1868–1869) L.R. 4 H.L. 226 at 237 per Blackburn J.; *Woolwich* [1993] A.C. 70 at 165 per Lord Goff.

[117] *South of Scotland Electricity Board v British Oxygen Co Ltd (No.2)* [1959] 1 W.L.R. 589; the earlier action is reported in [1956] 1 W.L.R. 1069. For an analysis of the *South of Scotland* case, see Ralph Gibson L.J's judgment in the CA in *Woolwich* [1993] A.C. 70 at 133–134.

[118] Electricity Act 1947 s.37(8); Hydro-Electric Development (Scotland) Act 1943 s.10A(5). See now the Electricity Act 1989.

that there should be proof before answer on the question of "undue discrimination", because there could be held to be such discrimination although the price charged to the respondents was lower than that charged to low voltage consumers. Moreover, although no right of recovery was specifically conferred by statute, an action would lie to recover the overcharges. For, in the words of Willes J. in *Great Western Railway Co v Sutton*[119]:

> "[W]hen a man pays more than he is bound to do by law for the performance of a duty which the law says is owed to him for nothing, or for less than he has paid, there is a compulsion or concussion in respect of which he is entitled to recover the excess by *condictio indebiti*, or action for money had and received."[120]

10–37   This principle is potentially one of great importance, as can be seen from the United States cases in which the courts have allowed claimants to recover excessive payments to public utility companies. As the Supreme Court of Michigan said in *Saginaw v Consumers Power Co*[121]:

> "To deny recovery would mean depriving consumers of gas until by the institution of legal proceedings they could establish the fact that the charges were illegal. This would be a 'kind of execution of judgment'."

In such circumstances it seems that recovery will be allowed even though no actual threat was made to cut off an essential service. As was said in the same case, the "latent threat that the gas company would shut off the gas was constantly before the consumer."[122]

10–38   Three minor points remain to be mentioned. As in other cases of duress, the claimant is not necessarily entitled to recover all the money he has paid, but only the excess over and above the legal charge.[123] Secondly, the action will not only lie to recover money paid, but also to recover money retained as an excessive charge for services to which the claimant is entitled for less.[124] And thirdly, the claimant is entitled to recover from a public officer or other such person, even though the latter is acting as agent for a superior and has paid the money over into

---

[119] *Great Western Railway Co v Sutton* (1868–1869) L.R. 4 H.L. 226 at 249, cited with approval in *South of Scotland* [1959] 1 W.L.R. 589 at 607 per Lord Merriman. See also Viscount Kilmuir L.C. at 596.

[120] *South of Scotland* was cited by Lord Goff with apparent approval in *Woolwich* [1993] A.C. 70 at 177. As the Privy Council said in *Waikato Airport* [2003] UKPC 50; [2004] 3 N.Z.L.R. 1 at [79]–[80], those who paid the charges in *South of Scotland* and *Waikato Airport* "obtained no commercial benefit from doing so ... There was no consideration in any normal commercial sense, and their Lordships can see no reason to deny a restitutionary remedy on that ground."

[121] *Saginaw v Consumers Power Co* 8 N.W. 2d 149 at 153 (1943) per Butzel J. There are many such cases; but it appears that a claimant must first exhaust any administrative remedy that he may have: see, generally, Palmer, *The Law of Restitution*, vol.II, 9.15. For a comparable Australian decision, see *Criterion Theatres Ltd v Melbourne and Metropolitan Board of Works* [1945] V.R. 267; cf. *South Australian Cold Stores* (1957) 98 C.L.R. 65.

[122] *Saginaw* 8 N.W. 2d 149 at 152 per Butzel J.

[123] *Lovell* (1800) 3 Esp. 153; 170 E.R. 570; *Dew v Parsons* (1819) 2 B. & Ald. 562; 106 E.R. 471.

[124] *Longdill v Jones* (1816) 1 Stark 345; 171 E.R. 492.

public funds,[125] though probably the superior is liable if he has received the money so paid.[126]

6. ECONOMIC DURESS

(a) *General Principles*

Closely allied with the examples of duress of goods are those cases where a **10–39** person obtains a benefit from another by exerting economic or commercial pressure on him. This may take many forms. For example, D refuses to deliver a crane unless C pays him £1,000 above the contract price; or C promises D to accept £500 as a total payment for a debt of £1,500, D having refused to pay the whole debt, with the knowledge that C is in financial difficulties; or D refuses to enter into a new contract with C unless C admits liability for defective workmanship under an existing contract.[127]

It has long been accepted in the United States that, in certain circumstances, a **10–40** contract may be set aside and restitution obtained if the contract has been made or benefits have been conferred in consequence of the exercise of illegitimate economic pressure, which is characterised as economic duress.[128] In recent years English courts have also recognised that commercial pressure *may* be illegitimate and constitute duress.[129] Even though it is "not a tort *per se*, the form that the duress takes may, or may not, be tortious'."[130] It is:

---

[125] *Steele* (1853) 8 Exch. 625; 155 E.R. 1502.

[126] *Brocklebank Ltd v R.* [1925] 1 K.B. 52 at 68 per Scrutton L.J. Contrast the decisions on duress of goods.

[127] But it has been said that only in exceptional circumstances will economic duress be successfully alleged in employment law: *Hennessy v Craigmyle & Co Ltd* [1986] I.C.R. 461.

[128] Early American cases are collected in J. Dalzell, "Duress by Economic Pressure" (1942) 20 N.C.L.R. 237, p.341. For later cases, see Palmer, *The Law of Restitution* vol.II, 9.12. See also J.P. Dawson, "Economic Duress: An Essay in Perspective" (1947) 45 Michigan L.R. 253; R.J. Sutton, "Economic Duress" (1974) 20 McGill L.J. 554; M.H. Ogilvie, "Economic Duress, Inequality of Bargaining Power and Threatened Breach of Contract" (1981) 26 McGill L.J. 289.

[129] *The Siboen and The Sibotre* [1976] 1 Lloyd's Rep. 293; *The Atlantic Baron* [1979] A.C. 704; *Pao On* [1980] A.C. 614; *Burmah Oil Co v Bank of England* [1980] A.C. 1090 at 1140 per Lord Scarman; *The Universe Sentinel* [1983] 1 A.C. 366 at 383–384 per Lord Diplock, and at 400–401 per Lord Scarman; *The Evia Luck* [1992] 2 A.C. 152 at 165 per Lord Goff; *Kolmar Group AG v Traxpo Enterprises P.V.T. Ltd* [2010] EWHC 113 (Comm); [2011] 1 All E.R. (Comm.) 46 at [92].

[130] *The Universe Sentinel* [1983] 1 A.C. 366 at 385 per Lord Diplock; see also *The Evia Luck* [1983] 2 A.C. 152 at 169 per Lord Goff; *Investec Bank (Channel Islands) Ltd v Retail Group Plc* [2009] EWHC 476 (Ch) at [122] per Sales J.; *Berezovsky v Abramovich* [2010] EWHC 647 (Comm) at [190] per Sir Antony Colman, regarding it as "extremely doubtful" whether "a threat of conduct towards a claimant which is neither a crime, nor a tort, nor a breach of contract or of fiduciary duty, is capable of founding a claim in tort, even if made for the purpose of damaging the claimant, with the effect that he is induced to act in such a way that he suffers loss". On this topic, see too E. McKendrick, "The Further Travails of Duress" in A. Burrows and Lord Rodger, *Mapping the Law* (Oxford: OUP, 2006) 181, pp.196–198; J. Edelman and E. Bant, *Unjust Enrichment in Australia* (Melbourne: OUP, 2006), pp.214–216.

"now accepted that economic pressure may be sufficient to amount to duress, . . . provided at least that the economic pressure may be characterised as illegitimate and has constituted a significant cause inducing the claimant to enter into the relevant contract"[131]

or to make a payment. However, "commercial pressure, in some degree, exists wherever one party to a commercial transaction is in a stronger bargaining position than the other party"[132]; so that economic duress should not, therefore, be found lightly.[133] For this reason the courts ask a further question, namely, whether the innocent party, although subjected to illegitimate pressure which was a "significant cause" of his actions, "nevertheless had a real choice and could have, if he had wished, equally well have resisted the pressure and, for example, pursued alternative legal redress."[134]

10–41   These three questions—what is illegitimate pressure; is that pressure a "significant cause" of the innocent party's actions; and did he have a "real choice"? —shade into one another.[135] With that in mind, we now turn to examine the three questions.

(i) What is Illegitimate Pressure?

10–42   Most important is the nature of the pressure.[136] It will often take the form of a threat, although a threat is not a necessary requirement.[137] "The law regards the

---

[131] *The Evia Luck* [1992] 2 A.C. 152 at 165 per Lord Goff. Contrast the case law on duress to the person (see para.10–06), where it is enough that it is *"a"* reason for the claimant acting as he did.

[132] *The Universe Sentinel* [1983] 1 A.C. 366 at 384 per Lord Diplock.

[133] *Moyes & Groves Ltd v Radiation New Zealand Ltd* [1982] 1 N.Z.L.R. 368 (NZCA).

[134] *Huyton SA v Peter Cremer GmbH & Co* [1999] 1 Lloyd's Rep. 620 at 636 per Mance J. For a Canadian decision holding that this is the *only* question that the courts should investigate, see *Greater Fredericton Airport Authority Inc v N.A.V. Canada* (2008) 290 D.L.R. (4th) 405 (New Brunswick CA), applauded in M.H. Ogilvie, "Economic Duress: An Elegant and Practical Solution" [2011] J.B.L. 229; however we doubt that this radically simplified test is sufficiently fine-grained to produce satisfactory answers in every case.

[135] Cf. *Carillion Construction Ltd v Felix (UK) Ltd* (2000) 74 Con. L.R. 144 at [24] per Dyson J.: "In determining whether there has been illegitimate pressure, the court takes into account a range of factors. These include whether there has been an actual or threatened breach of contract; whether the person allegedly exerting the pressure has acted in good or bad faith; whether the victim had any realistic practical alternative but to submit to the pressure; whether the victim protested at the time; and whether he affirmed and sought to rely on the contract ." These words were quoted with approval in *G.M.A.C. Commercial Credit Ltd v Dearden* Unreported, May 28, 2002 at [18] and in *Adam Opel GmbH v Mitras Automotive (UK) Ltd* [2007] EWHC 3481 (QB) at [25]–[26].

[136] It has been said that a threat which may be illegitimate must be distinguished from a mere *warning* or a frank indication of a contracting party's position; for example, that his economic circumstances may prevent him performing his contractual obligations. But the line can be a thin one, perhaps impossible to draw in practice: Beatson, "Duress, Restitution and Contractual Negotiation" in Beatson, *The Use and Abuse of Unjust Enrichment*, pp.118–120; P. Birks, "The Travails of Duress" [1990] L.M.C.L.Q. 342, p. 346; *Equiticorp Finance Ltd v Bank of New Zealand* (1992) 29 N.S.W.L.R. 260 at 298–299. See too R. Bigwood, *Exploitative Contracts* (Oxford: OUP, 2003), pp.295–301, arguing that it is more useful to distinguish threats and offers: an offer is a proposal to make the claimant is better off if he accepts the proposal (or no worse off if he rejects it), whereas a threat is a proposal to make the claimant worse off if he rejects the proposal.

[137] e.g. *Borrelli* [2010] UKPC 21; [2010] Bus. L.R. 1718.

threat of unlawful action as illegitimate, whatever the demand."[138] "Action" is manifestly unlawful if it is criminal or tortious, or, possibly, immoral or unconscionable.[139] Moreover, an illegitimate threat is not legitimatised by the fact that it is accompanied by a threat to institute legal proceedings.[140]

In some circumstances a threat to break a contract may be characterised as **10–43** illegitimate. But not all threats to do so are illegitimate.[141] A threat may be[142] illegitimate if the person making the threat knew that he would be in breach of contract if it were implemented.[143] But what if the person who made the threat believed that it was commercially reasonable for him to ask for a variation of an existing contract? In the United States, some jurisdictions have upheld agreements which were subsequently varied, without fresh consideration, when unexpected difficulties, physical or economic, made one party's performance unduly onerous, in circumstances when it could not be said that the contract was discharged by impossibility or frustration.[144] The *Restatement of Contracts 2d* accepts that such a variation, even if induced by the threat of non-performance, is binding in the absence of consideration if it is "fair and equitable."[145] It is not surprising that lower English courts have not been required to consider such a submission. The pre-existing duty rule has hitherto been an insurmountable barrier. In any event, it is debatable whether a court is in the best position to determine whether a variation is "fair and equitable" and whether it is wise to shift commercial risks which a party originally undertook.[146] Exceptionally the court may find that a party did not exert any illegitimate pressure; for example, if it is the promisor who takes the initiative and offers him the extra douceur.[147]

A more difficult question arises if the person who made the threat thought he **10–44** was entitled in law to make it and did not believe that the threat, if carried out,

---

[138] *The Universe Sentinel* [1983] 1 A.C. 366 at 401 per Lord Scarman (dissenting).

[139] *Alf Vaughan & Co Ltd v Royscot Trust Plc* [1999] 1 All E.R. (Comm.) 856 at 863 per Judge Rich QC, sitting as a High Ct judge, and *Crescendo Management* (1988) 19 N.S.W.L.R. 40 at 46 per McHugh J.A.

[140] *J&S Holdings Pty Ltd v N.R.M.A. Insurance Ltd* (1982) 41 A.L.R. 539 (Full Ct of the Fed Ct of Aus), overruled on other grounds in *David Securities Pty Ltd v Commonwealth Bank of Australia* (1992) 175 C.L.R. 353 at 378.

[141] *B&S Contracts and Design Ltd v Victor Green Publications Ltd* [1984] I.C.R. 419. See too *Atlas Express Ltd v Kafco (Importers and Distributors) Ltd* [1989] Q.B. 833; and R. Halson, "Opportunism, Economic Duress and Contractual Modifications" (1991) 107 L.Q.R. 649, pp.662 and following.

[142] *B&S Contracts* [1984] I.C.R. 419 at 428 per Kerr L.J.

[143] *B&S Contracts* [1984] I.C.R. 419; *The Atlantic Baron* [1979] Q.B. 704 at 719 per Mocatta J.; *The Evia Luck* [1992] 2 A.C. 152 at 166 and 168 per Lord Goff.

[144] The cases are collected in E.A. Farnsworth, *Contracts*, 2nd edn (Boston, Mass.: Little, Brown & Co, 1990) § 4.22.

[145] American Law Institute, *Restatement of Contracts 2d* (St Paul, Minn.: American Law Institute, 1981) 176, comment e.

[146] Cf. Beatson, "Duress, Restitution and Contractual Negotiation" in Beatson, *The Use and Abuse of Unjust Enrichment*, pp.126–129; Halson, "Opportunism, Economic Duress and Contractual Modifications", pp.661–664.

[147] Cf. *Williams v Roffey Bros & Nicholls (Contractors) Ltd* [1991] 1 Q.B. 1; *The Atlantic Baron* [1979] Q.B. 705, discussed at paras 10–63—10–64; *Pao On* [1980] A.C. 614, discussed at paras 10–77—10–79. But see *T. A. Sundell & Sons Pty v Emm Yannoulatos (Overseas) Pty Ltd* (1956) 56 S.R. (NSW) 323.

would be a breach of contract.[148] In such circumstances, the position of the "coerced" party does not change. The pressure on him is just the same whatever the threatener believes. But it is then open to the court to conclude that the threat was not illegitimate, inducing the claimant to act, and that the parties had entered into a compromise of a genuine dispute.[149] In *Huyton SA v Peter Cremer GmbH & Co*[150] Mance J. rejected counsel's submission that the right to restitution should arise only where one party sought in bad faith to exploit the weaknesses of another.[151] The judge accepted that it is "questionable" whether a "compromise" achieved by one party who does not believe that he has an arguable case is a compromise at all, "though it may be upheld if there is other consideration". On the other hand, he continued, it is[152] "difficult to accept that illegitimate pressure applied by a party who believes *bona fide* in his case can never give grounds for relief against an apparent compromise."

10–45 In *Universe Tankships Inc of Monrovia v I.T.W.F. (The Universe Sentinel)*[153] the House of Lords concluded that a threat to black a ship would be legitimate if it was an act done in contemplation or furtherance of a trade dispute. But the House held that a threat to black the ship unless the owners paid, inter alia, $6,480 to the I.T.W.'s Welfare Fund was a threat which was not made in furtherance or contemplation of a trade dispute and was not therefore legitimate.[154] Consequently, the owner could recover that sum; to allow recovery would not circumvent legislative policy.[155] In the view of Lord Diplock, ss.13, 14 and 29 of the Trade Union and Labour Relations Act 1974, which gave immunities from liability in tort[156]:

> "are not directly applicable to the shipowners' cause of action for money had and received. Nevertheless, these, sections, together with the definition of trade dispute in section 29, afford an indication, which your Lordships should respect, of where public policy requires that the line should be drawn between what kind of commercial pressure by a trade union upon an employer in the field of industrial relations ought to be treated

---

[148] Cf. *D.S.N.D. Subsea Ltd v Petroleum Geo-Services ASA* [2000] B.L.R. 530, where the claimant sub-contractor was concerned about the adequacy of the insurance arrangements and told the defendant contractor that it would not resume work until the matter was settled. There was no contractual provision allowing it to do so. At [134] Dyson J. held that even if the claimant would have been in breach if the threat had been implemented, and the threat constituted pressure, it was not illegitimate pressure, because it was "reasonable behaviour by a contractor acting *bona fide* in a very difficult situation". Hence the memorandum of understanding which the parties then entered into had not been procured by duress.

[149] *The Evia Luck* [1992] 2 A.C. 152 at 165 per Lord Goff.

[150] *Huyton SA v Peter Cremer GmbH & Co* [1999] 1 Lloyd's Rep. 620.

[151] Following P. Birks, *An Introduction to the Law of Restitution* (Oxford: Clarendon Press, 1985), p.183.

[152] *Huyton* [1999] 1 Lloyd's Rep. 620 at 637. Contrast *Carillion Construction* (2000) 74 Con. L.R. 144 at [37], where Dyson J. appeared to consider that it was an important, but not a critical, consideration that the defendants genuinely but mistakenly believed that they were entitled to withhold deliveries pending agreement of a final account. See also *C.T.N. Cash and Carry Ltd v Gallaher Ltd* [1994] 4 All E.R. 714 at 717 per Steyn L.J.

[153] *The Universe Sentinel* [1983] 1 A.C. 366.

[154] Lord Diplock (at 395) concluded that "economic duress is not a tort *per se*" (contra Lord Scarman at 400). Further cases on this point see fn.130.

[155] The House of Lords rejected the submission that the money was held on a trust which was void, its object being a non-charitable purpose. The money was paid because the owners had contracted to make the payments.

[156] *The Universe Sentinel* [1983] 1 A.C. 366 at 385. See also Lord Scarman at 401.

as legitimised despite the fact that the will of the employer is thereby coerced, and what kind of commercial pressure in that field does amount to economic duress that entitles the employer victim to restitutionary remedies."

As the law then stood, these statutory provisions recognised that it was **10–46** desirable to protect a trade union from tortious claims which could cripple its legitimate activities. But it does not follow that because it is wise to enact that a trade union should be insulated from tortious claims for loss suffered that it should be allowed to retain an enrichment which was gained from an act which was at common law wrongful, if not necessarily tortious.[157] For that reason it is debatable whether the concession that payments of back pay were irrecoverable, being sums paid in furtherance of a trade dispute, was a wise one, although a claim against an individual seaman might not have been worth pursuing even though he may have accepted his money with the knowledge that it was the product of the Federation's wrongful act.

As has been seen,[158] a threat of action, though lawful if carried out, may **10–47** amount to illegitimate pressure. Such is blackmail. But are there any other circumstances when it is illegitimate to utter a threat when it is legitimate to do what one threatens to do? Here it is sufficient to say that there are dicta of the Court of Appeal which contemplate this possibility if a party acts "unconscionably",[159] although their context was not D threatening wrongfully to repudiate his contract with C, but D's assertion that he would enter a new contract with C only if C accepted his terms. We return to this question later in this chapter.[160]

(ii) Was the Threat a "Significant Cause"?

In *Huyton*[161] Mance J., obiter, was not prepared to accept, at least in the context **10–48** of economic duress, that it was enough that the illegitimate pressure was "a" cause or "a" reason why the threatened party acted as he did.[162] He preferred to follow the dicta of Lord Goff in *The Evia Luck*,[163] namely, that the cause must be a "significant cause" of the threatened party's acts. Mance J. concluded that the "minimum basic test" should be a "but for test"[164]:

> "The illegitimate pressure must have been such as actually caused the making of the agreement, in the sense that it would not otherwise have been made either at all or, at least, in the terms in which it was made. In that sense the pressure must have been decisive or clinching."

---

[157] In obiter dicta in *The Evia Luck* [1992] 2 A.C. 152 at 160–161 and 166–167, Lord Templeman and Lord Goff appeared to accept Lord Diplock's reasoning and conclusion.
[158] See para.10–03.
[159] *C.T.N. Cash and Carry* [1994] 4 All E.R. 714; discussed at paras 10–82—10–83. This is so-called "lawful-act duress".
[160] See para.10–81.
[161] *Huyton* [1999] 1 Lloyd's Rep. 620.
[162] *Barton v Armstrong* [1976] A.C. 104.
[163] *The Evia Luck* [1992] 2 A.C. 152 at 165.
[164] *Huyton* [1999] 1 Lloyd's Rep. 620 at 636. The judge accepted that on occasions a "common sense relaxation" of the "but for test" may be made, for example, if there were two concurrent causes each of which may have induced the agreement.

10–49   **The onus of proof**   In principle, the burden of proof should be on the claimant. However, in *Barton v Armstrong*[165] Lord Cross expressed the view, taking the analogy of dispositions induced by fraud, that the burden was not on the innocent party but on the threatener to prove that the illegitimate pressure contributed nothing to the innocent party's decision to enter into the transaction. *Barton v Armstrong* was a case of threats to kill. There will rarely be any doubt that such threats achieved their purpose. Moreover:

> "[T]here are sound reasons of policy why those who threaten to murder or who set out to deceive should bear a liability even if it might well have been the case that, but for such behaviour, the contract would still have been made."[166]

These do not apply to other types of duress, and in *Huyton*[167] Mance J. declined to apply the rule established by *Barton v Armstrong* to a case of economic duress. Threats to the person must therefore be differentiated from other kinds of duress. Not only is the onus of disproving duress to the person on the threatener but also, as has been seen, the threats need only be "a", as distinct from "the significant cause" of the claimant's succumbing to the illegitimate pressure.

10–50   **Was there a reasonable alternative?**   This conceals two distinct but related questions. First, it must be asked whether the threatened party agreed, say, to the variation of the contract despite the existence of the threat. If the answer is yes, then, as has just been seen, a court should conclude that the threat was not a "significant cause" in inducing him to agree to the variation. He acted "voluntarily".[168] However, if the answer to this question is no, then, it must secondly be asked whether the threatened person had an alternative course of action, which a reasonable person would have followed. The courts have been asking this second question since the beginning of the 18th century. We begin by analysing the old case law on duress of goods.

10–51   In many of the old books it is said that the threatened harm must be such that a person of ordinary courage would yield to it.[169] But this requirement, which suggests an objective assessment of duress,[170] has most probably been abandoned. The modern view of duress is that a transaction will be set aside when one party capitulates because of illegitimate pressure.[171]

10–52   In the past it was suggested that a person has no right to avoid a contract or recover money paid under duress where he had an adequate legal remedy to

---

[165] *Barton v Armstrong* [1970] A.C. 104 at 120; followed in *Antonio v Antonio* [2010] EWHC 1199 (QB). See too *Crescendo Management Pty* (1998) 1 N.S.W.L.R. 40 at 46 per McHugh J.
[166] *Raiffeisen Zentralbank Osterreich AG v Royal Bank of Scotland Plc* [2010] EWHC 1392 (Comm); [2011] 1 Lloyd's Rep. 123 at [198] per Christopher Clarke J.
[167] *Huyton* [1999] 1 Lloyd's Rep. 620.
[168] *Pao On* [1980] A.C. 614 at 635; discussed at paras 10–77—10–79. For a jurisprudential analysis, see S. Smith, "Contracting Under Pressure: A Theory of Duress" [1997] C.L.J. 343.
[169] Bracton, 48.21.1; Co2 Inst. 483; 1 Bl. Comm. 131.
[170] *Skeate* (1841) 11 Ad. & El. 983 at 990; 113 E.R. 688 at 691.
[171] *Scott* (1886) 12 P.D. 21 at 24 per Butt J.; *Kaufman v Gerson* [1903] 2 K.B. 114 at 119 per Wright J.; [1904] 1 K.B. 591 at 597 per Collins M.R.; *H v H* [1954] P. 258 at 266 per Karminski J.; *The Siboen and The Sibotre* [1976] 1 Lloyd's Rep. 296 at 336 per Kerr J. See also *Astley* (1731) 2 Str. 915 at 916; 93 E.R. 939 at 940 per curiam ("where the rule *volenti non fit injuria* is applied, it must be where the party had his freedom of exercising his will"), and the well known judgment of Holmes J. in *Silsbee v Webber*, 50 N.E. 555 (1898).

recover compensation for the threatened harm.[172] Such a rule can only be justified on the ground that a person of reasonable courage would not be coerced by such duress. This justification is hardly tenable, and indeed there is doubt whether the rule exists. In some, but not all, of the cases on duress, it is accepted that the mere existence of a remedy at law for compensation would not give adequate protection to the person under pressure. Thus, in *Astley*,[173] recovery was allowed of money paid under duress of goods even though the claimant could, instead of paying the money, have brought an action of trover, because he "might have such an immediate want of his goods, that an action of trover would not do his business."[174] Indeed the delay, expense and uncertainty of legal process would prevent practically any legal remedy from being called adequate in this context. In any case, as Williston has pointed out, "so far as it would require a person threatened with injury necessarily to endure the injury because the law provides a remedy for it, [the rule] cannot be accepted."[175]

However, in the law of distress, statements are to be found in the old cases to the effect that where the claimant has a remedy at law he cannot pay the money and afterwards recover it in an action for money had and received.[176] There is considerable doubt, however, whether these cases can now be said to represent the law.[177] The principal objection to allowing an action for money had and received was that the defendant "might be surprised at the trial . . . ; he could not tell what sort of right of common or other justification the plaintiff might set up."[178] But this objection applies equally in other cases where the action is allowed, and it can be met today by the defendant's right to apply for particulars of the claim. Moreover, the mere existence of a remedy which will enable the claimant to claim compensation for the threatened wrong will not normally affect his right to bring an action for money had and received. It is true that, in these cases, replevin may be available and that it is a more summary remedy than many others. Nevertheless, it still suffers from sufficient doubts and delays to make it more efficacious for the claimant to recover his goods by the simple expedient of payment and reservation of rights, seeking later to recover the money in an action at law. In our view, the action for money had and received should be available in these cases; and the later authorities support this view.[179]

10–53

---

[172] See *Thoroughgood's case* 2 Co Inst. 483; 1 Bl.Comm. 131; *Ashmole v Wainwright* (1842) 2 Q.B. 837 at 845; 114 E.R. 325 at 329 per Lord Denman. This rule was used by older writers to justify the distinction between duress to the person and duress of goods in relation to setting aside contracts (see paras 10–20—10–23).

[173] *Astley* (1731) 2 Str. 915; 93 E.R. 939.

[174] *Astley* at 2 Str. 916; 93 E.R. 940; see also *Close* (1844) 7 Man. & G. 586 at 590; 135 E.R. 236 at 239; per Tindal C.J.

[175] S. Williston and G.J. Thompson, *A Treatise on the Law of Contracts*, revised edn (New York, NY: Baker Voorhis & Co, 1936–1938), 1620.

[176] *Lindon v Hooper* (1776) 1 Cowp. 414 at 418; 98 E.R. 1160 at 1163–1164 per Lord Mansfield; *Anscomb v Shore* (1808) 1 Camp. 285; 170 E.R. 959; *Gulliver v Cosens* (1845) 1 C.B. 788; 135 E.R. 753. Cf. *Hills v Street* (1828) 5 Bing. 37; 130 E.R. 973; and see G.L. Williams, *Liability for Animals* (Cambridge: CUP, 1939), pp.115–118. A similar rule was laid down in old cases on distress of rent: see *Knibbs v Hall* (1794) 1 Esp. 84; 170 E.R. 287; *Glynn v Thomas* (1856) 11 Ex. 870; 156 E.R. 1085.

[177] See C. Dodd and T.J. Bullen, *A Practical Treatise on the Law of Distress for Rent*, 2nd edn (London: Butterworth & Co, 1899), pp.223–224.

[178] *Lindon* (1776) 1 Cowp. 414 at 418; 98 E.R. 1160 at 1163–1164 per Lord Mansfield.

[179] *Loring v Warburton* (1858) El. Bl. & El. 507; 120 E.R. 598; *Green v Duckett* (1883) 11 Q.B.D. 275 at 279 per Denman J.; *Maskell v Horner* [1915] 3 K.B. 106 at 122 per Lord Reading C.J.

10–54   The case law just discussed is authority for this proposition: when an owner's goods are wrongly seized, there appears to be an almost irrebuttable presumption that the illegitimate pressure, the defendant's refusal to return the goods unless his demand was met, compelled the owner to pay. He "can only release them from seizure by payment"; for he has no other remedy.[180] In contrast, when confronted with allegations of economic duress the courts appear to proceed more cautiously. In *Huyton*[181] Mance J. rejected the submission that the "reasonable alternative" question is simply the "significant cause" question differently formulated. In his opinion, this could[182]:

> "lead too readily to relief being granted. It would not, for example, cater for the obvious possibility that, although the innocent party would never have acted as he did, but for the illegitimate pressure, he nevertheless had a real choice and could if he had wished, equally well have resisted the pressure and, for example, pursued alternative legal redress."

Hence, while the absence of a reasonable alternative was not an "inflexible third essential requirement of economic duress", it was "self-evident" that relief would be inappropriate if an innocent party "decides, as a matter of choice, not to pursue an alternative remedy which a reasonable person in his circumstances would have pursued".[183] Relief might also be refused if there was an absence of protest and conduct which suggested that the innocent party was "prepared to accept and live with the consequences, however unwelcome".[184]

10–55   Understandably, the courts do not wish to enter into the market place and direct what are and what are not proper bargaining tactics. "Illegitimate pressure" must be fenced in firmly. For it is in the general commercial interest, as recognised in the Uniform Commercial Code § 2–209, that good faith modifications and variations of contracts should be upheld. As Lord Scarman said in *The Universe Sentinel*[185]:

> "The absence of choice can be proved in various ways, e.g. by protest, by the absence of independent advice, or by a declaration to go to law to recover the money paid or the property transferred."

However, it is debatable whether it is right to resurrect the "reasonable person test". The earlier case law properly asks whether the threatened (not a reasonable) person has been coerced. If *he* irrationally fails to seek an alternative reasonable remedy, then a court may conclude, on the evidence, that he was not coerced. By and large businessmen are rational actors (if they are not they will

---

[180] *Maskell v Horner* [1915] 3 K.B. 106 at 122 per Lord Reading C.J.

[181] *Huyton* [1999] 1 Lloyd's Rep. 620.

[182] *Huyton* [1999] 1 Lloyd's Rep. 620 at 636.

[183] *Huyton* [1999] 1 Lloyd's Rep. 620 at 638. These were obiter dicta, for Mance J. held that the parties had entered into a compromise which was not voidable for duress. Any pressure imposed on the claimant was of its own making; and, even assuming that there was a threatened breach of contract, it was not a significant cause inducing the claimant to enter into the compromise. Cf. *B&S Contracts* [1984] I.C.R. 419 at 425 per Kerr J. The American cases ask if there is a suitable substitute product readily available in the market: Halson, "Opportunites, Economic Duress and Contractual Modifications", pp.668–673.

[184] *Huyton* [1999] 1 Lloyd's Rep. 620 at 638.

[185] *The Universe Sentinel* [1983] 1 A.C. 366 at 400.

fail). They will succumb to a threat only if no other reasonable course of action, including seeking speedy legal redress, is open to them.[186]

Significantly, there is no case in the books where a party has failed because a reasonable person in his position would have sought some other remedy. On the contrary, the case law demonstrates, more often than not, that no other remedy "would do his business." In *North Ocean Shipping Co Ltd v Hyundai Construction Co Ltd (The Atlantic Baron)*,[187] in determining whether the ship owners had acted under compulsion, Mocatta J. concluded that it would be "unreasonable" to hold that they should have claimed damages against the defendant shipyard, given the existence of their profitable time-charter with Shell. Failure to seek an injunction will rarely defeat a claim based on economic duress. So, in *The Universe Sentinel* the claimants had been properly advised that their prospects of obtaining an injunction to prevent the blacking of their ship were minimal, and they promptly sought to recover their money once the duress had terminated. Moreover, the facts may make it plain that it is highly unlikely that the court would grant an injunction. For that reason, in *Carillion Construction Ltd v Felix (UK) Ltd*.[188] Dyson J. said that it was "impossible to say with any confidence" that a court would have granted a mandatory injunction to compel the defendants to complete the cladding works which they had contracted to do. Furthermore, the matter was one of urgency and even expedited proceedings would have taken weeks, perhaps months, to come before the court.[189]

10–56

In previous editions of this work, it was contended that "submission to an honest claim" is a defence to claims in duress, so that relief should be denied in cases where a defendant demands a benefit from a claimant, in good faith but in fact without right, and the claimant submits to the claim and pays.[190] *Maskell v Horner*[191] was identified as such a case, and it was noted that even where there is duress, a person may submit to a claim which he knows to be unfounded, simply because he cannot be bothered to dispute it, or cannot produce the evidence necessary to unmask its falsehood,[192] or wishes "to avoid the inconvenience attendant on disputing the demand and to put an end to the matter".[193] However, we share Ewan McKendrick's view that the notion of "submission to

10–57

---

[186] For further discussion of the question whether the courts should assess the availability of alternatives as an objective rather than subjective matter, see P. Chandler, "Economic Duress: Clarity or Confusion?" [1989] L.M.C.L.Q. 270, pp.275–277; D. Nolan, "Economic Duress and the Availability of a Reasonable Alternative" [2000] R.L.R. 105, pp.110–114.

[187] *North Ocean Shipping Co Ltd v Hyundai Construction Co Ltd (The Atlantic Baron)* [1979] Q.B. 705 at 719, citing *Astley v Reynolds* (1731) 2 Str. 915; 93 E.R. 939. *The Atlantic Baron* is discussed at paras 10–63—10–64.

[188] *Carillion Construction Ltd v Felix (UK) Ltd* (2000) 74 Con. L.R. 144.

[189] See similarly *Adam Opel GmbH v Mitras Automotive (UK) Ltd* [2007] EWHC 3481 (QB) at [32].

[190] e.g. G. Jones, *Goff & Jones: The Law of Restitution*, 7th edn (London: Sweet & Maxwell, 2006), paras 10–52—10–56.

[191] *Maskell v Horner* [1915] 3 K.B. 106. Also *Twyford v Manchester Corp* [1946] Ch. 236.

[192] See, e.g. *Spragg v Hammond* (1820) 2 Brod. & B. 59 at 62; 129 E.R. 880 at 882 per Dallas C.J.; *Slater v Burnley Corp* (1888) 59 L.T. 636.

[193] *Deacon v Transport Regulation Board* [1958] V.R. 458 at 460 per Lowe J.; see also *Mason* (1959) 102 C.L.R. 108 at 143 per Windeyer J.; *Woolwich* [1993] A.C. 70 at 98–99 per Glidewell L.J., and at 165 per Lord Goff. The fact that the claimant has passed on to his customers a tax which he allegedly paid under coercion "might help to show that the person who paid the charges in the first instance did so voluntarily because he would not be out of pocket by doing so": *Mason*, above, at 136 per Menzies J. For discussion of the passing on defence, see Ch.32.

an honest claim" is not a helpful aid to analysis of these cases, and that a better way to understand them lies in "the notion of a 'choice' between reasonable alternatives", i.e. the question that matters is whether the claimant, "faced with a choice between reasonable alternatives, chose to agree the to the terms put forward by the defendant rather than pursue the alternative course of action".[194]

(b) *The Factual Settings*

10–58 The law on economic duress is still in the course of development; whether or not economic duress is found to exist turns on the facts of each case. The following discussion is divided according to the factual settings of the cases.

(i) *Where C Confers a Benefit on D because of D's Threat that Otherwise He Will not Carry out His Obligations under a Contract*

10–59 Whether C can recover money paid or obtain recompense for other benefits conferred in consequence of such threats may depend, as has been seen, on a number of factors.

10–60 If D threatens not to perform his part of the contract, knowing that this will amount to a breach of the contract, the threat may be characterised as an illegitimate or wrongful act, which amounts in law to duress. To take one example, in *B&S Contracts and Design Ltd v Victor Green Publications Ltd*,[195] the claimant company agreed to erect exhibition stands for the defendant company at Olympia, under a contract with a force majeure clause. The claimant decided to deploy employees who had already been given redundancy notices. On arriving at Olympia they threatened to strike unless they were paid £9,000 severance pay, to which they were not entitled; later they rejected the claimant's offer of £4,500. The claimant told the defendant about the employees' threat, and the defendant offered the balance of £4,500 "on account." The claimant refused that offer and told the defendant, "if you will give us £4,500 we will complete the contract". The defendant paid because, in the words of its director, it was "over the barrel". In this action the claimant sued to recover the £4,500 which the defendant subsequently deducted from the contract sums that were due to it. The Court of Appeal agreed with the trial judge that the claimant had made a "veiled threat," namely, that it would walk off the job unless the defendant paid the £4,500. The threatened breach of contract amounted to duress for the defendants had been influenced against their will "to pay money under the threat of unlawful damage to [their] economic interest".[196] It was faced with no alternative course of action but to pay the sum demanded.[197] It could not be said that the claimant's threat was lawful. The claimant could not have taken advantage of the force majeure clause to cancel the contract; it would have been reasonable for it to have paid the £9,000 demanded, there being no evidence that

---

[194] McKendrick, "The Further Travails of Duress", p.192.
[195] *B&S Contracts and Design Ltd v Victor Green Publications Ltd* [1984] I.C.R. 419. See also *The Alev* [1989] 1 Lloyd's Rep. 138; *Atlas Express Ltd v Kafco (Importers and Distributors) Ltd* [1989] Q.B. 833; *Carillion Construction* (2000) 74 Con. L.R. 144.
[196] *B&S Contracts* [1984] I.C.R. 419 at 423–424 per Eveleigh L.J.
[197] *B&S Contracts* [1984] I.C.R. 419 at 426 per Griffiths L.J.

it could not have afforded to have done so. Consequently, the defendant was entitled to make the deduction which it had made.

A more difficult case is *T.A. Sundell & Sons Pty Ltd v Emm Yannoulatos   **10–61**
(Overseas) Pty Ltd*,[198] for the appellant might well have thought that the partic- ular demand was a reasonable one. The appellant, an importer, had agreed to sell galvanised iron to the respondent at £104.15s. a ton. The iron was to come from France. Subsequently there was a sharp rise in the world price of zinc which led the appellant to demand an extra £31 a ton. The respondent increased his letter of credit, reserving his rights under the original contract,[199] because of the appellant's threat that if he failed to do so "no iron at all would be delivered". The appellant delivered the iron and had recourse in full to the letter of credit. The respondent, who had sub-contracted to sell to a third party, sued to recover the amount paid in excess of the original contract price. The Supreme Court of New South Wales found that the respondent had not willingly agreed to pay the increased price. Even if he had, the promise was not binding since the appellant had provided no fresh consideration. The court accepted[200] that a "compulsive threat . . . to refrain from performing merely a contractual duty" may amount in law to duress and denied that duress embraces only "a threat to refrain from performing a statutory duty or a threat to interfere with a proprietary right of the payer".

In *Sundell* the appellant believed that it was reasonable to pass on the price   **10–62**
increase to the respondent; indeed he offered to assist the respondent, by giving him access to his files in order to explain to the sub-purchaser why the increase was necessary. The court did not consider these factors to be decisive. As a matter of law the appellant's threat could amount to duress, and the trial judge had found duress. But on such facts a court could hold that the defendant had made no threat but had simply pointed out that he could not perform his side of the bargain.[201] The line between an implicit threat and a statement of "my position" is a very thin one.

In *The Atlantic Baron*,[202] Mocatta J. also accepted that the threat not to carry   **10–63**
out a contract amounted to duress, but held that the claimant had nonetheless affirmed the contract. In this case the defendant shipyard had contracted with the claimant company to build a tanker for a fixed price in US dollars, payable in five instalments. After the claimant had paid the first instalment, the dollar was devalued by 10 per cent. The defendant then demanded that the claimant increase its remaining instalments by 10 per cent. The claimant realised that the yard would not accept anything other than an unqualified agreement to the increase. At the time the claimant was negotiating a very lucrative time-charter of the tanker with Shell, a contract that was later finalised. Consequently it agreed to make the payments "without prejudice to our rights" because it did not wish to default in the performance of the time-charter with Shell. In turn the defendant

---

[198] *T.A. Sundell & Sons Pty Ltd v Emm Yannoulatos (Overseas) Pty Ltd* (1956) 56 S.R. (N.S.W.) 323. See also *Carr v Gilsenan* [1946] S.R. (Qd.) 44.
[199] The appellant had stated that the respondent knew that it could not deliver at the contract price. The respondent continued to assert that its increase of the letter of credit was without prejudice.
[200] *Sundell* (1956) 56 S.R. (N.S.W.) 323 at 328, per curiam.
[201] Cf. *Williams v Roffey Bros & Nicholls (Contractors) Ltd* [1991] 1 Q.B. 1, on which see para.10–72. See too Beatson, *The Use and Abuse of Unjust Enrichment*, pp.126–129.
[202] *The Atlantic Baron* [1979] Q.B. 705.

agreed, at the claimant's request, to a corresponding increase in letters of credit which had been provided as security for any default in its performance. The remaining instalments were paid without protest; the claimant took delivery of the tanker, again without protest, and took no further action for seven months, when it made a claim for the return of the excess payments.

10–64   Mocatta J. held that, although the defendant had given consideration for the varied agreement by increasing its letters of credit, the agreement had been induced by a threat to break the contract which amounted to economic duress.[203] It was immaterial that the shipyard was ignorant of the time-charter. Nonetheless, the judge dismissed the claim. The claimant's conduct amounted to an affirmation of the varied agreement to pay the extra 10 per cent. At the time of taking delivery of the tanker it had made no protest when there was no danger at that time that the shipyard would refuse to deliver if they had done so; and the final instalment payments were made "without qualification" and were followed by a delay of seven months before the claim was made.[204] Here is a rare example of a situation where a party realises that he has been coerced into paying more than was agreed, but went on with the contract, as varied, because it was in his best economic interests so to do.[205]

10–65   In *The Atlantic Baron* the defendant knew that its threat, if carried out, would be a breach of its contractual obligations. But in *The Siboen and The Sibotre* counsel[206] argued that the[207]:

> "defence of duress is made out whenever one party to a contract threatens [whether in good faith or not] to commit a breach of it and the other party agrees to vary or cancel the contract under this threat because it has no effective legal remedy in respect of the threatened breach . . . Duress must *a fortiori* be a defence when the party threatening to break the contract is putting forward some justification for doing so without any *bona fides*."

10–66   Kerr J. thought this proposition "much too wide", probably because it implied that an honest settlement, made with the intention of settling a claim, could subsequently be avoided, even if the party making the threat was acting in good faith or, if not, the other party was aware of his lack of bona fides but still wished to dispose of the matter by settlement. The judge did not think that bad faith had any relevance at all. In *The Siboen and The Sibotre* the owner had agreed to vary the charter rates because of the charterers' representation that they would go bankrupt if this were not done, so that the owner would be without any commercial redress. The charterers' representation was found to be fraudulent and the case was ultimately decided on that ground.[208] But it was argued that, even if there were no misrepresentation, the charter agreement, as varied, was voidable for duress. There was a threatened breach of the charter, and "if the charterers were liable to go bankrupt if the owners did not reduce their rates, then the owners would be left without any effective legal remedy in the face of these

---

[203] *The Atlantic Baron* [1979] Q.B. 705 at 719.
[204] *The Atlantic Baron* [1979] Q.B. 705 at 720.
[205] Cf. *Pao On* [1980] A.C. 614; discussed at paras 10–75——10–79.
[206] Robert Goff QC.
[207] *The Siboen and The Sibotre* [1976] 1 Lloyd's Rep. 293 at 334.
[208] *The Siboen and The Sibotre* [1976] 1 Lloyd's Rep. 293 at 321 and following.

threatened breaches."[209] Kerr J. rejected that argument. The owner had voluntarily agreed to vary the terms of the charter; there had been no protest and the owner had later sought to uphold the varied charter by subsequent arbitration. The owner "was acting under great pressure, but only commercial pressure, and not under anything which could in law be regarded as a coercion of his will so as to vitiate his consent".[210]

A bona fide compromise which is entered into with the intention of closing a **10–67** transaction is binding on the parties.[211] Conversely, as has been seen, money paid because of a "compulsive threat . . . to refrain from performing merely a contractual duty" may amount to duress.[212] A finding that both parties acted in good faith should not, however, lead to an inevitable conclusion that they had agreed to compromise a claim; indeed in the other categories of duress, such as duress of goods it is "not necessary to show that the defendant acted in bad faith".[213] A compromise is upheld because it is proper to threaten litigation if bona fide demands are not met and because it is desirable to uphold settlements made in consequence of such a threat. But a compromise can be set aside for duress.[214]

Was the benefit exacted by the mere threat of legal proceedings, or was it **10–68** exacted by illegitimate pressure which went beyond the threat of legal proceedings?[215] This is often a difficult question to answer when the defendant honestly believes that he was entitled to refuse to perform his part of the contract. In Australia it has arisen in the context of disputes between vendors and purchasers,[216] where one of the parties maintained that he was not liable under the contract to bear certain charges, such as a water rate. The purchaser protested but capitulated when the vendor honestly, but, as it was later determined, without right, threatened not to complete. The courts held that it was not conclusive that the:

> "vendor honestly believed that he was legally entitled . . . to the price which he asked . . . The withholding of another's legal right [to completion] is . . . itself treated as a 'practical compulsion'."[217]

The purchaser could not then be said to have acted voluntarily, with the intention of closing the transaction. On the contrary, he was "endeavouring to the utmost of [his] ability to preserve [his] legal rights as regards the question in issue so far as [he] could without jeopardising [his] rights under the contract as against the

---

[209] *The Siboen and The Sibotre* [1976] 1 Lloyd's Rep. 293 at 334.
[210] *The Siboen and The Sibotre* [1976] 1 Lloyd's Rep. 293 at 336. For other facts which gave rise to a genuine variation, see *Moyes & Groves Ltd v Radiation New Zealand Ltd* [1982] 1 N.Z.L.R. 368 NZ CA.
[211] See para.10–76.
[212] *Sundell* (1956) 46 S.R. (N.S.W.) 323 at 328.
[213] *Mason* (1959) 102 C.L.R. 108 at 141 per Windeyer J.; *Huyton* [1999] 1 Lloyd's Rep. 620 at 637.
[214] *Deacon v Transport Regulation Board* [1958] V.R. 458 at 459–460 per Lowe J.
[215] Cf. *Re Hooper and Grass' Contract* [1949] V.R. 269.
[216] See, e.g. *Nixon v Furphy* (1925) 25 N.S.W.(S.R.) 151; *Re Hooper* [1949] V.R. 269. Cf. *Knutson v Bourkes Syndicate* [1941] S.C.R. 419.
[217] *Re Hooper* [1949] V.R. 269 at 272 per Fullagar J.

[vendor]".[218] It is true that the equitable title to land had passed to the purchaser when the contract was made, so that there was also present a threat of an unauthorised interference with property as well as a threat to withhold "another's legal right". But the Australian cases suggest that the refusal to complete the contract, even though the vendor acted in good faith, may be, in some circumstances, "practical compulsion"[219] if it caused the coerced party to act as he did.

10–69   In determining whether the claimant had a choice between reasonable alternatives, it may also be significant to inquire whether the defendant has relied on contractual or statutory provisions which impose a penalty or a forfeiture of property. The problem may arise if an insurance company claims that a premium is due under a personal injury policy; the insured asserts that he is totally disabled, in which case he is not bound, under the terms of the policy, to pay a premium. But he pays under protest because he realises that if he fails to do so and he is not totally disabled the policy will lapse. This question has not yet arisen in an English reported case. But in the United States, where it frequently has, the jurisdictions are divided, some allowing and some denying recovery.[220] Possibly an English court might treat the insured's payment as having been made as a precautionary measure pending the resolution of the dispute,[221] although such a convenient interpretation would be impossible if the insurance company had refused to accept it on those terms. Then the court may have to decide whether the insured made the payment intending to close the transaction or whether a penal provision in the policy, that it would lapse if the premium was not paid promptly, led the insured to make the payment.

10–70   The decision of the High Court of Australia in *Mason*[222] suggests that the existence of a provision, providing for penalties and forfeitures, may be enough to persuade a court to find that a payment was then not made voluntarily, but under compulsion, although in *Mason* the penalty provisions were embodied in a statute rather than a contract. In *Mason* the claimant paid for a statutory licence because he knew that, if he did not do so, he could not carry on as an inter-state carrier; for the statute would impose on him severe penalties, including the seizure of his vehicles and books of account, if he attempted to work without a licence. The statute was held, in independent litigation, to be ultra vires. The High Court of Australia allowed the claimant to recover. The majority of the court held that the payments had been made under duress.[223]

---

[218] *Nixon* (1925) 25 N.S.W. (S.R.) 151 at 158 per Long Innes J. Other Australian cases include *White Rose Flour Milling Co Pty v Australian Wheat Board* (1944) 18 A.L.J.R. 324; *Carr v Gilsenan* [1946] S.R. (Qd.) 44.

[219] *Re Hooper* [1949] V.R. 269 at 272 per Fullagar J.; *Sundell* (1956) S.R. (N.S.W.) 323.

[220] Cf. *Still v Equitable Life Assurance Co*, 54 S.W.2d (1932), where recovery was allowed and which represents the majority view, with *Rossenfeld v Boston Mutual Life Insurance Co*, 110 N.E. 304 (1915).

[221] Cf. *Sebel Products Ltd v C&E Commissioners* [1949] Ch. 409. In practice payments are made under similar conditions if there is a dispute as to the liability to pay instalments under a time-charter.

[222] *Mason* (1959) 102 C.L.R. 108.

[223] Contrast *Atchison Topeka and Santa Fe Railway Co v O'Connor*, 223 U.S. 280 (1911) at 285–286 per Holmes J., and the judgments of Dixon C.J. and Kitto J. in *Mason*.

(ii) *Where C Promises to Confer a Benefit on D to Make D Perform His Obligations under a Contract*

It has been an established principle of the common law,[224] which has stood for hundreds of years, that a promise made by one contracting party to the other contracting party to fulfil his existing contractual obligation is not a promise supported by valuable consideration. The principle has been much criticised,[225] but it has been justified on the ground that it enables the court to protect one contracting party from the illegitimate demands made on him by the other. If that is its justification, it operates capriciously and may result in the court refusing to uphold a contractual variation which has been freely entered into between the parties. **10–71**

In *Williams v Roffey Bros & Nicholls (Contractors) Ltd*,[226] the Court of Appeal recognised this to be so, and enforced a promise to pay more than the promisor, a contractor, was contractually bound to pay. The promisee, his sub-contractor, was said to have conferred a benefit on the promisor, namely the performance of the existing contract, for the promisor did not have to find another sub-contractor and also avoided the payment of penalties for delay under the main contract. These distinctions are, given the precedents, hardly persuasive.[227] But the decision is to be welcomed, and the court's concern to uphold the promise is readily understandable. For there was no suggestion that the promisee had made an illegitimate threat; indeed it was the promisor who had made the offer to pay a larger sum to induce the promisee to go on with the contract. If the existing duty rule was rejected, and only Parliament or the House of Lords is free to do so, then the courts would be free to uphold a genuine variation, which is not the product of illegitimate pressure, and yet protect a contracting party from such pressure through the development of the law of duress. **10–72**

In *D&C Builders Ltd v Rees*,[228] Lord Denning M.R., possibly realising the strength of the authorities, relied on a concept more akin to that of equitable estoppel or the civilian concept of abuse of rights. But in 1965 when that case was decided economic duress was still a concept which lurked largely unrecognised in the case law. The defendant owed the claimants £482 odd for work done. The claimants pressed the defendant for months to settle the bill. The defendant's wife knew that the claimants were in financial difficulties and offered £300 in final settlement, saying that if this was not accepted nothing would be paid. The claimants accepted her cheque and gave a receipt "in completion of the account". The claimants then sued for the balance of £182 odd. The Court of Appeal held that the claimants could recover. **10–73**

Lord Denning M.R., with whose judgment Danckwerts L.J. agreed, found the solution in the equitable doctrine that a party will not be allowed to enforce his legal rights under a contract "where it would be inequitable, having regard to the **10–74**

---

[224] *Harris v Watson* (1791) Peake 102; *Stilk v Meyrick* (1809) 2 Camp. 317.

[225] Cf. Lord Blackburn's famous, if tantalising, dissent in *Foakes v Beer* (1884) 9 App. Cas. 605 at 622.

[226] *Williams v Roffey Bros & Nicholls (Contractors) Ltd* [1991] 1 Q.B. 1. Contrast *Re Selectmove Ltd* [1995] 1 W.L.R. 474.

[227] *Adam Opel GmbH v Mitras Automotive (UK) Ltd* [2007] EWHC 3481 (QB) at [41]–[42].

[228] *D&C Builders Ltd v Rees* [1966] 2 Q.B. 617, followed in *Tiney Engineering Ltd v Amods Knitting Machinery Ltd* [1986] B.T.L.C. 324; and *Ferguson v Davies* [1997] 1 All E.R. 315. Cf. *Ormes v Beadel* (1860) 2 Giff. 166; 66 E.R. 70; reversed (1860) 2 De G.F. & J. 333; 45 E.R. 649.

dealings which have taken place between the parties",[229] to do so. The defendant's wife was:

> "putting undue pressure on the creditor. She was making a threat to break the contract (by paying nothing) and she was doing it so as to compel the creditor to do what he was unwilling to do."[230]

Winn L.J. decided the case on the more orthodox ground that the accord was not binding in law, for it was neither under seal nor supported by consideration.[231]

10–75   *Pao On v Lau Yiu Long*[232] suggests that the courts may be unwilling to accept Lord Denning M.R.'s flexible and unorthodox principle. For in that case where the court found that there was no duress, the Privy Council rejected the argument that public policy may:

> "invalidate the consideration if there has been a threat to repudiate a pre-existing contractual obligation or an unfair use of a dominating bargaining position . . . Where businessmen are negotiating at arms' length it is unnecessary for the achievement of justice, and unhelpful in the development of the law, to invoke such a rule of public policy."[233]

Businessmen should be held to their bargains in the absence of fraud, mistake or duress. The uncertainty inherent in the adoption of a defence of public policy was said to be most undesirable. Moreover, to accept that the consideration was illegal, as being against public policy, would "create unacceptable anomaly"; "[it] would be strange if conduct less than duress could render a contract void, whereas duress does no more than render a contract voidable."[234]

10–76   In other situations, however, D may give fresh consideration for C's agreement to vary the contract. For example, C and D agree to cancel their original contract and to release each other from their executory obligations under it. Do their mutual promises supply the necessary consideration for the variation? While a genuine variation of contractual terms will undoubtedly be upheld, a variation which is induced simply by one party's claim to an extra payment or by his threat not to perform the contract may be entered into under pressure which amounts in law to duress. It is then voidable at the election of the injured party.

10–77   It is not always easy to determine whether a person willingly agreed to a variation supported by fresh consideration or whether that variation was the product of illegitimate pressure. Certainly it is not conclusive that a party provides "some purely nominal but legally sufficient consideration".[235] But, as

---

[229] *D&C Builders* [1966] 2 Q.B. 617 at 624, quoting Lord Cairns in *Hughes v The Metropolitan Railway Co* (1877) 2 App. Cas. 439 at 448.
[230] *D&C Builders* [1966] 2 Q.B. 617 at 625.
[231] *D&C Builders* [1966] 2 Q.B. 617 at 627 and following.
[232] *Pao On* [1980] A.C. 614 [1980] A.C. 614.
[233] *Pao On* [1980] A.C. 614 at 634. But query if the parties in *D&C Builders* were negotiating "at arms' length."
[234] *Pao On* [1980] A.C. 614 at 634. Contrast *Harris v Watson* (1791) Peake 102; 170 E.R. 94 with *Stilk v Meyrick* (1809) 6 Esp. 129; 170 E.R. 851; 2 Camp. 317; 170 E.R. 1168; on this, see Lord Scarman's comments in *Pao On* at 632–633.
[235] *The Siboen and The Sibotre* [1976] 1 Lloyd's Rep. 293 at 336 per Kerr J. Contrast *The Alev* [1989] 1 Lloyd's Rep. 138 at 147 per Hobhouse J.

the history of the litigation in *Pao On*[236] illustrates, judges may disagree on whether there is any real consideration to support a variation and whether it was voluntarily entered into. The claimants agreed ("the main agreement") with a company (F.C.) to sell their shares in another company to F.C. In exchange the claimants were to receive shares in F.C. The claimants also agreed not to sell 60 per cent of these shares for a year or so, in order to prevent the market price of F.C. shares from being depressed by the claimants' sale of their shares. In consideration for that promise the defendants, who were the majority share-holders in F.C., agreed ("the subsidiary agreement") to buy back the shares at the end of the year for $2.50 a share which was their deemed value at the date of the agreement. On reflection, the claimants formed the view that the subsidiary agreement was a commercial blunder since they anticipated that the price of an F.C. share would be more than $2.50 in a year's time. So, they refused to complete the main agreement unless and until the subsidiary agreement was varied so as to guarantee them, by way of indemnity, the price of $2.50 if the market price was less than that figure. The defendants yielded. They were not prepared to tolerate the delay which would follow if they sued for specific performance, although they were advised that the claimants had no defence to such a claim; and they were afraid that the public would lose confidence in F.C. if the news broke that the claimants had refused to complete the main agreement. Moreover, they thought that the risk which they were now required to bear was more academic than real since everyone expected F.C. shares to continue to rise over the year. In fact they did not; and at the end of the year F.C. shares had fallen to 36 cents. The claimants sued on the subsidiary agreement as varied. The defendants contended that neither the original subsidiary agreement nor the subsidiary agreement as varied had any legal effect.

The Privy Council, reversing the Hong Kong Court of Appeal, held that the **10–78** subsidiary agreement as varied was enforceable. Lord Scarman described the defendants' argument as "remarkable". If it were accepted it would mean that the claimants, having accepted, at the defendants' request, restrictions on their power to sell F.C. shares, would have not been safeguarded in the event of a fall in the market. "If the law really compels such a conclusion, one may be forgiven for thinking that the time has come to reconsider it."[237] The law did not compel such a conclusion. There was valuable consideration to support the subsidiary agree-ment as varied; it was not past consideration. The defendants' promise of an indemnity was not independent of the claimants' antecedent promise to F.C. to sell the shares for a year or so.[238] Extrinsic evidence was admissible to show that the real consideration for the defendants' promise was the claimants' promise to the defendants to complete their contract with F.C., and that consideration was valuable in law.[239] Moreover the claimants' threats did not amount to economic duress. There was commercial pressure but no improper coercion. As the trial judge had found,[240] the defendants "considered the matter thoroughly, chose to

---

[236] *Pao On* [1980] A.C. 614.
[237] *Pao On* [1980] A.C. 614 at 628.
[238] *Lampleigh v Braithwaite* (1615) Hobart 105, 80 E.R. 255; *Re Casey's Patents* [1892] 1 Ch. 104 at 115–116 per Bowen L.J.
[239] A promise by C to D to carry out his contract with T is given for valuable consideration: *New Zealand Shipping Co Ltd v A.M. Satterthwaite & Co Ltd (The Eurymedon)* [1975] A.C. 154 (PC).
[240] *Pao On* [1980] A.C. 614 at 634–635.

avoid litigation, and formed the opinion that the risk in giving the guarantee was more apparent than real".[241]

10-79 Here is yet another case[242] where economic duress was not found to exist even though the claimants must have known that they could not have resisted an action on the main agreement if they refused to complete. Unlike the Hong Kong Court of Appeal, the Privy Council was not prepared to strike down a subsidiary agreement which was commercially reasonable, and which formed part of a bargain which had been made for the defendants' benefit.

(iii) *Where C Confers a Benefit on D because D Threatens to Interfere with C's Business Relations with T*

10-80 If C confers a benefit on D because D threatens[243] to persuade T to break his contract with C, that threat should, in our view, be characterised as an illegitimate act and amount in law to duress, even if the defendant's conduct is not tortious.[244] Moreover it should be irrelevant that D thought he was justified in so acting.

(iv) *Where C Confers a Benefit on, or Contracts with, D because of D's Threat that He Will Not Contract with Him in the Future or that He Will Exercise Some Legal Privilege to C's Detriment*

10-81 A person who obtains a benefit from another by threatening not to contract with him in the future is generally not liable to restore that benefit. His threat is not illegitimate. As a general rule, he may contract with whom he pleases and upon what terms he pleases; it cannot be said that the benefit has been obtained through a wrongful act. Consequently if the claimant enters into a contract with the defendant because "there was no one else with whom he could contract for the supply of the particular commodity he required," he cannot escape its provisions.[245] As Singleton L.J. said in *Eric Gnapp Ltd v Petroleum Board*,[246] "there is here no question of force or threat of force or fear of personal suffering or abuse of legal proceedings. None of the essential elements of duress is present".

10-82 The common law does not recognise any principle of inequality of bargaining power.[247] To do so, as Lord Scarman said in *Pao On*, would be "unhelpful because it would render the law uncertain".[248] Although, as has been seen, the fact that "the defendants have used lawful means does not mean that economic duress" has not been exercised,[249] conduct which some may regard as morally or socially unacceptable may not amount in law to duress, as *C.T.N. Cash and Carry*

---

[241] *Pao On* [1980] A.C. 614 at 635.
[242] Cf. *The Siboen and The Sibotre* [1976] 1 Lloyd's Rep. 293, discussed at para.10–66, and the facts of *Huyton* [1999] 1 Lloyd's Rep. 620.
[243] Such a threat may be implicit: *Ross Systems v Linden Deri-Delite Inc*, 173 A. 2d 258 (1961).
[244] Cf. *Ellis v Barke* (1871) 40 L.J. Ch. 603; L.R. 2 Ch. 104 and *Rookes v Barnard* [1964] A.C. 1129.
[245] *Eric Gnapp Ltd v Petroleum Board* [1949] 1 All E.R. 980 at 986 per Singleton L.J.
[246] *Eric Gnapp* [1949] 1 All E.R. 980 at 986.
[247] As suggested by Lord Denning M.R. in *Bundy* [1975] Q.B. 326 at 336.
[248] *Pao On* [1980] A.C. 614 at 634.
[249] *C.T.N. Cash and Carry* [1994] 4 All E.R. 714 at 718 per Steyn L.J.

Ltd v Gallaher Ltd demonstrates.[250] The claimant company purchased consignments of cigarettes from the defendant company, which was the sole distributor in England of many popular brands. Each sale was under a separate contract. The defendant also arranged credit facilities, which it had an absolute discretion to withdraw. The defendant mistakenly delivered a consignment of cigarettes to the claimant's warehouse in Burnley and not to Preston as requested. Subsequently, the claimant agreed to arrange for their transfer to the warehouse in Preston, but before it could do so the cigarettes were stolen. The defendant believed that the goods were at the claimant's risk, and demanded payment. The claimant paid after the defendant had made it clear that unless it did so its credit facilities would be withdrawn; to pay was the lesser of two evils. The claimant subsequently sued for the return of the money, arguing that it had been paid under economic duress.

10–83 The Court of Appeal held that the claim failed. The dispute was an arm's-length dispute between two trading companies. "The fact that the defendants were in a monopoly position cannot therefore by itself convert what is not otherwise duress into duress".[251] They were entitled to refuse to provide future credit facilities for the claimants. It was an "important" fact that the defendants thought in good faith that the goods were at the claimants' risk. Echoing Lord Scarman in the *Pao On* case, Steyn L.J. concluded that the extension of duress to embrace[252]:

> "'lawful act duress' in a commercial context in pursuit of a *bona fide* claim, would be a radical one with far reaching implications. It would introduce a substantial and considerable element of uncertainty in the commercial bargaining process. Moreover, it will often enable *bona fide* settled accounts to be reopened when parties to commercial dealings fall out".

If the claimants could have shown that when the defendants made their threat they knew that the goods were at the defendants' risk, then the claimants would surely have succeeded, for the money would then have been extorted from them, and commercial self-interest is not unbridled. But as it stands, the case illustrates the point that the courts will not interfere in the "rough and tumble of the pressures of normal commercial bargaining".[253]

10–84 Other common law jurisdictions have also reached the conclusion that a threat not to enter into a contract with another is generally not an illegitimate act. In the Australian case of *Smith v William Charlick Ltd*[254] the Australian Wheat Harvest Board sold and delivered wheat to respondents, some at 5s. and some at 6s. 6d. per bushel. Having found at a later date that the respondents had a large amount

[250] *C.T.N. Cash and Carry* [1994] 4 All E.R. 714.
[251] *C.T.N. Cash and Carry* [1994] 4 All E.R. 714 at 717 per Steyn L.J.
[252] *C.T.N. Cash and Carry* [1994] 4 All E.R. 714 at 719. Cf. *G.M.A.C. Commercial Credit Ltd v Dearden* Unreported, May 28, 2002, at [15].
[253] *D.S.N.D. Subsea Ltd v Petroleum Geo-Services ASA* [2000] B.L.R. 530 at [131] per Dyson J. Cf. *Leyland Daf Ltd v Automotive Products Plc* [1994] 1 B.C.L.R. 249–250 per Nicholls V.C.: "In general, in the absence of a contractual or statutory obligation, one person is not compelled to trade with another. He cannot be forced to supply goods to someone else if he does not wish to do so."
[254] *Smith v William Charlick Ltd* (1924) 34 C.L.R. 38. Cf. *Paul v Wheat Commission* [1937] A.C. 139 (where the restitutionary claim was statute barred).

of this wheat still in their possession, it demanded from them a further sum of money, calling it a surcharge.

> "The demand was made, admittedly, not by reason of any legal obligation, but on the ground that, as the controlled price of flour was increased in correspondence with the higher price of wheat, the wheat-growers were morally entitled to the advanced price, inasmuch as the wheat had originally been sold for weekly requirements only, and the actual retention of wheat or flour proved overstatement of requirements at the time."[255]

The Board threatened not to do any further business with the respondents unless the demand was met. Having paid £1,952 under protest, the respondents sued for its recovery. The High Court of Australia dismissed their claim. There was no mistake and no wrongful threat. The payment was made with:

> "full knowledge of all material facts . . . It was paid, not in order to have that done which the Board was legally bound to do, but in order to induce the Board to do that which it was under no legal obligation to do."[256]

The respondents had simply chosen to pay a "further sum for wheat already sold to them rather than to be shut out from further trade with the mandatary of the owners of wheat."[257]

10–85 In contrast, in the US the *Restatement of Contracts 2d*[258] states that in exceptional circumstances a threat not to contract may amount to duress. For example, A intentionally misleads B into thinking that he will deliver goods at the "usual price," as he has done in the past. B does not attempt to buy them elsewhere. A then refuses to deliver unless B pays a price greatly in excess of the price usually charged. B has urgent need of the goods and agrees to pay the excess.

> "If the court concludes that the effectiveness of A's threat in inducing B to make the contract was significantly increased by A's prior unfair dealing, A's threat is improper and the contract is voidable by B."

Abuse of a long-standing commercial relationship may possibly be characterised as an illegitimate or wrongful act.

10–86 Whether a threat to do what one is entitled to do is improper depends on the nature of the threat. So, it has been held that a party may properly threaten another that his membership of a trade association will be terminated unless a fine is paid.[259] But other threats to exercise a privilege may amount in law to blackmail[260]; and any criminal threat should be illegitimate for the purpose of the law of unjust enrichment.[261] Indeed, a threat may not amount in law to blackmail

---

[255] *Charlick* (1924) 34 C.L.R. 38 at 51–52 per Isaacs J.
[256] *Charlick* (1924) 34 C.L.R. 38 at 51 per Knox C.J.
[257] *Charlick* (1924) 34 C.L.R. 38 at 70 per Starke J.
[258] *Restatement of Contracts* 176, illustration 13. There is some support for this principle in the cases. The Reporter collects the cases in his note, at pp.489–490.
[259] Cf. *Hardie and Lane Ltd v Chilton* [1928] 2 K.B. 306.
[260] Theft Act 1968 s.21.
[261] Cf. *The Universe Sentinel* [1983] 1 A.C. 366 at 401 per Lord Scarman.

but may nevertheless amount in law to duress because it is made for an illegitimate purpose. In the New Jersey case of *Wolf v Marlton Corp*,[262] the purchasers, having contracted to buy a house, demanded the return of their deposit, accompanying the demand with a threat that otherwise they would resell the property to a "purchaser who would be undesirable in our tract, and that the [vendors] would not be happy with the results". The Superior Court of New Jersey held that the threat amounted in law to duress, in that it involved an abuse of legal remedies, and was wrongful in a moral sense. The threat was malicious and unconscionable and "fundamental fairness requires the conclusion that his conduct in making this threat be deemed 'wrongful'".[263] The doctrine of abuse of rights is not known to the English common law, and the defendant's threat may not be tortious in England. Nevertheless an English court may conclude that such a threat is illegitimate, and that the deposit may be retained by the vendor.[264]

(c) *Conclusions*

English courts now recognise that in certain circumstances commercial pressure **10–87** may constitute duress. The nature of the threat is critical. A threat of unlawful action should always be illegitimate, whatever the nature of the demand.[265] So, a threat to commit a crime or a tort should be an illegitimate (or wrongful) threat.

A person puts commercial pressure on another, by threatening not to perform **10–88** an existing contractual obligation, or by threatening not to enter into a contract with the other person except on certain terms. Whether that threat amounts to duress depends on a number of factors.[266]

First, a threat which a person knows he is not entitled in law to make, for **10–89** example, consciously refusing to perform his side of a bargain, will normally be characterised as illegitimate. But whether it is found as a fact to have been "a significant cause" which induced the threatened person to confer a benefit upon the threatener may depend on a number of factors: the existence of a vigorous protest; the absence of independent advice; (possibly) knowledge of the other party's financial or personal circumstances; prompt repudiation of the transaction as soon as the pressure of the threat is removed. The courts are also required to ask whether the threatened person had an adequate, alternative legal or equitable remedy, although this has not proved in practice a formidable hurdle.

As the law now stands, it appears that an English court may not be ready to **10–90** accept as legitimate a threat which was made in the belief that it was commercially reasonable for the threatener to make a new demand (for example, to vary the terms of an existing contract).[267]

Secondly, a person makes a threat not to perform his side of the bargain, **10–91** believing that he is entitled in law not to do so. The other party gives in and makes an additional payment because he does not want to contest that honest

---

[262] *Wolf v Marlton Corp* 154 A. 2d 625 (1959).
[263] *Wolf* 154 A. 2d 625 (1959) at 630 per Freund J.A.D.
[264] See para.10–03.
[265] See para.10–03.
[266] See para.10–58 and following.
[267] Cf. *Sundell* (1956) 856 S.R. (N.S.W.) 323.

claim; he cannot then obtain restitution. But a court may conclude that a threat is illegitimate even if it was made in the honest belief that the person was entitled to make it.[268] For the other party may have given in because of that threat and not because he wished to enter into a compromise; whether it is found *as a fact* that the threat was coercive may depend on the presence of factors such as those outlined in the previous sub-paragraph.

10–92   Thirdly, special problems are presented if the consequence of C's threat not to perform a contract or pay a debt was simply the variation of the terms of an existing contract or debt. If D's promise to confer an additional benefit on C was not supported by fresh consideration, then C will not be able to enforce that promise.[269] Even if it was, the contract, as varied, may be voidable because a court may conclude that C's threat not to perform his side of the bargain was illegitimate and wrongful.[270] Whether a court will conclude that the threat was in fact coercive may depend on the presence of such factors as those outlined above.

10–93   Fourthly, as a general principle, it is legitimate for a person to take advantage of his position of economic strength to force a hard bargain on another. English courts have refused to rewrite contracts between the strong and the weak although by statute they now have power to do so in certain circumstances. Statutory jurisdiction apart, it has long been recognised that there may be exceptional circumstances where a contract may be set aside because its terms are unconscionable. We discuss this elsewhere.[271] It is sufficient here to emphasise that English courts have wisely not accepted any general principle that a threat not to contract with another, except on certain terms, may amount in law to duress.[272]

---

[268] *Huyton* [1999] 1 Lloyd's Rep. 620.
[269] See paras 10–71—10–79. But he may be able to do so if there is no finding that the promisee made an illegitimate threat; see para.10–71.
[270] Cf. *D&C Builders* [1966] 2 Q.B. 617.
[271] See paras 11–57—11–68.
[272] *National Westminster Bank Plc v Morgan* [1985] A.C. 686.

CHAPTER 11

UNDUE INFLUENCE AND UNCONSCIONABLE BARGAINS

1. INTRODUCTION

The Court of Chancery was always conscious that the common law conception **11–01**
of duress was so narrow that injustice could result. A person could be influenced
by subtle methods that lay outside the scope of duress. For example, he could be
persuaded by one standing in an intimate relationship with him to pursue a course
of conduct to his detriment and to the other's advantage. For this reason, the
Chancellor formulated the equitable doctrine of undue influence. The credit for
its formulation is usually given to Lord Hardwicke,[1] though its origins may be
older.[2]

Undue influence is an expression of "ambiguous purport".[3] Probate as well as **11–02**
Chancery judges have often used it, but identity of language conceals here a
diversity of meaning. The probate doctrine is distinct from equity's, and more
circumscribed.[4] In probate law, the undue influence must:

> "amount to force and coercion destroying free agency—it must not be the influence of
> affection and attachment—it must not be the mere desire of gratifying the wishes of
> another; for that would be a very strong ground in support of a testamentary act."[5]

---

[1] In *Morris v Burroughs* (1737) 1 Atk. 398; 26 E.R. 253.
[2] *Blunden & Hester v Barker* (1720) 1 P. Wms. 634 at 639–640; 24 E.R. 548 at 550 per Lord
Macclesfield; see W. Ashburner, *Principles of Equity* (London: Butterworth & Co, 1902),
pp.303–305.
[3] *Bullock v Lloyds Bank Ltd* [1955] Ch. 317 at 324 per Vaisey J.
[4] *Boyse v Rossborough* (1857) 6 H.L.C. 2 at 48–49; 10 E.R. 1192 at 1212 per Lord Cranworth L.C.;
Hindson v Weatherill (1854) 5 De G.M. & G. 301; 43 E.R. 886; *Parfitt v Lawless* (1872) L.R. 2 P.
& D. 462; *Baudains v Richardson* [1906] A.C. 169; *Craig v Lamoureux* [1920] A.C. 349; *Winter v
Crichton* (1991) 23 N.S.W.L.R. 116. Whether testators ought to be given the protection of the
equitable rules is discussed in R. Kerridge, "Wills Made in Suspicious Circumstances: The Problem
of the Vulnerable Testator" (2000) 59 C.L.J. 310, and P. Ridge, "Equitable Undue Influence and
Wills" (2004) 120 L.Q.R. 617.
[5] *Williams v Goude* (1828) 1 Hag. Ecc. 577 at 581; 162 E.R. 682 at 685 per Sir John Nicholl; *Hall
v Hall* (1865–69) L.R. 1 P. & D. 481 at 481 per Sir J.P. Wilde, and *Wingrove v Wingrove* (1885) 1
P.D. 81 at 82 per Sir James Hannen, both followed in *Carapeto v Good* [2002] EWHC 640 (Ch) at
[124]–[125] per Rimer J.; *Re Edwards (Deceased)* [2007] EWHC 1119 (Ch); [2007] W.T.L.R. 1387
at [47] per Lewison J. If the person who writes or prepares a will himself takes a benefit under it, then
even if no undue influence is alleged, the court must still be satisfied that the testator knew and
approved the contents of the will before executing it, and it will not rely on the signature of the
testator alone for that purpose: *Barry v Butlin* (1838) 2 Moo. P.C. 480 at 482–483; 12 E.R. 1089 at
1091 per Parke B; *Wintle v Nye* [1959] 1 W.L.R. 284 at 291 per Viscount Simonds. Some of the older
cases say that the onus on a person who takes a benefit under a will which he has been instrumental
in preparing or obtaining is "the onus of showing the righteousness of the transaction": e.g. *Fulton
v Andrew* (1875) L.R. 7 H.L. 448 at 471 per Lord Hatherley. But in *Fuller v Strum* [2001] EWCA
Civ 1879; [2002] 1 W.L.R. 1097 at [78], Longmore L.J. held that this is not "a separate onus from
that of dispelling the suspicion the testator may not have known or may not have approved the

11–03   The equitable doctrine, which is limited to the setting aside of transactions inter vivos, is wider than this. We discuss it in Part B, looking in turn at the nature of the doctrine, and the means by which a claimant can prove that there has been undue influence.

11–04   In Part C we consider the courts' jurisdiction to set aside unconscionable bargains. The basis of equity's intervention in these cases resembles the basis on which relief is granted in cases of undue influence, but the extent to which the two doctrines overlap depends on the nature of undue influence, a contested issue that we examine below.[6]

2. UNDUE INFLUENCE

(a) The Nature of the Doctrine

(i) Only One Doctrine

11–05   The leading case on undue influence is *Royal Bank of Scotland Plc v Etridge (No.2)*.[7] Prior to the House of Lords' decision in that case, the view had developed that there were two forms of undue influence: "actual undue influence", which comprised overt acts of coercion or improper pressure, and "presumed undue influence", which comprised unfair advantage taken of influence exercised by one party over another by reason of their relationship. Because these had come to be thought of as substantively different kinds of undue influence, the practice had grown up of pleading actual and presumed undue influence as alternative causes of action, and on occasion the courts had held that one type of undue influence had taken place but not the other.

11–06   In *Etridge*, the House of Lords held that this was a misunderstanding. They held that there is only one type of undue influence. There are two different ways of proving that undue influence has occurred, but what is being proved in either case is the same. "Actual undue influence" should therefore be seen as undue influence that is directly proved without the need to rely on presumptions, and "presumed undue influence" should be seen as undue influence that is proved with the help of presumptions. Actual and presumed undue influence are not mutually exclusive types of undue influence, nor are they alternatives, and so it would be inconsistent for a court to hold that a claimant had failed to establish actual undue influence, but that his claim should succeed because he had established presumed undue influence.[8]

---

contents of the will; it is merely a more grandiloquent way of expressing exactly the same concept."

[6] See paras 11–05—11–30, and especially para.11–28.

[7] *Royal Bank of Scotland Plc v Etridge (No.2)* [2001] UKHL 44; [2002] 2 A.C. 773.

[8] *Etridge* [2001] UKHL 44; [2002] 2 A.C. 773 at [210]–[228] per Lord Scott. See too Lord Clyde's comment at [92] that proceeding in this way is to confuse definition and proof. Cf. *Clarke v Marlborough Fine Art (London) Ltd (Amendments)* [2002] 1 W.L.R. 1731: if mutually inconsistent allegations of fact are made to support a case of actual undue influence, on the one hand, and a case of presumed undue influence, on the other, then the claimant cannot make a unified claim, but may make alternative claims; and note *Thompson v Foy* [2009] EWHC 1076 (Ch); [2010] 1 P. & C.R. 16 at [101] per Lewison J.: "it is highly unlikely on the facts that the court would ever be justified in finding that undue influence consisted both of coercion and abuse of trust and confidence. People do not usually trust those who coerce them."

This reconceptualisation of the doctrine of undue influence means that cases **11–07** decided prior to *Etridge* must be treated with caution when identifying the underlying nature of the doctrine. Judicial statements on this subject should be disregarded if they were explicitly or implicitly premised on the view that there are different types of undue influence, and were meant to describe only one type or the other. Following *Etridge*, any explanation of the doctrine must account for all of it: it must account for actual and presumed undue influence together, because in substance they are the same thing. There is no longer any scope for analyses of the law which would sub-divide undue influence into actual undue influence, the point of which is to prevent unconscientious exploitation by defendants, and presumed undue influence, the point of which is to protect vulnerable claimants. The Court of Appeal held this to be the law in *Etridge*,[9] but on appeal the House of Lords expressly held that this was incorrect.

(ii) *Understanding the Doctrine*

How, then, should we understand the doctrine? Since *Etridge*, different answers **11–08** have been given to this question. On several occasions the Court of Appeal has held that the primary focus of the doctrine is on the impairment of the claimant's intention. In *Pesticcio v Huet*, for example, Mummery L.J. emphasised that[10]:

> "Although undue influence is sometimes described as an 'equitable wrong' or even as a species of equitable fraud, the basis of the court's intervention is not the commission of a dishonest or wrongful act by the defendant, but that, as a matter of public policy, the presumed influence arising from the relationship of trust and confidence should not operate to the disadvantage of the victim, if the transaction is not satisfactorily explained by ordinary motives . . . The court scrutinises the circumstances in which the transaction, under which benefits were conferred on the recipient, took place and the nature of the continuing relationship between the parties, rather than any specific act or conduct on the part of the recipient. A transaction may be set aside by the court, even though the actions and conduct of the person who benefits from it could not be criticized as wrongful."

In other cases, however, the courts have conceptualised undue influence **11–09** differently, as a doctrine that responds to the defendant's unconscientious conduct. This is now the dominant judicial view. An example is Lord Nicholls' statement in *Etridge* that[11]:

---

[9] *Etridge* [1998] 4 All E.R. 705 at 711–712 per curiam. The same argument had previously been made in P. Birks and N.Y. Chin, "On the Nature of Undue Influence" in J. Beatson and D. Friedmann (eds), *Good Faith and Fault in Contract Law* (Oxford: Clarendon Press, 1994), 57.

[10] *Pesticcio v Huet* [2004] EWCA Civ 372 at [20]; discussed at para.11–15. See too *Hammond v Osborn* [2002] EWCA Civ 885; [2002] W.T.L.R. 1125 at [32] per Sir Martin Nourse, discussed at para.11–14; *Jennings v Cairns* [2003] EWCA Civ 1935; [2004] W.T.L.R. 361 at [40] per Arden L.J.; *Macklin v Dowsett* [2004] EWCA Civ 904; [2004] 2 E.G.L.R. 75 at [10] per Auld L.J.; *Hackett v Crown Prosecution Service* [2011] EWHC 1170 (Admin) at [64] per Silber J. Earlier days: *Inche Noriah v Bin Omar* [1929] A.C. 127 at 135 per Lord Hailsham; and note *Bridgeman v Green* (1757) Wilm. 58; 97 E.R. 22 and the other three-party cases cited at fn.32, discussed at paras 11–19—11–20.

[11] *Etridge* [2001] UKHL 44; [2002] 2 A.C. 773 at [6]–[7]. Lord Hobhouse also considered undue influence to be "an equitable wrong committed by the dominant party against the other which makes it unconscionable for the dominant party to enforce his legal rights": at [103].

"The objective [of the doctrine] is to ensure that the influence of one person over another is not abused. In everyday life people constantly seek to . . . persuade those with whom they are dealing to enter into transactions, whether great or small. The law has set limits to the means properly employable for this purpose. . . . If the intention was produced by an unacceptable means, the law will not permit the transaction to stand. The means used is regarded as an exercise of improper or 'undue' influence, and hence unacceptable."

Likewise, in *National Commercial Bank (Jamaica) Ltd v Hew*, a decision of the Privy Council, Lord Millett said that[12]:

"However great the influence which one person may be able to wield over another equity does not intervene unless that influence has been abused. Equity does not save people from the consequences of their own folly; it acts to save them from being victimised by other people. . . . it must be shown that the ascendant party has unfairly exploited the influence he is shown or presumed to possess over the vulnerable party. . . . Unless the ascendant party has exploited his influence to obtain some unfair advantage from the vulnerable party there is no ground for equity to intervene."

11–10   A similar diversity of opinion can be found in the academic literature. In previous editions of this work, stress was laid on the unconscientious nature of the defendant's conduct,[13] and a lead was taken from Lindley L.J.'s statement in *Allcard v Skinner* that the purpose of the doctrine is "to protect people from being forced, tricked or misled in any way by others into parting with their property."[14] This view of the doctrine identifies the prevention of exploitation as its core rationale. Another view, taken, for instance, by James Edelman and Elise Bant,[15] holds that what matters is not whether the defendant has behaved badly, but whether the claimant has been exposed to too much influence to exercise an independent judgment. Scholars who subscribe to this view are also apt to take

---

[12] *National Commercial Bank (Jamaica) Ltd v Hew* [2003] UKPC 51 at [28]–[33], discussed at para.11–16. See too *UCB Corporate Services Ltd v Williams* [2002] EWCA Civ 555; [2003] 1 P. & C.R. 12 at [86] per Jonathan Parker L.J., discussed at paras 11–23——11–24; *R. v Att Gen for England and Wales* [2003] UKPC 22; [2003] E.M.L.R. 24 at [21] per Lord Hoffmann, discussed at para.11–16; *Samuel v Wadlow* [2007] EWCA Civ 155 at [40] per Toulson L.J.; *Hewett v First Plus Financial Group Plc* [2010] EWCA Civ 312; [2010] 2 F.L.R. 177 at [34] per Briggs J.; *Royal Bank of Scotland Plc v Chandra* [2011] EWCA Civ 192 at [27]–[28] per Patten L.J., discussed at paras 11–17——11–18. See too Sir K. Lewison, "Under the Influence" [2011] R.L.R.I., p.3: "we are concerned . . . not with folly but with trickery, tyranny and fraud." Cf. *Louth v Diprose* (1992) 175 C.L.R. 621 at 627 per Brennan J.; *Contractors Bonding Ltd v Snee* [1992] 2 N.Z.L.R. 157 at 165 per Richardson J.; approved in *Hogan v Commercial Factors Ltd* [2006] 3 N.Z.L.R. 618 (NZCA); *Li Sau Ying v Bank of China (Hong Kong)* [2004] HKCFA 80; [2005] 1 H.K.L.R.D. 106 at [34] per Lord Scott. Earlier days: *Bank of Montreal v Stuart* [1911] A.C. 120 at 137 per Lord Macnaghten; *Poosathurai v Kannappa Chettiar* (1919) L.R. 47 I.A. 1 at 3 per Lord Shaw; *Re Craig (Deceased)* [1971] Ch. 95 at 104 per Ungoed-Thomas J.; *Re Brocklehurst* [1978] Ch. 14 at 42 per Bridge L.J.; *National Westminster Bank Plc v Morgan* [1985] A.C. 686 at 705–706 per Lord Scarman; *Barclays Bank Plc v O'Brien* [1994] A.C. 180 at 189 per Lord Browne-Wilkinson; *Dunbar Bank Plc v Nadeem* [1998] 3 All E.R. 876 at 883–884 per Millett L.J.

[13] G. Jones, *Goff & Jones: The Law of Restitution*, 7th edn (London: Sweet & Maxwell, 2006), Ch.11. See too W.H.D. Winder, "Undue Influence and Coercion" (1939–40) 3 M.L.R. 97; J. Cartwright, *Unequal Bargaining* (Oxford: OUP, 1991), pp.195–196.

[14] *Allcard v Skinner* (1887) 36 Ch. D. 145 at 183.

[15] J. Edelman and E. Bant, *Unjust Enrichment in Australia* (Melbourne: OUP, 2006), Ch.10. See too Birks and Chin, "On the Nature of Undue Influence"; P. Birks, "Undue Influence as Wrongful Exploitation" (2004) 120 L.Q.R. 35.

Allcard as a starting-point, but to highlight Cotton L.J.'s statement in that case, that relief for undue influence is not given:

> "on the ground that any wrongful act has in fact been committed by the donee, but on the ground of public policy, and to prevent the relations which existed between the parties and the influence arising therefrom being abused."[16]

A third, "relational", view, advocated by Mindy Chen-Wishart,[17] holds that it **11–11** misses the point to focus exclusively on the probity of the defendant's conduct, or on the claimant's ability to make independent decisions, as these are inter-dependent issues and neither can sensibly be understood in isolation. Rick Bigwood has also tried to steer a middle course between claimant- and defendant-sided explanations, arguing that undue influence is fault-based, but that the degree of fault sufficient to bring the doctrine into play is not deliberate exploitation but negligent failure to take reasonable precautions against the risk of foreseeable detriment to the claimant, where the parties were bargaining under conditions that the defendant knew would make exploitation possible. On this view, undue influence is a kind of passive wrongdoing.[18]

(iii) *Practical Implications*

It is to be hoped that the Supreme Court will soon decisively settle which of these **11–12** explanations is correct, as there are several reasons why the answer to this question can significantly affect the outcome of litigation.

First, and most obviously, a claimant seeking to establish that undue influence **11–13** has taken place needs to know whether it suffices to show that his relationship with the defendant disabled him from exercising a fully independent judgment, or whether he must also prove that the defendant was at fault, and if so, then to what extent.

Hammond v Osborn[19] holds that there is no need to prove fault against the **11–14** defendant. An elderly bachelor made a gift of £300,000 to his neighbour who had looked after him for over a year. He had come to repose much trust and confidence in her, and the sum represented around 90 per cent of his free assets. The burden of disproving undue influence therefore shifted onto the neighbour and she failed to discharge it.[20] The old man's decision to make the gift had been made without recourse to independent legal advice, and no other evidence was led to satisfy the court that he had made this decision freely and independently of her influence. Sir Martin Nourse questioned the neighbour's behaviour, but

---

[16] *Allcard* (1887) 36 Ch. D. 145 at 171. For discussion of the social and religious background of this case, and of the appellate judges' varying attitudes towards religion that fed into their different statements of the governing legal principle, see C. Smith, *"Allcard v Skinner* (1887)" in C. Mitchell and P. Mitchell (eds), *Landmark Cases in the Law of Restitution* (Oxford: Hart, 2006), 183.

[17] M. Chen-Wishart, "Undue Influence: Beyond Impaired Consent and Wrongdoing towards a Relational Analysis" in A. Burrows and Lord Rodger (eds), *Mapping the Law* (Oxford: OUP, 2006), 210; M. Chen-Wishart, "Undue Influence: Vindicating Relationships of Influence" [2006] C.L.P. 231.

[18] R. Bigwood, "Contracts by Unfair Advantage: From Exploitation to Transactional Neglect" (2005) 25 O.J.L.S. 65.

[19] *Hammond v Osborn* [2002] EWCA Civ 885; [2002] W.T.L.R. 1125.

[20] See paras 11–37—11–52 for discussion of the presumptions made in "presumed undue influence" cases.

would have set the gift aside even if he had thought that her "conduct was unimpeachable and that there was nothing sinister in it"[21]; Ward L.J. agreed that the gift should be set aside although he was "quite prepared to accept" that the neighbour "was not guilty of any reprehensible conduct".[22]

11–15   A similar finding was made in *Pesticcio*.[23] A man gave a house to his sister but later claimed that the gift was procured by undue influence. The trial judge held that he was a party "of significantly lower than average intelligence and understanding", that he had placed trust and confidence in his sister, and that the gift called for an explanation. On these facts, the burden of disproving undue influence shifted onto his sister, and she could not discharge this burden by showing that her brother had been advised by a solicitor, because the solicitor's advice had been negligent. On appeal, she argued that there could not have been any undue influence because she had done nothing wrong: she had acted in good faith and was not responsible for the solicitor's mistakes. This was emphatically rejected by the Court of Appeal, which held that the issue was not whether: "she could have done anything more"[24]—all that mattered was whether the nature and effect of the transaction had been fully explained to her brother; it had not been, and it made no difference whether this was through the sister's fault, because a transaction "may be set aside . . . even though the actions and conduct of the person who benefits from it could not be criticized as wrongful".[25]

11–16   These cases cannot be reconciled with others where the courts have held that there was no undue influence because the defendant was not at fault. Two decisions of the Privy Council illustrate the point. In *R v Att Gen for England and Wales*,[26] a soldier sought to resist the enforcement of a confidentiality agreement which prevented him from publishing an account of his service in the SAS. The court accepted that the Army had exercised influence over the soldier but did not accept that this had been undue. The Army had not unfairly exploited its influence when it had required him to sign the agreement as a condition of continued service in the regiment. If the contract had been hard to understand then it would have been unfair for the Army to have insisted on this without allowing him access to independent legal advice, but the contract had been easy to understand and the soldier had understood it. Again, in *Hew*,[27] a bank lent money to an elderly customer to finance a property development and the court denied that he should be able to escape liability for the debt on the ground of undue influence. The bank's officers had been in a relationship of influence with the customer but they had not exploited this to extract any special advantage that they would not have obtained in the ordinary course of commercial lending.

11–17   The Court of Appeal's decision in *Royal Bank of Scotland Plc v Chandra*[28] also forms part of this line of authority requiring fault by the defendant. Mrs Chandra guaranteed repayment of a loan made by a bank to a company of which she and her husband were the shareholders and directors. The money was needed

---

[21] *Hammond* [2002] EWCA Civ 885; [2002] W.T.L.R. 1125 at [32].
[22] *Hammond* [2002] EWCA Civ 885; [2002] W.T.L.R. 1125 at [61].
[23] *Pesticcio* [2004] EWCA Civ 372; and see the other cases cited at fn.10.
[24] *Pesticcio* [2004] EWCA Civ 372 at [22].
[25] *Pesticcio* [2004] EWCA Civ 372 at [20].
[26] *R v Att Gen for England and Wales* [2003] UKPC 22; [2003] E.M.L.R. 24
[27] *Hew* [2003] UKPC 51.
[28] *Royal Bank of Scotland Plc v Chandra* [2011] EWCA Civ 192.

to cover cost overruns on a hotel development project, but in spite of the extra funds the project ran into problems and the hotel was sold at a loss. Mrs Chandra resisted payment under the guarantee on the grounds of undue influence and misrepresentation, claiming that her husband had inaccurately told her that the project would be brought to a profitable conclusion with the extra money. The trial judge held that Mr Chandra had honestly believed this to be true, although he might have been negligent in forming this view. The Court of Appeal held that on these facts Mr Chandra had not unduly influenced his wife; even if he had been negligent, he had acted in good faith and his behaviour did not amount to the "conscious deception" or "abuse of confidence" that was required.[29]

Patten L.J. observed that the courts can also set aside guarantees given by **11–18** wives on the ground that they have been procured by misrepresentations, including innocent misrepresentations, by their husbands. Comparing this with the courts' jurisdiction to rescind transactions on the ground of undue influence, he said[30]:

> "The two are not the same, although in certain cases they may overlap. Undue influence is concerned with the abuse of a relationship of trust and confidence by the husband exercising control over the will of the wife in order to procure her consent to the guarantee. In a case of misrepresentation that consent has been procured not by the exercise of some form of pressure or domination but by the making of a false statement which the wife . . . has relied upon."

On the facts, however, there was no misrepresentation on which Mrs Chandra could rely to have the guarantee set aside[31]:

> "Mr Chandra did not give his wife an inaccurate explanation of the transaction. The most he can be accused of is an over-optimistic assessment of the chances of a future overspend. This might be said to give rise to a claim for a breach of a duty of care but that is not relied upon in this case and does not . . . amount to undue influence."

The second reason why it matters whether fault is a necessary component of **11–19** undue influence is that this can affect the liability of defendants who receive benefits from claimants who have been unduly influenced by a third party. An old line of cases holds that a defendant who receives such a gift must make restitution of the benefit whether or not he had actual knowledge or notice of the undue influence. These authorities cannot be reconciled with the view that fault must be proved against defendants; the passive receipt of a gift in good faith is not unconscientious conduct.

An example is *Bridgeman v Green*.[32] The plaintiff's servant took advantage of **11–20** his "weak understanding", and caused him to make substantial gifts both to the

---

[29] *Chandra* [2011] EWCA Civ 192 at [27]–[28]. Cf. *Hewett* [2010] EWCA Civ 312; [2010] 2 F.L.R. 177 (husband's deliberate concealment of affair was sufficient abuse of wife's confidence to constitute undue influence).

[30] *Chandra* [2011] EWCA Civ 192 at [32].

[31] *Chandra* [2011] EWCA Civ 192 at [39].

[32] *Bridgeman v Green* (1757) Wilm. 58; 97 E.R. 22; followed in *Huguenin v Baseley* (1807) 14 Ves. Jun. 273 at 288–289; 33 E.R. 526 at 533 per Lord Eldon L.C.; and *Cooke v Lamotte* (1851) 15 Beav. 234 at 250; 51 E.R. 527 at 534 per Sir John Romilly M.R. See too *Morley v Loughnan* [1893] 1 Ch. 736; *Liles v Terry* [1895] 2 Q.B. 679; *Barron v Willis* [1900] 2 Ch. 121; and cf. *Bullock v Lloyds Bank Ltd* [1955] Ch. 317 (settlement for father and brother procured by father's undue influence; set aside against both).

servant and to his relatives and friends. Lord Commissioner Wilmot held that these friends and relations were strictly liable to make restitution of the benefits they had received, observing that[33]:

> "There is no pretence that Green's brother, or his wife, was party to any imposition, or had any due or undue influence over the plaintiff; but does it follow from thence, that they must keep the money? No: whoever receives it, must take it tainted and infected with the undue influence and imposition of the person procuring the gift; his partitioning and cantoning it out amongst his relations and friends, will not purify the gift, and protect it against the equity of the person imposed upon. Let the hand receiving it be ever so chaste, yet if it comes through a corrupt polluted channel, the obligation of restitution will follow it . . . "

11–21   This may be contrasted with *Goodchild v Bradbury*.[34] An elderly farmer made a gift of land to his great-nephew, who immediately sold it on to another man who was aware of all the facts. The Court of Appeal rescinded both transactions, and laid particular emphasis on the fact that although the purchaser had not been a conscious wrongdoer, he had taken the property with notice of the fact that the farmer and his great-nephew were in a relationship of influence, and of the fact that this relationship might be abused. Presumably the significance of these facts was that they prevented him from relying on a defence of bona fide purchase.[35]

11–22   These cases may also be compared with the House of Lords' decisions in *Barclays Bank Plc v O'Brien*[36] and *Etridge*,[37] that a bank cannot enforce a guarantee given by a wife to secure her husband's business borrowing if the guarantee was procured by undue influence, if the bank had notice of the fact that the couple were in a relationship of influence that might potentially be abused, and if the bank failed to take certain steps to satisfy itself that the wife had been independently advised.[38] These rules were overtly designed to strike a balance between the courts' wish to protect wives who place their trust in their husbands, and the policy objective of ensuring that the flow of loan capital is not reduced because the matrimonial home has become an unacceptable security for financial institutions.

11–23   A third issue that turns on the role of fault within the doctrine of undue influence is the test that should be applied to determine whether the undue influence to which the claimant was subject caused him to enter the impugned transaction. In *Bank of Credit and Commerce International SA v Aboody*, the Court of Appeal considered that[39]:

---

[33] *Bridgeman* at Wilm. 64–65; 97 E.R. 25.
[34] *Goodchild v Bradbury* [2006] EWCA Civ 1868; [2007] W.T.L.R. 463.
[35] For which see Ch.29.
[36] *Barclays Bank Plc v O'Brien* [1994] 1 A.C. 180.
[37] *Etridge* [2001] UKHL 44; [2002] 2 A.C. 773.
[38] For a summary of the steps that must be taken, see *Mahon v F.B.N. Bank (UK) Ltd* [2011] EWHC 1432 (Ch) at [52] per Judge Simon Barker QC, sitting as a deputy High Court judge; for discussion, see J. Devenney, L. Fox O'Mahony, and M. Kenny, "Standing Surety in England and Wales: The Sphinx of Procedural Protection" [2008] L.M.C.L.Q. 527; J.C. Phillips and J. O'Donovan, *The Modern Contract of Guarantee*, 2nd English edn (London: Sweet & Maxwell, 2010), paras 4–194—4–241.
[39] *Bank of Credit and Commerce International SA v Aboody* [1990] 1 Q.B. 923 at 971 per curiam.

"[A]t least in ordinary circumstances, it would not be appropriate for the court to exercise this jurisdiction [to rescind a contract for undue influence] in a case where the evidence establishes that on balance of probabilities the complainant would have entered into the transaction in any event."

In *UCB Corporate Services Ltd v Williams*,[40] however, the Court of Appeal declined to follow *Aboody* on this point, and held that although undue influence must have been "a" cause of the claimant's entering the transaction, it need not have been a "but for" cause, i.e. it is not open to the defendant to argue that the claimant would have entered the transaction anyway. Jonathan Parker L.J. considered this to follow from Lord Browne-Wilkinson's characterisation of (actual) undue influence as a species of "fraud" in *CIBC Mortgages Plc v Pitt*.[40a] In Jonathan Parker L.J.'s words[41]:

"I cannot see any reason in principle why (for example) a husband who has fraudulently procured the consent of his wife to participate in a transaction should be able, in effect, to escape the consequences of his wrongdoing by establishing that had he not acted fraudulently, and had his wife had the opportunity to make a free and informed choice, she would have acted in the same way."

Lord Browne-Wilkinson did not define "fraud" in this context, but must have **11–24** meant something wider than common law deceit, and probably meant equitable fraud, an uncertain concept beloved of Chancery lawyers that was said by Viscount Haldane L.C. in *Nocton v Lord Ashburton* to be wider than an "actual intention to cheat", because a defendant "may misconceive the extent of the obligation which a Court of Equity imposes on him" and then his "fault is that he has violated, however innocently because of his ignorance, an obligation which he must be taken by the Court to have known."[42] But the gist of Jonathan Parker L.J.'s reasoning is clear enough: the defendant has acted unconscientiously, and so a claimant-friendly causation test should be used in cases of undue influence. He did not say whether this test should be used in cases of presumed as well as actual undue influence, but this must follow from the finding in *Etridge* that the only difference between these types of case is the method by which undue influence is proved: the defendant must have behaved as badly in one class of case as in the other.

A fourth reason why the role of fault matters is that this may affect the **11–25** question whether a defendant should be able to rely on the defence of change of position. It may be that a defendant who exerts undue influence on a claimant should be denied the defence because he is a "wrongdoer" in the sense that Lord Goff employed this term in *Lipkin Gorman (A Firm) v Karpnale Ltd*.[43] Another possibility is that the defence should not be available to claims founded on undue

---

[40] *UCB Corporate Services Ltd v Williams* [2002] EWCA Civ 555; [2003] 1 P. & C.R. 12.

[40a] *CIBC Mortgages Plc v Pitt* [1984] 1 A.C. 200, quoted at para.11–36, fn.81.

[41] *Williams* [2002] EWCA Civ 555; [2003] 1 P. & C.R. 12 at [86]. This finding was subsequently assumed to be correct in *UCB Group Ltd v Hedworth (No.2)* [2003] EWCA Civ 1717; [2003] 3 F.C.R. 739 at [68] and [77] per Jonathan Parker L.J.

[42] *Nocton v Lord Ashburton* [1914] A.C. 932 at 954; followed in *Pitt v Holt* [2011] EWCA Civ 197; [2011] 3 W.L.R. 19 at [165] per Lloyd L.J. See too *Earl of Aylesford v Morris* (1873) L.R. 8 Ch. App. 484 at 490–491 per Lord Selborne L.C.; *Hart v O'Connor* [1985] A.C. 1000 at 1024 per Lord Brightman, quoted in the text to fn.139.

[43] *Lipkin Gorman (A Firm) v Karpnale Ltd* [1991] 2 A.C. 548 at 580.

influence, whether or not the defendant has behaved badly, because this would stultify the protective policies that that underpin the doctrine.[44]

11–26   A fifth issue is whether undue influence is not only a ground for rescinding contracts and a ground for restitution in the law of unjust enrichment, but also an equitable wrong, the commission of which triggers a liability to pay compensation to the injured party. In *Mahoney v Purnell*,[45] an agreement between the claimant and his son-in-law was set aside for undue influence and abuse of fiduciary relationship, rescission was impossible and an account of profits would have been valueless. The parties had operated an hotel business in a partnership that was later incorporated as a company. The claimant surrendered his 50 per cent holding in the company for £200,000, to be paid in ten annual instalments of £20,000. This did not represent the fair value of his shareholding and loan account.[46] The company subsequently sold the hotel for over £3 million. However, the company was now in liquidation, the son-in-law having invested the proceeds of the sale in an unsuccessful business venture. Consequently, rescission was held to be impossible,[47] and there was no quantifiable profit in the hands of the son-in-law. May J. held that "practical justice in this case requires an award which is akin to compensation", founded "on abuse of trust", namely, the difference in value between what the claimant surrendered and what he received.[48]

11–27   *Mahoney* has been applauded by those who consider that undue influence is focused on wrongful conduct by the defendant,[49] and deplored by those who do not.[50] The claim was founded on "abuse of trust", which May J. equated with breach of fiduciary duty. But we doubt that every incidence of undue influence is a breach of fiduciary duty per se,[51] and May J. did not decide whether undue influence by non-fiduciaries triggers liability for compensation. We also note that breach of fiduciary duty has been identified in recent years as a wrong that can trigger a liability for compensation, but that this marks a departure from the traditional conceptualisation of the fiduciary dealing rules, which were not originally understood to impose duties, breach of which led to compensatory

---

[44] See para.27–47.
[45] *Mahoney v Purnell* [1996] 3 All E.R. 61. See too *Treadwell v Martin* (1976) 67 D.L.R. (3d) 493; *Dusik v Newton* (1985) 62 B.C.L.R. 1.; and cf. *Paroz v Paroz* [2010] QSC 41 at [134]–[138] per Peter Lyons J. (equitable compensation available for unconscionable dealing). But cf. *Derksen v Pillar (No.2)* [2003] EWHC 3050 (Ch) at [38] per Hart J., quoted in fn.58.
[46] *Mahoney* [1996] 3 All E.R. 61 at 81.
[47] For discussion of the tests used to determine when counter-restitution is impossible, see paras 31–05—31–12.
[48] *Mahoney* [1996] 3 All E.R. 61 at 87–91, following *Nocton* and *O'Sullivan v Management Agency and Music Ltd* [1985] Q.B. 428 at 464–467 per Fox L.J.
[49] J.D. Heydon, "Equitable Compensation for Undue Influence" (1997) 113 L.Q.R. 113; L. Ho, "Equitable Compensation and Undue Influence" in P. Birks and F. Rose (eds), *Restitution and Equity* (London: Mansfield Press/LLP, 2000), 193. See also T. Akkouh, "Equitable Compensation Where Rescission is Impossible" (2002) 16 Tru. L.I. 151 and V.J. Vann, "Equitable Compensation Where Rescission is Impossible: A Response" (2003) 17 Tru. L.I. 66.
[50] P. Birks, "Unjust Factors and Wrongs: Pecuniary Rescission for Undue Influence" [1997] R.L.R. 72. Cf. *Agnew v Länsförsäkringsbolagens* [2001] 1 A.C. 223 at 264 per Lord Millett: "there is no 'obligation' not to exercise undue influence in order to persuade a party to enter into a contract."
[51] See para.11–30.

liability, but were rather seen as rules that disabled fiduciaries from entering certain types of transaction and rendered their attempts to do so voidable at the principals' option.[52] For the courts to hold that undue influence is an equitable wrong would constitute a similar shift of understanding.

Sixthly, and finally, the role of fault within the doctrine of undue influence may affect the relationship between the doctrine and other areas of law. For example, it has been suggested that the courts' equitable jurisdiction to rescind transactions on the ground of undue influence is sufficiently similar in its objectives and effects to their equitable jurisdiction to relieve claimants from unconscionable bargains for the two doctrines to be merged into one.[53] As we discuss below in Part C, the rules governing relief from unconscionable bargains clearly demand that the defendant must have behaved unconscientiously, but it is unclear that this is true of the rules on undue influence.[54] **11–28**

It has also been suggested that the doctrine of undue influence should be seen as part of the law preventing self-dealing by fiduciaries, affording prophylactic protection to claimants who enter particular types of transaction, regardless of whether those with whom they deal intend to exploit them.[55] The relationship between these two bodies of law was considered by Lord Browne-Wilkinson in *Pitt*, where he noted that[56]: **11–29**

> "The abuse of confidence principle is founded on considerations of general public policy, *viz.* that in order to protect those to whom fiduciaries owe duties as a class from exploitation by fiduciaries as a class, the law imposes a heavy duty on fiduciaries to show the righteousness of the transactions they enter into with those to whom they owe such duties. This principle is in sharp contrast with the view of this House in *National Westminster Bank plc v Morgan*[57] that in cases of presumed undue influence . . . the law is not based on considerations of public policy."

To this we would add that although fiduciary relationships are evidently relationships of trust and confidence, the converse proposition is not true: not every relationship of trust and confidence is a fiduciary relationship, because one party must voluntarily undertake responsibility for another party's affairs before **11–30**

---

[52] See the cases cited in D. Hayton et al., *Underhill & Hayton's Law Relating to Trusts and Trustees*, 18th edn (London: LexisNexis, 2010), paras 27.09, fnn.1 and 2, 27.10, fn.1, and 27.11, fn.6.

[53] D. Capper, "Undue Influence and Unconscionability: A Rationalisation" (1998) 114 L.Q.R. 479; J. Phillips, "Protecting Those in a Disadvantageous Negotiating Position: Unconscionable Bargains as a Unifying Doctrine" (2010) 45 *Wake Forest Law Review* 837 especially at pp.852–857. See too N. Bamforth, "Unconscionability as a Vitiating Factor" [1995] L.M.C.L.Q. 538; A. Phang, "Undue Influence: Methodology, Sources and Linkages" [1995] J.B.L. 532.

[54] Cf. *Commercial Bank of Australia Ltd v Amadio* (1983) 151 C.L.R. 447 at 474 per Deane J.: "The two doctrines are . . . distinct. Undue influence, like common law duress, looks to the quality of the consent or assent of the weaker party . . . Unconscionable dealing looks to the conduct of the stronger party in attempting to enforce, or retain the benefit of, a dealing with a person under a special disability in circumstances where it is not consistent with equity or good conscience that he should do so."

[55] R. Bigwood, *Exploitative Contracts* (Oxford: OUP, 2003), Ch.8. Cf. P. Millett, "Equity's Place in the Law of Commerce" (1998) 114 L.Q.R. 214, p.219.

[56] *Pitt* [1994] A.C. 200 at 209.

[57] *National Westminster Bank Plc v Morgan* [1985] A.C. 686.

the courts will find that they are in a fiduciary relationship.[58] Moreover, not every finding of undue influence depends on a finding that the parties were in a relationship of trust and confidence: there is no need to show this when making out a case of "actual undue influence",[59] and yet such cases must be accounted for in any explanation of the doctrine as it must now be understood in the wake of *Etridge*.[60]

(b) *Proving Undue Influence*

11–31 In the following discussion we follow the courts' current practice of distinguishing cases of "actual undue influence" from cases of "presumed undue influence". These labels serve to differentiate the two modes of proof that can be used to establish undue influence. However, we are alive to the danger identified in *Etridge* by Lord Clyde that this classificatory approach may "add mystery rather than illumination" because "the names used to identify the [different classes of case] do not bear their actual meaning".[61] We would therefore emphasise here that there is no difference between the undue influence that is being proved in either type of case. The labels used here merely describe "different ways of proving the same thing".[62]

(i) *"Actual Undue Influence"*

11–32 Cases of "actual undue influence" are those in which the claimant is able to prove, without the aid of presumptions, that the defendant exerted undue influence on him which caused him to enter the impugned transaction.[63] Claimants most commonly succeed in doing this by leading evidence of "overt acts of improper pressure or coercion".[64] For example, a finding of undue influence was made in *Bank of Scotland v Bennett*,[65] on the basis of evidence that a woman had been told by her husband that their marriage would be over if she did not agree

---

[58] J. Edelman, "When Do Fiduciary Duties Arise?" (2010) 126 L.Q.R. 302. For this reason we doubt that Patten L.J. was correct to say in *Chandra* [2011] EWCA Civ 192 at [24] that "a relationship of trust and confidence between two parties is recognised in equity as being fiduciary in nature". See too his comments in *Johnson v E.B.S. Pensioner Trustees Ltd* Unreported Ch.D., March 6, 2001 at [33] (affirmed [2002] EWCA Civ 164; [2002] Lloyd's Law Rep P.N. 309). And cf. *Derksen (No.2)* [2003] EWHC 3050 (Ch) at [38] per Hart J.: "The proposition that the pleading of a relationship which is sufficient to give rise to presumed undue influence is *ipso facto* also a sufficient basis on which to plead fiduciary duties in respect of the breach of which the court may award equitable compensation is, so far as I am aware, a novel one in this jurisdiction."

[59] *Etridge* [2001] UKHL 44; [2002] 2 A.C. 773 at [103] per Lord Hobhouse.

[60] See paras 11–05—11–07. This difficulty with the argument is conceded in Bigwood, "Contracts by Unfair Advantage", p.93, fn.133 and text. See too L. Sealy, "Fiduciary Relationships" [1962] C.L.J. 69 at pp.78–79; and W.H.D. Winder, "Undue Influence and the Fiduciary Relationship" (1940) 4 Conv. (N.S.) 274 especially at p.288 where he concludes that the doctrine of undue influence is distinct from that of fiduciary relationship because "the one is based on the misuse of influence, the other on the abuse of confidence".

[61] *Etridge* [2001] UKHL 44; [2002] 2 A.C. 773 at [92].

[62] *Thompson* [2009] EWHC 1076 (Ch); [2010] 1 P. & C.R. 16 at [100] per Lewison J.

[63] *Lancashire Loans Ltd v Black* [1934] 1 K.B. 380; *Goldsworthy v Brickell* [1987] Ch. 378 at 400 per Nourse L.J.; *Aboody* [1990] 1 Q.B. 923 at 967 per curiam. For discussion of the causation test used in these cases, see paras 11–23—11–24.

[64] *Etridge* [2001] UKHL 44; [2002] 2 A.C. 773 at [8] per Lord Nicholls.

[65] *Bank of Scotland v Bennett* [1997] 1 F.L.R. 801.

to the transaction. James Munby QC, sitting as a deputy High Court judge, held that this was evidence that directly supported his finding of "moral blackmail amounting to coercion and victimisation".[66] Undue influence has also been established in cases where the claimant was blackmailed by a defendant who threatened to prosecute or sue the claimant or a member of his family.[67] Cases of the latter kind might also be pleaded as duress.[68] Findings of undue influence have also been made on the basis of evidence that a man induced his wife to agree to a transaction by misrepresenting its nature to her.[69]

Although such cases are comparatively rare, pleas of "actual undue influence" **11–33** have also succeeded in cases where there was "no direct evidence of influence" such as the making of overt threats.[70] "Neither coercion, nor pressure, nor deliberate concealment is a necessary element"[71] of an "actual undue influence" case, and there is:

> "a vast penumbra of facts which [might potentially] bear upon the question whether . . . undue influence was exerted. The vulnerability of one party must feature in that analysis. So does the forcefulness of the personality of the other."[72]

As we have already discussed, some recent cases suggest that the facts established by the claimant must support the inference that the defendant acted with a degree of fault greater than negligence, although other cases suggest that this is unnecessary.[73]

In *Re Craig (Deceased)*,[74] an elderly man with assets worth about £40,000 **11–34** made gifts of about £30,000 to his secretary and companion in the years before his death. These were set aside on the ground of undue influence by Ungoed-Thomas J., who held that the claimants had made out a case of "presumed undue

---

[66] *Bennett* [1997] 1 F.L.R. 801 at 827; reversed on a different point [1999] 1 F.L.R. 1115 (CA), but upheld on further appeal in *Etridge* [2001] UKHL 44; [2002] 2 A.C. 773. See too *Aboody* [1990] 1 Q.B. 923; *Bank of Credit and Commerce International SA v Hussain* Unreported Ch. D., December 15, 1999; *Bradshaw v Hardcastle* [2002] EWHC 2816 (QB).

[67] e.g. *Williams* (1866) L.R. 1 H.L. 200 at 209–210 per Lord Cranworth L.C.; *Kaufman* [1904] 1 K.B. 591; *Mutual Finance* [1937] 2 K.B. 389 at 396 per Porter J.; *Drew v Daniel* [2005] EWCA Civ 507; [2005] W.T.L.R. 807.

[68] See para.10–15. For the fusionist view that such cases *should* be pleaded as duress cases to avoid perpetuating needless distinctions between equitable and common law claims, see A. Burrows, "We Do This At Common Law But That In Equity" (2002) 22 O.J.L.S. 1, p.6.

[69] *Bank of Cyprus (London) Ltd v Markou* (1999) 78 P. & C.R. 208. See too *Broadway v Clydesdale Bank Plc (No.2)*, 2003 S.L.T. 707 at [20] per Lord Macfadyen. Cf. *Hewett* [2010] EWCA Civ 312; [2010] 2 F.L.R. 177 at [27]–[37] per Briggs J. (husband's concealment of affair amounted to misrepresentation of nature of transaction and thus to undue influence).

[70] *Goldsworthy v Brickell* [1987] 1 Ch. 378 at 400 per Nourse L.J.

[71] *Dunbar Bank* [1998] 3 All E.R. 876 at 883 per Millett L.J.

[72] *Drew v Daniel* [2005] EWCA Civ 507; [2005] W.T.L.R. 807 at [32] per Ward L.J. Cf. *Re Pauling's Settlement Trusts* [1964] Ch. 303 at 337 per Willmer L.J.: "it may not be difficult for a spinster daughter living at home to prove a case of actual undue influence for many years after she has attained the age of 21."

[73] See the discussion at paras 11–08—11–18.

[74] *Re Craig (Deceased)* [1971] Ch. 95. See too *Morley v Loughnan* [1893] 1 Ch. 736 at 752–756 per Wright J.; *Bank of Montreal v Stuart* [1911] A.C. 120 at 136–137 per Lord Macnaghten; *Langton v Langton* [1995] 2 F.L.R. 890; *Public Trustee v Bailey* [2005] EWHC 3524 (Ch) at [56]–[64] per His Honour Judge Weeks QC.

influence", but that they had also made out a case of "actual undue influence". His remarks on the latter aspect of the claim are worth quoting at length[75]:

> "[There is no] requirement that evidence of a gift being obtained by undue influence has to be established by some special species of evidence which distinguishes it from the ordinary evidential methods of discharging burdens of proof. The onus of establishing such behaviour as the exercise of undue influence is heavy, because the more objectionable the behaviour the more unlikely normally is it to occur, and, therefore, the heavier the onus of establishing it. But at the end of the day the finder of fact . . . has to review the evidence as a whole and conclude whether undue influence, unlikely though it normally be, is established. The absence of direct evidence of a gift being obtained by undue influence in circumstances such as those in this case is far from indicating that it did not occur. For my part, the amount of the gifts, the circumstances in which they were made, the vulnerability of Mr Craig to pressure by Mrs Middleton, the evidence of the direct exercise of that pressure on other occasions and for other purposes, the knowledge of Mr Craig and Mrs Middleton of his utter dependence on her, and the whole history of the relationship of Mr Craig and Mrs Middleton persuade me that were it not for undue influence by Mrs Middleton the gifts would never have been made. This is my conclusion even if, contrary to my view, this case does not fall within those of relations of trust and confidence in which the presumption of undue influence arises . . . "

11–35   As *Re Craig* shows, the evidence relied on in undue influence cases can be used in two different ways: to support a finding of undue influence made by direct inference from the facts, and to support a finding of undue influence made with the assistance of a presumption engendered by the parties' relationship and the nature of the transaction. It does not follow from the fact that the evidence might support the latter type of claim that a claimant is debarred from relying on it to support the former type of claim.[76] Indeed, a decision that a claimant has made out a case of "actual undue influence" makes it unnecessary for the court to consider whether the claimant might alternatively have made out a case of "presumed undue influence". Lord Scott made this point in *Etridge* in connection with the appeal in *Bennett*, where a wife had agreed to guarantee her husband's business debts, and the trial judge had held that the facts supported a finding of undue influence both with and without the help of presumptions. Lord Scott said[77]:

> "The discussion about the presumption of undue influence was unnecessary. Once actual undue influence has been found at trial, the question whether, if the evidence had been confined to the relationship between the parties and the nature of the impugned transaction, undue influence would have been presumed and, if it would, whether it had been rebutted, becomes irrelevant. And if, after a full trial, the judge concludes that undue influence has not been established, that conclusion means either that there never was a presumption of undue influence or, if there was, that it has been rebutted."

11–36   In "actual undue influence" cases there is no need to show that an ordinary person would have been influenced to enter the impugned transaction in the

---

[75] *Re Craig* [1971] Ch. 95 at 121.
[76] A contrary view is hinted at in A. Burrows, *The Law of Restitution*, 3rd edn (Oxford: OUP, 2010), p.293, fn.47.
[77] *Etridge* [2001] UKHL 44; [2002] 2 A.C. 773 at [316].

circumstances: all that matters is whether the particular claimant was influenced to do so.[78] Nor is there a need to show that the defendant acted with malign intent.[79] Nor is there a need to show a prior relationship of influence between the parties, although this is often present.[80] Nor is there a need to show that the transaction is disadvantageous to the claimant, according to Lord Browne-Wilkinson in *Pitt* because undue influence is a species of "equitable fraud", and a "man guilty of fraud is no more entitled to argue that the transaction was beneficial to the person defrauded than is a man who has procured a transaction by misrepresentation".[81] This was reaffirmed by Lord Nicholls in *Etridge*, although he considered that "in the nature of things, questions of undue influence will not usually arise, and the exercise of undue influence is unlikely to occur, where the transaction is innocuous."[82]

(ii) *"Presumed Undue Influence"*

Cases of "presumed undue influence" are those in which the claimant is able to prove with the aid of presumptions that the defendant exerted undue influence on him that caused him to enter the impugned transaction. In *Etridge* Lord Nicholls explained that a claimant may be able to take advantage of two different presumptions. One arises when the claimant can prove two facts: first, that he placed trust and confidence in the defendant, or was dependant on him, so that the parties were in a relationship of influence; and, secondly, that he entered a transaction at the defendant's behest that was not readily explicable by reference to the "ordinary motives of ordinary persons". When these facts have been proved[83]: **11–37**

> "the stage is set for the court to infer that, in the absence of a satisfactory explanation, the transaction can only have been procured by undue influence. In other words, proof of these two facts is *prima facie* evidence that the defendant abused the influence he acquired in the parties' relationship. . . . [The] evidential burden then shifts to him. It is for him to produce evidence to counter the inference which otherwise should be drawn."

Lord Nicholls described this rule as a "rebuttable evidential presumption",[84] language that was also used by Lord Scott.[85] Lord Hobhouse disliked this term and preferred to say that proof of the two facts identified by Lord Nicholls will lead the court to infer the existence of undue influence in the absence of contrary evidence.[86] But there was no difference between them, since Lord Nicholls also said that[87]: **11–38**

---

[78] *Re Brocklehurst Estate* [1978] Ch. 14 at 40 per Bridge L.J.; *Drew v Daniel* [2005] EWCA Civ 507; [2005] W.T.L.R. 807 at [41] per Ward L.J.

[79] *Aboody* [1990] 1 Q.B. 923 at 969–970 per curiam.

[80] *Goldsworthy* [1987] 1 Ch. 378 at 400 per Nourse L.J.; *Etridge* [2001] UKHL 44; [2002] 2 A.C. 773 at [103] per Lord Hobhouse.

[81] *Pitt* [1994] 1 A.C. 200 at 209.

[82] *Etridge* [2001] UKHL 44; [2002] 2 A.C. 773 at [12]; see also Lord Scott's comments at [156]; and *Turkey v Awadh* [2005] EWCA Civ 382; [2005] 2 P. & C.R. 29 at [36] and [38]–[39] per Chadwick L.J.

[83] *Etridge* [2001] UKHL 44; [2002] 2 A.C. 773 at [13]–[14].

[84] *Etridge* [2001] UKHL 44; [2002] 2 A.C. 773 at [16].

[85] *Etridge* [2001] UKHL 44; [2002] 2 A.C. 773 at [219].

[86] *Etridge* [2001] UKHL 44; [2002] 2 A.C. 773 at [104].

[87] *Etridge* [2001] UKHL 44; [2002] 2 A.C. 773 at [16].

"When a plaintiff succeeds by this route he does so because he has succeeded in establishing a case of undue influence. The court has drawn appropriate inferences of fact upon a balanced consideration of the whole of the evidence at the end of a trial in which the burden of proof rested upon the plaintiff. The use, in the course of the trial, of the forensic tool of a shift in the evidential burden of proof should not be permitted to obscure the overall position."

11–39 Writing extra-judicially, Sir Kim Lewison later put the point in this way[88]:

"[T]he nature of an evidential presumption . . . was never better explained than by Denning J. in an article he wrote in the Law Quarterly Review in 1945.[89] An evidential presumption, he said, is a presumption in the sense that from the presumption the fact in issue may be inferred, but not in the sense that it must be inferred. As the case proceeds the evidence may first weigh in favour of the inference and then against it; thus producing a burden sometimes apparent, sometimes real, which may shift from one party to the other as the case proceeds or may remain suspended between them. At the end of the day the court has to decide as a matter of fact whether the inference should be drawn or not. These presumptions are provisional only. It is a mistake to raise these provisional presumptions into propositions having the force of law. They are recognised by the law but their force depends on good sense rather than on law. They are only guides to the court in deciding whether to infer the fact in issue or not."

11–40 In some, though not all, cases of "presumed undue influence", the claimant can also take advantage of a second presumption, at the preliminary stage of proving that the parties were in a relationship of influence. This is a legal presumption[90] that certain types of relationship are always relationships of influence. We return to this below.[91] In *Etridge*,[92] Lord Nicholls stressed that this legal presumption is quite separate from the evidential presumption, or shifting of evidential onus, described in the foregoing paragraphs; this comes into play later on, once the claimant has proved that the parties were in a relationship of influence and that the transaction calls for an explanation.

11–41 In the following account of "presumed undue influence" cases we look in turn at the means by which a claimant may prove that the parties were in a relation-ship of influence, the means by which a claimant may prove that the impugned transaction was not readily explicable by reference to the ordinary motives of ordinary people, and the means by which a defendant may prove that even so there was no undue influence. Note that all these matters must be tested by[93]:

"looking at the situation at the time the impugned transaction was entered into, rather than at subsequent events, save in so far as subsequent events cast light on what was happening before and at the time of the impugned transaction. A transaction into which someone enters of their own free will does not retrospectively become tainted by undue

---

[88] Lewison, "Under the Influence", p.5, para.20. See too *Annulment Funding Co Ltd v Cowey* [2010] EWCA Civ 711; [2010] B.P.I.R. 1304 at [50] per Morgan J.: "an issue as to whether there was undue influence involves an issue of fact. The party asserting that there has been undue influence can call direct evidence which supports such a finding. Alternatively, that party can call evidence of other matters which justify the inference that undue influence was used."

[89] A.T. Denning, "Presumptions and Burdens" (1945) 61 L.Q.R. 379.

[90] So described in Lewison, "Under the Influence", p.8.

[91] See paras 11–42—11–46.

[92] *Etridge* [2001] UKHL 44; [2002] 2 A.C. 773 at [18].

[93] *Thompson v Fey* [2009] EWHC 1076 (Ch); [2010] P. & C.R. 16 at [101] per Lewison J.

influence merely because the counter-party fails to perform his or her side of the bargain."

Note, too, that it is a controversial issue whether the facts that the claimant is able to establish by these means must support the inference that the defendant acted unconscientiously when he exerted undue influence on the claimant. Some cases hold that a finding of undue influence necessarily entails a finding that the defendant acted with a degree of fault greater than negligence, but others suggest that it makes no difference whether the defendant was at fault.[94]

Relationship of influence There are two ways in which a claimant may be able to prove that he and the defendant were in a relationship of influence. First, he may be able to rely on evidence that they were in a relationship of a kind that the law presumes always to be a relationship of influence. Secondly, he may be able to rely on evidence from which the court can directly infer that the parties were in a relationship of influence. **11–42**

It should be emphasised that the presumption made in cases of the first sort is only a presumption of influence. It is not a presumption of *undue* influence. To establish undue influence, the claimant must also prove that the transaction was one that called for explanation, and if no such explanation is forthcoming, then the court will infer the existence of undue influence unless there are other facts to which the defendant can point that support the opposite conclusion.[95] **11–43**

In *Etridge* Lord Nicholls explained cases of the first sort in the following way[96]: **11–44**

"The law has adopted a seriously protective attitude towards certain types of relation-ships in which one party acquires influence over another who is vulnerable and dependent and where, moreover, substantial gifts by the influenced or vulnerable are not normally to be expected. Examples of relationships within this special class are parent and child, guardian and ward, trustee and beneficiary, solicitor and client, and medical advisor and patient.[97] In these cases the law presumes, irrebuttably, that one party had

---

[94] See the discussion at paras 11–08—11–18.

[95] *R v Att Gen for England and Wales* [2003] UKPC 22; [2003] E.M.L.R. 24 at [22] per Lord Hoffmann; *Markham v Karsten* [2007] EWHC 1509 (Ch); [2007] B.P.I.R. 1109 at [34] per Briggs J. See too Lewison, "Under the Influence", pp.8–9.

[96] *Etridge* [2001] UKHL 44; [2002] 2 A.C. 773 at [18].

[97] [Authors' note:] Parent and child: *Archer v Hudson* (1844) 7 Beav. 551; 49 E.R. 1180; *Wright v Vanderplank* (1855) 2 K. & J. 1; 69 E.R. 669; *Bainbrigge v Browne* (1881) 18 Ch. D. 188; *Berdoe v Dawson* (1865) 34 Beav. 603; 55 E.R. 768; *Lancashire Loans Ltd v Black* [1934] 1 K.B. 380; *Re Pauling's Settlement Trusts* [1964] Ch. 303 at 336 per curiam. Cf. *Avon Finance Co Ltd v Bridger* [1985] 2 All E.R. 281; *Coldunell Ltd v Gallon* [1986] 2 W.L.R. 466 (educated child over elderly parents). Aunt and niece: *Jennings v Cairns* [2003] EWCA Civ 1935; [2004] W.T.L.R. 361. Solicitor and client: *Tomson v Judge* (1855) 3 Dr. 306; 61 E.R. 920; *Wright v Carter* [1903] 1 Ch. 27. Doctor and patient: *Ahearne v Hogan* (1844) Dr.t.Sug. 310; *Mitchell v Homfray* (1881) 8 Q.B.D. 587; *Radcliffe v Price* (1902) 18 T.L.R. 446; *Goldsworthy v Brickell* [1987] Ch. 378 at 404. Spiritual advisers and followers: *Huguenin v Baseley* (1807) 14 Ves. Jun 273; 33 E.R. 526; *Lyon v Home* (1868) L.R. 6 Eq. 655; *Allcard v Skinner* (1887) 36 Ch. D. 145; *Roche v Sherrington* [1982] 2 All E.R. 426. Trustee and beneficiary: *Ellis v Barker* (1871) 7 Ch. App. 104; *Thomson v Eastwood* (1877) 2 App. Cas. 215; *Plowright v Lambert* (1885) 52 L.T. 646; *Beningfield v Baxter* (1886) 12 App. Cas. 167; *Tito v Waddell (No.2)* [1977] Ch. 106 at 241. Guardian and ward: *Hylton v Hylton* (1754) 2 Ves. Sen. 547; 28 E.R. 349; *Hatch v Hatch* (1804) 9 Ves. Jun. 292; 32 E.R. 615; *Taylor v Johnston* (1882) 19 Ch. D. 603 at 608. Superior officers and other ranks in the armed services: *R v Att Gen for England and Wales* [2003] UKPC 22; [2003] E.M.L.R. 24.

influence over the other. The complainant need not prove that he actually reposed trust and confidence in the other party. It is sufficient for him to prove the existence of the type of relationship."

11–45   In English law the relationship of husband and wife is not presumed to be a relationship of influence, although the court will take into account the fact that there are "opportunities for abuse which flow from a wife's confidence in her husband".[98] Nor is the relationship between siblings presumed to be a relationship of interest.[99] Some cases hold that the relationship of fiancé and fiancée is presumed to be a relationship of interest[100]; this anomalous and chauvinistic rule should be discarded.

11–46   Although Lord Nicholls said that an "irrebuttable" presumption is raised in respect of the special categories of relationship,[101] we share Sir Kim Lewison's extra-judicial view that this is unnecessary and unprincipled, and that a rebuttable presumption would be preferable.[102] Why should a solicitor, for example, be precluded from rebutting the presumption that he is in a relationship of influence with a client who is a successful businessman with much greater experience of transactions of the relevant kind? As Sir Kim observes, an irrebuttable presumption:

> "could only be justified if either it was a foregone conclusion that, if the evidence were to be called, the court's finding of fact would inevitably accord with the presumption; or that there are powerful reasons of policy for not allowing the truth to be found."[103]

Neither of these are compelling reasons for having such a rule in the present context.

11–47   If a claimant's relationship with the defendant does not fall into one of the special categories, then what evidence might he rely on to establish a relationship of influence? The answer will depend on the circumstances of the case, all of which must be taken into account.[104] In *Tufton v Sperni*,[105] Sir Raymond Evershed M.R. refuted "the suggestion that, to create the relationship of confidence, the person owing the duty must be found clothed in the recognisable garb of a guardian, trustee, solicitor, priest, doctor, manager, or the like"; and in *Morgan*,[106] Lord Scarman said that the "relationships which may develop a dominating influence of one over another are infinitely various. There is no substitute in this branch of the law for a 'meticulous examination of the facts'."

---

[98] *Etridge* [2001] UKHL 44; [2002] 2 A.C. 773 at [19] per Lord Nicholls; see also *Bank of Montreal v Stuart* [1911] A.C. 120 at 137 per Lord Macnaghten; *O'Brien* [1994] 1 A.C. 180 at 191 per Lord Browne-Wilkinson.

[99] *Pesticcio* [2003] EWHC 2293 (Ch); [2003] W.T.L.R. 1327 at [80] per Neuberger J.

[100] *Leeder v Stevens* [2005] EWCA Civ 50 at [18] per Jacob L.J.; regarding *Re Lloyd's Bank Ltd* [1931] 1 Ch. 289 at 302 as good law, although it had a "1930s redolence about it". Cf. *Zamet v Hyman* [1961] 1 W.L.R. 1442.

[101] See too *Markham* [2007] EWHC 1509 (Ch); [2007] B.P.I.R. 1109 at [34] per Briggs J.

[102] Lewison, "Under the Influence", p.9, paras 40–42. See too J. Edelman and E. Bant, *Unjust Enrichment in Australia* (Melbourne: OUP, 2006), p.221.

[103] Lewison, "Under the Influence", p.9.

[104] *Bundy* [1975] Q.B. 326 at 341–342 per Sir Eric Sachs.

[105] *Tufton v Sperni* [1952] 2 T.L.R. 516 at 522.

[106] *Morgan* [1985] A.C. 686 at 709.

Often a claimant will lead evidence going to the strength of his reliance on the **11–48**
defendant and to the extended duration of their relationship. Wives have successfully rested their arguments on evidence of this kind in cases where they have
guaranteed their husbands' business debts.[107] So too have a wide variety of other
claimants.[108] Note, though, that evidence of this sort is only relevant if it
establishes that the defendant "was in a position to influence the will of the
[claimant] in relation to a transaction of the relevant nature"[109]: establishing that
a defendant:

> "enjoyed a relation of trust and confidence with the [claimant] . . . is almost mean-
> ingless, unless the particular kind of trust and confidence is clearly established in
> relation to the impugned transaction."[110]

The nature of the impugned transaction may also be evidence from which the **11–49**
court can infer a relationship of influence between the parties, if it is "so
extravagantly improvident that it is virtually inexplicable"[111] except on the basis
that it was procured by undue influence. The improvident nature of the transaction performs two separate evidential roles in such a case, establishing both that
the parties were in a relationship of influence and that the transaction called for
explanation. Note that a high threshold of improvidence must be passed to
engage the principle,[112] and there is no general rule that the recipients of large
gifts must always prove that these were freely made.[113]

Transaction calling for an explanation In addition to establishing a rela- **11–50**
tionship of influence, the claimant must also establish that the impugned transaction "cannot readily be accounted for by the ordinary motives of ordinary
persons in that relationship".[114] Conversely, if the defendant can explain the
transaction to the court's satisfaction, then no presumption of undue influence
will arise.[115]

---

[107] e.g. *Aboody* [1990] 1 Q.B. 923; *Barclays Bank Plc v Coleman* [2001] Q.B. 21; affirmed in *Etridge* [2001] UKHL 44; [2002] 2 A.C. 773.
[108] e.g. *Tufton* [1952] 2 T.L.R. 516 (vendor and purchaser); *Re Craig* [1971] Ch. 95 (secretary/ companion and employer), discussed at para.11–34; *Bundy* [1975] Q.B. 326 (bank and customer); *O'Sullivan v Management Agency and Music Ltd* [1985] Q.B. 428 (manager and pop singer); *Goldsworthy* [1987] Ch. 378 (farm manager and farm owner); *Crédit Lyonnais Nederland NV v Burch* [1997] 1 All E.R. 144 (employer and junior employee); *Hew* [2003] UKPC 51 (bank and customer); *Abbey National Plc v Stringer* [2006] EWCA Civ 338 (son and mother); *Goodchild* [2006] EWCA Civ 1868; [2007] W.T.L.R. 463 (great-nephew and great-uncle); *Murphy v Rayner* [2011] EWHC 1 (Ch) (carer and employer).
[109] *Awadh* [2005] EWCA Civ 382; [2005] 2 P. & C.R. 29 at [38] per Chadwick L.J.
[110] Lewison, "Under the Influence", p.8.
[111] *Crédit Lyonnais Nederland N.V. v Burch* [1997] 1 All E.R. 144 at 154–155 per Millett L.J. See too *Huguenin v Baseley* (1807) 14 Ves. Jun. 273 at 296; 33 E.R. 526 at 536 per Lord Eldon L.C.; *Hyman* [1961] 1 W.L.R. 1442 at 1449 per Lord Evershed M.R.; *Alec Lobb (Garages) Ltd v Total Oil Great Britain Ltd* [1985] 1 W.L.R. 173 at 181–183 per Dillon L.J.
[112] *Tufton* [1952] 2 T.L.R. 516 at 530 per Sir Raymond Evershed M.R.
[113] *O'Brien* [1994] 1 A.C. 180 at 193–194 per Lord Browne-Wilkinson; rejecting *Hoghton v Hoghton* (1852) 15 Beav. 278 at 298; 51 E.R. 543 at 553 per Lord Romilly M.R. See too *Yerkey v Jones* (1939) 63 C.L.R. 649 at 678 and following per Dixon J.
[114] *Etridge* [2001] UKHL 44; [2002] 2 A.C. 773 at [13] per Lord Nicholls.
[115] *Awadh* [2005] EWCA Civ 382; [2005] 2 P. & C.R. 29 at [15] per Chadwick L.J. This suggests that Patten J. was wrong to defer consideration of the defendant's explanation of the claimant's gift until after the burden of proof had been reversed, in *De Wind v Wedge* [2008] EWHC 514 (Ch); [2010] W.T.L.R. 795 at [52].

11-51   Prior to *Etridge*, this requirement had come to be described as a requirement that the transaction should be "manifestly disadvantageous" to the claimant, but some doubts had developed about the content of this rule, and its underlying rationale.[116] In *Etridge* Lord Nicholls therefore discarded the language of "manifest disadvantage" while preserving the rule's substantive content. He also explained that the rule is "a necessary limitation upon the width of the first prerequisite" (namely that the parties should be in a relationship of influence), continuing that[117]:

> "It would be absurd for the law to presume that every gift by a child to a parent, or every transaction between a client and his solicitor or between a patient and his doctor, was brought about by undue influence unless the contrary is affirmatively proved. Such a presumption would be too far-reaching. The law would be out of touch with everyday life if the presumption were to apply to every Christmas or birthday gift by a child to a parent, or to an agreement whereby a client or patient agrees to be responsible for the reasonable fees of his legal or medical adviser. The law would be rightly open to ridicule, for transactions such as these are unexceptionable. They do not suggest that something may be amiss. So something more is needed before the law reverses the burden of proof, something which calls for an explanation. When that something more is present, the greater the disadvantage to the vulnerable person, the more cogent must be the explanation before the presumption will be regarded as rebutted."

11-52   When determining whether a transaction calls for explanation, the courts must take a range of factors into account: the relationship between the parties, the nature of the transaction, the size of the transaction, the amount of value transferred or risks assumed by the claimant relative to his assets, the benefits that the claimant would receive in exchange, and so on.[118] Many gifts may be "reasonably accounted for on the ground of friendship, relationship, charity, or other ordinary motives on which ordinary men act."[119] But some may not be.[120] Whether a guarantee can be reasonably accounted will turn on "(a) the seriousness of the risk of enforcement to the giver, in practical terms; and (b) the benefits gained by the giver in accepting the risk."[121] "In the ordinary course", a guarantee by a wife of her husband's business debts does not call for explanation, because it is "reasonably accounted for on the ground of . . . [the] relationship" between spouses, whose fortunes are normally "bound up together."[122] The purchase of property at the market price may not call for explanation,[123] but the sale of property at an undervalue might do so,[124] as might the joint purchase of

---

[116] *Morgan* [1985] A.C. 686; *Goldsworthy* [1987] Ch. 378; *Pitt* [1994] 1 A.C. 200; *Barclays Bank Plc v Coleman* [2001] Q.B. 20; result affirmed in *Etridge* [2001] UKHL 44; [2002] 2 A.C. 773.

[117] *Etridge* [2001] UKHL 44; [2002] 2 A.C. 773 at [24].

[118] *Pesticcio* [2004] EWCA Civ 372 at [20] per Mummery L.J., quoted in the text to fn.10.

[119] *Allcard* (1887) 36 Ch. D. 145 at 185 per Lindley L.J.; quoted in *Etridge* [2001] UKHL 44; [2002] 2 A.C. 773 at [22] per Lord Nicholls.

[120] *Rhodes v Bate* (1866) L.R. 1 Ch. App. 252 at 258 per Turner L.J.; *Hammond* [2002] EWCA Civ 885; *Aldridge v Turner* [2004] EWHC 2768 (Ch) at [63]–[65] per Michael Briggs QC, sitting as a deputy High Court judge; *Watson v Huber* Unreported Ch. D., March 9, 2005; *De Wind v Wedge* [2008] EWHC 514 (Ch); [2010] W.T.L.R. 795; *Smith v Cooper* [2010] EWCA Civ 722; [2010] 2 F.L.R. 1521; *Murphy v Rayner* [2011] EWHC 1 (Ch).

[121] *Aboody* [1990] 1 Q.B. 923 at 965 per curiam.

[122] *Etridge* [2001] UKHL 44; [2002] 2 A.C. 773 at [28] per Lord Nicholls.

[123] *Dailey v Dailey* [2003] UKPC 65; [2003] 3 F.C.R. 369 at [24]–[25] per Lord Hope.

[124] *Vale v Armstrong* [2004] EWHC 1160; [2004] W.T.L.R. 1471 at [50] per Evans-Lombe J.

a house by a defendant and an elderly claimant who uses "all his money . . . in buying a right which [is] seriously insecure and which [ties] him to this particular house."[125]

Countervailing evidence   If the court finds that the parties were in a relation-   **11–53**
ship of influence and that the transaction was not readily explicable by ordinary motives, then the evidential burden shifts onto the defendant to prove that even so the transaction was not procured by undue influence. "Unless the defendant introduces evidence to counteract the inference of undue influence that the complainant's evidence justifies, the complainant will succeed."[126] The defendant must satisfy the court that the claimant entered the transaction after "full, free and informed thought" about it.[127]

Evidence that the claimant knew what he was doing will not suffice for this   **11–54**
purpose, as in a case of undue influence the claimant "will always know what he . . . is doing; the question is why".[128] Nor will it suffice to show that the claimant previously said that he was not acting under improper pressure.[129]

Although this is not the only way of proving the claimant's independence of   **11–55**
mind,[130] defendants often seek to disprove undue influence by showing that the claimant received advice from an independent third party, commonly a lawyer. In *Etridge*, Lord Nicholls said that[131]:

"The weight, or importance, to be attached to such advice depends on all the circumstances. In the normal course, advice from a solicitor or other outside adviser can be expected to bring home to a complainant a proper understanding of what he or she is about to do. But a person may understand fully the implications of a proposed transaction, for instance, a substantial gift, and yet still be acting under the undue influence of another. Proof of outside advice does not, of itself, necessarily show that the subsequent completion of the transaction was free from the exercise of undue influence. Whether it will be proper to infer that outside advice had an emancipating effect, so that the transaction was not brought about by the exercise of undue influence, is a question of fact to be decided having regard to all the evidence in the case."

Legal advice "will not be independent if the solicitor is acting for both the   **11–56**
claimant and the defendant".[132] Where independent advice is given, "it must be given with knowledge of all relevant circumstances and must be such as a competent and honest advisor would have given if acting solely in the interests of the donor."[133] Inadequate advice, particularly negligent inadequate advice, is

---

[125] *Cheese v Thomas* [1994] 1 W.L.R. 129 at 134 per Nicholls V.C.
[126] *Etridge* [2001] UKHL 44; [2002] 2 A.C. 773 at [161] per Lord Scott.
[127] A phrase that seems to have originated in *Hyman* [1961] 1 W.L.R. 1442 at 1446 per Lord Evershed M.R., and which has been much repeated in the cases: see e.g. *Goodchild* [2006] EWCA Civ 1868; [2007] W.T.L.R. 463 at [36] and [42] per May L.J.; *Smith v Cooper* [2010] EWCA Civ 722; [2010] 2 F.L.R. 1521 at [61] per Lloyd L.J.
[128] *Stevens* [2005] EWCA Civ 50 at [19] per Jacob L.J. See too *Smith v Cooper* [2010] EWCA Civ 722; [2010] 2 F.L.R. 1521 at [61] per Lloyd L.J.: "the problem is lack of independence, not lack of understanding".
[129] *Goodchild* [2006] EWCA Civ 1868; [2007] W.T.L.R. 463 at [18]–[28] per Chadwick L.J.
[130] *Inche Noriah* [1929] A.C. 127 at 135 per Lord Hailsham; *Re Brocklehurst's Estate* [1978] Ch. 141.
[131] *Etridge* [2001] UKHL 44; [2002] 2 A.C. 773 at [20].
[132] *Smith v Cooper* [2010] EWCA Civ 722; [2010] 2 F.L.R. 1521 at [71] per Lloyd L.J.
[133] *Inche Noriah* [1929] A.C. 127 at 135–136 per Lord Hailsham L.C.

unlikely to have an emancipating effect.[134] Advice given to the claimant and the defendant together is also unlikely to have an emancipating effect: for example, where the facts support an inference that a wife was unduly influenced by her husband, an interview with a solicitor in the presence of the husband is unlikely to achieve the objective of establishing that she acted freely in knowledge of the true facts.[135] Note, however, that:

> "even where a presumption of influence is raised, that influence does not necessarily turn into undue influence merely because the person with the influence does not advise his counter-party to take independent legal advice."[136]

3. Relief from Unconscionable Bargains

(a) *Statutory Measures*

11–57   The legislature has sought to protect claimants from exploitation of their need for credit by enacting the Consumer Credit Act 1974 ss.140A–140D (inserted by the Consumer Credit Act 2006). More general legislation has also been enacted to protect claimants from exploitation of their bargaining position, namely the Unfair Contract Terms Act 1977 and the Unfair Terms in Consumer Contracts Regulations 1999. Discussion of these statutory provisions can be found in specialist texts and will not be undertaken here.[137]

(b) *Equitable Relief*

11–58   The source of the courts' equitable jurisdiction to set aside unconscionable bargains is that equitable fraud can be:

> "presumed or inferred from the circumstances or conditions of the parties contracting: weakness on one side, usury on the other, or extortion or advantage taken of that weakness. There has always been an appearance of fraud from the nature of the bargain."[138]

Speaking for the Privy Council in *Hart v O'Connor*, Lord Brightman said that[139]:

> "'Fraud' in an equitable context does not mean, or is not confined to, deceit: 'it means an unconscientious use of the power arising out of these circumstances and conditions' of the contracting parties . . . It is a victimisation, which can consist either of the active

---

[134] *Pesticcio* [2004] EWCA Civ 372, discussed at para.11–15. See too *De Wind* [2008] EWHC 514 (Ch); [2010] W.T.L.R. 795 at [54]–[55] per Patten J.

[135] *Etridge* [2001] UKHL 44; [2002] 2 A.C. 773 at [113] per Lord Hobhouse.

[136] *Wollenberg v Casinos Austria International Holding GMBH* [2011] EWHC 103 (Ch) at [207] per Lewison J., following *R v Att Gen for England and Wales* [2003] UKPC 22; [2003] E.M.L.R. 24 at [23] per Lord Hoffmann.

[137] See e.g. H. Beale (gen. ed.), *Chitty on Contracts*, 30th edn (London: Sweet & Maxwell, 2008), vol.1, Ch.15; E. Lomnicka and P. Dobson (gen. eds), *Encyclopedia of Consumer Credit Law*, looseleaf edn (London: Sweet & Maxwell, August 2011 issue).

[138] *Earl of Chesterfield v Janssen* (1751) 2 Ves. Sen. 125 at 157; 28 E.R. 82 at 102 per Lord Hardwicke.

[139] [1985] A.C. 1000 at 1024, quoting *Earl of Aylesford v Morris* (1873) L.R. 8 Ch. App. 484 at 490–491 per Lord Selborne L.C.

extortion of a benefit or the passive acceptance of a benefit in unconscionable circumstances."

Equity presumes bargains with expectants to be unconscionable.[140] The person **11–59** claiming the benefit of the bargain can rebut the presumption by showing that it is fair, just and reasonable. The *onus probandi* is a heavy one and will not easily be discharged; for example, it is not enough to show that the father, or other person on whose death the expectancy was to mature, was a party to the bargain.[141] Independent professional advice[142] is important evidence of fairness, as is adequacy of the consideration.[143] Since the bargain is voidable, it can be affirmed expressly or impliedly by the expectant party after coming into his inheritance.[144]

It is not only bargains with expectants that equity may presume to be uncon- **11–60** scionable. Equity will intervene to prevent any "unconscientious use of power", when there is weakness on the one side and extortion on the other, and will set aside improvident bargains, made with any "poor or ignorant person acting without independent advice, which cannot be shown to be a fair and reasonable transaction".[145] Equity does not intervene simply because the bargain is hard, unreasonable or foolish: it must be oppressive to the complainant in its overall terms, and although Lord Brightman contemplated in *Hart* that the doctrine might be triggered by the "passive acceptance of a benefit", recent cases insist that the party benefiting from the transaction must have actively imposed oppressive terms on the other party in a morally reprehensible manner.[146] Consequently the English doctrine remains a narrow one by comparison with the law of Australia, Canada and New Zealand, where the courts have been more willing to find unconscionable conduct in the absence of active oppression.[147]

---

[140] Expectants include not only heirs apparent and presumptive, but those who have either a vested or a contingent remainder or any reversionary interest. Relief has been granted against usurious loans: see *Benyon v Cooke* (1875) L.R. 10 Ch. 389 at 391 per Jessel M.R. The patriarchal attitudes that inform many of the C19 cases on expectant heirs are discussed in C. MacMillan, "*Earl of Aylesford v Morris* (1873)" in C. Mitchell and P. Mitchell (eds), *Landmark Cases in Equity* (Oxford: Hart, 2012).

[141] *King v Hamlet* (1834) 2 My. & K. 456 at 473–475; 39 E.R. 1018 at 1025–1026 per Lord Brougham; *Savery v King* (1856) 5 H.L.C. 627; 10 E.R. 1046; *Talbot v Staniforth* (1861) 1 J. & H. 484; 70 E.R. 837 .

[142] *O'Rorke v Bolingbroke* (1877) 2 App. Cas. 814; *Fry v Lane* (1888) 40 Ch.D. 312.

[143] *Shelly v Nash* (1818) 3 Madd. 232; 56 E.R. 494; *Perfect v Lane* (1861) 3 De G.F. & J. 369; 45 E.R. 921.

[144] Cf. *Levin v Roth* [1950] 1 All E.R. 698n.

[145] *Hart* [1985] A.C. 1000 at 1023–1024 per Lord Brightman.

[146] *Multiservice Bookbinding Ltd v Morden* [1979] Ch. 84 at 110; *Boustany v Pigott* (1995) 69 P. & C.R. 298 at 303 per Lord Templeman; *Portman Building Society v Dusangh* [2000] 2 All E.R. 221 at 229 per Simon Brown L.J., and at 232 per Ward L.J.; *Kalsep Ltd v X-Flow BV* (2001) 24(7) I.P.D. 24044 per Pumfrey J.; *Strydom v Vendside Ltd* [2009] EWHC 2130 (QB); [2009] 6 Costs L.R. 886 at [39] per Blair J.

[147] D. Capper, "The Unconscionable Bargain in the Common Law World" (2010) 126 L.Q.R. 403. Significant cases from these systems include the following. Australia: *Blomley v Ryan* (1956) 99 C.L.R. 362; *Commercial Bank of Australia Ltd v Amadio* (1983) 151 C.L.R. 447; *Louth v Diprose* (1993) 175 C.L.R. 621; *Bridgewater v Leahy* (1998) 194 C.L.R. 457. Canada: *Morrison v Coast Finance Ltd* (1965) 55 D.L.R. (2d) 710 (British Columbia CA); *Harry v Kreutzinger* (1978) 95 D.L.R. (3d) 231 (British Columbia CA); *Cain v Clarica Life Insurance Co* [2005] ABCA 437; (2005) 263 D.L.R. (4th) 368; *Lydian Properties Inc v Chambers* [2009] ABCA 21; (2009) 457 A.R. 211; New Zealand: *Nichols v Jessup* [1986] 1 N.Z.L.R. 226; *Gustav & Co Ltd v Macfield Ltd* [2008] NZSC 47; [2008] 2 N.Z.L.R. 735.

11-61   In *Alec Lobb (Garages) Ltd v Total Oil Great Britain Ltd*, Peter Millett QC, sitting as a deputy High Court judge, summarised the English governing equitable relief from unconscionable bargains in this way[148]:

> "It is probably not possible to reconcile all the authorities, some of which are of great antiquity, on this head of equitable relief, which came into greater prominence with the repeal of the usury laws in the nineteenth century. But if the cases are examined, it will be seen that three elements have almost invariably been present before the court has interfered. First, one party has been at a serious disadvantage to the other, whether through poverty, or ignorance, or lack of advice, or otherwise, so that circumstances existed of which unfair advantage could be taken: see, for example, *Blomley v Ryan*,[149] where, to the knowledge of one party, the other was by reason of his intoxication in no condition to negotiate intelligently. Second, this weakness of the one party has been exploited by the other in some morally culpable manner: see, for example, *Clark v Malpas*,[150] where a poor illiterate man was induced to enter into a transaction of an unusual nature, without proper independent advice, and in great haste. And third, the resulting transaction has been, not merely hard or improvident, but overreaching and oppressive. Where there has been a sale at an under-value, the undervalue has almost always been substantial, so that it calls for an explanation, and is in itself indicative of the presence of some fraud, undue influence, or other such feature. In short, there must, in my judgment, be some impropriety, both in the conduct of the stronger party and in the terms of the transaction itself (though the former may often be inferred from the latter in the absence of an innocent explanation) which in the traditional phrase 'shocks the conscience of the court', and makes it against equity and good conscience for the stronger party to retain the benefit of a transaction he has unfairly obtained."

11-62   There are many examples of cases where bargains have been set aside on these grounds: bargains with the seriously ill,[151] the old and eccentric,[152] the young and inexperienced,[153] the ill-educated and illiterate,[154] the poor and ignorant,[155] and persons unfamiliar with the English language.[156] Moreover, the jurisdiction was said by Nourse L.J. in *Crédit Lyonnais Nederland NV v Burch* to be "in good heart and capable of adaptation to different transactions entered into in changing circumstances."[157]

---

[148] *Alec Lobb (Garages) Ltd v Total Oil Great Britain Ltd* [1983] 1 W.L.R. 87 at 94–95, reversed in part [1985] 1 W.L.R. 173.

[149] *Blomley v Ryan* (1954) 99 C.L.R. 362.

[150] *Clark v Malpas* (1862) 4 De G.F. & J. 401; 25 E.R. 1238.

[151] *Clarke v Malpas* (1862) 4 De G.F. & J. 401 at 405; 45 E.R. 1238 at 1240; cf. *Irvani v Irvani* [2000] 1 Lloyd's Rep. 412 (heroin addiction not a special disability).

[152] *Longmate v Ledger* (1860) 2 Giff. 157; 66 E.R. 67; *Watkin v Watson-Smith, The Times*, July 3, 1986; *Boustany v Pigott* (1995) 69 P. & C.R. 298

[153] *Earl of Aylesford v Morris* (1873) L.R. 8 Ch. App. 484; *O'Rorke v Bolingbroke* (1877) 2 App. Cas. 814; *Multiservice Bookbinding Ltd v Morden* [1979] Ch. 84 at 110.

[154] *Clarke v Malpas* (1862) 4 De G.F. & J. 401; 45 E.R. 1238; *Baker v Monk* (1864) 4 De G. J. & S. 388; 46 E.R. 968; *Mountford v Scott* [1974] 1 All E.R. 248 at 252–253; *Singla v Bashir* [2002] EWHC 883 (Ch).

[155] *Evans v Llewellin* (1787) 1 Cox 333; 29 E.R. 1191; *Fry v Lane* (1888) 40 Ch. D. 312; *Cresswell v Potter* (1968) [1978] 1 W.L.R. 255; *Chagos Islanders v Att Gen* [2003] EWHC 2222 (QB) at [580].

[156] *Singla v Bashir* [2002] EWHC 883 (Ch); *Chagos Islanders v Att Gen* [2003] EWHC 2222 (QB) at [545]; cf. *Amadio* (1983) 151 C.L.R. 447; *Barclays Bank Plc v Schwarz, The Times*, August 2, 1995.

[157] *Crédit Lyonnais Nederland NV v Burch* [1997] 1 All E.R. 144 at 151.

In *Lloyds Bank Ltd v Bundy*,[158] Lord Denning M.R. was prepared to set aside   **11-63**
a "poor gentleman's" guarantee of his son's loan to the claimant bank, although
he knew what he was doing; in his Lordship's view the case law impliedly
recognised that a bargain could be set aside because of "inequality of bargaining
power". However Lord Scarman, in *Morgan*, doubted whether it was necessary
to create any "general principle of relief against inequality of bargaining power"
and suggested that it was a legislative task to impose "restrictions on freedom of
contract".[159] In our view, in this area of the law, judicial restraint is a wise policy
in the absence of any evidence of any wrongful conduct on the part of one of the
contracting parties. At the same time it should be recognised that relief may be
granted in exceptional circumstances. So, equity may grant relief against forfeiture, may relieve against penalties, and may exceptionally order the return of
earnest payments.[160] And in *Macaulay*[161] Lord Diplock contemplated that standard form contracts in restraint of trade, where the terms were not the product of
arm's-length negotiations, could be set aside and declared to be unconscionable.

We think it undesirable that the courts should enjoy an unfettered power to   **11-64**
rewrite contracts simply because the substantive terms *appear* to be unfair.[162] To
create and to exercise such power will involve the courts in the solution of
problems which litigation inter partes is not equipped to solve.[163] Unconscionability and inequality of bargaining power are elusive and mercurial concepts
which mean different things to different people. It is "seldom in any negotiation
that the bargaining powers of the parties are absolutely equal" and it should not
suffice to show that a contractual provision "is objectively unreasonable".[164]

(c) *In Admiralty*

Salvage agreements are liable to be set aside if the court regards their terms as   **11-65**
inequitable. In *Akerblom v Price, Potter, Walker & Co* Brett L.J. stated that[165]:

> "The fundamental rule of administration of maritime law in all courts of maritime
> jurisdiction is that, whenever the Court is called upon to decide between contending
> parties, upon claims arising with regard to the infinite number of marine casualties,
> which are generally of so urgent a character that the parties cannot be truly said to be

---

[158] *Lloyd's Bank Ltd v Bundy* [1975] 1 Q.B. 326 at 331.
[159] *Morgan* [1985] A.C. 686 at 708. The other members of the House of Lords agreed with Lord
Scarman. The facts, which were similar to those of *Bundy*, gave rise to a claim of undue influence.
See also *Hart* [1985] A.C. 1000 at 1023–1024.
[160] cf. *Stockloser v Johnson* [1954] 1 Q.B. 476 at 490 and 492 per Denning L.J.; *The Scaptrade* [1983]
2 A.C. 694 at 702 per Lord Diplock; *Sport International Bussum BV v Inter-Footwear Ltd* [1984] 1
W.L.R. 777; *B.I.C.C. Plc v Burndy Corp* [1985] Ch. 232. These cases are all discussed in Ch.14.
[161] *Schroeder Music Publishing Co Ltd v Macaulay* [1974] 1 W.L.R. 1308 at 1326, applauded by Lord
Denning M.R. in *Clifford Davis Management Ltd v W.E.A. Records Ltd* [1975] 1 W.L.R. 61 at 64. See
too *Silvertone Records Ltd v Mountfield* [1993] E.M.L.R. 152; *Panayiotou v Sony Music Enter-
tainment (UK) Ltd* [1994] E.M.L.R. 229; *Proactive Sports Management Ltd v Rooney* [2010] EWHC
1807 (QB).
[162] Cf. *Shiloh Spinners Ltd v Harding* [1973] A.C. 691 at 723 per Lord Wilberforce; and see S.M.
Waddams, "Unconscionability in Contracts" (1976) 39 M.L.R. 369.
[163] Cf. *Pao On* [1980] A.C. 614 at 634 per Lord Scarman: "it would render the law uncertain".
[164] *Alec Lobb (Garages) Ltd* [1985] 1 W.L.R. 173 at 183 per Dillon L.J.
[165] *Akerblom v Price, Potter, Walker & Co* (1881) 7 Q.B.D. 129 at 132–133.

on equal terms as to any agreement they may make with regard to them, the Court will try to discover what in the widest sense of the terms is under the particular circumstances of the particular case fair and just between the parties. If the parties have made no agreement, the Court will decide primarily what is fair and just . . . If the parties have made an agreement, the Court will enforce it, unless it be manifestly unfair and unjust; but if it be manifestly unfair and unjust, the court will disregard it and decree what is fair and just."

11–66   In the majority of cases where salvage agreements have been set aside, it has been because the reward stipulated for by the salvor in the agreement has been exorbitantly high. The court will be particularly ready to set aside such an agreement if the circumstances of the case and the conduct of the salvor were such as to give the owner of the salved property or his representative no option but to enter into the agreement. Thus, in *The Port Caledonia and The Anna*,[166] a vessel in difficulty requested assistance from a tug, and the tugmaster's terms were: £1,000 or no rope. The master of the distressed vessel had no option but to accept. The agreement was set aside and the tug was awarded £200.

11–67   But it is not only in cases of compulsion, such as these, that agreements are liable to be set aside. As appears from the passage from Brett L.J.'s judgment, quoted above, salvage agreements will be set aside whenever they are manifestly unfair and unjust.[167] Thus an agreement to render salvage services for a sum which is extravagantly small has been set aside as inequitable,[168] even when the agreement constituted a settlement made after the services had been rendered.[169] Again, agreements relating to the apportionment of a salvage reward among salvors may also be set aside if they are inequitable.[170]

11–68   It is, however, no part of the court's duty to set aside an agreement merely because it disagrees with the reward fixed by that agreement. Only if the amount stipulated is so exorbitantly large or so extravagantly small that, in all the circumstances of the case, the agreement must be regarded as inequitable, will the court interfere. Moreover, an agreement will not be set aside merely because the service agreed to be performed proved to be more arduous than was expected[171]; an agreement "cannot become fair or unfair by reason of circumstances which happened afterwards".[172]

---

[166] *The Port Caledonia and The Anna* [1903] P. 184.
[167] *The Mark Lane* (1890) 15 P.D. 135.
[168] *The Phantom* (1866) L.R. 1 A. & E. 58 (£10 substituted for 8s.6d.).
[169] *The Case of Silver Bullion* (1854) 2 E. & A. 70 (£50 substituted for 11s.).
[170] *The Enchantress* (1860) Lush. 93.
[171] *The True Blue* (1843) 2 W.Rob. 176.
[172] *The Strathgarry* [1895] P. 264 at 271 per Bruce J.

CHAPTER 12

FAILURE OF BASIS: GENERAL PRINCIPLES

1. FAILURE OF BASIS AS A GENERAL PRINCIPLE OF LIABILITY

This chapter and the next five chapters are concerned with failure of basis as a **12–01** ground for restitution, and with claims which, although not grounded on failure of basis, are closely related to it.[1] The core underlying idea of failure of basis is simple: a benefit has been conferred on the joint understanding that the recipient's right to retain it is conditional. If the condition is not fulfilled, the recipient must return the benefit. The condition might take one of a variety of forms. For instance, it might consist in the recipient doing or giving something in return for the benefit (hereafter referred to as "counter-performance"). Alternatively, the condition might be the existence of a state of affairs, or the occurrence of an event, for which the recipient has undertaken no responsibility. Failure of basis is, therefore, to be distinguished from unjust factors that focus on whether the payment is truly voluntary (such as mistake, duress, etc). In failure of basis cases, the claimant's intention to confer the benefit is genuine, but it is conditional.[2]

2. HISTORICAL DEVELOPMENT OF FAILURE OF BASIS

(a) *General*

The recognition of a general principle of failure of basis as a ground for **12–02** restitution has been made possible by relatively recent judicial and academic restatements of the law of unjust enrichment. Prior to these restatements, cases which can now be seen to be based on the same underlying unjust factor were categorised separately, which resulted in their fundamental similarities being obscured. For instance, the recovery of payments made in anticipation of a contract which did not materialise was formerly thought to be governed by whether a contract containing a term providing for recovery could be implied.[3] The implication of such a contract was, however, a highly artificial exercise, which had little reference to what had actually been agreed between the parties,

---

[1] The claims distinct from, but closely related to, failure of basis are (1) those arising from contracts which have been frustrated (see Ch.15); and (2) those arising from free acceptance (Ch.17). Claims arising from anticipated contracts that do not materialise rest partly on failure of basis, and partly on other kinds of claim (Ch.16).
[2] *McDonald v Dennys Lascelles Ltd* (1933) 48 C.L.R. 457 at 477.
[3] *Way v Latilla* [1937] 3 All E.R. 759.

and tended to conceal that the real basis of recovery was an obligation imposed by law.[4]

(b) *Historical Distinction between Money and Non-Money Benefits*

12–03   The development of the law of failure of basis was also profoundly affected by a fundamental procedural distinction, which turned on whether the benefit conferred was a money payment. Where the benefit took the form of money, the correct form of action was a claim for money had and received on the ground of total failure of consideration. Where the benefit conferred consisted of goods or services, however, a claim would succeed only if it was shown that they were requested (or freely accepted), and the claimant asked for a quantum meruit or a quantum valebat award. As a consequence of this procedural distinction, there was no reason to develop any general principles of failure of basis, that could be applied to all kinds of benefits.

12–04   Where an unusual fact pattern invited the consideration of a broader approach to failure of basis, the judges indicated that an underlying general principle could be identified. Thus, in *Pulbrook v Lawes*[5] a comparison of the principles governing money and services was prompted by the parties agreeing to alter the form of benefit that the claimant agreed to confer on the defendant. Initially it had been agreed that the claimant would pay £75 to the defendant so that the defendant could carry out some improvement works on his house, of which the claimant intended to take a lease. Subsequently the parties agreed that the claimant should carry out the work himself, which he did. The defendant, however, failed to carry out his share of the improvement works, which prevented the claimant from being able to occupy the premises. The agreement failed to satisfy the requirements of the Statute of Frauds, and so the claimant brought a quantum meruit claim for the value of the benefit that his work had conferred on the property. Blackburn J. held that the claimant doing the work:

> "was equivalent as between the parties to payment . . . when the contract goes off it is exactly the same thing as if the consideration had failed, and the plaintiff is entitled to recover the value of what the defendant received under a *quantum meruit*".[6]

Lush J. agreed, commenting that "what the plaintiff did was very much as if he had paid the £75 into the hands of the defendant after the making of the agreement, in which case he would clearly be entitled to recover back the money".[7]

12–05   The asymmetry between money claims and claims for non-monetary benefits was purely the product of now extinct forms of action[8] and the language of their pleaders; as such, it has no place in the present law of unjust enrichment.[9] Clearly

---

[4] For early acknowledgements that the implied contract was, in reality, an obligation imposed by law see *Craven-Ellis v Canons Ltd* [1936] 2 K.B. 403 at 411 per Greer L.J.; and *Re Cleadon Trust Ltd* [1939] 1 Ch. 286 at 312–315 per Scott L.J.

[5] *Pulbrook v Lawes* (1876) 1 Q.B.D. 284.

[6] *Pulbrook v Lawes* (1876) 1 Q.B.D. 284 at 289.

[7] *Pulbrook v Lawes* (1876) 1 Q.B.D. 284 at 290.

[8] Common Law Procedure Act 1852 ss.2–3.

[9] See further, Ch.1.

there is a substantive difference between the two types of benefit, in that a money payment obviously enriches the recipient, whilst goods delivered and services rendered may, or may not, enrich. However, whilst it is, of course, accepted that the valuation of goods received or services rendered presents difficulties in relation to the assessment of enrichment, which do not arise where a money payment is concerned, the difference between the two types of claim seems to be confined to the issue of enrichment.[10] It is now coming to be recognised that, leaving the enrichment issue aside, both types of claims are governed by the same underlying unjust factor.[11]

3. ALTERNATIVES TO A CLAIM IN UNJUST ENRICHMENT FOR FAILURE OF BASIS

(a) *Claims in Contract*

An action in unjust enrichment for failure of basis may not be the only action   **12–06** available. The basis for the transfer may have been receipt of counter-performance under a contract, in which case the claimant may have a claim for damages for breach of contract or even for specific performance. The impact of a contract on the claim in unjust enrichment is discussed in detail in Ch.3.

(b) *Claims in Unjust Enrichment Using Different Unjust Factors*

Since different unjust factors focus on different aspects of any given transaction,   **12–07** it may be possible, in some factual situations, to analyse a claim using several different unjust factors. Thus, for instance, where a payment has been induced by a mistake of fact, and the claimant has received no part of a counter-performance expected from the recipient of that payment, a claim could be formulated either in terms of mistake, or in terms of failure of basis. The courts' general approach to such overlaps is to permit the claimant to express the claim in whatever form is preferred. Thus, in *Kleinwort Benson Ltd v Lincoln CC*[12] payments had been made by a bank to a local authority under an interest rate swap transaction. The transactions were ultra vires the authority's powers,[13] and one way of formulating the bank's claim, which had been pursued by other banks in similar cases,[14] would have been to say that the basis for the payments had failed, since the authority could not lawfully perform its part of the bargain. The claimants, however, chose to formulate their claim in terms of paying under a mistake of law and their claim succeeded.

Whilst a broad approach to failure of basis is generally appropriate, it should   **12–08** be emphasised that if the concept is stretched too far, it loses its analytical utility.

---

[10] See further Chs 4 and 5.

[11] *Cobbe v Yeoman's Row Management Ltd* [2008] UKHL 55; [2008] 1 W.L.R. 1752 at [43]. For a Canadian illustration see *Deglman v Guaranty Trust Co. of Canada* [1954] S.C.R. 725, particularly at 728 per Rand J., Rinfret C.J., and Taschereau J.

[12] *Kleinwort Benson Ltd v Lincoln CC* [1999] 2 A.C. 349.

[13] *Hazell v Hammersmith and Fulham LBC* [1992] 2 A.C. 1.

[14] e.g. *Westdeutsche Landesbank Girozentrale v Islington LBC* [1994] 4 All E.R. 890; *Guinness Mahon & Co Ltd v Kensington and Chelsea RLBC* [1999] Q.B. 215.

Failure of basis identifies situations where a transfer of value has been made both voluntarily and conditionally, and the condition for its retention by the recipient has failed. Where a transfer is made under compulsion, it follows that failure of basis has no role. For instance, where money is paid under a court judgment, and the judgment is subsequently reversed, it is not helpful to explain the liability to return the payment as grounded on failure of basis.[15] In such cases the more accurate explanation is that the courts' powers to compel payments are partly justified by the existence of procedural mechanisms for the correction of errors.[16]

12–09   Furthermore, analysis in terms of failure of basis may place an inappropriate emphasis on the voluntary nature of the transfer, thereby obscuring the existence of a different unjust factor applicable to both voluntary and non-voluntary transfers. Thus, in *Woolwich Equitable Building Society v IRC*[17] Lord Goff and Lord Browne-Wilkinson highlighted the possibility that liability to repay tax which had been paid pursuant to ultra vires demands could be explained on the ground that there was "no consideration" for the payment.[18] However, as Lord Browne-Wilkinson went on to say, payment of tax pursuant to an ultra vires demand was not precisely the same as payment on a basis that fails, rather there is "a close analogy".[19] Other members of the House of Lords focused their analyses on whether a payment of tax made, in the absence of any threat of enforcement action by the tax authorities, could be truly regarded as voluntary.[20] This analytical focus on the voluntary nature of such payments distracted from the underlying question, which was whether, irrespective of whether the authorities happened to have threatened enforcement action, money paid as tax pursuant to an ultra vires demand was recoverable.[21]

4. Terminology

12–10   A variety of phrases are used in cases concerned with failure of basis, the most common being "failure of consideration". Others include "a consideration that happens to fail",[22] "absence of consideration"[23] and "no consideration".[24] The language of failure of basis has been preferred for four reasons.

12–11   First, it accurately identifies the essence of the claim being pursued. As was said in *Wilson v Church*, the claim arises when there has been "a total failure of

---

[15] *Vasailes v Robertson* [2002] NSWCA 177 at [5].
[16] B. McFarlane, "The Recovery of Money Paid Under Judgments Later Reversed" [2001] R.L.R. 1. See further Ch.26.
[17] *Woolwich Equitable Building Society v IRC* [1993] A.C. 70.
[18] *Woolwich* [1993] A.C. 70 at 166 and 197 respectively. See also *Steele v Williams* (1853) 8 Exch. 625 at 622–623; 155 E.R. 1502 at 1506 per Martin B.; *Campbell v Hall* (1774) 1 Cowp. 204; 98 E.R. 1045.
[19] *Woolwich* [1993] A.C. 70 at 197.
[20] See particularly Lord Slynn at 201–204 and Lord Jauncey (dissenting) at 192.
[21] See further, Ch.22.
[22] *Moses v Macferlan* (1760) 2 Burr. 1005 at 1012; 97 E.R. 676 at 682.
[23] e.g. *Westdeutsche* [1994] 4 All E.R. 890 at 924.
[24] e.g. *Friends Provident Life Office v Hillier Parker May & Rowden (A Firm)* [1997] Q.B. 85 at 98–99.

the original enterprise—a total subsidence, so to speak, of the common ground".[25]

Secondly, it avoids potential confusion with the doctrine of consideration in **12–12** contract. In contract "consideration" refers to the benefit conferred or detriment suffered by a promisee which makes a promise enforceable.[26] "Consideration" in unjust enrichment, by contrast, refers to the basis for making a payment. Thus, for instance, in the leading case of *Fibrosa Spolka Akcyjna v Fairbairn Lawson Combe Barbour Ltd*[27] there was a sale of machinery, under which the seller promised to manufacture and deliver it by a specified date, and the buyer paid in advance. The seller's promise provided consideration (in the contractual sense) for the payment. However, once the contract became frustrated and no delivery was possible, the buyer could successfully assert that there had been a failure of consideration in the unjust enrichment sense: the basis of making the payment was that he would receive the machinery and that had not been fulfilled.[28] It may be that when the terminology was originally introduced in the 18th century, there was not the same potential for misunderstandings[29]: but, today, the double meaning of "consideration" creates an obvious risk of confusion. For instance, in the leading case of *Westdeutsche Landesbank Girozentrale v Islington LBC*, Hobhouse J. asserted that "The phrase 'failure of consideration' is one which in its terminology presupposes that there has been at some stage a valid contract which has been partially performed by one party".[30] In the House of Lords, Lord Goff expressed the obiter view that "the concept of failure of consideration need not be so narrowly confined",[31] and the incorrectness of Hobhouse J.'s assertion can be seen from cases where, despite there being no contractual arrangement between the parties, payment was recovered by a claimant on the ground of failure of consideration.

For instance, in *Martin v Andrews*[32] the claimant had subpoenaed the defen- **12–13** dant to give evidence at a trial, and, as required by statute, had paid 6*l* to the defendant for travel expenses that would be incurred in attending the hearing. The case settled before the hearing, but the defendant refused to return the 6*l*. The claimant successfully recovered it, with Lord Campbell C.J. stating that "The consideration has failed".[33] The double meaning of "consideration" has been

---

[25] *Wilson v Church* (1879) 13 Ch. D. 1 at 26. For the later proceedings in the case see *National Bolivian Navigation Co v Wilson* (1880) 5 App. Cas. 176.

[26] H. Beale (gen. ed.), *Chitty on Contracts*, 30th edn (London: Sweet & Maxwell, 2008), Ch.3.

[27] *Fibrosa Spolka Akcyjna v Fairbairn Lawson Combe Barbour Ltd* [1943] A.C. 32.

[28] Recovery of payments under contracts which become frustrated is now governed by Law Reform (Frustrated Contracts) Act 1943; see Ch.15.

[29] B. Kremer, "Recovering Money Paid Under Void Contracts: 'Absence of Consideration' and Failure of Consideration" (2001) 17 J.C.L. 37, p.53.

[30] *Westdeutsche Landesbank Girozentrale* [1994] 4 All E.R. 890 at 924. Other examples include: *Dies v British and International Mining and Finance Corp Ltd* [1939] 1 K.B. 724 at 744: "it was not the consideration that failed but the party to the contract"; *McRae v Commonwealth Disposals Commission* (1951) 84 C.L.R. 377 at 406: "If there were no contract, there could be no failure of consideration".

[31] *Westdeutsche* [1996] A.C. 669 at 683. See too P. Birks, "No Consideration: Restitution After Void Contracts" (1993) 23 U.W.A.L.R. 195, p.209.

[32] *Martin v Andrews* (1856) 7 E. & B. 1; 119 E.R. 1148.

[33] *Martin v Andrews* at 7 E. & B. at 4; 119 E.R. at 1150. See also *Chillingworth v Esche* [1924] 1 Ch. 97; *Roxborough v Rothmans of Pall Mall Australia Ltd* [2001] HCA 68; (2001) 208 C.L.R. 516 at [16] and [102]; *Close v Wilson* [2011] EWCA Civ 5 at [31] (unenforceable nature of agreement no bar to recovery of payments made under it).

described as "a cross which the common law of unjust enrichment has to bear",[34] but there is no necessity for this unsatisfactory situation to continue: since "failure of consideration" no longer describes the essence of the claim accurately, better language should be used.

12–14   Thirdly, the phrase "failure of consideration" is associated with the action for money had and received on the ground of failure of consideration, which was available only in respect of money payments[35]; the general principle being analysed in this section applies to benefits of all kinds.

12–15   Fourthly, failure of basis language has already attracted powerful judicial and academic support.[36] In *Roxborough*[37] Gleeson C.J., Gaudron J. and Hayne J. encapsulated the principle in the following terms:

> "Failure of consideration is not limited to non-performance of a contractual obligation, although it may include that . . . the concept embraces payment for a purpose which has failed, as, for example, where a condition has not been fulfilled, or a contemplated state of affairs has disappeared."[38]

Gummow J. stated that " 'failure of consideration' identifies the failure to sustain itself of the state of affairs contemplated as a basis for the payments".[39] It should be noted that, by our use of this uniform terminology, we are deliberately treating cases decided using the language of "failure of consideration" and those using the language of "absence of consideration" as belonging to the same substantive category. As Aikens L.J. put it in *Haugesund Kommune v Depfa ACS Bank*, the debate about whether to use the language of failure or absence of consideration is "a question of which is the more apt terminology; it does not have any legal significance".[40]

5. The Requirement of Total Failure

(a) *Failure Must Be Total Where Money Has Been Paid*

12–16   Where the benefit conferred takes the form of money, the failure of basis must be total. There is no equivalent requirement where the benefit is non-financial.[41] If even a very small part of the benefit which formed the basis for the payment has

---

[34] P. Birks, "Failure of Consideration" in F. Rose (ed.), *Consensus ad Idem* (London: Sweet & Maxwell, 1996), 179, p.191.

[35] See above, para.12–02.

[36] Judicial: *David Securities Pty Ltd v Commonwealth Bank of Australia* (1992) 175 C.L.R. 353 at 382; *Roxborough* [2001] HCA 68; (2001) 208 C.L.R. 516. Academic: P. Birks and C. Mitchell, "Unjust Enrichment" in A. Burrows (ed.), *English Private Law*, 2nd edn (Oxford: OUP, 2007), paras 18–88—18–92; R. Stevens and B. McFarlane, "In Defence of *Sumpter v Hedges*" (2002) 118 L.Q.R. 569, pp. 575–576.

[37] *Roxborough* [2001] HCA 68; (2001) 208 C.L.R. 516.

[38] *Roxborough* [2001] HCA 68; (2001) 208 C.L.R. 516 at [16].

[39] *Roxborough* [2001] HCA 68; (2001) 208 C.L.R. 516 at [104].

[40] *Haugesund Kommune v Depfa ACS Bank* [2010] EWCA Civ 579; [2011] 1 All E.R. 190 at [62]. See similarly *Guinness Mahon* [1999] Q.B. 215 at 239–240 per Robert Walker L.J.

[41] e.g. *Powell v Braun* [1954] 1 W.L.R. 401; *Lusty v Finsbury Securities Ltd* (1991) 58 B.L.R. 66.

been conferred, no action will lie. Thus, in *Whincup v Hughes*[42] a payment was made for an apprenticeship, which was to last six years. The master died after only 11 months, and it was held that, since part of the benefit had been conferred, the basis had not totally failed. Various reasons have been given to justify this strict rule. The main reason given in *Whincup* was the difficulty of apportioning the premium. As the Court of Common Pleas explained, the premium could not simply be allocated to the six-year period pro rata. Rather, the value of the benefit received by the apprentice would vary during the course of the apprenticeship. At the start of the apprenticeship the apprentice would be receiving intensive tuition, and would be able to contribute little by way of useful service to the master's business; towards the end of the apprenticeship less tuition would be required and the apprentice could be expected to have become a valuable assistant. A second reason suggested in *Whincup*'s case was that returning a proportion of the payment would override the intentions of the parties as expressed in the contract of apprenticeship.[43] A third reason relates to the concern that, if a claim for unjust enrichment is allowed where there has only been a partial failure of consideration, parties will opt for that claim wherever it will yield a higher award than a claim for damages for breach of contract. In other words, the unjust enrichment claim would be used as the way to escape a bad bargain. Each of these arguments shall now be examined in turn.

(b) *Reasons for the Rule*

(i) *Difficulty of Valuation*

Difficulty of valuation is not a problem unique to the law of unjust enrichment.   **12–17**
In other areas of law, such as damages for personal injury, or for breach of contract, judges manage (often with the help of expert evidence) to overcome the difficulty of valuing benefits, and it is accepted that their findings cannot always be scientifically precise. In situations closely analogous to failure of basis, the difficulty of making an accurate valuation has not prevented a claim from arising. Thus, where a contract is frustrated, the statutory regime now directs courts to value benefits received; what little case law there is indicates that this can often be a difficult, but not impossible, task.[44] Similarly, where a local authority had granted a building lease for a fixed term, which contained an ultra vires option to renew, it was held that the lessee's right to property under art.1, Protocol 1 of the European Convention on Human Rights had been violated, and that a sum was to be awarded, by way of just satisfaction for that violation.[45] The court acknowledged that there was no indication in the lease of the value which the parties put on the option to renew, but observed that:

> "this may be regarded as the element which would most appropriately reflect the loss suffered by the applicant when he entered into the lease agreement containing an unenforceable option clause".[46]

---

[42] *Whincup v Hughes* (1871) L.R. 6 C.P. 78. See also *Ferns v Carr* (1885) 28 Ch. D. 409.
[43] *Whincup* (1871) L.R. 6 C.P. 78 at 83.
[44] Law Reform (Frustrated Contracts) Act 1943. See further, Ch.15.
[45] *Stretch v United Kingdom* (2004) 38 E.H.R.R. 12.
[46] *Stretch v UK* (2004) 38 E.H.R.R. 12 at [50].

It proceeded to estimate the value of the option and awarded that sum as just satisfaction.

12–18   As well as being out of line with current approaches to the valuation of benefits, the approach taken in *Whincup* also seems to have been peculiarly cautious when seen in a historical context. Courts going back to the 17th century had been far less reluctant to enter into the assessment of benefits received for a payment. For instance, in *Newton v Rowse*[47] the claimant had apprenticed his son to an attorney, paying £120. The articles of apprenticeship recorded that if the attorney died within a year, £60 was to be repaid. The attorney died within three weeks and the court decreed that £100 should be returned. The decision was later said to have "carried the jurisdiction as far as could be, by returning a larger sum than that agreed for",[48] but it was not seen as being objectionable in principle. The issue was whether it was for the Court of King's Bench or the Mayor's Court, to determine what proportion of a premium should be repaid.[49] Just over 20 years before the decision in *Whincup*, the Court of Chancery, in *Hirst v Tolson*,[50] had clearly explained that, where a master died before the end of an apprenticeship, a part of the premium paid should be returned, on the ground that "the consideration failing, the money must be paid back again".[51] Even as late as 1860, the court's ability to apportion the premium where a master had died or become bankrupt was treated as self-evident.[52] There was also a line of 19th century cases supporting the apportionment of premiums in cases concerning lawyers, which suggested that the courts had a special jurisdiction over attornies and officers of the court that allowed them to make such an adjustment.[53] This possibility was left open in *Whincup*,[54] only to be overruled shortly afterwards in *Ferns v Carr.*[55]

(ii) Inconsistency with the Contractual Terms

12–19   The concern that a remedy in unjust enrichment would be inconsistent with the terms of the parties' agreement is difficult to understand. If it is agreed that a payment shall be retained, whether or not performance occurs, there has been no failure of basis for the payment and no claim in unjust enrichment can arise. In such circumstances the payment is unconditional. Express terms providing for the retention of payment irrespective of performance should, therefore, present no analytical difficulty for the law of unjust enrichment—any legal difficulty is likely to revolve around the construction of the term. An implied term (which would have been the only possibility on the facts of *Whincup*) to the same effect is likely to be very rare; indeed it is quite hard to imagine when such terms would

---

[47] *Newton v Rowse* (1687) 1 Vern. 460; 23 E.R. 586.
[48] *Hale v Webb* (1786) 2 Bro. C.C. 78 at 80; 29 E.R. 44 at 46.
[49] For further examples of apprenticeship premiums being apportioned see *Soam v Bowden* (1678) Reports temp. Finch 396; 23 E.R. 216 (merchant); *Therman v Abell* (1688) 2 Vern. 64; 23 E.R. 650 (apothecary); *Ex p. Sandby* (1745) 1 Atk. 149; 26 E.R. 97 (bookseller).
[50] *Hirst v Tolson* (1850) 2 Mac. & G. 134; 42 E.R. 52.
[51] *Hirst* 2 Mac. & G at 137; 42 E.R. at 54.
[52] *Webb v England* (1860) 29 Beav. 44 at 55; 54 E.R. 541 at 547.
[53] *Ex p. Prankerd* (1819) 3 B. & A. 257; 106 E.R. 658; *Ex p. Bayley, in the matter of Harper* (1829) 9 B. & C. 691; 109 E.R. 257; early doubts about the jurisdiction can be seen in *Re Thompson* (1848) 1 Ex. 864; 154 E.R. 369.
[54] *Whincup* (1871) L.R. 6 C.P. 78 at 81 per Bovill C.J., and at 86 per Brett J.
[55] *Ferns v Carr* (1885) 28 Ch. D. 409.

be so obviously intended that they could be implied as a matter of fact. Whether such terms could be implied in law raises different questions, such as whether the term is necessary for the operation of the relationship between the parties.[56] Again, this would be a matter for the law of contract. It may be that the objection about inconsistency with contractual terms, as raised in *Whincup*, was inspired by the then prevalent theory that unjust enrichment remedies were part of quasi-contract.[57] According to that theory, the law of quasi-contract could not create liability where the law of contract would deny it; it would follow that, where no contractual term requiring repayment could be found, no remedy in unjust enrichment lay either. Fortunately, a clearer understanding of the free-standing nature of unjust enrichment remedies now prevails: to the extent that the concern about inconsistency with the contractual terms is based on the assumption that quasi-contract is a valid category, it can no longer be supported.

(iii) *Escaping from a Bad Bargain*

The concern about the use of unjust enrichment to escape from bad bargains **12–20** requires careful consideration. The law rightly recognises that unjust enrichment claims should not be permitted where they would, in effect, subvert the parties' contractual bargain. Thus, a claim for unjust enrichment on the ground of failure of basis cannot be brought whilst the contract under which the payment was made is still subsisting.[58] It is also appropriate that parties should not be permitted to obtain awards of damages for breach of contract that put them in a better position than if the contract had been fully performed—hence the principle that where a party claims reliance losses as damages for breach of contract, it is open to the party in breach to prove that the expectation losses would inevitably have been lower. If the party in breach succeeds in doing so, the damages award is limited to those expectation losses.[59] The requirement of total failure of basis derives some support from both of these broad principles, but it is doubtful whether that is sufficient to justify it.

First, the rule against allowing an unjust enrichment claim whilst the contract **12–21** is still subsisting already protects contractual agreements against subversion. Further protection for contracts might arguably be justifiable, but, as Peter Birks explained, the total failure requirement offers only a partial protection, which turns on whether the failure of basis happens to be total.[60] If contracts require protection against subversion, even where they no longer exist, there is no good reason to protect only those bargains where there has been both a money payment and some counter-performance. If protection is needed, it should extend to all contracts, irrespective of whether anything has been received in return for the payment.

Secondly, it is questionable whether making an award for unjust enrichment **12–22** which exceeds the expectation losses really does subvert the parties' contract. The situation is not exactly the same as where expectation damages are allowed

---

[56] For the tests for implying terms see: H. Beale (gen. ed.), *Chitty on Contracts*, Ch.13.
[57] See para.3–02 and following.
[58] See para.3–13 and following.
[59] *C&P Haulage Ltd v Middleton* [1983] 1 W.L.R. 1461; *C.C.C. Films (London) Ltd v Impact Quadrant Films Ltd* [1985] 1 Q.B. 16.
[60] P. Birks, "Failure of Consideration" in F. Rose (ed.), *Consensus Ad Idem*, 179, p.189.

to prevail over reliance damages. There, in a cause of action which is aimed at enforcing the contract, two possible measures of damages are in conflict; not inappropriately, the courts refuse to make an award that puts the innocent party in a better position than if the contract had been performed. The award in unjust enrichment, by contrast, relates to a distinct cause of action, which is aimed at reversing a transfer of benefit. Undoubtedly the practical result of the option to pursue a claim in unjust enrichment is that the innocent party escapes the consequences of a bad bargain; but whether this is regarded as objectionable or not depends on whether it is thought that the law of unjust enrichment should be systematically subordinated to the law of contract; it has nothing to do with whether there has been a total or only a partial failure of basis.[61]

(iv) *Symmetry*

12–23   A further argument against the requirement of total failure of basis in relation to money payments is that no similar requirement is imposed in respect of claims where non-monetary benefits have been given on a basis that has subsequently failed. For instance, in *Lusty v Finsbury Securities Ltd*[62] an architect claimed in unjust enrichment for the value of work done at the request of the defendants for a project which the defendants ultimately decided not to pursue. The defendants had already paid the architect an interim fee of £10,000, but the fact that the architect had received part payment was no bar to his claim—he was simply required to give credit for the part payment.[63] One explanation for this more flexible approach when work has been done and only part-payment for it received may be based on the ease of counter-restitution. Unlike services, money is readily restored, and it may be that in cases like *Lusty* the courts are operating on the basis that counter-restitution could easily take place, but that it is unnecessarily cumbersome and literal-minded to require it to be done. If this explanation is correct, then the difference in treatment between cases where money is paid first and cases where work is done first comes back to the difficulty of valuing the work done. As argued above,[64] the difficulty in valuing performance should not be exaggerated, and is certainly not sufficient to justify denying a claim altogether. A further argument from symmetry is that, where a claim for unjust enrichment is based on a different unjust factor, such as mistake, there is no requirement that the claimant must have received nothing in return for the benefit he has transferred.

(c) *Application of the Total Failure Requirement*

12–24   Taken literally, the requirement of *total* failure of basis would suggest that wherever a claimant has received anything at all in return for the payment, no claim in unjust enrichment can lie. However, the courts have not adopted a literal

---

[61] See further para.3–40 and following.

[62] *Lusty* (1991) 58 B.L.R. 66.

[63] See also *Whittle Movers Ltd v Hollywood Express Ltd* [2009] EWCA Civ 1189; [2009] 2 C.L.C. 771, where the Court of Appeal assumed that a similar exercise would be permissible in an inquiry to ascertain the extent of any unjust enrichment. On this case see further P.S. Davies, "Contract and Unjust Enrichment: A Blurry Divide" (2010) 126 L.Q.R. 175, pp.178–179.

[64] See paras 12–17——12–18.

approach. Three qualifications have emerged. First, although the claimant might have received some benefit, if that benefit does not form part of what was understood to be given for the payment, the claim for total failure of basis remains intact.[65] The principles that the courts have used in identifying the bases of payments are examined in detail in the next chapter. Secondly, the courts disregard benefits potentially forming part of the basis for payment where the claimant has exercised his or her legal rights so as to reject those benefits. Thirdly, it may be possible to sever the payment, and allocate parts of it to distinct elements of the benefit in return for which the payment was made; if only part of that expected benefit has been conferred, it is said that there has been a total failure of basis in relation to the severable part of performance which has not been achieved. These last two qualifications will now be analysed in detail.

(i) *Exercise of a Legal Right to Reject any Benefit Conferred*

Where a claimant has exercised a legal right to reject a benefit conferred by the **12–25** defendant, the receipt of that benefit is disregarded for the purposes of assessing whether the basis of payment has totally failed. The most common instance is where a buyer exercises the right to reject goods that are defective or unfit for their purpose.[66] For instance, in *Baldry v Marshall*[67] the purchaser of a Bugatti car, who had stipulated that it must be "comfortable and suitable for the ordinary purposes of a touring car" rejected the car delivered once it transpired that it was neither comfortable nor suitable for touring. His claim for the price succeeded. Whilst it may sometimes be immediately obvious whether goods comply with the seller's obligations (and, therefore, little benefit can be gained by a buyer who promptly exercises the right to reject), the nature of the obligations imposed on a seller may mean that considerable use has been made of the goods before they are validly rejected. For instance, one aspect of the implied condition of satisfactory quality is "durability"[68]; if the goods are of a kind where the buyer is entitled to expect significant longevity, the buyer may legitimately take considerable benefit from the goods before rejecting them once the lack of durability becomes apparent. For example, in *Rogers v Parish (Scarborough) Ltd*[69] a Range Rover was driven for 5,500 miles over a few months, then validly rejected.[70] As these examples make clear, significant benefits are disregarded when no account is taken of the position prior to the exercise of a right to reject.

(ii) *Severability*

The practical significance of the requirement of total failure of basis is reduced **12–26** by the doctrine of severability. The doctrine of severability allows courts to split up the total payment made and allocate it to particular parts of the benefit

---

[65] *Comptoir d'Achat et de Vente du Boerenbond Belge S/A v Luis de Ridder Limitada (The Julia)* [1949] A.C. 293, discussed at para.13–05.
[66] The buyer's rights to reject are set out in Sale of Goods Act 1979 s.35.
[67] *Baldry v Marshall* [1925] 1 K.B. 260.
[68] Sale of Goods Act 1979 s.14.
[69] *Rogers v Parish (Scarborough) Ltd* [1987] Q.B. 933.
[70] Cf. *Bernstein v Pamson Motors (Golders Green) Ltd* [1987] 2 All E.R. 220 (car accepted by use for three weeks).

expected in return. Where only part of the expected benefit has been conferred, it can be said that there has been a total failure of basis in respect of that part of the payment relating to the benefit still outstanding. The clearest examples are provided by cases where the total amount paid has been calculated as a cost per unit. Thus, in *Biggerstaff v Rowatt's Wharf Ltd*[71] where a payment for 7,000 barrels of oil was expressed, in the parties' agreement, to be 3s. 6d. per barrel, and less than 3,000 barrels were delivered, the court held that there had been a total failure as regards the price attributable to the outstanding barrels. Similarly, in *Roxborough v Rothmans of Pall Mall Australia Ltd*,[72] although the price paid for consignments of cigarettes was expressed as a net total sum, the seller's invoice made it clear that this total consisted of two elements: the wholesale price plus a licence fee. The licence fee represented a sum which the seller was required, by legislation, to pay to the state government in respect of the sale. After the legislation was declared unconstitutional, the buyers sought to recover their licence fee payments, and it was held that the licence element could be severed from the total price.[73]

12–27   However, it is not necessary that the contract should expressly apportion the consideration between the different elements of counter-performance: all that is needed is that the court is able to identify distinct elements of payment in respect of which there has been a failure of basis.[74] Thus, in *Stevenson v Snow*[75] an insurance premium had been paid for a voyage from London to Halifax, Nova Scotia. The vessel sailed from London to Portsmouth and, before setting off to Halifax, the captain notified the insurer that the conditions imposed by the insurer for the transatlantic voyage to Halifax could not be met. It was held that the premium could be apportioned, and that the part of it attributable to the voyage from London to Portsmouth could be retained by the insurer; but the part attributable to the voyage from Portsmouth to Halifax had to be returned. Lord Mansfield C.J. was reported as saying that "this is not a contract so entire that there can be no apportionment".[76]

12–28   A similarly creative approach was taken by the Privy Council in *Goss v Chilcott*,[77] where it was held that payments of instalments of a mortgage could be severed into payments of interest and repayments of the principal sum. On the facts, the instalments had been credited against interest due, and there had, therefore, been a total failure of basis in relation to the loan of the principal sum, none of which had been repaid. The Privy Council also indicated that, had the

---

[71] *Biggerstaff v Rowatt's Wharf Ltd* [1896] 2 Ch. 93. For similar examples see *Devaux v Conolly* (1849) 8 C.B. 640; 137 E.R. 658 (where the situation was described—8 C.B. at 666; 137 E.R. at 670—as "a simple case of the partial failure of consideration"); *Behrend & Co Ltd v Produce Brokers Co Ltd* [1920] 3 K.B. 530; *Ebrahim Dawood Ltd v Heath (Est 1927) Ltd* [1961] 2 Lloyd's Rep. 512 (note McNair J.'s analysis of *Devaux v Conolly* at 519).
[72] *Roxborough v Rothmans of Pall Mall Australia Ltd* [2001] HCA 68; (2001) 208 C.L.R. 516.
[73] *Roxborough* [2001] HCA 68; (2001) 208 C.L.R. 516 at [9]–[13] per Gleeson C.J., Gaudron and Hayne JJ.; at [109] per Gummow J.; and at [195]–[196] per Callinan J. Kirby J. dissented (see [165]–[167]). See also *Johnson v Johnson* (1802) 3 B. & P. 162; 127 E.R. 89.
[74] *Giedo Van der Garde BV v Force India Formula One Team Ltd* [2010] EWHC 2373 (QB) at [302]–[304] and [323].
[75] *Stevenson v Snow* (1761) 1 Black. W. 315; 96 E.R. 176; 3 Burr. 1237; 97 E.R. 808.
[76] *Stevenson* (1761) 3 Burr. 1237 at 1240; 97 E.R. 808 at 811. Cf. *Tyrie v Fletcher* (1777) 2 Cowp. 666; 98 E.R. 1297. See now Marine Insurance Act 1906 s.84(2).
[77] *Goss v Chilcott* [1996] A.C. 788.

facts required, it would have been prepared to go further in its application of the severability doctrine. It observed that:

> "even if part of the capital had been repaid, the law would not hesitate to hold that the balance of the loan outstanding would be recoverable on the ground of failure of consideration; for at least in those cases in which apportionment can be carried out without difficulty, the law will allow partial recovery on this ground".[78]

(iii) *Limits of the Courts' Ability to Apportion*

12–29 The High Court's recent decision in *Giedo Van der Garde BV v Force India Formula One Team Ltd*[79] highlights the current limits of the courts' ability to apportion. There a contract provided for the claimant, an aspiring race driver, to act as a test driver for the defendant Formula One racing team. The claimant paid $3 million. In return the defendant promised to give the claimant 6,000 kilometres of testing, sponsorship space on the car and on his race suit, pit passes and—if the claimant obtained the necessary licence from the motor racing authorities—the opportunity to test the car in high-profile testing immediately before Grand Prix races and to act as a reserve driver on race days. In the event approximately only 2,000 kilometres of testing were made available. On the claimant's claim for unjust enrichment on the ground of failure of basis, Stadlen J. would have felt able to apportion the testing distance to the price paid, if it had not been for the contingent rights to high-profile testing and to act as a reserve driver. It was not possible to apportion a distinct value to those elements of the consideration and it was, therefore, impossible to make an award.

12–30 However, in the Court of Appeal's earlier decision in *D.O. Ferguson & Associates v Sohl*,[80] the severability doctrine had been applied in a way that had, and may still have, the potential to eradicate the requirement of total failure of basis altogether. There a builder had contracted to do building work on the claimant's premises for £32,194, but had repudiated the contract, leaving the work incomplete. A total of £26,738 had been paid: £20,470 before the repudiation, and a further payment of £6,268 afterwards. The trial judge valued the work done at £22,065. The Court of Appeal held that there had been a total failure of consideration in respect of £4,673, because that sum "was paid by the defendant for work that was never done at all".[81] Applying orthodox principles, the decision is difficult to justify[82]: since the final payment was of £6,268, and the difference between the total value of the work and the total paid was £4,673, it follows that the claimant received work to the value of £1,595 for that payment. The basis for the final payment had not totally failed, it had only failed partially.

12–31 Unfortunately, the Court of Appeal preferred not to consider the significance of its decision, with Nourse L.J. commenting that he did "not think that any useful purpose is served by making too elaborate an analysis of the legal

---

[78] *Goss v Chilcott* [1996] A.C. 788 at 798.
[79] *Giedo Van der Garde BV v Force India Formula One Team Ltd* [2010] EWHC 2373 (QB). The failure of basis claim is analysed at [233]–[375].
[80] *D.O. Ferguson & Associates v Sohl* (1992) 62 B.L.R. 95.
[81] *D.O. Ferguson* (1992) 62 B.L.R. 95 at 105.
[82] See the editor's commentary on the case in *D.O. Ferguson* (1992) 62 B.L.R. 95 at 100.

principles",[83] and appealing instead to "simple common sense". Certainly the result in the case is intuitively attractive, but the Court of Appeal's approach has left the law in an uncertain position. Stadlen J. in *Giedo Van der Garde* felt able to explain the case on the narrow basis that the trial judge found that particular items of work, the value of which was specified in the original contractual documents, had been completed; it was, therefore, legitimate to apportion the instalment paid between the items of work completed, and those which remained incomplete (and in respect of which no payment was due).[84] On the other hand, the case may be seen as establishing that severability of payments to the level of single units of currency is legitimate, and can be undertaken where (as with building work) the value of the benefit received is difficult to assess. If this latter interpretation is correct, the requirement of total failure of basis has, effectively, been overturned. However, because the Court of Appeal did not acknowledge the full significance of its decision, later courts have been unsure of the correct position. For instance, in *Ministry of Sound (Ireland) Ltd v World Online Ltd*[85] Nicholas Strauss QC only felt able to say that, following *D. O. Ferguson*, "there *may be* circumstances in which recovery for partial failure may be allowed"[86]; he held that the point was too complex to resolve on a summary application. This current state of uncertainty is unsatisfactory, and, given the level of the authorities supporting the total failure requirement, can only now be clarified by the Supreme Court.

---

[83] *D.O. Ferguson* (1992) 62 B.L.R. 95 at 106.
[84] *Giedo Van der Garde* [2010] EWHC 2373 (QB) at [318]–[319]. This interpretation of the case rests (heavily) on the fact that the original contractual documents included a price specification—the Court of Appeal's judgments do not give a detailed account of the method of valuation used by the county court judge.
[85] *Ministry of Sound (Ireland) Ltd v World Online Ltd* [2003] EWHC 2178 (Ch); [2003] 2 All E.R. (Comm.) 823.
[86] *Ministry of Sound* [2003] EWHC 2178 (Ch); [2003] 2 All E.R. (Comm.) 823 at [63] (emphasis added).

Chapter 13

FAILURE OF BASIS: BASES OF TRANSFER

1. Introduction

In order to identify the basis on which money is paid, or other benefits conferred, **13–01** the transaction must be closely analysed. It can often be said that the basis of the transfer was that the recipient would give or do something in return; if nothing has been done in return, the basis has failed. Hence Lord Simon L.C.'s remark in *Fibrosa Spolka Akcyjna v Fairbairn Lawson Combe Barbour Ltd* that "when one is considering the law of failure of consideration . . . it is, generally speaking, not the promise which is referred to as the consideration, but the performance of the promise".[1] However, as Lord Simon's use of the words "generally speaking" indicated, the possible bases of a transfer are not limited to counter-performance by the recipient.[2] Even where counter-performance has been made in full, a failure to confer legal rights (for instance, because the underlying agreement is ultra vires) may amount to a failure of basis for the transfer in question.[3] Precisely when failure of basis might consist in a failure to confer legal rights is explained in more detail below.[4]

2. Guiding Principles

(a) *Basis Must Be Joint*

The basis of the transfer must be jointly understood as such by both parties.[5] It **13–02** must be ascertained objectively, and the parties' uncommunicated subjective thoughts are irrelevant.[6] Hence, if only one of the parties has a particular basis in mind, and that basis fails, no claim arises in unjust enrichment. For example, in *Burgess v Rawnsley*[7] a man and a woman had contributed to the purchase price of a house, which was conveyed into their joint names. The man believed that he was going to marry the woman and that they would live in the house together (although he had not mentioned this to her). The woman had no intention of marrying and intended to live independently in the upper part of the house. A

---

[1] *Fibrosa Spolka Akcyjna v Fairbairn Lawson Combe Barbour Ltd* [1943] A.C. 32 at 48.
[2] Cf. *Westdeutsche Landesbank Girozentrale v Islington BC* [1994] 4 All E.R. 890 at 925 per Hobhouse J., and at 959 per Dillon L.J., who seem to have overlooked Lord Simon's use of the words "generally speaking".
[3] *Guinness Manhon & Co Ltd v Kensington and Chelsea RLBC* [1999] Q.B. 215.
[4] See para.13–14 and following.
[5] *Osborn v The Governors of Guy's Hospital* (1726) 2 Str. 728; 93 E.R. 812.
[6] *Guardian Ocean Cargoes Ltd v Banco do Brasil SA (Nos 1 and 3)* [1994] 2 Lloyd's Rep. 152 at 158–159.
[7] *Burgess v Rawnsley* [1975] 1 Ch. 429.

majority of the Court of Appeal held that there had not been a failure of basis, and, therefore, that there was no resulting trust in favour of the man's executor. Browne L.J. observed that[8]:

> "it seems . . . impossible to say that there has been a total failure of consideration or that the trust has failed where a trust is created by two people and where there is a failure of purpose for which one of them created the trust but which he did not communicate to the other party and which the other did not share."

Sir John Pennycuick gave judgment in similar terms, also emphasising that the man's intended basis had never been communicated to the woman. The majority's suggestion that the outcome would be different where a purpose is communicated by one party to the other is surely correct. The joint basis of the transfer should be assessed objectively—a purely subjective assessment would be both impractical and undermine the parties' legitimate expectations.[9] If, therefore, one party voices his understanding of the basis of a transfer, and the other apparently assents, that basis can be taken to be an agreed basis, whether or not the other party has some private reservations about it.

13–03   In *David Securities Pty Ltd v Commonwealth Bank of Australia*[10] a majority of the High Court of Australia advocated a different approach to ascertaining the basis of the transaction. They stated that "we must ask what these particular appellants, in all the circumstances, thought they were receiving as consideration".[11] This approach appeared to place the emphasis on the claimant's subjective understanding of the transaction. The majority claimed that this approach was supported by the judgment of Kerr L.J. in *Rover International Ltd v Cannon Film Sales Ltd.*[12] Kerr L.J. in that case did indeed cite, with approval, a passage from *Chitty on Contracts* in which it was said that the assessment had to be undertaken "from the payer's point of view".[13] However, that passage did not support the use later made of it by the High Court of Australia.[14] As was clear from the context of the passage (which was set out by Kerr L.J.), the point being made was that the fact that the contract between the parties had been supported by good consideration did not preclude a payer from claiming for "total failure of consideration". Rather, the question was whether the payer had received any part of what he had bargained for. No observations were made on how the basis of the transaction should be ascertained. Later Australian authority has declined to follow the subjective approach advocated by the High Court and has taken the objective approach set out in the previous paragraph.[15] As a matter of both

---

[8] *Burgess v Rawnsley* [1975] 1 Ch. 429 at 442.

[9] The same reasoning underpins the objective approach to contract formation. See further, H. Beale (gen ed.), *Chitty on Contracts*, 30th edn (London: Sweet & Maxwell, 2008), para.2–003.

[10] *David Securities Pty Ltd v Commonwealth Bank of Australia* (1992) 175 C.L.R. 353.

[11] *David Securities* (1992) 175 C.L.R. 353 at 382 per Mason C.J., and Deane, Toohey, Gaudron and McHugh JJ.

[12] *Rover International Ltd v Cannon Film Sales Ltd* [1989] 1 W.L.R. 912.

[13] *Rover* [1989] 1 W.L.R. 912 at 924.

[14] *Giedo Van der Garde BV v Force India Formula One Team Ltd* [2010] EWHC 2373 (QB) at [271].

[15] *Fostif Pty Ltd v Campbells Cash & Carry Pty Ltd* [2006] HCA 61; (2006) 229 C.L.R. 386; J. Edelman and E. Bant, *Unjust Enrichment in Australia* (Melbourne: OUP, 2006), pp.246–247.

principle and authority, the objective approach should continue to apply in England.[16]

(b) *Basis Need Not Be Express*

The basis for making a transfer cannot be ascertained purely by analysis of the **13–04** express words and conduct of the parties. Sometimes the basis for a payment may be implicit. For instance, *Rowland v Divall*[17] concerned the purchaser of a car who had used it for four months. At that point, it emerged that the seller of the car had had no title and the true owner reclaimed it. According to the Court of Appeal, the purchaser had paid for title to the car, and, since he had received no such title, he was entitled to recover his payment on the ground of total failure of basis. There was nothing to suggest that the buyer had said or done anything to indicate that payment for the car was conditional on him receiving good title, but transfer of title is such a fundamental feature of sale of goods, that such a basis for the payment could be implied.

(c) *Failure of Basis Distinct from Receipt of Benefit*

Failure of basis must not be confused with receipt of benefit. The transferor may **13–05** receive a benefit from the transferee, but it does not follow that the basis for the transfer has, therefore, been satisfied. The benefit must be (at least part of[18]) what was understood to be the basis of the transfer. As Lord Simonds commented in *Comptoir d'Achat et de Vente du Boerenbond Belge S/A v Luis de Ridder Limitada (The Julia)*,[19] "receipt by the promisee of something which the promisor did not promise will not prevent a total failure of consideration".[20] Lord MacDermott, in the same case, gave the following illustration:

> "If, for example, tea is bought and paid for at so much a pound, the delivery of an empty tea chest will not, in the absence of some special stipulation, amount for this purpose to a partial peformance of the seller's promise."[21]

Furthermore, even the receipt of a contractually promised benefit is not incon- **13–06** sistent with the basis of payment having failed. Thus, in *Warman v Southern Counties Car Finance Corp Ltd*[22] the claimant entered a hire-purchase agreement for a car with the defendants for 12 months, paying each monthly instalment promptly. The defendants were acting in good faith, but it subsequently emerged

---

[16] *Giedo Van der Garde* [2010] EWHC 2373 (QB) at [285]–[286]. See too *Killen v Horseworld Ltd* [2011] EWHC 1600 (QB) at [48].

[17] *Rowland v Divall* [1923] 2 K.B. 500.

[18] Where the transferor has paid money, the *total* failure rule applies (see para.12–16 and following)—hence, if the transferee has conferred some part of the agreed counter-performance, no claim in unjust enrichment arises.

[19] *Comptoir d'Achat et de Vente du Boerenbond Belge S/A v Luis de Ridder Limitada (The Julia)* [1949] A.C. 293.

[20] *The Julia* [1949] A.C. 293 at 316. See also *Stocznia Gdanska SA v Latvian Shipping Co* [1998] 1 W.L.R. 574 at 588.

[21] *The Julia* [1949] A.C. 293 at 322–323.

[22] *Warman v Southern Counties Car Finance Corp Ltd* [1949] 2 K.B. 576.

that they had no title to the car; they had, therefore, failed to perform their contractual obligation to offer the claimant an option to purchase. Despite the fact that he had received the substantial contractually promised benefit of the use of the car for 12 months, the claimant was able to recover his payments on the ground of failure of basis. The right to purchase, it was said, was "the whole basis of the agreement, the very foundation of it".[23]

13–07   Conversely, the basis for a transfer may be satisfied despite the transferor receiving nothing of benefit. Perhaps the most common example is the payment of a deposit, where the payer subsequently defaults: the basis of such a payment is that it shall be forfeited if the payer fails to proceed.[24] A further illustration is provided by the House of Lords' decision in *Stocznia Gdanska SA v Latvia Shipping Co*,[25] where the purchasers of six ships contracted to pay instalments of the price on the completion of certain stages of the design and construction. One such instalment fell due after the keel of the vessel had been laid. At this point the purchasers had no property in the part-built vessels. It was held that the basis for the payment of that instalment had not failed.

(d) *Basis and Motive*

13–08   The basis for making a payment is often to obtain a promised counter-performance. Under such circumstances the payer's basis for payment and motive coincide. However, where the basis and motive for payment do not coincide, it is important to emphasise that only a failure of basis suffices for a claim in unjust enrichment. Hence, for example, in *Rowland v Divall*,[26] where the claimant had purchased, and had the use of a car, which the defendant had no title to sell, the claimant's motive for entering the transaction was, at least in part, to have the use of the car. The (legal) basis for payment, however, was that good title to the car would be transferred. The seller's failure to give good title, therefore, meant that the basis for payment had failed.[27]

13–09   The distinction between basis and motive may have been overlooked by Kerr L.J. in *Rover*.[28] There the claimants had entered an agreement with the defendants under which the defendants would supply films to the claimants for dubbing and distribution in Italy. The gross receipts from distribution were to be shared between the parties, but the claimants were obliged to pay the defendants advances in anticipation of such gross receipts. If the amount of the advances exceeded the amount to which the defendants were entitled, the agreement provided that the excess was to be repaid to the claimants. After the defendants purported to terminate the agreement for a breach by the claimants, it came to light that the claimants had not been incorporated at the date of the agreement and the contract was, therefore, ineffective. In a claim for return of payments made by the claimants, the defendants argued that there had not been a failure of

---

[23] *Warman* [1949] 2 K.B. 576 at 582. For further illustrations see *Rowland v Divall* [1923] 2 K.B. 500 and *Barber v NWS Bank Plc* [1996] 1 W.L.R. 641.
[24] See detailed discussion in Ch.14.
[25] *Stocznia Gdanska SA v Latvia Shipping Co* [1998] 1 W.L.R. 574.
[26] *Rowland v Divall* [1923] 2 K.B. 500.
[27] See further, paras 13–14 and following.
[28] *Rover* [1989] 1 W.L.R. 912 [1989] 1 W.L.R. 912.

basis, since several films had been supplied to the claimants for dubbing work to begin. Kerr L.J. (with whom Nicholls L.J. agreed[29]) held, however, that receipt of the films was "merely incidental to the performance of the contract", and not the basis for the claimant's payments. "The relevant bargain", according to Kerr L.J., "was the opportunity to earn a substantial share of the gross receipts . . . with the certainty of at least breaking even by recouping their advance [under the terms of the agreeement]."[30] By characterising the basis of the transaction in this way, Kerr L.J. was able to hold that the claim in unjust enrichment succeeded, but it is not easy to understand how the delivery of the films—without which none of the dubbing or distribution work could have been done—could be regarded as "merely incidental". If the defendants had taken the money, but then failed to deliver any films, there would seem to be an obvious failure of basis. A better explanation for the result in the case may be that part of the basis for making the advance payments was that the claimants would have a legally enforceable right against the defendants to recover the difference between those payments and the defendants' share of the gross receipts from distribution. Since the contract was ineffective, that obligation to repay any excess failed to come into existence, and a basis for making the advance payments therefore failed.[31]

(e) *Unconditional Transfers*

It follows from the general principles set out in the foregoing paragraphs, that **13–10** where a transfer of benefit is made unconditionally, no claim for failure of basis can arise.[32] Thus, for instance, where an employee participates in industrial action short of a strike in circumstances where the contract of employment continues to govern the relationship between the employee and employer,[33] and the employer has made it clear that partial performance will not be accepted, any partial performance by the employee is done at the risk of receiving no pay for the work.[34] Similarly, benefits may be transferred on the basis that they can be retained whether or not the transaction in respect of which they were given is completed successfully. The two most common examples of such transfers are deposits and payments of advance freight. The principles governing the identification of deposits, and the additional rules that apply to deposits, are dealt with in the next chapter.

The principles governing the payment of freight in advance, which date back **13–11** to the 17th century,[35] can be summed up, simply, as being that the right to retain freight paid in advance is not conditional on the successful completion of the

---

[29] *Rover* [1989] 1 W.L.R. 912 at 938. At 933 Dillon L.J. preferred to analyse the situation in terms of money paid under a mistake of fact.

[30] *Rover* [1989] 1 W.L.R. 912 at 925.

[31] See the analogous cases on guarantees and ultra vires contracts, at paras 13–29—13–30 and 13–20—13–27 respectively.

[32] *Osborn* (1726) 2 Str. 728; 93 E.R. 812.

[33] For the position where the contract temporarily does not govern the relationship between the parties, see paras 3–20—3–22.

[34] *Spackman v London Metropolitan University* [2007] I.R.L.R. 744 at [61] (Cty Ct).

[35] *Anon* (1683) 2 Show. K.B. 283; 89 E.R. 941. In *Allison v Bristol Marine Insurance Co* (1876) 1 App. Cas. 209 at 226, Brett J. suggested that the rules governing advance freight emerged to meet the commercial needs of parties involved with Indian voyages.

voyage.[36] Thus, in *Andrew v Moorhouse*[37] the parties were negotiating a contract for the carriage of goods from London to the Cape of Good Hope. The ship-owner's agent offered the defendant a choice of prices: either £5 per ton paid in London, or £7 per ton paid at the Cape. The defendant opted for £5 per ton. The ship was lost on the voyage, and the Court of Exchequer held that the freight was due, since it was to be paid in London "absolutely".[38] Freight paid in advance, however, is not paid unconditionally: if the voyage is never undertaken, the shipowner is liable to return it.[39] Although the principles governing advance freight have been subjected to criticism,[40] they were preserved by the Law Reform (Frustrated Contracts) Act 1943 on the basis that they were too well-established in commercial practice to be altered.[41] When seen in the context of the general principles of failure of basis, however, the rules of advance freight appear unobjectionable—indeed, they are exactly what would be expected in a situation where the party transferring the benefit has taken the risk of counter-performance not materialising.[42]

3. FAILURE OF BASIS AS FAILURE OF COUNTER-PERFORMANCE

13–12   Where it is claimed that the transferee of a benefit has failed to render counter-performance, it is necessary to look closely at what passed between the parties, in order to identify precisely what was the basis of the original transfer of benefit.[43] Two leading cases may be contrasted. In *Fibrosa*[44] a contract for the purchase of machines provided for payment in advance and for the machines to be delivered to the buyer at Gdynia in Poland. The German occupation of Poland during the Second World War frustrated the contract, and it was held that, since the machines could not be delivered, there had been a total failure of basis for the advance payment. In *Stocznia Gdanska*[45] the contract was to "design, build, complete and deliver" six ships, with the price payable in instalments at specified stages of the work. After the keels of two of the vessels had been laid, the buyer

---

[36] *Andrew v Moorhouse* (1814) 5 Taunt. 435; 128 E.R. 758; *De Silvale v Kendall* (1815) 4 M. & S. 37; 105 E.R. 749; *Byrne v Schiller* (1871) L.R. 6 Ex. 319; *Allison v Bristol Marine Insurance Co* (1876) 1 App. Cas. 209; *Compania Naviera General SA v Kerametal Ltd (The Lorna I)* [1981] 2 Lloyd's Rep. 559; [1983] 1 Lloyd's Rep. 373.

[37] *Andrew* (1814) 5 Taunt. 435; 128 E.R. 758.

[38] *Andrew* at 5 Taunt. at 437; 128 E.R. at 760.

[39] S.C. Boyd et al. (eds), *Scrutton on Charterparties and Bills of Lading*, 21st edn (London: Thomson, Sweet & Maxwell, 2008), para.A162; G. Williams, *The Law Reform (Frustrated Contracts) Act 1943* (London: Stevens & Sons, 1944), p.74. The authority commonly cited for this proposition is *Ex p. Nyholm, Re Child* (1873) 29 L.T. (N.S.) 634, but the case appears to contain no statement of the principle attributed to it.

[40] *Byrne v Schiller* (1871) L.R. 6 Ex. 319; Law Revision Committee, *Seventh Interim Report (Rule in Chandler v Webster)* Cmd 6009 (1939) p.10.

[41] Law Reform (Frustrated Contracts) Act 1943 s.2(5). See further Law Revision Committee, *Seventh Interim Report*, p.10; A. McNair, "The Law Reform (Frustrated Contracts) Act 1943" (1944) 60 L.Q.R. 160 p.171.

[42] Cf. the American authorities cited (at length) by Butt QC in *Byrne* (1871) L.R. 6 Ex. 319 at 320–322.

[43] *A.C.G. Acquisition XX LLC v Olympic Airlines SA* [2010] EWHC 923 (Comm.) at [47]–[51].

[44] *Fibrosa* [1943] A.C. 32.

[45] *Stocznia Gdanska* [1998] 1 W.L.R. 574.

failed to pay the instalment due at that stage, and the shipbuilders exercised their option to terminate the contracts. The question was whether, if the instalments were paid as specified in the contract, they could be immediately recovered back on the ground of failure of basis. The House of Lords held that they would not be recoverable, because the basis for the payment of instalments was not solely the delivery of the vessels; the design and construction of the vessels also formed part of that basis, and, since some design and construction had been undertaken, the basis had not failed. Lord Lloyd acknowledged that this analysis contrasted with the approach in *Fibrosa*, saying that:

> "the distinction between a simple contract of sale, in which the only consideration is the transfer of title, and a contract of sale which also includes the provision of services prior to delivery, may sometimes be a fine one. But the distinction is sound in principle."[46]

The crucial distinction seems to be the terms of the parties' contract. Whilst it   **13–13** would have been obvious to the purchasers of machinery in *Fibrosa* that the sellers would have to undertake preparatory manufacturing work before the machines could be delivered, the contract attributed no significance to that preparatory work; in particular, the advance payment was not linked to the progress of work on the machines.[47] In *Stocznia Gdanska*, by contrast, the payment of instalments was conditional on progress in the design and construction of the vessels. The contractual structure showed that the basis of those payments was the completion of particular stages of the project. This emphasis on the contractual terms serves to distinguish *Fibrosa* from *Stocznia Gdanska*, but it may be questioned whether the contractual terms should be conclusive.[48] For instance, if in a case like *Fibrosa* it could be shown that the purpose of an advance payment was to allow the seller to purchase the raw materials needed in order to perform his side of the bargain, and the buyer understood this (even though nothing was said in the contract), in one sense it would be difficult to say that the basis for the advance payment failed if the seller did indeed spend that payment on purchasing raw materials. Alternatively, it could be said that where a payment is made under a contract, the contractual terms alone reflect the agreed basis of the payment as a matter of law, and supersede any other understanding between the parties. On balance, the latter view is more convincing, since it gives full effect to the allocation of risk created by the contract.

4. FAILURE OF BASIS AS FAILURE TO CONFER EXPECTED LEGAL RIGHTS

(a) *General Principle*

The failure of basis for a transfer may consist in a failure to achieve a particular   **13–14** legal result. For instance, a contractual obligation undertaken (and performed)

---

[46] *Stocznia Gdanska* [1998] 1 W.L.R. 574 at 600.
[47] See Lord Goff's speech in *Stocznia Gdanska* [1998] 1 W.L.R. 574 at 590. See also *Hyundai Heavy Industries Co Ltd v Papadopoulos* [1980] 1 W.L.R. 1129.
[48] J. Beatson, "Discharge for Breach: The Position of Instalments, Deposits and Other Payments Due Before Completion" (1981) 97 L.Q.R. 389, p.408.

may be ultra vires the party receiving the benefit[49]; or the party receiving the benefit of the transfer might be a seller of goods who has no title to them.[50] In such situations the failure of basis for the transfer is a failure to confer certain expected legal rights on the claimant. In addition to the examples discussed below, the cases concerned with work done under anticipated contracts that fail to materialise can be analysed in terms of the failure to confer expected legal rights on the claimant,[51] and an equivalent principle applies in subrogation cases where a lender advances money on the condition that it will be repaid with interest, that the borrower will be under a legally binding obligation to repay, that the lender will receive an interest securing repayment, and that this interest will be of a particular quality and priority; a failure of any of these conditions will result in a failure of basis triggering subrogation.[52]

(b) *Instances of Failure of Basis as Failure to Confer Legal Rights*

(i) *Basis Expressly Identified as the Conferral of Legal Rights*

13–15   Where the parties have expressly identified the basis of a transfer as the conferral of a legal right, failure to create that right will give rise to a claim in unjust enrichment. Thus, in *Kelly v Lombard Banking Co Ltd*[53] the first payment under a hire-purchase agreement was made "in consideration of [an] option to purchase" a car, which was to be exercised by paying the final instalment. The agreement was later (legitimately) terminated by the seller, thereby depriving the hirer of the opportunity to make the final payment. The Court of Appeal held that the basis for the initial payment had not failed, because the option to purchase came into existence immediately, even though the right to exercise it depended on the fulfilment of conditions, such as the prompt payment of every instalment.

(ii) *Basis Expressed in Terms of a Legal Concept*

13–16   Where the basis of a transfer is expressed in terms of a legal concept, two contrasting approaches have developed in the case law. The first approach, seen particularly in cases concerned with marriage, has been to insist strictly on all relevant legal obligations being created as a condition of the transfer being retained.[54] Thus, in *Re Ames' Settlement*[55] a valid marriage ceremony occurred, and the couple cohabited for nearly 20 years; the marriage was then annulled on the ground of the husband's incapacity to consummate it. It was held that a settlement on the husband in consideration of marriage had failed. Vaisey J. commented that "the case is, having regard to the wording of the settlement, a simple case of money paid on a consideration which failed."[56]

---

[49] e.g. *Guinness Mahon* [1999] Q.B. 215.
[50] e.g. *Rowland v Divall* [1923] 2 K.B. 500.
[51] See Ch.16.
[52] C. Mitchell and S. Watterson, *Subrogation: Law and Practice* (Oxford: OUP, 2007), para.6.73 and following.
[53] *Kelly v Lombard Banking Co Ltd* [1959] 1 W.L.R. 41.
[54] *Essery v Cowlard* (1884) 26 Ch. D. 191; *Re Ames' Settlement* [1946] 1 Ch. 213.
[55] *Re Ames' Settlement* [1946] 1 Ch. 217.
[56] *Re Ames' Settlement* [1946] 1 Ch. 217 at 223.

In cases relating to patents, by contrast, a less strict approach developed. **13–17**
Where a transfer was made in order to obtain the use and enjoyment of an
existing patent, later revocation of the patent did not make the basis of the
transfer fail. Thus, in *Taylor v Hare*[57] it was held that a claimant who had paid
for the use of the defendant's patent for five years could not recover his payment
when it emerged that the defendant was not the inventor of the apparatus
protected by the patent. As Wightman J. would later put it, "enjoyment by
permission of the patentee, while the patent was supposed to be valid, is consideration".[58]

The contrasting approaches in cases relating to marriage and patents makes it **13–18**
difficult to formulate a general principle to apply to situations where the basis for
a transfer is expressed in terms of a legal concept. It may, however, be possible
to explain the two different approaches by reference to the expectations of the
relevant parties in the two situations. Thus, in relation to patents, particularly in
the early to mid-19th century, it may be that the parties were presumed to be
aware of the notorious uncertainties inherent in the patent system when they
made their agreement.[59] Certainly the judges were aware of those uncertainties.[60]
Settlors making settlements in consideration of marriage, by contrast, would have
been concerned about questions of legitimacy of offspring, and anxious that their
property should not move out of their family. To such parties, a rigorous
insistence on compliance with the requirements of marriage would be likely to
form the genuine basis of any transfer they made. The decision in *Re Ames'
Settlement* illustrates that approach, and may also reflect a further nuance in the
identification of the basis of a transfer. On the facts, the husband had received
payments of income from the trust fund during his supposed marriage. Those
payments were made in consideration of marriage in just the same way as the
settlement of the trust fund, but the settlor's executors were not seeking to
recover them. That distinction between the fund and its income may well have
reflected an understanding that whilst the transfer of the fund was conditional on
a valid marriage in all senses, enjoyment of the income was conditional on the
continuation of an apparently valid marriage.

(iii) *Insurance Contracts*

In insurance contracts, the basis for the insured's payment of the premium is that **13–19**
the insurer runs the risk of having to indemnify the insured against losses
resulting from the insured event. Hence, if the insurer has never been on risk, the
basis for payment of the premium has failed.[61] As Lord Mansfield C.J. put it in
1777:

---

[57] *Taylor v Hare* (1805) 1 Bos. & Pul. (N.R.) 260; 127 E.R. 461.

[58] *Lawes v Purser* (1856) 6 E. & B. 930 at 935; 119 E.R. 1110 at 1113.

[59] Anon., review of Charles Babbage, *Reflexions on the Decline of Science in England, and on some
of its Causes* (London: B. Fellowes, 1830), (1830) 43:86 *Quarterly Review* 305, pp.333–340; B.
Sherman and L. Bently, *The Making of Modern Intellectual Property Law* (Cambridge: CUP, 1999),
pp.101–110.

[60] See the allusion by Chambre J. in *Taylor v Hare* to the public controversies surrounding Ark-
wright's patents: (1805) 1 Bos. & Pul. (N.R.) 260 at 262; 127 E.R. 461 at 463.

[61] *Stevenson v Snow* (1761) 1 Black. W. 315 at 318; 96 E.R. 176 at 178; 3 Burr. 1237; 97 E.R. 808;
Tyrie v Fletcher (1777) 2 Cowp. 666; 98 E.R. 1297; *Re Phoenix Life Assurance Co* (1862) 2 J. & H.
441; 70 E.R. 1131.

"the under-writer receives a premium for running the risk of indemnifying the insured, and whatever cause it be owing to, if he does not run the risk, the consideration for which the premium or money was put into his hands, fails, and therefore he ought to return it."[62]

In relation to marine insurance, the principle has been given statutory recognition.[63]

(iv) *Ineffective Contracts*

13–20   **General**   Where parties have transferred benefits under arrangements which were believed to be contractually binding, but those arrangements turn out to have been legally ineffective, a claim in unjust enrichment for the return of the benefits is recognised.[64] Thus, in *Westdeutsche Landesbank Girozentrale v Islington LBC*[65] the bank and the council had entered into an interest rate swap agreement. Each party promised to pay to the other, on set dates, differences between a fixed rate of interest and the current prevailing market rate on a notional principal sum. The swap began in 1987 and was due to run for 10 years. However, in 1989 the Divisional Court decided that such interest rate swap transactions were outside the powers of local authorities,[66] and the payments ceased. The Divisional Court's decision was later upheld by the House of Lords.[67] The bank, which had made a net loss on the transaction, sought to recover its payments (giving credit for payments it had received from the council), and succeeded. Hobhouse J. held that the basis of the transfers had failed,[68] and both the Court of Appeal and House of Lords (in obiter dicta) agreed.[69]

13–21   **Full performance of ineffective contract**   Where the counter-performance specified in an ineffective contract is made in full, a claim in unjust enrichment may still arise in relation to transfers made under it. Thus, in *Guinness Mahon & Co Ltd v Kensington and Chelsea RLBC*[70] the council had entered an interest rate swap agreement with the claimant, a bank. Under that agreement the bank agreed to pay to the council interest calculated at a fixed rate on a loan of £5 million. The council promised to pay to the bank interest on a notional loan of £5 million calculated at a floating rate. During periods where the fixed rate was higher than the floating rate the council benefited; conversely, when the floating rate was higher, the bank benefited from the arrangement. The arrangement was carried out in full. The Court of Appeal upheld the bank's claim in unjust enrichment.

---

[62] *Tyrie v Fletcher* (1777) 2 Cowp. 666 at 668; 98 E.R. 1297 at 1299.
[63] Marine Insurance Act 1906 s.84. See too *Re London County Commercial Reinsurance Office Ltd* [1922] 2 Ch. 67.
[64] *Branwhite v Worcester Works Finance Ltd* [1969] 1 A.C. 552.
[65] *Westdeutsche Landesbank Girozentrale v Islington LBC* [1994] 4 All E.R. 890.
[66] *Hazell v Hammersmith and Fulham LBC* [1990] 2 Q.B. 697.
[67] *Hazell v Hammersmith and Fulham LBC* [1992] A.C. 1.
[68] For criticism of Hobhouse J.'s interpretation of "failure of consideration" see above, para.12–12.
[69] *Westdeutsche* [1994] 4 All E.R. 890 (QB, CA); [1996] AC 669 (HL).
[70] *Guinness Mahon & Co Ltd v Kensington and Chelsea RLBC* [1999] Q.B. 215. See also the similar decision in *Kleinwort Benson Ltd v Sandwell BC*, heard with *Westdeutsche* [1994] 4 All E.R. 890 (QB, CA).

Morritt L.J., giving the leading judgment, rejected the council's argument that since the bank had received everything it was entitled to under the agreement, it could not be said that the basis had failed. In his view, "The bank did not get in exchange for that performance all it expected, for it did not get the benefit of the contractual obligation of the local authority".[71]

The decision in the *Guinness Mahon* case, with its emphasis on the legal **13–22** obligations of the parties, was controversial.[72] In one sense, it seems self-contradictory to assert that a party who has received everything promised under an agreement can claim for a failure of basis. However, a closer examination of the situation shows that the position is more complex. Whenever contracting parties make transfers pursuant to their obligations under a contract, they will generally do so on two inter-related bases: first, that counter-performance will be forthcoming; secondly, that, if counter-performance is not forthcoming they can have recourse to their rights under the contract in order to compel either counter-performance or its financial equivalent in damages. If both sides perform their obligations in full it becomes unnecessary to rely on the second basis for making the transfers; but that is not to say that the second basis for transfer never existed. Criticism of the failure of basis analysis in *Guinness Mahon* overlooks this distinction between the existence of a basis for transfer and the necessity to rely subsequently on that basis.

A further ground to support the decision in *Guinness Mahon* can be found in **13–23** the factual matrix of the case. Whilst it might be possible to envisage situations in which private individuals enter contractual arrangements being indifferent to the legal rights created,[73] it is difficult to imagine a company (such as the bank) ever entering a transaction on that agreed basis. By statute company directors owe duties to the company to exercise reasonable care, skill and diligence.[74] Indifference to the conferral of legal rights on the company is hardly compatible with taking reasonable care to protect its interests. Bodies such as the bank in *Guinness Mahon* are also more likely to insure against losses, or simultaneously to enter complementary transactions to hedge against the risk of losses being incurred. Liability under such arrangements is likely to be triggered by the bank's legal liability to pay. It would, therefore, be a very unusual situation in which a party such as the bank entered a transaction where receipt of the relevant legal rights was not an agreed basis of the transaction.

Wider issues arising from *Guinness Mahon* Whilst the analysis of failure **13–24** of basis in *Guinness Mahon* is analytically convincing, the decision raises wider questions about the availability of remedies in unjust enrichment.[75] The bank's claim in such circumstances has been described as "purely technical",[76] and the outcome conflicts with earlier, similar cases such as *Davis v Bryan*[77] where it was

---

[71] *Guinness Mahon* [1999] 2 Q.B. 215 at 230.
[72] For a powerful argument against allowing claims in unjust enrichment where the intended contract has been fully performed see P. Birks, "No Consideration: Restitution after Void Contracts" (1993) 23 U.W.A.L.R. 195.
[73] See para.13–27.
[74] Companies Act 2006 s.174. See too A. Dignam and J. Lowry, *Company Law*, 6th edn (Oxford: OUP, 2010), paras 14–45—14–52.
[75] See further, the discussion in paras 2–23 and 34–32—34–38.
[76] Birks, "No Consideration: Restitution After Void Contracts", p.206.
[77] *Davis v Bryan* (1827) 6 B. & C. 651; 108 E.R. 591.

said by Bayley J. that an action could not succeed since it was "against equity and good conscience that the money should be recovered".[78] It is also difficult to reconcile the decision with the underlying rationale of the ultra vires doctrine, which has been said to exist:

"for the better regulation of local authorities in the public interest and, in relation to their revenue-raising powers, for the protection of their ratepayers (or charge payers). It does not exist for those in the position of the banks."[79]

13-25   **Earlier authorities on ineffective contracts**   The decisions in *Westdeutsche* and *Guinness Mahon* establish the present law. Earlier authorities were not so consistent in recognising claims in unjust enrichment. For instance, in *Linz v Electric Wire Company of Palestine Ltd*[80] and *Steinberg v Scala (Leeds) Ltd*[81] it was held that purchasers of shares under ineffective contracts had no recourse in unjust enrichment. In both cases emphasis was given to the fact that the purchasers had received an asset of some value; no weight was given to the fact that neither purchaser had acquired the legal rights intended by the contract. The Court of Appeal in *Guinness Mahon*[82] disapproved the decision in *Linz*, and it is difficult to see how the decision in *Steinberg* can avoid the same fate. Both decisions can be criticised for failing to make a proper investigation of the basis on which transfers were made by the purchasers of those shares.

13-26   **Willingness to perform ineffective contract**   Where the contract that the parties have made is ineffective, but one of them is both willing and able to perform it in full, it was held in *Thomas v Brown*[83] that there is no failure of basis entitling the other party to recover benefits conferred under the agreement. In such circumstances, Quain J. observed:

"it cannot be said that the consideration has failed . . . the defendant has always been ready and willing to assign the purchased property to the plaintiff in pursuance of the contract; in short, to give the plaintiff all that was bargained for."[84]

However, the judgment of Quain J. stands alone. Mellor J. in the same case did not rely on failure of basis. Sir John Romilly M.R. had previously held, in *Casson v Roberts*,[85] that a payment made under a contract unenforceable due to the requirements of the Statute of Frauds was recoverable. Subsequently, in *Monnickendam v Leanse*,[86] Horridge J. reached the same result as Quain J. had done in *Thomas v Brown*, but on the basis that there was "a good contract between the parties, but one which could not be enforced under the Statute of Frauds".[87] The reasoning used by Horridge J., which seems opaque at first glance, hints at the

---

[78] *Davis v Bryan* 6 B. & C. at 655; 108 E.R. at 593.
[79] *Westdeutsche* [1994] 4 All E.R. 890 at 915. See paras 23–30—23–31 for further discussion.
[80] *Linz v Electric Wire Company of Palestine Ltd* [1948] A.C. 371.
[81] *Steinberg v Scala (Leeds) Ltd* [1923] 2 Ch. 452.
[82] *Guinness Mahon* [1999] Q.B. 215 at 240 per Robert Walker L.J.
[83] *Thomas v Brown* (1876) 1 Q.B.D. 714.
[84] *Thomas v Brown* (1876) 1 Q.B.D. 714 at 723, discussed in A. Burrows, *The Law of Restitution*, 3rd edn (Oxford: OUP, 2011), p.326.
[85] *Casson v Roberts* (1862) 31 Beav. 613; 54 E.R. 1277.
[86] *Monnickendam v Leanse* (1923) 39 T.L.R. 445.
[87] *Monnickendam* (1923) 39 T.L.R. 445 at 447.

conceptual complexities created by the Statute of Frauds requirements, and indicates, significantly, that contracts failing to satisfy the Statute of Frauds criteria were regarded as having an underlying validity.[88] Any attempt to derive from the cases on the Statute of Frauds a general principle about the availability of claims in unjust enrichment where contracts are ineffective should, therefore, be avoided. Furthermore, even if such a general principle could be regarded as established, it would contradict the reasoning used in the more authoritative swaps contract cases discussed in the previous paragraphs.[89] If *full performance* of an ultra vires contract is insufficient to prevent a claim arising on the ground of failure of basis, then a fortiori mere readiness and willingness to perform the agreed obligations must also be insufficient.

Where legal rights not a basis for transfers under an intended con-   **13–27**
tract Situations might be imagined where the parties to an agreement were genuinely indifferent to the legal rights it created. Such situations shall, however, be extremely unusual. One rare example is provided by *Begbie v Phosphate Sewage Co Ltd*,[90] where the claimant wished to obtain a document which he knew had no legal validity, in order to induce a third party to enter a further transaction. There the Court of Appeal rightly held that the basis for the claimant's transfer under the agreement had not failed when the legally ineffective document was delivered. Both the *Guinness Mahon* and *Begbie* cases highlight the importance of careful scrutiny of the transaction in order to identify the basis of any transfer.

(v) *Documents Having no Legal Effect*

Where a transfer has been made on the basis that the transferor will receive a   **13–28**
document, if the transferor receives that document, but the document lacks its intended legal effectiveness, the basis of the transfer will be held to have failed.[91] Thus, in *Young v Cole*[92] the claimant had paid for, and received certain Guatemala bonds. The bonds were genuine, but had not been stamped as required by an order of the Guatemala Government and were, therefore, unenforceable. Whilst Bosanquet and Coltman JJ. held that the bonds "were not Guatemala

---

[88] *Crosby v Wadsworth* (1810) 6 East. 602 at 610; 102 E.R. 1419 at 1424. See too M. Lobban "The Formation of Contracts: Offer and Acceptance" in W.R. Cornish et al, *The Oxford History of the Laws of England, vol. XII, 1820–1914: Private Law* (Oxford: OUP, 2010), 329, p.330. For a critical commentary on the operation of the Statute of Frauds, see J. Stephen and F. Pollock, "Section Seventeen of the Statute of Frauds" (1885) 1 L.Q.R. 1. An analysis of the practical application of the statute is undertaken by R. Ferguson, "Commercial Expectations and the Guarantee of the Law: Sales Transactions in Mid-Nineteenth Century England" in G.R. Rubin and D. Sugarman (eds), *Law, Economy and Society: Essays in the History of English Law 1750–1914* (Abingdon: Professional Books, 1984), 192.
[89] See para.13–21 and following.
[90] *Begbie v Phosphate Sewage Co Ltd* (1875) L.R. 10 Q.B. 491; (1876) 1 Q.B.D. 679.
[91] *Jones v Ryde* (1814) 5 Taunt. 488; 128 E.R. 779; *Young v Cole* (1837) 3 Bing. (N.C.) 724; 132 E.R. 589; *Gompertz v Bartlett* (1853) 2 E. & B. 849; 118 E.R. 985; *Gurney v Womersley* (1854) 4 E. & B. 133; 119 E.R. 51; *Bradford Advance Co Ltd v Ayers* [1924] W.N. 152; *North Central Wagon Finance Co Ltd v Brailsford* [1962] 1 W.L.R. 1288.
[92] *Young v Cole* (1837) 3 Bing (N.C.) 724; 132 E.R. 589.

bonds",[93] Tindal C.J. took a more careful approach, saying that the claimant's payment had been made "on the understanding that the bonds [the claimant] had received from the Defendant were real Guatemala bonds, such as were saleable on the Stock Exchange."[94] As Tindal C.J. appreciated, the real ground of the claimant's claim was that the counter-performance had failed to confer the legal rights that both parties expected.[95]

(vi) *Securities*

13-29   Where a security for counter-performance is unenforceable, the basis of the transfer may be held to have failed. The point is illustrated by several cases decided under the legislation requiring the registration of annuities.[96] That legislation was extended, first by judicial interpretation,[97] then by Parliament, to require the registration of securities that guaranteed payment of such annuities. Where securities were unregistered and, therefore, unenforceable, the courts consistently held that the basis for the purchase of the associated annuities had failed.[98] Perhaps the clearest demonstration is given by *Scurfield v Gowland*,[99] where an annuity had been purchased secured by a deed, a bond and a warrant of attorney. Only the warrant was registered. The purchaser sought to recover his purchase money, and succeeded, Lord Ellenborough C.J. holding that:

> "The plaintiff contracted for one entire assurance consisting of several securities, and he has a right to have that assurance entire or to have back his money. The defendant has taken away one of his securities, and therefore the consideration for the money has failed."[100]

13-30   The recognition that failure of a security for counter-performance could amount to a failure of basis was not confined to annuities cases. In *National Bolivian Navigation Co v Wilson*[101] the claimants were bondholders, who had invested their money in a scheme to construct an ambitious transport link between Bolivia and the Atlantic Ocean. The terms of the scheme provided for bondholders to be compensated out of the profits made by the railway sector of the link, and repayments were guaranteed by a charge granted by the Bolivian Government over certain customs duties. Following very unsatisfactory progress

---

[93] *Young v Cole* 3 Bing (N.C.) at 731; 132 E.R. at 593 per Bosanquet J., and 3 Bing (N.C.) at 732; and 132 E.R. at 593–594 per Coltman J.

[94] *Young v Cole* at 3 Bing (N.C.) at 730; 132 E.R. at 593.

[95] See also *Gompertz v Bartlett* (1853) 2 E. & B. 849 at 854; 118 E.R. 985 at 988.

[96] For more detail see P. Mitchell, "Artificiality in Failure of Consideration" (2010) 29 U.Q.L.J. 190, pp.202–304; W. Lumley, *A Treatise Upon the Law of Annuities and Rent Charges* (London: Saunders & Benning, 1833), pp.94–95.

[97] The point appears to be assumed in *Shove v Webb* (1787) 1 T.R. 732; 99 E.R. 1348 and *Straton v Rastall* (1788) 2 T.R. 366; 100 E.R. 197. It was expressly decided in *Hood v Burlton* (1792) 2 Ves. Jun. 29 at 34–35; 30 E.R. 507 at 511.

[98] *Shove v Webb* (1787) 1 T.R. 732; 99 E.R. 1348; *Straton v Rastall* (1788) 2 T.R. 366; 100 E.R. 197; *Este v Broomhead* (1801) 3 Esp. 261; 170 E.R. 608; *Scurfield v Gowland* (1805) 6 East. 241; 102 E.R. 1279; *Cowper v Godmond* (1833) 9 Bing. 748; 131 E.R. 795; *Huggins v Coates* (1843) 5 Q.B. 432; 114 E.R. 1313.

[99] *Scurfield v Gowland* (1805) 6 East. 241, 102 E.R. 1279.

[100] *Scurfield* 6 East. at 244; 102 E.R. at 1281.

[101] *National Bolivian Navigation Co v Wilson* (1880) 5 App. Cas. 176. For proceedings in the lower courts, reported as *Wilson v Church*, see (1879) 13 Ch. D. 1.

with the construction of the railway, the Bolivian Government revoked the charge over the customs duties. The House of Lords held that this revocation was, in itself, enough to destroy the basis on which the investors' money had been paid.[102] A very similar approach is taken in the law of subrogation, where a lender's right to subrogate may be triggered by the failure to confer on him a security interest of the quality and priority for which he bargained.[103]

(vii) *Title in Sale of Goods*

The purchaser of goods pays for them on the basis that he shall receive good title **13–31** to the goods sold.[104] Thus, in *Rowland v Divall*,[105] where the purchaser of a car had not received good title to the car, it was held that the basis for payment had failed. It was no bar to recovery that the purchaser had had use of the car for four months. As Bankes L.J. put it:

> "It is true that a motor car was delivered to him, but the person who delivered it to him had no right to sell it, and therefore he did not get what he paid for—namely, a car to which he would have title."[106]

The award in *Rowland v Divall* gave no credit for the benefit that the claimant had had from the car for four months. It seems that the point was not argued, but it was later shown that the Court of Appeal's conclusion was correct. Any benefit received by the purchaser was at the expense of the true owner, not the seller; the purchaser could not be made to give credit to the seller for the use of someone else's car.[107]

(viii) *Satisfactory Quality in Sale of Goods*

Where goods obtained under a contract of sale are not of satisfactory quality, and **13–32** the buyer has not exercised his right to reject them, the basis for payment of the price remains intact. Thus, in *Yeoman Credit Ltd v Apps*,[108] where the purchaser of a car that was both unsafe and unroadworthy had driven it for three months, the Court of Appeal held that the price could not be recovered by a claim in unjust enrichment. If the purchaser has exercised his right to reject the goods, however, the assessment of whether the basis of payment has failed takes place after that right has been implemented.[109] In such circumstances, since the purchaser has received nothing for this payment, there is a failure of basis.[110]

---

[102] *National Bolivian Navigation* [1880] 5 App.Cas. 176 at 183 per Earl Cairns L.C.; at 190 per Lord Hatherley; at 196 per Lord Penzance; at 200–201 per Lord O'Hagan; at 205 per Lord Selborne; and at 209 per Lord Blackburn.

[103] e.g. *Anfield (UK) Ltd v Bank of Scotland Plc* [2010] EWHC 2374 (Ch); [2011] 1 All E.R. 708. See further C. Mitchell and S. Watterson, *Subrogation: Law and Practice* (Oxford: OUP, 2007), paras 6.73 and following. Subrogation to extinguished rights is discussed in Ch.41.

[104] *Rowland v Divall* [1923] 2 K.B. 500; *Butterworth v Kingsway Motors* [1954] 1 W.L.R. 1286; *Barber v NWS Bank Plc* [1996] 1 W.L.R. 641.

[105] *Rowland v Divall* [1923] 2 K.B. 500.

[106] *Rowland v Divall* [1923] 2 K.B. 500 at 504.

[107] *Warman* [1949] 2 K.B. 576; *Barber* [1996] 1 W.L.R. 641.

[108] *Yeoman Credit Ltd v Apps* [1962] 2 Q.B. 508.

[109] See para.12–25.

[110] e.g. *Baldry v Marshall* [1925] 1 K.B. 260; *Rogers v Parish (Scarborough) Ltd* [1987] Q.B. 933.

5. Failure of Basis as Failure to Discharge the Transferor from Legal Liability

(a) General Principle

13–33   Failure of basis as a failure to achieve a particular legal result can also arise where both parties understand the basis of the transfer to be the performance of a legal obligation. For instance, both parties might understand that a payment is due in respect of tax, or pursuant to a valid contractual obligation. If the tax is not due, or the contractual obligation is a penalty (and, therefore, void), there is also a failure of basis, but, unlike in the examples relating to ultra vires contracts and sellers of goods given above, the failure of basis consists in the failure of the transfer to discharge the claimant from certain legal obligations. The same broad principle of failure of basis can be used to justify recovery in this type of situation as in the situation where there is a failure to confer expected legal rights. The key question is to distinguish between legal results that are the basis of the transfer, and legal results that are merely ancillary to the basis of the transaction. As highlighted in the previous chapter, however, although situations in which a party believes that he is discharging a legal obligation can be analysed in terms of failure of basis (and are so analysed in the cases), failure of basis is not really the best way to deal with situations where the transfer is made under compulsion.[111]

(b) Instances of Failure of Basis as Failure to Discharge Legal Liability

(i) Payment of Tax and Similar Charges

13–34   The basis of a transfer fails where both parties understand that the transfer is made in order to discharge a tax (or similar) liability, but no such liability in fact exists.[112] For instance, where a plantation owner in Grenada paid duty on sugar exports which had been demanded by the authorities pursuant to an ineffective royal proclamation, he was entitled to reclaim the money on the ground that the basis of his payment had failed.[113] Similarly, in *Steele v Williams*[114] a parish clerk insisted on receiving a payment for searches of the parish registers in excess of the amount prescribed by statute. Martin B. regarded the case as being "like the case of money paid without consideration".[115] This was a convincing analysis, since the agreed basis on which the payment was made was that it was required by statute; that turned out not to be correct. In *Woolwich Equitable Building Society v IRC*[116] the House of Lords recognised a new principle of unjust enrichment, under which money paid by a citizen to a public authority in the form of taxes or other levies, which is paid pursuant to an ultra vires demand by

---

[111] See paras 12–07—12–09.
[112] *Westdeutsche* [1994] 4 All E.R. 890 at 959–960.
[113] *Campbell v Hall* (1774) 1 Cowp. 204, 98 E.R. 1045. See also Lord Browne-Wilkinson's speech in *Woolwich* [1993] A.C. 70 at 197.
[114] *Steele v Williams* (1853) 8 Exch. 625; 155 E.R. 1502.
[115] *Steele v Williams* 8 Exch. at 632; 155 E.R. at 1506.
[116] *Woolwich Equitable Building Society v IRC* [1993] A.C. 70.

the authority, is prima facie recoverable.[117] Most cases of money paid on the understanding that it is made to discharge a tax, or similar, liability, will now fall under this new principle.[118]

(ii) *Payment of Contractual Penalty*

Where a transfer is made as required by the terms of a contract, the agreed basis **13–35** of the transfer will generally be that it is to discharge a legal liability. If the contractual provisions requiring the transfer are void, so that no legal liability to make the transfer exists, the basis for the payment has failed. Thus, in *Commissioner of Public Works v Hills*[119] a railway company contracted with the South African government to construct a railway line, and paid £50,000, as stipulated in the contract, as security for performance. The contract also provided for the government to retain sums it owed to the company from the earlier construction of two other lines as part of a "guarantee fund" for the third line. The line was not completed on time, and the government claimed to forfeit both the £50,000 and the guarantee fund. The Privy Council held that the total paid by the company was not a genuine pre-estimate of loss likely to be suffered on breach, and, therefore, that the contractual terms requiring it to be paid were void under the rule against penalties. The payments were ordered to be returned to the company. Although no analysis of the legal basis for returning the payments was made, one explanation for the result is that the basis for making those payments had failed (another explanation could be mistake). In *Union Eagle Ltd v Golden Achievement Ltd*[120] the Privy Council described the remedy available to a person who had made payments which fell foul of the rule against penalties as "a restitutionary form of relief against forfeiture, which gives the court a discretion to order repayment of all or part of the retained money".[121] This statement was not necessary for the decision in the case, and it is respectfully submitted that it was not accurate to describe the remedy as turning on "a discretion": the claimant has a claim for unjust enrichment under such circumstances as of right.

(iii) *Payments Made to Close a Transaction*

Where a payment is made voluntarily in order to close a transaction, the payment **13–36** will not be recoverable despite it not having been required by law. In such circumstances the basis of the payment is the satisfaction of the payor's liabilities, whatever those might be. Thus, in *Brisbane v Dacres*[122] the captain of a naval vessel made a substantial payment to the admiral to whom he reported, believing that there was a binding naval custom that he must do so. The payment was held to be irrecoverable, having been made voluntarily to close the transaction.[123] By contrast, if the payment has been coerced, it may be recovered on the

---

[117] *Woolwich* [1993] A.C. 70 at 177.
[118] See further, Ch.23.
[119] *Commissioner of Public Works v Hill* [1906] A.C. 368.
[120] *Union Eagle Ltd v Golden Achievement Ltd* [1997] A.C. 514.
[121] *Union Eagle Ltd* [1997] A.C. 514 at 520.
[122] *Brisbane v Dacres* (1813) 5 Taunt. 143; 128 E.R. 641.
[123] *Brisbane* 5 Taunt. at 152; 128 E.R. at 646 per Gibbs J.

ground of duress or undue influence.[124] It should also be noted that, if a payment is made in the mistaken belief that it is legally due, it can now be recovered on the ground of mistake.[125] It may be that if the facts of *Brisbane* arose today, recovery would be allowed on this ground (although it is not entirely clear from the report of the case whether the claimant believed that the admiral had a legal entitlement to receive the payment).

6. Relationship between Failure to Achieve Legal Results and Requirement of Total Failure of Basis

13–37   Where the failure of basis for a transfer is alleged to consist in the failure to achieve particular legal results, the party making the transfer may have received something that looks like counter-performance. If the transfer in question was a payment of money, a claim in unjust enrichment requires that the basis has failed totally.[126] In such circumstances the requirement of *total* failure of basis might appear to conflict with the possibility that a failure of basis might consist in the failure to achieve particular legal results. For instance, in *Rowland v Divall*[127] the claimant purchased a car from the defendant, to which the defendant had no title. Four months after the sale the defendant's lack of title came to light, and the claimant was compelled to surrender the car to its true owner. The claimant's use of the car for four months persuaded the trial judge that there had not been a total failure of consideration for the payment of the price. The Court of Appeal, however, disagreed. As Atkin L.J. put it, "He paid the money in order that he might get the property and he has not got it."[128]

13–38   The Court of Appeal's analysis in *Rowland v Divall* has troubled some commentators. Burrows, for instance, regards it as manifesting "artificiality",[129] and as showing that the courts do not rigorously apply the total failure requirement. However, the case is best seen as an illustration of the careful scrutiny of a transaction that is required in order to identify the basis for transfers of benefit made pursuant to it. In the simple case of a sale of goods, it is clear that one important aspect of the transaction is that the buyer should obtain the use of the goods sold. Hence, if no goods are delivered, the basis for the payment of the price fails.[130] However, simply receiving the goods is not the sole basis for payment of the price. As the Court of Appeal rightly pointed out in *Rowland v Divall*, transfer of title is also fundamental to a sale of goods. It follows that there may be more than one basis for making a transfer of benefit. A failure of any one of those bases for the transfer will give rise to a claim in unjust enrichment.[131]

---

[124] *Dew v Parsons* (1819) 2 B. & Ald. 562; 106 E.R. 471; *Morgan v Palmer* (1824) 2 B. & C. 729; 107 E.R. 554. See further Chs 10 (on duress) and 11 (on undue influence).
[125] See paras 9–71——9–94.
[126] See para.12–16 and following.
[127] *Rowland v Divall* [1923] 2 K.B. 500.
[128] *Rowland v Divall* [1923] 2 K.B. 500 at 506.
[129] A. Burrows, *The Law of Restitution*, p.324.
[130] e.g. *Fibrosa* [1943] A.C. 32.
[131] See further, P. Mitchell, "Artificiality in Failure of Consideration" (2010) 29 U.Q.L.J. 190.

CHAPTER 14

FAILURE OF BASIS: DEPOSITS

1. COMMON LAW PRINCIPLES

(a) *Definition and General Rule*

A deposit is a sum of money paid (or, less commonly, some other benefit **14–01** transferred)[1] at the time of entering a contractual agreement. The basis of paying the deposit is that it provides security against the payer's failing to perform his future contractual obligations.[2] Thus, for instance, in relation to a sale of land (where deposits are a characteristic feature), the purchaser pays the deposit to the vendor at the time the contract of purchase is entered as security for him completing the contract. The condition of the payment being retained by the vendor is that the purchaser defaults on his obligations.[3] If the transaction fails due to default by the vendor, the payment must be returned. It is, therefore, essential to examine the parties' agreement closely, so as to identify what they have undertaken to do.[4] Where both parties have performed their obligations, the vendor is no longer technically entitled to retain the deposit as security. However, rather than having the vendor return the payment, and the purchaser simultaneously making a cross-payment of the full purchase price, the parties will typically agree that that the deposit is also to serve as an instalment of the purchase price,[5] so that, when the purchaser does proceed with the transaction, he will simply pay the difference between the purchase price and the deposit.

The conditions under which deposits will be forfeited are frequently expressed **14–02** as contractual terms, and it has been said that what happens to a deposit is "a question of the conditions of the contract".[6] However, those contractual terms simply serve to identify what the parties have agreed should be the basis of the payment, and a non-contractual articulation of the basis of payment is equally effective. Thus, in *Chillingworth v Esche*[7] where a deposit was paid in respect of an agreement to purchase land "subject to a proper contract being prepared by the vendor's solicitors", and there was no binding contract between the parties, Pollock M.R. observed that it was necessary[8]:

---

[1] e.g. *Omar v El-Wakil* [2001] EWCA Civ 1090; [2002] 2 P. & C.R. 3 at [24].
[2] *Ex p. Barrell* (1875) 10 Ch. App. 512; *Howe v Smith* (1884) 27 Ch. D. 89; *Soper v Arnold* (1889) 14 App. Cas. 429.
[3] *Depree v Bedborough* (1863) 4 Giff. 479; 66 E.R. 795; *Collins v Stimson* (1883) 11 Q.B.D. 142.
[4] *Re Scott and Alvarez's Contract* [1895] 2 Ch. 603.
[5] e.g. *Palmer v Temple* (1839) 9 Ad. & E. 508; 112 E.R. 1304 ("by way of deposit and in part of the sum of £5500"); *Howe v Smith* (1884) 27 Ch. D. 89 ("as a deposit and in part-payment of the purchase-money").
[6] *Howe v Smith* (1884) 27 Ch. D. 89 at 97 per Bowen L.J.
[7] *Chillingworth v Esche* [1924] 1 Ch. 97.
[8] *Chillingworth* [1924] 1 Ch. 97 at 108.

"[T]o ask ourselves whether this deposit was by those documents [that had passed between the parties] intended to pass irrevocably to the vendor if the purchaser did not carry out the transaction . . . There was no provision made in the documents which would justify the vendor in declining to return it, though if he had, by appropriate words, made provision for that in the document, such a provision could have been upheld."

It was later suggested that Pollock M.R. intended to refer in this passage only to contractual documents,[9] but the better view is that he was not intending to introduce such a limitation, and was simply illustrating that the basis of the payment had to be identified by examining everything that had passed between the parties.[10]

(b) Default by Both Parties

14–03   If the transaction fails due to default by both parties, it has been held that the payer's default should take precedence and the deposit is forfeited. Thus, in *Omar v El-Wakil*[11] the purchaser of a house had paid a deposit, but was unable to find the funds to complete the purchase; the vendor was also unable to complete, since the agreed purchase price was insufficient to redeem an outstanding mortgage on the property and he had no other funds available. Pill L.J., with whom Lord Phillips M.R. agreed, held that "the principle that the deposit was paid as a security for the performance of the contract by the claimant should prevail". Although the right to recover the deposit was based on default by the vendor, and such default had also occurred, "the availability of the right to recover required the existence of an ability and willingness on the part of the purchaser to complete".[12]

(c) Distinguishing Part Payments from Deposits

14–04   The consequences of a payment being treated as a part payment are very different to the consequences if the payment is a deposit. Whilst part payments may be recoverable where the payer repudiated the contract in respect of which they were made,[13] a deposit will be irrecoverable under such circumstances. Thus, in *Mayson v Clouet*,[14] a contract for the sale of land provided for payment of a deposit of 10 per cent immediately, one instalment of 10 per cent after three months, a second instalment of 10 per cent after six months, and the balance once certain building work had been completed. The buyer paid the deposit and both instalments, but defaulted on paying the balance. The vendor accepted this repudiatory breach, and it was held that the defaulting purchaser could recover the two instalments, but had forfeited the deposit. The factor determining

---

[9] *Gribbon v Lutton* [2001] EWCA Civ 1956; [2002] Q.B. 902 at [31]–[33] per Laddie J.
[10] *Gribbon* [2001] EWCA Civ 1956 at [61]–[64] per Robert Walker L.J., citing P. Birks, *Introduction to the Law of Restitution* (Oxford: OUP, 1985), pp.223–224.
[11] *Omar v El-Wakil* [2001] EWCA Civ 1090; [2002] 2 P. & C.R. 3.
[12] *Omar* [2001] EWCA Civ 1090 at [49].
[13] *Palmer* (1839) 9 Ad. & E. 508; 112 E.R. 1304; *Dies v British and International Mining and Finance Corp Ltd* [1939] 1 K.B. 724. See paras 3–35—3–38.
[14] *Mayson v Clouet* [1924] A.C. 980.

whether a payment is a deposit or a part payment is what the parties have agreed should happen to the payment.[15] Generally it is not necessary for the parties to spell out all the legal consequences in order to make a payment a deposit: it is sufficient to state that the payment is a "deposit". In the absence of any description of the payment, it will be assumed to be a part-payment only.[16]

However, a court might, exceptionally, conclude that, even though a payment **14–05** was described as a deposit, other provisions of the contract indicated that it was to be treated as a part payment.[17] In *Palmer v Temple*[18] an agreement for a lease provided that £300 was to be paid "by way of deposit, and in part of the sum of £5500". The agreement also provided that if either party should neglect or refuse to perform, he must pay to the other £1,000 as liquidated damages. The Court of King's Bench held that the intention of the parties, as collected from the whole of their agreement, showed that the only consequence of non-performance should be the payment of £1,000. The initial payment was, therefore, simply a part payment, which had to be returned when the agreement to grant a lease was repudiated by its payer. *Palmer* was an exceptional case, which the Court of Appeal subsequently held turned on its own particular facts[19]; it was also suggested that more attention should have been paid to the description of the payment as a deposit.[20] Certainly a payment described as a "deposit" does not lose its character as a deposit merely because the contract also contains provisions for the payment of liquidated damages on breach.[21]

(d) *Pre-Contract Deposits*

A pre-contract deposit, paid before any binding contract has been entered, is **14–06** essentially an expression of seriousness of intention on the part of the prospective purchaser. It is not subject to the same principles as deposits paid at the time of making a contract. Part of the basis of payment of a pre-contract deposit is that the contract will subsequently come into existence. If, therefore, no contract materialises, the basis of the payment has failed, and the deposit must be returned. Thus, for instance, in *Lloyd v Nowell*[22] a purchaser paid a deposit of £100 under an agreement stated to be "subject to the preparation by [the vendor's] solicitor and completion of a formal contract". No formal contract was ever prepared. The purchaser later repudiated the agreement, and it was held that the deposit was recoverable. It was not open to the vendor to waive the condition relating to a formal agreement so as to make his right to retain the deposit unconditional.

A party paying a deposit in relation to a future contract is not under any **14–07** obligation to help bring the contract into existence, and may reclaim the deposit

---

[15] *Howe v Smith* (1884) 27 Ch. D. 89 at 97 per Bowen L.J.; *Mayson* [1924] A.C. 980 at 985 per Lord Dunedin.
[16] *Dies* [1939] 1 K.B. 724 at 743.
[17] *Linggi Plantations Ltd v Jagaseethan* [1972] 1 M.L.J. 89.
[18] *Palmer v Temple* (1839) 9 Ad. & E. 508; 112 E.R. 1304 (PC).
[19] *Howe v Smith* (1884) 27 Ch. D. 89 at 93 per Cotton L.J.
[20] *Howe* (1884) 27 Ch. D. 89 at 100 per Fry L.J.
[21] *Howe* (1884) 27 Ch. D. 89 at 93 per Cotton L.J.
[22] *Lloyd v Nowell* [1895] 2 Ch. 744.

at any time before a binding contract is entered. [23] Thus, in *Chillingworth*,[24] a purchaser agreed to buy land subject to a proper contract being prepared by the vendor's solicitors. A deposit of 5 per cent of the purchase price was paid, and a formal contract was prepared, which offered the purchaser all that he could reasonably ask for.[25] The purchaser initially approved the formal contract, but changed his mind before it was executed and withdrew from the sale. His claim to recover the deposit succeeded. As Sargant L.J. explained, "the parties were not agreeing that they would enter into a reasonable contract, but that they would enter into such a contract, if any, as they might ultimately agree and sign."[26]

(e) *Limitation on Size of Deposit*

14–08   If the sum paid as a deposit exceeds what is reasonable, it falls outside the principles governing deposits, and the contractual term requiring payment of it is treated like any other provision for payment of a liquidated sum on breach of contract. Such obligations can only be enforced (and payments made under them retained[27]) if the sums payable (or paid) are genuine pre-estimates of the loss anticipated on breach. Where a contract term requires a payment to be made on breach which is not a genuine pre-estimate, the term is a penalty clause and void.[28]

14–09   In assessing whether a deposit is "reasonable as earnest money"[29] for the performance of the contract, an "objective" approach is used. Thus, in *Workers Trust & Merchant Bank Ltd v Dojap Investments Ltd*,[30] a Jamaican bank sold land at auction and required a deposit of 25 per cent of the purchase price, which the purchasers paid. On the purchasers defaulting, the bank claimed that it was entitled to retain the sum as a reasonable deposit, since banks selling premises at auction in Jamaica demanded anywhere between 15 per cent and 50 per cent as a deposit. The Privy Council, however, held that it was not sufficient to demonstrate that the size of the deposit was reasonable by reference to the behaviour a particular class of vendor. Rather, the starting point was that both in the United Kingdom and, formerly, in Jamaica, the customary deposit was 10 per cent. Special circumstances would be required to justify a deposit above this amount. The bank sought to establish such special circumstances by claiming that the high percentage was needed to deter frivolous bidding at the auction. It also relied on the liability of vendors, under Jamaican legislation, to pay transfer tax at the rate of 7.5 per cent of the purchase price within 30 days of the contract.[31] The taxation position, it argued, made the appropriate starting point in Jamaica 17.5 per cent. The Privy Council rejected both factors, giving no weight to the importance of

---

[23] *Potters (A Firm) v Loppert* [1973] 1 Ch. 399; *Gribbon* [2001] EWCA Civ 1956; [2002] Q.B. 902.
[24] *Chillingworth* [1923] 1 Ch. 576; [1924] 1 Ch. 97.
[25] *Chillingworth* [1923] 1 Ch. 576 at 584.
[26] *Chillingworth* [1924] 1 Ch. 97 at 114–115. Cf. *Moeser v Wisker* (1871) L.R. 6 C.P. 120.
[27] *Commissioner of Public Works v Hills* [1906] A.C. 368.
[28] For a full account of this doctrine see H. Beale (ed.), *Chitty on Contracts*, 30th edn (London: Sweet & Maxwell, 2008), paras 26.125–26.156.
[29] *Workers Trust & Merchant Bank Ltd v Dojap Investments Ltd* [1993] A.C. 573 at 579.
[30] *Dojap Investments* [1993] A.C. 573.
[31] Transfer Tax Act 1971.

deterring frivolous bids. So far as the taxation position was concerned, it held that there was no necessity for including the amount due as transfer tax in a deposit, since no tax was due where a contract was not completed. Furthermore, tax paid on a sale which subsequently fell through could be recovered from the authorities. The underlying theme of the Privy Council's advice seemed to be that a deposit in excess of 10 per cent would be justifiable only where a failure to perform the contract was likely to result in loss to the innocent party above that amount.[32]

(f) *Competing Explanations for the Principles Governing Deposits*

The principles governing deposits have sometimes been explained by reference **14-10** to concepts other than failure of basis. For instance, in *Collins v Stimson*[33] Pollock B. asserted that a deposit was forfeited on non-performance by the payer as "damages for breach of the agreement".[34] Lopes J., in the same case, suggested that the explanation was that the deposit was "a payment the necessary consequence of which was to induce the vendor to alter his position and to incur expenses".[35] However, neither explanation is convincing. Where a deposit is forfeited, courts do not enter into an assessment of whether the amount of the deposit reflects a loss actually suffered by the recipient, whether by way of expectation damages or reliance loss. It is not even necessary to show that the deposit represented an estimate of the damage that might be suffered if the payer defaulted: as the Privy Council commented in *Dojap Investments*, the deposit can be validly forfeited, "even though the amount of the deposit bears no reference to the anticipated loss".[36] In *Hinton v Sparkes*,[37] for example, a deposit of £50 was payable by the purchaser of a public house, who neither paid it nor completed the purchase. The vendor's only loss was £10, but the Court of Common Pleas held that the entire deposit was to be paid. If a deposit is forfeited, credit is given for that amount in a claim for damages for breach of contract against the defaulting party.[38]

A further possible alternative explanation may be suggested by the advice in **14-11** *Mayson*,[39] where it was said that the question of forfeiture of a deposit "must always depend on the particular terms of the contract".[40] To the extent that this, and similar remarks, might suggest that the principles applying to deposits are a matter of contractual construction, the explanation is tenable, but rather artificial. It requires the word "deposit" to take on a complex legal meaning which both parties are taken to have intended. The more convincing approach is to see the

---

[32] See particularly at 581. Cf. *Omar* [2001] EWCA Civ 1090; [2002] 2 P. & C.R. 3 (forfeiture of deposit of 31%; no argument that the payment was a penalty: see at [31]).
[33] *Collins v Stimson* (1883) 11 Q.B.D. 142.
[34] *Collins* (1883) 11 Q.B.D. 142 at 144.
[35] *Collins* (1883) 11 Q.B.D. 142 at 144.
[36] *Dojap Investments* [1993] A.C. 573 at 578. See also *Linggi Plantations* [1972] 1 M.L.J. 89 (PC).
[37] *Hinton v Sparkes* (1868) L.R. 3 C.P. 161.
[38] *Ockenden v Henly* (1858) El. Bl. & El. 485; 120 E.R. 590; *Linggi Plantations* [1972] 1 M.L.J. 89 (PC); *Ng v Ashley King (Developments) Ltd* [2010] EWHC 456 (Ch); [2011] Ch. 115, following *Carpenter v McGrath* [1996] NSWSC 411 and *Polyset Ltd v Panhandat Ltd* [2002] HKCFA 15.
[39] *Mayson* [1924] A.C. 980.
[40] *Mayson* [1924] A.C. 980 at 985.

principles governing deposits as an application of the more general principles of failure of basis.[41]

2. EQUITABLE RELIEF AGAINST FORFEITURE

14-12 Equity may provide relief against the forfeiture of deposits and part payments, despite such sums having been paid on the basis that they would be forfeited in the events that have happened.[42] The following two alternative approaches have been used: restraining the payee from exercising his strict legal rights, and returning the payments made to the payer.[43] Both approaches require it to be shown that, inter alia, it is unconscionable for the defendant to forfeit the asset in question.[44]

(a) Restraining the Payee

14-13 Where the payee seeks to exercise an option to terminate the contract and forfeit payments made, the payee may be restrained from insisting on his strict legal rights. For instance under Law of Property Act 1925 s.146(2), the court has the power to relieve against forfeiture of a lease on whatever terms it thinks fit. The doctrine is not confined to statute, however—it has been applied as a general equitable principle to sales of land and transfers of other property.[45] For instance, in *Re Dagenham (Thames) Dock Co, Ex p. Hulse*[46] a contract for the sale of land provided that the purchase price was £4,000, of which £2,000 was to be paid immediately, and the balance within two months. The contract also provided that, if payment was not made within two years, time being of the essence, the vendor was entitled to resume possession, and was to be under no obligation to refund any of the price paid. The balance was never paid and the purchaser company was eventually wound up. The vendor sought to rely on the term entitling him to resume possession and retain the part payment, but the Court of Appeal granted relief against such forfeiture. James L.J. described the situation as "an extremely clear case of a mere penalty for non-payment of the purchase-money",[47] and held that the company should be relieved against forfeiture of the land "on payment of the residue of the purchase-money with interest".

(i) Restrictions on Relief in Equity: Time of the Essence

14-14 Authorities subsequent to *Re Dagenham* indicate that equitable relief of the kind awarded in that case is only available in limited situations.[48] One very important

---

[41] *Gribbon* [2001] EWCA Civ 1956; [2002] Q.B. 902 at [61]–[64] per Robert Walker L.J.

[42] *Linggi Plantations* [1972] 1 M.L.J. 89 (PC)

[43] *Else (1982) Ltd v Parkland Holdings Ltd* [1994] 1 B.C.L.C. 130 at 145 per Hoffmann L.J.

[44] See paras 14–24—14–28.

[45] *Re Dagenham (Thames) Dock Co, Ex p. Hulse* (1873) L.R. 8 Ch. 1022; *Kilmer v British Columbia Orchard Lands Ltd* [1913] A.C. 319; *BICC Plc v Burndy Corp* [1985] 1 Ch. 232.

[46] *Re Dagenham (Thames) Dock Co, Ex p. Hulse* (1873) L.R. 8 Ch. 1022.

[47] *Re Dagenham* (1873) L.R. 8 Ch. 1022 at 1025.

[48] *Scandinavian Trading Tanker Co AB v Flota Petrolera Ecuatoriana (The Scaptrade)* [1983] 2 A.C. 694; *Sport Internationaal Bussum v Inter-Footwear Ltd* [1984] 1 W.L.R. 776; *Union Eagle Ltd v Golden Achievement Ltd* [1997] A.C. 514 at 519.

limitation (which would have applied on the facts of *Re Dagenham*) is that it is not available where the parties have stipulated that time is of the essence. In such circumstances the parties are seen as having "expressly intimated in their agreement" that the equitable relief is not to apply.[49] Thus, in *Union Eagle Ltd v Golden Achievement Ltd*[50] a purchaser of a flat was 10 minutes late tendering the purchase price under a contract that provided that time was to be of the essence; the vendor rescinded the contract, and retained the deposit. The Privy Council held that he was entitled to do so, and emphasised the importance of "practical considerations of business", in particular, certainty[51]: the vendor of the flat should be able to be confident that he is entitled to resell the property under such circumstances.

(ii) *Equitable Relief Unavailable Where Specific Performance Would Be Denied*

It seems that equitable relief against forfeiture, at least in the form of restraining   **14–15**
the payee from exercising his full legal rights, is not available where specific performance would be denied. Thus, in *Scandinavian Trading Tanker Co AB v Flota Petrolera Ecuatoriana (The Scaptrade)*[52] the House of Lords refused to grant equitable relief against a shipowner's exercise of his contractual right to withdraw his vessel following the charterer's failure to make punctual payment of an instalment of hire. The main reason that the House of Lords gave was that under a time charter no proprietary or possessory right is transferred to the charterer—it is simply a contract for services to be performed by the shipowner through the use of his vessel. Such a contract for services could not be subject to specific performance; yet, if equitable relief against the shipowner's exercise of his right of withdrawal were granted, the court would effectively be decreeing specific performance. The equitable relief, "though negative in form, is pregnant with an affirmative order to the shipowner to perform the contract".[53]

The relationship between equitable relief against forfeiture and specific per-   **14–16**
formance was further emphasised in *Sport Internationaal Bussum v Inter-Footwear Ltd*.[54] The case concerned an agreement to settle outstanding litigation, under which the defendant promised to pay £105,000 in three equal instalments;

---

[49] *Steedman v Drinkle* [1916] A.C. 275 at 279–280. This limitation was not apparent on the facts of the Privy Council's earlier decision in *Kilmer v British Columbia Orchard Lands Ltd* [1913] A.C. 319, where relief had been granted despite the contract providing that time was of the essence. It was said in *Steedman* [1916] A.C. 275 at 280 that the parties in the *Kilmer* case had agreed to waive the provision as to time being of the essence. For a sceptical comment on this reinterpretation see *Union Eagle* [1997] A.C. 514 at 521. However, the explanation seems to be provided by Kitto J. in *Tropical Traders Ltd v Goonan* (1964) 111 C.L.R. 41 at 53–55, on which see J. Heydon, "Equitable Aid to Purchasers in Breach of Time-Essential Conditions" (1997) 113 L.Q.R. 385, pp.386–387. For criticism of the rule see C. Harpum, "Relief Against Forfeiture and the Purchaser of Land" [1984] C.L.J. 134, pp.143–144.

[50] *Union Eagle Ltd v Golden Achievements Ltd* [1997] A.C. 514 (noted by J. Heydon, "Equitable Aid to Purchasers in Breach of Time-Essential Conditions" and J. Stevens (1998) 61 M.L.R. 255).

[51] *Union Eagle* [1997] A.C. 514 at 519. See similarly *Scandinavian Trading Tanker Co AB v Flota Petrolera Ecuatoriana (The Scaptrade)* [1983] 2 A.C. 694 at 703.

[52] *Scandinavian Trading Tanker Co AB v Flota Petrolera Ecuatoriana (The Scaptrade)* [1983] 2 A.C. 694.

[53] *The Scaptrade* [1983] 2 A.C. 694 at 701.

[54] *Sport Internationaal Bussum v Inter-Footwear Ltd* [1984] 1 W.L.R. 776.

the agreement provided that the payment of the second instalment was to be accompanied "immediately" by a guarantee to pay the third instalment. In return, the defendant was to receive a licence to use certain trademarks owned by the claimant. However, if the guarantee was not provided, the contract stipulated that the entire sum of £105,000 was to fall due immediately and the licence to use the trademarks was to terminate immediately. The defendants paid the second instalment punctually but failed to provide the guarantee. The claimants sought to enforce their contractual rights, terminating the licence agreement and suing for the balance of £105,000. The defendants sought equitable relief against forfeiture, but their claim was rejected by both the Court of Appeal and House of Lords. Oliver and Ackner L.JJ. gave as their main reason that the case did not concern property rights (see further below), but they also added that the only effective relief on the facts would be to order the claimants to regrant the licence to use the trademarks. This would be equivalent to specific performance. However, whilst—unlike in *The Scaptrade*—such an agreement was capable of specific enforcement, specific performance would not be granted to a party in breach of the contract and it therefore followed that relief against forfeiture was not available either.

(iii) *Property Rights*

14–17   In *The Scaptrade*[55] the House of Lords indicated that equitable relief was unavailable where no proprietary or possessory rights were concerned. This indication was confirmed and taken further in *Sport Internationaal Bussum*, where Oliver L.J. (with whom Ackner L.J. agreed) said that "the jurisdiction [to grant equitable relief] never was, and never has been up to now, extended to ordinary commercial contracts unconnected with interests in land".[56] In the House of Lords, Lord Templeman (who gave the only reasoned speech) indicated that relief should not be extended beyond "the recognised boundaries", although he did not indicate what those boundaries were.[57] A less restrictive attitude, however, could be seen in the slightly later decision of the Court of Appeal in *BICC Plc v Burndy*, where Dillon L.J. stated that:

> "Relief is only available where what is in question is forfeiture of proprietary or possessory rights, but I see no reason in principle for drawing a distinction as to the type of property in which the rights subsist".[58]

Kerr L.J. and Ackner L.J. agreed with this analysis,[59] with Ackner L.J. apparently retreating from his earlier insistence in *Sport Internationaal Bussum* that interests in land must be concerned. Similarly, in *Else (1982) Ltd v Parkland Holdings Ltd*[60] Evans L.J. defined the jurisdiction as applying where the party seeking relief might otherwise lose "property",[61] and the Court of Appeal discussed the

---

[55] *The Scaptrade* [1983] 2 A.C. 694.
[56] *Sport Internationaal Bussum* [1984] 1 W.L.R. 776 at 788.
[57] *Sport Internationaal Bussum* [1984] 1 W.L.R. 776 at 794.
[58] *BiCC Plc v Burndy* [1985] 1 Ch. 232 at 252.
[59] *Burndy* [1985] 1 Ch. 232 at 253 and 260 respectively. See also *Stockloser v Johnson* [1954] 1 Q.B. 476 at 499 per Romer L.J.: relief against forfeiture available on purchase of plant and machinery.
[60] *Else (1982) Ltd v Parkland Holdings Ltd* [1994] 1 B.C.L.C. 130.
[61] *Else* [1994] 1 B.C.L.C. 130 at 135.

application of the jurisdiction to a sale of shares. The less stringent approach can also be seen in the most recent appellate authority. In *On Demand Information Plc v Michael Gerson (Finance) Plc*[62] the House of Lords indicated that a party with a merely possessory right over movables would be able to invoke the doctrine. A narrower rule, Lord Millett commented, "would restrict the exercise of a beneficent jurisdiction without any rational justification".[63]

(iv) *Commercial Contracts*

A further restriction, suggested by the Court of Appeal in *Sport Internationaal Bussum* is that relief is not available for "ordinary commercial contracts".[64] However, in *Union Eagle* the Privy Council rejected the argument that agreements could simply be classified as commercial or not, with the consequence that some were subject to equitable relief and others not.[65] Whilst the status and bargaining power of the parties is undoubtedly relevant to the availability of relief, the better view is that this forms part of the broader assessment of whether it is inequitable in the circumstances to allow the forfeiture to take place.[66]   **14–18**

(v) *Summary of Limitations*

The courts have not been consistent in their exposition of the limitations on equitable relief against forfeiture. The balance of authority indicates that relief is only available to restrain forfeiture of property rights, but there seems to be no compelling reason of principle to go as far as the Court of Appeal in *Sport Internationaal Bussum* in requiring those property rights to relate to land. The principle that equitable relief against forfeiture will be denied where the type of agreement in question could not be specifically enforced has the support of the House of Lords, but it is respectfully questioned whether the additional limitation proposed by the Court of Appeal in *Sport Internationaal Bussum* can be correct. The whole essence of equitable relief against forfeiture is that the applicant for relief has failed to perform his obligations, and is, therefore, exposed to the risk of forfeiture. Taken literally, the Court of Appeal's limitation would eliminate the doctrine of equitable relief against forfeiture altogether.   **14–19**

(b) *Restitution as Equitable Relief*

(i) *General*

The power of courts to give equitable relief against the forfeiture of deposits and part payments by ordering that money be repaid (whether wholly or in part) was   **14–20**

---

[62] *On Demand Information Plc v Michael Gerson (Finance) Plc* [2002] UKHL 13; [2003] 1 A.C. 368.
[63] *On Demand Information* [2002] UKHL 13 at [29].
[64] *Sport Internationaal Bussum* [1984] 1 W.L.R. 776 at 788.
[65] *Union Eagle* [1997] A.C. 514 at 519.
[66] See paras 14–24—14–28. See also Harpum, "Relief Against Forfeiture and the Purchaser of Land", p.169 fn.6, commenting that some of the observations in the *Sport Internationaal* case "seem to be a little too cautious".

recognised in *Steedman v Drinkle*[67] and *Mussen v Van Diemen's Land Co.*[68] Both cases concerned contracts for the sale of land under which the price was to be paid in instalments. Both contracts provided that in the event of the purchaser defaulting on an instalment, the vendor was entitled to rescind the contract and to retain all instalments paid; and in both cases the purchaser did so default. The potential for such equitable relief to be available beyond sales of land was asserted by Somervell and Denning L.JJ. in *Stockloser v Johnson*,[69] a case concerned with the purchase of machinery by instalments. Romer L.J., however, was of the opinion that the only equitable relief available under such circumstances was to allow the purchaser extra time to complete, and this view has been followed on the ground that "it appears most to accord with established authority".[70] On the other hand, dicta of the House of Lords in *The Scaptrade* regarded *Stockloser* as authority for the following proposition:

> "[M]oney paid by one party to the other under a continuing contract prior to an event which under the terms of the contract entitled that other party to elect to rescind it and to retain the money paid might be treated as money paid under a penalty clause, and recovered to the extent that it exceeded to an unconscionable extent the value of any consideration that had been given for it."[71]

14–21   As a matter of principle, once it is accepted that equity can relieve against forfeiture, and that the courts can grant applicants extra time to perform their obligations, there seems to be little sense in denying that forfeited payments can be reclaimed. Both forms of equitable relief derive from the same underlying principle. Whilst it has been said that any jurisdiction to restore forfeited payments would require the contract "to be remodelled",[72] that objection applies with equal, if not greater, force, to the discretion to allow extra time. Indeed, in *Union Eagle*[73] the Privy Council contrasted the "objectionable uncertainty" of a power to allow extra time to complete a purchase with "the existence of a restitutionary form of relief against forfeiture, which gives the court a discretion to order repayment of all or part of the retained money".[74] Furthermore, the availability of a jurisdiction to restore forfeited payments offers the courts greater remedial flexibility and furthers their ability to do justice on the facts of the case.

(ii) *Readiness to Complete*

14–22   Where a party is seeking equitable relief against the forfeiture of payments, there is some authority to support the rule that he must be ready and willing to complete the contract.[75] However, in *Stockloser* Somervell and Denning L.JJ. indicated that readiness and willingness to complete the contract was not a

---

[67] *Steedman v Drinkle* [1916] A.C. 275.
[68] *Mussen v Van Diemen's Land Co* [1938] 1 Ch. 253. See also Heydon, "Equitable Aid to Purchasers in Breach of Time-Essential Conditions", pp.389–390.
[69] *Stockloser v Johnson* [1954] 1 Q.B. 476.
[70] *Galbraith v Mitchenall Estates Ltd* [1965] 2 Q.B. 473.
[71] *The Scaptrade* [1983] 2 A.C. 694 at 702.
[72] *Galbraith* [1965] 2 Q.B. 473 at 485 per Sachs J.
[73] *Union Eagle* [1997] A.C. 514.
[74] *Union Eagle* [1997] A.C. 514 at 520.
[75] *Mussen* [1938] 1 Ch. 253 at 263.

prerequisite for equitable relief against forfeiture of payments,[76] and this seems to be the better view. There seems to be no reason to insist on the claimant showing a readiness and willingness to complete when his claim, by its very nature, accepts that the contract is at an end.[77]

(iii) *Improvements to Land by Purchaser*

Where, in a contract for the acquisition of an interest in land, the price is to be paid in instalments and the purchaser has been permitted to go into possession of the land, the vendor may perhaps be liable for the value of any improvements made if the contract is subsequently terminated opportunistically for non-payment of an instalment.[78] Whilst this remedy has been described as "restitutionary relief",[79] it would not fall within any of the categories of liability in unjust enrichment under English law. Leaving aside problematic issues of subjective devaluation, it would seem to be impossible to identify an appropriate unjust factor as a ground for recovery. In particular, it would seem impossible to attribute the liability to the failure of a jointly understood basis for the conferral of benefits,[80] since the parties' understanding must surely be that the purchaser is making improvements for his own account, and that he takes the risk of not being able to make the required payments, thereby losing the land. Furthermore, liability could not be explained on the basis of free acceptance, since the vendor did not freely choose to accept the improvements—rather, if he was to resume possession of his own land, he had no choice but to take possession of any improvements to that land.[81]

14–23

(c) *Whether Enforcement of the Parties' Agreement Would Be Penal and Unconscionable*

(i) *General*

In *Stockloser* Denning L.J. stated that, for the jurisdiction to return forfeited payments to be exercised:

14–24

> "Two things are necessary: first, the forfeiture clause must be of a penal nature, in this sense, that the sum forfeited must be out of all proportion to the damage, and, secondly, it must be unconscionable for the seller to retain the money."[82]

---

[76] *Stockloser* [1954] 1 Q.B. 476 at 487–488 per Somervell L.J., and at 491 per Denning L.J.

[77] See further, Harpum, "Relief Against Forfeiture and the Purchaser of Land", pp.158–161.

[78] *Union Eagle* [1997] A.C. 514 at 521, where the Privy Council commented on the fact that no adequate restitutionary remedy was available at the time of the events in *Re Dagenham* (1873) L.R. 8 Ch. App. 1022, and drew attention to "a feature" of the *Re Dagenham* case that the purchasers had constructed a dock on the land purchased. See also, Harpum, "Relief Against Forfeiture and the Purchaser of Land", pp.165–166.

[79] Heydon "Equitable Aid to Purchasers in Breach of Time-Essential Conditions", p.389.

[80] See Chs 12–13 for the requirements of failure of basis.

[81] See Ch.17 for the requirements of free acceptance.

[82] *Stockloser* [1954] 1 Q.B. 476 at 490; *Else* [1994] B.C.L.C. 130 at 146 per Hoffmann L.J. Cf. the paraphrase of this principle in *The Scaptrade* [1983] 2 A.C. 694 at 702 (quoted in para.14.20), where the two requirements are—inaccurately—elided: money was recoverable if it "exceeded to an unconscionable extent the value of any consideration that had been given for it".

Although Denning L.J. was concerned with the forfeiture of payments, his statement of principle is equally applicable to the forfeiture of property rights. The first criterion is self-explanatory, although it leaves a wide discretion in ascertaining how much of a difference between the forfeited payments and the loss incurred will be objectionable. Denning L.J.'s reference to the clause being "penal" suggests a comparison with the analogous principles governing penalty clauses—that is, clauses which require a party in breach of contract to pay a liquidated sum to the innocent party. However, such a comparison is not straightforward, since the focus of the rule against penalties is on whether the amount to be paid represents a genuine pre-estimate of the loss likely to be suffered by the innocent party. In equitable relief against forfeiture, there is no similar question of estimation of loss. Nor would it be appropriate simply to ask whether, if the amount forfeited had been expressed as a payment to be made on breach, it would have been unenforceable as a penalty. Where the purchaser is benefiting from paying by instalments, and has the use of the subject matter of the contract before having paid for it in full, these benefits may be legitimately reflected in the machinery for forfeiture.

(ii) *Context of the Transaction*

14–25   Whether it is unconscionable for a payee to retain a payment that is out of all proportion to the loss suffered depends on the context of the transaction. As Farwell J. pointed out in *Mussen*, where both parties are experienced business people, and the applicant is aware of the content of the term, it will not ordinarily be inequitable for the payments to be retained.[83] Similarly, where the claimant has knowingly gambled on being able to satisfy the stringent forfeiture provisions, it is unlikely to be inequitable for the applicant to be deprived of payments made before the date of default.[84] It may also be important to examine whether the instalments already paid could be regarded as payments for the use of the subject matter of the contract (akin to rental fees): in *Stockloser* the court was concerned with the purchase of machinery by instalments, but, in his illustration of unconscionability Denning L.J. used the example of the purchaser of a necklace on terms that on default both the necklace and the instalments paid should be forfeited. One explanation for this choice of example is that with the necklace its value is as an object in itself, rather than being derived from the use that could be made of it during the period that the instalments were being paid.

(iii) *Benefits Obtained*

14–26   More broadly, the fact that a purchaser has received a substantial benefit under the contract will count against his application for relief against forfeiture. Thus, in *Else*,[85] a controlling shareholding in a Premier League football club was sold, the price to be paid in instalments. As soon as the deposit was paid, the purchaser became entitled to appoint its nominee as the chairman of the club. The purchaser subsequently defaulted in paying the instalments and the vendor sought to

---

[83] *Mussen* [1938] 1 Ch. 253 at 262–263. See also *The Scaptrade* [1983] 2 A.C. 694 at 703.
[84] *Stockloser* [1954] 1 Q.B. 476 at 492.
[85] *Else* [1994] 1 B.C.L.C. 130.

exercise a contractual right to terminate the contract and retain half of the instalments paid. The Court of Appeal held that no equitable relief against forfeiture was appropriate because, inter alia, the parties regarded the transaction as being about the right to be chairman of the club, and the purchaser had held that position for two years before the contract was terminated.[86]

(iv) *Nature of the Transaction*

The nature of the transaction may also reveal legitimate reasons for the forfeiture **14–27** provisions. For instance, the shipowner under a time charter contracts to provide expensive services to the charterer; the provision for payment of hire in advance is designed to provide a fund out of which such expenses can be met. It follows, therefore, that a term giving the shipowner the option to withdraw the vessel from the charterer's service for failure to pay an instalment of the hire reflects the nature of the obligations assumed by the shipowner; it is not merely a means of pressurising the charterer to pay promptly.[87]

(v) *The Parties' Conduct*

The parties' conduct is considered broadly. Thus, for instance, in *Else* it was **14–28** relevant to the refusal of relief that the applicant had been found not to be a credible witness at the trial.[88] A similarly broad approach has been taken to the vendor's conduct. Thus, where a vendor "somewhat sharply" exercised a right to rescind, relief was granted.[89] Similarly, if the vendor had led the purchaser to believe that he would not strictly enforce his legal rights, although falling short of estoppel, this conduct might prevent the payments being forfeited.[90] Conversely, the applicant may have made improvements to the forfeited property that would lead to the vendor being unjustly enriched if he were able to rely on his strict legal rights. This factor may well explain the Court of Appeal's decision in *Re Dagenham*,[91] where it allowed the claimant extra time to complete, despite the contractual stipulation that time was to be of the essence. On the facts, the company had undertaken extensive works, constructing a dock and, as the Privy Council commented, at the time of the decision in the *Re Dagenham* case, the English law of unjust enrichment was not sufficiently well developed to offer a remedy.[92] The Court of Appeal may well have felt that allowing extra time for completion was preferable to allowing the vendor to take the benefit of the dock.

---

[86] *Else* [1994] 1 B.C.L.C. 130 at 140 per Evans L.J.; at 143 per Russell L.J.; and at 143 and 146 per Hoffmann L.J.
[87] *The Scaptrade* [1983] 2 A.C. 694 at 702.
[88] *Else* [1994] B.C.L.C. 130 at 140 per Evans L.J.
[89] *Steedman* [1916] A.C. 275, as interpreted by Denning L.J. in *Stockloser* [1954] 1 Q.B. 476 at 492.
[90] *Legione v Hateley* (1983) 152 C.L.R. 406.
[91] *Re Dagenham* (1873) L.R. 8 Ch. 1022.
[92] *Union Eagle* [1997] A.C. 514 at 521. The Privy Council may have been hinting that a remedy for the increase in value of the land would be available today—see para.14–23.

3. STATUTORY REGULATION OF DEPOSITS IN SALES OF LAND

14–29   Section 49(2) of the Law of Property Act 1925 states that:

> "Where the court refuses to grant specific performance of a contract, or in any action for the return of a deposit, the court may, if it thinks fit, order the repayment of any deposit."

The subsection creates a statutory jurisdiction applying to parties claiming the return of a deposit when they themselves have been in default. It does not affect the common law principles entitling a party not in default to recover his deposit.[93] Hence, a party seeking to recover a deposit where the other party has defaulted does not need to rely on s.49(2).[94]

(a) *Scope of Section 49(2)*

14–30   The subsection, it has been said, "confers upon the judge a discretion which is unqualified by any language of the subsection"[95], and the courts have rejected attempts to introduce implicit qualifications. Thus, although the draftsman of the subsection had a very specific aim,[96] and the provision seems most obviously relevant to situations where the vendor has been refused specific performance, but the purchaser is unable to rescind the contract, its application is not confined to that situation.[97] Nor is it necessary to show that the conduct of the party retaining the deposit has been open to criticism in some way.[98] Rather, "repayment must be ordered in any circumstances which make this the fairest course between the two parties".[99] The courts have also interpreted the subsection as authorising the repayment of part of the deposit where that seems the fairest outcome.[100]

(b) *Exercise of the Discretion under Section 49(2)*

(i) *General*

14–31   The current leading case on the exercise of the discretion in s.49(2) is *Omar*.[101] There it was said that in ascertaining whether the return of the deposit is the fairest course between the parties, the starting-point is that the payment of a

---

[93] *Schindler v Pigault* (1975) 30 P. & C.R. 328 at 336; *Dimsdale Developments (South East) Ltd v de Haan* (1983) 47 P. & C.R. 1 at 11.
[94] *Country and Metropolitan Homes Surrey Ltd v Topclaim Ltd* [1996] Ch. 307.
[95] *Universal Corp v Five Ways Properties Ltd* (1978) 38 P. & C.R. 687.
[96] Harpum, "Relief Against Forfeiture and the Purchaser of Land", pp.169–171.
[97] *Michael Richards Properties Ltd v Wardens of St Saviour's Parish Southwark* [1975] 3 All E.R. 416; *Universal Corp* (1978) 38 P. & C.R. 687; followed with regret in *Dimsdale Developments* (1983) 47 P. & C.R. 1.
[98] *Universal Corp* (1978) 38 P. & C.R. 687; *Schindler* (1975) 30 P. & C.R. 328 at 336.
[99] *Universal Corp* (1978) 38 P. & C.R. 687 at 691.
[100] *Dimsdale Developments* (1983) 47 P. & C.R. 1.
[101] *Omar* [2001] EWCA Civ 1090; [2002] 2 P. & C.R. 3; *Midill (97 PL) Ltd v Park Lane Estates Ltd* [2008] EWCA Civ 1227; [2009] 1 W.L.R. 2460 at [51]. See also *Bidaisee v Sampath* [1995] 2 L.R.C. 446.

deposit is an earnest for performance. The fact that the contract was not completed does not, therefore, raise a presumption that the deposit should be returned. Furthermore, in the conveyancing context to which s.49(2) applies, it is important that there should be certainty as to the consequences of making such a payment.[102] It follows that the circumstances under which the court will exercise its discretion will be "exceptional".[103]

(ii) *Difficulties in Obtaining Finance*

Whether the circumstances are exceptional will be assessed on the facts of the **14–32** individual case. Difficulties in obtaining the finance necessary for completion will not generally make the situation exceptional; on the contrary, this is the "classic circumstance in which a deposit is liable to be forfeited".[104] However, if the difficulty has been caused by a change in the law—as, for instance, where a Nigerian purchaser was unable to obtain funds in time due to changes in the Nigerian exchange control laws—it seems that the courts may be more sympathetic.[105]

(iii) *Resale Price*

The overall economic impact of the purchaser's breach on the vendor is a **14–33** relevant factor to take into account when considering whether the deposit should be returned.[106] Hence, where, as a result of a drop in property prices, a vendor has had to resell the property below the contract price, it is unlikely to be fair to require the vendor to return the deposit, particularly if the difference in value between the contract price and market price is close to the amount of the deposit paid.[107] However, it does not follow that the fact that a vendor has been able to resell the property at the same price, or at a higher price than that stipulated in the contract, automatically makes it inequitable for the deposit to be retained.[108] Such a situation is not exceptional,[109] and "there is no obvious reason why the purchaser should have the benefit of any such price rise".[110] It is also important to emphasise that the legitimacy of deposit payments is not based on them being estimates of likely loss in the event of the purchaser defaulting.[111] If, however, the higher price on resale has been achieved (at least partly) as a result of the purchaser's efforts, there is more to be said for exercising the discretion to return the deposit. For instance, in *Bidaisee v Sampath*[112] the purchaser had, with the vendor's agreement, begun to develop the land before the date set for completion.

---

[102] *Omar* [2001] EWCA Civ 1090 at [35]–[36].
[103] *Omar* [2001] EWCA Civ 1090 at [37].
[104] *Tennaro Ltd v Majorarch Ltd* [2003] EWHC 2601 (Ch) at [84]–[85] (Flat 37); *Cole v Rose* [1978] 3 All E.R. 1121.
[105] *Universal Corp* (1978) 38 P. & C.R. 687.
[106] *Arbisala v St James' Homes (Grosvenor Dock) Ltd (No.2)* [2008] EWHC 456 (Ch); [2009] 1 W.L.R. 1089.
[107] *Tennaro* [2003] EWHC 2601 (Ch) at [85].
[108] *Midill* [2008] EWCA Civ 1227; [2009] 1 W.L.R. 2460. At [53] Carnwath L.J. "respectfully question[ed]" the decision in *Dimsdale Developments* (1983) 47 P. & C.R. 1.
[109] *Michael Richards* [1975] 3 All E.R. 416 at 425.
[110] *Midill* [2008] EWCA Civ 1227; [2009] 1 W.L.R. 2460 at [54].
[111] *Arbisala* [2008] EWHC 456 (Ch); [2009] 1 W.L.R. 1089 at [14].
[112] *Bidaisee v Sampath* [1995] 2 L.R.C. 446.

Following the purchaser's default, the seller resold the land for significantly more than the original contract price. The Privy Council refused to order the return of the deposit, holding that the increase in price was, in itself, insufficient to make the circumstances exceptional, and emphasising that there was no evidence of the extent to which the development works had increased the land's value. The implication was that, had there been such evidence, the purchaser would have had a stronger case.

(iv) *Vendor's Conduct*

14–34   Although, as shown above,[113] it is not a necessary condition for the exercise of the discretion under s.49(2) that the vendor's conduct is open to criticism in some way, the vendor's conduct is a relevant factor to consider in deciding whether the deposit ought to be returned. As was said in *Arbisala v St James' Homes (Grosvenor Dock) Ltd (No.2)*[114]:

> "[W]hat needs to be looked at is how close the purchaser came to performing the contract, what alternatives he was able to propose to the vendor and how advantageous they would be compared with the actual performance of the contractual terms. Where the purchaser simply could not perform the contract or offer any such alternative, then it would be exceptional . . . for the deposit to be returned."

Thus, for instance, where a vendor had promptly rescinded the contract on the purchaser's failing to complete on time, but the purchaser was ready to complete a fortnight later, the purchaser had an arguable claim to recover the deposit. The delay was due to changes to the Nigerian exchange control laws and the vendor, it was alleged, knew that the funds for the purchase were to be transferred from Nigeria.[115]

14–35   The clearest example of the significance of the vendor's conduct can be seen in *Tennaro Ltd v Majorarch Ltd.*[116] There the parties had contracted for the grant of long leases of three flats, with the purchaser paying three deposits. None of the sales had been completed. The entitlement to retain the deposit on the first flat was straightforward. In relation to the second and third flats (Flats 31 and 32), however, the position was more difficult. Flat 32 had been sold for £841,259, and a deposit of £44,084 had been paid. At the time of rescission it was worth £1,075,000. The purchaser had assigned the benefit of the contract relating to Flat 32 to an individual who offered to purchase it from the vendors for £1,100,000. The vendors, however, refused. Neuberger J. held that the deposit should be returned: the vendor had had an opportunity to sell the flat at a price higher than that specified in the contract and had given no explanation for its refusal to do so.[117] Flat 31 was sold for £443,740, with a deposit of £44,084. After the date for completion, the purchaser offered to complete at the contract price but the vendors refused, again giving no explanation. The current value of the flat (which remained unsold) was £525,000. Neuberger J. also ordered the return of the

---

[113] See para.14–30.
[114] *Arbisala v St James' Homes (Grosvenor Dock) Ltd (No.2)* [2008] EWHC 456 (Ch); [2009] 1 W.L.R. 1089 at [13].
[115] *Universal Corp* (1978) 38 P. & C.R. 687.
[116] *Tennaro Ltd v Majorarch Ltd* [2003] EWHC 2601 (Ch).
[117] *Tennaro* [2003] EWHC 2601 (Ch) at [88]–[90].

deposit paid for this flat.[118] Whilst the Court of Appeal in *Midill (97 PL) Ltd v Park Lane Estates Ltd*[119] approved Neuberger J.'s approach to Flat 32,[120] it was not entirely convinced by his approach to Flat 31. As Carnwath L.J. pointed out, the agreements between the parties in *Tennaro* had provided for the transfer of all three flats; it was not clear whether the vendor's offer to complete the sale of one of only one of those flats, at the contract price, was not commercially disadvantageous for the vendor.[121] It could also be said that it was not obvious why the vendors should have been obliged to give the purchasers a further opportunity to perform the contract: the purchasers had already had one attempt and failed, and there was little to suggest that things would be different the second time round.[122]

(v) *Broader Factors*

The language of s.49(2), as interpreted by the courts, seems to permit considera-   **14–36** tion of all factors bearing on whether it is "fit" to return the deposit. There is some authority to support the proposition that these factors include a general assessment of the conduct and position of the parties. Thus, in *Omar* one ground given for refusing to exercise the discretion under s.49(2) was that the purchaser's conduct, in having failed to honour other obligations under the agreement between the parties, "does not excite sympathy".[123] Similarly, in *Arbisala*, it was said that the purchaser in that case being enormously wealthy "does not assist him in the exercise of the discretion."[124] However, the purchaser in *Arbisala* had also made several fraudulent misrepresentations about his financial readiness to complete the transaction, yet these seem to have been given no weight in the assessment of whether the deposit should be returned. The purchaser's conduct would seem to be more obviously relevant than his wealth to whether it is "fit" to return the deposit.

---

[118] *Tennaro* [2003] EWHC 2601 (Ch) at [98].
[119] *Midill (97 PL) Ltd v Park Lane Estates Ltd* [2008] EWCA Civ 1227; [2009] 1 W.L.R. 2460.
[120] *Midill* [2008] EWCA Civ 1227 at [53].
[121] *Midill* [2008] EWCA Civ 1227 at [53].
[122] Cf. *Universal Corp* (1978) 38 P. & C.R. 687, where the reason for the delay in completion would not recur.
[123] *Omar* [2001] EWCA Civ 1090; [2002] 2 P. & C.R. 3 at [37].
[124] *Arbisala* [2008] EWHC 456 (Ch); [2009] 1 W.L.R. 1089 at [47].

CHAPTER 15

FRUSTRATED CONTRACTS

1. INTRODUCTION

The law on the recovery of benefits conferred under a contract that has subse- **15–01** quently been frustrated is now set out in Law Reform (Frustrated Contracts) Act 1943. As its name suggests, the Act aimed to reform the applicable common law principles. Very shortly before the Act was passed, those principles had been settled as being the general principles of failure of basis.[1] Prior to 1942, however, the law on the recovery of benefits conferred under a frustrated contract had been very different. It had been seen predominantly in terms of whether the parties' contract provided, either expressly or impliedly, for what was to happen in the event of frustration.[2] Whilst the main focus of this chapter is on the current statutory provisions, a brief sketch of the background to the Act is given first, in order to give a context for the Act, and to cast light on what its provisions were designed to achieve.[3]

2. THE BACKGROUND TO THE 1943 ACT

(a) *The Position at Common Law*

Until the early 1940s, a variety of approaches to the recovery of benefits **15–02** conferred under frustrated contracts could be seen. The dominant approach was that the consequences of frustration were governed by the parties' contract.[4] Whilst the courts were prepared to adopt a liberal approach to the construction of express terms governing the consequences of frustration,[5] there was great reluctance to imply terms.[6] The result of this approach, as Atkin L.J. noted, was that the law risked being at odds with commercial expectations, since businessmen

---

[1] *Fibrosa Spolka Akcyjna v Fairbairn Lawson Combe Barbour Ltd* [1943] A.C. 32. For the general principles of failure of basis, see Chs 12–13.

[2] *Chandler v Webster* [1904] 1 K.B. 493.

[3] For a fuller account, see P. Mitchell, "*Fibrosa Spolka Akcyjna v Fairbairn Lawson Combe Barbour, Limited*" in C. Mitchell and P. Mitchell (eds), *Landmark Cases in the Law of Restitution* (Oxford: Hart Publishing, 2006), 246.

[4] *Chandler* [1904] 1 K.B. 493. See too E. McKendrick, "Frustration, Restitution, and Loss Apportionment" in A. Burrows (ed.), *Essays on the Law of Restitution* (Oxford: OUP, 1991), 147, p.149.

[5] e.g. *Elliott v Crutchley* [1904] 1 K.B. 565.

[6] *Blakeley v Muller & Co* [1903] 2 K.B. 760n.; *Russkoe Obschestvo D'Lia Izgsbovlenia Snariadov I'Voennick Pripassov v John Stirk & Sons Ltd* (1922) 10 Ll. L. Rep. 214 (CA).

"would be practically certain to try to make some arrangement as to the adjustment of their rights".[7]

15–03 In the maritime context, by contrast, a more flexible approach to the consequences of frustration could be seen. One technique developed by the common law courts was the doctrine of freight *pro rata itineris*, under which the owner of a vessel who had contracted to carry goods to a particular destination was entitled to recover a portion of the agreed freight if the goods were delivered short of the destination due to a frustrating event.[8] The precise analytical basis of the doctrine fluctuated between contract and unjust enrichment, eventually coming to be settled as contractual.[9] In applying it, however, the courts showed considerably more flexibility than they had in implying terms into non-maritime contracts.[10] They also left open the possibility that the common law courts might administer "some of that 'larger equity' . . . as exercised by Courts of Admiralty in similar cases".[11]

(b) *Admiralty Jurisdiction*

15–04 The "larger equity" administered by the Courts of Admiralty flowed from the fact that those courts were not limited to enforcing the parties' contracts. On the contrary, it was said that "the Prize Courts deal with claims in accordance with the law of nations, and upon equitable principles freed from contracts".[12] Whilst the common law courts were confined by the parties' agreement[13]:

> "[T]he Prize Court takes all the circumstances into consideration, and may award, as it has done in decided cases, the whole, or a moiety of the freight, or a sum pro rata itineris, or it may discard the contract rate altorgether, even as a basis for assessment or calculation . . . ; or it may withold or diminish the sum by reason of misconduct, as, e.g. by resistance to search, or spoliation, or non-disclosure of papers."

Thus, it was open to the court simply to share the loss between the parties, despite there being no contractual provision to that effect.[14] A more detailed assessment was also possible, which could take account of factors such as expenses incurred and benefits conferred by the parties.[15] Whatever the detailed approach taken, the underlying justification for the court's exercise of this discretion was that, rather than enforcing the parties' agreement, it was adjusting the parties' rights in the aftermath of a legally imposed dissolution of their contract.[16]

---

[7] *Russkoe* (1922) 10 Ll. L. Rep. 214 (CA) at 217.
[8] *Luke v Lloyd* (1759) 1 W. Bl. 190; 96 E.R. 102; *Osgood v Groning* (1810) 2 Camp. 466; 170 E.R. 1220.
[9] *Metcalfe v Britannia Ironworks Company* (1876) 1 Q.B.D. 613 (DC); (1877) 2 Q.B.D. 423 (CA); *St Enoch Shipping Co Ltd v Phosphate Mining Co* [1916] 2 K.B. 624.
[10] e.g. *The Soblomsten* (1866) L.R. 1 Ad. & Ecc. 293, where an implied promise to accept goods at an intermediate port was inferred from silence and inactivity on the part of the shipper.
[11] *Metcalfe* (1876) 1 Q.B.D. 613 at 635 per Quain and Mellor JJ.
[12] *The Corsican Prince* [1916] P. 195 at 202.
[13] *The Corsican Prince* [1916] P. 195.
[14] *The Friends* (1810) Edw. 246; 165 E.R. 1098.
[15] *The Juno* [1916] P. 169.
[16] *The Teutonia* (1871) L.R. 3 Ad. & Ecc. 394; affirmed on different grounds (1872) L.R. 4 P.C. 171.

(c) *Scotland*

Like the Admiralty jurisdiction, Scots law did not confine itself to enforcing the   **15–05**
parties' contract in the aftermath of a frustrating event. However, unlike the
Admiralty jurisdiction, Scots law did not adopt an open-ended discretionary
approach. As the House of Lords explained in *Cantiare San Rocco SA v Clyde
Shipbuilding and Engineering Co Ltd*,[17] Scots law made use of the Roman
condictio. The basis of this remedy, the House of Lords added, was that:

> "[A] person had received from another some property, and . . . by reason of circum-
> stances existing at the time, or arising afterwards, it was or became contrary to honesty
> and fair dealing for the recipient to retain it".[18]

Lord Shaw highlighted the contrast with English law: leaving the loss to lie
where it fell unless the contract provided otherwise was, he said, appropriate only
"among tricksters, gamblers and thieves".[19]

(d) *The Law Revision Committee*

In 1937 "the rule laid down or applied in *Chandler v Webster*" was referred to   **15–06**
the Law Revision Committee. The Committee reported in favour of reforming
the rule, and replacing it with a "positive rule" that:

> "The payer should be entitled to the repayment of all monies he has paid to the payee,
> less the amount of any loss directly incurred by the payee for the purpose of performing
> the contract".[20]

The Committee had, at one stage, supported a proposal under which either the
expenses incurred by the payee or the benefit received by the payor would be
deducted, whichever was the larger.[21] A note at the end of the Report signed by
Rayner Goddard and Egerton Mortimer drew attention to the fact that the
Committee did not consider what was to happen where non-pecuniary benefits
were conferred, or, indeed where no benefits had been conferred at all. This was
a point that had troubled the Committee's chairman, Lord Wright, mid-way
through the Committee's deliberations, and he had sought advice from the Lord
Chancellor. The Lord Chancellor's instructions were to focus on money payments, and this may well have allowed the Report to appear more quickly.[22]

---

[17] *Cantiare San Rocco SA v Clyde Shipbuilding and Engineering Co Ltd* [1924] A.C. 226.
[18] *Cantiare San Rocco* [1924] A.C. 226 at 234 per Earl of Birkenhead. As a matter of Roman law,
the *condictio* analysis appears to have been mistaken, because the *condictio* was used only for
agreements that did not fall within the recognised contractual categories. See further W. Buckland,
"*Casus* and Frustration in Roman and Common Law" (1932–1933) 46 Harvard L.R. 1281,
pp.1284–1286; R. Evans-Jones, "Roman Law in Scotland and England and the Development of One
Law for Britain" (1999) 115 L.Q.R. 605, p.612.
[19] *Cantiare San Rocco* [1924] A.C. 226 at 259.
[20] Law Revision Committee, *Seventh Interim Report (Chandler v Webster)* (HMSO, 1939), Cmd 6009
pp.6–7.
[21] For the development of the Committee's proposals through successive drafts of its report, see P.
Mitchell in Mitchell and Mitchell, *Landmark Cases in the Law of Restitution*, pp.259–264.
[22] P. Mitchell in Mitchell and Mitchell, *Landmark Cases in the Law of Restitution*, p.263; McKendrick in Burrows, *Essays on the Law of Restitution*, pp.153–154.

However, it also meant that, when the Committee's recommendations came to be enacted, there was an obvious gap in the scheme of liabilities.

15–07   Despite the Cabinet approving the Law Revision Committee's report "in principle", shortly after its publication in May 1939, the timing of the Report proved unfortunate. A Bill was drafted, but by the time it was ready for presentation to Parliament, the Second World War had begun and the government was unwilling to become embroiled in a wide-ranging debate about giving relief to contracting parties whose contracts might have become more onerous as a result of wartime conditions, although they had not been frustrated. Only the fortuitous combination of a new Lord Chancellor (Lord Simon replacing Lord Caldecote), pressure from a Member of Parliament, and the decisions at first instance and the Court of Appeal in *Fibrosa Societe Anonyme* (sic) *v Fairbairn Lawson Combe Barbour Ltd*[23] restarted the legislative process.[24] Once it became apparent that *Fibrosa* would be appealed to the House of Lords, the Lord Chancellor realised that there were two potential options for reform and expressed a slight preference for the common law route.

15–08   In the event, the House of Lords in *Fibrosa*[25] did reform the law, but not to the extent that the Law Revision Committee had recommended. It was held that the principles of failure of consideration applied where payments had been made in advance under contracts that were subsequently frustrated; whether the payment was recoverable or not turned on whether the basis for making the payment had totally failed. In other words, the payer would recover the payment in full where he had received none of the contractual performance promised in exchange for that payment. As Lord Simon L.C., and other members of the House of Lords, observed, whilst this development made the law more coherent than it had been under the rule in *Chandler v Webster*, it was not an ideal solution, because it took no account of expenditure incurred by the recipient of the payment in performance of the contract. Their Lordships agreed that apportionment was the ideal solution, but that only the legislature could introduce it.

15–09   After their decision in the *Fibrosa* case, Lord Simon consulted the Law Lords about the content of such legislation. The possibility of liability where no benefits had been conferred, but expense had been incurred in relation to performance was briefly considered, only to be dismissed shortly afterwards.[26] The Law Lords also considered what the appropriate principles should be where non-pecuniary benefits had been conferred. Again, the initiative was taken by Lord Simon, who drafted the initial proposals, and commented on the draftsman's later versions. Parliamentary involvement in the reform was limited to passing it without amendment.

15–10   Several important themes emerge from the background and events immediately preceding the enactment of the Law Reform (Frustrated Contracts) Act 1943. First, whilst there was a general dissatisfaction with the rule in *Chandler*

---

[23] *Fibrosa Societe Anonyme (sic) v Fairbairn Lawson Combe Barbour Ltd* [1942] 1 K.B. 12.
[24] P. Mitchell in Mitchell and Mitchell, *Landmark Cases in the Law of Restitution*, pp.267–271.
[25] *Fibrosa* [1943] A.C. 32 (noted by P. Winfield, (1942) 58 L.Q.R. 442 and G. Williams, "The End of *Chandler v Webster*", [1942] M.L.R. 46).
[26] P. Mitchell in Mitchell and Mitchell, *Landmark Cases in the Law of Restitution*, pp.277–279. See also G. Williams, "The End of *Chandler v Webster*", p.52 fn.6. For a careful discussion of the issue see McKendrick in Burrows, *Essays on the Law of Restitution*, pp.165–170.

that the consequences of frustration should be regulated by the parties' agreement, there was no general agreement on what the law should be. Secondly, there were a variety of possibilities for reform, ranging from the Roman-inspired *condictio* of Scots law to the open-ended discretionary approach of Admiralty. The Law Revision Committee did not commit itself to implementing any one of these distinct possibilities, and, even if it had done, significant additions were made to its proposals in the legislation. Thirdly, the manner in which the statutory provision dealing with non-money benefits was created was less than ideal, in that the Law Revision Committee's own terms of reference seemed to leave it in doubt whether non-pecuniary benefits should be considered; when the issue was addressed, it was at the Lord Chancellor's individual initiative and consultation was very limited. Finally, and perhaps most importantly, it must be remembered that in 1943 the law of unjust enrichment was still at a very formative stage. There was certainly no established independent category into which the 1943 Act could be fitted. Nor do the terms of the 1943 Act indicate that it was an attempt to codify the law of unjust enrichment as it applied to frustrated contracts. On the contrary, the House of Lords' decision in *Fibrosa* had already introduced the classic unjust enrichment solution of recovery on the ground of failure of basis; the 1943 Act was a deliberate reaction to the perceived inadequacies of that solution. In short, whilst the 1943 Act governs a situation where the law of unjust enrichment would otherwise apply, it should not be seen as being a part of the law of unjust enrichment.[27]

3. THE 1943 ACT

(a) *Scope of the Act*

Section 1(1) of the Act provides that: **15–11**

"Where a contract governed by English law has become impossible of performance or been otherwise frustrated, and the parties thereto have for that reason been discharged from the further performance of the contract, the following provisions of this section shall, subject to the provisions of section two of this Act, have effect in relation thereto."

This subsection makes it clear that the Act has no application to situations where a contract has been terminated for breach. The Act provides no definition of "impossible of performance" or "frustrated", leaving those terms to be interpreted by reference to the common law.[28] Earlier attempts to define the doctrine of frustration in the section had proved unsatisfactory. This lack of definition had concerned Arnold MacNair,[29] who was careful to point out in an article published after the Act had been passed that "frustration" should be interpreted broadly,

---

[27] Cf. *BP Exploration Co (Libya) Ltd v Hunt (No.2)* [1979] 1 W.L.R. 783 at 799. McKendrick in Burrows, *Essays on the Law of Restitution*, p.154 describes the claim that the 1943 Act creates a scheme of "mutual restitution" as "controversial".

[28] For the common law on impossibility of performance and frustration see H. Beale (ed.), *Chitty on Contracts*, 30th edn (London: Sweet & Maxwell, 2008), Ch.23.

[29] P. Mitchell in Mitchell and Mitchell, *Landmark Cases in the Law of Restitution*, pp.264–265.

and not limited to changes in circumstances which had not been contemplated by the parties. In particular, supervening illegality (whether contemplated or not) should be included.[30] This broad reading of the subsection seems compelling.

(b) *Common Law Remedies*

15–12   It is nowhere stated expressly that common law rights which would otherwise apply to the situations for which the Act makes provision are abolished. An intention to abolish common law rights might, perhaps, be inferred from the preamble to the Act, which states that it is "an Act to amend the law relating to the frustration of contracts", although that statement seems to be equally consistent with a statutory intention to create additional rights, rather than an intention to replace existing rights with new ones. However, the intention to abolish common law rights must be at least implicit in the creation of statutory rights that are less favourable to claimants than their common law rights.[31] Thus, s.1(2) of the Act provides for the recovery of pre-payments subject to a discretion to deduct expenses incurred by the recipient of the payment. If the common law rights of a party making a prepayment have not been abolished by the Act, such a party could simply choose to have recourse to the common law principles of failure of basis—as expounded in *Fibrosa*[32]—and effectively shut out the court's discretion. Such an option cannot have been intended by the legislature.[33]

(c) *Money Payments*

(i) *Section 1(2)*

15–13   Section 1(2) states that:

> "All sums paid or payable to any party in pursuance of the contract before the time when the parties were discharged (in this Act referred to as 'the time of discharge') shall, in the case of sums so paid, be recoverable from him as money received by him for the use of the party by whom the sums were paid, and, in the case of sums so payable, cease to be so payable:
>
>   Provided that, if the party to whom the sums were so paid or payable incurred expenses before the time of discharge in, or for the purpose of, the performance of the contract, the court may, if it considers it just to do so, having regard to all the circumstances of the case, allow him to retain or, as the case may be, recover the whole or any part of the sums so paid or payable, not being an amount in excess of the expenses so incurred."

Under the first paragraph of this subsection, payments made are to be returned; and payments due under the contract, but remaining unpaid at the time of the frustrating event, are no longer payable. The latter provision can be explained on

---

[30] A. McNair, "The Law Reform (Frustrated Contracts) Act 1943" (1944) 60 L.Q.R. 160, pp.162–164.

[31] See para.2–15.

[32] *Fibrosa* [1943] A.C. 32.

[33] G. Williams, *The Law Reform (Frustrated Contracts) Act 1943* (London: Stevens & Sons, 1944), pp.34–35.

the basis that, although frustration only excuses the parties from performance of obligations falling due in the future,[34] if the debtor had paid as required by the contract, the payment would be immediately recoverable back under s.1(2).

(ii) *No Requirement of Total Failure of Basis*

The first paragraph of the subsection confers rights that resemble a claim in **15–14** unjust enrichment on the ground of failure of basis. However, it should be noted that the claims are not identical. In a claim in unjust enrichment the payer would only be able to recover if the basis for the payment had totally failed—in other words, if the condition under which he paid remained unfulfilled. Under the Act, by contrast, it is not a requirement of liability that the party making the payments has received nothing in return for those payments.[35] The point can be illustrated by comparing the results under a contract such as that involved in *Stocznia Gdanska SA v Latvian Shipping Co*.[36] There the contract was for the design, construction and delivery of a ship, with payment to be made in instalments. If the contract was frustrated after the design stage, at which point the buyer had already paid an instalment of the price, the buyer would have no claim for the recovery of that instalment in unjust enrichment, since the basis for that payment had not failed; however, he would have a claim under s.1(1) of the 1943 Act.

(iii) *Risk*

A further difference between a claim in unjust enrichment and a claim under **15–15** s.1(2) of the 1943 Act is that whilst a claim in unjust enrichment requires a careful analysis of the basis on which the payment was made,[37] the claim under s.1(2) requires no such analysis. Rather, the assumption is that any pre-payment should be returned in the event of the contract becoming frustrated. As Glanville Williams commented, the Act "speculates as to the object for which the advance was obtained".[38] In this respect, the 1943 Act follows the tenor of the Law Revision Committee's Report,[39] but the assumption is not obviously correct. The payment might be made on the basis that it was security against the occurrence

---

[34] *Hirji Mulji v Cheong Yue SS Co Ltd* [1926] A.C. 497.

[35] G. Williams, "The Law Reform (Frustrated Contracts) Act 1943" [1944] M.L.R. 66, p.67; Williams, *The Law Reform (Frustrated Contracts) Act 1943*, pp.30–31; A. Stewart and J. Carter, "Frustrated Contracts and Statutory Adjustment: The Case for a Reappraisal" [1992] C.L.J. 66, p.79; G. Treitel, *Frustration and Force Majeure*, 2nd edn (London: Sweet & Maxwell, 2004), para.15–050.

[36] *Stocznia Gdanska SA v Latvian Shipping Co* [1998] 1 W.L.R. 574. For a detailed discussion of this case in the context of failure of basis, see paras 13–10—13–11.

[37] See Ch.13.

[38] Williams, *The Law Reform (Frustrated Contracts) Act 1943*, p.10. Cf. *Lobb v Vasey Housing Auxiliary (War Widows Guild)* [1963] V.R. 239 at 245, where it seems to have been assumed that the identical provisions of the Frustrated Contracts Act 1959 (Victoria) required there to have been a failure of basis before a claim could be brought under the Act.

[39] Law Revision Committee, *Seventh Interim Report*. See, in particular, the committee's highly critical comments on the doctrine of advance freight at p.10 ("unsatisfactory in principle but it has been regarded as settled law for a long time past and the business practice of shipowners and insurers is to some extent based on it"). In fact, the doctrine is an excellent illustration of a pre-payment where the payer deliberately takes the risk of a frustrating event occurring in order to obtain a cheaper contract price. See further para.13–11.

of the frustrating event.[40] For instance, in *Fibrosa*[41] the contract for supply of machinery to a Polish firm was made a mere two months before the outbreak of the Second World War, when international relations in Europe were already in an ominous condition. The pre-payment was a departure from the sellers' usual practice, and it was, in any event, unnecessary for them to obtain security against the buyers' insolvency, because the contract had been made by an agent: under the then prevailing rules of the law of agency, the agent of a foreign principal was personally answerable on the contract. There was, therefore, strong evidence that the pre-payment was not conditional on the contract being fully performed.[42] Similarly, in *Clark v Lindsay*,[43] where a contract had been made to hire a room to view the coronation procession of Edward VII at a time when the King's ill-health was publicly known, it was held that a pre-payment could not be recovered, since "The doubt was known, and each party took his chance".[44] A further illustration is provided by the cases on advance freight discussed above.[45] Whilst such an analysis is central to recovery in unjust enrichment on the ground of failure of basis, it has no place in the statutory scheme created by the 1943 Act. The 1943 Act does allow for contracts with terms governing the consequences of frustration, and that may extend to implied terms[46]; however, if a term cannot be implied (or the Act is interpreted as applying only to express terms), the 1943 Act may well have the curious effect that prepayments must be returned despite the basis on which they were paid not having failed.

(iv) *Payments Made "in Pursuance of the Contract"*

15–16   Nothing in the wording of s.1(2) excludes payments of money made in advance of the contract being concluded (so long as those payments are made in, or for the purpose of, performance of the contract). Nor is there anything to limit the payments governed by the Act to those made as required by the parties' contract. For instance, if, in response to a seller's temporary cashflow problems, a buyer voluntarily pays in advance (despite the contract not calling for payment until delivery), such payment would seem to fall within s.1(2). However, if money were paid under the mistaken belief that it was due under the contract, such a payment would not truly be made "in pursuance of the contract", and would therefore be recoverable under the general principles of the law of unjust enrichment (on the ground of mistake).[47]

(v) *Expenses*

15–17   Where the recipient of a payment has incurred expenses "in, or for the purpose of the performance of the contract" the court has a discretion to allow the recipient of the payment to retain some or all of it, and—where payments due were not made—to claim an appropriate sum from the debtor. The subsection

---

[40] Williams, *The Law Reform (Frustrated Contracts) Act 1943*, p.9, particularly at fn.33.
[41] *Fibrosa* [1943] A.C. 32.
[42] P Mitchell in Mitchell and Mitchell, *Landmark Cases in the Law of Restitution*, p.274.
[43] *Clark v Lindsay* (1903) 88 L.T. 198.
[44] *Clark* (1903) 88 L.T. 198 at 202 per Channell J.
[45] See para.13–11.
[46] See the discussion at paras 15–56—15–58.
[47] See further Ch.9.

thus provides both a "shield and a sword" to the recipient.[48] The court's discretion comes into effect when expenses have been incurred by the recipient. "Expenses" are not directly defined in the Act, although some guidance may be derived from s.1(4), which provides as follows:

> "In estimating, for the purposes of the foregoing provisions of this section, the amount of any expenses incurred by any party to the contract, the court may, without prejudice to the generality of the said provisions, include such sum as appears to be reasonable in respect of overhead expenses and in respect of any work or services performed personally by the said party."

It may, therefore, be the case that a recipient can be regarded as incurring "expenses in or for the purpose of the performance of the contract" when, although work has not yet begun on the subject matter of the contract, overhead costs in relation to the facilities where the work is to be carried out have been incurred. Such costs must be referable to the performance of the contract, and it is suggested that this requirement would be satisfied where the recipient of the payment had earmarked the facilities for carrying out the contractual work at a set time, or has purchased machinery with which the contractual work is to be carried out. There is nothing in the statutory language to indicate that it is a condition of the discretion arising that the expenditure was either reasonable or foreseeable. However, the reasonableness of the expenses may well be a factor that influences the court's exercise of its discretion.[49]

Pre-contractual expenses   The statutory language permits expenses to be   **15–18** taken into account that have been incurred "for the purpose of the performance of the contract". There is nothing in this phrase that necessarily excludes expenses incurred before the contract was concluded. Thus, for instance, where the parties are negotiating towards a contract which subsequently materialises, and one party incurs expenditure in order to be able to perform his anticipated obligations, such expenditure should be taken into account under s.1(2). However, it would seem that the party incurring the expenditure must have "the contract" in contemplation. For instance, it was surely not intended that a professional person could claim a deduction under s.1(2) for the expenses incurred in obtaining the qualifications necessary to allow him to practice his profession.[50] Whilst this expenditure was incurred for the purpose of being able to perform future contracts generally, it was not incurred for the purpose of the particular contract under consideration.[51] A difficult intermediate situation arises where the expenses have been incurred before the identity of the other contracting party or parties is known. For instance, a person might put up a grandstand with a view of the route of a proposed procession and then sell tickets to members of the public. If the procession is cancelled, the price paid for the tickets must be returned to the purchasers, but could a deduction be made for the expense of erecting the grandstand? Glanville Williams argued that, because no contract was in existence at the time of the expenses being incurred, such

---

[48] McNair, "The Law Reform (Frustrated Contracts) Act 1943", p.165.
[49] See paras 15–21—15–22.
[50] Williams, *The Law Reform (Frustrated Contracts) Act 1943*, p.44.
[51] Williams, *The Law Reform (Frustrated Contracts) Act 1943*, pp.43–44.

expenses could not be said to be incurred "for the purpose of the performance of the contract".[52] In our view, however, that reads the statutory language too narrowly. It would exclude the operation of s.1(2) for expenses incurred even where two parties were negotiating towards a contract which subsequently materialised. Furthermore, there is no reason why the identity of the other contracting party must be definite in order for any expenses to be incurred "for the purpose of the performance of the contract". In the grandstand example, the expenses are incurred purely for the purpose of performing a group of immediate, identical contractual obligations arising under contracts to purchase tickets. Those expenses should, therefore, be admitted under s.1(2). Of course, it would not follow that the defendant should retain the entirety of his expenses: the court must exercise its discretion so as to identify the appropriate sum to be retained.[53]

15–19   **Expenses and net loss**   Although the statutory language refers to "expenses", we agree with Glanville Williams that this should be taken to mean "expenses after deduction of gains resulting from those expenses". In other words, the recipient's "net loss".[54] Thus, for instance, in a factual situation such as that which arose in *Fibrosa*,[55] where machinery had been manufactured, but the frustrating event prevented it from being delivered, the recipient of the payment has incurred expenses, but also has a valuable asset that can be sold to another buyer. It would be entirely at odds with the subsection's emphasis on justice if the existence of that valuable asset were disregarded. If, however, it is preferred to use a literal meaning of "expenses", having no regard to whether the defendant has acquired a valuable asset as a result of the expenditure, the existence of a valuable asset should be taken into account at the stage of assessing the just sum.[56]

15–20   This latter approach was adopted in in *Lobb v Vasey Housing Auxiliary (War Widows Guild)*,[57] where the claimant's testator had paid £1,250 in return for the right to be granted a lifetime lease of a flat which had not yet been built. The parties agreed that the lease would be granted as soon as the testator went into occupation. The testator died before the flat was completed and the claimant sought to recover the payment made. The defendant sought to retain part of the sum paid, having incurred expenses by entering a contract with a third party to have the flat built. Hudson J. applied s.3(2) of the Frustrated Contracts Act 1959 (Victoria), which is in identical terms to s.1(2) of the 1943 Act. He held that if it was shown that the flat had been completed, and had been disposed of to another tenant for £1,250 or more, the defendant would have "suffered no loss, and justice would not demand that the defendant should be allowed to retain any part of the sum of £1250".[58]

---

[52] Williams, *The Law Reform (Frustrated Contracts) Act 1943*, p.44.
[53] See paras 15–21—15–25.
[54] Williams, *The Law Reform (Frustrated Contracts) Act 1943*, p.39.
[55] *Fibrosa* [1943] A.C. 32.
[56] See paras 15–21—15–25.
[57] *Lobb v Vasey Housing Auxiliary (War Widows Guild)* [1963] V.R. 239.
[58] *Lobb* [1963] V.R. 239 at 248.

(vi) *Discretion*   **15–21**

Once it is shown that the recipient has incurred expenses, the court has a discretion as to the extent to which it permits the recipient to retain (or claim) payments made (or due). Although it has been suggested that the proviso "is probably best rationalised as a statutory recognition of the defence of change of position",[59] this seems to be unconvincing. As commentators have pointed out, the proviso to s.1(2) is limited to expenses incurred in relation to the contract, whilst the defence of change of position would be available (in principle) for any extraordinary expenditure that the recipient of the payment would not otherwise have undertaken.[60] Furthermore, the expenses need not have been incurred as a result of the payment[61]—indeed, the Act expressly provides a remedy where expenses have been incurred despite the other party's failure to make the payments required under the contract. The change of position defence, by contrast, could only apply where a payment had been made. [62] Nor is there any requirement that the recipient show that the receipt (or anticipated receipt) of the payment caused it to incur expenses. In the defence of change of position, by contrast, causation is a fundamental requirement.[63]

Where expenses have been incurred by the recipient, the statutory language   **15–22**
permits the court to reduce the amount to be repaid if it considers it "just" to do so. In *Gamerco SA v ICM/Fair Warning (Agency) Ltd* Garland J. held that these words "clearly confer a very broad discretion", adding that[64]:

> "I see no indication in the Act, the authorities or the relevant literature that the court is obliged to incline towards either total retention or equal division. Its task is to do justice in a situation which the parties had neither contemplated nor provided for, and to mitigate the possible harshness of allowing all loss to lie where it has fallen."

On the facts of the case before him, Garland J. had to decide how to exercise this discretion where a contract to promote and organise a concert in Madrid was frustrated by the Spanish authorities' decision to revoke the permit it had previously granted. The claimants had paid the defendants $412,500, and the defendants had incurred expenses of approximately $50,000. Garland J. held that justice would be done by making no deduction from the prepayment. He seems to have been guided to this conclusion by two main factors. First, that the onus was on the defendant to show that any deduction for expenses should be made.[65] Secondly, that the claimant's own wasted expenses under the transaction were $450,000. In accordance with the instructions in s.1(6) of the 1943 Act, Garland

---

[59] *BP v Hunt* [1979] 1 W.L.R. 783 at 800. See also R. Goff, "The Search for Principle" (1983) 69 *Proceedings of the British Academy* 169, p.181.

[60] A. Haycroft and D. Waksman, "Frustration and Restitution" [1984] J.B.L. 207, p.215; McKendrick in Burrows, *Essays on the Law of Restitution*, p.156. On the defence of change of position, see Ch.27.

[61] *BP v Hunt* [1979] 1 W.L.R. 783 at 800.

[62] Stewart and Carter, "Frustrated Contracts and Statutory Adjustment: The Case for a Reappraisal", p.78.

[63] See further, para.27–25 and following.

[64] *Gamerco SA v ICM/Fair Warning (Agency) Ltd* [1995] 1 W.L.R. 1226 at 1237. See also, the assessment of s.1(2) by Haycroft and Waksman, "Frustration and Restitution", p.216: "a device for the adjustment of loss". Cf. Williams, *The Law Reform (Frustrated Contracts) Act 1943*, pp.35–36, arguing for a sharing of losses between the parties.

[65] *Lobb* [1963] V.R. 239 at 248 (interpreting the identical language in s.3(2) of the Frustrated Contracts Act 1959 (Victoria)).

J. disregarded the parties' insurance position, and he also gave no weight to an "unguarded remark at a time of great anxiety" by one of the directors of the defendant company, who had said that the claimants would get all of their money back. If, however, there had been a "question of estoppel or change of position", that might have been relevant. Since Garland J. went on to award the amount of the prepayment in full, an estoppel or change of position would have made no difference to the outcome of the particular case. But, particularly given the paucity of authority on s.1(2), Garland J.'s remarks provide a valuable insight into what may be relevant when the court exercises its broad discretion under the subsection.

15–23   **Purpose of payment**   A further relevant factor should be the purpose for which the advance payment was made. As explained above, a remedy under the 1943 Act (in contrast to the common law), does not require that the basis for which the payment was made has failed.[66] However, the Act does acknowledge the significance of the basis of the payment in the sense that a contractual term expressly providing for the payment to be retained in the event of frustration will be given effect.[67] Where there is no express provision, the purpose of the payment should similarly be taken into account when exercising the discretion under s.1(2). Thus, if the purpose of the payment was to protect the seller against the contract becoming frustrated, it would be appropriate for the discretion to be exercised in the seller's favour.[68]

15–24   **Expenses exceeding prepayment**   Under s.1(2), the amount of the prepayment imposes a ceiling on the payer's potential liability. If the expenses incurred by the payee have exceeded the amount of the prepayment, the payee's only recourse under the Act is to bring a claim under s.1(3), alleging that the payer has received a non-financial benefit from the payee's expenditure.[69]

15–25   **Prior breach**   The fact that one of the parties has committed a breach of the contract before the frustrating event occurs is not relevant to the assessment under s.1(2). As Robert Goff J. explained in *BP Exploration Co (Libya) Ltd v Hunt (No.2)*, under s.1(2) "the court has (subject to an allowance for expenses, or the effect of section 2(3), or a cross-claim or set-off) no option but to order repayment in an appropriate case".[70] It might, on the wording of the subsection, be technically possible to consider prior breaches at the stage of assessing the "just sum" to be repaid, but the view of Robert Goff J. is more convincing. There would be obvious injustice if prior breaches were relevant where expenses had been incurred, but not relevant where there had been no expenses.

(vii) *Payments Made after the Frustrating Event*

15–26   Section 1(2) is limited to payments made or due *before* the contract was discharged by frustration. If a payment is made after the frustrating event whether

---

[66] See para.15–15.
[67] Law Reform (Frustrated Contracts) Act 1943 s.2(3); discussed at paras 15–52—15–58.
[68] Treitel, *Frustration and Force Majeure*, para.15–072.
[69] Haycroft and Waksman, "Frustration and Restitution", pp.216–217.
[70] *BP Exploration Co (Libya) Ltd v Hunt (No.2)* [1979] 1 W.L.R. 783 at 808.

it can be recovered will be governed by the general rules of unjust enrichment.[71] Thus, a payment made in the mistaken belief that the frustrating event had not occurred, or in the mistaken belief that the contract remained binding despite the frustrating event, would be recoverable on the ground of mistake.[72] A payment made to close the transaction, by contrast, would not be recoverable.

(viii) *Use Value of Money*

Where there has been a significant lapse of time between a payment and the **15–27** frustrating event, the recipient will have received a benefit greater than the face value of the payment—he will have had the use of the money and may well have profited by that use. However, under s.1(2) only "sums paid . . . in pursuance of the contract" are recoverable and no account can be taken of the opportunity to profit.[73] Awards of interest in claims under the 1943 Act are dealt with below.[74]

(d) *Benefits other than Money Payments*

(i) *Section 1(3)*

Section 1(3) of the Act deals with benefits other than money payments. It **15–28** provides as follows:

> "Where any party to the contract has, by reason of anything done by any other party thereto in, or for the purpose of, the performance of the contract, obtained a valuable benefit (other than a payment of money to which the last foregoing subsection applies) before the time of discharge, there shall be recoverable from him by the said other party such sum (if any), not exceeding the value of the said benefit to the party obtaining it, as the court considers just, having regard to all the circumstances of the case and, in particular,—
>
> (a) the amount of any expenses incurred before the time of discharge by the benefited party in, or for the purpose of, the performance of the contract, including any sums paid or payable by him to any other party in pursuance of the contract and retained or recoverable by that party under the last foregoing subsection, and
>
> (b) the effect, in relation to the said benefit, of the circumstances giving rise to the frustration of the contract."

(ii) *The Conditions for Exercising the Discretion*

Before the court can exercise its discretion under this subsection, it must be **15–29** shown that one of the parties has "obtained a valuable benefit . . . before the time of discharge"; such benefit must have been obtained "in, or for the purpose of, the performance of the contract". There is some similarity between these requirements and the requirements for the exercise of the discretion under s.1(2) in relation to money payments, and similar points can be made to those made above

---

[71] Williams, *The Law Reform (Frustrated Contracts) Act 1943*, p.34.
[72] *Oom v Bruce* (1810) 12 East. 225; 104 E.R. 87. For general discussion, see Ch.9.
[73] *BP v Hunt* [1979] 1 W.L.R. 783; [1981] 1 W.L.R. 232 at 244.
[74] See para.15–66.

in relation to s.1(2). Thus, a party conferring a valuable benefit after the time of discharge must seek a remedy in the general law of unjust enrichment, by invoking an unjust factor such as mistake.[75] Furthermore, nothing in the terms of the subsection would exclude a benefit conferred in advance of the conclusion of the contract (provided that it was conferred in, or for the purpose of, performance of the contract subsequently agreed), nor is there anything to limit the subsection strictly to benefits conferred as required by the contractual provisions. For instance, a seller who knew that goods were needed as soon as possible, and had agreed to deliver them on a set date, might make an early delivery. Such a benefit would fall within the statutory scheme.

(iii) *Unperformed Obligation to Transfer Non-Money Benefit*

15–30 As Sir Guenter Treitel has pointed out, there is a discrepancy in the way that s.1(2) and s.1(3) deal with unperformed obligations.[76] Under s.1(2) a party who has failed to perform an obligation to pay money, which fell due before the frustrating event occurred, is relieved from performance. Section 1(3), by contrast, contains no such provision. It follows that, if a contractual obligation to transfer a non-money benefit has fallen due before the frustrating event occurred, and remains unperformed, the party subject to that obligation is liable in damages for having failed to perform it. Any damages award obtained falls outside the scheme of the Act. It is not a payment made "in pursuance of the contract" (s.1(2)), nor, being made after the frustrating event, is it a benefit conferred "before the time of discharge". This seems to be an unfortunate oversight in the legislative scheme.[77]

(iv) *Two Distinct Stages*

15–31 In *BP v Hunt* Robert Goff J. interpreted s.1(3) as calling for "two distinct stages" of analysis.[78] First, the valuable benefit must be identified; then, the just sum must be assessed.

(v) *"Benefit"*

15–32 **General** The 1943 Act provides no method for identifying or valuing non-financial benefits, nor does it impose the contract price as an upper limit on the value that might be given to the benefit concerned.[79] As can be seen from the general principles of the law of unjust enrichment, there is no obvious or universally accepted technique for assessing enrichment, and the issue is particularly difficult where services are rendered to the defendant.[80] In *BP v Hunt*

---

[75] See para.15–26. Cf. the statutory schemes in New South Wales and South Australia, which bring into account benefit-conferring acts done after frustration in the belief that the contract is still ongoing: Stewart and Carter, "Frustrated Contracts and Statutory Adjustment: The Case for a Reappraisal", p.89 fn.104.
[76] Treitel, *Frustration and Force Majeure*, para.15–066.
[77] Stewart and Carter, "Frustrated Contracts and Statutory Adjustment: The Case for a Reappraisal", pp.84–85 highlight the way the problem is dealt with in New South Wales and British Columbia.
[78] *BP v Hunt* [1979] 1 W.L.R. 783 at 801.
[79] *Rover International Ltd v Cannon Film Sales Ltd* [1989] 1 W.L.R. 912 at 928 per Kerr L.J. For the potential relevance of the contractual provisions under s.1(3), see paras 15–42—15–44.
[80] See paras 5–21—5–37.

Robert Goff J. construed s.1(3) as requiring "that the benefit should in an appropriate case be identified as the end product of the services".[81] He reached this conclusion for two reasons. First, that s.1(3) distinguishes between the performance of the contract and the benefit received by the defendant. Secondly, that s.1(3)(b) refers to the effect of the frustrating circumstances on the benefit obtained. However, Robert Goff J. went on to state that in some situations it would not be possible to identify the benefit as the end product of services, since some services had no end product as such. He gave as examples surveying work and the transportation of goods.[82] It seems that, with such services, the benefit can legitimately be assessed differently, probably in terms of the value of the services performed.

Where a service led to an end product, Robert Goff J. indicated that the end   **15–33** product would be the "benefit"; however, if it did not occur, it would be possible to regard the service itself as the end product. Thus, where prospecting work was done, if that led to the discovery of a valuable mineral deposit, the mineral deposit was (it seems) to be regarded as the benefit.[83] However, if the prospecting work resulted in no mineral being found:

> "[T]here is always (whether the prospecting is successful or not) the benefit of the prospecting itself, i.e. of knowing whether or not the land contains any deposit of the relevant minerals".[84]

It is not obvious why the judge felt that the surveying example he had given earlier, as an illustration of where services might result in no end product, could not be explained in a similar way. Robert Goff J. made it clear that he felt compelled by the statutory language to adopt this approach to identifying the benefit conferred in terms of the end product of the services. It would have been more satisfactory, in his view, "to treat the services themselves as the benefit". "After all", he explained, "the services in question have been requested by the defendant, who normally takes the risk that they may prove worthless, from whatever cause".[85]

The approach that Robert Goff J. felt compelled to take to the identification of   **15–34** the benefit bristles with difficulties, as the judge himself pointed out. As explained above,[86] the genesis of s.1(3) was highly unusual, in that it was neither proposed nor even considered by the Law Revision Committee, but was formulated hurriedly in order to complement the proposal that the Committee had made in respect of money payments. There is nothing in the relevant working papers to suggest that any method as complicated as that expounded by Robert Goff J. was intended by the draftsman. Furthermore, it may be respectfully questioned whether the statutory language really does compel the approach that the judge adopted. The subsection does indeed use the words "performance" and "benefit", but not by way of contrast—rather, the reference to "performance"

---

[81] *BP v Hunt* [1979] 1 W.L.R. 783 at 801.
[82] *BP v Hunt* [1979] 1 W.L.R. 783 at 801–802.
[83] *BP v Hunt* [1979] 1 W.L.R. 783 at 803.
[84] *BP v Hunt* [1979] 1 W.L.R. 783 at 802.
[85] *BP v Hunt* [1979] 1 W.L.R. 783 at 802.
[86] See paras 15–06—15–10.

describes how the benefit must have been conferred.[87] Furthermore, the reference in s.1(3)(b) to the effect of frustrating circumstances on the benefit does not require that the benefit of services must be conceived in terms of its end product. Section 1(3)(b) seems to be more obviously directed at situations where the benefit consisted in the receipt of goods, which have been destroyed or damaged by the frustrating event.[88] Robert Goff J., by contrast, appears to have assumed that s.1(3)(b) should be applied in the widest circumstances possible. The statutory language does not require that assumption to be made, and, given the difficulties that the judge's assumption created, it would seem preferable to adopt a less difficult approach to the identification of the benefit of services.

15–35   A more straightforward approach to valuing the benefit for the purposes of s.1(3) was taken in *Atwal v Rochester*,[89] where a building contract had been frustrated, mid-way through the building work, by the supervening illness of the builder. The court held that under s.1(3) the builder should receive the value of the materials used in carrying out the work, the value of the labour expended and a profit element.[90] Unfortunately, the court does not appear to have been referred to the analysis of Robert Goff J. in *BP v Hunt*, nor was it invited to consider the point that, on the facts of the case before it, there was little value in half-completed building works.

15–36   **Apportionment of benefit**   Where a benefit has resulted as a combination of the work of the claimant and some other source, the court must apportion the benefit and decide how much is attributable to the claimant. Thus, to take the example Robert Goff J. gave of the prospector who discovers a valuable mineral deposit on the defendant's land, it would be incorrect to attribute the entire value of the deposit to the prospector. Rather, the prospector could be said to have unlocked the potential value that the land had.[91]

15–37   **Valuation of benefit**   In *BP v Hunt* Robert Goff J. held that the benefit was to be valued "as at the date of frustration",[92] that is, after the frustrating event had occurred. He reached this conclusion on the basis of his construction of the Act, in particular, s.1(3)(b), which, he said "makes it plain that the plaintiff is to take the risk of depreciation or destruction by the frustrating event." "If the effect of the frustrating event upon the value of the benefit is to be measured", he continued, "it must surely be measured upon the benefit as at the date of frustration."[93]

15–38   Robert Goff J. regarded himself as compelled to reach this conclusion by the language of the Act, but, as Haycroft and Waksman have pointed out, the Act seems to be less dogmatic than Robert Goff J. understood it to be.[94] Section 1(3) refers to "a valuable benefit [obtained] *before* the time of discharge" (emphasis

---

[87] Haycroft and Waksman, "Frustration and Restitution", p.218.
[88] e.g. *Appleby v Myers* (1867) L.R. 2 C.P. 651.
[89] *Atwal v Rochester* [2010] EWHC 2338 (TCC).
[90] *Atwal* [2010] EWHC 2338 (TCC) at [37].
[91] *Cobbe v Yeoman's Row Management Ltd* [2008] UKHL 55; [2008] 1 W.L.R. 1752.
[92] *BP v Hunt* [1979] 1 W.L.R. 783 at 803.
[93] *BP v Hunt* [1979] 1 W.L.R. 783 at 803.
[94] Haycroft and Waksman, "Frustration and Restitution", p.220. See also Williams, *The Law Reform (Frustrated Contracts) Act 1943*, pp.48–50; Stewart and Carter, "Frustrated Contracts and Statutory Adjustment: The Case for a Reappraisal", p.99.

added) and continues that the sum recoverable shall not exceed "the value of the *said* benefit" (emphasis added). Furthermore, s.1(3)(b) identifies the effect of the frustrating event on the benefit conferred as being a circumstance to take into account in assessing the "just sum", not as a factor determining the assessment of the value of the benefit. It does not follow from the fact that the effect of the frustrating event is relevant to assessing the "just sum" that the claimant must always take the risk of destruction by the frustrating event. Rather, it is a matter for the judge's discretion whether, and to what extent, he should bear that risk.[95] In addition, since, under s.1(3), the value of the benefit conferred imposes a ceiling on the amount recoverable by the claimant, valuing the benefit at the date of frustration would effectively exclude from the Act any situations in which the frustrating event has destroyed the benefit conferred. It is difficult to believe that the Act was intended to have such a narrow scope, and it would seem, therefore that Andrew Burrows is correct in his criticism that Robert Goff J. drew an "unnecessarily sharp distinction" between identifying and valuing the benefit.[96]

Benefits flowing from performance The recipient of a benefit under a   **15–39**
contract may have made use of that benefit in a way that has enhanced his position. For instance, the recipient of goods under a contract might have sold those goods and thereby had the use of the price up to the time that the contract was frustrated. Similarly, the benefit conferred may have saved the recipient an otherwise necessary expense—for instance, he may have received services that he would otherwise have had to purchase by borrowing money at a commercial rate of interest. In *BP v Hunt* Robert Goff J. said that it was "very tempting" to take into account such an additional benefit or saving, as it would "lead to a more realistic valuation".[97] He held, however, that he was precluded from doing so, for two reasons with which the Court of Appeal agreed.[98] First, by the terms of s.1(2) only "sums paid" were recoverable, with no allowance for the use value of money received in the meantime.[99] It would be inconsistent with the terms of s.1(2) to take account under s.1(3) of either the use value of money obtained, or the saving of borrowing costs. Secondly, s.1(3)(a) itself referred to "the amount of any expenses", which indicated that only *actual* expenses were relevant. It would create an unfair inconsistency in the application of that subsection if the claimant was allowed to claim for the time value of benefits conferred, whilst the time value of the expenditure incurred by the defendant was disregarded.

(vi) *Just sum*

General Section 1(3) instructs courts to make an award that they consider   **15–40**
"just", having regard to "all the circumstances". As the Court of Appeal commented in *BP v Hunt*, "the subsection gives no help as to how, or upon what principles, the court is to make its assessment or as to what factors to take into

---

[95] Treitel, *Frustration and Force Majeure*, para.15–064.
[96] A Burrows, "Free Acceptance and the Law of Restitution" (1988) 104 L.Q.R. 576, p.591.
[97] *BP v Hunt* [1979] 1 W.L.R. 783 at 803–804.
[98] *BP v Hunt* [1981] 1 W.L.R. 232 at 244.
[99] See para.15–26.

account".[100] Nor is there any guidance as to the weight to give to the factors identified in subss.1(3)(a) and (b). In *BP v Hunt* Robert Goff J. solved the difficulty by asserting that "the principle underlying the Act is prevention of the unjust enrichment of the defendant at the claimant's expense",[101] but the Court of Appeal did not endorse this approach, commenting that "We get no help from the use of words which are not in the statute".[102] The Court of Appeal, however, did not go on to give any substantive guidance as to the principles on which the "just sum" should be assessed. Its approach to s.1(3) placed great emphasis on the discretion given to the trial judge: "What is just is what the trial judge thinks is just".[103] It was, therefore, open to a trial judge to assess the sum to be paid in whatever way he thought appropriate, so long as the decision was not unjust. Thus, s.1(3) did not require a judge to perform the "accountancy exercise" of adding up all the benefits received by each party under the contract and making an award that equalised the benefits received.[104] However, if a trial judge decided to take that approach, the award could not be overturned, since "the balancing of benefits is another way of assessing a just sum".[105] Similarly, there was no single correct method for valuing the benefits conferred.

15–41   Whilst the categorical statement by Robert Goff J. that the Act was intended to reverse unjust enrichment is not borne out by the terms of the Act, or the intentions of its creators, the potential for unjust enrichment to occur as the result of frustration of a contract must surely be at least one relevant factor to take into account. Other potentially relevant principles could include the sharing of losses inflicted by the frustrating event (as occurs in general average), the balancing of benefits resulting from the contract in the circumstances prevailing after frustration, whether one party was better placed to protect himself against the consequences of the frustrating event, and that the frustrating event should not be used as an opportunity to renegotiate the basis on which benefits were previously agreed to be conferred.

15–42   **Relevance of contract terms**   The terms of the parties' contract will often be relevant to the assessment of the just sum. In *BP v Hunt* Robert Goff J. identified three ways in which this might occur.[106] First, the contract terms "may serve to indicate the full scope of the work done".[107] If, he explained, the contractual terms provide for payment of a substantial prize if the claimant successfully completes the work, but for nothing if he fails to do so, and he has already conferred a substantial benefit on the defendant, "the element of risk taken by the plaintiff may be held to have the effect of enhancing the amount of any sum to be awarded". The facts of the *BP v Hunt* case did not quite fit within this example, since, although the claimants took the risk of an oil concession being unprofitable, and would enjoy large profits if their efforts to develop it succeeded, the contract did not provide for "a substantial prize" to be paid by the defendant.

[100] *BP v Hunt* [1981] 1 W.L.R. 232 at 238.
[101] *BP v Hunt* [1979] 1 W.L.R. 783 at 805.
[102] *BP v Hunt* [1981] 1 W.L.R. 232 at 243.
[103] *BP v Hunt* [1981] 1 W.L.R. 232 at 238.
[104] *BP v Hunt* [1981] 1 W.L.R. 232 at 242.
[105] *BP v Hunt* [1981] 1 W.L.R. 232 at 243.
[106] *BP v Hunt* [1979] 1 W.L.R. 783 at 805–806.
[107] *BP v Hunt* [1979] 1 W.L.R. 783 at 805.

When the case was decided in the Court of Appeal, however, a different approach was adopted. Responding to a submission that, because under the contract BP had taken the risk of physical failure of the project, the just sum should be reduced, the Court of Appeal observed that:

> "[T]he fact that the plaintiffs were willing in the early days of the joint enterprise to take risks with their money is of little, if any, significance to the assessment of the just sum".[108]

This would suggest, equally, that taking a risk should not enhance the just sum either. In any event, it is clear that where the contract terms provide that one of the parties bears certain risks, and the contract has become frustrated due to the materialisation of a different risk, which was not in contemplation at the time the contract was made, the distribution of those other risks does not prevent the award of a just sum under s.1(3).[109]

Secondly, "the contract consideration is always relevant as providing some **15–43** evidence of what will be a reasonable sum to be awarded in respect of the plaintiff's work".[110] For example, the agreement between the parties may show whether it is more appropriate to base the just sum on a fee for the work done or on a share of the (anticipated) profits from the venture.[111]

Thirdly, "the contract consideration, or a rateable part of it, may provide a **15–44** limit to the sum to be awarded".[112] In most cases, Robert Goff J. explained, "the defendant will only have been prepared to contract for the goods or services on the basis that he paid no more than the contract consideration".[113] Thus, in *Atwal*,[114] where the price due under a building contract was significantly below the market rate, the parties appear to have assumed that the contract price formed the upper limit for a claim under s.1(3). This third use of the contract price illustrates a further factor that is appropriately taken into account in assessing the just sum, namely, that it would be unjust to allow one party to exploit the occurrence of the frustrating event so as to revalue benefits he had previously agreed to confer at a lower price. It may, however, be doubted whether a rateable part of the contract price should act as a ceiling on recovery. As explained elsewhere, there are strong reasons against using a rateable part of the contract price as a ceiling in claims in unjust enrichment.[115] These reasons apply with equal force to claims under s.1(3) of the 1943 Act.

Expenses incurred   Section 1(3)(a) directs a court exercising its discretion to **15–45** consider "the amount of any expenses incurred before the time of discharge by the benefited party in, or for the purpose of, the performance of the contract". As with the corresponding provision relating to money payments, there is nothing in the statutory language to exclude expenses not reasonably or foreseeably incurred. However, if it is accepted that the contract price constitutes a limit on

---

[108] *BP v Hunt* [1981] 1 W.L.R. 232 at 242.
[109] *BP v Hunt* [1983] 2 A.C. 352 at 373.
[110] *BP v Hunt* [1979] 1 W.L.R. 783 at 805.
[111] e.g. *Way v Latilla* [1937] 3 All E.R. 759.
[112] *BP v Hunt* [1979] 1 W.L.R. 783 at 806.
[113] *BP v Hunt* [1979] 1 W.L.R. 783 at 806.
[114] *Atwal* [2010] EWHC 2338 (TCC).
[115] See paras 3–55—3–56.

the possible award under s.1(3), expenses exceeding the contractual remuneration will be irrecoverable.

15–46   **Effect of the frustrating event**   The second matter to which s.1(3) directs a court to have regard is the effect of the frustrating event on the benefit. This might be an increase in value (for instance, if the frustrating event causes the market price to go up) or a decrease (for instance, if the frustrating event damages or destroys work done under the contract).[116] As explained above, in *BP v Hunt* Robert Goff J. regarded this part of subsection (3) as particularly significant, since it demonstrated the intention to regard the "benefit" conferred as the end product of services.[117] The judge also took the view that the value of the benefit was to be assessed after the frustrating event had taken place.[118] This effectively made the importance of the effect of the frustrating event a mandatory rather than discretionary factor. In our view Robert Goff J.'s interpretation limited the court's discretion to a greater extent than was required by the statutory language. The effect of the frustrating event should be a matter for the judge's discretion not a mandatory rule for assessing the value of the benefit conferred.

15–47   **Prior breaches**   Despite the reference in s.1(3) to "all the circumstances", breaches of contract committed prior to the frustrating event have been held to be irrelevant to the assessment of the just sum. As Robert Goff J. put it in *BP v Hunt*[119]:

> "[T]he basis of such an award is that the defendant has been unjustly enriched at the plaintiff's expense, and the mere fact that the plaintiff has committed a prior breach of contract does not affect the question whether the defendant has been unjustly enriched, which depends upon the quite separate question whether he has received a benefit in respect of which he ought, in justice, to make restitution."

As can be seen from this analysis, Robert Goff J. reached his conclusion by relying on the assumption that s.1(3) was designed to reverse unjust enrichment. There is no support for this assumption either in the wording of the Act, or in the genesis of the subsection, and this has prompted commentators to question whether Robert Goff J.'s conclusion was correct.[120] However, although we share the doubts that the Act was designed to reverse unjust enrichment, Robert Goff J.'s decision to exclude prior breaches from the assessment of the just sum under s.1(3) can be supported on the ground that consistency with s.1(2) requires it. As shown above,[121] the wording of s.1(2) excludes consideration of prior breaches (or, indeed, any other factor) where a payment has been made and no expenses have been incurred by the other party. Under such circumstances the sum received must simply be repaid. Where the party receiving the payment has incurred expenses, the court's discretion comes into play, but there is no good

---

[116] Williams, *The Law Reform (Frustrated Contracts) Act 1943*, pp.54–55.
[117] See para.15–31.
[118] See para.15–36.
[119] *BP v Hunt* [1979] 1 W.L.R. 783 at 808.
[120] Haycroft and Waksman, "Frustration and Restitution", p.222.
[121] See para.15–25.

reason why prior breaches should suddenly become relevant at that point. If prior breaches were to be made relevant under s.1(3) there would, therefore, be an unfortunate asymmetry in the treatment of money and non-money benefits.

Relationship between s.1(2) and (3)   Section 1(3)(a) expressly contemplates   **15–48** that claims under s.1(2) and under s.1(3) will arise on the same facts. Where claims are brought under both subsections, s.1(3)(a) indicates that, in assessing the just sum under s.1(3), the court should take account of payments made by the recipient of the benefit and retained (or recoverable) under s.1(2). In other words, a party should not be permitted to recover for both expenses incurred (under s.1(2)) and for the benefit that his expenditure has conferred on the other party (under s.1(3)).

The provisions of s.1(2) and (3) have the potential to present parties with a   **15–49** choice about how to formulate their claims to their best advantage. Thus, where a party has received a prepayment under a contract that is subsequently frustrated, if that party has incurred expenses in doing work under the contract, he could either seek to have his expenses taken account of in reducing the payer's claim under s.1(2); or, if the work undertaken has conferred a benefit on the payer, the payee could claim under s.1(3).[122] The Act imposes no restriction on the payee's choice, so the decision is likely to turn on whether the benefit to the payer has exceeded the cost of providing it.

Insurance   Section 1(5) of the 1943 Act directs the court not to take into   **15–50** account any sums which have "become payable" to either contracting party, as a result of the frustrating circumstances, under contracts of insurance. However, the subsection makes an exception where there is either an "express term" of the frustrated contract that imposes an obligation to insure or an obligation to insure imposed by statute. The general exclusion of insurance payments can be explained on the basis that such payments are *res inter alios acta*, and that any other rule would interfere with the insurer's right of subrogation.[123] The exceptions are readily comprehensible, as relating to situations where the obligation to insure indicates that the risk of the frustrating event was to be borne by the party bearing that obligation. Indeed, it may be that, where one of the parties was under an obligation to insure, it would not even be necessary for a court to examine whether insurance had actually been obtained, and whether any sums had "become payable" under it. In such circumstances, it may well be that the existence of the obligation to insure would be, in itself, sufficient to justify awards under s.1(2) and (3) that placed the risk of the frustrating event on the party subject to the insurance obligation.

(e) *Limitations on the Application of the Act*

Section 2 of the Act sets out certain limits on its operation. The following three   **15–51** subsections call for substantive comment. Section 2(3) disapplies the Act where

---

[122] Cf. Stewart and Carter, "Frustrated Contracts and Statutory Adjustment: The Case for a Reappraisal", p.80, where the authors state that "It seems implicit . . . that where the expenses result in a benefit to the other party the claim in respect of those expenses must be brought under section 1(3)."

[123] Williams, *The Law Reform (Frustrated Contracts) Act 1943*, p.56. For general discussion of insurers' subrogation rights, see Ch.21.

the contract in question "contains any provision" dealing with frustration. Section 2(4) deals with the courts' powers to sever partly performed contracts, and s.2(5) excludes specific kinds of contracts, including charterparties. Subsections (1) and (2) are simpler: subs.(1) specifies the date of the Act coming into force, and subs.(2) states that the Act applies to the Crown.

(i) *Contractual Provisions Intended to Have Effect Despite Frustration*

15–52   **General**   Subsection (3) provides as follows:

> "Where any contract to which this Act applies contains any provision which, upon the true construction of the contract, is intended to have effect in the event of circumstances arising which operate, or would but for the said provision operate, to frustrate the contract, or is intended to have effect whether such circumstances arise or not, the court shall give effect to the said provision and shall only give effect to the foregoing section of this Act to such extent, if any, as appears to the court to be consistent with the said provision."

In *BP v Hunt*, Robert Goff J. held that there was no need for a term to be "*clearly* intended to have effect in the event of the frustrating circumstances".[124] Rather, it was simply a matter of applying the ordinary principles of construction to the term in question. Robert Goff J. made it clear that it was not necessary for the term to make express reference to frustration by giving an example of a loan of money on terms that it was to be repaid out of the profits of the debtor's business. If that business consisted of a ship, which subsequently struck a reef and sank, Robert Goff J. remarked that: "it may be that the court, having regard to the terms of the contract and the risk taken thereunder by the lender, would make no award".[125] The underlying principle, he said, was that "the court should not act inconsistently with the contractual intention of the parties applicable in the events which have happened".[126]

15–53   This does, indeed, seem to be the underlying principle of s.2(3), but it may be that Robert Goff J. formulated it too expansively—particularly in the example of the loan to the shipowner—and was too quick to reject the submission that any term should "clearly" be intended to apply in the event of frustration. Indeed, when he came to apply s.2(3) to a contract term that stated that the defendant "shall have no personal liability to repay the sums required in the operating agreement", he seems to have taken a more cautious approach.[127] In holding that the term should not be given effect, he remarked that:

> "[W]here there is no clear indication that the parties did intend the clause to be applicable in the event of frustration, the court has to be very careful before it draws the inference that the clause was intended to be applicable in such radically changed circumstances".[128]

---

[124] *BP v Hunt* [1979] 1 W.L.R. 783 at 806.
[125] *BP v Hunt* [1979] 1 W.L.R. 783 at 807.
[126] *BP v Hunt* [1979] 1 W.L.R. 783 at 807.
[127] *BP v Hunt* [1979] 1 W.L.R. 783 at 828–832.
[128] *BP v Hunt* [1979] 1 W.L.R. 783 at 829. See, similarly, the approach of the Court of Appeal and the House of Lords at [1981] 1 W.L.R. 232 at 241 and [1983] 2 A.C. 352 at 372 respectively.

This remark should be seen as a gloss on his rejection of the argument that only "clear" terms were within s.2(3). Robert Goff J. also observed that:

> "[T]he mere fact that the parties had agreed that the plaintiff should receive his contractual consideration in a certain form is unlikely to preclude an award of resitution in the event of frustration".[129]

This would suggest that the shipowner example he had discussed earlier in his judgment was an exceptional case.

In our view, the more limited approach to s.2(3) is more convincing. As **15–54** explained further below (in relation to whether implied terms come within s.2(3)),[130] there is a fundamental tension between the policy of the Act and the principle of s.2(3)—indeed, the Act was prompted by universal dissatisfaction with an approach that gave too much emphasis to the parties' contractual allocation of risk. Section 2(3) should, therefore, be seen as an exception to the general principles of the Act, not as a broad principle to be given equal importance with the rules set out in s.1. [131] On this approach, it would be very unusual for a term to have effect after frustration unless it is expressly stated that it is to have such effect. The most obvious example of such a term would be a procedural term, such as a provision for the reference of disputes to arbitration; another example might be an employee's obligation to keep confidential any information obtained in the course of employment.[132]

Entire obligations   Robert Goff J. acknowledged that there must be limits to **15–55** the application of the principle that the courts should not act inconsistently with the contractual intention of the parties. Where there is an entire obligation, under which payment is not to be made for work until the work is complete, the contractual risk of frustration is on the worker.[133] Such an obligation would surely not, in itself, be regarded as a "provision intended to have effect in the event of circumstances arising which operate . . . to frustrate the contract". As Robert Goff J. commented, if it were so regarded, "there would be few awards under s.1(3)".[134] Some additional contractual language, however, might be sufficient to bring such an obligation within the remit of s.2(3).

Implied terms   Whether implied terms fall within s.2(3) is a difficult and **15–56** finely balanced question. In 1944, Arnold McNair, who had been deeply involved in the drafting discussions, wrote that s.2(3):

> "[F]ollows logically from the view, now believed to be generally accepted, that the doctrine of frustration rests upon an implied term and that the Court is seeking to give effect to the intentions of the parties".[135]

---

[129] *BP v Hunt* [1979] 1 W.L.R. 783 at 832.

[130] See paras 15–56—15–58.

[131] See *BP v Hunt* [1983] 2 A.C. 352, where counsel for BP successfully submitted (at 360) that s.2(3) was "a qualification of section 1 . . . Only in exceptional cases will any clause survive the frustration . . . "

[132] Stewart and Carter, "Frustrated Contracts and Statutory Adjustment: The Case for a Reappraisal", pp.70–71.

[133] e.g. *Cutter v Powell* (1795) 6 T.R. 320; 101 E.R. 573.

[134] *BP v Hunt* [1979] 1 W.L.R. 783.

[135] McNair, "The Law Reform (Frustrated Contracts) Act 1943", p.169.

It seems that he envisaged that the "provision" in the subsection would be an express term which, as a matter of conventional contract doctrine, could not be contradicted by an implied term.[136]

15–57　　McNair's rationale for s.2(3) is not tenable today, because it is no longer assumed that frustration rests on an implied term.[137] However, there remains the alternative rationale for the sub-section, as expounded by Goff J. in *BP v Hunt*, namely that it prevents either party from subverting the contractual bargain and from re-allocating risks that had originally been placed on it.[138] Similar considerations are accepted elsewhere in the law of unjust enrichment as good reasons for excluding non-contractual claims.[139] This alternative rationale for s.2(3) would not depend on the relevant contractual provision being an express term, indeed, the subsection would more effectively prevent the subversion of contractual bargains if implied terms were included as well. It is not entirely clear whether the statutory language could be made to extend to implied terms —"provision" might seem to suggest an express term[140]—but the potential for the subsection to prevent the subversion of bargains would be undermined if a more flexible interpretation was not adopted. In the House of Lords' decision in the *BP v Hunt* case Lord Brandon (with whom the other members of the House agreed), seemed to contemplate that implied terms could be included in s.2(3), when he observed that there was nothing in the contract "to indicate either expressly or by necessary implication" that the parties had intended a contractual clause to apply after BP's interest had been expropriated.[141]

15–58　　Although it is attractive to interpret s.2(3) so as to prevent the parties' allocation of risk being undermined, this approach is not without difficulty. The concern with respecting the parties' allocation of risk is indeed an important theme in the law of unjust enrichment, but, as pointed out in the introduction to this chapter, the 1943 Act does not fit easily into the general category of unjust enrichment.[142] Furthermore, emphasis on the parties' allocation of risk under their contract was precisely what prompted the reforms that culminated in the 1943 Act itself. Indeed, it could be said that there is a fundamental tension between the underlying policy of the Act and s.2(3). It is not a perfect solution, but in order to reduce this fundamental tension as far as possible, the best approach may be to regard s.2(3) as an exception to the underlying policy of the Act. That would entail interpreting s.2(3) narrowly by confining it to express terms relating to frustration.[143] Furthermore, once it is appreciated that the underlying policy of the Act is in conflict with s.2(3), the broad approach to express terms advocated by Robert Goff J. in *BP v Hunt* looks less convincing[144];

---

[136] McNair, "The Law Reform (Frustrated Contracts) Act 1943", p.169 places his discussion of s.2(3) under the heading: "Express Provision".

[137] H. Beale (ed.), *Chitty on Contracts*, paras 23–010—23–011.

[138] See para.15–51.

[139] See Ch.3.

[140] Cf. s.1(5), which refers to "an express term of the frustrated contract".

[141] *BP v Hunt* [1983] 2 A.C. 352 at 372.

[142] See paras 15–02—15–10.

[143] Cf. Williams, *The Law Reform (Frustrated Contracts) Act 1943*, pp.60–61, who regards s.2(3) as showing that "the intention of the parties is paramount" and relies on dicta of Lord Simon L.C. in *Fibrosa* [1943] A.C. 32 at 43 that the common law remedy in unjust enrichment may be excluded either expressly or by proper implication.

[144] For the approach to express terms, see para.15–52.

there may be more merit in the argument that terms should "clearly" be intended to operate in the event of frustrating circumstances than the judge was prepared to allow.

Contract price   The prevailing approach to the assessment of the just sum   **15–59**
under s.1(3) regards the contract price as evidence of the value of the benefits conferred, and will often use the contract price as a limit on the sum to be awarded.[145] In *BP v Hunt* Robert Goff J. held that the use of the contract price as a limit on the amount payable under s.1(3) "may properly be said to arise by virtue of the operation of section 2(3) of the Act".[146] Slightly later in his judgment, he made the same point less categorically, admitting that s.2(3) might be "inapplicable".[147] Although the better view is that s.2(3) should be applied narrowly,[148] it may doubtless be possible to conclude, in some situations, that the parties intended that their agreement on price should continue to apply after the frustrating event.[149] However, this seems to be an unnecessarily elaborate route by which to justify making use of the contractual price in assessing the just sum. The more straightforward, and compelling, route is simply to say that what the defendant had agreed to pay for the contractual performance is clearly relevant to what it is "just" to require him to pay for the part performance he has received.

(ii) *Severance*

Section 2(4) provides that: **15–60**

> "Where it appears to the court that a part of any contract to which this Act applies can properly be severed from the remainder of the contract, being a part wholly performed before the time of discharge, or so performed except for the payment in respect of that part of the contract of sums which are or can be ascertained under the contract, the court shall treat that part of the contract as if it were a separate contract and had not been frustrated and shall treat the foregoing section of this Act as only applicable to the remainder of that contract."

This provision is likely to be of particular significance in relation to long-term contracts where periodical payments have been made. For instance, if a contract of employment were frustrated, the general provisions of the Act would seem to require (or, at the very least, present the opportunity for) a debate about whether the employee's services were worth more or less than the payments he had received under the contract of service. There would be the potential for the parties' entire bargain to be subverted. However, applying s.2(4) would permit a court to sever the period during which the employee earned his contractual remuneration and to focus solely on the period during which the frustrating event prevented the remuneration from being earned. The Act makes no alteration to the circumstances under which severance is permitted. It would seem, therefore,

---

[145] See para.15–43.
[146] *BP v Hunt* [1979] 1 W.L.R. 783 at 806.
[147] *BP v Hunt* [1979] 1 W.L.R. 783 at 806.
[148] See para.15–53.
[149] Robert Goff J. gives a possible example in *BP v Hunt* [1979] 1 W.L.R. 783 at 806: a poor householder, who contracts for building work to be done at below the market rate.

that the existing limits on severability continue to apply: for instance, the inability to sever payments made under an apprenticeship contract would still be good law.[150]

(iii) *Excluded contracts*

15–61   Section 2(5) disapplies the statutory scheme for the return of payments and benefits from three categories of contract. It states that:

"This Act shall not apply—

(a) to any charter party, except a time charterparty or a charterparty by way of demise, or to any contract (other than a charterparty) for the carriage of goods by sea; or

(b) to any contract of insurance, save as is provided by subsection (5) of the foregoing section; or

(c) to any contract to which section 7 of the Sale of Goods Act 1979 (which avoids contracts for the sale of specific goods which perish before the risk has passed to the buyer) applies, or to any other contract for the sale, or for the sale and delivery, of specific goods, where the contract is frustrated by reason of the fact that the goods have perished."

15–62   **Advance freight**   Section 2(5)(a) preserves the common law rules on payment of freight in advance under voyage charterparties, under which the right to retain such freight was not conditional on the successful completion of the voyage.[151] In this respect, the Act follows the recommendations of the Law Revision Committee, which, despite being highly critical of the advance freight rules, regarded them as being too well established to be abolished.[152] Strong criticism of the rules seems to be misplaced, because they actually reflect the agreed basis on which the payment was made and are, therefore, consistent with the general principles of failure of basis.[153] However, by enacting the 1943 legislation after the House of Lords' decision in *Fibrosa*,[154] the decision was taken to replace failure of basis as the test for the return of payments following a frustrating event.[155] The retention of failure of basis for advance payments of freight in voyage charterparties is, therefore, open to criticism as creating an anomaly.[156]

15–63   **Insurance**   The 1943 Act does not apply to contracts of insurance. The relevant common law rules governing the recovery of insurance premiums are

---

[150] e.g. *Whincup v Hughes* (1871) L.R. 6 C.P. 78. See further, discussion at para.12–16 and following, and Williams, *The Law Reform (Frustrated Contracts) Act 1943*, pp.62–72.

[151] *Anon* (1683) 2 Show. K.B. 283; 89 E.R. 941; *Andrew v Moorhouse* (1814) 5 Taunt. 435; 128 E.R. 758; *De Silvale v Kendall* (1815) 4 M. & S. 37; 105 E.R. 749; *Byrne v Schiller* (1871) L.R. 6 Ex. 319; *Allison v Bristol Marine Insurance Co* (1876) 1 App. Cas. 209.

[152] Law Revision Committee, *Seventh Interim Report*, p.10. See too McNair, "The Law Reform (Frustrated Contracts) Act 1943", pp.170–171.

[153] See para.13–11.

[154] *Fibrosa* [1943] A.C. 32.

[155] See paras 15–14——15–15 for a discussion of the ways in which the 1943 legislation differed from the principles of failure of basis.

[156] For a discussion of changes in the pattern of usage of voyage charterparties since the 1943 Act was passed see M. Howard, "Frustration and Shipping Law—Old Problems, New Contexts" in McKendrick, *Force Majeure and Frustration*, pp.127–129.

discussed elsewhere.[157] In the absence of any discussion in the report of the Law Revision Committee it is difficult to know why the regime introduced by the 1943 Act was thought to be unsuitable. Possibly, as with the exception for payment of advance freight under voyage charterparties, it was thought that commercial practice in relation to insurance was too well settled to be disturbed by legislative reform. At any rate, there is no obvious reason of principle why insurance contracts would be unsuitable for the kind of treatment that the 1943 Act gives to other types of contract.[158]

Sale of goods   Contracts governed by the Sale of Goods Act 1979 s.7 are **15–64** excluded from the 1943 Act, as are contracts for the sale of specific goods where the contract has been frustrated by the perishing of the goods. Section 7 of the 1979 Act provides that:

"Where there is an agreement to sell specific goods and subsequently the goods, without any fault on the part of the seller or buyer, perish before the risk passes to the buyer, the agreement is avoided".

As Glanville Williams observed, s.2(5)(c) of the 1943 Act "seems to be a somewhat involved way of saying that the Act does not apply to any contract for the sale of specific goods that perish, whether the risk passed to the buyer before the date of the perishing or not".[159] Discussion of the precise extent of this exception is beyond the scope of this work,[160] but its effect is that, where such contracts are frustrated by the perishing of the goods, the general common law principles of failure of basis will apply.[161] Contracts for the sale of generic goods, or for the sale of specific goods where the goods have not perished, by contrast, fall within the 1943 Act.

(f) Additional Points

(i) Currency

The court's discretion as to the just sum to be awarded extends to the currency **15–65** in which such an award should be made. Where the award is made under s.1(2), the presumption is that the currency of the award will be the same as the currency in which the money was originally paid.[162] Where the award is under s.1(3), the appropriate currency will depend on the circumstances of the case. Thus, in *BP v Hunt* the benefit of receipt of barrels of oil was valued in United States dollars, as that was the currency of the international oil industry. The benefit of the development work undertaken by the claimant, however, was valued in pounds

---

[157] See para.13–19.
[158] G Williams, "The Law Reform (Frustrated Contracts) Act 1943", p.69 (describing the exclusion as "puzzling"); Williams, *The Law Reform (Frustrated Contracts) Act 1943*, pp.80–81 (giving illustrations of where the Act's application to contracts of insurance would be beneficial).
[159] Williams, *The Law Reform (Frustrated Contracts) Act 1943*, p.81.
[160] See M. Bridge (ed.), *Benjamin's Sale of Goods*, 8th edn (London: Sweet & Maxwell, 2010), para.6.035.
[161] See Chs 12 and 13.
[162] *BP v Hunt* [1981] 1 W.L.R. 232 at 245.

sterling, since the claimant was an English company which had used sterling resources in order to finance the development work.[163]

(ii) *Interest*

15–66   The Senior Courts Act 1981 s.35A provides that the High Court may award interest in proceedings for the recovery of "a debt or damages". An award made under s.1(2) or s.1(3) of the 1943 Act was held to be such an award for the purposes of the Law Reform (Miscellaneous Provisions) Act 1934 s.3(1), which was the predecessor of s.35A.[164] Section 35A confers a wide discretion on the court in relation to the rate of interest and the time from which interest should be charged. An indication of how that discretion might be exercised in cases falling under the 1943 Act is provided by *BP v Hunt*, where Robert Goff J. rejected the submission that interest should fall due from the moment that the parties' contract became frustrated, and held, instead, that the appropriate time was the date when the claimants notified the defendant of their intention to bring a claim against him.[165] Both the Court of Appeal and the House of Lords upheld the trial judge's exercise of his discretion on this point.[166]

(iii) *Appellate Courts*

15–67   On current authority, there is very little role for appellate courts in cases where the discretion under s.1(2) or s.1(3) has been exercised. The Court of Appeal in *BP v Hunt* remarked, in relation to s.1(3), that "The responsibility lies with the judge: he has to fix a sum which he, not an appellate court, considers just."[167] Slightly later, it added that "what is just is what the trial judge thinks is just", and observed that the Court of Appeal could only interfere with an assessment where it was "so plainly wrong that it cannot be just".[168] The Court of Appeal also made it clear that trial judges should be allowed considerable freedom of choice in the principles they applied. For instance, the Court of Appeal disagreed with the statement of Robert Goff J. that the underlying principle of the 1943 Act was the prevention of unjust enrichment[169]; however, it still upheld the award that he had made, despite the fact that the reasoning leading to that award had been heavily reliant on principles drawn from the law of unjust enrichment. Although these observations were made in relation to s.1(3), they are equally applicable to the wide discretion conferred by s.1(2). Whilst the Court of Appeal's approach avoids constraining trial judges in their exercise of the discretion, it may be questioned whether its approach allows for too much freedom and has the potential to create inconsistency. As Goff L.J. (as he had become) commented in a lecture given in 1983, "This is surely no case for the Chancellor's foot . . . ."[170]

---

[163] *BP v Hunt* [1981] 1 W.L.R. 232 at 245.
[164] *BP v Hunt* [1983] 2 A.C. 352 at 373.
[165] *BP v Hunt* [1979] 1 W.L.R. 783 at 848.
[166] *BP v Hunt* [1981] 1 W.L.R. 232 at 245; [1983] 2 A.C. 352 at 374.
[167] *BP v Hunt* [1981] 1 W.L.R. 232 at 238.
[168] *BP v Hunt* [1981] 1 W.L.R. 232 at 238.
[169] *BP v Hunt* [1981] 1 W.L.R. 232 at 243.
[170] R. Goff, "The Search for Principle" (1983) 69 *Proceedings of the British Academy* 169, p.181.

CHAPTER 16

ANTICIPATED CONTRACTS THAT DO NOT MATERIALISE

1. INTRODUCTION

Where benefits are transferred in anticipation of a contractual agreement which **16–01** is intended to provide for payment for those benefits, and the contractual agreement does not materialise, the situation seems to lend itself to analysis in terms of failure of basis.[1] The same principles that govern liability where the contract is void or unenforceable would seem to be equally applicable where the contract does not come about. As Barry J. commented in *William Lacey (Hounslow) Ltd v Davis*[2]:

> "I am unable to see any valid distinction between work done which was to be paid for under the terms of a contract erroneously believed to be in existence, and work done which was to be paid for out of the proceeds of a contract which both parties erroneously believed was about to be made."[3]

It is now acknowledged that the potential for the law of unjust enrichment to **16–02** provide appropriate remedies where anticipated contracts do not materialise has reduced the pressure to find a solution to such problems within the law of contract.[4] However, as several of the decisions examined in this chapter demonstrate, the courts have not consistently analysed situations of this kind by applying the principles of failure of basis. Doubtless part of the reason for that inconsistency is that, where the benefit conferred consisted in the performance of

---

[1] A Burrows, "Free Acceptance and the Law of Restitution" (1988) 104 L.Q.R. 576, pp.581 and 595–597; E. McKendrick, "Work Done in Anticipation of a Contract Which Does Not Materialise" in W.R. Cornish, et al. (eds), *Restitution: Past, Present, and Future* (Oxford: Hart, 1998), 163, pp.181–184.

[2] *William Lacey (Hounslow) Ltd v Davis* [1957] 1 W.L.R. 932 at 939. In the previous edition of this work, the decision in *William Lacey* was explained by reference to the principle of free acceptance: G. Jones, *Goff & Jones: The Law of Restitution*, 7th edn (London: Sweet & Maxwell, 2006), para.26–009. In our view, however, Burrows, "Free Acceptance and the Law of Restitution", pp.595–598 provides a compelling criticism of this approach. See also P. Birks and C. Mitchell, "Unjust Enrichment" in A. Burrows (ed.), *English Private Law*, 2nd edn (Oxford: OUP, 2007), para.18.121 (treating *William Lacey* as an illustration of failure of basis).

[3] Cf. McKendrick in Cornish et al, *Restitution: Past, Present and Future*, p.181, where the passage quoted in the text is interpreted (and criticised) as imposing liability on the ground of mistake. If this is the correct interpretation of Barry J.'s observation, then we agree with McKendrick's criticism.

[4] E. McKendrick, "The Battle of Forms and the Law of Restitution" (1988) 8 O.J.L.S. 197, p.207, cited with approval in *Whittle Movers Ltd v Hollywood Express Ltd* [2009] EWCA Civ 1189; [2009] 2 C.L.C. 771 at [15] (noted P. Davies, "Contract and Unjust Enrichment: A Blurry Divide" (2010) 126 L.Q.R. 175); *Benourad v Compass Group Plc* [2010] EWHC 1882 (QB) at [106](c). Cf. *T.T.M.I. Sarl v Statoil ASA* [2011] EWHC 1150 (Comm) at [53], where Beatson J. stresses the "limits" of the law of unjust enrichment by comparison with the law of contract.

a service, it was not clearly appreciated that an analysis in terms of failure of basis was appropriate.[5] As a result, some of the cases—even those decided recently—fail to identify the unjust factor on which liability is based.[6] Furthermore, as was pointed out in *Countrywide Communications Ltd v ICL Pathway Ltd*, on some occasions courts have awarded claimants the amount of their wasted expenditure, rather than a sum representing the enrichment enjoyed by the defendant.[7] Such awards cannot be explained in terms of the law of unjust enrichment. They may sometimes be justified on other grounds.[8]

2. The Basis of the Transfer

16–03 A claimant who relies on failure of basis to recover benefits transferred in anticipation of a future contract must first identify the basis of the transfer. In accordance with the general principles that govern failure of basis as a ground of recovery,[9] the basis must be ascertained by an examination of the dealings between the parties. The objectively understood joint basis of the transfer must be identified,[10] and, as with the position in failure of basis more generally, there may be several conditions to which the transfer is subject. For instance, in *Cobbe v Yeoman's Row Management Ltd*,[11] an experienced property developer entered an oral agreement to purchase a site for development, which was conditional on the developer successfully obtaining planning permission. It was understood between the parties that if the application for planning permission was unsuccessful, the developer was not to be paid for his efforts; but that, if the vendor pulled out before a grant of planning permission was made, the developer would be reimbursed.[12] In the event, the vendor pulled out after planning permission had been obtained and the House of Lords held that the developer was entitled to recover the value of the benefit he had conferred on the vendor.[13]

---

[5] See para.12–03 and following.

[6] e.g. *Countrywide Communications Ltd v ICL Pathway Ltd* [2000] C.L.C. 324 at 349: "an obligation will be imposed only if justice requires it, or, which comes to the same thing, if it would be unconscionable for the plaintiff not to be recompensed"; *Vedatech Corp v Crystal Decisions (UK) Ltd* [2002] EWHC 818 (Ch) at [69], where the unjust factor is said to be that "it would be unjust for [the defendant] to have it for nothing"; *M.S.M. Consulting Ltd v United Republic of Tanzania* [2009] EWHC 121 (QB) at [171]: "the modern approach is to determine whether or not the circumstances are such that the law should, as a matter of justice, impose upon the defendant an obligation to make payment".

[7] *Countrywide Communications Ltd v ICL Pathway Ltd* [2000] C.L.C. 324. One such decision is Denning L.J.'s judgment in *Brewer Street Investments Ltd v Barclays Woollen Co Ltd* [1954] 1 Q.B. 428, discussed at para.16–19.

[8] K. Barker, "Coping with Failure—Reappraising Pre-Contractual Remuneration" (2003) 19 J.C.L. 105. See also J. Dietrich, "Classifying Precontractual Liability: A Comparative Analysis" (2001) 21 L.S. 153, which would locate (all) precontractual liability between contract and tort; S. Hedley, "Work done in Anticipation of a Contract Which Does Not Materialise: A Response" in Cornish et al., *Restitution: Past, Present, and Future*, 195, which argues that the cases should be accommodated within contract.

[9] See Chs 12 and 13 above.

[10] *Killen v Horseworld Ltd* [2011] EWHC 1600 (QB) at [48].

[11] *Cobbe v Yeoman's Row Management Ltd* [2008] UKHL 55; [2008] 1 W.L.R. 1752 (noted by A. Goymour [2009] C.L.J. 37).

[12] *Cobbe* [2008] UKHL 55; [2008] 1 W.L.R. 1752 at [6] and [12].

[13] *Cobbe* [2008] UKHL 55; [2008] 1 W.L.R. 1752 at [40]–[43].

(a) *Expedited Performance*

Where the parties have indicated to each other that they are negotiating towards   **16–04**
a binding contract, and one party commences performance in advance of that
binding contract, it is generally the case that the basis of any transfer is not
gratuitous. Thus, in *British Steel Corp v Cleveland Bridge and Engineering Co
Ltd*[14] the defendants had notified the claimants of their intention to enter a
contract with the claimants for the purchase of steel nodes, which were to be of
a specified quality and to be delivered in a particular order. Whilst the parties
were negotiating towards a contractual agreement, the claimants, at the defendant's request, began to manufacture and supply the nodes. No contract was ever
concluded. Robert Goff J. held that the defendant was liable to pay "a reasonable
sum for such work as has been done pursuant to that request".[15]

It was implicit in the analysis of Robert Goff J. in *British Steel* that when the   **16–05**
buyers refused to pay for the nodes that had been delivered, the basis for
conferring the benefit of the nodes on the buyer had failed. However, as Ewan
McKendrick has pointed out, the transaction involved in the case was more
complicated than a simple exchange of money for steel: the buyers did not give
the sellers "carte blanche" to produce whatever nodes they wanted to and to
deliver them in any order. Rather, a particular size, quality and sequence was
requested.[16] Robert Goff J. observed that the buyer's claim for "damages in
respect of late delivery or delivery out of sequence" could only be sustained if
there was a binding contract between the parties,[17] but it seems not to have been
argued in the case that delivery in a particular order, within a reasonable time,
constituted part of the understood condition for payment. We agree with McKendrick, that a "more sensitive" approach to ascertaining the basis on which
benefits are conferred, in line with the general principles of failure of basis, is
desirable.[18] Applying such an approach to the facts of the *British Steel* case, the
defendants' liability for such materials as he had used would be governed by the
principle of free acceptance.[19]

(b) *Preparatory Work*

Where the claimant's activity consists not in performance of the anticipated   **16–06**
contract but in preparations necessary for a hoped-for contract, any benefits
transferred by that activity are normally conferred at the claimant's risk. As
Christopher Clarke J. put it in *M.S.M. Consulting Ltd v United Republic of
Tanzania*[20]:

---

[14] *British Steel Corp v Cleveland Bridge and Engineering Co Ltd* [1984] 1 All E.R. 504. The decision
was approved in *Regalian Properties Plc v London Docklands Development Corp* [1995] 1 W.L.R.
212 at 230.
[15] *British Steel* [1984] 1 All E.R. 504 at 511.
[16] E McKendrick, "The Battle of Forms and the Law of Restitution" (1988) 8 O.J.L.S. 197,
pp.212–214.
[17] *British Steel* [1984] 1 All E.R. 504 at 506.
[18] McKendrick, "The Battle of Forms and the Law of Restitution", p.212.
[19] See Ch.17.
[20] *M.S.M. Consulting Ltd v United Republic of Tanzania* [2009] EWHC 121 (QB) at [171](b). See
also *Benourad* [2010] EWHC 1182 (QB) at [106] (l).

"Generally speaking a person who seeks to enter into a contract with another cannot claim to be paid the cost of estimating what it will cost him, or of deciding on a price, or bidding for the contract. Nor can he claim the cost of showing the other party his capability or skills even though, if there was a contract or retainer, he would be paid for them."

Thus, in *Regalian Properties Plc v London Docklands Development Corp*,[21] Rattee J. distinguished the decision in *British Steel*,[22] holding that there was no liability where a claimant incurred expense in order to satisfy conditions imposed by the defendants for the grant of a building lease.[23] Similarly, in *M.S.M. Consulting*[24] the claimant organised viewings of premises, and prepared estimated budgets for refurbishment, in the hope that it would be appointed as the defendant's agent for the purchase. Christopher Clarke J. held that the value of this work, done "in the hope that M.S.M. would be awarded a contract", could not be recovered.[25]

(c) *Basis May Be Revealed by the Nature of the Transaction*

16–07 The nature of the transaction may indicate that the basis of the transfer is that it is not to be paid for unless a contract is concluded. Perhaps the best illustration concerns builders' estimates. As Barry J. put it, in *William Lacey*[26]:

"[I]f a builder is invited to tender for certain work, either in competition or otherwise, there is no implication that he will be paid for the work . . . involved in arriving at his price: he undertakes this work as a gamble, and its cost is part of the overhead expenses of his business, which he hopes will be met out of the profits of such contracts as are made as a result of tenders which prove to be successful."

However, if the estimating work done by a builder goes beyond what is "normal", the customary assumption that estimates are gratuitous ceases to apply.[27] The same analysis applies to work done by property consultants in the hope of obtaining a contract to act as agents for the prospective purchaser.[28]

(d) *Dealings Expressly Subject to Contract*

16–08 The dealings between the parties may show that the basis of any transfer is that it shall not be paid for unless a binding contract is entered. Thus, in *Regalian*

---

[21] *Regalian Properties Plc v London Docklands Development Corp* [1995] 1 W.L.R. 212.

[22] *British Steel* [1984] 1 All E.R. 504.

[23] *Regalian Properties* [1995] 1 W.L.R. 212 at 230, approved in *Vedatech Corp* [2002] EWHC 818 (Ch) at [76]. See similarly *Cobbe* [2008] UKHL 55; [2008] 1 W.L.R. 1752 (agreement to sell land conditional on property developer obtaining planning permission; developer's costs in applying for planning permission understood not to be recoverable if application unsuccessful).

[24] *M.S.M. Consulting* [2009] EWHC 121 (QB).

[25] *M.S.M. Consulting* [2009] EWHC 121 (QB) at [174].

[26] *William Lacey* [1957] 1 W.L.R. 932 at 934. This example was cited with approval in *Countrywide Communications* [2000] C.L.C. 324 at 340–341.

[27] *British Steel* [1984] 1 All E.R. 504 at 935.

[28] *M.S.M. Consulting* [2009] EWHC 121 (QB).

Properties,[29] the claimant successfully tendered for the development of several sites owned by the defendant. The defendant's acceptance of the claimant's tender was stated to be "subject to contract", and also subject to the claimant's scheme "achieving the desired design quality". The defendants were unimpressed by the designs subsequently submitted by the claimant, and the claimant then spent large sums commissioning new designs and experts' reports. Eventually the redevelopment fell through and the claimant sought to recover the expenses he had incurred. Rattee J. held that, by entering negotiations that were expressly subject to contract, each party:

> "[M]ust be taken to know... that pending the conclusion of a binding contract any cost incurred by him in preparation for the intended contract will be incurred at his own risk, in the sense that he will have no recompense for those costs if no contract results."[30]

(e) *Risk*

An alternative way of approaching the issue of whether benefits have been **16–09** conferred on the basis that they are to be paid for, is to ask who took the risk of a contract failing to materialise.[31] For instance, where a builder has prepared estimates for a potential customer, the builder takes the risk that the customer will engage a different builder to undertake the work. Similarly, it should be considered whether the basis of the claimants' provision of services was that they were only to be paid for if they bring about a desired result. Thus, in *M.S.M. Consulting* Christopher Clarke J. took into account that the claimant's services as a property consultant had not been the effective cause of the defendant's subsequent property purchase, although he did not consider this to be a decisive factor.[32]

However, it cannot be assumed that, simply because benefits have been **16–10** conferred on the understanding that they are to be paid for under the anticipated contract, the party conferring those benefits takes the risk of the contract not materialising *for any reason*. For instance, the dealings between the parties and the nature of the transaction may well show that it was not intended that the recipient of a benefit should be entitled to retain it where the reason that the anticipated contract has not materialised is that the recipient of the benefit has simply changed his mind about proceeding. Thus, in *Brewer Street Investments Ltd v Barclays Woollen Co Ltd*,[33] a landlord and prospective tenant had been negotiating towards a lease of premises and certain alterations had been undertaken at the prospective tenants' request. No lease was ever agreed, because the

---

[29] *Regalian Properties* [1995] 1 W.L.R. 212.

[30] *Regalian Properties* [1995] 1 W.L.R. 212 at 231. See also *Countrywide Communications* [2000] C.L.C. 324; *Easat Antennas Ltd v Racal Defence Electronics Ltd* Unreported Ch D, June 21, 2000 at [69].

[31] *Hosking v Legal & General Ventures Ltd* Unreported CA February 12, 1999; *Stephen Donald Architects Ltd v King* [2003] EWHC 1867 (TCC); *M.S.M. Consulting* [2009] EWHC 121 (QB). But for the view that risk-taking reasoning is a redundant and harmful distraction, see F. Wilmot-Smith, "Replacing Risk-Taking Reasoning" (2011) 127 L.Q.R. 000.

[32] *M.S.M. Consulting* [2009] EWHC 121 (QB) at [176]. See also *Benourad* [2010] EWHC 1882 (QB) at [131].

[33] *Brewer Street Investments Ltd v Barclays Woollen Co Ltd* [1954] 1 Q.B. 428.

prospective tenants had insisted on being granted an option to purchase the premises, which the landlord had never been prepared to offer. At the trial, Morris L.J. strongly emphasised the reason for the failure of the negotiations, remarking that there would have been no liability if the landlord had simply changed its mind about granting a lease at all or had decided to offer a tenancy to someone else. All the members of the Court of Appeal agreed with this approach.[34]

16–11   Similarly, in *Cobbe*,[35] the parties had entered an oral agreement for a conditional sale of land, which both of them fully appreciated was not legally binding. The agreement provided that if the claimant, an experienced property developer, obtained planning permission for the residential redevelopment of the land, a binding contract would be entered for the sale of the land for £12 million. The land would then be redeveloped, the residential units sold, and any receipts above £24 million were to be shared between the parties. The claimant succeeded in obtaining permission, but the vendor then refused to honour the agreement, insisting on a higher price. It was held that, although the claimant could have had no claim if the application for development had been unsuccessful (thereby preventing a binding contract for the sale of the land being entered), he was entitled to recover where the reason for the contract failing to materialise was the vendor's unilateral decision to withdraw.[36]

(f) *Fault*

16–12 In his judgment in *Brewer Street*,[37] Denning L.J. used the language of fault to make the point that a party would not be entitled to retain benefits where the reason for the anticipated contract not materialising was that that party had simply changed his mind. Thus, he said that[38]:

> "If it was the landlords' fault, as for instance, if they refused to go on with the lease for no reason at all, or because they demanded a higher rent than that which had already been agreed, then they would not be allowed to recover any part of the cost of the alterations... On the other hand, if it was the prospective tenants' fault that the negotiations broke down, as, for instance, if they sought a lower rent than that which had been agreed upon, then the prospective tenants ought to pay the cost of the alterations up to the time they were stopped."

16–13 The use of the language of fault was endorsed in *Sabemo Pty Ltd v North Sydney MC (Sabemo)*,[39] where Sheppard J. held that the defendant authority was liable to pay for work undertaken by the claimant in anticipation of a building lease being granted. The claimant had successfully tendered for the grant of the lease, and had prepared three different schemes for the redevelopment of the land

---

[34] *Brewer Street* [1954] 1 Q.B. 428 at 434 per Somervell L.J.; at 436 per Denning L.J.; and at 439 per Romer L.J. See also *Jennings and Chapman Ltd v Woodman, Matthews & Co* [1952] 2 T.L.R. 409 at 415 per Denning L.J.; *Sabemo Pty Ltd v North Sydney MC* [1977] 2 N.S.W.L.R. 880.

[35] *Cobbe* [2008] UKHL 55; [2008] 1 W.L.R. 1752.

[36] Cf. *Hosking* Unreported CA, February 12, 1999, where one of the conditions on which the claimant was to receive a reward for his services to an investment syndicate was that the members of the syndicate would not exclude him from participation.

[37] *Brewer Street* [1954] 1 Q.B. 428.

[38] *Brewer Street* [1954] 1 Q.B. 428 at 436.

[39] *Sabemo Pty Ltd v North Sydney MC* [1977] 2 N.S.W.L.R. 880.

concerned. After more than three years of work, however, the council decided to drop the scheme. Sheppard J. held that the crucial feature of the case was that the council had decided to drop the proposal for reasons that had nothing to do with the claimants. "In looking at the matter in this way", he explained, "I am imputing a degree of fault to the defendant".[40] He went on to lay down a general principle in the following terms[41]:

> "[W]here two parties proceed upon the joint assumption that a contract will be entered into between them, and one does work beneficial for the project, and thus in the interests of the two parties, which work he would not be expected, in other circumstances, to do gratuitously, he will be entitled to compensation or restitution, if the other party unilaterally decides to abandon the project, not for any reason associated with bona fide disagreement concerning the terms of the contract to be entered into, but for reasons which, however valid, pertain only to his own position and do not relate at all to that of the other party."

Despite Sheppard J.'s description of the claim as being for "restitution", on the facts of the case before him the defendant had received no identifiable benefit from the claimant.[42] However, it has been assumed by English courts that the principles enunciated in *Sabemo* may be equally applicable to claims in unjust enrichment.

Thus, in *Countrywide Communications* Nicholas Strauss QC indicated that,   **16–14** although he was not entirely convinced by the decision in *Sabemo*:

> "[W]hat may often be decisive [in finding liability] are the circumstances in which the anticipated contract does not materialise and in particular whether they can be said to involve 'fault' on the part of the defendant".[43]

This statement was included in a passage approved by Christopher Clarke J. in *M.S.M. Consulting*[44]; Christopher Clarke J. went on to address the issue of fault on the facts of the case before him.[45] Further support for the approach taken in *Sabemo* may also be found in the fact that, in *Regalian Properties*, Rattee J. distinguished *Sabemo* on the facts, rather than declining to apply it.[46]

Despite this limited judicial support, however, we share the doubts expressed   **16–15** in previous editions of this work and elsewhere about the use of fault in this context.[47] As Gareth Jones has put it, "Fault is a slippery and pejorative concept",[48] which is likely to create more difficulties than it solves. To take a

---

[40] *Sabemo* [1977] 2 N.S.W.L.R. 880 at 900.
[41] *Sabemo* [1977] 2 N.S.W.L.R. 880 at 902–903.
[42] G Jones, *Goff and Jones: The Law of Restitution, Countryside Communications*, para.26–011; Birks and Mitchell in Burrows, *English Private Law*, para.18–120, fn.230.
[43] *Countryside Communications* [2000] C.L.C. 324 at 349.
[44] *M.S.M. Consulting* [2009] EWHC 121 (QB) at [170]–[171].
[45] *M.S.M. Consulting* [2009] EWHC 121 (QB) at [177].
[46] *Regalian Properties* [1995] 1 W.L.R. 212 at 228 and 231.
[47] G Jones, "Claims Arising Out of Anticipated Contracts Which Do Not Materialize" (1980) 18 U.W.O.L.R. 447; Jones, *Goff and Jones: The Law of Restitution*, para.26–011, describing fault as "a shadowy sign-post which may point in more than one direction".
[48] Jones, "Claims Arising Out of Anticipated Contracts Which Do Not Materialize", p.454. Cf. Dietrich, "Classifying Pre-Contractual Liability: A Comparative Analysis", pp.167–170 particularly at p.169 (but note that Dietrich makes no distinction between English and Australian law in his analysis).

simple example, should the decision to withdraw as a result of a financial reversal be regarded as fault? Should it make a difference why such a reversal had been suffered? At a broader level, it is not even clear that it is convincing to describe a party who capriciously decides to withdraw from contractual negotiations as being at "fault", since there is no enforceable legal obligation to negotiate in good faith.[49] Furthermore, fault, at least as used by Sheppard J. in *Sabemo*[50] seems to have a peculiar meaning, since it extends—it seems—to a decision to withdraw from the anticipated contract for a "valid" reason.[51] The *Sabemo* case also highlights the particular difficulty in applying the concept of fault to situations involving public authorities. There the point was raised that a public authority, such as the defendant, might change its plans as a result of changes in its elected officials. Sheppard J. dismissed the point, emphasising that, on the facts of the case, the council's policy in favour of the development had been consistent for three years.[52] It seems misleading, however, to regard a newly elected council's decision to reverse its predecessors' policies as involving "fault". In short, use of the concept of fault tends to obscure the analysis, and distract from the real question, which is whether the basis on which the benefits were conferred permits them to be retained when the anticipated contract fails to materialise.

(g) *Unconscionability*

16–16   In earlier editions of this work it was suggested that, in order to identify when a party who has incurred reliance loss in anticipation of a contract that does not materialise is entitled to recover that reliance loss, an analogy should be made with the law of estoppel. The proposed test would be whether it was unconscionable to permit the defendant to deny an obligation to compensate the claimant.[53] However, as was judicially noted, this was, in effect, a proposal for what the law ought to be rather than an account of what it was.[54] One of the difficulties with the proposal was that estoppel was not traditionally used to reverse unjust enrichment—it either protected expectations or permitted the recovery of detrimental reliance.[55] Even where a claim is genuinely concerned with the reversal of unjust enrichment, the estoppel analogy would not seem to be helpful. Of course, issues concerning estoppel may well arise in situations where there is also a question about the obligation to make restitution in the absence of an anticipated contract, but it is important that the distinctive requirements of the two remedies should be kept separate. In particular, it would be unfortunate if the

---

[49] *Walford v Miles* [1992] 2 A.C. 128. This was a point admitted by Sheppard J. in *Sabemo* [1977] 2 N.S.W.L.R. 880 at 900: "To some this may seem to be, at least in English law, somewhat strange".

[50] *Sabemo* [1977] 2 N.S.W.L.R. 880.

[51] *Sabemo* [1977] 2 N.S.W.L.R. 880 at 903.

[52] *Sabemo* [1977] 2 N.S.W.L.R. 880 at 901.

[53] Jones, *Goff and Jones: The Law of Restitution*, paras 26–011—26–012. For an expanded exposition of the argument see Jones, "Claims Arising Out of Anticipated Contracts Which Do Not Materialize".

[54] *Aragona v Alitalia Linee Aeree Italiane SpA* Unreported QBD, April 9, 2001.

[55] See para.16–21. See too E McKendrick in Cornish et al, *Restitution: Past, Present and Future*, p.180.

availability of a remedy in unjust enrichment was to be seen as turning on whether it was "unconscionable" for the defendant to retain the benefit.[56] The current law of unjust enrichment has reached a stage of development where reliance on such generalisations is counter-productive, as tending to obscure the true reason for recovery. Furthermore, the circumstances in which an estoppel will be granted are not identical to those under which a remedy in unjust enrichment would be granted. That is inevitable, since the question in estoppel is whether a party should be precluded from denying that he had entered a binding contract; in unjust enrichment, the question is very different—should the defendant be entitled to retain benefits conferred? For instance, it would not be unconscionable to allow one party to deny that there was a binding agreement where both parties had been careful to stop short of reaching a binding agreement, and no agreement had ultimately been reached[57]: benefits conferred by way of expedited performance of their anticipated agreement, by contrast, would be recoverable.

3. ENRICHMENT

(a) *General*

Several leading authorities in this area have been concerned with the assessment **16–17** of the defendant's enrichment. Hence, where no enrichment is shown claims have been denied.[58] Where enrichment can be shown the courts have acted consistently with the general principles governing the quantification of enrichment,[59] by making their assessment either on the basis of an hourly rate,[60] or, where this reflects the parties' understanding of the value of the benefit, on the basis of a commission.[61] A combination of the two is also possible.[62] One leading case that has proved controversial is *William Lacey*,[63] in which a firm of builders prepared extensive estimates for the owner of premises, which enabled the owner to obtain steel and timber licences, and also allowed him to negotiate a grant for the building work from the War Damage Commission. Before any of the work began the owner sold the premises. The judgment of Barry J. did not clearly identify the benefit received by the defendant, and it has been doubted (including in the previous edition of this work) whether the defendant was truly enriched.[64] However, the better view is that there was enrichment, since the defendant used the claimant's estimates to obtain a larger payment from the War Damage

---

[56] See also the concerns expressed by McKendrick in Cornish et al, *Restitution: Past, Present and Future*, p.189. Cf. *M.S.M. Consulting* [2009] EWHC 121 (QB) at [171] (e).

[57] *Att Gen of Hong Kong v Humphreys Estate (Queen's Gardens) Ltd* [1987] A.C. 114.

[58] e.g. *Regalian Properties* [1995] 1 W.L.R. 212 at 225.

[59] See paras 5–27—5–37.

[60] e.g. *Countrywide Communications* [2000] C.L.C. 324.

[61] e.g. *Way v Latilla* [1937] 3 All E.R. 759.

[62] *Vedatech Corp* [2002] EWHC 818 (Ch) at [90].

[63] *William Lacey* [1957] 1 W.L.R. 932.

[64] Jones, *Goff and Jones: The Law of Restitution*, para.26–009; *Benourad* [2010] EWHC 1882 (QB) at [130]. In *Sabemo* [1977] 2 N.S.W.L.R. 880 at 902, Sheppard J. commented that the increased "permissible amount" obtained from the War Damage Commission did not "go to the root" of the decision.

Commission than he would otherwise have obtained.[65] On the other hand, it would not have been appropriate to quantify the enrichment as the increase in value of the premises as a result of the War Damage Commission's grant, because the claimant's estimates did not create that increased value, they merely unlocked the site's potential.[66] It follows that, applying orthodox principles of assessing enrichment, it was appropriate to value the benefit received by the defendant in terms of the value of the claimant's services.[67]

(b) A Discretion to Allow Recovery Where No Benefit Has Been Conferred?

16–18 In *Countrywide Communications*[68] Nicholas Strauss QC stated that a factor to consider when deciding whether to permit recovery, was:

> "the nature of the benefit which has resulted to the defendant . . . and in particular whether such benefit is real (either 'realised' or 'realisable') or a fiction . . . Plainly, a court will at least be more inclined to impose an obligation to pay for a real benefit . . . ".

This statement would seem to indicate that a court has a discretion to allow recovery for fictitious benefits.[69] However, we would regard such a discretion as a regrettable development, since it would obscure the real basis for the remedy. For the same reason, we would also question the approach to this issue taken in *Sabemo*,[70] where it was said that, although the case was not one of unjust enrichment,[71] recovery was allowed on the basis that work had been done "beneficial for the project, and thus in the interests of the two parties".[72] It would be preferable to address directly the issue whether remedies should be available outside the law of unjust enrichment in such circumstances.

4. CLAIMS OUTSIDE UNJUST ENRICHMENT

16–19 Where a claim has succeeded despite the fact that the defendant has not been enriched, liability cannot be explained in terms of unjust enrichment. The most prominent example where this has occurred is *Brewer Street*.[73] There the claimants owned premises, of which the defendants wished to become tenants. The parties were confident that a lease would be agreed in due course, and the

---

[65] *Countrywide Communications* [2000] C.L.C. 324; *Aragona* Unreported QBD, April 9, 2001; Jones, "Claims Arising Out of Anticiapted Contracts Which Do Not Materialize", p.456; McKendrick, "The Battle of Forms and the Law of Restitution", p.211.

[66] Applying *Cobbe* [2008] UKHL 55; [2008] 1 W.L.R. 1752 at [40]–[41].

[67] The basis of the award in *William Lacey* was approved in *Vedatech Corp* [2002] EWHC 818 (Ch) at [76].

[68] *Countrywide Communications* [2000] C.L.C. 324 at 349.

[69] See similarly, the comment by Christopher Clarke J. in *M.S.M. Consulting* [2009] EWHC 121 (QB) at [171] (c), that an obligation is "likely" where the defendant has received a clear benefit; the implication seems to be that an obligation is still possible where no benefit has been received.

[70] *Sabemo* [1977] 2 N.S.W.L.R. 880.

[71] *Sabemo* [1977] 2 N.S.W.L.R. 880 at 897.

[72] *Sabemo* [1977] 2 N.S.W.L.R. 880 at 902–903.

[73] *Brewer Street* [1954] 1 Q.B. 428.

defendants requested that certain alterations be made to the premises in anticipation of their occupation. The defendants undertook responsibility for payment for the work, and the claimants engaged contractors who began the task. The parties, however, failed to agree a lease because the defendants insisted on being granted an option to purchase the premises. The claimants ordered the contractors to stop work, and paid them; they then sought to recover the cost from the defendants. Somervell and Romer L.JJ. based their analysis on the contractual undertaking by the defendants to pay for the work. Denning L.J., however, regarded that basis of claim as unavailable, because he regarded the prospective tenants as having promised to pay only on completion of the work. In his view, the claim had to be expressed as being "in restitution",[74] for the value of the wasted work. There are formidable problems with explaining the case in terms of unjust enrichment, because there seems to be no benefit received by the defendant.[75] The building works were carried out on the claimant's premises, which the defendants never occupied. Even if that objection could be overcome (perhaps by emphasising that the works had been done at the defendant's request), the works were incomplete.[76] Nor had the claimants' payment to the contractors saved the defendants a necessary expense, because the contractors' agreement was with the claimants not the defendants.

Although Denning LJ was in the minority in *Brewer Street*,[77] his decision **16–20** indicates the potential for precontractual liability outside the law of unjust enrichment. Several possible sources for such claims could be envisaged, some more straightforward than others. The straightforward options would include claims in deceit[78] or for a constructive trust.[79] A more difficult possibility is the law of negligence, in relation to which Joachim Dietrich has argued that some features of the existing case law on anticipated contracts already bear a striking similarity to the requirements for liability in the tort of negligence.[80] For instance, both discuss a requirement of fault. However, it is difficult to see how one party to an anticipated contract could be under a duty of care to the other party under current English law.[81] There are two alternative tests—the assumption of responsibility test derived from *Hedley Byrne & Co Ltd v Heller and Partners Ltd*,[82] and the three-stage test derived from *Caparo Industries Plc v Dickman*.[83] The two parties' opposing economic interests would seem to preclude a finding that one party had implicitly assumed responsibility to protect the other, and, although there is a direct relationship between the parties (which might satisfy the requirement of proximity in the *Caparo* test), any duty of care

---

[74] *Brewer Street* [1954] 1 Q.B. 428 at 436.

[75] McKendrick in Cornish et al, *Restitution: Past, Present and Future*, p.178.

[76] Cf. A Burrows, "Free Acceptance and the Law of Restitution" (1988) 104 L.Q.R. 576, p.598, which seems to be based on the misapprehension that the work had been completed. The position was different in *Jennings and Chapman Ltd v Woodman, Matthews & Co* [1952] 2 T.L.R. 409.

[77] *Brewer Street* [1954] 1 Q.B. 428.

[78] See further K. Oliphant (ed.), *The Law of Tort*, 2nd edn (London: Butterworths, 2007) Ch.28. The possibility of a claim in deceit in such circumstances was expressly considered by Lord Scott in *Cobbe* [2008] UKHL 55; [2008] 1 W.L.R. 1752 at [3]–[4] and [38].

[79] e.g. *Pallant v Morgan* [1953] Ch. 43.

[80] Dietrich, "Classifying Pre-Contractual Liability: A Comparative Analysis", pp.167–170.

[81] *Customs and Excise Commissioners v Barclays Bank Plc* [2006] UKHL 28; [2007] 1 A.C. 181.

[82] *Hedley Byrne & Co Ltd v Heller and Partners Ltd* [1964] A.C. 465.

[83] *Caparo Industries Plc v Dickman* [1990] 2 A.C. 605.

would be at odds with the parties' precontractual autonomy. There is also the difficulty that the claimant would be asserting that the defendant had a duty to take positive steps to protect him, which English law is notoriously reluctant to recognise, even in relation to physical injury, let alone for purely economic loss.[84]

16–21   A further potential ground of precontractual liability, where the dealings between the parties relate to the acquisition of rights relating to land, is the doctrine of proprietary estoppel. A detailed account of this doctrine is beyond the scope of this work,[85] but in essence the doctrine comes into play where a party has acted to his detriment in the belief that he either already had the relevant rights over the land,[86] or that he was the beneficiary of a binding obligation to confer such rights on him,[87] and the defendant has been somehow complicit in the mistake or expectation. Where the conditions for the application of proprietary estoppel are present, the remedy is discretionary. It will often consist in making good the claimant's expectation,[88] or there may be a financial remedy taking the form of compensation for expenditure.[89] Thus, in *The Unity Joint Stock Mutual Banking Association v King*,[90] where two sons had been let into possession of land owned by their father, in the expectation of a future transfer of that land, and had built several buildings on the land, it was held that the father would not be entitled to resume possession "without allowing to his sons the amount of the money they had laid out upon it".[91] It should be noted that a remedy assessed by reference to what the disappointed party has spent is likely to give a different award to one assessed by reference to the defendant's enrichment. For instance, under the former there is no element of profit, and no question of subjective devaluation, whereas an assessment of unjust enrichment would reflect the value of what the defendant had received, and might be subject to subjective devaluation.

---

[84] *Stovin v Wise* [1996] A.C. 923.

[85] For a detailed account, see K. Gray and S. Gray, *Elements of Land Law*, 5th edn (Oxford: OUP, 2008), Ch.9.2.

[86] *Pilling v Armitage* (1805) 12 Ves. Jun. 78 at 85; 33 E.R. 31 at 34; *Dillwyn v Llewellyn* (1862) 4 De G. F. & J. 517; 45 E.R. 1285 (although it should be noted that the court's analysis was in terms of detrimental reliance amounting to valuable consideration for the promise to give the land: see P. Atiyah, "Consideration: A Restatement" in *Essays on Contract* (Oxford: OUP, 1990) 179, pp.226 and following); *Ramsden v Dyson* (1866) L.R. 1 H.L. 129 at 140–141 per Lord Cranworth L.C., and at 168 per Lord Wensleydale; *Willmott v Barber* (1880) 15 Ch. D. 96.

[87] *Gregory v Mighell* (1811) 18 Ves. Jun. 328; 34 E.R. 341; *Ramsden v Dyson* (1866) L.R. 1 H.L. 129; *Plimmer v The Mayor, Councillors and Citizens of the City of Wellington* (1884) 9 App. Cas. 699; *Cobbe* [2008] UKHL 55; [2008] 1 W.L.R. 1752.

[88] *Thompson v Foy* [2009] EWHC 1067 (Ch); [2010] 1 P. & C.R. 16 at [98].

[89] *Plimmer* (1884) 9 App. Cas. 699 at 711.

[90] *The Unity Joint Stock Mutual Banking Association v King* (1858) 25 Beav. 72; 53 E.R. 563.

[91] *The Unity Joint Stock* at 25 Beav.77; 53 E.R. at 566.

Chapter 17

FREE ACCEPTANCE

1. Introduction

The recognition of a principle of free acceptance was one of the most striking, **17–01** and widely noted, features of previous editions of this work.[1] However, previous editions did not devote a separate chapter to free acceptance as a ground of liability.[2] The decision to create this new chapter on the subject was partly prompted by a sense that the subject was significant enough to call for such treatment, and was also partly a response to the case law which has relatively recently emerged in this area.[3]

The principle of free acceptance has a (unique) dual role in the law of unjust **17–02** enrichment, since it provides both a test for assessing enrichment, and also articulates an independent unjust factor.[4] This chapter is concerned solely with free acceptance as a ground of liability. The principles of free acceptance applicable to enrichment and to free acceptance as an unjust factor are not necessarily interchangeable.[5]

2. The Principle of Free Acceptance

The principle of free acceptance may be articulated as follows[6]: **17–03**

> "[A defendant] will be held to have benefited from the services rendered if he, as a reasonable man, should have known that the claimant who rendered the services expected to be paid for them, and yet did not take a reasonable opportunity open to him

---

[1] See, for instance, the opening sentences of A Burrows, "Free Acceptance and the Law of Restitution" (1988) 104 L.Q.R. 576.

[2] The discussion of free acceptance in the seventh edition of this work appears as part of a section dealing with enrichment: G. Jones, *Goff & Jones: The Law of Restitution* (London: Sweet & Maxwell, 2006), paras 1–019—1–022. Burrows, "Free Acceptance and the Law of Restitution", p.577 fn.8, comments that earlier editions of Goff and Jones did not make it "clear beyond doubt" that they conceptualised free acceptance as an unjust factor as well as a test of enrichment.

[3] e.g. *Becerra v Close Brothers* Unreported QBD, June 25, 1999; *R. (Rowe) v Vale of White Horse DC* [2003] EWHC 388 (Admin); [2003] 1 Lloyd's Rep 418; *Chief Constable of the Greater Manchester Police v Wigan Athletic AFC Ltd* [2008] EWCA Civ 1449; [2009] 1 W.L.R. 1580; *Benedetti v Sawaris* [2009] EWHC 1330 (Ch) at [572]–[575]; [2010] EWCA Civ 1427.

[4] For discussion of free acceptance as a test for enrichment see paras 4–29—4–33.

[5] E. McKendrick, "The Battle of Forms and the Law of Restitution" (1988) 8 O.J.L.S. 197, p.207.

[6] Jones, *Goff and Jones: The Law of Restitution*, para.1–019. Quoted with approval in *Becerra* Unreported QBD (Comm Ct), June 25, 1999; *R. (Rowe)* [2003] EWHC 388 (Admin); [2003] 1 Lloyd's Rep 418 at [13]; *Wigan Athletic* [2008] EWCA Civ 1449; [2009] 1 W.L.R. 1580 at [38].

to reject the proffered services. Moreover, in such a case, he cannot deny that he has been unjustly enriched."

As can be seen from this formulation of the principle, free acceptance is not like other unjust factors such as mistake, duress and undue influence (which are concerned with vitiation of the claimant's will), nor with factors like failure of basis (which is concerned with conditions of the claimant's will). Rather, free acceptance focuses on the defendant's will.[7] Given that in situations involving free acceptance, the claimant's intentions have been both freely formed and fully carried out, it has not been straightforward to identify why exactly it is unjust to allow the defendant to retain the benefit he has received. Unfortunately, recent authorities recognising the principle of free acceptance have tended not to explain the point, assuming that because a benefit has been freely accepted, it must, therefore, be unjust for the defendant to retain it. Thus, for instance, in *Benedetti v Sawaris*[8] Patten J. observed that:

"The question whether there has, properly speaking, been a free acceptance of the services is likely in practice to be the determining factor as to whether it is regarded as unjust for a defendant to retain the benefit of the services without paying for them".[9]

17–04   Despite its prominent position in leading works on the law of unjust enrichment,[10] the principle of free acceptance had virtually no express support in the authorities until recently,[11] and had been subjected to powerful criticisms. Authoritative support had been claimed for the principle by seeking to elucidate the underlying reasons for liability in certain cases where the courts had implied a contract in law, despite the absence of an agreement between the parties.[12] Thus, for instance, in *Lamb v Bunce*[13] a surgeon had been permitted to claim for his fees against the overseer of a parish in circumstances where there had been no agreement between the parties, but the overseer had stood by whilst the surgeon treated one of the paupers of the parish. Lord Ellenborough C.J. held that:

"if the parish officer stands by and sees that obligation [to treat paupers] performed by those who are fit and competent to perform it, and does not object, the law will raise a promise on his part to pay for the performance".[14]

---

[7] P. Birks, *An Introduction to the Law of Restitution*, revised edn (Oxford: OUP, 1989), p.265.
[8] *Benedetti v Sawaris* [2009] EWHC 1330 (Ch).
[9] *Benedetti* [2009] EWHC 1330 (Ch) at [574].
[10] In addition to Goff and Jones, the principle of free acceptance was prominent in Peter Birks' work: Birks, *An Introduction to the Law of Restitution*, Ch.8. See also, P. Birks, "In Defence of Free Acceptance" in A. Burrows (ed.), *Essays on the Law of Restitution* (Oxford: OUP, 1991) 105. However, Birks later changed his position: P. Birks, *Unjust Enrichment*, 2nd edn (Oxford: OUP, 2005), p.144.
[11] See, however, *Leigh v Dickeson* (1884) 15 Q.B.D. 60 at 64–65, per Brett M.R.
[12] *Falcke v Scottish Imperial Insurance Co* (1886) 34 Ch. D. 234 at 241; per Cotton L.J.; and at 249; per Bowen L.J.
[13] *Lamb v Bunce* (1815) 4 M. & S. 275; 105 E.R. 836.
[14] *Lamb v Bunce* 4 M. & S. at 277; 105 E.R. at 838.

Similarly, in *Taylor v Laird*,[15] where Pollock C.B. said "One cleans another's shoes; what can the other do but put them on?",[16] the issue being discussed was whether a contract could be implied. Indeed, in the very next sentence, Pollock C.B. asked, rhetorically, "Is that evidence of a contract to pay for the cleaning?" The problem with implying a contract as a matter of law, in the absence of an agreement between the parties, was that the contract was a fiction. The legal analysis was concealing rather than explaining the true grounds for the decision.[17] The principle of free acceptance was an attempt to identify the fundamental reason behind the imposition of liability in those cases.

Perhaps the most compelling of the criticisms of the principle of free acceptance was made by Andrew Burrows, who argued that, both as a matter of principle and authority, there was no place for free acceptance in the law of unjust enrichment.[18] Burrows examined the example used by Peter Birks to illustrate the claim that free acceptance was an unjust factor—in which a window cleaner starts to clean the defendant's windows, without prior request by the defendant, and the defendant, realising what is happening, refrains from telling the window-cleaner that he is not prepared to pay for the work.[19] This example indicated that the principled justification for recognising free acceptance as an unjust factor was simply that a party who had conferred a benefit on another, in the absence of any understanding that it was to be paid for, but hoping for some payment, should be able to recover if the defendant forebore from objecting. In such cases, it was said, the defendant's failure to reject the benefit "estops him from making the sweeping answer that the plaintiff ought to have looked before he leaped."[20] However, as Burrows pointed out, the window-cleaner was taking the risk that he would not be paid for the work, and "surely on any common sense view there would be no injustice in my not paying a risk-taker".[21] This is a powerful argument, which draws on concepts familiar from the courts' decisions in cases concerning anticipated contracts and failure of basis more generally,[22] and it highlights the need for a close analysis of situations where free acceptance is alleged as the ground of liability. Such an analysis might lead to the conclusion, which Burrows favours, that the risk is on the claimant.[23] However, it is crucial to identify accurately what risk is actually being taken by a claimant like the speculative window cleaner. Certainly such a claimant takes the risk that, having cleaned the windows without the householder's knowledge, the householder will refuse to pay; but it is not so clear that he also takes the risk that a householder who realises that his windows are being cleaned will not warn him that he is

17–05

---

[15] *Taylor v Laird* (1856) 25 L.J. Ex. 329.

[16] *Taylor* (1856) 25 L.J. Ex. 329 at 332.

[17] See further Birks, *An Introduction to the Law of Restitution*, pp.268–270.

[18] Burrows, "Free Acceptance and the Law of Restitution".

[19] Birks, *An Introduction to the Law of Restitution*, p.265.

[20] Birks, *An Introduction to the Law of Restitution*, p.276.

[21] Burrows, "Free Acceptance and the Law of Restitution", p.578. See also Burrows' summary of the debate in A. Burrows, *The Law of Restitution*, 3rd edn (Oxford: OUP, 2011), pp.334–339.

[22] See paras 16–09—16–11 (anticipated contracts) and 13–01—13–11 (failure of basis).

[23] See also *Becerra* Unreported QBD (Comm Ct), June 25, 1999, where Thomas J., having been referred to Burrows' article, commented that he saw "great force" in this analysis "in the context of dealings in the financial markets and the City".

wasting his time.[24] In other words, the window cleaner could be said only to take the risk of the work being rejected once the recipient is aware of what is happening.

3. THE SCOPE OF FREE ACCEPTANCE

17–06   The situations in which recourse to the principle of free acceptance will be necessary will partly depend on where the boundaries of other unjust factors are drawn. In particular, the need to rely on a principle of free acceptance will depend on how broadly the principle of failure of basis is understood. Thus, in *Aragona v Alitalia Linee Aeree Italiane SpA*[25] Judge Hegarty QC expressed the view that, where parties anticipated entering a contract, and one of them commenced performance of its anticipated obligations in advance of the contract being concluded, the ground of recovery of any benefits conferred would depend on whether an express request for those benefits had been made. Where no specific request had been made, the judge was of the opinion that recovery would be on the ground of free acceptance. This analysis assumed a narrow scope for failure of basis. On a broader interpretation of failure of basis, the basis on which the benefit is conferred need not be express.[26] Thus, in the situation being considered in the *Aragona* case it could be said that the basis on which the benefits were conferred was the shared anticipation of a contract providing for payment for those benefits; when no contract materialised the basis for conferring the benefits failed.[27]

17–07   The strongest examples of free acceptance can be seen in situations where recovery cannot be explained on another ground.[28] For instance, in *Sumpter v Hedges*[29] a builder had defaulted on his obligations under a building contract and had abandoned the site with the work half-finished. He had also left behind some materials which the landowner used to complete the building work. At the trial Bruce J. found the landowner liable for the value of the materials he had used and there was no appeal against that finding. The trial judge's reasoning was not reported, but it can be explained as an application of the principle of free acceptance. Certainly, where the defendant makes use of the claimant's materials in ways that were never contemplated by the parties, and of which the claimant is unaware, it is artificial to claim that some implied joint basis for payment has arisen.[30]

---

[24] The reasoning in *Cobbe v Yeoman's Row Management Ltd* [2008] UKHL 55; [2008] 1 W.L.R. 1752 offers a parallel: there the claimant property developer took the risk of the application for planning permission being refused, but he did not take the risk of the landowner acting capriciously.

[25] *Aragona v Alitalia Linee Aeree Italiane SpA* Unreported QBD, April 9, 2001.

[26] See para.13–04.

[27] For a wider-ranging argument that many supposed cases of free acceptance are better explained in terms of failure of basis, see Burrows, "Free Acceptance and the Law of Restitution".

[28] Birks argued that free acceptance should only be used in such situations: Birks, *An Introduction to the Law of Restitution*, p.466.

[29] *Sumpter v Hedges* [1898] 1 Q.B. 673.

[30] The result of the claim for materials used may also be explained as damages for conversion. See Burrows, "Free Acceptance and the Law of Restitution", p.590.

Further examples of free acceptance can be seen in situations where the parties **17–08** had had some prior dealings, and the claimant had tendered a benefit which did not conform to the defendant's requirements, but which the defendant elected to retain anyway. For instance, in *Munro v Butt*[31] the Court of Queen's Bench discussed the example of a claimant who had tendered incomplete contractual performance under a contract where complete performance was a condition of payment. If the incomplete performance consisted in having supplied "an independent chattel, a piece of furniture for example", and "the party for whom it was made had yet accepted it, an action might, upon obvious grounds, be maintained".[32] The court contrasted the situation where building work not conforming to the contractual specification was done on the claimant's land; there, it was held, no action would lie. Unfortunately the court did not explain what it meant by the "obvious grounds" giving rise to an action against the party accepting defective furniture. The court might, perhaps, in line with the analysis adopted in later cases such as *Sumpter v Hedges*,[33] have meant that a new, implied contract had come into existence, under which the customer agreed to pay a fair price for the furniture. Such an analysis would probably not be acceptable today, as relying too heavily on ideas of quasi-contract, and an unjust factor would need to be identified. Failure of basis seems a difficult ground to sustain, since the dealings between the parties indicated that the defendant only agreed to pay for furniture conforming to the contractual specification. It might, perhaps, be said that there was an additional understanding between the parties that any non-conforming contractual performance was not to be retained gratuitously. However, it is difficult to explain why a similar understanding would not arise in respect of building work. Free acceptance is also problematic, since the recipient of the furniture is likely to have received it on the basis that he was bound to receive it as contractual performance,[34] and free acceptance is assessed at the time of receipt of the benefit.[35] What seems to give rise to the claim is the decision to retain the furniture after its defectiveness has been discovered (when it could have been rejected). This would not be so much free acceptance as free retention.[36]

4. ELEMENTS OF FREE ACCEPTANCE

(a) *Acceptance*

(i) *Defendant's Knowledge*

If a benefit is conferred on the defendant without his knowledge, he cannot be **17–09** said to have accepted it at all. The knowledge required for liability to arise is

---

[31] *Munro v Butt* (1858) 8 El. & Bl. 738; 120 E.R. 275.
[32] *Munro v Butt* 8 El. & Bl. at 752–753; 120 E.R. 281.
[33] *Sumpter v Hedges* [1898] 1 Q.B. 673.
[34] See the analysis in R. Stevens and B. McFarlane, "In Defence of *Sumpter v Hedges*" (2002) 118 L.Q.R. 569, pp.574–577.
[35] Birks, *An Introduction to the Law of Restitution*, p.287.
[36] Another example would be the liability in *British Steel Corp v Cleveland Bridge and Engineering Co Ltd* [1984] 1 All E.R. 504, if the factual situation was analysed in accordance with the suggestion in para.16–05.

"knowledge which will lead to the possibility of effective action by refusing to accept liability".[37] Thus, it will be necessary for the defendant to be given sufficient notice of the impending benefit to enable a free choice to be made to refuse it. The defendant's state of knowledge will often be a question of fact, but where the defendant is a legal person (such as a company), or it is alleged that the defendant's agent knew of the receipt of the benefit, it will be necessary to establish that, as a matter of law, the knowledge of the individual concerned is to be attributed to the defendant.[38]

(ii) *Express Refusal of Benefit*

17–10   Where a defendant has informed the claimant that he does not wish to receive a benefit from the claimant, which the claimant then proceeds to confer, the defendant comes under no obligation to pay for that benefit.[39] The benefit has not, in such circumstances, been truly accepted at all. Thus, in *Bookmakers' Afternoon Greyhound Services Ltd v Wilf Gilbert (Staffordshire) Ltd*[40] it was held that there was no liability to pay for a greyhound betting service provided by the claimant, and made use of by the defendant, because the defendant had consistently made clear that it did not want the service, and would not pay for it.

(b) *Acceptor Appreciates that the Benefits Are Not Conferred Gratuitously*

17–11   The defendant must know, or ought to have known, that the claimant expected to be paid for his services. Thus, there is no liability where a defendant freely accepts services which he was led to believe were being conferred gratuitously. In *R. (Rowe) v Vale of White Horse DC*,[41] a council sought to recover the value of sewerage services that had been supplied to the owner of a former council house. The conveyance from the council to the owner's predecessor in title had contained no covenant for payment for sewerage services, and the council had adopted a deliberate silence on the issue for 18 years, as a result of a combination of administrative oversight and legal uncertainty. Lightman J. held that, in the circumstances, the owner of the house, as a reasonable person, could not have known that the council expected to be paid for the services; the services had not, therefore, been freely accepted and the council could not claim for them in unjust enrichment.[42]

17–12   Free acceptance will also fail where the defendant believes, as a reasonable person, that the services he is being offered are to be paid for by a third party.[43] Thus, in *Becerra v Close Brothers*,[44] the defendant merchant bank was organising the sale of a business through a controlled auction, under which bidders would be selected and invited to make a bid. The defendant's fee for conducting

---

[37] *Re Cleadon Trust Ltd* [1939] 1 Ch. 286 at 299.
[38] e.g. *Re Cleadon Trust* [1939] 1 Ch. 286.
[39] *Leigh v Dickeson* (1884) 15 Q.B.D. 60 at 64–65.
[40] *Bookmakers' Afternoon Greyhound Services Ltd v Wilf Gilbert (Staffordshire) Ltd* [1994] F.S.R. 723 at 742–744.
[41] *R. (Rowe) v Vale of White Horse DC* [2003] EWHC 388 (Admin); [2003] 1 Lloyd's Rep. 418.
[42] *R. (Rowe)* [2003] EWHC 388 (Admin); [2003] 1 Lloyd's Rep. 418 at [14].
[43] e.g the facts in *Brown and Davis Ltd v Galbraith* [1972] 3 All E.R. 31.
[44] *Becerra v Close Brothers* Unreported QBD (Comm Ct) June 25, 1999.

the auction was to be calculated by reference to a percentage of the final purchase price achieved. The claimant, a merchant banker, heard about the sale, and contacted the defendant, requesting permission to interest a Japanese financial institution in making a bid. The defendant granted permission and agreed to send the claimant certain information about the business being sold. It told the claimant that he was acting "off his own bat". The Japanese financial institution was interested in making a purchase and eventually became the highest bidder in the auction. The claimant's attempt to recover a reasonable fee from the defendants failed, both in contract and in unjust enrichment. Thomas J. held that the requirements of free acceptance had not been satisfied, since the defendant had told the claimant that he was acting on his own account. He also found that not only had the defendant understood that the claimant would look to the bidder for any payment for his services, but that had also been the claimant's own expectation as well.

(c) *Acceptance Must Be by Choice*

(i) *General Rule*

Where a defendant has had no option about whether to accept the benefit the **17–13** principle of free acceptance does not apply.[45] In other words, there must have been an opportunity to reject the benefit. Thus, in *Munro*,[46] the Court of Queen's Bench contrasted two examples of a claimant tendering incomplete performance of his contractual obligations. In the first example, the claimant supplies the defendant with "an independent chattel, a piece of furniture for example", which the defendant chooses to retain. In the second example, the incomplete performance consists of building work on the defendant's own land. Liability would arise in the first case but not the second. In the circumstances of the second example, the landowner had little choice but to resume possession, in order to attempt to rectify the situation. As (successful) counsel had put it in argument, "the owner of a house cannot reject his house".[47] It would seem to follow from the underlying principle of *free* acceptance that a defendant should not be obliged to undertake onerous activity, or to incur expense, in order to avail himself of an opportunity to reject.[48]

(ii) *Combination of Desired and Undesired Benefits*

Where a defendant has received a combination of desired and undesired benefits, **17–14** he will not be held to have freely accepted the undesired benefits merely because he did not reject everything. In *Chief Constable of the Greater Manchester Police*

---

[45] *Taylor* (1856) 25 L.J. Exch 329 at 332 per Pollock C.B.; *Leigh* (1884) 15 Q.B.D. 60.
[46] *Munro* (1858) 8 E. & B. 738; 120 E.R. 275.
[47] *Munro* 8 E. & B. at 747; 120 E.R. at 279. Cf. the factual situation in *Burn v Miller* (1813) 4 Taunt. 745; 128 E.R. 523, where a landlord encouraged his tenant to carry out improvements to the premises, which fell outside a prior agreement for improvements to be made. The tenant's claim succeeded. For further discussion of this case, see para.3–31.
[48] G. Mead, "Free Acceptance: Some Further Considerations" (1989) 105 L.Q.R. 460, pp.464–466.

v Wigan Athletic[49] the defendant was a football club which, in order to hold matches at its home ground, had to comply with a statutory safety certificate. The terms of that certificate included a condition that the club must secure "such number of police officers as in the opinion of the chief constable is sufficient to ensure orderly behaviour of spectators". Following the club's promotion to a higher division of the football league, the chief constable and the club disagreed about the appropriate level of policing needed. The chief constable specified a significant increase (with corresponding increase in costs), whilst the club insisted that policing should continue at its previous level. The club refused to pay for anything more. The chief constable however, provided policing at the higher level over the course of two seasons and then sought to recover the cost from the club. The Court of Appeal held that there had been no implied request by the club for the higher level of policing, so any claim in contract failed. A majority of the Court of Appeal also held that there was no claim in unjust enrichment. Sir Andrew Morritt C., in considering whether the club could be considered as having freely accepted the higher level of policing for the purposes of assessing whether a benefit had been conferred, emphasised that it would have been impossible for the club to reject the extra police services without also rejecting policing services at the lower level that it had consistently requested. To have rejected all of the proffered services, he continued:

> "[W]ould have meant that the club could not play its home matches at the stadium at all . . . it is clear that there was not free acceptance of the services in dispute because the club was, in practice, unable to reject them alone."[50]

When he came to consider whether there was an unjust factor present on the facts of the case, he referred back to this analysis of free acceptance at the benefit stage, observing that "for the club it was all or nothing", and that the club was faced with "Hobson's Choice".[51] Smith L.J., the other member of the majority, expressed her agreement with Sir Andrew Morritt C.'s reasoning, also adding that she did "not see why the club should pay for services which it did not ask for".[52]

17–15   The analysis in the *Wigan Athletic* case was applied and developed in *Benedetti*.[53] There the claimant had acted as a facilitator in the highly profitable acquistion by the defendant of a telecommunications company. At a relatively late stage in the deal, the financing arrangements had changed and two additional investors had become involved. The claimant claimed against both of those additional investors in unjust enrichment. His claim succeeded before Patten J., but was denied by the Court of Appeal. The crucial point was that, although the investors made a free choice to enter the transaction, they never had the choice to participate without the benefit of the claimant's services. As Arden L.J. (with whom Etherton and Rimer L.JJ. agreed) explained[54]:

---

[49] *Chief Constable of the Greater Manchester Police v Wigan Athletic AFC Ltd* [2008] EWCA Civ 1449; [2009] 1 W.L.R. 1580.
[50] *Wigan Athletic* [2008] EWCA Civ 1449; [2009] 1 W.L.R. 1580 at [47].
[51] *Wigan Athletic* [2008] EWCA Civ 1449; [2009] 1 W.L.R. 1580 at [50].
[52] *Wigan Athletic* [2008] EWCA Civ 1449; [2009] 1 W.L.R. 1580 at [59].
[53] *Benedetti* [2009] EWHC 1330 (Ch); [2010] EWCA Civ 1427.
[54] *Benedetti* [2010] EWCA Civ 1427 at [118].

"[I]t is not enough merely to know that the services are being provided or to have the option of not engaging the activity that would mean that the benefit of other services was rejected. A person in general owes no obligation to take steps to desist from an activity on which he is currently engaged by reason only that it might lead him to benefit from the services being provided to him without his consent, express or implied."

Although Arden L.J. appears not to have drawn a clear distinction between **17–16** free acceptance as a test of benefit and free acceptance as an unjust factor,[55] it would seem that the general principles set out above are applicable to both types of free acceptance. It would therefore appear that free acceptance by conduct requires proof that the defendant had a clear choice to proceed either with or without the claimant's services and opted for the former course. However, it may be questioned whether the defendants in *Wigan Athletic* and *Benedetti* had really not been given a free choice. They had, of course, been influenced by the opportunity to gain a further advantage from receipt of the services, but it is difficult to see why that should prevent their decision from being described as having been made "freely".[56]

(iii) *The Limits of "Free" Acceptance*

It does not follow from the requirement that the acceptance of benefits must be **17–17** "free" that the choice must be made under no constraints whatsoever. Thus, in *Wigan Athletic*[57] Maurice Kay L.J. interpreted the factual situation differently from the majority. In his view, the level of policing specified by the chief constable was to be taken as the minimum necessary to satisfy the requirements of the safety certificate.[58] It therefore followed that the benefit conferred by the claimants in policing the matches at the higher level was a benefit that the defendant wanted to receive. As Maurice Kay L.J. explained:

"[W]hen the chief constable refused to give way, [the club] wanted [the extra officers] not in the sense of preference or desire but because it needed them in order to avoid the unacceptable alternative of cancelling its home matches".[59]

The analysis of Maurice Kay L.J. indicates that the limits of free acceptance will require further clarification. One potential source of principles would be the law of duress, where the courts are similarly faced with issues about whether a party's freedom of action was illegitimately constrained.[60]

---

[55] See in particular *Benedetti* [2010] EWCA Civ 1427 at [116], where the example of a cobbler conferring additional benefits on a customer turns on mistake, and at [120], where it is said that the claimant could have succeeded on the alternative basis that an incontrovertible benefit had been conferred on the investors.

[56] See further, paras 4–30—4–31.

[57] *Wigan Athletic* [2008] EWCA Civ 1449; [2009] 1 W.L.R. 1580. For the facts see para.17–14.

[58] *Wigan Athletic* [2008] EWCA Civ 1449; [2009] 1 W.L.R. 1580 at [65] and [69]. Cf. the approaches of Sir Andrew Morritt C. at [46] and Smith L.J. at [58].

[59] *Wigan Athletic* [2008] EWCA Civ 1449; [2009] 1 W.L.R. 1580 at [69].

[60] See Ch.10.

5. Conclusion

17–18   Free acceptance as an unjust factor has now been recognised in the case law, although it often seems that no systematic distinction is drawn between free acceptance as a test for enrichment and free acceptance as an unjust factor. It is also a matter for concern that the underlying arguments against free acceptance have not been engaged with in the cases. In our view, there is a role for free acceptance as an unjust factor, which can take account of the argument that the claimant takes the risk of not being paid. That role needs to be carefully delineated. We would suggest that the core example of free acceptance as an unjust factor is the situation envisaged in *Munro*,[61] where the claimant tenders a non-conforming contractual performance, gambling on the defendant being prepared to accept it. In such circumstances, the claimant only takes the risk of the benefit being rejected once its non-conformity is detected.

---

[61] *Munro* (1858) 8 El. & Bl. 738; 120 E.R. 275, as discussed in paras 17–08 and 17–13.

CHAPTER 18

NECESSITY

1. INTRODUCTION

In Roman law a stranger who undertook the unsolicited management of another **18–01**
person's affairs was entitled in some circumstances to recover his reasonable
costs. *Negotiorum gestio*—"the management of affairs"—was a bilateral legal
relationship that created rights and obligations on both sides, and although the
Romans viewed the action of the party assisted *against* the intervener (the *actio
negotiorum gestorum directa*) as the main action arising out of the parties'
relationship, they also held that the intervener could bring an action to recover his
expenses (the *actio (negotiorum gestorum) contraria*).[1] Modern civilian and
mixed legal systems typically have a similar doctrine under which benevolent
interveners are entitled not only to recover benefits conferred on the party
assisted but also to recover their expenses, and possibly also a reward for their
intervention.[2]

In contrast, many common law jurisdictions, including England, have tended **18–02**
to reject any doctrine of *negotiorum gestio*, seemingly fearful that this would
"breed overnight a nation of busy-bodies anxious to perform useless and med-
dlesome services for others and to try their luck with the courts",[3] and contend-

---

[1] E.G. Lorenzen, "The *Negotiorum Gestio* in Roman and Modern Civil Law" (1928) 13 Cornell L.Q.
190; F. Schulz, *Classical Roman Law* (Oxford: Clarendon Press, 1951) p.624; P.G. Stein (ed.), W.W.
Buckland, *Text Book of Roman Law from Augustus to Justinian*, 4th edn (Cambridge: CUP, 2003),
p.537; J. Kortmann, *Altruism in Private Law: Liability for Nonfeasance and Negotiorum Gestio*
(Oxford: OUP, 2004), pp.44–47.

[2] J.P. Dawson, "*Negotiorum Gestio*: The Altruistic Intermeddler" (1961) 74 Harvard L.R. 817 and
1073; R. Zimmermann, *The Law of Obligations: Roman Foundations of the Civilian Tradition*
(Oxford: OUP, 1996), Ch.14 and pp.875–878; R.D. Leslie "*Negotiorum Gestio* in Scots Law: The
Claim of the Privileged Gestor" [1983] J.R. 12; S.J. Stoljar, "*Negotiorum Gestio*" in E. von
Caemmerer and P. Schlechtriem (eds), *International Encyclopedia of Comparative Law, vol.10:
Restitution—Unjust Enrichment and Negotiorum Gestio* (Tübingen, Mohr, The Hague: Nijhoff, 1984)
Ch.17; D.H. Van Zyl, *Negotiorum Gestio in South African Law* (Durban: Butterworths, 1989); N.R.
Whitty, "*Negotiorum Gestio*", in *The Laws of Scotland: Stair Memorial Encyclopaedia* vol.15
(Edinburgh: Butterworths and the Law Society of Scotland, 1996); Kortmann, *Altruism in Private
Law*, Ch.10. See too C. von Bar et al (eds), *Principles, Definitions and Model Rules of European
Private Law, Draft Common Frame of Reference, Book V: Benevolent Intervention in Another's
Affairs*, interim outline edn (Munich: Sellier, 2008), critiqued in N. Jansen, "*Negotiorum Gestio* and
Benevolent Intervention in Another's Affairs: Principles of European Law?" (2007) 15 Z.Eu.P.
958.

[3] E.W. Hope, "Officiousness" (1930) 15 Cornell L.Q. 25, p.36, regarding this outcome as unlikely.
Cf. J.P. Dawson, "Rewards for the Rescue of Human Life?" in K. Nadelmann et al (eds), *Twentieth
Century Comparative and Conflicts Law: Legal Essays in Honour of Hessel E. Yntema* (Leyden:
A.W. Sythoff, 1961) 142, p.142: "official sources of American law have done their best to discourage
good Samaritans".

ing that virtue should be its own reward.[4] In *Nicholson v Chapman* Eyre C.J. suggested that: "it is better for the public that these voluntary acts of benevolence from one man to another, which are charities and moral duties, but not legal duties, should depend altogether for their reward upon the moral duty of grati- tude",[5] and thought that a generalised right of recovery would encourage "the wilful attempts of ill-designing people to turn . . . floats and vessels adrift, in order that they may be paid for finding them".[6] In *Falcke v Scottish Imperial Insurance Co Ltd*, Bowen L.J. stated that "liabilities are not to be forced on people behind their backs", and that:

> "the general principle is, beyond all question, that work or labour done or money expended by one man to preserve or benefit the property of another do not according to English law create any lien upon the property saved or benefited, nor even, if standing alone, create any obligation to repay the expenditure".[7]

In *Morrison Steamship Co Ltd v Greystoke Castle (Cargo Owners) (The Chel- dale)*, Lord Uthwatt held that "the principle involved in general average con- tribution is peculiar to the law of the sea", and that on land a contribution cannot "be obtained on the ground that loss incurred by one person has delivered another from a common danger."[8] In *Bureau Wijsmuller NV v Owners of the Tojo Maru (The Tojo Maru) (No.2)*, Lord Reid said that "on land a person who interferes to save property is not in law entitled to any reward".[9] And in *The Goring*, in the Court of Appeal, Ralph Gibson L.J. thought that the English courts' reluctance to acknowledge a generalised right of recovery "has not rested . . . only on a lack of prior authority and the fear of innovation but can be supported by reasons",[10] while, in the House of Lords, Lord Brandon considered this view to be quite as "forceful"[11] as Sir John Donaldson M.R.'s dissenting opinion in the Court of Appeal, that salvage awards in respect of rescues undertaken on non-tidal waters should be allowed pursuant to a general policy of encouraging rescuers.[12]

18–03   Notwithstanding these authorities, however, there are cases where English law has recognised the rights of a person who acts in an emergency to help another. In the past these have been treated as isolated exceptions to a general rule against recovery, but we consider that the time has come for the courts to recognise that the exceptions have swallowed up the general rule. They should recognise that

---

[4] C.K. Allen, "Legal Duties" (1931) 40 Yale L.J. 331, pp.373–377.
[5] *Nicholson v Chapman* (1793) 2 H. Bl. 254 at 259; 126 E.R. 536 at 539.
[6] *Nicholson* (1793) 2 H. Bl. 254, following *Binstead v Buck* (1777) 2 W. Bl. 1117; 96 E.R. 660 (no lien on straying dog for costs of upkeep).
[7] *Falcke v Scottish Imperial Insurance Co Ltd* (1886) 34 Ch. D. 234 at 248.
[8] *Morrison Steamship Co Ltd v Greystoke Castle (Cargo Owners) (The Cheldale)* [1947] A.C. 265 at 310.
[9] *Bureau Wijsmuller NV v Owners of the Tojo Maru (The Tojo Maru) (No.2)* [1972] A.C. 242 at 268.
[10] *The Goring* [1987] Q.B. 687 at 708.
[11] *The Goring* [1988] A.C. 831 at 857.
[12] *The Goring* [1987] Q.B. 687 at 706–707.

the "exceptional" cases are all underpinned by a policy of encouraging (or of not discouraging) intervention in emergency situations,[13] and they should generalise the principles disclosed by these cases into a coherent and rational doctrine analogous to the civilian doctrine of *negotiorum gestio*. This doctrine would only belong in part to the law of unjust enrichment, as the remedies awarded would include, but would not be limited to, the restitution of benefits. In appropriate cases, necessitous interveners might also be entitled to a reward or an indemnity for their costs.

In the following discussion we describe the cases in which recovery has been **18–04** allowed. We look in turn at salvage claims, claims for general average contribution, other claims by those who preserve another person's property, claims by those who preserve another person's credit, claims by those who care for the sick and the mentally incapable, and claims by those who bury the dead. Drawing on this body of case law, we then consider the limits that might apply to a generalised right of action and the remedies to which successful claimants might be entitled.

2. SALVAGE

(a) *The Nature of the Right*

A salvage service may be briefly described as a necessary service voluntarily **18–05** rendered which assists in saving a recognised subject of salvage from danger at sea.[14] The salvor's right to reward for such a service has long been enforced in the Court of Admiralty as part of the maritime law; in modern times, this right been extended by statute, most recently by the Merchant Shipping Act 1995, which gives force of law in the UK to the International Convention on Salvage 1989.[15]

---

[13] Jeroen Kortmann rightly observes that the present general rule disallowing interveners' claims "does not *actively* discourage intervention but *merely fails to neutralize* the discouraging effect of the prospect that an intervention might prove costly": Kortmann, *Altruism in Private Law*, p.91; see too A. Honoré, "Law, Morals, and Reason" in J. Ratcliff (ed.), *The Good Samaritan and the Law* (New York, NY: Anchor Books, 1966), p.234. For discussion of the theoretical arguments for and against a general principle supporting recovery, see Dawson "*Negotiorum Gestio*: The Altruistic Intermeddler", and "Rewards for the Rescue of Human Life"; F.D. Rose, "Restitution for the Rescuer" (1989) 9 O.J.L.S. 167; H. Dagan, "In Defense of the Good Samaritan" (1999) 97 Michigan L.R. 1152; Kortmann, *Altruism in Private Law*, Chs 8 and 9; and cf. W.M. Landes and R.A. Posner, "Salvors, Finders, Good Samaritans, and Other Rescuers: An Economic Study of Law and Altruism" (1978) 7 J.L.S. 83; S. Levmore "Waiting for Rescue: An Essay on the Evolution and Incentive Structure of the Law of Affirmative Obligations" (1986) 72 Virginia L.R. 879.

[14] This is a description of civil salvage, with which we are here concerned. Civil salvage should be distinguished from military salvage, which is the rescue of property from an enemy in wartime and which gives rise to a claim for reward in a prize court. On civil salvage generally, see F.D. Rose, *Kennedy and Rose on Civil Salvage*, 7th edn (London: Sweet & Maxwell, 2010); J. Reeder QC, *Brice on the Maritime Law of Salvage*, 5th edn (London: Sweet & Maxwell, 2011).

[15] Merchant Shipping Act 1995 s.224 and Sch.1.

18–06   By maritime law, the only property which could be the subject of salvage was a ship, her apparel and cargo, the wreck of these, and freight at risk. Statute has, however, extended the law of salvage to cover aircraft and hovercraft, and has also empowered the courts to make awards of "special compensation" for the provision of services designed to prevent or minimise environmental damage.[16] Common examples of salvage services are towing or piloting a ship in peril; raising a sunken ship or cargo; rescuing cargo or passengers from a ship in peril; and refloating a ship which has been stranded. But the classes of salvage service are not closed and new categories are recognised from time to time.

18–07   Although the parties may (and generally do) regulate the rendering of salvage services by agreement, the right to reward for salvage services is not, in origin, contractual. Admiralty judges successfully resisted the temptation to invoke the fiction of "implied contract" as a basis of the right. In the words of Sir Francis Jeune P.[17]:

> "To rest the jurisdiction of the Admiralty Court upon an implied request from the owner of the property in danger to the salvors, or on an implied contract between the salvors and owner with the relinquishment of the *res* for consideration, is, I think, to confuse two different systems of law and to resort to a misleading analogy. The true view is, I think, that the law of Admiralty imposes on the owner of property saved an obligation to pay the person who saves it simply because in the view of that system of law it is just he should . . . "

The court does not, therefore, usually[18] inquire whether the master of the salved vessel has requested the services[19]; indeed salvage may be awarded even where the services have been accepted under protest.[20] It is, however, essential that the services should have been of such a kind and rendered in such circumstances that

---

[16] Whether the courts have a statutory power to reward life salvage is considered below at para.18–12.

[17] *The Cargo ex Port Victor* [1901] P. 243 at 249.

[18] Exceptionally, the fact that the services have been requested may be relevant. Thus, if the services have been rendered at the request of the master of the salved vessel, the salvor may be entitled to a reward even though the vessel is salved through some other cause (see *The Undaunted* (1860) Lush. 90; 167 E.R. 47); and if such services are not completed because they are stopped or prevented by the master of the salved vessel, the salvor may be entitled not only to a reward for services he has rendered but also to some compensation for having lost the opportunity of completing his services and, therefore, of reaping a greater reward (see *The Maude* (1876) 3 Asp. M.L.C. 338; *The Hassel* [1959] 2 Lloyd's Rep. 82). These cases should not, however, be rationalised as being akin to common law claims on a quantum meruit basis; for part, at least, of the property in danger must in fact be saved, and the right is to reward, and not to remuneration, although the grant of the reward is a recognition of the fact that "if men are engaged by a ship in distress . . . they are to be paid according to their efforts made, even though the labour and services may not prove beneficial to the vessel": *The Undaunted* (1860) Lush. 90 at 92; 167 E.R. 47 at 49 per Dr Lushington; see too *The Orelia* [1958] 1 Lloyd's Rep. 441.

[19] *The Vandyck* (1881) 7 P.D. 42.

[20] Provided that the master of the salved vessel would have acted unreasonably with regard to the safety of his ship and the other property in his charge if he had not accepted the services: *The Kangaroo* [1918] P. 327. Cf. the cases at common law where services are rendered against the will of the defendant and yet there is a right to reimbursement, e.g. *Great Northern Railway Co v Swaffield* (1874) L.R. 9 Ex. 132; *Matheson v Smiley* [1932] 2 D.L.R. 787 (Manitoba CA).

a reasonably prudent owner would have accepted them.[21] It is this requirement which, coupled with the further requirement that the subject of salvage must have been in danger, indicates that the courts' jurisdiction to make salvage awards rests on the policy consideration that it is desirable to provide a positive incentive to "seafaring folk to take risks for the purpose of saving property".[22]

This policy often results in substantial awards. Liberality is particularly **18–08** encouraged in the case of services rendered by tugs specially maintained for purposes of salvage,[23] and in the case of salvage of passenger vessels.[24] It is a concomitant to the rule that a salvor receives a reward, rather than remuneration, for his services, that the services must have been successful before any reward is given.[25] They need not have been completely successful but they must have at least contributed to part of the property being saved. In assessing the amount of the reward, the court will remember that in other cases great efforts, though undeservedly unsuccessful, may reap no reward at all.[26] There may, however, be exceptional cases. By special agreement, remuneration may be payable even though the services are unsuccessful; and where services are rendered at the specific request of the vessel in distress, a reward will be payable in respect of such services irrespective of their success.[27]

Although the origin of salvage is not contractual, in most cases nowadays **18–09** salvage is regulated by a salvage agreement, which is frequently in Lloyd's standard form.[28] Since, however, salvage is based on principles of equity, the court has the power to set aside a salvage agreement on the grounds that it is fraudulent or induced by misrepresentation or non-disclosure, or even because the court considers its terms to be "manifestly unfair and unjust".[29] In particular, an agreement is likely to be regarded as inequitable if it stipulates for an exorbitant reward which the master was forced to agree to on account of the necessitous position in which he found himself.[30] An agreement may, however, also be set aside on the ground that the agreed sum was far too small.[31]

---

[21] *The Emilie Galline* [1903] P. 106.
[22] *The Sandefjord* [1953] 2 Lloyd's Rep. 557 at 561 per Willmer J. See too *The Jane* (1831) 2 Hag. Adm. 338 at 343–344; 166 E.R. 267 at 270; *The Industry* (1835) 3 Hag. Adm. 203 at 204; 166 E.R. 381 at 383; *Owners of the Beaverford v Owners of The Kafiristan* [1938] A.C. 136 at 147; *Ministry of Trade of Iraq v Tsavliris Salvage (International) Ltd (The Altair)* [2008] EWHC 612 (Comm); [2008] 2 Lloyd's Rep. 90 at [57] ("the strong maritime policy interest in rewarding salvors").
[23] See, e.g. *The Glengyle* [1898] A.C. 519.
[24] *The Ardincaple* (1834) 3 Hag. Adm. 151 at 153; 166 E.R. 362 at 363.
[25] See para.18–18.
[26] *The City of Chester* (1884) 9 P.D. 182 at 202.
[27] Provided that some part of the property in danger is saved, as it may be through the efforts of some other salving vessel: *The Undaunted* (1860) Lush. 90; 167 E.R. 47. If this condition is fulfilled, a reward may be given for requested services even though such services have been of no benefit to the salved vessel: *The Undaunted* (1860) Lush. 90; 167 E.R. 47; *The Orelia* [1958] 1 Lloyd's Rep. 441.
[28] Lloyd's Standard Forms of Salvage Agreement (LOF 1995) and (LOF 2000) are both reproduced in *Kennedy and Rose on Civil Salvage*, Appendix A.
[29] *Akerblom v Price, Potter, Walker & Co* (1881) 7 Q.B.D. 129 at 132–133. For further discussion, see O. Lennox-King, "Laying the Mark to Port and Starboard: Salvage under Duress and Economic Duress at Contract Law" (2007) 21 A.N.Z.M.L.J. 32.
[30] As in e.g. *The Port Caledonia and The Anna* [1903] P. 184.
[31] As in e.g. *The Phantom* (1886) L.R. 1 A. & E. 58.

(b) *Conditions of the Right to Salvage Reward*

(i) *Location of the Salvage Operation*

18–10 By maritime law, salvage is only awarded for services rendered on the high seas and may not be awarded for services to vessels in non-tidal waters.[32] By statute, salvage can be recovered where a salvage operation takes place on inland waters, provided that at least one vessel is involved that is not a vessel of inland navigation.[33]

(ii) *The Thing Salved Must Be a Recognised Subject of Salvage*

18–11 It was the rule of maritime law that the only property which could be the subject of salvage was a ship, her apparel and cargo, the wreck of these, and freight at risk.[34] The law of salvage has, however, been extended by statute to cover hovercraft[35] and aircraft, their apparel and cargo, and the wreck of these.[36] By incorporating art.14 of the International Convention on Salvage 1989 into English law, the Merchant Shipping Act 1995 has also empowered the courts to make awards where the salvor's actions have prevented environmental damage. The effect of such services is not to preserve the salvee's property, but to restrict his legal liability to others (a doubtful subject of salvage under maritime law in the absence of legislation[37]).

18–12   Traditionally, the subject of salvage has been property not lives. Some concession was made by the maritime law under which those who salved lives as well as property could expect a greater reward for their services.[38] Moreover, those who salve human life while property is salved in the same operation are entitled by statute "to a fair share of the payment awarded to the salvor for salving the vessel".[39] However, the law has never rewarded those who salved lives alone. The historical reason was that in such cases "no property could be arrested applicable to the purpose. There could be no proceeding *in rem*, the ancient foundation of the salvage suit."[40] Actions in personam can now be brought,[41] but it remains the law that no salvage reward is payable where life alone is salved, and although the Secretary of State has a discretionary power to award sums out

---

[32] *The Goring* [1988] A.C. 831.
[33] Merchant Shipping Act 1995 Sch.11 Pt 2 para.2(1). Under para.2(2) "'inland waters' does not include any waters within the ebb and flow of the tide at ordinary spring tides or the waters of any dock which is directly or (by means of one or more other docks) indirectly, connected with such waters."
[34] *Wells v The Owners of the Gas Float Whitton No.2 (The Gas Float Whitton No.2)* [1896] P. 42, especially at 63–64, affirmed [1897] A.C. 337. *Cf. The Silia* [1981] 2 Lloyd's Rep. 534 (bunker oil, part of the ship).
[35] Hovercraft Act 1968; Hovercraft (Application of Enactments) Order 1972 (SI 1972/971) art.8(1).
[36] Civil Aviation Act 1982 s.87.
[37] See the discussion in *Kennedy and Rose on Civil Salvage*, paras 5.016–5.022.
[38] *Bligh, Harbottle & Co v Simpson (The Fusilier)* (1865) 3 Moo. N.S. 51 at 74; 16 E.R. 19 at 29 per Lord Chelmsford.
[39] Merchant Shipping Act 1995 s.224 and Sch.11 Pt 1, giving force of law in the UK to the International Convention on Salvage 1989 art.16. In English law this rule dates back to the Merchant Shipping Act 1854 s.458.
[40] *The Fusilier* (1865) 3 Moo. N.S. 51 at 55.
[41] See para.18–39.

of public funds to "pure" life salvors,[42] this power does not appear to have been exercised in recent times.

(iii) *Entitlement to Claim*

In previous editions of this work, it was stated that a claim for salvage would lie **18–13** only if it were brought by a claimant who fell within a legally recognised category of salvor.[43] However, the better view is that claimants need not bring themselves within such a classification, for "there are no rigid categories of salvor. They include any volunteer who renders services of a salvage nature."[44] Hence it is more accurate to say that although claims are typically brought by salvors of particular kinds, there is no legal requirement that claimants should conform to this description. Most typically, claims are successfully made either by parties who are entitled to reward by reason of their ownership of the salving vessel, or by parties who are so entitled by having personally rendered salvage services. The first group is not limited to the true owner or owners of the salving vessel; for sometimes a charterer is *pro hac vice* owner in respect of salvage, in which event it will be he, and not the true owner, who is entitled to the reward. A charterer is, however, only *pro hac vice* owner where he is rendered so by the terms of the charter,[45] or where the charter is by demise.[46] In the second group of salvors, the usual claimants are the master and crew of the salving vessel; but anybody who has personally rendered salvage services may claim.

A claim can be made by the owner of the salving vessel against a salved **18–14** vessel of which he is also owner[47]; and he can claim against cargo carried on his own vessel, unless he would, but for the salvage services, have been liable to the cargo for loss or damage which would have been caused by the danger so averted.[48] The crew of a salving vessel can claim salvage against a salved vessel in the ownership of their employers,[49] unless their services were such that they were bound to perform them under their contract of employment.[50]

(iv) *The Services Must Not Have Been Rendered under a Pre-Existing Duty*

No award will be made to a salvor who owes a pre-existing duty to the owner of **18–15** the salved property, for such a person does not need the bait of a prospective award to induce him to intervene. The pre-existing duty may have been undertaken by contract, or it may have fallen within the salvor's official duties or have

---

[42] Merchant Shipping Act 1995 Sch.11 Pt 2 para.5.
[43] G. Jones, *Goff & Jones: The Law of Restitution*, 7th edn (London: Sweet & Maxwell, 2006), para.18.006.
[44] *The Sava Star* [1995] 2 Lloyd's Rep. 134 at 151 per Clarke J.
[45] *The Scout* (1872) L.R. 3 A. & E. 512 at 515 per Sir Robert Phillimore.
[46] *Elliott Steam Tug Co Ltd v Lord High Admiral Executing Office Commissioners* [1921] 1 A.C. 137.
[47] Merchant Shipping Act 1995 s.224(1) and Sch.11, giving force of law in the UK to the International Convention on Salvage 1989 art.12.3. However, sister-ship salvage is nowadays extremely rare as the great majority of vessels are owned by one-ship companies.
[48] *The Glenfruin* (1885) 10 P.D. 103.
[49] *The Sappho* (1871) L.R. 3 P.C. 690.
[50] *The Maria Jane* (1850) 14 Jur. 857.

been imposed by general law[51] or by custom. The general principle is that, where the salvor acted under any such pre-existing duty, he is only entitled to receive a salvage award if his services went beyond the ordinary scope of his duty. So, for example, to entitle a pilot on board the salved vessel to receive a salvage reward, he must show that the vessel was in such distress as to:

> "call upon him to run such unusual danger, or incur such unusual responsibility, or exercise such unusual skill, or perform such an unusual kind of service, as to make it unfair and unjust that he should be paid otherwise than upon the terms of salvage reward."[52]

Similarly, where there is a pre-existing towage contract, an award of salvage will be justified "if the services rendered are beyond what can be reasonably supposed to have been contemplated by the parties entering into such a contract."[53] This principle has been applied to many different classes of people,[54] including foyboatmen,[55] harbourmasters,[56] port authorities,[57] and various other officials.

18–16 One effect of the principle is that the crew of the salved vessel are debarred from recovering salvage, unless they rendered salvage services after their contracts of service had already been determined[58]; for the crew of a ship "are to be taken as pledging the last ounce of strength and service to their ship when they sign their articles and enter upon the voyage."[59] Officers and men of the Royal Navy can recover no reward for matters within their ordinary duties, such as, for example, repressing mutinies on vessels,[60] or protecting ships or cargo from pirates[61]; moreover, any claim by the commander or crew or part of the crew of any of Her Majesty's ships is subject to the consent of the Secretary of State to the prosecution of the claim.[62] The crews of lifeboats, which are provided by the Royal National Life-Boat Institution for the saving of life, are only permitted by the Institution's regulations to intervene to salve property if other craft are not available or, if available, are inadequate for the purpose. If a salvage award is made in favour of a lifeboat crew, the Institution will have a first charge on the

---

[51] Certain statutory duties, which require masters of vessels to go to the assistance of other vessels in distress, exceptionally do not affect the right to salvage; see Merchant Shipping Act 1995 s.93.
[52] *Akerblom v Price* (1881) 7 Q.B.D. 129 at 135 per Brett L.J.; see also *The Driade* [1959] 2 Lloyd's Rep. 311.
[53] *Five Steel Barges* (1890) 15 P.D. 142 at 144 per Sir James Hannen.
[54] Its application in the case of ships' agents has been unusually lenient.
[55] *The Macgregor Laird* [1953] 2 Lloyd's Rep. 259; *The Southwark* [1962] 2 Lloyd's Rep. 62.
[56] *The Corcrest* (1946) 80 Lloyd's List Rep. 78.
[57] *The Citos* (1925) 22 Lloyd's Rep. 275; *The Mars and Other Barges* (1948) 81 Lloyd's Rep. 452; *Owners, Master and Crew of the Bostonian v Owners of the Gregerso* [1971] 1 Lloyd's Rep 220 at 225–227. See too *Transnet Ltd (t/a National Ports Authority) v The MV Cleopatra Dream* [2011] ZASCA 12; and cf. *The Mbashi* [2002] 2 Lloyd's Rep. 602 (SA High Ct).
[58] e.g. by being discharged by the master (see *The Warrior* (1862) Lush. 476; 167 E.R. 214), or by the proper abandonment of the ship at sea (see *The Florence* (1852) 16 Jur. 572).
[59] *The Albionic* (1941) 70 Lloyd's List Rep. 257 at 263 per Langton J. See too *The Sava Star* [1995] 2 Lloyd's Rep. 134 at 142.
[60] *The Francis and Eliza* (1816) 2 Dods. 115; 165 E.R. 1433.
[61] *The Cargo ex Ulysses* (1888) 13 P.D. 205 at 208 per Sir James Hannen.
[62] Merchant Shipping Act 1995 s.230. Where salvage services have been rendered by or on behalf of the Crown, the Crown is entitled to claim salvage in respect of those services to the same extent as any other salvor; see also s.230(2).

award for expenses involved in launching the boat, etc. in the cost of stores used, and in any repairs rendered necessary by the intervention.[63]

(v) *There Must Have Been a Danger at Sea from which the Salved Property or Lives were Saved*

The element of danger gives rise to the necessity that is the foundation of all salvage claims. But in the context of salvage the test of what constitutes danger is probably not so stringent as in general average.[64] Salvage will be awarded in a case "in which there was no immediate risk, no immediate danger; but there was a possible contingency that serious consequences might have ensued."[65] As in general average, however, the danger must have in fact existed[66]; a supposed, but non-existent, danger will not found a salvage award.[67] **18–17**

(vi) *The Services Must Have Achieved Some Success*

It is essential to an award of salvage that some part at least of the property in danger should in fact be saved.[68] The salvor, who takes the risk that he will receive nothing if nothing is saved, has the corresponding opportunity of gaining a substantial reward if his efforts are successful. This reward is payable by the owner of the salved property because he has been benefited by the salvor's services. In the words of Dr Lushington[69]: **18–18**

"I apprehend that, upon general principles, a mere attempt to save the vessel and cargo, however meritorious that attempt may be, or whatever degree of risk or danger may have been incurred, if unsuccessful, can never be considered in this court as furnishing any title to a salvage reward. The reason is obvious, *viz.* that salvage reward is for benefits actually conferred, not for a service attempted to be rendered."

If, however, some part of the property in danger is saved, every person who contributed to the saving of the property will be entitled to receive a reward, even though his own efforts would not, without assistance from others, have been successful.[70]

---

[63] For examples of awards to lifeboatmen, see *The Harold Brown and The SHM 1* [1959] 2 Lloyd's Rep. 187; and *The Boston Lincoln* [1980] 1 Lloyd's Rep. 481.
[64] For the test in general average contribution, see *Industrie Chimiche Italia Centrale and Cerealfin SA v Tsavliris (Alexander G.) Maritime Co (The Choko Star)* [1990] 1 Lloyd's Rep. 516.
[65] *The Ella Constance* (1864) 33 L.J. Adm. 189 at 193 per Dr Lushington; see also *The Phantom* (1866) L.R. 1 A. & E. 58 at 60. A particularly generous view is taken in cases of towage: *Troilus (Cargo Owners) v Glenogle (Owners, Master and Crew) (The Troilus and the Glenogle)* [1951] A.C. 820.
[66] *Owners and/or Demise Charterers of the Tug Sea Tractor v Owners of the Tramp (The Tramp)* [2007] EWHC 31 (Admiralty); [2007] 2 Lloyd's Rep. 363 at [19].
[67] *The Ranger* (1845) 3 Notes of Cases 589; *The British Inventor* (1933) 45 Lloyd's List Rep. 263.
[68] *The Renpor* (1883) 8 P.D. 115. To save a vessel from one danger only to leave her exposed to another equivalent danger does not, however, constitute success in this context: see *The Melanie (Owners) v The San Onofre (Owners)* [1925] A.C. 246.
[69] *The Zephyrus* (1842) 1 W. Rob. 329 at 330–331; 166 E.R. 596 at 597.
[70] *The Jonge Bastiaan* (1804) 5 C. Rob. 322; 165 E.R. 791.

(vii) *The Claimant Must Not Have Been at Fault*

18–19   **Where the salvage services were made necessary by the salvor's fault** It has been held that, where salvage services to ship A were made necessary by the fault of ship B, not merely those members of the crew of ship B who were actually at fault, but also the remaining members of the crew[71] and, indeed, the owners of ship B[72] are precluded from recovering reward for salvage services rendered to ship A by them or their vessel consequent upon the faulty action. The foundation of this rule has been said to be the principle that no man should profit from his own wrong[73]; and the owners of the vessel at fault have been held to be precluded from recovering any reward because the fault was committed by persons for whom they were vicariously responsible.[74]

18–20   Nevertheless, in *Owners of the Beaverford v Owners of The Kafiristan*,[75] the House of Lords held that the fact that salvage services to ship A were rendered necessary by the fault of ship B would not prevent the owners of ship C, which had rendered salvage services, from recovering reward, even though the owners of ship C were also the owners of ship B. It is obviously difficult, on principle, to reconcile this decision with the earlier cases in which owners were unable to recover because of their vicarious responsibility for those at fault; for the owners of ship C must have been vicariously responsible for the fault of their servants on ship B, and yet were able to recover. Moreover, the manner in which Lord Wright, who delivered the principal speech, approached the problem indicated that he had serious doubts as to the correctness of the earlier cases. He said[76]:

> "The maritime law of salvage is based on principles of equity. There does not seem to be any reason in equity why the salved vessel . . . should not pay the appropriate salvage remuneration merely because the salving vessel belongs to the same owners as the other colliding vessel. That fact seems to be irrelevant so far as concerns the usefulness and meritorious character of the actual services rendered.
>   . . . The rubric 'that no man can profit by his own wrong' . . . in my opinion is wholly inapplicable. The claim to salvage is not based on the fact that the *Empress of Britain* was guilty of negligent navigation. It is based on a separate fact, that the *Beaverford* rendered salvage services. It is for these meritorious services and not for the negligence of the crew of the *Empress of Britain* that the appellants claim the right to have salvage awarded. They are not seeking to profit by their own wrong, for which in the final account they will make the appropriate compensation by, among other things, bearing their proper share of the salvage award."

18–21   He went on to declare[77] that, even:

> "if the rule laid down in *Cargo ex Capella*[78] is at all sound, it is at any rate excluded where the ship which is the instrument of the salvage is a different ship from that which is the instrument of the negligent collision."

---

[71] *The Duc d'Aumale (No.2)* [1904] P. 60.
[72] *The Duc d'Aumale (No.2)* [1904] P. 60.
[73] *The Cargo ex Capella* (1867) L.R. 1 A. & E. 356 at 357 per Dr Lushington.
[74] *The Duc d'Aumale (No.2)* [1904] P. 60.
[75] *Owners of the Beaverford v Owners of The Kafiristan* [1938] A.C. 136; applying *The Glengaber* (1872) L.R. 3 A. & E. 534.
[76] *The Beaverford* [1938] A.C. 136 at 147–149.
[77] *The Beaverford* [1938] A.C. 136 at 149.
[78] *The Cargo ex Capella* [1867] L.R. 1 A. & E. 356.

It follows that, in the light of Lord Wright's reasoning, the earlier cases may **18–22** yet be overruled, despite the long period for which they have been accepted as good law. Moreover, it cannot, at least in ordinary cases, be accepted that the claimant's claim should be barred on principles of circuity of action, even where the claimant vessel was solely to blame.[79] Circuity of action: "can only be pleaded when the rights of the litigants are such that the defendants would be entitled to recover back from the plaintiffs the same amount of damages which the plaintiffs sought to recover from the defendants"[80]; and where, as will usually be the case, the wrongdoing vessel is able to limit her liability for her wrongdoing, the principle of circuity of action cannot have the effect of altogether defeating that vessel's claim to salvage.

Where the salvors were guilty of fault after rendering the salvage **18–23** **services**   Where, after rendering the salvage services, the salvors have been guilty of wilful or criminal misconduct, as, for example, where they have stolen part of the salved property,[81] or where they have wrongfully prevented the master and crew of the salved vessel from returning on board,[82] they will be deprived of any right to reward. They may also lose their right to reward if, by their subsequent gross negligence, they bring the salved vessel into danger at least as great as that she was saved from[83]; but where the salvors' negligence or misconduct is not of a serious nature, they will not be deprived of all right to reward,[84] unless the loss arising from the negligence or misconduct is equal to or exceeds the potential loss from which the salved property was rescued.[85] Moreover, the owners are entitled to maintain an action for negligence against the salvors by way of counterclaim and are not restricted to setting off their loss against the amount of any salvage award.[86]

In *The St Blane*, Brandon J. formulated the following principles as governing **18–24** "the general approach of the Court to charges of negligence against persons who render or try to render assistance at sea"[87]:

"As to this, it is well established that the Court takes a lenient view of the conduct of salvors and would-be salvors, and is slow to find that those who try their best, in good faith, to save life or property in peril at sea, and make mistakes or errors of judgement in doing so, have been guilty of negligence. Nevertheless it is not in doubt that the Court may, in a proper case, after making all allowances, find negligence against salvors and, having done so, award damages against them in respect of it.[88] In deciding such matters

---

[79] *Owners of the Susan V. Luckenbach v Admiralty Commissioners (The Susan V. Luckenbach)* [1951] P. 197.

[80] *The Beaverford* [1937] P. 63 at 69 per Bucknill J., cited with approval by the Court of Appeal in *The Susan V. Luckenbach* [1951] P. 197 at 203.

[81] *The Kedah* (1948) 81 Lloyd's List Rep. 217.

[82] *The Capella* [1892] P. 70.

[83] *Shersby v Hibbert (The Duke of Manchester)* (1846) 2 W. Rob. 470; 166 E.R. 833; affirmed (1847) 6 Moo. P.C. 90; 13 E.R. 618.

[84] *The Atlas* (1862) Lush. 518 at 528; 16 E.R. 235 at 242 per Sir John Coleridge. The authorities are fully discussed in *The Tojo Maru* [1972] A.C. 242.

[85] *The Yan-Yean* (1883) 8 P.D. 147.

[86] *The Tojo Maru* [1972] A.C. 242.

[87] *The St Blane* [1974] 1 Lloyd's Rep. 557 at 560–561.

[88] *The Rene (Owners) v The Alenquer (Owners)* [1955] 1 W.L.R. 263; *The Tojo Maru* [1972] A.C. 242.

the Court looks at all the circumstances of the case, including the status of the salvors—whether amateur or professional—and the question whether they have acted at request or on their own initiative. This principle of the lenient approach to mistakes is an important one. It derives from the basic policy of the law relating to salvage services, which is always to encourage, rather than discourage, the rendering of such services. The principle is especially important in cases involving life salvage, where its application demands that salvors should not in general be criticised if, faced with an actual or potential conflict between saving life on the one hand, and preserving property on the other, they err on the side of the former at the expense of the latter. I approach the charges of negligence in this case in the light of the principle of leniency stated above."

(viii) *The Services Must Not Have Been Rendered Against the Owner's Will*

18–25 The services must not have been rendered against the will of the owner of the thing in danger, or of his representative (usually the master of the ship in danger),[89] unless the owner or his representative is guilty of unreasonable disregard to the safety of the ship or other property in his charge.[90]

(c) *The Award*

(i) *Assessment of the Award*

18–26 The amount of the salvage award may be fixed by agreement. Such an agreement may, however, be set aside on the grounds that it is inequitable, either because the agreed sum is exorbitantly high or because it is inadequate. But if it is not inequitable or otherwise liable to be avoided, e.g. for misrepresentation or non-disclosure, then the agreement will be enforced, and the mere fact that the court might have awarded a different sum, whether higher or lower, than the sum agreed will not prevent the court from upholding the agreement.[91]

18–27 Where there is no enforceable agreement as to the amount of the salvage award, assessment of the award is a matter for the court's discretion. In the words of Dr Lushington[92]:

"The amount of salvage reward due is not to be determined by any rules; it is a matter of discretion, and probably in this, or in any other case no two tribunals would agree."

18–28 In exercising this discretion, the court is not concerned to calculate reasonable remuneration for work done.[93] The court's task is to assess the amount of a reward which will, in the interests of public policy, encourage others to act as salvors, but which at the same time will not bear too harshly on the owners of the

---

[89] *The Black Boy* (1837) 3 Hag. Adm. 386n.; 166 E.R. 449; *The Barefoot* (1850) 14 Jur. 841; *The Samuel* (1851) 15 Jur. 407.
[90] *The Kangaroo* [1918] P. 327.
[91] *The Africa* (1880) 5 P.D. 192 at 196 per Sir Robert Phillimore.
[92] *The Cuba* (1860) Lush. 14 at 15; 167 E.R. 8 at 8.
[93] But see *Semco Salvage and Maritime Pte Ltd v Lancer Navigation Co Ltd (The Nagasaki Spirit)* [1996] 1 Lloyd's Rep. 449 (CA); [1997] A.C. 455 (HL) (salvor's remuneration under the International Convention on Salvage 1989 arts 13 and 14.) For discussion of the rules governing the identification and quantification of benefit in claims to recover the value of services on the ground of unjust enrichment, see paras 5–21—5–37.

salved property.[94] In *Owners of the Tantalus v Owners of the Telemachus*, Willmer J. stated "the underlying principle upon which all awards of salvage must be based" as follows[95]:

> "I have to arrive at such an award as will fairly compensate the master and crew of the salving vessel, without injustice to the salved interests, and such an award as will, in the interests of public policy, encourage other mariners in like circumstances to perform like services."

The award incorporates elements of reimbursement, remuneration and **18–29** reward.[96] Thus, when the court came to make its award in *The Mbashi*,[97] it noted that previous cases provided little helpful guidance as every case had to turn on its own facts, that the services rendered were completely successful, there was a risk to the environment, neither the master nor crew were accustomed to the sea conditions, the services were rendered promptly, and the claimant's equipment on board operated efficiently, performing necessary functions. In fixing the award the court held that, while it should grant rewards that encouraged intervention, the rewards should not be unduly burdensome to shipowners and the cargo interests. The expenses incurred were around R18,300. Striking a balance between all these factors, it was appropriate to make an award of around R3,200,000, which was 2.5 per cent of the value of the salved properties (around R128,500,000).

It is usually said that a reward will not be made of more than half the value of **18–30** the property salved. Generally, this is true and on occasions the award may be much less than half. But there are circumstances in which an award of more than half may be made,[98] as, for example, where the property is derelict; or where the salvors have rendered services which are particularly deserving of high reward; or where the value of the salved property is very low. Thus, in *The Boiler Ex Elephant*,[99] five men found a derelict marine boiler from the *SS Elephant* (which had been lost with all hands five years before) floating on the high seas about three miles off Eastbourne. With some difficulty they succeeded in towing it ashore and, with the aid of men and horses, for whose assistance they paid £10, they hauled it up the beach above the high-water mark. The proceeds of sale of the boiler were only £58 3s. 4d. and the five salvors were awarded a sum of £50 with costs. It is significant that, in that case, nobody appeared to defend the action, which is another factor tending to increase the amount of the award. But

---

[94] "It must always be remembered that the underlying purpose of salvage is to confer a benefit on the owner of the salved property: if the amount of the award is such a high percentage of a salved fund that the owner of the salved property in effect receives close to nothing out of it then he will not have benefited": Reeder, *Brice on the Maritime Law of Salvage*, para.2.154, quoted with approval in *R. (S.R.M. Global Master Fund L.P.) v Treasury Commissioner* [2009] EWCA Civ 788; [2010] B.C.C. 558 at [66].

[95] *Owners of the Tantalus v Owners of the Telemachus* [1957] P. 47 at 49.

[96] F.D. Rose, "Restitution and Maritime Law", in E.J.H. Schrage (ed.), *Unjust Enrichment and the Law of Contract* (The Hague: Kluwer, 2011), 367, p.378.

[97] *The Mbashi* [2002] 2 Lloyd's Rep. 602 (SA High Ct, Durban and Coast Local Division, exercising its Admiralty Jurisdiction).

[98] Until the turn of the 19th century, the salvor's only remedy was in rem against the vessel saved. "This itself disabled him from recovering more than its value": *The Tojo Maru* [1972] A.C. 242 at 293 per Lord Diplock.

[99] *The Boiler Ex Elephant* (1891) 64 L.T. 543.

the court will never make an award amounting to the whole value of the salved property, unless the parties fix in advance a sum of salvage remuneration greater than the salvaged fund.[100]

18–31 A case exemplifying the problems which may face a court when assessing a salvage award is *The Queen Elizabeth*.[101] In that case Willmer J. had to assess an award for services rendered by tugs to a very large ship of exceptional value. The services were rendered when *The Queen Elizabeth* went aground outside Southampton Water. The sound value of the vessel was £6,000,000; making allowance for the cost of repairs and for the value of cargo on board, the salved value of ship and cargo was £6,208,000. Willmer J. made an award of £43,500 in all, in respect of the 12 tugs represented before him. He took into account matters such as that, although the services only lasted about a day, they were skilfully and efficiently rendered; that the danger to the ship was continuous and increasing, and there was a chance, though very remote, of total loss; and that it was essential to the owners of the ship that she should be refloated as soon as possible. On the exceptionally high value of the salved property, he had this to say[102]:

> "I am not saying that you can measure salvage awards as sums in arithmetical proportion in relation to the salved property when you have values of the magnitude that you have in this case, but equally it would not, I think, be right to say that, where you have a value of this size, the addition of a few millions or the subtraction of a few millions would make no difference whatsoever. So long as even an outside chance of anything in the nature of total loss remains, then I think that the increase of value must involve some, although possibly not great, increase in the salved award over and above what might have been awarded had the value been much smaller."

18–32 The criteria for fixing rewards under the International Convention on Salvage 1989 are set out in art.13. This provides that rewards shall be fixed "with a view to encouraging salvage operations", taking account of various criteria, including the salved value of the vessel and other property, the skill and efforts of the salvor, the measure of success obtained by the salvor, the nature and degree of the danger, etc. Article 14 further provides for the award of "special compensation" for services that prevent or minimise environmental damage.

18–33 The leading case on the interpretation of these articles is *Semco Salvage and Marine Pte Ltd v Lancer Navigation Co Ltd (The Nagasaki Spirit)*,[103] where Lord Mustill held that the promoters of the Convention did not choose to create an entirely new and distinct category of environmental salvage in order to finance

---

[100] *The Lyrma (No.2)* [1978] 2 Lloyd's Rep. 30 at 33. There is a conflict of judicial opinion whether the incidence of taxation should be taken into account when assessing an award: see *The Tantalus* [1957] P. 47; *Makedonia (Cargo Owners) v Makedonia (Owners) (The Makedonia)* [1958] 1 Q.B. 365; and the dicta in *The Frisia* [1960] 1 Lloyd's Rep. 90 at 94 and 96.

[101] *The Queen Elizabeth* (1949) 82 Lloyd's List Rep. 803. For other awards, see *The Orelia* [1958] 1 Lloyd's Rep. 441 (towage); *The Amity* [1959] 1 Lloyd's Rep. 328 (towage); *The Bosworth (No.1)* [1960] 1 Lloyd's Rep. 163 (vessel listing, crew taken off and vessel towed into port); *The Santa Alicia and the Gorm* [1961] 2 Lloyd's Rep. 20 (towage); and *The Southwark* [1962] 2 Lloyd's Rep. 62 (vessel drifting, towed into berth); *The Evaine* [1966] 2 Lloyd's Rep. 413 (yacht on fire, award increased on appeal); *The Boston Lincoln* [1980] 1 Lloyd's Rep. 481 (lifeboat refloats the casualty).

[102] *The Queen Elizabeth* (1949) 82 Lloyd's List Rep. 803 at 821.

[103] *Semco Salvage and Marine Pte Ltd v Lancer Navigation Co Ltd (The Nagasaki Spirit)* [1997] A.C. 455.

owners of vessels and gear to enable them to be ready to prevent environmental damage. The right to special compensation depends on the performance of salvage operations to assist a vessel in distress,[104] and the phrase "fair rate" in art.14.3 means a fair rate of expenditure (the amount attributable to the equipment and personnel used), including indirect or overhead expenses and taking into account the additional cost of having resources instantly available,[105] but does not include any element of profit. The ascertainment of the "fair rate" must necessarily be performed with a "fairly broad brush".[106]

Following this decision, some dissatisfaction was felt by salvors over the **18–34** levels of remuneration to which they were entitled for environmental services, and accordingly a special clause was devised that could be added to Lloyd's Form: the "Special Compensation P. & I. Clause" ("SCOPIC"). When this clause applies, art.14 is excluded and SCOPIC remuneration is payable according to a detailed scheme set out in an appendix to the clause.

The court has power to award interest on a salvage award. A claim for salvage **18–35** is a claim for the recovery of a debt within the Law Reform (Miscellaneous Provisions) Act 1934 s.3(1).[107]

(ii) *Apportionment of the Award among Salvors*

Like the amount of the award, the apportionment of the award among the salvors **18–36** can be regulated by agreement, though again such an agreement may be set aside if it is inequitable.[108] Where no valid agreement regulating apportionment has been entered into, the Merchant Shipping Act 1995 s.229 empowers the court to make an apportionment "in such manner as it thinks just". However the section also provides that the court should exercise its discretionary power in accordance with the criteria for assessing an award that are contained in the International Convention on Salvage 1989 art.13.[109] Certain other accepted methods of apportionment are also generally acted upon.[110] If more than one salving vessel is involved, then the ship which was first on the scene may receive a more generous award than one which arrived later. And as between owner, master and crew of the salving vessel, it is usual to award three-quarters to the owner; to award one-third of what remains to the master; and to divide the remainder rateably among the crew.[111]

---

[104] *The Nagasaki Spirit* [1997] A.C. 455 at 468.
[105] See the judgment of Staughton L.J. in the Court of Appeal: *The Nagasaki Spirit* [1996] 1 Lloyd's Rep. 449.
[106] Given the clarity of the articles, resort to the *travaux preparatoires* was unjustified. But they had been referred to in argument without objection, and according to Lord Mustill (at 469) their analysis supported the House's interpretation of art.14.
[107] *Tyne Tugs v Owners of the MV Aldora (The MV Aldora)* [1975] Q.B. 748; *The Rilland* [1979] 1 Lloyd's Rep. 455; *The Ilo* [1982] 1 Lloyd's Rep. 39; *The Helenus and Montagua* [1982] 2 Lloyd's Rep. 261.
[108] *The Enchantress* (1860) Lush. 93; 167 ER 49.
[109] See para.18–32.
[110] For examples of apportionment between salvors, see *The New Australia* [1958] 2 Lloyd's Rep. 35; *The Driade* [1959] 2 Lloyd's Rep. 311; *The Frisia* [1960] 1 Lloyd's Rep. 90.
[111] There is no "general rule" that the master is entitled to one-third; he may be awarded more: *The Golden Falcon* [1990] 2 Lloyd's Rep. 366.

(iii) *Contribution to Payment of the Award by Those Interested in the Salved Property*

18–37 The liability to pay salvage falls on every person interested in the property benefited by the salvage services[112]; but in the case of life salvage, the reward is payable not by those whose lives have been saved but by the owners of the vessel, cargo or apparel preserved.[113] Each interest, therefore, contributes rateably towards the payment of the reward, the amount of each interest's contribution being dependent on the value of the property saved.[114] In the absence of agreement to the contrary, no one interest is liable for more than its rateable proportion of the reward.[115] Hence if a salvor proceeds only against one of the salved interests, he can recover only the proportion of the salvage reward for which that interest is liable.[116] However, the ship may contract an obligation to the salvor to pay the reward in full. Indeed, if the owner or the master of the ship enters into a valid salvage agreement in which the amount of the reward is fixed, the ship will become liable to the salvor for the whole reward so fixed.[117]

(d) *Remedies*

18–38 A salvor's usual and most effective remedy is his maritime lien on the property salved, including freight if this has been saved.[118] The lien arises as soon as the salvage services have been rendered and ranks before all previous liens on the property. In furtherance of this lien, the court has power to arrest the property and, if necessary, sell it to raise the funds needed to satisfy the award[119]; but often an arrest is avoided by an undertaking by those interested in the property to give security.[120]

18–39 In addition to his lien, a salvor has the right to proceed in personam,[121] which he may wish to do if the salved property has not been available for arrest within the jurisdiction.[122] A salvor may also seek a freezing order against the assets within the jurisdiction of the owner of the salved property.[123]

---

[112] *The Fusilier* (1865) B. & L. 341 at 352; 167 E.R. 391 at 398; *Five Steel Barges* (1890) 15 P.D. 142.

[113] International Convention on Salvage 1989 art.11, given force of law in the UK by the Merchant Shipping Act 1995 s.224 and Sch.11 Pt 1.

[114] *The Longford* (1881) 6 P.D. 60.

[115] If there is no such agreement, the rule should not be departed from: *The M. Vatan* [1990] 1 Lloyd's Rep. 336.

[116] *The Mary Pleasants* (1857) Sw. 224; 166 E.R. 1107.

[117] *The Cumbrian* (1887) 6 Asp. M.L.C. 151.

[118] *The Tolten* [1946] P. 135 at 150.

[119] Senior Courts Act 1981 s.21.

[120] See also *Stellar Chartering and Brokerage Inc v Efibanca-Ente Finanziario Interbancario SpA (The Span Terza) (No.2)* [1982] 1 Lloyd's Rep. 225 (CA); [1984] 1 W.L.R. 27 (HL).

[121] *Five Steel Barges* (1890) 15 P.D. 142.

[122] Other ships in the same ownership as the salved vessel may be arrested in order to found jurisdiction and obtain security.

[123] Senior Courts Act 1981 s.37.

3. General Average Contribution

(a) *The Nature of the Liability*

The principle of general average contribution,[124] which requires parties to a **18–40** common maritime adventure to contribute towards losses incurred for the preservation of ship or cargo, has as old a history as any part of the law. Its origin lies in the Rhodian sea law, later embodied in the Digest of Justinian under the title *De Lege Rhodia de Iactu*,[125] which governed mercantile transactions in the Mediterranean and the Adriatic for a millennium before the advent of Christianity. The extant Admiralty records suggest that that court adopted the principles of Rhodian sea law, and compelled parties to maritime adventures to contribute "towards the losses or damages susteyned"[126]; and the English common lawyers, having pirated from the Admiralty much of its mercantile jurisdiction, were content to adopt these principles. In one of the earliest and most influential cases at law, *Birkley v Presgrave*,[127] Lawrence J. propounded a definition of general average loss which closely followed ancient precedent. This definition, which has provided the foundations of the modern English law of general average, runs as follows[128]:

> "All loss which arises in consequence of the extraordinary sacrifices made or expenses incurred for the preservation of the ship and cargo come within general average, and must be borne proportionately by all those who are interested."

The Rhodian law, the Digest of Justinian, the Court of Admiralty, and the **18–41** majority of common law judges have all accepted that general average contribution is based upon "common principles of justice".[129] "Natural justice" requires that those whose property has been saved should indemnify those whose property has been sacrificed for the whole adventure.[130] The liability is not compensatory, however, since mere loss with intention to benefit is insufficient to found a claim,

---

[124] See, generally, F. D. Rose, *General Average: Law and Practice*, 2nd edn (London: LLP, 2005); J.H.S. Cooke and R.R. Cornah, *Lowndes & Rudolf: The Law of General Average and The York-Antwerp Rules*, 13th edn (London: Sweet & Maxwell, 2008). General average (loss to be shared by all) should be distinguished from particular average (loss to be borne by a particular interest).

[125] R.G. Marsden, *Select Pleas in the Court of Admiralty*, vols 1 and 2; (1892) 6 Selden Society 95 (citing *Whitefield v Garrarde* (1540)), and (1897) 11 Selden Society 39 (citing *The Elizabeth* (1575)). But cf. G.O. Sayles, *Select Cases in the Court of King's Bench* (1936) 55 Selden Society 156–157, citing a case decided in 1285.

[126] W.S. Holdsworth, *History of English Law*, vol.1 (London: Methuen, 1903), p.553 and following.

[127] *Birkley v Presgrave* (1801) 1 East. 220; 102 E.R. 86.

[128] *Birkley* 1 East. 228–229; 102 E.R. 90 per Lord Kenyon C.J. Cf. Marine Insurance Act 1906 s.66(1): "A general average loss is a loss caused by or directly consequential on a general average act. It includes a general average expenditure as well as a general average sacrifice." And cf. York-Antwerp Rules 2004 r.A: "There is a general average act when, and only when, any extraordinary sacrifice or expenditure is intentionally and reasonably made or incurred for the common safety for the purpose of preserving from peril the property involved in a common maritime adventure".

[129] *Birkley* 1 East. 227; 102 E.R. at 89.

[130] *Burton v English* (1883) 12 Q.B.D. 218 at 221 per Brett M.R. See also the declaration in *The Elizabeth* (1575), (1897) 11 Selden Society 39 ("ought by lawe and equity to make contribution").

and recovery is allowed only where the defendant's property has been successfully preserved.[131] A better explanation may therefore lie in the law of unjust enrichment,[132] a restitutionary liability being imposed on each owner of a saved interest to pay a proportionate part of the value of the claimant's sacrificed property because this was the necessary cost of rescue and so this is the value of his saved expense.[133]

(b) *The York-Antwerp Rules*

18–42 Although trading nations throughout the world have generally adopted the principle of general average contribution as part of their municipal law, important differences have developed in the application of the principle in various countries. Since the middle of the 19th century, efforts have been made to eliminate these differences. Proposals have varied from a universally adopted code to the total abolition of general average contribution. Neither of these extremes has as yet found acceptance. Instead, a series of rules has been developed with the purpose of resolving differences and, more recently, of reaching agreement on matters of principle. These are known as the York-Antwerp Rules. These rules were first agreed in 1864 and have been reviewed and amended from time to time, most recently in 2004.[134] They have no statutory force, but have found wide acceptance among ship-owning and mercantile interests, and are frequently incorporated into contracts of affreightment by standard clauses which usually also provide for the place of adjustment, often London or New York. Hence the rules are of great importance in practice, since a claimant's right to general average contribution arising at common law may well be modified by the York-Antwerp Rules incorporated into the parties' contract.[135] References will be made here to the 2004 Rules, but it should be borne in mind that if an earlier version has been incorporated into a contract between the parties, then this will govern their relationship and the 2004 Rules will not apply.

---

[131] *Pirie & Co v Middle Dock Co* (1881) 44 L.T. 426 at 430; *Chellew v Royal Commission on the Sugar Supply* [1921] 2 K.B. 627.

[132] F.D. Rose, "General Average as Restitution" (1997) 113 L.Q.R. 569, p.570.

[133] It was unfortunate, though perhaps inevitable in the prevailing intellectual climate, that attempts were made at the end of the 19th century to rationalise general average contribution in terms of implied contract: e.g. *Wright v Marwood* (1881) 7 Q.B.D. 62 at 67 per Bramwell L.J.; cf. *Strang, Steel & Co v A. Scott & Co* (1889) 14 App. Cas. 601 at 608, where Lord Watson left the point open. However, this rationalisation has been rejected by many judges: e.g. *Burton v English* (1883) 12 Q.B.D. 218 at 220–221 per Brett M.R.; *Price* (1881) 44 L.T. 426 at 428 per Williams J.; *Milburn & Co v Jamaica Fruit Transporting and Trading Co of London* [1900] 2 Q.B. 540 at 546 and 550.

[134] For the history and development of the rules, see Cornah, *Lowndes & Rudolf*, pp.43–65; the York Rules 1864 and the York-Antwerp Rules 1877, 1890, 1924, 1950, 1974 (and as amended 1990), 1994 and 2004 are given in *Lowndes & Rudolf* Appendix 2.

[135] *Alma Shipping Corp v Union of India (The Astrea)* [1971] 2 Lloyd's Rep. 494 at 501 per Roskill J.; *Union of India v E.B. Aaby's Rederi A/S (The Evje)* [1975] A.C. 797. General average clauses are not construed narrowly and their normal effect is that general average liability is based on the common law rules as amended by the stated version of the York-Antwerp Rules: *Castle Insurance Co Ltd v Hong Kong Islands Shipping Co (The Potoi Chau)* [1984] A.C. 226 at 238. Where the York-Antwerp Rules apply, however, they will do so to the exclusion of any inconsistent law and practice: e.g. York-Antwerp Rules 2004, Rule of Interpretation.

(c) *Reasonable Action Intentionally Taken in Response to a Real Danger*

A general average act must have been done with the intentional object of   **18–43**
preserving the defendants' interests from peril, the requisite mental state having
been described by Tucker J. as "the exercise by someone of his reasoning powers
and discretion applied to a particular problem with freedom of choice to decide
to act in one out of two or more possible ways."[136] The act must also have been
a reasonable response to the circumstances.[137] American authority holds that the
master alone is the proper person to do a general average act, and that a claim
will not lie in respect of acts which have been done by others[138]; such English
authority as touches on the point agrees that acts done by the master or with his
sanction will certainly suffice, but also suggests that general average acts may be
done by others.[139]

The peril in response to which action is taken must be a real and imminent   **18–44**
danger to the safe prosecution of the common adventure that creates "a necessity
for the sacrifice",[140] although precautionary measures may qualify as general
average acts if the danger is sufficiently imminent.[141] If no danger exists then a
claim may be disallowed although the master acted in the reasonable and honest
belief that his actions were necessary.[142]

(d) *Sacrifice and Expenditure*

The burden is on the claimant to show that he has suffered damage as a direct   **18–45**
consequence of a general average act,[143] either as a result of making an extraordinary sacrifice or incurring extraordinary expenditure. A general average sacrifice
may consist of loss of or damage to ship, including her stores, furniture and
tackle; or loss of or damage to cargo, or loss of freight which would otherwise
have been earned by the shipowner. Familiar examples of sacrifice are the
jettison of cargo or ship's stores; damage to ship or cargo in extinguishing a fire;
use of ship's stores as fuel; cutting away the ship's mast or cables.[144] Liability

---

[136] *Athel Line Ltd v Liverpool & London War Risks Insurance Association Ltd* [1944] K.B. 87 at
94.
[137] *Anglo-Grecian Steam Trading Co Ltd v T. Benyon & Co* (1926) 24 Lloyd's List L.R. 122; York-
Antwerp Rules 2004, Rule Paramount.
[138] *Ralli v Troop*, 157 U.S. 386 (1894); *Minneapolis SS Co v Manistee Co*, 156 F. 424 (1907); *The
Andree Moran* [1930] A.M.C. 631.
[139] *Mouse's Case* (1609) 12 Co. Rep. 63; 77 E.R. 1341 (passenger); *Price v Noble* (1811) 4 Taunt.
123; 128 ER 275 (prize-master); *Papayanni v Grampian SS Co* (1896) 1 Com. Cas. 448 (port
captain). For discussion, see Rose, *General Average*, pp.31–35.
[140] *Pirie & Co v Midland Dock Co* (1881) 44 L.T. 426 at 430. See too *Société Nouvelle d'Armement
v Spillers & Baker Ltd* [1917] 1 K.B. 865.
[141] *Lawrence v Minturn* (1854) 17 How. 100; *Vlassopoulos v British and Foreign Marine Insurance
Co (The Makis)* [1929] 1 K.B. 187 at 199.
[142] *Joseph Watson & Son Ltd v Fireman's Fund Insurance Co of San Francisco* [1922] 2 K.B. 355.
Cf. *The West Imboden* [1936] A.M.C. 696. See too York-Antwerp Rules 2004, Rule VII: "in a
position of peril".
[143] *Corfu Navigation Co v Mobil Shipping Co Ltd (The Alpha)* [1991] 2 Lloyd's Rep. 515. See too
York-Antwerp Rules 2004, Rule E (1).
[144] Although these are not relevantly "sacrificed" if they are in a state of wreck and would therefore
have been lost in any case: *Shepherd v Kottgen* (1877) 2 C.P.D. 578 at 585; York-Antwerp Rules
2004, Rule IV.

incurred under an indemnity clause in a towage contract may be held to be a general average loss.[145] An accident subsequent to the general average act, such as the breaking of a towline and the subsequent liability to tugowners under the indemnity clause, does not break the chain of causation if at the time of the general average act that accident was foreseeable.[146] Hence those losses, damages or expenses which should reasonably have been foreseen as flowing from the general average act constitute "a general average loss ... caused by and directly consequential on a general average act."[147]

18–46   General average expenditure is normally incurred in the first instance by the ship. In the past, important examples have been the cost of salvage operations and port of refuge expenses, but under the York-Antwerp Rules 2004, salvage has been excluded from general average (except where one party to the salvage has paid all or any of the proportion of salvage due from another party),[148] and crew wages and maintenance at a port of refuge are no longer allowed.[149]

(e) *Benefit to Defendant*

18–47   The law of unjust enrichment holds that a defendant's benefit must be valued at the time of receipt.[150] Yet the law of general average, and the York-Antwerp Rules 2004, Rules XVI and XVII, hold that the value of the property sacrificed and of the interests benefited must be assessed at the port of adjustment, which is normally at the end of the voyage.[151] Consequently the effect of events occurring between the general average act and the termination of the adventure must be taken into account. For example, in *Chellew v Royal Commission on the Sugar Supply*,[152] a ship sustained damage to her hull and engines, and so the master put into a port of refuge where he incurred expenses. After the ship left the port of refuge, a fire then broke out and the ship and cargo were lost. The shipowners claimed a general average contribution from the cargo owners for the port of refuge expenses but their claim failed. In our view the best explanation for this result is that the cargo owners were enriched when the expenses were

---

[145] But see *Sea-Land Services Inc v Aetna Insurance Co (The Beauregard)* [1977] 2 Lloyd's Rep. 84 (US CCA, 2nd Circuit).

[146] *Australian Coastal Shipping Commission v Green* [1971] 1 Q.B. 456.

[147] Within the Marine Insurance Act 1906 s.66(1): *Green* [1971] 1 Q.B. 456 at 481. See also *Federal Commerce & Navigation Co Ltd v Eisenerz GmbH (The Oak Hill)* [1970] 2 Lloyd's Rep. 332; [1975] 1 Lloyd's Rep. 105.

[148] York-Antwerp Rules 2004, Rule VI(a). Compare York-Antwerp Rules 1994, Rule VI. Prima facie, expenditure on salvage operations does not give rise to a right of general average contribution in any case, because each interest benefited is only severally liable for its own proportion of such expenditure. But where salvage expenditure is incurred under a salvage agreement, the ship may be liable for the full amount of the expenditure under the agreement.

[149] York-Antwerp Rules 2004, Rules X and XI. Compare York-Antwerp Rules 1994, Rules X and XI.

[150] See paras 4–34——4–42.

[151] *Simonds v White* (1824) 2 B. & C. 805; 107 E.R. 582; *Wavertree Sailing Ship Co Ltd v Love* [1897] A.C. 373.

[152] *Chellew v Royal Commission on the Sugar Supply* [1921] 2 K.B. 627; affirmed [1922] 1 K.B. 12. See too *Tate & Lyle Ltd v Hain Steamship Co* (1934) 151 L.T. 249 at 256; *Green Star Shipping Co Ltd v London Assurance (The Andree)* [1933] 1 K.B. 378 at 390; *The Cheldale* [1947] A.C. 265 at 283, 285 and 312.

incurred, but were entitled to a change of position defence following the loss of their property.[153]

(f) *Remedies*

According to Lord Watson in *Strang, Steel & Co v A. Scott & Co*[154]: **18–48**

"Each owner of jettisoned goods becomes a creditor of ship and cargo saved, and has a direct claim against each of the owners of ship and cargo, for a *pro rata* contribution towards his indemnity, which he can enforce by a direct action."

Shipowners also have a personal claim to recover the value of sacrifices and expenditure from cargo owners, and the common law also gives them a possessory lien over the cargo to support this claim. As noted by Clarke L.J. in *Mora Shipping Inc v Axa Corporate Solutions Assurance SA*[155]:

"Cargo owners have no such lien because they do not have possession of cargo which is laden on board the vessel but owned by others. However, it is the duty of the shipowner to exercise a lien on the cargo, not only for his own contribution but also for that of cargo owners who may be entitled to contribution. Failure to do so exposes the shipowner to liability and damages."

The shipowner's lien is normally released in exchange for the defendant's **18–49** giving an average bond[156] and security in the form of a cash deposit[157] or (more usually) a guarantee from his insurer. An average adjuster will then be appointed to assess the rights and liabilities of all the parties and at the conclusion of this (often lengthy) process, the defendant's insurer will generally pay the contribution that is found to be due.[158] If a shipowner refuses to deliver cargo to a consignee who has offered to pay a reasonable sum by way of deposit or to put up a reasonable security, he may be liable in conversion.[159]

---

[153] As argued in Rose, "General Average as Restitution", p.572. For the view that reliance on receipt of the enrichment is not a prerequisite for the change of position defence, see para.27–28. An alternative explanation suggested in Rose, *General Average*, p.50 is that the cargo owners' restitutionary liability crystallised at the time of the general average act, but that the valuation of this liability was postponed to the end of the voyage, by which time the value of the cargo had decreased to zero. However, this is inconsistent with the general rule governing the timing of benefits, and also seems wrongly to assume that the benefit received by the cargo owners was the value of the cargo rather than the value of their saved expense at the time when the expenditure was incurred. On this view, the value of the defendant ship and cargo owners' respective interests at the end of the voyage is only relevant because this information is needed in order to apportion responsibility for paying the claimant.

[154] *Strang, Steel & Co v A. Scott & Co* (1889) 14 App. Cas. 601 at 606.

[155] *Mora Shipping Inc v Axa Corporate Solutions Assurance SA* [2005] EWCA Civ 1069; [2005] 2 Lloyd's Rep. 769 at [25]. See too *Strang* (1889) 14 App. Cas. 601 at 606.

[156] With the result that a new contractual relationship is created between the parties that supersedes their previous rights and obligations: *The Potoi Chau* [1984] A.C. 226 at 239–241.

[157] On which, see the York-Antwerp Rules 2004, Rule XXII.

[158] Though N.B. the adjustment is not generally binding on the parties: *Wavertree Steamship Co Ltd v Love* [1897] A.C. 373; *Attaleia Marine Co Ltd v Bimeh Iran (The Zeus)* [1993] 2 Lloyd's Rep. 497; *Sameon Co SA v NV Petrofina (The World Hitachi Zosen)* Unreported CA, April 30, 1997.

[159] *Anderson Tritton & Co v Ocean Steamship Co* (1884) 10 App. Cas. 107 at 115.

4. OTHER CASES OF PRESERVATION OF PROPERTY

(a) *Problems with "Agency of Necessity" Reasoning*

18–50 Besides salvage awards and awards of general average contribution, other awards have also been made to claimants who have intervened to preserve another's property in an emergency. Historically, many of these awards have been made on the basis that emergencies can generate an "agency of necessity". However, there are good reasons for doubting the coherence of this supposed doctrine, and for thinking that the cases in which it has been invoked are now best understood in other ways.[160]

18–51 One reason is that the idea of "agency of necessity" derives from two different groups of cases arising out of situations where one party acted for another party's benefit in necessitous circumstances. The first group concerned the question whether the intervener had the power to bind another party to a contract with a third party who agreed to supply the intervener with the means of rescue. The second group concerned the question whether the intervener had the right to recover his own expenditure from the other party. In *China Pacific SA v Food Corp of India (The Winson)*,[161] Lord Diplock considered that it would be "an aid to clarity of legal thinking" if the term "agency of necessity" were only used in cases which were concerned with the first of these questions, because:

> "where reimbursement is the only relevant question all of those conditions that must be fulfilled in order to entitle one person to act on behalf of another in creating direct contractual relationships between that other person and a third party may not necessarily apply".

18–52 We would add that many cases falling within the first group concerned the actions of an intervener who had previously been appointed to act as the other party's agent, whose actions went beyond the scope of his express actual authority, but who would now be said to have had the power to bind his principal to a contract with a third party either because he had implied actual authority to do so,[162] or because he had apparent authority—a type of authority that was not fully recognised until some time after many of the relevant cases were decided.[163]

18–53 Turning to the second group of cases, we also find that "agency of necessity" reasoning requires the courts to ask, first, whether the necessitous circumstances of the case make it appropriate for the law to deem the intervener to have acted as the defendant's agent, and, secondly, whether he is therefore entitled to

---

[160] For general discussion, see P.G. Watts (ed.), *Bowstead and Reynolds on Agency*, 19th edn (London: Sweet & Maxwell, 2010), Ch.4. See too G. McMeel, "Philosophical Foundations of the Law of Agency" (2000) 116 L.Q.R. 387, pp.408–410.

[161] *China Pacific SA v Food Corp of India (The Winson)* [1982] A.C. 939 at 958.

[162] Cf. *Walker v Great Western Railway Co* (1867) L.R. 2 Exch. 228 (implied actual authority to engage doctor to attend employee); *De Bussche v Alt* (1878) 8 Ch.D. 286 (implied actual authority to delegate powers); *Montaignac v Shitta* (1890) 5 App. Cas. 357 (implied actual authority to lend on unusual terms); *Gokal Chand-Jagan Nath v Nand Ram Das-Atma Ram* [1939] A.C. 106 (implied actual authority to give credit in unusual circumstances).

[163] In Diplock L.J.'s seminal decision in *Freeman & Lockyer v Buckhurst Park Properties (Mangal) Ltd* [1964] 2 Q.B. 480.

recover his costs pursuant to the general rule of agency law that every agent is entitled to be reimbursed expenses incurred in the execution of his authority.[164] This is an unnecessarily complex and roundabout way of explaining why a necessitous intervener should be entitled to recover his expenditure. The same result could be reached more simply, without interposing a deemed agency relationship of doubtful authenticity, by holding that necessitous interveners have a general right of recovery under English law.

For all of these reasons we shall not concern ourselves too closely with the   **18–54** question whether or not "agency of necessity" reasoning was used in the cases discussed in the rest of this chapter.

(b) *Shipmasters*

The master of a ship has long had the power to take extraordinary steps to deal   **18–55** with the ship or her cargo in an emergency. For example, he may, to preserve the ship for the remainder of the cargo, dispose of part, and sometimes even the whole, of the cargo in various ways: he may jettison the goods to lighten the ship[165]; he may sell[166] part, or hypothecate[167] part or even the whole of the cargo to raise money to pay for such repairs as are necessary to enable the ship to continue her voyage; and he may enter into a salvage agreement on the part of the cargo owner.[168] The master also has an extensive power in cases of necessity to deal with the ship herself.[169] But in all these cases, whether he is dealing with the ship or with her cargo, it is essential for the master to show not only that his actions were necessary,[170] but also that they were wise and prudent in the circumstances and that it was impracticable for him to communicate with the owner of the ship or her cargo as the case may be.[171] Where he can establish these things, he is entitled to charge the owners with expenses properly incurred by him.[172]

(c) *Bailees*

Bailees have also been entitled to recover expenses they have incurred in   **18–56** preserving the bailor's property. An example is *Great Northern Railway Co v*

---

[164] Reasoning of this sort underpinned e.g. *Tetley v British Trade Corp* (1922) 10 Lloyd's List L.R. 678 and *The Argos* (1873) L.R. 5 P.C. 134 at 165.

[165] *The Gratitudine* (1801) 3 Ch. Rob. 240 at 258; 167 E.R. 450 at 457 per Lord Stowell.

[166] *Gunn v Roberts* (1874) L.R. 9 C.P. 331 at 337 per Brett J.

[167] *The Gratitudine* (1801) 3 Ch. Rob. 240; 167 E.R. 450.

[168] *The Winson* [1982] A.C. 939. And see now International Convention on Salvage 1989 art.6, given force of law in the UK by the Merchant Shipping Act 1995 s.224 and Sch.1, which gives the master or owner the power to sign a salvage contract for cargo.

[169] *Robertson v Carruthers* (1819) 2 Stark. 571; 171 E.R. 739; *The Glasgow* (1856) Swab. 145; *The Australia* (1859) Swab. 480; *Atlantic Mutual Insurance Co v Huth* (1880) 16 Ch.D. 474.

[170] *Australasian Steam Navigation Co v Morse* (1872) L.R. 4 P.C. 222 at 230; *Phelps, James & Co v Hill* [1891] 1 Q.B. 605 at 610; *Prager v Blatspiel, Stamp & Heacock Ltd* [1924] 1 K.B. 566 at 571–572; *John Koch Ltd v C&H Products Ltd* [1956] 2 Lloyd's Rep. 59 at 69; *The Choko Star* [1990] 1 Lloyd's Rep. 516.

[171] *Beldon v Campbell* (1851) 6 Exch. 886 at 890; *Australasian Steam* (1872) L.R. 4 P.C. 222; *The Choko Star* [1990] 1 Lloyd's Rep. 516.

[172] *The Argos* (1873) L.R. 5 P.C. 134 at 165 per Sir Montagu Smith; *Notara v Henderson* (1872) L.R. 7 Q.B. 225; *Hingston v Vent* (1876) 1 Q.B.D. 367.

Swaffield,[173] where the defendant sent his horse by railway but failed to collect it from the station. The stationmaster arranged for the horse to be kept at a nearby livery stable, but the defendant refused to pay the livery charges and after four months the plaintiff railway company therefore paid the charges itself and delivered the horse to the defendant. According to Kelly C.B. in the Court of Exchequer the company[174]:

> "had no choice, unless they would leave the horse at the station or in the high road to his own danger and the danger of other people, but to place him in the care of a livery stable keeper, and as they are bound by their implied contract with the livery stable keeper to satisfy his charges, a right arises in them against the defendant to be reimbursed those charges which they have incurred for his benefit."

18–57   In *The Winson*[175] the Indian Government chartered a vessel to take a cargo of wheat from US ports to Bombay but the vessel stranded on a reef and the master retained salvors on behalf (severally) of the ship and cargo interests. Over a period of two and one-half months the salvors salved six parcels of wheat and stored them in warehouses at the salvors' expense. The shipowners then notified the cargo owners that they were abandoning the voyage and the contract of carriage came to an end. The cargo owners accepted liability for the warehouse storage charges thereafter but submitted that until that time the shipowners were responsible for the charges rather than the cargo owners because the master, when making the salvage agreement, had only been acting on the shipowners' behalf.

18–58   The House of Lords held that possession had been transferred from the shipowners to the salvors when the cargo was off-loaded into barges, and that the direct bailment relationship thereby created between the cargo owners and the salvor had continued to exist until the cargo owners took possession of the wheat from the warehouse owners (who had become sub-bailees of the salvors). According to Lord Diplock[176]:

> "[S]o long as that relationship of bailor and bailee continued to subsist the salvors . . . owed a duty of care to the cargo owner to take such measures to preserve the salved wheat from deterioration by exposure to the elements as a man of ordinary prudence would take for the preservation of his own property. For any breach of such duty the bailee is liable to his bailor in damages for any diminution in value of the goods consequent upon his failure to take such measures; and if he fulfils that duty he has . . . a correlative right to charge the owner of the goods with the expenses reasonably incurred in doing so."

18–59   This dictum was noted in *Guildford BC v Hein*.[177] The defendant was disqualified from having custody of dogs for a particular period and so the claimant

---

[173] *Great Northern Railway Co v Swaffield* (1874) L.R. 9 Ex. 132. See too *Notara v Henderson* (1872) L.R. 7 Q.B. 225; *Garriock v Walker* (1873) 1 R. 100 (Ct of Sess); *Sims & Co v Midland Railway Co* [1913] 1 K.B. 103 at 112; *Coldman v Hill* [1919] 1 K.B. 443 at 456; *Springer v Great Western Railway Co* [1921] 1 K.B. 257; *Sachs v Miklos* [1948] 2 K.B. 23 at 35–36; *Munro v Wilmott* [1949] 1 K.B. 295 at 297.

[174] *Great Northern Railway* (1874) L.R. 9 Ex. 132 at 136.

[175] *The Winson* [1982] A.C. 939; distinguished in *E.N.E. 1 Kos Ltd v Petroleo Brasileiro SA Petrobras (The Kos)* [2010] EWCA Civ 772; [2010] 2 Lloyd's Rep. 409.

[176] *The Winson* [1982] A.C. 939 at 960.

[177] *Guildford BC v Hein* [2005] EWCA Civ 979; [2005] L.G.R. 797.

council lawfully removed them from her custody, becoming bailees of the dogs for the relevant period. When the court orders expired the council sought to retain possession because it was concerned that the defendant would commit further offences and it obtained an injunction prohibiting her from keeping dogs. Clarke L.J. said that the council could not have recovered the costs of keeping the dogs before obtaining the injunction because, once the orders expired, they were obliged to return them to the defendant. After the injunction had been granted, however, they became "bailees of necessity" because they would not be allowed to redeliver the dogs and so they would have a correlative right to the reasonable cost of looking after them "and, perhaps, to a reasonable remuneration for doing so".[178]

Note, finally, that recovery services which remove vehicles from the public   **18–60**
highway and store them at the request of the police may be entitled to recover their costs from the owners. For example, in *Surrey Breakdown Ltd v Knight*,[179] a garage pulled a stolen car out of a pond at the request of the police. Sir Christopher Staughton was prepared to accept that it could recover its costs from the owner *if* necessity compelled its intervention. But the Court of Appeal rejected its claim on the ground that "it cannot reasonably be said that [the garage] in taking the car out of the pond [was] doing so because necessity compelled them to do so without the authority . . . of the owner." There is also a statutory power to levy charges for the removal, storage and disposal of vehicles in the Road Traffic Regulation Act 1984 s.102.

(d) *Tenants*

In *Weigall v Waters*,[180] a lease contained a covenant by the tenant to keep the   **18–61**
property in good repair, "casualties by fire and tempest excepted". The property was damaged in a storm and the tenant paid for the costs of repair. He sought to set off his expenditure against subsequent rent payments, but in decisions that were "heavy [with] procedural and jurisdictional content",[181] the set-off was refused both by the Court of Exchequer (exercising its equity jurisdiction) and by the Court of King's Bench. For both courts the problem was that the amount laid out had to be assessed by a jury and was therefore an uncertain sum. However, they would both have allowed the tenant to set off his expenditure as money paid to the landlord's use if the amount spent had been certain (or had not been challenged), and this is how a case of this kind would now be decided, following *Lee-Parker v Izzet*,[182] and *British Anzani (Felixstowe) Ltd v International Marine Management (UK) Ltd*.[183]

---

[178] *Hein* [2005] EWCA Civ 979; [2005] L.G.R. 797 at [51].
[179] *Surrey Breakdown Ltd v Knight* [1999] R.T.R. 84. See too *White v Troups Transport* [1976] C.L.Y. 33 (County Ct); *Service Motor Polices at Lloyd's v City Recovery Ltd* [1997] EWCA Civ 2073; *Lambert (t/a Lambert Commercials) v Fry* [2000] C.L.Y. 113 (County Ct). And cf. *R. v Howson* (1966) 55 D.L.R. (2d) 582 at 593 (Ontario CA); *Suburban Towing and Equipment Pty Ltd v Suttons Motor Finance Pty Ltd* [2008] NSWSC 1346.
[180] *Weigall v Waters* (1795) 6 T.R. 488; 101 E.R. 663. Earlier proceedings at (1795) 2 Anst. 575; 145 E.R. 971.
[181] *Eller v Grovecrest Investments Ltd* [1995] Q.B. 272 at 276 per Hoffmann L.J.
[182] *Lee-Parker v Izzet* [1971] 1 W.L.R. 1688.
[183] *British Anzani (Felixstowe) Ltd v International Marine Management (UK) Ltd* [1980] Q.B. 137 at 146–148.

(e) *Trustees and Liquidators*

18–62   Unless there is a charging clause in the trust deed, trustees are required to act gratuitously,[184] but the courts have an inherent jurisdiction to make remuneration awards in cases where trustees have gone to unusual lengths to preserve or enhance the value of the trust property, and the power to make such awards also finds statutory expression in the Trustee Act 2000 s.29. The courts' inherent jurisdiction "should be exercised only sparingly and in exceptional cases",[185] and the court should[186]:

> "balance two influences which are to some extent in conflict. The first is that the office of trustee is, as such, gratuitous; the court will accordingly be careful to protect the interests of the beneficiaries against claims by the trustees. The second is that it is of great importance to the beneficiaries that the trust should be well administered. If therefore the court concludes, having regard to the nature of the trust, the experience and skill of a particular trustee and to the amounts which he seeks to charge when compared with what other trustees might require to be paid for their services and to all the other circumstances of the case, that it would be in the interests of the beneficiaries to increase the remuneration, then the court may properly do so."

18–63   In *Foster v Spencer*,[187] remuneration was awarded to the trustees of a decaying cricket ground that they were finally able to sell with planning permission after 20 years of work that went far beyond their contemplation when they were appointed as unpaid trustees. The court held that retrospective remuneration was appropriate because the true extent of the trustees' services could not be known until it was possible to market and sell the land, and because no money was available to pay them any remuneration for a long period.

18–64   The principles governing special trustee remuneration have also been applied in cases involving company liquidators. For example, in *Re Berkeley Applegate (Investment Consultants) Ltd*,[188] a liquidator was remunerated and reimbursed out of the company's own assets and assets which it held on trust for others, the

---

[184] The underlying reason for this rule is to ensure that the interest and duty of a trustee are not put into conflict: *Bray v Ford* [1896] A.C. 44 at 51–52.

[185] *Re Worthington (Deceased)* [1954] 1 W.L.R. 526 at 530 per Upjohn J.

[186] *Re Duke of Norfolk's ST* [1982] 1 Ch. 61 at 79 per Fox L.J. Note that the beneficiaries' consent is not required, but their objections will be considered, as in e.g. *Polly Peck International Plc v Henry* [1999] 1 B.C.L.C. 407.

[187] *Foster v Spencer* [1996] 2 All ER 672. See too *Robinson v Pett* (1734) 3 P. Wms 249; 24 E.R. 1049; *Marshall v Holloway* (1820) 2 Swan. 432; 36 E.R. 681; *Forster v Ridley* (1864) 4 De G. J. & S. 452; 46 E.R. 993; *Re Freeman's ST* (1887) 37 Ch. D. 148; *Re Masters* [1953] 1 W.L.R. 81; *Re Drexel Burnham Lambert UK Pension Plan* [1995] 1 W.L.R. 32; *Pearson v Parklane Holdings Ltd* Unreported NZ CA, November 26, 1997; *Rathbone Trust Co (Jersey) Ltd v Kane* [2004] JRC 041 at [28]; *HSBC Trustees (CI) Ltd v Rearden* [2005] JRC 130; *Landau v Anburn Trustees Ltd* [2007] J.L.R. 250 (Royal Ct of Jersey); *Regent Trust Co Ltd v RJD* [2009] JRC 117.

[188] *Re Berkeley Applegate (Investment Consultants) Ltd* [1989] 1 Ch. 32. See too *Ontario (Securities Commission) v Consortium Construction Inc* (1992) 93 D.L.R. (4th) 321 (Ontario CA); *Re G. B. Nathan & Co Pty Ltd (In Liquidation)* (1991) 24 NSWLR 674; *13 Coromandel Place Pty Ltd v CL Custodians Pty Ltd (In Liquidation)* [1999] FCA 144; (1999) 30 A.C.S.R. 377; *Re Application of Sutherland* [2004] NSWSC 798; (2004) 50 A.C.S.R. 297; *Dean-Willcocks v Nothintoohard Pty Ltd (In Liquidation)* [2006] NSWCA 311; *Coad v Wellness Pursuit Pty Ltd (In Liquidation)* [2009] WASCA 68; *Trio Capital Ltd (Admin. App.) v ACT Super Management Pty Ltd* [2010] NSWSC 941; (2010) 79 A.C.S.R. 425. And cf. *Monks v Poynice Pty Ltd* (1987) 8 N.S.W.L.R. 662, where an award was made to an invalidly appointed receiver.

court holding that if "the liquidator had not done this work, it is inevitable that the work, or at all events a great deal of it, would have had to be done by someone else".[189]

5. PRESERVATION OF CREDIT

A third party may accept a bill of exchange for the honour of the drawer.[190] But   **18–65** his acceptance can only be made after a protest for non-acceptance[191] and it is subject to the consent of the holder of the bill,[192] for the latter may wish to exercise his right of recourse which arises on non-acceptance.

The acceptor for honour undertakes that he will: **18–66**

> "on due presentment, pay the bill according to the tenor of his acceptance, if it is not paid by the drawee, provided it has been duly presented for payment, and protested for non-payment, and that he receives notice of these facts."[193]

If the bill is so paid, the payer for honour is subrogated to, and succeeds to, both the rights and duties of the holder as regards the party for whose honour he pays and all parties liable to that party.[194] This appears to be another manifestation of necessitous intervention.[195] The stranger's intervention takes the form of fulfilment of the contractual duty of the person assisted; and since his action preserves the latter's commercial credit which would otherwise be endangered, he is entitled to reimbursement in respect of his expenditure.

6. CARE OF THE SICK AND MENTALLY INCAPABLE

The courts have often made awards to claimants who have provided medical and   **18–67** nursing care or the necessaries of life to the sick and incapacitated, sometimes against the people to whom they have supplied these benefits, and sometimes against third parties who were under a legal duty to provide them. An example

---

[189] *Re Berkeley* [1989] 1 Ch. 32 at 47.
[190] Bills of Exchange Act 1882 s.65(1). On notice of dishonour, see *Eaglehill Ltd v J. Needham Builders Ltd* [1973] A.C. 992.
[191] *Vandewall v Tyrrell* (1827) M. & M. 87; 173 E.R. 1090; *Geralopulo v Wieler* (1851) 10 C.B. 690; 138 E.R. 272; Bills of Exchange Act 1882 s.65(1).
[192] *Mitford v Walcot* (1700) 12 Mod. 410; 88 E.R. 1416; Bills of Exchange Act 1882 s.65(1).
[193] Bills of Exchange Act 1882 s.66(1).
[194] Bills of Exchange Act 1882 s.68(5).
[195] Cf. *Hawtayne v Bourne* (1841) 7 M. & W. 595 at 599; 151 E.R. 905 at 908, where Parke B., although he took a most restricted view of the rights of the necessitous intervener, accepted the link between the rights of the acceptor for honour and of the master of a ship who deals with the ship or cargo in an emergency.

of the first type of case is *Matheson v Smiley*,[196] where a surgeon unsuccessfully treated a man who had intentionally shot himself in order to commit suicide, and was permitted by the Manitoba Court of Appeal to recover a fee from the dead man's estate. The case was argued in the now-outmoded language of implied contract, and the executrix argued that there could be no liability because the deceased had not requested the surgeon's services—indeed, by his actions he had shown that he did not want them. However the court rejected this argument, citing Lord Blackburn's judgment in *Metropolitan Asylum District Managers v Hill (No.2)* for the proposition that[197]:

> "Those who have the charge of a sick person, if he is helpless (whether the disease be infectious or not) are, at common law, under a legal obligation to do, to the best of their ability, what is necessary for the preservation of the sick person. And the sick person, if not helpless, is bound to do so for his own sake."

Matheson was decided at a time when suicide was an offence, and it may be doubted whether Lord Blackburn's second proposition is still good law in the light of modern ideas about patient self-determination and freedom to reject medical treatment, now embodied in English law by the Mental Capacity Act 2005 ss.24–26.[198] Nevertheless, his first proposition was effectively treated as good law in a more recent Canadian case, *Skibinski v Community Living British Columbia*,[199] which exemplifies the second type of case referred to above.

18–68   *Skibinski* concerned a 48-year-old woman with serious medical problems and developmental disabilities. For 16 years she lived with her mother, and was provided with a day programme of care by the claimant, who was a professional caregiver. This care was paid for by the defendant, which is a quasi-autonomous organisation funded by the provincial government that provides services to adults with developmental disabilities. Following an episode when the patient attacked her mother's neighbours, she was compulsorily detained in a psychiatric hospital, and following her discharge, the claimant took her into residential care at her

---

[196] *Matheson v Smiley* [1932] 2 D.L.R. 787. It may be that this category also takes in a series of Canadian cases where claims against a deceased person's estate have been allowed by relatives or friends who provided or paid for medical and nursing care (along with companionship and domestic services) at the end of the deceased person's life. See e.g. *Clarkson v McCrossen Estate* (1995) 122 D.L.R. (4th) 239 (British Columbia CA); *Norland v Phillips Estate* Unreported Ontario Sup Ct, January 18, 2006; *Gould v Royal Trust Corp of Canada* [2009] BCSC 1528. In cases of this kind the carer frequently acts to her detriment in reliance on a representation that she will receive a share of the deceased person's estate, and for this reason the English cases are generally resolved under the doctrine of proprietary estoppel, as in e.g. *Jennings v Rice* [2002] EWCA Civ 159; [2003] 1 P. & C.R. 100.

[197] *Metropolitan Asylum District Managers v Hill (No.2)* (1881) 6 App. Cas. 193 at 204.

[198] See too *Re T (Adult: Refusal of Treatment)* [1993] Fam. 95; *Airedale NHS Trust v Bland* [1993] A.C. 789 at 864 and 891–894; *Re C (Adult: Refusal of Treatment)* [1994] 1 W.L.R. 290; *Re AK (Medical Treatment: Consent)* [2001] 1 F.L.R. 129 at 136. For a recent discussion see A.R. Maclean, "Advance Directives and the Rocky Waters of Anticipatory Decision-Making" (2008) 16 Medical Law Rev. 1. And cf. *Soldiers Memorial Hospital v Sanford* [1934] 2 D.L.R. 334 (Nova Scotia Sup Ct).

[199] *Skibinski v Community Living British Columbia* [2010] BCSC 1500; (2010) 13 B.C.L.R. (5th) 271. See too *Simmons v Wilmott* (1800) 3 Esp. 91; 170 E.R. 549; *Lamb v Bunce* (1815) 4 M. & S. 275; 105 E.R. 836; *Tomlinson v Bentall* (1826) 5 B. & C. 738; 108 E.R. 274; *Hastings v Seman's Village* [1946] 4 D.L.R. 695 (Sasketchewan CA); *Mollgaard v ARCIC* [1999] 3 N.Z.L.R. 735 (NZ High Ct).

mother's request. She expected that the defendant would also pay for this additional care, but in the event the parties could not agree on the amount to be paid and she provided care for three years without payment. The judge held that her action in taking the patient into residential care was a necessitous intervention, taking into account all the circumstances of the patient's committal and discharge from hospital, her exigent needs, the claimant's skills and experience, the claimant's existing close relationship with her, and the lack of ready suitable care alternatives.

Following *Matheson* this finding was open to the judge although the defendant **18–69** had told the claimant that it would not pay for the care following the breakdown of their contractual negotiations. However, the claimant could only recover the reasonable costs of eight months' care on the ground of necessity because[200]:

> "[T]he law of necessitous intervention affirms assistance in pressing circumstances. It was not conceived to govern situations spanning years. Sometimes an extended period of critical medical care, for example after a serious accident, might extend for months. But the law of necessitous intervention cannot encompass the three year time period in the case at bar. While C.L.B.C.'s duty to provide funding for Ms Savone's care, combined with the lengthy history of its provisioning of funds for Ms Savone's care and other considerations renders the cost of Ms Savone's care needs an inevitable expense . . . the plaintiff cannot base a claim for unjust enrichment for the entire period of her care on the fact that her care for a time can be characterized as a necessitous intervention."

This finding may be compared with a series of English cases following the **18–70** House of Lords' decision in *Hunt v Severs*,[201] that the voluntary carers of tort victims have the right to participate in the fruits of tort actions in which damages have been awarded to reflect the cost of the care.[202] This rule produces the same effect as would be achieved if the tort damages recoverable by the victim from the tortfeasor were reduced by the value of the care, and the carer were given a direct claim against the tortfeasor on the ground of necessitous intervention. This effect is also achieved by the Health and Social Care (Community Health and Standards) Act 2003 Pt 3, which sets up an Injury Costs Recovery Scheme that requires tortfeasors to reimburse the NHS for the costs of treating their victims.[203] In none of these cases, however, have carers been debarred from recovering because their interventions have ceased to be needed with the passing of time. Possibly there is a factual difference between these cases, where there is

---

[200] *Skibinski* [2010] BCSC 1500; (2010) 13 B.C.L.R. (5th) 271 at [299].
[201] *Hunt v Severs* [1994] 2 A.C. 350 at 358–363. See too *H v S* [2002] EWCA 792; [2003] Q.B. 965; *Hughes v Lloyd* [2007] EWHC 3133 (Ch); [2008] W.T.L.R. 473; *Drake v Foster Wheeler Ltd* [2010] EWHC 2004 (QB); [2011] 1 All E.R. 63 at [31]–[43]. For detailed discussion, see S. Degeling, *Restitutionary Rights to Share in Damages: Carers' Claims* (Cambridge: CUP, 2003). Note that the principle does not apply in cases where the carer is herself the tortfeasor.
[202] This portion of the damages must be held on trust for the carer. Legislation was proposed to replace this trust with a personal liability: Department of Constitutional Affairs, *The Law on Damages* (CP 9/07, 2007) pp.48–50; Ministry of Justice, *Civil Law Reform Bill: Consultation* (CP 53/09, 2009) p.64 and Annex A, Draft Civil Law Reform Bill, cl.7. But it was subsequently decided not to proceed with this legislation: Ministry of Justice, *Civil Law Reform Bill: Response to Consultation* (CP(R.) CP 53/09 2011) p.40.
[203] See paras 19–42—19–44 for discussion.

no alternative carer available, and *Skibinski*, where different care arrangements could have been made after eight months had elapsed.

18–71   Note, finally, that the Mental Capacity Act 2005 s.8, provides that a person intervening on behalf of a mentally incapacitated person has the power to pledge his credit and use his money for acts in connection with his or her care or treatment; the person intervening may also be entitled to an indemnity for expenditure incurred.[204]

7. BURIAL OF THE DEAD

18–72   The personal representatives of the deceased are primarily responsible for his burial[205]; and for this expenditure they will be reimbursed out of the estate before all other claims.[206] Two special cases require mention. Before 1883 a husband was responsible, at common law, for the burial of his wife.[207] This responsibility now[208] falls on her personal representatives, who are entitled to be reimbursed out of her estate before all other claims.[209] Presumably, if she does not leave a sufficient estate, her husband is responsible under the old common law rule. Secondly, a parent is probably responsible for the burial of a deceased child, at least if the parent has sufficient means.[210]

18–73   Apart from these primary rules, it has been suggested that at common law any householder under whose roof the body lies is responsible for the decent burial of that body.[211] But under modern legislation, it is the duty of local authorities to bury or cremate the body of any person found dead in their area, if it appears that no suitable arrangements for the disposal of the body are being made.[212]

18–74   In the past, cases have occurred where those primarily responsible have not carried out their duty to bury the deceased and others have intervened to carry out this task. It may not be known in time who are the personal representatives, or

---

[204] Earlier days: *Howard v Digby* (1834) 2 Cl. & F. 634; 6 E.R. 1293; *Williams v Wentworth* (1842) 5 Beav. 325; 49 E.R. 603; *Nelson v Duncombe* (1846) 9 Beav. 211; 50 E.R. 323; and cf. *Guardians of West Ham Union v Pearson* (1890) 62 L.T. 638 (where the defendant was not a lunatic but was incapacitated by *delirium tremens*).

[205] 2 Bl. Com. 508. How far this duty is enforceable at law is uncertain; see *Rogers v Price* (1829) 3 Y. & J. 28 at 35–36; 148 E.R. 1080 at 1083–1084 per Hullock B.

[206] Administration of Estates Act 1925 ss.33(2) and 34(3), Sch.1 Pt 1; see also *Edwards v Edwards* (1834) 2 C. & M. 612 at 615 per Parke B.

[207] *Jenkins v Tucker* (1788) 1 H. Bl. 90; 126 E.R. 55. This was so even where she had a separate estate. Equity would not allow a husband to throw on to that estate the expense of burial: see *Bertie v Chesterfield* (1722) 9 Mod. 31; 88 E.R. 296; *Gregory v Lockyer* (1821) 6 Madd. 90; 56 E.R. 1024.

[208] *Rees v Hughes* [1946] K.B. 517.

[209] *Re M'Myn* (1886) 33 Ch.D. 575; *Rees v Hughes* [1946] K.B. 517.

[210] *R. v Vann* (1851) 2 Den. 325; 169 E.R. 523; *Clarke v London General Omnibus Co* [1906] 2 K.B. 648 at 659 per Lord Alverstone C.J.; cf. Farewell L.J. at 663.

[211] *R. v Stewart* (1840) 12 Ad. & El. 773 at 778; 113 E.R. 1007 at 1010 per Lord Denman C.J.

[212] Public Health (Control of Disease) Act 1984 ss.46–48; local authorities arrange for a few thousand welfare funerals under this statute each year, but it is now much more common for funeral grants to be made out of the social fund to pay for the burial of those on income-related benefits, under the Social Security (Contributions and Benefits) Act 1992 s.138, as discussed in *Stewart v Secretary of State for Work and Pensions* [2011] EWCA Civ 907 at [1]–[8]. If a seaman dies abroad then the person who last employed him shall be liable to pay the expenses of his burial or cremation: Merchant Shipping Act 1995 s.73(2).

the husband of a deceased woman may be abroad or otherwise inaccessible. In these circumstances, it has generally been held that the stranger may recover his reasonable expenses from the person primarily responsible for the burial. The cases form a common pattern. From them the elements of necessitous intervention plainly emerge. The stranger is justified by the necessity of prompt action, the public interest in the disposal of the body and the impracticability of communicating with the person on whom lies the primary responsibility to bury the body.

An example is provided by *Shallcross v White*.[213] A testator died of typhus   **18–75** while staying in the house of a friend. On the doctor's advice, the friend and his family were then obliged to remove themselves into a hotel while the house was fumigated, cleansed and whitewashed, and the bed and furniture of the room in which the testator died were destroyed and burnt to prevent infection. The costs of all this were recovered out of the testator's estate, Lord Langdale M.R. stating that there was "both a necessity to do it, in order to prevent the probable mischief, and there was also a duty on the persons surrounding this gentleman to perform it".[214]

8. TOWARDS A GENERAL DOCTRINE

(a) *Limits of the Claim*

As we said at the start of this chapter, it remains to be seen whether the English   **18–76** courts will forge a general doctrine from the foregoing cases, but in our view this would be a desirable step for them to take. The limits of any claim should, however, be carefully defined; and the nature of these limits will inevitably reflect the extent to which courts wish to encourage (or to refrain from discouraging) interventions to preserve the lives and property of others in an emergency. It seems likely that some or all of the following limits would be placed on a general doctrine.

First, the likelihood of imminent harm to the defendant's property or person   **18–77** must have been great.[215] The analogy of maritime law suggests that the courts will hold that there was an emergency if there was "no immediate risk, no immediate danger; but there was a possible contingency that serious consequences might have ensued".[216]

---

[213] *Shallcross v White* (1850) 12 Beav. 558; 50 E.R. 1174. See too *Besfich v Coggil* (1628) 1 Palm. 559; 81 E.R. 1219; cf. *Church v Church*, cited in T. Raym. 260, and Vin. Abr. Executors B a 24. (In cases of necessity a stranger may direct the funeral, and defray the expenses out of the deceased's effects, without rendering himself liable as executor *de son tort*). Later decisions include *Jenkins v Tucker* (1788) 1 H. Bl. 90; 126 E.R. 55; *Ambrose v Kerrison* (1851) 10 C.B. 776; 138 E.R. 307; *Tugwell v Heyman* (1812) 3 Camp. 298; 170 E.R. 1389; *Rogers v Price* (1829) 3 Y. & J. 28; 148 E.R. 1080; *Green v Salmon* (1838) 8 Ad. & El. 348; 112 E.R. 869; *Davey v Rural Municipality of Cornwallis* [1931] 2 D.L.R. 80 (Manitoba CA); *Croskery v Gee* [1957] N.Z.L.R. 586 at 588–589.
[214] *Shallcross* 12 Beav. at 561; 50 E.R. at 1176.
[215] *The Bona* [1895] P. 125 (CA); *Sachs v Miklos* [1948] 2 K.B. 23 at 36 (CA); *Surrey Breakdown* [1999] R.T.R. 84 at 88 (CA).
[216] *The Elia Constance* (1864) 33 L.J. Adm. 189 at 193 per Dr Lushington. A cautious court may well conclude that the contingency should be *probable* rather than *possible*.

18–78   Secondly, it must have been impracticable for the claimant to communicate with the defendant,[217] and recovery should not generally be allowed where intervention "was contrary to the known wishes of the assisted person".[218] However, in the latter case recovery might exceptionally be allowed if the defendant's rejection of the claimant's intervention was against the public interest.[219]

18–79   Thirdly, the claimant must have been an appropriate person to act in the circumstances,[220] although at the same time he must not have owed a pre-existing duty to intervene, for example because he was a member of the emergency services.[221]

18–80   Fourthly, a claimant should be able to recover only in respect of expenses reasonably incurred in the circumstances.[222]

18–81   Fifthly, it should be a bar to recovery that a claimant has acted for his own benefit and only incidentally conferred a benefit on the defendant in the course of doing so.[223]

18–82   Finally, there is some authority to suggest that the intervener must also show that he intended to charge for his services.[224] In our view, however, it is illogical to conclude from the fact that it is good public policy to encourage intervention, that the burden of proving an intention to charge should be imposed on the intervener; the burden should rather lie on the assisted person to prove that the intervener intended to act gratuitously.[225]

(b) *Remedies*

18–83   As and when this issue falls to be considered, it will be necessary to distinguish three possible measures of recovery: reward, restitution of enrichment and reimbursement of expenses.

18–84   It seems possible that rewards will remain confined to maritime salvors, who are rewarded in order to provide a real and positive incentive to "seafaring folk

---

[217] *Springer v Great Western Railway Co* [1921] 1 K.B. 257; *The Winson* [1982] A.C. 939 at 961; *The Choko Star* [1990] 1 Lloyd's Rep. 516 at 525. Cf. *Gwilliam v Twist* [1895] 2 Q.B. 84 (drunken bus driver ordered to stop driving and owner of bus could have been contacted before replacement driver asked to take over).

[218] *Re F (Mental Patient: Sterilisation)* [1990] 2 A.C. 1 at 75.

[219] As in e.g. *Great Northern Railway* (1874) L.R. 9 Exch. 132; *The Kangaroo* [1918] P. 327; *Matheson* [1932] 2 D.L.R. 787 (Manitoba CA); *Hein* [2005] EWCA 979; *Skibinski* [2010] BCSC 1500; (2010) 13 B.C.L.R. (5th) 271. Cf. BGB § 679, and other sources cited in R. Zimmermann, *The Law of Obligations: Roman Foundations of the Civilian Tradition* (Oxford: OUP, 1996), p.448 fn.118.

[220] *Re Rhodes* (1890) 44 Ch. D. 94 at 107 (CA); *Macclesfield Corp v Great Central Railway Co* [1911] 2 K.B. 528 at 541; *Skibinski* [2010] BCSC 1500; (2010) 13 B.C.L.R. (5th) 271 at [308]. Cf. *Hardwicke v Hudson* [1999] 3 All E.R. 426 at 435–436 (CA).

[221] See paras 18–15—18–16.

[222] *Jenkins* (1788) 1 H. Bl. 90; 126 E.R. 55 (burial costs recoverable if suited to deceased's station in life); *Re Rhodes* (1890) 44 Ch. D. 94 at 105 (CA) (cost of necessaries supplied to an *incapax* recoverable if suited to her station in life); *White v Troups Transport* [1976] C.L.Y. 33 (County Ct) (only hire cost of smallest crane needed to remove lorry from highway can be recovered).

[223] Cf. *Tanguay v Price* (1906) 37 S.C.R. 657; *Warfel v Vondersmith*, 101 A. 2d 736 (1954).

[224] *Re Rhodes* (1884) 44 Ch.D. 94.

[225] cf. the Ulpian text D.3.5.4: *nisi donandi animo fideiussit.*

to take risks for the purpose of saving property",[226] but who are rewarded only if their services are successful.[227] In our view the courts are correct to think that it is essential to encourage individuals to salvage property on the high seas, but we doubt that there is the same need to encourage intervention in other situations.

In previous editions of this work, it was argued that other types of intervener **18–85** should not be awarded restitution of enrichment and should be restricted to recovery of their reasonable costs.[228] These costs should be recoverable even if the rescue attempt was unsuccessful, on the basis that a reasonable defendant would have authorised the claimant's expenditure, accepting the risk that it might not be successful. However, the costs that an intervener can recover should be limited to those expenses which were reasonably incurred in, and which actually contributed to, the intervener's attempts to preserve the property in an emergency, nor should he be entitled to recover any damage that he suffers through his intervention. Suppose, for example, that a man runs into a collapsing building to rescue a child, that his scarf is ruined when he uses it to bind the child's wounds, that he suffers a broken arm when he is hit by falling masonry and that his suit is also ruined during the rescue. On the approach previously advocated in this book, only the cost of the scarf would be recoverable.

However, we share Jeroen Kortmann's view that there is no good reason to **18–86** limit the claim in this way, and that a better approach would be to follow French and German law in aiming to neutralise the whole cost of the intervention by awarding compensation for the full loss.[229] We should also add that in the event that the English courts chose instead to award restitution of benefits rather than compensation for loss, the relevant benefit should usually be the saved cost of employing another person to perform the relevant service, rather than, for example, the value of preserved property that already belonged to the defendant.[230]

---

[226] *The Sandefjord* [1953] 2 Lloyd's Rep. 557 at 561 per Willmer J.
[227] See para.18–18.
[228] *Goff & Jones: The Law of Restitution*, 7th edn, para.17.014. See too G. Jones, *Restitution in Public and Private Law* (London: Sweet & Maxwell, 1991), pp.164–165.
[229] Kortmann, *Altruism in Private Law*, pp.179–183. See too RGZ 167, 83 (May 7, 1941) and other cases discussed in Dawson, "Rewards for the Rescue of Human Life", pp.148–154.
[230] Cf. discussion at para.5–26.

CHAPTER 19

SECONDARY LIABILITY: OVERVIEW

1. INTRODUCTION

It often happens that a claimant and a defendant are both legally liable to pay a **19–01** third party in respect of the same debt or damage. The third party may not accumulate recoveries by enforcing his rights against both of them in full, but to maximise his chances of recovery he is allowed to recover in full from either of them. If his choice falls on the claimant, who pays him in full, the claimant may be entitled to recover some or all of his payment from the defendant on the ground that the defendant is the person who should ultimately bear some or all of the burden of paying the third party: in the language of the cases, the defendant is "primarily" and the claimant only "secondarily" liable for the defendant's share of their common obligation.[1]

The type of action brought in this situation varies according to whether the **19–02** claimant's payment discharges the defendant's liability to the third party. The rules on discharge are discussed in Ch.5.[2] If the defendant's liability is not discharged, then the claimant may be entitled to take over the third party's subsisting right of action against the defendant by subrogation, and to enforce this right for his own benefit. There is only one situation where claimants regularly exercise rights of this kind, namely where an indemnity insurer pays its insured in respect of an insured loss and acquires the insured's subsisting rights against a third party who was also liable for this loss.[3] Indemnity policies usually contain subrogation clauses entitling the insurer to do this, but indemnity insurers are also given subrogation rights as a pre-emptive measure by the law of unjust enrichment. Where the insured is paid by the insurer, but can still recover from the third party in respect of the same loss, the insured can choose whether to enforce his rights against the third party, or to forbear from suing him. If he enforces his rights, then he may obtain more than a full indemnity for his loss by accumulating recoveries from the insurer and the third party. If he does not, then the third party will effectively be exonerated from liability. Neither outcome is generally regarded as satisfactory by the courts, and so they transfer the insured's rights to the insurer as a prophylactic measure.

---

[1] *Duncan, Fox & Co v North and South Wales Bank* (1880) 6 App. Cas. 1 at 11 (HL); *Brook's Wharf and Bull Wharf Ltd v Goodman Bros* [1937] 1 K.B. 534 at 544 (CA); *Niru Battery Manufacturing Co v Milestone Trading Ltd (No.2)* [2004] EWCA Civ 487; [2004] 2 All E.R. (Comm.) 289 at [68]; *Berghoff Trading Ltd v Swinbrook Developments Ltd* [2009] EWCA Civ 413; [2009] 2 Lloyd's Rep. 233 at [24]–[26].

[2] See paras 5–38—5–60.

[3] A further example arises in the law of bills of exchange. Under the Bills of Exchange Act 1882 s.59(2), the acceptor of a bill is not discharged from liability when the holder is paid by the drawer or indorser; and s.52(4) provides that when the bill is paid the holder must deliver it up to the party paying it who can then enforce the bill as the new holder.

19–03   Where the defendant's liability is discharged, the claimant can bring an action in his own right for contribution or reimbursement. These are restitutionary remedies which reverse unjust enrichment.[4] There is no substantial difference between contribution claims and reimbursement claims, and it is only the quantum of the claimant's right which distinguishes them.[5] If the defendant has charged his property to secure his obligation to the third party, and this obligation is extinguished by the claimant's payment, then the law may also generate a new right in the claimant's favour which mirrors the third party's extinguished rights as holder of the securities: the claimant is treated, by a fiction, as though the securities have not been discharged but have instead been assigned to the claimant. Confusingly, this remedy is also termed subrogation, but it differs from the subrogation remedy given to indemnity insurers, which entails a transfer of subsisting rights.

19–04   For historical reasons, the law in this area is fragmented into several sets of rules deriving from the common law and statute. Ultimately, these rules are all explicable by reference to a single set of principles, but a claimant needs to know which rules govern his claim. Different pleading rules may govern his proceedings, according to the type of action that he brings. Some recovery regimes are also exclusive: most importantly the Civil Liability (Contribution) Act 1978 s.7(3) states that rights conferred by the statute supersede any rights which the claimant would otherwise have at common law. Also different limitation rules may apply to different types of claim: for example, the Limitation Act 1980 s.2 provides that a claimant has only two years within which to claim under the 1978 Act, rather than the six years that he would otherwise have at common law. In the rest of this chapter we therefore examine the different recovery regimes and the interplay between them. In Ch.20 we discuss the principles that underpin all

---

[4] English cases locating the claimant's right in the law of unjust enrichment are: *Westdeutsche Landesbank Girozentale v Islington LBC* [1996] A.C. 669 at 727; *Grupo Torras SA v Al-Sabah (No.5)* [2001] Lloyd's Rep. Bank. 36 at 64 (CA); *Société Eram Shipping Co Ltd v Compagnie Internationale de Navigation* [2001] 2 All E.R. (Comm.) 721 at 735–736 (CA); *Dubai Aluminium Co Ltd v Salaam* [2002] UKHL 48; [2003] 2 A.C. 366 at [72] and [76]; *Berghoff Trading* [2009] EWCA Civ 413; [2009] 2 Lloyd's Rep. 233 at [24]. Canadian and Scottish cases to this effect are: *County of Carleton v City of Ottawa* [1965] S.C.R. 663 at 668; *Regional Municipality of Peel v Ontario* (1990) 75 D.L.R. (4th) 523 at 525 (Ontario CA); affirmed [1992] 3 S.C.R. 762; *Caledonia North Sea Ltd v London Bridge Engineering Ltd*, 2000 S.L.T. 1123 at 1141 (Ct of Sess. IH); affirmed on a different point [2002] 1 Lloyd's Rep. 553 (HL); *Strata Plan LMS 1751 v Scott Management Ltd* [2010] BCCA 192; (2010) 3 B.C.L.R. (5th) 326. Australian courts formerly took the same view: *A.M.P. Workers' Compensation Services (NSW) Ltd v Q.B.E. Insurance Ltd* (2001) 53 N.S.W.L.R. 35 at 40 (NSWCA); *Burke v L.F.O.T. Pty Ltd* [2002] HCA 17; (2002) 209 C.L.R. 282 at [38]; but see now *Friend v Brooker* [2009] HCA 21; (2009) 239 C.L.R. 129.

[5] *Edmunds v Wallingford* (1885) 14 Q.B.D. 811 at 814–815 (CA); *Whitham v Bullock* [1939] 2 All E.R. 310 at 315 (CA); *Dawson v Bankers and Traders Insurance Co Ltd* [1957] V.R. 491 at 502 (Victoria Sup Ct); *Re Downer Enterprises Ltd* [1974] 1 W.L.R. 1460 at 1468–1469; *Ronex Properties Ltd v John Laing Construction Ltd* [1983] Q.B. 398 at 407 (CA); *Aetna Insurance Co v Canadian Surety Co* (1994) 114 D.L.R. (4th) 577 at 622 (Alberta CA); *Cockburn v G.I.O. Finance Ltd (No.2)* (2001) 51 N.S.W.L.R. 624 at 631 (NSWCA). Cf. *Caledonia v London Bridge* 2000 S.L.T. 1123 at 1141 (Ct of Sess, IH) not considered on appeal: *Caledonia North Sea Ltd v British Telecommunications Plc* [2002] 1 Lloyd's Rep. 553 (HL). Consistently with this, the courts can make 100% contribution awards, which are essentially identical with reimbursement awards: e.g. *Baynard v Woolley* (1855) 20 Beav. 583 at 585–586; 52 E.R. 729 at 730; *Bahin v Hughes* (1886) 31 Ch. D. 390 at 395 (CA); *Beswick v Kirby* Unreported QBD, January 29, 1985; *Nelhams v Sandells Maintenance Ltd* [1996] P.I.Q.R. 52 (CA); *The Sincerity S* [1996] 2 Lloyd's Rep. 503.

claims for contribution and reimbursement, and in Ch.21 we discuss insurers' subrogation claims. Claims to acquire extinguished security rights via subrogation are considered in Ch.39.

2. MAPPING THE LAW OF CONTRIBUTION AND REIMBURSEMENT

In this part we describe the different sets of rules that govern claims for contribution and reimbursement. In Part 3 we discuss the interplay between all these claims and claims for subrogation.   **19–05**

The law of contribution and reimbursement is fragmented into several parts. First, claims by those who pay more than their share of a common liability for the same debt lie in equity and at common law. Secondly, claims by those who pay more than their share of a common liability for the same damage are generally governed by the Civil Liability (Contribution) Act 1978. But, thirdly, claims by carriers who pay more than their share of a common liability for damage to cargo carried by road are governed by the Carriage of Goods by Road Act 1965 (which gives force of law in the UK to the Geneva Convention on the Contract for the International Carriage of Goods by Road 1956, known as CMR). And, fourthly, claims by ship owners who have paid more than their share of a common liability for death or personal injuries caused by collisions at sea are governed by the Merchant Shipping Act 1995 (which gives force of law in the UK to the Brussels Collision Convention 1910). Fifthly, claims against tortfeasors by the Department of Social Security to recover the value of social security benefits paid to tort victims are governed by the Social Security (Recovery of Benefits) Act 1997, and similar claims against tortfeasors to recover the costs of National Health Service treatment received by tort victims are governed by the Health and Social Care (Community Health and Standards) Act 2003.   **19–06**

In the following account, we describe the scope of these different recovery regimes, and consider several problem areas where it is currently unclear which rules govern a claim. In particular, we note that some recent cases on the meaning of the word "damage" in s.1(1) of the Civil Liability (Contribution) 1978 Act have failed to clarify the extent of the courts' jurisdiction under the statute.   **19–07**

(a) *Claims in Equity and at Common Law*

Here we describe the equitable and common law rules governing claims between parties under a common liability for the same debt. The equitable and common law rules governing claims between parties under a common liability for the same damage, which existed prior to the enactment of the Law Reform (Married Women and Tortfeasors) Act 1935 and the Civil Liability (Contribution) Act 1978, are briefly considered below.[6]   **19–08**

(i) *Contribution Claim*

Contribution claims at common law have a long history. Sir John Baker writes that it was long possible "to bring special assumpsit for a contribution, but there   **19–09**

---

[6] See para.19–22.

is no indication in the earlier cases that [the defendant's promise to pay a contribution to the claimant] might be fictitious".[7] This development, which enabled claimants to bring what we would now characterise as a claim in unjust enrichment, seems to have been the work of Lord Mansfield in the mid-18th century.[8] Previously, in the 16th and 17th centuries, common law claims in assumpsit between co-sureties had been rejected, as a "great cause of suits",[9] and it may be that Lord Mansfield imported the principle of contribution between co-sureties into the English common law from Scots law,[10] which itself derived this principle from Roman law.[11]

19–10   In equity, contribution claims between co-sureties date back at least to the 17th century.[12] It has been said of these equitable rules, too, that their origins lie in the "control and direction, by the courts of equity, of the causes of action arising under deeds or contracts and not with the creation of independent and separate causes of action",[13] but independent equitable claims for contribution in what we would now call unjust enrichment had appeared by the end of the 18th century,[14] and their appearance may also have fed into the development of the common law rules.[15]

19–11   As a consequence of this long history, many rules which now govern contribution claims between co-sureties are at least 200 years old, although of course many have been reaffirmed in the intervening period. These rules provide that a surety can recover a contribution from his co-sureties both at common law and in equity, although the common law action in this context has fallen into disuse since the Judicature Acts 1873 and 1875, since when the normal course has been

---

[7] J.H. Baker, "The History of Quasi-Contract in English Law", in W.R. Cornish et al. (eds), *Restitution: Past, Present and Future* (Oxford: Hart, 1998), 37, p.46.

[8] *Decker v Pope* (1757) Selw. N.P. (1812 edn), vol.1, pp.71–72, fn.27. Other early cases are: *Turner v Davies* (1796) 2 Esp. 478; 170 E.R. 425; *Cole v Saxby* (1800) 3 Esp. 159; 170 E.R. 572.

[9] *Wormleighton and Hunter's Case* (1614) Godb. 243 at 243; 78 E.R. 141 at 142. Cf. *Offley and Johnson's Case* (1584) 2 Leon. 166; 74 E.R. 448, where the court held that although a contribution claim lay between co-sureties according to the custom of the city of London, such a claim did not lie at common law.

[10] Baker, "The History of Quasi-Contract in English Law", p.46, fn.42 and text, noting D.M. Walker (ed.), Viscount Stair, *Institutions of the Laws of Scotland* (Edinburgh: University Presses of Edinburgh and Glasgow, 1981), p.168; Lord Bankton, *Institute of the Laws of Scotland* vol.1 (Edinburgh: printed by R. Fleming, for A. Kincaid, 1751), p.237.

[11] For which see F. Schulz, *Classical Roman Law* (Oxford: Clarendon Press, 1951), pp.499–505; P. Stein (ed.), W.W. Buckland, *A Textbook of Roman Law*, 3rd edn (Cambridge: CUP, 1963), pp.449–450; R. Zimmermann, *The Law of Obligations: Roman Foundations of the Civilian Tradition*, paperback edn (Oxford: OUP, 1996), pp.129–137.

[12] *Fleetwood v Charnock* (1629) Nelson 10; 21 E.R. 776; *Peter v Rich* (1629/1630) 1 Chancery Reps 34; 21 E.R. 499; *Morgan v Seymour* (1637/1638) 1 Chancery Reps 120; 21 E.R. 525. Baker has also observed that "contribution in equity has an earlier history in the procedure called *audita querela*": J.H. Baker, "The Use of Assumpsit for Restitutionary Money Claims 1600–1800", in E.J.H. Schrage (ed.), *Unjust Enrichment: The Comparative Legal History of the Law of Restitution*, 2nd edn (Berlin: Duncker und Humblot, 1999), 31, p.44, fn.69, citing *Ross v Pope* (1551) Plowd. 72; 75 E.R. 114; Sir R. Brooke, *La Graunde Abridgement* (London, 1573), tit. "*Audita querela*", para.2; W Sheppard, *Grand Abridgement* (London: G. Sawbridge et al, 1675), Pt III, pp.326–327.

[13] *Legal and General Assurance Society Ltd v Drake Insurance Co Ltd* [1992] QB 887 at 900 (CA).

[14] *Deering v Earl of Winchelsea* (1787) 2 Bos. & Pul. 270; 126 E.R. 1276. This case was heard in the Court of Exchequer, sitting in Equity.

[15] *Craythorne v Swinburne* (1807) 14 Ves. Jun. 160 at 164 and 169; 33 E.R. 482 at 484 and 485.

to bring an action in the Chancery Division founded upon equitable principles.[16] The question has arisen whether contribution claims between co-sureties now fall within the courts' jurisdiction under the Civil Liability (Contribution) Act 1978, and it seems that some do, while others do not. This is discussed below.[17]

At common law and in equity a surety can recover a contribution from his **19–12** co-sureties whether they were bound jointly, jointly and severally, or severally,[18] whether or not they were bound by separate instruments,[19] whether or not he was aware of their existence at the time of giving his guarantee,[20] whether or not their liabilities arose at different times,[21] and whether they are bound in the same sum or different sums.[22] A surety can recover interest from a co-surety on sums paid to the creditor in excess of his own share of their common liability, whether or not the principal debt carried interest, the interest to run from the date of the surety's payment.[23]

At common law, a surety could recover no larger sum from a co-surety than the **19–13** total amount owed by the principal debtor, divided by the number of sureties, and no adjustment was made if one or more of the other co-sureties had become insolvent.[24] In equity, however, the amount recoverable was calculated by reference to the number of solvent co-sureties remaining at the time when contribution was sought, and this is the rule which has been applied since 1873 in all

---

[16] *Lowe & Sons v Dixon & Sons* (1885) 16 Q.B.D. 455 at 458 per Lopes J.; *Kent v Abrahams* [1928] W.N. 266; *Hay v Carter* [1935] Ch. 397; *Re a Debtor (No.627 of 1936)* [1937] 1 Ch. 156 at 165 (CA).

[17] See para.19–33.

[18] *Stirling v Forrester* (1821) 3 Bli. 575 at 590–591; 4 E.R. 712 at 717 (HL); *Ward v National Bank of New Zealand* (1883) 8 App. Cas. 755 at 765 (PC); *McLean v Discount & Finance Ltd* (1939) 64 C.L.R. 312 at 328; *Mahoney v McManus* (1981) 180 C.L.R. 370 at 376; *Stimpson v Smith* [1999] Ch. 340 at 348 (CA).

[19] *Deering* (1787) 2 Bos. & Pul. 270; 126 E.R. 1276; *Ware v Horwood* (1807) 14 Ves. Jun. 28 at 31; 33 E.R. 432 at 433; *Craythorne* (1807) 14 Ves. Jun. 160 at 165; 33 E.R. 482 at 484; *Ellesmere Brewery Co v Cooper* [1896] 1 Q.B. 75 at 79; *Molson's Bank v Kovinsky* [1924] 4 D.L.R. 330 at 336 (Ontario CA); *McLean* (1939) 64 C.L.R. 312 at 328; *Mahoney* (1981) 180 C.L.R. 370 at 376; *Stimpson v Smith* [1999] Ch. 340 at 348 (CA).

[20] *Deering* (1787) 2 Bos. & Pul. 270; 126 E.R. 1276; *Craythorne* (1807) 14 Ves. Jun. 160 at 165, 33 E.R. 482 at 484; *Whiting v Burke* (1871) 6 Ch. App. 342; *Molson's Bank* [1924] 4 D.L.R. 330 at 336 (Ontario CA); *McLean* (1939) 64 C.L.R. 312 at 328; *Mahoney* (1981) 180 C.L.R. 370 at 376; *Stimpson* [1999] Ch. 340 at 348 (CA). If a surety agrees to be bound by a guarantee which shows on its face that other joint and several sureties are also intended to be parties to it, then he will only be bound on the footing that the others are bound as well: *Evans v Bremridge* (1855) 25 L.J. Ch. 102; affirmed (1856) 25 L.J. Ch. 334 (where the intended co-surety never executed the deed of guarantee); *Ellesmere Brewery* [1896] 1 Q.B. 75 at 82–83 (CA) (where the intended co-sureties were discharged from liability by the surety's own variation of the limit to which he would be liable); *James Graham & Co (Timber) Ltd v Southgate-Sands* [1986] Q.B. 80 (where the intended co-surety's signature on the deed of guarantee was forged).

[21] *Whiting* (1871) 6 Ch. App. 342; *Grobb v Darling* (1907) 17 Man. R. 211 at 215 (Manitoba CA); *Stimpson* [1999] Ch. 340 at 348 (CA).

[22] *Stimpson* [1999] Ch. 340 at 348 (CA).

[23] *Swain v Wall* (1641) 1 Ch. Rep. 149; 21 E.R. 534; *Lawson v Wright* (1786) 1 Cox 275; 29 E.R. 1164; *Hitchman v Stewart* (1855) 3 Drew. 271; 61 E.R. 907; *Re Swan's Estate* (1869) 4 Ir. Eq. 209; *Ex p. Bishop* (1880) 15 Ch. D. 400; *Re Hunt* (1902) 86 L.T. 504; *A.E. Goodwin Ltd (In Liquidation) v A.G. Healing Ltd (In Liquidation)* (1979) 7 A.C.L.R. 481 at 492 (NSW Sup Ct (Eq Div)).

[24] *Cowell v Edwards* (1800) 2 Bos. & Pul. 268; 126 E.R. 1275; *Browne v Lee* (1827) 6 B. & C. 689; 108 E.R. 604; *Batard v Hawes* (1853) 2 E. & B. 287; 118 E.R. 775; noted in *Re a Debtor (No.627 of 1936)* [1937] Ch. 156 at 164–165 (CA).

contribution actions by sureties[25] (and in actions by other types of claimant as well[26]). A further difference between the approaches taken by the common law and Chancery courts is that the former required a claimant to sue one defendant at a time in an action for money paid, while the latter would permit the rights of all the parties to be settled at the same enquiry, allowing an equitable accounting between them if that were the remedy sought.[27]

19–14   Since at least the middle of the 19th century, various other types of co-debtor have also had the right at common law to bring an action for money paid to recover a contribution from their co-debtors,[28] and they have also enjoyed a corresponding right in equity.[29] Such claimants include joint contractors[30] and indemnity insurers which have insured the same risk[31]—although as we shall see, the courts have sometimes found it hard to understand the interplay between

---

[25] *Peter v Rich* (1629/1630) 1 Chancery Reps 34; 21 E.R. 499; *Morgan v Seymour* (1637/1638) 1 Chancery Reps 120; 21 E.R. 525; *Hitchman v Stewart* (1855) 3 Drew. 271; 61 E.R. 907; *Lowe & Sons* (1885) 16 Q.B.D. 455 at 458; *Re Price* (1978) 85 D.L.R. (3d) 554 (Nova Scotia Sup Ct); *Mahoney* (1981) 180 C.L.R. 370 at 376; *De Sousa v Cooper* (1992) 106 Fed. L.R. 79 at 81 (Northern Territory Sup Ct).

[26] Partners: *Wadesdon v Richardson* (1812) 1 V. & B. 103; 35 E.R. 40; *Oldaker v Lavender* (1833) 6 Sim. 239; 58 E.R. 583; *Cruikshank v M'Vicar* (1844) 8 Beav. 106 at 118; 50 E.R. 42 at 47. All discussed in R.C. I'Anson Banks (ed.), *Lindley & Banks on Partnership*, 18th edn (London: Sweet & Maxwell, 2002), paras 20.07–20.08. Tortfeasors: *Fisher v C.H.T. Ltd (No.2)* [1966] 2 Q.B. 475 (CA), noted in *Renaissance Leisure Group Inc v Frazer* (2001) 197 D.L.R. (4th) 336 at 355–356 (Ontario Sup Ct). Co-obligants generally: *Edwards v Proprius Holdings Ltd (No.2)* [2009] NZHC 689 at [22]; *Primary Healthcare Centres (Broadford) Ltd v Humphrey* [2010] CSOH 129 at [18].

[27] Cf. *Tucker v Bennett* (1927) 2 D.L.R. 42 at 47 (Ontario Sup Ct); *Manufacturers Mutual Insurance Ltd v G.I.O.* Unreported NSW Sup Ct (Eq Div), February 2, 1993.

[28] For the rule that the action for money laid out or paid to the defendant's use was the appropriate common law action to recover a contribution during this period, see: *Abbott v Smith* (1774) 2 W. Bl. 947 at 949; 96 E.R. 559 at 560; *Garnons v Swift* (1809) 1 Taunt. 507; 127 E.R. 930; *Maxwell v Johnson* (1818) 2 B. & Ald. 51; 106 E.R. 286; *Edger v Knapp* (1843) 5 Man. & G. 753 at 758; 134 E.R. 763 at 765; *Kemp v Finden* (1844) 12 M. & W. 421 at 423–424; 152 E.R. 1262 at 1262–1263; *Batard v Douglas* (1852) 2 El. & Bl. 287 at 296; 118 E.R. 775 at 778.

[29] Cf. *Albion Insurance Co Ltd v Government Insurance Office of NSW* (1969) 121 C.L.R. 342 at 350 per Kitto J.: "the basic concept was accepted by both law and equity as one of natural justice".

[30] *Abbott* (1774) 2 W. Bl. 947 at 949; 96 E.R. 559 at 560; *Holmes v Williamson* (1817) 6. M & S. 158; 105 E.R. 1202; *Edger* (1843) 5 Man. & G. 753; 134 E.R. 763; *Boulter v Peplow* (1850) 9 C.B. 493 at 507–508; 137 E.R. 984 at 989–990; *Batard v Hawes* (1853) 2 El. & Bl. 287; 118 E.R. 775; *Spottiswoode's Case* (1855) 6 De G. M. & G. 345; 43 E.R. 1267; *Sedgwick v Daniell* (1857) 2 H. & N. 319; 157 E.R. 132; *Marsack v Webber* (1860) 6 H. & N. 1; 158 E.R. 1; *Davitt v Titcumb* [1990] Ch. 110 at 117; *Lumley v Robinson* [2002] EWCA Civ 94 at [12]. See too *Petrie v Petrie* [1944] S.C.R. 246; *Capita Financial Group Ltd v Rothwells Ltd* (1993) 30 N.S.W.L.R. 619 (NSW CA); *Duke Nominees Pty Ltd v D&S Group of Companies Pty Ltd* Unreported Fed Ct of Aus, June 10, 1998.

[31] *Godin v London Assurance Co* (1758) 1 Burr. 489; 97 E.R. 419; *Newby v Reed* (1763) 1 W. Bl. 416; 96 E.R. 237; *Davis v Gildart* (1777), discussed in J.A. Park, *System of the Law of Marine Insurance*, 2nd edn (London: T. Whieldon, 1790), p.282; *British & Mercantile Insurance Co v London, Liverpool & Globe Insurance Co* (1877) 5 Ch. D. 569 at 583 and 587 (CA); *Sickness and Accident Assurance Association Ltd v General Accident Assurance Corp Ltd* (1892) 19 R. 977 at 980 (Ct of Sess OH); *American Surety Co of New York v Wrightson* (1910) 103 L.T. 663; *Dawson v Bankers' and Traders' Insurance Co Ltd* [1957] V.R. 491 at 502–503 (Sup Ct of Victoria); *Albion Insurance Co Ltd v Government Insurance Office of NSW* (1969) 121 C.L.R. 342; *Government Insurance Office of NSW v Crowley* [1975] 2 N.S.W.L.R. 78 (NSW Sup Ct (Eq Div); *Commercial Union Assurance Co Ltd v Hayden* [1977] Q.B. 804 (CA); *Legal & General Assurance Soc Ltd v Drake Insurance Co Ltd* [1992] 1 Q.B. 887 at 892 (CA); *Eagle Star Insurance Co Ltd v Provincial Insurance Plc* [1994] 1 A.C. 130 at 138–139 (PC); *A.M.P. Workers'* (2001) 53 N.S.W.L.R. 35 (NSWCA). See too the Marine Insurance Act 1906 ss.32 and 80.

double insurers' contribution rights and their subrogation rights,[32] and it is also uncertain whether contribution claims between insurers now fall within the scope of the Civil Liability (Contribution) Act 1978.[33] The Chancery courts also enabled partners to recover a contribution from fellow partners when they paid the whole of a jointly owed debt,[34] but contribution actions by partners who paid a debt were not generally permitted at common law,[35] as a partner seeking a contribution from fellow partners had to ask for an equitable taking of accounts.[36] This remains the method by which partners' contribution claims must usually be determined, whether "during the continuance of the relationship [or] after its termination".[37] Note, too, that contribution claims by partners who have paid more than their share of a jointly owed liability for damage, rather than debt, now fall within the scope of the 1978 Act.

The categories of claimant by whom contribution can be claimed at common **19–15** law or in equity are not closed,[38] and further types of successful claimant include: (1) occupiers of land in a manor under a common liability to pay for building work[39]; (2) tavern guests under a common liability to pay for their dinner[40]; (3) beneficiaries under a will[41]; (4) parties under a common statutory liability to pay for building work[42]; (5) joint tenants under a common liability to repair property[43]; (6) part owners of a ship under a common liability for debts incurred with their authority by the master[44]; (7) tithe owners under a common statutory

---

[32] See paras 19–45—19–47.

[33] See para.19–34.

[34] *Re The Royal Bank of Australia* (1856) 6 De G. M. & G. 572, 43 E.R. 1356; *Matthews v Ruggles-Brise* [1911] 1 Ch. 194. Cf. *Gye v Davies* (1995) 131 A.L.R. 723 (NSWCA).

[35] Although an action for money paid would lie where two or more partners had jointly engaged in a particular transaction which was distinct and separate from their partnership business: *Sedgwick* (1857) 2 H. & N. 319; 157 E.R. 132.

[36] *Sadler v Nixon* (1834) 5 B. & Ad. 936; 110 E.R. 1038.

[37] *Hurst v Bryk* [2002] 1 A.C. 185 at 197, followed in subsequent proceedings, sub nom. *Hurst v Bennett* [2001] EWCA Civ 182, esp. at [43] and following.

[38] *Trade Practices Commission v Manfal Pty Ltd (No.3)* (1991) 33 F.C.R. 382 at 385 (Fed Ct of Aus); *Austotel Management Pty Ltd v Jamieson* Unreported Fed Ct of Aus, December 20, 1995; *Burke v L.F.O.T. Pty Ltd* [2002] HCA 17; (2002) 209 C.L.R. 282 at [49] (McHugh J., dissenting, but not on this point).

[39] *Dimes v Arden* (1836) 6 N. & M. K.B. 494. Cf. *Att Gen v Mewtis* (1627) and *Williams' Case* (1635), in W.H. Bryson (ed.), *Cases Concerning Equity and the Courts of Equity 1550–1660* vol.2 (Selden Soc vol. 118, 2001), pp.530 and 664.

[40] *Child v Morley* (1800) 8 T.R. 610 at 614; 101 E.R. 1574 at 1576 per Lord Kenyon C.J.: "I remember a case in Rolle's Abridgment, where a party met to dine at a tavern, and after dinner all but one of them went away without paying their quota of the Reckonings and that one paid for all the rest; and it was holden that he might recover from the others their aliquot proportions."

[41] *Tombs v Roch* (1846) 2 Coll. 490; 63 E.R. 828; *Hensman v Fryer* (1867) L.R. 3 Ch. App. 420; *Lancefield v Iggulden* (1874) L.R. 10 Ch. App. 136; *Re John* [1933] 1 Ch. 370; *Re Cohen (Deceased)* [1960] Ch. 179.

[42] *Hunt v Harris* (1865) 34 L.J.C.P. (N.S.) 249; *Spiers & Son Ltd v Troup* (1915) 84 L.J.K.B. 1986 at 1992 per Scrutton J.

[43] *Leigh v Dickeson* (1884) 15 Q.B.D. 60 at 66–67 per Cotton L.J., citing Sir A. Fitzherbert, *Natura Brevium* pp.127 (writ *de reparatione facienda*) and 162 (writ of contribution). But NB following the Law of Property Act 1925, property occupied by joint tenants was normally held on a trust for sale, and since the Trusts of Land and Appointment of Trustees Act 1996 property of this kind has normally been held on a trust of land; in either case, one might therefore expect that the expense of repairs would be borne by the trustees.

[44] *French v Foulston* (1771) 5 Burr. 2727 at 2729–2730; 98 E.R. 431 at 431–432; *Von Freeden v Hull* (1907) 76 L.J.K.B. 715 (CA).

liability to pay for repairing a chancel[45]; (8) parties under a common statutory liability to pay a tax debt[46]; (9) company directors under a common statutory liability to pay the debts of a company.[47]

(ii) *Reimbursement Claims*

19–16 Like contribution claims, reimbursement claims can be traced back to claims which most strongly resemble a contractual claim to recover an indemnity. From at least the 15th century, where a principal debtor had expressly promised to save the surety harmless, the common law courts would permit him to sue on this promise if he was obliged to pay the creditor.[48] The common law count for money laid out (or paid) to the defendant's use, through which such claims came to be mediated, alleged that the defendant was indebted to the claimant for money laid out and spent at the defendant's "special instance and request", and that in consideration thereof he promised to pay the claimant the relevant sum. Sir John Baker states that this count "was in regular use from at least 1610", but that although the defendant's promise to repay the claimant could be fictitious, his initial request originally could not.[49] Hence, at this time, "the contours of the obligation to indemnify, like those of the obligation to make contribution, were essentially contractual".[50]

19–17 In the early 17th century, the Chancery courts began to let sureties recover their payments from the principal debtors even in the absence of a counter-bond or express promise to save harmless,[51] and the first clear case of a common law court allowing recovery on an action for money paid in these circumstances came about a century later.[52] However, while the defendants in such cases made no express promise to indemnify the claimant, we cannot confidently characterise the claims made in these cases as claims in unjust enrichment. The reason is that the courts developed a rule, which remains part of the English law of contract,[53]

---

[45] *Wickhambrook PCC v Croxford* [1935] 2 K.B. 417 (CA); *Chivers & Sons Ltd v Air Ministry* [1955] 1 Ch. 585.

[46] *Armstrong v Commissioner of Stamp Duties* [1967] 2 N.S.W.R. 63 (NSW CA); *Gadsen v Commissioner of Probate Duties* [1978] V.R. 653 at 657 (Sup Ct of Victoria).

[47] *Spika Trading Pty Ltd v Harrison* (1990) 19 N.S.W.L.R. 211 (NSW Sup Ct (Comm Div)), considered in *Street v Retravision* (1995) 16 A.C.S.R. 780 (Fed Ct of Aus).

[48] W.T. Barbour, "The History of Contract in Early English Equity" (1914) 4 *Oxford Studies in Social and Legal History* 1, p.137.

[49] Baker, "The History of Quasi-Contract in English Law", pp.44–45, adding that "the averment of a request was needed to prevent the argument that the consideration was past, by showing that the payment had only been made in response to an implied undertaking to reimburse".

[50] D. Ibbetson, "Unjust Enrichment in England before 1600" in Schrage (ed.), *Unjust Enrichment*, 146.

[51] J.B. Ames, *Lectures on Legal History* (Cambridge, Mass: Harvard University Press, 1913), p.156. For examples of equitable claims to reimbursement by a surety against a principal debtor, see *Ford v Stobridge* (1632) Nels. 24; 21 E.R. 780; *Layer v Nelson* (1687) 1 Vern. 456; 23 E.R. 582 (where the Lord Chancellor enforced the custom of the City of London); *Hungerford v Hungerford* (1708) Gilb. Eq. Rep. 67 at 69; 25 E.R. 47 at 48; *Re Melton* [1918] 1 Ch. 37 (CA).

[52] *Morrice v Redwyn* (1731) 2 Barn K.B. 26· 94 E.R. 333.

[53] *Betts v Gibbins* (1834) 2 Add. & E. 57; 111 E.R. 22; *Toplis v Grane* (1839) 5 Bing (NC) 636 at 650; 132 E.R. 1245 at 1250; *Brittain v Lloyd* (1845) 14 M. & W. 762 at 773; 153 E.R. 683 at 686–687; *Dugdale v Lovering* (1875) L.R. 10 C.P. 196 at 200; *Sheffield Corp v Barclay* [1905] A.C. 392 at 397; *Secretary of State v Bank of India Ltd* [1938] 2 All E.R. 797 (PC); *Yeung Kai Yung v Hong Kong and Shanghai Banking Corp* [1981] A.C. 787 (PC); *Royal Bank of Scotland Plc v Sandstone Properties Ltd* [1988] 2 B.C.L.C. 429; *Honorable Society of the Middle Temple v Lloyd's Bank Plc* [1999] 1 All E.R. (Comm.) 193 at 232–233.

that if a defendant requests a claimant to incur expenditure on his behalf, and does not expressly promise to repay him, then such a promise will be implied in fact.[54] The English courts did not clearly distinguish between contractual claims to an indemnity and claims in unjust enrichment to reimbursement during the 18th and 19th centuries, and at common law both types of claim came to be mediated through the same action: the action for money laid out or paid to the defendant's use. As a result, it is now impossible to tell of many old cases where the defendant asked the claimant to pay the creditor, whether the claim lay in contract (because the defendant had expressly or impliedly promised to repay the claimant[55]) or unjust enrichment (because the claimant had relieved the defendant of the burden of paying the creditor in circumstances where this burden should properly have been borne by the defendant).

Hence, although we now know that these are the "two possible legal bases for   **19-18** the right of reimbursement by a surety against the principal debtor",[56] we cannot confidently identify the ground for recovery in many older cases concerning actions for money paid brought by sureties against principal debtors.[57] The same can also be said of many analogous actions by accommodation acceptors of bills of exchange,[58] joint debtors who had previously agreed that another joint debtor would pay the whole debt,[59] agents who paid their principals' debts while acting within the scope of their authority,[60] and tenants who were obliged to abate a nuisance emanating from the leased property, for the abatement of which the landlord was primarily liable.[61]

In other 19th century cases, however, claimants recovered in an action for   **19-19** money paid even though their payments had not been requested by the defendants—and these cases we would now assign to the law of unjust enrichment. The earliest is *Exall v Partridge*,[62] where the claimant's goods were distrained for the

---

[54] Cf. H.J. Stephen, *A Treatise on the Principles of Pleading in Civil Actions*, 2nd edn (London: J. Butterworth & Son, 1827) p.312.

[55] Cf. *Re a Debtor (No.627 of 1936)* [1937] 1 Ch. 156 at 166 (CA).

[56] *Anson v Anson* [1953] 1 Q.B. 636 at 641 per Pearson J.

[57] *Morrice v Redwyn* (1731) 2 Barn. K.B. 26; 94 E.R. 333; *Woffington v Sparks* (1754) 2 Ves. Sen. 569; 28 E.R. 363; *Taylor v Mills* (1777) 2 Cowp. 525; 98 E.R. 1221; *Davies v Humphreys* (1840) 6 M. & W. 153 at 167; 151 E.R. 361 at 367; *Clark v Chipman* (1866) 26 Upper Canada Queen's Bench Reports 170 (Upper Canada Court of Queen's Bench); *Gough v Godwin* [1931] 1 D.L.R. 701 (Nova Scotia Sup Ct).

[58] *Bleaden v Charles* (1831) 7 Bing. 246; 131 E.R. 95; *Reynolds v Doyle* (1840) 1 M. & G. 753; 133 E.R. 536; *Hawley v Beverley* (1843) 6 M. & G. 221 at 227; 134 E.R. 873 at 875; *Asprey v Levy* (1847) 16 M. & W. 851; 153 E.R. 1436; *Driver v Burton* (1852) 17 Q.B. 989; 117 E.R. 1560; *McKindsey v Stewart* (1871) 21 Upper Canada Common Pleas Reports 226 (Upper Canada Court of Error and Appeal); *Re Chetwynd's Estate* [1938] 3 Ch. 13 (CA). See too Bills of Exchange Act 1882 ss.28 and 59(3).

[59] *Hutton v Eyre* (1815) 6 Taunt. 289; 128 E.R. 1046.

[60] *Bayliffe v Butterworth* (1847) 1 Exch. 425; 154 E.R. 181; *Chapman v Shepherd* (1867) L.R. 2 C.P. 228 at 239; See too *Anglo Overseas Transport Ltd v Titan Industrial Corp (UK) Ltd* [1959] 2 Lloyd's Rep. 152; *Perishables Transport Co Ltd v N. Spyropoulos (London) Ltd* [1964] 2 Lloyd's Rep. 379.

[61] *Gebhardt v Saunders* [1892] 2 Q.B. 452; *Thompson & Norris Manufacturing Co v Hawes* (1895) 73 L.T. 369; *Andrew v St Olave's Board of Works* [1898] 1 Q.B. 775; *North v Walthamstow UDC* (1898) L.J. Q.B. 972; *Haedicke v Friern Barnet UDC* [1904] 2 K.B. 807 at 814–815; reversed on another point [1905] 1 K.B. 110 (CA); *Wilson's Music & General Printing Co v Finsbury BC* [1908] 1 K.B. 563 at 569–570; *Rhymney Iron Co v Gelligaer DC* [1917] 1 K.B. 589 at 594, 596–597, and 597.

[62] *Exall v Partridge* (1799) 8 T.R. 308; 101 E.R. 1405.

defendant's rent, and he recovered the value of his payment to the landlord even though the defendant had neither requested him to pay the landlord nor promised to indemnify him against the cost of doing so.[63] Likewise, in *Brown v Hodgson*,[64] the claimant carrier mistakenly delivered a consignment of butter to the defendant, who sold it and kept the proceeds; the claimant admitted his mistake and without reference to the defendant paid the third party to whom the butter should have been delivered; the claimant recovered this payment as money paid to the defendant's use. In a Canadian case, *Ashford v Hack*,[65] the claimant tenant recovered money paid to the landlord from a subsequent assignee of the lease, and the judge expressly stated that he "did not enter into any contract with the defendant, so that he could establish no action founded on contract".[66] And in *Re a Debtor (No.627 of 1936)*,[67] Greene L.J. identified *Brook's Wharf and Bull Wharf Ltd v Goodman Bros*[68] as "a case where the law [raised] an obligation to indemnify irrespective of any actual antecedent contractual relationship between the parties". The claimant in the *Brook's Wharf* case was a bonded warehouseman which recovered the amount of the customs duties which it had been obliged to pay on goods imported by the defendant, even though the defendant had not requested the claimant to make this payment.[69]

---

[63] See too *Bevan v Waters* (1828) 3 Car. & P. 520; 172 E.R. 529; *Rodgers v Maw* (1846) 15 M. & W. 444; 153 E.R. 924; *Johnson v Royal Mail Steam Packet Co* (1867) L.R. 3 C.P. 38; *Johnson v Skafte* (1869) L.R. 4 Q.B. 700 at 705; *The Orchis* (1890) 15 P.D. 38 (CA); *The Heather Bell* [1901] P. 143 at 154–156; *Re Button* [1907] 2 K.B. 180 (CA).

[64] *Brown v Hodgson* (1811) 4 Taunt. 189; 128 E.R. 301.

[65] *Ashford v Hack* (1849) 6 Upper Canada Queen's Bench Reports 541.

[66] *Ashford* (1849) 6 Upper Canada Queen's Bench Reports 541 at 542. For actions brought by the assignors of leases against subsequent assignees, see too: *Stone v Evans* (1796) Peake Add Cas 94; 170 E.R. 206; *Burnett v Lynch* (1826) 5 B. & C. 589 at 602, 108 E.R. 220 at 224–225; *Moule v Garrett* (1872) L.R. 7 Ex. 101; *McKerrow v Tattle* (1905) 25 N.Z.L.R. 881 (NZ High Ct); *Beckton Dickinson UK Ltd v Zwebner* [1989] 1 Q.B. 208; *Cale v Assidoman K.P.S. (Harrow) Ltd*; *Re a Debtor (No.21 of 1995)* Unreported Ch D, November 3, 1995. For actions brought by subtenants obliged to pay the tenant's rent on the threat of distress or eviction, see: *Sapsford v Fletcher* (1792) 4 T.R. 511; 100 E.R. 1147; *Graham v Tate* (1813) 1 M. & S. 609; 105 E.R. 228; *Taylor v Zamira* (1816) 6 Taunt. 524; 128 E.R. 1138; *Graham v Allsopp* (1848) 3 Ex. 186; 154 E.R. 809; *Jones v Morris* (1849) 3 Exch. 72; 154 E.R. 1044; *Gregory v Stanway* (1860) 2 F. & F. 309; 175 E.R. 809; *Noyes v Ellis* (1877) 3 V.L.R. 307 (Sup Ct of Victoria); *Murphy v Davey* (1884) 14 L.R. Ir. 28 (Irish High Ct, Common Pleas Div); *Underhay v Read* (1887) 20 Q.B.D. 209. For an action by the assignor of a lease against the immediate assignee to recover money paid to the rating authority, see *Sydney Real Estate Bank v Weiss* (1891) 12 L.R. (N.S.W.) L. 170 (NSW CA). Much of the old law governing the relationships between landlords, tenants, and assignees has been superseded by the Landlord and Tenant (Covenants) Act 1995.

[67] *Re a Debtor (No.627 of 1936)* [1937] 1 Ch. 156 at 166 (CA). See too *D&J Motors Ltd v Ellis* (1972) 7 N.B.R. (2d) 516 at 519 (New Brunswick Sup Ct).

[68] *Brook's Wharf and Bull Wharf Ltd v Goodman Bros* [1937] 1 K.B. 534 (CA).

[69] For claims by those who have been compelled to pay tax for the payment of which the defendant was primarily liable, see also: *Hales v Freeman* (1819) 1 Brod. & B. 391; 129 E.R. 773; *Dawson v Linton* (1822) 5 B. & Ald. 521; 106 E.R. 1281; *Foster v Ley* (1835) 2 Bing. N.C. 269; 132 E.R. 106; *Spencer v Parry* (1835) 3 Ad. & E. 331; 111 E.R. 439; *Bate v Payne* (1849) 13 Q.B. 900; 116 E.R. 1507; *Foster v Lamie* (1878) 12 N.S.R. 269 (Nova Scotia CA); *Eastwood v McNab* [1914] 2 K.B. 361; *Gemmell v Brienesse* (1933) 33 S.R. (N.S.W.) 472 (NSW CA); *Bernard & Shaw Ltd v Shaw* [1951] 2 All E.R. 267 at 270; *James More & Sons Ltd v University of Ottawa* (1974) 49 D.L.R. (3d) 666 (Ontario High Ct); *Steele Excavating Ltd v British Columbia Forest Products Ltd* Unreported British Columbia CA, October 9, 1987; *Canada Trust Co v Parfeniuk* [1989] 5 W.W.R. 554 (Manitoba QB); *Halgido Pty Ltd v D.G. Capital Co Ltd* Unreported Fed Ct of Aus, December 20, 1996.

In *Duncan, Fox & Co v North and South Wales Bank* Lord Selborne L.C. said **19–20** that a reimbursement claim will lie wherever[70]:

"there is a primary and a secondary liability of two persons for one and the same debt, the debt being, as between the two, that of one of those persons only, and not equally of both, so that the other, if he should be compelled to pay it, would be entitled to reimbursement from the person by whom (as between the two) it ought to have been paid."

This formulation echoed the statements in *Leake on Contracts*[71] which was adopted by Cockburn C.J. in *Moule v Garrett*, that[72]:

"Where the plaintiff has been compelled by law to pay, or being compellable by law, has paid money which the defendant was ultimately liable to pay, so that the latter obtains the benefit of the payment by the discharge of his liability; under such circumstances the defendant is held indebted to the plaintiff in the amount."

These broad statements of principle indicate that the categories of those who can recover reimbursement at common law or in equity are not closed.

Support for this conclusion can also be drawn from *Niru Battery Manufactur-* **19–21** *ing Co v Milestone Trading Ltd (No.2)*,[73] where money was mistakenly paid on Niru's behalf to CAI (which therefore owed Niru a liability in unjust enrichment) after the negligent issue of an inspection certificate by SGS (for which SGS was liable to Niru in tort). Judgment was entered against CAI and SGS jointly and severally, which SGS paid. SGS then sought to recover the full amount of its payments from CAI. It was a controversial question whether the Civil Liability (Contribution) Act 1978 gave SGS a claim, because CAI's liability to Niru lay in the law of unjust enrichment rather than the law of wrongs.[74] However, the Court of Appeal did not need to decide this point, because they considered that in any case a claim for reimbursement would lie at common law because SGS and CAI had owed a common liability to Niru which SGS had discharged in circumstances where CAI was primarily liable to pay.[75]

---

[70] *Duncan, Fox & Co v North and South Wales Bank* (1880) 6 App. Cas. 1 at 10; followed in: *Re Downer Enterprises Ltd* [1974] 1 W.L.R. 1460 at 1468; *Selous Street Properties Ltd v Oronel Fabrics Ltd* [1984] 1 E.G.L.R. 50 at 61; *Reid v Royal Trust Corp of Canada* (1985) 20 D.L.R. (4th) 223 at 235–236 (Prince Edward Island CA); *Becton Dickinson* [1989] Q.B. 208 at 215–218.

[71] S M Leake, *The Elements of the Law of Contract* (London: Stevens, 1867), p.41.

[72] *Duncan, Fox* (1872) L.R. 7 Ex. 101 at 104. See too *Brook's Wharf* [1937] 1 K.B. 534 at 544 (CA); *General Security Insurance Co of Canada v Howard Sand & Gravel Co Ltd* [1954] S.C.R. 785 at 798; *County of Carleton v City of Ottawa* [1965] S.C.R. 663 at 668; *Electricity Supply Nominees Ltd v Thorn EMI Retail Ltd* (1991) 63 P. & C.R. 143 at 148–149 (CA); *Land Hessen v Gray* Unreported QBD, July 31, 1998; *Lumley General Insurance Ltd v Oceanfast Marine Pty Ltd* [2001] NSWCA 479 at [3]–[5] and at [160]–[163].

[73] *Niru Battery Manufacturing Co v Milestone Trading Ltd (No.2)* [2004] EWCA Civ 487; [2004] 2 All E.R. (Comm.) 289.

[74] See para.19–30.

[75] *Niru Battery* [2004] EWCA Civ 487; [2004] 2 All E.R. (Comm.) 289 at [66]–[72]. Cf. *Altimarloch Joint Venture Ltd v Moorhouse* [2009] NZHC 1569; followed in *Lee, Kim and Beveridge as Trustees of the Roy Family Trust v North Shore CC* [2010] NZHC 498 at [58]–[60]: a contribution claim lies in equity between a tortfeasor and a contract-breaker although no such claim lies under the NZ Law Reform Act 1936.

(b) *Claims under the Civil Liability (Contribution) Act 1978*

19–22   Claims for contribution and reimbursement formerly lay in equity between wrongdoers liable for the same damage—for example, between trustees under a common liability for breach of trust,[76] and between company directors under a common liability for breach of an equitable duty to the company.[77] But the common law courts generally refused to allow such claims between tortfeasors,[78] and this was considered unsatisfactory by the Law Revision Committee in its *Third Interim Report* of 1934, which recommended that the common law rule should be altered so as to allow tortfeasors a right of contribution among themselves.[79] Parliament accepted this recommendation and enacted the Law Reform (Married Women and Tortfeasors) Act 1935 s.6(1)(c), which provided that:

> "Where damage is suffered by any person as a result of a tort . . . any tortfeasor liable in respect of that damage may recover contribution from any other tortfeasor who is, or would if sued have been, liable in respect of the same damage, whether as a joint tortfeasor or otherwise . . . "

19–23   It came to be felt that the scope of this section was too narrow, for several reasons: it did not allow for claims between wrongdoers who were not tortfeasors,[80] it did not apply if one wrongdoer was a tortfeasor but another was not, even though their wrongs had caused the same damage; and it did not allow for claims between equitable wrongdoers. The latter omission was believed to be undesirable because the equitable rules were thought to be insufficiently flexible because they only allowed for an equal apportionment between wrongdoers even if one was more to blame than another, unless the balance of responsibility was so heavily tipped against one that he should be made to bear the whole burden of compensating the victim.[81]

---

[76] *Connock v Rowe* (1611), in Bryson (ed.), *Cases Concerning Equity and the Courts of Equity 1550–1660*, p.602; *Lingard v Bromley* (1812) 1 V. & B. 114; 35 E.R. 45; *Bahin* (1886) 31 Ch. D. 390 (CA); *Bacon v Camphausen* (1888) 55 L.T. 851; *Wynne v Tempest* [1897] 1 Ch. 110; *Re Linsley* [1904] 2 Ch. 785. Cf. *MacDonald v Hauer* (1977) 72 D.L.R. (3d) 110 (Saskatchewan CA); *Goodwin v Duggan* (1996) 41 N.S.W.L.R. 158 (NSW CA).

[77] *Ashurst v Mason* (1875) L.R. 20 Eq. 225; *Ramskill v Edwards* (1885) 31 Ch. D. 100; *Jackson v Dickinson* [1903] 1 Ch. 947. Cf. *Cummings v Lewis* (1993) 41 F.C.R. 559 at 594–549 (Full Ct of Fed Ct of Aus).

[78] Cases denying recovery to joint tortfeasors were: *Merryweather v Nixan* (1799) 8 T.R. 186; 101 E.R. 1337; *Farebrother v Ansley* (1808) 1 Camp. 343; 170 E.R. 979; *Wilson v Milner* (1810) 2 Camp. 452; 170 E.R. 1215; *Weld-Blundell v Stephens* [1920] A.C. 956 (HL). The bar was extended to several concurrent tortfeasors in: *Horwell v London General Omnibus Co Ltd* (1877) 2 Ex. D. 365 at 379 (CA); *The Koursk* [1924] P. 140 at 158 (CA). But there were exceptions to the common law principle: *Wooley v Batte* (1826) 2 C. & P. 417; 172 E.R. 188; *Betts v Gibbins* (1834) 2 Ad. & E. 57; 1110 E.R. 22; *Pearson v Skelton* (1836) 1 M. & W. 504; 150 E.R. 533; and for general discussion, see G. Williams, *Joint Torts and Contributory Negligence* (London: Stevens & Sons, 1951), pp.80–84.

[79] Law Revision Committee, *Third Interim Report* (Cmd 4637, 1934).

[80] *McConnell v Lynch-Robinson* [1957] N.I. 70, construing the identically worded Law Reform (Miscellaneous Provisions) Act (Northern Ireland) 1937 s.16(1)(c).

[81] Law Commission, *Report on Contribution* (1977) Law Com. No.79, para.28, citing *Bahin* (1886) 31 Ch. D. 390 (CA); *Robertson v Southgate* (1847) 6 Hare 536; 67 E.R. 1276. They seem to have had in mind the special rules governing contribution claims between trustees, whom the Chancery courts wished to keep up to the mark by refusing to acknowledge that a "passive" trustee might delegate his functions to an "active" trustee, and then escape the blame for the "active" trustee's breaches of

In 1977, the Law Commission therefore recommended that the courts' juris-   **19–24**
diction under the 1935 Act should be extended by legislation to take in "wrongdoers other than tortfeasors",[82] and that the new Act would govern claims
between persons who were liable for damage suffered as a result of a "tort,
breach of contract, breach of trust, or other breach of duty".[83] The wording of the
corresponding section in the 1978 Act—s.6(1)—differs slightly from this, replacing the words "or other breach of duty" with the words "or otherwise". Nevertheless it is clear that the Law Commission did not envisage that the courts' new
statutory jurisdiction would take in claims between parties who were not wrongdoers, and they expressly recommended that the legislation should leave
untouched the common law and equitable rules governing claims between parties
under a common liability for debt.[84]

The Law Commission's recommendations with regard to the scope of the new   **19–25**
legislation were fully accepted by Parliament. In the House of Commons Standing Committee that reviewed the Civil Liability (Contribution) Bill 1978, the Bill
was said to be "substantially on the lines of the Law Commission's original
recommendations",[85] and in the House of Lords, the Bill was introduced by Lord
Scarman, who said that it was "drafted so as to give effect, with certain
modifications, to the report and recommendations of the Law Commission".[86]
He also specifically stated that:

"[T]he purpose of this Bill is to extend [the 1935 Act] to persons who are not tortfeasors
[and] who do not fall within the limited categories . . . of those who have the right of
contribution at common law".[87]

Hence, as Lord Hope noted in *Royal Brompton NHS Trust v Hammond*[88]:

"the Act is concerned only with liability for damage, so the rules which apply to
contribution between two or more persons who are liable for the same debts are not
affected by it."

Section 1(1) of the 1978 Act provides that: **19–26**

"Subject to the following provisions of this section, any person liable in respect of any
damage suffered by another person may recover contribution from any other person
liable in respect of the same damage (whether jointly with him or otherwise)."

---

trust. However, it should not be supposed that there is a *general* rule debarring unequal apportion-
ments in equity, and in fact the equitable rules clearly permit the courts to make an unequal
apportionment where this seems appropriate: see e.g. *Re Steel* [1979] Ch. 218 at 226; *Hampic Pty Ltd
v Adams* [1999] NSWCA 455; *Burke v L.F.O.T. Pty Ltd* [2002] HCA 17; (2002) 209 C.L.R. 282 at
[119].

[82] Law Commission, *Report on Contribution* at para.58.
[83] Law Commission, *Report on Contribution* at para.81.
[84] Law Commission, *Report on Contribution* at paras 26–29 and 80(a). See too Law Commission,
Working Paper on Contribution (1975) LCWP No.59, para.45(a).
[85] *Hansard*, Standing Committees Session 1997–8, vol.II, Standing Committee C: Civil Liability
(Contribution) Bill, col.67 (June 14, 1978) (G. Pattie M.P.).
[86] *Hansard*, HL Debs, 5th series, vol.395, col.245 (July 18, 1978).
[87] *Hansard*, HL Debs, 5th series, vol.395, col.249.
[88] *Royal Brompton NHS Trust v Hammond* [2002] 1 W.L.R. 1397 at 1414 (HL). At 1415 Lord Hope
adds that the 1978 Act extended the 1935 Act "so as to provide for relief by way of contribution
between wrongdoers whatever the basis of their liability".

And s.6(1) provides that:

> "A person is liable in respect of any damage for the purposes of this Act if the person who suffered it . . . is entitled to recover compensation from him in respect of that damage (whatever the legal basis of his liability, whether tort, breach of contract, breach of trust or otherwise)."

19–27   Like the 1935 Act, the 1978 Act therefore provides for contribution claims between tortfeasors.[89] Unlike the earlier legislation, and unlike the many Commonwealth contribution statutes whose wording is derived from the 1935 Act, the 1978 Act also takes in the following situations: where one party is liable in tort and another is liable for breach of contract,[90] or breach of trust,[91] or knowing receipt of misdirected trust funds,[92] or breach of confidence[93]; where two parties are both liable for breach of contract,[94] or for breaches of statutory duty[95]; where one party is liable for breach of statutory duty and another in tort[96] or breach of contract[97]; where one party is liable for breach of statutory duty and another for breach of trust[98]; where trustees are jointly and severally liable for breach of trust[99]; and where one party is liable for breach of fiduciary duty and another for dishonestly assisting in the breach or knowingly receiving trust funds.[100] Note, too, that a public authority liable to pay damages under the Human Rights Act 1998 is relevantly liable for "damage" according to s.8(5)(b).

19–28   Where two parties would each be liable to pay identical damages in an action for tort or breach of contract, that is a strong indicator that the "damage" for

---

[89] Joint tortfeasors under the 1935 Act: *Ronex Properties* [1983] Q.B. 398 (CA); *Harper v Gray & Walker (A Firm)* [1985] 1 W.L.R. 1196. Joint tortfeasors under the 1978 Act: *Lampitt v Poole BC* [1991] 2 Q.B. 545 at 552 (CA). Several concurrent tortfeasors under the 1935 Act: *Pride of Derby and Derbyshire Angling Association Ltd v British Celanese Ltd* [1953] Ch. 159 (CA). Several concurrent tortfeasors under the 1978 Act: *K v P* [1993] Ch. 140; *Diboll v City of Newcastle-upon-Tyne* [1993] P.I.Q.R. 16 (CA).

[90] *Thomas Saunders Partnership v Harvey* (1989) 30 Con. L.R. 103 at 121; *The Carnival* [1994] 2 Lloyd's Rep. 14 (CA); *Heaton v AXA Equity and Law Life Assurance Society Pty Plc* [2002] 2 A.C. 329 at [3], [4] and [85].

[91] *K v P* [1993] Ch. 140 at 148; *Friends' Provident Life Office v Hillier Parker May & Rowden (A Firm)* [1997] Q.B. 85 at 94–104 (CA).

[92] *Charter Plc v City Index Ltd* [2007] EWCA Civ 1382; [2008] Ch. 313.

[93] *Magical Marking Ltd v Holly* [2008] EWHC (Ch) 2428; [2009] E.C.C. 10 at [65].

[94] *Co-operative Retail Services Ltd v Taylor Young Partnership* [2002] 1 W.L.R. 1419 (HL) (where the contribution claim failed because the defendants had contracted out of their liability to the third party). See too the Landlord and Tenant (Covenants) Act 1995, s. 13(3), which extends the scope of the 1978 Act to parties under a common liability for breaches of covenant in a lease. To the extent that this includes a common liability to pay the rent, rather than a common liability to pay damages for non-performance of another obligation, e.g. to repair, the 1995 Act exceptionally deems the 1978 Act to take in parties under a common liability for debt.

[95] *Nolan v Merseyside CC* (1982) 133 N.L.J. 616.

[96] *Morris v Breaveglen Ltd (t/a Anzac Construction Co)* Unreported CA, May 9, 1997; *Thames Water Utilities Ltd v Videotron Corp* Unreported QBD (Official Referees' Business), July 2, 1998; *Crowley t/a Crowley Civil Engineers v Rushmoor BC* [2009] EWHC 2237 (TCC).

[97] *Davis v Earldene Maintenance Ltd* Unreported CA, February 23, 1999; *Anglian Water Services Ltd v Crawshaw Robbins & Co Ltd* [2001] Building L.R. 173.

[98] *West Wiltshire DC v Garland* [1993] Ch. 409 at 418.

[99] *K v P* [1993] Ch. 140 at 148.

[100] *Dubai Aluminium* [2002] UKHL 48; [2003] 2 A.C. 366.

which they are both liable is also the same.[101] However, as the cases on breach of trust suggest,[102] liability to pay "compensation" for "damage" under s. 6(1) is not synonymous with liability to pay "damages",[103] and consistently with this, it has also been held that a claim lies under the 1978 Act where the claimant has paid the third party's costs.[104]

There are some situations where the Act clearly does not apply: first, where **19–29** one of the parties is a wrongdoer who is liable for restitutionary damages or an account of profits (because in these circumstances he is not liable to pay "compensation")[105]; secondly, where one of the parties is liable to pay a fine following the commission of a criminal offence[106]; and, thirdly, where one of the parties is liable to a company liquidator under the Insolvency Act 1986 ss.214, 217, 238 or 239 (although the Act may apply where one of the parties has incurred a liability under s.212).[107]

There are other situations where it is less certain whether or not the Act **19–30** applies. Various cases have considered the question whether it follows from the fact that the word "damage" in ss.1 and 6 is not synonymous with the word "damages", that the Act covers claims between parties whose liabilities are not wrong-based, but are liabilities for debt or for unjust enrichment. In our view, claims of this kind do not fall within the scope of the Act, because the Law Commission's 1977 Report and *Hansard* indicate that Parliament's intention was solely to enact a scheme for contribution between wrongdoers. For this reason, we believe that judicial findings to the contrary are mistaken—most notably, the Court of Appeal's decision in *Howkins & Harrison (A Firm) v Tyler*,[108] that the 1978 Act takes in parties whose liability arose in debt, and the Court of Appeal's decision in *Friends' Provident Life Office v Hillier Parker May & Rowden (A Firm)*,[109] that the Act takes in parties whose liability arose in unjust enrichment.

---

[101] *Greene Wood & McLean LLP v Templeton Insurance Ltd* [2009] EWCA Civ 65; [2009] 1 W.L.R. 2013 at [25].

[102] Liability for breach of trust does not sound in damages, and is mediated through proceedings for an account. For discussion see D. Hayton et al., *Underhill & Hayton: Law Relating to Trusts and Trustees*, 18th edn (London: LexisNexis Butterworths, 2010), art.85.

[103] e.g. *Birse Construction Ltd v Haiste Ltd* [1996] 1 W.L.R. 675 at 682 (CA); *Royal Brompton* [2002] 1 W.L.R. 1397 at 1401 (HL).

[104] *Parkman Consulting Engineers (An Unlimited Company) v Cumbrian Industrials Ltd* (2001) 79 Con. L.R. 112 at 137–140 (CA); affirming (2000) 78 Con. L.R. 18, at 109–111, and distinguishing *J Sainsbury Plc v Broadway Malyan (A Firm)* (1998) 61 Con. L.R. 31 at 60–64. A previous decision to the contrary, not cited in *Parkman*, is *Eastwood v Rider, The Times*, July 31, 1990, which was, however, doubted in *Adams v Associated Newspapers Ltd* [1999] E.M.L.R. 26. *Parkman* was followed on this point in *Nationwide Building Society v Dunlop Haywards (DHL) Ltd* [2009] EWHC 254 (Comm); [2010] 1 W.L.R. 258 at [81]–[83] and *Mouchel Ltd v Van Oord (UK) Ltd (No.2)* [2011] EWHC 1516 (TCC); [2011] P.N.L.R. 26 at [8]–[25]. Cf. *C.S.R. Ltd v Amaca Pty Ltd* [2007] NSWCA 107.

[105] *Magical Marking* [2008] EWHC (Ch) 2428; [2009] E.C.C. 10 at [65]. For the same reason the 1978 Act cannot apply where one of the parties is liable to pay exemplary damages, a point overlooked by Lord Woolf M.R. in *Thompson v Metropolitan Police Commissioner* [1998] Q.B. 498 at 517 (CA).

[106] *Customs and Excise Commissioners v Bassimeh* [1995] S.T.C. 910.

[107] *Re International Championship Management Ltd* [2006] EWHC 768 (Ch); [2007] B.C.C. 95; *HMRC v Yousef* [2008] EWHC 423 (Ch), [2008] B.C.C. 805.

[108] *Howkins & Harrison (A Firm) v Tyler* [2001] P.N.L.R. 634 at 638–639 and 641 (CA); followed in *Bovis Lend Lease Ltd v Saillard Fuller & Partners* (2001) 77 Con. L.R. 134 at 184–185; but doubted and distinguished in *Yousef* [2008] EWHC 423 (Ch); [2008] B.C.C. 805 at [24].

[109] *Friends' Provident Life Office v Hillier Parker May & Rowden (A Firm)* [1997] Q.B. 85.

The latter case has been considered in several further authorities, in some of which the opposite view has been taken,[110] but neither case has been over-ruled.

19–31   Given the unsettled state of the law on this point, it seems likely that it will be revisited in future cases. In that event, the courts need not take an expansive view simply in order to provide a deserving claimant with a remedy, since he will probably be able to claim at common law in any case, as the Court of Appeal recognised in *Niru Battery*.[111]

19–32   Do claims between co-sureties, and between indemnity insurers who have insured the same risk, fall within the scope of the 1978 Act? Our conclusion that the Act does not extend to claims by parties under a common liability for debt does not settle this question, because it may be that sureties and indemnity insurers do not owe liabilities for debt, and are liable instead to pay damages for breach of a primary contractual obligation other than an obligation to pay money.

19–33   Claims between co-sureties were considered in *Hampton v Minns*,[112] where the judge held that the answer depends on the terms of the guarantee. If the surety has undertaken that "in case the debtor is in default of payment I will forthwith make the payment on behalf of the debtor",[113] then his liability is in debt, and his contribution claim will fall outside the scope of the Act. On the other hand, if he has guaranteed "the performance of all the terms and conditions of the contract", then his liability is to pay damages for failing to ensure that the principal debtor performs his obligations, and his contribution claim will fall within the scope of the Act. Many guarantees roll these forms of wording together, however, in which case it is impossible to be sure whether or not a court will find the contribution claim to fall within the statute.

19–34   Similar points can be made with respect to indemnity insurers: it is often said that actions by insureds against indemnity insurers "sound in unliquidated damages rather than debt".[114] However, one line of English authority considers that in this context "the word 'damages' is used in a somewhat unusual sense", and should not be taken literally because the primary contractual promise made by an indemnity insurer is that the insured shall enjoy "the right to be indemni-fied by a payment of money".[115] This suggests that the insurer's liability is closer to a primary liability in debt than to a secondary liability to pay damages for

---

[110] See especially *Royal Brompton* [2002] 1 W.L.R. 1397 at 1412–1413 (HL). Further discussion in *Niru Battery* [2004] EWCA Civ 487; [2004] 2 All E.R. (Comm.) 289; *Charter* [2007] EWCA Civ 1382; [2008] Ch. 313. And cf. *Henderson v Amadio Pty Ltd (No.2)* (1995) 62 F.C.R. 221 at 236 (Fed Ct of Aus); affirmed (1998) 81 F.C.R. 149 at 202 (Full Ct of Fed Ct of Aus).

[111] *Niru Battery* [2004] EWCA Civ 487; [2004] 2 All E.R. (Comm) 289. See para.19–21.

[112] *Hampton v Minns* [2002] 1 W.L.R. 1, esp. at 26. See too *McGuinness v Norwich and Peterborough BS* [2011] EWCA Civ 1286, for discussion of the same point in a different context.

[113] As in e.g. *Hyundai Heavy Industries Ltd v Papadopoulos* [1980] 1 W.L.R. 1129.

[114] *Forney v Dominion Insurance Co Ltd* [1969] 1 Lloyd's Rep. 502 at 509. See too *Irving v Manning* (1847) 1 H.L.C. 287 at 307; 9 E.R. 766 at 774–775; *Chandris v Argo Insurance Co Ltd* [1963] 2 Lloyd's Rep. 65 at 74; *Edmunds v Lloyd Italico e L'Ancora Cia di Assicurazioni e Riassicurazioni SpA* [1986] 2 All E.R. 249 at 250; *The Fanti* [1991] 2 A.C. 1 at 35; *Odyssey Re (Bermuda) Ltd v Reinsurance Australia Corp Ltd* [2001] NSWSC 266 (NSW Sup Ct (Eq Div)).

[115] *Jabbour v Custodian of Israeli Absentee Property* [1954] 1 W.L.R. 139 at 144–145. See too *Pickersgill & Sons Ltd v London & Provincial Marine & General Insurance Co* [1912] 3 K.B. 614 at 622.

breach of a primary contractual obligation.[116] However, a second line of cases maintains that an indemnity insurer's primary contractual promise is to prevent the insured risk from materialising, with the result that "as soon as the loss has occurred . . . the primary obligation is broken, giving rise to the secondary obligation to pay damages".[117] Whether contribution claims between indemnity insurers fall within the scope of the Act must depend upon which of these views is preferred, and, as in the case of co-sureties, the answer may well turn on the wording of the relevant policies.

(c) *Claims under the Carriage of Goods by Road Act 1965*

The Carriage of Goods by Road Act 1965 s.1, gives force of law in the UK to the   **19–35**
Geneva Convention on the Contract for the International Carriage of Goods by Road 1956, which is commonly referred to by the acronym CMR.[118] Articles 37 to 40 of CMR provide for contribution claims between principal and successive carriers of goods shipped by road, where the claimant carrier has been obliged to pay compensation under art.23 for total or partial loss of the goods to the consignor or consignee. Under s.5(1) of the 1965 Act,[119] the regime of the Civil Liability (Contribution) Act 1978 is disapplied, "so as to leave the way clear for the operation of the special provisions of CMR relating to such matters".[120]

Article 37 of CMR states that: **19–36**

> "[A] carrier who has paid compensation in compliance with the provisions of this Convention, shall be entitled to recover such compensation . . . from the other carriers who have taken part in the carriage".

This reference to "other carriers" is not to all carriers who have taken part in the carriage, but to a potentially smaller class of "successive carriers", as defined by art.34.[121] Article 34 effectively provides that carriers must have been bound by a single contract of carriage in order to count as "successive carriers" under the Convention, so that some carriers will fall outside the scope of the art.34, for example because they are sub-contractors who are not party to the single contract for the whole of the carriage, because they have not accepted the goods and the

---

[116] *England v Guardian Insurance Ltd* [2000] Lloyd's Rep. I.R. 404 at 422; *Bovis Lend Lease Ltd v Saillard Fuller & Partners* [2001] 77 Con. L.R. 134 at 184–185.

[117] *The Italia Express (No.2)* [1992] 2 Lloyd's Rep. 281 at 286 per Hirst J. See too *Halvanon Insurance Co Ltd v Compania de Seguros do Estado de Sao Paolo* [1995] L.R.L.R. 303 at 306 (CA); *Callaghan v Dominion Insurance Co Ltd* [1997] 2 Lloyd's Rep. 541; *Coakley v Argent Credit Corp Plc* Unreported Ch D, June 4, 1998; *Sprung v Royal Insurance Co (UK) Ltd* [1999] Lloyd's Rep. I.R. 111 (CA).

[118] Derived from the French title for the Convention: *Convention Relative du Contrat de Transport International de Marchandises par Route.*

[119] As amended by the Civil Liability (Contribution) Act 1978 s.9(1) and Sch.1 para.7.

[120] *Cummins Engine Co Ltd v Davis Freight Forwarding (Hull) Ltd* [1981] 2 Lloyd's Rep. 402 at 405 (CA); *I.T.T. Schaub-Lorenz Vertriebgesellschaft mbH v Birkart Johann Internationale Spedition GmbH* [1988] 1 Lloyd's Rep 487 at 494 (CA).

[121] *I.T.T. Schaub-Lorenz Vertriebgesellschaft mbH v Birkart Johann Internationale Spedition GmbH* [1988] 1 Lloyd's Rep. 487 at 493 (CA); cited in *Coggins v L.K.W. Walter International Transportorganisation AG* [1999] 1 Lloyd's Rep. 255 (Central London County Court). The *I.T.T.* case was overlooked in the decision to the contrary in *Harrison & Sons Ltd v R.T. Steward Transport* (1993) 28 E.T.L. 747 at 754–756.

consignment note.[122] Since contribution claims against carriers who fall outside the scope of art.34 are not governed by CMR they must be governed by national law instead, which in this case would be the Civil Liability (Contribution) Act 1978.

(d) *Claims under the Merchant Shipping Act 1995*

19–37   Questions of apportionment and contribution arising out of collisions at sea caused by the fault of two or more ships were formerly governed by the Maritime Conventions Act 1911, which gave force of law in the United Kingdom to the Brussels Collision Convention 1910. The relevant sections of the 1911 Act were then re-enacted as the Merchant Shipping Act 1995 ss.187–190. However, where death or personal injury result from a collision caused through the fault not of a ship but of a person, such as a harbour master,[123] for example, or the senior officer in charge of the escorts of a convoy,[124] then the rights and liabilities of the parties fall outside the scope of the statute, and the parties' rights and liabilities are governed by the rules of common law, as amended by statute[125] —which would mean the rules contained in the Civil Liability (Contribution) Act 1978.

19–38   The Merchant Shipping Act 1995 distinguishes the situation where a collision caused by the fault of two or more ships causes damage or loss to property (which is covered by s.187), from the situation where such a collision causes death or personal injury (which is covered by ss.188 and 189). Under s.187(1) and (4), liability to make good damage caused to the ships at fault, their cargo or freight, "shall be in proportion to the degree in which each ship was in fault",[126] and "nothing in this section shall operate to render any ship liable for any damage to which the fault of the ship has not contributed". In contrast, s.188(1) provides that:

> "[W]here loss of life or personal injuries are suffered by any person on board a ship owing to the fault of that ship and of any other ship or ships, the liability of the owners shall be joint and several."

And s.189(1) provides that where:

> "a proportion of the damages [payable for such loss of life or personal injuries] is recovered against the owners of one of the ships which exceeds the proportion in which the ship was at fault, they may recover by way of contribution the amount of the excess from the owners of the other ship or ships to the extent to which those ships were respectively in fault."

19–39   Hence the 1995 Act exposes shipowners to joint and several liability for death and personal injury and gives them contribution rights against one another in the

---

[122] But cf. *Flegg Transport Ltd v Brinor International Shipping and Forwarding Ltd* [2009] EWHC 3047 (QB).

[123] As in e.g. *The Homefire and the Sandwich* (1935) 52 Lloyd's List Rep. 105.

[124] As in e.g. *The Sobieski* (1949) 82 Lloyd's List Rep. 370 (CA).

[125] See e.g. *The Sobieski* (1949) 82 Lloyd's List Rep. 370 at 383–385 per Bucknill L.J.

[126] Applied in e.g. *The Antares II and Victory* [1996] 2 Lloyd's Rep. 482; *Miom 1 Ltd v Sea Echo ENE* [2010] EWHC 3180 (Admlty); *Owners or Charterers of the Ship Samco Europe v Owners or Charterers of the Ship MSC Prestige* [2011] EWHC 1580 (Admiralty).

event that one of them is obliged to pay in full. But the Act generally absolves shipowners from liability to make payments in respect of damage to other vessels and their cargoes for which other ship owners are properly liable, and in this situation the statute effectively operates a proportionate liability system, with the result that questions of contribution do not generally arise.[127]

There is an exception to this general rule. The wording of s.187(1) cannot be taken to cover the case where a wholly innocent ship is damaged by the fault of two others. This seems to be the result of bad draftsmanship, as art.4 of the Brussels Collision Convention 1910 provides that even as against a third party, each of two or more ships at fault should be liable for no more than her own share of the damage.[128] But as matters now stand, this situation is not covered by the 1995 Act, with the result that the two ships at fault are subject to the common law rule that they are jointly and severally liable to the innocent ship for the whole of her damage: i.e. the innocent ship can recover the whole damage from either of the ships at fault.[129]   **19–40**

This situation was considered in *The Cairnbahn*,[130] where it was held that if one of the owners at fault was obliged to pay the whole damage to the owners of the innocent vessel, then he could recover a contribution from the other owner at fault under the Maritime Conventions Act 1911 s.1(1)—which was re-enacted as the Merchant Shipping Act 1995 s.187(1). The Court of Appeal reasoned that the common law bar against contribution claims between tortfeasors which generally prevailed at that time[131] had not been applied by the Admiralty courts prior to the enactment of the 1911 Act in cases where two ships at fault had damaged a third, and there was no reason to think that the legislature had intended the 1911 Act to prevent the owner from recovering a contribution by abrogating the old Admiralty rule which allowed recovery.[132] Since *The Cairnbahn* was decided, the common law bar against contribution claims between tortfeasors has itself been abrogated by the Law Reform (Married Women and Tortfeasors) Act 1935, which in turn was replaced and extended by the Civil Liability (Contribution) Act 1978. So the question arises, whether the owner at fault should bring his contribution claim under the 1995 Act or under the 1978 Act? We believe that the claimant must claim under the 1978 Act, s.7(3) of which provides that the right to contribution under the statute "supersedes any right, other than an express contractual right, to recover contribution . . . otherwise than under [the] Act in corresponding circumstances".   **19–41**

(e) *Claims under the Social Security (Recovery of Benefits) Act 1997 and the Health and Social Care (Community Health and Standards) Act 2003*

In 1942, the Beveridge Report first drew official attention to the situation where an accident victim receives welfare payments from the state and then recovers   **19–42**

---

[127] For general discussion of proportionate liability systems, see paras 20–72—20–76.

[128] Sir H.V. Brandon, "Apportionment of Liability in the British Courts Under the Maritime Conventions Act of 1911" (1977) Tulane L.R. 1025, p.1034.

[129] *The Devonshire* [1912] A.C. 634. See too *The Homefire and the Sandwich* (1935) 52 Lloyd's List Rep. 105 at 109; *The Juno and the Bannprince* [1957] 2 Lloyd's Rep. 399 at 416.

[130] *The Cairnbahn* [1914] P. 25 (CA).

[131] See para.19–22, fn.78 and text.

[132] *The Cairnbahn* [1914] P. 25 at 32, 33–34, and 38–39, all approving *The Frankland* [1901] P. 161.

tort damages from a tortfeasor responsible for injuring him.[133] In Beveridge's view, an injured person should always be entitled to receive social security benefits immediately, whether or not he has an overlapping tort claim, but he should not be entitled to have his needs met twice over. The Law Reform (Personal Injuries) Act 1948 sought to prevent double recovery of this kind by requiring the deduction of welfare benefits from tort damages, but a different strategy was adopted by Parliament when it enacted the Social Security Act 1989. Like the 1948 Act, the 1989 Act required the deduction of welfare benefits from the tort damages payable in personal injury cases, but it also required the tortfeasor to pay an equivalent sum to the Department of Social Security. In effect, the DSS could seek reimbursement from the tortfeasor for the payments that it was legally obliged to make to the victim.

19–43   The relevant parts of the 1989 Act were amended and re-enacted as the Social Security (Recovery of Benefits) Act 1997, and two years later the recovery regime established by the 1997 Act was extended by the Road Traffic (N.H.S. Charges) Act 1999, which enabled the cost of NHS treatment received by those who had been tortiously injured in road traffic accidents to be recovered from the tortfeasors. The 1999 Act was itself superseded by the Health and Social Care (Community Health and Standards) Act 2003 Pt 3, under which an Injury Costs Recovery Scheme was set up. This scheme came into force on January 29, 2007 and it requires tortfeasors to pay a fixed sum per day of treatment or ambulance journey, the amount payable being fixed by a statutory tariff.

19–44   The 1997 and 2003 Acts work in essentially the same way. They require a tortfeasor, or more usually, his insurer, to apply for a certificate of recoverable Social Security benefits or NHS charges for the care received by the victim. Some Social Security benefits are not recoverable, essentially because they have no causal connection with the tortious injury. The certificate states the value of the benefits or care which the victim has received. The tortfeasor or insurer can then deduct this amount from the amount which he must pay to the victim as tort damages, but he must pay an equivalent amount to the Compensation Recovery Unit, which is the body charged with administering the recovery regimes created by the legislation.[134] These rules effectively give the NHS and the (renamed) Department for Work and Pensions a right to reimbursement from tortfeasors who would otherwise be unjustly enriched at their expense if the damages that they were liable to pay were reduced by the amount of benefit or care received by their victims.[135]

3. Claims for Contribution and Reimbursement and Subrogation Claims

19–45   To understand the interplay between claims for contribution and reimbursement and claims for subrogation, it must be appreciated that there are two different types of subrogation. The first entails a transfer of subsisting rights of action

---

[133] Report by Sir William Beveridge, *Social Insurance and Allied Services*, (1942) Cmd 6404.
[134] Detailed information is available online at: *http://www.dwp.gov.uk/other-specialists/compensation-recovery-unit/*.
[135] As noted in Law Commission, *Damages for Personal Injury: Medical, Nursing and Other Expenses; Collateral Benefits*, paras 3.22–3.23.

following a payment that does not extinguish these rights: the best example is the case where an indemnity insurer pays its insured and then acquires his subsisting rights against a third party.[136] The second entails treating a claimant, by a fiction, as though rights have been transferred to him following his payment, although the effect of the payment was to extinguish the rights.[137] Since contribution and reimbursement claims are predicated on the claimant having discharged the defendant's liability to a third party (and having extinguished the third party's corresponding rights), no question can arise of the claimant also bringing a subrogation claim of the first kind. However he may well be entitled to bring a subrogation claim of the second kind to supplement his claim for contribution or reimbursement.

The Mercantile Law Amendment Act 1856 s.5, confers this right on sureties,   **19–46** and also on "every person who, . . . being liable with another for any debt or duty, shall pay such debt or perform such duty". Thus various types of claimant besides sureties[138] have been able to bring a subrogation claim to supplement a claim for contribution and reimbursement, including accommodation acceptors of bills of exchange,[139] sub-sureties,[140] assignors of leases[141] and payers of tax.[142] It was also said by Lord Selborne L.C. in *Duncan, Fox*, that claimants are entitled to do this whenever[143]:

> "there is, strictly speaking, no contract of suretyship, but in which there is a primary and secondary liability of two persons for one and the same debt, by virtue of which, if it is paid by the person who is not primarily liable, he has a right of reimbursement or indemnity from the other."

Notwithstanding these authorities, the mistaken view has been formed by the   **19–47** courts over the past century, that an insurer entitled to contribution from a second insurer who has insured the same risk is not entitled to be treated as though it has acquired its insured's (extinguished) rights against the second insurer by subrogation.[144] These cases fail to distinguish properly between the two types of

---

[136] See Ch.21.
[137] See Ch.39.
[138] For surety cases see e.g. *Aylwin v Whitty* (1861) 30 L.J. Ch. 860; *Re M'Myn* (1886) 33 Ch. D. 575; *Leicestershire Banking Co Ltd v Hawkins* (1900) 16 T.L.R. 317; *Smith v Wood* [1929] 1 Ch. 14.
[139] *Bechervaise v Lewis* (1972) L.R. 7 C.P. 372; *Gray v Seckham* (1872) L.R. 7 Ch. App. 680.
[140] *Fox v Royal Bank of Canada* [1976] 2 S.C.R .2.
[141] *Re Downer Enterprises Ltd* [1974] 1 W.L.R. 1460. The assignor of a lease has also been enabled to sue the assignee's surety: *Selous Street Properties Ltd v Oronel Fabrics Ltd* (1984) 270 E.G. 643 at 644; *Kumar v Dunning* [1989] Q.B. 193 at 201; *Becton Dickinson* [1989] Q.B. 208; *Coronation Street Industrial Properties Ltd v Ingall Industries Plc* [1988] 2 E.G.L.R. 44.
[142] *Dimdore v Leventhal* (1936) 36 S.R. (N.S.W.) 378 at 385 (NSW CA); *Resource Plastics Inc v W. Pickett & Bros Customs Brokers Inc* Unreported Ontario High Ct, October 18, 1995.
[143] *Duncan, Fox* (1880) 6 App. Cas. 1 at 13 (HL). See too *Ruabon Steamship Co v London Assurance Co* [1900] A.C. 6 at 12; *Re Downer Enterprises Ltd* [1974] 1 W.L.R. 1460 at 1468.
[144] *Sickness and Accident Assurance Association v General Accident Assurance Corp Ltd* (1892) 19 R. 979n. at 980–1n. (Ct of Sess. (OH)); affirmed (1892) 19 R. 977, (Ct of Sess (IH)); *Austin v Zurich General Accident and Liability Insurance Co Ltd* [1945] 1 K.B. 250; *Dawson v Bankers and Traders Insurance Co Ltd* [1957] V.R. 491 at 503 (Victoria Sup Ct); *Albion Insurance Co Ltd v Government Insurance Office (NSW)* (1969) 121 C.L.R. 342; *Sydney Turf Club v Crowley* (1972) 126 C.L.R. 420; *Bovis Construction Ltd v Commercial Union Assurance Co Plc* [2001] Lloyd's Rep. I.R. 321 at 324; *Speno Rail Maintenance Pty Ltd v Metals & Minerals Insurance Pte Ltd* [2009] WASCA 91; (2009) 226 F.L.R. 306 at [176]–[227] (not considered on appeal sub nom. *Zurich Australian Insurance Ltd v Metals & Minerals Insurance Pte Ltd* [2009] HCA 50; (2009) 240 C.L.R. 391); *Cameco Corp v Insurance Co of State of Pennsylvania* [2010] SKCA 95; [2010] 10 W.W.R. 385.

subrogation referred to above, and are out of line with earlier authorities,[145] as well as the Marine Insurance Act 1906 s.80(2). An insurer which is entitled to this type of subrogation remedy may sue the second insurer in its own name if it wishes to do so, although, in common with other claimants who are legally compelled to discharge a defendant's liability to a third party, the insurer also has the right to use the insured's name in litigation against the second insurer under the Mercantile Law Amendment Act 1856 s.5.[146] In contrast, where the insurer's payment to the insured does not extinguish the insured's rights against a third party, he must bring any subrogated action against the third party in the name of the insured.[147]

---

[145] *Godin v London Assurance Co* (1758) 1 Burr. 489 at 492; 97 E.R. 419 at 421; *Morgan v Price* (1849) 4 Ex. 615 at 620–621; 154 E.R. 1360 at 1362; *North British and Mercantile Insurance Co v London, Liverpool and Globe Insurance Co* (1877) 5 Ch. D. 569 at 575–576 and 587.

[146] *Caledonia v London Bridge* 2000 S.L.T. 1123 (CS (IH)), affirmed on a different point sub nom *Caledonia v BT* [2002] UKHL 4; [2002] 1 Lloyd's Rep. 553; discussed in C. Mitchell. "Claims in Unjustified Enrichment to Recover Money Paid Pursuant to a Common Liability" (2001) 5 Edin. L.R. 186.

[147] See para.21–114.

CHAPTER 20

SECONDARY LIABILITY: CONTRIBUTION AND REIMBURSEMENT

1. INTRODUCTION

To make out a claim for contribution or reimbursement, the claimant must show **20–01** that he discharged the defendant's liability to a third party and that: (1) the claimant and the defendant were both liable to the third party, (2) who was forbidden to accumulate full recoveries from both of them, but (3) who could choose to recover in full from either of them, and that (4) some or all of the burden of paying him should ultimately be borne by the defendant. Each of these four requirements is discussed here in turn.

2. CLAIMANT AND DEFENDANT BOTH LIABLE TO THE THIRD PARTY

(a) *The Basic Rule*

The claimant must prove[1] that he paid the third party pursuant to an existing legal **20–02** liability.[2] He does not have to show that his liability arose under English law: it is enough that he was liable under foreign law.[3] Nor does he have to show that he paid under pressure of legal process: it is enough that at the time of the payment he was legally compellable to pay.[4] Nor is it automatically fatal that his liability to the third party was voluntarily assumed without any prior request from

---

[1] It is not enough for him to assert or "concede" the point: *Patterson v Campbell* (1910) 44 N.S.R. 214 at 216 (Nova Scotia CA); *N.M.F.M. Property Ltd v Citibank Ltd (No.10)* [2000] FCA 1558 at [490].

[2] *Pawle v Gunn* (1838) 4 Bing N.C. 445 at 448; 132 E.R. 859 at 860; *Mackreth v Walmesley* (1884) 51 L.T. 19; *Re Moss* [1905] 2 K.B. 307; *McLean v Discount & Finance Co Ltd* (1939) 64 C.L.R. 312 at 335; *Thomas v Nottingham Inc Football Club Ltd* [1972] Ch. 596; *Good Motel Co Ltd (In Liquidation) v Rodeway Pacific International Ltd* (1988) 94 Fed. L.R. 84 (Full Ct of Fed Ct of Aus). But NB if a surety pays the creditor before the due date, he can recover from the principal debtor when the due date arrives: *Drager v Allison* [1959] S.C.R. 661. See too Civil Liability (Contribution) Act 1978 s.1(1); Merchant Shipping Act 1995 s.189(3).

[3] *Liberian Insurance Agency v Mosse* [1977] 2 Lloyd's Rep. 560 at 562; affirmed in *Société Eram Shipping Co Ltd v Compagnie Internationale de Navigation* [2001] 2 All E.R. (Comm.) 721 at 735–736 (CA).

[4] *Broughton's Case* (1599) 5 Co. Rep. 24a; 77 E.R. 86; *Cordron v Lord Masserene* (1792) Peake 194; 170 E.R. 126; *Hutton v Eyre* (1815) 6 Taunt. 289 at 296; 128 E.R. 1046 at 1048; *Hales v Freeman* (1819) 1 Brod. & B. 391 at 399; 129 E.R. 773 at 776; *Carter v Carter* (1829) 5 Bing. 406 at 409; 130 E.R. 118 at 119; *The Heather Bell* [1901] P. 143 at 155; affirmed [1901] P. 272 at 279 (CA); *Stimpson v Smith* [1999] Ch. 340 (CA); *Burke v L.F.O.T. Pty Ltd* [2002] HCA 17; (2002) 209 C.L.R. 282 at [42].

the defendant: this is merely one factor which may bear on the court's decision whether to allow a claim.[5]

20-03   The claimant must also show that the defendant was liable to the third party, for if he was not then the defendant can say that he has not benefited by the claimant's dealings: as Lindley L.J. once said, "If I ask a person to reimburse the money which I have spent, but not on his behalf, why should he?"[6] For example, in *Bonner v Tottenham and Edmonton Permanent Investment Building Society*,[7] the claimants assigned their lease to an assignee who mortgaged it to the defendant building society. The assignee became bankrupt and the defendant took possession of the property as subtenant. Breaching its contract with the assignee, the defendant failed to pay the rent, and the landlord could not sue the defendant as no privity of estate existed between them.[8] The landlord therefore recovered the rent from the claimants under a covenant in the lease. The claimants sued the defendant for the value of the payment, but the claim failed because the defendant had never been liable to the landlord.[9]

20-04   For a contribution or reimbursement claim to lie, the defendant must have been liable to the third party *at the time of* the claimant's payment. This is borne out by various cases which hold that for limitation purposes the claimant's cause of action accrues at the time of his payment.[10] It is also consistent with *Liberian*

---

[5] Sureties: *Re a Debtor (No.627 of 1936)* [1937] 156 at 166 (CA). Co-sureties: *Deering v Earl of Winchelsea* (1787) 2 Bos. & Pul. 270; 126 E.R. 1276; *Smith v Wood* [1929] 1 Ch. 14 at 21 (CA). Double insurers: *Limit (No.3) Ltd v A.C.E. Insurance Ltd* [2009] NSWSC 514 at [259]–[303]. See too Mercantile Law Amendment Act 1856 s.5. And compare the position of insurers who are legally entitled to subrogation although they have contracted with their insureds voluntarily: *Mason v Sainsbury* (1782) 3 Doug. K.B. 61; 99 E.R. 538; *Caledonia North Sea Ltd v British Telecommunications Plc* [2002] UKHL 4; [2002] 1 Lloyd's Rep. 553; and for general discussion see Ch.21. These authorities all cast serious doubt on statements to the contrary in *England v Marsden* (1866) L.R. 1 C.P. 529 and *Owen v Tate* [1976] 1 Q.B. 402 (CA).

[6] *Thompson and Norris Manufacturing Co v Hawes* (1895) 73 L.T. 369 at 371 (CA).

[7] *Bonner v Tottenham and Edmonton Permanent Investment Building Society* [1899] 1 QB 161 (CA). See too *Griffinhoofe v Daubuz* (1855) 5 El. & Bl. 746; 119 E.R. 659, explained in *Edmunds v Wallingford* (1885) L.R. 14 Q.B.D. 811 at 815; *An Bord Bainne Co-operative Ltd v Milk Marketing Board* [1988] 1 C.M.L.R. 605; *State Bank of Victoria v Parry* (1990) 2 A.C.S.R. 15 (Sup Ct of Western Aus); *Regional Municipality of Peel v Ontario* [1992] 3 S.C.R. 762; *Wessex Regional Health Authority v John Laing Construction Ltd* (1994) 39 Con. L.R. 56; *O.L.L. Ltd v Secretary of State for Transport* [1997] 3 All E.R. 987; *Cockburn v G.I.O. Finance Ltd (No.2)* [2001] NSWCA 177; (2001) 51 N.S.W.L.R. 624; *Desmond v Cullen* [2001] NSWCA 238; (2001) 34 M.V.R. 186; *Man Nutzfahrzeuge AG v Freightliner Ltd* [2007] EWCA Civ 910; [2008] P.N.L.R. 6; *Fortis Bank SA/NV v India Overseas Bank* [2011] EWHC 538 (Comm); [2011] 2 Lloyd's Rep. 190 at [54]–[68].

[8] Cf. *Electricity Supply Nominees Ltd v Thorn E.M.I. Retail Ltd* (1991) 63 P. & C.R. 143 (CA), where the original tenant's claim against the assignee's subtenant was allowed because the subtenant had covenanted with the landlord to observe the obligations of the head lease.

[9] The defendant was liable to the assignee, from whom in turn the claimants could have recovered their payment but for the fact that the assignee was insolvent. Conceivably the claimants might therefore have been subrogated to the assignee's rights against the defendant, though this would have meant giving them an advantage over the assignee's other creditors of a kind that the courts refused to give claimants in the analogous cases of *Re Harrington Motor Co Ltd* [1928] Ch. 105 and *Hood's Trustees v Southern Union General Insurance Co of Australasia Ltd* [1928] Ch. 793 (triggering the enactment of the Third Parties (Rights against Insurers) Act 1930).

[10] *Davies v Humphreys* (1840) 6 M. & W. 153 at 168–169; 151 E.R. 361 at 367–368; *Wolmershausen v Gullick* [1893] 2 Ch. 514; *Walker v Bowry* (1924) 35 C.L.R. 48; *Hawrish v Peters* [1982] 1 S.C.R. 1083; *Grego v D. Club Pty Ltd* [2011] WASC 55 at [44]–[45]. See too CMR art.39(4); Merchant Shipping Act 1995 s.190; Limitation Act 1980 s.10.

Insurance Agency v Mosse,[11] where the claimant paid an insured on the defendant insurers' behalf, but the claim failed because by then the defendants could have avoided the policy for the insured's breach of the duty of utmost good faith and in these circumstances they could not have been enriched by the claimant's payment.

This rule creates a problem in cases of double insurance where the insured   **20–05** claims from one insurer but not the other, and then loses his right against the second insurer by the time of the first insurer's payment, for example because he does not comply with a claims notification clause. To avoid the conclusion that the first insurer cannot recover a contribution from the second insurer, some courts have held that the time for determining whether the second insurer was liable is the time of the insured loss rather than the time when the first insurer pays the insured.[12] But this has not been accepted by other courts,[13] and even if one agrees that contribution should be available in this situation, another approach might be to draw an analogy with cases which hold a defendant to have been enriched not because his liability was discharged by the claimant's payment, but because the imposition of liability on the claimant prevented the defendant's liability from arising in the first place.[14]

It has been said that common law and equitable claims for contribution and   **20–06** reimbursement do not lie unless the claimant and defendant were "liable to a common demand", meaning that they must have owed a joint, or a joint and several, liability.[15] However, these dicta are suspect,[16] and the better view is that several concurrent liabilities will also suffice. This is borne out by *Exall v Partridge*,[17] where the claimant's goods were distrained for the defendant's rent, and he recovered the value of his payment to the landlord; also, by the many cases permitting contribution between sureties who were severally liable to a creditor on separate guarantees,[18] and by the many cases allowing contribution between double insurers who were severally liable for the same loss.[19] The view that liability *in solidum* is required has also been rejected by the Scottish and Australian courts.[20]

---

[11] *Liberian Insurance Agency v Mosse* [1977] 2 Lloyd's Rep. 560.
[12] *Legal & General Assurance Society Ltd v Drake Insurance Co Ltd* [1992] Q.B. 887 (CA); *O'Kane v Jones* [2003] EWHC 3470; [2004] 1 Lloyd's Rep. 389.
[13] *Eagle Star Insurance Co v Provincial Insurance Plc* [1994] A.C. 130 (PC); *Bolton MBC v Municipal Mutual General Insurance Ltd* [2006] EWCA Civ 50; [2006] 1 W.L.R. 1492.
[14] e.g. *A.M.P. Workers Compensation Services (NSW) Ltd v Q.B.E. Insurance Ltd* (2001) 53 N.S.W.L.R. 35 (NSW CA), discussed at para.4–25.
[15] *Johnson v Wild* (1889) 4 Ch. D 146 at 150; *Bonner v Tottenham and Edmonton Permanent Investment BS* [1899] 1 Q.B. 161 at 174 (CA); *Smith v Cock* [1911] A.C. 317 at 326 (PC); *Karori Properties Ltd v Jelicich* [1969] N.Z.L.R. 698 at 703 (NZ High Ct).
[16] The determining factor in the cases was either that the defendant owed no liability (as in *Johnson* and *Bonner*), or that the parties' liabilities were unconnected, so that the third party could have recovered from both of them in full (as in *Smith*).
[17] *Exall v Partridge* (1799) 8 T.R. 308; 101 E.R. 1405.
[18] See cases cited at para.19–12 fn.19.
[19] See cases cited at para.19–14 fn.31.
[20] Scotland: *Belmont Laundry Co Ltd v Aberdeen Steam Laundry Co Ltd* (1895) 1 F. 45 (Ct of Sess (IH)); *Rose Street Foundry and Engineering Co Ltd v John Lewis & Sons Ltd*, 1917 S.C. 341 (Ct of Sess (IH)); *Grunwald v Hughes*, 1965 S.L.T. 209 (Ct of Sess (IH)) 215; *BP Petroleum Development Ltd v Esso Petroleum Co Ltd*, 1987 S.L.T. 345 at 348 (Ct of Sess (OH)). Australia: *Street v Retravision (NSW) Pty Ltd* (1995) 56 F.C.R. 588 at 597 (Fed Ct of Aus); *Bialkower v Acohs Pty Ltd*

(b) *Disproving the Claimant's Liability to the Third Party*

20–07 Where a claimant is sued by a third party and joins the defendant to the proceedings by issuing a Pt 20 claim, the Pt 20 claim will fall away if judgment goes against the third party in the main proceedings.[21] However, three questions arise with respect to the defendant's ability to argue that the claimant was not liable to the third party. First, can he raise defences on the claimant's behalf, either where they are both joined as defendants to the main proceedings, or where the claimant has issued a Pt 20 claim? Secondly, where the claimant is found liable in proceedings by the third party, and then brings new proceedings against the defendant, can the defendant challenge the finding in the first proceedings that the claimant was liable? Thirdly, where the defendant is sued by a claimant who has settled a third party's claim, can he dispute that the claimant was liable to pay so much, or anything at all?

(i) *Raising Defences on the Claimant's Behalf*

20–08 Before the introduction of the Civil Procedure Rules, the law held that a person joined to proceedings as a third party was not a defendant to the main proceedings.[22] Hence he was not entitled as of right and without a special order of the court to take an active part in opposing the main claim.[23] It was recognised, however, that a defendant sued for contribution by this mechanism had a legitimate interest in the main proceedings, and so he was allowed to take an active role in these, subject to the court's directions, if he could show that the claimant was making inadequate efforts to defend himself.[24] He could cross-examine the witnesses in the main proceedings on the question whether the claimant was liable,[25] call witnesses of his own to testify on this point,[26] and raise defences on the claimant's behalf that he would not raise for himself.[27] He could also be substituted as the defendant to the main proceedings with the consent of the person who had brought them.[28]

20–09   Where he was not substituted as a defendant in the main proceedings, it was unclear whether an order allowing him to participate made him a party, with the results, first, that he was bound by the court's finding against the claimant for the purposes of the claimant's action against him, and, secondly, that he could appeal from a judgment against the claimant. Canadian authority suggested this to be

---

(1998) 83 F.C.R. 1 at 12 (Full Ct of Fed Ct of Aus); *James Hardie & Co Pty Ltd v Wyong Shire Council* (2000) 48 N.S.W.L.R. 679 at 687–688 (NSW CA).

[21] As in e.g. *Football League Ltd v Edge Ellison (A Firm)* [2006] EWHC 1462 (Ch); [2007] P.N.L.R. 2.

[22] *Edison & Swan United Electric Light Co v Holland* (1889) 41 Ch. D. 28 at 32 (CA).

[23] *Barton v London & North Western Railway Co* (1888) 38 Ch. D. 144 at 150–151 and 153–154 (CA); *Gillespie v Anglo-Irish Beef Processors Ltd* [1994] B.N.I.L. 68 (CA).

[24] RSC Ord.16 r.4(4); CCR Ord.12 r.3(1).

[25] *Barton* (1888) 38 Ch. D. 144 at 150 and 154 (CA); *Re Salmon* (1889) 42 Ch. D. 351 at 362 (CA). See too *Eden v Weardale Iron and Coal Co* (1887) 35 Ch. D. 287; followed in *Pioneer Concrete (N.T.) Pty Ltd v Watkins Ltd* (1983) 66 F.L.R. 279 at 291 (Full Ct of Fed Ct of Aus).

[26] *Barton* (1888) 38 Ch. D. 144 at 150 and 154 (CA).

[27] *Witham v Vane* (1880) 49 L.J. Ch. 242; *Callender v Wallingford* (1884) L.J. Q.B. 569 at 570; *Barton* (1888) 38 Ch. D. 144 at 150 and 154 (CA); *Barclays Bank v Tom* [1923] 1 K.B. 221 at 224 (CA).

[28] *Matthey v Curling* [1922] A.C. 180 at 198 (CA); affirmed on a different point by HL.

so,[29] and this was consistent with the Senior Courts Act 1981 s.151(1), which states that for the purposes of construing English statutes and other documents, the term "party" in relation to any proceedings, "includes any person who pursuant to or by virtue of rules of court . . . has been served with, or has intervened in, those proceedings." However, the English cases which touched on the point suggested that the defendant would only be bound by the court's decision if he had agreed to this at the time when the court ordered that he could participate in the main proceedings.[30] Otherwise, he would have no right to appeal from a judgment against the claimant.[31]

Under the Civil Procedure Rules, if a defendant is joined to a set of proceed- **20–10** ings by the issue of a Pt 20 claim, he is a party to these proceedings by dint of CPR r.20.10(1). Also, under CPR r.20.13, where a defence is filed to a Pt 20 claim, the court must consider the future conduct of proceedings, and must give directions which ensure that the Pt 20 claim and the main claim are managed together, so far as this is practicable. These rules suggest that the court can still permit a defendant to raise defences on a claimant's behalf in the main proceedings, provided that this would be just, proportionate to the expense that might be entailed, and consistent with the goal of enabling the parties to reach a speedy resolution of their dispute.

(ii) *Previous Court Orders*

A claimant may not bring new proceedings for contribution or reimbursement if **20–11** he and the defendant have already been sued to judgment as co-defendants to an action by the third party and a contribution order has been made in those proceedings.[32] Nor may he relitigate the quantum of his entitlement if the court has already apportioned the burden of paying the third party in earlier proceedings.[33]

In contrast, where a claimant alone is sued to judgment by the third party, and **20–12** brings separate proceedings against a defendant who was not a party to the first proceedings, either as a co-defendant or as defendant to a Pt 20 claim, the defendant can challenge the findings made in the first action. This appears from a series of dicta, stating that the whole point of third-party proceedings (as opposed to successive sets of independent proceedings) is to prevent the same question from being tried twice over with possibly different results,[34] and from the fact that there is nothing in the Civil Procedure Rules to stop a defendant from reopening the question of the claimant's liability.[35]

---

[29] *McFall v Vancouver Exhibition Association* [1943] 3 D.L.R. 39 at 40 per MacDonald C.J.B.C. (British Columbia CA): "Respondent had brought in appellants under a creditor notice, claiming indemnity; appellants had leave to contest the main action and were accordingly bound by the judgment."
[30] *Benecke v Frost* (1876) 1 Q.B.D. 419; *Coles v Civil Service Supply Association* (1884) 26 Ch. D. 529 at 531; *Edison* (1889) 41 Ch. D. 28 at 33 (CA).
[31] *Asphalt & Public Works Ltd v Indemnity Guarantee Trust Ltd* [1969] 1 Q.B. 465 at 470–471 and 472–473 (CA), distinguishing *The Millwall* [1905] P. 155 at 165–166 (CA).
[32] *Bell v Holmes* [1956] 1 W.L.R. 1359.
[33] *Wall v Radford* [1991] 2 All E.R. 741; *Talbot v Berkshire CC* [1994] Q.B. 290 (CA).
[34] *Benecke* (1876) 1 Q.B.D. 419 at 422; *Barclays Bank v Tom* [1923] 1 K.B. 221 at 224 (CA); *Standard Securities Ltd v Hubbard* [1967] Ch. 1056 at 1059.
[35] *Powell v Pallisers of Hereford Ltd* [2002] EWCA Civ 99 especially at [14].

20–13   This is unsatisfactory. When a single incident gives rise to several sets of proceedings in which the courts make inconsistent findings of fact, the parties may rightly feel that justice has not been done.[36] Note, in particular, that a claimant who is found liable to a third party in one set of proceedings remains liable even if a different court holds otherwise in a later set of proceedings. This follows from the principle that a competent court has jurisdiction to decide wrongly as well as rightly[37]: if it makes a mistake, then the mistake will be conclusive between the parties unless and until it is corrected by an appellate court.[38] Sixty years ago, these considerations led Glanville Williams to argue that the English rules of civil procedure should be altered to oblige claimants to use the machinery of third-party proceedings to recover contribution and to prevent them from issuing separate sets of proceedings with this end in mind.[39] However this excellent suggestion has never been implemented.[40]

(iii) *Settlements*

20–14   If a claimant settles a third party's claim, and then sues a defendant, the defendant may wish to argue that the settlement figure was too high or that the claimant should not have settled at all. Such arguments are open to defendants in some situations.

20–15   For example, where several sureties have guaranteed a debt, and the debt falls due, one can give notice to the others that they should take steps to defend the creditor's claim, make terms, or pay their due shares of the debt, and if they do nothing after receiving this notice, they cannot complain if he settles with the creditor on their behalf. If he fails to give notice, however, then they can object that the creditor's claim was unfounded or that the settlement could have been made on better terms.[41]

---

[36] See Lord Neuberger M.R.'s comments in *Wright (A Child) v Cambridge Medical Group* [2011] EWCA Civ 669 at [86]–[87]. And cf. *Johnson v Cartledge and Matthews* [1939] 3 All E.R. 654, where the incident with which the case was concerned gave rise to five separate sets of proceedings in which the courts had reached inconsistent findings on the question of liability.

[37] *Philips v Bury* (1694) Skin. 447 at 485; 90 E.R. 198 at 216.

[38] *Meyers v Casey* (1913) 17 C.L.R. 90 at 115.

[39] G. Williams, *Joint Torts and Contributory Negligence* (London: Stevens, 1951), pp.185–186, allowing for exceptions where third-party proceedings are impossible.

[40] Though note CMR art.39. For discussion by law reform bodies of the question whether claimants should be compelled to seek contribution by third party proceedings, see University of Alberta, Institute of Law Research and Reform, *Contributory Negligence and Concurrent Wrongdoers* (Report No.31, 1979) p.74; Ontario Law Reform Commission, *Report on Contribution Among Wrongdoers and Contributory Negligence* (1988) pp.215–216; Scottish Law Commission, *Report on Civil Liability: Contribution* (Scot Law Com. No.115, 1988) paras 3.78–3.79; New Zealand Law Commission, *Apportionment of Civil Liability* (NZLC PP 19, 1992) para.256; New South Wales Law Reform Commission, *Contribution Between Persons Liable for the Same Damage* (Discussion Paper No.38, 1997) paras 7.3–7.11.

[41] *Duffield v Scott* (1789) 3 T.R. 374; 100 E.R. 628; *Smith v Compton* (1832) 3 B. & Ad. 407; 110 E.R. 146 (doubted for other reasons in *Great Western Railway v Fisher* [1905] 1 Ch. 316 at 324); *Jones v Williams* (1841) 7 M. & W. 493 at 501; 151 E.R. 860 at 864; *Pettmann v Keble* (1850) 9 C.B. 701; 137 E.R. 1067; *Stewart v Braun* [1925] 2 D.L.R. 423 (Manitoba KB); *B.S.E. Trading Ltd v Hands* (1998) 75 P. & C.R. 138.

Under the Civil Liability (Contribution) Act 1978 s.1(4), a claimant "who has **20–16**
made or agreed to make any payment in bona fide settlement or compromise"[42]
of a third party's claim[43]:

> "shall be entitled to recover contribution in accordance with this section without regard
> to whether or not he himself is or ever was liable in respect of the damage, provided,
> however, that he would have been liable assuming that the factual basis of the claim
> against him could be established."

This subsection was enacted to overcome the problems created by *Stott v West
Yorkshire Road Car Co Ltd*,[44] where it was held that a claimant who settled a
third party's claim could not recover contribution from a defendant unless he
could prove that he would have been held liable if the third party had sued him
to judgment. The Law Commission thought that a claimant who settled a third
party's claim might find this hard to prove, particularly where he had denied
liability in order to negotiate a more favourable settlement,[45] suggesting that the
Stott rule discouraged the settlement of claims.[46] Hence, s.1(4) was enacted to
relieve a settling claimant of the need to show that the third party would have
been able to prove the factual basis of his claim.

However, the claimant still has to show that he would have been liable in law[47] **20–17**
if the alleged facts were made out, and so a claimant who settles with a creditor
although his liability is legally doubtful may still be unable to recover a contribution. This was tested in *B.R.B. (Residuary) Ltd v Connex South Eastern Ltd*.[48]
The parties both inherited rights and liabilities from the British Railways Board.
The claimant settled an action by the widow of one of the Board's former
employees in the mistaken belief that it had inherited the Board's liability
towards her when in fact this liability had been inherited by the defendant.
Judgment was entered against the claimant by consent and it sought reimbursement under the 1978 Act. The defendant denied liability on the basis that the
claimant had never been legally liable to the widow, but Cranston J. found for the
claimant for two reasons: first, because the entry of judgment had itself conclusively rendered the claimant liable to the widow, regardless of the underlying
legal merits of her claim, and, secondly, because the question whether the
claimant would have escaped liability on the legal merits had to be tested against

---

[42] The word "payment" includes "payment in kind", and so the subsection applies where a claimant
does work to repair damage to property: *Baker & Davies Plc v Leslie Wilks Associates (A Firm)*
[2005] EWHC 1179 (TCC); [2005] 3 All E.R. 603.
[43] See too the Defamation Act 1996 s.3(8)(a): where a claimant offers to make amends for defaming
a third party by paying him compensation, and the offer is accepted, "the amount of compensation
paid under the offer shall be treated as paid in bona fide settlement or compromise of the claim" for
the purposes of the 1978 Act.
[44] *Stott v West Yorkshire Road Car Co Ltd* [1971] 2 Q.B. 651, especially at 657 (CA). See too *James
P. Corry & Co Ltd v Clarke* [1967] N.I. 62 at 71. And cf. *Baylis v Waugh* [1962] N.Z.L.R. 44 at 49
(NZ High Ct).
[45] As was subsequently the case in e.g. *Thomas Saunders Partnership v Harvey* (1989) 30 Con. L.R.
103 at 120–121.
[46] Law Commission, *Report on Contribution* (1977) Law Com. No.79, paras 44–57.
[47] Whether English or foreign law. Propositions of foreign law do not comprise part of the "factual
basis" of the third party's claim for the purposes of s.1(4): *Arab Monetary Fund v Hashim (No.8)*,
The Times, June 17, 1993 (Chadwick J.).
[48] *B.R.B. (Residuary) Ltd v Connex South Eastern Ltd* [2008] EWHC 1172 (QB); [2008] 1 W.L.R.
2867.

the pleadings in the widow's action, and these had disclosed no defence to her claim. The problem with both of these findings is that they make the defendant's liability to the claimant turn on issues that should not make a difference, namely whether the settlement agreement has led to the making of a consent order, and whether the parties have pleaded their statements of case sufficiently fully to lay down the factual substratum needed for a legal defence.[49]

20–18   Section 1(4) refers to claimants who have entered "bona fide" settlements, and unlike the Irish Civil Liability Act 1961 s.22, it does not say that the settlement must have been "reasonable" before the claimant is entitled to contribution. Nor does it empower the courts to fix the amount at which an "unreasonable" settlement should have been settled for the purposes of assessing contribution. The Law Commission chose the "bona fide" wording because it wished to prevent dishonest collusion between a claimant and a third party.[50] An attempt was made in Parliament to add a requirement that the settlement must have been reasonable, but the amendment was withdrawn when critics objected that it would enable the defendant to reopen the merits of the third party's claim against the claimant, which they took to be undesirable.[51] This suggests that Parliament's intention when enacting the statute was to prevent defendants from challenging settlement agreements unless they can prove fraudulent intent. Nevertheless, the courts have assumed that even where the other parties have acted in good faith, the defendant can argue that the claimant acted unreasonably in settling for too large a sum.[52] This has prompted the further questions, whether it is relevant that the claimant acted on legal advice, and if so, whether the defendant should have discovery of communications between the claimant and his legal adviser? The weight of authority suggests that such legal advice is usually irrelevant to the question whether the settlement was reasonable, as this is something for the court alone to decide.[53]

(c) Disproving the Defendant's Liability to the Third Party

20–19   A defendant will escape liability to the claimant if he can show that he was not liable to the third party. Alternatively, if he can show that he had a partial

---

[49] This is not to say that the wrong result was reached, since a claim grounded on mistake should have succeeded.

[50] Law Commission, *Report on Contribution*, paras 55–57. For a case where an arrangement was allegedly reached in bad faith between the third party and the claimant, see *Abbey National Plc v Gouldman* [2003] EWHC 925 (Ch); [2003] 1 W.L.R. 2042 at [14].

[51] *Hansard, Reports of Standing Committees for 1977–1978 Session, vol.2: Standing Committee C: Sittings on the Civil Liability (Contribution) Bill*, especially cols 23–24 and 43 (I. Percival MP) and cols 40–41 (P. Mayhew MP) (June 7, 1978).

[52] e.g. *Oxford University Press v John Stedman Design Group* (1990) 34 Con. L.R. 1; *Society of Lloyd's v Kitsons Environmental Services Ltd* [1994] C.I.L.L. 940; *D.S.L. Group Ltd v Unisys International Services Ltd* [1994] C.I.L.L. 942; *J Sainsbury Plc v Broadway Malyan (A Firm)* (1998) 61 Con. L.R. 31. Cf. *Nesbitt v Beattie* [1955] 2 D.L.R. 91 at 94 (Ontario CA); *Bakker v Joppich* (1980) 25 S.A.S.R. 468 at 475 (Sup Ct of South Aus); *Saccardo Constructions Pty Ltd v Gammon* (1991) 56 S.A.S.R. 552 at 559–560 (Full Ct of Sup Ct of South Aus); *Dowthwaite Holdings Pty Ltd v Saliba* [2006] WASCA 72 at [89]–[95].

[53] *Oxford University Press* (1990) 34 Con. L.R. 1 at 101–102; *D.S.L. Group* (1994) 41 Con. L.R. 33 at 39–43; *J Sainsbury* (1998) 61 Con. L.R. 31 at 64. Contra, *Society of Lloyd's* (1994) 41 Con. L.R. 20 at 29–30; *P&O Developments Ltd v Guy's and St Thomas' NHS Trust* (1998) 62 Con L.R. 38 at 55.

defence to the third party's claim, his liability to the claimant will be correspondingly reduced.

(i) *Previous Court Orders*

Where a defendant defeats a claim by a third party, and the third party successfully sues a claimant instead, can the claimant then relitigate the defendant's liability to the third party in new proceedings? This question was considered by the Law Commission in the Working Paper[54] which preceded their 1977 *Report on Contribution,*[55] which led in turn to the enactment of the Civil Liability (Contribution) Act 1978. In the Working Paper, the Law Commission suggested that the claimant should be able to reopen the question of the defendant's liability to the third party, if he can show that he has evidence conclusive of the defendant's liability, of which the third party was unaware at the time of the first action.[56] Following its consultation process, however, the Law Commission concluded that it was better that the claimant should be bound by the previous decision in the defendant's favour than that the defendant should have to defend himself twice. Hence they recommended that a defendant should not be liable for contribution once he has defeated an action by a third party on its merits.[57] **20–20**

However, the Law Commission also thought that a defendant who defeats a third party's claim by relying on the expiry of a limitation period should not be relieved from liability to pay contribution. Otherwise, an inconsistency would be created with the rule that a defendant is liable to pay contribution where the third party never sues him at all, although he would have been liable on the merits if he had been sued in time. In the Law Commission's view, a defendant "ought to be no better off if the [third party's] proceedings against [him] fail on a 'limitation' point than if they are never brought"[58]—and they drew the same conclusion with regard to the situation where a defendant has the third party's proceedings against him dismissed for want of prosecution.[59] Hence they proposed that the contribution legislation should provide that where a defendant has defeated a third party's claim, this should amount to conclusive evidence that he is not liable to pay contribution, but they also wished to add this proviso to the relevant section of their bill[60]: **20–21**

> "[P]rovided that the judgment in his favour rested on a determination of the merits of the claim against him in respect of the damage (and not, for example, on the fact that the action was brought after the expiration of any period of limitation applicable thereto)."

In the event, this wording was not incorporated into the 1978 Act, s.1(5) of which simply states that: **20–22**

---

[54] Law Commission, *Working Paper on Contribution*, (1975) LCWP No.59.
[55] Law Commission, *Report on Contribution*.
[56] Law Commission, *Working Paper on Contribution*, para.39.
[57] Law Commission, *Report on Contribution*, paras 63–65.
[58] Law Commission, *Report on Contribution*, at para.60.
[59] Law Commission, *Report on Contribution*, at para.61.
[60] Draft Civil Liability (Contribution) Bill cl.3(7).

"[A] judgment given in any action brought in any part of the United Kingdom by or on behalf of the person who suffered the damage in question against any person from whom contribution is sought under this section shall be conclusive in the proceedings for contribution as to any issue determined by that judgment in favour of the person from whom the contribution is sought."

Taken at face value, s.1(5) therefore allows a defendant to rely on a technical determination in his favour in a previous action by a third party, but the cases suggest that the courts are reluctant to interpret the subsection in this way.[61] Note, though, that there are stronger reasons for allowing a defendant the protection of a previous judgment in his favour where the third party's proceedings were time-barred than where they were dismissed for want of prosecution. In the former case, judgment against the third party is final, but dismissal for want of prosecution is an interim order that does not bar further proceedings on the same facts.[62]

20–23   In *Moy v Pettman Smith (A Firm),*[63] the question arose whether s.1(5) prevents a claimant from appealing against a decision that a defendant is not liable to a third party, where the third party has sued the claimant and defendant as joint defendants, and has won against the claimant but lost against the defendant. In the Court of Appeal, Latham L.J. held that this is not prohibited by the subsection. Although this was enacted "to ensure that a person is not exposed to the risks of further litigation after the issues have *prima facie* been resolved", he thought that the "same considerations do not apply where, as in this case, all the relevant parties were present at, and took a full part in, the trial of those issues."[64] This finding was confirmed on appeal,[65] but it may be questioned whether the fact that the parties appeared in court together as defendants provides sufficient justification for this result, given that the opposite rule still governs the case where the parties have been sued in separate proceedings. In both situations, the claimant may have a legitimate complaint that his chances of recovery have been destroyed by the third party's failure to make out his claim against the defendant. If the interests of finality dictate that this complaint must be overridden in the one case, then why is it not also overridden in the other?

(ii) Settlements

20–24   The Civil Liability (Contribution) Act 1978 s.1(3), states that a defendant is liable for contribution under the 1978 Act "notwithstanding that he has ceased to

---

[61] *R.A. Lister & Co Ltd v E.G. Thomson (Shipping) Ltd (No.2)* [1987] 1 W.L.R. 1614 at 1623; *Nottingham Health Authority v Nottingham CC* [1988] 1 W.L.R. 903 at 906 (CA).
[62] A point made by Callinan J. in *James Hardie & Co Pty Ltd v Seltsam Pty Ltd* (1998) 196 C.L.R. 53 at 96, considering *Hart v Hall & Pickles Ltd* [1969] 1 Q.B. 405 (CA), where it was held that a contribution claim would lie under the Law Reform (Married Women and Tortfeasors) Act 1935 s.6, where the third party's previous action against the defendant had been dismissed for want of prosecution. The 1935 Act contained no provision equivalent to s.1(5), and so the *Hart* case only has persuasive authority when construing the latter subsection.
[63] *Moy v Pettman Smith (A Firm)* [2002] EWCA Civ 875; [2002] P.N.L.R. 961.
[64] *Moy v Pettman Smith (A Firm)* [2002] EWCA Civ 875; [2002] P.N.L.R. 961 at [10].
[65] *Moy* [2005] UKHL 7; [2005] 1 W.L.R. 581, where Lord Carswell also noted Goddard L.J.'s finding in *Hanson v Wearmouth Coal Co Ltd* [1939] 3 All E.R. 47 at 55 (CA), that the claimant should be entitled to appeal a decision in the defendant's favour. Note, though, that this was a case decided under the Law Reform (Married Women and Tortfeasors) Act 1935.

be liable in respect of the damage in question since the time when the damage occurred". The main purpose of this subsection is to render defendants liable for contribution although the third party has lost his ability to sue them by the time of the claimant's payment, through the expiry of a limitation period.[66] However, it has been held that the subsection also renders a defendant liable to pay contribution although he has previously settled the third party's claim.[67]

Where there is no evidence of dishonest collusion between the defendant and **20–25** the third party,[68] it seems arguable that the defendant should not have to pay more by way of contribution than he agreed to pay the third party. Such a rule would be consistent with s.2(3)(a) of the 1978 Act, which states that where the defendant's liability to a third party is limited by a pre-existing contract, he is not liable for a greater sum by way of contribution.[69] The rule has also been adopted by the Defamation Act 1996 s.3(8)(b), which states that where a defendant offers to make amends for defaming a third party by paying him compensation, and the third party accepts this offer, but then recovers from the claimant instead, the defendant is not liable for a larger sum by way of contribution than the amount he agreed to pay.[70] However, it might be said that the defendant should not be allowed to prejudice the claimant's position by settling with the third party for less than his true share of their common liability.

This issue was considered in *Jameson v Central Electricity Generating* **20–26** *Board*,[71] where the questions arose whether a third party is debarred from suing a claimant where the claimant and the defendant are several concurrent tortfeasors and the third party has settled his claim against the defendant, and if not, whether the claimant can recover contribution from the defendant if the third party wins judgment against him? Jameson was exposed to asbestos dust at different locations, including premises owned by CEGB, during his employment by Babcock. He contracted mesothelioma, and sued Babcock for negligence and breach of statutory duty. This action was settled shortly before he died of the disease. The settlement figure, paid "in full and final settlement and satisfaction" of his claim, was around £80,000, which was assumed to have been less than two-thirds of his actual loss. After his death, Jameson's widow brought a claim against CEGB under the Fatal Accidents Act 1976, making similar allegations of negligence and breach of statutory duty. The CEGB brought third party proceedings against Babcock seeking a contribution under the Civil Liability (Contribution) Act 1978. The Court of Appeal held that Babcock was liable under the 1976 Act and that Babcock was entitled to recover a contribution from CEGB.[72]

---

[66] See paras 20–41—20–42.
[67] *Watts v Aldington, The Times*, December 16, 1993 (CA); *Guinness Plc v C.M.D. Property Developments Ltd* (1995) 76 B.L.R. 40; *British Racing Drivers' Club Ltd v Hextall Erskine & Co (A Firm)* [1996] 3 All E.R. 667 at 683; *Jameson v Central Electricity Generating Board* [2000] 1 A.C. 455 at 471; *Heaton v AXA Equity and Law Life Assurance Society Plc* [2002] 2 A.C. 329 at 356.
[68] As in *Corvi v Ellis*, 1969 S.L.T. 350 (Ct of Sess (IH)), where a man sued his own daughter and then abandoned his suit with a view to having judgment ordered in her favour and a contribution claim precluded.
[69] For discussion of the relevant part of the 1978 Act s.2(3)(a), see paras 20–38—20–40.
[70] Discussed in *Veliu v Mazrekaj* [2006] EWHC 1710 (QB); [2007] 1 W.L.R. 495.
[71] *Jameson v Central Electricity Generating Board* [2000] 1 A.C. 455 (HL).
[72] *Jameson* [1998] Q.B. 323 (CA).

20–27   The first of these findings was reversed by the House of Lords for reasons that are discussed below. So far as the contribution claim was concerned, Lord Hope accepted that in principle CEGB would have been entitled to a contribution from Babcock if it had been liable to Jameson's widow in the main proceedings, and he also thought that Babcock would have been "exposed to a claim for a contribution . . . which [would have been] calculated as if [its settlement with Jameson] had not been entered into".[73] In other words, he did not think that a defendant's liability to pay contribution to a claimant should generally be capped at the amount which the defendant has previously agreed to pay in settlement of the third party's claim.

20–28   The reasons why Lord Hope held that CEGB was not liable to Jameson's widow were as follows. He considered that[74]:

> "The liability which is in issue in this case is that of [several] concurrent tortfeasors, because the acts of negligence and breach of statutory duty which are alleged against Babcock and the defendant respectively are not the same. So the plaintiff has a separate cause of action against each of them for the same loss. But the existence of damage is an essential part of the cause of action in any claim for damages. It would seem to follow . . . that once the plaintiff's claim has been satisfied by any one of several tortfeasors, his cause of action for damages is extinguished against all of them."

It was therefore necessary to decide whether Jameson's agreement with Babcock had relevantly "satisfied" Jameson's claim for damages, by examining the terms of the agreement and comparing them with what his widow was now claiming. The relevant question was not whether he had been fully compensated for his loss, but whether he had accepted that the settlement figure should be taken to fix the full measure of his loss, with the result that he had accepted Babcock's payment in full satisfaction. On the facts, Lord Hope considered that Jameson had accepted Babcock's payment as representing the full measure of his loss, and it followed that his widow was debarred from recovering from CEGB.

20–29   This reasoning was reaffirmed and extended by the House of Lords in two further cases, to take in situations where the same damage has been caused to a victim by two wrongdoers who have not committed a tort, but who have instead committed a breach of contract, breach of statutory duty, or an equitable wrong such as a breach of fiduciary duty.[75] Their Lordships distinguished *Jameson* in both cases, holding that on the facts the victim in each case had not accepted the settlement payment as fixing the full measure of the loss which he had suffered.

20–30   As we discuss below,[76] joint tortfeasors and several concurrent tortfeasors are both liable for the same damage, but there is a significant difference between

---

[73] *Jameson* [2000] 1 A.C. 455 at 471.
[74] *Jameson* [2000] 1 A.C. 455 at 472.
[75] *Heaton* [2002] 2 A.C. 329; *Cape and Dalgliesh (A Firm) v Fitzgerald* [2002] UKHL 16; [2003] 1 C.L.C. 65. Further cases in which the case has been considered are: *Rawlinson v North East Essex Health Authority* [2000] Lloyd's Rep. Med. 54; *Kenburgh Investments (Northern) Ltd v Minton* [2000] 1 Lloyd's Rep. 736 (CA); *Allison v K.P.M.G. Peat Marwick* [2000] 1 N.Z.L.R. 560 (NZ CA); *Mehta v Reid* Unreported CA, December 19, 2000; *Ogle v Chief Constable of Thames Valley Police* [2001] EWCA Civ 598; *John v Price Waterhouse (A Firm)* Unreported Ch. D., April 11, 2001, at [384]–[391].
[76] See paras 20–65—20–66.

them, namely that joint tortfeasors, unlike several concurrent tortfeasors, commit a single wrong, notwithstanding the procedural rule that they can be sued in separate actions.[77] Because of this, the rules governing the release of several concurrent tortfeasors differ from those which govern the release of joint tortfeasors, and there is nothing in the *Jameson* case to cast doubt on the proposition that the release of one joint tortfeasor, whether under seal or by way of accord and satisfaction,[78] automatically releases all the others, whatever the terms of the settlement agreement pursuant to which the release is granted[79]—although a covenant not to sue a joint tortfeasor does not have the same effect.[80] The same is also true of joint debtors—because they owe a single obligation, the release of one joint debtor releases all, although a covenant not to sue a joint debtor does not.[81] Less logically,[82] this is also true of joint and several debtors[83] but not of several concurrent debtors.[84]

(iii) *Contributory Negligence*

The Civil Liability (Contribution) Act 1978 s.2(3)(b) states that where a defendant's liability to a creditor is reduced by virtue of the Law Reform (Contributory Negligence) Act 1945 s.1, the defendant is not liable to pay any larger sum by way of contribution than the amount which he would have been liable to pay the third party. Where all the parties have contributed to the damage suffered by the third party, including the third party himself, any reduction in the amount of damages recoverable by the third party to reflect his contributory negligence is

20–31

---

[77] Cf. *Watts v Aldington, The Times*, December 16, 1993 (CA) per Steyn L.J.: "These appeals illustrate the absurdity of the rule that the release of one of two joint and several tortfeasors operates as a release of the other. In Victorian times judges of great distinction reasoned that in a case involving joint and several liability of joint tortfeasors there is only a single cause of action and accordingly a release of one of two joint tortfeasors extinguishes that single cause of action or, as it was usually put, releases the other joint tortfeasors. The rule has been relaxed by statute. The fact that joint tortfeasors can be sued successively heavily compromised the procedural logic but the old rule apparently still survives." Note, too, that it is unsettled whether the doctrine of res judicata applies to joint tortfeasors: *Cooper Tire & Rubber Co v Shell Chemicals UK Ltd* [2009] EWHC 2609 (Comm); [2009] 2 C.L.C. 619 at [78]–[80]; considering *House of Spring Gardens Ltd v Waite (No.2)* [1991] 1 Q.B. 241 (not discussed on appeal: [2010] EWCA Civ 864; [2010] Bus. L.R. 1697).
[78] *Gardiner v Moore* [1969] 1 Q.B. 55 at 92.
[79] *Thurman v Wild* (1840) 11 Ad. & El. 453; 113 E.R. 487; *Cutler v McPhail* [1962] 2 Q.B. 292.
[80] *Duck v Mayou* [1892] 2 Q.B. 511 (CA); *Apley Estates Co Ltd v De Bernales* [1947] Ch. 217 (CA); *Gardiner* [1969] 1 Q.B. 55. But cf. *Bryanston Finance Ltd v De Vries* [1975] Q.B. 703 at 723 (CA) per Lord Denning M.R., describing the distinction between a release and a covenant not to sue as "an arid and technical distinction without any merits".
[81] *Hutton v Eyre* (1815) 6 Taunt. 289; 128 E.R. 1046; *Johnson v Davies* [1999] Ch. 117 (CA).
[82] Cf. *Jenkins v Jenkins* [1928] 2 K.B. 501 at 508, falling in with the view espoused in *North v Wakefield* (1849) 13 Q.B. 536 at 541; 116 E.R. 1368 at 1370, that the reason for extending the rule governing the release of joint debtors to joint and several debtors is that "otherwise the co-debtors, if not released could, by recovering contributions from the one who was released, defeat his release". As observed in H.G. Beale (ed.), *Chitty on Contracts*, 30th edn (London: Sweet & Maxwell, 2010), para.17–017 fn.48, this reasoning will not do, because "it assumes what requires to be proved, *viz.* that the creditor intends to protect the debtor released against claims from co-debtors".
[83] *Nicholson v Revill* (1836) 4 Ad. & El. 675; 111 E.R. 941; *Deanplan Ltd v Mahmoud* [1993] Ch. 151 at170; *Pollak v National Australia Bank Ltd* [2002] FCA 237.
[84] *Sun Life Assurance Society Plc v Tantofex (Engineers) Ltd* [1999] 2 E.G.L.R. 135.

made before the court assesses the respective contributions of the claimant and the defendant.[85]

20–32 Can a defendant rely on the third party's contributory negligence as a defence to a contribution claim, where his liability to the third party was for breach of contract rather than tort? The best view is that at least where the defendant owed concurrent duties in contract and tort, the third party's contributory negligence can be raised as a defence to the claim for contribution.[86] But there are conflicting authorities on the point, which awaits definitive resolution by the House of Lords.[87] The Law Commission reviewed this area of the law in 1993, and recommended that legislation should be enacted under which contributory negligence is made a defence to a claim for damages for breach of contract, and that s.2(3)(b) of the 1978 Act should be amended to take such new legislation into account.[88]

(iv) *Statutory Defences*

20–33 The Civil Liability (Contribution) Act 1978, s. 2(3)(a) states that where a defendant's liability to a third party would have been limited (or even, by implication, excluded) by "any enactment", the defendant need pay no more by way of contribution than he would have had to pay the third party.[89] A trustee defending a contribution claim by another trustee where both were liable for breach of trust could therefore ask the court to reduce his contribution liability on the basis that it would have reduced his liability under the Trustee Act 1925 s.61; a company director might invoke the Companies Act 2006 s.1157 with the same end in mind.

(v) *Contractual Exclusion of Liability*

20–34 Under the Civil Liability (Contribution) Act 1978 s.2(3)(a), where a defendant's liability to a third party is reduced or excluded by "any agreement made before the damage occurred", the defendant need pay no larger sum by way of contribution than the amount of his maximum liability to the third party, as specified by the contract.

---

[85] *Fitzgerald v Lane* [1989] A.C. 328 at 336–345; deriving assistance from the judgment of Samuels J.A. in *Barisic v Devenport* [1978] 2 N.S.W.L.R. 111 (NSW CA), and refusing to follow *The Miraflores and the Abadesa* [1967] 1 A.C. 826 at 846. See too *The Volvox Hollandia (No.2)* [1993] 2 Lloyd's Rep. 315; *Nelhams v Sandells Maintenance Ltd* [1996] P.I.Q.R. 52 (CA); *Henderson v Merrett Syndicates* [1996] 1 P.N.L.R. 32; *West v Wilkinson* [2008] EWCA Civ 1005.

[86] *Forsikringsaktieselskapet Vesta v Butcher* [1989] A.C. 852.

[87] *Sayers v Harlow Urban DC* [1958] 1 W.L.R. 623; *Quinn v Burch Brothers (Builders) Ltd* [1966] 2 Q.B. 370 at 380–381 (left open on appeal); *Artingstoll v Hewen's Garages Ltd* [1973] R.T.R. 197 at 201; *De Meza v Apple* [1974] 1 Lloyd's Rep. 508 (left open on appeal: [1975] 1 Lloyd's Rep. 498); *Basildon DC v J.E. Lesser (Properties) Ltd* [1985] Q.B. 839; *Victoria University of Manchester v Wilson* (1985) 2 Con. L.R. 43; *A.B. Marintrans v Comet Shipping Co Ltd* [1985] 1 W.L.R. 1270; *Tennant Radiant Heat Ltd v Warrington Development Corp* [1988] 1 E.G.L.R. 41; *Barclays Bank Plc v Fairclough Building Ltd (No.1)* [1995] Q.B. 214; *Secretary of State for the Environment, Transport and Regions v Unicorn Consultancy Services* Unreported Ch. D. October 19, 2000 at [123].

[88] Law Commission, *Contributory Negligence as a Defence in Contract* (1993) Law Com. No.219, paras 4.38 and 5.6–5.9.

[89] Commonwealth cases to the same effect are: *Unsworth v Commissioner for Railways* (1958) 101 C.L.R. 73; *Calderwood v Nominal Defendant* [1970] N.Z.L.R. 296 (NZ CA); *Commonwealth of Australia v Flaviano* (1996) 40 N.S.W.L.R. 199 (NSW CA).

Co-operative Retail Services Ltd v Taylor Young Partnership Ltd[90] illustrates   **20–35**
the operation of this rule.[91] CRS entered a standard form building contract with
Wimpey for the construction of offices. It also engaged TYP and HLP as
architects and engineers on the project. Wimpey engaged an electrical subcontractor, Hall, under a standard form subcontract, and Hall entered a warranty
agreement with CRS and Wimpey, under which it promised to exercise reasonable skill and care when carrying out the subcontract works. The main building
contract excluded Wimpey from liability for damage to the works before practical completion, if this was caused by Wimpey's negligence or breach of statutory duty, and Wimpey was required to take out and maintain a joint names
all-risks insurance policy for the benefit of CRS, Wimpey and the subcontractors.
The main contract and the subcontract also provided that if damage was caused
to the works through negligence, then this should be disregarded in computing
amounts payable under the contract, and that Wimpey (or Hall) would reinstate
the works in full, additional time for which was to be granted, and the costs of
which were to be met from the insurance moneys.

Before practical completion, a fire occurred which damaged the works. Since   **20–36**
fire was an insured risk under the joint names policy, the insurer paid for the costs
of reinstatement, and the works were reinstated by Wimpey in accordance with
the terms of the main building contract. The insurer then brought subrogated
proceedings in CRS's name against TYP and HLP, seeking to recover the
reinstatement costs, on the ground that the fire had been caused by their negligence and breach of contract. TYP and HLP issued Pt 20 proceedings against
Wimpey and Hall, seeking contribution or reimbursement on the ground that they
had all been liable for the same damage suffered by CRS. This claim failed,
essentially because the terms of the main contract between CRS and Wimpey
excluded Wimpey and Hall's liability for damage to CRS. This being so, in Lord
Hope's words[92]:

> "[A]s Wimpey and Hall are not persons from whom C.R.S. is entitled to recover
> compensation in respect of the fire damage, it is not open to T.Y.P. and H.L.P. to recover
> contribution from either Wimpey or Hall in respect of the fire damage for which they
> are said to be liable."

This result was argued to be inequitable by TYP and HLP because it left them
bearing the whole cost of a disastrous fire, for which they had only been partially
responsible. In Lord Bingham's view, however:

> "[T]his is the effect of the standard form contract which C.R.S., Wimpey and Hall
> made, and it is a standard form of which T.Y.P., H.L.P. and their professional indemnity
> insurers must be taken to have been aware."[93]

---

[90] *Co-operative Retail Services Ltd v Taylor Young Partnership Ltd* [2002] 1 W.L.R. 1419 (HL).
[91] See too *Southern Water Authority v Carey* [1985] 2 All E.R. 1077 at 1086; *Plant Construction Plc
v Clive Adam Assocs (A Firm)* (1997) 55 Con L.R. 42 at 70; *B.M.T. Marine and Offshore Survey Ltd
v Lloyd Werft Bremerhaven GmbH* [2011] EWHC 32 (Comm). And cf. *Herrick v Leonard and
Dingley Ltd* [1975] 2 N.Z.L.R. 566 at 572 (NZ High Ct); *Giffels Association Ltd v Eastern
Construction Co* [1978] 2 S.C.R. 1346 at 1355–1356; *Orange Julius Canada Ltd v City of Surrey*
[2000] BCCA 467; *Farstad Supply A/S v Enviroco Ltd* [2010] UKSC 18; [2010] Bus. L.R. 1087 (a
Scottish appeal).
[92] *Co-operative* [2002] 1 W.L.R. 1419 at 1434.
[93] *Co-operative* [2002] 1 W.L.R. 1419 at 1423.

20–37   Insurance policies sometimes contain a clause cancelling cover in the event that there is another insurance covering the same loss. The question has arisen, what the effect of such a clause might be where an insured is covered by two policies, both of which contain the clause. The answer is that the clauses cancel each other out, leaving the insured to recover in full against either insurer, assuming that there is no limit on their respective liabilities and leaving the insurers to their rights inter se.[94]

(vi) *Contractual Limitation of Liability*

20–38   If a defendant's liability is not excluded by his contract with the third party, but is limited to an agreed amount, then again the Civil Liability (Contribution) Act 1978 s.2(3)(a) comes into play. In this situation, several methods could be used to apportion liability between the parties. The Law Commission used the following example to illustrate them in its report which led to the enactment of the statute.[95] Suppose that the amount of damages payable to the third party is £1,000, that a clause in the contract between the third party and the defendant sets a ceiling of £400 on any claim which the third party might make for breach of contract, and that the defendant and the claimant are held to be equally responsible for the third party's damage. Method 1 is to find the defendant liable for £400 and the claimant liable for £500, the balance to be irrecoverable by the third party.[96] Method 2 is to apportion only the common extent of liability between the claimant and the defendant—in this example, £400—and to leave the claimant liable for the balance. Applying this method to the example, the defendant is liable for £200 and the claimant for £800. Method 3 is to apportion the total amount of the damage between the claimant and the defendant, but then to limit the defendant's liability to the extent provided for in his contract with the third party. This produces the result that the claimant is liable for £600 and the defendant for £400. The Law Commission favoured this final method and recommended that provision should be made for it in the 1978 Act.[97] However, s.2(3)(a), which follows the wording of the Law Commission's draft clause, neither requires that Method 3 be used nor precludes the adoption of another method.

20–39   In *Nationwide Building Society v Dunlop Haywards (DHL) Ltd*.[98] Christopher Clarke J. applied Method 3, as he thought that "in implementing the Commission's draft Bill . . . [Parliament] must be taken to have intended to adopt the policy option favoured by the Commission",[99] but he doubted that this was the fairest outcome. The Law Commission rejected Method 2 as:

---

[94] *Waddell v Road Transport General Insurance Co Ltd* [1932] 2 K.B. 563; *National Employers' Mutual General Insurance Association Ltd v Haydon* [1980] 2 Lloyd's Rep. 149; *Poland v Zurich Insurance Co* Unreported QBD (Comm Ct), November 21, 1983.

[95] Law Commission, *Report on Contribution*, paras 71–73.

[96] This method is proscribed by the Irish Civil Liability Act 1961 s.35(1)(g).

[97] Law Commission, *Report on Contribution*, para.74. Cf. Scottish Law Commission, *Report on Civil Liability—Contribution* (Scot. Law Com. No.115, 1988) para.3.67, where the same conclusion is drawn.

[98] *Nationwide Building Society v Dunlop Haywards (DHL) Ltd* [2009] EWHC 254 (Comm); [2010] 1 W.L.R. 258.

[99] *Nationwide BS v DHL* [2009] EWHC 254 (Comm); [2010] 1 W.L.R. 258 at [60].

"unduly favourable to [the defendant, since] he has caused £1,000 worth of damage for which he was ready to assume liability up to £400 but at the end of the day his liability is further reduced to £200".

In the judge's view, however: "[T]he fact that [the defendant] was ready to assume liability to the [third party] for up to £400 is no good reason for requiring him to pay up to that sum in contribution proceedings" in cases where the claimant's liability to the third party is greater than the defendant's on account of his own deceitful conduct, for example because the remoteness rules governing his liability in deceit are more favourable to the third party than the rules governing the defendant's liability in negligence.[100]

Finally, note that indemnity insurers often insert rateable proportion clauses   **20–40** into their policies, which provide that if the insured risk is also covered by another policy, the insurer is liable only for a rateable proportion of any loss or damage.[101] In *Legal and General Assurance Society Ltd v Drake Insurance Co Ltd*,[102] the Court of Appeal held that where an insured loss is covered by two such policies, the insured can recover no more than a rateable proportion from each insurer, so that neither can sue the other for contribution, because neither is obliged to pay the insured for more than its own share of the loss. This case was distinguished in *Drake Insurance Plc v Provident Insurance Plc*,[103] on the ground that the claimant insurer had protested against the defendant insurer's refusal to contribute both before and after paying the insured. It is hard to see why this made a difference. Many cases hold that contribution and reimbursement claims do not lie unless the claimant pays under a legal liability, and since the claimant owed no liability in respect of the defendant's share, that should have determined the case. Matters might have been different if the claimant had made a mistake but it seems to have been aware of its legal position.

(vii) *Expiry of Limitation Periods*

In *George Wimpey & Co Ltd v British Overseas Airways Corp*,[104] the House of   **20–41** Lords held that a claimant could not recover a contribution under the Law Reform (Married Women and Tortfeasors) Act 1935 s.6, where the defendant had previously been sued by a third party and had escaped liability because the claim was time-barred. Illogically, however, it was decided in other cases that a claim lay under the 1935 Act where the third party had never sued the defendant but

---

[100] *Nationwide BS v DHL* [2009] EWHC 254 (Comm); [2010] 1 W.L.R. 258 at [69]–[70]. These were essentially the facts of *Nationwide*, although it was the claimants who could rely on the limitation clause and the defendants whose fraud meant that they owed a much more extensive liability to the third party. See paras 20–57—20–58 for further discussion.

[101] In Australia clauses of this kind are invalidated by the Insurance Contracts Act 1984 (Cth) s.45, considered in *Speno Rail Maintenance Pty Ltd v Metals & Minerals Insurance Pte Ltd* [2009] WASCA 91; (2009) 226 F.L.R. 306; affirmed sub nom. *Zurich Australian Insurance Ltd v Metals & Minerals Insurance Pte Ltd* [2009] HCA 50; (2009) 240 C.L.R. 391.

[102] *Legal and General Assurance Society Ltd v Drake Insurance Co Ltd* [1992] Q.B. 887. Cf. *NFU Mutual Insurance Society Ltd v HSBC Insurance (UK) Ltd* [2010] EWHC 773 (Comm); [2011] Lloyd's Rep. I.R. 86 (no double insurance where one policy contains rateable proportion clause and another contains excess clause).

[103] *Drake Insurance Plc v Provident Insurance Plc* [2003] EWCA Civ 1834; [2004] 2 All E.R. (Comm.) 65 at [123]–[127] and [158].

[104] *George Wimpey & Co Ltd v British Overseas Airways Corp* [1955] A.C. 169.

had lost the right to do so by the time the contribution claim was made by reason of a time bar.[105]

20–42   The rule in the *Wimpey* case was abrogated by the Civil Liability (Contribution) Act 1978 s.1(3), which provides that:

> "[A] person shall be liable to make contribution [under the 1978 Act] notwithstanding that he has ceased to be liable in respect of the damage in question since the time when the damage occurred, unless he ceased to be liable by virtue of the expiry of a period of limitation or prescription which extinguished the right on which the claim against him in respect of the damage was based."

Thus, a defendant cannot escape liability for contribution on the ground that the third party's remedy against him has become time-barred by the time of the contribution claim, but he can escape liability for contribution if the expiry of a limitation period has extinguished the underlying right upon which the third party's claim is based.[106] In most cases the third party's underlying right is preserved despite the fact that his remedy has become statute-barred, but there are a few exceptions to this general rule: under the Limitation Act 1980 s.3(2), the owner's title to a chattel is extinguished six years after its conversion; and under the Limitation Act 1980 s.11A, a tort victim's right to sue for damage caused by a defect in a product is extinguished 10 years after the "relevant time" defined in the Consumer Protection Act 1987 s.4(2).

(viii) *Discharge of Co-Sureties*

20–43   If a surety pays a principal debt, then he may have the right to recover contribution from co-sureties in addition to his right to be reimbursed by the principal debtor. If he wishes to recover contribution from his co-sureties, however, then he must take care not to prejudice *their* rights to reimbursement by the principal debtor, as if he does so, the courts may absolve them from liability to pay contribution. So, if one of several sureties pays off the principal debt, and is entitled to be treated as though he has acquired the creditor's rights against the principal debtor via subrogation, then he may decide to release the principal debtor.[107] But if he does this, his co-sureties will be discharged from liability to pay him contribution, as he will have prejudiced their rights to be reimbursed by the principal debtor.[108] The same principle applies where the surety fails to preserve any securities over the principal debtor's property, to which the other sureties are also entitled.[109]

---

[105] *Morgan v Ashmore, Benson, Pease & Co Ltd* [1953] 1 W.L.R. 418; *Harvey v R.G. O'Dell Ltd* [1958] 2 Q.B. 78; *Fortes Service Areas* v *Department of Transport* (1985) 31 Building LR 1 at 12–13 (CA). These decisions rested on the premise that the phrase "if sued", as used in s.6, meant "if sued at any time", contrary to Lord Reid's obiter view in *Wimpey* that the words "if sued" must refer to a hypothetical action brought by the third party against the defendant at the time of the contribution claim. Lord Reid's view has since been preferred in *Dormer v Melville Dundas & Whitson Ltd*, 1990 S.L.T. 186 at 189 (Ct of Sess (IH)), when a similar question of construction arose with regard to the Law Reform (Miscellaneous Provisions) (Scotland) Act 1940 s.3(2).

[106] *Nottinghamshire Health Authority v Nottingham CC* [1988] 1 W.L.R. 903 at 911–912 (CA); *Société Commerciale de Réassurance v Eras International Ltd* [1992] 1 Lloyd's Rep. 570 at 601 (CA).

[107] *Griffiths v Wade* (1966) 60 D.L.R. (2d) 62 at 68 (Alberta CA).

[108] *Sword v Victoria Super Service Ltd* (1958) 15 D.L.R. (2d) 217 (British Columbia Sup Ct); *Griffiths v Wade* (1966) 60 D.L.R. (2d) 62 (Alberta CA).

[109] *Greenwood v Francis* [1899] 1 Q.B. 312 at 322 and 324 (CA).

3. THIRD PARTY MAY NOT ACCUMULATE RECOVERIES

If a third party can accumulate recoveries from the claimant and defendant, and **20–44** the claimant pays his own liability, this will have no effect on the defendant's liability, and no question can arise of the defendant having been enriched at the claimant's expense. When deciding whether the creditor can accumulate recoveries, the court must consider whether the liabilities owed by the claimant and defendant are assumed or imposed. Where they were assumed by agreement with the third party, the court must look to the terms of the agreements to decide this question. Where their liabilities are imposed by law, the court must ask whether it would be consistent with the policy underpinning their liabilities to allow the third party to accumulate recoveries.

(a) *Assumed Liabilities*

Where a claimant and a defendant have both assumed their liabilities by agree- **20–45** ment, the courts' starting point when deciding whether to let the third party accumulate recoveries is the terms of the parties' agreements. If a third party lends money to a claimant and a defendant in separate and unconnected transactions, then he can obviously recover from both of them in accordance with the terms of the two loans. But if he lends them money in a single transaction, pursuant to an agreement under which they undertake joint, or joint and several, liability to repay him, then it will lie in the nature of the agreement that the third party cannot recover more than the amount of the debt.

Similarly, where two sureties guarantee different debts, or distinct parts of the **20–46** same debt, the creditor can recover from both of them and a contribution claim will not lie between them.[110] But where they guarantee the same debt, but to different limits, the creditor cannot recover more than the amount of the debt by suing both of them, and a contribution claim will lie between them to the extent that their liabilities overlap.[111]

Similarly, where two insurers have provided coverage in respect of different **20–47** risks, both of which materialise, the insurers must both pay in full.[112] It is only where one or more insureds decide[113] to buy coverage from different indemnity

---

[110] *Coope v Twynam* (1823) T. & R. 426 at 429; 37 E.R. 1164 at 1166; *Pendlebury v Walker* (1841) 4 Y. & C. Ex. 424 at 441–442; *Ellis v Emmanuel* (1876) 1 Ex. D. 157 at 162; *Molson's Bank v Kovinsky* [1924] 4 D.L.R. 330 (Ontario CA).

[111] *Ellis* (1876) 1 Ex. D. 157 at 162; *Cornfoot v Holdenson* [1932] V.L.R. 4 at 6–7 (Victoria Sup Ct).

[112] *Glasgow Provident Insurance Society v Westminster Fire Office* (1887) 14 R. 947 at 964 (Ct of Sess (IH)); affirmed (1888) 15 R. 89 (HL); *Boag v Standard Marine Insurance Co Ltd* [1937] 2 K.B. 113 at 123 (CA). Cf. *Collyear v C.G.U. Insurance Ltd* [2008] NSWCA 92; (2008) 227 F.L.R. 121.

[113] There is nothing to prevent an insured from taking out as many insurances as he chooses against the same risk, and in the absence of any rateable proportion clause, he may claim payment from the insurers in any order he pleases: *Godin v London Assurance Co* (1758) 1 Burr. 489 at 492; 97 E.R. 419 at 420–421; *Newby v Reed* (1763) 1 W. Bl. 416 at 416; 96 E.R. 237 at 237; *British & Mercantile Insurance Co v London, Liverpool & Globe Insurance Co* (1877) 5 Ch. D. 569 at 583 and 587 (CA); *Bank of British North America v Western Assurance Co* (1884) 7 Ontario Reports 166 (Ontario High Ct); *Albion Insurance Co Ltd v Government Insurance Office (NSW)* (1969) 121 C.L.R. 343 at 348.

insurers in respect of the same risk[114] to the same interests[115] in the same subject matter,[116] that they are forbidden to recover in full from both insurers, pursuant to the "well established principle that in a case where there are two promises of indemnity in respect of the same liability the promisee can only recover once and not twice".[117] Note, though, that if an insured takes out two contingency policies (i.e. policies such as life policies, under which the insurer promises to pay a fixed sum on the happening of an event regardless of the actual loss suffered), then he can accumulate recoveries provided that he does not recover more than the amount of his insurable interest.[118]

20–48   Note, too, that the "nature of the obligation undertaken by an original tenant and his assignees" when they give separate contractual undertakings to pay the rent "is that they will perform in so far as the [obligation is] not performed by any other party", and it follows that "payment (or deemed payment) of the rent by any one of them prevents the landlord from suing any of the others."[119]

(b) Imposed Liabilities

20–49   Where a claimant or defendant owes a liability to a third party which he has not assumed, but which has been imposed by operation of law, the courts must look to the underlying policy of the law, to determine whether it would be consistent with this policy to allow the third party to accumulate recoveries.

20–50   For example, the main purpose of imposing tort liabilities is to compensate tort victims for the harm which they suffer at the hands of tortfeasors, but it is not to make them better off than they were before the tort was committed. So tort victims who are harmed by joint and several concurrent tortfeasors may not recover more than the amount of their damage by accumulating recoveries from the tortfeasors.[120]

---

[114] *American Surety Co v Wrightson* (1910) 27 T.L.R. 91; *State Government Insurance Commission v Switzerland Insurance Australia Ltd* (1995) 8 A.N.Z. Ins. Cas 61–267 (Full Ct of Sup Ct of South Aus).

[115] *Scottish Amicable Heritable Securities Association Ltd v Northern Assurance Co* (1883) 11 R. 287 (Ct of Sess (IH)); *Nichols v Scottish Union* (1885) 2 T.L.R. 190; *Andrews v Patriotic Assurance Co of Ireland (No.2)* (1886) 18 L.R. Ir. 355; *Port Avon Cinema v Price* [1939] 4 All E.R. 601.

[116] *British & Mercantile* (1877) 5 Ch. D. 569 (CA); *Wrightson* (1910) 27 T.L.R. 91.

[117] *Commercial & General Insurance Co Ltd v Government Insurance Office (NSW)* (1973) 129 C.L.R. 374 at 380 per Barwick C.J. Cf. *Godin* (1758) 1 Burr. 489 at 492; 97 E.R. 419 at 421; *British & Mercantile* (1877) 5 Ch D 569 at 581 (CA).

[118] *Hebdon v West* (1863) 3 B. & S. 579; 122 E.R. 218; *Simcock v Scottish Imperial Insurance Co* (1902) 10 S.L.T. 286 (Ct of Sess (OH)); both applying the Life Assurance Act 1774 s.3.

[119] *Sun Life Assurance* [1999] 2 E.G.L.R. 135 at 136–137; considering *Deanplan* [1993] Ch. 151. Under the Landlord and Tenant (Covenants) Act 1995 ss.3 and 5, the original tenant of a lease granted after 1995 is now generally released from covenants in the lease once it has been assigned. But it can happen under the scheme of the 1995 Act that two parties are bound by the same covenant to a landlord, in which case they are deemed to owe him a joint and several liability by s.13.

[120] *Clark v Newsam* (1847) 1 Exch. 131 at 140; 154 E.R. 55 at 59; followed in *Smith v Streatfeild* [1913] 3 K.B. 764 at 769; *Bell v Thompson* (1934) 34 S.R. (N.S.W.) 431 at 435 (NSW Sup Ct); *Dougherty v Chandler* (1946) 46 S.R. (N.S.W.) 370 at 375 (NSW Sup Ct); *Spiers v Caledonian Collieries Ltd* (1956) 57 S.R. (N.S.W.) 483 at 511–512 (NSW Sup Ct); *Dingle v Associated Newspapers Ltd* [1961] 2 Q.B. 162 at 188–189 (CA); not considered on appeal: [1964] A.C. 371; *Martin v Listowel Memorial Hospital* Unreported Ontario CA, November 1, 2000, at [35]; *Crooks v Newdigate Properties Ltd* [2009] EWCA Civ 283; [2009] C.P. Rep. 34 at [19], citing *Tang Man Sit v Capacious Investments Ltd* [1996] A.C. 514 at 522 (PC).

Again, the purpose of the law of unjust enrichment is to enable claimants to   **20–51**
recover benefits which defendants have unjustly received at their expense, but it
is not to enable them to make a profit by recovering twice over. Authority for this
is *Trustor AB v Smallbone*,[121] where Scott V.C. discussed the following hypothetical situation. A defendant is unjustly enriched by the receipt of money from a
claimant. Because he knows of the circumstances making his enrichment unjust,
he cannot rely on a change of position defence if he pays the money to someone
else.[122] The defendant pays the money to a third party who also knows of the
circumstances which made it unjust for the defendant to have received the money
from the claimant. Here the claimant can recover from the defendant or the third
party, but he cannot recover from both in full: in Scott V.C.'s words, "there can
be no double recovery".[123]

As in the case of assumed liabilities, it is a question of fact whether the policies   **20–52**
underlying the imposition of each party's liability preclude double recovery. For
example, where two wrongdoers cause separate injuries to the same third party
there is no reason why he should not recover from both of them,[124] but where
they cause him a single indivisible injury this is not permitted. The same point
is expressed in a different way in cases turning on the question whether a
claimant and defendant are liable for the "same damage" for the purposes of the
Civil Liability (Contribution) Act 1978. Section 1(1) provides that "any person
liable in respect of any damage suffered by another person may recover contribution [under the statute] from any other person liable in respect of the same
damage". To escape liability under the statute, defendants therefore sometimes
argue that the damage for which they are liable to a third party is not the "same
damage" as the damage for which the claimant was liable, with the result that the
third party can accumulate recoveries and no contribution claim will lie.

Some guidance on the meaning of this phrase was given by Scott V.C. in   **20–53**
Howkins & Harrison (A Firm) v Tyler.[125] The appellant firm valued property for
a building society, and in reliance on this valuation the building society lent
money to the respondent borrowers against the security of the property. The borrowers defaulted, the property was sold for less than the amount of the loan, and
without admitting liability, the firm settled the building society's claim in negligence. The firm then sought contribution from the respondents under the 1978
Act, a claim that should have been dismissed on the basis that Parliament
confined the scope of the 1978 Act to claims between wrongdoers, so that a claim

---

[121] *Trustor AB v Smallbone* Unreported CA, May 9, 2000. See too subsequent proceedings, reported
sub nom *Trustor AB v Smallbone (No.2)* [2001] 1 W.L.R. 1177 esp. at 1186 per Morritt V.C.
[122] Since he cannot make such a payment in good faith: *Lipkin Gorman (A Firm) v Karpnale Ltd*
[1991] 2 A.C. 548 at 579; discussed at paras 27–32—27–35.
[123] *Trustor (No.2)* [2001] 1 W.L.R. 1177 at [70]. See too *S.C.E.G.S. Redlands Ltd v Barbour* [2008]
NSWCA 928 at [8]: where defendants are jointly enriched the amount recoverable from one must be
reduced by the value of the amount recovered from the other.
[124] As in e.g. *Great North Eastern Railway Ltd v J.L.T. Corporate Risks Ltd* [2006] EWHC 1478
(QB).
[125] *Howkins & Harrison (A Firm) v Tyler* [2001] P.N.L.R. 634 (CA). Cf. *British and Commonwealth
Holdings Plc v Quadrex Holdings Inc* Unreported QBD (Comm Ct), May 8, 1991, where Gatehouse
J. noted counsel's argument that the phrase "same damage" should be interpreted by looking at the
"overlap of damages" payable to a creditor by a claimant and a defendant, "in the sense that for each
pound recovered by [the creditor] from one of the [parties] it could not recover that pound from the
other".

cannot lie where one of them was liable in debt.[126] However, Scott V.C. was prepared to assume that the respondent borrowers had relevantly owed a liability for "damage" because the building society had suffered a loss when they breached their contractual promise to pay the debt, and he went on to consider the question whether this was the "same damage" as the damage suffered by the building society as a result of the appellant firm's negligence.

20–54   Scott V.C. held that it was not, because the liabilities owed by the parties did not satisfy a test which he formulated to determine when the "same damage" requirement is satisfied. In effect, he considered that this requirement breaks down into two parts. First, the parties must have been liable to a third party who is forbidden to accumulate recoveries from both of them. Secondly, this third party's rights against the defendant must have been extinguished when he is paid by the claimant, and it must also be possible to say that if the defendant had paid the third party instead, then again the claimant's liability would have been discharged.[127]

20–55   Applying this test to the facts, Scott V.C. held that it was not satisfied, because it could not be said that the appellant firm's payment of damages to the building society had discharged the respondent borrowers' contractual liability to pay the debt. This did not mean, of course, that the building society could accumulate recoveries from the firm and the borrowers. It simply meant that the situation was not one which could be resolved by holding the debt to have been discharged and allowing a contribution claim. Instead, to prevent the building society from recovering twice over, Scott V.C. would have ordered it to account to the appellant firm for the fruits of its action against the borrowers, to the extent that it would otherwise make a profit.[128]

20–56   Scott V.C.'s "mutual discharge" test has been applied in several cases, including *Eastgate Group Ltd v Lindsey Morden Group Inc*,[129] where a vendor of company shares was sued for breach of warranty by the purchaser when there turned out to be a difference in the value of the company's business as warranted and the value of the business in fact. The vendor joined the purchaser's accountants as Pt 20 defendants, claiming a contribution under the 1978 Act, and the question arose whether they were liable for the "same damage". Longmore L.J. held that they were, because the vendor's liability on the warranty was not a liability in debt, but a liability to compensate the purchaser for loss actually suffered, and so it would have been discharged if the purchaser had been paid by the accountants.

---

[126] See para.19–30.

[127] *Howkins* [2001] P.N.L.R. 634 at 639–640.

[128] *Howkins* [2001] P.N.L.R. 634 at 641. For discussion of this remedy in the context of insurance law, where it is often inaccurately said to be a type of subrogation, see paras 21–11—21–13 and 21–93—21–106.

[129] *Eastgate Group Ltd v Lindsey Morden Group Inc* [2002] 1 W.L.R. 642 at 648–651 (CA). See too *Hurstwood Developments Ltd v Motor & General & Andersley & Co Insurance Services Ltd* [2002] Lloyd's Rep. I.R. 185 (CA). But cf. *Royal Brompton Hospital NHS Trust v Hammond* [2002] UKHL 14; [2002] 1 W.L.R. 1397 at [28] where Lord Steyn thought that the usefulness of the "mutual discharge" test might vary with the circumstances of individual cases. On the same general point see also *Greene Wood & McClean LLP v Templeton Insurance Ltd* [2009] EWCA Civ 65; [2009] 1 W.L.R. 2013 especially at [21]–[23]; further proceedings [2010] EWHC 2679 (Comm); [2011] 2 Costs L.R. 205 esp. at [67]–[79].

A different point arose in *Nationwide BS v DHL*,[130] where a building society   **20–57**
lost some £21 million on loans made in reliance on fraudulently overstated
valuations of property. It sued its valuers for deceit and its solicitors for negligence. The solicitors settled the claim against them for £5 million, relying on a
contractual limitation clause, and could also have reduced their liability by
invoking rules on remoteness and contributory negligence that could not have
been invoked by the valuers. The solicitors then sought a contribution from the
valuers, which argued that the damage for which the parties had been commonly
liable was the whole £21 million loss. The point of this argument was that the
contribution payable would be reduced if it could be shown that the solicitors had
only paid a small, rather than a large, part of the damage for which the parties had
been commonly liable.

The valuers' argument was rejected by Christopher Clarke J., who held that   **20–58**
any category of loss for which only one of the parties was liable should be
ignored when identifying the "same damage". The remoteness rules meant that
the solicitors would have been liable only for £13.2 million, and the contributory
negligence rules would further have reduced their liability to £6.6 million. The
judge held that the latter rules should be taken into account when identifying the
"same damage" because the only reason why the valuers could not also have
invoked them was that their liability lay in deceit. Ignoring them for the purpose
of the contribution proceedings would therefore be "to visit on [the solicitors] the
approach taken by the court, partly for reasons of deterrence, against fraudsters,
when [they were] innocent of any fraud."[131] Reluctantly, however, the judge
thought that he was bound to ignore the contractual limitation because this had
been the intention of the Law Commission when drafting the clause of the bill
that later came to be enacted in the 1978 Act as s.2(3)(a).[132]

4. THIRD PARTY CAN RECOVER IN FULL FROM CLAIMANT OR DEFENDANT

Where a third party is forbidden to accumulate recoveries from a claimant and a   **20–59**
defendant, English law almost always gives him the right to recover from either
party in full, in order to maximise his chances of recovery. In this part we
describe some of the situations in which a third party is given such a right. We
also consider why English law generally operates a system of joint and several
liability, rather than a proportionate liability system which would limit the
amount payable by the claimant and defendant to their proper shares.

(a) *Joint and Several Liabilities*

(i) *General Incidents of Joint and Several Liability*

Two points must be made at the outset regarding the consequences of character-   **20–60**
ising liabilities as joint and several. One is that where liabilities are several, or

---

[130] *Nationwide BS v DHL* [2009] EWHC 254 (Comm); [2010] 1 W.L.R. 258.
[131] *Nationwide BS v DHL* [2009] EWHC 254 (Comm); [2010] 1 W.L.R. 258 at [71].
[132] See paras 20–38—20–39.

joint and several, the party to whom they are owed can choose whether to sue all of the liable parties in one set of proceedings, or to bring separate proceedings against one or more of them, suing each for the whole of the relevant debt or damage, until he recovers in full.[133] In contrast, where contractors are jointly liable to a promisee he must generally join them all to proceedings to enforce their joint promise,[134] and one might have expected that this rule would also apply to joint tortfeasors, since they also owe a single, joint obligation. However, English law has long held that the victims of joint torts can sue any or all of the tortfeasors, at their option, and for this reason the courts often say—confusingly —that joint tortfeasors are jointly *and severally* liable to their victims.[135]

20-61   The second point to note is that the Civil Liability (Contribution) Act 1978 s.3, which replaced and extended the Law Reform (Married Women and Tortfeasors) Act 1935 s.6(1)(a) and (b),[136] abrogates the common law rule that recovery of judgment against any one of a number of joint tortfeasors[137] or joint contractors[138] bars further action against the others, even where the judgment has not been satisfied.[139] However, in *Morris v Wentworth-Stanley*,[140] the court held that s.3 does not apply to a judgment obtained by consent against a joint debtor, where the consent judgment embodies a release by accord and satisfaction (rather than a covenant not to sue), because an accord and satisfaction with one joint debtor releases the others from liability. Consistently with this, the Court of

---

[133] *Isaacs & Sons v Salbstein* [1916] 2 K.B. 139 at 143 (CA); *Bucknell v O'Donnell* (1922) 31 C.L.R. 40; *Freshwater v Bulmer Rayon Co Ltd* [1933] Ch. 162; *United Australia Ltd v Barclays Bank Ltd* [1941] A.C. 1. For further cases on joint and several contracts, see G. Williams, *Joint Obligations* (London: Butterworth, 1949), p.60 fn.2, but note that in the case of a joint and several contract, the promisee cannot sue the promise as joint by suing some but not all of the promisors in a single set of proceedings without also joining the others: see cases cited by Williams, above, p.61 fn.3.

[134] *Kendall v Hamilton* (1879) 4 App. Cas. 504; *Wegg Prosser v Evans* [1895] 1 Q.B. 108 at 111 (CA); *Norbury, Nazio & Co Ltd v Griffiths* [1918] 2 K.B. 369 (CA). There are some exceptions to this rule, which does not apply in the county court: County Courts Act 1984 s.48. For earlier cases, and general discussion, see Williams, *Joint Obligations*, pp.51–60.

[135] See e.g. *Wah Tat Bank Ltd v Chan Cheng Kum* [1975] A.C. 507 at 516 (PC); *C.B.S. Songs Ltd v Amstrad Consumer Electronics Plc* [1988] A.C. 1013 at 1058 (HL); *McCullagh v Lane Fox & Partners Ltd* [1996] 1 E.G.L.R. 35 at 42 (CA); *Kuwait Oil Tanker Co SAK v Al Bader* [2000] 2 All E.R. (Comm.) 271 at 317 (CA); *Baxter v Obacelo Pty Ltd* (2001) 205 C.L.R. 635 at [25]. Earlier examples are in Williams, *Joint Torts and Contributory Negligence*, p.50, n. 4; and earlier authorities for the propositions (i) that joint tortfeasors can be joined as co-defendants, (ii) that the victim can instead sue one only, and (iii) that the victim can instead sue some but not all of them in a single set of proceedings, are in Williams, *Joint Torts and Contributory Negligence*, pp.49–50 fnn.1, 2, and 3.

[136] The 1978 provision extends the 1935 provision because: (1) it applies not to tortfeasors, but to "any person liable in respect of any debt or damage"; and (2) it makes it clear that the provision applies not only to successive actions but also to a single action against two or more persons, confirming the view taken of the 1935 provision in *Bryanston Finance* [1975] Q.B. 703 at 722 (CA).

[137] *Brinsmead v Harrison* (1872) L.R. 7 C.P. 547; *London Association for the Protection of Trade v Greenlands Ltd* [1916] 2 A.C. 15 at 21 (HL); *Ash v Hutchinson & Co (Publishers) Ltd* [1936] Ch. 489; see also the cases collected in Williams, *Joint Torts and Contributory Negligence*, p.36 fn.2.

[138] *King v Hoare* (1844) 13 M. & W. 494; 153 E.R. 206; *Kendall v Hamilton* (1879) 4 App. Cas. 504 (HL); *Parr v Snell* [1923] 1 K.B. 1. For discussion, see Williams, *Joint Obligations*, pp.94–103.

[139] See too *Shapland v Palmer* [1999] 1 W.L.R. 2068 at 2071 (CA).

[140] *Morris v Wentworth-Stanley* [1999] Q.B. 1004 (CA).

Appeal held in *Crooks v Newdigate Properties Ltd*,[141] that where a consent judgment embodies a covenant by the claimant not to sue the defendant, while retaining the right to sue some other party, the consent judgment does not release this other party from liability, save to the extent that recovery from him would leave the claimant more than fully satisfied.

(ii) *Debt*

When two parties join together in making a promise to a third, their promise may be joint, or it may be joint and several. If it is a joint promise, then the parties make only one promise which is binding on them both: together, they owe a single liability.[142] If it is a joint and several promise, then again the parties make one promise which is binding on them both, but each also makes a separate promise which is binding on him alone: together, they owe a single liability, but each also owes another liability of his own. If the parties wish to characterise their liabilities as joint and several rather than joint, then they must use express words, as English law presumes that when two parties join in making a promise to a third they intend to create a joint liability.[143] Joint promises are now much less common than joint and several promises, but where two parties join in making a promise to a third, it remains a question of construction whether their words are sufficient to create a joint and several liability.[144] **20–62**

It often happens that several parties assume different contractual liabilities to the same person,[145] but for present purposes, it is more significant that several parties can also separately assume liabilities to the same creditor for the same debt, in circumstances where he may not recover twice. For example, the "nature of the obligation undertaken by an original tenant and his assignees" when they give separate contractual undertakings to the landlord that the rent will be paid "is that they will perform in so far as the [obligation to pay rent is] not performed by any other party liable to do so".[146] Hence the landlord cannot recover from all **20–63**

---

[141] *Crooks v Newdigate Properties Ltd* [2009] EWCA Civ 283; [2009] C.P. Rep. 34. See too *Watts v Aldington, The Times*, December 16, 1993 (CA); *Johnson v Davies* [1999] Ch. 117; *Baxter v Obacelo Pty Ltd* (2001) 205 C.L.R. 635 especially at [51]–[55]; *Itek Graphics Pty Ltd v Elliott* [2002] NSWCA 442 at [173]–[182].

[142] *King* (1844) 13 M. & W. 494 at 505; 153 E.R. 206 at 210; *Re Hodgson* (1885) 31 Ch. D. 177 at 188 (CA).

[143] *Levy v Sale* (1877) 37 L.T. 709; *White v Tyndall* (1883) 13 App. Cas. 263; *The Argo Hellas* [1984] 1 Lloyd's Rep. 296 at 300; *Johnson v Davies* [1999] Ch. 117 at 127 (CA).

[144] The words "we promise jointly and severally" suffice for this purpose, and indeed any other express statement that the parties' liabilities are joint and several: *Leggatt v National Westminster Bank Ltd* [2001] 1 F.L.R. 563 at 565 (CA); *A.I.B. Group (UK) Plc v Martin* [2002] 1 W.L.R. 94 (HL). See too Lord Millett (editor-in-chief), *Encyclopaedia of Forms and Precedents*, Vol.4(3), 5th edn (1997); s.v. "Boilerplate Clauses", paras 81–82 and 256–257; Vol.17(2), 5th edn reissue (2000), s.v. "Guarantees and Indemnities", paras 3291, 3303, 3321 and 3351; and for general discussion, see Williams, *Joint Obligations*, pp.38–41.

[145] Different parties also sometimes assume different contractual liabilities in the same document, e.g. Lloyd's slips: *General Reinsurance Corp v Forsakringsaktiebolaget Fennia Patria* [1983] Q.B. 856 at 864 (CA); *Touche Ross & Co v Baker* [1992] 2 Lloyd's Rep. 207 at 209 (HL). See too Lloyd's Act 1982 s.8(1).

[146] *Sun Life Assurance* [1999] 2 E.G.L.R. 135 at 136–137, considering *Deanplan* [1993] Ch. 151. Under the Landlord and Tenant (Covenants) Act 1995 ss.3 and 5, the original tenant of a lease granted after 1995 is now generally released from covenants in the lease once it has been assigned. But it can happen under the scheme of the 1995 Act that two parties are bound by the same covenant to a landlord, in which case they are deemed to owe him a joint and several liability by s.13.

of them in full. Again, two sureties may separately agree to guarantee the same principal debt,[147] or two indemnity insurers may separately agree to indemnify the insured in respect of the same loss—and in these circumstances, the creditor or the insured[148] can choose which of them to sue but may not recover twice over.[149]

(iii) *Breach of Contract*

20–64 "If two or more defendants have each committed breaches of the same or different contracts with the plaintiff and as the result of each defendant's breach the plaintiff has suffered the same damage he may recover the whole amount of it from any of the defendants."[150] So, in *Woolford v Liverpool CC*,[151] the defendant public authorities jointly and severally warranted that they would take out personal accident insurance for participants in a venture course. They all failed to do this, and damages for breach of contract were awarded against them jointly and severally in favour of a participant who was accidentally injured and had no insurance cover.

(iv) *Tort*

20–65 The law governing joint liability for torts is difficult and obscure. The courts have used terminology when describing this liability which makes it hard for them to distinguish two issues. The first is a question of substantive law: is there a sufficient connection between two defendants to justify holding one liable for damage that has been tortiously caused by the other? The second is a procedural question: must two tortfeasors who have caused the same damage be sued together in a single set of proceedings or can the victim sue them separately?

20–66 Using the term "joint tortfeasors" to denote parties who are sufficiently connected with one another to justify holding one liable for the damage tortiously caused by another, we can follow Glanville Williams in distinguishing such tortfeasors from "several concurrent tortfeasors" and "several non-concurrent tortfeasors".[152] Joint tortfeasors are all deemed to be liable for the same damage because one or more of them causes this damage by his tortious actions or omissions, and they are all connected by some relational or participatory link. Together they are deemed to commit a single wrong resulting in a single injury. Several concurrent tortfeasors each cause the same damage by their tortious actions but they are not connected in a way that could lead to a finding of joint

---

[147] *Legal and General Assurance* [1992] 1 Q.B. 887 at 900 (CA).

[148] Marine Insurance Act 1906 s.32(2)(a).

[149] Since an insured cannot recover more than a full indemnity for his loss under an indemnity policy, he will not usually intend to buy more than one policy to cover the same risk, although if he obtains "layered" coverage from separate insurers then they will be liable for different parts of his loss and so their liabilities will not overlap. However he may find himself doubly insured by coincidence: e.g. where the driver of another person's car is covered by the owner's policy and his own.

[150] *Victoria University of Manchester v Hugh Wilson & Lewis Womersley (A Firm)* (1985) 2 Con. L.R. 43 at 87; considering *Burrows v The March Gas and Coke Co* (1870) L.R. 5 Exch. 67.

[151] *Woolford v Liverpool CC* [1968] 2 Lloyd's Rep. 256. See too *Bilodeau v A. Bergeron & Fils Ltee* [1975] 2 S.C.R. 345; *London Electricity Plc v B.I.C.C. Supertension Cables Ltd* Unreported QBD (Official Referees' Business), May 5, 1993; *Heaton* [2002] 2 A.C. 329.

[152] Williams, *Joint Torts and Contributory Negligence*, especially Ch.1. "Concurrent" effectively means "liable in respect of the same damage". Hence joint tortfeasors might equally well be described as "joint concurrent tortfeasors", but in practice this term is not used as joint tortfeasors can only ever be liable in respect of the same damage, and so the word "concurrent" is taken as read.

tortfeasance. Each commits a different wrong, but their different wrongs cause a single injury.[153] Several non-concurrent tortfeasors each cause different damage by their tortious actions, perhaps to the same victim, but perhaps not, and they are not connected in a ways that would make them joint tortfeasors. Each commits a different wrong, and their different wrongs cause different injuries.

Several concurrent tortfeasors cannot be joined as defendants to one action **20–67** because they are severally liable "on separate causes of action",[154] and a fortiori this rule also applies to several non-concurrent tortfeasors. It is tempting to assume that joint tortfeasors must all be joined as defendants to a single set of proceedings, because this is the procedural rule which generally applies to parties who owe a single joint liability. But this is not the case: joint tortfeasors can be sued jointly in a single set of proceedings, but they can also be sued separately, and recovery of judgment against one does not operate as a bar to proceedings against the others. This is why the liability of joint tortfeasors is commonly but confusingly said to be "joint and several", and this is why Lord Denning M.R. said in *Egger v Viscount Chelmsford* that "no tortfeasors can truly be described solely as joint tortfeasors [because they] are always several tortfeasors as well".[155]

Where several non-concurrent tortfeasors have caused different damage to the **20–68** same victim, the victim can recover from each tortfeasor in full, and payment by one does not affect the position of the others. In contrast, in the case of both joint tortfeasors and several concurrent tortfeasors, "each tortfeasor is liable in full to compensate the [victim] for the whole of the damage",[156] but the victim cannot recover more than the full amount of his loss by accumulating recoveries from both of them.[157] Hence, if the victim recovers the whole of his loss from one tortfeasor, his rights are exhausted and he can recover nothing more from the others.[158]

(v) *Unjust Enrichment*

Claims in unjust enrichment are usually brought against a single defendant who **20–69** alone receives a benefit from the claimant. But it can happen that a single benefit is received by more than one defendant—for example, where a payment is made

---

[153] Cf. *Thompson v Australian Capital Television Pty Ltd* (1996) 186 C.L.R. 574 at 580.
[154] *Sadler v Great Western Railway Co* [1896] A.C. 450 at 454 (HL), quoted with approval in *Baxter v Obacelo Pty Ltd* (2001) 205 C.L.R. 635 at [25].
[155] *Egger v Viscount Chelmsford* [1965] 1 Q.B. 248 at 264 (CA).
[156] *Rahman v Arearose Ltd* [2001] Q.B. 351 at 361 (CA); *Hackney LBC v Sivanandan* [2011] I.R.L.R. 740 at [15]–[17]. But cf. *Barker v Corus (UK) Plc* [2006] UKHL 20; [2006] 2 A.C. 572, discussed below at para.20–76. Note that the principle stated in the text overrides the general duty owed by tort victims to mitigate their loss; i.e. where a victim claims the whole loss from one of several tortfeasors, it is no answer that he should have mitigated his loss by claiming against one or more of the others: *Steamship Enterprises of Panama Inc v Owners of the SS Ousel, The Liverpool (No.2)* [1963] P. 64; *International Factors Ltd v Rodriguez* [1979] Q.B. 351; *London and South of England Building Society v Stone* [1983] 3 All E.R. 105; *Standard Chartered Bank v Pakistan National Shipping Corp* [2001] EWCA Civ 55; [2001] 1 All E.R. (Comm.) 822; *Peters v East Midlands Strategic Health Authority* [2009] EWCA Civ 145; [2010] Q.B. 48. See too H. McGregor QC, *McGregor on Damages*, 18th edn (Londons: Sweet & Maxwell, 2009), para.7–085, approved in *Haugesund Kommune v Depfa ACS Bank (No.2)* [2010] EWHC 227 (Comm); [2010] 1 All E.R. (Comm) 1109 at [21].
[157] See cases cited at para.20–50 fn.120.
[158] *D'Angola v Rio Pioneer Gravel Co Pty Ltd* [1979] 1 N.S.W.L.R. 495 at 499 (NSW CA).

into a joint bank account,[159] or where a debt owed by several debtors is discharged.[160] In such cases, the law generally holds that all the defendants are jointly and severally enriched, with the result that a claim for the whole amount of the enrichment lies against any or all of them, but the principle against double recovery prevents the claimant from recovering from every defendant in full.[161]

20–70   An obligation to pay contribution is itself usually a several obligation. So, for example, if there are three joint debtors, and one discharges the debt in full, the court will not fix each of the others with a joint and several liability to pay a contribution of two-thirds of the debt, but will instead make each of them severally liable to pay a contribution of one-third.[162] However, there seems to be an exception to this rule. Suppose that a claimant and two defendants are all liable to a third party, and that the defendants have received benefits from the third party, while the claimant has not. This fact may lead the court to apportion liability between the parties in a way which prevents the defendants from continuing to enjoy the benefits at the claimant's expense, and the court may also fix them with joint and several liability to pay contribution to the claimant, as a device to ensure that they meet their contribution liabilities out of their receipts from the third party.[163]

(vi) *Combinations of Liabilities*

20–71   It often happens that two parties are severally liable on different grounds to a third, but that their liabilities overlap, in the sense that he may not recover twice over by accumulating recoveries from them both. For example, one may be liable in tort and the other in unjust enrichment.[164] In such a case, because their liabilities are several, the third party is free to choose which of them to sue, and to recover from one in full without troubling to sue the other.

(b) *Proportionate Liabilities*

20–72   Where two parties freely assume joint or several liabilities for the whole of a debt, there is no room to argue that it would be fairer to them if they were made severally liable for different parts of the debt. That would obviously be a less burdensome arrangement, but assuming that they are free to contract on the terms

---

[159] *Euroactividade AG v Moeller* Unreported CA, February 1, 1995; *O.E.M. Plc v Schneider* [2005] EWHC 1072 (Ch).

[160] *Filby v Mortgage Express (No.2) Ltd* [2004] EWCA Civ 759 at [45]; *Brasher v O'Hehir* [2005] NSWSC 1194.

[161] *Trustor* Unreported CA, May 9, 2000 at [63]–[66] per Scott V.C. See too *Smith v Moneymart Co* (2006) 266 D.L.R. (4th) 275 (Ontario CA); *Tracy v Instaloans Financial Solution Centres (BC) Ltd* [2008] BCSC 699; (2008) 293 D.L.R. (4th) 60; affirmed [2009] BCCA 110; (2009) 309 D.L.R. (4th) 236.

[162] *Cowell v Edwards* (1800) 2 Bos. & Pul. 268; 126 E.R. 1275; *Earl of Mountcashell v Barber* (1853) 14 C.B. 53; 139 E.R. 23; *Benson v McKone* (1919) 45 D.L.R. 83 at 91 (Manitoba CA).

[163] *Dubai Aluminium Co Ltd v Salaam* [2003] 2 A.C. 366 at [62]–[64] and [167]; affirming [1999] 1 Lloyd's Rep. 415 at 477.

[164] As in e.g. *Shuman v Coober Pedy Tours Pty Ltd* [1994] SASC 4401 (Full Ct of Sup Ct of South Aus); *Niru Battery Manufacturing Co v Milestone Trading Ltd (No.2)* [2004] EWCA Civ 487; [2004] 2 All E.R. (Comm) 289; *Haugesund* [2010] EWHC 227 (Comm); [2010] 1 All E.R. (Comm.) 1109; *Bank of Ireland v Pexxnet Ltd* [2010] EWHC 1872 (Comm) at [68].

which they choose, there is nothing unfair about holding them to their promises. They could have chosen instead to create a proportionate liability system—as, for example, insurers often do by inserting rateable proportion clauses into their policies. These typically provide that:

> "If at the time of any claim . . . there shall be any other insurance covering the same risk or any part thereof the insurer shall not be liable for more than its rateable proportion thereof."

The purpose of such clauses is not to prevent an insured from recovering the full amount of his insured loss, but they can have this effect, since they limit the insured to recovering a share from each insurer,[165] and if one insurer is insolvent, then the insured will recover nothing from that source.

Turning to joint and several liability for wrongdoing, we find that there is **20–73** greater scope for arguments that the imposition of shared liability is unfair to the wrongdoers, and that the law should avoid this outcome by adopting a system of proportionate liability, i.e. by saying that each is liable only for a share of the damage which they have all caused. These arguments have led some overseas jurisdictions to enact legislation which either selectively or wholly abolishes joint and several liability for tort and other wrongs, and with it, rights of contribution and reimbursement between the relevant wrongdoers.[166] But they have not persuaded the law reform bodies of other jurisdictions,[167] and they were rejected by the Common Law Team of the English Law Commission, when it undertook a study of joint and several liability in tort law in 1996.[168] Hence, joint and several liability for the same damage generally continues to be imposed on wrongdoers in England, although there are a few exceptions to this rule,[169] and it is also possible to contract out of the rule, as is done, for example, by the insertion of net contribution clauses into construction contracts and collateral warranty agreements entered by participants in construction projects: these essentially provide that where two or more parties are jointly liable for the same

---

[165] *British & Mercantile* (1877) 5 Ch. D. 569 at 588 (CA).
[166] See e.g. Irish Civil Liability Act 1961 s.38; British Columbia Negligence Act 1979 ss.1 and 2(c), as interpreted in *Leischner v West Kootenay Power and Light Co Ltd* (1984) 150 D.L.R. (3d) 242 at 244–246 (British Columbia Sup Ct); affirmed (1986) 24 D.L.R. (4th) 641 at 665–667 (British Columbia CA); Development Act 1993 (South Australia) s.72; Building Act 1993 (Victoria) ss.129–133; Corporate Law Economic Reform Program (Audit Reform and Corporate Disclosure) Act 2004 (Cth). Australian legislation in this area is discussed in B. Macdonald, "Proportionate Liability in Australia: The Devil in the Detail" (2005) 26 Aus. Bar Rev. 29. Some American states have persisted with joint and several liability for multiple tortfeasors, while others have moved to a pure system of proportionate liability, and still others have adopted a hybrid system of proportionate liability and joint and several liability. For a summary of the position in 35 states, see American Law Institute, *Third Restatement of the Law of Torts, Apportionment of Liability* (2000), §17, Comment a, Tables.
[167] Ontario Law Reform Commission, *Report on Contribution Among Wrongdoers and Contributory Negligence* (1988); New Zealand Law Commission, *Apportionment of Civil Liability* (Report 47, 1998).
[168] Department of Trade and Industry, *Feasibility Investigation of Joint and Several Liability* (1996). But cf. Sir Michael Latham et al, *Constructing the Team: Final Report of the Government/Industry Review of Procurement and Contractual Arrangements in the UK Construction Industry* ("The Latham Report") (1994), which recommended the introduction of a proportionate liability system to resolve construction industry disputes.
[169] See e.g. the Merchant Shipping Act 1995 s.187.

loss, the liability of the party with the benefit of the clause will be limited to the amount that it would have had to bear if another party had paid in full and then brought contribution proceedings.[170]

20-74   There are three main arguments which favour the retention of a general joint and several liability system, supplemented by a contribution and reimbursement regime. First, a system of this sort aims to ensure so far as possible that the victims of multiple wrongdoing should be fully compensated, by putting the risk of a wrongdoer's insolvency onto the other wrongdoers rather than the victim. Secondly, a joint and several liability system relieves the victim of the burden of managing and funding complex multi-party litigation, and shifts this burden onto the wrongdoers who are often better able to bear it. Thirdly, where each wrongdoer causes the same indivisible damage to a victim, it is just that each should be fully liable for the damage he has caused, and this is not altered by the further fact that other wrongdoers have also caused the same damage.

20-75   The main argument against the imposition of joint and several liability is that it encourages victims to target wrongdoers on the basis of their ability to pay, rather than their moral blameworthiness, or the causative potency of their actions, or the benefits which they have derived from their wrongdoing. In the final analysis, however, this does not clinch the argument for the proponents of proportionate liability, because the further question still remains to be answered, whether making one of many defendants pay the claimant in full is *more unfair* than pushing the burden of paying for the company's loss back onto the claimant by reducing the defendants' respective liabilities to parts of the damage. The Common Law Team of the Law Commission thought not, and we agree.

20-76   In *Barker v Corus (UK) Plc*,[171] the House of Lords held that the defendants' negligent exposure of an employee to asbestos dust was the legal cause of his mesothelioma. The employee, who had also exposed himself to asbestos dust during periods of self-employment, could not prove that any particular exposure had been the cause in fact of his disease, but he could prove that at least one exposure must have been. The majority held that the defendants were liable in negligence, but were only proportionately liable for a share of the damage, because one or more of them might not have caused his injury in fact.[172] This decision provoked a public outcry because it meant that employees suffering from mesothelioma that had been negligently caused by successive employers, some of whom had become insolvent or had ceased to exist by the time of the

---

[170] See e.g. the net contribution clause in the Association of Consulting Engineers Conditions of Engagement 1995, 2nd Edition 1998, Agreement B1, reliance on which would have been fair and reasonable for the purposes of the Unfair Contract Terms Act 1977, had the statute applied in *Langstane Housing Association Ltd v Riverside Construction (Aberdeen) Ltd* [2009] CSOH 52; (2009) 124 Con. L.R. 211.

[171] *Barker v Corus (UK) Plc* [2006] UKHL 20; [2006] 2 A.C. 572, following *Fairchild v Glenhaven Funeral Services Ltd* [2002] UKHL 22; [2003] 1 A.C. 32.

[172] The court left it to the lower courts to develop principles for apportioning liability between the employers. Cf. *E.M. Baldwin & Son Pty Ltd v Plane* (1999) Australian Torts Reports T91–499; *James Hardie & Co Pty Ltd v Roberts* [1999] NSWCA 314; (1999) 47 N.S.W.L.R. 425; *Bitupave Ltd v McMahon* [1999] NSWCA 330; *Patrick Operations Pty Ltd v Comcare* [2006] NSWCA 142. See now the Compensation Act 2006 s.3(4); and also R. Merkin, "Tort and Insurance: Some Insurance Law Perspectives" [2010] P.N. 194 pp.215–218, observing that apportionment remains necessary —and difficult—following the enactment of the 2006 Act, since contribution claims will inevitably be brought between employers (and their insurers).

action, would be denied full recovery. Parliament responded by enacting the Compensation Act 2006 s.3, which fixes every employer in such cases with joint and several liability for the whole of the employee's damage.[173]

5. ULTIMATE BURDEN PROPERLY BORNE BY DEFENDANT

Several principles emerge from the cases in which the courts have decided how **20–77** much of the burden of paying a third party should ultimately be borne by the defendant. First, where the claimant and the defendant's relationship is governed by a contract that allocates responsibility for paying the third party, effect is usually given to this allocation. Secondly, where there is no contractual allocation, the courts have adopted a default rule of equal apportionment. But, thirdly, this rule may be departed from, and an unequal apportionment made, where the causative potency of the parties' actions was unequal. Fourthly, the same result follows where the moral blameworthiness of the parties' actions was unequal. Fifthly, the same result follows where one party gains a larger benefit than the other from the transactions which gave rise to their respective liabilities. After some comments on the apportionment process, we consider each principle in turn and assess their relative weight.

(a) *The Apportionment Process*

(i) *Independence of the Apportionment Rules*

The apportionment rules are independent of the rules which imposed liability on **20–78** the claimant and the defendant towards the third party. This can produce results which seem odd at first sight: for example, the courts may take the relative causative potency of the parties' actions into account, although their liabilities to the third party were determined by the application of a "but-for" causation test[174]; and the relative moral blameworthiness of their actions may be taken into account, although their underlying liabilities were strict.[175]

(ii) *Apportionment Must Be Exhaustive*

When deciding the proportions in which the parties must bear the burden of **20–79** paying the third party, the court must allocate the whole of this burden between them, and must not create a "gap", by holding that some part of the burden should be borne by another person who is not a party to the proceedings.[176] This is not to say that the court must assess the parties' liabilities without reference to the role played by others: if other parties' actions are a significant part of the

---

[173] As discussed in *Sienkiewicz v Greif (UK) Ltd* [2011] UKSC 10; [2011] 2 W.L.R. 523.

[174] *J (A Child) v Wilkins* [2001] R.T.R. 19.

[175] *Rippon v Port of London Authority* [1940] 1 K.B. 858 at 866–867, which should be preferred to *Nolan v Merseyside CC* (1982) 133 N.L.J. 616 at 621 (CA).

[176] *Maxfield v Llewellyn* [1966] 1 W.L.R. 1119 (CA); followed in *Rolls Royce Industrial Power (Pacific) Ltd v James Hardie & Co Pty Ltd* (2001) 53 N.S.W.L.R. 626 at 641–642 (NSW CA).

factual matrix then it may be appropriate to consider them.[177] The point is rather that the parties to contribution and reimbursement claims necessarily owe a common liability which must be apportioned between the two of them and nobody else.[178]

(iii) *Irrelevance of the Parties' Financial Resources*

20–80   Whether one or more of the parties lacks the resources to pay his share of their common liability is irrelevant to the apportionment process.[179] Whether one or more of the parties is insured is also immaterial.[180]

(iv) *100 per cent Apportionment*

20–81   It is open to the court to hold that either a claimant or a defendant should bear the whole burden of paying the third party. If the court decides that the claimant should bear the whole of burden then his claim will fail.[181] If the court decides that the defendant should bear the whole of burden, then the claimant will be entitled to 100 per cent contribution, or reimbursement, which is the same thing.[182]

(v) *Appealing from Apportionment Decisions*

20–82   Unlike the trial judge, an appellate court does not usually have the opportunity to see and hear the witnesses in a case. For this reason an apportionment decision by the trial judge is only altered in exceptional circumstances[183]: where there has been a clear mistake of legal principle[184] or fact.[185] Hence, in most cases it is

---

[177] *Renaissance Leisure Group Inc v Frazer* (2001) 197 D.L.R. (4th) 336 at 355–357 (Ontario Sup Ct).
[178] *Martin v Listowel Memorial Hospital* (2000) 192 D.L.R. (4th) 250 at 264 (Ontario CA).
[179] *Way v Crouch* [2005] UKEAT 0614_04_0306; [2005] I.C.R. 1362 at 1371–1372; *Hackney LBC v Sivanandan* [2011] UKEAT 0075_10_2705; [2011] I.R.L.R. 740 at [22].
[180] *West London Pipeline & Storage Ltd v Total UK Ltd* [2008] EWHC 1296 (Comm); [2008] Lloyd's Rep. I.R. 698 at [10].
[181] As in e.g. *Walsh v Bardsley* (1931) 47 T.L.R. 564 at 565 (CA); *Bilodeau v A. Bergeron & Fils Ltee* [1975] 2 S.C.R. 345; *Blair v Canada Trust Co* (1986) 32 D.L.R. (4th) 515 (British Columbia Sup Ct); *Rolls Royce* (2001) 53 N.S.W.L.R. 626 (NSW CA); *Burke v L.F.O.T. Pty Ltd* [2002] HCA 17; (2002) 209 C.L.R. 282. See too *K v P* [1993] Ch. 140 at 149.
[182] In equity: *Baynard v Woolley* (1855) 20 Beav. 583 at 585–586; 52 E.R. 729 at 730; *Bahin v Hughes* (1886) 31 Ch. D. 390 at 395 (CA). See too the Civil Liability (Contribution) Act 1978 s.2(2). 100 per cent contribution awards were made under the 1978 Act in e.g. *Nelhams v Sandells Maintenance Ltd* [1996] P.I.Q.R. 52 (CA); *Henderson v Merrett Syndicates Ltd* [1997] Lloyd's Rep. I.R. 247 at 261; *Thames Valley Housing Association Ltd v Elegant (Guernsey) Ltd* [2011] EWHC 1288 (Ch) at [114]–[120]. 100 per cent contribution awards were made under the Law Reform (Married Women and Tortfeasors) Act 1935 s.6, in e.g. *Ryan v Fildes* [1938] 3 All E.R. 517; *Semtex Ltd v Gladstone* [1954] 1 W.L.R. 945; *Lister v Romford Ice and Cold Storage Co Ltd* [1955] A.C. 555 at 579–580 and 585.
[183] *The MacGregor* [1943] A.C. 197 esp. at 199–200; disapproving *The Testbank* [1942] P. 75 (CA); *Ingram v United Automobile Service Ltd* [1943] K.B. 612 (CA); *Quintas v National Smelting Co Ltd* [1961] 1 W.L.R. 401 at 418 (CA); *Steel Structures Ltd v Rangitikei County* [1974] 2 N.Z.L.R. 306 at 309–310 (NZ CA); *Diboll v City of Newcastle-upon-Tyne* [1993] P.I.Q.R. 16 at 20 (CA); *J (A Child)* [2001] R.T.R. 283 at [12].
[184] See e.g. *Fitzgerald v Lane* [1989] A.C. 328 at 340; *Hayes v Leo Scaffolding Ltd* Unreported CA, December 3, 1997; *Andrews v Initial Cleaning Services Ltd* [2000] I.C.R. 166 (CA); *Webb v Barclays Bank Plc* [2001] EWCA Civ 1141; [2002] P.I.Q.R. 8.
[185] See e.g. *Worlock v S.A.W.S. (A Firm)* (1982) 22 Building L.R. 66 at 84 (CA); *Roads and Traffic Authority of NSW v Fletcher & Leighton Contractors* [2001] NSWCA 63.

"not the point" that "some may not agree with [the trial judge's] emphasis on particular matters" or that "some may have come to a result other than [the trial judge's apportionment]".[186] Moreover, "it is insufficient for an appellant to persuade an appeal court that . . . the trial judge's apportionment is different from that which the appeal court would have decided", as an appeal court "is not entitled to interfere if the trial judge's apportionment was reasonably open".[187] A trial judge should usually set out his reasons for an apportionment decision,[188] but it seems that he need not do so if his assessment of the claimant and defendant's positions towards one another sufficiently appears from his assessment of their positions towards the third party.[189]

(b) *Principles of Apportionment*

(i) *Contractual Allocation of Responsibility*

A claimant and defendant may agree that although they are both legally liable to   **20–83**
a third party, one of them should ultimately bear some or all of the burden of paying him and the other should not.[190] The court will give effect to the parties' agreement by allowing a claim for contribution or reimbursement where some or all of the responsibility for paying the third party was undertaken by the defendant, and by the same token the claim will be disallowed, or reduced, where some or all of this responsibility was undertaken by the claimant.[191] So, in *Hutton v Eyre*,[192] a joint debtor was compelled to pay the creditor, even though he had previously agreed with another joint debtor that the other should pay the whole debt, and he successfully recovered the amount of his payment as money paid to the other's use.

If the defendant agrees to indemnify the claimant against loss if he pays the   **20–84**
third party, then the claimant can enforce his contractual right to an indemnity without resorting to the law of unjust enrichment. However, there is nothing to stop him from bringing an action for reimbursement on the ground of unjust enrichment if he wishes to do so. On the other hand, if the claimant agrees to indemnify the defendant against loss in the event that he pays the third party, then the courts will interpret this to mean that the parties have allocated responsibility for paying the third party to the claimant, with the result that he will have no right to be reimbursed.[193]

---

[186] *Rolls Royce* (2001) 53 N.S.W.L.R. 626 at 638 per Stein J.A. (NSW CA).
[187] *Rolls Royce* (2001) 53 N.S.W.L.R. 626 at 653 per Fitzgerald A.J.A.
[188] *West v Wilkinson* [2008] EWCA Civ 1005 at [9].
[189] *Adcock v Norfolk Line Ltd* [1993] B.L.M. (Sept.) 6; *Rolls Royce* (2001) 53 N.S.W.L.R. 626 at 648 (NSW CA).
[190] The parties' right to do this is recognised by various statutes, e.g. the Partnership Act 1890 s.24; the Civil Liability (Contribution) Act 1978 s.7(3)(b); and see too CMR art.40.
[191] *Official Trustee in Bankruptcy v Citibank Savings Ltd* (1995) 38 N.S.W.L.R. 116 at 120 (NSW Sup Ct (Eq Div)); *Berghoff Trading Ltd v Swinbrook Developments Ltd* [2009] EWCA Civ 413; [2009] 2 Lloyd's Rep. 233.
[192] *Hutton v Eyre* (1815) 6 Taunt. 289; 128 E.R. 1046.
[193] See e.g. *Majlis Perbandaran Pulau Pinang v Lim Soo Seng* [1991] M.L.J. 162 (Malaysian CA); *Mawson v Cassidy* Unreported CA, January 26, 1995; *Morris v Breaveglen Ltd* Unreported CA, May 9, 1997; *M.M.I. General Insurance Ltd v Copeland* [2000] NSWSC 317.

(ii) *Equal Apportionment*

20–85   Where there is no contract allocating responsibility between the parties, the courts apply a default rule that they are equally responsible for paying the third party. The courts then ask whether they should depart from this rule, and make an unequal apportionment in accordance with one or more of the three rules discussed in the next three sections. It can happen that a court arrives back at an equal apportionment after applying these further rules.[194] But the point to note here is that a court will always apportion liability equally where none of these other rules applies, or if it possesses insufficient information to apply any of them clearly.[195]

20–86   The maxim "equity is equality" is often invoked in contribution cases,[196] but it means little. The courts may invoke the maxim to justify a mathematically equal apportionment where no other rule dictates a different outcome, but they may also invoke it to justify a mathematically unequal but "proportionately equal" apportionment—and they would not let a party rely on the maxim to argue for a mathematically equal apportionment where the parties have contracted otherwise, or where an unequal apportionment is otherwise appropriate.[197]

(iii) *Causative Potency*

20–87   The courts "are no longer constrained as they were to find a single cause for a consequence and to adopt the 'effective cause' formula"; nowadays they "readily recognize that there are concurrent and successive causes of damage on the footing that liability will be apportioned as between the wrongdoers."[198] They also recognise that "material causes, contributing to the same actionable damage, may be several in number and differ in degrees of significance".[199] In cases where they make an unequal apportionment because the actions of one party were more causatively potent than those of another, they often also held that this party acted in a more morally blameworthy way. However, while the ideas of causative potency and moral blameworthiness are closely linked,[200] there have

---

[194] As in e.g. *Downs v Chappell* [1997] 1 W.L.R. 426 at 445 (CA); *Secretary of State for the Environment, Transport and Regions v Unicorn Consultancy Services* Unreported Ch. D., October 19, 2000, at [131]; *Shellharbour CC v Rigby* [2006] NSWCA 308; [2006] Aust. Torts Reports 81–864 at [112]–[119]. And cf. *Miom 1 Ltd v Sea Echo E.N.E.* [2010] EWHC 3180 (Admlty) at [84]–[96].

[195] Trustees: *Lingard v Bromley* (1812) 1 V. &. B 114; 35 E.R. 45; *Jesse v Bennett* (1856) 6 De G. M. & G. 609; 43 E.R. 1370; *Robinson v Harkin* [1896] 2 Ch. 415 at 426. Tortfeasors: *Bank View Mill Ltd v Nelson Corp* [1942] 2 All E.R. 477 at 483; reversed on a different point [1943] 1 K.B. 337 (CA); *Chelsea Building Society v Goddard and Smith (A Firm)* Unreported QBD, October 10, 1996. See too Partnership Act 1890 s.24(1); and cf. Merchant Shipping Act 1995 s.187(2).

[196] See e.g. *Craythorne v Swinburne* (1807) 14 Ves. Jun. 160 at 165; 33 E.R. 482 at 484; *Scholefield Goodman & Sons Ltd v Zyngier* [1986] A.C. 562 at 575 (PC); *Hampton v Minns* [2002] 1 W.L.R. 1 at 15.

[197] *Re Steel* [1979] Ch. 218 at 226. See too *Bialkower v Acohs Pty Ltd* (1998) 83 F.C.R. 1 at 12–13 (Full Ct of Fed Ct of Aus); *Burke* [2002] HCA 17; (2002) 209 C.L.R. 282 at [119].

[198] *March v Stramare (E&MH) Pty Ltd* (1991) 171 C.L.R. 506 at 512 per Mason C.J.

[199] *Roads and Traffic Authority v Royal* [2008] HCA 19; (2008) 245 A.L.R. 653 at [91] per Kirby J.

[200] *Miraflores v Owners of the George Livanos (The Miraflores, The Abadesa and The Livanos)* [1967] 1 A.C. 826 at 845. See too H.L.A. Hart and A.M. Honoré, *Causation in the Law*, 2nd edn (Oxford: Clarendon, 1985) p.234.

been cases where the courts have differentiated between the two and have focused on the relative causative potency of the parties' actions when apportioning liability between them.

For example, in *Schott Kem Ltd v Bentley*,[201] claims were made against various   **20–88** defendants, for breach of fiduciary duty, knowing receipt of funds paid in breach of fiduciary duty and dishonest assistance in a breach of fiduciary duty. The trial judge ordered the defendants to make interim payments into court, and an appeal was successfully made to vary this order so as to indicate the nature of the apportionment made between them more clearly. One defendant, who had acted just as dishonestly as the others, was nevertheless ordered to pay less than them, because although he was a "full party" to their dishonest scheme, he was in a "subordinate position" by comparison with the others.[202] Again, in *Crowley t/a Crowley Civil Engineers v Rushmoor BC*[203] the judge held that there were six tortious causes of the third party's damage, each of which contributed equally to the damage. The parties were equally responsible for two of these, and the defendant solely responsible for the rest, leading the judge to apportion overall responsibility on an 80:20 split.

In *Brian Warwicker Partnership Plc v H.O.K. International Ltd*,[204] the claim-   **20–89** ant engineers and the defendant architects were both liable in negligence for causing the same damage to a developer. The engineers paid the developer and brought a claim under the Civil Liability (Contribution) Act 1978 against the architects. In the course of apportioning liability between the parties, the trial judge took into account various breaches of the architects' duty of care towards the developer, which were not causally connected with the damage for which the parties were commonly liable. This led him to make an apportionment that was more heavily weighted against the architects than it would otherwise have been. They appealed, arguing that the court cannot consider such matters under s.2, which provides that:

"[T]he amount of the contribution recoverable from any person shall be such as may be found by the court to be just and equitable *having regard to the extent of that person's responsibility for the damage in question*".[205]

The architects argued that the court can only consider those features of the parties' conduct which bear on their responsibility for the third party's damage. However, this construction of the section was rejected and the judge's approach upheld by the Court of Appeal. The court followed an earlier decision of the Court of Appeal, *Re-Source America International Ltd v Platt Site Services Ltd*, where Tuckey L.J. had held that the section[206]:

---

[201] *Schott Kem Ltd v Bentley* [1991] 1 Q.B. 61 (CA).
[202] *Schott* [1991] 1 Q.B. 61 at 76 per Neill L.J.
[203] *Crowley t/a Crowley Civil Engineers v Rushmoor BC* [2009] EWHC 2237 (TCC) at [133]–[134]. Further cases include: *Arab Monetary Fund v Hashim*, *The Times*, October 11, 1994; *Australian Breeders Co-operative Society v Jones* (1997) 150 A.L.R. 488 (Full Ct of Fed Ct of Aus); *Hampic Pty Ltd v Adams* [1999] NSWCA 455; *Webb* [2001] EWCA Civ 1411; [2002] P.I.Q.R. 8 at [59].
[204] *Brian Warwicker Partnership Plc v H.O.K. International Ltd* [2005] EWCA Civ 962; [2006] P.N.L.R. 5; followed in *Furmedge v Chester-Le-Street DC* [2011] EWHC 1226 (QB) at [177]–[178].
[205] Emphasis added.
[206] *Re-Source America International Ltd v Platt Site Services Ltd* [2004] EWCA Civ 665; (2004) 95 Con. L.R. 1 at [51].

"is not expressed exclusively in terms of causative responsibility for the damage in question, although obviously the court must have regard to this, as the section directs, and it is likely to be the most important factor in the assessment of relative responsibility which the court has to make. But in the result the court's assessment has to be just and equitable and this must enable the court to take account of other factors as well as those which are strictly causative."

20–90   *Re-Source* and *Brian Warwicker* are out of line with the well-established rule that the damages recoverable from a negligent defendant will be reduced under the (similarly worded) Law Reform (Contributory) Negligence Act 1945 s.1(1), only where the claimant's fault has been a cause of the claimant's damage.[207] They also produce the anomalous result that where a defendant commits two breaches of duty, one that causes no damage and one that causes damage for which a claimant is also liable, the claimant can point to the defendant's first breach as a reason for increasing the defendant's contribution liability, even though the third party to whom the defendant's duty was owed could not have sued him for it.

(iv) *Moral Blameworthiness*

20–91   Although the relative moral blameworthiness of the parties' actions is often intertwined with their relative causative potency, there are other reasons why a court might conclude that one party has behaved more culpably than another. Most obviously, where one party has committed a wrong deliberately and another has not, this fact may well lead the courts to tip the balance in the "innocent" party's favour. So, to give some examples, an unequal apportionment might be made between parties who were jointly and severally liable for defamation, "if one tortfeasor was malicious and the other was merely infected by that other's malice"[208]; where a trustee commits a fraudulent breach of trust, and his co-trustees also commit breaches of trust by failing to act jointly with him in matters of trust administration, but without any fraudulent intent, then they can shift the burden of making good the trust losses onto him[209]; and if a claimant is induced by a defendant's misrepresentation to commit a tort against a third party, then he can look to the defendant for reimbursement[210]—although it may be that this rule is qualified by the proviso that the claimant's actions must not have been "apparently illegal".[211] An unequal apportionment might also be made where one tortfeasor has actual knowledge of the risk of harm to the victim, while another merely ought to have known of the danger.[212]

---

[207] *Davies v Swan Motor Co (Swansea) Ltd* [1949] 1 All E.R. 620; *Jones v Livox Quarries Ltd* [1952] 2 Q.B. 608.

[208] *Belan v Casey* [2002] NSWSC 58 at [33] per Young C.J. in Eq.

[209] *Baynard* (1855) 20 Beav. 583 at 585–586; 52 E.R. 729 at 730; *Elwes v Barnard* (1865) 13 L.T. 426; *Bellemore v Watson* (1885) 1 T.L.R. 241 at 242 (CA); *Re Smith* [1896] 1 Ch. 71; *Deloitte Haskins & Sells v Coopers and Lybrand Ltd* Unreported Alberta QB, November 29, 1996, at [92].

[210] *Adamson v Jarvis* (1827) 4 Bing. 66; 130 E.R. 693; *Betts v Gibbins* (1834) 2 Ad. & El. 57; 111 E.R. 22; *Toplis v Grane* (1839) 5 Bing. N.C. 636; 132 E.R. 1245.

[211] *Dugdale v Lovering* (1875) L.R. 10 C.P. 196 at 201 per Grove J.

[212] *B.I. (Contracting) Pty Ltd v Myer Emporium Ltd* [2005] NSWCA 305 at [18]; citing *Higgins v William Inglis & Son Pty Ltd* [1978] 1 N.S.W.L.R. 649; *Downs v Chappell* [1997] 1 W.L.R. 426; and *Rolls Royce* (2001) 53 N.S.W.L.R. 626.

When assessing the relative moral blameworthiness of the parties' actions, the **20–92** courts should not strive to achieve arithmetical perfection, or a "nicely calculated less or more", as Willmer L.J. said in a maritime collision case, *The Koningin Juliana*, where he also said that the "inquiry must be qualitative rather than quantitative" and that it is "necessary to look at the over-all picture".[213] In *Dubai Aluminium Co Ltd v Salaam*,[214] Rix J. took it to be a relevant factor going to the moral blameworthiness of the parties' actions that some had settled the third party's claims quickly, while others had reprehensibly held out until after the initiation of proceedings. However, obstructive (or co-operative conduct) when defending a third party's claim should more properly be dealt with as a factor going to the apportionment of costs[215] and should be ignored when apportioning liability.[216]

Another issue in *Dubai Aluminium* was whether a claimant who was vic- **20–93** ariously liable for another party's fraudulent wrongdoing should be treated as having acted in bad faith for the purposes of its contribution claim, although the claimant was personally innocent of any dishonesty. At first instance Rix J. held not,[217] but the Court of Appeal held the opposite,[218] and so did the House of Lords, Lord Nicholls worrying that otherwise the employer of a dishonest employee would be placed "in a better position, vis-à-vis the co-defendants, than the employee for whose wrong the employer is vicariously liable."[219] However, there would be nothing wrong with such an outcome if the employee and the co-defendants were dishonest conspirators. The policy which dictates that an innocent principal should be vicariously liable to the innocent victim of his agent's wrongdoing does not also dictate that the principal should be vicariously liable to pay a contribution to his agent's dishonest co-conspirators. A principal is vicariously liable to the innocent victim of his agent's wrongdoing although he is no less innocent than the victim, because he has placed the agent in a position to commit the wrong. But where the agent has conspired with another fraudster to commit a wrong against a fourth party, the principal and the other fraudster are not equally innocent, and the fact that the principal has placed the agent in a position to commit the wrong is less reprehensible than the fraudster's dishonest decision to participate in the conspiracy.

---

[213] *The Koningin Juliana* [1974] 2 Lloyd's Rep. 353 at 364 (CA). See too Lord Wilberforce and Lord Simon's comments on appeal: [1975] 2 Lloyd's Rep. 111 at 113 and 116 (HL); also *The Oropesa* (1940) 68 Lloyd's List Rep. 21 at 27; and *The Portslade* (1948) 81 Lloyd's List Rep. 395 at 400.

[214] *Dubai Aluminium Co Ltd v Salaam* [1999] 1 Lloyd's Rep. 415.

[215] As in *Price v Price* (1880) 42 L.T. 626. Cf. *Connor & Labrum v Regocz-Ritzman* (1995) 70 P. & C.R. D41.

[216] *Furmedge* [2011] EWHC 1226 (QB) at [173]: "the mere fact that there has been a (correct) admission of liability at an early stage by the Council and, on my finding, an (incorrect) denial of liability by B.I.L. does not mean that some 'weighting' to the apportionment should follow from this state of affairs." See too *Rexstraw v Johnson* [2003] NSWCA 287, where it was held to be an irrelevant consideration that one defendant had had "the courage and honesty to acknowledge his shortcomings", while the other had "still not given any credible explanation for so completely abandoning any commitment to the welfare of the investors who had trusted him".

[217] *Dubai Aluminium* [1999] 1 Lloyd's Rep. 415 at 472–477.

[218] *Dubai Aluminium* [2001] 1 Q.B. 113 at 136 (CA).

[219] *Dubai Aluminium* [2002] UKHL 48; [2003] 2 A.C. 366 at [45].

(v) *Retention of Gains*

20–94 In *Bonner v Tottenham & Edmonton Permanent Benefit BS*, Vaughan Williams L.J. held that in a reimbursement claim[220]:

> "[T]he plaintiff may be entitled to recover . . . [if] he can establish that the defendant has such an interest or benefit as to make the maxim apply '*Qui sentit commodum sentire debet et onus*'."

This maxim may be translated as "he who takes the benefit must bear the burden". The principle which it encapsulates has been applied in many cases, to allocate responsibility between the parties by reference to the benefits which they have derived from the transactions which have given rise to their respective liabilities.[221]

20–95 For example, where responsibility between principal and successive carriers of goods by road cannot be apportioned by reference to the relative causative potency of their actions, each carrier will be liable for damage to a cargo interest in proportion to his share of the payment for carriage[222]; again, a trustee who wrongfully applies trust funds to his own exclusive use must reimburse his co-trustees if they must make good the trust losses out of their own pockets[223]; where a surety enjoys the whole benefit of a guarantee, he is not entitled to reimbursement from the principal debtor,[224] or to a contribution from the co-surety,[225] because it is he, rather than they, who derives the benefit from the guarantee; and where directors have distributed company funds to the shareholders in breach of the capital maintenance rules, and have been ordered to pay the company's losses out of their own pockets, they are entitled to be reimbursed by the shareholders to the extent that they have benefited by receipt of the money.[226]

---

[220] *Bonner v Tottenham & Edmonton Permanent Benefit BS* [1899] 1 Q.B. 161 at 176 (CA). See too *Deering* (1787) 1 Cox 318 at 323–324; 29 E.R. 1184 at 1186; *Burnett v Lynch* (1826) 5 B. & C. 589 at 607; 108 E.R. 220 at 226; *Bater v Kare* [1964] S.C.R. 206 at 211; *Albion Insurance Co Ltd v Government Insurance Office of New South Wales* (1969) 121 C.L.R. 342 at 351; *Legal and General Assurance* [1992] Q.B. 887 at 891–892 (CA); *Morgan Equipment Co v Rodgers (No.2)* (1993) 32 N.S.W.L.R. 467 (NSW Sup Ct (Comm Div)) 482.

[221] But cf. *Amaca Pty Ltd v State of New South Wales* [2003] HCA 44; (2003) 199 A.L.R. 596 at [19]: "That [one defendant] was a commercial enterprise pursuing profit and [the other party was] a polity raising revenue by taxation are not considerations relevant to their respective responsibilities to contribute to the damage sustained by the injured plaintiff."

[222] See generally *Walek and Co v Chapman and Ball (International) Ltd* [1980] 2 Lloyd's Rep. 279; and cf. CMR art.38 which provides for a similar method of apportionment in the event that one of the carrier's becomes insolvent.

[223] *Trafford v Boehm* (1746) 3 Atk. 440 at 444; 26 E.R. 1054 at 1056; *Lord Montford v Lord Cadogan* (1810) 17 Ves. Jun. 485 at 489–490; 34 E.R. 188 at 190; *Booth v Booth* (1838) 1 Beav. 125 at 130; 48 E.R. 886 at 888; *Raby v Ridehalgh* (1855) 7 De G. M. & G. 104; 44 E.R. 41; *Chillingworth v Chambers* [1896] 1 Ch. 685 (CA); *Re Pauling's ST (No.2)* [1963] 2 Ch. 576.

[224] *Erskine v Cormack* (1842) 4 D. 1478; *McMurray v McFarlane* (1894) 31 S.L.R. 531; both considered in *Martin v Sinclar Group Ltd* [2011] CSOH 54 at [24].

[225] *Bater v Kare* [1964] S.C.R. 206; *Woolmington v Bronze Lamp Restaurant Pty Ltd* [1984] 2 N.S.W.L.R. 242 (NSW Sup Ct (Eq Div); *Morgan Equipment Co v Rodgers (No.2)* (1993) 32 N.S.W.L.R. 467 at 477 (NSW Sup Ct (Comm Div)); *Official Trustee in Bankruptcy v Citibank Savings Ltd* (1995) 38 N.S.W.L.R. 116 at 127–128 (NSW Sup Ct (Eq Div)). Cf. *Trotter v Franklin* [1990] 2 N.Z.L.R. 92 (NZ High Ct); *Hampton* [2002] 1 W.L.R. 1 at 17–18.

[226] *Re National Funds Assurance Co* (1878) 10 Ch. D. 118; *Re Alexandra Palace Co* (1882) 21 Ch. D. 149; *Moxham v Grant* [1900] 1 Q.B. 88 (CA).

(c) *The Relative Weight of the Apportionment Rules*

As noted already, the courts give pre-eminence to any contractual arrangements   **20–96**
between the parties when apportioning liability between them, and where there
is no contract, they apply a default rule of equal apportionment unless one or
more of the remaining three rules come into play, in which case, these rules
govern the outcome. The question arises, though, whether each of these three
rules carries equal weight? Much turns on the facts of individual cases, and so
generalisation is dangerous, but it seems that the rule on retention of gains has
greater weight than the other two rules.

So far as the relative weight of causative potency and moral blameworthiness   **20–97**
are concerned, the courts will certainly make a fraudulent party bear a greater
share of the responsibility for a loss than a party who was merely negligent,
where the causative impact of their actions was roughly the same.[227] But they
will not necessarily view one party's dishonesty as a reason to make him bear a
greater share than another party who has acted in good faith, if the actions of this
other party have had a greater causative impact.[228] However, the rule on retention
of gains is generally accorded priority over the other two because a defendant
who has received a benefit might otherwise be enabled to keep the benefit at the
expense of a claimant who has acted in a more causatively potent or morally
blameworthy way. This outcome would usually entail giving the defendant an
unjustifiable windfall, and punishing the claimant, something that is not generally
the business of the civil law.

The view that the courts will allocate a greater share of responsibility to a party   **20–98**
who has received a benefit, than to a party who has received nothing, even if he
has acted in bad faith, is borne out by *Eaves v Hickson*.[229] Here, trustees were
fraudulently induced to pay trust property to the wrong persons, in reliance on a
forged marriage certificate that was presented to them by the recipients' father.
The trustees, the recipients and the recipients' father were all joined as defendants to an action by the beneficiaries, and Romilly M.R. ordered that the recipients should repay the sums they had received, that their father should then be
liable for so much of the trust fund as could not be recovered from the recipients,
and that the trustees should finally have to pay any amount that was still
outstanding. This case illustrates not only that the recipients of property paid to
them in breach of trust should ultimately have to bear the burden of making good
the trust losses, but also that a person who dishonestly induces a breach of trust
bears a greater responsibility for making good the trust losses than "innocent"
trustees whom he has dishonestly induced to commit the breach.

In *Dubai Aluminium*,[230] the House of Lords agreed with Rix J.'s finding at first   **20–99**
instance that two fraudsters who had received all the money extracted from a
third party by a fraudulent scheme should reimburse the other defendants as "it

---

[227] See e.g. *Thomas Saunders Partnership v Harvey* (1989) 30 Con. L.R. 103 at 122.
[228] *The Savina* [1976] 2 Lloyd's Rep. 123 at 134 (HL); *Downs v Chappell* [1997] 1 W.L.R. 426 at 445
(CA); *Dairy Containers Ltd v N.Z.I. Bank Ltd* [1995] 2 N.Z.L.R. 30 at 126 (NZ High Ct).
[229] *Eaves v Hickson* (1861) 30 Beav. 136; 54 E.R. 840.
[230] *Dubai Aluminium* [2002] UKHL 48; [2003] 2 A.C. 366 at [50]–[54] and [162]–[164], followed in
Pulvers (A Firm) v Chan [2007] EWHC 2406 (Ch); [2008] P.N.L.R. 9 at [401], and *Cherney v
Neuman* [2011] EWHC 2156 (Ch) at [324]–[325]. See too *Cook v Green* [2009] BCC 204 at
[75]–[77].

cannot be just and equitable to require one party to contribute in a way which would leave another party in possession of his spoils."[231] Similar findings were made by the High Court of Australia in *Burke v L.F.O.T. Pty Ltd*,[232] and by the Court of Appeal in *Cressman v Coys of Kensington (Sales) Ltd*[233] and *Niru Battery*, where Clarke L.J. held that the principle applies both where the recipient still has the money, and where he pays it away other than in good faith.[234] In *Charter Plc v City Index Ltd*,[235] Morritt C. was led by this dictum to conclude that there was no prospect of the claimant recovering a contribution and therefore struck out the claim. On appeal, Carnwath L.J. disagreed because he thought that a claimant who receives money and then pays it away is in a "similar position" to a claimant who had never received anything.[236] However, this can only be true if the claimant has acted in good faith. If he has not (and in *Charter* the claimant had not), then it would surely be inequitable to let him recover a portion of his bad faith expenditure from the defendant.

---

[231] *Dubai Aluminium* [1999] 1 Lloyd's Rep. 415 at 475, following Ferris J.'s observations to the same effect in *K v P* [1993] Ch. 140 at 149.
[232] *Burke v L.F.O.T. Pty Ltd* [2002] HCA 17; (2002) 209 C.L.R. 282.
[233] *Cressman v Coys of Kensington (Sales) Ltd* [2004] EWCA Civ 47; [2004] 1 W.L.R. 2775 at [48].
[234] *Niru Battery* [2004] EWCA Civ 487; [2004] 2 All E.R. (Comm.) 289 at [50].
[235] *Charter Plc v City Index Ltd* [2006] EWHC 2508 (Ch); [2007] 1 W.L.R. 26 at [33]–[53].
[236] *Charter* [2007] EWCA Civ 1382; [2008] Ch. 313 at [59].

Chapter 21

SECONDARY LIABILITY: INSURERS' SUBROGATION RIGHTS

1. Introduction

It often happens that an insured suffers a loss in respect of which he has two **21–01** claims: one against an indemnity insurer and one against a third party. In these circumstances he can generally choose which claim to pursue first.[1] If he claims against the insurer, then the insurer must pay him to the full extent of its liability, and may not object that he should first have exhausted his rights against the third party.[2]

If the insurer pays the loss, then the question arises whether the third party's **21–02** liability is discharged by the insurer's payment. The rules on discharge were discussed in Ch.5.[3] They provide that the third party's liability is discharged in a few cases: for example, where he is another indemnity insurer.[4] More often, though, his liability is not discharged, whether it arose in contract,[5] tort[6] or unjust enrichment,[7] or under a statute.[8] Another way of putting this is to say that the insurer's payment is ignored when the extent of the third party's liability is decided.[9]

Where the third party's liability is discharged, the insurer may have a direct **21–03** claim against him for contribution or reimbursement. The Mercantile Law Amendment Act 1856 s.5, and the Marine Insurance Act 1906 s.80(2), may also give the insurer the right to be treated, by a fiction, as though it has acquired the

---

[1] The policy may provide otherwise: *London Guarantee Co v Fearnley* (1880) 5 App. Cas. 911.

[2] *Cullen v Butler* (1816) 5 M. & S. 461 at 466; 105 E.R. 1119 at 1122; *Dickenson v Jardine* (1868) L.R. 3 C.P. 639 at 644; *North British and Mercantile Insurance Co v London, Liverpool & Globe Insurance Co* (1877) 5 Ch. D. 569 at 575 (CA); *Collingridge v Royal Exchange Assurance Co* (1877) 3 Q.B.D. 173 at 176–177; *Darrell v Tibbitts* (1880) 5 Q.B.D. 560 at 562 (CA); *Fifth Liverpool Starr-Bowkett Building Society v Travellers Accident Insurance Co Ltd* (1893) 9 T.L.R. 221; *Bovis Lend Lease Ltd v Saillard Fuller & Partners* (2001) 77 Con. L.R. 134 at [120]. By the same token, a defendant may not object if an insured chooses to pursue him first, in preference to claiming against the insurer: *Stace & Francis Ltd v Ashby* [2001] EWCA Civ 1655.

[3] See paras 5–47—5–56.

[4] e.g. *British and Mercantile* (1877) 5 Ch. D. 569 (CA); *Austin v Zurich General Accident and Liability Insurance Co Ltd* [1945] 1 K.B. 250.

[5] e.g. *Darrell v Tibbitts* (1880) 5 Q.B.D. 561 at 563 (CA).

[6] e.g. *Bradburn v Great Western Railway Co.* (1874) L.R. 10 Ex. 1; *Parry v Cleaver* [1970] A.C. 1 (HL).

[7] e.g. *Dickenson* (1868) L.R. 3 C.P. 639.

[8] e.g. *Mason v Sainsbury* (1782) 3 Doug. K.B. 61; 99 E.R. 538; *Ellerbeck Collieries Ltd v Cornhill Insurance Co* [1932] 1 K.B. 401 at 411 (CA).

[9] e.g. *Horton v Evans* [2007] EWHC 315 (QB) at [11]–[17]; *Bee v Jenson (No.2)* [2007] EWCA Civ 923; [2008] R.T.R. 7 at [9]; *Banfield v Leeds BS* [2007] EWCA Civ 1369 at [48]; *Shulman v S.H. Simon (Electrical) Ltd* [2010] EWHC 2762 (QB) at [2]–[12].

insured's extinguished rights against the third party via subrogation.[10] However the insurer would usually derive no advantage from this, because the insured's rights are usually personal rights and the insurer has its own personal right for contribution or reimbursement.

21–04   In the more common case where the insured's rights against the third party subsist despite the insurer's payment, the insurer may be entitled to take over the insured's rights of action and to insist that the insured lends his name to proceedings to enforce these for the insurer's benefit. Indemnity insurance policies often contain subrogation clauses entitling the insurer to do this, but indemnity insurers are also frequently given subrogation rights by operation of law.[11]

21–05   The reasons for this are as follows. Where the insured has been paid by the insurer, but can still recover from the third party in respect of the same loss, the insured can choose whether to enforce his rights against the third party or to forbear from suing him. If he enforces his rights of action, then he may obtain more than a full indemnity for his loss by accumulating recoveries from the insurer and the third party. If he does not, then the third party will effectively be exonerated from liability. Neither outcome is generally regarded as satisfactory by the courts.

21–06   Allowing the insured to make a profit would be inconsistent with the liabilities owed by the insurer and the third party, assuming that they are liable to restore the insured to the position which he occupied prior to the loss but not put him into a better position. Thus, the courts often say that one reason for transferring the insured's rights to the insurer via subrogation is to prevent "double recovery" by the insured, or to prevent him from being "more than fully indemnified",[12] and make the additional point that disallowing double recovery reduces the moral risk of dishonesty by the insured.[13] On the other hand, allowing the third party to escape liability would be inconsistent with the courts' usual assumption that it is he rather than the insurer who is the appropriate person to bear the burden of paying for the insured loss. Thus, the courts also say that the law gives the insurer subrogation rights as a means of ensuring that it is the "primarily liable" third party rather than the "secondarily liable" insurer who pays for the loss.[14]

---

[10] See paras 19–45—19–47.

[11] For discussion of the differences between subrogation rights conferred by policy terms and subrogation rights acquired by law, see C. Mitchell and S. Watterson, *Subrogation: Law and Practice* (Oxford: OUP, 2007), paras 10.168–10.181.

[12] e.g. *Castellain v Preston* (1883) 11 Q.B.D. 380 at 387 (CA); *Dane v Mortgage Insurance Corp* [1894] 1 Q.B. 54 at 61 (CA); *A.F.G. Insurances Ltd v City of Brighton* (1972) 126 C.L.R. 655 at 664; *Arab Bank Plc v John D. Wood Commercial Ltd* [2000] 1 W.L.R. 857 at [95] (CA); *Somersall v Friedman* [2002] SCC 59; [2002] 3 S.C.R. 109 at [50]; *Caledonia North Sea Ltd v British Telecommunications Plc* [2002] UKHL 4; [2002] 1 Lloyd's Rep. 553 at [92]; *Insurance Commission of Western Australia v Kightly* [2005] WASCA 154; (2005) 30 W.A.R. 380 at [26].

[13] e.g. *Condominium Corp No.9813678 v Statesman Corp* [2007] ABCA 216 at [27].

[14] e.g. *Mason* (1782) 3 Doug. K.B. 61 at 64; 99 E.R. 538 at 540; *British and Mercantile* (1877) 5 Ch. D. 565 at 587 (CA); *John Edwards & Co v Motor Union Insurance Co* [1922] 2 K.B. 239 at 253; *Speno Rail Maintenance Australia Pty Ltd v Hammersley Iron Pty Ltd* [2000] WASCA 408; (2000) 23 W.A.R. 291 at [167]–[168]; *Caledonia North Sea* [2002] UKHL 4; [2002] 1 Lloyd's Rep. 553 at [16] and [62].

2. HISTORICAL DEVELOPMENT OF SUBROGATION IN INSURANCE LAW

(a) *Subrogation and Abandonment*

The rules which now entitle an indemnity insurer to acquire its insured's subsist-   **21–07**
ing rights of action via subrogation ultimately derive from 18th century cases on
abandonment. As developed by the common law courts in the 18th and 19th
centuries, the doctrine of abandonment provided that a marine insurer which paid
its insured for a total loss was entitled to acquire whatever remained of the
insured subject matter (termed the "salvage"). Where the insured subject matter
was completely lost there was nothing left for the insurer to acquire, but an
insurer sometimes had to pay an actual total loss although something remained
of the insured subject matter. Moreover, an associated rule provided that an
insured who suffered a partial loss could sometimes claim for a constructive total
loss if he gave timely notice of abandonment which was accepted by the
insurer.[15] In either case, giving the insurer the right to the salvage was viewed as
a means of preventing the insured from making a profit to which he was not
entitled under an indemnity policy.[16]

As the law evolved, the theory emerged that abandonment took effect as   **21–08**
though the salvage were assigned to the insurer by way of sale immediately after
the event causing the insured loss.[17] Consistently with this, the courts held that
if an insured vessel were abandoned during a voyage, but then completed the
voyage and earned freight, the freight should go to the insurer.[18] For the same
reason, the insurer could also bring proceedings in its own name where its rights
as owner of the salvage were infringed by a third party after the abandonment.
For example, in *Cammell v Sewell*,[19] Martin B. accepted that an insurer had
standing to maintain an action in trover when the salvage was sold to a third party
without the insurer's consent after notice of abandonment had been given.

The situation where a defendant interfered with the insurer's rights as owner   **21–09**
of the salvage after abandonment differed from the situation where a defendant
interfered with the *insured's* rights as owner of the insured subject matter before
abandonment. The latter situation most obviously arose where the defendant's

---

[15] This notice requirement prevented the insured from delaying his decision whether to claim for a
partial or a constructive total loss in order to take account of shifts in the market: *Gernon v Royal
Exchange Assurance Co* (1815) 6 Taunt. 383 at 387; 128 E.R. 1083 at 1084–1085 per Gibbs C.J.
[16] *Roux v Salvador* (1835) 1 Bing. (N.C.) 526 at 539; 131 E.R. 1220 at 1225; and subsequent
proceedings: *Roux v Salvador* (1836) 3 Bing. (N.C.) 267 at 282–283; 132 E.R. 413 at 420–421. These
dicta echo the discussion in J.A. Park, *A System of the Law of Marine Insurance* (London:
T. Whieldon, 1787), pp.161–162.
[17] *Davidson v Case* (1820) 2 Brod. & B. 379 at 387; 129 E.R. 1013 at 1016; *Miller v Woodfall* (1857)
8 El. & Bl. 493 at 503; 120 E.R. 184 at 188; *Rankin v Potter* (1873) L.R. 6 H.L. 83 at 144. This theory
resembles, and may well have been influenced by, the Roman law theory that the *beneficium
cedendarum actionum* by means of which a surety acquired a creditor's rights against a principal
debtor operated by way of a deemed contract of sale: Paul D. 46.1.36; Mod. D. 46.3.76; C. 8.40.2 pr.
(Sev. et Ant.); Nov. 4.1 *in fine*. Further discussion: R. Zimmermann, *The Law of Obligations: Roman
Foundations of the Civilian Tradition* (Oxford: OUP, 1996), pp.129–137.
[18] *Davidson* (1820) 2 Brod. & B. 379 at 387; 129 E.R. 1013 at 1017; *Stewart v Greenock Marine
Insurance Co* (1848) 2 H.L.C. 159 at 183; 9 E.R. 1052 at 1059; *Simpson & Co v Thomson* (1877) 3
App. Cas. 279 at 292 (HL). See now the Marine Insurance Act 1906 s.63(2).
[19] *Cammell v Sewell* (1858) 3 H. & N. 617 at 644; 157 E.R. 615 at 627.

wrongful actions were the cause of the insured loss. In cases of this kind, the right to sue the defendant was personal to the insured. Once abandonment had taken place, however, the law held that the insured's accrued right should pass to the insurer along with the salvage. This rule was given effect by the Chancery courts, which could act in personam against a recalcitrant insured by ordering him to surrender his rights of action against the defendant, and to lend his name to proceedings brought by the insurer to enforce these rights.[20] Thus, in *London Assurance Co v Johnson*,[21] Lord Hardwicke L.C. accepted that he had jurisdiction to order an insured who had been paid on a total loss to permit the insurer to "stand in his place" for the purpose of bringing an action against a defendant. Acknowledging the existence of the equitable rule in *Mason v Sainsbury*, Lord Mansfield remarked that it was an everyday occurrence that in abandonment cases "the insurer uses the name of the insured".[22] Likewise in *Yates v Whyte*,[23] Tindal C.J. held that an insurer could "recover in the name of the assured after he [had] been satisfied" and had "the plainest equity to institute such a suit"; and in the same case, Park J. held that "the insurers could not sue in their own names" but "had the clearest equity to use the name of the assured, in order to reimburse themselves".

21–10   The view that subrogation was an incident of the doctrine of abandonment persisted into the 20th century, as evidenced by the Marine Insurance Act 1906 s.79, which remains in force, and which purported to codify the law of subrogation as it then stood. Section 79(1) reads as follows:

> "Where the insurer pays for a total loss . . . he thereupon becomes entitled to take over the interest of the assured in whatever may remain of the subject-matter so paid for, and he is thereby subrogated to all the rights and remedies of the assured in and in respect of that subject-matter as from the time of the casualty causing the loss."

Section 79(2) provides for subrogation rights following payment of a partial loss where no abandonment has taken place, but even so the wording of s.79(1) suggests that Sir Mackenzie Chalmers, the draftsman of the Act, did not fully grasp the significance of *Simpson & Co v Thomson*,[24] where the House of Lords held that although subrogation and abandonment are both designed to prevent the insured from recovering more than a full indemnity, they are separate doctrines that operate in different ways.[25] Since 1906 it has become easier to see this, as

---

[20] *Yorkshire Insurance Co Ltd v Nisbet Shipping Co Ltd* [1962] 2 Q.B. 330 at 339; *Morris v Ford Motor Co* [1973] QB 792 at 800–801 (CA).
[21] *London Assurance Co v Johnson* (1737) West T. Hard. 266; 25 E.R. 930. The action failed for other reasons.
[22] *Mason v Sainsbury* (1782) 3 Doug. K.B. 61 at 64; 99 E.R. 538 at 540.
[23] *Yates v Whyte* (1838) 4 Bing. N.C. 272 at 283; 132 E.R. 793 at 797. Tindal C.J. and Park J. both cited *Randal v Cockran* (1748) 1 Ves. Sen. 98; 27 E.R. 916, but it is unclear from this report of *Randal* whether it concerned an action brought by the insurer in the insured's name, or an action brought by the insured for his own benefit, for the fruits of which the insured was subsequently ordered to account to the insurer.
[24] *Simpson & Co v Thomson* (1877) 3 App. Cas. 279 (HL).
[25] In *Yorkshire Insurance* [1962] 2 Q.B. 330 at 343, Diplock J. thought that *Simpson* was the first case in which the English courts had clearly noted the distinction between "the insurer's rights in the subject-matter of the insurance [arising under the doctrine of abandonment] and his rights of subrogation to the remedies of the assured". See too *Allgemeine Versicherungs-Gesellschaft Helvetia v Administrator of German Property* [1931] 1 K.B. 672 at 687 (CA).

the two doctrines have developed differently in one important respect. Consistently with the theory that abandonment operates as a deemed sale of the salvage, the law has long provided, and still provides, that if an insurer accepts an abandonment,[26] then it can keep any profit deriving from the fact that the salvage is worth more than the amount paid under the policy.[27] In contrast, the rule was laid down in the 20th century that a subrogated insurer which recovers money from a defendant may keep no more than the amount of its payment to the insured and must hand over any excess,[28] which is impressed with a trust in the insured's favour.[29]

(b) Subrogation Confused with Other Rights

Five years after the House of Lords disentangled subrogation from abandonment **21–11** in *Simpson*, the Court of Appeal tangled it up with other rights in *Castellain v Preston*.[30] This case is now widely regarded as the "leading case" on insurers' subrogation rights,[31] but the court's reasoning is seriously flawed. The problem is that the court failed to draw a clear distinction between three different rights that are given to indemnity insurers in three different situations in order to prevent insureds from becoming more than fully indemnified. Instead, the court conflated all three rights and described them collectively as incidents of the "doctrine of subrogation". Properly speaking, "subrogation" only means the right given to an insurer which has paid its insured to take over the insured's subsisting rights of action against a third party in respect of the insured loss. It is confusing and misguided to use the term to describe the other two rights as well.[32]

The first of these other rights arises where the insurer pays an insured loss and **21–12** the insured afterwards receives a payment in diminution of the same loss from a third party, which takes the cumulative total of the insured's recoveries above the amount of his loss. In these circumstances, the law places the insured under a duty to account for the excess to the insurer. Authorities supporting the existence

---

[26] Insurers have the right to refuse abandonment, and in practice they rarely accept it, as ownership of the salvage brings with it liabilities as well as benefits: see e.g. *River Weir Commissioners v Adamson* (1877) 2 App. Cas. 743; *Arrow Shipping Co v Tyne Improvement Commissioners* [1894] A.C. 508; *The Mostyn* [1928] A.C. 57.

[27] *Roux* (1836) 3 Bing. (N.C.) 267 at 286; 132 E.R. 413 at 421; *Rankin v Potter* (1873) L.R. 6 H.L. 83 at 119; *Thames and Mersey Marine Insurance Co v British and Chilian Steamship Co* [1915] 2 K.B. 214 at 220–221; *Page v Scottish Insurance Corp* (1929) 140 L.T. 571 at 575 (CA); *Glen Line Ltd v A.G.* (1930) 36 Com. Cas. 1 at 14 (HL); *L. Lucas Ltd v Export Credits Guarantee Dept* [1973] 1 W.L.R. 914 at 924 (CA).

[28] *Glen Line* (1930) 36 Com. Cas. 1 at 14 (HL); *Boag v Standard Marine Insurance Co* [1937] 2 K.B. 113 at 122–123 (CA).

[29] *Lonrho Exports Ltd v Export Credits Guarantee Dept* [1999] Ch. 158 at 181–182.

[30] *Castellain v Preston* (1883) 11 Q.B.D. 380.

[31] e.g. *Yorkshire Insurance Co* [1962] 2 Q.B. 330 at 339; *Esso Petroleum Ltd v Hall Russell & Co Ltd (The Esso Bernicia)* [1989] A.C. 713 at 744; *Caledonia North Sea* [2002] UKHL 4; [2002] 1 Lloyd's Rep. 553 at [11].

[32] As noted in *British Traders' Insurance Co Ltd v Monson* (1964) 111 C.L.R. 86 at 94. For a full discussion of *Castellain* and the problems it has created, see Mitchell and Watterson, *Subrogation: Law and Practice*, paras 10.17–10.28.

of this duty stretch back for two and a half centuries,[33] and the leading case on the subject is now *Lord Napier and Ettrick v Hunter*.[34] There the House of Lords held that the relevant portion of the third party's payment is subject to an equitable lien in the insurer's favour. This is discussed further in Part 7.

21-13   The insurer's right of recovery in this class of case can be explained as a right deriving from the law of unjust enrichment. The reason why the insured's retention of the third party's payment is relevantly unjust derives from a combination of policy factors: first, the nature of the insured's relationship with the insurer and third party makes it inappropriate for him to accumulate recoveries from both of them, and secondly, the law deems the third party rather than the insured to be the appropriate person to bear the burden of paying for the insured loss. The same considerations underpin the insurer's subrogation right, as discussed in Part 3.

21-14   The insurer may also be entitled to a different right where the insured suffers a loss and then receives a third party payment which diminishes the loss before the insurer does anything. In this case the insurer's liability is reduced by the amount of the third party's payment, and so it is only liable to pay the net amount.[35] However, the insurer may pay the insured without making a deduction because it does not know of the third party's payment. In these circumstances, the insurer can recover its payment to the extent that the two payments, taken together, leave the insured more than fully indemnified. Because it paid in full in the mistaken belief that it was liable to do so,[36] it has a personal claim in unjust enrichment to recover its overpayment on the ground of mistake.[37] An alternative ground for recovery may also be the combination of policy factors which also underpin the insurer's right of recovery where its payment to the insured predates rather than post-dates the third party's payment.[38]

---

[33] *Randal* (1748) 1 Ves. Sen. 98; 27 E.R. 916; *Blaauwpot v Da Costa* (1758) 1 Eden 130; 28 E.R. 633; *White v Dobinson* (1844) 14 Sim. 273; 60 E.R. 363; *Commercial Union Assurance Co v Lister* (1874) LR 9 Ch. App. 483 at 484n; *Burnand v Rodocanachi Sons & Co* (1882) 7 App. Cas. 333 at 339 (HL); *Dane v Mortgage Insurance Corp* [1894] 1 Q.B. 54 at 61 (CA); *King v Victoria Insurance Co Ltd* [1896] A.C. 250 at 255–256 (PC); *Re Miller, Gibb & Co Ltd* [1957] 1 W.L.R. 703; *Re Palmdale Insurance Ltd (In Liquidation) (No.3)* [1986] V.R. 439 at 446–447 (Sup Ct of Victoria); *Horton v Evans* [2007] EWHC 315 (QB) at [16]; *Bee v Jenson (No.2)* [2007] EWCA Civ 923; [2008] R.T.R. 7 at [24].

[34] *Lord Napier and Ettrick v Hunter* [1993] A.C. 713.

[35] *Burnand* (1882) 7 App. Cas. 333 at 339 (HL); *Yorkshire Insurance Co* [1962] Q.B. 330 at 340; *Kern Corp Ltd v Walter Reid Trading Pty Ltd* (1987) 163 C.L.R. 181. Where the quantum of damages paid by a defendant has been assessed in a mediated settlement the insurer may obtain disclosure of documents relating to the settlement negotiations in order to discover what proportion of the damages were paid in relation to the insured loss: *Dos Santos v Sun Life Assurance Co of Canada* (2005) 249 D.L.R. (4th) 416 (British Columbia CA).

[36] It makes no difference whether the insurer's mistake was a mistake of fact or a mistake of law following abolition of the mistake of law bar in *Kleinwort Benson Ltd v Lincoln CC* [1999] 2 A.C. 349; see paras 9–71—9–94.

[37] *Re Miller, Gibb & Co Ltd* [1957] 1 W.L.R. 703 at 710–711 and *Lord Napier* [1993] A.C. 713 at 751 (HL), both explaining *Stearns v Village Main Reef Gold Mining Co Ltd* (1905) 10 Com. Cas. 89 (CA); *Yorkshire Insurance Co* [1962] 2 Q.B. 330 at 341. See too *Darrell v Tibbitts* (1880) 5 Q.B.D. 560 at 567–568 per Thesiger L.J.

[38] For dicta suggesting that the insurer's right of recovery depends on these considerations in both types of case, see *Yorkshire Insurance* [1962] Q.B. 333 at 341; *Lord Napier* [1993] 1 Lloyd's Rep. 10 at 12 (not considered on appeals to the CA and HL).

3. RATIONALES FOR SUBROGATION

The courts have given two reasons for giving an indemnity insurer the right to **21–15** bring subrogated proceedings against a defendant who has caused an insured loss. The first is that the insured would otherwise be able to recover more than a full indemnity by accumulating recoveries from the insurer and the defendant. The second is that the defendant would otherwise escape the burden of paying the insured in the event that the insured forbore from suing him, and thereby take the benefit of insurance for which he had not paid.

(a) *The Insured Should Not Accumulate Recoveries*

This first argument has only ever been made in cases where the insurer has paid **21–16** the insured an indemnity, i.e. a payment which is designed to compensate the insured for loss which he has actually suffered. Where the insured has been paid under a contingency policy, i.e. a policy under which the insurer agrees to pay a fixed sum on the happening of a specified event, regardless of the measure of loss actually suffered by the insured, no objection has ever been raised to the insured accumulating recoveries. Hence, subrogation has never been available in cases of the latter sort. However, it is doubtful that the distinction between indemnity and contingency policies is particularly clear-cut, a point to which we shall return below, in Part 4.[39]

Should the law give indemnity insurers subrogation rights where the insured **21–17** has been paid under the policy and has no intention of enforcing his right of action against a defendant or has put it beyond his power to do so? A situation of the first kind might arise, for example, where the defendant belongs to the insured's family[40]; a situation of the second kind might arise where the insured has settled his claim against the defendant for the amount of his uninsured losses only.[41] In such cases there is no risk that the insured will recover twice over in respect of his loss. Hence one might have thought that the courts would decline to let the insurer bring subrogated proceedings.

However, this argument never seems to have been pursued in the English **21–18** courts, which have, on the contrary, developed a rule that the insured owes a duty to preserve his rights of action against defendants for the insurer's benefit, breach of which duty will sound in an action for damages.[42] Thus, an insured who settles his claim against a defendant at an undervalue may be liable to the insurer for prejudicing its ability to bring subrogated proceedings, and indeed the damages payable by the insured may exceed the amount which he has recovered from the defendant. Many insurance policies place insureds under a contractual obligation to preserve their rights of action against defendants, and in cases of this kind, the insureds' liability to pay damages may be explained on normal contractual principles. However, to the extent that the law imposes a duty on an insured to protect his insurer's subrogation rights, it seems to have lost sight of the main

---

[39] See paras 21–25—21–27.
[40] See cases cited at para.21–57, fnn.126 and 127.
[41] See cases cited at para.21–89, fn.181.
[42] See paras 21–107—21–113.

reason why the law gives these rights to the insurer in the first place. In other words, the courts' decisions on this point cannot be justified by reference to the policy against over-indemnification. They can only be justified on the basis that the insured should not be allowed to compromise the insurer's ability to shift the burden of paying for the loss onto another party who is thought to be a more appropriate person to bear this burden.

21–19   In this context, the Supreme Court of Canada's decision in *Somersall v Friedman*[43] merits attention. The Somersalls were injured in a motor accident caused by Friedman who was under-insured. Without telling their own insurer, the Somersalls settled their claim against Friedman, on the basis that he would admit liability at trial, and they would not sue him for more than the amount of his liability coverage. The Somersalls then looked to their insurer for the remainder of their loss, and the insurer refused to pay, arguing that the Somersalls had committed a repudiatory breach of contract by interfering with its contractual subrogation right so extensively as to deprive it of the substantial benefit of performance.

21–20   This argument was rejected by the majority of the court, whose judgment was delivered by Iacobucci J. In his view[44]:

> "[I]t is important to keep in mind the underlying objectives of the doctrine of subrogation which are to ensure (i) that the insured receives no more and no less than a full indemnity, and (ii) that the loss falls on the person who is legally responsible for causing it . . . . Consequently, if there is no danger of the insured's being overcompensated and the tortfeasor has exhausted his or her capacity to compensate the insured there is no reason to invoke subrogation. Similarly, if the insured enters into a limits agreement or otherwise abandons his or her claim against an impecunious tortfeasor the insurer has lost nothing by his inability to be subrogated."

21–21   On the facts, the Somersalls would not be overcompensated if their insurer paid them the difference between their actual loss and the amount which they had recovered from Friedman. Moreover, it seemed that Friedman's capacity to pay for their loss had effectively been exhausted once his liability insurer had paid over the sum due under the settlement as he had few if any assets of his own.[45] Hence, Iacobucci J. concluded that the insurer's argument should fail because the objectives "that the doctrine of subrogation are intended to advance [were] not prejudiced by the [insurer's] inability to be subrogated."[46]

(b) *The Burden of Paying the Insured Should Fall on the Defendant*

21–22   In *Somersall* Iacobucci J. made it clear that preventing the insured from recovering more than a full indemnity is not the law's only objective in giving the insurer

---

[43] *Somersall v Friedman* [2002] SCC 59; [2002] 3 S.C.R. 109.
[44] *Somersall* [2002] SCC 59; [2002] 3 S.C.R. 109 at [50].
[45] In dissent, Binnie J. expressed strong concerns that the majority's assumption that Friedmann was impecunious was unwarranted by the evidence (*Somersall* [2002] SCC 59; [2002] 3 S.C.R. 109 at [98]–[100]), and also took exception to Iacobucci J.'s statement that subrogation rights in general are of "near-negligible value" to insurers, pointing out (*Somersall* [2002] SCC 59; [2002] 3 S.C.R. 109 at [117]) that if that were true then insurers would not spend millions of dollars a year pursuing subrogated claims.
[46] *Somersall* [2002] SCC 59; [2002] 3 S.C.R. 109 at [51].

subrogation rights. The law also aims to ensure that the burden of paying the insured should ultimately fall on the defendant rather than the insurer. However, this objective also seems questionable in some circumstances: it is not always clear that a defendant rather than an insurer should be the person who ultimately pays for the insured loss.

Where the defendant has committed a tort, it is intuitively easily to character-   **21–23**
ise him as the person who should pay, and who ought not to be allowed to escape liability simply because his victim happens to be insured. The fault principle suggests that the defendant should pay, as does the notion that negligent behaviour is deterred by the threat of litigation, whether subrogated or otherwise.[47] However it is empirically unproven that the tort system deters negligent behaviour, and many would agree with Lord Hoffmann that "there must be better ways" of making defendants more careful than forcing them to pay damages to insurers via subrogated proceedings (particularly public authority defendants).[48] Moreover the fault principle has no bite where the defendant does not owe a fault-based liability, for example because he, like the insurer, is contractually bound to indemnify the insured for the relevant loss. In this sort of case the courts should not simply assume that the defendant rather than the insurer ought to pay for the loss. All must depend on the proper interpretation of the parties' contractual arrangements, but a better result might be to make the defendant and the insurer share this burden.[49]

4. PRECONDITIONS FOR THE EXERCISE OF SUBROGATION RIGHTS

An insurer can acquire its insured's subsisting rights of action via subrogation   **21–24**
only where the insurer has agreed to indemnify the insured for a loss, where the insured has been fully indemnified in accordance with the policy terms, and where the exercise of the insured's right against the defendant would diminish the loss for which he has been indemnified. Each of these preconditions for the exercise of subrogation rights will be discussed in turn.

(a) *Indemnity*

"The doctrine of subrogation in insurance ... gives effect to the principle of   **21–25**
indemnity embodied in the contract".[50] However, the question whether an insurance contract embodies the indemnity principle is not always straightforward. The traditional picture of insurance contracts is that they can be divided into two types: indemnity policies, under which the insurer promises to compensate the insured for specified types of loss, and contingency policies, under which the insurer agrees to pay a fixed sum of money on the happening of a specified event,

---

[47] *Lister v Romford Ice & Cold Storage Co* [1957] A.C. 555 at 579 (HL).
[48] *Stovin v Wise* [1996] A.C. 923 at 954–955 (HL). Cf. Law Commission, *Remedies against Public Bodies: A Scoping Report* (Law Commission, 2006) para.3.35
[49] S.I. Langmaid, "Some Recent Subrogation Problems in the Law of Suretyship and Insurance" (1934) 47 Harvard L.R. 976, pp.987–995.
[50] *Banque Financière de la Cité SA v Parc (Battersea) Ltd* [1999] 1 A.C. 221 at 231 per Lord Hoffmann.

no matter what loss the insured suffers. In this picture, the main types of indemnity policy are policies of marine insurance, property insurance, liability insurance, insurance against theft and reinsurance; and the main types of contingency policy are life policies and personal accident policies. The traditional view also holds that insurers are given subrogation rights as a means of preventing their insureds from accumulating recoveries only where the policy belongs to the former, and not to the latter group.[51] The reason is that an indemnity insurer promises to hold the insured harmless against loss, so that the amount of the insured's loss is the measure of the insurer's liability,[52] whereas a contingency insurer promises to pay the insured regardless of his loss.[53]

21–26   This account of the law remains broadly accurate, but as Steytler P. observed in an Australian case, *Insurance Commission of Western Australia v Kightly*,[54] it needs some refinement. His point was that the generic labels traditionally applied to policies do not always accurately reflect whether or not they are meant to compensate the insured for actual loss on the happening of an insured event. Thus, for example, there is a strong argument that "keyman" policies taken out by companies on the lives of employees, and life policies taken out by creditors on the lives of their debtors, are designed to serve this purpose. Similarly, personal accident policies may or may not be intended to compensate the insured for his actual loss. Where a policy provides for the payment of a lump sum for loss of life or limb, or for the payment of regular sums during a period of incapacity, regardless of the financial loss actually suffered by the insured, is rightly regarded as a contingency policy. But in Steytler P.'s words, "a policy which compensates the insured for actual financial loss suffered as a consequence of an injury caused by accident is one of indemnity".[55] Hence he concluded that the insurer in the case was entitled to subrogation following payment under a personal accident policy of medical expenses, rehabilitation expenses, travel expenses and lost salary.

21–27   The parties' own characterisation of a policy does not automatically determine its character: the issue is whether the policy, or the relevant parts of it, are in fact designed to compensate the insured for loss. Thus, in *Meacock v Bryant & Co*,[56] cover was provided against the eventuality that the insured was not paid money owed by Spanish debtors by a particular date. The policy described itself as an

---

[51] *Dalby v India and London Life Assurance Co* (1854) 15 C.B. 365 at 387; 139 E.R. 465 at 474 per Parke B.; *Solicitors' & General Life Assurance Society v Lamb* (1864) 2 De G. J. & S. 251; 46 E.R. 372; *Bradburn v Great Western Railway Co* (1874) L.R. 10 Exch. 1; *National Insurance Co of New Zealand Ltd v Espagne* (1961) 105 C.L.R. 569 at 588; *State Government Insurance Office (Queensland) v Brisbane Stevedoring Pty Ltd* (1969) 123 C.L.R. 228 at 240–241; *Wollington v State Electricity Commission of Victoria (No.2)* [1980] V.R. 91 at 97.

[52] This is so whether an indemnity insurer owes a secondary liability to pay damages for breach of its promise to prevent the insured risk from materialising (as held in e.g. *Ventouris v Mountain (The Italia Express) (No.2)* [1999] 2 Lloyd's Rep. 281 at 286), or a primary liability to pay the amount of the indemnity as a debt (as held in e.g. *England v Guardian Insurance Ltd* [2000] Lloyd's Rep I.R. 404 at 422).

[53] *Gould v Curtis* [1913] 3 K.B. 84 at 95–96 (CA); *Glynn v Scottish Union & National Insurance Co Ltd* (1963) 40 D.L.R. (2d) 929 at 938 (Ontario CA).

[54] *Insurance Commission of Western Australia v Kightly* [2005] WASCA 154; (2005) 30 W.A.R. 380.

[55] *Insurance Commission* [2005] WASCA 154; (2005) 30 W.A.R. 380 at [29]. See too *Wollington* [1980] V.R. 91 (Full Ct of Sup Ct of Victoria); *Wilson v Great West Life Assurance Co* [2008] NBCA 57; (2008) 297 D.L.R. (4th) 325.

[56] *Meacock v Bryant & Co* [1942] 2 All E.R. 661.

insurance against the "contingency" that the debts would not be paid, but Atkinson J. held that in reality this was a contract of indemnity, designed to compensate the insured for loss. Once it had been paid by the insurer, it would therefore have to account for money received from Spain when this was eventually paid, to the extent that it was more than fully indemnified by its receipt of both payments.

(b) *Full Indemnification*

Subrogation clauses often give the insurer subrogation rights "before or after" payment under the policy.[57] But the law does not give an insurer the right to bring subrogated proceedings until after the insured has been fully indemnified in line with the terms of the policy[58]—meaning that it must have satisfied all of his claims arising in relation to the event causing the insured loss.[59] The insurer's legal subrogation right does not arise at any earlier time, for example, when the insured claims under the policy or when the insurer agrees to pay.[60] However, the making of the policy does confer a "latent" or "contingent" subrogation right on the insurer, which can be protected by orders pending payment under the policy, for example by an injunction preventing the insured from entering a settlement agreement with a defendant.[61]

21–28

It formerly seemed that the insurer's right did not arise until after the insured had been fully compensated for his loss. Hence, when an insurer fully indemnified its insured under the policy but did not fully compensate him for his loss, for example because there was an excess clause, it was thought that the insured would generally be entitled to remain *dominus litis* of any litigation brought against a defendant[62]—although an exception to this rule was established in a

21–29

---

[57] The International Hull Clauses (01/11/03) cl.49 is drafted even more widely, giving the underwriters subrogation rights "whether or not [they] have paid a claim or agreed to pay a claim or potential claim".

[58] *Dickenson* (1868) L.R. 3 C.P. 639 at 644; *City Tailors Ltd v Evans* (1922) 91 L.J.K.B. 379 at 385 (CA); *Brisbane Stevedoring* (1969) 123 C.L.R. 228 at 240–241; *A.F.G Insurances Ltd v City of Brighton* (1972) 126 C.L.R. 655 at 663; *Hammer Waste Pty Ltd v Q.B.E. Mercantile Mutual Ltd* [2002] NSWSC 1106. See too Marine Insurance Act 1906 s.79(1) and (2), which premise the insurer's subrogation right on payment of a total or partial loss. And cf. *Scottish Union and National Insurance Co v Davis* [1970] 1 Lloyd's Rep. 1 at 5 (CA) (insured owes no duty to account to insurer for third party recoveries until after the insurer has indemnified him under the policy).

[59] *Page v Scottish Insurance Corp* (1929) 140 L.T. 571 at 576 and 577 (CA).

[60] *Primetrade AG v Ythan* [2005] EWHC 2399 (Comm); [2006] 1 All E.R. (Comm.) 157 at [88].

[61] *John Edwards* [1922] 2 K.B. 249 at 254–255; *Boag* [1937] 2 K.B. 113 at 122 (CA); *Brisbane Stevedoring* (1969) 123 C.L.R. 228 at 241 (disliking the word "contingent" but affirming the principle). See too *Commercial Union Assurance Co v Lister* (1874) L.R. 9 Ch. 483, discussed below at para.21–110. In practice, the insurer's position prior to payment of a claim is generally protected by an express provision in the policy, requiring the insured to take reasonable steps to preserve his rights for the insurer's benefit.

[62] This issue was left undecided in *Page* (1929) 140 L.T. 571 at 576 (CA), but the statement in the text is borne out by: *Commercial Union Assurance* (1874) L.R. 9 Ch. 483; *National Fire Insurance Co v McLaren* (1886) 12 O.R. 682; especially 687; *Andrews v Patriotic Assurance Co of Ireland (No.2)* (1886) 18 L.R. Ir. 355 at 365; *Driscoll v Driscoll* [1918] 1 I.R. 152 at 159; *Globe & Rutgers Fire Insurance Co v Truedell* [1927] 2 D.L.R. 659; *Arthur Barnett Ltd v National Insurance Co of NZ Ltd* [1965] N.Z.L.R. 874 at 883 (NZCA); *Ledingham v Ontario Hospital Services Commission* (1974) 46 D.L.R. (3d) 699 (Sup. Ct of Canada); *Farrell Estates Ltd v Canadian Indemnity Co* (1990) 69 D.L.R. (4th) 767 (British Columbia CA); *Zurich Insurance Co Ltd v Ison T.H. Auto Sales Inc* [2011] ONSC 1870.

series of marine insurance cases on valued policies, which held that an insured was estopped from denying that a full indemnity paid under a valued policy constitutes full compensation for his loss.[63]

21–30   However, in *Lord Napier*,[64] which is discussed in Part 7, the House of Lords took a different approach to the question of when an insurer should become entitled to remedies against its insured. Their Lordships reasoned that the indemnity principle is inseparably linked to the terms of the policy, and that clauses which exclude types and amounts of loss from coverage can vary the insured's position not only with regard to the amount which he can recover from the insurer, but also with regard to the total sum which he can accumulate from the insurer and third parties before it can be said that he has been more than fully indemnified. Consistently with this reasoning, it now seems that under English law,[65] an insurer can become *dominus litis* from the moment that the insured has been paid to the full extent of the insurer's liability under the policy, even though he has not been fully compensated for his loss. *Lord Napier* suggests that this outcome should follow wherever the reason for the shortfall is an excess clause in the policy—although not when it derives from a limitation clause, for reasons discussed in Part 7.

21–31   There is no rule stating that an insurer must indemnify its insured in a particular way before its subrogation right will arise. So, in *Page v Scottish Insurance Corp*,[66] no objection was made to the fact that the insurer paid the insured for the cost of repairs to his damaged car which had been carried out by the insured himself. Likewise, in *Brown v Albany Construction Co Ltd*,[67] the court rejected the defendant's argument that the insurer had not relevantly indemnified its insureds, where it had bought their damaged house at its full market value prior to the damage, rather than paying them the difference between that amount and its current market value. Stuart-Smith L.J. held that this was "a perfectly straightforward case where the liability under the policy was discharged in a way which was agreeable to [both parties]".

21–32   Whatever method of indemnification is used, the insured must receive an actual benefit. In *Scottish Union & National Insurance Co v Davis*,[68] the insured's car was damaged by a tortfeasor. With the insurer's consent the car was sent to a garage for repairs, but the insured was dissatisfied with the garage's work, and took the car away to be repaired elsewhere. The garage sent its bill to the insurer which paid without getting the insured to sign a satisfaction note. The

---

[63] *North of England Steamship Insurance Association v Armstrong* (1870) L.R. 5 Q.B. 244; *Thames & Mersey Marine Insurance* [1915] 2 K.B. 214; affirmed [1916] 1 K.B. 30; *Goole & Hull Steam Towing Co Ltd v Ocean Marine Insurance Co Ltd* [1928] 1 K.B. 589; *Yorkshire Insurance* [1962] 2 Q.B. 330 at 343. See too Marine Insurance Act 1906 s.27(2): where an insured is fully insured under a valued policy, the agreed value is conclusive between the insurer and insured as to the value of the subject matter in the absence of fraud.

[64] *Lord Napier* [1993] A.C. 713.

[65] Canadian authorities continue to provide that an insurer's right of subrogation does not arise until the insured has been fully compensated for his loss: e.g. *Mayer v 1314312 Ontario Inc* (2002) 58 O.R. (3d) 226 (Ontario Sup Ct of Justice); *Somersall* [2002] SCC 59; [2002] 3 S.C.R. 109 at [53]. But cf. *Affiliated F.M. Insurance Co v Quintette Coal Ltd* (1998) 156 D.L.R. (4th) 507 (British Columbia CA).

[66] *Page v Scottish Insurance Corp* (1929) 140 L.T. 571 (CA).

[67] *Brown v Albany Construction Co Ltd* Unreported CA, June 16, 1995.

[68] *Scottish Union & National Insurance Co v Davis* [1970] 1 Lloyd's Rep. 1 (CA).

insured then recovered damages from the tortfeasor and used these to pay the costs of repair at another garage. The insurer claimed that the insured owed it a duty to account for this money, but the claim was rejected on the basis that the insurer had never indemnified the insured.[69]

(c) *Rights in Diminution of the Insured Loss*

In *Castellain*, Cotton L.J. held that[70]:   **21–33**

> "[I]f there is a money or any other benefit received which ought to be taken into account in diminishing the loss or in ascertaining what the real loss is against which the contract of indemnity is given, the indemnifier ought to be allowed to take advantage of it in order to calculate what the real loss is, even although the benefit is not a contract or right of suit which arises and has its birth from the accident insured against."

There is therefore a normative element to the question whether a third party's payment to the insured is one that relevantly diminishes the insured loss: the issue is whether the payment "ought to be taken into account" when calculating the amount of the insurer's liability, or whether the insured ought to be allowed to keep it in addition to the policy proceeds.

The law clearly allows the insured to keep both payments where the third party   **21–34**
pays him pursuant to a liability in respect of a loss other than the insured loss.[71] So, for example, if property is insured against fire, and the defendant wrongfully causes a fire which damages the property and also causes the insured a personal injury, the insurer can be subrogated to the insured's rights of action in respect of the property damage, but not to his rights in respect of the injury.[72] However the insured cannot keep both payments where the third party owed him a liability, the performance of which reduces his insured loss. So, in *Dickenson v Jardine*,[73] it was held that an insurer can acquire its insured's right to recover a general average contribution from other cargo interests; in *Assicurazioni Generali de Trieste v Empress Assurance Corp Ltd*,[74] it was held that a reinsured which is paid by a reinsurer must account for the fruits of an action against the insured for damages for fraudulent misrepresentation which induced the reinsured to enter the underlying policy and/or pay out on a claim; and in *Winterthur Swiss*

---

[69] *Scottish Union* [1970] 1 Lloyd's Rep. 1 at 5.

[70] *Castellain* (1883) 11 QBD 380 at 395 (CA).

[71] *South British Insurance Co Ltd v Brown's Wharf Pty Ltd* [1966] 1 N.S.W.R. 80 at 85 (NSW CA).

[72] *Law Fire Assurance Co v Oakley* (1888) 4 T.L.R. 309. Nor can an insurer which pays for the loss of a vessel acquire the owner's rights against a third party for lost freight: *Sea Insurance Co v Hadden* (1884) 13 Q.B.D. 706 (CA); *Glen Line Ltd* (1930) 36 Com. Cas. 1 at 14 and 16 (HL); *C.T. Bowring Reinsurance Ltd v M.R. Baxter (The M. Vatan and M. Ceyhan)* [1987] 2 Lloyd's Rep. 416 at 423.

[73] *Dickenson v Jardine* (1868) L.R. 3 C.P. 639. See too *Price v A1 Ships' Small Damage Insurance Association Ltd* (1889) 22 Q.B.D. 580 at 590 (CA).

[74] *Assicurazioni Generali de Trieste v Empress Assurance Corp Ltd* [1907] 2 K.B. 814. Cf. *Insurance Co of Africa v Scor (UK) Reinsurance Co Ltd* [1985] 1 Lloyd's Rep. 312 at 330 (CA); *H.I.H. Casualty and General Insurance Ltd v New Hampshire Insurance Co* [2001] EWCA Civ 735; [2001] Lloyd's Rep. I.R. 596 at [219].

Insurance Co v AG (Manchester) Ltd,[75] it was held that a legal expenses insurer could be subrogated to its insured's rights against a negligent solicitor in respect of the solicitor's fees and also in respect of the costs payable by the insured to the other side owing to the solicitor's mishandling of litigation.

21-35   This principle applies regardless of whether the third party's liability to pay the insured is itself a compensatory liability. This follows from *Castellain*,[76] where the question arose whether an insured property vendor's loss was relevantly diminished when the purchaser paid the full purchase price with no reduction made for the fact that the property had been damaged by fire. At first instance, Chitty J. held that it was not. He was influenced by the decision of the US Supreme Court in *King v State Mutual Fire Insurance Co*,[77] where a fire insurer paid a mortgagee and then sought to recoup itself out of the mortgage debt. The action was disallowed on the ground that the property itself was not insured under the policy: rather, the insurance was a personal contract which provided that those with a proprietary interest during the currency of the policy should suffer no loss by way of fire. Since the mortgagee had separate contracts with the mortgagor and the insurer, there was no danger that he would be paid twice for the same thing, as the two contracts were unconnected. However, when *Castellain* went to the Court of Appeal, Chitty J.'s analysis was rejected as narrow and over-technical. Whatever the exact legal nature of a fire insurance contract, the reality was that an insured vendor who was paid the full purchase price would be more than fully indemnified were he allowed to keep this money and the insurance proceeds as well.

21-36   In *Castellain* Bowen L.J. also considered that if a man's house were damaged by fire, and his brother gave him money to help him, then this payment would only threaten the indemnity principle if the money were given to reduce the insured loss.[78] Later cases have developed this principle, holding that if a third party's ex gratia payment is intended to diminish the insured loss then the total amount which the insured can accumulate will be correspondingly reduced, but if he intends the payment as a gift over and above anything recoverable from the insurer then the insured can accumulate recoveries from them both.[79]

---

[75] *Winterthur Swiss Insurance Co v AG (Manchester) Ltd* [2006] EWHC 839 (Comm) at [101]. The same principle underlies *Commercial Finance Corp v Merchants Casualty Insurance Co* [1931] 1 D.L.R. 212 (Ontario Sup Ct), affirmed [1931] 4 D.L.R. 210 (Ontario CA), affirmed [1932] S.C.R. 33.

[76] *Castellain* (1882) 8 Q.B.D. 613; reversed (1883) 11 Q.B.D. 380. For an analogous case concerning the sale of goods, see *Gill v Yorkshire Insurance Co* (1913) 24 W.L.R. 389. Other rights which diminish an insured loss, and which may therefore be acquired by subrogation, include a creditor's right to recover a debt from the principal debtor and sureties (*Parr's Bank Ltd v Albert Mines Syndicate Ltd* (1900) 5 Com. Cas. 116) and a creditor's rights under a scheme of arrangement: *Dane v Mortgage Insurance Corp* [1894] 1 Q.B. 54 (CA).

[77] *King v State Mutual Fire Insurance Co* 7 Cush. 1 (Mass., 1851).

[78] *Castellain* (1883) 11 Q.B.D. 380 at 405.

[79] *Burnand* (1882) 7 App. Cas. 333 (HL); *Stearns v Village Main Reef Gold Mining Co* (1905) 10 Com. Cas. 89; *Merrett v Capitol Indemnity Corp* [1991] 1 Lloyd's Rep. 169; *Colonia Versicherung AG v Amoco Oil Co (The Wind Star)* [1995] 1 Lloyd's Rep. 570, affirmed [1997] Lloyd's Rep. I.R. 261 (CA); *Insurance Australia Ltd v H.I.H. Casualty & General Insurance Ltd (In Liquidation)* [2007] VSCA 223 at [159]–[177].

5. LIMITS TO SUBROGATION

An insurer which brings subrogated proceedings against a defendant occupies the **21–37**
same position as the insured would have been occupied, had he brought the
action for his own benefit. Hence the defendant can raise the same defences to the
proceedings as he could have raised against the insured's action. This is discussed in Part 6.

In this Part, we discuss other limits on the insurer's subrogation right. It is **21–38**
unclear whether the defendant, as opposed to a recalcitrant insured, can rely on
every one of these as a means of defending a subrogated claim. There is
Australian authority for the general proposition that "the defendant may raise the
absence or inadequacy of [the insurer's subrogation right] in its defence [and] it
is then for the insurer to justify its right to proceed in the name of the insured."[80]
However, it seems likely that an English court would only permit a defendant to
rely on limits to the insurer's subrogation rights to the extent that these affected
its authority to bring proceedings in the insured's name.[81] The defendant's
argument would otherwise be met by the objection that the court should not go
behind the form of subrogated proceedings to consider matters which are irrelevant to the question which the proceedings are constituted to address, namely
whether the defendant is liable to the insured.[82]

(a) *Insured Has Ceased to Exist*

In *M.H. Smith (Plant Hire) Ltd v D.L. Mainwaring (t/a Inshore)*,[83] an insurer was **21–39**
prevented from bringing subrogated proceedings in the name of an insured
company which had been wound up and dissolved. In these circumstances, the
insurer might still succeed if it obtained an order under the Companies Act 2006
s.1029, restoring the company to the register for the purposes of the subrogated
proceedings.[84] However, if it can foresee that its insured's liquidation is imminent, it would do better to take an assignment of the insured's rights of action.

(b) *Insurer Cannot Sue Himself*

In *Simpson*,[85] the insured owned two ships, one of which collided with the other. **21–40**
The insurer sought to bring subrogated proceedings in the insured's name in his

---

[80] *Woodside Petroleum Development Pty Ltd v H&R-E&W Pty Ltd* [1999] WASCA 1024; (1999) 20
W.A.R. 380 at 387 (Full Ct of Sup Ct of Western Aus), affirmed in *Anthanasopoulos v Moseley*
(2001) 52 NSWCA 266; (2001) 52 N.S.W.L.R. 262 at 278, itself followed and applied in *Australian
Associated Motor Insurers Ltd v N.R.M.A. Insurance Ltd* [2002] FCA 1061.
[81] An insurer will generally obtain its insured's express authority to use the insured's name in
litigation by having him sign a subrogation form when his claim is paid.
[82] Cf. *New Zealand Society of Accountants v A.N.Z. Banking Group (New Zealand) Ltd* [1996] 1
N.Z.L.R. 283 (NZCA) (defendant cannot raise insurer's contributory negligence as defence to
subrogated proceedings); *Zurich Indemnity Co of Canada v Matthews* (2005) 254 D.L.R. (4th) 97
(Ontario CA) (defendant cannot raise insurer's improvident underwriting as defence).
[83] *M.H. Smith (Plant Hire) Ltd v D.L. Mainwaring (t/a Inshore)* [1986] 2 Lloyd's Rep. 244 (CA).
[84] Cf. *Re Alan Meek Wagstaff & Co* Unreported Ch D, December 11, 2000 (where an order was made
for the benefit of an insurer under the Companies Act 1985 s.653(2B)).
[85] *Simpson* (1877) 3 App. Cas. 279 (HL).

capacity as owner of the "innocent" vessel against the insured in his other capacity as owner of the "negligent" vessel. The House of Lords would not allow this, reasoning that the insured had no right of action against himself which the insurer could acquire via subrogation.[86] To deal with this situation, marine policies now often contain a "Sistership Clause" under which questions of liability for the collision are referred to arbitration.[87]

(c) Co-insurance

21-41   As a general rule an insurer may not bring a subrogated claim against a defendant who is found on construction of the policy to be a co-insured. Where there is a joint insurance of an identical interest, for example where a husband and wife jointly insure their jointly owned property, this rule might plausibly be explained in line with the rule in *Simpson*.[88] However, most of the cases barring subrogated proceedings against co-insureds are concerned with composite policies covering the different interests of participants in construction projects, purchased by an employer or a head contractor not only for its own benefit, but for the benefit of contractors and/or subcontractors and/or suppliers as well.[89] The courts have given various reasons for the rule which are considered here in turn.

(i) Reasons for the Subrogation Bar

21-42   **Co-insureds should be treated as one**   According to de Grandpré J. in *Commonwealth Construction Co Ltd v Imperial Oil Ltd*,[90] where the different insured interests are pervasive and relate to the entire subject matter of the policy, subrogated proceedings are barred against a co-insured, just as in the case of joint

---

[86] See too *Ellerbeck Collieries Ltd v Cornhill Insurance Co* [1923] 1 KB 401 at 411 (CA); *Brouwer v Grewal* (1995) 30 Alta L.R. (3d) 244 at 266. But cf. *Montgomery & Co v Indemnity Mutual Marine Insurance Co* [1902] 1 K.B. 734 especially at 739–740 (CA), declining to extend the principle to a case where a general average loss is suffered by a shipowner who also owns cargo.

[87] e.g. Institute Time Clauses, Hulls (1/1/95) cl.9; Institute Voyage Clauses, Freight (1/11/95) cl.7; International Hull Clauses (1/11/03) cl.7.

[88] *General Accident Fire and Life Assurance Corp Ltd v Midland Bank Ltd* [1940] 2 K.B. 388 at 404–405 per Greene M.R.

[89] Cases where negligent contractors or subcontractors have successfully defended subrogated actions on the basis that they are co-insureds include: *Commonwealth Construction Co Ltd v Imperial Oil Ltd* (1977) 69 D.L.R. (3d) 558 (Sup Ct of Can); *Petrofina (UK) Ltd v Magnaload Ltd* [1984] 1 Q.B. 127; *National Oilwell (UK) Ltd v Davy Offshore Ltd* [1993] 2 Lloyd's Rep. 582 at 612–615; *Sylvan Industries Ltd v Fairview Sheet Metal Ltd* (1993) 96 D.L.R. (4th) 277; affirmed (1994) 113 D.L.R. (4th) 493; *Madison Developments Ltd v Plan Electric Co* (1997) 152 D.L.R. (4th) 653 (Ontario CA); *Condominium Corp No.9813678* [2007] ABCA 216. Similar cases where this argument has not succeeded include: *Stone Vickers Ltd v Appledore Ferguson Shipbuilders Ltd* [1992] 2 Lloyd's Rep. 578 (CA); reversing [1991] 2 Lloyd's Rep. 288 on construction of the policy; *Stuart Olson Construction Ltd v Allan Forest Sales Ltd* (1995) 161 A.R. 6; *Hopewell Project Management Ltd v Ewbank Preece Ltd* [1998] 1 Lloyd's Rep. 448; *Deepak Fertilisers and Petrochemicals Corp v ICI Chemicals & Polymers Ltd* [1999] 1 Lloyd's Rep. 387 especially at 400 (CA); *Daishowa-Marubeni International Ltd v Toshiba International Corp* (2003) 231 D.L.R. (4th) 495 (Alberta CA); *Secunda Marine Services Ltd v Fabco Industries Ltd* [2006] 3 F.C.R. 3 (Fed Ct of Canada); *Brookfield Homes (Ontario) Ltd v Nova Plumbing & Heating Ltd* [2010] ONCA 791; (2010) 90 C.C.L.I. (4th) 189.

[90] *Commonwealth Construction Co Ltd v Imperial Oil Ltd* (1976) 69 D.L.R. (3d) 558 at 561 (Sup Ct of Canada).

insurance, because the insured and the co-insured should be regarded as one, triggering the rule in *Simpson*.[91]

This analysis presupposes that every co-insured has an identical insurable **21–43** interest in the whole of the insured subject matter. Where the insured subject matter is jointly owned property, this is not a problem, but in most construction cases the interests of co-insureds are evidently not the same—and indeed, it requires a stretch to say that some have an insurable interest at all, given that they have no legally recognised property interest in the contract works.[92] Nevertheless the courts have often chosen to adopt the fiction that each of the multiple participants in construction projects have a "pervasive insurable interest" in the entire contract works, for reasons of commercial convenience: namely, that it is desirable to enable a head contractor to take out a single policy covering all the risks of the project, rather than leaving all the participants to insure their separate interests.[93]

However, different reasoning can produce the same commercially desirable **21–44** effect, and the courts' decisions on "pervasive insurable interest" have had the unfortunate effect of destabilising the concept of insurable interest in property.[94] For example, in *Deepak Fertilizers Corp v ICI Chemicals and Polymers Ltd*,[95] the Court of Appeal held that a co-insured engineering firm had a "pervasive insurable interest" in the contract works whilst a construction project was under way, but that this interest came to an end after the work was completed. Hence a subrogated action would lie against the firm in respect of an explosion that took place after completion, but it would not have lain while the project was ongoing. This is an unnecessarily complex rule whose effects are uncertain.

Circuity of action   In *The Yasin*,[96] Lloyd J. ruled out subrogated proceedings **21–45** against a co-insured, because if they were successful, the co-insured could pass his loss back to the insurer by claiming under the policy, rendering the action futile. As Lloyd L.J. he reaffirmed this analysis in the Court of Appeal, in *Petrofina Ltd v Magnaload Ltd*.[97] However his reasoning was rejected by Brooke

---

[91] *Simpson* (1877) 3 App. Cas. 279.
[92] This is so even if one takes the wider view of insurable interest in property espoused by Lawrence J. in *Lucena v Craufurd* (1806) 2 Bos. & Pul. N.R. 269 rather than the narrower view espoused by Lord Eldon in the same case: see, respectively, their comments at 302 and 321 (127 E.R. 630 at 643 and 650). A vogue for Lawrence J.'s wider view can be detected in recent case law, e.g. *Mark Rowlands Ltd v Berni Inns Ltd* [1986] Q.B. 211 at 228 (CA); *Glengate-K.B. Properties Ltd v Norwich Union Fire Insurance Society Ltd* [1996] 1 Lloyd's Rep. 614 (CA); *Feasey v Sun Life Assurance Co of Canada* [2003] EWCA Civ 885; [2003] 2 All E.R. (Comm.) 587.
[93] *Petrofina* [1984] QB 127 (CA); *Stone Vickers* [1991] 2 Lloyd's Rep. 288; reversed on a different point [1992] 2 Lloyd's Rep. 578 (CA); *National Oilwell (UK) Ltd v Davy Offshore Ltd* [1993] 2 Lloyd's Rep. 582.
[94] J. Birds, "Insurable Interests" in N. Palmer and E. McKendrick (eds), *Interests in Goods*, 2nd edn (London: LLP, 1998), 91, pp.101–107; A.T. Olubajo, "Pervasive Insurable Interest: A Reappraisal" (2004) 20 Construction L.J. 45.
[95] *Deepak Fertilizers Corp v ICI Chemicals and Polymers Ltd* [1999] 1 Lloyd's Rep. 387; followed in *Daishowa-Marubeni* (2003) 231 D.L.R. (4th) 495 (Alberta CA).
[96] *The Yasin* [1979] 2 Lloyd's Rep. 45 at 55.
[97] *Petrofina Ltd v Magnaload Ltd* [1984] Q.B. 127 at 140.

L.J., in *Co-operative Retail Services Ltd v Taylor Young Partnership*, whose comments on the point were affirmed by the House of Lords.[98] In Brooke L.J.'s view, circuity of action[99]:

> "is an inappropriate plea if the insurer has provided a full indemnity to one co-assured because it will have discharged its liability under the policy in respect of the losses in question and a second co-assured cannot look to it to pay him those losses a second time."

21–46   **Scope of cover**   In *Stone Vickers Ltd v Appledore Ferguson Shipbuilders Ltd*,[100] and again in *National Oilwell (UK) Ltd v Davy Offshore Ltd*,[101] Colman J. held that an implied term should be read into an insurance policy covering, for example, negligence liability incurred by several co-insureds, that the insurer accepts the risk of their negligence not only towards third parties but also towards one another. Colman J. reasoned that if the insurer were permitted to bring subrogated proceedings in respect of a loss caused by the negligence of one co-insured, it would be enabled to recover in respect of a loss against which it had previously agreed to insure him, which would be inconsistent with the terms of the policy.

21–47   **Benefit of insurance agreements between insured and co-insured**   In *Co-operative Retail*, Brooke L.J. in the Court of Appeal,[102] and Lord Hope in the House of Lords,[103] preferred another explanation. This focuses on the co-insured defendant's relationship with the insured rather than his relationship with the insurer, and says that where an insured agrees to effect insurance for the defendant, he impliedly also agrees to exempt the defendant from liability for causing an insured loss, with the result that neither he, nor the subrogated insurer acting through him, can sue the defendant for such a loss. This argument is discussed further below.[104]

(ii) Fraudulent Misconduct by a Co-insured

21–48   Where a co-insured has acted fraudulently with the result that he is disabled from claiming under the policy—and indeed is strictly speaking no longer a "co-insured" at all—a second, "innocent" co-insured may still be able to claim under

---

[98] *Co-operative Retail Services Ltd v Taylor Young Partnership* [2000] EWCA Civ 207; (2000) 74 Con. L.R. 12; affirmed [2002] UKHL 17; [2002] 1 W.L.R. 1419 at [64]–[65].
[99] *Co-operative Retail* [2000] EWCA Civ 207; (2000) 74 Con. L.R. 12 at [72]; drawing on Colman J.'s analysis in *National Oilwell* [1993] 2 Lloyd's Rep. 582 at 613–615.
[100] *Stone Vickers Ltd v Appledore Ferguson Shipbuilders Ltd* [1991] 2 Lloyd's Rep. 288, reversed on a different point [1992] 2 Lloyd's Rep. 578 (CA).
[101] *National Oilwell (UK) Ltd v Davy Offshore Ltd* [1993] 2 Lloyd's Rep. 582.
[102] *Co-operative Retail* [2000] EWCA Civ 207; (2000) 74 Con. L.R. 12 at [72].
[103] *Co-operative Retail* [2002] UKHL 17; [2002] 1 W.L.R. 1419 at [65], approving *Hopewell Project Management* [1998] 1 Lloyd's Rep. 448 at 458. See too *Tate Gallery Board of Trustees v Duffy* [2007] EWHC 361 (TCC); [2007] 1 All E.R. (Comm.) 1004.
[104] See paras 21–78—21–88.

the policy provided that the other's fraud is not imputed to him.[105] In this event, the insurer can clearly take over any rights of action which the "innocent" co-insured may have against the other.[106]

(d) *Contractual Waivers*

Subrogated proceedings might also be barred following a payment under a **21–49** contractors' all-risk policy because the insurer has agreed to include a subrogation waiver clause in the policy. Standard construction industry terms require the employer or head contractor, as the case may be, to arrange for such a clause when purchasing insurance coverage for the other contracting party. It is also common to find clauses in such policies—and indeed in many other policies—waiving the insurer's right to bring subrogated proceedings against co-insureds,[107] against an insured company's subsidiary or affiliated companies,[108] or against an insured's employees.[109] Employee waiver clauses often carry the proviso that the insurer shall not waive its subrogation rights in cases of serious or wilful misconduct.[110]

(i) *Waiver Clauses and Co-Insureds*

The function of a subrogation waiver clause is not to extend the benefits of **21–50** coverage to the parties named in the clause, but simply to give them immunity from subrogated proceedings by the insurer. However, a defendant named in a subrogation waiver clause may fall within a class of co-insureds described elsewhere in the policy, and in this case basic contractual principles indicate that the defendant has standing to enforce the clause against the insurer. However, reliance on the clause would be superfluous, to the extent that the defendant has subrogation immunity as a co-insured in any event.[111] And to the extent that he does not, for example because he is not covered for the relevant loss, he would

---

[105] Where there is a joint policy the fraud of one co-insured will be imputed to another: *Woolcott v Sun Alliance and London Insurance Ltd* [1978] 1 Lloyd's Rep. 629; *New Hampshire Insurance Co v M.G.N. Ltd* [1997] L.R.L.R. 24; *Direct Line Insurance Ltd v Khan* [2001] EWCA Civ 1794; [2002] Lloyd's Rep. I.R. 364. But where there is a composite policy the innocent co-insured is not tainted by the other's fraud, and New Zealand authorities hold that where domestic assets are the subject matter insured, a presumption is made that the policy is composite rather than joint: L. Cunningham, "The Right of an Innocent Co-Insured Spouse to Recover Under a 'Joint' Insurance Policy" (1994) 8 *Otago Law Review* 169.
[106] *P. Samuel & Co v Dumas* [1924] A.C. 431 at 445.
[107] As in e.g. the policies considered in *National Oilwell* [1993] 2 Lloyd's Rep. 582; and *Scottish & Newcastle Plc v G.D. Construction (St Albans) Ltd* [2003] EWCA Civ 16, (2003) 86 Con. L.R. 1.
[108] See too International Hull Clauses (1/11/03), cl.28; and on clauses protecting affiliated companies in business interruption policies see D. Cloughton, *Riley on Business Interruption Insurance*, 8th edn (London: Sweet & Maxwell, 1999); pp.363–364.
[109] As in e.g. the policy in *Woodside Petroleum* [1999] WASCA 1024; (1999) 20 W.A.R. 380. Subrogation waivers in favour of an insured's employees are also commonly encountered in professional indemnity policies, as in e.g. *Arab Bank Plc* [1999] 1 Lloyd's Rep. 262; and see too Lloyd's Form N.M.A. 1088 (10/10/57), reproduced in Sir P. Millett (ed.), *Encyclopedia of Forms and Precedents*, 5th edn (London: Butterworths, 1998), vol.20, para.[1795].
[110] See e.g. *Ingham v Vita Pacific Ltd* (1995) 8 A.N.Z. Ins. Cas. 61–272 (Sup Ct of South Aus); *Tradigrain SA v Intertek Testing Services (I.T.S.) Canada Ltd* [2007] EWCA Civ 154; [2007] 1 C.L.C. 188.
[111] See paras 21–41—21–47.

still be unable to rely on the waiver clause, were the court to hold that the effect of the clause is simply to give him subrogation immunity that is co-extensive with his entitlement to coverage.

21-51   This was the approach taken by Colman J. in *National Oilwell*,[112] when construing a clause which provided for waiver against "any assured and any person . . . whose interests are covered by this policy". As the judge recognised, this meant that the subrogation waiver clause was effectively redundant. However, Colman J.'s analysis was subsequently doubted in an Australian case, *Woodside Petroleum Development Pty Ltd v H&R-E&W Pty Ltd*,[113] where Ipp J. considered that a similarly worded clause in a construction policy was intended to provide the named parties with immunity from subrogated actions in respect of uninsured as well as insured losses. From the insured employer's point of view, "obvious commercial benefits" flowed from this, since it lay in the employer's interest that none of its co-insured contractors and subcontractors should be tied up in litigation while the construction project was ongoing.

(ii) *Waiver Clauses and Strangers to the Contract*

21-52 Where the party named in a subrogation waiver clause is a not a party to the insurance contract, the question arises whether he can enforce the clause against the insurer, or is debarred from doing so by the rules on privity of contract? In other Commonwealth jurisdictions, the courts have made significant inroads into the rules on privity, to enable third parties to enforce the terms of insurance contracts to which they are not privy.[114] For present purposes, the most significant of these is *Fraser River Pile & Dredge Ltd*,[115] in which the Supreme Court of Canada followed its own guidelines laid down in *London Drugs Ltd v Kuhne & Nagel International Ltd*,[116] to hold that a defendant can rely on a waiver clause against subrogated proceedings where the insurer and insured intended him to have the benefit of the clause, and where his activities were the very activities which they contemplated as coming within the scope of the clause.

---

[112] *National Oilwell* [1993] 2 Lloyd's Rep. 582 at 616. In *BP Exploration Operating Co Ltd v Kvaerner Oilfield Products Ltd* [2004] EWHC 999 (Comm); [2005] 1 Lloyd's Rep. 307, it was common ground that the subrogation waiver clause gave the co-insured defendant an immunity that was co-extensive with cover.

[113] *Woodside Petroleum Development Pty Ltd v H&R-E&W Pty Ltd* [1999] WASCA 1024; (1999) 20 W.A.R. 380 at 392–394, preferring the analysis of Judge Rubin in *Marathon Oil Co v Mid Continent Underwriters*, 786 F. 2d 1301 (US Court of Appeals 5th Circuit, 1986). The broad approach taken by the court when construing the subrogation waiver clause in *Woodside Petroleum* was also favoured in *G.P.S. Power Pty Ltd v Gardiner Willis Associations Pty Ltd* [2000] QCA 475; [2001] Qd 586; and *Larson-Juhl Australia LLC v Jaywest International Pty Ltd* [2001] NSWCA 260; (2001) 11 A.N.Z. Ins. Cas. 61–499.

[114] Besides the Canadian authorities cited in the next note, note these Australian cases: *Trident Insurance Co v McNiece Brothers Pty Ltd* [1988] HCA 44; (1988) 165 C.L.R. 107; *Barroora Pty Ltd v Provincial Insurance (Australia) Ltd* (1992) 26 N.S.W.L.R. 170 (NSW Sup Ct); *Co-operative Bulk Handling Ltd v Jennings Industries Ltd* (1997) 9 A.N.Z. Ins. Cas. 61–335 (Full Ct of Sup Ct of Western Aus). Note, too, that the Insurance Contracts Act 1984 (Cth) s.48 abrogates the doctrine of privity in respect of insurance contracts coming within the ambit of the statute.

[115] *Fraser River Pile & Dredge Ltd* (1999) 176 D.L.R. (4th) 257. Earlier cases to the same effect included: *J. Clark & Son Ltd v Finnamore* (1973) 32 D.L.R. (3d) 236; *Mumford v Casey Mercury Sales Ltd* (1980) 108 D.L.R. (3d) 551; *Esagonal Construction Ltd v Traina* [1994] I.L.R. 2695 at 2971; *Tony & Jim's Holdings Ltd v Silva* (1999) 170 D.L.R. (4th) 193 (Ontario CA).

[116] *London Drugs Ltd v Kuhne & Nagel International Ltd* [1992] 3 S.C.R. 299.

English common law might have developed along similar lines,[117] but a   **21–53**
stranger to the insurance contract who seeks to enforce a subrogation waiver
clause in his favour against the insurer would now be likely to invoke the
Contracts (Rights of Third Parties) Act 1999.[118] In accordance with s.1(3) he
would have to be "expressly identified in the contract by name, as a member of
a class or as answering a particular description but need not be in existence when
the contract is entered into". He could enforce the clause in his own right under
s.1(1)(a) if "the contract expressly provides that he may", or under s.1(1)(b) and
(2) if "the term purports to confer a benefit on him" and provided that a contrary
intention by the contracting parties does not appear in the agreement.

(e) *Waivers by Conduct/Laches*

In various American cases, insurers have been denied the right to share in the   **21–54**
fruits of subrogated proceedings where they have failed to participate in the
litigation and have failed to take any other steps to enforce or protect their
subrogated interest.[119]

Whether an insurer's inaction constitutes a waiver of rights is a question of fact   **21–55**
which varies from case to case. In *Health Cost Controls v Wardlow*,[120] the insurer
lost its subrogation rights because it failed to request the insured's written
agreement to account for the fruits of litigation (as required by the policy) until
long after its payment. Again, in *Valora ex rel. Valora v Pennsylvania Employees
Benefit Trust Fund*,[121] the insurer lost its subrogation right through inaction for
five years after it began paying policy benefits, including three years in which the
insured pursued his action against a third party through to a settlement. By way
of contrast, in *Zych v Unidentified Vessel*,[122] an insurer was held not to have
surrendered its ownership of an abandoned wreck notwithstanding the lapse of
130 years, during which time it had taken no steps to recover the wreck. Rovner
D.J. held that the insurer's failure to engage in recovery efforts did not constitute
a waiver of its ownership rights because the technology needed to find the wreck
had only recently become available.[123] Others had looked for the vessel in the
past, but it would have been unreasonable to expect the insurer to do so when its
chances of success would have been minimal.

---

[117] A process seemingly started by *Enimont Supply SA v Chesapeake Shipping Inc (The Surf City)* [1995] 2 Lloyd's Rep. 242.
[118] But note that an insurer and insured can contract out of the 1999 Act, as is done e.g. in the International Hull Clauses (1/11/03) cl.36.
[119] See the cases digested in R.J. Sutton "Conduct or Inaction by Insurer Constituting Waiver of, Or Creating Estoppel to Assert, Right of Subrogation" (2005) 125 A.L.R. 5th 1. An insurer which has lost its subrogation right in this way may not complain if the insured settles his claim against a defendant in breach of policy terms: *Shawnee Fire Insurance Co v Cosgrove*, 116 P. 819 (1911); affirmed 121 P. 488 (1912); *Powers v Calvert Fire Insurance Co* 57 S.E. 2d 638 (1950).
[120] *Health Cost Controls v Wardlow* 825 F. Supp. 152 (W.D. Kentucky, 1993); affirmed on other grounds 47 F. 3d 1169 (6th Circuit, 1995).
[121] *Valora ex rel. Valora v Pennsylvania Employees Benefit Trust Fund* 847 A. 2d 681 (PA Super, 2004).
[122] *Zych v Unidentified Vessel* 1991 A.M.C. 1254.
[123] *Zych* 1991 A.M.C. 1254 at 1259.

(f) *Clean Hands*

21–56   As discussed in Part 2, the courts' jurisdiction to order a recalcitrant insured to lend his name to subrogated proceedings ultimately derives from the Chancery courts. This suggests that an insured who wishes to resist lending his name to proceedings on the ground that the insurer has treated him improperly can argue that the insurer should be denied the court's assistance on equitable grounds, because it has failed to come to court with "clean hands".

21–57   The leading English authority for this proposition is *Morris v Ford Motor Co*[124] There Lord Denning M.R. invoked an equitable discretion to deny an indemnifier the right to acquire its payee's right of action against the payee's negligent employee, where the payee did not wish to enforce this right of action, for fear of upsetting industrial relations in its factory. This case is probably inconsistent with the House of Lords' decision in *Lister*,[125] where a subrogated claim against a negligent employee was successful. Moreover, it seems doubtful whether a court would be justified in refusing an insurer subrogation on equitable grounds simply because the insured's personal relationship with the defendant is such that he would prefer not to sue. There is no danger of the insured being more than fully indemnified in this situation, as he does not intend to enforce his rights of action; but the court may wish to prevent the insured from shifting the burden of paying the loss onto the insurer. Thus, in Canada, insurers have been subrogated to a parent's right to sue a child,[126] and a spouse's right to sue the other spouse,[127] and in Australia, legislation was considered necessary to prevent insurers from bringing subrogated actions against their insureds' families.[128]

21–58   It seems, too, that subrogation will not be denied on equitable grounds because the insurer has declined liability until a late stage in proceedings brought by the

---

[124] *Morris v Ford Motor Co* [1973] Q.B. 792 at 800–801 (CA).

[125] *Romford Ice* [1957] A.C. 555. See too *Dawson v Bankers & Traders Insurance Co Ltd* [1957] V.R. 491 at 507; *Northern Assurance Co v Coal Mines Insurance* [1970] 2 N.S.W.R. 223 at 226; *Jovanovic v Broers* (1979) 45 Fed. L.R. 453. Following *Lister*, members of the British Insurance Association and Lloyd's voluntarily undertook not to pursue subrogated claims in an insured employer's name against a negligent employee (BIA Circular No.89/59), and from time to time the (renamed) Association of British Insurers continues to reissue circulars to its members reminding them of the agreement (the most recent was sent out on October 21, 1994). In Australia insurers are now denied the right to bring such proceedings by the Insurance Contracts Act 1984 (Cth) s.66, unless the employee's negligence amounts to "serious or wilful misconduct"—on this proviso, see *Boral Resources (Queensland) Pty Ltd v Pyke* (1992) 2 Qd R. 25; *Morning Vale Pty Ltd v Pennefather* (1992) 8 S.R. (W.A.) 114.

[126] *Makowsky v Makowsky* (1979) 7 Alta L.R. (2d) 69; *Morawietz v Morawietz* (1986) 18 C.C.L.I. 108; *Wade v Northern Shield Insurance Co* (1986) 5 B.C.L.R. (2d) 62. In Australia, insurers are denied subrogation rights where their insureds have rights of action against family members by the Insurance Contracts Act 1984 (Cth) s.65(1)(c)—unless the family member's wrongdoing amounts to "serious or wilful misconduct", or occurs in the course of employment by the insured: s.65(2).

[127] *Sainas v Sainas* (1968) 66 D.L.R. (2d) 753; *Liberty Mutual Insurance Co v Partridge* (1976) 67 D.L.R. (3d) 603. Cf. *National Trust Co Ltd v Allan* (1999) 141 Man. R. (2d) 94 (Manitoba QB) (insurer may bring subrogated proceedings in name of trustee insured against beneficiary's wife).

[128] Insurance Contracts Act 1984 (Cth) s.65(1)(c). Under s.65(2), a subrogated action is allowed where the family member's wrongdoing amounts to "serious or wilful misconduct", or occurs in the course of employment by the insured. There currently seems to be little likelihood of similar legislation being enacted in the UK, following the Law Commission's decision not to investigate changes to the law of subrogation as part of its ongoing review of insurance contract law: Law Commission and Scottish Law Commission, *Insurance Contract Law: Analysis of Responses and Decisions on Scope* (2006) para.3.27.

insured against a third party. These were the facts of *England v Guardian Insurance Ltd*,[129] where the insureds brought proceedings against various defendants in respect of damage to their house, and the insurer not only declined liability for this damage for a long period, but also declined to contribute to the costs of the insureds' litigation prior to the time when it eventually accepted liability, and wrote a letter to the Legal Aid Board questioning why the insureds' proceedings against some of the defendants were being legally aided. Judge Thornton QC refused to hold that the insurer's conduct was sufficiently bad to disentitle it from exercising subrogation rights. For much of the relevant period it had been engaged in bona fide negotiations with the insured to settle the claim, and although the letter had been "unfortunate", it had not affected the insureds as it had only been received by the Board after judgment had been reserved, and the Board had not acted on it.

Nonetheless, the possibility remains that subrogation might be withheld on equitable grounds where an insurer has behaved badly in other ways. Examples can be found in the Canadian and American courts. In *Arendas v Rich & Co Inc*,[130] subrogation was denied to an employer which paid workmen's compensation benefits, and then refused to assist its employee's widow in bringing an action against a defendant, and deliberately withheld information that she needed to make out her case. In *Re Halifax Insurance Co*,[131] an insurer refused to join its (property) insureds in bringing an action against a defendant who happened to be insured by the insurer as well, under a separate (liability) policy, and the insurer was not permitted to share in the settlement monies which the property insureds recovered from the defendant. Again, in *Home Insurance Co v Pinski Bros Inc*,[132] an insurer was prevented from bringing subrogated proceedings against a defendant who was insured by the insurer under a separate policy. The common feature of the latter cases is that in each the insurer failed to act evenhandedly between its two insureds, one of whom had a right of action against the other. It provided one, but not the other, with resources, information and access to its regular legal counsel.

21-59

These cases raise the question whether an insurer should automatically be denied subrogation wherever it has insured the competing parties to litigation under separate policies, regardless of whether there is any evidence of it acting

21-60

---

[129] *England v Guardian Insurance Ltd* [2000] Lloyd's Rep. I.R. 404. Cf. *Morley v Moore* [1936] 2 K.B. 359 (CA); *Bourne v Stanbridge* [1965] 1 W.L.R. 189 (CA); *Hobbs v Marlowe* [1978] A.C. 16; *Ingersoll Milling Machinery Co v M/V Bodena* 829 F. 2d 293 (2nd Circuit, 1987) (insurer retains subrogation right even though it denies coverage and only pays insured pursuant to court order following litigation).

[130] *Arendas v Rich & Co Inc* 220 F. Supp 957 (1963). See too *Powers v Calvert Fire Insurance Co*, 57 S.E. 2d 638 (1950); *Burnaby v Standard Fire Insurance Co*, 20 Cal. Rep. 2d 44 (1993).

[131] *Re Halifax Insurance Co* (1964) 44 D.L.R. (2d) 339 at 342 (reasoning that the insurer had impliedly waived its right to share in recoveries by the property insureds from the liability insureds). Cf. *Baio v Commercial Union Insurance Co* 410 A. 2d 502 (1979) (insurer denied right to share in money recovered by insured from tortfeasor whom the insurer had assisted).

[132] *Home Insurance Co v Pinski Bros Inc* 500 P. 2d 945 esp. at 950 (1972). See too *Stafford Metal Works Inc v Cook Paint & Varnish Co*, 418 F. Supp 56 especially at 63 (1976); *Royal Exchange Assurance of America Inc v SS President Adams*, 510 F. Supp. 581 (1981). Sed contra *Counts v General Motors Corp*, 1988 W.L. 32066 (Del. Super Ct, 1988), order modified 1988 W.L. 67804 (Del. Super Ct, 1988) (no conflict although insurer appointed same law firm to act for both sides of dispute, provided that insurer does not use information or material obtained from one insured to assist the other in his conduct of the litigation).

more favourably to one than another.[133] There are strong arguments against allowing subrogation in this situation—in particular, that it wastes resources and sets up potential conflicts of interest where the insurer has been made privy to information regarding the strengths and weaknesses of either side to the dispute. However, automatic denial of subrogation can produce the effect that a wrongdoing insured receives the benefit of coverage he has not paid for, a result which may sometimes be equally undesirable.

(g) Voluntary Payments by Insurer

21-61 The courts have been inconsistent in their attitude towards subrogated proceedings by insurers who have paid their insureds although they are not legally obliged to do so. In various cases, they have allowed such proceedings to go ahead, prompted by a disinclination to allow a defendant to raise matters as between the insurer and the insured in the context of subrogated proceedings, a desire to encourage insurers to pay disputed claims, and a desire to make wrongdoing defendants pay for losses which they have caused.[134] Yet in other cases they have held that an insurer which acts gratuitously has no subrogation rights. Some, though not all, of these cases can be explained on the basis that allowing subrogated recovery would have subverted the public policy underlying a rule of law which rendered the insurance contract void.

21-62 A well known example of the latter type of case is *John Edwards & Co v Motor Union Insurance Co Ltd*,[135] where McCardie J. refused subrogation to an insurer which had paid a claim under a PPI policy which was deemed to be void by the Marine Insurance Act 1906 s.4.[136] However, the same explanation cannot be used for *Canwest Geophysical Ltd v Brown*,[137] a Canadian case where the insurer was denied subrogation following payment on motor policy to which it had gratuitously added death benefits, nor for *Wellington Insurance Co v Armac Diving Services Ltd*, another Canadian case where the insurer compromised the insured's claim but denied liability and was not permitted to recoup itself out of third party recoveries.[138]

---

[133] Different considerations apply where an insurer wishes to bring subrogated proceedings in the name of an innocent co-insured against a negligent co-insured: see paras 21–41—21–47.

[134] *King v Victoria Insurance Co* [1896] A.C. 250 (PC); *Leduc v British Canadian Insurance Co* [1924] 1 D.L.R. 196; *Austin v Zurich General Accident & Liability Insurance Co Ltd* [1944] 2 All E.R. 243 at 246, not disapproved in principle by CA, although the court thought that this was not a subrogation case (for reasons that are doubted at paras 19–45—19–47): [1945] K.B. 250 at 258; *Sydney Turf Club v Crowley* [1971] 1 N.S.W.L.R. 724 at 730 (NSW CA); *Q.B.E. Insurances Ltd v G.R.E. Insurance Ltd* (1983) 2 A.N.Z. Ins. Cas. 60–533; *McAll v Brooks* [1984] R.T.R. 99; *Manitoba Public Insurance Corp v D (K)* [1995] 2 W.W.R. 206; *Clark v Ardington Electrical Services* [2002] EWCA Civ 510; [2003] Q.B. 36; *Ideal Waterproofing Pty Ltd v Buildcorp Australia Pty Ltd* [2004] NSWSC 765 at [38]; *Wabbits Pty Ltd v Godfrey* [2009] NSWSC 1299.

[135] *John Edwards & Co v Motor Union Insurance Co Ltd* [1922] 2 K.B. 249.

[136] Non-marine policies, to which the Act does not apply, are valid although they contain a PPI clause, provided that the insured does in fact have an insurable interest: *Re London County Commercial Reinsurance Office* [1922] 2 Ch. 67.

[137] *Canwest Geophysical Ltd v Brown* [1972] 3 W.W.R. 23.

[138] *Wellington Insurance Co v Armac Diving Services Ltd* (1987) 37 D.L.R. (4th) 462.

(h) *Public Policy*

In exceptional circumstances, such as wartime, for example, public policy con- **21–63**
siderations may lead the courts to deny subrogation rights to an insurer. Thus, in
The Palm Branch,[139] enemy underwriters were prevented from bringing subrogated proceedings in the name of their insureds in the Prize Court.

(i) *Quantum of Insurer's Recovery*

An insurer which successfully brings subrogated proceedings cannot keep the **21–64**
whole fruits of the action for itself if these exceed the amount of its payment to
the insured. In Lord Atkin's words "subrogation will only give the insurer rights
up to twenty shillings in the pound on what has been paid"[140]: any surplus
belongs to the insured.

This principle was applied in *Yorkshire Insurance Co Ltd v Nisbet Shipping Co* **21–65**
Ltd.[141] An insured vessel was lost in a collision in 1945, and the insurer paid the
agreed value of £72,000. With the insurer's consent, the insured began proceedings against the owners of the other vessel and 10 years later won damages of
£75,000. These were properly converted into Canadian dollars at the rate of
exchange which applied at the time of the collision. When this sum was transmitted to England, and converted back into pounds, the amount realised was
around £126,000, the pound having been devalued in 1949. The insurer claimed
to be entitled to the whole of this sum, but Diplock J. ruled that the insured need
only account for £72,000.

A further rule affecting the insurer's entitlement to recoup itself out of the **21–66**
fruits of subrogated proceedings is that the insured can deduct the amount of his
unrecovered costs from the proceeds of successful litigation before these are
turned over to the insurer.[142] This rule was reviewed in *England*,[143] where Judge
Thornton QC held that reasonable costs can be deducted provided that they are
linked to attempts to reduce the loss for which the insured had been indemnified,
that costs can be deducted even though they are incurred in connection with
litigation that fails, and that deductible expenditure is not confined to costs and
expenses incurred during the pursuit of legal proceedings but can extend to pre-
trial investigations etc.

6. DEFENCES

As Denning L.J. once observed, "the insurers who stand behind [a subrogated] **21–67**
action take their plaintiff as they find him, and if he is, for some reason or other,
debarred from making a claim, they fall with him."[144] In this part we describe
various defences that have been raised against subrogated actions.

---

[139] *The Palm Branch* [1916] P. 230; varied [1919] A.C. 272.
[140] *Glen Line* (1930) 36 Com. Cas. 1 at 14 (HL).
[141] *Yorkshire Insurance Co Ltd v Nisbet Shipping Co Ltd* [1962] 2 Q.B. 330.
[142] *Assicurazioni Generali de Trieste* [1907] 2 K.B. 814.
[143] *England* [2000] Lloyd's Rep I.R. 404 at 423–426.
[144] *Romford Ice* [1956] 2 Q.B. 180 at 191 (CA). See too *Sydney Turf Club* [1971] 1 N.S.W.L.R. 724
at 734 (NSW CA).

(a) *Factual Defences*

21–68   If the defendant is not liable to the insured on the facts of a case, then subrogated proceedings against him will fail.[145]

(b) *Contributory Negligence*

21–69   If the defendant can raise the defence of contributory negligence to an insured's claim, then he can raise the same defence against subrogated proceedings brought in the insured's name.[146]

(c) *Illegality*

21–70   Subrogated proceedings can be defeated by an ex turpi causa defence founded on the illegality of the insured's actions.[147]

(d) *Statute*

21–71   Where a defendant's liability to an insured is limited by statute, the insurer's subrogated proceedings will be subject to the same limitation.[148]

(e) *Delay*

21–72   If an insured's action against a defendant has become time-barred, then subrogated proceedings will fail for the same reason, and the insurer cannot argue, for example, that the limitation period for the subrogated action should run from

---

[145] *Otter Mutual Fire Insurance Co v Rand* (1913) O.W.R. 568; *Traders General Insurance Co v Noel* (1957) 8 D.L.R. (2d) 341; *Heckbert v Wye Electricity Ltd* (1984) 9 C.C.L.I. 72; *Dept of National Heritage v Steensen Varning Mulchay* [1998] EWHC Tech 305; *North King Lodge Ltd v Gowlland Towing Ltd* [2005] BCCA 557; (2005) 47 B.C.L.R. (4th) 20; *Ericsson Ltd v K.L.M. Royal Dutch Airlines* [2005] HKCU 1815 (where some of the multiple defendants were liable on the facts but others were not); *HSBC Rail (UK) Ltd v Network Rail Infrastructure Ltd* [2005] EWCA Civ 1437; [2006] 1 W.L.R. 643; *Vicar of Spalding v Chubb Fire Ltd* [2010] EWCA Civ 981; [2010] 2 C.L.C. 277.
[146] *General Animals Insurance Co v Montreal Tramways Co* (1918) 45 Que. S.C. 425; *Thames & Mersey Marine Insurance* [1915] 2 K.B. 244; affirmed [1916] 1 K.B. 30; *Brown v British Columbia Electric Railway Co* [1925] 3 D.L.R. 734 (where insured was not contributorily negligent on the facts); *Goole & Hull Steam Towing* [1928] 1 K.B. 589; *Phoenix Assurance Co of Hartford v City of Montreal* (1942) 10 I.L.R. 308; *Traders General Insurance Co v Segal* (1963) Que. Q.B. 740; *Deutz Australia Pty Ltd v Skilled Engineering Ltd* [2001] VSC 194.
[147] *Euro-Diam Ltd v Bathurst* [1990] 1 Q.B. 1 at 38–39 (CA).
[148] *North of England Iron Steamship* (1870) L.R. 5 Q.B. 244 especially at 245n (defendant's liability limited by Merchant Shipping Act 1862 s.54). Several cases also establish that a defendant's liability might be limited by the Warsaw Convention arts 22 and 23, as amended by the Hague Protocol 1955, which are given force of law in the UK by the Carriage by Air Act 1961: *Bland v British Airways Board* [1981] 1 Lloyd's Rep. 289 (CA); *Collins v British Airways Board* [1982] Q.B. 734 at 745 (CA); *Antwerp United Diamonds BVBA v Air Europe* [1995] 2 Lloyd's Rep. 224 (where the relevant limitation was inapplicable because the insured's loss was caused through the misconduct of the defendant's employees).

the time when it paid the insured rather than the time when the insured's right of action accrued.[149]

In *Graham v Entec Europe Ltd (t/a Exploration Associates)*,[150] the Court of **21-73** Appeal held that where subrogated proceedings are brought in respect of latent damage, the insurer as well as the insured is a person whose knowledge of the relevant damage can start time running for limitation purposes. This case turned on the wording of the Limitation Act 1980 s.14A(5), which provides that the starting date for reckoning the limitation period under s.14A is the earliest date when the claimant "or any person in whom the cause of action was vested before him" first had the requisite knowledge. This subsection was designed to catch assignees, but the court held that the policy reasons for its enactment extend to subrogated proceedings.

(f) *Set-Off*

The question whether a defendant should be entitled to rely on a right of set-off **21-74** against subrogated proceedings has been considered in several Canadian cases. In *Best Buy Carpets Ltd v 281856 British Columbia Ltd*,[151] Hogarth J. found in the defendant's favour on this issue, reasoning that the defendant was entitled to "raise any defence that was open to it as if the action had been brought by the insured",[152] including an equitable set-off. However, in *Lewenza v Ruszczak*,[153] the opposite conclusion was drawn by the Ontario Court of Appeal, and this decision was affirmed by another Ontario Court of Appeal, in *Colonial Furniture Co (Ottawa) Ltd v Saul Tanner Realty Ltd*,[154] where Rosenberg J.A. noted that a defendant's inability to set off a claim against the insured "does not deprive it of the benefit of its [rights]" as it can still "demand payment . . . or take whatever other steps are available to it in its execution [of judgment]".[155] Allowing the defendant to exercise a right of set-off against the insured would deprive the insurer of any chance of recovery, whereas the only disadvantage incurred by the defendant would be the increased cost of enforcing its rights against the insured in a separate action.

(g) *Exclusion Clauses*

Subrogated proceedings will fail if the defendant's liability to the insured is **21-75** excluded by a term of a pre-existing contract between the defendant and the

---

[149] *London Assurance Co v Johnson* (1737) West T. Hard. 266 at 269; 25 E.R. 930 at 932; *R.B. Policies at Lloyds v Butler* (1949) 65 T.L.R. 436; *Manitoba Public Insurance Corp v R.W. From Ltd* (1982) 12 M.R. (2d) 27; *Central Insurance Co Ltd v Seacalf Shipping Corp (The Aiolos)* [1983] 2 Lloyd's Rep. 25 at 30 (CA); *Royal Insurance Co of Canada v Aguiar* (1985) 16 D.L.R. (4th) 477 at 479 (Ontario CA); *Republic of India v India Steamship Co (The Indian Grace) (No.2)* [1994] 2 Lloyd's Rep. 331 at 336.
[150] *Graham v Entec Europe Ltd (t/a Exploration Associates)* [2003] EWCA Civ 1177; [2003] 4 All E.R. 1345.
[151] *Best Buy Carpets Ltd v 281856 British Columbia Ltd* (1987) 28 C.C.L.I. 311 (British Columbia Sup Ct).
[152] *Best Buy* (1987) 28 C.C.L.I. 311 at 313.
[153] *Lewenza v Ruszczak* (1959) 22 D.L.R. (2d) 167.
[154] *Colonial Furniture Co (Ottawa) Ltd v Saul Tanner Realty Ltd* (2001) 196 D.L.R. (4th) 1.
[155] *Colonial Furniture* (2001) 196 D.L.R. (4th) 1 at [22].

insured[156] or by trade usage.[157] An exclusion clause in a contract between the defendant and the insured will be ineffective against the insured (and thus against the subrogated insurer), if the defendant commits a breach of contract of a kind which disentitles him from relying on the clause.[158]

21–76   The existence of a term or trade usage excluding the defendant's liability may be a material fact which the insured should have disclosed to the insurer when taking out the policy, and if its existence was not disclosed, the insurer may be entitled to avoid liability.[159] But if the insurer knows of its existence and pays the insured nonetheless, then the insurer will be taken to have affirmed the validity of the policy,[160] and will presumably be estopped from denying that it was liable to pay.

(h) Arbitration Clauses

21–77   An insurer may not initiate subrogated proceedings if this would put the insured in breach of an arbitration agreement with the defendant.[161] Indeed, the courts will issue an anti-suit injunction to restrain the insurer from bringing proceedings in a foreign court even though the insurer "would not commit an actionable breach of contract *vis-à-vis* [the defendant] by commencing the court proceeding".[162]

---

[156] *Thomas & Co v Brown* (1899) 4 Com. Cas. 186 (implied term); *Coupar Transport (London) Ltd v Smith's (Acton) Ltd* [1959] 1 Lloyd's Rep. 369 at 380–381 (express term). Note, too, that the UK Standard Conditions for Towage and Other Services (revised 1986) cll. 3 and 4 go even further, and render a ship owner liable for events brought about by a third party without the owner's fault: these clauses have disastrous effects for the subrogation rights of the owner's P & I Club.

[157] *Tate & Sons Ltd v Hyslop* (1885) 15 Q.B.D. 368.

[158] *Levison v Patent Steam Carpet Cleaning Co Ltd* [1978] Q.B. 69 (defendant cannot enforce clause); *Photo Production Ltd v Securicor Transport Ltd* [1980] A.C. 827 (defendant can enforce clause); *Rose v Borisko Bros Ltd* (1982) 125 D.L.R. (3d) 671 at 679; affirmed (1983) 147 D.L.R. (3d) 191 (defendant cannot enforce clause).

[159] *Société Anonyme d'Intermédiaires Luxembourgeois v Farex Gie* [1995] L.R.L.R. 116 at 142 (CA), citing *Tate & Sons* (1885) 15 Q.B.D. 368. See too *Canadian National Railway Co v Canadian Industries Ltd* [1941] S.C.R. 591 at 599; *Brisbane Stevedoring* (1969) 123 C.L.R. 228 at 248. But cf. *Marc Rich & Co A.G. v Portman* [1996] 1 Lloyd's Rep. 430 at 440 per Longmore J.: "I do not consider underwriters have discharged the onus of showing that in the comparatively new and rarely used market in which demurrage was insured it was material for a prudent underwriter to be informed about either actual or assumed irrecoverability from third parties."In Australia, the Insurance Contracts Act 1984 (Cth) s 68(2) provides that an insured is not required as part of his general duty of disclosure to inform his insurer of the existence of any contract with a third party which may affect the insurer's ability to recover from that third party via a subrogated action.

[160] *The Auditor* (1924) 18 Lloyd's List Rep. 402 and 464 at 468.

[161] *Schiffahrtsgesellschaft Detlev von Appen GmbH v Voest Alpine Intertrading GmbH (The Jay Bola)* [1997] 2 Lloyd's Rep. 279 at 291 (CA); *Starlight Shipping Co v Tai Ping Insurance Co Ltd (The Alexandros T)* [2007] EWHC 1893 (Comm); [2008] 1 All E.R. (Comm) 593 at [12]–[15]. As observed in *Phoenix Finance Ltd v Federation Internationale de l'Automobile* [2002] EWHC 1028 (Ch) at [83], this is consistent with the Arbitration Act 1996 s.82(2), which treats as a party to the arbitration agreement a person claiming under or through such a party.

[162] *West Tankers Inc v Ras Riunione Adriatica di Sicurta (The Front Comor)* [2005] EWHC 454 (Comm); [2005] 2 Lloyd's Rep. 257 at [68]. A leapfrogged appeal was made to the HL, which made a reference to the ECJ on a different issue: [2007] UKHL 4; [2007] 1 All E.R. (Comm.) 794; for the ECJ's decision see [2009] 1 A.C. 1138.

(i) *Benefit of Insurance Clauses*

As a general rule, an insurer may not bring subrogated proceedings against a **21–78** defendant where the insured has previously agreed with the defendant that the insurance should enure to the defendant's benefit. It follows by necessary implication from the fact that the insured agreed to this that he intended to exempt the defendant from liability for loss covered by the policy.[163]

The key question in cases of this kind is obviously whether the insured has **21–79** agreed that the benefit of the insurance should enure to the defendant. In some cases, the insured and the defendant have a contract which contains an express term to this effect.[164] Even in the absence of an express term, however, the courts will imply such a term into a contract between an insured and a defendant in some situations. Two common examples are[165]: (1) where the insured peril is fire damage to leased property caused by the tenant's negligence; and (2) where the insured peril is damage to the works caused by the negligence of a participant in a building project. There are obviously differences between these situations, but one broad conclusion can be drawn from all the cases: namely, that the courts are unlikely to find that an insured has agreed to exempt a defendant from liability for an insured loss where the agreement between the insured and the defendant does not oblige the insured to take out insurance.

(i) *Two Common Situations*

Leases The cases on subrogated actions by landlords' insurers against negli- **21–80** gent tenants suggest that a court is most likely to hold that the parties intended the tenant to have the benefit of the landlord's fire insurance where the lease contains all of these terms: that the landlord will insure the premises against fire; that the tenant will pay for the cost of this insurance; that the tenant's obligation to keep the property in good repair will not extend to repairing fire damage; and that in the event of a fire the landlord will use any insurance proceeds to repair the property.[166] Even if a lease does not contain all these terms, a court may still hold that the tenant was meant to have the benefit of the insurance where the lease obliges the landlord to insure against fire damage and also modifies the

---

[163] *Mark Rowlands Ltd v Berni Inns Ltd* [1986] 1 Q.B. 211 at 232–233 (CA).
[164] As in e.g. *The Auditor* (1924) Lloyd's List Rep. 464; *Canadian Transport Co Ltd v Court Line Ltd* [1940] A.C. 934.
[165] Other cases have concerned: (1) mortgage indemnity guarantees: *Mortgage Corp v McNicholas* Unreported CA, September 22, 1992; *Woolwich BS v Brown, The Independent*, January 22, 1996; *Bradford & Bingley BS v Marachanda* Unreported CA, October 16, 1997; cf. *Banfield v Leeds BS* [2007] EWCA Civ 1369; (2) leases of machinery: *D'Amours v Manitoba Forestry Resources Ltd* (1981) 9 Man. R. (2d) 91; *Bow Helicopters Ltd v Bell Helicopters Textron* (1982) 125 D.L.R. (3d) 386; *Western Drill-Dredging Manufacturing Ltd v Suncor Inc* [1995] 4 W.W.R. 69; (3) towing contracts: *St Lawrence Cement Inc. v Wakeham & Sons Ltd* Unreported Ontario CA, October 30, 1995; reversing (1992) 8 O.R. (3d) 340; (4) offloading contracts: *L&B Construction Ltd v Northern Canada Power Commission* [1984] 6 W.W.R. 598.
[166] *Mark Rowlands* [1986] 1 Q.B. 211 (CA); *Alberta Importers and Distributors (1993) Inc v Phoenix Marble Ltd* [2008] ABCA 177; (2008) 62 C.C.L.I. (4th) 175 (finding for the tenant even though the lease also required the tenant to acquire general liability coverage). The same principle can also apply where it is the tenant rather than the landlord who has covenanted to insure: *Majestic Theatres Ltd v NA Properties Ltd* (1985) 57 A.R. 210; *Jarski v Schmidt* (1987) 26 C.C.L.I. 94; and cf. *Laing Property Corp v All Seasons Display Inc* [2000] BCCA 467; (2000) 190 D.L.R. (4th) 1 (benefit of insurance enures to landlord's employees).

tenant's covenant to repair, to exempt him from liability to repair fire damage. A similar conclusion may also be drawn, in the absence of an express covenant to insure, where the tenant must pay an amount which is stated to correspond to the cost of premiums[167]; and even the absence of a term requiring the tenant to pay for the premiums may not be fatal if the other terms are present and the landlord in fact pays for the premiums out of rental income.[168]

21–81   On the other hand, a covenant to insure by the landlord, without more, will not found an inference that the landlord has agreed not to sue the tenant,[169] and where the lease does not require the landlord to insure, this is likely to prove fatal to the tenant's defence.[170]

21–82   Note that the tenant is not precluded from relying on his agreement with the landlord by the fact that he has no insurable interest in the property. This point was made in the Ontario Court of Appeal, in *Amexon Realty Inc v Comcheq Services Ltd*,[171] where Goudge J.A. stressed that it is the agreement between the landlord and the tenant that disables the insurer from recovering via a subrogated action, and it makes no difference whether the tenant himself would have been able to claim under the policy.

21–83   **Construction contracts**   Just as the terms of leases vary from one case to another, so too do the terms of the different JCT agreements which it has fallen to the courts to consider. Hence much turns on the precise wording of the relevant clauses and any overview of the subject must be read with this in mind. However, some general comments will be offered here in relation to a paradigm case: a subrogated action brought by an employer's insurer against a negligent contractor.

21–84   Typically in a case of this sort, the court must decide how two clauses of the construction contract were intended by the parties to interact, one stipulating that the contractor should be liable to the employer for loss caused by the contractor's negligence, the other requiring the employer to insure against the risk of damage to the works. The court must first decide whether it was the parties' intention to arrange matters so that they should both have to bear (and thus be obliged to insure against) the same risk, i.e. that the works would be damaged by the contractor's negligence. Generally speaking, the courts have tended to hold that the parties did not intend to put themselves in this position. This seems realistic, given the commercial context of the parties' dealings.

---

[167] *Tsolon Investments Pty Ltd v Waffle Pod Footing Systems NSW Pty Ltd* [2002] NSWCA 302.
[168] *Agnew-Surpass Shoe Stores Ltd v Cummer-Yonge Investments Ltd* (1973) 55 DLR (3d) 676; *Ross Southward Tire Ltd v Pyrotech Products Ltd* (1975) 57 DLR (3d) 248; *T. Eaton Co v Smith* [1978] 2 S.C.R. 749 especially at 754–755; *Marlborough Properties Ltd v Marlborough Fibreglass Ltd* [1981] 1 N.Z.L.R. 464; *North Newton Warehouses Ltd v Alliance Woodcraft Manufacturing Inc* [2005] BCCA 309; (2005) 44 B.C.L.R. (4th) 227.
[169] *Marlborough Properties* [1981] 1 N.Z.L.R. 464; *Leisure Centre Ltd v Babylon* [1984] 1 N.Z.L.R. 318; *Lambert v Keymood Ltd* [1997] 2 E.G.L.R. 70 (where the tenant's actions were in any case reckless rather than merely negligent). Cf. *Wisma Development Pte Ltd v Sing-The Disc Shop Pte Ltd* [1994] 3 S.L.R. 295 (where a covenant to insure by a tenant without more constituted insufficient evidence from which the court could infer an agreement that the tenant would not sue the negligent landlord).
[170] *Matthews v Andrew* (1986) 25 D.L.R. (4th) 452; *Yale Properties Ltd v Pianta* (1987) 13 B.C.L.R. (2d) 242; *Lee-Mar Developments Ltd v Monto Industries Ltd* (2000) 18 C.C.L.I. (3d) 224 (Ontario Sup Ct); affirmed (2001) 146 O.A.C. 360; *Sooter Studios Ltd v 74963 Manitoba Ltd* [2006] MBCA 12; (2006) 34 C.C.L.I. (4th) 1.
[171] *Amexon Realty Inc v Comcheq Services Ltd* (1998) 37 O.R. (3d) 573 at 576.

The courts must next decide whether the parties intended the employer or the **21-85** contractor to bear the relevant risk. Two approaches to this question emerge from the cases. The first, which puts the risk of damage caused by the contractor's negligence onto the contractor, is to construe the clause obliging the employer to insure as placing him under an obligation to insure only in respect of damage caused by a reason other than the contractor's negligence.[172] The second, which puts the risk onto the employer, is to hold that the clause obliging the employer to insure obliges him to insure against damage caused by the contractor's negligence, and hence that the employer intended to exempt the contractor from liability for causing such damage.[173]

In *Scottish & Newcastle Plc v G.D. Construction (St Albans) Ltd*,[174] the Court **21-86** of Appeal held that the latter construction of the parties' agreement produces the result that the insured is debarred from suing the defendant whether or not he actually obtains the benefit of coverage for the defendant. Note, though, that the insured must have assumed a contractual obligation to do this, and that "a mere intention to do so in the future is insufficient", as Colman J. observed in *BP Exploration Operating Co Ltd v Kvaerner Oilfield Products Ltd*.[175]

(ii) *Inconsistent Policy Terms*

Insurers sometimes insert an express term into their policies, stipulating that the **21-87** policy coverage is not intended to enure to the benefit of third parties.[176] The question arises whether such a term is effective to prevent a defendant from relying on a benefit of insurance clause in his contract with the insured? When answering this, the court should bear in mind that the key question is what the insured and the defendant intended and not what the insurer intended. However, where the insured and the defendant are both aware that the insurer has expressly prohibited the insured from extending the benefit of coverage to third parties, this may suggest that they did not intend the defendant to be protected.

This is the best explanation of *Court Line Ltd v Canadian Transport Co Ltd*,[177] **21-88** which concerned a charterparty which provided that the owner should give the

---

[172] As in e.g. *Barking and Dagenham LBC v Stamford Asphalt Co Ltd* (1997) 54 Con. L.R. 1 (CA). See too *National Trust v Haden Young Ltd* (1994) 72 B.L.R. 1; affirming (1993) 66 B.L.R. 88; *European and International Investments Inc v McLaren Building Services Ltd* [2001] Scot CS 67; *Casson v Ostely P.J. Ltd* [2001] EWCA Civ 1013; (2001) 85 Con. L.R. 18; *Tyco Fire & Integrated Solutions (U.K.) Ltd v Rolls-Royce Motor Cars Ltd* [2008] EWCA Civ 286; [2008] 2 All E.R. (Comm.) 584.

[173] As in e.g. *James Archdale & Co Ltd v Comservices Ltd* [1954] 1 W.L.R. 459 (CA); *Coleman Street Properties Ltd v Denco Miller Ltd* (1982) 31 B.L.R. 32; *Scottish Special Housing Association v Wimpey Construction (UK) Ltd* [1986] 1 W.L.R. 995 (HL). Similar cases on subcontractors are: *Norwich CC v Harvey* [1989] 1 W.L.R. 828; *British Telecommunications Plc v James Thomson & Sons (Engineers) Ltd* (1996) 82 B.L.R. 1; *John F. Hunt Demolition Ltd v A.S.M.E. Engineering Ltd* [2007] EWHC 1507 (TCC); [2008] Bus. L.R. 558. And cf. *Madison Developments Ltd v Plan Electric Co* (1997) 152 D.L.R. (4th) 653 (Ontario CA).

[174] *Scottish & Newcastle Plc v G.D. Construction (St Albans) Ltd* [2003] EWCA Civ 16; (2003) 86 Con. L.R. 1 at [11], also noting that in these circumstances the insured's failure to obtain coverage for the defendant might constitute a breach of contract for which damages are recoverable.

[175] *BP Exploration Operating Co Ltd v Kvaerner Oilfield Products Ltd* [2004] EWHC 999 (Comm); [2005] 1 Lloyd's Rep. 307 at [99].

[176] e.g. Institute Cargo Clauses (1/1/82) cl.15; Institute Container Clauses, Time (1/1/87) cl.17; International Hull Clauses (1/11/03) cl.36.

[177] *Court Line Ltd v Canadian Transport Co Ltd* [1940] A.C. 934 at 938–941. See too *Canadian National Railway* [1941] S.C.R. 591.

time-charterer "the benefit of their protection and indemnity club insurance as far as the club rules allow". Charterparties, especially time charters, often contain a clause of this kind, the wording of which reflects the fact that most P. & I. Clubs provide in their rules that ship owners may not give such benefits to charterers[178]—and so it was in the case. Hence the House of Lords held that the time-charterer could not rely on the benefit of insurance clause in its contract with the owner.

(j) *Settlements and Releases*

21–89 If an insured agrees to settle or relinquish his claim against a defendant, the defendant may well be able to rely on this agreement in defence to subrogated proceedings,[179] even though the insured entered the agreement without consulting the insurer.[180] Where the settlement is clearly intended to refer only to the insured's uninsured losses, the insurer's subrogated action to recover for insured losses will be unaffected by the settlement.[181] Although the matter is not free from controversy, it has also been held that subrogated proceedings are not affected by a settlement entered after the insurer has paid the insured, if the defendant was aware of the fact that the insurer accordingly had subrogation rights.[182] Otherwise, the defendant should be able to rely on a settlement,[183] and

---

[178] S.J. Hazelwood, *P. & I. Clubs: Law and Practice*, 3rd edn (London: LLP, 2000) pp.89–90, adding that although "P. & I. clubs do assume charter risks by means of accepting so-called 'Special Entries' . . . these entries are separate insurances and the club prohibition remains intact."

[179] By the same token an insured will be unable to recover for uninsured losses from a defendant if the insurer releases him from all liability in the course of exercising its subrogated right to negotiate with the defendant: *Kitchen Design and Advice Ltd v Lee Valley Water Co Ltd* [1989] 2 Lloyd's Rep. 333.

[180] Cf. *Long v Brown* [1996] 1 W.W.R. 280: insurer's adjuster authorises insured to sign release which adjuster and insured both mistakenly believe to refer to property damage only; in fact defendant drafted release as a general release; release not void for mutual mistake and so binding on insured and subrogated insurer.

[181] *Smidmore v Australian Gas Lights Co* (1881) 2 N.S.W.L.R. 219; *Dufourcet & Co v Bishop* (1886) 18 Q.B.D. 373; *McDonell v Brebric* (1966) 52 D.L.R. (2d) 502; *Taylor v O. Wray & Co Ltd* [1971] 1 Lloyd's Rep. 497; *Le v Williams* [2004] NSWSC 645 at [34]–[39].

[182] *Haigh v Lawford* (1964) 114 L.J. 208; *Brisbane Stevedoring* (1969) 123 C.L.R. 228 at 241; *Ware Chemical of Canada Ltd v Cosmos Chemical Ltd* (1973) 36 D.L.R. (3d) 483 at 494; *Lord Napier and Ettrick v R.F. Kershaw Ltd* [1993] 1 Lloyd's Rep. 10 at 13 (not considered on appeals to CA and HL); *Baltic Shipping Co v Merchant "Mikhail Lermontov"* (1994) 36 N.S.W.L.R. 361 at 370 (NSW CA). The same view was also taken in *Morganite Ceramic Fibres Pty Ltd v Sola Basic Australia Ltd* (1987) 11 N.S.W.L.R. 189 (NSW Sup Ct), but on appeal (Unreported NSW CA, May 11, 1989), Meagher J.A. denied that any such principle existed (the other members of the court did not need to decide the question on the view which they took of the case).

[183] *West of England Fire Insurance Co v Isaacs* [1897] 1 Q.B. 226; *Phoenix Fire Assurance Co v Spooner* [1905] 2 K.B. 753; *Kirton v British America Assurance Co.* (1907) 10 O.W.R. 498; *Horse, Carriage & General Insurance Co Ltd v Petch* (1916) 33 T.L.R. 131; *Globe & Rutgers Fire Insurance Co v Truedell* [1927] 2 D.L.R. 659; *Yorkshire Insurance* [1962] 2 Q.B. 330 at 340; *Corbett v Rolfe* (1964) 47 D.L.R. (2d) 222; *Sweigard v Kardash* (1966) 56 W.W.R. 129; *Leibel v Derkach* (1975) 63 D.L.R. (3d) 176; *Manitoba Public Insurance Corp v Sam's Enterprises Ltd* [1978] 2 W.W.R. 658; *Broadlands Properties Ltd v Guardian Assurance Co* (1984) 3 A.N.Z. Ins. Cas. 60–552; *McCourt Cartage Ltd v Fleming Estate* (1997) 152 D.L.R. (4th) 179; *Dwyer v Liberty Insurance Co of Canada* [2002] NLCA 75; (2002) 219 Nfld & P.E.I.R. 308 at [36]–[44].

the insurer will be left to its remedies against the insured for prejudicing its subrogation right.[184]

(k) *Unilateral Discontinuances*

If an insured begins proceedings against a defendant independently of the insurer, **21–90** and then unilaterally discontinues the proceedings under CPR Pt 38,[185] then the question arises whether the insurer can later bring a second subrogated set of proceedings against the same defendant relying on the same set of facts? In *The Millwall*,[186] it was held that a subrogated action would not lie to pursue a right of appeal that had been lost through a discontinuance. But a discontinuance does not normally render an action res judicata,[187] and it is open to the insurer acting through the insured to apply to the court under CPR r.38.7 for permission to make another claim against the defendant.[188] The court would be most unlikely to grant such permission if any costs of the first action remained payable by the insured under CPR r.38.6.[189]

(l) *Judgments and Stays*

It sometimes happens that an insurer pays an insured loss, and that, acting **21–91** independently of the insurer, the insured then sues a defendant for his uninsured loss only. If the insured recovers judgment from the defendant, or accepts a payment into court with the result that further pursuit of the action is stayed,[190] then the insurer will not be permitted to bring a second, subrogated, action to recover the insured loss as this would constitute an abuse of court process.[191]

In some circumstances the insurer can have the judgment reopened[192] or the **21–92** stay lifted,[193] but the courts will only exercise their discretion to do this if the insurer can produce clear evidence of wrongful behaviour by the defendant, such

---

[184] See paras 21–107—21–113.

[185] i.e. without having agreed with the defendant that he will do so.

[186] *The Millwall* [1905] P. 155 at 163.

[187] *The Ardanhu* (1887) 12 App. Cas. 256 at 262 (HL).

[188] Under the former practice of the old RSC Ord.21, r.3, leave to discontinue was required and the courts would often impose terms as a condition of granting leave, including a term that no new action would be brought in respect of the same set of facts. Such an order would have debarred subrogated proceedings. However, leave to discontinue is no longer required, and defendants are protected instead by the stipulation in CPR r.38.7 that the burden lies on the claimant to seek permission to make another claim.

[189] Cf. *Re Payne* (1883) 23 Ch. D 288; *Martin v Earl Beauchamp* (1883) 25 Ch. D 12; *M'Cabe v Bank of Ireland* (1889) 14 App. Cas. 413.

[190] CPR r.36.15. In several Canadian cases, an insurer and insured have simultaneously brought proceedings in respect of different losses caused by the same act of a defendant, and the courts have ordered joinder of their actions, or else that they be set for trial consecutively and disposed of together: *Arrow Transit Lines Ltd v Tank Truck Transport Ltd* [1968] 1 O.R. 154; *Provencher v Temelini* (1987) 27 C.P.C. 9; *Rachansky v Walker* (1993) 9 Alta L.R. 433. An English court might deal with this situation by making a Group Litigation Order under CPR r.19.11.

[191] *Derrick v Williams* [1939] 2 All E.R. 559; *Buckland v Palmer* [1984] 1 W.L.R. 1109 (CA), considered in *Kahl v Holderness BC* [1995] P.I.Q.R. 401 at 414–416 (CA).

[192] *Buckland* [1984] 1 W.L.R. 1109 at 1115 (CA); *Burn v Cotton* Unreported CA, February 3, 1987.

[193] *Lambert v Mainland Market Deliveries Ltd* [1977] 1 W.L.R. 825.

as deliberately submitting to the insured's attenuated claim in order to disadvantage the insurer. The fact that the insurer's position has been prejudiced is not enough in itself.[194]

7. THE INSURED'S DUTY TO ACCOUNT FOR THIRD PARTY RECOVERIES

21–93   Where an insured is paid by his indemnity insurer, and then receives another payment in respect of the same loss from a third party, whether via legal action or otherwise, the insured must account to the insurer for the third party's payment, to the extent that it leaves him more than fully indemnified.[195] The leading case on this topic is *Lord Napier and Ettrick v Hunter*.[196] Stop Loss insurers paid Lloyd's Names for losses flowing from allegedly negligent underwriting. The Names then sued Outhwaite Underwriting Agencies and Members' Agents for their losses and the claim was settled for £116 million. A dispute arose between the Stop Loss insurers and the Names with regard to the allocation of this settlement money. They disagreed about two issues. The first was whether the Names should have to account to the Stop Loss insurers once they had been fully indemnified under the terms of the policy, or whether they could first recoup themselves for their uninsured losses out of the settlement money. The second was whether the Stop Loss insurers had a personal or a proprietary right to their share of the money.

(a) *Full Indemnity or Full Compensation?*

21–94   This issue arose because the Stop Loss policies contained both excess and limitation clauses, so that the Stop Loss insurers were liable to the Names only for losses above and below fixed amounts. Obviously no problem would have arisen if the settlement money had been sufficient to compensate the Names for all of their losses, insured and uninsured, as the parties could then simply have shared out the money proportionately. However, there was a shortfall, which meant that the Stop Loss insurers would have been left out of pocket if the court had accepted the Names' argument that they were entitled to recoup themselves for all of their uninsured losses before the Stop Loss insurers could take anything.

21–95   At first instance, Saville J. found for the Names, holding that the Stop Loss insurers' entitlement to recoup themselves out of the settlement money did not arise until after the Names had been fully compensated for their loss. However, his decision was overturned by the Court of Appeal,[197] whose own decision was affirmed by the House of Lords. In Lord Jauncey's view, the reason was that[198]:

---

[194] *Hayler v Chapman* [1989] 1 Lloyd's Rep. 490.
[195] And subject to the rule that if the value of the third party recoveries exceeds the amount of the loss then the excess goes to the insured rather than the insurer: see para.21-10, fnn.28 and 29.
[196] *Lord Napier* [1993] A.C. 713.
[197] *Lord Napier and Ettrick v R.F. Kershaw Ltd* [1993] 1 Lloyd's Rep. 10.
[198] *Lord Napier* [1993] A.C. 713 at 747.

"[I]n the context of recoveries subrogation is concerned only with the loss against which the assured is insured rather than any general loss . . . . If an insured has suffered an insured loss and an uninsured loss full indemnification of the former subrogates the insurers irrespective of the fact that the assured has not yet recovered the uninsured loss."

On this approach, the Stop Loss insurers should have been entitled to recoup themselves before the Names took anything—i.e. their claim should have taken priority over the Names' claims to recoup themselves for both the top and bottom "layers" of their loss. However, it was common ground between the parties that before the Stop Loss insurers could recover anything the Names could recoup themselves in respect of the top layer—i.e. for that portion of their uninsured loss which exceeded the policy limits. The only disputed question was whether the Stop Loss insurers should next be entitled to recoup themselves in respect of the insured loss, or whether the Names should next be entitled to recover in respect of the bottom layer—i.e. for the excess. The court decided this issue in favour of the Stop Loss insurers. However, the logic of Lord Templeman's reasoning confirms that the Names were entitled to recoupment for the top layer of their loss before the Stop Loss insurers' rights arose.

21–96   To explain this, it is helpful to refer to a set of hypothetical facts considered by the court. Assume that a Name is issued a policy with an excess of £25,000 and a limit of £125,000, giving him a layer of coverage for £100,000. He suffers a loss of £160,000, and his Stop Loss insurer pays him £100,000. He then recovers £130,000 from a third party in diminution of the loss. At first instance, Saville J. held that the Name should retain so much of the third party's payment as would be needed to compensate him for his total uninsured loss—i.e. the £25,000 excess added to the £35,000 top slice, making £60,000 in all, and leaving £70,000 for the Stop Loss insurer.[199] However, the Court of Appeal[200] and the House of Lords[201] both held that the £130,000 should be applied on a "top-down" basis—i.e. the first £35,000 should go to the Name in respect of the top slice and the remaining £95,000 should go to the Stop Loss insurer for the middle layer, leaving it only £5,000 out of pocket and leaving nothing to compensate the Name for the bottom layer.

21–97   The reason, in Lord Templeman's view,[202] was that the Name agreed to bear the top and bottom layers, with the result that he should occupy the same position as would have been occupied by the insurers of the top and bottom layers if separate policies had been issued for each of the three layers. In this case, the insurer of the top layer would have been "entitled to be the first to be subrogated because he [would] only [have] agreed to pay if the first two insurances did not cover the total loss". Likewise, the insurer of the middle layer would have been "entitled to be the second to be subrogated because he [would] only [have] agreed to pay if the first insurance cover proved insufficient".

21–98   It may have come as a surprise to the Names that the excess clauses in their Stop Loss policies did not merely render a portion of their loss irrecoverable from their insurers, but also disabled them from recovering from third parties in

[199] *Lord Napier and Ettrick v R.F. Kershaw Ltd* [1993] 1 Lloyd's Rep. 10 at 16–17.
[200] *Lord Napier and Ettrick v R.F. Kershaw Ltd* [1993] 1 Lloyd's Rep. 10 at 17–19.
[201] *Lord Napier* [1993] A.C. 713 at 730–731.
[202] *Lord Napier* [1993] A.C. 713 at 730–731.

respect of the excess until after their insurers had recouped themselves. They might have thought that agreeing to the former did not necessarily entail agreement with the latter, and that they, rather than their insurers, should have taken priority when the settlement money was allocated, or at least that their respective claims should have been prorated.

21–99   However the court's reasoning was correct, as we can demonstrate by slightly varying the facts of the hypothetical situation discussed above.[203] Suppose that the insurer issues a policy containing an excess clause of £25,000 and a limit of £125,000. Suppose, further, that the insured suffers a loss of £50,000 and that he recovers £20,000 from a third party in respect of the same loss before the insurer pays him anything. As a result, his net loss is £30,000 and because of the excess clause the insurer only need pay him £5,000. Now compare the situation where the insurer pays the insured before he recovers anything from the third party. The insurer is liable to pay £50,000 less £25,000 making £25,000. If the insured then receives £20,000 from the third party, and is permitted to put the whole of this towards his £25,000 shortfall, then the insurer would end up having paid him £20,000 more than it paid him in the previous case. There is no justification for this discrepancy, and it must follow that in the second case the insured should account to the insurer for the £20,000—as the court held in *Lord Napier*.

21–100   Although it has been said that the rules of indemnity and subrogation are the same for marine and non-marine insurance,[204] it is unclear where *Lord Napier* has left the rules of marine insurance with regard to the allocation of third party recoveries in cases of under-insurance. This point was not addressed in *Lord Napier* itself, but in *Kuwait Airways Corp v Kuwait Insurance Co SAK*, Rix J. thought that the position in marine insurance "may well be different" notwithstanding the House of Lords' decision.[205]

21–101   The Marine Insurance Act 1906 s.81 provides that:

"Where the assured is insured for an amount less than the insurable value or, in the case of a valued policy, for an amount less than the policy valuation, he is deemed to be his own insurer in respect of the uninsured balance."

This was considered in *The Commonwealth*.[206] A ship with an agreed value of £1,350 was insured for £1,000. The vessel sank following a collision, and the underwriters paid a total loss of £1,000 under the policy. The insured then recovered £1,000 from the other vessel's owners. The Court of Appeal held that this payment should be allocated between the insured and the underwriters on a pro rata basis, reasoning that the risk which each had undertaken should be reflected in their respective entitlements to share in the money. This is obviously inconsistent with the approach taken in *Lord Napier*, but we doubt whether the House of Lords intended to overrule the approach taken in the marine insurance

---

[203] *Lord Napier and Ettrick v R.F. Kershaw Ltd* [1993] 1 Lloyd's Rep 10 at 22 per Staughton L.J.
[204] e.g. *Burnand* (1882) 7 App. Cas. 333 at 339 (HL); *Darrell* (1880) 5 Q.B.D. 560 at 563 (CA); *Page* (1929) 140 L.T. 571 at 575 (CA); *H. Cousins & Co Ltd v D&C Carriers Ltd* [1971] 2 W.L.R. 85 at 92 (CA).
[205] *Kuwait Airways Corp v Kuwait Insurance Co SAK* [1996] 1 Lloyd's Rep. 664 at 695; not considered on appeal [1997] 2 Lloyd's Rep. 687 (CA).
[206] *The Commonwealth* [1907] P 216.

cases, which are of long standing and are reflected in the language of the 1906 Act.

Luckily, this question may not matter much in practice, as many hull policies **21–102** make express provision for the allocation of recoveries which decisively settle the question one way or the other. Until recently, standard forms adopted the "top-down" approach,[207] but market practice favoured the pro rata approach, and this is now reflected in cl.49.4 of the International Hull Clauses (1/11/03).

(b) *Personal or Proprietary Right?*

The House of Lords found for the Stop Loss insurers on this issue as well. **21–103** Reviewing the historical development of the doctrine of subrogation, they found ample evidence in the older cases to support the view that the Chancery courts had recognised an insurer's interest in the outcome of proceedings by an indemnified insured against third parties.[208] Although some early cases spoke of giving the insurer an interest under a trust, the House of Lords would not go so far as that, since they thought it unnecessary and commercially undesirable to impose fiduciary duties on the Names. Instead, they contented themselves with impressing the settlement money with an equitable lien in favour of the Stop Loss insurers.[209] It followed that the insurers could have an injunction against the Names' solicitors restraining them from paying the settlement money over to their clients without first providing for the insurers.[210]

There are good reasons for thinking that the House of Lords went too far in **21–104** *Lord Napier* when it gave the Stop Loss insurers a proprietary claim. It is a difficult question when the law should give a proprietary remedy to a claimant who makes out a claim in unjust enrichment, but the law does not often give such a remedy to a claimant who has paid money under a contract which gives him no security interest although he was free to bargain for such an interest. Lord Templeman thought it appropriate to place the Stop Loss insurers into a stronger position than the Names' unsecured creditors because "the insurers could not resist payment whereas an unsecured creditor may choose whether to advance moneys or not".[211] But an insurer chooses to enter an insurance contract with an insured in the same way that a lender chooses to enter a loan contract with a borrower. Once either contract has been entered its terms must be performed. The element of compulsion is the same for both, and both should take the consequences if they fail to stipulate for security and the other party becomes insolvent.

There is a further reason why the Stop Loss insurers should have been confined **21–105** to a personal remedy. If an insured receives a payment from a defendant which

---

[207] See e.g. Institute Time Clauses, Hulls (1/1/95) cl.12.3; Institute Voyage Clauses, Hulls (1/11/95) cl.0.3.
[208] *Randal* (1748) 1 Ves. Sen. 98; 27 ER 916; *Blaauwpot v Da Costa* (1758) 1 Eden. 130; 28 E.R. 633; *White v Dobinson* (1844) 14 Sim. 273; 60 E.R. 363; *Commercial Union Assurance Co v Lister* (1874) L.R. 9 Ch. App. 483; *King* [1896] A.C. 250; *Re Miller, Gibb & Co Ltd* [1957] 1 W.L.R. 703.
[209] *Lord Napier* [1993] A.C. 713 at 737–738 (Lord Templeman), at 744 (Lord Goff), and 750–751 (Lord Browne-Wilkinson).
[210] See too *England* [2000] Lloyd's Rep. I.R. 404 (insurer's equitable lien takes priority over Legal Aid Board's statutory lien on recoveries).
[211] *Lord Napier* [1993] A.C. 713 at 737.

diminishes his insured loss, then the insurer's liability is correspondingly reduced. If the insurer then overpays him, the law gives it a personal action to recover the overpayment.[212] Why, then, should the law give the insurer a proprietary, rather than a personal claim, simply because it paid the insured before rather than after he is paid by the defendant? The effect of giving a proprietary claim in the second case, but restricting him to a personal claim in the first, is to create an anomaly for which there is no justification. One way of resolving this anomaly would be to give the insurer a proprietary claim in both cases, but this still would not meet the previous objection to the House of Lords' decision, suggesting that the court would have done better to restrict the insurer to a personal claim in both situations.

21–106   Although *Lord Napier* decides that the insurer has a proprietary interest in the fruits of the insured's claim against the third party, their Lordships did not decide whether the insurer has a similar interest in the claim itself.[213] This point later arose in *Re Ballast Plc*.[214] The insured engineering company built a defective road and was obliged to do remedial works, the cost of which it recovered from its insurer. The company alleged that the damage was caused by the negligence of another company which had designed the road, but before it could pursue a claim for breach of contract, it went into insolvent liquidation. The liquidators disclaimed their interest in the company's claim, which they considered to lack merit, and the insurer applied for a vesting order under the Insolvency Act 1986 s.181(3). Lawrence Collins J. dismissed the application, holding that the insurer needed a proprietary interest in the claim before a vesting order would be made and that it had no such interest. To hold otherwise would have been inconsistent with the rule that a subrogated insurer can recover no more than the amount of its payment to the insured, and with various procedural rules which are predicated on the view that any rights of action exercised by a subrogated insurer belong to the insured.[215]

8. THE INSURED'S DUTY TO PROTECT THE INSURER'S POSITION

21–107   An insurer's subrogated proceedings will fail if the insured has previously released the defendant from liability, or settled his claim, or pursued an action in his own right for less than the whole loss. For this reason, insurers often protect themselves by inserting clauses into their policies, stating that the insured owes a duty to ensure that all rights against third parties are properly preserved and exercised and/or prohibiting them from compromising or releasing claims against

---

[212] See para.21–14.
[213] *Lord Napier* [1993] A.C. 713 at 740, 745 and 752–753.
[214] *Re Ballast Plc* [2006] EWHC 3189 (Ch); [2007] Lloyd's Rep. I.R. 742.
[215] *Re Ballast* [2006] EWHC 3189 (Ch); [2007] Lloyd's Rep. I.R. 742 at [91]–[109]. For previous dicta to the same effect, see *The Aiolos* [1983] 2 Lloyd's Rep. 25 at 30; *Lonrho Exports Ltd v Export Credits Guarantee Dept* [1999] Ch. 158 at 181. For the relevant procedural rules, see para.21–118.

third parties. Moreover, various authorities indicate that the law may imply such terms as an incident of the insurer's subrogation right.[216]

Several English cases are explicable on this basis.[217] In *West of England Fire* **21–108** *Insurance Co v Isaacs*,[218] for example, the defendant tenant of premises insured them against fire. The premises were damaged by fire and the insurer paid him £100 to cover the cost of repairs. The landlord then sued the defendant for breach of his covenant to repair, and he settled the claim by paying the landlord £140 and agreeing to release him from his own obligation to reinstate the premises in the event of fire damage. The insurer then sued the defendant to recover the amount of the insurance payment, arguing that its subrogation rights against the landlord had been lost as a result of the settlement agreement. The Court of Appeal upheld the claim and ordered the defendant to repay the £100.

A different aspect of the principle is illustrated by *Horse, Carriage and* **21–109** *General Insurance Co v Petch*,[219] where an insured brought proceedings against a defendant in respect of a motor accident in which he had been injured and in which his car had been damaged. The claim was settled for £1,250 without any apportionment between the personal injury and the property damage. The question then arose whether the insurer, which had previously paid the insured £80 for his personal injury, was entitled to a share of the settlement money. The court held that it could recoup itself in full, the court deeming the insured to have complied with his duty to act in the insurer's best interests by recovering the whole £80 loss for which the insurer had paid him.

In *Commercial Union Assurance Co v Lister*,[220] the owner of a silk mill in **21–110** Halifax suffered property damage and loss of profits when the mill was blown up, allegedly through the negligence of the Halifax Corporation, which had supplied gas to the mill. The owner's insurer paid his claim for the property damage but the lost profits were uninsured. The insurer sought a declaration that it was "entitled to the benefit of any right of action" against the corporation, and an injunction restraining the mill-owner "from prosecuting the action other than for the full amount". No injunction was issued as the owner gave an undertaking that he would claim the whole damage, but Sir George Jessel M.R. made it plain that the owner owed a duty not to prejudice the insurer's interest, and would be in breach of this duty if he compromised the action "otherwise than bona fide".[221]

Some of the foregoing cases might appear to suggest that an insurer can always **21–111** recover the full amount of the indemnity in action for breach, but in fact this is not so. As Judge Thornton QC observed in *England*[222]:

---

[216] *Boag* [1937] 2 K.B. 113 at 128 (CA); *Brisbane Stevedoring* (1969) 123 C.L.R. 228 at 241; *Arthur Barnett Ltd v National Insurance Co of NZ Ltd* [1965] N.Z.L.R. 874 at 885 (NZ CA); *Levesque v Co-operative Fire & Casualty Co* (1976) 68 D.L.R. (3d) 553 at 556–558; *Sola Basic Australia Ltd v Morganite Ceramic Fibres Pty Ltd* Unreported NSW CA, May 11, 1989; *French v Fish* (1995) 128 D.L.R. (4th) 364 at 382.

[217] See too *Phoenix Assurance Co v Spooner* [1905] 2 K.B. 753. And cf. *Davies v MacRitchie* [1938] 4 D.L.R. 187; *Broadlands Properties Ltd v Guardian Assurance Co* (1984) 3 A.N.Z. Ins. Cas. 60–552.

[218] *West of England Fire Insurance Co v Isaacs* [1896] 2 Q.B. 377; [1897] 1 Q.B. 226 (CA).

[219] *Horse, Carriage and General Insurance Co v Petch* (1916) 33 T.L.R. 131.

[220] *Commercial Union Assurance Co v Lister* (1874) L.R. 9 Ch. App. 483 (CA).

[221] *Commercial Union Assurance Co v Lister* (1874) L.R. 9 Ch. App. 483 at 484. See too James L.J.'s comments at 486.

[222] *England* [2000] Lloyd's Rep. I.R. 404 at [68].

"If [an] insured settles . . . third party litigation without due regard to the subrogation interests of the insurer . . . [the] recoverable damages would be the value of the damage occasioned to those subrogation rights by the inappropriate settlement."

It follows that an insurer can only recover the whole amount of its payment if it would have been able to recoup itself in full from the third party and the insured's actions have made that impossible. But it would recover less where its ability to recover has only been partially prejudiced because it could not have recovered in full from the third party in any event, because he would have had a partial defence to the subrogated claim. And the insurer will recover nothing if the subrogated action would have failed outright,[223] or if it would have succeeded but it would have been impossible to enforce judgment owing to the defendant's lack of funds.[224]

21–112   In a claim for breach of the insured's duty the burden is on the insurer to establish that he acted unreasonably or in bad faith.[225] The insured's duty is to act reasonably and bona fide with due regard to the insurer's interests. Where the insured loss is incapable of precise quantification and is disputed by the defendant, all that the insured must do when negotiating a settlement is to fix a sum which he reasonably believes could fairly and justly be sought, given the insurer's recoupment right.[226] Although the most obvious harm that an insured might cause his insurer "occurs where the insured settles a claim he may have against a third party for an indemnity and so deprives the insurer of its benefit in whole or in part", he may also cause harm in other ways, for example, "the documents necessary to establish such claim may be destroyed".[227]

21–113   Finally, note that the insurer also probably owes a duty to the insured when bringing subrogated proceedings not to prejudice his interest in their outcome.[228] It seems likely that this duty closely resembles the duty owed by the insured, and that it would be breached, for example, if the insurer were to settle the proceedings on terms that required payment only of the insured loss and left the insured's interest in recovering uninsured losses out of account.

9. PROCEDURAL RULES

21–114   Subrogated proceedings by an insurer to enforce its insured's subsisting rights of action against a defendant must be brought in the insured's name,[229] and the

---

[223] *Traders General Insurance Co v Noel* (1957) 8 D.L.R. (2d) 341. American cases to the same effect are: *Chapman v Hoage*, 296 U.S. 526 (1936); *Century Insurance Co Ltd v Joachim* 8 A. 2d 191 (1939); *Washington Fire & Marine Insurance Co v Williamson* 100 So. 2d 852 (1958); *Gibbs v Hawaiian Eugenia Corp* 1993 A.M.C. 43 at 49.

[224] *Somersall* [2002] SCC 59; [2002] 3 S.C.R. 109, discussed in paras 21–19—21–21.

[225] *Willumsen v Royal Insurance Co Ltd* (1975) 63 D.L.R. (3d) 112 at 116 (Alberta CA).

[226] *Commercial Union Assurance Co v Lister* (1874) L.R. 9 Ch. App. 483 at 484; *Arthur Barnett* [1965] N.Z.L.R. 874 at 883 and 885 (NZ CA).

[227] *Horwood v Land of Leather Ltd* [2010] EWHC 546 (Comm); [2010] Lloyd's Rep. I.R. 453 at [67].

[228] *England* [2000] Lloyd's Rep. I.R. 404 at 418.

[229] *Simpson* (1877) 3 App. Cas. 279 at 286 and 293 (HL); *Union Assurance Co v British Columbia Electric Railway Co* (1915) 21 D.L.R. 62 (British Columbia CA); *Gough v Toronto & York Radial Railway Co* (1918) 42 O.L.R. 415 (Ontario CA); *The Esso Bernicia* [1989] A.C. 643 at 663 (HL); *Metz v Breland* (1990) 47 C.C.L.I. 107 (Alberta CA); *Graham* [2003] EWCA Civ 1177; [2003] 4 All E.R. 1345 at [37].

insurer's name should not appear on the record as a party to the action.[230] If an insurer brings subrogated proceedings in its own name the claim will be struck out.[231] An insurer will usually obtain its insured's authority to commence proceedings in his name by having him sign a subrogation form after settlement of his claim. This procedure differs from assignment, insofar as an insurer which takes an assignment of its insured's rights must enforce these in its own name.[232] Insurers generally prefer to use their subrogation rights for this reason, as they dislike the unfavourable publicity which flows from their names appearing on the record as parties to litigation.

If an insured refused to lend its name to his insurer's subrogated proceedings, **21–115** the insurer could formerly bring an action against the insured in the Chancery court, seeking an order compelling him to do so. Since the Supreme Court of Judicature Act 1873, the correct procedure has been for the insurer to start proceedings against the defendant in its own name and to join the insured to these as a co-defendant, seeking an order that the insured should allow his name to be used.[233]

Because costs will be awarded against the insured, rather than the insurer, in **21–116** the event that the action fails, it is usual for the insurer to undertake to indemnify the insured against liability for costs before commencing subrogated proceedings, and it is most unlikely that a court would compel an insured to allow his name to be used unless such an undertaking had been given.[234] On the other hand, where the insured actively participates in the proceedings alongside the insurer and has a financial interest in their outcome, for example because he was under-insured and wishes to recover for his uninsured loss, then liability for costs will be apportioned in line with their respective interests in the litigation.[235]

An insurer is entitled to subrogation by operation of law only after it has paid **21–117** the insured in accordance with the terms of the policy. If the insurer purports to bring subrogated proceedings prematurely, without the insured's authority, then the insured can apply for an order that his name be removed and the claim struck out as an abuse of court process under CPR r.3.4(2)(b).[236] Furthermore, an insurer which commences subrogated proceedings prematurely cannot cure the

---

[230] *Wilson v Raffalovich* (1881) 7 Q.B.D. 553 at 558 (CA).
[231] *The Aiolos* [1983] 2 Lloyd's Rep. 25 (CA); *Jubilee Motor Policies Syndicate 1231 at Lloyd's v Volvo Truck & Bus (Southern) Ltd* [2010] EWHC 3641 (QB) (where the insurer repudiated liability under the policy but was obliged to pay under the Road Traffic Act 1988 s.151(5)).
[232] *King* [1896] A.C. 250; *Compania Columbiana de Seguros v Pacific Steam Navigation Co* [1965] 1 Q.B. 101. Note too that an assignee may (subject to the terms of the assignment) keep all the fruits of the litigation, even if these exceed what has been paid for the assigned rights: *Compania Columbiana* [1965] 1 Q.B. 101, at 121 per Roskill J.; in contrast a subrogated insurer can keep no more than the amount of its payment to the insured: see cases cited in para.21–10, fn.28.
[233] *Yorkshire Insurance* [1962] 2 Q.B. 330 at 339; *M.H. Smith* [1986] 2 Lloyd's Rep. 244 at 246 (CA); *The Esso Bernicia* [1989] A.C. 643 at 663 (HL).
[234] Cf. *Netherlands Insurance Co Est. 1845 Ltd v Karl Ljunberg & Co A.B. (The Mammoth Pine)* [1986] 2 Lloyd's Rep 19 at 22 (PC); *Thornton v Hendricks* (1992) 32 Con. L.R. 123 at 131; *Cox v Bankside Members Agency Ltd* [1995] 2 Lloyd's Rep. 437 at 463 (CA).
[235] *Duus Brown & Co v Binning* (1906) 11 Com. Cas. 190.
[236] Cf. *Coleman and Biedman v Davis* (1849) 7 C.B. 871, 137 E.R. 345 (indorser of promissory note paid holders, then brought action against maker in their names without their permission; action stayed for abuse of court process).

defect simply by paying the insured an indemnity at a later date,[237] although the defect can be cured if the insured ratifies the proceedings after the insurer has paid him.[238] It seems that the insured can do this even after the lapse of a limitation period that would have prevented him from initiating proceedings himself by the time when he ratifies the insurer's action.[239]

21–118　　　When dealing with subrogated proceedings the courts generally ignore the insurer's interest in the outcome of the litigation and treat the proceedings as though these had been brought by the insured for his own benefit.[240] This general approach is reflected in the following rules[241]:

- the insured is liable to make standard disclosure of documents as a party to subrogated proceedings under CPR Pt 31, but the insurer is not.[242] However it may be that in some cases the insurer could be ordered to make disclosure as a non-party under CPR r.31.17.

- judgment against the defendant must be entered in the name of the insured, and so the defendant must pay the insured in order to obtain discharge.[243] Presumably, however, this requirement will be satisfied if the defendant pays another party at the insured's direction, for example, the insurer[244];

- costs are awarded to the insured in the event that the action is successful, although they have been incurred at the insurer's direction,[245] and this principle applies even where the costs awarded to an insured include a success fee payable to a solicitors' firm under a collective conditional fee agreement entered by the insurer on the insured's behalf.[246] Once awarded,

---

[237] *Page* (1929) 140 L.T. 571 (CA).

[238] *Victoria Teachers' Credit Union v KPMG (A Firm)* [2000] VSCA 23. Cf. *Adams v London Improved Motor Coach Builders Ltd* [1921] 1 K.B. 495 at 502 (CA); *Danish Mercantile Co Ltd v Beaumont* [1951] Ch. 680 (CA); *Alexander Ward & Co v Samyung Navigation Co Ltd* [1975] 1 W.L.R. 678 (HL); *Caulfield (A Minor) v Trustees of Lurgan Baptist Church* [2007] NIQB 110.

[239] *The Frotanorte* [1995] 2 Lloyd's Rep. 254 at 261, referring to *Presentaciones Musicales SA v Secunda* [1994] Ch. 271.

[240] Cf. HMRC Notice 701/36 (May 2002) para.5.2: for VAT purposes "supplies of legal services in connection with [subrogated] claims are made to the insured party and not to the insurer." But note Sales J.'s doubts about this in *R. (Medical Protection Society Ltd) v HMRC* [2009] EWHC 2780 (Admin); [2010] S.T.C. 555 at [8].

[241] See also *Nguyen v Cosmopolitan Homes* [2008] NSWCA 246 (insured's affidavit evidence inadmissible in his absence for cross-examination, and it makes no difference that proceedings are brought by subrogated insurer).

[242] *Wilson* (1881) 7 Q.B.D. 553 (CA); *J. Nelson & Sons Ltd v Nelson Line (Liverpool) Ltd* [1906] 2 K.B. 217.

[243] *Yorkshire Insurance* [1962] 2 Q.B. 330 at 341; *England* [2000] Lloyd's Rep. I.R. 404 at [11].

[244] Cf. *William Brandt's Sons & Co v Dunlop Rubber Co Ltd* [1905] A.C. 454.

[245] *R. v Archbishop of Canterbury* [1903] 1 K.B. 289 at 295 (CA); *Gough* (1918) 42 O.L.R. 415; *H. Cousins & Co* [1971] 2 Q.B. 230 at 242 (CA); *Halliday v High Performance Personnel Pty Ltd (In liquidation)* (1993) 113 A.L.R. 637 at 640 (HCA).

[246] *Sousa v Waltham Forest LBC* [2011] EWCA Civ 194; [2011] 1 W.L.R. 2197. At [23]–[25] Ward L.J. reached this conclusion on the basis that he had to treat the CFA entered by the insurer as having been entered by the insured, but at [26]–[31] he also held that the same conclusion would follow even if he looked at the realities of the situation.

the insurer can recover the costs from the insured to the extent that their receipt leaves him over-indemnified[247];

- costs are awarded against the insured if the action fails,[248] although the insurer will be obliged to reimburse him under an express or implied term of the policy. If the insured were unable to comply with the costs order, then the court could exercise its jurisdiction under the Supreme Court Act 1981 s.51, to make a costs order against the insurer[249];

- if the action is successful, then interest can be awarded on the judgment sum for periods both before and after the insured was indemnified by the insurer, although the insured was not actually out of pocket following the insurer's payment.[250] The insured will keep the interest for the period before, and the insurer will take the interest for the payment after, indemnification, as the insured would otherwise be more than fully indemnified in respect of the later period. Where the insured was under-insured and the whole loss along with interest is recovered in subrogated proceedings, the insured is entitled to a proportionate share of the interest along with the amount of his uninsured loss.[251] The allocation of interest between the parties may also be the subject of an express clause in the policy[252];

- interest can also be awarded on top of a costs order in favour of the insured, even though these costs were paid for by the insurer.[253] Again, the insured must account to the insurer for the interest;

- the fact that an insurer and its insured have previously agreed the amount of the insured's losses between themselves is irrelevant to the calculation of damages payable by the defendant[254];

---

[247] *Sea Insurance Co v Hadden* (1884) 13 Q.B.D. 706 (CA).

[248] *Morris* [1973] QB 792 at 800 (CA); *Wates Construction Ltd v H.G.P. Greentree Allchurch Evans Ltd* [2005] EWHC 2174 (TCC); [2006] B.L.R. 45 (where indemnity costs were awarded following the insured's pursuit of an obviously doomed claim on its insurer's insistence).

[249] See too CPR r.48.2.

[250] *H. Cousins & Co* [1971] 2 Q.B. 230 (CA); *Metal Box Co Ltd v Currys Ltd* [1988] 1 W.L.R. 175; *Clark v Ardington Electrical Services Ltd* [2002] EWCA Civ 510; [2003] Q.B. 36 at [157]–[162]. The insured will keep the interest for the period before, and the insurer will take the interest for the payment after, indemnification, as the insured would otherwise be over-indemnified; cf. *Angas Securities Ltd v Valcorp Australia Pty Ltd* [2011] FCA 190 at [219]. The allocation of interest may be the subject of an express clause in the policy: see e.g. Institute Time Clauses, Hulls (1/1/95) cl.12.4.

[251] *Re Miller Gibb & Co Ltd* [1957] 1 W.L.R. 703.

[252] e.g. Institute Time Clauses, Hulls (1/1/95) cl.12.4.

[253] *Hogan v Trustees of the Roman Catholic Church for the Archdiocese of Sydney (No.2)* [2006] NSWSC 74 at [39].

[254] *Brown* [1995] N.P.C. 100 per Stuart-Smith L.J. (quoted from LEXIS transcript): "the mechanics by which [an insurer chooses to settle its insured's claim] is neither here nor there and is no concern of the third party." See too *Crayden's Pharmacy Ltd v Standard Paving Co* (1973) 37 D.L.R. (3d) 167 at 168; *Verlysdonk v Premier Petrenas Construction Co Ltd* (1987) 60 O.R. (2d) 65; *Grosvenor Fine Art Furniture (1982) Ltd v Terrie's Plumbing & Heating Ltd* (1994) 113 Sask. R. 105 at 138–145 per Wakeling J.A., whose dissenting judgment on this point is to be preferred to the views of the majority of the Saskatchewan CA.

- nor may the court refer to the terms of such an agreement for the purpose of deciding the appropriate track for a subrogated claim by reference to its financial value under CPR r.26.8[255];

- an insurer sued in its own name cannot counter-claim for damages to which it can only be entitled via subrogation to the insured's rights.[256]

21–119   Against the trend of these rules, a number of other rules have been laid down which require the courts to look behind the form of subrogated proceedings and take notice of the insurer's interest in their outcome:

- if subrogated proceedings are unsuccessful, and a costs order is made against the insured, but the insured becomes insolvent before it is satisfied, then the court may make an order for costs directly against the insurer under the Supreme Court Act 1981 s.51. The insurer must previously have agreed to indemnify the insured against the costs, and the use of this summary procedure must not unfairly prejudice the insurer's position, given the existence of an alternative route to recovery under the Third Parties (Rights against Insurers) Act 1930[257];

- it is a relevant consideration when deciding whether to award security for costs against a foreign claimant that he is insured by an insurer within the court's jurisdiction, out of whose resources a costs order could be met[258];

- an insurer can intervene in its own name in a subrogated Admiralty action in rem to seek a distribution of funds held by the court, which can order payment directly to the insurer.[259]

---

[255] *Khiaban v Beard* [2003] EWCA Civ 358; [2003] R.T.R. 28. The judge at first instance had wished to look behind the sum claimed in order to prevent an insurer from using the fast-track system as a means of obtaining speedy judgment on liability prior to recovering the full amount of the insured's loss from the defendant's insurer. But see now *Beaumont Premier Properties Ltd v Jones* [2006] EWHC 1143 (QB) (following judgment for insured on liability in fast-tracked claim for £13,000, insured applied to increase sum claimed to £55,000 at direction of insurer; application denied). And cf. *Russell v Wilson, The Times*, May 26, 1989 (CA) (fact that subrogated proceedings funded by legal expenses insurer was no reason to disapply a procedural rule remitting the claim to arbitration, the costs of which would not follow the event but would be borne by each party).
[256] *Page* (1929) 140 L.T. 571 at 576 (CA); *Rap Industries Pty Ltd v Royal Insurance Australia Ltd* (1988) 5 A.N.Z. Ins. Cas. 75,516; *Red Sea Insurance Co Ltd v Bouyges SA* [1995] A.C. 190.
[257] *Tharros Shipping Co Ltd v Bias Shipping Ltd (No.3)* [1995] 1 Lloyd's Rep. 541 at 555–556.
[258] *The Seaspeed Dora* [1988] 1 Lloyd's Rep. 36.
[259] *Worsley Hall v Ioannis Vatis* (1921) Lloyd's List Rep. 120 and 489.

CHAPTER 22

MONEY PAID AS TAXES AND OTHER LEVIES THAT ARE NOT DUE

1. INTRODUCTION

This chapter is primarily concerned with the recovery of money paid as taxes that **22–01** are not due. This might happen, for example, because a mistake of fact is made when calculating the claimant's tax liability, or because the claimant pays money as tax under legislation that is ultra vires, or contrary to European law. In these circumstances, the claimant may have a statutory right to recover his payment. Alternatively, a claim may lie at common law: following *Woolwich Equitable Building Society v IRC*,[1] money paid as tax that is not due can be recovered by reason of the constitutional principle laid down in art.4 of the Bill of Rights 1689, that there shall be no taxation without Parliament; depending on the circumstances, a claim may also lie on the ground of mistake or duress.

Statutory claims are discussed in Part 2, and common law claims are discussed **22–02** in Part 3. It is noted that many statutory claims are subject to restrictions that do not apply to common law claims, so that the question arises for many claimants whether they are free to choose between their statutory and common law rights, or are confined to their more limited statutory rights. The extent of the *Woolwich* principle is also discussed, and it is noted that in addition to the recovery of money paid as tax, the case also mandates the recovery of money paid to public bodies as fees, charges and other levies that are not due. It is also considered whether a case that does not fall within any statutory scheme, but does fall within the scope of the *Woolwich* rule, must be pleaded as a *Woolwich* claim, or may be pleaded as a claim resting on some other ground for recovery, such as mistake of law or duress. The substance of these other grounds for recovery is discussed elsewhere,[2] and here we focus only on their relationship with the *Woolwich* ground.

2. STATUTORY RECOVERY REGIMES

Money paid as tax that is not due can be recovered under various statutes, **22–03** including the Taxes Management Act 1970 s.33, and the Finance Act 1998 Sch.18 para.51 (money paid as income tax, capital gains tax (CGT), and corporation tax); the Customs and Excise Management Act 1979 s.137A (money paid as excise duties); the Inheritance Tax Act 1984 s.241 (money paid as inheritance tax); the Finance Act 1989 s.29 (money paid as car tax); the Value Added Tax Act

---

[1] *Woolwich Equitable Building Society v IRC* [1993] A.C. 70 at 176.
[2] For mistake of law, see paras 9–71—9–94; for duress *ex colore officii* see paras 10–25—10–38.

1994 s.80 (money paid as VAT); the Finance Act 1994 Sch.7 para.8 (money paid as insurance premium tax); and the Finance Act 1996 Sch.5 para.14 (money paid as landfill tax). Specialist works should be consulted for detailed discussion of these provisions, but some comments are made here about the Taxes Management Act 1970 s.33, and the Value Added Tax Act 1994 s.80. Note, too, that many of the foregoing sections forbid claims to be made otherwise than under the statute,[3] and also require claims to be brought within a shorter time period than would apply at common law.[4] However, not all of these periods are of the same length,[5] and some other defences are also available to some types of statutory claim that do not apply to other statutory or common law claims.[6] In 1994 the Law Commission recommended that these rules should be rationalised, but unfortunately their recommendations have not been implemented.[7]

(a) The Taxes Management Act 1970 s.33

22–04   Prior to April 1, 2010, the Taxes Management Act 1970 s.33(1) provided that[8]:

> "If a person who has paid income tax or capital gains tax under an assessment (whether a self-assessment or otherwise) alleges that the assessment was excessive by reason of some error or mistake in a return, he may by notice in writing at any time not more than four years after the end of the year of assessment to which the return relates, make a claim to the Board for relief."

On receiving such a claim, HMRC was required by s.33(2) and (3) to investigate all the circumstances and then to give such relief by way of repayment as was reasonable and just. For the purposes of s.33(1), an "error or mistake" included "errors of omission and commission, errors arising from a misunderstanding of the law, and erroneous statements of fact", and the burden was on the taxpayer to establish the error or mistake on the balance of probabilities.[9]

22–05   The rights conferred by s.33 were less advantageous to claimants than their common law rights for two reasons. First, the limitation rule in s.33(1) gave claimants less time than the rule contained in the Limitation Act 1980 s.32(1)(c), which provides that the six-year limitation period governing claims to recover

---

[3] For discussion of the question whether such provisions are vulnerable to attack under the Human Rights Act 1998, for infringement of the taxpayer's rights under art.1 of the First Protocol of the ECHR, see M. Chowdry and C. Mitchell, "Tax Legislation as a Justifying Factor" [2005] R.L.R. 1, p.20, comparing *National & Provincial Building Society v UK* [1997] S.T.C. 1466 (ECHR), and *Buffalo Srl (In Liquidation) v Italy* Unreported ECHR, July 2, 2004.

[4] e.g. the Customs and Excise Management Act 1979 s.137A (4) and (5); the Finance Act 1994 Sch.7 para.8(4) and (7); and the Finance Act 1996 Sch.5 para.14(4) and (6). These all provide for a limitation period of three years from the date of payment.

[5] In contrast with the sections in the previous note, taxpayers have four years to claim under the Inheritance Tax Act 1984 s.241; and the Taxes Management Act 1970 s.33.

[6] e.g. the Taxes Management Act 1970 Sch.1AB para.2(8) gives a "prevailing practice" defence which is not available against claims under many other sections.

[7] Law Commission, *Restitution: Mistakes of Law and Ultra Vires Public Authority Receipts and Payments* (1994), Law Com. No.227.

[8] These words were substantially reproduced in the Finance Act 1998, Sch.18 para.51, which provided for the recovery of money paid as corporation tax.

[9] *Thompson v IRC* [1995] S.T.C. (S.C.D.) 320 at [4].

money paid by mistake does not start to run until the claimant knew of the mistake or could have discovered it with reasonable diligence.[10] In contrast, s.33(1) gave claimants no more than four years after the end of the year of assessment to which their return related. Secondly, s.33(2A) denied recovery where payment was made in accordance with generally prevailing practice at the time, whereas the common law holds that it is no defence to a claim for money paid by mistake of law that the payment was made pursuant to a "settled view of the law".[11]

The existence of these differences prompted the question of whether claimants **22–06** were confined to their rights under s.33 or could claim at common law instead? In the *Woolwich* case,[12] and in *Deutsche Morgan Grenfell Goup Plc v IRC*,[13] the House of Lords held that it did not follow from the fact that claimants have a right of recovery under s.33 that Parliament intended to exclude common law recovery in cases where the section does not apply. In *Monro v HMRC*,[14] however, the Court of Appeal held that Parliament did intend to exclude common law recovery in cases where s.33 does apply—subject to the proviso that Parliament cannot have intended to deprive taxpayers of their wider common law rights where this is required by European law.[15] A similar conclusion was drawn by the Court of Appeal in *Test Claimants in the F.I.I. Litigation v HMRC*,[16] but there the court invoked the *Marleasing* principle[17] to read a restriction on claimants' rights under s.33 as "subject to the limitation that it applies only if and to the extent that the United Kingdom can consistently with its Treaty obligations impose such a restriction". In other words, the court held that where a case falls within s.33, a claimant may only bring proceedings under the section, and may not rely on his common law rights, but that if statutory restrictions on his s.33 rights are contrary to European law then the English courts can effectively construe these restrictions out of existence.[18]

Against the view that taxpayers were confined to their s.33 rights in cases **22–07** falling within the section, it might have been objected that such rights have

---

[10] Parliament sought to disapply s.32(1)(c) in relation to mistakes of law relating to taxation matters by enacting the Finance Act 2004 s.320, and the Finance Act 2007 s.107. But no transitional arrangements were made when these sections were enacted and so the question has arisen whether they are compliant with EU law. This was one of the issues in *Test Claimants in the F.I.I. Litigation v HMRC* [2008] EWHC 2893 (Ch); [2009] S.T.C. 254; reversed in part [2010] EWCA Civ 103; [2010] S.T.C. 1251; currently on appeal to the Supreme Court. For discussion, see paras 33–30—33–36.

[11] *Kleinwort Benson Ltd v Lincoln CC* [1999] 2 A.C. 349 at 381–383, 401 and 414–415; *Deutsche Morgan Grenfell Group Plc v IRC* [2006] UKHL 49; [2007] 1 A.C. 558 at [145].

[12] *Woolwich* [1993] AC 70 at 169 and 199–200.

[13] *Deutsche Morgan Grenfell Group Plc v IRC* [2006] UKHL 49; [2007] 1 A.C. 558 at [19], [55] and [135].

[14] *Monro v HMRC* [2008] EWCA Civ 306; [2009] Ch. 69; affirming Morritt C.'s decision at first instance: [2007] EWHC 114 (Ch); [2007] S.T.C. 1182.

[15] *Monro* [2008] EWCA Civ 306; [2009] Ch. 69 at [34].

[16] *Test Claimants in the F.I.I. Group Litigation v HMRC* [2010] EWCA Civ 103; [2010] S.T.C. 1251 at [261]. Arden L.J. was a member of both courts.

[17] Named for *Marleasing v La Comercial Internacional de Alimentación* (C–106/89) [1990] E.C.R. I–4135.

[18] Provided that this does not "go against the grain of the legislation", a proviso that does not seem hard to satisfy, going by the approach taken by the court in *F.I.I.* [2010] EWCA Civ 103; [2010] S.T.C. 1251 at [264].

existed in the legislation since 1923,[19] while claims based on mistake of law were not recognised until 1999,[20] and that it is hard to say that Parliament's intention in 1923 was to oust a common law claim that would not exist for another 75 years. However it could have been countered that Parliament cannot have meant to create rights that would never be used once wider rights became available at common law, and it is also notable that when the statutory recovery scheme was first introduced in 1923, some objections were made in Parliamentary debate to the limitations placed on claimants' statutory rights,[21] and yet these were retained on the basis that a balance had to be struck between the rights of the taxpayer and the Revenue. Whatever the rights and wrongs of these arguments, however, the matter has now been dealt with by legislation. The Taxes Management Act 1970 s.33 has been substantially amended by the Finance Act 2009 s.100 and Sch.52 Pt 1,[22] which have created a new statutory scheme for the recovery of money paid as income tax or CGT on or after April 1, 2010. They insert a new s.33 and Sch.1AB into the 1970 Act, and Sch.1AB para.1(6) stipulates that HMRC is not liable to give relief in cases falling within s.33 except as provided by the 1970 Act or other statutes governing income tax and CGT.

22–08   Controversially, the 2009 amendments have left intact the "prevailing practice" defence to claims under s.33.[23] They have also placed limits on a claimant's right to recover under the section by specifying that HMRC shall not be liable to give effect to a claim in various cases set out in Sch.1AB para.2. In essence these feature claimants who have failed to exhaust other avenues of appeal or recovery (some of which may be subject to very tight time limits, e.g. 30 days[24]). It is also provided by para.3 that the time during which claims can be made is limited to four years after the end of the relevant tax year.

22–09   The 2009 amendments also bring a wider class of claimants within the ambit of s.33 than was previously the case, with the result that their claims are subject to restrictions that would not previously have affected them. Under the old wording of the section it applied only to "a person who has paid income tax or capital gains tax under an assessment". Payments of income tax and CGT (and corporation tax) are almost always made under an assessment,[25] and so most claims to recover money paid as income tax or CGT (or corporation tax) fell within this wording. But there were two notable exceptions to this. First, in *Woolwich* Lord Goff and Lord Slynn held that there is no assessment where payments are made under ultra vires legislation,[26] and in *Deutsche Morgan*

---

[19] The section was originally enacted as the Finance Act 1923 s.24.

[20] *Kleinwort Benson* [1999] 2 A.C. 349. See paras 9–71—9–94.

[21] *Hansard*, HC Debs, July 2, 1923, col.225.

[22] See also Sch.52, Pt 2, which similarly amends the provisions governing claims to recover money paid as corporation tax under the Finance Act 1998 Sch.18 para.51.

[23] Taxes Management Act 1970 Sch.1AB para.2(8). M. Jones, "Finance Act Notes: Section 100 and Schedule 52—Recovery of Overpaid Tax" [2009] BTR 635, p.636, gives three reasons why this rule is unsatisfactory: tax should be levied according to the law, not according to mistaken but prevailing practice; whether or not a mistaken payment was made in accordance with prevailing practice, the claimant would not have paid but for his mistake; and "prevailing practice" is a nebulous concept, making it hard to know when claims will lie.

[24] Consider the Taxes Management Act 1970 Sch.1AB, para.2(6) ("Case E").

[25] A person taxed under the PAYE system may apply for an assessment under the Income Tax and Corporation Taxes Act 1988 s.205(3).

[26] *Woolwich* [1993] A.C. 70 at 169 and 199–200.

Grenfell Lord Walker said that the same is true of payments under legislation that is unlawful under EU law.[27] Secondly, the House of Lords also noted in *Deutsche Morgan Grenfell* that advance corporation tax was anyway never paid under an assessment, for technical reasons relating to the machinery by which it was collected.[28] Hence, s.33 did not affect the claim in that case, nor any of the other claims brought in the wake of *Metallgesellschaft Ltd v IRC*, a decision of the ECJ which held that aspects of the statutory regime governing the payment of corporation tax on dividends paid within corporate groups were contrary to EU law.[29]

The first of these findings meant that some significant classes of claim fell   **22–10** outside the section, prompting calls for reform on the basis that a more principled statutory remedy would focus on "whether the tax was due or whether there had been an error rather than on the procedural mechanism for the payment".[30] Following the 2009 changes, it is now provided that the statutory recovery regime contained in the 1970 Act applies to cases where "a person has paid an amount by way of income tax or capital gains tax but the person believes that the tax was not due".[31] The fact that "assessment" is not mentioned here means that claims will henceforth fall within the scope of the statutory regime whether or not an assessment has been made.

(b) *The Value Added Tax Act 1994 section 80*

The Value Added Tax Act 1994 s.80(1) provides that a taxable person who   **22–11** accounts to HMRC for output tax that is not due shall be entitled to a credit for the relevant amount. Section 80(1A) states that the same result will follow where HMRC assesses a taxable person to VAT and brings an amount into the account as output tax which was not due. Section 80(1B) states that a taxable person who otherwise pays an amount as output tax that is not due shall be entitled to repayment. Section 80(3) provides that it is a defence to a claim under the section that crediting or repaying an amount to the taxable person would "unjustly enrich" him because he passed the cost of paying HMRC on to a third party. This is discussed in Ch.32.[32] Section 80(4) gives the taxable person four years to claim under the section (to run from the date specified in s.80(4ZA) and (4ZB)). Moreover, while s.81(3A) does not allow a taxpayer to offset overpaid but out-of-time output tax against an assessment, it does allow HMRC to adjust a taxpayer's claim to recover overpaid output tax so as to reduce it for what would have been an out-of-time, over-credited input tax.[33] Section 80(7) states that

---

[27] *Deutsche Morgan Grenfell* [2006] UKHL 49; [2007] 1 A.C. 558 at [135].
[28] *Deutsche Morgan Grenfell* [2006] UKHL 49; [2007] 1 A.C. 558 at [19], [54] and [135]. See too *F.I.I.* [2010] EWCA Civ 103; [2010] S.T.C. 1251 at [250].
[29] *Metallgesellschaft Ltd v IRC* [2001] Ch. 620.
[30] J. Beatson, "Restitution of Taxes, Levies and Other Imposts: Defining the Extent of the *Woolwich* Principle" (1993) 109 L.Q.R. 401, pp.420–421. See too Law Commission, *Restitution: Mistakes of Law and Ultra Vires Public Authority Receipts and Payments* (1994), Law Com. No.227, para.7.8.
[31] Taxes Management Act 1970 Sch.1AB para.1(1)(a).
[32] See paras 32–02—32–10.
[33] *Birmingham Hippodrome Theatre Trust Ltd v HMRC* [2011] UKFTT 117 (TC) at [75], rejecting counsel's argument that "such a lopsided effect is so manifestly unfair that it either cannot have been intended by Parliament or else must be in breach of Community law principles of fairness."

HMRC shall not be liable to repay money paid as output tax which is not due except as provided by the section. Claims to recover money under s.80 are choses in action which can be freely assigned from one person to another.[34]

22–12   In *F.J. Chalke Ltd v HMRC*[35] the claimant motor dealers paid VAT pursuant to demands that were later held by the ECJ to have been contrary to EU law. The claimants accepted that their s.80 recovery right was intended by Parliament to be exclusive, insofar as it enabled them to recover the face value of the money they had paid, but they argued that their common law right to recover compound interest as the user value of this money[36] was not ousted by the statutory scheme. Henderson J. held that, as a matter of domestic law, the statutory scheme for the recovery of overpaid VAT contained in s.80 is exhaustive, and that interest may only be recovered on a repayment of overpaid VAT if it is awarded by the VAT and Duties Tribunal under its statutory power to do so, or pursuant to the VAT Act 1994 s.78. However, the claimants would have been entitled to compound interest under EU law, but for the fact that any such claims were time-barred.[37] The question whether the VAT Act 1994 creates an exhaustive code for the payment of interest was then revisited in *Littlewoods Retail Ltd v HMRC*.[38] After careful analysis of the wording of ss.78 and 80, Vos J. concluded as a matter of domestic law that it does.[39] However, there remained the question whether repayment of the principal amount of the sums overpaid together with simple interest was an adequate remedy in EU law or whether compound interest was payable as a matter of EU law to reflect the use value of the overpayment in the hands of HMRC. On this point Vos J. made a reference to the CJEU.[40]

3. Common Law Claims

(a) *Woolwich Equitable Building Society v IRC*

22–13   In *Woolwich*[41] the claimant building society paid money in response to a tax demand issued under regulations that were later held in judicial review proceedings to have been ultra vires and void.[42] The claimant had disputed the validity of the regulations from the start but had paid because it wished to avoid penalties and unfavourable publicity.[43] Following the outcome of the judicial review proceedings, the Revenue returned the capital sum together with interest from the date of judgment, but stated that it made this payment ex gratia, and refused to

---

[34] *Midland Co-operative Society Ltd v HMRC* [2008] EWCA Civ 305; [2008] Bus. L.R. 1187.
[35] *F.J. Chalke Ltd v HMRC* [2009] EWHC 952 (Ch); [2009] S.T.C. 2027; affirmed [2010] EWCA Civ 313; [2010] S.T.C. 1640.
[36] Following *Sempra Metals Ltd v IRC* [2007] UKHL 34; [2008] A.C. 561; discussed at paras 5–05—5–10.
[37] See para.33–22.
[38] *Littlewoods Retail Ltd v HMRC* [2010] EWHC 1071 (Ch); [2010] S.T.C. 2072.
[39] *Littlewoods* [2010] EWHC 1071 (Ch); [2010] S.T.C. 2072 at [45]–[62].
[40] The wording of which was settled in later proceedings: *Littlewoods* [2010] EWHC 2771 (Ch); [2011] S.T.C. 171.
[41] *Woolwich* [1993] A.C. 70.
[42] In *R. v IRC Ex p. Woolwich Building Society* [1990] 1 W.L.R. 1400 (HL).
[43] The building society's reasons for paying were summarised by Nolan J. at first instance: *Woolwich* [1989] 1 W.L.R. 137 at 142–143.

pay interest for the period running from the date of receipt to the date of judgment. To make good its claim to this interest under the Supreme Court Act 1981 s.35A,[44] the claimant therefore had to show that it had been entitled as of right to the return of the money from the date of payment. As the law then stood, payments made in response to an ultra vires public demand were recoverable only if they were made under a mistake of fact[45] or illegitimate compulsion,[46] and the claimant had made no mistake, nor had it been subjected to illegitimate pressure. However, a majority of the House of Lords held that the law should be reformulated to allow recovery of money paid as tax pursuant to an ultra vires demand,[47] and concluded that the claimant had therefore been entitled to recover its money as of right from the moment of payment.

One policy justification for this finding, identified by Lord Goff, was that a **22–14** general right to recover payments of tax levied without Parliamentary authority is needed to give full effect to the constitutional principle enshrined in the Bill of Rights 1689 art.4, that the Crown may not impose direct or indirect taxes without parliamentary authority.[48] Another, broader, ground for recovery was also identified by Lord Browne-Wilkinson, namely that administrative action must be constrained by the rule of law, and bodies invested with state power must adhere to the limits of the jurisdiction conferred on them, to protect citizens from state depredations:

> "[W]here the parties are on an unequal footing so that money is paid by way of tax or other impost in pursuance of [an *ultra vires*] demand by some public officer, these moneys are recoverable since the citizen is, in practice, unable to resist the payment

---

[44] Now the Senior Courts Act 1981 s.35A. Only simple interest can be recovered under s.35A, and following *Westdeutsche Landesbank Girozentrale v Islington LBC* [1996] A.C. 669, no claim in unjust enrichment lay at common law to recover compound interest as the use value of the money; this finding was later reversed in *Sempra* [2007] UKHL 34; [2008] A.C. 561; discussed at para.5–05 and following.

[45] As in e.g. *Meadows v Grand Junction Waterworks Co* (1905) 21 T.L.R. 538. Note that *Woolwich* preceded the abrogation of the bar against recovery on the ground of mistake of law in *Kleinwort Benson* [1999] 2 A.C. 349, on which see paras 9–71—9–94.

[46] As in e.g. *Morgan v Palmer* (1824) 2 B. & C. 729; 107 E.R. 554; *Steele v Williams* (1853) 8 Exch. 625; 155 E.R. 1502; *Hooper v Exeter Corp* (1887) 56 L.J.Q.B. 457; *Queens of the River SS Co Ltd v River Thames Conservators* (1899) 15 T.L.R. 474; *T&J Brocklebank Ltd v R.* [1925] 1 K.B. 52; *South of Scotland Electricity Board v British Oxygen Co Ltd (No.2)* [1959] 2 All E.R. 225. Payment in response to an ultra vires demand could not be recovered if the demand was merely accompanied by a threat to sue—something stronger than this was needed for it to be said that the claimant was illegitimately compelled to pay: *William Whiteley Ltd v R.* (1909) 101 L.T. 741; cf. *Woolwich* [1993] A.C. 70 at 173, where Lord Goff stated that on the facts of *Woolwich* "the possibility of distraint by the Revenue was very remote".

[47] For previous dicta supporting recovery on this ground, see *Steele v Williams* (1853) 8 Exch. 625 at 633; 155 E.R. 1502 at 1505; *A.G. v Wilts United Dairies Ltd* (1921) 37 T.L.R. 884 at 887; *Mason v New South Wales* (1959) 102 C.L.R. 108 at 117; *Air Canada v British Columbia* [1989] 1 S.C.R. 1161 at 1215. In his dissenting speech in *Woolwich* [1993] A.C. 70 at 192–193, Lord Jauncey considered that this reformulation of the law would be a "particularly inappropriate" piece of judicial legislation, "having regard to the considerable number of instances which exist of Parliament having legislated in various fields to define the circumstances under which payments of tax not lawfully due may be recovered, and also in what situations and upon what terms interest on overpayments of tax may be paid." Cf. Lord Slynn's contrary view at 200, and note, too, that there was no statutory provision, e.g. the Taxes Management Act 1970 s.33, on which the claimant could have relied to recover its money: [1993] A.C. 70 at 169 per Lord Goff, and at 199 per Lord Slynn, noted in the text to para.22–09, fn.26.

[48] *Woolwich* [1993] A.C. 70 at 172.

save at the risk of breaking the law or exposing himself to penalties or other disadvantages."[49]

(b) *The Scope of the Woolwich Rule*

22–15   Although the collection of tax in the UK is now heavily dependent on self-assessment mechanisms, the submission of a self-assessment to HMRC is generally followed by some sort of demand for payment. However, this is not always the case, and so the question arises whether the *Woolwich* principle applies in situations where money has not been collected through the machinery of demand? In *Boake Allen Ltd v HMRC*[50] the obiter view was expressed in the Court of Appeal that the *Woolwich* rule does not apply unless there was a demand. However, provided that a claimant's money has been paid *as tax*—i.e. to discharge a supposed tax liability—it should make no difference in principle whether HMRC demanded the payment. After all, the *Woolwich* case itself was expressly fought and decided on the basis that the building society's payment was not made in response to illegitimate pressure exerted by the Revenue,[51] and as Bastarache J. has observed in the Supreme Court of Canada:

> "The right of [a claimant] to obtain restitution for taxes paid under *ultra vires* legislation does not depend on the behaviour of each party but on the objective consideration of whether the tax was exacted without proper legal authority."[52]

Consistently with these authorities, the Court of Appeal subsequently concluded in *F.I.I.*[53] that there is no need for claimants to show that they paid pursuant to a demand in order to bring themselves within the scope of the *Woolwich* rule; this finding is currently under appeal to the Supreme Court.

22–16   If the rule in *Woolwich* is underpinned by broadly conceived rule of law considerations, then this suggests that claims should lie not only against governmental bodies who have demanded tax but also against any other sort of public authority which has acted beyond its powers to demand duties, fees and other

---

[49] *Woolwich* [1993] A.C. 70 at 198. See too *Gosling v Veley* (1850) 12 Q.B. 328 at 407; 116 E.R. 891 at 922 per Wilde C.J.: "no pecuniary burden can be imposed upon the subjects of this country, by whatever name it may be called, whether tax, due, rate or toll, except upon clear and distinct legal authority, established by those who seek to impose the burthen"; *British Sky Broadcasting Group Plc v Customs and Excise Commissioners* [2001] S.T.C. 437 at [34] per Elias J.: "the underlying rationale of the *Woolwich* case was . . . that the Revenue would have benefited from receiving moneys they ought never to have received if they had acted lawfully." Cf. Holmes J.'s comments in *Atchison, Topeka & Santa Fe Railway Co v O'Connor*, 223 U.S. 280 at 285–286 (1912), endorsed in *Woolwich* at [1993] A.C. 70 at 172–173, 198 and 203; also Dixon C.J.'s comments in *Mason v New South Wales* (1959) 102 C.L.R. 108 at 116.

[50] *Boake Allen Ltd v HMRC* [2006] EWCA 25; [2006] S.T.C. 606 at [84], [89] and [140]–[147]; not considered on appeal: [2007] UKHL 25; [2007] 1 W.L.R. 1386.

[51] Cf. Law Commission, *Restitution of Payments Made under a Mistake of Law* (1991), LCCP No.120, para.3.90. And cf. *F.M.C. Plc v Intervention Board for Agricultural Produce* (C–212/1994) [1996] E.C.R. I–389 at [72] (ECJ): a rule of national law, by virtue of which a sum paid to a public authority under a mistake law may be recovered only if it was paid under protest, is contrary to the principle of effectiveness.

[52] *Kingstreet Investments Ltd v New Brunswick (Department of Finance)* [2007] SCC 1; [2007] 1 S.C.R. 3 at [53].

[53] *F.I.I.* [2010] EWCA Civ 103; [2010] S.T.C. 1251 at [152]–[173].

levies.[54] It also suggests that the concept of a "public authority" should be given a wide connotation in this context, to embrace not only governmental bodies but also bodies such as public service providers and universities whose authority to charge is subject to and limited by public law principles.[55]

Consistently with this, a broad view of the rule in *Woolwich* was taken by the **22–17** Privy Council in *Waikato Regional Airport Ltd v Att Gen of New Zealand*.[56] Under the New Zealand Biosecurity Act 1993, certain airports could not operate international flights without border control services provided by the Ministry of Agriculture and Fishery (MAF). The cost of these was partly met from central government funding, and the balance was recovered from regional but not from metropolitan airports, under a policy which the regional airports successfully challenged in judicial review proceedings. Speaking for the court, Lord Nicholls and Lord Walker held that restitution should be awarded under the *Woolwich* principle, although MAF's charges did not constitute a tax.[57] Nor did it matter that the airports had received services in exchange for their money, since these had been of no commercial benefit to them.[58] Nor (probably) would it have mattered if the services had been of commercial benefit to the airports, following *South of Scotland Electricity Board v British Oxygen Co Ltd*,[59] where the House of Lords ordered restitution of excessive charges for electricity supplies.

The *Woolwich* principle applies not only where money is paid under invalid **22–18** legislation, but also where payment is made because a valid statute is misconstrued or misapplied.[60] This follows from *British Steel Plc v Customs and Excise Commissioners (No.1)*,[61] where the Court of Appeal held that the claimant would be entitled to recover money paid as excise duty on oil used in its blast furnaces if it had qualified for relief from this duty. Scott V.C. held that restitution would be awarded because:

---

[54] Cf. *Steele* (1853) Ex. 625; 155 E.R. 1502 (charges to take extracts from a parish register); *Queens of the River* (1889) 15 T.L.R. 474 (charges for the use of pier facilities); *R v Birmingham CC Ex p. Dredger* (1993) 91 L.G.R. 532 (stallage). But see too *Norwich CC v Stringer* (2001) 33 H.L.R. 15 (CA), where the claimant received housing benefit that was not due, repaid some of this on receipt of a demand that failed to comply with statutory notice provisions, and then sought to recover his repayment; this unmeritorious claim was rightly rejected.

[55] Cf. *South of Scotland Electricity Board* [1959] 1 W.L.R. 587 (HL); *Barbour v University of British Columbia* [2009] BCSC 425; (2009) 310 D.L.R. (4th) 130 at [69] (reversed on a different point [2010] BCCA 63; (2010) 316 D.L.R. (4th) 354). See too Law Commission, *Restitution: Mistakes of Law and Ultra Vires Public Authority Receipts and Payments*, paras 6.42–6.45; J. Beatson, "Restitution of Taxes, Levies and Other Imposts", pp.417–418.

[56] *Waikato Regional Airport Ltd v Att Gen of New Zealand* [2003] UKPC 50; [2004] 3 N.Z.L.R. 1.

[57] *Waikato* [2003] UKPC 50; [2004] 3 N.Z.L.R. 1 at [80].

[58] Cf. *Att Gen v Wilts United Dairies Ltd* (1921) 37 T.L.R. 884 at 887 per Atkin L.J.: "It makes no difference that the obligation to pay . . . is expressed in the form of an agreement . . . [if it was illegal for the defendant] to require such an agreement . . . [or] to enter into such an agreement."

[59] *South of Scotland Electricity Board v British Oxygen Co Ltd* [1959] 1 W.L.R. 587.

[60] Canadian law previously distinguished between (irrecoverable) payments made pursuant to unlawful legislation and (recoverable) payments made pursuant to a mistake of law as to the proper interpretation of valid legislation: *Air Canada v British Columbia* [1989] 1 S.C.R. 1161; *Canadian Pacific Airlines Ltd v British Columbia* [1989] 1 S.C.R. 1133. However these cases have been superseded by *Kingstreet Investments* [2007] SCC 1; [2007] 1 S.C.R. 3; see para.22–27.

[61] *British Steel Plc v Customs and Excise Commissioners (No.1)* [1997] 2 All E.R. 336. In subsequent proceedings the CA held that the claimant had qualified for relief from the duty: *British Steel Plc v Customs and Excise Commissioners (No.2), The Times*, May 12, 1999.

"whether the demand is based on *ultra vires* regulations, or on a mistaken view of the facts of the case, it will ... be a demand outside the taxing power conferred by the empowering legislation."[62]

Another case in point is *British Sky Broadcasting Group Plc v Customs and Excise Commissioners*,[63] where the *Woolwich* principle was said to mandate recovery of money paid following a breach of the Commissioners' duty to act fairly between different classes of taxpayer (although a breach of this duty was not established on the facts).

22–19   Note, however, that a claimant who unsuccessfully appeals from an assessment relating to the tax payable in one year, but successfully appeals on the same grounds from an assessment relating to the tax payable in a later year, may not afterwards recover the money paid following the failure of his first appeal, on the basis that it was paid under a mistaken assessment.[64] The doctrine of res judicata does not apply to decisions by HMRC in relation to the tax due in respect of one year of assessment so as to preclude either the taxpayer or HMRC from contesting the same issue of fact or law on an appeal in relation to the tax due in a subsequent year.[65] The corollary of this is that decisions in relation to the tax due in respect of one year do not retrospectively falsify decisions made in relation to the tax due in respect of an earlier year.

22–20   The *Woolwich* principle does not apply where a tax or levy has been lawfully raised for, and expended upon, purposes prescribed in the empowering legislation, merely because the relevant public authority has not complied with rules governing its expenditure.[66]

22–21   Whether common law claims against public bodies under the *Woolwich* rule are subject to special defences is discussed elsewhere.[67]

(c) *Procedural Issues*

22–22   Since May 1, 2004 the High Court has had the power to order restitution in judicial review proceedings under CPR r.54.3.[68] Hence a claimant wishing to invoke the *Woolwich* principle could bring judicial review proceedings under CPR Pt 54 to establish the invalidity of the defendant's receipt and ask for a restitutionary award in these proceedings. However Pt 54 proceedings are subject to a tight three-month time limit,[69] and the question arises whether a claimant might alternatively bring a private law claim in unjust enrichment without first establishing the ultra vires nature of the defendant's receipt in proceedings for

---

[62] *British Steel* [1997] 2 All E.R. 336 at 376.
[63] *British Sky Broadcasting Group Plc v Customs and Excise Commissioners* [2001] S.T.C. 437 at [33]–[35].
[64] *Carvill v IRC* [2002] EWHC 1488 (Ch); [2002] S.T.C. 1167.
[65] *Barnett v Brabyn* [1996] S.T.C. 716; *Caffoor v C.I.T., Colombo* [1961] A.C. 584 at 598 (PC); approved in *MacNiven v Westmoreland Investments Ltd* [2001] UKHL 6; [2003] 1 A.C. 311 at [89]; *King v Walden* [2001] S.T.C. 822 at [14]–[27].
[66] *Saxmere Co Ltd v Wool Board Disestablishment Co Ltd* [2005] NZHC 342 at [138]; affirmed [2010] NZCA 513 at [177].
[67] See para.27–51 (change of position); para.32–15 (passing on); and paras 33–32——33–36 (limitation).
[68] Civil Procedure (Amendment No.5) Rules 2003 (SI 2003/3361) r.13.
[69] CPR r.54.5.

judicial review? In the *Woolwich* case,[70] Lord Slynn suggested that a claimant should be able to do this, and this was confirmed by the Court of Appeal in *British Steel*.[71] This finding was consistent with the relaxation of the *O'Reilly v Mackman*[72] exclusivity doctrine that has gathered pace since the introduction of the Civil Procedure Rules.[73]

However, the *British Steel* case pre-dates the 2004 changes to the procedural rules affecting public law proceedings, and it seems that its application may not always be a straightforward matter, following *Jones v Powys Local Health Board*.[74] There Plender J. held that it was an abuse of process for the claimant to bring a private law action for restitution of sums paid towards the costs of his deceased father's care and accommodation in a nursing home, when the primary focus of his action was to challenge the defendant's decision that his father was not entitled to the free provision of these benefits. The judge considered that allowing the claimant to frame his action in this way would deprive the defendant of the protection afforded by the requirement for permission in CPR r.54.4. He also suggested that the courts should test a claimant's right to invoke the *Woolwich* principle in private law proceedings without first bringing an action for judicial review by asking whether he is "asserting an entitlement to a subsisting right in private law" that might "incidentally involve the examination of a public law issue", or whether the "primary focus" of the proceedings is to challenge a public law act or decision.[75]

22–23

As matters now stand, it is difficult for claimants to know how to constitute their proceedings and how much time they have. We share Rebecca Williams's view that this is unsatisfactory and that it would be preferable for the law to make a decisive choice between one procedure and the other.[76] She argues that on balance the private law procedure should be chosen, i.e. that a claimant relying on the *Woolwich* rule to recover money paid as tax that was not due should always frame his claim as a private law action. This would be consistent with the *British Steel* case, and would be consistent with the choice that the law has made with regard to claims against public authorities in tort. Private law proceedings are also better suited to the efficient management of group litigation where many claimants seek restitution of money as tax that is not due.[77]

22–24

---

[70] *Woolwich* [1993] A.C. 70 at 200.
[71] *British Steel* [1997] 2 All E.R. 336.
[72] *O'Reilly v Mackman* [1983] 2 A.C. 337.
[73] *Clark v University of Lincolnshire and Humberside* [2000] 1 W.L.R. 1988 (CA); *Rhondda Cynon Taff CBC v Watkins* [2003] EWCA Civ 129; [2003] 1 W.L.R. 1864; *Bunney v Burns Anderson Plc* [2007] EWHC 1240 (Ch); [2008] Bus. L.R. 22.
[74] *Jones v Powys Local Health Board* [2008] EWHC 2562 (Admin).
[75] *Jones* [2008] EWHC 2562 (Admin) at [28], using the language of Lord Steyn's speech in *Boddington v British Transport Police* [1999] 2 A.C. 143 at 172. Without deciding that this is the correct test, Hamblen J. held that it was satisfied on the facts of *Bloomsbury International Ltd v Sea Fish Industry Authority* [2009] EWHC 1721 (QB); [2010] 1 C.M.L.R. 12 at [35]–[41] (reversed on a different point by the CA, but restored on further appeal: [2010] EWCA Civ 263; [2010] 1 W.L.R. 2117; [2011] UKSC 25; [2011] 1 W.L.R. 1546). Compare the Canadian doctrine of "collateral attack" which prevents claimants from attacking executive decisions in "proceedings other than those whose specific object is the reversal, variation, or nullification of the order or judgment": *Wilson v R.* [1983] 2 S.C.R. 594 at 599, considered in *Garland v Consumers' Gas Co* [2004] SCC 25; [2004] 1 S.C.R. 629; and *Att Gen of Canada v TeleZone Inc* [2010] SCC 62; [2010] S.C.R. 585.
[76] R. Williams, *Unjust Enrichment and Public Law* (Hart: Oxford, 2010), pp.49–52.
[77] See para.1–35.

(d) *Relationship between the Woolwich Principle and Other Grounds for Recovery*

22–25   These procedural considerations are linked to a deeper question going to the juridical nature of *Woolwich* claims and their relationship with other common law claims to recover money paid as tax which is not due. It can be argued that all common law claims to recover money paid as tax should be treated as public law claims and litigated exclusively in the Administrative Court, because this court is best able to deal with the competing concerns to which such claims give rise.[78] According to this view, it is undesirable to squeeze the *Woolwich* principle into the bipolar private law framework of a claim for unjust enrichment, because this leaves the court with no choice whether to treat an ultra vires government act as a nullity, with the result that restitution must inevitably follow unless a defence can be established. By contrast, in public law proceedings the court has a more flexible discretion as to the consequences that should be attributed to an ultra vires act. This argument suggests not only that claimants should be prevented from bringing private law claims in unjust enrichment founded on the *Woolwich* principle, but also that they should be prevented from bringing private law claims on other grounds, e.g. mistake or duress.

22–26   A different approach, persuasively argued by Rebecca Williams, is to treat *Woolwich*-type claims as hybrids, governed by rules which derive both from constitutional and administrative law and from the law of unjust enrichment.[79] On this view, claims to recover ultra vires tax payments, and other ultra vires receipts or payments, should all be dealt with by allowing the (private) law of unjust enrichment to define the enrichment and expense elements of the claim, while the reason for restitution, or unjust factor, should be simply the existence of the ultra vires event. This should not be considered as a special "policy motivated" private law unjust factor; instead it should be recognised that the reason for restitution is provided wholly by public law, while the remaining elements of the unjust enrichment claim are dealt with by the usual private law rules. This approach would be preferable for various reasons, including: conceptual accuracy—there are two relevant events (the ultra vires receipt or payment, and the defendant's unjust enrichment) and so the law should be able to respond to both of them; consistency of treatment of ultra vires receipts and ultra vires payments (as to which see Ch.23); and improved chances of recovery for taxpayers, given that public law remedies are discretionary, whereas an entitlement to restitution arises as a matter of right once a private law claim in unjust enrichment has been made out.

22–27   The first of these approaches was effectively adopted by the Supreme Court of Canada in *Kingstreet Investments Ltd v New Brunswick (Department of*

---

[78] J. Alder, "Restitution in Public Law: Bearing the Cost of Unlawful State Action" (2002) 22 L.S. 165. See too Ho Hock Lai, "Beyond Restitution and into Public Law" [1993] *Singapore Journal of Legal Studies* 582; R.B. Grantham and C.E.F. Rickett. *Enrichment and Restitution in New Zealand* (Oxford: Hart, 2000), p.240.

[79] Williams, *Unjust Enrichment and Public Law*, especially Chs 2 and 3. See too J. Beatson, "Finessing Substantive 'Public Law' Principles into 'Private Law' Relations" [1997] *Acta Juridica* 1, pp.16–19; J.D. McCamus, "Restitutionary Liability of Public Authorities in Canada" in C. Rickett and R. Grantham (eds), *Structure and Justification in Private Law* (Oxford: Hart, 2008), 291, p.316.

Finance),[80] where the claimant paid money as tax under a statute that was later held to be unconstitutional and void, and brought proceedings to recover its money. The court allowed the claim, but in the course of doing so departed from several previous Supreme Court decisions,[81] to hold that claims to recover money paid as tax which was not due should not be understood as claims in unjust enrichment. Rather they should be seen as a sui generis type of restitutionary claim "based on the constitutional principle that taxes should not be levied without proper authority".[82] Bastarache J. considered this to be a more apt characterisation because such claims raise "important constitutional principles which would be ignored by treating the claim [as a private law restitutionary claim founded on unjust enrichment or wrongdoing]".[83] He considered that "the unjust enrichment framework adds an unnecessary layer of complexity to the real legal issues".[84]

A parallel can be drawn between this development and the evolution of German law in the first quarter of the 20th century.[85] Until 1920, the *Reichsgericht* held that claims by citizens to recover money and goods from the state were justiciable in the civil courts.[86] However the court then changed its mind in a case concerned with goods requisitioned by the German government during the First World War, holding that the dispute should be resolved by the administrative court because the legality of the seizure had to be tested by public law rules.[87] This prompted Gerhard Lassar to argue in an influential *Habilitation* thesis that the private law rules of unjustified enrichment contained in the BGB are a self-contained interlocking set of principles which may not work in the public law sphere without adjustment, not least because the administrative laws of Germany are the responsibility of the states.[88] He concluded that a "special public law claim" for restitution should be recognised and the *Reichsgericht* subsequently took this course in 1923.[89] This "special public law claim" is now well established in German law and has been recognised in various statutes. It is subject to tighter time limits than an ordinary private law claim, but in other ways it has been developed to treat citizens more favourably than they would be if they brought a private law claim in unjust(ified) enrichment.[90]

22–28

---

[80] *Kingstreet Investments Ltd v New Brunswick (Department of Finance)* [2007] SCC 1; [2007] 1 S.C.R. 3. This case post-dated *Deutsche Morgan Grenfell* [2006] UKHL 49; [2007] 1 A.C. 558, discussed at paras 22–29—22–31, but the HL's decision seems not to have been cited to the SCC. In *Alberta v Elder Advocates of Alberta Society* [2011] SCC 24; (2011) 331 D.L.R. (4th) 257 at [91] it was held to be arguable that *Kingstreet* might not apply where money paid to a public body is not due for a reason other than the fact that it is paid under an ultra vires tax statute.
[81] *Air Canada* [1989] 1 SCR 1161; *Canadian Pacific Airlines* [1989] 1 SCR 1133; *Air Canada v Ontario (Liquor Control Board)* [1997] 2 SCR 581; *Re Eurig Estate* [1998] 2 SCR 565.
[82] *Kingstreet Investments* [2007] 1 S.C.R. 3 at [33].
[83] *Kingstreet Investments* [2007] 1 S.C.R. 3 at [34].
[84] *Kingstreet Investments* [2007] 1 S.C.R. 3 at [35].
[85] Discussed in T. Krebs, *Restitution at the Crossroads: A Comparative Study* (London: Cavendish Press, 2001), pp.192–197.
[86] e.g. RGZ 72, 152 (October 29, 1909).
[87] RGZ 99, 41 (April 30, 1920).
[88] G. Lassar, *Der Erstattungsanspruch im Verwaltungs- und Finanzrecht* (Berlin: 1921).
[89] RGZ 107, 189 (June 12, 1923).
[90] e.g. VGH Mannheim NVw.Z. 1991, 583 (October 18, 1990), refusing to apply the (private law) rule in § 814 II BGB, that claimants cannot recover money paid in the knowledge that it is not due; B.Verw.G.E. 36, 108 (September 17, 1970), confirmed B.Verw.G., 2 B. 84/89 (December 27, 1989), refusing to allow a change of position defence.

22–29   In *Deutsche Morgan Grenfell*,[91] the claimant paid tax under a statute, parts of which were later held by the European Court of Justice to infringe the EC Treaty because they allowed some taxpayers to defer payment but withheld this advantage from others including the claimant. The claimant sought to recover the use value of the money between the date of payment and the date when the money would have been paid, had payment been deferred.[92] The claimant pleaded that it had paid under a "retrospective" mistake of law, relying on *Kleinwort Benson Ltd v Lincoln CC*[93] for the proposition that payments can be deemed to have been mistaken when they are made under an understanding of the law that is later falsified by a court decision which retrospectively changes the relevant law. The claimant wished to found its action on the ground of mistake, rather than on the *Woolwich* rule, in order to take advantage of a limitation rule that applies only to claims to recover mistaken payments.

22–30   In its defence the Revenue argued that facts which would support an action on *Woolwich* grounds must be litigated as such, and may not be relied on to support an action on some other ground, such as mistake. This was rejected by the House of Lords, which held that claimants may rely on mistake as a reason for restitution when seeking to recover money paid as tax which was not due. Their Lordships recognised that significant differences exist between tax payments and "private transactions",[94] but held that their decision was mandated by "the constitutional principle of equality", by which they meant that "under the rule of law, the Crown (that is the executive government in its various emanations) is in general subject to the same common law obligations as ordinary citizens."[95]

22–31   Counsel for the Revenue seem to have made no sustained attempt to argue in *Deutsche Morgan Grenfell* that a rule confining mistaken payers of tax to the *Woolwich* ground would be desirable in principle. Instead argument before their Lordships was focused on the question whether Lord Goff had previously laid down a binding rule to this effect in passages of his speeches in *Woolwich*[96] and *Kleinwort Benson*.[97] This was a simple question for their Lordships to answer in the negative, not only because the Revenue's reading of the relevant passages was strained, but also because Lord Goff's remarks were obiter.[98] This follows from the fact that *Woolwich* was argued and decided on the basis that the claimant had made no mistake, and from the fact that the money mistakenly paid in *Kleinwort Benson* was not paid as tax. To approach the issue as though everything turned on the meaning of Lord Goff's dicta was therefore misguided. No doubt counsel were encouraged to take this approach by the fact that it was

---

[91] *Deutsche Morgan Grenfell* [2006] UKHL 49; [2007] 1 A.C. 558.
[92] This was recognised as a form of benefit recoverable in an action for unjust enrichment in an associated case: *Sempra* [2007] UKHL 34; [2008] Bus. L.R. 49, discussed at paras 5–05—5–10.
[93] *Kleinwort Benson Ltd v Lincoln CC* [1999] 2 A.C. 349, discussed at paras 9–71—9–94.
[94] *Deutsche Morgan Grenfell* [2007] 1 A.C. 558 at [13], [33] and [49].
[95] *Kleinwort Benson* [1999] 2 A.C. 349 at [132]–[133] per Lord Walker, noting that this is recognised by the Crown Proceedings Act 1947 s.21(1). See also Lord Hope's statement at [39], citing P. Birks, "Restitution from the Executive: A Tercentenary Footnote to the Bill of Rights" in P.D. Finn (ed.), *Essays in Restitution* (Sydney: Law Book Co Ltd, 1990), 164, p.174: "unless displaced by statute, causes of action good against private citizens are no less good against public bodies".
[96] *Woolwich* [1993] A.C. 70 at 163–166 and 171–174.
[97] *Kleinwort Benson* [1999] 2 A.C. 349 at 381–384.
[98] As noted in *Boake Allen* [2006] EWCA 25; [2006] S.T.C. 606 at [160]; not considered on appeal: [2007] UKHL 25; [2007] 1 W.L.R. 1386.

endorsed by Jonathan Parker L.J. in the Court of Appeal. It is a pity, though, that more time was not spent arguing the point from first principles, given that the German and the Canadian courts have both held it to be desirable to confine claimants to public law proceedings.

CHAPTER 23

ULTRA VIRES PAYMENTS BY PUBLIC BODIES

1. INTRODUCTION

The previous chapter considered the situation where a claimant pays money to a **23–01** defendant public authority in the form of tax or other levy that is not due. This chapter concerns the opposite situation, where a claimant public authority makes an ultra vires payment to a defendant. This may happen, for example, because the public body miscalculates the amount of a social security benefit or tax credit or tax repayment owed to a defendant, or makes a payment out of public funds which has not been duly authorised by democratic process, or makes a payment which is prohibited by European law, or makes a payment under an ultra vires contract. In these circumstances, the public authority may have a statutory claim to recover the payment. Alternatively, a claim may lie at common law: following *Auckland Harbour Board v R.*,[1] payments made out of public funds without lawful authority are recoverable as of right by virtue of their ultra vires nature; depending on the facts, a claim may also lie on the ground of mistake or failure of consideration or pursuant to the policy underpinning the rule that renders the claimant public body incapable of entering certain types of transaction. Statutory claims are considered in Part 2, and common law claims in Part 3.

These claims all form part of a larger family of claims in which the claimant **23–02** relies on its own legal incapacity as a ground for recovery. In all these cases that fall into this group, there are underlying policy reasons why a human or artificial person is deemed to lack the legal capacity to enter certain transactions. If such a person enters such a transaction, and thereby benefits a defendant, then the law will award restitution if that would be consistent with the policy objectives of the rule that invalidated the transaction. Conversely, if it would stultify these objectives then restitution will be denied. Other claims founded on legal incapacity are discussed in Ch.24. A similar policy-based calculation is undertaken in cases where benefits have been transferred under transactions that are illegal, and cases of this sort are discussed in Ch.25.

2. STATUTORY CLAIMS

(a) *Overpaid Social Security Benefits*

The Social Security Administration Act 1992 s.71 gives the Secretary of State for **23–03** Work and Pensions a right to recover overpayments of various types of social

---

[1] *Auckland Harbour v R.* [1924] A.C. 318 (PC).

security benefit.[2] The section provides that the money must be repaid when the overpayment was caused by a misrepresentation of a material fact or by a failure to disclose relevant information. In this context a material fact "includes (but is not necessarily restricted to) any facts that the claimant is required to disclose and that if not disclosed would cause an overpayment".[3] A failure to disclose relevant information is premised on the statutory duty of disclosure placed on benefit claimants to notify the Secretary of State of such information as he may require in connection with the benefit, and of any changes in circumstances which they might reasonably be expected to know might affect the continuance of their entitlement to benefit.[4]

23–04   The burden of proof in overpayment cases is on the Secretary of State to show that he is entitled to recovery.[5] Money is not recoverable under s.71 unless the initial decision to award benefit has been validly taken away, by being reversed or varied on an appeal, or by a further decision that is effective to revise or supersede it under the Social Security Act 1998 ss.9 or 10.[6] Prior to July 1996, the decision reversing or superseding the initial decision to award benefit had to be made at the same time as the overpayment decision; following the enactment of the Social Security (Overpayments) Act 1996, these decisions may be taken separately. Thus:

> "[I]n any appeal against an overpayment decision alone (i.e. where the question of entitlement is not itself directly under appeal as well) the tribunal is required to satisfy itself that a proper and complete, procedurally and substantively valid decision to remove the entitlement in question was in fact taken and already in place before the making of the determination as to recoverability".[7]

Once an overpayment determination has been made, the Secretary of State can choose whether to use court enforcement mechanisms to recover the money or to deduct the relevant sum from future benefit payments to which the recipient is

---

[2] The benefits to which s.71 applies are listed in subs.(11). They are: benefits as defined in the Social Security Contributions and Benefits Act 1992 s.122; jobseekers' allowance; state pension credit; employment and support allowances; income support; social fund payments mentioned in the Social Security Contributions and Benefits Act 1992 s.138(1)(a) or (2); health in pregnancy grants; and child benefit. This list does not include housing benefits and council tax benefits which are subject to a different regime that is discussed below in s.2. A useful but now outdated account of the statutory recovery regime is P. Stagg, *Overpayments and Recovery of Social Security Benefits* (London: LAG, 1996); see too N.J. Wikeley and A.I. Ogus, *The Law of Social Security*, 5th edn (London: Butterworths, 2002), pp.163–168.

[3] CPC/2021/2008; [2008] UKUT 15 (AAC) at [68].

[4] By the Social Security (Claims and Payments) Regulations 1987 (SI 1987/1968) reg.32. For a useful discussion of the different duties imposed by reg.32, see CDLA/2328/2006.

[5] CPC/2021/2008; [2008] UKUT 15 (AAC) at [72]; CIB/8/2008; [2009] UKUT 47 (AAC) at [35].

[6] Social Security Administration Act 1992 s.71(5A). The reason is that the adjudication of awards and the payment of awards were constitutionally separate functions at the time when the 1992 Act was enacted, adjudication officers being responsible for all decisions concerning the making of awards and the Secretary of State being responsible for their payment. These two functions were subsequently merged and placed in the hands of the Secretary of State by the Social Security Act 1998 ss.1 and 8.

[7] CIS/928/2009; [2009] UKUT 143 (ACC) at [22]. Scc too R(IS) 13/05; discussed in CIS/1726/2010; [2010] UKUT 291 (AAC).

entitled. The latter method is most often used in practice,[8] and in *R. (Balding) v Secretary of State for Work and Pensions*, Mummery L.J. observed that if[9]:

> "the Secretary of State exercise[s] his discretion to take the deduction route, which is tightly regulated by the Social Security (Payments on Account, Overpayments and Recovery) Regulations 1988 (S.I. 1988/664), he is not enforcing a liability against the claimant to pay money under the 1992 Act. He is actually exercising his statutory power to pay the recipient no more than the correct amount of *net* benefit due to him under the applicable social security legislation."

The 1988 Regulations to which Mummery L.J. refers in this passage place limits on the extent to which a recipient's future benefits can be reduced, to ensure that he continues to receive a reasonable amount of benefit notwithstanding his repayment obligation.[10]

The questions whether a recipient has misrepresented a material fact or failed **23–05** to disclose relevant information have often been considered by the social security appeal tribunals and higher courts.[11] They have not consistently taken a line for or against the Department when construing s.71, and their decisions often turn on the facts of individual cases. Examples of decisions favouring recipients are tribunal findings that statements of honest opinion on claim forms do not constitute misrepresentations or failures of disclosure for the purposes of the section,[12] that there is no continuing duty of disclosure on recipients once they have disclosed relevant information to the right person,[13] that "a failure to comment on a statement such as 'Please use this space to tell us anything else you think we might need to know' [cannot] amount to a misrepresentation",[14] and that "statements that in ordinary language are factually and objectively true [are not] 'misrepresentations', when they happen to conflict with restricted or artificial meanings imposed . . . by regulations for particular benefit purposes elsewhere."[15] In *Hooper v Secretary of State for Work and Pensions*[16] the Court of Appeal held that if the Secretary of State wishes to impose a mandatory duty to disclose information on recipients then he must do so in clear and unambiguous language. Hence no mandatory duty was imposed by the statements contained in a recipient's order book, that "you should tell the office . . . before you start

---

[8] In 1986, two-thirds of recoveries were effected in this way: NACRO Working Party *Enforcement of the Law Relating to Social Security* (1986) para.9.4.

[9] *R. (Balding) v Secretary of State for Work and Pensions* [2007] EWCA Civ 1327; [2008] 1 W.L.R. 564 at [21].

[10] On the 1988 Regulations, note *Brown v Secretary of State for Work and Pensions* [2007] EWCA 89; R(DLA) 2/07: reg.5 does not empower the Department to offset arrears of benefit, accumulated during a period of suspension, against an irrecoverable overpayment.

[11] Since November 2008 cases that were previously dealt with by the Social Security Commissioners have been dealt with by the Upper Tribunal (Administrative Appeals Chamber). Electronic copies of their decisions and earlier decisions by the Commissioners may be accessed at: *http://www.osscsc .gov.uk/Decisions/decisions.htm.*

[12] CDLA/5803/1999; CDLA/1823/2004.

[13] CIS/3529/2008; [2009] UKUT 52 (AAC).

[14] CJSA/3583/2007; [2008] UKUT 4 (AAC) at [17].

[15] CIS/928/2009; [2009] UKUT 143 (ACC) at [40].

[16] *Hooper v Secretary of State for Work and Pensions* [2007] EWCA Civ 494; R(IB) 4/07. For additional discussion of the form taken by requests for information in leaflets, fact sheets, notes, and instructions issued to recipients, see CDLA/2328/2006 and CIB/3823/2008; [2009] UKUT 120 (AAC).

work" and "you should fill in an application form before you do any permitted work". Because the word "must" was not used, there was "room for doubt in the mind of a sensible layperson as to whether the S.S.W.P. [was] imposing a mandatory requirement".[17]

23–06   Decisions which take a sterner line against recipients include *Jones v Chief Adjudication Officer*,[18] where Evans L.J. held that a representor need not know a material fact before he can misrepresent it for the purposes of the section, and *Chief Adjudication Officer v Sherriff*,[19] where Nourse L.J. held that a representor need not even know that he has made a representation. In *Sherriff* recovery was therefore allowed against an 80-year-old benefit claimant in a nursing home who had signed a claim form, the contents of which she did not understand, and which had been filled out for her by a member of staff. The court reasoned, rather dubiously, that if she had had the capacity to make a claim at all, then she must also have had the capacity to make a misrepresentation in her claim form. Similarly, in *B v Secretary of State for Work and Pensions*,[20] the Court of Appeal held that a person can fail to comply with his duty of disclosure, whether or not he has the mental capacity to understand what is required. These cases all illustrate that there is no fault requirement in s.71, which indeed provides for recovery where there has been a misrepresentation or failure of disclosure "whether fraudulently or otherwise". Prior to *B*, a line of Commissioners' decisions dating as far back as 1982 had held that a recipient who knew a fact could only be said to have failed to disclose this fact if disclosure was something that could reasonably have been expected of him.[21] However the Court of Appeal in *B* could find no warrant for this approach in the statute, Sedley L.J. stating that "the moral argument against fixing [a recipient] with the financial consequences of not reporting something which she did not appreciate she needed to report encounters a statutory provision which not only makes no such allowance but leaves room for none."[22]

23–07   Finally, in *Hinchy v Secretary of State for Work and Pensions*,[23] the respondent was entitled to income support and also to disability living allowance for a fixed period. These payments were administered through different offices, and when the respondent's entitlement to disability living allowance came to an end she did not inform the income support office of this fact. Through administrative error, this office paid her a severe disability premium to which she was not entitled for the next two years. The Court of Appeal held that no claim lay under s.71

---

[17] *Hooper* [2007] EWCA Civ 494; R(IB) 4/07 at [56].

[18] *Jones v Chief Adjudication Officer* [1994] 1 W.L.R. 62 at 65. See too *Page and Davis v Chief Adjudication Officer* Unreported CA, June 24, 1991.

[19] *Chief Adjudication Officer v Sherriff, The Times*, May 10, 1995.

[20] *B v Secretary of State for Work and Pensions* [2005] EWCA Civ 929; [2005] 1 W.L.R. 3796; R(IS) 9/06; affirming CIS/4348/2003. See too CIS/3846/2001; R(IS) 4/06 (misrepresentation made when illiterate recipient signed declaration on claim form that information given was complete).

[21] R(SB) 21/82; R(SB) 15/87; CG/4494/1999; R(IS) 5/03. There was some debate whether the "reasonably to be expected" test was objective or subjective: compare R(A) 1/95 and CIS/ 1769/1999.

[22] *B* [2005] EWCA Civ 929; [2005] 1 W.L.R. 3796 at [40].

[23] *Hinchy v Secretary of State for Work and Pensions* [2005] UKHL 16; [2005] 1 W.L.R. 967; reversing [2003] EWCA Civ 138; [2003] 1 W.L.R. 2018. See too CIS/1960/2007 at [14] (disclosure made in connection with claim for one type of benefit insufficient for purposes of claim for another type of benefit).

because she owed no duty to disclose information to the income support office that the Department already knew through the other office. This decision was reversed by the House of Lords, which held that the notes on her order books clearly stated that she must disclose changes in her rights to other benefits to the income support office, and that she could not assume that administrative action taken by another office would relieve her of the need to do this.[24]

Section 71 requires that an overpayment must have been caused by the **23–08** recipient's misrepresentation or failure of disclosure. The causation rules in this area were summarised by Mr Commissioner Jacobs as follows[25]:

"If the claimant's was the only evidence relied on [when the decision was taken to make the overpayment], the claimant caused the overpayment. If the claimant's evidence was part of the evidence relied on, it was a cause of the overpayment; it is irrelevant that there was also an additional cause: see the decision of the Court of Appeal in *Duggan v Chief Adjudication Officer*,[26] which has been followed in Scotland in *Riches v Secretary of State for Social Security*.[27] The only circumstance in which the claimant will not have caused the overpayment is if (a) the other evidence was the only evidence relied on and (b) it did more than merely report the claimant's evidence."

The effect of bankruptcy on liability under s.71 was discussed by the Court of **23–09** Appeal in *R. (Steele) v Birmingham CC*.[28] The court distinguished four situations:

1. where benefits are awarded and paid to the recipient before the date of the bankruptcy order, and the decision that the overpayment is recoverable is also issued before this date;

2. where benefits are awarded and paid to the recipient before the date of the bankruptcy order, and the decision that the overpayment is recoverable is issued after this date;

3. where benefits are awarded to the claimant before the date of the bankruptcy order, but paid to the recipient after this date, and the decision that the overpayment is recoverable is also issued after this date; and

4. where benefits are awarded and paid to the recipient after the date of the bankruptcy order and the decision that the overpayment is recoverable is also issued after this date.

---

[24] This principle does not apply where a recipient has had dealings with different members of staff in a single local office, unless they were physically separated as a matter of fact so as to constitute two distinct "offices" of the department albeit in the same building: CSB/677/1986; CIS/1887/2002; CIS/3700/2005; CIS 4422/2002.

[25] CDLA/5803/99 [36].

[26] Reported as an Appendix in R(SB) 13/89. *Duggan v Chief Adjudication Officer* was endorsed in *Morrell v Secretary of State for Work and Pensions* [2003] EWCA Civ 526; R(IS) 6/03, and followed in CIS/1960/2007 and in CIS/2710/2008; [2009] UKUT 98 (AAC). See too R(SB) 3/90: even if there has been disclosure, a later misrepresentation may be the cause of an overpayment if the adjudication officer relies on it, and it is not open to the claimant to say that the officer had the means of checking his misstatement.

[27] *Riches v Secretary of State for Social Security* [1994] S.L.T. 730 at 734.

[28] *R. (Steele) v Birmingham CC* [2005] EWCA Civ 1824; [2006] 1 W.L.R. 2380. See too *R. (Charlebois) v Social Security Commissioners* [2008] EWHC 2647 (Admin).

The court held that in cases 2., 3., and 4. the recipient owes no liability at all until after it has been determined that the overpayment is recoverable, and so he owes no contingent liability for the purposes of the Insolvency Act 1986. Hence his debt to the Department is not released on his discharge from bankruptcy.[29]

23–10   Case 1. was subsequently considered in *Balding*[30] where the court held that the overpaid benefit was recoverable by virtue of a determination made before the issuing of the bankruptcy order, so that there was a liability to pay money under an enactment for the purposes of the Insolvency Act 1986 s.382(4). It followed that the recipient's debt was a bankruptcy debt that would be released on discharge unless incurred by fraud.[31] Note, however, that the Department may continue to make deductions from ongoing benefits until the date of discharge.[32] Note, too, that the Department may not lawfully make deductions from social security benefits payable during the moratorium period of a debt relief order.[33]

23–11   Where a recipient has acted fraudulently by lying or suppressing relevant information then it is easy to agree that he should be ordered to repay the money,[34] but where the Department and a recipient have both made innocent mistakes it is more debateable where the equities of the situation lie. On the one hand, the Department has a limited budget, and it makes a large number of recoverable overpayments each year.[35] If it does not recover a significant proportion of these, then that will seriously disadvantage many people in need for whom better provision could be made with more resources. On the other hand, it may be unfair to the recipients of overpayments if they are forced to repay the money where they have limited means and have spent the money in good faith.[36]

---

[29] The same rule applies to overpayments of housing benefit and council tax benefit recoverable under the Social Security Administration Act 1992 ss.75 and 76 (as to which, see paras 23–15——23–18): CH/3495/2008; [2009] UKUT 70 (AAC).

[30] *Balding* [2007] EWHC 759 (Admin); [2007] 1 W.L.R. 1805; affirmed [2007] EWCA Civ 1327; [2008] 1 W.L.R. 564.

[31] Insolvency Act 1986 s.281(3).

[32] *R. v Secretary of State for Social Security Ex p. Taylor* [1997] B.P.I.R. 505.

[33] *R. (Cooper) v Secretary of State for Work and Pensions* [2010] EWCA Civ 1431; [2011] B.P.I.R. 223.

[34] He will also incur criminal penalties, under the Social Security Administration Act 1992 ss.111A and 112; on s.111A see *R. v Passmore* [2007] EWCA Crim 2053; [2008] 1 Cr. App. R. 12. On the progressive toughening of the criminal law relating to social security fraud, see G. McKeever, "Rights, Responsibilities and Social Security Fraud" (2009) 16 J.S.S.L. 139; P. Larkin, "The 'Criminalisation' of Social Security Law: Towards a Punitive Welfare State?" (2007) 24 J.L.S. 295.

[35] In 2007–2008 the Department made £558 million of overpayments; as at March 31, 2008 it had an identified debt stock of £1.8 billion resulting from the overpayment of benefits; and in 2007–2008 it collected over £272 million in debts from 1.6 million people: National Audit Office, Department of Work and Pensions, *Management of Benefit Overpayment Debt*, HC 294 (Session 2008–2009) para.1.1. In 2009–2010, the Department made £3.1 billion of overpayments: Comptroller and Auditor General, *Minimising the Cost of Administrative Errors in the Benefit System*, HC 569 (Session 2010–2011) para.2; Comptroller and Auditor General, *Reducing Losses in the Benefits System Caused by Customers' Mistakes*, HC 704 (Session 2010–2011) para.1.

[36] For further discussion, see NACRO Report, *Enforcement of the Law Relating to Social Security* Pt 9. At para.9.11 the point is made that "the writing off (remission) of debts due to the Crown is strictly controlled by general Civil Service rules and individual departments have little room for manoeuvre", but at para.9.13 it is noted that "waiver on compassionate grounds is unlikely to be opposed as a principle" although some of the tests used by the Department to determine whether overpayments should be recovered are criticised for being too stringent.

The Secretary of State has a discretion whether to enforce his statutory rights **23–12** and can waive recovery once an overpayment determination has been made.[37] The Department maintains a policy document setting out its approach to the waiver of overpayments, and in B,[38] Sedley L.J. thought that this document should be disclosed to interested parties, since it was "the antithesis of good government" for it to be kept "in the departmental drawer". In 2006 the document was duly disclosed and its contents made publically available.[39] Its key points were as follows:

1. the Department's policy is to pursue recovery whenever a recipient agrees to repay an overpayment; hence if a recipient wants to ask for an overpayment to be written off, then he should not agree to repay it;

2. only in exceptional cases will recovery be waived on compassionate grounds: where there is severe ill-health or the situation is particularly distressing. Moreover the Department is much more likely to consider waiver in such cases where the recipient has acted in good faith than where he has acted in a bad faith;

3. overpayments of less than a "small overpayment limit" can be waived by the local office. Otherwise the waiver must be considered centrally. The relevant limit was increased from £40 to £65 in 2008.[40] The Department has delegated authority to waive overpayments of up to £100,000 where there is severe hardship, but Treasury approval is needed for waiver of recovery of overpayments of more than £1,000 on other grounds, and also for waiver of recovery of any amount where there is a question of principle at stake;

4. cases are considered on their individual merits, and the following factors are taken into account: (1) the type of overpayment; (2) the culpability of the recipient; (3) the length of time since the overpayment was made; (4) whether recovery will have a bad effect on the recipient's personal circumstances; (5) defences against recovery; (6) cost-effectiveness of recovery; (7) where a group of people has been overpaid through the same mistake each person should be treated equally as regards recovery.

In its discussion of factor (5), the Department contemplated that both change **23–13** of position and estoppel would be defences to a statutory recovery claim on appropriate facts. However, it is unclear why the Department believed this to be so, given that the statute does not expressly provide for either defence, and given, too, that it is uncertain whether either defence is even available to common law claims grounded on the rule in *Auckland Harbour Board v R*.[41] In *R. (Child*

---

[37] *Steele* [2005] EWCA Civ 1824; [2006] 1 W.L.R. 2380 at [17].
[38] *B* [2005] EWCA Civ 929; [2005] 1 W.L.R. 3796 at [43].
[39] The document was disclosed at the request of the Child Poverty Action group, which published it online in 2006: *http://www.cpag.org.uk/cro/wrb/wrb190/Secretary-of-State-waiver-scanned.doc*. The Department also maintains a written document setting out its general policy and procedures for overpayment recovery which was published on-line following a Freedom of Information Act request by Citizens Advice Cymru in 2005: *http://www.rightsnet.org.uk/pdfs/DWP_ORG_Feb_2005.doc*.
[40] NAO Report, *Management of Benefit Overpayment Debt*, para.3.25.
[41] *Auckland Harbour Board v R.* [1924] A.C. 318. For discussion of this point, see para.27–52.

Poverty Action Group) v Secretary of State for Work and Pensions,[42] however, the appellate courts accepted that the change of position defence is not available to claims under s.71, and presumably the Department will adjust its waiver policy accordingly.

23–14   The *CPAG* finding also means that at least so far as defences are concerned, the Secretary of State's statutory recovery rights are stronger than common law rights of recovery grounded on mistake (and possibly also claims grounded on the rule in *Auckland Harbour Board*). However, his statutory recovery rights are weaker than any common law recovery rights that he might have in the sense that s.71 only enables him to recover overpayments made pursuant to a benefit award that were caused by the recipient's misrepresentation or failure of disclosure, and it does not allow for the recovery of overpayments which were made through uninduced administrative error. Furthermore, in *CPAG* the Supreme Court held that s.71 "constitutes a comprehensive and exclusive scheme for dealing with all overpayments of benefit made pursuant to awards".[43] Hence the Secretary of State is prevented from relying on any rights that he might otherwise have at common law, either in cases falling within the scope of the section or in cases falling outside it. This is discussed further elsewhere.[44]

(b) *Overpaid Housing Benefit and Council Tax Benefit*

23–15   Statutory claims lie to recover overpaid housing benefit and council tax benefit, under the Social Security Administration Act 1992 ss.75 and 76.[45] In contrast to claims under s.71, there is no requirement that such benefits must have been overpaid following a misrepresentation or failure of disclosure. Instead the Housing Benefit Regulations 2006 and Council Tax Benefit Regulations 2006 provide that overpaid benefits are always recoverable unless the payment has been made through an official error, and the recipient could not reasonably have been expected to realise, at the time of receipt of the payment or of any notice relating to that payment, that it was an overpayment.[46] The Regulations further provide that an overpayment is not relevantly made by official error if the recipient caused or materially contributed to the paying authority's mistake (e.g. by misrepresenting a material fact or failing to disclose relevant information).[47]

---

[42] *R. (Child Poverty Action Group) v Secretary of State for Work and Pensions* [2009] EWCA Civ 1058; [2010] 1 W.L.R. 1886 at [20]; [2010] UKSC 54; [2011] 2 A.C. 15 at [10] and [14].

[43] *CPAG* [2010] UKSC 54; [2011] 2 A.C. 15 at [12] per Lord Brown.

[44] See paras 2–17—2–19.

[45] For general discussion, see Department of Work and Pensions, "HB/CTB Overpayments Guide", published online at: *http://www.dwp.gov.uk/local-authority-staff/housing-benefit/claims-processing/operational-manuals/overpayments-guide/.*

[46] Housing Benefit Regulations 2006 (SI 2006/213) reg.100(1) and (2); Council Tax Benefit Regulations 2006 (SI 2006/215) reg.83(1) and (2).

[47] Housing Benefit Regulations 2006 reg.100(3); Council Tax Benefit Regulations 2006 reg.83(3). See e.g. *R. (Prince) v Social Security Commissioner* [2009] EWHC 1181 (Admin) at [10]; but cf. CH/2567/2007; CH/3586/2007; R(H) 10/08. A broad common sense approach should be used to determine what was the substantial cause of the overpayment: *R. (Sier) v Cambridge CC Housing Benefit Review Board* [2001] EWCA Civ 1523 at [30]–[31], considered in CH/3083/2005 at [38] and CH 2297/09; [2010] UKUT 57 (AAC) (where several overpayments were made at different times from different causes, with the result that some were recoverable and some were not).

If an overpayment has been made to a recipient who has supplied a benefit   **23–16**
provider with accurate information, then in some circumstances he might plausibly argue that he cannot reasonably be expected to have understood the
complex calculation by which the amount of his benefit was determined, and
hence to have realised that an overpayment might have been made—even if he
received a letter stating that an estimated payment was being made pending full
investigation of his entitlement.[48] Also, when determining what a recipient might
reasonably be expected to have realised, it is a relevant consideration what the
recipient was told by the benefit provider, including positive statements in
response to queries whether he is entitled to the amounts paid.[49] However "it is
not relevant whether the [recipient] could reasonably have been expected to
realise the *amount* by which she was being overpaid . . . what matters is whether
[she] could reasonably have been expected to realise that the amount she was
receiving definitely contained some element of overpayment".[50] Furthermore,
where a recipient has noticed an error and made a series of good faith efforts to
draw it to the benefit provider's attention, he cannot later resist repayment when
the benefit provider finally comes to its senses and asks for the money back,
because ex hypothesi the recipient did realise that an overpayment must have
been made in this situation.[51]

Overpaid benefits can be recovered both from the person to whom they were   **23–17**
paid,[52] and also, in circumstances prescribed in the Regulations, from some other
person, either as well as, or instead of, the person to whom they were paid.[53] In
practice housing benefit is often paid directly to landlords, and if an overpayment
has been made of which the landlord can reasonably be expected to have been
aware (e.g. because the benefit paid exceeds the amount of the rent or is paid after
termination of the tenancy), then the benefit provider can hold the landlord liable
either instead of, or in addition to, the tenant.[54] Where a landlord is required to
repay the overpayment the tenant will then owe him the overpayment sum but
this may be of little practical benefit to the landlord if the liability is treated as
a mere debt rather than rent arrears. In *R. v Haringey LBC Ex p. Ayub*,[55] the court
held that once the rent is paid by means of the housing benefit payment made
directly to the landlord, the rent liability for the relevant period is extinguished
once and for all, so that the landlord cannot treat the tenant's liability to
reimburse him for his expenditure as a liability for rent arrears. However this rule
was effectively reversed by the Housing Benefit Regulations 2006 reg.95(2).

---

[48] *R. v Liverpool CC Ex p. Griffiths* (1990) 22 H.L.R. 312.
[49] CH/1675/2005 at [12].
[50] CH/2554/2002 at [9]. See too CH/1909/2008; CH/628/2010; [2010] UKUT 316 (AAC).
[51] CH/3309/2006.
[52] Where the benefit provider is a council that provides accommodation to a recipient directly,
housing benefit will probably not be "paid", but will instead take the form of a credit to the
recipient's rent account. Thereafter "if the credit given was too much, it can only be recovered via
the statutory overpayment provisions, not by recreating the rent liability retrospectively": CH
2297/09; [2010] UKUT 57 (AAC) at [5].
[53] For discussion of the relevant provisions, see CH/4234/2004 and CH/3160/2007; [2008] UKUT 18
(AAC).
[54] An overpayment made directly to a landlord in respect of one tenant may be recovered out of
housing benefit payable to the landlord to discharge rent owed to the landlord by another tenant:
Godwin v Rossendale BC [2002] EWCA Civ 726; [2003] H.L.R. 9.
[55] *R. v Haringey LBC Ex p. Ayub* (1993) 25 H.L.R. 566.

23-18   As with claims under s.71, benefit providers are not legally required to exercise their rights under ss.75 and 76 to recover overpayments,[56] but they are expected by central government to make serious attempts to do so, and in practice recovery action is taken in most cases.[57] A research report undertaken for the Department of Work and Pensions in 2000 found that none of the local authorities visited maintained a formal written overpayments policy which not only set out their procedures for recovery, but also explained their reasons for choosing whether to enforce or waive recovery in particular cases.[58] Since then, the practice of maintaining and publishing policy documents containing both types of information has become much more widespread.

(c) Other Welfare Benefits

23-19   The National Assistance Act 1948 Pt III (along with other legislation) places local authorities under a duty to provide various welfare services, and s.45 of the 1948 Act provides that if a local authority incurs expenditure under Pt III in consequence of a person's misrepresentation or failure to disclose a material fact, then the authority can recover its expenditure from this person. In *West Sussex CC v Amberley (UK) Ltd*[59] the manager of a registered home run by the defendant company submitted invoices for the care of mentally ill residents which were correctly calculated but which were ignored by the claimant council. Instead, the council made its own mistaken calculations of the amounts owed, overlooking an increase in the contributions made towards their own care costs by the residents themselves. As a result the council overpaid the defendant for six years. The manager was aware of this fact but did not draw it to the council's attention as the parties were engaged in a long-running dispute over the council's fee scale,[60] and he put the overpayments towards the additional fees that he believed the council should have paid. Field J. held that the council could not recover its overpayments under s.45 as it had never asked for information relating to the contributions made by the residents, and the manager had been entitled to pursue a policy of insisting that the council pay the higher fees that he thought fair. In drawing this conclusion the judge seems to have accepted that it was a relevant question whether the council could reasonably have expected the manager to have disclosed the residents' increased contributions, analogising with the approach that was formerly taken towards disclosure of material facts in cases under the (similarly worded) Social Security Administration Act 1992 s.71.[61] As previously noted, however, the Court of Appeal has denied that this is the correct approach in s.71 cases, in *B*.[62]

---

[56] If a benefit provider chooses not to pursue its legal rights in court but instead brings pressure to bear on the recipients of an overpayment by other means, e.g. by refusing to rehouse him although he is priority listed for better accommodation, then such a refusal may be ultra vires: *R. (Joseph) v Newham LBC* [2008] EWHC 1637 (Admin).

[57] DSS Research Report No.119: "Local Authorities and Benefit Overpayments" (2000) para.4.10; published online at: *http://research.dwp.gov.uk/asd/asd5/rrep119.pdf*.

[58] DSS Report, "Local Authorities and Benefit Overpayments", Ch.2.

[59] *West Sussex CC v Amberley (UK) Ltd* [2010] EWHC 651 (QB).

[60] Field J. resolved this dispute in the council's favour and his findings on this point were upheld on appeal: *Amberley* [2011] EWCA Civ 11; (2011) 14 C.C.L. Rep. 178.

[61] *Amberley* [2011] EWCA Civ 11; (2011) 14 C.C.L. Rep. 178 at [14]–[15].

[62] *B* [2005] EWCA Civ 929; [2005] 1 W.L.R. 3796; R(IS) 9/06. See text to para.23–06, fn.20.

(d) *Overpaid Tax Credits*

Statutory claims lie to recover overpaid tax credits,[63] and HMRC has a discretion **23–20** whether to recover all or some of the overpayment or to waive recovery.[64] Because overpaid tax credits are deemed by statute to be unpaid tax, HMRC may not only enforce its right to recovery by reducing the amount of future tax credits paid to the recipient, but may also resort to any of the recovery mechanisms contained in the collection and recovery provisions of the Taxes Management Act 1970 Pt VI.[65]

When the tax credit system was introduced in 2003, the method by which tax **23–21** credits are calculated meant that a large number would inevitably be overpaid in the first year; in the event, though, many more were overpaid than expected —around 1.9 million, which was a third of the total—and many millions of pounds' worth of tax credits then had to be repaid by families on low incomes who struggled to find the money. HMRC's handling of these problems was criticised in a 2005 Report by the Parliamentary Ombudsman,[66] although she welcomed HMRC's exercise of a discretion not to demand repayment in cases of hardship and the introduction of discretionary "Additional Tax Credits" or "top-up payments". These can be paid, on request, on the grounds of hardship or where there are reasons to think that a possible overpayment should not be recovered.[67] In a follow-up 2007 Report, however, she was still not satisfied that HMRC's administrative practices were achieving fair outcomes and recommended some changes to the way in which its hardship measures were implemented.[68] Subsequent changes seem to have had a good effect, since the number of complaints received about tax credits by her office during 2008/2009 was much lower than in previous years.[69]

Under its Code of Practice 26,[70] HMRC previously waived its recovery rights **23–22** only when recipients could reasonably have believed that they were entitled to overpaid tax credits; this test has now been replaced by a test which asks whether HMRC and recipients have performed certain responsibilities.[71] HMRC must give correct advice, accurately record information, and correct mistakes when told about them; claimants must give accurate information, tell HMRC about changes, tell HMRC if their award notices are wrong or incomplete, and check the amounts stated on the notices against payments received and tell HMRC if there is a disparity. If HMRC does not meet all its responsibilities and this failure causes an overpayment, and the claimant meets all his responsibilities, then

---

[63] Income and Corporation Taxes Act 1988 s.813; Tax Credits Act 2002 s.28.

[64] Tax Credits Act 2002 s.28(1).

[65] Income and Corporation Taxes Act 1988 s.813(3); Tax Credits Act 2002 s.29(3).

[66] Parliamentary and Health Service Ombudsman, *Tax Credits: Putting Things Right*, HC 124 (Third Report for Session 2005–2006); discussed in R. Kirkham, "Auditing by Stealth? Special Reports and the Ombudsman" [2005] P.L. 740.

[67] Parliamentary Report, *Tax Credits: Putting Things Right*, Chs 2 and 5.

[68] Parliamentary and Health Service Ombudsman, *Tax Credits: Getting It Wrong?*, HC 1010 (Fifth Report for Session 2006–2007) Ch.3.

[69] Parliamentary and Health Service Ombudsman, *Every Complaint Matters: Annual Report 2008–9*, HC 786 (Fourth Report for Session 2008–2009) p.5.

[70] HMRC leaflet COP26, "What Happens If We've Paid You Too Much Tax Credit?" published online at: *http://www.hmrc.gov.uk/leaflets/cop26.pdf*.

[71] HMRC, "What Happens If We've Paid too Much Tax Credit?", pp.2–5.

HMRC should not seek to recover the overpayment. If HMRC fails to apply a change of circumstances correctly and this increases an overpayment, it should not seek to recover the amount of the overpayment caused by this mistake. But if HMRC meets its responsibilities and the claimant does not, then it will normally seek recovery.

(e) Overpaid Tax Repayments

23–23   Various statutes provide for the repayment of overpaid tax, and if a miscalculation is made when calculating the amount of the repayment so that HMRC repays too much, then it is typically given a statutory right to recover the overpayment.[72] However, since the money repaid by HMRC was ex hypothesi due as tax all along, the relevant statutory sections conceptualise HMRC's right not as a right to recover its overpayment but rather as a right to recover tax that was always due. So, for example, the Taxes Management Act 1970 s.30(1) provides that "Where an amount of tax has been repaid to any person which ought not to have been repaid to him, that amount of tax may be assessed and recovered as if it were unpaid tax." This permissive wording gives HMRC a discretion whether to make an assessment but does not require it to do so.[73]

3. COMMON LAW CLAIMS

(a) Auckland Harbour Board v R.

23–24   In *Auckland Harbour Board v R.*[74] the New Zealand Minister for Railways agreed to pay the Auckland Harbour Board money in consideration for the Board's granting a lease over part of its land to a third party. This agreement was sanctioned by legislation which authorised the payment only if the Board granted the lease, and this was never done, although the payment was made. The Minister later set off the amount of the payment against other money owed to the Board, on the ground that the payment had been illegal and void. The Board sued for the amount of the set-off and the Privy Council rejected its claim, Viscount Haldane observing that[75]:

> "It has been a principle of the British Constitution now for more than two centuries, a principle which their Lordships understand to have been inherited in the Constitution of New Zealand with the same stringency, that no money can be taken out of the

---

[72] See e.g. Taxes Management Act 1970 s.30 (mistaken repayment of income tax or capital gains tax); Customs and Excise Management Act 1979 s.167(4) (overpayment made in respect of any drawback, allowance, rebate or repayment of duty); Value Added Tax Act 1994 s.73(2) (mistaken repayment of VAT) (construed in *West Devon BC v C&E Commissioners* [2001] S.T.C. 1282; *C&E Commissioners v Laura Ashley Ltd* [2003] EWHC 2832 (Ch); [2004] S.T.C. 635; and cf. *C&E Commissioners v Croydon Hotel & Leisure Co Ltd* [1996] S.T.C. 1105); Finance Act 1997 Sch.5 para.14 (mistaken repayment of excise duty, landfill tax, insurance premium tax).

[73] HMRC's decision whether to exercise this discretion can be challenged in judicial review proceedings, but the General Commissioners have no power to hold that an inspector's exercise of the discretion was unreasonable, and to substitute their own decision for his: *Guthrie (Inspector of Taxes) v Twickenham Film Studios Ltd* [2002] EWHC (Ch) 1936; [2002] S.T.C. 1374.

[74] *Auckland Harbour Board* [1924] A.C. 318.

[75] *Auckland Harbour Board* [1924] A.C. 318 at 326–327.

consolidated Fund into which the revenues of the State have been paid, excepting under a distinct authorisation from Parliament itself. The days are long gone by in which the Crown, or its servants, apart from Parliament, could give such an authorisation or ratify an improper payment. Any payment out of the consolidated fund made without Parliamentary authority is simply illegal and *ultra vires*, and may be recovered by the Government if it can, as here, be traced."

In an obiter dictum in *Woolwich*[76] Lord Goff interpreted Viscount Haldane's **23–25** reference to "tracing" in this passage to mean that a claim under the *Auckland Harbour Board* principle is "proprietary in nature", and hence that it is a prerequisite for recovery that the money or its traceable proceeds must survive in the defendant's hands at the time of the claim. However there is no reason in principle why the government should not have a personal claim to the value of the money paid, and the better view, taken in the Australian courts,[77] is that Viscount Haldane used the word "traced" in a non-technical sense here, and simply meant that the recipient of the money must be identified before a claim will lie.[78]

Viscount Haldane's statement that ultra vires payments "may" be recovered **23–26** has also been the subject of judicial comment in an Australian case. In *Director-General of Social Services v Hales*,[79] Sheppard J. stressed that there are many reasons why those charged with public administration might sensibly choose not to pursue the recipients of ultra vires payments—most obviously because they no longer have any money or because the costs of recovery would be disproportionate to the sums at stake. He held that there was "no sense" in which the *Auckland Harbour Board* case can "be said to be one which decides that action must be taken to recover moneys paid without parliamentary authority". However, he also considered that "in ordinary circumstances" the "public duty" of an official who made an unauthorised payment "would require him to take steps" for its recovery, and that it would only be "if the circumstances of the case were such as to indicate a sound reason why recovery action should not be taken that he would be justified in not acting".[80]

The constitutional principle recognised by Viscount Haldane in the *Auckland* **23–27** *Harbour Board* case breaks down into two propositions: first, that all Crown revenues, not being revenues payable into some other public fund established for a specific purpose, must be paid as soon as they are received into a consolidated fund controlled by the Treasury (more specifically, by the Comptroller and Auditor-General)[81]; and, secondly, that only Parliament can authorise the appropriation of money out of this consolidated fund.[82] The mechanisms by which this

---

[76] *Woolwich* [1993] A.C. 70 at 177.
[77] *Commonwealth of Australia v Burns* [1971] V.R. 825 at 828.
[78] Cf. Law Commission, *Restitution: Mistakes of Law and Ultra Vires Public Authority Receipts and Payments* (1994) Law Com. No.227, para.17.12.
[79] *Director-General of Social Services v Hales* (1983) 78 F.L.R. 373 (Full Ct of Fed Ct of Aus).
[80] *Hales* (1983) 78 F.L.R. 373 at 411.
[81] *Re W's Application* [1998] N.I. 19 at 27. See too *Revere Jamaica Alumina Ltd v Att Gen* (1977) 26 W.I.R. 486 at 495; *Northern Suburbs General Cemetery Reserve Trust v Commonwealth of Australia* (1993) 176 C.L.R. 555; *Australian Tape Manufacturers Association v Commonwealth of Australia* (1993) 176 C.L.R. 480.
[82] See too *New South Wales v Bardolph* (1934) 52 C.L.R. 455; *Combet v Commonwealth of Australia* [2005] HCA 61; (2005) 224 C.L.R. 494 at [44] and [232]–[235]; *R. v Secretary of State for Foreign and Commonwealth Affairs Ex p. World Development Movement Ltd* [1995] 1 W.L.R. 836; *Pape v Commissioner of Taxation* [2009] HCA 23; (2009) 238 C.L.R. 1 at [54] and following.

is done were described by the Court of Appeal in *Hooper*, which observed that two types of statute are used to authorise expenditure by government departments[83]:

> "Statutes dealing with a particular area of government make provision for specific expenditure for a defined purpose. We shall here describe these as 'specific statutes'. . . . Such statutes do not, however, of themselves provide Ministers with access to the public funds. Revenues raised by taxation or otherwise are, in general, paid into the Exchequer Account at the Bank of England, where they constitute the Consolidated Fund. Parliamentary authorisation is required for issues from the Consolidated Fund and this is provided each year by the second type of statute. A series of Consolidated Fund Bills are brought before Parliament founded upon supply resolutions. The final such Bill is the Consolidated Fund (Appropriation) Bill, which becomes the Appropriation Act. We shall describe this type of legislation as appropriation legislation. Such legislation authorises the issue to Government Departments of the funds that they have demonstrated that they require to perform their executive functions. In some instances the funds will be required to make the payments already authorised by specific statutes. In other instances the funds will be required to enable the Government Departments to make payments pursuant to prerogative or common law powers which are not the subject of any specific statute."

23-28   The court went on to observe that the question whether legislation is needed to authorise an extension of the existing powers of a Government Department was addressed in a memorandum on November 2, 1945 by Granville Ram, First Parliamentary Counsel, that is still treated by ministers as setting out the position. He concluded, first, that legislation is not legally necessary except where an extension is precluded by a previous statute either expressly or by necessary implication; but, secondly, that if the extended powers involve an annual charge extended over a period of years then legislation is not required by law, but is required by established practice formally recorded in the transactions between the Public Accounts Committee and the Treasury.

23-29   The court concluded its review of the law with the following comments:

> "Where a Minister proposes to make a payment that has been authorised by a specific statute the Court can properly review his decision to see whether, on true interpretation of the statute, the payment falls within its authorisation. If it does not, the decision to make the payment will be unlawful.[84]
>
> Where a Minister proposes to make payments in circumstances where this conflicts with the intention of Parliament, as manifested in a specific statute, the decision will be

---

[83] *Hooper* [2002] EWCA Civ 813; [2003] 1 W.L.R. 2623 at [131]–[134]; not considered on appeal [2005] UKHL 29; [2005] 1 W.L.R. 1681. See too *Secretary of State for Trade and Industry v Frid* [2004] UKHL 24; [2004] 2 A.C. 506 at [27] per Lord Hoffmann: "The constitutional accountability of the Crown to Parliament for the expenditure of public money means that, as a matter of public law, the Crown may have to deal differently with money from different sources. Part XII of the Social Security Administration Act 1992 prescribes what may be paid out of the National Insurance Fund, what must be paid in, how it must be invested and so forth. But these provisions do not . . . create a trust in private law . . . In private law the Crown through its various emanations is the beneficial owner of all central funds. If it fails to comply with the provisions which require such funds to be segregated, the remedy lies in public law." For additional discussion see J. McEldowney, "The Control of Public Expenditure" in J. Jowell and D. Oliver (eds), *The Changing Constitution*, 6th edn (Oxford: OUP, 2007), 359; A.W. Bradley and K.D. Ewing, *Constitutional and Administrative Law*, 14th edn (Harlow: Pearson, 2007), Ch.17.

[84] Citing *R. v Foreign Secretary, Ex p. World Development Movement Ltd* [1995] 1 W.L.R. 836.

unlawful as an abuse of power, even, it seems, if Parliament has authorised the issue of funds for that purpose in an appropriation statute."[85]

These last comments bear out the point made by Evans L.J. in *R. v Criminal Injuries Compensation Board Ex p. P*,[86] that where ministerial expenditure is authorised by legislation it does not follow from this that the minister is exclusively accountable to Parliament for his spending. In Evans L.J.'s words, this would mean that:

"there is a kind of Parliamentary approval which, short of having statutory effect, protects executive action by the government from being subject to the jurisdiction of the courts. In my judgment, no such hybrid exists. If [a scheme under which payments were made] had statutory authority, the courts would have power to see that the statute was properly implemented in accordance with its terms, but the validity of the statute could not be queried, unless questions arose as to its validity under European law . . . That is because 'Parliamentary supremacy over the judiciary is only exercisable by statute'.[87] The fact that Parliament makes public funds available to [a minister] for the purposes of [a] scheme, which may be revised by him from time to time, does not mean . . . that the scheme itself has force and effect as a statute. Short of statutory authority for the scheme, as distinct from the costs of funding it, there is no constitutional bar . . . to the exercise of the court's powers of judicial review."

Although the *Auckland Harbour Board* case was itself directed only to pay-   **23–30**
ments made out of the Consolidated Fund, the Law Commission has observed that the rule stated in the case cannot rationally be confined in this way. It identified the underlying reason for the rule as "the protection of public funds from unlawful dissipation",[88] and contended that in line with this consideration, all unauthorised payments of central government funds should be recoverable as of right, by virtue of their ultra vires nature.[89] The Law Commission also thought it "unlikely" that the principle would apply to local authorities or semi-state bodies.[90] However, the rationale underlying the rule applies to such bodies just as forcefully as it does to central government bodies, and in *Charles Terence Estates Ltd v Cornwall Council*,[91] Cranston J. held that rent payments made by a local authority under an ultra vires tenancy agreement were accordingly recoverable (subject to defences). Hence it is curious that the *Auckland Harbour*

---

[85] Citing *R. v Home Secretary Ex p. Fire Brigades Union* [1995] 2 A.C. 513 at 554.
[86] *R. v Criminal Injuries Compensation Board Ex p. P* [1995] 1 All E.R. 870 at 885–886 (CA).
[87] Citing *M v Home Office* [1994] 1 A.C. 377 at 395 per Lord Templeman.
[88] Law Commission, *Restitution: Mistakes of Law and Ultra Vires Public Authority Receipts and Payments*, para.17.2.
[89] Law Commission, *Restitution: Mistakes of Law and Ultra Vires Public Authority Receipts and Payments*, para.17.11: "The limitation to payments out of the Consolidated Fund, as opposed to payments out of Departmental Budgets is probably anomalous. However, once a payment has been properly appropriated from the Consolidated Fund to the spending Department, the issue of the *vires* of the payment may become significantly more complex, as many areas of Departmental expenditure will be for the discretion of the relevant Minister, out of the funds provided by Parliament."
[90] Law Commission, *Restitution: Mistakes of Law and Ultra Vires Public Authority Receipts and Payments*, para.17.11.
[91] *Charles Terence Estates Ltd v Cornwall Council* [2011] EWHC 2542 (QB) at [97], *Tauranga Borough v Tauranga Electric-power Board* [1944] N.Z.L.R. 155, where the New Zealand Court of Appeal allowed a claim to recover the value of electricity supplied by one public body to another under an ultra vires agreement.

Board rule was never identified by the courts as a ground for recovery by local authorities in the litigation of the 1990s which followed *Hazell v Hammersmith & Fulham LBC*.[92] There, interest rate swap contracts between banks and local authorities were held to be void because they were beyond the councils' statutory borrowing powers, and in the wake of this decision many claims were made to recover payments that had been made under such contracts. Because many of the contracts provided for "upfront payments" by the banks, the councils were often the "winners" of their contracts at the time when *Hazell* declared them to be void, and thus the defendants to claims by banks. But in some cases the council was the "loser", and thus the claimant,[93] and in these cases the council should have been able to invoke the *Auckland Harbour Board* rule.[94]

23–31   In *Hazell* Lord Templeman stressed that the object of the rule rendering the contracts void was "the protection of the public",[95] and in one of the swaps cases, *Guinness Mahon & Co Ltd v Kensington and Chelsea RLBC*,[96] Morritt L.J. thought that the courts should develop the law of unjust enrichment in a way that was consistent with this policy. On the facts of *Guinness Mahon*, however, the council was the winner of the swap transaction and the defendant in the case, and as Waller L.J. said,[97] quoting Leggatt L.J.'s previous comments in *Westdeutsche Landesbank Girozentale v Islington LBC*,[98] "protection of council taxpayers from loss is to be distinguished from securing a windfall for them". That is, the rule laid down in *Hazell* was designed to protect taxpayers from unauthorised expenditure of public money, a rationale which does not obviously justify giving banks the right to recover money *received* by local authorities under ultra vires contracts. However, it might be said that if policy concerns demand that a local authority should recover money paid under a losing ultra vires swaps contract, then fairness demands that it should also have to repay money received from a bank under a winning contract.[99] Also, if local authorities knew that they could recover money paid under ultra vires contracts, but keep money received, then that would give them a perverse incentive to enter such contracts, subverting the policy of the rule rendering them ultra vires.[100]

23–32   The *Auckland Harbour Board* rule clearly does apply where a payment is made from central government funds, the purported authority for which is an ultra vires statute,[101] and still more straightforwardly, where no legislation has

---

[92] *Hazell v Hammersmith & Fulham LBC* [1992] 2 A.C. 1.
[93] e.g. *South Tyneside MBC v Svenska International Plc* [1995] 1 All E.R. 545.
[94] As argued in E. O'Dell, "Incapacity" in P. Birks and F.D. Rose (eds), *Lessons of the Swaps Litigation* (Oxford: Mansfield Press, 2000), 113.
[95] *Hazell* [1992] 2 A.C. 1 at 36.
[96] *Guinness Mahon & Co Ltd v Kensington and Chelsea RLBC* [1999] Q.B. 215 at 229.
[97] *Guinness Mahon* [1999] Q.B. 215 at 233.
[98] *Westdeutsche Landesbank Girozentrale v Islington LBC* [1994] 1 W.L.R. 938 at 951 (CA).
[99] T. Krebs, *Restitution at the Crossroads: A Comparative Study* (London: Cavendish, 2001), pp.183–184, observing that "otherwise the bank would be 'punished' twice, particularly if it had 'hedged' its exposure under one swap by entering into the mirror image of it with another local authority."
[100] For further discussion, see R. Williams, *Unjust Enrichment and Public Law* (Oxford: Hart, 2010) pp.56–69, arguing that the public law ultra vires event occurring when a local authority paid out under a void swaps contract was itself a reason for restitution.
[101] As in *Breckenridge Speedway Ltd v R.* [1970] S.C.R. 175.

ever been enacted that might expressly or impliedly[102] justify the payment. A striking example is *Foroma v Minister of Public Construction and National Housing*,[103] where money was diverted by corrupt Zimbabwean public officials from a government housing scheme into a "VIP housing scheme" for which there was no Parliamentary authority. Under the VIP scheme, loans were made on generous terms to favoured applicants, including the claimant, for the purpose of building themselves luxury houses. A new permanent secretary was then appointed to the housing ministry who questioned the legality of the VIP scheme and refused to hand over occupation of the house which had been built for the claimant until the loan money was repaid. The claimant boldly sued for occupation of the property and his claim was dismissed, Smith J. holding that[104]:

"[I]rrespective of the bona fides or lack thereof on the part of the beneficiaries [of the V.I.P. scheme] and despite the ostensible authority exhibited by the minister and the then permanent secretary of the ministry the law is clear. It is the duty of [the new permanent secretary] to collect, as soon as possible, all moneys paid out on behalf of the beneficiaries of the V.I.P. housing scheme."

The *Auckland Harbour Board* principle is more often invoked in cases where **23–33** legislation has been validly enacted, but imposes qualifying conditions that are not satisfied when payment is made. *Auckland Harbour Board* was itself a case of this kind, and the point was made there by Viscount Haldane that the money was recoverable even though the Controller and Auditor-General had passed the voucher for payment: "no merely executive ratification . . . could divest [the payment] of its illegal character."[105] Another example, from New South Wales, is *Att Gen v Gray.*[106] The defendant was employed on a casual basis by the Education Department to teach school children. He was paid at the rate specified for casual teachers with a university degree when he should have been paid at the lower rate for those without such a qualification. He argued that the case did not fall within the scope of the *Auckland Harbour Board* rule, because the amounts he had received did not exceed the amounts permitted by the relevant Appropriation Act. This was rejected because this statute was not the only relevant legislation, and "other statutory provisions to safeguard the financial stability of the State [could not] be disregarded". Under the Public Service Act 1902 (NSW), the salary payable to employees in the defendant's position had to be determined

---

[102] Cf. *Steele Ford & Newton v Crown Prosecution Service (No.2)* [1994] 1 A.C. 22; followed in *R. (C) v Sevenoaks Youth Court* [2009] EWHC 3088 (Admin); [2010] 1 All E.R. 735. In both cases the court rejected the argument that Parliament had impliedly authorised the courts to make costs orders out of central funds.

[103] *Foroma v Minister of Public Construction and National Housing* [1997] 4 L.R.C. 174 (Zimbabwe High Ct).

[104] *Foroma* [1997] 4 L.R.C. 174 at 188. At 191 he added that the Treasury also had a duty "to ensure that strenuous measures are taken to recover the moneys due to the state and that it concurs with the steps taken by the ministry to do so."

[105] *Auckland Harbour Board* [1924] A.C. 318 at 326 (PC).

[106] *Att Gen v Gray* [1977] 1 N.S.W.L.R. 406 (NSW CA). See too *Commonwealth of Australia v Hamilton* (1977) 139 C.L.R. 362, where the disputed payments had been authorised on the facts, but where McPherson A.C.J. stressed at 388 that recovery would follow in cases where the operation of a statutory authority "is made to depend on the fulfilment of a statutory condition that is not satisfied" or where the recipient does not possess "a particular statutory characteristic or qualification that would entitle him to payment."

from time to time by the Public Service Board, and the only salary properly payable to the defendant was at the lower rate which had been determined by the Board to be appropriate for teachers in his grading.

23–34   It may be that the scope of the *Auckland Harbour Board* rule will come to be considered in future cases where payments have been made contrary to the European law on state aid, contained in art.88 (ex art.93) of the EC Treaty.[107] Where the Commission finds that State aid has been unlawfully paid, it must order the relevant Member State to recover the payment plus interest,[108] and if the Member State fails to comply then this may lead to infraction proceedings.[109] The sums involved in state aid cases can be very large—for example, €3 billion plus compound interest in the German *Landesbanken* cases in 2004[110]—but by comparison with other major EU Member States, the United Kingdom has not been obliged to bring many actions to recover unlawful state aid payments to date.[111] In the event that it must bring such proceedings in the future, the courts may have to consider whether English law provides mechanisms to allow the immediate and effective implementation of the Commission's recovery decision,

---

[107] For general discussion see A. Jones, *Restitution and European Community Law* (London: LLP, 2000), Ch.5; T Köster, "Recovery of Unlawful State Aid" in M.S. Rydelski (ed.), *The EC State Aid Regime: Distortive Effects of State Aid on Competition and Trade* (London: Cameron May, 2006), 653; M. Angeli, "The European Commission's 'New Policy' on State Aid Control: Some Reflections on Public and Private Enforcement of Recovery of Illegal Aid" (2009) 30 E.C.L.R. 533.

[108] Council Regulation (EC) No.659/1999 of March 22, 1999 laying down detailed rules for the application of Article 93 [now Article 88] of the EC Treaty [1999] OJ L.83/1, art.14(1). Where unlawful State aid has been paid, the Commission need not give specific reasons to justify the exercise of its power to require Member States to order repayment: *Spain v Commission* (Joined Cases C–278/92, C–279/02 and C–280/92) [1994] E.C.R. I–4103 at [78]; *P&O European Ferries (Vizcaya) SA v and Diputacion Foral de Vizcaya v Commission* (Joined Cases T–116/01 and T–118/01) [2003] E.C.R. II–2957 at [224].

[109] The only defence to infraction proceedings is the "absolute impossibility" of recovering the money: e.g. *Commission v Italy* (C–280/95) [1998] E.C.R. I–259 at [13]; *Commission v Belgium* (C–378/98) [2001] E.C.R. I–5107 at [30]; *Commission v Greece* (C–415/03) [2005] E.C.R. I–3875. The risk of driving the recipient into insolvency cannot be invoked as a reason to escape the recovery obligation: *Commission v Belgium* (C–52/84) [1986] E.C.R. 89; *Commission v Spain* (C–499/99) [2002] E.C.R. I–6031; and for discussion see A. Fort, "State Aid Control and Insolvency", online at: *http://www.insol-europe.org/downloads/congress/2003/Insol_Cork_full_paper.pdf.*

[110] Commission Decision C(2004)3924/3 of October 20, 2004 (*L.B. Berlin*); Commission Decision C(2004)3925/3 of October 20, 2004 (*West L.B.*); Commission Decision C(2004)3926/3 of October 20, 2004 (*Nord L.B.*); Commission Decision C(2004)3927/3 of October 20, 2004 (*Bayern L.B.*); Commission Decision C(2004)3928/3 of October 20, 2004 (*Hamb. L.B.*); Commission Decision C(2004)3930/3 of October 20, 2004 (*L.B. Holstein*); Commission Decision C(2004)3931fin of October 20, 2004 (*He. La. Ba.*).

[111] Jones Day, Lovells, and Allen & Overy, "Study on the Enforcement of State Aid Law at National Level" (2006) p.467; this study for the DG Competition is published online at: *http://ec.europa.eu/competition/state_aid/studies_reports/studies_reports.html.* The best known example is *DTI v British Aerospace Plc* [1991] 1 C.M.L.R. 165, which was stayed while the ECJ examined the case; the ECJ found for British Aerospace on procedural grounds: *British Aerospace and Rover v Commission* (C–294/90) [1992] E.C.R. I–493; but the Commission then followed the art.88(2) procedure correctly and found that £44.4 million of illegal State aid had been paid; this money was repaid with interest and the initial High Court proceedings discontinued: *Hansard*, HC Debs, May 26, 1993, col.580. Another example is the Commission Decision of 11.02.2009 (*BT Group Plc*); appeal to General Court pending: (T–226/09) *British Telecommunications v Commission* and (T–230/09) *BT Pension Scheme Trustees v Commission*; and see too the Pension Protection Fund and Occupational Pension Schemes (Miscellaneous Amendments) Regulations 2010 (SI 2010/196), responding to the Commission's decision.

as required by art.14(3) of Regulation 659/1999. This might bring some out-standing questions about the scope of the *Auckland Harbour Board* rule into sharper focus—for example, whether recipients should be allowed a change of position defence. This question is discussed elsewhere,[112] but it may be noted here that EU law currently leaves the recipients of unlawful state aid with little room to argue that the principles of legitimate expectation and legal certainty entitle them to keep the money.[113]

(b) *Other Grounds for Recovery*

The common law of unjust enrichment provides several other grounds for recovery on which a public authority might conceivably rely to recover an ultra vires payment. Payments by mistake of fact have long been recoverable, and payments by mistake of law have been recoverable since the bar against recovery on this ground was removed in *Kleinwort Benson Ltd v Lincoln CC*.[114] Where benefits have been paid under an ultra vires contract, failure of basis is another possible ground, and there is some authority for the view that "absence of consideration" is a third,[115] although there are good reasons for thinking that this really amounts to failure of basis under another name.[116] **23–35**

It is generally assumed that a public body can rely on these reasons for restitution in exactly the same way as a private individual who has made a mistaken payment, or paid money on an agreed basis that has failed to materi-alise. However some doubt has been cast on this assumption by *Kingstreet Investments Ltd v New Brunswick (Department of Finance)*,[117] where the Supreme Court of Canada held that claims to recover money paid as tax which was not due should not be understood as claims in unjust enrichment, but as sui generis restitutionary claims "based on the constitutional principle that taxes should not be levied without proper authority".[118] Bastarache J. considered this to be a more apt characterisation because such claims raise "important constitu-tional principles which would be ignored by treating the claim [as a private law restitutionary claim founded on unjust enrichment or wrongdoing]".[119] *Kingstreet Investments* concerned a claim *against* a public authority, but the same **23–36**

---

[112] See para.27–52.
[113] See e.g. *Land Rheinland-Pfalz v Alcan Deutschland GmbH* (C–24/95) [1997] E.C.R. I–1591. But for the view that there is more scope for legitimate expectations arguments than has been thought, see A. Giraud, "A Study of the Notion of Legitimate Expectations in State Aid Recovery Proceedings: 'Abandon All Hope, Ye Who Enter Here'?" (2009) 45 *Common Market Law Review* 1399; P. Anestis and E. Psaraki, "State Aid: Some Issues with Regard to Execution of Commission's Recovery Decisions" [2009] *Global Competition Review*, Oct. Supp. (*The European Antitrust Review* 2009) 42.
[114] *Kleinwort Benson Ltd v Lincoln CC* [1999] 2 A.C. 349; discussed at paras 9–71—9–94.
[115] *Westdeutsche* [1994] 4 All E.R. 890 at 930; *Guinness Mahon* [1999] Q.B. 215 at 230 and 239–240 (CA).
[116] Cf. *Haugesund Kommune v Depfa ACS Bank* [2009] EWHC 2277 (Comm); [2010] Lloyd's Rep. P.N. 21 at [142]. Failure of basis as a ground for recovery where benefits have been transferred under a void contract is discussed at paras 13–20—13–27.
[117] *Kingstreet Investments* [2007] SCC 1; [2007] 1 S.C.R. 3.
[118] *Kingstreet Investments* [2007] SCC 1; [2007] 1 S.C.R. 3 at [33].
[119] *Kingstreet Investments* [2007] SCC 1; [2007] 1 S.C.R. 3 at [34].

reasoning might equally lead one to the conclusion that claims by public authorities to recover ultra vires payments should not form part of the private law of unjust enrichment either, and that the courts would do better to build on the *Auckland Harbour Board* case to develop a sui generis public law right of action, or at least a hybrid right of action where the (private) law of unjust enrichment defines the enrichment and expense elements of the claim, while the reason for restitution, or unjust factor, is simply the ultra vires event, as determined by public law principles.

23-37   It currently seems unlikely, however, that the English courts will develop the law in this way, given that in *Deutsche Morgan Grenfell*,[120] the House of Lords rejected the opportunity to make similar findings to those made in *Kingstreet Investments*. The claimant sought to recover the use value of money paid as tax that was not due, and to found its action on the ground of mistake, rather than on the rule in *Woolwich*,[121] so as to take advantage of a limitation rule that applies only to claims for mistaken payments. In its defence the Revenue argued that facts which would support an action on *Woolwich* grounds must be litigated as such, and may not be relied on to support an action on some other ground, such as mistake. This was rejected by the House of Lords, which held that the Revenue is subject to the same private law causes of action as a private individual. Their Lordships recognised that significant differences exist between tax payments and "private transactions",[122] but held that their decision was mandated by "the constitutional principle of equality", by which they meant that "under the rule of law, the Crown (that is the executive government in its various emanations) is in general subject to the same common law obligations as ordinary citizens."[123]

---

[120] *Deutsche Morgan Grenfell* [2006] UKHL 49; [2007] 1 A.C. 558.
[121] *Woolwich* [1993] A.C. 70.
[122] *Deutsche Morgan Grenfell* [2007] 1 A.C. 558 at [13], [33] and [49].
[123] *Deutsche Morgan Grenfell* [2007] 1 A.C. 558 at [132]–[133] per Lord Walker. *Kingstreet Investments* and *Deutsche Morgan Grenfell* are discussed further at paras 22–27—22–31.

CHAPTER 24

LEGAL INCAPACITY

1. INTRODUCTION

In everyday English, the word "person" generally means "human being" but in **24–01** legal usage, the word denotes a subject of legal rights and duties.[1] English law recognises two categories of persons in this legal sense: "natural persons" (now only human beings) and "artificial persons" (including states, international organisations, public bodies, religious bodies, and private associations). Many legal theorists have written on the nature of legal personality, and have considered such questions as whether this entails something more than the possession of a set of duty-owing, right-owning capacities, and whether the possession of such capacities is only a legal construct or can derive from some extra-legal source.[2]

The English courts and legislature have not committed themselves to any **24–02** particular jurisprudential theory of legal personality, and they often decide the question whether a particular human being or artificial entity possesses the capacity to own particular rights or owe particular duties on a case-by-case basis. However, they are apt to assume that certain capacities are "normally attendant on legal personality",[3] and this can lead them to hold that a human being or artificial entity known to possess some legal capacities, and therefore to be a legal person, must necessarily possess other legal capacities as well, when this is a question that should more properly be decided from first principles each time.[4]

Despite these problems, it is clear that Parliament and the courts have deemed **24–03** certain human and artificial persons to lack the capacity to enter certain types of transaction, as a means of implementing various protective policies. And in the event that such a person enters such a transaction, and thereby benefits a defendant, the court will order restitution of the benefit on the ground of unjust enrichment if that would serve the policy objectives of the rule invalidating the transaction.

In the previous chapter we discussed one group of claims conforming to this **24–04** pattern, namely claims by public bodies to recover ultra vires payments. In this

---

[1] *Deutsche Genossenschaftsbank v Burnhhope* [1995] 1 W.L.R. 1580 at 1588.
[2] For a clear summary of the standpoints that have been taken on these and other issues, see R.W.M. Dias, *Jurisprudence* (London: Butterworths, 1985), pp.265–270.
[3] *NUGMW v Gillian* [1946] K.B. 81 at 86 per Scott L.J. See too *Bonsor v Musicians Union* [1954] Ch. 479 at 507–508; *Clark v University of Lincolnshire and Humberside* [2000] 1 W.L.R. 1988 at [11]; *Shrewsbury & Atcham BC v Secretary of State for Communities & Local Government* [2008] EWCA Civ 148; [2008] 3 All E.R. 548 at [73].
[4] Examples are given in L. Sealy, "Perception and Policy in Company Law Reform" in D. Feldman and F. Meisel (eds), *Corporate and Commercial Law: Modern Developments* (London: LLP, 1996), 11, pp.16–20.

chapter we discuss further claims of the same type, namely claims by the mentally incapable, claims by minors, and claims by companies acting beyond their powers, to recover benefits conferred under contracts that they lacked the legal capacity to enter. We also discuss claims to recover payments by companies that are contrary to the capital maintenance rules or contrary to the rules of the statutory insolvency regime. It is convenient to examine these rules here, although they are not concerned with corporate capacity in a strict sense—i.e. they do not concern the extent of a company's powers in its memorandum, and are instead concerned with particular types of transaction which they deem to be legally ineffective.

24–05   It has been said that restitutionary recovery of benefits by a legally incapable claimant is based on the fact that the claimant "does not truly intend to benefit the defendant".[5] However it is not true of all the cases that the claimant cannot form an unimpaired intention to benefit the defendant—many minors are able to do this, for example. Hence a sounder approach is to ask whether the policy that underlies the rule deeming the claimant to lack legal capacity also dictates that he should have restitution, regardless of whether his intention to benefit the defendant was actually impaired.[6] This policy calculation is similar to that which is undertaken in cases where benefits have been transferred under illegal transactions, as discussed in Ch.25.

24–06   While this chapter concerns claims in unjust enrichment by legally incapable claimants, the situation can also arise, where a claimant confers benefits on a legally incapable defendant, and the defendant seeks to rely on his incapacity as a defence to a claim brought against him, for example, on the ground of mistake or failure of basis. This is discussed in Ch.34.

2. MENTAL INCAPACITY

24–07 Under the Mental Capacity Act 2005 s.16:

> "[A] person lacks capacity in relation to a matter if at the material time he is unable to make a decision for himself in relation to the matter because of an impairment of, or a disturbance in the functioning of, the mind or brain."

Early authority held that a contract entered by a mentally incapable person was void,[7] but the modern rule is that the contract is generally voidable at his instance, provided that the other contracting party knew of his mental incapacity. There is still one situation, though, where the contract is void, namely where the affairs of the mental incompetent have been placed in the hands of the Court of Protection or a "deputy" of the court appointed under the Mental Capacity Act 2005 s.16. In this case, it would interfere with the control exercised by the court

---

[5] A. Burrows, *The Law of Restitution*, 3rd edn (Oxford: OUP, 2011), p.310.
[6] J. Edelman and E. Bant, *Unjust Enrichment in Australia* (Melbourne: OUP, 2006), p.301.
[7] *Thompson v Leach* (1689) 3 Mod. 301; 87 E.R. 199; *Yates v Boen* (1739) 2 Str. 1104; 93 E.R. 1060; *Gore v Gibson* (1845) 13 M. & W. 623; 153 E.R. 260.

if the transaction were allowed to stand, even if it were entered at a time when the mentally incapable person understood what he was doing.[8]

Where a mentally incapable claimant retains control of his own affairs, the situation is governed by *Imperial Loan Co v Stone*, where Lord Esher M.R. said that he can only set aside a contract with a person of sound mind in the following circumstances[9]: **24–08**

> "When a person enters into a contract, and afterwards alleges that he was so insane at the time that he did not know what he was doing, and proves the allegation, the contract is as binding on him in every respect, whether it is executory or executed, as if he has been sane when he made it, unless he can prove further that the person with whom he contracted knew him to be so insane as not to be capable of understanding what he was about."

This rule is arguably too harsh to the mentally incapable person, and it can be contrasted with the rule governing minors' contracts, considered in the next part, where it makes no difference whether the defendant knows that the claimant is a minor.[10] The difference of approach taken in these two groups of cases might possibly be justified on the basis that mental incapacity is harder to detect than minority because it is a matter of medical opinion rather than an objectively verifiable fact.[11] However, it is noticeable that the Canadian courts hold contracts entered by a mental incapable person to be voidable, although the other party has no notice of his incapacity, when their terms are unfair.[12] This was also the position taken by the New Zealand Court of Appeal in *Archer v Cutler*[13] and *O'Connor v Hart*,[14] but in the latter case, the Privy Council overruled both decisions and affirmed Lord Esher's earlier statement of the law in *Imperial Loan*, Lord Brightman ruling that[15]: **24–09**

> "The validity of a contract entered into by a lunatic who is ostensibly sane is to be judged by the same standards as a contract by a person of sound mind, and is not voidable by the lunatic or his representatives by reason of 'unfairness' unless such unfairness amounts to equitable fraud which would have enabled the complaining party to avoid the contract even if he had been sane."

---

[8] *Re Walker* [1905] 1 Ch. 160; *Rourke v Halford* (1916) 31 D.L.R. 371 (Ontario CA); *Re Marshall* [1920] 1 Ch. 284; *Monticello State Bank v Baillee* (1922) 66 D.L.R. 494 (Alberta CA); and cf. *Re Oppenheim's WT* [1950] Ch. 633.

[9] *Imperial Loan Co v Stone* [1892] 1 Q.B. 599 at 601. See also *Neill v Morley* (1804) 9 Ves. Jun. 478; 32 E.R. 687; *Ball v Mannin* (1829) 3 Bli. N.S. 1; 4 E.R. 1241; *Selby v Jackson* (1843) 6 Beav. 192; 49 E.R. 799; *Molton v Camroux* (1848) 2 Ex. 487; 154 E.R. 584; *York Glass Co Ltd v Jubb* (1925) 134 L.T. 36; *Manches v Trimborn* (1946) 115 L.J.K.B. 305.

[10] H. Goudy, "Contracts by Lunatics" (1901) 17 L.Q.R. 147; cf. R. Wilson, "Lunacy in Relation to Contract, Tort and Crime" (1902) 18 L.Q.R. 21.

[11] Burrows, *The Law of Restitution*, pp.315–316.

[12] *Fyckes v Chisholm* (1911) 3 O.W.N. 21 (Ontario High Ct); *Wilson v R.* [1938] S.C.R. 317; *Hardman v Falk* [1955] 3 D.L.R. 128 (British Columbia CA).

[13] *Archer v Cutler* [1980] 1 N.Z.L.R. 386.

[14] *O'Connor v Hart* [1984] 2 N.Z.L.R. 754.

[15] *Hart v O'Connor* [1985] A.C. 1000, restrictively interpreting earlier English dicta, on which the New Zealand Court of Appeal had relied; see, in particular, *Molton* (1848) 2 Ex. 487 at 502–503; 154 E.R. 584 at 591 per Pollock C.B. See too *Gibbons v Wright* (1954) 91 C.L.R. 423.

24–10   Although *Imperial Loan* concerned a claim to rescind an executory contract, *Archer* and *Hart* were both claims to rescind an executed contract and recover benefits conferred thereunder, and it is clear that a restitutionary remedy is available provided that the defendant knew of the claimant's mental incapacity. An example from the Ontario Court of Appeal is *Rourke v Halford*,[16] where a mentally incapable person was able to recover money given to a niece and nephew, and it was also said that the money could be traced into land which they had bought and liens imposed on this land to secure their restitutionary liabilities.[17]

24–11   There is no requirement that the basis on which the benefit was transferred must have totally failed, as there is for claims by minors, as we discuss in the next section. However, where a mentally incapable person has the right to rescind, he must be able to make *restitutio in integrum*.[18]

24–12   A drunkard, who enters into a contract while drunk, is apparently in the same position as a mentally incapable person.[19]

3. MINORS

24–13   A minor, known in the past as an "infant", is a person who has not yet reached the age of 18.[20] There are two classes of minor. A minor who has not yet reached the "age of understanding" probably cannot make a contract at all.[21] But a minor who has reached such an age has a limited contractual capacity. It is with minors of the latter sort that the cases are principally concerned.

24–14   The general rule is that a contract does not bind a minor unless he ratifies it after he comes of age.[22] However the common law rule is subject to certain exceptions. First, contracts for necessaries and certain other cognate transactions impose some form of liability on minors. It is debatable whether this liability is contractual or derives from the law of unjust enrichment, a point that we consider immediately below. Secondly, contracts which confer an interest in property on the minor and which impose on him obligations of a continuous or recurring nature are regarded as binding on the minor, unless he repudiates them and disclaims the property either before or within a reasonable time of coming of age.[23]

---

[16] *Rourke v Halford* (1916) 31 D.L.R. 371.

[17] *Rourke* (1916) 31 D.L.R. 371 at 376.

[18] *Niell v Morley* (1804) 9 Ves. Jun. 478; 32 E.R. 687; *Molton* (1849) 4 Ex. 17; 154 E.R. 1107; *Wilson v R.* [1938] S.C.R. 317.

[19] There is very little authority, but see *Gore v Gibson* (1845) 13 M. & W. 623; 153 E.R. 260; *Molton* (1849) 4 Ex. 17 at 19; 154 E.R. 1107 at 1109 per Patteson J.; *Matthews v Baxter* (1873) L.R. 8 Ex. 132; *Bawlf Grain Co v Ross* (1917) 55 S.C.R. 232; *Gibbons* (1954) 91 C.L.R. 423 at 442; *Blomley v Ryan* (1956) 99 C.L.R. 362; Sale of Goods Act 1979 s.3(2).

[20] Family Law Reform Act 1969 s.1. By s.9 a person now attains a particular age at the commencement of the relevant anniversary of his or her birth.

[21] *Johnson v Clark* [1908] 1 Ch. 303 at 311–312 per Parker J. See too *R. v Oldham MBC Ex p. Garlick* (1992) 24 H.L.R. 726 at 741–742.

[22] *Nash v Inman* [1908] 2 K.B. 1 at 12 per Buckley L.J.

[23] *North Western Railway Co v M'Michael* (1850) 5 Ex. 114; 155 E.R. 49; *Lovell & Christmas v Beauchamp* [1894] A.C. 607 at 611 per Lord Herschell.

A minor is under some liability to pay for necessaries. These are goods and **24–15**
services that are "fit to maintain the [minor] in the state, station and degree in
life" in which he moves.[24] According to circumstances they can include food and
clothing,[25] shelter,[26] medical services[27] and the provision of education.[28] In the
case of necessary goods, as distinct from services, it has been said that his
liability only arises in the law of unjust enrichment.[29] If that is correct, then it
follows that the minor cannot be bound by an executory contract for necessary
goods. Those who argue for this interpretation of the law usually rely upon the
following dictum of Fletcher Moulton L.J. in *Nash v Inman*[30]:

> "An infant, like a lunatic,[31] is incapable of making a contract of purchase in the strict
> sense of the words; but if a man satisfies the need of the infant or lunatic by supplying
> to him necessaries, the law will imply an obligation to repay him for the services so
> rendered, and will enforce the obligation against the estate of the infant or lunatic. The
> consequence is that the basis of the action is hardly contract. Its real foundation is an
> obligation which the law imposes on the infant to make a fair payment in respect of
> needs satisfied. In other words, the obligation arises *re* and not *consensu*."

Fletcher Moulton L.J.'s dictum apparently derives support from the rule that a **24–16**
minor is only liable to pay a reasonable sum for necessary goods, as provided by
the Sale of Goods Act 1979 s.3(2). If the basis of his liability is contractual, then
he should have to pay the contract price. Section 3(2) does not, however, exclude
the possibility of liability being contractual. For it has long been the law that
contracts for necessaries only bind a minor if they are for his benefit.[32] If such
contracts contain terms onerous to him, then they will not bind him unless, in
spite of these terms, the contracts are beneficial to him. It follows that a minor
will not, in any case, be bound by a contract for necessaries for which more than
a reasonable price is charged. Nor does s.3(2) of the Sale of Goods Act 1979
affect the position. Its provisions are consistent with the view that a minor may
be liable on an executory contract for necessaries, provided that the terms are not
onerous to him. A minor's contract to buy necessary goods for less than a
reasonable price is surely valid.

The weight of authority is against the view that a minor's liability for neces- **24–17**
saries is always in unjust enrichment. Apart from two 17th century cases, in

---

[24] *Peters v Fleming* (1840) 6 M. & W. 42 at 47; 151 E.R. 314 at 315 per Parke B.
[25] *Russel v Lee* (1661) 1 Lev. 86 at 86–87; 83 E.R. 310 at 310.
[26] *Duncomb v Tickridge* (1648) Aleyne 94 at 94; 82 E.R. 933 at 933; *Soon v Watson* (1962) 33 D.L.R.
(2d) 428 at 434.
[27] *Dale v Copping* (1610) 1 Bulst. 39 at 39; 80 E.R. 743 at 743.
[28] *Minister for Education v Oxwell* [1966] W.A.R. 39.
[29] Sir J. Miles, "The Infant's Liability for Necessaries" (1927) 43 L.Q.R. 389; W.A. Keener, *A
Treatise on the Law of Quasi-Contracts* (New York, NY: Baker, Voorhis and Co, 1893), pp.20–22.
Winfield did not make up his mind: Sir P.H. Winfield, *The Law of Quasi-Contracts* (London: Sweet
& Maxwell, 1952), pp.108–109.
[30] *Nash v Inman* [1908] 2 K.B. 1 at 8; and his dicta in *Re J* [1909] 1 Ch. 574 at 577. See also
Pontypridd Union v Drew [1927] 1 K.B. 214 at 220 per Scrutton L.J.
[31] This reference to the "lunatic" is not altogether happy. It is probable that a mentally incapable
person can make a valid contract of purchase: see para.24–08. *Re Rhodes* (1890) 44 Ch. D. 94, upon
which Fletcher Moulton L.J. relies, is a case of necessitous intervention (for which, see generally
Ch.18).
[32] *Clements v London & North Western Railway Co* [1894] 2 Q.B. 482; *Fawcett v Smethurst* (1914)
84 L.J.K.B. 473.

which it was held that a minor would be liable on an executory contract for necessary goods,[33] in more recent years Buckley L.J. has said that[34]:

> "The plaintiff when he sues the defendant for necessary goods supplied during infancy, is suing him in contract on the footing that the contract was such as the infant, notwithstanding infancy, could make. The defendant, although he was an infant, had a limited capacity to contract. In order to maintain his action the plaintiff must prove that the contract sued on is within that limited capacity. The rule as regards liability for necessaries may, I think, be thus stated: an infant may contract for supply at a reasonable price of articles reasonably necessary for his support in his station in life if he has not already a sufficient supply."

24–18   It has also been usual since the time of Coke to speak of beneficial contracts of service together with contracts for necessary goods as contracts for necessaries[35]; and, more recently, the Court of Appeal has decided[36] that the two types of contract, for necessary services and goods, are similar, and that such contracts, though executory, are binding on a minor provided they are not onerous to him. Thus it is not easy to support a distinction between contracts for necessary goods and for necessary services. To do so, moreover, would introduce an anomaly into the law.[37]

24–19   The rule at common law appears, therefore, to be that a contract for necessaries, whether for goods or for services, will bind a minor provided that it is not on balance onerous to him.[38] If, however, it is burdensome to the minor, then it will not bind him, although he will be liable to pay a reasonable price for necessary goods or services received by him thereunder.

24–20   It has been held that a minor is only entitled to recover money paid under a contract which he elects to avoid if he can show that the the basis on which he made the payment has totally failed. In *Steinberg v Scala (Leeds) Ltd*[39] the claimant, a minor, was allotted shares in the defendant company, on which she paid the full amount due. Eighteen years later, while still a minor, she repudiated the contract for the purchase of the shares and sought to recover from the defendant company the money she had paid for them. The Court of Appeal held

---

[33] *Ive v Charter* (1619) Cro. Jac. 560; 79 E.R. 480; *Delavel v Clare* (1652) Latch. 156; see also Y.B. 18 Edw.II f. 2 pl. 7 (debt). The same view seems to have been taken by the court in *Dale* (1610) 1 Bulst. 39; 80 E.R. 743.

[34] *Nash* [1908] 2 K.B. 1 at 12. See also *Stocks v Wilson* [1913] 2 K.B. 235 at 242 per Lush J.; *Doyle v White City Stadium Ltd* [1935] 1 K.B. 110 at 122–124 per Lord Hanworth M.R.

[35] Co. Litt. f. 172a; *Walter v Everard* [1891] 2 Q.B. 369. See also *Manby v Scott* (1663) 1 Sid. 109 at 112; 82 E.R. 1000 at 1003; Sir W.S. Holdsworth, "Unjustifiable Enrichment" (1939) 55 L.Q.R. 37, p.47.

[36] *Roberts v Gray* [1913] 1 K.B. 520; see, particularly, Lord Cozens-Hardy M.R. at 525–526: "as early as Lord Coke . . . it has been held that an infant's contract for necessaries is binding, and it was laid down by him that that doctrine also applied not merely to bread, cheese and clothes, but to education and instruction." Cf. *Chaplin v Leslie Frewin (Publishers) Ltd* [1966] Ch. 71: para.24–24.

[37] P.H. Winfield, "Necessaries under the Sale of Goods Act 1893" (1942) 58 L.Q.R. 82, p.95.

[38] *Doyle v White City Stadium Ltd* [1935] 1 K.B. 110.

[39] *Steinberg v Scala (Leeds) Ltd* [1923] 2 Ch. 452. See also *Austern v Gervas* (1703) Hob. 77; 80 E.R. 226; *Holmes v Blogg* (1818) 8 Taunt. 508; 129 E.R. 481; *Re Burrows and Ruddock* (1856) 8 De G.M. & G. 254; 44 E.R. 388; *Everitt v Wilkins* (1874) 29 L.T. 846.

that she was not entitled to recover because there had been no total failure of basis.[40]

In our view, it is inappropriate for the court to require a minor to prove a total **24–21** failure of basis as a pre-requisite for recovery. As we discuss elsewhere, the total failure requirement should be jettisoned in all cases where recovery is sought on the ground of failure of basis[41]; but in any case we do not consider that a minor should need to rely on failure of basis as a ground of recovery in cases of this sort, as the protective policies that underlie the rule invalidating the contract should also provide the minor with a policy-based reason for restitution. As Lord Millett once wrote, extra-judicially, "If the transaction is *ultra vires* the party at whose expense the property was provided, then incapacity is a sufficient ground for restitution."[42] And in Andrew Burrows' words:

> "[T]he policy justification for allowing minors out of contracts—that the minor's consent should not count because one needs to protect the young against foolishness and poor judgement—should surely be fully carried over to restitution of an unjust enrichment."[43]

Hence we consider that the question in *Steinberg* should not have been whether the basis for the payments had totally failed, but whether the claimant could have made *restitutio in integrum*. A minor who cannot restore the status quo ante should be unable to avoid the contract; but if he has restored the status quo, then he should be able to avoid the contract and recover benefits conferred thereunder. Moreover, as we discuss in Ch.31, the courts should always take a flexible approach to the question whether counter-restitution is possible, allowing claimants to pay the money value of goods and services received without insisting on precise counter-restitution *in specie*.

Support for the first of these views can be found in *Valentini v Canali*,[44] where **24–22** the contract was void under s.1 of the Infants' Relief Act 1874.[45] The claimant, while a minor, agreed to become the tenant of the defendant's house and to pay £102 for the furniture. He paid £68 on account for the furniture and occupied the premises and used the furniture for some months. A Divisional Court held that

---

[40] cf. *Corpe v Overton* (1833) 10 Bing. 252 at 258; 131 E.R. 901 at 904 per Bosanquet J.; *Hamilton v Vaughan-Sherrin Electrical Engineering Co* [1894] 3 Ch. 589; doubted in *Steinberg* [1932] 2 Ch. 452 at 460, 462 and 465. Australian authorities requiring a total failure of basis are: *English v Gibbs* (1888) 9 L.R. (N.S.W.) 455; *Woolf v Associated Finance Pty Ltd* [1956] V.L.R. 51.

[41] See paras 12–16—12–23.

[42] P.J. Millett, "Restitution and Constructive Trusts" (1998) 114 L.Q.R. 399, p.411, adding that "If . . . [the transaction] is merely *ultra vires* the recipient, then some other ground must be found."

[43] Burrows, *The Law of Restitution*, pp.313–314. See too *Zouch v Parsons* (1765) 3 Burr. 1794 at 1801; 97 E.R. 1103 at 1107–1108 per Lord Mansfield: "miserable must the condition of minors be; excluded from the society and commerce of the world; deprived of necessaries, education, employment, and many advantages; if they could do no binding acts. Great inconvenience must arise to others, if they were bound by no act. The law, therefore, at the same time that it protects their imbecility and indiscretion from injury through their own imprudence, enables them to do binding acts, for their own benefit . . . "

[44] *Valentini v Canali* (1889) 24 Q.B.D. 166; see G.H. Treitel, "The Infants' Relief Act 1894" (1957) 73 L.Q.R. 194, pp.202–205; P.S. Atiyah, "The Infants' Relief Act 1894: A Reply" (1958) 74 L.Q.R. 97, pp.101–103.

[45] The 1874 Act was abrogated by the Minors' Contracts Act 1987.

he was not entitled to recover the £68. Lord Coleridge C.J., with whose judgment Bowen L.J. concurred, said[46]:

> "When an infant has paid for something and has consumed or used it, it is contrary to natural justice that he should recover back the money which he has paid. Here the infant plaintiff who claimed to recover back the money which he had paid to the defendant had had the use of a quantity of furniture for some months. He could not give back his benefit or replace the defendant in the position in which he was before the contract."

24–23   This passage seems to indicate that a restitutionary claim would have succeeded if the minor had not used or consumed the goods in such a way as to make restitutio in integrum impossible. Hence we would support the court's reasoning to the extent that it did not insist on a total failure of basis, although we consider that it took too narrow a view of the claimant's ability to make counter-restitution by paying the money value of benefits received. The court's approach was not, however, adopted in *Pearce v Brain*,[47] although the court purported to follow *Valentini*. The claimant, a minor, exchanged his motorcycle and sidecar for the defendant's motor car. The motor car only went 70 miles before it broke down. The claimant then repudiated the contract on the grounds of his minority and claimed the return of the motorcycle and sidecar or its value. A Divisional Court held that the contract of exchange was void under s.1 of the Act, and that, in this context, no distinction could be drawn between recovery of money and recovery of a chattel. In both cases there must be a total failure of consideration before recovery will be allowed; on the facts of the case, however, there was no total failure of consideration and the claimant's action therefore failed.

24–24   Further uncertainty has been caused by the Court of Appeal's decision in *Chaplin v Leslie Frewin (Publishers) Ltd.*[48] A minor contracted with the defendant publishers to deliver the manuscript of his memoirs. Having delivered it, he subsequently regretted his decision. He then sought an interlocutory injunction to restrain the defendants from publishing the manuscript on the grounds that the contract was not for his benefit and that the copyright of the manuscript was still vested in him. He succeeded before the trial judge but failed before the Court of Appeal. The Court of Appeal held that the contract was for his benefit and was therefore binding on him[49]; and that, even if it were not, he could not recover the copyright transferred under the contract. In Danckwerts L.J.'s opinion:

> "[I]f an infant revokes a contract, the property and interest which have been previously transferred by him cannot be recovered by the infant . . . The transfers of property made by [the infant] remain effective against him, even if the contract is otherwise revocable."[50]

---

[46] *Valentini* (1889) 24 Q.B.D. 166 at 167.
[47] *Pearce v Brain* [1929] 2 K.B. 310.
[48] *Chaplin v Leslie Frewin (Publishers) Ltd* [1966] Ch. 71. (The case was later compromised: *The Times*, February 16, 1966.)
[49] Lord Denning M.R. dissented on this point. The minor had in fact received some advance royalties.
[50] *Chaplin* [1966] Ch. 71 at 94, adopting counsel's argument.

Although Winn L.J. seemed to regard the matter as turning more on the construction of the Copyright Act 1956 ss.36 and 37, he expressed his general agreement with the judgment of Danckwerts L.J.

Lord Denning M.R., who dissented in part, did not regard the particular **24–25** contract as being for the minor's good. Moreover, he would have allowed the minor to recover the copyright transferred, seemingly on the terms that he returned the money received by him from the defendants.[51] In his view, *Steinberg, Valentini*, and *Pearce* could[52]:

> "have no application to a disposition [such as the transfer of copyright] which requires a deed or writing in order to be effective. They cannot be used so as to nullify the firmly established rule that such a disposition is voidable. For the protection of the young and the foolish, the law holds that a disposition by deed or writing can be avoided by the infant at any time before he comes of age. At any rate a disposition is voidable when it is made in pursuance of a contract which is not for the benefit of the infant."

The issue before the Court of Appeal in *Chaplin* was whether the trial judge **24–26** had acted correctly in granting the claimant an interlocutory injunction. It is unfortunate that Danckwerts and Winn L.JJ. should have been so ready to determine that the copyright which had been transferred could not have been recovered even if the minor could have elected to avoid the contract. In our view, Lord Denning M.R.'s conclusion that the minor could recover the copyright on terms is preferable, although it could have been more happily supported on the grounds that the minor had offered to restore, and was capable of restoring, the status quo ante. The adoption of the ancient common law rule which requires certain dispositions to be by deed or writing will result in an arbitrary distinction. If accepted, gifts or grants made by a minor by deed or writing will be voidable; in contrast, those which may be made by delivery without a deed or writing will not. Moreover, to explain *Steinberg, Valentini* and *Pearce* as cases where the property in the money or goods, which were handed over by a minor, passed on delivery and "where it is unjust that [the minor] should recover them back"[53] is unconvincing. These cases were not decided on that ground, although they are, as has been suggested, reconcilable with a narrow interpretation of the principle of restitutio in integrum—although as we have also said, we believe that the courts would do better to take a wide view of this principle.

Two final points remain to be made. First, the cases are divided over the **24–27** question whether a minor should be entitled to restitution in a case where he makes a gift to the defendant.[54] In our view, restitution should be ordered in such a case where that would be consistent with the policy objectives that deprive minors of the legal capacity to contract. Secondly, the Gambling Act 2005 s.83, provides that stakes and fees paid by children and young persons to licensed

---

[51] Counsel conceded this point: *Chaplin* [1966] Ch. 71 at 86 but the concession is not mentioned in Lord Denning's judgment.

[52] *Chaplin* [1966] Ch. 71 at 90.

[53] *Chaplin* [1966] Ch. 71 at 90 per Lord Denning M.R.

[54] Yes: *Hearle v Greenbank* (1749) 3 Atk. 695 at 712; 26 E.R. 1200 at 1208; *Re D'Angibau* (1880) 15 Ch. D. 228 at 241; *Burnaby v Equitable Reversionary Interest Soc* (1885) 28 Ch. D. 416 at 424. No: *Earl of Buckinghamshire v Drury* (1762) 2 Eden 60 at 72–73; 28 E.R. 818 at 821; *Taylor v Johnston* (1882) 19 Ch. D. 603; and cf. Latey Committee, *Report of the Committee on the Age of Majority* (1967) Cmnd 3342, p.98.

operators of gambling facilities must be repaid as soon as is reasonably practicable after the licensees become aware of their youth, but there is no obligation on the children and young persons to repay their winnings.

4. COMPANIES ACTING BEYOND THEIR POWERS

24–28   At common law a contract entered by a company that was beyond the powers expressly or impliedly conferred on the company by memorandum of association or constituting statute was void under the doctrine of ultra vires, as held by the House of Lords in *Ashbury Railway Carriage and Iron Co Ltd v Riche*.[55] The purpose of the ultra vires doctrine was to protect the company shareholders, and its intra vires creditors, who had contracted with the company on the basis that the money, goods or services they supplied to the company would only be used for its (published) purposes, and would not be used in the pursuit of different and possibly riskier ventures.

24–29   During the course of the 20th century, the ultra vires doctrine was widely circumvented by company draftsmen by the use of increasingly wide objects clauses. The doctrine was also progressively cut down by legislation, and it has now been largely abolished by the Companies Act 2006 s.39.[56] It is therefore unlikely that the question will any longer arise in practice, whether a company should be entitled to recover benefits transferred to a defendant under an executed ultra vires transaction. However, a handful of cases can be cited in which the recipients of benefits transferred by companies under ultra vires contracts were ordered to make restitution, as a means of furthering the goals of the ultra vires doctrine.[57]

24–30   In *Rover International Ltd v Cannon Film Sales Ltd*[58] the Court of Appeal awarded restitution of benefits conferred by a company under a contract that was void because it had been entered prior to the company's incorporation. However the claimant company did not rely on its own lack of capacity as a ground of recovery in this case, and the claim was founded either on mistake or on failure of basis. In an Irish case, *H.K.N. Invest Oy v Incotrade Pvt Ltd*,[59] payments were made into a company promoter's bank account under contracts that had been entered on the company's behalf prior to its incorporation. After the company was incorporated it immediately became insolvent and a dispute arose regarding the beneficial ownership of the money in the account. The judge ruled that the promoter had held the money on constructive trust for the company from the moment of receipt, a finding that can only be explained as a response to the

---

[55] *Ashbury Railway Carriage and Iron Co Ltd v Riche* (1875) L.R. 7 H.L. 653.
[56] There is an exception for companies that are charities in the Companies Act 2006 s.42.
[57] *Brougham v Dwyer* (1913) 108 L.T. 504; *Re K.L. Tractors Ltd* (1961) 106 C.L.R. 318 at 337–338; *Bell Houses Ltd v City Wall Properties Ltd* [1966] 2 Q.B. 656 at 694; *Caisse Populaire Notre Dame Ltée v Moyen* (1967) 61 D.L.R. (2d) 118 (Saskatchewan QB); *Breckenridge Speedway Ltd v Alberta* [1970] S.C.R. 175; *Caledonia Community Credit Union Ltd v Haldimand Feed Mill Ltd* (1974) 45 D.L.R. (3d) 676 (Ontario High Ct); *International Sales and Agencies Ltd v Marcus* [1982] 3 All E.R. 551 at 560.
[58] *Rover International Ltd v Cannon Film Sales Ltd* [1989] 1 W.L.R. 912; discussed at paras 3–41——3–43 and 13–09.
[59] *H.K.N. Invest Oy v Incotrade Pvt Ltd* [1993] I.R. 152 (Irish High Ct).

promoter's unjust enrichment at the company's expense if one accepts the difficult principle of "interceptive subtraction".[60] The judge's conclusion is also problematic in light of the fact that the company did not exist at the time when the payments were made.

5. Unlawful Returns of Capital to Company Shareholders

Creditors deal with a limited liability company on the basis that although the **24–31** shareholders do not owe unlimited liability for the company's debts, they are liable for these debts to the extent that they have contributed to the company's share capital. To protect creditors dealing with the company on this basis, shareholders are required to give full value when they are issued shares in the company, and the company may not buy its own shares back from the shareholders except in tightly defined circumstances. Companies are also prohibited from returning capital to shareholders and making dividend payments out of funds that do not fall within the statutory definition of distributable profits. Specialist works should be consulted for detailed discussion of all these rules.[61] Many are now contained in the Companies Act 2006 although some still arise at common law. Collectively they make up the doctrine of capital maintenance.

The courts formerly conceptualised the common law rules invalidating unlaw- **24–32** ful returns of share capital as part of the ultra vires doctrine, discussed in the previous part. However, the abolition of the ultra vires doctrine has made it easier to see that this was always a confusion of ideas. The capital maintenance doctrine continues to govern the dealings between limited liability companies and their shareholders, and there are strong reasons to think that the two doctrines have always been underpinned by different policy considerations, and that the courts' failure to distinguish between them clearly was a source of significant confusion.[62] For example, in a series of cases decided in the wake of *Re Lee, Behrens & Co*,[63] the courts made some unconvincing distinctions between gratuitous payments by companies that were "intra vires" because they were supposedly for the company's benefit and therefore impliedly authorised, and gratuitous payments that were "ultra vires" because they were not.[64] We share Eva Micheler's view[65] that a better explanation of these cases is that payments were held to be invalid in cases concerned with unlawful returns of capital to shareholders, while

---

[60] Discussed at paras 6–52—6–62.

[61] e.g. E. Ferran, *Principles of Corporate Finance Law* (Oxford: OUP, 2008), Ch.7.

[62] J. Armour, "Share Capital and Creditor Protection: Efficient Rules for a Modern Company Law?" (2000) 63 M.L.R. 355, pp.365–368; J. Armour, "Avoidance of Transactions as a 'Fraud on the Creditors' at Common Law" in J. Armour and H.N. Bennett (eds), *Vulnerable Transactions in Corporate Insolvency* (Oxford: Hart Publishing, 2003), 281, pp.290–295.

[63] *Re Lee, Behrens & Co* [1932] 2 Ch. 46.

[64] *Re W&M Roith Ltd* [1967] 1 All E.R. 427; *Ridge Securities Ltd v IRC* [1964] 1 All E.R. 275; *Charterbridge Corp v Lloyds Bank* [1970] Ch. 62; *Re Horsley and Weight Ltd* [1982] Ch. 442; *Re Halt Garage (1964) Ltd* [1982] 3 All E.R. 1016.

[65] E. Micheler, "Disguised Returns of Capital: An Arm's Length Approach" (2010) 69 C.L.J. 151, pp.153–161.

payments were upheld in cases concerned with payments to outsiders, where the capital maintenance doctrine was an irrelevant consideration.[66]

24–33   In *Progress Property Co Ltd v Moore*,[67] Lord Walker affirmed Mummery L.J.'s finding in the Court of Appeal that[68]:

> "The common law rule devised for the protection of the creditors of a company is well settled: a distribution of a company's assets to a shareholder, except in accordance with specific statutory procedures, such as a winding up of the company, is a return of capital, which is unlawful and *ultra vires* the company."

Lord Walker regarded this as: "a judge-made rule, almost as old as company law itself, derived from the fundamental principles embodied in the statutes by which Parliament has permitted companies to be incorporated with limited liability", and he stressed that Mummery L.J.'s reference to "ultra vires" should not be construed as a reference to the ultra vires doctrine in its strict sense, but should be understood to mean that companies cannot effectively enter transactions that are contrary to the capital maintenance doctrine by reason of limits imposed on their power to act by the general law rather than their memoranda of association.

24–34   How should the courts approach the task of characterising transactions between a company and its shareholders to decide whether the common law rule is engaged?[69] In *Progress Property* the judge at first instance rejected the submission that there is an unlawful return of capital "whenever the company has entered into a transaction with a shareholder which results in a transfer of value not covered by distributable profits, and regardless of the purpose of the transaction",[70] and Lord Walker agreed that[71]:

> "A relentlessly objective rule of that sort would be oppressive and unworkable. It would tend to cast doubt on any transaction between a company and a shareholder, even if negotiated at arm's length and in perfect good faith, whenever the company proved, with hindsight, to have got significantly the worse of the transaction."

24–35   Lord Walker went on to hold that[72]:

> "[I]n cases of this sort the court's real task is to inquire into the true purpose and substance of the impugned transaction. That calls for an investigation of all the relevant

---

[66] See too Armour, "Avoidance of Transactions as a 'Fraud on the Creditors' at Common Law", p.293, criticising Harman J.'s finding in *Barclays Bank Plc v British & Commonwealth Plc* [1995] B.C.C. 19 at 29, that a company cannot make a gratuitous disposition of its assets except out of distributable profits. This better view is that "the maintenance of capital principle only ever restricted transactions between a company and its shareholders . . . and did not extend to a principle that the capital of the company might only be expended for purposes within its objects."

[67] *Progress Property Co Ltd v Moore* [2010] UKSC 55; [2011] Bus. L.R. 260 at [15]. See too *Aveling Barford Ltd v Perion Ltd* [1989] B.C.L.C. 626.

[68] *Progress Property* [2009] EWCA Civ 629; [2009] Bus. L.R. 1535 at [23].

[69] Identified as the key question in e.g. *MacPherson v European Strategic Bureau Ltd* [2000] 2 B.C.L.C. 683 at [59]. Cf. *Davis Investments Pty Ltd v Commissioner of Stamp Duties (New South Wales)* (1958) 100 C.L.R. 392 at 406.

[70] *Progress Property* [2008] EWHC 2577 (Ch) at [39]–[41].

[71] *Progress Property* [2010] UKSC 55; [2011] Bus. L.R. 260 at [24].

[72] *Progress Property* [2010] UKSC 55; [2011] Bus.L.R. 260 at [27]–[29]. On the facts of the case the court concluded that the impugned transaction was not an unlawful return of capital.

facts, which sometimes include the state of mind of the human beings who are orchestrating the corporate activity.

Sometimes their states of mind are totally irrelevant. A distribution described as a dividend but actually paid out of capital is unlawful, however technical the error and however well-meaning the directors who paid it. The same is true of a payment which is on analysis the equivalent of a dividend, such as in ... *Re Walters' Deed of Guarantee*[73] and *British and Commonwealth Holdings plc v Barclays Bank plc.*[74] Where there is a challenge to the propriety of a director's remuneration the test is objective (*Re Halt Garage (1964) Ltd*[75]), but probably subject in practice to what has been called, in a recent Scottish case, a 'margin of appreciation': *Clydebank Football Club Ltd v Steedman.*[76] If a controlling shareholder simply treats a company as his own property, as the domineering master-builder did in *Re George Newman & Co. Ltd,*[77] his state of mind (and that of his fellow directors) is irrelevant. It does not matter whether they were consciously in breach of duty, or just woefully ignorant of their duties. What they do is enough by itself to establish the unlawful character of the transaction.

The participants' subjective intentions are however sometimes relevant, and a distribution disguised as an arm's length commercial transaction is the paradigm example. If a company sells to a shareholder at a low value assets which are difficult to value precisely, but which are potentially very valuable, the transaction may call for close scrutiny, and the company's financial position, and the actual motives and intentions of the directors, will be highly relevant. There may be questions to be asked as to whether the company was under financial pressure compelling it to sell at an inopportune time, as to what advice was taken, how the market was tested, and how the terms of the deal were negotiated. If the conclusion is that it was a genuine arm's length transaction then it will stand, even if it may, with hindsight, appear to have been a bad bargain. If it was an improper attempt to extract value by the pretence of an arm's length sale, it will be held unlawful. But either conclusion will depend on a realistic assessment of all the relevant facts, not simply a retrospective valuation exercise in isolation from all other inquiries."

Section 847 of the Companies Act 2006 provides that a shareholder who **24–36** receives a distribution made in contravention of Pt 23 is liable to repay the company the value of that part of the distribution which was unlawful, provided that he knew or had reasonable grounds to believe at the time of the distribution that it was unlawful.[78] This section was first enacted as the Companies Act 1980 s.44, in order to implement art.16 of the Second EC Directive on Company Law, but it echoes the common law rule (preserved by s.847(3)), that shareholders who knowingly receive unlawful returns of capital are personally liable to account as constructive trustees of the property,[79] if they receive it with a degree of

---

[73] *Re Walters' Deed of Guarantee* [1933] Ch. 321 (claim by guarantor of preference dividends).

[74] *British and Commonwealth Holdings Plc v Barclays Bank Plc* [1996] 1 W.L.R. 1 (claim for damages for contractual breach of scheme for redemption of shares).

[75] *Re Halt Garage (1964) Ltd* [1982] 3 All E.R. 1016.

[76] *Clydesbank Football Club Ltd v Steedman* 2002 S.L.T. 109 at [76].

[77] *Re George Newman & Co Ltd* [1895] 1 Ch. 674.

[78] The shareholder need not know the relevant law; it is enough that he knows facts which lead to the conclusion that the distribution is unlawful: *It's a Wrap (UK) Ltd (In Liquidation) v Gula* [2006] EWCA Civ 544; [2006] 2 B.C.L.C. 634.

[79] *Russell v Wakefield Waterworks Co* (1875) L.R. 20 Eq. 474 at 479; *Belmont Finance Corp Ltd v Williams Furniture Ltd* [1980] 1 All E.R. 393 at 405; *Precision Dippings Ltd v Precision Dippings Marketing Ltd* [1986] Ch. 447 at 457–458; *Rolled Steel Products (Holdings) Ltd v British Steel Corp* [1986] Ch. 246 at 297–298; *Heinl v Jyske Bank (Gibraltar) Ltd* [1999] Lloyd's Rep. Bank. 511 at 520–521; *Allied Carpets Group Plc v Nethercott* [2001] B.C.C. 81.

knowledge that makes it unconscionable on the facts for them to retain it.[80] This rule rests on the premise that directors who authorise a misapplication of company funds in breach of the capital maintenance rules are in a position analogous to that occupied by trustees who breach the terms of the trust by distributing trust property to persons other than the beneficiaries.[81]

24–37   As we discuss in Ch.8,[82] liability for knowing receipt of misdirected trust funds is not a restitutionary liability arising in response to the defendant's unjust enrichment, but a compensatory liability arising in response to the defendant's (equitable) wrongdoing. As we also discuss there, it remains to be seen whether the English courts will impose a concurrent liability in unjust enrichment on the recipients of misdirected trust funds that does not require proof of fault, as some legal writers have urged.[83] A similar argument has been made in the present context by Jennifer Payne, that strict liability in unjust enrichment should be imposed on shareholders who receive unlawful dividends contrary to the capital maintenance rules.[84] She envisages that this would run concurrently with their statutory liability under s.847, but that it would supersede their liability for knowing receipt because this rests on an analogy between company directors and trustees that she considers to be imperfect and unconvincing. She correctly observes that "incapacity" would be a problematic label for the ground of recovery if such a liability were to be imposed, since it would exacerbate the confusion between the ultra vires and capital maintenance doctrines that has already been described, and she concludes that the ground of recovery should instead be located in the policy underpinning the common law rule invalidating unlawful returns of capital, namely the protection of creditors.

24–38   Consistently with the view that we take in Ch.8, that the English courts should impose strict liability in unjust enrichment for the receipt of misdirected trust funds,[85] we agree that they should also impose strict liability in unjust enrichment for the receipt of company funds paid away in breach of the capital maintenance rules, and that the ground for recovery should lie in the policy considerations underpinning the rule that invalidates such transactions. However we consider that this liability should not supersede, but should run concurrently with, the fault-based, wrong-based liability that already exists at common law, the measure of recovery being different in some cases for the two types of liability, as we also discuss in Ch.8.[86]

---

[80] *Bank of Credit and Commerce International (Overseas) Ltd v Akindele* [2001] Ch. 437 at 455; reaffirmed in *Criterion Properties Plc v Stratford UK Properties LLC* [2002] EWCA Civ 1883; [2003] 1 W.L.R. 2108 at [20]–[39]; not reviewed on appeal [2004] UKHL 28; [2004] 1 W.L.R. 1846; *Charter Plc v City Index Ltd* [2007] EWCA Civ 1382; [2008] Ch. 313; *Uzinterimpex JSC v Standard Bank Plc* [2008] EWCA Civ 819; [2008] Bus. L.R. 1762.

[81] *Flitcroft's Case* (1882) 21 Ch. D. 519 at 527, 534 and 535; *Re Sharpe* [1892] 1 Ch. 154 at 165; *Moxham v Grant* [1900] 1 Q.B. 88; *Selangor United Rubber Estates Ltd v Cradock (No.3)* [1968] 1 W.L.R. 1555 at 1575; *Bairstow v Queen's Moat Houses Plc* [2000] 1 B.C.L.C. 549 at 557–560; affirmed [2001] EWCA Civ 712; [2001] 2 B.C.L.C. 531.

[82] See paras 8–123—8–130.

[83] See paras 8–50—8–68.

[84] J. Payne, "Unjust Enrichment, Trusts and Recipient Liability for Unlawful Dividends" (2003) 119 L.Q.R. 583.

[85] See paras 8–50—8–68.

[86] See para.8–130.

6. PAYMENTS MADE CONTRARY TO THE STATUTORY INSOLVENCY REGIME

A policy-based explanation for the award of restitutionary remedies can also be   **24–39**
given of certain provisions of the Insolvency Act 1986 that invalidate transactions entered by an insolvent company prior to insolvency, and empower the
courts to make orders requiring the recipients of benefits from the company to
repay them.[87] The policy goals of these statutory sections are (1) fostering the
collective insolvency process, (2) enabling the equal distribution of an insolvent
company's assets, and (3) deterring the dismemberment of companies on the
verge of insolvency.[88] Specialist works should be consulted for discussion of the
relevant provisions,[89] and only a brief account will be given here. The question
whether the innocent recipient of an infringing payment can invoke the change
of position defence is noted elsewhere.[90]

(a) *Insolvency Act 1986 s.127*

Section 127 provides that: **24–40**

"[I]n a winding up by the court, any disposition of the company's property . . . made
after the commencement of the winding up is, unless the court otherwise orders,
void."

Section 129 deems a winding-up to commence at the time when a petition for
winding-up is presented, unless the company resolves to undertake a voluntary
winding-up before the presentation of a petition.

In *Bank of Ireland v Hollicourt (Contracts) Ltd*,[91] a petition was presented for   **24–41**
a company's compulsory liquidation, but through an oversight its bank continued
to honour cheques drawn on its account for the next three months, the account
remaining in credit throughout this period. The liquidator sought a declaration
that all post-petition withdrawals from the account were void under s.127, and an
order requiring the bank to re-credit the account. It was common ground that
there had been a void "disposition" in favour of the payees, although the
liquidator had taken no steps to recover from them, and no validation order was
sought. Hence, the only issue was whether he was entitled to relief against the
bank. The Court of Appeal held that he was not, as there had been no "disposition" in the bank's favour. For the purposes of the section, a "disposition" could
only take place in favour of a party that received the company's property for its

---

[87] S. Degeling, "Restitution for Vulnerable Transactions" in Armour and Bennett (eds), *Vulnerable Transactions in Corporate Insolvency*, 385; Sir R. Goode, "The Avoidance of Transactions in Insolvency Proceedings and Restitutionary Defences" in A. Burrows and Lord Rodger, *Mapping the Law* (Oxford: OUP, 2006), 299.
[88] A. Keay, "The Recovery of Voidable Preferences: Aspects of Restoration" [2000] C.F.I.L.R. 1; M.G. Bridge, "Collectivity, Management of Estates and the *Pari Passu* Rule in Winding-up", in Armour and Bennett, *Vulnerable Transactions in Corporate Insolvency*, 1, pp.1–6.
[89] e.g. Sir R. Goode QC, *Principles of Corporate Insolvency Law*, 4th edn (London: Sweet & Maxwell, 2011), Ch.13.
[90] See para.27–53.
[91] *Bank of Ireland v Hollicourt (Contracts) Ltd* [2001] Ch. 555.

own benefit, and the bank had merely adjusted the account entries between itself and the company.[92]

24–42   According to Mummery L.J.:

> "[T]he policy promoted by s.127 is not aimed at imposing on a bank restitutionary liability to a company in respect of the payments made by cheques in favour of the creditors, in addition to the unquestioned liability of the payees of the cheques. . . .
> Section 127 only invalidates the dispositions by the company of its property to the payees of the cheques. It enables the company to recover the amounts disposed of, but only from the payees. It does not enable the company to recover the amounts from the bank, which has only acted in accordance with its instructions as the company's agent to make payments to the payees out of the company's bank account. As to the intermediate steps in the process of payment through the bank, there is no relevant disposition of the company's property to which the section applies."

24–43   *Rose v A.I.B. Group (UK) Plc*[93] also concerned a claim by a liquidator for an order against a bank, but in this case the company had paid money to its bank to clear its overdraft after a winding-up petition had been presented, and before it had been advertised. The judge had no doubt that the company's payments to the bank constituted "dispositions" for the purpose of s.127, following the Court of Appeal's finding to this effect in *Re Gray's Inn Construction Co Ltd*.[94] It was a more difficult question whether these dispositions should be validated, given that the petition had not been advertised at the time of the payments and the bank had been unaware of it, but the judge declined to validate them, reasoning that this would infringe the pari passu principle, and could not be justified on the basis that the payments helped keep the company's business going, to the benefit of all its creditors.

(b) *Insolvency Act 1986 ss.238 and 423*

24–44   Section 238 provides that an administrator or liquidator may apply to the court where the company has entered a "transaction at an undervalue" no more than two years prior to the onset of its insolvency, at a time when the company was unable to pay its debts or became unable to pay them as a consequence of that transaction. There is no need for the applicant to show that the company intended to sell its property at an undervalue with a view to defrauding its creditors.[95] A transaction is relevantly at an "undervalue" where the company makes a gift, or else receives consideration that is "significantly less" than the consideration supplied, a matter to be tested as at the date of the transaction.[96] The burden lies

---

[92] *Bank of Ireland* [2001] Ch. 555 at 563 and 565–566, rejecting suggestions to the contrary by Buckley L.J. in *Re Gray's Inn Construction Co Ltd* [1980] 1 W.L.R. 711 at 715–716.
[93] *Rose v A.I.B. Group (UK) Plc* [2003] EWHC 1737; [2003] 1 W.L.R. 2791.
[94] *Re Gray's Inn Construction Co Ltd* [1980] 1 W.L.R. 711.
[95] *Stanley v T.M.K. Finance Ltd* [2010] EWHC 3349 (Ch); [2011] B.P.I.R. 876 at [7].
[96] *Phillips v Brewin Dolphin Bell Lawrie* [2001] UKHL 2; [2001] W.L.R. 143 at [26]; followed in *Reid v Ramlort* [2002] EWHC 2416 (Ch); [2003] 1 B.C.L.C. 499 at [17], adding that "if at that date value is dependent on the occurrence or non-occurrence of some event and that event occurs before the assessment of value has been completed then the valuer may have regard to it".

on the applicant to prove this,[97] and the court should take an objective approach towards valuation.[98]

An example is provided by *Phillips v Brewin Dolphin Bell Lawrie*,[99] which **24–45** concerned the sale of a business coupled with a subletting of computer equipment under a collateral agreement in the face of an absolute bar in the head lease. The House of Lords held that the consideration included the collateral agreement, but that, as the collateral agreement was so precarious as to make it worthless, and the head lessors had almost immediately declared it to be a repudiatory breach, the burden of proof was discharged.

If the court accepts that a transaction at an undervalue has taken place, then it **24–46** is empowered to make such an order as it thinks fit to restore the company to its original position. However the court shall not make an order under s.238 if it is satisfied that the company acted in good faith and for the purpose of carrying on its business, and reasonably believed that the transaction would be for the company's benefit.

Transactions at an undervalue can also be attacked under s.423, which is **24–47** similar in form to s.238, but does not depend upon the transferor's insolvency, and does require evidence that the company intended to put assets beyond the reach of a creditor.[100] This need not mean that the company had a dishonest purpose,[101] although this inference may inevitably follow from some qualifying facts.[102] Again, in cases where the requirements of the section are met, the court is empowered to make such an order as it thinks fit to restore the company to its original position, although it cannot make an order to the prejudice of a person who has acquired property from the company in good faith for value and without notice of the relevant circumstances.[103]

According to Sales J.[104]: **24–48**

"A claim under s. 423 is a claim for some appropriate form of restorative remedy, to restore property to the transferor for the benefit of creditors, who may then seek to execute against that property in respect of obligations owed by the transferor to them. In an appropriate case, an order might be made to require the transferee to pay sums or transfer property direct to the creditors, if the position in relation to execution is clear and any further costs associated with execution ought to be avoided. But often the appropriate order will be for the transferee to pay sums or transfer property back to the transferor, leaving the distribution of those sums or property as between the creditors of the transferor to be governed by the general law. This may be particularly important if the transferor is bankrupt or in liquidation (or about to become bankrupt or go into

---

[97] *Stone & Rolls Ltd v Micro Communications Inc* [2005] EWHC 1052 (Ch) at [93].

[98] *Ailyan v Smith* [2010] EWHC 24 (Ch); [2010] B.P.I.R. 289 at [69] per H.H.J. David Cooke: "The court has to assess as best it can on the evidence what [the asset's] value in money or money's worth would be to a rational and reasonably well-informed purchaser, having knowledge of the actual characteristics of what it is he is buying."

[99] *Phillips v Brewin Dolphin Bell Lawrie* [2001] UKHL 2; [2001] W.L.R. 143; distinguished in *Delaney v Chen* [2010] EWHC 6 (Ch); [2010] B.P.I.R. 316.

[100] *National Westminster Bank Plc v Jones* [2001] EWCA Civ 1541; [2002] 1 B.C.L.C. 55 at [45].

[101] *Arbuthnot Leasing International Ltd v Havelet Leasing Ltd (No.2)* [1990] B.C.C. 637.

[102] *Banca Carige SpA Cassa di Risparmio di Genova e Imperia v Banco Nacional de Cuba* [2001] 1 W.L.R. 2039 at 2057.

[103] Insolvency Act 1986 s.425(2).

[104] *4 Eng Ltd v Harper* [2009] EWHC 2633 (Ch); [2010] 1 B.C.L.C. 176.

liquidation) and has a range of creditors not all of whom are before the court on the application made under s. 423."

24–49   A transaction can be attacked under s.423 where it has been undertaken in an attempt to prejudice future creditors, although there are no existing creditors, for in Jessel M.R.'s words[105]:

> "[A] man is not entitled to go into a hazardous business, and immediately before doing so, settle all his property voluntarily, the object being this: 'If I succeed in business, I make a fortune for myself. If I fail, I leave my creditors unpaid. They will bear the loss'."

In *Midland Bank Plc v Wyatt*[106] s.423 was held to cover the voluntary disposition of assets to avoid future but unknown creditors, regardless of whether the transferor was about to enter into a hazardous business. Likewise, in *Hill v Spread Trustee Co Ltd*,[107] the Court of Appeal held that the transferor need not have a particular creditor or group of creditors in mind, nor need they be creditors at the date of the impugned transaction.

24–50   In *Hashmi v IRC*[108] the Court of Appeal held that a claimant seeking to demonstrate that a transferor had the requisite statutory purpose of defrauding creditors did not need to establish that this was his sole or dominant purpose and that it would suffice for the claimant to show that this was his substantial purpose.

---

[105] *Re Butterworth* (1882) 19 Ch. D. 588 at 598.
[106] *Midland Bank Plc v Wyatt* [1995] 1 F.L.R. 697.
[107] *Hill v Spread Trustee Co Ltd* [2006] EWCA Civ 542; [2007] 1 W.L.R. 2404 at [101] and [125]. See too *Random House UK Ltd v Allason* [2008] EWHC 2854 (Ch) at [94]; *Curtis v Pulbrook* [2011] EWHC 167 (Ch); [2011] 1 B.C.L.C. 638 at [50]–[52].
[108] *Hashmi v IRC* [2002] EWCA Civ 981; [2002] B.P.I.R. 974; followed in *Barnett v Semenyuk* [2008] B.P.I.R. 1427.

CHAPTER 25

ILLEGALITY

1. INTRODUCTION

If a claimant transfers a benefit to a defendant under an illegal agreement, the fact **25–01** that the agreement is illegal might affect an unjust enrichment claim between them in several ways. If the claimant seeks restitution on a ground of recovery such as mistake or failure of basis, for example, then the defendant may plead the illegality of the transaction as a defence. This is discussed in Ch.35. But in some situations the claimant can rely on illegality itself as a ground of recovery. There are two types of case where this is possible, which are discussed here in turn.

The first is where protection of persons in the claimant's position is the very **25–02** reason for the rule rendering the transaction illegal: in such cases restitution may be ordered pursuant to the policy of the rule, it being an overriding principle that "if a transaction be objectionable on grounds of public policy, the parties to it may be relieved; the relief not being given for their sake, but for the sake of the public".[1] The policy calculation required in such cases resembles the calculation undertaken in cases where claimants rely on their own legal incapacity as a ground of recovery, as discussed in Ch.24.

The second class of case is where it is desirable to encourage a claimant to **25–03** withdraw from an illegal bargain. Hence the law allows him a *locus poenitentiae* or "space for repentance": provided that the scheme is not too far advanced, restitution is awarded pursuant to a policy of incentivising participants in illegal schemes to abandon them.

2. CLAIMANTS BELONGING TO A PROTECTED CLASS

In *Smith v Bromley*,[2] the claimant's brother had committed an act of bankruptcy. **25–04** But the defendant, his chief creditor, at first refused to sign his certificate of discharge. Later he authorised its signature, but only on condition that the bankrupt, or someone for him, would pay him £40 and give a note for £20 more. The claimant paid the £40 on behalf of her brother and she then sued the defendant for its recovery. Lord Mansfield held that her claim succeeded. He said[3]:

---

[1] *Vauxhall Bridge Co v Earl Spencer* (1821) Jac. 64 at 67, 37 E.R. 774 at 776 per Lord Eldon.
[2] *Smith v Bromley*—although decided in 1760, the case was not reported until 1781 in 2 Doug. 696n; 99 E.R. 441n; cf. *Sievers v Boswell* (1841) 3 Man. & G. 524; 133 E.R. 1250. Other statements of the doctrine by Lord Mansfield are found in *Clarke v Shee* (1774) 1 Cowp. 197 at 200; 98 E.R. 1041 at 1044; *Browning v Morris* (1778) 2 Cowp. 790 at 792; 98 E.R. 1364 at 1365–1366; *Lowry v Bourdieu* (1780) 2 Doug. 468 at 472; 99 E.R. 299 at 302.
[3] *Smith* (1760) 2 Doug. 696n at 697; 99 E.R. 441n at 443.

"If the act is in itself immoral, or a violation of the general laws of public policy, there, the party paying shall not have this action; for where both parties are equally criminal against such laws . . . the rule is, *potior est conditio defendentis*. But there are other laws, which are calculated for the protection of the subject against oppression, extortion, deceit, etc. If such laws are violated, and the defendant takes advantage of the plaintiff's condition or situation, there the plaintiff shall recover."

25–05   Claimants have been granted relief on similar grounds on a number of occasions.[4] An important illustration is *Kiriri Cotton Co Ltd v Dewani*.[5] In that case, the appellants had let a flat to the respondents. In consideration for the lease they had obtained from the respondents, contrary to the provisions of the Uganda Rent Restriction Ordinance 1949, a premium of 10,000 shillings. At the time of the demand and payment neither party realised that the demand was illegal. The respondents, who had occupied the flat, claimed that the premium was money received by the appellants to their use, a claim which the Court of Appeal for Eastern Africa upheld. In their argument before the Judicial Committee of the Privy Council, the appellants claimed that the payments were voluntary and therefore irrecoverable. Lord Denning, who delivered the advice of the Board, accepted the general principle, stated by Littledale J. in *Hastelow v Jackson*,[6] that "if two parties enter into an illegal contract, and money is paid upon it by one to the other, that may be recovered back before the execution of the contract, but not afterwards". But he held that, even if the contract was executed, as it was, the payer was entitled to recover provided that he was not *in pari delicto* with the payee; though if the parties were on equal terms, the claimant could not recover merely because he mistook the law.[7] Here the parties were not *in pari delicto*. The Rent Restriction Ordinance was passed with the object of protecting the tenant and the duty of observing the law was placed by that legislation on the shoulders of the landlord. The tenant was, therefore, entitled to recover his premium in an action for money had and received.

25–06   There are two possible limits to this right of recovery. The first originated in *Lodge v National Union Investment Co Ltd*.[8] The claimant sought to recover, in equity, policies deposited as security for a loan, the transaction being illegal under the Moneylenders Act 1900. Parker J. held that he was only entitled to recover the securities on repayment of the money advanced to him, stating that[9]:

---

[4] *Jaques v Golightly* (1776) 2 W.Bl. 1073; 96 E.R. 632; *Jacques v Withy* (1788) 1 H.Bl. 65; 126 E.R. 40; *Browning* (1778) 2 Cowp. 780; 98 E.R. 1364; *Williams v Hedley* (1807) 8 East 378; 103 E.R. 388; *Bloxsome v Williams* (1824) 3 B. & C. 232; 107 E.R. 270; *Barclay v Pearson* [1893] 2 Ch. 154.

[5] *Kiriri Cotton Co Ltd v Dewani* [1960] AC. 192; see also *Amar Singh v Kulubya* [1964] A.C. 142; *Rogers v Louth CC* [1981] I.R. 268. Cf. *Shelley v Paddock* [1980] Q.B. 348 (parties not *in pari delicto*; damages for fraud).

[6] *Hastelow v Jackson* (1828) 8 B. & C. 221 at 226; 108 E.R. 1026 at 1029.

[7] *Kiriri Cotton* [1960] A.C. 192 at 204.

[8] *Lodge v National Union Investment Co Ltd* [1907] 1 Ch. 300.

[9] *Lodge* [1907] 1 Ch. 300 at 312. It is doubtful how far such a restriction on recovery would be imposed in some actions at common law, e.g. trover: see *Fitzroy v Gwillim* (1786) 1 T.R. 153; 99 E.R. 1025 (doubted in *Tregoning v Attenborough* (1830) 7 Bing. 97; 131 E.R. 37; and *Hargreaves v Hutchinson* (1834) 2 Ad. & El. 12; 111 E.R. 5); *Hindle v O'Brien* (1809) 1 Taunt. 413; 127 E.R. 894 (distinguished in *Roberts v Goff* (1820) 4 B. & Ald. 92; 106 E.R. 872). The matter is discussed at some length by Parker J. in *Lodge*, at 307–311, and by Lord Radcliffe in *Kasumu v Baba-Egbe* [1956] A.C. 539 at 549.

"I do not think it either *aequum* or *bonum* that the plaintiff, who has had the benefit of the £1,075 and who is relying on the illegality of the contract and the exception enabling him to sue notwithstanding such illegality, should have relief without being put on terms by which both parties may be restored to the position they occupied before the transaction commenced."

The scope of this decision has been the subject of debate. "Its history is one **25–07** of being distinguished rather than applied".[10] In *Chapman v Michaelson*, the Court of Appeal held that Parker J.'s reasoning only applied if the claimant sought true equitable relief,[11] and in *Cohen v Lester (J.) Ltd*,[12] Tucker J. refused to impose terms when the particular contract was not illegal but simply unenforceable under the Moneylenders Act 1927 s.6. The point was again reconsidered in *Kasumu v Baba-Egbe*,[13] where the respondent had mortgaged land to the appellant, licensed moneylenders, as security for a loan. The transaction was unenforceable under the relevant Nigerian Ordinance because no book record had been kept. The sole question on the appeal was whether, as a condition of obtaining, inter alia, cancellation and delivery up of the mortgage deeds, the respondent should be compelled to repay the outstanding balance of the loan with interest. The Privy Council granted relief but refused to impose this condition. The Ordinance declared the particular transaction to be unenforceable; and to impose terms, as requested by the appellant, would be to enforce "directly or indirectly, a claim in respect of the transaction".[14] Lord Radcliffe, who delivered the Board's advice, accepted that *Lodge* did not establish "any wide general principle that governs the actions of courts in granting relief in money-lending cases".[15] The court would never grant equitable relief on terms if to do so would in effect reverse an Act of Parliament.[16]

The principle in *Lodge* has, therefore, been narrowly confined. The claim must **25–08** be a claim for "true equitable relief", whatever that precisely may mean,[17] and the exercise of the court's discretion must not conflict with the provisions of statutory enactments. Rarely will both these conditions be satisfied.[18]

The second limit to this head of recovery was laid down in *Green v Portsmouth* **25–09** *Stadium Ltd*.[19] In that case, the claimant, a bookmaker, alleged that he had, over a long period of time, been overcharged by the defendants each time he went on their course, contrary to the Betting and Lotteries Act 1934 s.13. He sought to recover the charges so paid, in excess of the amount allowed by the statute, as money had and received by the defendants to his use. Parker J. held,[20] following

---

[10] (1956) 72 L.Q.R. 481 [R.E.M.].
[11] *Chapman v Michaelson* [1909] 1 Ch. 238 at 242 and 243.
[12] *Cohen v Lester (J.) Ltd* [1939] 1 K.B. 504. Cf. *Colin Campbell v Pirie*, 1967 S.L.T. 49.
[13] *Kasumu v Baba-Egbe* [1956] A.C. 539.
[14] *Kasumu v Baba-Egbe* [1956] A.C. 539 at 551.
[15] *Kasumu v Baba-Egbe* [1956] A.C. 539 at 549.
[16] *Kasumu v Baba-Egbe* [1956] A.C. 539 at 549.
[17] (1956) 72 L.Q.R. 480–481 [R.E.M.].
[18] Australian cases considering this rule are *Mayfair Trading Co Ltd v Dwyer* (1958) 101 C.L.R. 428; *Deposit & Investment Co Ltd v Kaye* (1962) 63 S.R. (N.S.W.) 453 at 464; *Lejo Holdings Pty Ltd v Deutsche Bank (Asia) AG* [1988] 2 Qd R. 30; *Farrow Mortgage Services Pty Ltd v Edgar* (1993) 114 A.L.R. 1.
[19] *Green v Portsmouth Stadium Ltd* [1953] 2 Q.B. 190.
[20] *Green* [1953] 1 W.L.R. 487.

Lord Mansfield in *Browning v Morris*,[21] that the action would lie. The defendants appealed, and the Court of Appeal allowed their appeal. The statute was not a bookmakers' charter, but a law for the regulation of racecourses and other such matters in the interests of the general public, and did not contemplate the bringing of an action for money had and received at the suit of a person in the claimant's situation.[22] There was "nothing in this statute to authorise such an action".[23]

25–10   These decisions make it difficult to establish this right of recovery today. In Denning L.J.'s view, in modern statutes "one finds that if it is intended that an overcharge shall be recoverable the Act says so".[24] Accordingly, in the absence of such a statutory provision, it will no longer be easy to invoke the principle enunciated in *Smith v Bromley*. In the past, the imposition of a penalty on the defendant, but not on the claimant, was regarded as an indication that the claimant was to be protected and hence that he might have an action,[25] though that fact alone was never regarded as conclusive.[26] In *Green*, where penalties could have been imposed on the defendants under the Act, Denning L.J. took the view that "the presumption is that where the statute provides those consequences for a breach, no other remedy is available".[27] It may well be, however, that Denning L.J.'s interpretation of Lord Mansfield's judgment in *Smith* is too restrictive and that the courts may yet conclude that it is unnecessary to find express provision for restitution in the statute.[28]

25–11   This presumption is, in any event, displaced when the statutory provision is enacted specifically for the protection of persons in the claimant's position. In *Green*,[29] the statute was not passed for the protection of people in Green's position and there was no oppression. The claimant had, therefore, to find his remedy on the statute, and since the statute provided no remedy, his action could not succeed. In contrast, as has been seen, in *Kiriri Cotton*,[30] where the claimant recovered despite the fact that there was no statutory remedy specifically provided, it was held that the claimant belonged to that class of persons which the Ordinance was intended to protect. In such circumstances, though the Ordinance gave no remedy, the claimant could have an action at common law to recover his money.

---

[21] *Browning v Morris* (1788) 2 Cowp. 790.
[22] The House of Lords had already held that no action for damages would lie for breach of another section of the same statute: see *Cutler v Wandsworth Stadium Ltd* [1949] A.C. 398. No more, therefore, would an action for money had and received avail the claimant here.
[23] *Green* [1953] 2 Q.B. 190 at 196 per Denning L.J.
[24] *Green* [1953] 2 Q.B. 190 at 195. Cf. the suggestion of Lord du Parcq in *Cutler* [1949] A.C. 398 at 410, that the legislature should always state expressly that a civil action will lie, if that is the intention; this suggestion was approved by Lord Morton at 415. But see *Rickless v United Artists' Corp* [1988] Q.B. 40; applying *Lonrho Ltd v Shell Petroleum Co Ltd* [1982] A.C. 173 at 185.
[25] *Browning* (1788) 2 Cowp. 790 at 793; 98 E.R. 1364 at 1366 per Lord Mansfield.
[26] *Stokes v Twitchen* (1818) 8 Taunt 492; 129 E.R. 475.
[27] *Green* [1953] 2 Q.B. 190 at 195.
[28] See, in particular, *South Australia Cold Stores Ltd v Electricity Trust of South Australia* (1966) 115 C.L.R. 247 at 257–258 per Kitto J.; and cf. *Mistry Amar Singh v Kulubya* [1964] A.C. 142 PC.
[29] *Green* [1953] 2 Q.B. 190, at 195 and 196.
[30] *Kiriri Cotton* [1960] A.C. 192.

This principle has been applied in later cases. For example, in *Re Cavalier*   **25–12**
Insurance Co Ltd,[31] purchasers of household appliances bought extended warranty cover from a company that was not authorised to do insurance business in
the UK, as required by statute. When the company became insolvent they could
not enforce their contracts, but were able to recover their premiums because the
purpose of rule requiring insurance companies to obtain authorisation is the
protection of policyholders. Similarly, an Australian case, *A.S.I.C. v Karl Suleman Enterprizes*,[32] concerned an investment scheme promoted by the defendant
without registering disclosure documents with the statutory regulator, as required
by legislation. The question arose whether investors could recover their money
on the ground of illegality, and the judge held that they could because[33]:

"The prohibition imposed by [the statute] exists to protect persons from being enticed
by contravening behaviour into subscription contracts with respect to securities.
Accordingly, persons who are drawn into such contracts by the initiators of illegal offers
and invitations cannot be regarded as being *in pari delicto* unless they become knowing
participants in the illegal design. Absent such fault, they may therefore obtain restitution according to equitable principles. This is a case in which a duty not to solicit
investment without creation and lodgment of a disclosure document is imposed by
statute for the protection of investors as a section of society . . . The unjustness of the
enrichment represented by the soliciting party's receipt comes directly from the statutory illegality . . . "

A final example is *Murray Vernon Holdings Ltd v Hassall*.[34] A corporate   **25–13**
restructuring scheme fell foul of the prohibition against a company providing
financial assistance for the purchase of its own shares that was formerly contained in the Companies Act 1985 s.151.[35] Judge Hodge QC, sitting as a deputy
High Court judge, held that the company would be entitled to bring a claim in
unjust enrichment to recover the unlawful financial assistance it had provided in

---

[31] *Re Cavalier Insurance Co Ltd* [1989] 2 Lloyd's Rep. 430 esp. at 450. The rule was accepted in
principle, but held to be inapplicable on the facts, in: *Westdeutsche Landesbank Girozentrale v
Islington London BC* [1994] 4 All E.R. 890 at 931–932 (statute invalidating interest rate swap
contracts between banks and local authorities was not enacted for banks' protection); *Box v Barclays
Bank Plc* [1998] Lloyd's Rep. Bank. 185 (carrying on unauthorised deposit-taking business was
illegal, but deposit contracts were still enforceable under Banking Act 1987 s.3(3)); *Gibbs Mew Plc
v Gemmell* [1999] E.C.C. 97 at [44] (CA) (beer tie agreement was contrary to art.85 of the EC Treaty,
but purpose of art.85 was not publican's protection); *Aspinall's Club Ltd v Al-Zayat* [2008] EWHC
2101 (Comm) (statute prohibiting gaming on credit was designed to protect gamblers, but unlawful
credit had not been provided to enable the claimant to gamble and lose the money that was the subject
matter of the claim).
[32] *A.S.I.C. v Karl Suleman Enterprizes* [2003] NSWSC 400; (2003) 45 A.C.S.R. 401. See too *South
Australia Cold Stores* (1966) 115 C.L.R. 247 at 257–258; *David Securities Pty Ltd v Commonwealth
Bank of Australia* (1992) 175 C.L.R. 353 at 384; *Henderson v Amadio Pty Ltd (No.2)* (1996) 62
F.C.R. 221 at 231 (Fed Ct of Aus); affirmed (1998) 81 F.C.R. 149 (Full Ct of Fed Ct of Aus);
Fitzgerald v J.J. Leonhardt Pty Ltd (1997) 189 C.L.R. 215 at 229; *Estinah v Golden Hand Indonesian
Emploment Agency* [2001] HKEC 985 at [17]; *Kilroy v A OK Payday Loans Inc* (2007) 278 D.L.R.
(4th) 198 (British Columbia CA). And cf. the discussion of *Garland v Consumers' Gas Co* [1998] 3
S.C.R. 112 in P.D. Maddaugh and J.D. McCamus, *The Law of Restitution*, looseleaf edn (Aurora,
Ont.: Canada Law Book, August 2010 issue) para.15:300.20.
[33] *A.S.I.C.* [2003] NSWSC 400; (2003) 45 A.C.S.R. 401 at [17].
[34] *Murray Vernon Holdings Ltd v Hassall* [2010] EWHC 7 (Ch).
[35] See now the Companies Act 2006 s.678.

breach of s.151. He rejected the submission that such a claim would be precluded by a defence of illegality, ruling that[36]:

> "[S]uch a case clearly falls within the [principle] . . . which permits recovery where the transaction was rendered illegal under a law made for the protection of the party seeking to effect recovery. . . . By pursuing a restitutionary claim . . . for the recovery of the unlawful financial assistance, [the company] would merely have been seeking to undo the consequences of an illegal transaction, and not seeking to take advantage of it."

3. WITHDRAWAL FROM ILLEGAL TRANSACTIONS

25–14 Where money has been paid under an illegal contract, the payer is allowed a *locus poenitentiae*, i.e. a "space for repentance". So long as the contract remains wholly, or perhaps even substantially, executory, he may withdraw from his illegal bargain and recover the money he has paid, pursuant to a policy of incentivising participants in illegal schemes to abandon them.[37] As the Law Commission has stated[38]:

> "Illegality is being used to found a claim in restitution when the plaintiff relies on the doctrine of *locus poenitentiae*, that is, where the plaintiff claims to withdraw from the illegal transaction during 'the time for repentance'. Here one cannot analyse the illegality as constituting a defence to a standard restitutionary claim: rather the law grants restitution, where it otherwise would not, precisely in order to discourage illegality."

25–15 This doctrine originated in 1780 in *Lowry v Bourdieu*.[39] Then two distinct lines of authority developed. In the first, a claimant who innocently entered into an illegal contract was entitled on discovering the illegality to withdraw and recover the money paid thereunder, provided that the contract was substantially unperformed.[40] The second line was principally concerned with wagers. Here it was held that the claimant was allowed to withdraw even though he was aware of the illegality unless the illegality was *malum in se*.[41]

---

[36] *Murray* [2010] EWHC 7 (Ch) at [66].

[37] P. Birks, *An Introduction to the Law of Restitution*, revised edn (Oxford: Clarendon Press, 1989), pp.299–303 and 424–432; revisited and elaborated in P. Birks, "Recovering Value Transferred Under an Illegal Contract" [2000] *Theoretical Inquiries in Law* 155.

[38] Law Commission, *Illegal Transactions: The Effect of Illegality on Contracts and Trusts* (1999), LCCP No.154, para.2.49.

[39] *Lowry v Bourdieu* (1780) 2 Doug. 468 at 471; 99 E.R. 299 at 301–302 per Buller J.; followed in *Andree v Fletcher* (1789) 3 T.R. 266; 100 E.R. 567. Buller J. first advanced the idea in his *Nisi Prius*: Sir F. Buller, *An Introduction to the Law Relative to Trials at Nisi Prius* (London: C. Bathurst, 1772), p.132.

[40] *Tappenden v Randall* (1801) 2 B. & P. 467; 126 E.R. 1388; *Stainforth v Staggs* (1808) 1 Camp. 398 n., 170 E.R. 998 n; cf. *Watkins v Hewlett* (1819) 1 Brod. & B. 1; 129 E.R. 623; *Clark v Johnson* (1826) 3 Bing. 424; 130 E.R. 576; *Chappell v Poles* (1837) 2 M. & W. 867; 150 E.R. 1010.

[41] *Aubert v Walsh* (1810) 3 Taunt. 277; 128 E.R. 110; *Busk v Walsh* (1812) 4 Taunt. 290 at 292; 128 E.R. 340 at 342 per Mansfield C.J.; *Hastelow v Jackson* (1828) 8 B. & C. 221 at 224–225; 108 E.R. 1026 at 1028–1029 per Bayley J. See, generally, R.M. Jackson, *The History of Quasi-Contract in English Law* (Cambridge: CUP, 1936), pp.91–93.

For many years the doctrine was dormant until its revival in 1876 in the   **25–16**
controversial case of *Taylor v Bowers*.[42] The claimant was in embarrassed
circumstances. To prevent his creditors seizing his goods, he made over and
delivered all his stock-in-trade to one Alcock. Subsequently, meetings of the
claimant's creditors were held, but no compromise was reached with them.
Alcock then executed a bill of sale of the goods to the defendant, one of the
claimant's creditors, who had been aware of the original arrangement between
the claimant and Alcock. The alleged purpose of the bill was to secure the debt
owing by the claimant to the defendant, but the claimant did not sanction the bill,
nor was he even aware of it. After demand, he sued the defendant for detention
of the goods. The Court of Queen's Bench held that he was entitled to recover
because, as Lord Cockburn C.J. said:

> "Where money has been paid, or goods delivered, under an unlawful agreement, but
> there has been no further performance of it, the party paying the money or delivering
> the goods may repudiate the transaction, and recover back his money or goods."[43]

The Court of Appeal affirmed this decision. The judgment of Mellish L.J.,[44]   **25–17**
with which Baggallay J.A. agreed, was based on similar reasoning. These
judgments are open to criticism. The arrangement was not wholly executory, for
the goods had been handed over by the claimant to Alcock with the intention of
defrauding his creditors. Furthermore, the doctrine was here applied for the first
time, where there was not only illegality but immorality, of which the claimant
was aware, to which he was a party and out of which he intended to profit. The
remaining member of the Court of Appeal, James L.J., held that the claimant
could recover because he could prove his title to the goods independently of the
fraudulent transaction.[45]

The decision in *Taylor* was unsuccessfully invoked in *Kearley v Thomson*.[46]   **25–18**
The claimant offered to pay a sum of money to the defendants, solicitors to a
petitioning creditor, if they undertook neither to appear at the public examination
of the bankrupt nor to oppose his order of discharge. This, the defendants, with
their client's consent, agreed to do, and they received the sum of money. They did
not appear at the public examination; but, before any application for discharge
had been made, the claimant brought an action for the return of his money. His
action failed. The contract was illegal as tending to pervert the course of justice;
and where, as here:

> "there has been a partial carrying into effect of an illegal purpose in a substantial
> manner, it is impossible, though there remains something not performed, that the money
> paid under that illegal contract can be recovered back".[47]

Fry L.J., who delivered the unanimous judgment of the Court of Appeal, indicated[48] that the principle enunciated by the majority of the Court of Appeal in
Taylor required consideration by the House of Lords.

---

[42] *Taylor v Bowers* (1876) 1 Q.B.D. 291.
[43] *Taylor* (1876) 1 Q.B.D. 291 at 295.
[44] *Taylor* (1876) 1 Q.B.D. 291 at 297.
[45] *Taylor* (1876) 1 Q.B.D. 291 at 297–298.
[46] *Kearley v Thomson* (1890) 24 Q.B.D. 742.
[47] *Kearley* (1890) 24 Q.B.D. 742 at 747.
[48] *Kearley* (1890) 24 Q.B.D. 742 at 746.

25–19 Nevertheless, the *locus poenitentiae* doctrine was subsequently applied in various cases, culminating in *Tribe v Tribe*.[49] There a father transferred, for a consideration which was never paid, shares in his company to his son, in order to safeguard his assets from his creditors. He did this because the landlord of premises, of which he was the lessee and the company the licensee, had served notice of dilapidations, requiring him to carry out substantial and costly repairs. In the event, no repairs were carried out, and the father asked for the return of the shares. The son refused. The father then sued, claiming that the son was a bare trustee of the shares since he had agreed to surrender them on demand or at such time as the dispute as to dilapidations was settled. In his defence, the son pleaded that the illegal purpose could not be set up to rebut the presumption of advancement. The trial judge found as fact that the father did not intend to give the shares to his son and that the purpose of the transfer was to conceal them from his creditors. Despite this finding of fact, he found for the claimant since the illegal purpose had not been executed. The Court of Appeal held that the father was entitled to the delivery up of the share certificates. He could withdraw from the transaction before the illegal purpose had been carried into effect. It had not been carried out, for no creditor or creditors had been deceived by the transaction, and the court declined to hold that the *locus poenitentiae* rule "does not apply to a case where the presumption of advancement arises but the illegal purpose has not been carried into effect in any way".[50]

25–20 This conclusion is open to the criticism that it is one thing to allow recovery pursuant to a policy of encouraging withdrawal from illegal transactions, but another to allow recovery in cases where the only reason for the claimant's abandonment of his illegal enterprise is that a change in his circumstances has rendered the scheme unnecessary. Awarding restitution in the latter case does not promote withdrawal, and may even encourage those who contemplate entry into an illegal transaction by providing them with a safety net if they find that there is no longer anything to be gained from it.

25–21 Be that as it may, it seems that there are other limitations to the right to recover money paid under executory illegal contracts, one more established than the others. The first, as has been seen,[51] is that the illegal agreement must not have been substantially carried into effect; "some sort of *restitutio in integrum* on equitable terms" must still be possible.[52] The scope of this limitation was considered in *Q v Q*.[53] A man transferred ownership of a house to his sons with

---

[49] *Tribe v Tribe* [1996] Ch. 107. See too *Hermann v Charlesworth* [1905] 2 K.B. 123 at 131, 134 and 136; *Petherpermal Chetty v Muniandy Servai* (1908) 24 T.L.R. 462 at 463; *Perpetual Executors Trustees Association of Australia Ltd v Wright* (1917) 23 C.L.R. 185. Cf. *Wilson v Strugnell* (1881) 7 Q.B.D. 548 (though this case was overruled in *Herman v Jeuchner* (1885) 15 Q.B.D. 561, the particular point was left open); *Symes v Hughes* (1870) L.R. 9 Eq. 475; *South Western Mineral Water Co v Ashmmore* [1967] 1 W.L.R. 1110. Australian law recognises the same principle: *Payne v Macdonald* (1908) 6 C.L.R. 208; *Perpetual Executors and Trustees Association of Australia Ltd v Wright* (1917) 23 C.L.R. 185; *Martin v Martin* (1959) 110 C.L.R. 297 at 305.
[50] *Tribe* [1996] Ch. 107 at 121 per Nourse L.J.
[51] *Kearley* (1890) 24 Q.B.D. 742: see para.25–18. See also *Symes v Hughes* (1870) L.R. 9 Eq. 475; *Re Great Berlin Steamboat Co* (1884) 26 Ch.D. 616; *Apthorp v Neville & Co* (1907) 23 T.L.R. 575; *Re National Benefit Insurance Co* [1931] 1 Ch. 46.
[52] *South Western Mineral Water* [1967] 1 W.L.R. 1110 at 1127 per Cross J. Cf. *Zimmermann v Letkeman* [1978] 1 S.C.R. 1097 at 1105; *Ouston v Zurowski* (1985) 18 D.L.R. (4th) 563 (British Columbia CA).
[53] *Q v Q* [2008] EWHC 1874 (Fam); [2009] 1 F.L.R. 935.

a view to evading inheritance tax, and the question arose whether this illegal scheme had progressed sufficiently far to prevent him from recovering the property. Black J. referred to Nourse L.J.'s observation in *Tribe* that one must not confuse the transaction itself with the parties' purpose,[54] and held that "it is the purpose which has to have been carried into effect or partially carried into effect" and that the "transaction itself may be and often is entirely unexceptional, as it is here, and in those circumstances it is irrelevant".[55] She also observed that much can turn on how the parties' "illegal purpose" is defined. If it were defined in the *Q* case as having been "to save inheritance tax", then this would support the argument that nothing relevant could have happened until a false declaration respecting ownership of the house was made after the father's death. However, she preferred to define the purpose more widely as "to deceive the Revenue", and this led her to conclude that[56]:

> "considerable steps have been taken towards this which have gone beyond the mere creation of authentic looking documents which have been kept within the family and moved into the realms of actually presenting a false picture to the taxman. By falsely representing to the Revenue (by false omissions from his own tax return and/or false inclusions on those of [his sons]) that he was no longer the owner of the transferred assets, [the father] has, in my judgment, partly carried the illegal purpose into effect and deprived himself of the chance of withdrawing from it . . . "

As Black J. recognised herself, it is hard to define the scope of the limitation **25–22** that a claimant must not have passed the "point of no return" by substantially executing the illegal purpose. Whether a claimant has passed this point is a question of fact, the determination of which is open to judicial manipulation by adopting a wide or narrow definition of the illegal purpose. As a consequence the courts can make decisions which are plausible on the facts of the cases before them, but which sit alongside one another rather uncomfortably.[57] For this reason some legal writers have argued for the abandonment of the limitation altogether.[58]

Secondly, some judges have said that there must be genuine repentance on the **25–23** part of the claimant.[59] A distinction has been drawn between "repentance cases" where recovery was allowed, and "frustration cases" where it was not. *Bigos v*

---

[54] *Tribe* [1996] Ch. 107 at 121
[55] *Q v Q* [2009] 1 F.L.R. 935 at [127].
[56] *Q v Q* [2009] 1 F.L.R. 935 at [130].
[57] Compare *Taylor* (1876) 1 Q.B.D. 291; *Kearley* (1890) 24 Q.B.D. 742; *Hermann* [1905] 2 K.B. 123; *Scheuerman v Scheuerman* (1916) 52 S.C.R. 625 at [31]; *Donaldson v Freeson* (1934) 51 C.L.R. 185; *Taylor v Bhail* (1996) 50 Con. L.R. 7; *Collier v Collier* [2002] EWCA Civ 1095; (2002) 6 I.T.E.L.R. 270 at [46], [82] and [108]–[111]; *Q v Q* [2008] EWHC 1874 (Fam); [2009] 1 F.L.R. 935.
[58] J.K. Grodecki, "*In Pari Delicto Potior Est Condition Defendentis*" (1955) 71 L.Q.R. 254; R. Merkin, "Restitution by Withdrawal from Executory Illegal Contracts" (1981) 97 L.Q.R. 420, p.444.
[59] *Parkinson v College of Ambulance Ltd and Harrison* [1925] 2 K.B. 1 at 16; *Alexander v Rayson* [1936] 1 K.B. 190; *Berg v Sadler and Moore* [1937] 2 K.B. 158 at 165; *Harry Parker v Mason* [1940] 2 K.B. 590 at 608–609; *Bigos v Bousted* [1951] 1 All E.R. 92 at 95; *Chettiar v Chettiar* [1962] A.C. 294 at 302; *Sykes v Stratton* [1972] 1 N.S.W.L.R. 145 at 166. There are hints of some repentance theory in the early Chancery cases, e.g. *Birch v Blagrave* (1755) Amb. 264; 27 E.R. 176.

Bousted[60] is representative. The defendant wished to send his wife and daughter abroad for the sake of his daughter's health. In those days foreign currency was in short supply. He therefore made an arrangement, illegal by English law, under which the claimant agreed to provide Italian currency in Italy and the defendant promised to repay her in English money in England, depositing a share certificate with the claimant as security. The defendant's wife and daughter went to Italy but the claimant failed to provide the promised currency. The claimant claimed the balance of the loan, and the defendant counterclaimed for the return of the share certificate. Pritchard J. held that the defendant was unable to recover his share certificate from the claimant. The defendant had not repented. His scheme had merely been frustrated by events beyond his control. If this limit on the right of recovery is strictly enforced, then there will in the future be few cases in which the exception in favour of executory contracts can be successfully invoked.

25–24   In *Tribe*,[61] however, Millett L.J. was prepared to conclude that:

> "[G]enuine repentance is not required. Justice is not a reward for merit; restitution should not be confined to the penitent . . . voluntary withdrawal from an illegal transaction when it has ceased to be needed is sufficient."

The Lord Justice did not discuss the decisions which suggest that repentance is a necessary condition, but his conclusion has much to commend it. "Repentance" is a complex concept of uncertain meaning,[62] and as Millett L.J. said[63]:

> "[I]f the policy which underlies the primary rule is to discourage fraud, the policy which underlies the exception must be taken to encourage withdrawal from a proposed fraud before it is implemented, an end which is no less desirable. And if the former objective [a principle of policy] is of such overriding importance that the primary rule must be given effect even where it leads to a denial of justice, then in my opinion the latter objective justifies the adoption of the exception where this enables justice to be done."

25–25   Thirdly, it is doubtful whether the principle now applies in marine insurance. The Marine Insurance Act 1906 s.84, provides that a premium is returnable by the insurer if there is a total failure of consideration and, in particular:

> "[W]here the policy is void, or is avoided by the insurer as from the commencement of the risk, the premium is returnable, provided that there has been no . . . illegality on the part of the assured".

No distinction is drawn between executed and executory contracts, although this distinction was accepted at common law before the Act.[64]

---

[60] *Bigos v Bousted* [1951] 1 All E.R. 92. (The claimant's claim on the loan agreement was abandoned at the commencement of the hearing.) Cf. *United City Merchants (Investments) Ltd v Royal Bank of Canada* [1982] Q.B. 208 (CA); reversed [1983] 1 A.C. 168 (HL).

[61] *Tribe* [1996] Ch. 107 at 135. Cf. *McDonald v Fellows* (1979) 105 D.L.R. (3d) 434 (Alberta CA).

[62] For an interesting discussion written from the perspective of a moral philosopher, see I. Samet, "*Locus Poenitentiae*: Repentance, Withdrawal and Luck" in C. Mitchell (ed.), *Constructive and Resulting Trusts* (Oxford: Hart, 2010), p.335.

[63] *Tribe* [1996] Ch. 107 at 134.

[64] *Palyart v Leckie* (1817) 6 M. & S. 290; 105 E.R. 1251.

Finally, it was suggested in the old case of *Tappenden v Randall*[65] that relief **25–26** would only be given where the contract was not "too grossly immoral for the court to enter into any discussion of it". How far this limitation applies, if at all, to the doctrine in its modern form is debatable.

---

[65] *Tappenden v Randall* (1801) 2 B. & P. 467 at 471; 126 E.R. 1388 at 1391 per Heath J.

CHAPTER 26

BENEFITS CONFERRED UNDER JUDGMENTS AND ORDERS THAT ARE LATER REVERSED

1. INTRODUCTION

A court may order the unsuccessful party to a suit to pay money or transfer **26–01** property to the successful party,[1] and this order may be complied with before any appeal from the court's decision is heard. In this situation, the successful party's enrichment is justified by the court order,[2] and so there is generally no prospect of the unsuccessful party recovering the benefit for as long as the order subsists, even if there are good reasons for thinking that the court has made a mistake.[3]

If an appeal is heard, and the initial order is reversed, then the appellate court **26–02** will direct the respondent to restore to the appellant the money paid or the property transferred under the original order.[4] This rule is an old one,[5] and few recent English authorities touch on the point, which might seem to suggest that the principles governing recovery are settled and well understood. However, some questions remain about the nature and extent of the principle.[6]

---

[1] The court's order may be finally determinative the issues between the parties, or it may form part of a stay order pending an appeal, as in e.g. *Cai v Zheng (No.2)* [2009] NSWCA 317.

[2] See paras 2–32—2–40.

[3] But note the cases on wrongful application of process cited in para.26–03, fn.9.

[4] An order for recovery can be made in the appeal itself: *Nykredit Plc v Edward Erdman Ltd* [1997] 1 W.L.R. 1627 at 1636–1637. But a further order can also be applied for in new proceedings, if an unsuccessful respondent declines to repay what was received under the original order: *Lee v Mallam* (1910) 10 S.R. (N.S.W.) 876.

[5] *Eyre v Woodfine* (1590) Cro. Eliz. 278; 78 E.R. 533; *Buckley v Wilkinson* (1688) 2 Show. K.B. 68; 89 E.R. 798; *President and Scholars of St John's College, Oxford v Murcott* (1797) 7 T.R. 259; 101 E.R. 963; *Lozano v Janson* (1859) 2 El. & El. 160; 121 E.R. 61. *Indebitatus assumpsit* did not lie to recover money paid under a judgment later reversed on a writ of error: *Mead v Death and Pollard* (1700) 1 Ld. Ray. 742; 91 E.R. 1396. A writ of restitution was the appropriate and essential remedy: for the form of this writ see W. Tidd, *Queen's Bench Forms*, 8th edn (London: 1840), p.690. The plaintiff in this writ asked to be restored to all that he had lost and to what the plaintiff in the judgment had taken after the first judgment *colore judicii praedicti*: *Sympson v Juxon* (1625) Cro. Jac. 699; 79 E.R. 607. There was much abstruse learning as to when the plaintiff in the judgment was required to bring a *scire facias*: W. Tidd, *King's Bench Practice*, revised edn (London: 1828), Vol.2, pp.1033 and 1186. The writ of restitution has never been abolished, but it is now hardly ever used in this context.

[6] Further discussion: D.M. Gordon QC, "Effect of Reversal of Judgment on Acts Done Between Pronouncement and Reversal" (1958) 74 L.Q.R. 517 and (1959) 75 L.Q.R. 85; B. McFarlane, "The Recovery of Money Paid Under Judgments Later Reversed" [2001] 9 R.L.R. 1; A. Papamatheos, "What are the Juridical Bases of Reversal of Judgment Restitution?" [2004] 25 Aust. Bar Rev. 268.

2. The Nature of the Principle

26–03   In *Rodger v Comptoir d'Escompte de Paris*,[7] Lord Cairns said that money could be recovered from a defendant "who by mistake and by wrong obtained possession of the money under a judgment which has been reversed." However he cannot have meant that it is a civil wrong sounding in an action for compensatory damages to receive money under a judgment that is later reversed. Litigants are not responsible for the courts' mistakes unless they have intentionally misled them or have otherwise abused the court process: as Wilde C.J. observed:

> "The law allows every person to employ its process for the purpose of trying his rights, without subjecting him to any liability, unless he acts maliciously and without probable cause."[8]

Unless they have deliberately abused the court process, successful litigants therefore commit no wrong when they win a court order that is later held to have been mistaken.[9] It is for this reason that a claimant seeking an interim injunction must give a cross-undertaking as to damages as a precondition for the making of the order: otherwise the defendant would be left without a remedy if he suffered loss through compliance with the order and the issue between the parties was then resolved in his favour.[10]

26–04   The law of unjust enrichment therefore provides a better explanation of the claimant's right of recovery, as Swift J. held in *AB v British Coal Corp (AB)*.[11] However, some uncertainty attaches to the exact ground for recovery. Several possibilities have been suggested. Swift J. located the reason for restitution in the fact that a payer does not truly intend to benefit the recipients where he is compelled to pay by legal process, because his intention is vitiated in the same way that a payer's intention is vitiated in cases of duress.[12] Another possible

---

[7] *Rodger v Comptoir d'Escompte de Paris* (1871) L.R. 3 P.C. 465 at 475.

[8] *De Medina v Grove* (1847) 10 Q.B. 152 at 176; 116 E.R. 67 at 69.

[9] On the tort of malicious abuse of process, see *Grainger v Hill* (1838) 4 Bing. N.C. 212; 132 E.R. 769; *Varawa v Howard Smith Co Ltd* (1911) 13 C.L.R. 35; *Metall und Rohstoff AG v Donaldson Lufkin & Jenrette Inc* [1990] 1 Q.B. 391 at 467–473 (CA). An action for money had and received lay to recover money paid under a judgment obtained by improper means in *Duke de Cadaval v Collins* (1836) 4 Ad. & El. 858; 111 E.R. 1006; the facts of *Moses v Macferlan* (1760) 2 Burr. 1005; 97 E.R. 676, do not quite bring the case within the same category and it may be better understood as a claim founded on a breach of contract; cf. Eyre C.J.'s comments in *Phillips v Hunter* (1795) 2 H. Bl. 402 at 415–416; 126 E.R. 618 at 626.

[10] As Jacob L.J. observed in *SmithKline Beecham Plc v Apotex Europe Ltd* [2006] EWCA Civ 658; [2007] Ch. 71 at [25]. See too *National Australia Bank Ltd v Bond Brewing Holdings Ltd* [1991] 1 V.R. 386 at 597–604 per Brooking J. (Victoria CA); *Burger King Corp v Hungry Jack's Pty Ltd* [2001] NSWCA 187 at [487]–[500]. The requirement for a cross-undertaking to pay damages is set down in para.5.1 of PD 25A supplementing CPR Pt 25.

[11] *AB v British Coal Corp* [2007] EWHC 1948 (QB) at [34]. See too *Heydon v N.R.M.A. Ltd (No.2)* [2001] NSWCA 445; (2001) N.S.W.L.R. 600 at [14] per Mason P.

[12] *AB* [2007] EWHC 1948 (QB) at [14]–[15], citing a statement to this effect in the previous edition of this work: G. Jones, *Goff and Jones: The Law of Restitution*, 7th edn (London: Sweet & Maxwell, 2006), para.16.001. See too *Dr Drury's Case* (1610) 8 Co. 141b at 143a: recovery should be allowed because the appellant's "acts [were] done in the execution of justice, which are compulsive." Coke was contrasting acts which are compulsive, for example, payment in consequence of execution after the issue of the writ *fieri facias*, and acts which are voluntary. Note, however, that a claimant may recover even though he has satisfied a judgment voluntarily, without waiting for execution: *Rodger* (1871) 3 L.R. 3 P.C. 465 at 475 per Lord Cairns. Australian authorities identifying compulsion as the

explanation is that a claimant makes a "retrospective mistake" of the kind identified in *Kleinwort Benson Ltd v Lincoln CC*[13] when he pays pursuant to an understanding of the law that is retrospectively falsified by the appellate court's decision.[14] A third is that the basis of the transfer fails when the judgment or order is set aside.[15]

In our view, however, none of these explanations captures the essence of the **26–05** claimant's right, essentially for the reason given by Ben McFarlane, that in cases where benefits are transferred pursuant to a judgment[16]:

> "the normal unjust enrichment models designed to protect the freedom of choice of the transferor do not apply; the judgment has rendered [his] consent irrelevant and the transferor cannot pick and choose the conditions of the transfer."

In our view, the better explanation of the claimant's right lies in the policy consideration, also identified by McFarlane, that the courts' power to force litigants to transfer benefits to other litigants is partly justified by procedural mechanisms whose function is to reduce the risk of judicial error. These include the right to appeal, a necessary concomitant of which is the right to recover money paid under the initial judgment following a successful appeal.[17] Without this the legal system would be caught in self-contradiction and the appellate process would be rendered "nugatory".[18] Hence, as Lord Nicholls held in *Nykredit Plc v Edward Erdman Ltd*, appellate courts have an inherent jurisdiction to order repayment as a means of[19]:

> "unravelling the practical consequences of orders made by the courts below and duly carried out by the unsuccessful party. The result of [a successful appeal is] . . . that, to the extent indicated, orders made in the courts below should not have been made. This result could, in some cases, be an idle exercise unless the [appellate court] were able to

---

ground for restitution are *Commissioner for Railways (NSW) v Cavanagh* (1935) 53 C.L.R. 220 at 225, and *Caldwell v Hill* [2000] NSWCA 239 at [56].

[13] *Kleinwort Benson Ltd v Lincoln CC* [1999] 2 A.C. 349, discussed at paras 9–71—9–94.

[14] Lord Cairns mentions mistake, probably without meaning to identify it as the ground for recovery, in *Rodger* (1871) L.R. 3 P.C. 465 at 475. It was explicitly relied on as the ground of recovery in a more recent Australian case: *Palmer v Blue Circle Southern Cement Ltd* [1999] NSWSC 697.

[15] *Vasailes v Robertson* [2002] NSWCA 177 at [5]. See too P. Birks, *An Introduction to the Law of Restitution*, revised edn (Oxford: Clarendon Press, 1989), endnote 5, pp.451–452, discussing *Barder v Caluori* [1988] A.C. 20.

[16] McFarlane, "The Recovery of Money Paid Under Judgments Later Reversed", p.6, cited with approval in *Woolworths Ltd v Strong (No.2)* [2011] NSWCA 72 at [35].

[17] A similar principle gives a defence or justification to some defendants who are sued in the civil courts for acts that were legally validated by the initial judgment and were undertaken in reliance on the judgment. See e.g. *MacIntosh v Lobel* (1993) 30 N.S.W.L.R. 441 at 459–465 (defendant not liable for trespass to land awarded to him by a judgment that was later reversed); and see too *Wilde v Australian Trade Equipment Co Pty Ltd* (1981) 145 C.L.R. 590 at 603; *Battenberg v Union Club* [2005] NSWSC 242; (2005) 53 A.C.S.R. 263 at [41]–[67].

[18] *Commonwealth v McCormack* (1984) 155 C.L.R. 273 at 277.

[19] *Nykredit Plc v Edward Erdman Ltd* [1997] 1 W.L.R. 1627 at 1637. Cf. *National Australia Bank* (1991) 1 V.R. 386 at 594 per Brooking J. (Victoria CA): "The authorities I have mentioned rest the power of the court to direct repayment or to award interest on the duty of courts to strive to arrive at a perfect judicial determination which will avoid injustice and to take care that no act of the court does injury to a suitor . . . , or on the need to get at justice . . . , or on the general jurisdiction of the courts to act rightly and fairly . . . , or on the need to do complete justice between the parties".

make consequential orders which achieve, as nearly as is reasonably practicable, the restitution which this result requires."

26–06   One consequence of identifying this policy-based consideration as the ground for recovery is that defendants may be prevented from relying on the defence of change of position in response to claims if it were thought that this would stultify the policy objectives underpinning the claimant's right of recovery.[20]

3. THE EXTENT OF THE PRINCIPLE

(a) *Claims against Parties to the Litigation*

26–07   The principle applies not only in cases where an appellate court resolves the issues between the parties in the appellant's favour, but also in cases where the court orders a new trial and does not finally dispose of the proceedings.[21] In either case, if the unsuccessful respondent has received money then he must repay the face value of the money to the appellant.[22] He must also repay the user value of the money in the form of interest, as held by the Privy Council in *Rodger*,[23] where Lord Cairns said that otherwise the appellant would lose, and the respondent would gain, "the ordinary fruits which are derived from the enjoyment of money" during the relevant period. Note, however, that the benefit that the respondent is ordered to repay by an award of interest is not the profit that he makes from his use of the money, but the value of his saved borrowing costs during the relevant period. These saved costs were identified as the relevant benefit in claims to recover interest as the user value of money by the House of Lords in *Sempra Metals Ltd v IRC*.[24] Consistently with this characterisation of the benefit in issue, there is no need to investigate what the respondent actually did with the money when valuing his saved borrowing costs,[25] nor does it make

---

[20] The defence was allowed in *Palmer* [1999] NSWSC 697, but the ground of recovery identified there was mistake. For discussion, see para.27–54.

[21] *T.C.N. Channel 9 Pty Ltd v Antoniadis (No.2)* [1999] NSWCA 104; (1999) 48 N.S.W.L.R. 381 at 384, followed in *Ageas Insurance Co (Asia) v Lam Hau Wak Inneo* [2011] 1 H.K.L.R.D. 422 (HK CA).

[22] *Nykredit* [1997] 1 W.L.R. 1627 at 1636–1637. See too *Jim Ennis Construction Ltd v Premier Asphalt Ltd* [2009] EWHC 1906 (TCC); (2009) 125 Con. L.R. 141 at [28]–[29] (restitution of money paid in accordance with adjudicator's decision). And cf. *Commonwealth v McCormack* (1984) 155 C.L.R. 273; *National Australia Bank* [1991] 1 V.R. 386 at 591–592 (Victoria CA); *T.C.N. Channel 9* [1999] NSWCA 104; (1999) 48 N.S.W.L.R. 381 at 382; *Meerkin & Apel v Rossett Pty Ltd (No.2)* [1999] VSCA 10; [1999] 2 V.R. 31 at 32; *Heydon v N.R.M.A. Ltd (No.2)* [2001] NSWCA 445; (2001) 53 N.S.W.L.R. 600 at 603; *South Eastern Coalfields Ltd v State of M. P.* [2003] 8 S.C.C. 648 (India Sup Ct); *Easterday v State of Western Australia* [2005] WASCA 105 at [31].

[23] *Rodger* (1871) 3 L.R. 3 P.C. 465 at 475. See too *Bank of Australasia v Breillat* (1847) 6 Moo. P.C. 152 at 206; 3 E.R. 642 at 633; *Merchant Banking Co v Maud* (1874) L.R. 18 Eq. 659; *Commonwealth v McCormack* (1984) 155 CLR 273; *Evans v Kent General Insurance Corp* (1991) 100 N.S.R. (2d) 411 (Nova Scotia CA); *National Australia Bank* (1991) 1 VR 386 at 597 (Victoria CA); *Nykredit* [1997] 1 W.L.R. 1627 at 1636–1637 (PC); *Heydon* [2001] NSWCA 445; (2001) N.S.W.L.R. 600; *Man Ping Nam v Man Fong Hang (No.2)* (2007) 10 H.K.C.F.A.R. 140 at [23]; *Cai v Zheng (No.2)* [2009] NSWCA 317.

[24] *Sempra Metals Ltd v IRC* [2007] UKHL 34; [2008] A.C. 561, discussed at paras 5–05—5–10.

[25] Although this would obviously be relevant if a claim were brought to recover secondary profits, as permitted by the cases cited at fn.33.

a difference what the appellant would have done with it if he had not been ordered to pay it to the respondent.[26]

In *AB*,[27] the defendant was ordered to make periodic payments of costs to the claimants' solicitors, but it disputed the amounts and sought a stay of the costs orders pending appeal. The parties then reached an informal agreement that, if the appeal were successful, any overpayment would be refunded. The Court of Appeal held that there had been an error in calculating the costs and directed that they should be recalculated. When that was done it was found that £74 million had been overpaid. There was no dispute that restitution should be made of this capital sum but the claimants' solicitors declined to pay interest, arguing that the payments had been made voluntarily under the parties' informal agreement which made no provision for the repayment of interest.

26–08

Swift J. held that interest was payable on the payments made prior to the Court of Appeal's decision because these were made under compulsion of legal process. However there was no such compulsion to pay after the decision, and the payments thereafter were made voluntarily under the parties' agreement. Nevertheless interest was also payable on the later payments because a term should be implied into the agreement that any repayment should be made with interest as a mechanism for reversing the solicitors' unjust enrichment at the defendant's expense. The rate of interest was agreed by the parties to be 1 per cent above base rate, and the only remaining issue was whether the interest should be simple or compound. In a late submission, following the decision in *Sempra*,[28] the defendant argued that interest should be compounded. Surprisingly, however, Swift J. held that compound interest would not have been in the contemplation of the parties and should not be implied into the agreement, a conclusion that is inconsistent with her finding that the interest term was to be implied to reverse unjust enrichment, and the House of Lords' finding in *Sempra* that the reversal of unjust enrichment requires compound rather than simple interest to be awarded. It seems that Swift J. approached the issue as a question of terms implied in fact and that this led her to emphasise what the parties must have understood to be the law governing interest when they entered the agreement (when no one could have had *Sempra* in mind). But she could just as well have held that the parties must have intended that the general law should govern their transaction, so that if the payments had to be returned, interest should be calculated using the prevailing legal principles. Alternatively she could have held that a term had to be implied in law, which would necessarily have been informed by the prevailing law on recovery of the use value of money as compound interest.[29]

26–09

If a respondent has received rights to property, then these must be reconveyed, even where the property is registered land and he entered his title on the register

26–10

---

[26] Cf. *Heydon* [2001] NSWCA 445; (2001) N.S.W.L.R. 600 at [24]–[36], where Mason P. reaches a similar conclusion that the benefit transferred should be quantified by reference to market borrowing rates, but for the different, pragmatic reason, that otherwise "it would be intolerably burdensome if a court required evidence and argument in every case as to what rate or rates of interest would do justice" between the parties. See too *Roads & Traffic Authority v Ryan (No.2)* [2002] NSWCA 128 at [7]–[8] and [21]–[26]; *Cornwall v Rowan (No.2)* [2005] SASC 122 at [39].

[27] *AB* [2007] EWHC 1948 (QB).

[28] *Sempra* [2007] UKHL 34; [2008] A.C. 561; discussed at paras 5–05—5–10.

[29] Cf. *Bank of Credit and Commerce International v Ali* [2001] UKHL 8; [2002] 1 A.C. 251 (express general term construed by reference to legal rights existing at the time of the agreement).

following receipt of title from the appellant.[30] He is also liable to pay mesne profits,[31] which are awarded to reverse the transfer of the property's user value.[32] If the respondent has sold the property transferred, then he must make restitution of its proceeds,[33] and if he has made secondary profits, for example, by cutting timber on land that has been conveyed to him, then he must account for these profits to the appellant.[34]

(b) *Claims against Third Parties*

26–11   The general principle is that an appellate court can only order restitution against a party to the judgment.[35] The successful appellant must, therefore, bring separate proceedings against any third party who has received the appellant's property before the appeal was heard. If the third party has bought any property from an officer of the court then he will get a good title. Coke's reasoning in *Manning's Case*[36] is unimpeachable:

> "If the sale of the term should be avoided, the vendee would lose his term, and his money, too, and thereupon great inconvenience would follow, that none would buy of the sheriff goods or chattels in such cases, and so execution of judgments . . . would not be done."

26–12   However, if the third party did not buy from a court officer, then at law and in equity he bought at his peril.[37] He was bound by any decree that was made against the person from whom he derived title.[38] This still appears to be the law if the subject matter of the sale *pendente lite* is pure personalty.[39] However, the Land Charges Act 1972 s.5 provides that a pending land action may be registered in the register of pending actions,[40] and by s.5(7): "A pending land action shall

---

[30] *White v Tomasel* [2004] QCA 89; [2004] 2 Qd R. 438, where the majority held that an exception should be made to the principle of indefeasibility that underpins Torrens systems of land registration.

[31] *Kirkland v Modee Peston-jee Khoorsedjee* (1843) 3 Moo. Ind. App. 220; 18 E.R. 481; *Lindsay and Hadden v Oriental Bank Corp at Columbo* (1860) 8 Moo. P.C. 401; 15 E.R. 151; *Rajah Lelanund Singh v Maharajah Luckmissur Singh* Unreported PC, July 15, 1870 (noted by Lord Cairns in the course of argument in *Rodger* (1871) 3 L.R. 3 P.C. 465 at 471 fn.8).

[32] See paras 5–18—5–19.

[33] *Goodyere v Ince* (1590) Cro. Jac. 278; 79 E.R. 211; *Robertson v Miller* (1904) 3 N.B. Eq. 78.

[34] *Sympson v Juxon* (1624) Cro. Jac. 699; 79 E.R. 607; *Calthorpe v May* (1707) 3 E.R. 269; (1707) 7 Bro. P.C. 413.

[35] *R. v Lever* (1690) 1 Show. K.B. 261; 89 E.R. 560; 2 Salk. 587; 91 E.R. 492.

[36] *Manning's Case* (1609) 8 Co. Rep. 94b at 97a; 77 E.R. 618 at 624; see also *Hoe's Case* (1599) 5 Co. Rep. 89b; 77 E.R. 191; *Doe d. Emmett v Thorn* (1813) 1 M. & S. 425; 105 E.R. 160. And cf. *Zain-ul-abdin Khan v Muhammad Asghar Ali Khan* (1887) I.L.R. 10 All. 166 (PC). The sheriff is himself protected provided the writ of execution is not void on its face; see *Williams v Williams and Nathan* [1937] 2 All E.R. 559.

[37] *Bellamy v Sabine* (1857) 1 De G. & J. 566 at 584–585; 44 E.R. 842 at 850–851 per Turner L.J.

[38] *Bishop of Winchester v Paine* (1805) 11 Ves. Jun. 194 at 197–198; 32 E.R. 1062 at 1064–1065 per Sir W. Grant M.R.; *Metcalfe v Pulvertoft* (1813) 2 V. & B. 200; 35 E.R. 295; see also *Sorrell v Carpenter* (1728) 2 P. Wms. 482 at 483; 24 E.R. 825 at 826. W.H. Lyon (ed.), *Story's Equity Jurisprudence*, 14th edn (Boston, Mass: Little, Brown & Co, 1918), paras 536–537.

[39] It is said that any other conclusion would result in great inconveniences; see *Wigram v Buckley* [1894] 3 Ch. 483 at 494–495 per Lindley J.

[40] A "'pending land action' means any action or proceeding pending in court relating to land or any interest in or charge on land": Land Charges Act 1972 s.17.

not bind a purchaser without express notice of it unless it is for the time being registered under this section." If the title to the land is registered then a pending land action, being an interest affecting an estate in land,[41] may be protected by the entry of notice on the Land Register.[42]

(c) Claims by Third Parties

In *SmithKline Beecham Plc v Apotex Europe Ltd*,[43] Apotex resolved to import **26–13** products into the UK that were manufactured by its parent companies in Canada. GSK issued proceedings against Apotex for patent infringement and won an interim injunction after giving a cross-undertaking to pay damages to Apotex, but not to its parent companies which were not parties to the proceedings. Apotex could have asked for the cross-undertaking to be given for the benefit of the parent companies, but it failed to do this and by the time that the proceedings were resolved in Apotex's favour the parent companies had suffered substantial trading losses. They wished to recover these from GSK, but Lewison J. declined to hold either that the parent companies could retrospectively be joined as parties so as to take advantage of the cross-undertaking, or that the cross-undertaking should be retrospectively amended so as to extend to losses incurred by the parent companies as non-parties, or that they could recover GSK's trading profits by claiming in unjust enrichment.

The parent companies appealed from this last finding, arguing that they should **26–14** be entitled to restitution by analogy with the authorities that allow recovery of benefits transferred under judgments that are later reversed. These cases were said to embody a principle that the court has power to ensure that a litigant who has used its process to gain an advantage at the expense of another party must return the benefit if he loses on appeal. Furthermore this power was said to extend to making the respondent return a benefit gained at the expense of someone who was not party to the proceedings but who has suffered a loss as a result of the "wrongful" order. However, the parent companies could find no authority for the latter proposition and in his leading judgment in the Court of Appeal, Jacob L.J. rejected it. He considered that it had no clear limit and that it would produce undesirable results if pursued to its logical conclusion. It would mean that claims in unjust enrichment to recover a "wrongful" enjoiner's profits could be brought not only by the enjoinee but also by every other person who was caused to lose business profits by the "wrongful" grant of the injunction, e.g. the enjoinee's suppliers, wholesalers, distributors, carriers, etc.[44] Furthermore all these parties would also be able to recover from others in addition to the enjoiner who made a gain through the grant of the injunction, e.g. the enjoiner's suppliers, etc.[45] The undesirable result would be a hailstorm of claims and no reliable means of matching up claimants' losses with defendants' gains. To avoid all this,

---

[41] Land Registration Act 2002 s.87.
[42] Land Registration Act 2002 s.32.
[43] *SmithKline Beecham Plc v Apotex Europe Ltd* [2005] EWHC 1655 (Ch); [2006] 1 W.L.R. 872; affirmed [2006] EWCA Civ 658; [2007] Ch. 71.
[44] *SmithKline* [2006] EWCA Civ 658; [2007] Ch. 71 at [41].
[45] *SmithKline* [2006] EWCA Civ 658; [2007] Ch. 71 at [42].

Jacob L.J. therefore held that the enjoinee is the only party who might conceivably have a claim in unjust enrichment (and he will not usually need one since he can usually rely on the enjoiner's cross-undertaking).

26-15   Much of the argument in the Court of Appeal in *SmithKline* turned on the question whether GSK's gain had been made at the parent companies' expense. Jacob L.J. held that it had not, and rejected their argument that there was a sufficient link between their loss and GSK's gain to justify recovery, because they had lost, and GSK had gained, a quasi-proprietary right in the form of a business opportunity to sell a specific product in a specific market: in Jacob L.J.'s view, "a mere freedom to trade [cannot] fairly be regarded as property or anything in the nature of property".[46]

26-16   The rules determining whether a defendant has been enriched at a claimant's expense are discussed in Ch.6, where it is argued there that a "but for" causation test is used to decide whether there has been a transfer of value between the parties, but that this test may have to be qualified by a further rule that prevents the recovery of gains that are too remote a consequence of the claimant's loss. On this view, given that the parent companies' losses and GSK's gains would not have occurred but for the grant of the injunction, it could be argued that Jacob L.J. effectively denied them restitution (and would have denied restitution to any other party in the same position apart from Apotex) on the grounds that GSK's gains were too remote.

26-17   Note, finally, that Jacob L.J.'s reasons for denying the parent companies' claim in *SmithKline* also apply to the situation where a third party suffers a loss as a result of a court order, later reversed, that directs one litigant to transfer a benefit to another.

---

[46] *SmithKline* [2006] EWCA Civ 658; [2007] Ch. 71 at [71].

Part Six
DEFENCES

CHAPTER 27

CHANGE OF POSITION

1. INTRODUCTION

The modern English law governing the change of position defence began with **27–01**
Lipkin Gorman (A Firm) v Karpnale Ltd.[1] The defendant casino owed a prima
facie liability in unjust enrichment after receiving money paid as stakes from a
fraudulent solicitor. However, some of the fraudster's bets had been successful
and the House of Lords held that the casino's liability should be reduced by the
total amount which it had paid out as winnings.[2] Lord Goff held this to follow
from a general principle that a defendant can escape liability in unjust enrichment
where his "position has so changed that it would be inequitable in all the
circumstances to require him to make restitution, or alternatively restitution in
full."[3] He chose not to lay down a set of detailed rules about this defence, as he
thought it more appropriate for the courts to work matters out on a case-by-case
basis.[4] This process is now underway, but questions remain about the ambit and
operation of the defence and its relationship with other defences.[5]

In *Commerzbank AG v Price-Jones*,[6] Munby J. interpreted Lord Goff's speech **27–02**
to mean that the courts have a broad discretion to allow or to withhold the
defence according to the equities of a case. Hence he thought that there is no need
for the courts to "gloss or refine"Lord Goff's words to explain when the defence

---

[1] *Lipkin Gorman (A Firm) v Karpnale Ltd* [1991] 2 A.C. 548.
[2] *Lipkin Gorman* [1991] 2 A.C. 548 at 581–583. This was generous to the defendant, since the
fraudster had restaked much of this money and then lost it, but the court may have taken the
pragmatic view that a stricter approach would have called for an excessively complex calculation.
[3] *Lipkin Gorman* [1991] 2 A.C. 548 at 580. The Court of Appeal had previously rejected the defence
in *Durrant v Ecclesiastical Commissioners for Great Britain* (1880) 6 Q.B.D. 234 and *Bayliss v
Bishop of London* [1913] 1 Ch. 217; and see too *Standish v Ross* (1849) 3 Exch. 527 at 534; 154 E.R.
954 at 957; *Newall v Tomlinson* (1871) L.R. 6 C.P. 405; *Ministry of Health v Simpson* [1951] A.C.
251 at 276. But for previous judicial dicta supporting the defence, see *Kleinwort, Sons & Co v Dunlop
Rubber Co* (1907) 97 L.T. 263 at 267 (HL); *Larner v LCC* [1949] 2 KB 683 at 688 (CA); *National
Westminster Bank Ltd v Barclays Bank International Ltd* [1975] Q.B. 654 at 675–676; *Barclays Bank
v W.J. Simms, Son & Cooke (Southern) Ltd* [1980] Q.B. 677 at 695; *Rover International Ltd v Cannon
Film Sales Ltd (No.3)* [1989] 1 W.L.R. 912 at 925 (CA). And see too *BP Exploration Co (Libya) Ltd
v Hunt (No.2)* [1979] 1 W.L.R. 783 at 800 and 804, where Robert Goff J. rationalised the proviso to
the Law Reform (Frustrated Contracts) Act 1943 s.1(2) and (3)(a) as a statutory embodiment of the
change of position defence: on this, see para.15–21.
[4] *Lipkin Gorman* [1991] 2 A.C. 548 at 580. See too Lord Bridge's comments at 558; also *Haugesund
Kommune v Depfa ACS Bank* [2010] EWCA Civ 579; [2011] 1 All E.R. 190 at [152] per Etherton
L.J.: "The defence is not fixed in stone, and has developed and can be expected to develop further
over time on a case by case basis."
[5] Discussion of the latter can be found at paras 28–01—28–02 (ministerial receipt), 29–10—29–14
(bona fide purchase), 30–14—30–16 (estoppel) and 31–14—31–16 (counter-restitution impossible).
[6] *Commerzbank AG v Price-Jones* [2003] EWCA Civ 1664.

is available.[7] However, this was to misread *Lipkin Gorman*, where Lord Goff expressly stated that "the court [does not have] *carte blanche* to reject [a claim in unjust enrichment] simply because it thinks it unfair or unjust in the circumstances to grant recovery."[8] Hence the better view is that taken by Robert Walker L.J. in *Scottish Equitable Plc v Derby*, holding that:

> "[T]he court must proceed on the basis of principle, not sympathy, in order that the defence of change of position should not ... 'disintegrate into a case by case discretionary analysis of the individual facts, far removed from principle'."[9]

27-03 To develop the defence in a principled way the courts must understand its rationale. The point of the defence is essentially to strike a fair balance between the claimant's interest in restitution and the defendant's interest in making spending decisions freely, without fear that a claim in unjust enrichment might later invalidate the assumptions that he makes about the means at his disposal.[10] When undertaking this balancing exercise, the courts have a flexible discretion to reduce the defendant's liability pro tanto where his position has only partly changed,[11] and to make restitutionary orders on terms where the defendant's dealings with third parties can be unwound and where he has bought property, the immediate sale of which would create particular difficulties.[12] A consideration which the courts could also take into account, besides the protection of the defendant's autonomy in decision-making, is that placing defendants under a duty to take reasonable steps to check whether their receipts are impeachable would incentivise them to avoid litigation costs (both to themselves and to claimants).[13] However, the English cases do not clearly establish that defendants owe such a duty and some courts have held that they do not.[14]

---

[7] *Commerzbank* [2003] EWCA Civ 1664 at [56]. Emphasis was also placed on "inequitability" and "unconscionability" in *Barclays Private Bank Ltd v Austin* [2003] EWCA Civ 1502 at [8], and, to a lesser extent, in *Niru Battery Manufacturing Co v Milestone Trading Ltd (No.1)* [2003] EWCA Civ 1446; [2004] Q.B. 985 at [149] and [180].

[8] *Lipkin Gorman* [1991] 2 A.C. 548 at 578. Cf. *Kleinwort Benson Ltd v Birmingham CC* [1997] Q.B. 380 at 387 per Evans L.J.: the courts have no "discretionary power to order repayment in unjust enrichment cases whenever it seems in the circumstance of the particular case just and equitable to do so". In *Lipkin Gorman* Lord Goff was well aware that the change of position defence had been rejected by earlier courts precisely because they thought that it would entail the exercise of an unpredictable discretion: e.g. *Bayliss* [1913] 1 Ch. 127 at 140 per Hamilton L.J.: "we are not now free in the twentieth century to administer that vague jurisprudence which is sometimes attractively styled 'justice between man and man'."

[9] *Scottish Equitable Plc v Derby* [2001] 3 All E.R. 818 at [34] (CA), quoting A. Burrows, *The Law of Restitution* (London: Butterworths, 1993), p.426. See too *Philip Collins Ltd v Davis* [2000] 3 All E.R. 808 at 827; *Test Claimants in the F.I.I. Group Litigation v HMRC* [2008] EWHC 2893 (Ch); [2009] S.T.C. 254 at [313].

[10] *Kleinwort Benson Ltd v Lincoln CC* [1999] 2 A.C. 349 at 382: the defence is "concerned to protect the stability of closed transactions". See too *Dextra Bank & Trust Co Ltd v Bank of Jamaica* [2001] UKPC 50; [2002] 1 All E.R. (Comm.) 193 at [38]; and for an earlier expression of the same idea, see *Brisbane v Dacres* (1813) 5 Taunt. 143 at 152–153; 128 E.R. 641 at 645.

[11] *David Securities Pty Ltd v Commonwealth Bank of Australia* (1992) 175 C.L.R. 353 at 385; *Lipkin Gorman* [1991] 2 A.C. 548 at 580; *Dextra Bank* [2001] UKPC 50; [2002] 1 All E.R. (Comm.) 193 at [38].

[12] See paras 27–10—27–12, 27–17 and 27–57.

[13] E. Bant, *The Change of Position Defence* (Oxford: Hart, 2009), p.217; cf. H. Dagan, *The Law and Ethics of Restitution* (Cambridge: CUP, 2004), pp.46–47.

[14] See para.27–32.

2. Qualifying Detriment

Defendants might feel themselves worse off if they have to repay money which **27–04** they would rather keep, but their disappointment on this score is "is a hardship which every defendant to a restitution claim has to face, and by itself it is no defence."[15] According to Mummery L.J. in *Commerzbank*, a defendant most obviously suffers relevant detriment "where there has been a reduction in [his] assets", but "Lord Goff did not . . . restrict the scope of the defence to [such] cases" and it may also be founded on other types of detriment.[16] Hence the questions arise, what types of financial expenditure count and what other types of detriment count?

(a) *Financial Expenditure*

(i) *Extraordinary Expenditure*

In *Lipkin Gorman*, Lord Goff held that where a defendant has been paid **27–05** money:

> "the mere fact that [he] has spent the money, in whole or in part, does not of itself render it inequitable that he should be called upon to repay, because the expenditure might in any event have been incurred by him in the ordinary course of things."[17]

In *Dextra Bank & Trust Co Ltd v Bank of Jamaica*, he restated this point, observing (with Lord Bingham) that a defendant must have incurred "extraordinary expenditure".[18] This might seem to be a rule about the type of detriment that a defendant must have suffered, but in fact it is a rule about causation. The defendant need not show that he spent money on something that other people might think unusual, nor that he spent it in a way that he had never spent money before. The test is whether he entered a transaction that he would not have entered but for his enrichment.

Statements to the contrary have been made by the Australian and Canadian **27–06** courts, which have held that a defendant can never "resort to the defence of change of position where he or she has simply spent the money received on

---

[15] *Mahme Trust Reg v Tayeb* [2002] EWHC 1543 (Ch); [2003] W.T.L.R. 21 at [143]. Cf. *Scottish Equitable* [2001] 3 All E.R. 818 at [34]: the claimant's demand for repayment "must have come as a bitter disappointment" to the defendant, but this was no reason to deny restitution; *Filby v Mortgage Express (No.2) Ltd* [2004] EWCA Civ 759 at [67]: "there is no residual general discretion to withhold the remedy nor to modify it simply to avoid harsh reality." See too *Hydro Electric Commission of the Township of Nepean v Ontario Hydro* [1982] 1 S.C.R. 347 at 370: whether the defendant has the means to repay the claimant is an irrelevant consideration.

[16] *Commerzbank* [2003] EWCA Civ 1663 at [39]. But cf. *National Westminster Bank Plc v Somer International (UK) Ltd* [2001] EWCA Civ 970; [2002] Q.B. 1286 at [47]: the defence "only protects the actual reduction of the transferee's assets following receipt".

[17] *Lipkin Gorman* [1991] 2 A.C. 548 at 580; also emphasised in *F.I.I.* [2008] EWHC 2893 (Ch); [2009] S.T.C. 254 at [322].

[18] *Dextra Bank & Trust Co Ltd v Bank of Jamaica* [2001] UKPC 50; [2002] 1 All E.R. (Comm.) 193 at [38]. See too *Rural Municipality of Storthoaks v Mobil Oil Canada Ltd* [1976] 2 S.C.R. 147 at 164; *Alpha Wealth Financial Services Pty Ltd v Frankland River Olive Co Ltd* [2008] WASCA 119; (2008) 66 A.C.S.R. 594 at [202].

ordinary living expenses",[19] and that he must have undertaken a "special financial commitment" or "special project".[20] However, English law holds that a defendant who lets his standard of living drift upwards to match his new wealth can also rely on the defence. In *Philip Collins Ltd v Davis*,[21] two musicians with a "relaxed and philosophical" propensity to overspend their income escaped liability to the extent that increases in their everyday outgoings were referable to their receipts from the claimant. This was confirmed by the Court of Appeal in *Scottish Equitable*.[22] It is also consistent with some other Canadian cases: in *R.B.C. Dominion Securities Inc v Dawson*,[23] the defendant's position was held to have changed when he spent money entertaining his friends, expenditure which he could not have afforded but for his enrichment; and in *Social Services Appeal Board (Newfoundland) v Butler*,[24] a defendant who normally lived on the poverty line was held to have "changed her position to enjoy a more relaxed and enriched standard of living during the period when she was receiving the overpayments by mistake."

(ii) *Continuing Enrichment*

27–07   The causation rules which govern the change of position defence are discussed further below.[25] Even when a defendant can establish a causal link between his enrichment and his expenditure, however, there are some types of spending that still do not count as a detriment, because they do not reduce the defendant's overall wealth. These are the payment of debts and the purchase of assets which remain in his hands.

27–08   **Payment of debts** In *Scottish Equitable* Robert Walker L.J. held that "in general it is not a detriment to pay off a debt which will have to be paid off sooner or later", although he added that exceptionally "it might be if there were

---

[19] *David Securities* (1992) 175 C.L.R. 353 at 385–386. Cf. *Corporate Management Services (Australia) Pty Ltd v Abi-Arraj* [2000] NSWSC 361 at [21], distinguishing money spent on repairing property ("ordinary" expenditure) from money spent on improvements ("extraordinary" expenditure).

[20] *Rural Municipality of Storthoaks v Mobil Oil Canada Ltd* [1976] 2 S.C.R. 147 at 160; followed in: *Re Ottawa Board of Education and Federation of Women's Teaching Assocs* (1986) 25 L.A.C. (3d) 146; *Durrand v Highwood Golf & Country Club* (1998) 240 A.R. 320 (Alberta Provincial Ct); *Jones v Crane* (2001) 207 Nfld. & P.E.I.R. 343 (Newfoundland Sup Ct). Further cases are: *Monico Investments Ltd v Rebelcorp Financial Group Ltd* Unreported Ontario Sup Ct, October 20, 1994, at [69]; *Dalzell v Parnell* Unreported Ontario Sup Ct, January 6, 2005, at [73].

[21] *Phillip Collins Ltd v Davis* [2000] 3 All E.R. 808 at 827–830. See too *Kiel-Nootebos* Pensions Ombudsman Determination N00829, February 11, 2005, at [47]–[48].

[22] *Scottish Equitable* [2001] 3 All E.R. 818 at [33], itself followed in *F.I.I.* [2008] EWHC 2893 (Ch); [2009] S.T.C. 254 at [343]–[344], where Henderson J. held the principle to apply to government expenditure following the receipt of tax revenues; but we doubt that the defence should ever be available in response to claims to recover money paid as tax that is not due: see para.27–51.

[23] *R.B.C. Dominion Securities Inc v Dawson* (1994) 111 D.L.R. (4th) 230 at 240 (Newfoundland CA).

[24] *Social Services Appeal Board (Newfoundland) v Butler* (1996) 139 Nfld. & P.E.I.R. 282 at [29]–[30].

[25] See paras 27–25——27–30.

a long-term loan on advantageous terms".[26] A defendant's wealth is not reduced when he pays a debt because the detrimental effect of the payment is offset by the beneficial effect of his release from liability to the creditor.[27]

Note, though, that matters are different if the defendant pays a debt, and then   **27–09** incurs further expenditure, or forgoes earning opportunities, that he would not have incurred or forgone, had the debt still been outstanding. In *Gertsch v Atsas*,[28] the defendant innocently received a $100,000 legacy under a forged will, around $70,000 of which was used to extinguish a mortgage on her property. As a result of receiving the legacy, she gave up paid employment and became a student existing on state benefits; otherwise, she would have stayed in employment and reduced her mortgage debt to $10,000 by the time of the claim.[29] Hence the judge concluded that she should only have to repay $10,000 of the $70,000.

Robert Walker L.J.'s exceptional case was discussed in *Boscawen v Bajwa*,[30]   **27–10** where Millett L.J. reviewed the Court of Appeal's earlier decision in *Re Diplock*.[31] There executors paid money to charities under a void will trust. The testator's next-of-kin, to whom the money should have been paid, brought various claims against the charities, including a claim to be subrogated to a charge over property belonging to a hospital, which had used money from the estate to pay the chargee. The court dismissed this claim, holding that securities which have been extinguished by payment cannot be acquired by subrogation because they no longer exist.[32] Millett L.J. rejected this analysis in *Boscawen*, holding that in such cases the courts are able to treat the claimant, by a fiction, as though the security has been assigned to him.[33] He then gave a different explanation of the court's refusal to award subrogation in *Re Diplock*[34]:

> "The hospital had changed its position to its detriment. It had in all innocence used the money to redeem a mortgage held by its bank, which, no doubt, was willing to allow its advance to remain outstanding indefinitely so long as it was well secured and the interest was paid punctually. The next of kin were seeking to be subrogated to the bank's security in order to enforce it and enable a proper distribution of the estate to be made. This would have been unjust to the hospital. It may be doubted whether in its anxiety to avoid injustice to the hospital the court may not have done an even greater

---

[26] *Scottish Equitable* [2001] 3 All E.R. 818 at [35], followed in *Credit Suisse (Monaco) SA v Attar* [2004] EWHC 374 (Comm) at [98]. See too *Dominion Securities* (1994) 111 D.L.R. (4th) 230 at 240–241 (Newfoundland CA); *Sullivan v Lee* (1994) 95 B.C.L.R. (2d) 195 at 199 (British Columbia Sup Ct); *Cronan Estate v Hughes* (2000) 37 E.T.R. (2d) 27 (Ontario Sup Ct); *C.I.B.C. Trust Corp v Bayly* (2005) 15 E.T.R. (3d) 149 (British Columbia Sup Ct); *A.S.B. Securities Ltd v Geurts* [2005] 1 N.Z.L.R. 484 at [67] (NZ High Ct); *Datasat Communications Ltd v Swindon Town FC Ltd* [2009] EWHC 859 (Comm) at [109]; *Royal Bank of Canada v B.M.P. Global Distribution Inc* [2011] BCSC 458 at [153].
[27] German law has a similar rule: BGH NJW 1985, 2700.
[28] *Gertsch v Atsas* [1999] NSWSC 898; (1999) 10 B.P.R. 18,431.
[29] *Gertsch* [1999] NSWSC 898; (1999) 10 B.P.R. 18,431 at [98].
[30] *Boscawen v Bajwa* [1996] 1 W.L.R. 328 at 340–341 (CA).
[31] *Re Diplock* [1948] Ch. 465; affirmed sub nom. *Ministry of Health v Simpson* [1951] A.C. 251.
[32] *Re Diplock* [1948] Ch. 465 at 549–550.
[33] For further discussion, see paras 39–05—39–11.
[34] *Boscawen* [1996] 1 W.L.R. 328 at 341 (CA). Cf. *R.B.C. Direct Investing Inc v Khan* [2010] ONSC 3100 at [16]–[17] (defence available to extent that creditor would have been willing to accept part payment in full settlement, or to extent that terms of debt would have allowed payment over time, but no evidence of either on facts of case).

injustice to the next of kin, who were denied even the interest on their money. Justice did not require the withholding of any remedy, but only that the charge by subrogation should not be enforceable until the hospital had had a reasonable opportunity to obtain a fresh advance on suitable terms from a willing lender, perhaps from the bank which had held the original security."

27–11　　　Similarly, in *Gertsch*,[35] where money from the claimant was used to pay off the defendant's mortgage, the judge considered whether to make "an order allowing for the repayment of the whole sum by instalments, over a lengthy period of time".[36] He decided against this, because it would occasion the defendant "considerable financial hardship, having regard to her present uncertain earning situation", and decided instead to order the immediate repayment of a lesser sum. However, if this money were not repaid within seven days, then the claimant would be entitled to acquire a charge for the lesser sum over the defendant's property.[37]

27–12　　　These cases show that the change of position defence does not always operate as an absolute bar to recovery, as the courts can strike a more nuanced balance between the parties by allowing recovery on terms, to enable the defendant to regain the position which he previously occupied before requiring him to make restitution.[38]

27–13　　　**Surviving assets**　　　Where a defendant buys an asset which remains in his hands at the time of the action, the defence is disallowed to the extent that he is still enriched. In *Lipkin Gorman*, Lord Templeman said that a defendant who buys and retains a car suffers no greater detriment than the decline in value of the car between the date of purchase and the date of proceedings[39]; and in *Credit Suisse (Monaco) SA v Attar*, thedefence was denied to a defendant who had bought shares which had increased in value since the date of purchase, and which had in fact been sold by the time of the action.[40]

27–14　　　Contrast an Australian case, *Corporate Management Services (Aust) Pty Ltd v Abi-Arraj*,[41] where a complete defence was allowed to a defendant who had spent money on building works which were unfinished and deteriorating at the time of the action, and which would never be completed. Likewise, in a Jersey case, *Re the Esteem Settlement*,[42] Birt D.B. held that money spent on improving or repairing a house should be regarded as lost, to the extent that this expenditure

---

[35] *Gertsch* [1999] NSWSC 898; (1999) 10 B.P.R. 18,431.
[36] *Gertsch* [1999] NSWSC 898; (1999) 10 B.P.R. 18,431 at [95].
[37] *Gertsch* [1999] NSWSC 898; (1999) 10 B.P.R. 18,431 at [100].
[38] See too *Re Eurig Estate* [1998] 2 S.C.R. 565; *Re Gareau Estate* (1995) 9 E.T.R. (2d) 95 at [32] (Ontario Sup Ct), discussed at para.27–57.
[39] *Lipkin Gorman* [1991] 2 A.C. 548 at 560.
[40] *Credit Suisse (Monaco) SA v Attar* [2004] EWHC 374 (Comm) at [98]. The relevant transactions are described at [61] and [66]. See too *Re Gareau Estate* (1995) 9 E.T.R. (2d) 95 at [29] and [37] (Ontario Sup Ct) (no defence where money used to buy investments); *Campden Hill Ltd v Chakrani* [2005] EWHC 911 (Ch) at [87] (no defence where money used to buy an interest in land, and defendant would have bought the land anyway and was in bad faith); *Bisley v Richards* Unreported NZ High Ct, August 10, 2007 (no defence where money used to buy second hand car).
[41] *Corporate Management Services (Aust) Pty Ltd v Abi-Arraj* [2000] NSWSC 361 at [23]–[24].
[42] *Re the Esteem Settlement* 2002 J.L.R. 53 at 174–6. See also Birt D.B.'s comments at 105–106, on tracing money into improvements to property with a view to asserting a claim against the property.

fails to increase the value of the property. However, Birt D.B.'s conception of the value of residential property was too static. Houses which are not maintained fall into disrepair, and their value decreases. To the extent that repairs and improvements check such falls in value they should be regarded as leaving a valuable residue in the owner's hands.[43]

Most types of movable property can be sold with little personal inconvenience   **27–15** to their owners, but the same cannot generally be said of houses. What should the law do where a defendant buys and retains an asset, the value of which cannot easily be realised in cash? Forcing him to sell the asset might be unfair if this would mean forcing him to incur serious personal inconvenience and/or heavy transaction costs. This may not be a problem if the defendant can afford to pay a cash equivalent to the value locked up in the asset, but what if the defendant does not have the funds needed for this? In *R.B.C. Dominion Securities*, the Newfoundland Court of Appeal held that a defendant should not have to repay money which she had used to replace her old furniture with new furniture, stating that her case resembled that of a person "who lives at a higher standard of living because more money is available but would not have done so were it not for the windfall."[44] However, this reasoning ignored the fact that a defendant who buys consumables and consumes them is in a different position from a defendant who buys durables which remain in his hands. The enrichment received by the first defendant has gone; the enrichment received by the second survives. Why, then, should he be allowed to keep it? The best answer is that ordering restitution would be unfair if he has no other assets, and the financial and personal costs of realising its value would be disproportionately high. This seems to be the best way of distinguishing *R.B.C. Dominion Securities* from another Canadian case, *Sullivan v Lee*, where the judge ordered the defendant to hand over a motor-home and electronic goods, and declared that "upon conveying legal title to [the claimant], she will have no liability to him for the amounts expended in their purchase."[45]

These cases can also be contrasted with two others. In *Saunders & Co*   **27–16** *(A Firm) v Hague*,[46] the defendant knocked down his house and built a new one with funds received from the claimant. He argued that the only way that he could afford to repay the claimant would be to sell the new house and that this would be unfair. This was rejected because he produced no evidence of his financial position, including the amount of his mortgage (if any) and present income. In *Re Gareau Estate*,[47] two executrices mistakenly paid money to a good faith recipient who used it to build a house. She could not repay the money without losing her home, but she was enjoying the benefit of some $20,000 that should have gone to other people. Since their claim was "not pressing", the judge concluded that[48]:

---

[43] Cf. *Fea v Roberts* [2005] EWHC 2186 (Ch); (2005) 8 I.T.E.L.R. 231 at [112], where the defendant was not in good faith, but where the judge would otherwise have disallowed the defence in relation to money spent on "home improvements".
[44] *R.B.C. Dominion Securities* (1994) 111 D.L.R. (4th) 230 at 239–240.
[45] *Sullivan v Lee* (1994) 95 B.C.L.R. (2d) 195 at 199 (British Columbia Sup Ct).
[46] *Saunders & Co (A Firm) v Hague* [2004] 2 N.Z.L.R. 475 especially at [100] (NZ High Ct).
[47] *Re Gareau Estate* (1995) 9 E.T.R. (2d) 95 (Ontario Sup Ct).
[48] *Re Gareau Estate* (1995) 9 E.T.R. (2d) 95 at [32].

"[T]he equities of this situation can best be handled by imposing a constructive trust on the house and lot to secure the amount found due back to the estate, together with interest . . . with such constructive trust to be realized, if not sooner paid, at the time of disposition of the house and lot by [the defendant], or 20 years from now, whichever should first occur."

(iii) *Reversible Expenditure*

27–17   The foregoing cases suggest that a wider principle may be emerging that transactions entered by a defendant do not count as detriment if they can be unwound: in the words of an Australian judge, a qualifying change of position "must be legally or practically irreversible or there must be significant difficulties in reversing the change".[49] This principle also seems to be at work in several cases where the courts have refused the defence in respect of tax payments made on the defendant's receipts, reasoning that these could be recovered.[50] However, some questions arise with regard to this rule. How much time, effort and expense can be expected of a defendant in unwinding a transaction? Where he pays money to a third party in the mistaken belief that he has been validly enriched, should he be required to pursue legal proceedings against the third party? The answers will turn on the facts of individual cases, but it is notable that in analogous damages cases concerning the duty to mitigate, the courts have held that claimants need not undertake difficult litigation but may be required to act against third parties where this would be straightforward.[51] A further consideration is that in cases involving sequential transfers of value the law may allow claimants to recover from remote recipients of benefits, in which case it would seem to be unnecessarily complex to require an intermediate recipient to recover from his own payee in order to hand over the fruits of recovery to a claimant. This is discussed elsewhere.[52]

(b) *Other Types of Detriment*

27–18   Is the change of position defence available where the detriment suffered does not entail the expenditure of money? This question is pertinent to several situations: where the defendant delivers goods or performs services; where he foregoes an earning opportunity; and where he suffers mental or physical harm.

---

[49] *Alpha Wealth* [2008] WASCA 119; (2008) 66 A.C.S.R. 594 at [202] per Buss J.A. See too *Jaffer v Commonwealth Bank of Australia Ltd* [2001] SASC 191 at [58]–[64]; *Kiel-Nootebos* Pensions Ombudsman Determination N00829, February 11, 2005, at [46]; *Corp* Pensions Ombudsman Determination P00299, August 18, 2006, at [50]; *Fitzsimons v Minister for Liquor Gaming and Racing for the State of New South Wales* [2008] NSWSC 782 at [128]–[129]; *Glad Cleaning Service Pty Ltd v Vukelic* [2010] NSWSC 422 at [51].

[50] *Hillsdown v Pensions Ombudsman* [1997] 1 All E.R. 862 at 904; *Hinckley and Bosworth BC v Shaw* [2000] L.G.R. 9 at 51; *K&S Corp Ltd v Sportingbet Australia Pty Ltd* [2003] SASC 96; (2003) 86 S.A.S.R. 313 at [160]. Cf. *First National City Bank v McManus*, 223 S.E. 2d 544 (North Carolina CA, 1976); *Amsouth Investment Services Inc v Phillips*, 937 F. 2d 602 (4th Circuit CA, 1991). Cf. *Deutsche Bank v Beriro* (1895) 73 L.T. 671 (applying a similar principle in an estoppel case).

[51] *Pilkington v Wood* [1953] Ch. 770; *Western Trust & Savings Ltd v Clive Travers & Co* [1997] P.N.L.R. 295.

[52] See paras 6–35—6–51.

(i) *Goods and Services*

In *Lipkin Gorman*, Lord Goff observed that one reason why the bona fide **27-19**
purchase defence is not simply an example of the change of position defence is
that:

> "change of position will only avail a defendant to the extent that his position has been
> changed; whereas, where *bona fide* purchase is invoked, no enquiry is made (in most
> cases) into the adequacy of the consideration."[53]

Consistently with this, Rimer J. held in *Mahme Trust Reg v Tayeb* that a defendant who performs services for a claimant can rely on the change of position
defence only to the extent that he can prove the value of the services.[54] He also
said that "in effect, this head of defence comes down to one based on a claim for
a *quantum meruit*",[55] but this is not quite right. Where a defendant counterclaims
for a quantum meruit award on the ground of unjust enrichment, then it may be
that he can only recover the value of the services to the claimant, and cannot
recover the cost of performing the services if that is a greater amount.[56] But
where a defendant raises the change of position defence, the value of the services
to the claimant is beside the point, as the only relevant issue is the cost to the
defendant of performing the services, this being the measure of his detriment. Of
course, this distinction does not matter where the cost to the defendant and
benefit to the claimant are the same, as in *Maersk Air Ltd v Expeditors International (UK) Ltd*,[57] where the defendant had done virtually nothing, with the
result that it could not invoke the defence to justify its retention of a "service
fee" charged in respect of fictitious transactions billed to the claimant by the
defendant's fraudulent employee.

A defendant who parts with goods must also prove their value in order to make **27-20**
out the defence. In *National Westminster Bank Plc v Somer International (UK)
Ltd*[58] the defendant did this, and was held to have changed its position when it
sent computer equipment to a customer in the mistaken belief that the customer
was the source of money which had been credited to the defendant's account with
the claimant bank.

(ii) *Lost Earning Opportunities*

In principle, foregone opportunities for gains should count as a detriment, **27-21**
provided that the defendant can prove that he would have made the gain but for
his enrichment—something which may be difficult where the opportunity for
gain would have turned on the hypothetical actions of a third party. However,

---

[53] *Lipkin Gorman* [1991] 2 A.C. 548 at 580–581. The bona fide purchase defence is discussed in
Ch.29.
[54] *Mahme Trust Reg v Tayeb* [2002] EWHC 1543 (Ch); [2003] W.T.L.R. 21 at [145]. Cf. *Eastbourne
BC v Foster* [2001] EWCA 1091; [2002] I.C.R. 234 at [43].
[55] *Mahme* [2002] EWHC 1543 (Ch); [2003] W.T.L.R. 21 at [145].
[56] See paras 6–68—6–69.
[57] *Maersk Air Ltd v Expeditors International (UK) Ltd* [2003] 1 Lloyd's Rep. 491 at [45]–[46].
[58] *National Westminster Bank Plc v Somer International (UK) Ltd* Unreported Bristol County Court,
February 18, 2000. There was no appeal from this part of the judge's decision, the essence of which
was summarised by Potter L.J. in the CA: [2002] Q.B. 1286 at [1]–[10]. On goods, see too *Pearce
v Lloyds TSB Bank Plc* [2001] EWCA Civ 1907.

English cases on this point are inconclusive. In *Somer* Potter L.J. said in obiter dicta that[59]:

> "[T]he defence of 'change of position' only protects the actual reduction of the transferee's assets ... [and a] transferee who, in reliance upon a receipt, forgoes a realistic and quantifiable opportunity to increase his assets is not apparently protected."

However, dicta in other cases say the opposite[60]: in the *Scottish Equitable* case,[61] Robert Walker L.J. thought that a defendant might relevantly change his position if he gives up his job at an age when it will be hard to get new employment; and in *Commerzbank*,[62] Mummery L.J.said the same thing of a defendant who rejects a firm offer of a better paid job. Overseas authorities in point include *Gertsch*,[63] where a defendant who went to university rather than pursuing paid employment was allowed to set off her lost salaries against her restitutionary liability, and *Palmer v Blue Circle Southern Cement Ltd*,[64] where the defendant's omission to apply for social security benefits was held to be a relevant change of position.[65]

27–22   *Kinlan v Crimmin*[66] also holds that lost opportunities can constitute detriment. There the defendant was a shareholder and director of a company to which he sold his shares under an agreement that (unknown to the parties) was void for non-compliance with the Companies Act 1985 ss.164 and 159(3). The company's claim to recover its payment was defeated by the change of position defence, for these reasons[67]:

> "Had [the defendant] realised that the agreement was invalid and the payments made under it were made by mistake, [he] would obviously have wished to consider how his continuing interest in the company should be protected, either by his resuming his rights

---

[59] *Somer* [2002] Q.B. 1286 at [47].

[60] All obiter because in each case the defendant's assertion that he would have made a gain was not borne out by the facts.

[61] *Scottish Equitable* [2001] 3 All E.R. 818 at [32] (CA).

[62] *Commerzbank* [2003] EWCA Civ 1664 at [39]. Cf. *Brown* Pensions Ombudsman Determination 71981/2, September 10, 2009.

[63] *Gertsch* [1999] NSWSC 898; (1999) 10 B.P.R. 18,431 at [98]. See para.27–09.

[64] *Palmer v Blue Circle Southern Cement Ltd* [1999] NSWSC 697.

[65] See too *Morgan Guaranty Trust Co of New York v Outerbridge* (1990) 66 D.L.R. (4th) 517 (Ontario Sup Ct); *Sydney CC v Burns Philip Trustee Co Ltd (In Liquidation)* Unreported NSW Sup Ct, November 13, 1992; *Farmers' Mutual Insurance Ltd v Q.B.E. International Insurance Ltd* [1993] 3 N.Z.L.R. 305 at 316 (NZ High Ct); *Kilham v Banque Nationale de Paris* Unreported Victoria Sup Ct, June 28, 1994; *Toronto Dominion Bank v Bank of Montreal* Unreported Ontario Sup Ct, February 2, 1995, at [48]; *Ethnic Earth Pty Ltd v Quoin Technology Pty Ltd (In Liquidation) (No.3)* [2006] SASC 7; (2006) 94 S.A.S.R. 103 at [86]. And for cases where the principle was accepted, but the defendant would have made no gain, see *Ferram Inc v Three Dees Management Ltd* (1992) 7 O.R. (3d) 600 at [17] (Ontario Sup Ct); *Carter v Sabiston* [2007] W.W.R. 351 at [53]–[54] (Saskatchewan QB); *Moore v National Mutual Life Association of Australasia Ltd* [2011] NSWSC 416 at [100]; *T.R.A. Global Pty Ltd v Kabakasha* [2011] VSO 48 at [30]–[40].

[66] *Kinlan v Crimmin* [2006] EWHC 779 (Ch); [2007] 2 B.C.L.C. 67.

[67] *Kinlan* [2006] EHWC 779 (Ch); [2007] 2 B.C.L.C. 67 at [60] per Philip Sales, sitting as a deputy High Court judge.

to protect himself as a quasi-partner in the business or by seeking the reformulation of the agreement so as to ensure that it and the payments to him were valid. These opportunities which were denied him cannot be restored to him."

(iii) *Mental or Physical Harm*

In the *Commerzbank* case,[68] Munby J. denied that financial and non-financial **27–23** detriment should be treated differently, and stated that the defence can be founded on changes to a defendant's position which do not entail financial detriment, but which adversely affect him in other ways. Similarly in *Scottish Equitable*, Robert Walker L.J. said that the fact "that the recipient may have suffered some misfortune . . . such as a breakdown in his health . . . is not a defence unless the misfortune is causally linked [with his enrichment]".[69]

What kind of causally linked detriment might a defendant suffer, that does not **27–24** amount to financial loss? Munby J. gave the examples of a defendant who decides to marry, to divorce or to start a family, but these are all decisions with financial implications. Suppose, though, that a defendant can prove that he would not have suffered a breakdown in his health but for his enrichment at the hands of a claimant, as in the example suggested by Robert Walker L.J. Perhaps he has given up his job, and his change of lifestyle has caused him to become depressed. In such a case, the financial implications of the defendant's illness can be quantified easily enough (treatment costs, loss of earnings), but it will be hard to quantify his non-financial detriment. The example of personal injury damages in tort suggests that quantification difficulties should not lead the court to refuse to set a figure on the defendant's detriment, but still it cannot be ignored that this is unlikely to be an easy task.

3. CAUSATION

(a) *The "But For" Test*

A defendant who wishes to rely on a change of position defence must put it **27–25** forward "fairly and squarely" in his statement of case so that "its factual merits can be explored at the trial".[70] Where his defence is:

"based on the incurring of expenditure . . . after a payment was received from the [claimant], it is not essential that the money expended . . . [was] identical with the money . . . received from the [claimant]."[71]

---

[68] *Commerzbank* [2003] EWCA Civ 1664 at [65]–[72].
[69] *Scottish Equitable* [2001] 3 All ER 818 at [31] (CA). Cf. *Ewing v Stockham Value Ltd* [2000] NICA 30 (defendant knew that claimant had made a mistaken payment and so had no ground for complaint when "brusque and peremptory" letter of claim was sent).
[70] *Adrian Alan Ltd v Fuglers (A Firm)* [2002] EWCA Civ 1655; [2003] P.N.L.R. 14 at [16].
[71] *Abi-Arraj* [2000] NSWSC 361 at [12].

However the defendant must prove, at least on a "but for" basis, that his change of position was causally linked with his enrichment,[72] and no presumption to this effect will generally be made, although it has been held in the context of government expenditure that:

> "[T]here is no need to demonstrate a precise link between particular receipts and particular items of expenditure and . . . it is reasonable to infer that planned expenditure would not have taken place at the level which it did but for the availability of the tax receipts which were taken into account in fixing departmental budgets."[73]

The courts will make allowances for the fact that a good faith defendant may not keep an exact record of his spending, since he does not expect that he will have to account for his spending to anyone else.[74] But a mere assertion that money has been spent, without supporting evidence, does not suffice[75]; nor does evidence that an invoice was issued by the defendant's business associate, unaccompanied by evidence that this was ever paid.[76] By the same token, a defendant who contends that he has foregone an earning opportunity must furnish "precise" evidence of this.[77]

27–26   It has been suggested that a remoteness cap should be superadded to the "but-for" causation test in change of position cases, to stop defendants from relying

---

[72] *Scottish Equitable* [2001] 3 All E.R. 818 at [31] (CA). See too *Management Corporation Strata Title No.473 v De Beers Jewellery Pte Ltd* [2001] 4 S.L.R. 90 at [101] (Singapore High Ct); affirmed [2002] 2 S.L.R. 1 (Singapore CA); *Standard Bank London Ltd v Canara* [2002] EWHC 1574 (QB) at [104]; *National Bank of Egypt International Ltd v Oman Housing Bank SAOC* [2002] EWHC 1760 (Comm); [2003] 1 All E.R. (Comm.) 246 at [29]; *Parkway Properties Pte Ltd v United Artists Singapore Theatres Pte Ltd* [2003] 2 S.L.R. 103 (Singapore CA) at [46]; *Kiel-Nootebos* Pensions Ombudsman Determination N00829, February 11, 2005, at [46]; *Fea* [2005] EWHC 2186 (Ch); (2005) 8 I.T.E.L.R. 231 at [77]; *Saba Yachts Ltd v Fish Pacific Ltd* [2006] NZHC 1452 at [49]; *Abou-Rahmah v Abacha* [2006] EWCA Civ 1492; [2007] Bus. L.R. 220 at [56]; *Faulkner* Pensions Ombudsman Determination M00843, September 25, 2007, at [51]; *4Eng Ltd v Harper* [2009] EWHC 2633 (Ch); [2010] B.P.I.R. 1 at [14] and [85]–[86]; *F.I.I.* [2008] EWHC 2893 (Ch); [2009] S.T.C. 254 at [343].

[73] *Bloomsbury International Ltd v Sea Fish Industry Authority* [2009] EWHC 1721 (QB); [2010] 1 C.M.L.R. 1 at [137] (reversed on a different point by the CA, but restored on further appeal: [2010] EWCA Civ 263; [2010] 1 W.L.R. 2117; [2011] UKSC 25; [2011] 1 W.L.R. 1546). See para.27–51 for discussion of the larger question whether public body defendants should be allowed to rely on the defence in response to claims to recover payments that were not due.

[74] *R.B.C. Dominion Securities* (1994) 111 D.L.R. (4th) 230 at 238 (Newfoundland CA); *Gertsch* [1999] NSWSC 898; (1999) 10 B.P.R. 18,431 at [128]; *Scottish Equitable* [2001] 3 All E.R. 818 at [33] (CA), affirming *Philip Collins* [2000] 3 All E.R. 808 at 827–830; *Fea* [2005] EWHC 2186 (Ch); (2005) 8 I.T.E.L.R. 231 at [111]. A similar idea underpins *Corp* Pensions Ombudsman Determination P00299, August 18, 2006, at [60], and *Smith* Pensions Ombudsman Determination Q00734, May 4, 2007, at [34] (taking a "fair and pragmatic approach"); but cf. *X* Pensions Ombudsman Determination Q00275, March 29, 2007, at [44]–[49] (where the principle was accepted but could not be applied in the absence of any evidence of the recipient's income and expenditure).

[75] *Schonwetter v German Motorwerks (1995) Ltd* [2000] BCSC 393 at [28]; *Saunders* [2004] 2 N.Z.L.R. 475 at [100] (NZ High Ct); *T.D. Canada Trust Co v Mosiondz* [2005] SKQB 540; (2005) 272 Sask. R. 100 at [30]; *Lazeski v Lakeview School Division No.142* [2007] SKQB 109 at [71]; *M.G.N. Ltd v Horton* [2009] EWHC 1680 (QB) at [33]; *Five Star Finance Ltd (In Liquidation) v Williams* [2010] NZHC 404 at [57].

[76] *Saba Yachts* [2006] NZHC 1452 at [65].

[77] *Commerzbank* [2003] EWCA Civ 1664 at [40].

on losses which are too far removed from the defendant's enrichment.[78] One part of Hobhouse J.'s judgment in *Westdeutsche Landesbank Girozentrale v Islington LBC*[79] might be explained on this basis. He would not have let Westdeutsche rely on the defence against Islington's counterclaim for money paid under the parties' void contract, although Westdeutsche had made a back-to-back contract with Morgan Grenfell under which it had paid money each time it had received money from Islington. The Morgan Grenfell contract was said to be "wholly independent of Westdeutsche's transaction with Islington", even though Westdeutsche would not have entered this contract but for the supposed existence of its contract with Islington.

(b) *Reliance*

Must the defendant show that he relied on the claimant's payment? Australian   **27–27** and Canadian authorities hold that he must,[80] and so do the only English cases where the court's decision counts as ratio. In *Streiner v Bank Leumi (UK) Plc*,[81] money was paid into the defendant's account with a Maltese bank, which then paid the money over to his business associates pursuant to an order by the Maltese court. Leggatt J. held that the change of position defence was not available, because the defence:

> "cannot operate without some form of reliance on the payment by the person whose position is said to have changed. It is not enough that without his knowledge his position has been passively changed."

Likewise, in *Credit Suisse*,[82] money was paid into a joint bank account held by a husband and wife. The husband withdrew some of the money, and Gross J. held that the wife could not raise the change of defence in respect of these withdrawals because "the necessary causal link cannot be established".

As other English judges have observed,[83] however, these cases are unsat-   **27–28** isfactory because the reliance rule which they establish leaves a good faith defendant unprotected where he receives a benefit which is subsequently stolen or destroyed. This happened in a Hong Kong case, *Hua Rong Finance Ltd v Mega Capital Enterprises Ltd*,[84] where the claimant gave a cheque for $1.5

---

[78] P. Key, "Change of Position" (1995) 58 M.L.R. 505, p.512; R. Nolan, "Change of Position" in P. Birks (ed.), *Laundering and Tracing* (Oxford: OUP, 1995), 135, pp.149–151; A. Burrows, "Change of Position: The View from England" (2003) 36 *Loyola of Los Angeles Law Review* 803, pp.807–808.
[79] *Westdeutsche Landesbank Girozentrale v Islington LBC* [1994] 4 All E.R. 890 at 948 (not considered on subsequent appeals). Cf. *South Tyneside MBC v Svenska International Plc* [1995] 1 All E.R. 545, discussed at para.27–29, fn.88.
[80] *David Securities* (1992) 175 C.L.R. 353 at 386; *Storthoaks v Mobil* [1976] 2 S.C.R. 147 at 164; *State Bank of New South Wales Ltd v Swiss Bank Corp* (1995) 39 N.S.W.L.R. 350 (NSW CA), but note the wide reading of this case in *Perpetual Trustees Australia Ltd v Heperu Pty Ltd* [2009] NSW CA 84 at [137]–[140].
[81] *Streiner v Bank Leumi (UK) Plc* Unreported QBD, October 31, 1985.
[82] *Credit Suisse* [2004] EWHC 374 (Comm) at [98].
[83] *Scottish Equitable* [2001] 3 All E.R. 818 at [30]–[31] (CA); *Rose v A.I.B. Group (UK) Plc* [2003] EWHC 1737 (Ch); [2003] 1 W.L.R. 2791 at [49]; *Cressman v Coys of Kensington (Sales) Ltd* [2004] EWCA Civ 47; [2004] 1 W.L.R. 2774 at [41].
[84] *Hua Rong Finance Ltd v Mega Capital Enterprises Ltd* [2000] HKCFI 1310.

million to a fraudster who purported to act for the defendant. The fraudster deposited the cheque into the defendant's bank account, and then withdrew all the money eight minutes later and disappeared. Recovery was denied because the defendant's position was held to have changed. Another authority in point is *National Bank of New Zealand Ltd v Waitaki International Processing (NI) Ltd.*[85] The defendant deposited money with a finance company that became insolvent, and was allowed the defence at common law although it had known that it was not entitled to the money and so could not have acted in reliance on the validity of the payment.[86] The English courts should follow the example of these cases, and of German law,[87] to hold that reliance is unnecessary provided that a causal link can be established.

(c) Anticipatory Changes of Position

27-29　　Provided that the defendant's enrichment and detriment are causally linked, there is no need for the enrichment to precede the detriment: the defence is available where detriment has been incurred in anticipation of an enrichment that subsequently arrives. This was established by the Privy Council's decision in *Dextra Bank.*[88] Dextra Bank sent the Bank of Jamaica a cheque for $3 million. Both were the victims of a fraud. The Bank of Jamaica thought that it was buying foreign currency and Dextra Bank thought that it was making a foreign currency loan. Even before it received Dextra Bank's cheque, the Bank of Jamaica paid third parties whom it mistakenly believed had paid Dextra Bank for the dollars on its behalf. This payment gave the Bank of Jamaica a complete defence to Dextra Bank's claim for the value of the cheque.

27-30　　In *Commerzbank*, the Court of Appeal accepted the finding in *Dextra Bank* that the change of position defence is available "in cases of 'anticipatory reliance' where a recipient of an overpayment has already changed his position in good faith in the expectation of receiving a future benefit".[89] The defence was also

---

[85] *National Bank of New Zealand Ltd v Waitaki International Processing (NI) Ltd* [1999] 2 N.Z.L.R. 211 at 228–229 (NZ CA).

[86] As required by the statutory change of position defence given to recipients of mistaken payments by the New Zealand Judicature Act 1908 s.94B.

[87] The disenrichment rule under BGB §818 III applies, for example, where money received by a defendant is embezzled by his employee (RGZ 68, 269) or seized by a foreign power in wartime (RGZ 120, 297, 299).

[88] *Dextra Bank* [2001] UKPC 50; [2002] 1 All E.R. (Comm.) 193 at [38]. See too *Thomas v Houston Corbett & Co* [1969] N.Z.L.R. 151 at 164 (NZ CA); *Fitzsimons v McBride* [2008] NSWSC 782 at [123]–[132]; *F.I.I.* [2008] EWHC 2893 (Ch); [2009] S.T.C. 254 at [344]; *Charles Terence Estates Ltd v Cornwall Council* [2011] EWHC 2542 (QB) at [98]. In *Dextra Bank* at [39] the court declined to follow Clarke J.'s decision in *South Tyneside v Svenska* [1995] 1 All E.R. 545, that a defendant could not point to anticipatory expenditure incurred in reliance on the supposed validity of a void interest swap contract. In the court's view, the "exclusion of anticipatory reliance in [*Svenska*] depended on the exceptional facts of the case." The defendant there had paid money under a back-to-back contract with another bank, and it may be that this was too remote a form of expenditure: cf. *Westdeutsche* [1994] 4 All E.R. 890 at 948; discussed at para.27–26.

[89] *Commerzbank* [2003] EWCA Civ 1664 at [38] per Mummery L.J. The defence failed on the facts because the defendant failed to prove that his position had changed.

allowed by the Court of Appeal in *Abou-Rahmah v Abacha*,[90] where the defendant bankpermitted withdrawals from an account before receiving the claimant's money. In *Dextra Bank* the court attached no particular significance to the fact that the defendant had expected the claimant's payment because of its own mistaken assessment of the situation, and in principle it should make no difference whether the reason for the defendant's expectation is a misrepresentation by the claimant or the claimant's self-induced misapprehension. The Court of Appeal held otherwise in *Commerzbank*,[91] but this was to introduce extraneous considerations of fault into a causal inquiry. Note too that in all three cases the defendants argued that they had consciously decided to change their positions, and so the question did not arise whether the defence is available where a third party decides to change a defendant's position for him, for example by stealing his money in the expectation that the loss will be made good by a forthcoming payment by the claimant. In principle, the defence should be available in this situation as well.

4. DISQUALIFYING CONDUCT

In *Lipkin Gorman* Lord Goff held that the change of position defence: **27–31**

> "[I]s not open to one who has changed his position in bad faith as where the defendant has paid away the money with knowledge of the facts entitling the plaintiff to restitution; and it is commonly accepted that the defence should not be open to a wrong-doer."[92]

Hence there are two types of conduct that can disqualify a defendant from relying on the defence: changes of position in "bad faith" and "wrongdoing".

(a) *Bad Faith*

(i) *The Fault Spectrum*

In *Niru Battery Manufacturing Co v Milestone Trading Ltd (No.1)*,[93] Moore-Bick **27–32**
J. considered the degree of fault needed to disqualify a defendant, and his comments were approved by the Court of Appeal.Unsurprisingly he thought that bad faith takes in dishonesty, and it seems that this includes both "self-conscious" dishonesty of the kind identified in *Twinsectra Ltd v Yardley*,[94] and

---

[90] *Abou-Rahmah v Abacha* [2006] EWCA Civ 1492; [2007] Bus. L.R. 220. The court did not explicitly address the point, but the timing of the payments is clear from Rix L.J.'s comments at [34], and at [56] he found that there was "a relevant causal connection between the change of position and the circumstances in which payment [was] effected".

[91] *Commerzbank* [2003] EWCA Civ 1664 at [41]–[44] and [78]–[83].

[92] *Lipkin Gorman* [1991] 2 A.C. 548 at 580.

[93] *Niru Battery Manufacturing Co v Milestone Trading Ltd (No.1)* [2002] EWHC 1425 (Comm); [2002] 2 All E.R. (Comm.) 705 at [135]; affirmed [2003] EWCA Civ 1446; [2004] Q.B. 985 at [164]; and see too *Abou-Rahmah* [2006] EWCA Civ 1492; [2007] Bus. L.R. 220 at [48]–[49].

[94] *Twinsectra Ltd v Yardley* [2002] UKHL 12; [2002] 2 A.C. 164. For a case where the defence was denied to a defendant who "knew perfectly well that [his actions] . . . were dishonest" see *Colliers CRE Plc v Pandya* [2009] EWHC 211 (QB) at [94].

"objective" dishonesty of the kind described in *Barlow Clowes International Ltd (In Liquidation) v Eurotrust International Ltd*.[95] He also thought that bad faith is "capable of embracing a failure to act in a commercially acceptable way and sharp practice of a kind that falls short of outright dishonesty as well as dishonesty itself".[96] Note, though, that this formulation appears to exclude negligence,[97] suggesting that a defendant can rely on the defence although he has negligently failed to recognise the flawed nature of the transfer by which he has been benefited.[98] Defendants can also rely on the defence although they have changed their position by making foolish investment decisions: if they honestly believe that money is theirs to spend as they choose, then they cannot be criticised for spending it unwisely.[99]

27–33   Moore-Bick J. went on to say that where a defendant "knows that the payment he has received was made by mistake, the position is quite straightforward: he must return it."[100] This was borne out by *Cressman v Coys of Kensington (Sales) Ltd*[101] where the Court of Appeal held that the defendant had not given away the right to a personalised number plate in good faith, because he had known from the moment of receipt that he had received the right by mistake.However, it would be wrong to conclude that a defendant can *never* plead change of position where he has suffered detriment after becoming aware of the circumstances entitling the claimant to restitution. In *National Bank of New Zealand*,[102] the defendant warned the claimant that it had made a mistaken payment, and when the claimant obstinately denied this, deposited the money with afinance company whichbecame insolvent. The court resolved the case by assessing the relative fault of the parties, an exercise that was later held to be unsound in *Dextra Bank*,[103] butthe court was surely right to hold that knowledge and bad faith do not always go hand in hand.

---

[95] *Barlow Clowes International Ltd (In Liquidation) v Eurotrust International Ltd* [2005] UKPC 37; [2005] 1 W.L.R. 1453.

[96] *Niru (No.1)* [2002] 2 All E.R. (Comm.) 705 at [135]. See too *Haugesund* [2010] EWCA Civ 579; [2011] 1 All E.R. 190 at [122]: lack of good faith is "not the same thing as having acted dishonestly".

[97] As noted in *Abou-Rahmah* [2005] EWHC 2662; [2006] 1 All E.R. (Comm.) 247 at [88].

[98] For an argument to the contrary, that English law requires a defendant to have some reasonable basis for the assumptions that he makes about the basis of his enrichment, see Bant, *The Change of Position Defence*, pp.151–155. Bant asserts (at p.153) that "a requirement of reasonable reliance . . . underpins a number of English decisions", citing *Rose* [2003] EWHC 1737 (Ch); [2003] 1 W.L.R. 2791, *Maersk Air* [2003] 1 Lloyd's Rep. 491; and *Fea* [2005] EWHC 2186 (Ch); (2005) 8 I.T.E.L.R. 231. However, these do not provide particularly clear support for her proposition and she concedes that their reasoning is "obscured under the label of 'good faith'". By way of analogy she also cites cases on estoppel (discussed at pp.43–47) and payment over by an agent (discussed at pp.76–78).

[99] *Haugesund* [2010] EWCA Civ 579; [2011] 1 All E.R. 190 at [125]: "the [defendants] acted in good faith in making the investments and . . . any question of negligence or other criticism of those investments is irrelevant to this defence." It follows that Cranston J. was incorrect to think that it mattered whether the defendant had been "negligent or foolish in the way it changed its position" in *Charles Terence Estates* [2011] EWHC 2542 (QB) at [98].

[100] *Niru (No.1)* [2002] 2 All E.R. (Comm.) 705 at [135].

[101] *Cressman v Coys of Kensington (Sales) Ltd* [2004] EWCA Civ 47; [2004] 1 W.L.R. 2774 at [21] and [41]. See too *Guertin v Metics* Unreported Ontario Sup Ct, November 12, 2002; *R.B.C. v Khan* [2010] ONSC 3100.

[102] *National Bank of New Zealand* [1999] 2 N.Z.L.R. 211 (NZ CA).

[103] *Dextra Bank* [2002] 1 All E.R. (Comm.) 193 at [40]–[45].

In *Niru (No.1)*, Moore-Bick J. also thought that difficulties might arise in cases   **27–34**
where the defendant does not know for sure, but "has grounds for believing that
the payment may have been made by mistake".[104] In such cases, his Lordship
thought that "good faith may well dictate that an enquiry be made of the payer,"
an assessment that is borne out by several other authorities,[105] although obviously much will turn on the facts of individual cases.[106]

In *Abou-Rahmah*[107] the defendant was a Nigerian bank which suspected "in a   **27–35**
general way" that two customers were involved in money laundering. As
required by Nigerian law, the bank reported movements in the account to the
Nigerian Drugs and Law Enforcement Agency, but continued to operate the
account. The claimants were defrauded of money that was paid into the account
and then paid out on the customers' instructions. The bank had no particular
reason to think that these transactions were tainted, and so Arden and Pill L.JJ.
allowed the bank a change of position defence when it was sued by the claimants
for restitution.[108] Rix L.J. thought that the bank should not be entitled to the
defence, taking the firm line that it is not "commercially acceptable for banks
who suspect 'in a general way' would-be customers of being involved in money
laundering to open up accounts for them."[109] However he did not press this
opinion to the point of dissent.

(ii) *Relative Fault*

The New Zealand Court of Appeal has twice held that where a claimant's money   **27–36**
is lost through the combined carelessness of the claimant and the defendant, the
court should weigh up the relative fault of the parties when determining the
extent to which the defendant's liability is reduced under the New Zealand
Judicature Act 1908 s.94B (which establishes a statutory change of position
defence for recipients of mistaken payments). In *Thomas v Houston Corbett &
Co*,[110] the claimant solicitors and the defendant doctor were both the victims of
a fraud perpetrated by the claimants' clerk. The clerk caused the firm to pay
money to the defendant, who was induced by receipt of this money to make a
payment to the clerk. The court held that the defendant was one-third at fault, and

---

[104] *Niru (No.1)* [2002] 2 All E.R. (Comm.) 705 at [135].
[105] *Mercedes Benz (NSW) Pty Ltd v A.N.Z. and National Mutual Royal Savings Bank Ltd* Unreported
NSW Sup Ct May 5, 1992; *Ellis* Pensions Ombudsman Determination K00694, June 8, 2001, at
[9]–[10]; *Port of Brisbane Corp v A.N.Z. Securities Ltd* [2002] QCA 158; *Maersk Air* [2003] 1
Lloyd's Rep. 491; *Fea* [2005] EWHC 2186 (Ch); (2005) 8 I.T.E.L.R. 231; *Jones v Churcher* [2009]
EWHC 772 (QB); [2009] 2 Lloyd's Rep. 94; *Kenny* Pensions Ombudsman Determination 28034/5,
February 24, 2010, at [15]; *Royal Bank of Canada v B.M.P. Global Distribution Inc* [2011] BCSC 458
at [154]. See too *Heperu* [2009] NSWCA 84 at [136]: "lack of reasonable enquiries of the payer
before money is paid away may be a factual foundation for lack of good faith ... [and] some
knowledge of 'tell tale' signs [may] likewise found such an argument." These cases should be
preferred to *Bisley v Richards* Unreported NZ High Ct, August 10, 2007, at [24], where the judge
asserted that actual knowledge is always required and denied that "good faith would require that
where a payee is unsure as to whether a mistake has been made, she should inquire further."
[106] For cases where defendants who failed to make enquiries were held to have acted in good faith
nevertheless, see e.g. *Seagate Technology Pte Ltd v Goh Han Kim* [1995] 1 S.L.R. 17 (Singapore
CA); *Perfect Auto Lease & Sales Inc v Gagnier Trucking (Fingal) Ltd* [2008] ONCA 61.
[107] *Abou-Rahmah* [2006] EWCA Civ 1492; [2007] Bus. L.R. 220.
[108] *Abou-Rahmah* [2006] EWCA Civ 1492; [2007] Bus. L.R. 220 at [82] and [101]–[102].
[109] *Abou-Rahmah* [2006] EWCA Civ 1492; [2007] Bus. L.R. 220 at [52].
[110] *Thomas v Houston Corbett & Co* [1969] N.Z.L.R. 151.

that the firm was two-thirds at fault, for the defendant's payment to the clerk, and so his liability was reduced by two-thirds of this amount. Again, in *National Bank of New Zealand*,[111] the claimant negligently ignored the defendant's warnings that it had paid the defendant money by mistake, and the defendant negligently took insufficient security when it deposited the money with a finance house which became insolvent. The court declined to allow the defence in full, but reduced the defendant's liability by 90 per cent.

27–37　　These cases were reviewed in *Dextra Bank*,[112] where the Privy Council declined to introduce the concept of "relative fault" into the common law version of the defence. They gave two reasons for this. One was that the process of comparing the degrees of fault displayed by the parties was too uncertain. The other was that a claimant's carelessness does not prevent him from establishing a cause of action, and that it would therefore be "very strange" if "the defendant should find his conduct examined to ascertain whether he had been negligent". The first of these reasons is more persuasive than the second. The claimant's fault is irrelevant when asking whether he has a claim, because this enquiry assumes that the benefit still exists and asks which of the parties has the better right to it. At the later stage when the defence of change of position is considered, this assumption no longer holds good. Ex hypothesi, the benefit has been lost and a different question must be addressed, namely which of the parties should bear the loss. Hence there would be no inconsistency if the court ignored the claimant's fault at the first stage, but took it into account at the second stage.[113]

(iii) *Attributed Fault*

27–38　In *Credit Suisse*,[114] money was paid into a joint bank account held by two defendants, who were husband and wife. Gross J. held that the wife was debarred from relying on the defence because her husband had acted in bad faith, reasoning that in the case of joint accounts, bad faith by one account-holder should be attributed to the other. He would have done better to treat the defendants separately when considering their states of mind, given that their liabilities were joint and several.[115] This was done in a similar case, *Euro-actividade AG v Moeller*,[116] where Simon Brown L.J. found the argument "not unappealing" that Mrs Moeller's position had been changed for her by her husband's withdrawals from their joint account, but did not believe that she had actually acted in good faith, the only evidence offered on this point having been the "totally and absolutely worthless" assertions of her husband that she had known nothing of his fraudulent activities.

(b) *Wrongdoing*

27–39　Lord Goff did not say in *Lipkin Gorman* whether a defendant should be characterised as a "wrongdoer" because he has committed a criminal offence, and/or

---

[111] *National Bank of New Zealand* [1999] 2 N.Z.L.R. 211.
[112] *Dextra Bank* [2002] 1 All E.R. (Comm.) 193 at [45].
[113] J. McCamus, "Wrongful Conduct and Change of Position" in S. Degeling and J. Edelman (eds), *Unjust Enrichment in Commercial Law* (Sydney: Lawbook Co, 2008), 385; Bant, *The Change of Position Defence*, p.179.
[114] *Credit Suisse* [2004] EWHC 374 (Comm) at [98].
[115] See para.4–54.
[116] *Euroactividade AG v Moeller* Unreported CA, February 1, 1995.

because he has committed a civil wrong, and/or because he has behaved in a morally shabby way.

Many of the cases that have considered whether a defendant's "wrongdoing"   **27–40**
should debar him from raising the defence have been concerned with illegality.
In *Equiticorp Industries Group Ltd v R. (No.47)*,[117] Smellie J. held that the New Zealand government could not raise the defence in respect of payments which had been made pursuant to a share purchase and buy-back scheme that infringed the New Zealand Companies Act 1955 s.62, which prohibits the purchase by a company of its own shares. In *Garland v Consumers' Gas Co Ltd*,[118] the Supreme Court of Canada held that a regulated gas utility could not raise the defence against a claim to recover money which it had collected from customers as "late payment penalties", contrary to s.347 of the Canadian Criminal Code, which prohibits receiving interest at a criminal rate.[119] In *Barros Mattos Junior v General Securities & Finance Ltd*,[120] Laddie J. held that the defendants could not raise the defence because they had converted US dollars which had been stolen from the claimant into Nigerian naira before paying the money away to third parties, contrary to the Nigerian Foreign Exchange (Monitoring and Miscellaneous Provisions) Decree 1995: this requires forex dealings in Nigeria to be conducted through authorised intermediaries.

The offences committed by each of these defendantswere notably different, as   **27–41**
were the circumstances of each case. In *Garland*, the defendant's enrichment at the expense of its customers was itself the illegal act which forestalled the change of position defence; in *Equiticorp*, both the government's receipt of benefits and its subsequent disposal of these benefits were illegal because they formed part of a larger scheme, the whole of which fell foul of the companies legislation; in *Barros*, the illegality in issue was not the defendants' receipt of money, nor their actions in paying it on to third parties, but their actions in converting the US dollars into Nigerian naira through an unauthorised intermediary. In *Equiticorp*, officers of the New Zealand government discovered late in the day that the share purchase scheme which they had devised was illegal, but decided to press ahead regardless[121]; in *Garland*, the gas utility implemented the late payment penalty with the approval and authority of its regulator, the Ontario Energy Board, and some 20 years elapsed before the legality of this penalty was challenged in the courts[122]; in *Barros*, the defendants were presumably aware of the Nigerian forex regulations, but regarded them as a dead letter in light of the fact that the Nigerian authorities never enforce them in practice.[123]

---

[117] *Equiticorp Industries Group Ltd v R. (No.47)* [1998] 2 N.Z.L.R. 481 at 654 and 730 (NZ High Ct).

[118] *Garland v Consumers' Gas Co Ltd* [2004] SCC 25; [2004] 1 S.C.R. 629 at [63]–[66]; followed in *Kilroy v A OK Payday Loans Inc* (2006) 273 D.L.R. (4th) 255 (British Columbia Sup Ct).

[119] The Supreme Court had previously held that the defendant's actions in charging late payment penalties amounted to charging a criminal rate of interest under s.347, in *Garland* [1998] 3 S.C.R. 112.

[120] *Barros Mattos Junior v General Securities & Finance Ltd* [2004] EWHC 1188 (Ch); [2004] 2 Lloyd's Rep. 475.

[121] *Equiticorp* [1998] 2 N.Z.L.R. 481 at 553–620.

[122] *Garland* [2004] 1 S.C.R. 629 at [5]–[6].

[123] Or so the defendants alleged: no evidence seems to have been led on the point, and Laddie J. held that even if it were true that that the "Nigerian authorities have . . . 'under-prioritised' the pursuit of breaches of the Decree, that does not alter the fact that it is existing criminal legislation in that country": *Barros* [2004] 2 Lloyd's Rep. 475 at [36].

27–42   These observations suggest that the courts would do best to take a flexible attitude towards the question whether the gravity of the defendant's illegal actions should debar him from raising the change of position defence. However, in *Barros*, Laddie J. denied that they have any such discretion, and held that, subject to a de minimis threshold, the courts must always disallow the change of position defence in accordance with the maxim *ex dolo malo non oritur actio* ("an action does not arise out of fraud")—even if this effectively means imposing an arbitrarily heavy penalty on a defendant for a comparatively minor breach of the law.[124] Thus, the defendants in *Barros* were liable to repay US \$8 million because they changed the money into naira before paying it on to third parties, a liability they would not have incurred if they had paid over the money in dollars. The maxim invoked by Laddie J. to justify this harsh result encapsulates a rule that debars *claims* founded on evidence of illegality, and there is no reason to think that it should be extended to knock out *defences*—even assuming that the rule for claimants works well, something which has been widely doubted.[125]

27–43   The question whether a defendant was relevantly a "wrongdoer" also arose in *Test Claimants in the F.I.I. Group Litigation v HMRC*,[126] where Henderson J. held that the defence is not available in response to claims in unjust enrichment that are "founded on" wrongdoing. By this he did not mean a wrong-based claim in tort or breach of contract, for example, where the claimant seeks restitution rather than compensation. He meant claims in unjust enrichment where the fact that the defendant has committed a legal wrong forms a necessary part of the factual substratum of the claim. Applying this test, he held that the claims in *F.I.I.* resting on the rule in *Woolwich Equitable BS v IRC*[127] were relevantly "founded on" wrongdoing because the claimants had to plead that HMRC had unlawfully levied tax in breach of EU law; in contrast the claims in *F.I.I.* resting on mistake were not "founded on" wrongdoing because the claimants merely had to plead that they had paid the money mistakenly thinking that the tax was due.[128]

27–44   This reasoning is suspect for several reasons. First, it is unclear why Henderson J.'s distinction should make a difference in principle. Secondly, he seems to have thought that all *Woolwich* claims would fall within the scope of his rule because he thought that receipt of money paid as tax which is not due is always a "recognised legal wrong".[129] However, while a legal wrong was committed on the facts of *F.I.I.*, because the defendant committed a breach of EU law, the receipt of money paid as tax that is not due is not always wrongful, in the sense that the defendant must always commit a breach of legal duty when receiving such payments. Finally, Henderson J.'s approach is out of line with the *Barros* case, where there was no need for the claimants to found their claim on the illegal act that led to the denial of the defence (dealings with an unauthorised forex intermediary).[130]

---

[124] *Barros* [2004] 2 Lloyd's Rep. 475 at [22]–[30] and [42]–[43].
[125] See Ch.35 for discussion.
[126] *Test Claimants in the F.I.I. Group Litigation v HMRC* [2008] EWHC 2893 (Ch); [2009] S.T.C. 254.
[127] *Woolwich Equitable BS v IRC* [1993] A.C. 70. For discussion see Ch.21.
[128] *F.I.I.* [2009] S.T.C. 254 at [339].
[129] *F.I.I.* [2009] S.T.C. 254 at [337]. This aspect of *F.I.I.* was affirmed in *Littlewoods Retail Ltd v HMRC* [2010] EWHC 1071 (Ch); [2010] S.T.C. 2072 at [107]–[108].
[130] On appeal the Court of Appeal found it unnecessary to discuss this aspect of the *F.I.I.* case: [2010] EWCA Civ 103; [2010] S.T.C. 1251 at [189]–[193].

5. Special Cases

In *Haugesund Kommune v Depfa A.C.S. Bank* Aikens L.J. stated that "the   **27–45**
defence of change of position is a general defence to all restitution claims (for
money or other property) based on unjust enrichment".[131] However, other cases
hold that the defence is not available in response to certain types of claim. Good
reasons can be advanced for some, but not for all, of these findings.

(a) *Lack of Consent and Want of Authority*

In *Ministry of Health v Simpson*,[132] Lord Simonds held that the Court of   **27–46**
Chancery would make no decree against a defendant unless he behaved in an
unconscientious manner, but said that this rule "did not excuse the wrongly paid
legatee from repayment because he had spent what he had been wrongly paid."
This was followed in *Gray v Richards Butler*,[133] where the defendant solicitors
were not allowed to raise the change of position defence against a claim to
recover money paid as fees by the executors of an invalid will. In principle,
though, there is no good reason to withhold the defence from the good faith
recipients of misdirected money, and it is telling that in *Lipkin Gorman* Lord Goff
attributed Lord Simonds' hostility towards the defence to "the mistaken assumption that mere expenditure of money may be regarded as amounting to a change
of position".[134]

(b) *Undue Influence*

Where a wife is induced to give domestic security for business borrowing, the   **27–47**
lender usually acts in good faith, since it has no more than an attenuated
constructive notice of the fact that she has been unduly influenced by her
husband. The lender inevitably changes its position by lending money or not
calling in existing debts, but if it were allowed to invoke the defence, then the
wife's protection would be destroyed. This has led some writers to rationalise the
line of cases exemplified by *Barclays Bank Plc v O'Brien*[135] and *Royal Bank of
Scotland Plc v Etridge (No.2)*[136] on the basis that the bank cannot invoke its
change of position because this would subvert the protective policies implemented by the cases.[137]

---

[131] *Haugesund Kommune v Depfa A.C.S Bank* [2010] EWCA Civ 579; [2011] 1 All E.R. 190 at
[122].
[132] *Ministry of Health v Simpson* [1951] A.C. 251 at 276.
[133] *Gray v Richards Butler* [2001] W.T.L.R. 625.
[134] *Lipkin Gorman* [1991] 2 A.C. 548 at 580.
[135] *Barclays Bank Plc v O'Brien* [1994] 1 A.C. 180.
[136] *Royal Bank of Scotland Plc v Etridge (No.2)* [2002] 2 A.C. 773.
[137] M. Bryan, "Change of Position: Commentary" in M. McInnes (ed.), *Restitution: Developments in
Unjust Enrichment* (Sydney: Law Book Co, 1996), 75, pp.79–80; M. Chen-Wishart, "In Defence of
Unjust Factors: A Study of Recission for Duress, Fraud and Exploitation" in D. Johnston and
R. Zimmermann (eds), *Unjustified Enrichment: Key Issues in Comparative Perspective* (Cambridge:
CUP, 2002), 159, pp.170–173.

(c) *Legal Incapacity*

27-48   Similar considerations may also underlie the rule that the defence cannot be raised against a claim to recover benefits on the ground that the claimant lacked legal capacity to confer them. In *Williams v Williams*[138]the defendants gave up their secure council accommodation in reliance on the fact that the claimant had conveyed his house to himself and them on a trust for sale as tenants in common. The deed of gift was declared void for want of capacity and the defendants' change of position was no bar to the making of this declaration, although they had acted in good faith.

(d) *Failure of Basis*

27-49   When value is transferred to a recipient on an agreed basis, he knows that he may have to repay a like sum if the basis fails to materialise, suggesting that he cannot spend the money in the honest belief that the transferor had an unqualified intention to benefit him. So, for example, if a claimant pays a defendant money to build a garage, and the defendant spends it on a holiday that he would not otherwise have bought, the law will almost certainly not permit him to rely on this fact in the event that the garage is not built and the claimant sues to recover his money. *Goss v Chilcott*[139] was like this. The defendants borrowed money from the claimant under a void agreement, which was paid to a third party at the defendants' request. This arrangement did not constitute a change of position because the defendants knew that if the third party failed to repay the money then the claimant would require the defendants to repay it themselves. This decision was affirmed and followed by the Court of Appeal in *Haugesund*,[140] where the defendant local authorities could not raise the defence in response to claims by a bank from which they had received money under void interest swap agreements that they used to invest in financial instruments that subsequently declined in value.

27-50   An exception to this principle is that payments to meet preparatory expenses will constitute expenditure on which a defendant can rely: in *BP Exploration Co (Libya) Ltd v Hunt (No.2)*[141] Robert Goff J. held that the statutory allowance for such expenses given by the Law Reform (Frustrated Contracts) Act 1943 s.1(2), should be seen as a statutory example of the change of position defence. However, a defendant cannot invoke the defence if he spends money on materials which will not actually help him to perform his agreement. These were the facts

---

[138] *Williams v Williams* [2003] EWHC 742 (Ch).
[139] *Goss v Chilcott* [1996] A.C. 788 esp. at 799 (PC). See too *Gilsan (International) Ltd v Optus Networks Pty Ltd* [2004] NSWSC 1077 at [381] where McDougall J. found it "difficult conceptually to see how there can be a relevant change of position" where benefits are rendered on an agreed basis that they will be paid for. Cf. *Ford v Perpetual Trustees Victoria Ltd* [2009] NSWCA 186; (2009) 75 N.S.W.L.R. 42, where the mentally incompetent defendant was held not to have been enriched when the claimant paid money to his son at the defendant's request.
[140] *Haugesund* [2010] EWCA Civ 579; [2011] 1 All E.R. 190 at [127] and [155] per Aikens and Pill L.JJ.; cf. Etherton L.J.'s comments at [153]. See too Tomlinson J.'s finding at first instance that it was "completely fatal" to the defence that "the municipalities knew from the start that the amounts advanced by Depfa were to be repaid": [2009] EWHC 2227 (Comm); [2010] Lloyd's Rep. P.N. 21 at [163].
[141] *BP Exploration Co (Libya) Ltd v Hunt (No.2)* [1979] 1 W.L.R. 783 at 800 and 804.

of a New Zealand case, *Saba Yachts Ltd v Fish Pacific Ltd*,[142] where the defendant commissioned plans for a boat that fell outside the specification of the boat which it had agreed to build for the claimant.

(e) *Money Paid as Tax that Is Not Due*

In *F.I.I.*,[143] Henderson J. held that HMRC cannot rely on change of position as **27–51** a defence to a claim founded on the rule established by *Woolwich*,[144] because claims of this kind, unlike claims for mistake, are "founded on wrongdoing". This analysis has been doubted above,[145] and it is submitted that in principle the better view is that public bodies should never be allowed to plead change of position in response to a claim to recover money paid as tax, whatever the ground on which the claim rests. The reason is that allowing them the defence would seriously undermine the constitutional principle that taxation must not be levied without Parliamentary authority, and the wider principle that public bodies are constrained by the rule of law. It would also unfairly cast the burden of paying for the government's unlawful act onto an innocent taxpayer when this should properly be borne by the public at large. These are the reasons given in Canada for rejecting a defence of fiscal chaos,[146] and in Germany for denying public bodies the change of position defence.[147] The English courts would do well to follow suit, and it is telling that in *F.J. Chalke Ltd v HMRC*,[148] Henderson J. held that the defence cannot be raised in cases where restitution of mistaken payments to public bodies is mandated by EU law, because this would be contrary to the principle of effectiveness.[149]

(f) *Ultra Vires Payments by Public Bodies*

In *Att Gen v Gray*[150] the defendant teacher was paid salary at a higher rate than **27–52** the one to which he was entitled, and the New South Wales Court of Appeal held that the state Education Department had no authority to certify his entitlement to salary at the higher rate, with the result that he could not raise an estoppel defence, although representations were made to him that he was entitled to the

---

[142] *Saba Yachts Ltd v Fish Pacific Ltd* [2006] NZHC 1452 at [58]–[63].
[143] *F.I.I.* [2008] EWHC 2893 (Ch); [2009] S.T.C. 254 at [335]–[348].
[144] *Woolwich* [1993] A.C. 70.
[145] See para.27–44.
[146] *Kingstreet Investments Ltd v New Brunswick (Department of Finance)* [2007] SCC 1; [2007] 1 S.C.R. 3 at [28], approving Wilson J.'s dissenting judgment in *Air Canada v British Columbia* [1989] 1 S.C.R. 1161 at 1215.
[147] B.Verw.G. 17.09.1970, B.Verw.G.E. 36, 108, confirmed B.Verw.G. 27.12.1989, 2 B 84/89.
[148] *F.J. Chalke Ltd v HMRC* [2009] EWHC 952 (Ch); [2009] S.T.C. 2027 at [171]–[178]. On appeal the CA found it unnecessary to consider this finding: see Etherton L.J.'s comments at [2010] EWCA Civ 313; [2010] S.T.C. 1640 at [73]–[74]. HMRC conceded the point in *Test Claimants in the Thin Cap Group Litigation v HMRC* [2009] EWHC 2908 (Ch); [2010] S.T.C. 30 at [236] and *F.I.I.* [2010] EWCA Civ 103; [2010] S.T.C. 1251 at [191].
[149] Vos J. proposed making a reference on this point to the CJEU, in *Littlewoods* [2010] EWHC 1071 (Ch); [2010] S.T.C. 2072 at [138]–[139]; but was later persuaded not to: [2010] EWHC 2771 (Ch); [2011] S.T.C. 171 at [7].
[150] *Att Gen v Gray* [1977] 1 N.S.W.L.R. 406.

money.[151] Similarly in *Commonwealth of Australia v Burns*,[152] the defendant received pension payments on her father's behalf, which continued after her father's death. When the defendant asked whether she was entitled to these payments she was incorrectly told that she was, and in reliance on this statement, she spent the money. Nevertheless she was ordered to make restitution. These cases were consistent with the principle laid down by the House of Lords in *Howell v Falmouth Boat Construction Co Ltd*,[153] that the doctrine of estoppel cannot prevent the Crown from repudiating an ultra vires act or statement, or government officials could subvert the ultra vires doctrine by acting beyond their powers and falsely telling the public that their actions are authorised. Against this, however, it might be said that the injustice caused by placing good faith recipients in a worse position than they occupied prior to payment outweighs the public interest in ensuring the proper application of public funds. This suggests that there was a good reason to depart from the *Falmouth Boat* rule in *Gray* and *Burns*. It also suggests that the recipients of ultra vires payments by public bodies should also be allowed the defence of change of position. This is borne out by *Charles Terence Estates Ltd v Cornwall Council*,[154] where the defence was successfully invoked by a company which had been paid rent by a local authority under an ultra vires tenancy agreement, but which had spent equivalent sums on purchasing and refurbishing the relevant properties.[155]

(g) *Claims under the Insolvency Act 1986*

27–53   It seems that the change of position defence can be raised against a claim to recover benefits transferred under a transaction that is void by reason of the Insolvency Act 1986 s.127,[156] and also against a claim to recover benefits conferred under a transaction defrauding creditors contrary to s.423.[157] Several Commonwealth jurisdictions with statutory regimes analogous to the regime

---

[151] *Gray* [1977] 1 N.S.W.L.R. 406 at 410–411. Cf. *Dodington's Case* (1596) Cro. Eliz. 545 at 545; 78 ER 792 at 792: "this payment of the money, by the appointment of the Lord Treasurer, was not allowable: for the Privy Seal is not sufficient authority to dispose of the Queen's treasure, unless where it is due; and, he disposing of it otherwise, it is out of his authority."

[152] *Commonwealth of Australia v Burns* [1971] V.R. 825 at 829.

[153] *Howell v Falmouth Boat Construction Co Ltd* [1951] A.C. 837 at 844–845 (HL). See too *Western Fish Products Ltd v Penwith DC* [1981] 2 All E.R. 204 at 219 (CA); *Minister for Immigration & Ethnic Affairs v Kurtovic* (1990) 21 FCR 193 at 208 (Fed Ct of Aus).

[154] *Charles Terence Estates Ltd v Cornwall Council* [2011] EWHC 2542 (QB) at [97]–[99] and [102].

[155] The defence has also been allowed to claims made by local councils on the ground of failure of basis to recover money paid under ultra vires redundancy agreements: *Hinckley & Bosworth BC v Shaw* [2000] L.G.R. 9; *Eastbourne BC v Foster* Unreported QBD, December 20, 2000, varied on a different point [2001] L.G.R. 529. See too Law Commission, *Restitution: Mistakes of Law and Ultra Vires Public Authority Receipts and Payments* (1994), Law Com. No.227, para.17.20, where the Law Commission assumed that the defence would be available. And cf. Law Reform Commission of British Columbia, *Report on the Recovery of Unauthorised Disbursements of Public Funds* (LRC, 1980), L.R.C. 48, recommending statutory recognition of estoppel and change of position defences; this recommendation was implemented by the British Columbia Financial Arbitration Act 1981 s.67.

[156] *Rose* [2003] EWHC 1737; [2003] 1 W.L.R. 2791.

[157] *4Eng* [2009] EWHC 2633 (Ch); [2010] B.P.I.R. 1 at [14].

contained in ss.239–241 provide for such a defence in general terms.[158] However, it is arguable that the defence is contrary to the purpose of these sections, namely to claw back funds for the general body of creditors and to maintain proper priority between them, and that the scheme of the 1986 Act is to place their interests above those of recipients who may have given little or nothing in exchange for the benefits they receive.[159]

(h) *Money Paid under Judgments that Are Later Reversed*

Australian authority holds that the change of position defence can be raised by   **27-54**
defendants who receive benefits pursuant to judgments or court orders that are later reversed.[160] The English courts may wish to consider whether this would undermine the policy supporting recovery in such cases to an unacceptable degree.[161]

6. PROPRIETARY CLAIMS

In an Australian case, *Gertsch*,[162] Foster J.A. held that the imposition of a   **27-55**
constructive trust on assets held by a defendant "is based upon some degree of blameworthiness on the part of the defendant", that "the defence of change of position is based upon the innocence of the defendant" and that it followed that "the defence is not available to resist a claim for constructive trust". To the extent that the English courts require proof of fault before awarding a proprietary remedy for unjust enrichment, they can be expected to take the same line.[163] However, it is far from clear that proprietary awards are contingent upon proof of fault under English law,[164] and to the extent that they are not, there is no

---

[158] T. O'Sullivan, "Defending a Liquidator's Claim for Repayment of a Voidable Transaction" (1997) 9 Otago Law Rev. 111; also *Re Ernst and Young Inc* (1997) 147 D.L.R. (4th) 229 (Alberta CA); *Countrywide Banking Corp Ltd v Dean* [1998] A.C. 338 (PC); *Re Excel Freight Ltd (In Liquidation)* (1999) 8 N.Z.C.L.C. 261 at 827 (NZ High Ct); *Cripps v Lakeview Farm Fresh Ltd (In Receivership)* [2006] 1 N.Z.L.R. 238 (NZ High Court). A line of Canadian authority denies the defence to the recipients of fraudulent preferences because the moneys received were the proceeds of fraud: *Principal Group Ltd (Bankrupt) v Anderson* (1994) 164 A.R. 81 at [180] (Alberta QB); affirmed (1997) 200 A.R. 169 (Alberta CA); *Re Titan Investments Ltd Partnership* [2005] ABQB 637; (2005) 383 A.R. 323 at [45]–[47]; *Haag Capital LLC v Correia* [2010] ONSC 5339 at [65]–[70]. However we do not consider that these authorities should be followed to the extent that they deny the defence to defendants who were not at fault but were merely the innocent "winners" of Ponzi schemes perpetrated by others.
[159] S. Davenport, "*4Eng v Harper*: Restitution and Insolvency" (2011) 24 *Insolvency Intelligence* 91.
[160] *Palmer* [1999] NSWSC 697.
[161] For which, see para.26–05.
[162] *Gertsch* [1999] NSWSC 898; (1999) 10 B.P.R. 18,431 at [25]; followed in *K&S Corp* [2003] SASC 96; (2003) 86 S.A.S.R. 313 at [157].
[163] Cf. Nourse L.J.'s comments in relation to personal liability for knowing receipt in *Bank of Credit and Commerce International Ltd v Akindele* [2001] Ch. 437 at 456: "if the circumstances of the receipt are such as to make it unconscionable for the recipient to retain the benefit of it, there is an obvious difficulty in saying that it is equitable for a change of position to afford him a defence."
[164] See paras 37–21—37–22.

compelling reason why the defence should not be raised in reply to a claim for a proprietary award.

27-56   Where the claim relates to an enrichment that traceably survives in a particular asset, it may seem odd to allow the defence because it may seem that the defendant is still enriched. However the change in a defendant's position need not relate to the disposal of a particular asset: it is enough for him to show a causal link between his enrichment and a decrease in his overall wealth. Hence the defence should be available where the recipient of a mistaken payment invests that money in securities and then dissipates other money in the honest belief that his total wealth has been increased.

27-57   How should the defence be implemented in such a case? Where the proprietary interest awarded to the claimant is a lien over the securities there is no problem: the amount secured by the lien can be reduced by the amount of the defendant's detriment. However, matters are more complex where the claimant is entitled to an order that he is the beneficial owner of the property. Here, the claimant can rightly assert that the securities belong to him, but it is also true that the defendant has incurred expense which he would not have incurred but for the bona fide belief that they were his. At common law, except in relation to land, the court does not have to order specific delivery,[165] and any money judgment can easily allow for the defendant's change of position. In equity, the court can resolve the impasse between the parties by making a declaration on terms. This was done in a Canadian case which is discussed above, *Re Gareau Estate*,[166] where a constructive trust was imposed on the defendant's house "to secure the amount found due [to the claimant, and] . . . to be realized, if not sooner paid, at the time of disposition of the house and lot by [the defendant], or 20 years from now, whichever should first occur." In a simpler case, the court could simply make a declaration of trust in the claimant's favour, to be realised on payment by the claimant to the defendant of an amount corresponding to the defendant's detriment.[167]

27-58   Special problems also arise where the claimant's money is used to extinguish a charge over the defendant's property and a subrogation claim is made asserting the claimant's right to be treated, by a fiction, as though the charge-holder's rights have not been extinguished but have instead been assigned to the claimant.[168] In *Boscawen*,[169] Millett L.J. stated that the defence could be raised by a defendant debtor whose position is changed when his compliant creditor willing to wait for repayment is replaced by a subrogated claimant seeking immediate repayment: the solution to this problem, again, is to make an order on terms, allowing the defendant time to renegotiate his original loan agreement. More straightforwardly, a defendant might alternatively plead that, as a result of having used the claimant's money to discharge his debt, he changed his position by incurring expenditure or forgoing earning opportunities. In this case the court can

---

[165] Torts (Interference with Goods) Act 1977 s.5.

[166] *Re Gareau Estate* (1995) 9 E.T.R. (2d) 95 at [32] (Ontario Sup Ct); discussed at para.27–16.

[167] Cf. BGH NJW 1980, 1789: the claimant rescinded the gift of a plot of land after the defendant had started building on the land, and the *Bundesgerichtshof* held that the defendant was only obliged to retransfer the land if the claimant reimbursed him for his expenditure.

[168] For general discussion of subrogation to extinguished rights, see Ch.39.

[169] *Boscawen* [1996] 1 W.L.R. 328 at 340–341 (CA); discussed at para.27–10.

create a new charge over his property to secure his restitutionary liability to the claimant after the amount of the defendant's detriment has been subtracted.[170]

Less obviously, where a claimant asserts the right to acquire a security interest **27–59** with priority over those who held junior security interests in the same property at the time when the claimant paid off a senior security,[171] these junior charge-holders can also invoke the defence. Subrogation rights in this form arise in part to reverse the secondary enrichment accruing to such parties as a result of the discharge of the senior security interest.[172] An example is where a junior charge-holder, believing that a senior charge has been discharged, advances further sums on the security of the same property. The junior charge-holder may be able to show that he would not have made these further advances but for the discharge of the senior charge. If so, then he may be able to raise the defence of change of position against a claimant who seeks to be treated as though he has acquired the senior charge by subrogation with priority over the junior security.[173]

---

[170] *Gertsch* [1999] NSWSC 898; (1999) 10 B.P.R. 18,431.
[171] Cf. *Banque Financière de la Cité v Parc (Battersea) Ltd* [1999] 1 A.C. 221 (HL) (junior charge-holder); *Eagle Star Insurance Co Ltd v Karasiewicz* [2002] EWCA Civ 940 (beneficial owner of property bound by senior charge).
[172] See paras 39–13—39–15.
[173] *Redman v Rymer* (1889) 60 L.T. 385; *McCullough v Elliott* (1922) 62 D.L.R. 257 at 262–263 (Alberta CA), referring to *Home Savings Bank of Chicago v Bierstadt*, 48 N.E. 161 (1897). These cases, along with the more complex situation that arose in *Armatage Motors Ltd v Royal Trust Corp of Canada* (1997) 34 O.R. (3d) 599 (Ontario CA), are all discussed in C. Mitchell and S. Watterson *Subrogation: Law and Practice* (Oxford: OUP, 2007), paras 7.62–7.85.

CHAPTER 28

MINISTERIAL RECEIPT

1. INTRODUCTION

Suppose that an agent receives a benefit from a claimant for the value of which **28-01** he must immediately account to his principal. Suppose, further, that the agent actually pays this value to the principal in good faith. If the claimant sues the agent in unjust enrichment, then the agent can now rely on the change of position defence,[1] following recognition of this defence by the House of Lords in *Lipkin Gorman (A Firm) v Karpnale Ltd.*[2] Even prior to *Lipkin Gorman*, however, a defence was given to an agent who paid the value of such a benefit over to his principal,[3] or applied it in accordance with his instructions,[4] provided that he acted in good faith and without notice of the claim.[5]

On one view, this "payment over" defence should be understood as an early **28-02** version of the change of position defence, which has now been subsumed by the wider version of the defence that was recognised in *Lipkin Gorman* (wider in the sense that is not restricted to agents and is generally available).[6] On another view, which we prefer, an agent who receives a benefit for which he must account to his principal should have a defence of "ministerial receipt" to claims in unjust enrichment whether or not he pays the value of the benefit to his principal, and whether or not he takes good title to property which he then uses as his own, because his obligation to account means that the agent never takes the value of the benefit for himself, and that the principal alone is enriched by the transaction.[7] On this view, a claim in unjust enrichment lies against the principal, and no claim lies against the agent, because the law holds that the principal is enriched at the claimant's expense and the agent is not. If this is correct, then the results

---

[1] As noted in *Jones v Churcher* [2009] EWHC 722 (QB); [2009] 2 Lloyd's Rep. 94 at [67]. See too *Niru Battery Manufacturing Co v Milestone Trading Ltd (No.1)* [2003] EWCA Civ 1446, [2004] Q.B. 985; and *Abou-Rahmah v Abacha* [2006] EWCA Civ 1492; [2007] 1 All E.R. (Comm.) 827, in both of which change of position was the only defence discussed by the court.
[2] *Lipkin Gorman (A Firm) v Karpnale Ltd* [1991] 2 A.C. 548.
[3] *Owen & Co v Cronk* [1895] 1 Q.B. 265; *Kleinwort & Co v Dunlop* (1907) 97 L.T. 26; *Admiralty Commissioners v National Provincial and Union Bank* (1922) 127 L.T. 452; *Gower v Lloyds and National Provincial Bank* [1938] 1 All E.R. 766; *Transvaal and Delagoa Bay Investment Co Ltd v Atkinson* [1944] 1 All E.R. 579; *Australia and New Zealand Banking Group Ltd v Westpac Banking Corp* (1987) 164 C.L.R. 662. See too *Jones* [2009] EWHC 722 (QB); [2009] 2 Lloyd's Rep. 94.
[4] *Holland v Russell* (1861) 1 B. & S. 424; 121 E.R. 773; affirmed (1863) 4 B. & S. 14; 122 E.R. 365.
[5] *Continental Caoutchouc & Gutta Percha Co v Kleinwort, Sons & Co* (1904) 90 L.T. 474 at 477; *Nizam of Hyderabad v Jung* [1957] Ch. 185 at 239 and 248.
[6] A. Burrows, *The Law of Restitution*, 3rd edn (Oxford: OUP, 2010), p.565.
[7] This argument is ably developed in J.P. Moore, *Restitution from Banks* (unpublished D Phil thesis, Oxford University, 2000). See too P. Birks, "The Burden on the Bank" in F.D. Rose (ed.), *Restitution and Banking Law* (Oxford: Mansfield Press, 1998), 189, pp.209–210.

(though not the reasoning) of the cases where the "payment over" defence was allowed can be explained on the basis that the agent came under an immediate accounting duty when he received the benefit and should therefore have had a defence, whether or not he actually paid the value of the benefit over to the principal.

28–03   The proposition that an agent is not enriched for the purposes of a claim in unjust enrichment when he receives a benefit for which he must account to his principal is consistent with the view taken by some scholars that it is conceptually impossible for more than one defendant to be enriched at a claimant's expense at the same time.[8] However, we do not share this view, and our understanding of the requirement that a defendant's benefit must have been gained at the claimant's expense does not preclude the conclusion that a principal and agent are both enriched when the agent receives a benefit for which he must account. This is discussed further in Ch.6.[9]

28–04   In our view the defence of ministerial receipt is allowed for a different reason, namely that it is desirable to protect agents from being caught in the middle of disputes between their principals and third parties. An agent will be faced with an impossible dilemma if he is sued by a claimant to recover a benefit but is also called upon to account for this benefit by his principal (who may incur consequential losses if the agent fails to comply). Agents perform a valuable function as intermediaries with the power to create legal relations between others, and it enhances their ability to perform this function if they are allowed then to "drop out" when disputes arise between their principals and third parties over transfers of value.[10] Allowing this also makes the law simpler and reduces multiplicity of suits.

28–05   Robert Stevens has objected to this explanation, arguing that there is no special rule general to "agency law" according to which agents can escape liabilities in private law pursuant to these policy goals.[11] We agree that it would be an oversimplification to say that agents can generally do this—many cases in contract and tort show that they cannot, and these cases clearly give rise to a range of different considerations which may or may not suggest that shielding the agent from liability should be an overriding policy objective in each case. Nevertheless we consider that the rule argued for here is appropriate to the context of claims in unjust enrichment.

28–06   Support for the view that English law gives agents the defence of ministerial receipt described here can be drawn from a series of cases decided in equity where agents have escaped liability for knowing receipt although they have not actually paid the value of the benefits they have received to their principals; liability for knowing receipt is not itself a liability in unjust enrichment, but the logic of the courts' reasoning also applies to unjust enrichment claims. The

---

[8] e.g. L.D. Smith, "Three-Party Restitution: A Critique of Birks' Theory of Interceptive Subtraction" (1991) 11 O.J.L.S. 481, p.483.
[9] See paras 6–36 and following.
[10] As recognised in German law: H Dörner, "Change of Position and *Wegfall der Bereicherung*" in W.J. Swadling (ed.), *The Limits of Restitutionary Claims: A Comparative Analysis* (London: UKNCCL, 1997) 64, pp.65–66.
[11] R. Stevens, "Why Do Agents 'Drop Out'?" [2005] L.M.C.L.Q. 101. See too P.G. Watts (ed.), *Bowstead and Reynolds on Agency*, 19th edn (London: Sweet & Maxwell, 2010) para.9.102; Burrows, *The Law of Restitution*, pp.566–568.

defence of ministerial receipt has also been recognised in some common law cases, but the predominant view at common law is that payment over is required in order for the agent to escape liability. In the following account we review these two lines of authority in turn. In our view the courts would do well to develop the law by dropping the requirement for payment over at common law. This would eliminate inconsistency between the rules of common law and equity and further the policy goal of insulating agents from liability.

2. IN EQUITY

A defendant is not liable for knowing receipt if he acts in a ministerial capacity   **28–07**
when he knowingly receives misdirected trust property or property that has been paid away in breach of fiduciary duty,[12] i.e. if he receives the property as agent for a principal to whom he owes an immediate duty to account for the property (or an equivalent sum), and who himself incurs a liability to the claimant at the moment when the defendant receives the property.[13] As we discuss in Ch.8, liability for knowing receipt is not a liability for unjust enrichment,[14] but as we also discuss there, certain other equitable claims (such as the personal claim recognised in *Re Diplock*[15]) should be seen as claims in unjust enrichment to recover the value of property to which the claimant had an equitable right, and it may be that further claims of this kind will be recognised in the future.[16] The courts' reasoning in the knowing receipt cases applies with equal force to all of these claims.

In a series of cases against banks which have received and dealt with mis-   **28–08**
applied trust property, the question has arisen whether the bank has received the property for its own benefit or has acted ministerially. To understand the authorities on this issue properly, it must be appreciated that the situation where the misapplied property has been deposited by the account holder differs from the situation where the property has been deposited by a third party.

In the first situation, the bank always receives the money beneficially, and   **28–09**
never receives it ministerially: there is simply a loan of money from the account holder to the bank, or if the account is overdrawn, a repayment of the debt owed to the bank by the account holder. Hence, the bank is potentially liable to claims that are predicated on the basis that it has received misapplied property for its own benefit, where a trustee or fiduciary himself deposits trust money into his

---

[12] *Barnes v Addy* (1874) 9 Ch. App. 244 at 254–245; *Adams v Bank of New South Wales* [1984] 1 N.S.W.L.R. 285 at 290–292; *Westpac Banking Corp v Savin* [1985] 2 N.Z.L.R. 41 at 69; *Agip (Africa) Ltd v Jackson* [1990] Ch. 265 at 291–292; *Cukurooa Celik Enduustrisi AS v Hill Taylor Dickinson (A Firm)* Unreported QBD (Comm Ct), June 1, 1996; *Trustor AB v Smallbone (No.2)* [2001] 3 All E.R. 987 at 994; *Twinsectra Ltd v Yardley* [2002] UKHL 12; [2002] 2 A.C. 164 at [106].

[13] In these circumstances the agent may be liable for dishonest assistance: see e.g. *British North American Elevator Co v Bank of British North America* [1919] A.C. 658, but note that this case predates the modern law governing the mental element required for liability as a dishonest assistant established by *Royal Brunei Airline Sdn Bhd v Tan* [1995] 2 A.C. 378 and subsequent decisions.

[14] See paras 8–123—8–130.

[15] *Re Diplock* [1948] Ch. 465 (CA); affirmed [1951] A.C. 251.

[16] See paras 8–50—8–68.

personal account.[17] Certain cases to the contrary, which suggest that in this situation a bank can only be liable as a dishonest assistant, are incorrect in principle.[18]

28–10   In the second situation, where cash is deposited with a bank by a person other than the account holder, or the bank's own account with a central clearing bank is credited as result of instructions from such a person, the bank will almost always take the proceeds of the transaction ministerially as agent for the account holder.[19] It has been hard for the courts and legal scholars to accept this proposition although cases can be marshalled in its support. One reason for their reluctance may be that they have not always clearly understood that a bank which receives a third-party deposit on its customer's behalf does not receive "beneficially" simply because it takes good title to the money and then uses the money as its own: "beneficial receipt" as distinguished from "ministerial receipt" of money entails not merely that a defendant takes good title to the money, but also that the defendant does not have to account for an equivalent sum to a principal who is himself legally liable to the claimant from the moment of the defendant's receipt. A second, related reason may be that it is not immediately obvious what happens when a bank receives a third-party deposit on a customer's behalf, particularly where the account is overdrawn. Properly understood, though, such transactions always work in the same way, regardless of the state of the account between the bank and the customer: first, the bank receives the deposit ministerially, as agent for its customer; then, in a separate transaction, the bank either borrows the money from its customer and credits the amount in its books as a debt which it owes to the customer, or where his account is overdrawn, applies the amount on his behalf in reduction of his debt to the bank.[20]

28–11   Authority for this, at least where the customer's account is in credit, can be found in *Agip (Africa) Ltd v Jackson (Agip)*, where Millett J. stated that[21]:

> "The essential feature of [claims in knowing receipt] . . . is that the recipient must have received the property for his own use and benefit. This is why neither the paying nor the collecting bank can normally be brought within it."

---

[17] As in e.g. *Director, Real Estate and Business Brokers v N.R.S. Mississauga Inc* (2001) 194 D.L.R. (4th) 527.

[18] e.g. *Polly Peck International Plc v Nadir (No.2)* [1993] B.C.L.C. 187.

[19] An exception to this rule arises where the bank has some prior right of its own to be paid by the third party, pursuant to an arrangement previously entered by the third party and the bank: *Continental Caoutchouc* (1904) 90 L.T. 474 at 476 per Collins M.R.; *Uzinterimpex JSC v Standard Bank Plc* [2008] EWCA Civ 819; [2008] Bus. L.R. 1762 at [38]–[42] per Moore-Bick L.J. In *Standard Bank London Ltd v Canara Bank* [2002] EWHC 1032 (Comm) at [99], Moore-Bick J. thought that Collins M.R.'s observations on this point were irreconcilable with *Barclays Bank Ltd v W. J. Simms, Son & Cooke (Southern) Ltd* [1980] Q.B. 677 at 695 and *Lloyds Bank Plc v Independent Insurance Co Ltd* [2000] Q.B. 110. However these two lines of authority do not concern the same issue.

[20] Cf. M. Bryan, "Recovering Misdirected Money from Banks: Ministerial Receipt at Law and in Equity" in F.D. Rose (ed.), *Restitution and Banking Law*, 161, pp.181–187; L.D. Smith, "Unjust Enrichment, Property, and the Structure of Trusts" (2000) 116 L.Q.R. 412, p. 433. Although he does not take the points made in the text, Bryan does criticise the distinction drawn in *Agip* [1990] Ch. 265 between receipt by a bank into an account that is in credit and receipt into an account that is overdrawn on the grounds that the nature of the relationship between banker and customer is such that the bank always has the benefit of using the customer's money for its own purposes until such time as it is called upon to repay the debt. In *Uzinterimpex* [2008] EWCA Civ 819; [2008] Bus. L.R. 1762 at [40], Moore-Bick L.J. thought that there was "a good deal of force" in this criticism.

[21] *Agip (Africa) Ltd v Jackson* [1990] Ch. 265 at 291; affirmed [1991] Ch. 547.

It can also be found in a Scottish case, *Compagnie Commerciale Andre SA v Artibell Shipping Co Ltd*, where Lord Macfadyen held that[22]:

> "There is, no doubt, a sense in which money paid to a bank to the credit of the account of one of its customers becomes, on receipt, the bank's money—as Lord Mackay said in *Royal Bank of Scotland v Skinner*[23] it is 'simply consumed by the banker.' But in that simple situation, the bank is not thereby enriched, because it grants an immediate obligation of corresponding amount to its customer. Receipt by the bank in that way would not . . . afford the necessary foundation for an argument that in the event of the money becoming repayable by the customer to the payer, the bank had been unjustly enriched."

Earlier cases indicate that the same analysis applies where misdirected money **28–12** is credited to an overdrawn account by a third party. In *Continental Caoutchouc and Gutta Percha Co v Kleinwort Sons & Co*,[24] Collins M.R. considered that a bank can rely on the defence of ministerial receipt where it has not received money in its own right pursuant to some prior agreement between the bank and the third party, but has instead received the money in its capacity as the customer's agent, and has then credited the money to the customer's overdrawn account, as in these circumstances the bank will have "constructively sent [the money on] and received it back, and [will have] done nothing incompatible with [its] position as a conduit-pipe or intermediary". In *British North American Elevator Co v Bank of British North America*,[25] the Privy Council held a bank liable as an accessory to a breach of trust, but not as a beneficial recipient of trust property, where the bank had "knowingly [become a party] to a misapplication of what were trust funds"[26] paid into an overdrawn account by a person other than the bank's customer. Finally, in *Bank of New South Wales v Vale Corp (Management) Ltd*,[27] the corporate manager of a unit trust wrongfully deposited money it had received as subscriptions for units into the overdrawn account of companies belonging to the same corporate group, and the New South Wales Court of Appeal considered that "it was not the [defendant] bank, but rather it was the [corporate group] which was the recipient of almost the entirety of the moneys paid out of [the manager's] account."

Against this line of authority are a number of decisions and dicta, which **28–13** include Millett J.'s further statement in *Agip* that "if the collecting bank uses the money to reduce or discharge the company's overdraft . . . it receives the money for its own benefit."[28] He later shifted his position, and wrote extra-judicially that a bank can only be said to have received third-party deposits beneficially where

---

[22] *Compagnie Commerciale Andre SA v Artibell Shipping Co Ltd* 2001 S.C. 653 at 661–662.

[23] *Royal Bank of Scotland v Skinner*, 1931 S.L.T. 382 at 384.

[24] *Continental Caoutchouc and Gutta Percha Co v Kleinwort Sons & Co* (1904) 90 L.T. 474 at 476.

[25] *British North American Elevator Co v Bank of British North America* [1919] A.C. 658.

[26] *British North American Elevator Co* [1919] A.C. 658 at 663.

[27] *Bank of New South Wales v Vale Corp (Management) Ltd* Unreported NSWCA, October 21, 1981.

[28] *Agip* [1990] Ch. 265 at 292; affirmed [1991] Ch. 547. See too *Foxton v Manchester and Liverpool District Banking Co* (1881) 44 L.T. 406; *Coleman v Bucks and Oxon Union Bank* [1897] 2 Ch. 243; *Citadel General Assurance Co v Lloyds Bank Canada* [1997] 3 S.C.R. 805; *Evans v European Bank Ltd* [2004] NSWCA 82; (2004) 61 N.S.W.L.R. 75 at [167]; *B.M.P. Global Distribution Inc v Bank of Nova Scotia* [2009] SCC 15; [2009] 1 S.C.R. 504 at [77].

there has been "some conscious appropriation of the sum paid into the account in reduction of the overdraft".[29] However, when a bank receives a payment from a third party it has no choice but to credit the account designated by the third party, and so it is uncertain what his Lordship meant by this.

3. AT COMMON LAW

28–14 There are some cases at common law that gave agents a defence to unjust enrichment claims although they did not pay their principals the value of the benefits which they received. For example, in *Sadler v Evans*[30] the plaintiff paid money to the agent of Lady Windsor, in the mistaken belief that he owed it to her. Perrot B. non-suited his action for money had and received against the agent and held that the action should have been brought against Lady Windsor, a decision that was affirmed on appeal, in Lord Mansfield's words because[31]:

> "The money was paid to the known agent of Lady W. He is liable to her for it; whether he has actually paid it over to her, or not: he received it for her ... Where 'tis to a known agent ... the action ought to be brought against the principal, unless in special cases [such as where the agent receives the money in bad faith]."

28–15 However, 12 years later, in *Buller v Harrison*,[32] Lord Mansfield changed his mind. The plaintiff underwriters paid money to their insured's agent in the mistaken belief that it was due under the policy. The agent credited this sum against a debt that was owed him by the insured, but this gave him no defence. Lord Mansfield said[33]:

> "[T]he law is clear, that if an agent pay over money which has been paid to him by mistake, he does no wrong; and the plaintiff must call on the principal ... [But in] this case, there was no new credit, no acceptance of new bills, no fresh goods bought or money advanced. In short, no alteration in the situation which the defendant and his principals stood in towards each other [at the time of the payment] ... Is it conscientious then, that the defendant should ... say, though there is no alteration in my account with my principal, this is a hit, I have got the money and I will keep it? If there had been any new credit given, it would have been proper to have left it to the jury to say, whether any prejudice had happened to the defendant by means of this payment: but here no prejudice at all is proved, and none is to be inferred. Under these circumstances ... the defendant has no defence."

28–16 This decision has been followed in a series of later cases which also hold that an agent has no defence where he has simply credited his principal with money

---

[29] Sir P. Millett, "Tracing the Proceeds of Fraud" (1991) 107 L.Q.R. 70, p.83, fn.46, noted without deciding the issue by the NZCA in *Westpac Banking Corp v M. M. Kembla New Zealand Ltd* [2001] 2 N.Z.L.R. 298 at 316–317.

[30] *Sadler v Evans* (1766) 4 Burr. 1984; 98 E.R. 34. See too *Greenway v Hurd* (1794) 4 T.R. 553 at 555; 100 E.R. 1171 at 1173–1174 per Lord Kenyon C.J.; *Miller v Arris* (1800) 3 Esp. 231 at 233; 170 E.R. 589 at 599; *Duke of Norfolk v Worthy* (1808) 1 Camp. 337 at 339; 170 E.R. 977 at 979 per Lord Ellenborough; *Ellis v Goulton* [1893] 1 Q.B. 350 at 353–354 per Bowen L.J.

[31] *Sadler* at 4 Burr. at 1986; 98 E.R. 35.

[32] *Buller v Harrison* (1777) 2 Cowp. 565; 98 E.R. 1243.

[33] *Buller* 2 Cowp. at 568; 98 E.R. at 1245–1246.

received on his behalf and the money is not actually paid.[34] The predominant position at common law was therefore summarised in the following terms by Millett L.J. in *Portman Building Society v Hamlyn Taylor Neck (A Firm)*[35]:

> "[W]here the plaintiff has paid money under (for example) a mistake to the agent of a third party . . . [and] the agent still retains the money . . . the plaintiff may elect to sue either the principal or the agent, and the agent remains liable if he pays the money over to his principal after notice of the claim. If he wishes to protect himself, he should interplead. But once the agent has paid the money to his principal or to his order without notice of the claim, the plaintiff must sue the principal."

---

[34] *Cox v Prentice* (1815) 3 M. & S. 344; 105 E.R. 601; *Bavins & Sims v London & South Western Bank Ltd* [1900] 1 Q.B. 270; *Kleinwort, Sons & Co v Dunlop Rubber Co* (1907) 97 L.T. 263; *Scottish Metropolitan Assurance Co Ltd v P. Samuel & Co Ltd* [1923] 1 K.B. 348; *British American Continental Bank v British Bank for Foreign Trade* [1926] 1 K.B. 328.

[35] *Portman Building Society v Hamlyn Taylor Neck (A Firm)* [1998] 4 All E.R. 202 at 207; followed in *Jones v Churcher* [2009] EWHC 722 (QB); [2009] 2 Lloyd's Rep. 94 at [69] per Judge Havelock-Allan QC, stating that the critical point in claims against banks is "the point at which the crediting of funds to the customer's account can no longer be reversed".

CHAPTER 29

BONA FIDE PURCHASE AND GOOD CONSIDERATION

1. INTRODUCTION

In some situations a purchaser of property can acquire clear legal title to the **29–01** property although the vendor's title is defective, provided that he gives value and acts in good faith and without notice of the defects in the vendor's title. This rule applies in cases where the vendor's legal title is void or voidable, for example because he has stolen the property or obtained it by fraud; it also applies where the vendor holds the legal title subject to an equitable interest in the property. The effect of the rule is to favour the purchaser's security of purchase over the rights of those from whom the vendor has acquired the property. This effect would be subverted, and the policy of the rule stultified, if they were able to recover the value of the property from the purchaser in an action for unjust enrichment, and so the law gives the purchaser a defence to such a claim. In the following account we summarise the rules governing the acquisition of clear legal title by bona fide purchase in Part 2, and we consider the operation and rationale of bona fide purchase as a defence to claims in unjust enrichment in Part 3.

In Part 4, we consider the defence to claims in unjust enrichment that the **29–02** claimant's payment "is made for good consideration, in particular if the money is paid to discharge, and does discharge, a debt owed to the payee (or a principal on whose behalf he is authorised to receive the payment) by the payer or by a third party by whom he is authorised to discharge the debt".[1]

It is open to question whether this defence has separate work to do within the law of unjust enrichment that is not done by the defence of bona fide purchase as it is understood here, by the bar against recovery of benefits to which the claimant is contractually entitled, and by the defence of change of position defence.

2. BONA FIDE PURCHASE AS A METHOD OF ACQUIRING CLEAR LEGAL TITLE TO PROPERTY

The law generally holds that no one can pass a better title to property than the **29–03** title he possesses. At common law, this principle is encapsulated in the rule *nemo dat quod non habet* ("no one gives what he does not have")[2]; in equity the principle informs the operation of the rule *qui prior est tempore potior est jure*

---

[1] *Barclays Bank Ltd v W.J. Simms Son & Cooke (Southern) Ltd* [1980] Q.B. 677 at 695 per Robert Goff J., applied in *Lloyds Bank Plc v Independent Insurance Co Ltd* [2000] Q.B. 110.
[2] Embodied in the Sale of Goods Act 1979 s.21.

("he who is first in time is stronger in law").[3] However, the law also provides that in some exceptional situations a purchaser of legal title from a vendor whose title is defective will acquire legal title free of defects if he gives value and acts in good faith and without notice.

29–04   At common law the *nemo dat* rule invalidates many purported conveyances of property to which the vendor has no valid title, but the bona fide purchase exception operates in one frequently occurring case, namely where money passes into currency.[4] When a bona fide purchaser provides goods or services in exchange for stolen money he acquires legal title to the money, and the original owner loses his legal title, even where the notes and coins are still identifiable in the purchaser's hands. An early decision to this effect is *Miller v Race*, where Lord Mansfield emphasised that "trade and commerce ... would be much incommoded by a contrary determination".[5] Hence the policy of the rule is to preserve the effectiveness of money as currency in the interests of maintaining an efficient market economy.[6]

29–05   Constructive notice is not known at common law and so a purchaser of money who acts honestly will take clear legal title even where a reasonable person would have known that the vendor's title was defective[7]; if, however "there be anything which excites the suspicion that there is something wrong in the transaction, the [purchaser] is not acting in good faith if he shuts his eyes to the facts presented to him and puts the suspicions aside without further inquiry."[8] Consideration does not need to have been provided at the time when the purchaser receives the money, but must have been provided by the time when he

---

[3] *Phillips v Phillips* (1862) 4 De G. F. & J. 208 at 215–216; 45 E.R. 1164 at 1167 per Lord Westbury L.C.: "every conveyance of an equitable interest is an innocent conveyance, that is to say, the grant of a person entitled merely in equity passes only that which he is justly entitled to and no more. If, therefore, a person seised of an equitable estate (the legal estate being outstanding), makes an assurance by way of mortgage or grants an annuity, and afterwards conveys the whole estate to a purchaser, he can grant to the purchaser that which he has, *viz.*, the estate subject to the mortgage or annuity, and no more. The subsequent grantee takes only that which is left in the grantor. Hence grantees and incumbrancers claiming in equity take and are ranked according to the dates of their securities; and the maxim applies, *'Qui prior est tempore potior est jure'*."

[4] For a detailed discussion, see D. Fox, *Property Rights in Money* (Oxford: OUP, 2008), paras 8.20–8.83. Three further examples are set out in the Sale of Goods Act 1979 ss.23–25: these concern conveyances by a seller with a voidable title to goods (s.23), by a seller of goods who remains in possession after he has sold them (s.24), and by a buyer who acquires possession with the seller's consent before he has acquired the seller's title (s.25). Historically, another exception was the sale of property in a market overt: B. Davenport and A. Ross, "Market Overt" in N. Palmer and E. McKendrick (eds.), *Interests in Goods*, 2nd edn (London: LLP, 1998), Ch.14; this rule was abolished by the Sale of Goods (Amendment) Act 1994.

[5] *Miller v Race* (1758) 1 Burr. 452 at 457; 97 E.R. 398 at 402. See too *Clarke v Shee* (1774) 1 Cowp. 197 at 200; 98 E.R. 1041 at 1044 per Lord Mansfield: "Where money or notes are paid *bona fide*, and upon a valuable consideration, they never shall be brought back by the true owner." See also *Wookey v Pole* (1820) 4. B & Ald. 1; 106 E.R. 839; *Orton v Butler* (1822) 5 B. & Ald. 652; 106 E.R. 1329; *Foster v Green* (1862) 7 H. & N. 881; 158 E.R. 726; *Lipkin Gorman (A Firm) v Karpnale Ltd* [1991] 2 A.C. 548 at 572–574.

[6] Fox, *Property Rights in Money*, paras 8.01–8.09.

[7] *Bank of Bengal v Fagan* (1849) 7 Moo. P.C. 61; *Raphael v Bank of England* (1855) 17 C.B. 161. See too the Bills of Exchange Act 1882 s.90: "a thing is done in good faith within the meaning of this Act, where it is in fact done honestly, whether it is done negligently or not".

[8] *London Joint Stock Bank v Simmons* [1892] A.C. 201 at 221 per Lord Herschell. See too *Jones v Gordon* (1877) 2 App. Cas. 616 at 629 per Lord Blackburn.

becomes aware that the vendor's title is defective.[9] Common law does not generally enquire whether the proffered consideration is adequate consideration.[10] However value given under a void contract has been held to be no consideration at all, because it is not given pursuant to a valid legal obligation.[11]

According to Lord Templeman and Lord Goff in *Lipkin Gorman (A Firm) v* **29–06** *Karpnale Ltd*,[12] executory consideration, in the form of a promise to repay money in the future, is not good consideration either. However, their Lordships' comments on this point were obiter, and they are out of line with older authorities which hold that a bank that accepts the deposit of a cheque from its customer and irrevocably credits his account may qualify as a holder for value of the instrument.[13] As argued by David Fox, the best view is therefore that executory consideration can be good consideration for the purposes of the bona fide purchase rule at common law, and their Lordships' comments in *Lipkin Gorman* should be understood to mean only that a bank gives no consideration where it accepts money on deposit but merely makes a provisional credit entry to its customer's account.[14]

In equity, the rule that a bona fide purchaser of legal title takes free of any **29–07** equitable title or interest in the property was largely settled during the Chancellorship of Lord Nottingham, in the late 17th century.[15] As at common law, the rule protects purchasers of legal title provided that they have given value,[16] but no enquiry is normally made into the adequacy of the consideration provided.[17] If the purchase is for money consideration, then the money must have been paid in full before the purchaser receives notice of the equitable interest, since an obligation to pay will be unenforceable once the purchaser has notice.[18] The purchaser must also have acted in good faith[19] and must have had no actual,

---

[9] *Sarkis v Watfa* [2006] EWHC 374 (QB) at [54].

[10] *Lipkin Gorman* [1991] 2 A.C. 548 at 581.

[11] *Lipkin Gorman* [1991] 2 A.C. 548 at 560–562 and 575–577; citing *Clarke v Shee* (1774) 1 Cowp. 197; 98 E.R. 1041. See too *Banque Belge pour l'Etranger v Hambrouck* [1921] 1 K.B. 321 at 326 and 329: money paid to a mistress for past or future cohabitation is paid in exchange for an immoral consideration that is not recognised by law. Note that *Lipkin Gorman* concerned a gaming contract and that the old rule rendering such contracts void was later abrogated by the Gambling Act 2005 ss.334 and 335.

[12] *Lipkin Gorman* [1991] 2 A.C. 548 at 562 and 577.

[13] *Pease v Hirst* (1829) 10 B. & C. 122; 109 E.R. 396; *Hulse v Hulse* (1856) 17 C.B. 711; 139 E.R. 1256; *Ex p. Richdale* (1881) 19 Ch. D. 409 at 417 and 418; *Capital and Counties Bank Ltd v Gordon* [1903] A.C. 240 at 245. See too Bills of Exchange Act 1882, ss.27 and 29.

[14] Fox, *Property Rights in Money*, paras 8.33–8.38.

[15] See, generally, the *Introduction* to D.E.C. Yale (ed.), *Lord Nottingham's Chancery Cases* (Vol.II) (Selden Society, Vol.79 for 1961). For detailed discussion of the current law, see C. Harpum et al., *Megarry & Wade: The Law of Real Property*, 7th edn (London: Sweet & Maxwell, 2008), paras 8.05–8.25; D. Hayton et al., *Underhill and Hayton: Law Relating to Trusts and Trustees*, 18th edn (London: Butterworths, 2010), paras 99.14–99.58.

[16] The rule does not protect volunteers: *Mansell v Mansell* (1732) 2 P. Wms 678; 24 E.R. 913; *Re Strachan* (1876) 4 Ch. D. 123; *Banque Belge* [1921] 1 K.B. 321; *Wu Koon Tai v Wu Yau Loi* [1997] A.C. 179 at 184 and 189–190 (PC).

[17] *Basset v Nosworthy* (1673) Rep. temp. Finch 102; *Midland Bank Ltd v Green* [1981] A.C. 513.

[18] *Tourville v Naish* (1734) 3 P. Wms 307; 24 E.R. 1077; *Taylor Barnard v Tozer* [1984] 1 E.G.L.R. 21 at 22.

[19] "A separate test which may have to be passed even though absence of notice is proved": *Midland Bank* [1981] A.C. 513 at 528 per Lord Wilberforce. There are, however, no clear examples of the test operating independently in the case law.

constructive or imputed notice of the equitable title or interest.[20] The burden of proof lies on the purchaser to establish the provision of value, good faith and lack of notice.[21]

29–08 The bona fide purchase rule does not protect purchasers of equitable title, the parties being assumed to have intended that the purchaser should receive nothing more than the vendor has to give.[22]

3. BONA FIDE PURCHASE AS A DEFENCE TO CLAIMS IN UNJUST ENRICHMENT

29–09 It is clear from the House of Lords' discussion of bona fide purchase in *Lipkin Gorman*[23] that it can operate as a defence to personal claims in unjust enrichment, although it was not available to the defendant on the facts of that case.[24] Cass, a partner in the claimant firm of solicitors, withdrew cash from the firm's client account and spent this cash gambling at the defendant casino. Their Lordships declined to hold that the defendant relevantly gave consideration in exchange for the money that Cass paid, as this was paid pursuant to a void gaming contract.[25] However it is clear that they would have allowed the defendant a complete defence to the firm's common law claim in unjust enrichment if Cass had instead been provided with goods or services pursuant to a legally valid contractual obligation. Bona fide purchase has also been held to operate as a defence to equitable claims in unjust enrichment—for example, in response to

---

[20] *Pilcher v Rawlins* (1872) L.R. 7 Ch. App. 259; *Cave v Cave* (1880) 15 Ch. D. 639; *Northern Counties of England Fire Insurance Co v Whipp* (1884) 26 Ch. D. 482 at 495–496; *Earl of Sheffield v London Joint Stock Bank Ltd* (1888) 13 App. Cas. 333; *Thomson v Clydesdale Bank Ltd* [1893] A.C. 282; *Carl Zeiss Stiftung v Herbert Smith & Co (No.2)* [1969] 2 Ch 276; *Kingsnorth Finance Co Ltd v Tizard* [1986] 1 W.L.R. 783. Note that the doctrine of notice now has only a very limited role to play in registered conveyancing. For discussion of the extent to which the registration of interests in land can operate as a defence to claims in unjust enrichment under English law, see E. Bant, "Registration as a Defence to Claims in Unjust Enrichment: Australia and England Compared" [2011] Conv. 309, pp.322–326.
[21] *Pilcher* (1873) L.R. 7 Ch. App. 259 at 268–269; *A.G. v Biphosphated Guano Co* (1879) 11 Ch D 327; *Re Nisbet and Potts' Contract* [1906] 1 Ch. 386 at 404, 409 and 410; *G. L. Baker v Medway Supplies Ltd* [1958] 1 W.L.R. 1217 at 1220 (reversed on a different point [1958] 1 W.L.R. 1225); *Barclays Bank Plc v Boulter* [1998] 1 W.L.R. 1 at 8.
[22] *Rice v Rice* (1854) 2 Drew 73; 61 E.R. 646; *Phillips* (1861) 4 De G. F. & J. 208 at 215–216; 45 E.R. 1164 at 1166 (quoted in fn.3); *Cave v Cave* (1880) 15 Ch. D. 639 at 646–647; *Latec Investments Ltd v Hotel Terrigal (In Liquidation)* (1965) 113 C.L.R. 265 at 278.
[23] *Lipkin Gorman* [1991] 2 A.C. 548; discussed at paras 8–22 and following. See too *Clarke v Shee* (1774) 1 Cowp. 197; *Nelson v Larholt* [1948] 1 K.B. 339 at 342, obiter.
[24] In *Foskett v McKeown* [2001] 1 A.C. 102 at 129, Lord Millett said that that "a claim in unjust enrichment is subject to a change of position defence, which usually operates by reducing or extinguishing the element of enrichment . . . [but an] action like the present is subject to the *bona fide* purchaser for value defence, which operates to clear the defendant's title." In *Papamichael v National Westminster Bank Plc* [2003] EWHC 164 (Comm); [2003] 1 Lloyd's Rep. 341 at [253], Judge Chambers Q.C. interpreted this to mean that a bona fide purchase defence "is not available where the claim is a personal one for unjust enrichment". However, this is not what Lord Millett said, both comments were obiter, and Judge Chambers's conclusion is inconsistent with the House of Lords' reasoning in *Lipkin Gorman*.
[25] The old rule rendering gaming contracts void was abrogated by the Gambling Act 2005 ss.334 and 335.

personal claims of the kind recognised in *Re Diplock*,[26] to recover the value of misapplied assets in respect of which the claimant was owed a fiduciary duty[27]; and in response to proprietary claims following the defendant's use of the claimant's equitable property to acquire a new asset for himself without the claimant's authority or consent.[28]

It has been said that the defence of bona fide purchase is "simply the paradigm   **29–10** change of position defence", and that "the true rule is that equity will not permit a defendant to set up title to property in which the plaintiff has a beneficial interest unless he has given value or otherwise changed his position to his detriment without notice, actual or constructive, of the plaintiff's interest".[29] The better view is that these are distinct defences. One reason, identified by Lord Goff in *Lipkin Gorman*,[30] is that "change of position will only avail a defendant to the extent that his position has been changed; whereas, where *bona fide* purchase is invoked, no inquiry is made (in most cases) into the adequacy of the considera-tion." In other words, the change of position defence only operates pro tanto, to the extent that the defendant has suffered detriment, whereas the bona fide purchase defence always operates as an absolute bar: provided that the defendant has given some consideration in exchange for the relevant property, the claim will fail completely, whatever the value of the consideration given.

This difference reflects the different rationales of the two defences. The change   **29–11** of position defence aims to protect the defendant's interest in making spending decisions freely, without fear that a claim in unjust enrichment might later invalidate the assumptions that he makes about the means at his disposal. The bona fide purchase defence aims to protect the security of certain classes of purchase transaction.

Two versions of this explanation of the bona fide purchase defence have been   **29–12** advanced by legal scholars. On one view,[31] the purpose of the defence is to prevent claims in unjust enrichment from stultifying the choices made by the law when deciding the correct balance to be struck between the rights of property owners and the public interest in protecting particular classes of transaction in the interests of market efficiency. On this view, the defence is a narrow one and is confined to those cases where an exception to the *nemo dat* principle needs to be preserved.

On another view, the defence has the wider purpose of preventing claims in   **29–13** unjust enrichment from subverting the contractual arrangements made between

---

[26] *Re Diplock* [1948] Ch. 465 (CA); affirmed [1951] A.C. 251; discussed at para.8–51 and follow-ing.
[27] See too *G.L. Baker Ltd v Medway Building and Supplies Ltd* [1958] 3 All E.R. 540 at 543; *Re J. Leslie Engineers Co Ltd* [1976 1 W.L.R. 292 at 299.
[28] *Foskett* [2001] 1 A.C. 102 at 130. In *Foskett* the House of Lords denied that the law of unjust enrichment generates equitable proprietary rights in unauthorised substitutes. As discussed at paras 8–83 and following, however, their Lordships' reasons for making this assertion do not stand up to scrutiny.
[29] Sir P. Millett, "Tracing the Proceeds of Fraud" (1991) 107 L.Q.R. 71, p.82. Cf. P. Key, "*Bona Fide* Purchase as a Defence in the Law of Restitution" [1994] L.M.C.L.Q. 421, pp.425–426.
[30] *Lipkin Gorman* [1991] 2 A.C. 548 at 580–581.
[31] P. Birks, *Unjust Enrichment*, 2nd edn (Oxford: OUP, 2005), pp.240–244; W. Swadling, "Ignorance and Unjust Enrichment: The Problem of Title" (2008) 28 O.J.L.S. 627, pp.656–657.

the defendant and the vendor from whom the defendant has received the claimant's property.[32] Understood in this way, the defence is a manifestation of the principle, discussed in Ch.3, that contracts can operate as a justifying ground not only in two-party cases where the claimant and defendant agree that the defendant should receive a benefit from the claimant, but also in three-party cases where a third party agrees with the defendant that the defendant should receive a benefit emanating from the claimant. If this understanding of the bona fide purchase defence is correct, then there is no reason to limit the availability of the defence to those situations where an exception to the *nemo dat* principle is engaged. However, while there may well be situations where it is appropriate for a court to hold that a contract between a third party and a defendant should override the claimant's right in unjust enrichment, there are others where the contract should not have this effect. The courts must investigate the relationships between all of the parties, their intentions and the surrounding circumstances, in order to decide which is the appropriate outcome.[33]

29–14   Whichever of these two explanations of the bona fide purchase defence is correct, both support the view that the defence can be raised against personal claims in unjust enrichment. The latter explanation is also consistent with the view that the defence effectively applies in two-party as well as three-party cases, though not as a separate defence but as part of a general rule against recovery if that would undermine contractual agreements between the parties. If either view is correct, then it also reinforces the argument that there is no separate role to be played within the law of unjust enrichment by a defence of "good consideration". To this we shall now turn.

4. GOOD CONSIDERATION

29–15   In *Barclays Bank Ltd v W.J. Simms Son & Cooke (Southern) Ltd*,[34] the defendant presented a cheque for payment to the claimant bank, which mistakenly overlooked a stop order placed on the cheque and paid the defendant. Robert Goff J. would have denied recovery of the bank's mistaken payment if this had been authorised by the customer who had issued the cheque, as the customer's debt to the defendant would then have been discharged, and the defendant would have given "good consideration" for the money, in the form of the discharge of its debt. However, since the payment was not authorised, the debt was not discharged and the defence was not available.[35]

---

[32] K. Barker, "After Change of Position: Good Faith Exchange in the Modern Law of Restitution" in P. Birks (ed.), *Laundering and Tracing* (Oxford: Clarendon Press, 1995), 191, p.192: unlike the change of position defence, which "aims to protect individual recipients against unfair losses caused by a given receipt", the defence of bona fide purchase "deploys a broad policy of transactional security in exchange dealings, with the primary (economic) objective of facilitating the free transfer of wealth." See too K. Barker, "*Bona Fide* Purchase as a Defence to Unjust Enrichment Claims: A Concise Restatement" [1999] R.L.R. 75; A. Burrows, *The Law of Restitution*, 3rd edn (Oxford: OUP, 2010), pp.577–580.

[33] See para.3–58 and following for further discussion.

[34] *Barclays Bank Ltd v W.J. Simms Son & Cooke (Southern) Ltd* [1980] Q.B. 677 at 695.

[35] See too *Jones* [2009] EWHC 722 (QB); [2009] 2 Lloyd's Rep. 94 at [48]–[55]. For the (unfortunately inconsistent) law governing the discharge of debts by unauthorised interveners who have paid them by mistake, see paras 5–45—5–46.

Robert Goff J. relied for his analysis on the Court of Exchequer's decision in **29–16**
Aiken v Short.[36] There George Carter borrowed £200 from Francis Short, who
took as security an equitable mortgage over property which was to come to
George under Edward Carter's will. Edward changed his will; under the new will
George was entitled to a modest annuity which was to cease upon assignment, as
he well knew. Subsequently, George obtained another loan from the plaintiff
bank, conveying as security his "property" under Edward's will. The bank
agreed to discharge Francis Short's debt. After Francis Short's death, his widow
and sole executrix, Elizabeth, demanded payment of the debt from George who
"referred" her to the plaintiff bank, which paid off the debt. On discovering that
George's security was worthless, the plaintiff bank claimed to recover its payment from Elizabeth on the ground of mistake.

The Court of Exchequer held that the claim failed. The three Barons of the **29–17**
Exchequer spoke with somewhat different voices. Bramwell B. said that the
claim failed because the plaintiff's mistake was not sufficiently fundamental.[37]
But Pollock C.B. and Platt B. held that the "money which the defendant got from
her debtor was actually due to her, and there can be no obligation to refund it".[38]
In *R.E. Jones v Waring and Gillow Ltd*, Scrutton L.J. later explained this as
follows[39]:

> "[W]here the defendant has no legal relationship with the plaintiff but receives money
> which has in fact come from the plaintiff *bona fide* and for valuable consideration from
> a third party with whom he has a legal relationship, he can keep the money so obtained
> from the plaintiff under a mistake of fact if he, the defendant, was not a party to the
> mistake and did not contribute to it."

This principle was applied by the Court of Appeal in *Lloyds Bank Plc v* **29–18**
Independent Insurance Co Ltd.[40] A company owed a debt to the defendant and
told its bank to pay the defendant the amount that was owed. The bank made the
payment in the mistaken belief that three cheques deposited in the company's
account had cleared. However, one cheque was dishonoured and so the agent's
account was substantially overdrawn. The bank claimed to recover its mistaken
payment from the defendant and the Court of Appeal held that the claim must
fail. The money had been paid with the company's authority to discharge its debt
to the defendant, and so the defendant had given good consideration for the
money.

In previous editions of this work, good consideration was treated as a distinct **29–19**
defence within the law of unjust enrichment.[41] However, we doubt that it has a
role to perform that cannot be performed by other principles. In two-party cases,
where a claimant pays money to a defendant to discharge a legal obligation that
he owes the defendant, any claim to recover the money could be met by the

---

[36] *Aiken v Short* (1856) 1 H. & N. 210; 156 E.R. 1180.
[37] *Aiken* at 1 H. & N. at 215; 156 E.R. at 1183.
[38] *Aiken* 1 H. & N. at 215; 156 E.R. at 1183 per Platt B.; see also Pollock C.B., 1 H. & N. at 214;
156 E.R. at 1182.
[39] *R.E. Jones v Waring and Gillow Ltd* [1925] 2 K.B. 612 at 640; see too *Re J. Leslie Engineers Co
Ltd* [1976] 2 All E.R. 85 at 91 per Oliver J.
[40] *Lloyds Bank Plc v Independent Insurance Co Ltd* [2000] Q.B. 110.
[41] e.g. G. Jones, *Goff & Jones: The Law of Restitution*, 7th edn (London: Sweet & Maxwell, 2006),
Ch.41.

response that the defendant's enrichment is justified by the legal right that he had to receive the money. Hence the case would fall within the scope of the principles outlined in Chs 2 and 3. Moreover, even if that were not enough to bar the claim, the defendant would also be entitled to rely on the change of position defence discussed in Ch.27, having released his legal right against the claimant in exchange for the payment.

29–20   In three-party cases, where a claimant pays money to a defendant to discharge a legal obligation that the claimant owes to a third party, the change of position defence would again be available, for the reason already given—and indeed, this is the basis on which Waller L.J. would have decided the *Independent Insurance* case,[42] although Peter Gibson L.J. thought otherwise, noting that Robert Goff J. had treated good consideration as a separate defence from change of position in *Barclays Bank v Simms*.[43]

29–21   It also seems possible that the defendant in a three-party case would be entitled to rely on the defence of bona fide purchase. This is easiest to justify if one takes the broader view of the defence, that extends it beyond a limited rule that reflects the law's title-clearing rules, and enables it to encompass the acquisition of any form of benefit for value and in good faith. On the narrow view of the defence, that it is only available where the defendant receives flawed title to an asset, one might say that it should not be available in cases where there is no title-clearing to be done because the defendant receives full legal title to the money paid by the claimant. Even on this view, however, it might be argued that the law's concern to ensure the currency of money that underpins the defence as a title-clearing device should carry over into cases where the defendant receives good title, but needs protection from claims in unjust enrichment.

29–22   Finally, it may be that the three-party cases are also amenable to analysis as cases where recovery was denied because the defendant's enrichment was justified by his contract with the third party. This is suggested by the approach taken by Peter Gibson L.J. in the *Independent Insurance* case,[44] which he rested on Lord Hope's statement in *Kleinwort Benson Ltd v Lincoln CC*,[45] that a defendant:

> "cannot be said to have been unjustly enriched if he was entitled to receive the sum paid to him. The payer may have been mistaken as to the grounds on which the sum was due to the payee, but his mistake will not provide a ground for its recovery if the payee can show that he was entitled to it on some other ground."

Whether this is a viable explanation of the three-party cases depends on the view that is taken of the way that contract can operate as a justifying ground in cases with multiple parties, a matter that is discussed in Ch.3.[46]

---

[42] *Independent Insurance* [2000] Q.B. 110 at 127.
[43] *Independent Insurance* [2000] Q.B. 110 at 130.
[44] *Independent Insurance* [2000] Q.B. 110 at 132.
[45] *Kleinwort Benson Ltd v Lincoln CC* [1999] 2 A.C. 349 at 407–408.
[46] See para.3–58 and following. Cf. Burrows, *The Law of Restitution*, p.213, who argues that "this does not appear to provide a sound justification where, as on the facts of *Lloyds Bank*, the payee has no legal entitlement *against the payor* to be paid." This is inconsistent with some of the cases discussed in Ch.3.

CHAPTER 30

ESTOPPEL

1. INTRODUCTION

The defence of estoppel generally depends on the claimant having made a **30-01** representation of fact to the defendant, that he is entitled to the benefit he has received, and on the defendant having changed his position to his detriment in reliance on this representation, making it inequitable for the claimant to resile from it. The payment of money is not generally a representation in itself, and in many situations no other representation can be discovered on the facts, with the result that the defence is unavailable. Where the defence can be established, the courts' starting point is that the claimant should be held to his undertaking with the result that the defence operates as a complete bar to the claim. However in recent times the courts have held that the defence should only operate pro tanto, and should not bar the claim completely, where this would be a disproportionately favourable outcome to the defendant, given the amount of detriment that he has suffered. It is difficult to reconcile these findings with the stated rationale of the defence, which is to hold claimants to their promises where defendants have detrimentally relied on them.

2. REPRESENTATION

The claimant must generally have made a representation of fact which led the **30-02** defendant to believe that he was entitled to treat the money as his own. Sometimes a representation may be implicit in the payment itself in the light of the surrounding circumstances,[1] for example, where it is made in response to a claim by the defendant, or follows upon an account showing the money as due to the defendant.[2] In contrast, a paying bank does not impliedly represent, by honouring a cheque, that it is genuine or that its customer's signature is genuine, even if the cheque is presented for special collection.[3] A payment is not normally a representation in itself which can found an estoppel, and there must normally be some

---

[1] *National Westminster Bank Plc v Somer International (UK) Ltd* [2001] EWCA Civ 970; [2002] 1 All E.R. 198. See also Scrutton L.J.'s view of the facts in *Holt v Markham* [1923] 1 K.B. 504; and Asquith J.'s apparent acceptance of the second representation in *Weld-Blundell v Synott* [1940] 2 K.B. 107; and cf. *Sidney Bolsom Investment Trust Ltd v E. Karmios & Co Ltd* [1956] 1 Q.B. 529 at 540–541 per Denning L.J.
[2] A representation is more readily found if it is made fraudulently: see *Hirschfeld v London Brighton and South Coast Railway Co* (1876) L.R. 2 Q.B.D. 1.
[3] *National Westminster Bank Ltd v Barclays Bank Ltd* [1975] Q.B. 654.

further indication by the claimant that the defendant is entitled to receive the money.[4]

30–03   In cases where there is no express representation, a claimant may still be estopped where he has breached a duty of accuracy owed to the defendant.[5] Such a duty arises only in exceptional circumstances, and whether or not it exists is a question of law. For example, there is "no basis for any suggestion that a bank owes a duty of care to a payee in deciding to honour a customer's cheque, at any rate when this appears to be regular on its face".[6] In *R.E. Jones Ltd v Waring & Gillow Ltd*[7] Lord Sumner stated that establishing a breach of a duty of accuracy is *essential* to raise an estoppel defence, and a similar observation was made by Asquith J. in *Weld-Blundell v Synott*.[8] But it is hard to reconcile these findings with the judgments in *Deutsche Bank (London Agency) v Beriro & Co*[9] and *Holt v Markham*,[10] in both of which estoppel was successfully invoked without any breach of duty having been committed by the claimant. Moreover we consider that the only discernible ratio decidendi of that part of the *R.E. Jones* case concerned with estoppel is that on the facts there was no sufficient representation by the appellants leading the respondents to change their position.[11] Hence the best view is that a breach of duty need not be shown in order to make out the estoppel defence,[12] but that a payment made by a claimant who owes a duty of accuracy entails an implied representation that the money is due.[13]

3. DETRIMENTAL RELIANCE

30–04   The defendant, acting in good faith and without notice of the claim, must have changed his position to his detriment. Examples of detrimental changes in position include: being in receipt of payments over a period of time and spending them in such a manner as to have altered the defendant's mode of living[14]; paying money to a third party to whom the defendant believes that he is obliged to pay

---

[4] *R.E. Jones Ltd v Waring & Gillow Ltd* [1926] A.C. 670. In *Transvaal & Delagoa Bay Investment Co v Atkinson* [1944] 1 All E.R. 579, Atkinson J. suggested (at 585) that the claimant must have "expressly or impliedly represented to the defendant that the money paid was truly due and owing to the defendant".
[5] The leading cases are: *Skyring v Greenwood* (1825) 4 B. & C. 281 at 290–291; 107 E.R. 1064 at 1068 per Bayley J.; *Coventry, Sheppard & Co v Great Eastern Railway Co* (1883) 11 Q.B.D. 776; *Mercantile Bank of India Ltd v Central Bank of India Ltd* [1938] A.C. 287; *Avon CC v Howlett* [1983] 1 W.L.R. 605 at 611 and 621, obiter.
[6] *National Westminster Bank* [1975] Q.B. 654 at 662 per Kerr J.
[7] *R.E. Jones Ltd v Waring and Gillow Ltd* [1926] A.C. 670 at 693.
[8] *Weld-Blundell v Synott* [1940] 2 K.B. 107 at 114–115.
[9] *Deutsche Bank (London Agency) v Beriro & Co* (1895) 1 Com. Cas. 123 and 255.
[10] *Holt v Markham* [1923] 1 K.B. 504.
[11] We also find Lord Sumner's reasoning less persuasive than that of the dissentients, Viscount Cave and Lord Atkinson, to support their conclusion that there had been a representation in the case.
[12] Cf. *Lipkin Gorman (A Firm) v Karpnale Ltd* [1991] 2 A.C. 548 at 579, where Lord Goff did not mention any need to establish a breach of duty to make out the defence.
[13] P. Birks, *An Introduction to the Law of Restitution*, revised edn (Oxford: OUP, 1989), pp.402–407. See too A. Burrows, *The Law of Restitution*, 3rd edn (Oxford: OUP, 2010), pp.551–553.
[14] *Skyring* (1825) 4 B. & C. 281; 107 E.R. 1064; *Lloyds Bank Ltd v Brooks* (1950) 6 *Legal Decisions Affecting Bankers* 161; *Avon CC v Howlett* [1983] 1 W.L.R. 605.

it, and from whom there is no practical means of recovering it[15]; and investing the money in a company which later goes into liquidation.[16]

The courts have allowed defendants some latitude when proving changes of **30–05** position for the purposes of the estoppel defence. In *Skyring v Greenwood*,[17] for example, Abbott C.J. was willing to presume that "every prudent man accommodates his mode of living to his income", and in *Avon CC v Howlett*,[18] Slade L.J. recognised that a bona fide defendant who receives a benefit may find it "very difficult . . . subsequently to recall and identify retrospectively" in what way its receipt has led him to alter his mode of living and to incur burdensome extra commitments and expenditure.

An example of a case in which the defendant failed to discharge the burden of **30–06** proving that he incurred detriment in reliance on the claimant's representation is *United Overseas Bank v Jiwani*.[19] The claimant bank mistakenly credited the defendant's account with money that he used to buy a hotel. Mocatta J. did not accept that the defendant had honestly been misled by the bank's representation that the money was his to spend as he wished. Moreover, the defendant would have bought the hotel in any case, and it was a profitable investment that was still in his hands at the time of the claim, and so it could not be said that he had changed his position to his detriment.

The claimant's payment must not have been primarily caused by the defen- **30–07** dant's fault.[20] For example, the defence will not be available if the defendant has knowledge of unusual and exceptional circumstances surrounding a particular transaction, such as the presentation of a cheque, which could not have been known to the claimant.[21] Nor will the defence be available if the defendant obtains possession of money by a wrongful act or misleads the claimant by a misrepresentation that the money is due.

4. THE EFFECT OF THE DEFENCE

In *Avon*[22] the Court of Appeal held that estoppel cannot operate pro tanto. In that **30–08** case the claimant mistakenly paid instalments amounting to £1,007 to the defendant. The defendant argued that the claimant was estopped from recovering any of the money. The claimant had made a representation of fact which led the defendant to believe that he was entitled to the money, and in good faith he had changed his position relying on that representation. It was specifically pleaded in his defence that he had only spent about £546 of the £1,007. The trial judge, Sheldon J., held that the claimant was estopped. He also found as a fact that by the date of the hearing the defendant had spent all the overpaid money. Yet his counsel declined an invitation to amend the pleadings to put the defence on a

---

[15] *Deutsche Bank* (1895) 1 Com. Cas. 123 and 255.
[16] *Holt* [1923] 1 K.B. 504.
[17] *Skyring v Greenwood* (1825) 4 B. & C. 281 at 289; 107 E.R. 1064 at 1068.
[18] *Avon CC v Howlett* [1983] 1 W.L.R. 605, 621–622.
[19] *United Overseas Bank v Jiwani* [1976] 1 W.L.R. 964.
[20] *Larner v London County Council* [1949] 2 K.B. 683 at 689 per Denning L.J.
[21] *National Westminster Bank* [1975] Q.B. 654 at 676–677 per Kerr J.
[22] *Avon* [1983] 1 W.L.R. 605.

broader basis.[23] Consequently, the judge held that it would not be inequitable to require the defendant to make restitution of the balance of £460, but the Court of Appeal reversed that decision, holding that estoppel should be deemed to be a rule of evidence which defeats a claim *in limine*.

30–09   In Slade L.J.'s view[24]:

> "[T]he authorities suggest that, in cases where estoppel by representation is available as a defence to a claim for money had and received, the courts do not treat the operation of the estoppel as being restricted to the precise amount of the detriment which the representee proves he has suffered in reliance on the representation."

Eveleigh and Slade L.JJ. concluded that the question whether estoppel could operate pro tanto had already been decided in *Greenwood v Martins Bank Ltd*,[25] where a bank's customer was[26]:

> "estopped from asserting that a cheque with which he has been debited is a forgery, because of his failure to inform the bank in due time, so that it could have recourse to the forger, the debit will stand for the whole amount and not merely that which could have been recovered from the forger."

Slade L.J. also regarded *Skyring*[27] and *Holt*[28] as further authority for the proposition that estoppel cannot operate pro tanto: the fact that in these cases there was no exact inquiry into the alteration of each defendant's financial position suggested that such an inquiry was irrelevant and inappropriate.[29]

30–10   It is doubtful whether these decisions support Eveleigh and Slade L.JJ.'s statement of principle. In *Greenwood* the bank had not received any benefit but had suffered loss, which it could not recoup from the forger and which it recouped by debiting its customer's accounts; in contrast, in *Avon* the claimant sought to recover money from a defendant who had been enriched by the receipt of the payment. In *Skyring* and *Holt* there was no judicial statement that estoppel by representation cannot operate pro tanto, and it is reading a great deal into the uncertain facts of these cases to say that the courts there thought it immaterial whether all the money had been spent or not.[30]

30–11   All members of the Court of Appeal accepted that the rule that estoppel does not operate pro tanto could give rise to injustice. Consequently, all three members were prepared to recognise that exceptionally it could operate pro tanto. Slade L.J. thought that this "might be the case, for example, where the sums sought to be recovered were so large as to bear no relation to any detriment which the recipient could possibly have suffered".[31] But it was Eveleigh L.J.'s judgment which "most clearly pointed the way to the future", according to Clarke L.J.

---

[23] *Avon* [1983] 1 W.L.R. 605 at 616.
[24] *Avon* [1983] 1 W.L.R. 605 at 622.
[25] *Greenwood v Martins Bank Ltd* [1932] 1 K.B. 371; [1933] A.C. 51.
[26] *Avon* [1983] 1 W.L.R. 605 at 622 per Slade L.J.
[27] *Skyring* (1825) 4 B. & C. 281.
[28] *Holt* [1923] 1 K.B. 504; [1933] A.C. 51 HL.
[29] *Avon* [1983] 1 W.L.R. 605 at 624 per Slade L.J.
[30] See *Somer* [2001] EWCA Civ 970; [2002] 1 All E.R. 198 at [45]–[46].
[31] *Avon* [1983] 1 W.L.R. 605 at 624–625.

when he reviewed this area of the law in the later case of *National Westminster Bank plc v Somer International (UK) Ltd.*[32] Eveleigh L.J. said that[33]:

> "while there might have been a representation there may be circumstances which would render it unconscionable for the defendant to retain a balance in his hands."

Avon was considered in two cases decided in 2001 by the Court of Appeal. In **30–12** *Scottish Equitable Plc v Derby*,[34] the claimant mistakenly over-stated the value of his pension policy by some £172,000, and paid him this excess amount when he cashed in the policy. He used around £42,000 to reduce his mortgage debt, around £121,000 to buy a new pension policy, and around £9,000 to effect some modest improvements to his lifestyle. The reduction in the defendant's mortgage debt did not count as a detrimental change in his position because he would have had to pay this debt anyway, and the provider of the new pension policy agreed to unwind the transaction without enforcing any of the penalties written into the contract. Moreover the claimant conceded that it could not recover the £9,000 and only sought to recover the balance. The question before the court was therefore whether the defendant could nevertheless argue that the £9,000 expenditure constituted detriment incurred in reliance on the claimant's representation that the whole £172,000 was due, with the result that he had a complete defence to the claim. The Court of Appeal held that the defence could only operate pro tanto because the facts brought it within the unconscionability exception identified in *Avon*.

In *Somer*,[35] the claimant bank mistakenly credited the defendant's account by **30–13** around US$77,000. The defendant was expecting to be paid by a business customer and was led by the bank to believe that the sum mistakenly credited to its account represented this payment. The defendant therefore sent goods worth around £13,000 to the customer. The question arose whether the defendant was entitled to a complete defence of estoppel, and again the Court of Appeal held that it was not because the case fell within the unconscionability exception. Hence the claimant could recover the difference between US$77,000 and £13,000.

Two points should be made about these decisions. First, Robert Walker L.J. **30–14** was attracted to the "ingenious and convincing" argument made by counsel in the *Scottish Equitable* case,[36] that the court should assess the detriment suffered by the defendant at the date of trial, and that application of the change of position defence at this date would always negative the defendant's detriment, leaving him unable to raise the defence of estoppel. However, we consider that this argument was misconceived because it makes the application of the estoppel defence conditional on the prior application of the change of position defence. There is no justification for this. It is a matter for the defendant to decide which defences he chooses to rely upon, and it does not follow from the fact that a defendant could invoke the change of position defence if he chose to do so that

---

[32] *Somer* [2001] EWCA Civ 970; [2002] 1 All E.R. 198 at [56].
[33] *Avon* [1983] 1 W.L.R. 605 at 611–612.
[34] *Scottish Equitable Plc v Derby* [2001] EWCA Civ 369; [2001] 3 All E.R. 818.
[35] *Somer* [2001] EWCA Civ 970; [2002] 1 All E.R. 198.
[36] *Scottish Equitable* [2001] EWCA Civ 369; [2001] 3 All E.R. 818 at [45]–[47].

he *must* invoke it, and *must* therefore be disabled from invoking the defence of estoppel instead.[37]

30–15   Secondly, and more importantly, it is hard to think that there are any limits (other then the de minimis principle) to the unconscionability exception identified in *Avon* and applied in *Scottish Equitable* and *Somer*. Unless the difference between the value of the benefit received by the defendant and the value of the detriment incurred by the defendant is vanishingly small, the courts can always be expected to hold that it would be "unconscionable" for the defendant to keep this windfall. Andrew Burrows concludes that: "the *Avon* exception [therefore] swallows up its all or nothing rule" and argues that the "cleaner approach would be to recognise this and to clarify that . . . the all or nothing estoppel defence is in this context inapt and should be excised."[38]

30–16   In practical terms, taking this approach would leave no work for the estoppel defence to do what is not done by the change of position defence, which is moreover easier to prove since there is no need to show a representation. The defence of estoppel would therefore be eliminated. In our view, however, the two defences are different and estoppel has a role to play that is not performed by change of position. Change of position is about the fair allocation of loss where the value transferred from the claimant to the defendant has been dissipated through no fault of the defendant's, while estoppel is about holding the claimant to his undertakings where these have been detrimentally relied upon by the defendant.[39] Before brushing the estoppel defence to one side on the basis that it always produces the same outcome as the change of position defence, one would need to be certain that a court would never think it appropriate to fulfil the defendant's expectations rather than merely reversing his detriment, or to achieve some combination of the two. There is an unspoken assumption in recent judicial discussions of the estoppel defence that this would never be appropriate, but no explanation has been offered of why this should be so.

---

[37] As argued in E. Bant, *The Change of Position Defence* (Oxford: Hart Publishing, 2009), pp.226–227, whose analysis was affirmed in *T.R.A. Global Pty Ltd v Kebakoska* [2011] VSC 480 at [37].

[38] A. Burrows, *The Law of Restitution*, p.557.

[39] P. Birks, *Unjust Enrichment*, 2nd edn (Oxford: OUP, 2005), pp.235–236. Birks argues that "the legitimate way to prevent overkill is . . . to construe [the claimant's representations] as prospectively revocable in the event of the representor's making a mistake." However, we share the doubts expressed by Bant, *The Change of Position Defence*, pp.228–229, that the courts would be willing to find implied terms of this kind.

CHAPTER 31

COUNTER-RESTITUTION IMPOSSIBLE

1. INTRODUCTION

A claimant who seeks restitution of an unjust enrichment must make counter- **31–01**
restitution of benefits received from the defendant in exchange. If counter-
restitution is impossible then the claim is barred. This rule has most often been
applied in cases where the claimant has sought rescission of a contract on the
grounds of undue influence or misrepresentation, for example, and has sought to
recover benefits conferred on the defendant under the contract.[1] But the rule has
also been applied where there was never a contract between the parties, for
example because they transferred benefits to one another under a contract that
turned out to be void.

The common law courts formerly applied this rule very fiercely, insisting on **31–02**
precise counter-restitution of non-money benefits *in specie*, but the Chancery
courts permitted substitutionary counter-restitution of non-money benefits by the
payment of money, and the courts have now begun to take this more flexible
approach across the board. This is discussed in Part 2. In Andrew Burrows'
words, it means that it has become "a nonsense to talk of restitution being
impossible given that, assuming solvency, it is always possible for the claimant
to pay the defendant a sum of money for the value of the benefit received."[2] If
this is correct, then it has become inaccurate to say that "counter-restitution
impossible" is a defence to claims in unjust enrichment; it is, rather, a pre-
condition for recovery that the amount recoverable by a claimant should be
reduced by the amount of the benefits that he received from the defendant.[3]

This view of the way in which the law has developed has a number of **31–03**
implications. First, it means that the older common law cases demanding
counter-restitution *in specie* must now be treated with great caution, as it has
become increasingly likely that the courts will refuse to follow them.

Secondly, it casts significant doubt on the rule, discussed in Ch.12, that claims **31–04**
to recover benefits transferred on a basis that fails will only lie where the failure
is total: if the claimant transfers a benefit to the defendant on the basis that he will
receive a benefit in return, and if he can always make counter-restitution of any
part of this benefit that he receives from the defendant, then the main reason for

---

[1] It is debateable whether rescission is a remedy for unjust enrichment only when it leads to the return
of benefits conferred under a wholly or partially executed contract, or whether rescission of a wholly
executory contract can also be understood as a remedy for unjust enrichment; see para.40–15.
[2] A. Burrows, *The Law of Restitution*, 3rd edn (Oxford: OUP, 2010), p.250. For a modern case in
which the relationship between the parties would have made counter-restitution very difficult to
quantify, see *Crystal Palace (2000) Ltd v Dowie* [2007] EWHC 1392 (QB); [2007] I.R.L.R. 682 at
[210]–[218].
[3] *Dunbar Bank Plc v Nadeem* [1998] 3 All E.R. 876 at 884 per Millett L.J. See too P. Birks, *Unjust
Enrichment*, 2nd edn (Oxford: OUP, 2005), p.228.

the law's insistence that he must not have received anything falls away.[4] In the previous edition of this work, the point was put in this way[5]:

> "The proper enquiry is whether the claimant who claims restitution [on the ground of failure of consideration] has received any part of the bargained for performance (consideration). If he has and he is not in a position to make counter-restitution, then his restitutionary claim must fail. Conversely, if he has received no part of the consideration, or *if it is still possible for him to make counter-restitution in respect of the part which he received*, then his restitutionary claim should succeed."

31–05   Thirdly, if the law makes counter-restitution a pre-condition for claims in unjust enrichment, then there are two ways in which this rule might be understood. It might be a rule that claim and counterclaim must be netted off, imposed with the pragmatic purpose of reducing multiplicity of suits. Or it might be a rule that enrichments transferred and received in a process of exchange must be netted off, imposed to ensure that the mutual reciprocity of the parties' performances is duly reflected in the unwinding process that must follow failure of the basis for the parties' exchange. English authority on this point is sparse, but in *Kleinwort Benson Ltd v Sandwell BC*,[6] Hobhouse J. took the latter view. If that is correct, then it means that the rules governing the identification and quantification of benefit discussed in Chs 4 and 5 may need some qualification.

2. OPERATION OF THE RULE

31–06   Until at least the beginning of the 20th century, the counter-restitution requirement was more strictly applied at common law than in equity. Rescission was denied at common law if precise counter-restitution was impossible, in which case a defrauded party had to fall back on his action for damages for deceit. In *Clarke v Dickson*,[7] for example, the claimant was refused rescission of a contract to buy shares in a partnership on the ground that in the meantime the partnership had been converted into a limited liability company. The claimant bought "shares in a partnership with others. He cannot return those . . . Still stronger, he has changed their nature."[8] Nor was a claimant entitled to rescission where he had received a benefit under the contract which of its very nature could not be restored, such as services[9] or which he had consumed or disposed of, so that the purchaser of a mine could not rescind the contract of purchase after the mine had been worked out.[10]

---

[4] See paras 12–16—12–31.

[5] G. Jones, *Goff & Jones: The Law of Restitution*, 7th edn (London: Sweet & Maxwell, 2006) at para.19.005 (emphasis added). This argument was noted in *Giedo Van der Garde BV v Force India Formula One Team Ltd* [2010] EWHC 2373 (QB) at [260] per Stadlen J., but after lengthy consideration of the authorities he concluded at [367], "with regret", that he was bound not to accede to it.

[6] *Kleinwort Benson Ltd v Sandwell BC* [1994] 4 All E.R. 890.

[7] *Clarke v Dickson* (1858) El. Bl. & El. 148; 120 E.R. 463.

[8] *Clarke* El. Bl. & El. at 154–155; 120 E.R. 467 per Crompton J. See also *Street v Blay* (1831) B. & Ad. 456; 109 E.R. 1212; *Western Bank of Scotland v Addie* (1867) L.R. 1 Sc. 145 (HL).

[9] *Glasgow and South Western Railway Co v Boyd & Forrest* [1915] A.C. 526

[10] *Vigers v Pike* (1842) 8 Cl. & F. 562; 8 E.R. 220. See also *Sheffield Nickel and Silver Plating Co Ltd v Unwin* (1877) 2 Q.B.D. 214, considered in *Capcon Holdings Plc v Edwards* [2007] EWHC 2662 (Ch) at [45]–[54].

Even at common law, however, rescission was not barred merely because   **31–07**
property transferred under the contract had deteriorated or depreciated in
value:

> "To hold otherwise would be to say that where a losing and insolvent business is sold
> by means of the representation that it is solvent and profitable, rescission could never
> be obtained if the loss were increased prior to the discovery of the true state of
> affairs."[11]

Depreciation which would have occurred in any event was therefore disregarded.
Thus in *Armstrong v Jackson*[12] a contract for the purchase of shares was set aside,
despite a substantial intervening fall in their value. In other cases, compensation
was ordered. "Where compensation can be made for any deterioration of the
property, such deterioration shall be no bar to rescission, but only a ground for
compensation."[13] In the Canadian case of *Wiebe v Butchart's Motors Ltd*,[14] a
contract for the sale of a motor-car was induced by a misrepresentation by the
seller, and the buyer was entitled to rescind the contract on paying the seller $600
for the deterioration of the car, which had been used continuously since the sale.
Moreover, where property was improved as a result of bona fide expenditure of
the party who, if rescission took place, would have to restore it, rescission could
be ordered on the terms that such expenditure was to be repaid by the other
party.[15]

The courts were also willing to take a more flexible approach in common law   **31–08**
cases where the defendant has committed a fraud. In *Hulton v Hulton*,[16] a
separation deed obtained by the husband by fraudulent misrepresentation was
rescinded, and the wife did not have to repay sums that she had received under
the deed because the husband had received corresponding benefits, such as
freedom from proceedings by the wife for restitution of conjugal rights. The deed
had also required certain letters to be destroyed, and the fact that they could not

---

[11] *Adam v Newbigging* (1888) 13 App. Cas. 308 at 330 per Lord Herschell; this dictum is inconsistent
with Thesiger L.J.'s comments in *Waddell v Blockey* (1879) 4 Q.B.D. 678 at 683, which was
moreover a case of fraud, and therefore out of line with the cases discussed at paras 31–08—31–09.
In *Adam* the claimant was entitled to rescind a contract of partnership for non-fraudulent misrepresentation, although the firm had become insolvent in the meantime. Another reason for the
result, given by Lord Watson at 322, lay in the distinction between partnerships and limited liability
companies that became insolvent between the time when the claimant contracted to become a partner
or shareholder, and the time when he sought rescission: a firm's insolvency did not affect the
claimant's liability to third-party creditors, and so rescission was allowed, but a company's insolvency altered the quality of the claimant's shares and so rescission was barred. On this, see also
Senanayake v Cheng [1966] A.C. 63 at 80–81 (PC).

[12] *Armstrong v Jackson* [1917] 2 K.B. 822. See too *Gillette v Peppercorn* (1840) 3 Beav. 78 at 85;
49 E.R. 31 at 33; *Blake v Mowatt* (1856) 21 Beav. 603; 52 E.R. 993; *Addie* (1867) L.R. 1 Sc. 145 at
166; *Cheese v Thomas* [1994] 1 W.L.R. 129 at 135. Cf. *O'Sullivan v Management Agency and Music
Ltd* [1985] Q.B. 428 at 449 and following per Dunn L.J.

[13] *Lagunas Nitrate Co v Lagunas Syndicate* [1899] 2 Ch. 392 at 456 per Rigby L.J.; see also *Erlanger
v New Sombrero Phosphate Co* (1878) 3 App. Cas. 1218 at 1278–1279 per Lord Blackburn.

[14] *Wiebe v Butchart's Motors Ltd* [1949] 4 D.L.R. 838; see also *Addison v Ottawa Auto and Taxi Co*
(1914) 16 D.L.R. 318.

[15] *Bellamy v Sabine* (1847) 2 Ph. 425; *Davey v Durrant* (1857) 1 De G. & J. 535; *Stepney v Biddulph*
(1865) 13 W.R. 576; cf. *Greenwood v Bennett* [1973] Q.B. 195; Torts (Interference with Goods) Act
1977 s.6(1).

[16] *Hulton v Hulton* [1917] 1 K.B. 813.

be restored to the husband was held to be no bar to rescission, because, in the words of Scrutton L.J.:

> "[I]t was the defendant who was anxious that those letters should be destroyed. I cannot in those circumstances treat the letters as so important to him that there can be no rescission because they cannot be brought back into existence."[17]

31–09   Again, in the Scottish case of *Spence v Crawford*,[18] a purchaser of shares attempted to resist the vendor's action for reduction of the contract, which had been induced by the purchaser's fraudulent misrepresentation, on the grounds that restitutio in integrum was impossible. Under the contract of purchase the vendor had, at the purchaser's expense, been discharged from a guarantee of the company's debt and had had restored to him securities which had secured that guarantee. Moreover, the company's constitution had been altered, and there had been some change in the individual shareholdings in the company, including that of the purchaser. The House of Lords rejected these submissions and allowed reduction (i.e. rescission ab initio) on terms. Lord Wright stated that[19]:

> "A case of innocent misrepresentation may be regarded rather as one of misfortune than as one of moral obliquity. There is no deceit or intention to defraud. The court will be less ready to pull a transaction to pieces where the defendant is innocent, whereas in the case of fraud the court will exercise its jurisdiction to the full in order, if possible, to prevent the defendant from enjoying the benefit of his fraud at the expense of the innocent plaintiff."

31–10   Unlike the common law courts, the Chancery courts were able to take a more flexible approach in all cases, as they had "the power to take accounts of profits and to direct inquiries as to allowances proper to be made for deterioration", and so were always able to do what was "practically just between the parties, and by so doing [to] restore them substantially to the *status quo*."[20] In *Erlanger v New Sombrero Phosphate Co*,[21] a company that had bought and worked a mine was entitled to rescind the purchase contract for non-disclosure, on the terms that it would return ownership of the mine and account to the vendor for the profits it had made. And in *O'Sullivan v Management Agency and Music Ltd*,[22] the claimant singer was entitled to avoid a management contract for undue influence

---

[17] *Hulton* [1917] 1 K.B. 813 at 825.

[18] *Spence v Crawford* [1939] 3 All E.R. 271.

[19] *Spence* [1939] 3 All E.R. 271 at 288–289, citing Lindley M.R.'s previous statement in *Lagunas* [1899] 2 Ch. 392 at 433–434, that: "if this were a case of fraud, the court would be justified in making an order for repayment of the purchase-money (including the amount realized by the sale of the shares) on the plaintiffs accounting for all their profits. The defendants could not effectually set up their own wrong as a reason for not giving such relief against them. But, there being in this case no fraud, the reasoning which in a case of fraud would justify such an order is inapplicable." See also *Root v Badley* [1960] N.Z.L.R. 756; *O'Sullivan* [1985] Q.B. 428 at 451 and 454 per Dunn L.J.

[20] *Alati v Kruger* (1955) 94 C.L.R. 216 at 223–224 per Dixon C.J., Webb, Kitto and Taylor JJ. Lord Blackburn made the same point in *Erlanger* (1878) 3 App Cas 1218 at 1278–1279.

[21] *Erlanger v New Sombrero Phosphate Co* (1878) 3 App. Cas. 1218. See too *South Western Mineral Water Co Ltd v Ashmore* [1967] 1 W.L.R. 1110; *Cheese* [1994] 1 W.L.R. 129; *Midland Bank Plc v Greene* [1995] 1 F.C.R. 374.

[22] *O'Sullivan v Management Agency and Music Ltd* [1985] Q.B. 428.

under which he had assigned the copyrights in his songs and recordings, on the terms that he would make counter-restitution of the value of the promotion and management services performed for his benefit by the defendant. According to Dunn L.J.[23]:

"[T]he principle of *restitutio in integrum* is not applied with its full rigour in equity in relation to transactions entered into by persons in breach of a fiduciary relationship, and ... such transactions may be set aside even though it is impossible to place the parties precisely in the position in which they were before, provided that the court can achieve practical justice between the parties".

It appears that the courts are now starting to permit substitutionary counter- **31–11** restitution in common law as well as equitable claims. This development should be applauded since the strict approach traditionally taken at common law in the absence of fraud could produce unjust results.[24] In *Atlantic Lines & Navigation Co Inc v Hallam Ltd (The Lucy)*,[25] Mustill J. suggested that a contract for services, which in their nature cannot be restored *in specie*, might be rescinded despite part performance of the services by the misrepresentor. In *D. O. Ferguson & Associates v Sohl*[26] contractors failed to finish the fitting out of a shop, their repudiatory breach was accepted by the owner, who had already paid a large sum, and the Court of Appeal held that the incomplete work which had been done could be valued and set off against the amount he had paid. Hence he was permitted to recover the difference. In *Smith New Court Securities Ltd v Scrimgeour Vickers (Asset Management) Ltd* it was accepted in the Court of Appeal that rescission of a contract for the sale of shares was no longer possible because the claimant had disposed of the shares it had bought, although Nourse L.J. thought this rule "a hard one" in relation to fungible assets.[27] In the House of Lords, however, Lord Browne-Wilkinson said that since "identical shares can be purchased on the market, the defrauded purchaser can offer substantial *restitutio in integrum* which is normally sufficient",[28] and that if a sale of shares cannot be rescinded once the specific shares purchased have been sold, then "the law will need to be looked at closely hereafter".[29]

---

[23] *O'Sullivan* [1985] Q.B. 428 at 458.
[24] As stressed in E McKendrick, "Total Failure of Consideration and Counter-Restitution: Two Issues or One?" in P. Birks (ed.), *Laundering and Tracing* (Oxford: Clarendon Press, 1995) 217.
[25] *Atlantic Lines & Navigation Co Inc v Hallam Ltd (The Lucy)* [1983] 1 Lloyd's Rep. 188 at 202.
[26] *D. O. Ferguson & Associates v Sohl* (1992) 62 Build. L.R. 95.
[27] *Smith New Court Securities Ltd v Scrimgeour Vickers (Asset Management) Ltd* [1994] 1 W.L.R. 1271 at 1280.
[28] A point previously made in *Re International Contract Co* (1872) L.R. 7 Ch. App. 485 at 487 per Mellish L.J.: "one share, an incorporeal right to a certain portion of the profits of the company, is the same as another, and ... share No. 1 is not distinguishable from share No. 2, in the same way as a grey horse is distinguishable from a black horse."
[29] *Smith New Court* [1997] A.C. 254 at 262. Note, however, that if a claimant has sold shares in a falling market and is permitted to return substitute shares purchased at a lower value (or their equivalent in money), then he will gain a windfall at the expense of the defendant: R. Halson, "Rescission for Misrepresentation" [1997] R.L.R. 89, pp.91–92.

31-12   In *Halpern v Halpern (No.2)*,[30] the parties compromised a dispute relating to their father's will, and documents and notes relating to the claim were allegedly destroyed in accordance with the compromise agreement. The defendants refused to perform the compromise agreement, claiming that it was voidable, and had been avoided, for duress, and the question arose whether the alleged destruction of the documents precluded rescission for duress. This issue was tried separately from others that arose in the litigation, and the trial judge held that the contract could not be rescinded because, even on a liberal approach, counter-restitution was impossible. On appeal, Carnwath L.J. held that the issue was "abstract" because it was a question of fact to be determined at trial whether the documents had indeed been destroyed. However, because of the importance of the issue for the development of the law, Carnwath L.J. addressed the defendants' argument that the "counter-restitution impossible" bar no longer exists either for duress or for undue influence because counter-restitution is never impossible.[31] He said that "a definitive response is not possible or appropriate, until the facts have been found",[32] but was "inclined to agree" that rescission for duress should be no different in principle from rescission for other vitiating factors, and thought that "if the defendants were able to establish that their consent to the compromise agreement was procured by improper pressure (whether that is characterised as duress or undue influence), it would be surprising if the law could not provide a suitable remedy".[33]

31-13   Note, finally, that there are situations where the claimant is exempt from making counter-restitution, so that, having made restitution, the defendant is left to bring an independent claim for unjust enrichment. Such exemptions arise in respect of benefits which the defendant ought never to have transferred to the claimant. For example, in *Rowland v Divall*[34] the Court of Appeal held that a party who sold a car that did not belong to him should make restitution of the price but could not insist on counter-restitution of the months of use which the buyer enjoyed before the true owner came on the scene. Again, in *Guinness Plc v Saunders*,[35] the House of Lords held that a company could recover money paid to a director for special services in connection with a takeover bid without making counter-restitution in respect of the services which it had received. The services should have been performed by the director qua director, and he was in breach of fiduciary duty in taking special payment for them. The court was anxious to give no encouragement to those who breach their fiduciary duties, but it is hard to reconcile its approach in this case with the allowance for work and

---

[30] *Halpern v Halpern (No.2)* [2007] EWCA Civ 291; [2008] Q.B. 195; reversing [2006] EWHC 1728 (Comm); [2007] Q.B. 88.
[31] *Halpern* [2007] EWCA Civ 291; [2008] Q.B. 195 at [64]: "Just as in *Erlanger v New Sombrero Phosphate Co* the value of depreciation of a phosphate mine could be measured in order to make counter-restitution in equity, so, it is argued, the court can in the present case put an appropriate monetary value on the loss of the documents, even if this is represented by a reduction in the claimant's prospects of success in the arbitration (cf. *Kitchen v Royal Air Force Association* [1958] 1 W.L.R. 563)."
[32] *Halpern* [2007] EWCA Civ 291; [2008] Q.B. 195 at [75].
[33] *Halpern* [2007] EWCA Civ 291; [2008] Q.B. 195 at [75].
[34] *Rowland v Divall* [1923] 2 KB 500.
[35] *Guinness Plc v Saunders* [1990] 2 A.C. 663.

skill that is sometimes made in favour of fiduciaries who are ordered to disgorge unauthorised profits in actions founded on breach of fiduciary duty.[36]

3. NATURE OF THE RULE

There is an overlap between the counter-restitution requirement and the change **31–14** of position defence, to the extent that both rules enable a defendant to escape liability where he has incurred the cost of conferring a benefit on the claimant. A defendant who receives a benefit from a claimant and pays him £1,000 in exchange might either plead that he has changed his position by spending £1,000, or else that he should not have to make restitution of the benefit he has received unless the claimant makes counter-restitution of the £1,000 benefit that he has had from the defendant.

However, there are differences between the two rules that make it impossible **31–15** to say that the counter-restitution requirement is simply a manifestation of the change of position defence.[37] One is that a defendant who has induced a claimant to transfer a benefit by a threat or a fraudulent misrepresentation is entitled to counter-restitution of benefits that he has conferred on the claimant,[38] although he would be disqualified from pleading the change of position defence.[39] Another is that in cases where the cost to the claimant of conferring a benefit on the defendant is greater than the value of the benefit to the defendant, the claimant's cost will count as detriment for the purposes of the change of position defence, but he cannot require the defendant to make counter-restitution of more than the value of the benefit.

It follows that the best explanation of the counter-restitution requirement does **31–16** not go to the defendant's disenrichment in the same way as the change of position defence. Instead the rule rests on the fact that, where there has been an exchange between the parties, and the claimant recovers that the benefit he has conferred on the defendant, the basis on which he received the benefit from the defendant must fail. Were he to recover without making counter-restitution, the defendant

---

[36] As in e.g. *Boardman v Phipps* [1967] 2 AC 46. Following Lord Goff's statement in the *Guinness* case, [1990] 2 A.C. 663 at 701, that allowances should be restricted to cases where an award would not encourage fiduciaries to put themselves in a position of conflict, the English courts have become less generous: see e.g. *Quarter Master UK Ltd (In Liquidation) v Pyke* [2004] EWHC 1815 (Ch); [2005] 1 B.C.L.C. 245 at [76]–[77]; *Cobbetts LLP v Hodge* [2009] EWHC 786 (Ch); [2010] 1 B.C.L.C. 30 at [118]; and see too *Imageview Management Ltd v Jack* [2009] EWCA Civ 63; [2009] Bus. L.R. 1034 at [54]–[61], but cf. *Nottingham University v Fishel* [2000] I.C.R. 1462 at 1499–1500. The Australian and New Zealand courts have been more generous: see e.g. *Llewellyn v Derrick* (1999) 33 A.C.S.R. 213; *Say-Dee Pty Ltd v Farah Constructions Pty Ltd* [2005] NSWCA 309 at [252]; *Chirnside v Fay* [2006] NZSC 68; [2007] 1 N.Z.L.R. 433 at [103]–[154] per Blanchard and Tipping JJ.; but cf. Elias C.J.'s comments at [24]–[38]. For general discussion, see M. Harding, "Justifying Fiduciary Allowances" in A. Robertson and Tang Hang Wu (eds), *The Goals of Private Law* (Oxford: Hart, 2009), 341.
[37] Burrows, *The Law of Restitution*, p.570.
[38] *Halpern* [2007] EWCA 291; [2008] Q.B. 195 at [55]–[75], denying the existence of a special common law rule excluding the defence where a claimant has been induced to enter a transaction by duress.
[39] See paras 27–32 and following.

would therefore have a claim against him on the ground of failure of basis. Lord Wright had this in mind when held in *Spence* that[40]:

> "Restoration . . . is essential to the idea of restitution. To take the simplest case, if a plaintiff who has been defrauded seeks to have the contract annulled and his money or property restored to him, it would be inequitable if he did not also restore what he had got under the contract from the defendant. Though the defendant has been fraudulent, he must not be robbed, nor must the plaintiff be unjustly enriched, as he would be if he both got back what he had parted with and kept what he had received in return."[41]

31-17   However, this does not explain why the law makes counter-restitution a pre-condition for the claimant's right of recovery, rather than simply allowing the claim and leaving the defendant to bring a counterclaim. Should this be seen as a pragmatic rule of convenience that understands the parties to have a claim and counterclaim, and requires these claims to be set off against one another, taking account of any defences that might be raised against them, in order to avoid a multiplicity of suits? Or should it be seen as a special rule applying to benefits acquired in exchange for other benefits, that requires these benefits to be netted off, with the result that as they go back and forth between the parties, there is only ever one single rolling enrichment consisting in the difference between the value of the benefits, and consequently only ever one possible claim?

31-18   The difference between these approaches has been extensively discussed by German scholars in their analysis of analogous German law.[42] According to their "two claims theory" (*Zweikondiktionentheorie*), transactions under which a mutual exchange of benefits has taken place should be unwound by giving the parties independent claims, each of which is potentially vulnerable to defences. In contrast, their "difference theory" (*Saldotheorie*) holds that there is only one enrichment and one party enriched: a claim will lie against the party who received the greater value on the basis that he has been enriched by the difference between what he received and what he gave, and the claimant is not considered to have been enriched at all. (*"Saldo"* means "balance" or, here, "difference".)

---

[40] *Spence* [1939] 3 All E.R. 271 at 288–289. See too *National Commercial Bank (Jamaica) Ltd v Hew* [2003] UKPC 51 at [43]; *Halpern* [2007] EWCA 291; [2008] Q.B. 195 at [74] per Carnwath L.J., citing G.H. Treitel, *The Law of Contract*, 11th edn (London: Sweet & Maxwell, 2003), p.380: "the essential point is that the representee should not be unjustly enriched at the representor's expense; that the representor should not be prejudiced is a secondary consideration, which is only taken into account when some benefit has been received by the representee." But cf. D. O'Sullivan, S. Elliott and R. Zakrzewski, *The Law of Rescission* (Oxford: OUP, 2008), paras 18.05–18.06 and 18.103–18.117, arguing that this cannot be the only consideration in play because the rule bars rescission in some rare cases where the claimant can return the benefit he has received but circumstances have changed in such a way that rescission would unjustifiably prejudice the defendant.

[41] An exception to the principle that even a fraudster is entitled to counter-restitution is established by the Marine Insurance Act 1906 s.84, which provides that an insurer which avoids a policy for fraud need not return any premium paid by the insured. Whether this punitive rule is justified by the special circumstances of insurance business seems questionable.

[42] See the works cited and discussed in R. Zimmermann and J. du Plessis, "Basic Features of the German Law of Unjustified Enrichment" [1994] R.L.R. 14, pp.41–42; P. Hellwege, "Unwinding Mutual Contracts: *Restitution in Integrum* v. Change of Position" in D. Johnston and R. Zimmermann (eds), *Unjustified Enrichment: Key Issues in Comparative Perspective* (Cambridge: CUP, 2002), 243, pp.258–260; B.S. Markesinis, W. Lorenz, and G. Dannemann, *The German Law of Obligations Vol I: The Law of Contracts and Restitution* (Oxford: OUP, 1997), pp.764–766; B. Häcker, *Consequences of Impaired Consent Transfers* (Tübingen: Mohr Siebeck, 2009), pp.71–77.

On this theory, no attention is paid to losses suffered by the claimant other than those which correspond to the benefits received by the defendant.

To illustrate the difference between these approaches, Birke Häcker posits a **31–19** situation in which a claimant and a defendant agree to an exchange of paintings under which the claimant swaps his Constable for the defendant's Corot.[43] Following transfer of the paintings, the Corot is destroyed while in the claimant's possession. The claimant then discovers a ground for rescission, avoids the contract, and demands the return of the Constable. Under the "two-claims theory", the parties' mutual claims are independent, and each party therefore bears the risk that the other may be able to raise a defence such as change of position to the claim. On this theory, the claimant can therefore recover the Constable, and need not to pay the value of the Corot to the defendant unless it was destroyed through his own fault; otherwise he will be entitled to raise a change of position defence to the defendant's (counter)claim.[44]

This outcome is widely regarded by German scholars as unsatisfactory **31–20** because they consider that the unwinding process which takes place when the contract is rescinded should reflect the fact that the parties enriched one another in a process of exchange. The "difference" theory was therefore developed in order to take account of the mutual reciprocity of the parties' performances. On this approach, the value of the paintings would be netted off to discover which of them is enriched at the other's expense at the time of the exchange. If the Constable were worth £500,000 and the Corot £300,000, for example, then the value of the defendant's enrichment at the claimant's expense would be £200,000. The risk of the Corot's destruction would be borne by the claimant, and to recover the Constable he would therefore have to pay the defendant £300,000. This could either be seen as the value of the Corot, or as the difference between the value of the Constable (£500,000) and the value of the defendant's enrichment (£200,000). Conversely, if the Constable were worth £300,000 and the Corot were worth £500,000, then the claimant would have been enriched at the defendant's expense (to the tune of £200,000), and so no claim would lie to recover the Constable; moreover the claimant could only rely on the change of position defence in reply to a counterclaim by the defendant for £200,000 if the Corot had been lost through a reason other than his own fault.[45]

In *Kleinwort Benson*,[46] Hobhouse J. conceptualised the English rule requiring **31–21** counter-restitution as a pre-condition for recovery in "exchange cases" as acting in accordance with the "difference theory". The case concerned an interest rate swap contract that had been performed for more than six years before the commencement of the action. The question arose whether the claimant bank should have to make counter-restitution of payments received more than six years previously, given that an independent claim by the defendant council to

---

[43] Häcker, *Consequences of Impaired Consent Transfers*, pp.71 and following.
[44] For the proposition that a defendant should not have to show that he has taken positive action to change his position in reliance on his receipt, see paras 27–27—27–28. For the proposition that the change of position defence is not available to defendants who are at fault, see paras 27–32—27–38.
[45] The latter feature of the "difference theory" is regarded as unsatisfactory by some scholars, who have therefore argued in favour of a modified form of the "two-claims theory" under which the parties can rely on the change of position defence only in a limited range of circumstances: Häcker, *Consequences of Impaired Consent Transfers*, pp.75–77.
[46] *Kleinwort Benson* [1994] 4 All E.R. 890.

recover these payments would now be time-barred. Hobhouse J. held that all payments both ways should be taken into account when quantifying the claim, proceeding on the basis that, as interest rates fluctuated and payments went back and forth between the parties, there was one single rolling enrichment consisting in the difference between the value of their performances. It followed that the bank's claim was only for the net amount that it was owed following the most recent payment under the contract (which had been made within the limitation period).[47]

---

[47] *Kleinwort Benson* [1994] 4 All E.R. 890 at 941. See too his subsequent comments in *Kleinwort Benson Ltd v South Tyneside MBC* [1994] 4 All E.R. 972 at 978–979; also *Goss v Chilcott* [1996] A.C. 788 at 798, where Lord Goff accepted that in a case where a borrower defaulted on a loan after having made an interest payment to a lender, the basis for the payments made by both parties would have failed, and that "the capital sum would be recoverable by the lender, and the interest payment would be recoverable by the borrower; and doubtless judgment would, in the event, be given for the balance." The facts of this case are discussed at para.12–28. Note that the use value of money (quantified as interest) is not objectively enriching in the same way as its face value: see paras 5–05 and following.

CHAPTER 32

PASSING ON

1. INTRODUCTION

The defence of passing on asserts that the claimant has lost his title to sue the **32–01** defendant in unjust enrichment because he has made good the loss which the defendant's enrichment inflicted on him by passing this loss on to a third party. Passing on has been recognised as a defence to various statutory claims to recover money paid as tax that was not due, but it has not been recognised by the English courts as a defence to common law claims in unjust enrichment.

2. PASSING ON AS A STATUTORY DEFENCE

Several statutes give HMRC a defence to statutory claims to recover money paid **32–02** as tax that was not due, in cases where the claimant has passed the cost of the payment on to a third party.[1] This is described in the legislation as the defence of "unjust enrichment", language which denotes that HMRC generally has a defence where repayment to the claimant would lead to his unjust enrichment at the expense of the third party to whom he passed on his loss, and where there is no realistic prospect that the claimant will return this benefit to the third party.[2]

The most frequently litigated statutory passing-on defence is contained in the **32–03** Value Added Tax Act 1994 s.80(3).[3] VAT is an indirect tax on consumers which is collected from traders who can choose whether to include a VAT element in the

---

[1] Customs & Excise Management Act 1979 s.137A(3) (money paid as excise duty); Value Added Tax Act 1994 s.80(3) (money paid as VAT); Finance Act 1994 Sch.7 para.8(3) (money paid as insurance premium tax); Finance Act 1996 Sch.5 para.14(3) (money paid as landfill tax); Finance Act 2001 s.32(2) (money paid as aggregates levy).

[2] M. Chowdry, "Unjust Enrichment and Section 80(3) of the Value Added Tax Act 1994" [2004] B.T.R. 620.

[3] Under European law the VAT legislation of each Member State must comply with Council Directive 2006/112/EC of November 28, 2006 on the common system for value added tax [2006] OJ L347/1, which sets out the basic framework for national VAT legislation, but allows Member States some flexibility in their implementation of such legislation. There is nothing in the Directive which requires or expressly authorises Member States to enact a statutory passing on defence to claims to recover money paid as VAT that is not due, but the ECJ has held that they may enact such a defence provided that the evidential burden of disproving it is not practically impossible for claimants to discharge: *Amministrazione delle Finanze delle Stato v San Giorgio SpA* (199/82) [1983] E.C.R. 3595; *Kapniki Michaïlidis AE v Idryma Kinonikon Asphaliseon* (Joined Cases C–441/98 and C–442/98) [2000] ECR I–7145; *Weber's Wine World v Abgabenberufungskommission Wien* (C–147/01) [2003] E.C.R. I–11365. See too A. Jones, *Restitution and European Community Law* (London: LLP, 2000), pp.87–92.

charges that they make for their products or services. If a trader does this, and it later transpires that the VAT was not due, then allowing him to recover his payment would generally unjustly enrich him at the expense of his customers who effectively provided the money: he would be better off than he was before he paid HMRC because his payment would then have been recouped both from HMRC and from the customers,[4] and this would usually be an outcome to which the customers did not consent,[5] their payments having been made either in the mistaken belief that equivalent sums were legally payable as tax to HMRC, or else on the failed basis that these amounts were legally payable.[6]

32–04 In cases where the trader has put secure mechanisms in place to ensure that HMRC's repayment will be passed back to the customers, these mechanisms will undo his unjust enrichment at their expense and so the statutory defence is not available.[7] It may also be that the court can impose this outcome in cases where the customers are identifiable, by denying the defence and ordering restitution, but stipulating that the money repaid by HMRC should be held on constructive trust for the customers.[8] However, if no mechanisms have been put in place by the trader, and the court cannot impose a constructive trust on the fruits of recovery from HMRC, because the customers cannot be identified, then the defence will generally be allowed in order to prevent the trader from accumulating recoveries.[9]

32–05 There is one exception to this general rule, namely where the trader has suffered consequential loss through reduced sales as a result of having been obliged to charge his customers a higher price for his products or services in order to recover the cost of the incorrectly levied VAT element. The courts are permitted to take such loss into account by s.80(3A)–(3C). The rationale for these subsections is that once it has been established that repayment would unjustly enrich the trader at the customers' expense, and that this enrichment will not actually be passed back to them although they are legally entitled to recover it, the money necessarily represents a windfall to which neither the trader nor

---

[4] *Marks & Spencer Plc v C&E Commissioners (No.5) (Referral to ECJ)* [2005] UKHL 53; [2005] S.T.C. 1254 at [25]: "reimbursement would amount to double recovery by, and unjust enrichment of, the trader."

[5] But cf. *Newcastle Theatre Royal Trust Ltd v C&E Commissioners* [2005] UKVAT V18952 at [15], where it was found as a fact that the customers paid for theatre tickets on the basis that if the VAT element included in the price were found not to be due then the theatre could keep the money and apply it to its general purposes.

[6] For general discussion of mistake and failure of basis as grounds for recovery in unjust enrichment, see Chs 9 and 12. Cf. *Roxborough v Rothmans of Pall Mall Australia Ltd* [2001] HCA 68; (2001) 208 C.L.R. 516 (failure of basis); but contrast *Cauvin v Philip Morris Ltd* [2002] NSWSC 736 (neither mistake not failure of basis properly pleaded and so claim struck out).

[7] *Lamdec Ltd v C&E Commissioners* [1991] V.A.T.T.R. 296; *C&E Commissioners v McMaster Stores (Scotland) Ltd*, 1996 S.L.T. 935; *C&E Commissioners v National Westminster Bank Plc* [2003] EWHC 1822; [2003] S.T.C. 1072. And note the Value Added Tax Act 1994 s.80A, which empowers HMRC to make regulations governing the reimbursement arrangements made by a claimant seeking to rely on s.80(3). This power has been exercised: Value Added Tax Regulations 1995 (SI 1995/2518). For discussion, see *Portsmouth City Football Club Ltd v HMRC* [2010] EWHC 75 (Ch); [2011] S.T.C. 683.

[8] Cf. *K.A.P. Motors Pty Ltd v Commissioner of Taxation* [2008] FCA 159; (2008) 168 F.C.R. 319 at [41]–[42].

[9] S. Degeling, "The Defence of Passing on and Policies against Accumulation" [2004] R.L.R. 25.

HMRC are entitled. Allowing HMRC to keep it would then usually be the best option, since letting the gain lie where it falls would avoid scarce judicial resources being used to transfer a benefit from one undeserving party to another,[10] and would also lead to the money being applied to the public good.[11] However, if the trader can prove that he has suffered a loss, then the scales are tipped the other way and the defence is disallowed.[12]

Proving consequential loss can be a complex and difficult matter. In *Marks &* **32–06** *Spencer Plc v C&E Commissioners (No.1)*,[13] expert economic evidence was heard on the question whether Marks & Spencer had suffered a loss of sales and profits due to paying VAT at the standard rate on teacakes that should have been zero-rated. The tribunal and higher courts all held that customers had borne the cost of the VAT paid on the teacakes, as this was included as a factor in setting margins. They also held that Marks & Spencer had only suffered a loss in profits and sales corresponding to 10 per cent of the claimed sum. Marks & Spencer had contended that by maintaining prices and selling the same number of teacakes as were actually sold it would have increased its profits by at least as much as its VAT payments. However, this argument was rejected. It had to be assumed that customers would have known that no VAT was chargeable on teacakes and also that, as a rational retailer operating in a competitive market, Marks & Spencer would therefore have reduced the sale price of the teacakes in order to maintain or increase sales. After a delay of a year or two (reflected in a reduction of the claimed sum by 10 per cent), prices would have dropped and the same profit margin would have been achieved.

If a trader who pays or accounts for output tax that is not due does not adjust **32–07** his prices to include the VAT element when selling his products or services, but instead absorbs the cost of paying output tax into his overheads, then ordering

---

[10] Cf. *Devenish Nutrition Ltd v Sanofi-Aventis SA* [2007] EWHC 2394 (Ch); [2009] Ch. 390 at [147] per Longmore L.J.: if the victim of an illegal price-fixing cartel has passed on his loss to his customers, then he cannot recover an account of profits for the defendants' breach of statutory duty because "there is no very obvious reason why the profit made by the defendants (albeit undeserved and wrongful) should be transferred to the claimant without the claimant being obliged to transfer it down the line to those who have actually suffered the loss. Neither the law of restitution nor the law of damages is in the business of transferring monetary gains from one undeserving recipient to another undeserving recipient."

[11] But cf. R. Williams, *Unjust Enrichment and Public Law* (Oxford: Hart, 2010), p.155: in principle the defence could be disallowed even in this situation on the basis that "it is more important that the public body be stripped of the *ultra vires* tax than that the tax ends up in the right hands"; i.e. the unjust enrichment of the trader should be seen as the price to be paid for binding HMRC to the rule of law.

[12] As in e.g. *Marks & Spencer Plc v C&E Commissioners (No.1)* [1997] V. & D.R. 85; affirmed [1999] S.T.C. 205; affirmed on this point [2000] S.T.C. 16 (CA). In several cases, the courts have found there to have been no consequential loss on the facts: *Grantham Cricket Club v C&E Commissioners* [1998] B.V.C. 2272; *C&E Commissioners v National Westminster Bank Plc* [2003] S.T.C. 1072; *King (t/a Barbury Shooting School) v C&E Commissioners* [2003] UKVAT V18313. Note that the receipt of money paid as tax that is not due is not generally a civil wrong, but that in cases where VAT is levied in breach of EU law, the trader could sue HMRC for compensatory damages, following *R. v Secretary of State for Transport Ex p. Factortame Ltd (No.4)* [1996] Q.B. 404; and *(No.5)* [2000] 1 A.C. 524.

[13] *Marks & Spencer Plc v C&E Commissioners (No.1)* [1997] V. & D.R. 85; affirmed [1999] S.T.C. 205; affirmed on this point [2000] S.T.C. 16.

restitution would not unjustly enrich him at his customers' expense, since they would not then have been the effective source of the money paid to HMRC. This was discussed in *Baines & Ernst Ltd v HMRC*,[14] where the claimant accounted for VAT in respect of debt management services provided to its customers for several years. The VAT and Duties Tribunal held in an unconnected case that services of this kind are exempt for VAT purposes, and so the claimant brought proceedings under the Value Added Tax Act 1994 s.80 to recover the difference between the output tax which it had paid and the input tax which it had incorrectly reclaimed on its purchases. HMRC invoked s.80(3), arguing that the claimant had incorporated a VAT element into the charge which it had made for its services, but the claimant denied this, asserting that it would have charged its customers at the same rate even if it had known that it was an exempt body.

32–08   The VAT and Duties Tribunal held that the defence had been made out because the price formula used in the claimant's contracts had included a VAT element.[15] However, Warren J. held that the terms of the claimant's contracts were not conclusive and that the question whether the claimant had actually passed on the cost of its VAT payments had to be determined in the light of other evidence as well, e.g. the extent to which the claimant would have increased its rates to recoup itself for its inability as an exempt body to reclaim input tax, and the extent to which its pricing strategy had been affected by the prices charged by its competitors. Hence he remitted the case to the Tribunal for reconsideration in the light of this additional evidence.[16] However, the Court of Appeal was not satisfied with this either, holding that the burden of proof was on HMRC to establish a s.80(3) defence, that the evidence upon which it had relied was insufficient, and that the defence accordingly failed.

32–09   HMRC ran into difficulties in this case because they argued that the claimant would have reduced its charges by the entire amount of the output tax which had been paid. The Court of Appeal did not accept that this was borne out by the evidence, which merely suggested that the claimant would have reduced its charges to a lesser extent. If HMRC had pleaded a more limited defence they might therefore have enjoyed greater success. But even then, they might have found it difficult to establish the exact extent to which the claimant had passed on its loss to its customers, and it seems that this is what they are now expected to do. This suggests that future cases in which they seek to rely on the Value Added Tax Act 1994 s.80(3) will reach a new level of complexity.[17]

32–10   Finally, the question arises whether customers can ever sue HMRC directly where they have effectively borne the burden of paying indirect taxation that is not due because the cost of this has been passed onto them by a trader? A recent

---

[14] *Baines & Ernst Ltd v HMRC* [2006] EWCA 1040; [2006] S.T.C. 1632. See too *Tayside Numbers Ltd v C&E Commissioners* [1992] VATTR 406; *National Provincial Building Society v C&E Commissioners* [1996] V. & D.R. 153.

[15] *Baines & Ernst* [2004] UKVAT 18769.

[16] *Baines & Ernst* [2005] EWHC 2300 (Ch); [2006] S.T.C. 653.

[17] Cf. the position in Australia, where equivalent legislation places the onus of proof on the taxpayer, who must prove that money paid as sales tax has been absorbed, rather than passed on to his customers, before he can recover it on the ground that it was not due: Sale Tax Assessment Act 1992 s.51, considered in *Avon Products Pty Ltd v Commissioner of Taxation* [2006] HCA 29; (2006) 230 C.L.R. 356.

line of authority from the European Court of Justice suggests that in principle they should be able to do this. These cases are discussed elsewhere.[18]

3. PASSING ON AS A DEFENCE AT COMMON LAW

The question whether passing on is a defence to common law claims in unjust enrichment arose in the litigation spawned by the House of Lords' finding in *Hazell v Hammersmith & Fulham LBC*[19] that interest rate swap contracts entered by many local authorities and banks during the late 1980s and early 1990s were void because they were beyond the councils' powers. To cover their payments out on interest swaps which later turned out to be void, some banks had entered valid back-to-back swap contracts with other banks in which the risks were reversed. These hedge contracts ensured that money lost under the void swap contract came back to the bank under the hedge. In response to claims in unjust enrichment by certain banks which had entered hedge contracts, some defendant councils sought to persuade the courts that the claims should fail because the banks' losses had been passed on. **32–11**

In *Kleinwort Benson Ltd v Birmingham CC*[20] the Court of Appeal rejected this argument for two reasons: first, because the payments received by the claimant bank from another bank under the hedge contract were not relevantly causally connected with the payments made by the claimant to the defendant under the swaps contract[21]; and, secondly, because a claimant in unjust enrichment need not show that the defendant's gain corresponds to a loss in the claimant's hands.[22] The first of these reasons was essentially a finding of fact that the claimant bank had not passed on its loss to its counter-party under the hedge contract, and if that was the ground for the court's decision then its second, broader reason for denying the defence cannot have been the ratio of the case.[23] Moreover, the proposition that a claimant need not show that he has suffered a loss that corresponds to the defendant's gain has not been universally accepted by the courts, some of which have held instead that a claimant's entitlement should be capped at the amount of his loss if this is lower than the amount of the defendant's gain. There are also good reasons of principle for thinking that this narrower rule should be preferred, which are discussed in Ch.6.[24] **32–12**

---

[18] See para.6–50.

[19] *Hazell v Hammersmith & Fulham LBC* [1992] 2 A.C. 1.

[20] *Kleinwort Benson Ltd v Birmingham CC* [1997] Q.B. 380. See too *Kleinwort Benson Ltd v South Tyneside Metropolitan BC* [1994] 4 All E.R. 972 at 984–985 and 987 per Hobhouse J.

[21] *Kleinwort Benson* [1997] Q.B. 380 at 399 per Morritt L.J.

[22] *Kleinwort Benson* [1997] Q.B. 380 at 394–395 per Saville L.J. The same reason was given for rejecting the defence in *Commissioner of State Revenue (Victoria) v Royal Insurance Ltd* (1994) 182 C.L.R. 51 at 75 per Mason C.J. following Windeyer J. in *Mason v New South Wales* (1959) 102 C.L.R. 108 at 146; *Roxborough* (2001) 208 C.L.R. 516 at [25]–[26]; *K.A.P. Motors* [2008] FCA 159; (2008) 168 F.C.R. 319 at [44].

[23] As noted in M. Rush, *The Defence of Passing On* (Oxford: Hart, 2006), p.39.

[24] See paras 6–63—6–74. And cf. R. Grantham and C. Rickett, "Disgorgement for Unjust Enrichment" [2003] C.L.J. 159, pp.168–171 especially p.169 where they argue that the reasons given by the courts for rejecting the defence of passing on, including the notion that there is no need to show a correspondence between the claimant's loss and the defendant's gain, are "misguided and confused".

32–13   It follows that the courts may yet revisit the question whether passing on is a defence to claims in unjust enrichment at common law, and in the event that this question arises for further consideration, some lessons can be learnt from the statutory versions of the defence discussed in the previous section. One is that evidential problems undoubtedly arise in practice around issues such as whether a claimant has absorbed his loss or passed it on to third parties, but these have not proved to be insuperable.[25]

32–14   The example of the statutory regimes also suggests that if the English courts ever revisit the availability of the passing on defence at common law, then they would do well to investigate the reason why the third party has borne the claimant's loss, since this may affect the question whether the claimant or the defendant has a better claim to the money. For example, if a claimant mistakenly pays a defendant and then works harder at his business to generate extra sales to make up the deficit, then he will no longer be out of pocket, but he will surely have a stronger claim to the mistakenly paid money than the defendant.[26] But if a claimant mistakenly pays a defendant on a third party's behalf, and the third party indemnifies him because he mistakenly thinks that he must, then neither the claimant nor the defendant deserves to keep the benefit which has been unjustly gained at the third party's expense. In the first case the claim should be allowed, but in the second it should not be, unless the claimant is required to account for the fruits of his action to the third party.

32–15   In *Kleinwort Benson*, Evans L.J. left open the possibility that the defence of passing on might be available at common law "in taxation cases", where an element of public law is involved[27]; and in *Waikato Regional Airport Ltd v Att Gen of New Zealand*,[28] the Privy Council hinted that if the claimant had passed on its loss then the defendant public authority could not be said to have been enriched at his expense. In Canada, passing on was formerly a defence to common law claims to recover money paid as tax that was not due, following the Supreme Court's decision in *Air Canada v British Columbia*, where La Forest J. held that "the law of restitution is not intended to provide windfalls to plaintiffs who have suffered no loss."[29] However, the Supreme Court drew the opposite conclusion in *Kingstreet Investments Ltd v New Brunswick (Department of Finance)*, Bastarache J. holding that the defence creates great evidential problems, and more fundamentally, that "restitution law is not concerned by the possibility of the plaintiff obtaining a windfall precisely because it is not founded on the concept of compensation for loss."[30] For the reasons that we have already given, we doubt that either of these is a convincing argument for rejecting the defence, and the English courts may yet allow it in response to a claim founded

---

[25] For additional discussion of this point, see Rush, *The Defence of Passing On*, pp.194–207; F.D. Rose, "Passing On" in P. Birks (ed.), *Laundering and Tracing* (Oxford: Clarendon Press, 1995), 261, pp.284–285. Note that similar problems are overcome in US anti-trust cases where claims for compensatory damages by the victims of cartels are defended on the basis that their losses were passed on to their customers.

[26] An example taken from Rush, *The Defence of Passing On*, p.188.

[27] *Kleinwort Benson* [1996] 4 All E.R. 733 at 738–741.

[28] *Waikato Regional Airport Ltd v Att Gen of New Zealand* [2003] UKPC 50; [2004] 3 N.Z.L.R. 1 at [77]–[78].

[29] *Air Canada v British Columbia* [1989] 1 S.C.R. 1161 at 1202.

[30] *Kingstreet Investments Ltd v New Brunswick (Department of Finance)* [2007] SCC 1; [2007] 1 S.C.R. 3 at [47].

on the rule in *Woolwich Equitable BS v IRC*.[31] There is a strong similarity between such claims and the statutory claims to recover money paid as tax in response to which the defence is available, and the Law Commission has recommended that the defence should be available in response to claims of this kind.[32]

---

[31] *Woolwich Equitable BS v IRC* [1993] A.C. 70, discussed in Ch.22.
[32] Law Commission, *Restitution: Mistakes of Law and Ultra Vires Public Authority Receipts and Payments* (1994) Law Com No.227, paras 10.44–10.48.

CHAPTER 33

LIMITATION

1. INTRODUCTION

There are several rationales for the defence of limitation in the law of unjust **33–01** enrichment. Claims become harder to prove, and to defend, with the passing of time as memories fade and documents disappear. This makes the court's fact-finding task more difficult and increases the risk of arbitrary decision making. Fairness to the defendant also demands that he should no longer have to face the threat of litigation after a certain period of time has elapsed. Conversely, however, fairness to the claimant demands that time should not start to run until he knows, or ought reasonably to know, that he has a cause of action; and where he has been unable to exercise his independent judgment owing to minority, mental incapacity or pressure, then in principle time should not start to run until he is able to make his own free decisions, or dies so that responsibility for concluding his affairs passes to a legally capable person.[1]

The law of limitation affecting claims in unjust enrichment is unfortunately in **33–02** a poor state. Its shortcomings were highlighted by the Law Commission in a report on limitation of actions published 10 years ago. They observed that the law is a ragged patchwork of rules emanating from common law, equity and statute, and that these do not clearly provide for all claims in unjust enrichment in a fair and consistent way. They recommended that various problems with the existing law of limitation should be resolved by the introduction of a single, core limitation regime, which would apply, as far as possible, to all private law claims, including claims in unjust enrichment.[2] This welcome recommendation was accepted in principle by the government in 2002[3]; in 2007, the government announced that it would consult on the content of a draft Bill to implement the Law Commission's recommendations[4]; in 2009, the government then announced that reform of the law of limitation would not after all be taken forward.[5] It seems, therefore, that the law will remain in its present unsatisfactory state for the foreseeable future and that the courts must make such sense of the rules as they can.

---

[1] A. Burrows, *The Law of Restitution*, 3rd edn (Oxford: OUP, 2010), p.605. Cases concerning mistake and concealment of facts may fall within the Limitation Act 1980 s.32, discussed at paras 33–23—33–36. Cases concerning mental incapacity and minority may fall within the Limitation Act 1980 s.28, discussed at para.33–19. Claims to reverse transactions on the ground of undue influence are purely equitable and so are governed only by the doctrine of laches, with the result that there is scope for the courts to postpone the running of time that they do not have in connection with common law claims founded on duress; see para.33–39.

[2] Law Commission, *Limitation of Actions* (2001) Law Com. No.270.

[3] *Hansard, H.L. Deb.*, July 16, 2002, col.127 WA.

[4] *Hansard, H.L. Deb.*, January 9, 2007, col.8 WS.

[5] *Hansard, H.C. Deb.*, November 19, 2009, col.13 WS.

33–03   The following account deals in turn with the limitation periods that are applicable to different claims in unjust enrichment, with the dates when these periods commence, and with the circumstances in which these commencement dates may be postponed.

2. LIMITATION PERIODS

33–04   The primary criterion for the application of statutes of limitation was originally procedural. All claims in *assumpsit* were deemed to fall within the Limitation Act 1623 s.3, and had to be brought "within six yeares next after the cause of such accions or suit". Because this statute applied only to particular "writs" and forms of "action" proceedings in equity, which were initiated by bill (not writ) and prosecuted in a suit (not an action),[6] were not within its terms.[7] Nevertheless, in certain cases, for example where the equitable remedy was similar to the legal remedy or where the equitable remedy was in aid of legal rights, the Court of Chancery applied the analogy of the statute and its successors[8] to bar claims in equity that were not expressly barred at law.[9] A principal's suit for an account against a non-fiduciary agent was therefore barred after six years,[10] as was a claim by one beneficiary against another beneficiary who had been overpaid because of the mistake of the trustees.[11]

33–05   Subject to some exceptions, purely equitable claims were and are barred only by laches, a term that is most commonly used to "comprehend that degree of delay, which when coupled with prejudice to the defendant or third parties, will operate as a defence in equity".[12] It is unclear whether mere delay can constitute laches or whether some conduct by the claimant is also needed.[13] Equity adopts

---

[6] *Re Richardson* [1920] 1 Ch. 423 at 440.

[7] Equity noticed and applied the statutes indirectly. Thus equity would not assist in the prosecution of legal proceedings where it was clear that such proceedings would be statute-barred: *Jermy v Best* (1819) 1 Sim. 373 at 375; 57 E.R. 617 at 618; *Widdowson v Harrington* (1820) 1 J. & W. 533 at 548; 37 E.R. 471 at 476.

[8] For example, the Real Property Limitation Acts 1833 and 1874, and the Civil Procedure Act 1833.

[9] *Hovenden v Lord Annesley* (1806) 2 Sch. & Lef. 607.

[10] *Lockey v Lockey* (1719) Prec. Ch. 518; 24 E.R. 232; *Knox v Gye* (1871) L.R. 5 H.L. 656.

[11] *Re Robinson* [1911] 1 Ch. 502; and cf. *Baker v Courage & Co* [1910] 1 K.B. 56.

[12] *Hughes v La Baia Ltd* [2011] UKPC 9 at [36] per Lord Walker, endorsing R.P. Meagher, W.M.C. Gummow and J.R.F. Lehane, *Equity: Doctrine and Remedies*, 4th edn (Sydney: Butterworths LexisNexis, 2002), para.36.050. See too W. Ashburner, *Principles of Equity* (London: Butterworth & Co, 1902), pp.721–729; J. L. Brunyate, *Limitation of Actions in Equity* (London: Stevens & Sons, 1932), pp.1–23.

[13] The commentators are divided: compare Meager, Gummow & Lehane, *Equity, Doctrine and Remedies*, paras 36.005 and 36.065–36.080 and J. McGhee (ed.), *Snell's Equity*, 32nd edn (London: Sweet & Maxwell, 2010), para.5.016; with J.M. Lightwood, *The Time Limit on Actions* (London: Butterworth & Co, 1909), pp.255–256 and 261–262. There are cases supporting the idea that mere delay can constitute laches: *Hercy v Dinwoody* (1793) 2 Ves. Jun. 87; 30 E.R. 536; *Baker v Read* (1854) 18 Beav. 398; 52 E.R. 157; *Harcourt v White* (1860) 28 Beav. 303; 54 E.R. 382; *Archbold v Scully* (1861) 9 H.L.C. 360 at 383; 11 E.R. 769 at 778; *Brooks v Muckleston* [1909] 2 Ch. 519; *P&O Nedlloyd BV v Arab Metals Co (The U.B. Tiger) (No.2)* [2006] EWCA Civ 1717; [2007] 1 W.L.R. 2288 at [61]. There is also case law inconsistent with that idea: see the cases collected in Meager, Gummow and Lehane, *Equity, Doctrine and Remedies*, para.36.070.

no fixed time-bar but considers the circumstances of each case to determine whether they amount to laches. "Two circumstances, always important in such cases, are the length of the delay and the nature of the acts done during the interval, which might affect either party and cause a balance of justice or injustice in taking the one course or the other".[14] Of particular importance is the prejudice to the defendant caused by the conduct of the claimant.[15] However, there is no mechanical test to determine whether a claim should be barred by laches and it lies in the discretion of the court to decide on the facts whether the doctrine is engaged.[16]

The old law of limitations, and to some extent the equitable doctrine of **33–06** laches,[17] were profoundly affected by the Limitation Acts 1939 and 1975. The 1975 statute is now consolidated in the Limitation Act 1980. These statutes, however, do not solve a significant number of the limitation problems to which claims in unjust enrichment give rise. Indeed, there is not even a general section, akin to s.3 of the Act of 1623, which previously governed all *assumpsit* claims. In their quest for consistency, the courts have therefore been compelled to adopt generous interpretations of the legislation in order to bring claims for unjust enrichment within the statutory regime.

An example is the Court of Appeal's finding in *Re Diplock*,[18] that actions for **33–07** money had and received fell within s.2(1)(a) of the 1939 Act (now s.5 of the Limitation Act 1980), which states that "actions founded on simple contract" are barred after six years. Lord Greene M.R. was prepared to assume that these words "must be taken to cover actions for money had and received, formerly actions on the case. . . . The assumption must, we think, be made, though the words used cannot be regarded as felicitous."[19] Again, in *Kleinwort Benson Ltd v Sandwell BC*[20] Hobhouse J. held that the words "action founded on simple contract", within the Limitation Act 1980 s.5, "are sufficiently broad to cover an action for money had and received". In reaching this conclusion the ambiguity of the statutory provision enabled him to look to *Hansard* for guidance as to its meaning.[21] In the debate on the Limitation Act 1939, the precursor of the 1980 Act, the Solicitor-General stated that the statute was intended to implement the recommendations of the *Fifth Interim Report* of the Law Revision Committee and, in particular, the recommendation "that the period for all actions founded in tort or simple contract (including quasi-contract) . . . should be six years".

It seems, therefore, that common law claims in unjust enrichment are generally **33–08** barred after six years, unless a different period is laid down by the Limitation Act 1980 or another statute. In contrast, purely equitable claims for which no period

---

[14] *Lindsay Petroleum Co v Hurd* (1874) L.R. 5 P.C. 221 at 239–240 per Sir Barnes Peacock; approved in *Erlanger v New Sombrero Phosphate Co* (1878) 3 App. Cas. 1218 at 1279 per Lord Blackburn.
[15] As emphasised by Lord Neuberger in *Fisher v Brooker* [2009] UKHL 41; [2009] Bus. L.R. 1334 at [64] and [79].
[16] *Nelson v Rye* [1996] 1 W.L.R. 1378 at 1392–1395 per Laddie J.
[17] The doctrine of laches is expressly preserved by the Limitation Act 1980 s.36(2).
[18] *Re Diplock* [1948] Ch. 465.
[19] *Re Diplock* [1948] Ch. 465 at 514.
[20] *Kleinwort Benson Ltd v Sandwell BC* [1994] 4 All E.R. 890 at 942–943.
[21] *Pepper v Hart* [1993] A.C. 593.

is prescribed by statute,[22] such as claims to avoid transactions for undue influence, are barred only by laches,[23] although where an equitable claim is similar to a common law claim governed by a statutory limitation period, the court has a discretion to proceed by way of analogy by applying the statutory limitation period.[24] The rationale for applying statutory limitation periods to equitable claims by analogy is obscure, and it is unpredictable when the courts will decide to do this.[25]

33–09   Statutory limitation periods are expressly laid down for the following claims:

- claims under the Law Reform (Frustrated Contracts) Act 1943 have a limitation period of six years by operation of the Limitation Act 1980 s.9 (which applies to actions to recover any sum recoverable by virtue of any enactment other than the Civil Liability (Contribution) Act 1978);

- claims under the Civil Liability (Contribution) Act 1978 have a limitation period of two years by operation of the Limitation Act 1980 s.10[26];

- claims for restitution of a deceased person's estate have a limitation period of 12 years by operation of the Limitation Act 1980 s.22(a)[27];

- claims by beneficiaries to recover trust property transferred to third parties in breach of trust have a limitation period of six years by operation of the Limitation Act 1980 s.21(3)[28];

---

[22] Where no period of limitation is prescribed by statute for an equitable claim the claim may still be debarred by laches: *Re Loftus (Deceased)* [2006] EWCA Civ 1124; [2007] 1 W.L.R. 591 at [40].

[23] As in e.g. *Wright v Vanderplank* (1856) 8 De G.M. & G. 133; 44 E.R. 340; *Turner v Collins* (1871) L.R. 7 Ch. 329; *Allcard v Skinner* (1887) 36 Ch. D. 145; *Smith v Smith* Unreported NSW Sup Ct, July 12, 1996; *Azaz v Denton* [2009] EWHC 1759 (QB) at [106]–[122]; *Goldie v Getley (No.3)* [2011] WASC 132 at [202].

[24] See e.g. *Molloy v Mutual Reserve Life Insurance Co* (1906) 94 L.T. 756 at 762 (CA); *Re Diplock* [1948] Ch. 465 at 514 (CA); *Kleinwort Benson* [1994] 4 All E.R. 890 at 943; *Hampton v Minns* [2002] 1 W.L.R. 1 at [115]. For an argument that the court should take a similar approach to determining the limitation period that governs a claim for subrogation to extinguished rights, as part of an "autonomous" approach that looks at the substance of the claim rather than a "parasitic" approach that looks at the rights which have been paid off with the claimant's money, see C. Mitchell and S. Watterson, *Subrogation: Law and Practice* (Oxford: OUP, 2007), paras 7.132–7.167.

[25] For discussion, see C. Daly and C. Mitchell, *"Paragon Finance plc v D B Thakerar & Co (a firm)"* in C. Mitchell and P. Mitchell (eds), *Landmark Cases in Equity* (Oxford: Hart, 2012).

[26] Note that this rule does not apply to contribution claims at common law which are governed by the usual six-year rule, nor to contribution claims in equity which are governed by the same rule by way of analogy: *Hampton* [2002] 1 W.L.R. 1 at [115]. Hence claimants need to know whether or not their claims fall within the scope of the statute, a matter that is discussed in Ch.19. In principle there is no good reason for statutory and common law claims for contribution and reimbursement to be governed by different limitation rules.

[27] Considered in *Davies v Sharples* [2006] EWHC 362 (Ch); [2006] W.T.L.R. 839; *Re Loftus* [2006] EWCA Civ 1124; (2006) 9 I.T.E.L.R. 107.

[28] The subsection does not apply to an action by the Attorney-General to enforce a charitable trust: *Att Gen v Cocke* [1988] Ch. 414. It has been argued that where the trustee has acted dishonestly, claims of this kind might fall within s.21(1)(a) (so that no statutory limitation period applies), because they are claims "in respect of . . . fraud . . . to which the trustee was a party or privy". This argument was rejected in *Cattley v Pollard* [2006] EWHC 3130 (Ch); [2007] Ch. 353, which should be preferred to *Statek Corp v Alford* [2008] EWHC 32 (Ch); [2008] W.T.L.R. 1089 (where the opposite view was taken), for the reasons given in C. Mitchell, "Dishonest Assistance, Knowing Receipt, and the Law of Limitation" [2008] Conv. 226, pp.234–235. The argument was also rejected by Lord Hoffmann in the Hong Kong Final Court of Appeal when construing equivalent legislation in *Peconic*

- claims in respect of salvage have a limitation period of two years running from the date when the salvage operations are terminated, under art.23(1) of the International Convention on Salvage 1989, which is incorporated into English law by the Merchant Shipping Act 1995 s.224 and Sch.11.

Claimants should also be alert to the fact that statutory restitutionary regimes **33–10** often make special provision for limitation that differs from the usual six-year rule at common law. For example, a four-year period governs claims to recover money paid as tax that was not due under the Inheritance Tax Act 1984 s.241, and the Taxes Management Act 1970 s.33; and a three-year period governs similar claims under the Customs and Excise Management Act 1979 s.137A (4) and (5), the Value Added Tax Act 1994 s.80, and the Finance Act 1996 Sch.5 para.14 (4) and (6).

3. DATE OF COMMENCEMENT

Limitation periods generally run from the date when the claimant's cause of **33–11** action accrues, and a cause of action in unjust enrichment normally accrues at the date when the defendant receives a benefit from the claimant. This rule applies, for example, where the claimant has transferred a benefit by mistake,[29] where he has transferred a benefit on a basis that immediately fails,[30] where he has paid money as tax that is not due,[31] and where he has discharged a debt for which he was secondarily and the defendant was primarily liable.[32] However, this rule probably does not apply in cases where benefits are transferred on a basis that subsequently fails: here the cause of action is not complete until the failure of basis occurs, and so this is most probably the date at which time starts to run.[33] Note, too, that the Limitation Act 1980 s.10(3) and (4) contain special rules for ascertaining the date when time starts to run on a claim under the Civil Liability (Contribution) Act 1978.[34]

A complicating issue is the question whether it is a necessary prerequisite for **33–12** a claim in unjust enrichment that the claimant must demand repayment, or

---

Industrial Development Ltd v Chio Ho Cheong [2009] HKFCA 16; [2009] W.T.L.R. 999 at [17]–[26]. Further litigation on this point seems likely, following Supperstone J.'s finding in *Williams v Central Bank of Nigeria* [2011] EWHC 876 (QB) at [22]–[26], that it cannot be resolved on a summary application.

[29] *Baker v Courage & Co* [1910] 1 K.B. 56; *Kleinwort Benson Ltd v Lincoln CC* [1999] 2 A.C. 349 at 386 and 409; *Fuller v Happy Shopper Markets Ltd* [2001] EWHC 702 (Ch); [2001] 2 Lloyd's Rep. 49 at [12]–[18]; *Fea v Roberts* [2005] EWHC 2186 (Ch); (2005) 8 I.T.E.L.R. 231 at [61].

[30] *Kleinwort Benson Ltd v South Tyneside MBC* [1994] 4 All E.R. 972 at 978.

[31] *Woolwich Equitable BS v IRC* [1993] A.C. 70 at 171.

[32] *Davies v Humphreys* (1840) 6 M. & W. 153 at 168–169; 151 E.R. 361 at 367–368; *Wolmershausen v Gullick* [1893] 2 Ch. 514; *Walker v Bowry* (1924) 35 C.L.R. 48; *Hawrish v Peters* [1982] 1 S.C.R. 1083. See too Merchant Shipping Act 1995 s.190.

[33] *Guardian Ocean Cargoes Ltd v Banco do Brasil* [1994] 2 Lloyd's Rep. 152 (CA). Cf. *BP Exploration Co (Libya) Ltd v Hunt (No.2)* [1983] 2 A.C. 352 at 373 per Lord Brandon: "The date on which B.P.'s cause of action [under the Law Reform (Frustrated Contracts) Act 1943] arose was the date when the contract between the parties was frustrated . . . ".

[34] Considered in *Knight v Rochdale Healthcare NHS Trust* [2003] EWHC 1831 (QB); [2004] 1 W.L.R. 371; *Baker & Davies Plc v Leslie Wilks Associates* [2005] EWHC 1179 (TCC); [2006] P.N.L.R. 3; *Aer Lingus Plc v Gildacroft Ltd* [2006] EWCA Civ 4; [2006] 1 W.L.R. 1173.

communicate his intention to rescind a contract with the defendant before seeking restitution, and if so, whether time should start to run against him before his demand has been made, or his intention to rescind has been communicated. In principle, claims in unjust enrichment should not depend on the making of a demand, since a defendant's duty to make restitution arises because he has received a benefit that the law deems to be unjust, and not because he has refused to return the value of this benefit when the claimant asks him to do so. Furthermore, even if the claimant were required to make a demand, this should not mean that time only started to run when the demand is made, for otherwise the claimant could postpone the date from which time started to run for as long as he wished[35]—a bad effect that would also result from holding that time does not start to run on a claim for restitution contingent on rescission of a contract until the claimant's intention to rescind is communicated to the defendant.

33–13   The cases which touch on these points contain contrary dicta which have left the law in a confused state. In *Freeman v Jeffries*,[36] the amount which the incoming tenant of a farm was to pay the outgoing tenant was referred to two valuers for valuation. The incoming tenant gave the outgoing tenant a promissory note for the amount so found due which he subsequently paid. He later discovered that certain errors had been made in the valuation and that he had, therefore, paid too much. Without giving the outgoing tenant any information as to the nature of his complaint, he sought to recover from him the alleged overpayment. The Court of Exchequer gave judgment for the defendant on various grounds, one of which[37] was that the plaintiff had made no demand before action. Martin B. considered that the plaintiff could not recover the money unless the arrangement between the parties was rescinded and this could not be achieved "unless some communication has been made by the plaintiff".[38] Bramwell B. relied on the analogy of trover and on the authority of *Wilkinson v Godefroy*.[39] In trover, however, demand and refusal were only evidence that the tort has been committed; and *Wilkinson* was concerned with recovery of money from a stakeholder to whom it had been entrusted, when a demand was necessary to throw upon the depositee a duty to repay.

33–14   In *Baker v Courage & Co*[40] Hamilton J. held that no demand was needed for a claim to lie for restitution of money paid under a mistake that was shared by both parties. However, if a demand is ever necessary, then it should surely be in exactly that case rather than where the payer alone is mistaken. Hamilton J. also considered that *Freeman* could be distinguished on the ground that the mistake there was unilateral,[41] but if any action could have been maintained in *Freeman* on the ground of mistake, such mistake must have been shared by the payee.

---

[35] G. Virgo, *The Principles of the Law of Restitution*, 2nd edn (Oxford: OUP, 2006), pp.749–750, quoted with approval in *Fuller v Happy Shopper Markets Ltd* [2001] EWHC 702 (Ch); [2001] 1 W.L.R. 1681 at [18].
[36] *Freeman v Jeffries* (1869) L.R. 4 Ex. 189.
[37] Martin and Bramwell BB., but not Kelly C.B. and Pigott B., who held for the defendant on this ground.
[38] *Freeman* (1869) L.R. 4 Ex. 189 at 200.
[39] *Wilkinson v Godefroy* (1839) 9 Ad. & El. 536; 112 E.R. 1315.
[40] *Baker v Courage & Co* [1910] 1 K.B. 56.
[41] *Baker* [1910] 1 K.B. 56 at 65–66.

Subsequently, in *Fuller v Happy Shopper Markets Ltd*,[42] Lightman J. distin-   **33–15**
guished *Freeman* as a case where rescission was sought, and held that although
notice is required in such a case, it is not required where a simple claim is made
for the repayment of money. In his Lordship's view:

> "[T]here is no reason why a demand for payment of moneys had and received should
> be required before a right to repayment arises, for the right of restitution arises at the
> moment that unjust enrichment takes place."[43]

And he considered that[44]:

> "[W]hen *Freeman v Jeffries* is properly understood, the law is clear: if the rescission of
> a contract gives rise to a right on the part of a party to repayment of moneys had and
> received, the due exercise of the right of rescission by giving notice of rescission must
> precede the accrual of the right of action for money had and received. In the absence
> of some such special consideration, in particular where no question of rescission arises,
> e.g. where the contract is void or (as on the facts of this case) where there is an
> overpayment, the general rule is that no notice or demand is required."

The view that time starts to run against a claimant in a rescission case from the   **33–16**
date when the claimant communicates to the defendant his intention to rescind
was also taken by the Privy Council in *Lakshmijit v Sherani*.[45] The facts of that
case, were, however, unusual. The claimant had contracted to sell land to the
defendant by instalments. The defendant defaulted. Under the terms of the
contract, the claimant was permitted to elect either to sue for the purchase money
or to rescind and retake possession, retaining the instalments already paid. He did
nothing; and the defendant remained in possession of the land for over 12 years.
The claimant then sought to rescind the contract and sued for possession. The
defendant pleaded that he had acquired the title by adverse possession. The Privy
Council rejected this defence and gave judgment for the claimant. The analogy
of *Car and Universal Finance Co Ltd v Caldwell*[46] persuaded the court that time
did not run against the claimant until he had unequivocally communicated to the
defendant that he was rescinding the agreement. Communication was necessary
because rescission "alters the rights and obligations of both parties to the sale
agreement, since it puts an end to the purchaser's right to possession of the land
and prevents any further instalment of the purchase price becoming due".[47] Until
such communication was made the defendant remained entitled to possession.

In our view, however, there is much force in the dissent of Viscount Dilhorne.   **33–17**
He distinguished *Caldwell* on the ground that it concerned a contract voidable for
fraud, where the defrauded party was not able to communicate his intention to
rescind, and concluded that time should run against the claimant as soon as his
right to rescind arose. On the facts, this was when there was the requisite default
under the agreement.[48] English courts are traditionally reluctant to allow the

---

[42] *Fuller v Happy Shopper Markets Ltd* [2001] EWHC 702 (Ch); [2001] 1 W.L.R. 1681.
[43] *Fuller* [2001] EWHC 702 (Ch); [2001] 1 W.L.R. 1681 at [13], citing *Kleinwort Benson v Tyneside* [1994] 4 All E.R. 972 at 978 per Hobhouse J.
[44] *Fuller* [2001] EWHC 702 (Ch); [2001] 1 W.L.R. 1681 at [18].
[45] *Lakshmijit v Sherani* [1974] A.C. 605.
[46] *Car and Universal Finance Co Ltd v Caldwell* [1965] 1 Q.B. 525.
[47] *Lakshmijit* [1974] A.C. 605 at 616, per curiam (Lord Cross).
[48] *Lakshmijit* [1974] A.C. 605 at 616–618.

claim of a squatter that he has acquired a good title by adverse possession. The Privy Council's decision in *Lakshmijit* is such a case.

4. POSTPONEMENT OF THE DATE OF COMMENCEMENT

(a) *The Limitation Act 1980*

33–18 Although the accrual of the claimant's cause of action is generally the date when time starts to run on claims in unjust enrichment, the Limitation Act 1980 postpones this date in some classes of case.

(i) *Section 28*

33–19 The Limitation Act 1980 s.28 makes special provision for persons who are legally incapable by reason of mental incapacity or minority: in such cases the six-year limitation period normally runs from the date the person ceases to be under a disability or dies, whichever event occurs first. A claimant can only take advantage of s.28 where he is legally incapable at the time when his cause of action accrues: the section does not apply where he becomes mentally incapable at some later date.[49]

(ii) *Section 29(5)*

33–20 The Limitation Act 1980 s.29(5) provides that where a right of action has accrued to recover a debt or other liquidated pecuniary claim, or a claim to the personal estate of a deceased person or to any share or interest in any such estate, and the person liable or accountable for the claim acknowledges the claim in signed writing, or makes any payment in respect of it, the right shall be treated as having accrued on and not before the date of the acknowledgment or payment.

33–21 Claims in unjust enrichment to recover the face value of money payments clearly fall within subs.(5), but it is less obvious whether it also takes in claims to recover the value of goods or services, or claims for the use value of money. In *Amantilla Ltd v Telefusion Plc*,[50] Judge Davies QC, held that a quantum meruit claim for building services fell within s.29(5). He reasoned that the claim had a sufficiently certain description to count as an action for a liquidated sum because it was for a contractual remedy and was therefore based on the parties' intentions. This reasoning does not apply to a claim in unjust enrichment for the value of services. On policy grounds, however, it may be desirable to adopt a purposive construction of subs.(5) in order to bring all claims in unjust enrichment for non-monetary benefits within its scope. The policy underlying subs.(5) is that a defendant's apparent acceptance of a claim should not work to the disadvantage of a claimant who is misled into failing to issue a claim form, and this policy applies as forcefully to claims for non-monetary benefits as it does to claims to recover the face value of money.[51]

---

[49] *Azaz v Denton* [2009] EWHC 1759 (QB) at [43]–[49].
[50] *Amantilla Ltd v Telefusion Plc* (1987) 9 Con. L.R. 139.
[51] A. Burrows, *The Law of Restitution*, 3rd edn (Oxford: OUP, 2010), p.611.

Section 29(5) was also considered in *F.J. Chalke Ltd v HMRC*.[52] The claimant **33–22**
paid money as VAT that was not due, and recovered the face value of its
payments under the VAT Act 1994 s.80. It then brought a common law claim in
unjust enrichment to recover compound interest on its payments as the user value
of the money, in line with the finding in *Sempra Metals Ltd v IRC*[53] that such
claims are possible under English law. The question arose whether the claimant
could invoke s.29(5) to argue that HMRC's payment of its statutory claim
postponed the time at which the limitation period started to run on its common
law claim for the user value of the money. This required Henderson J. to decide
whether a cause of action in unjust enrichment to recover the use value of money
is a right to recover a "debt or other liquidated pecuniary claim" within the
meaning of s.29(5). It also required him to decide whether the claimant had a
single claim mandated by European law to recover both the face value and the
use value of its money, with the result that HMRC's payment should be construed as a part-payment of this single claim for the purposes of the subsection.
He gave a negative answer to the latter question, a finding that was later upheld
by the Court of Appeal, which also considered that for the domestic purposes of
the 1980 Act the statutory claim for the face value of the money and the common
law claim for the user value of the money were not different facets of a single
claim, but "different claims . . . based on different causes of action."[54] Because
of the answer he gave to the second question, it was unnecessary for Henderson
J. to decide the first question, but even so he expressed the view that claims in
unjust enrichment for the use value of money do fall within s.29(5) because[55]:

> "They are wholly dependent on the right to recover the principal sums, and their
> quantification takes the principal sums as its starting point. The claims are restitutionary
> in nature, not compensatory, and following *Sempra* their quantum falls to be calculated
> on a conventional basis which the court can apply whether or not the parties agree. In
> short, the claims appear to me more closely akin to the *quantum meruit* claim in
> *Amantilla* than to a claim for damages in tort or contract."

(iii) *Section 32(1)(a)*

Section 32(1) provides that where an action is brought for which a limitation **33–23**
period is prescribed by the Act and (1) the action is based upon the fraud of the
defendant or his agent, or (2) any fact relevant to the claimant's right of action
has been deliberately concealed from him by the defendant or his agent, or (3) the
action is for relief from the consequences of a mistake, the limitation period does
not start to run until the claimant has discovered the fraud, concealment or
mistake, or could with reasonable diligence have discovered it. Section 32(2)
provides that for the purposes of the section the deliberate commission of a

---

[52] *F.J. Chalke Ltd v HMRC* [2009] EWHC 952 (Ch); [2009] S.T.C. 2027; affirmed [2010] EWCA Civ 313; [2010] S.T.C. 1640.
[53] *Sempra Metals Ltd v IRC* [2007] UKHL 34; [2008] A.C. 561; discussed at paras 5–05 and following. The claimant successfully contended that European law enabled it to bring this common law claim notwithstanding the exclusive nature of the recovery regime created by the VAT Act 1994 s.80; see para.22–12.
[54] *F.J. Chalke* [2010] EWCA Civ 313; [2010] S.T.C. 1640 at [51]; affirming [2009] EWHC 952 (Ch); [2009] S.T.C. 2027 at [149].
[55] *F.J. Chalke* [2009] EWHC 952 (Ch); [2009] S.T.C. 2027 at [157]. The Court of Appeal preferred to express no view on this issue: [2010] EWCA Civ 313; [2010] S.T.C. 1640 at [52].

breach of duty where it is unlikely to be discovered for some time amounts to deliberate concealment of the facts involved in the breach of duty. Section 32(3) and (4) provide protection for purchasers for value without notice of the fraud, concealment or mistake.

33–24   A claimant relying on sub-s.(1) must prove that he could not have discovered the relevant fraud, concealment or mistake[56] earlier than he did without taking exceptional measures that he could not reasonably have been expected to take.[57]

33–25   In *Beaman v A.R.T.S. Ltd*[58] the Court of Appeal held that the statutory precursor of s.32(1)(a) required fraud to be an essential ingredient of the cause of action, from which it followed that an action alleging a "dishonest" conversion was not relevantly an "action based on fraud" because it was not essential to plead fraud in an action for conversion. Thus, s.32(1)(a) applies only to actions in deceit or actions where the pleading would be defective without an allegation of fraud, and fraud here "connotes at the minimum an intention on the part of the [defendant] to pursue a particular course of action, either knowing that it is contrary to the interests of the [claimant] or being recklessly indifferent whether it is contrary to their interests or not".[59]

(iv) Section 32(1)(b)

33–26   Section 32(1)(b) postpones the running of time wherever there is a deliberate concealment, whether such concealment was contemporaneous with or subsequent to the accrual of the cause of action.[60] At first sight subs.(1)(b) might seem very broad since it appears to allow a claimant to rely on the concealment of "any fact relevant to [his] right of action". However, the Court of Appeal held in *A.I.C. Ltd v I.T.S. Testing Services (UK) Ltd (The Kriti Palm)*[61] that the concealed fact must have been a fact which the claimant needs to know in order to plead his case.

---

[56] What must be discovered or known are all the facts which together constitute the cause of action: *Official Assignee of Collier v Creighton* [1993] 2 N.Z.L.R. 534 at 538–540.

[57] *Paragon Finance v D.B. Thakerar & Co (A Firm)* [1999] 1 All E.R. 400 at 418; followed in *Schulman v Hewson* [2002] EWHC 855 (Ch) at [42]; *Biggs v Sotnicks* [2002] EWCA Civ 272 at [71]–[72]. Construing equivalent legislation in the Hong Kong Court of Final Appeal Lord Hoffmann left open the question whether it required the court to apply an objective test of reasonableness, or whether it could subjectively focus on the actual claimant, given that the section refers to time not running until the "plaintiff could with reasonable diligence" have discovered the fraud or mistake: *Peconic Industrial Development Ltd v Lan Kwok Fai* [2009] HKFCA 16; [2009] W.T.L.R. 999 at [30]–[32]. On reasonable diligence, see too *Peco Arts Inc v Hazlitt Gallery Inc* [1983] 1 W.L.R. 1315; *Davies v Sharples* [2006] EWHC 362 (Ch); [2006] W.T.L.R. 839 at [57]–[59]; *Bloomsbury International Ltd v Sea Fish Industry* [2009] EWHC 1721 (QB); [2010] 1 C.M.L.R. 12 at [129]–[132] (reversed on a different point by the CA, but restored on further appeal: [2010] EWCA Civ 263; [2010] 1 W.L.R. 2117; [2011] UKSC 25; [2011] 1 W.L.R. 1546).

[58] *Beaman v A.R.T.S. Ltd* [1949] 1 K.B. 550 at 558.

[59] *Armitage v Nurse* [1998] Ch. 241 at 251. See too *Att Gen of Zambia v Meer Care & Desai (A Firm)* [2007] EWHC 952 (Ch) at [384]–[386].

[60] *Sheldon v R.H.M. Outhwaite (Underwriting Agencies) Ltd* [1996] A.C. 102.

[61] *A.I.C. Ltd v I.T.S. Testing Services (UK) Ltd (The Kriti Palm)* [2006] EWCA Civ 1601; [2007] 1 All E.R. (Comm) 667 at [307] and [453].

In *Cave v Robinson Jarvis & Rolf (A Firm)*, Lord Scott considered that[62]:   **33–27**

"[D]eliberate concealment for section 32(1)(b) purposes may be brought about by an act or an omission and that, in either case, the result of the act or omission, i.e. the concealment, must be an intended result. A claimant . . . [can] prove the facts necessary to bring the case within the paragraph . . . if he can show that some fact relevant to his right of action has been concealed from him either by a positive act of concealment or by a withholding of relevant information, but, in either case, with the intention of concealing the fact or facts in question."

There are, however, two possible interpretations of the mental element   **33–28** required under s.32(1)(b). The limited reading requires deliberate concealment of a fact which the defendant knew to be relevant to a claim against him or was reckless as to its potential relevance. The wider reading says that any deliberate concealment of a relevant fact prevents the running of time even where the defendant did not know that the fact was relevant and was not reckless as to its potential relevance. In *Williams v Fanshaw Porter & Hazelhurst (A Firm)*[63] Park J., with whose judgment Brooke L.J. agreed, preferred the wide interpretation, holding that s.32(1)(b) "does not require, that the defendant must have known that the fact was relevant to the right of action."

Note that s.32(1)(b) does not help a claimant where facts relevant to his claim   **33–29** have been suppressed by some third party other than the defendant or his agent.[64]

(v) *Section 32(1)(c)*

At common law, if money was paid under mistake then time ran from the date   **33–30** when the payment was made and not from the date when the mistake was, or ought reasonably to have been, discovered.[65] Equity adopted the same rule if the equitable claim was strictly analogous to a common law claim.[66] But if the claimant was seeking purely equitable relief, such as rescission or rectification, then time did not normally run until he had, or ought reasonably to have, discovered the mistake.[67]

This conflict has been largely resolved by the Limitation Act 1980 s.32(1)(c),   **33–31** which "applies a general principle as to the postponement of time running, until the maker of the mistake actually does know of his mistake, with an exception where he ought, with due diligence, to have discovered it earlier", although not

---

[62] *Cave v Robinson Jarvis & Rolf (A Firm)* [2002] UKHL 18; [2003] 1 AC 384 at [60].

[63] *Williams v Fanshaw Porter & Hazelhurst (A Firm)* [2004] EWCA Civ 157; [2004] 1 W.L.R. 3185 at [39] Mance L.J. left open the question whether the wider or the narrower meaning should be preferred.

[64] *Compagnie Noga D'Importation et D'Exploration SA v Australia & New Zealand Banking Group Ltd* [2005] EWHC 225 (Comm) at [51]; *Att Gen of Zambia v Meer Care & Desai (A Firm)* [2007] EWHC 952 (Ch) at [399] and [402] (not considered on appeal: [2008] EWCA Civ 1007; [2008] Lloyd's Rep. F.C. 587).

[65] *Baker* [1910] 1 K.B. 56.

[66] *Re Robinson* [1911] 1 Ch. 502; *Re Mason* [1928] Ch. 385 at 392–393 per Romer J.; affirmed [1929] 1 Ch. 1.

[67] *Brooksbank v Smith* (1836) 2 Y. & C. Ex. 58; 160 E.R. 311; *Denys v Shuckburgh* (1840) 4 Y. C. Ex. 42; 160 E.R. 912.

where he "ought, with due diligence, to have avoided making [his mistake] in the first place".[68]

33–32   It was to obtain the benefits of the extended limitation period under s.32(1)(c) that the claimants in both *Kleinwort Benson Ltd v Lincoln CC*[69] and *Deutsche Morgan Grenfell Plc v IRC* [70] sought to ground their claims on mistake of law. Both cases were fought on the basis that the claimant could only take advantage of the provision if mistake were a necessary component of its cause of action. When *Deutsche Morgan Grenfell* reached the House of Lords, however, the claimant amended its pleadings to make the alternative argument for the first time that mistake did not need to be an essential element of its cause of action for the subsection to apply, provided that a mistake could be discovered in the facts of the case.[71] On this reading of s.32(1)(c), claimants could rely on it although the ground of recovery on which they relied was some ground other than mistake, for example the rule in *Woolwich Equitable Building Society v IRC*.[72] In the event, the court did not have to decide this point, although Lord Walker and Lord Hoffmann both favoured the claimant's contention,[73] while Lord Scott preferred Pearson J.'s previous finding in *Phillips-Higgins v Harper*,[74] that the subsection "applies only where the mistake is an essential ingredient of the cause of action".[75]

33–33   The point was then revisited in *Test Claimants in the F.I.I. Group Litigation v HMRC*,[76] where the Court of Appeal followed Aldous L.J.'s earlier finding in *Malkin v Birmingham CC*[77] that the subsection only applies in cases "where the plaintiff can establish that the mistake was part of or an element of the cause of action." The court was influenced to adopt this rule by the consideration that any broader formulation would lead to "undesirable uncertainty as to its scope" and "extending the scope of liabilities of indefinite duration, the existence of which after the expiration of the normal limitation period may be unknown to the obligor, is not obviously desirable."[78] Against this, it might be said that the policy underlying the rule in s.32(1)(c) is to prevent time running against claimants who have honestly mistaken their legal rights in circumstances where these are not reasonably discoverable, and that this policy applies as strongly to claimants who do not need to plead mistake in order to make out their claim as it does to those who do.

---

[68] *Fea* [2005] EWHC 2186 (Ch); (2005) 8 I.T.E.L.R. 231 at [64].

[69] *Kleinwort Benson v Lincoln* [1999] 2 A.C. 349, discussed at paras 9–71 and following.

[70] *Deutsche Morgan Grenfell Plc v IRC* [2006] UKHL 49; [2007] 1 A.C. 558, discussed at paras 22–29—22–31.

[71] Prompted by J. Edelman, "Limitation Periods and the Theory of Unjust Enrichment" (2005) 68 M.L.R. 848.

[72] *Woolwich Equitable Building Society v IRC* [1993] A.C. 70; discussed at para.22–13 and following.

[73] *Woolwich* [2006] UKHL 49; [2007] 1 A.C. 558 at [22] and [147].

[74] *Phillips-Higgins v Harper* [1954] 1 Q.B. 411 at 419, considering the statutory precursor to s.32(1)(c), the Limitation Act 1939 s.26(c).

[75] *Woolwich* [2006] UKHL 49; [2007] 1 A.C. 558 at [91]–[92].

[76] *Test Claimants in the F.I.I. Group Litigation v HMRC* [2010] EWCA Civ 103; [2010] S.T.C. 1251.

[77] *Malkin v Birmingham CC* Unreported CA, January 12, 2000, at [23].

[78] *F.I.I.* [2010] EWCA Civ 103; [2010] S.T.C. 1251 at [245]; followed in *F.J. Chalke* [2010] EWCA Civ 313; [2010] S.T.C. 1640 at [44].

Deutsche Morgan Grenfell was one of many claims brought against the   **33-34**
Revenue following the ECJ's decision in *Metallgesellschaft Ltd v IRC*[79] that
advance corporation tax paid by many corporate groups had not been due
because the statutory scheme under which the tax was levied had infringed the
EC Treaty. Following Park J.'s decision for the claimant at first instance in
2003,[80] the government became alarmed by the prospect that many valuable
claims would be brought by claimants relying on s.32(1)(c),[81] whose mistake had
not been reasonably discoverable until the date of the ECJ's decision.[82] It
therefore brought forward legislation to disapply s.32(1)(c) in relation to mistakes of law relating to taxation matters under the care and management of the
Revenue: the Finance Act 2004 s.320, which applied prospectively to actions
brought on or after September 8, 2003, and the Finance Act 2007 s.107, which
extended the disapplication retrospectively to any action brought before September 8, 2003 for relief from the consequences of such a mistake of law.

In *F.I.I.*,[83] the validity of these sections was challenged on the basis that they   **33-35**
prevented claims by taxpayers who were entitled under EU law to recover
benefits received by HMRC, by curtailing the limitation period applicable to their
claims in mistake without making transitional arrangements, contrary to the
principles of legitimate expectations and effectiveness.[84] The facts of *F.I.I.* were
the reverse of those in *Deutsche Morgan Grenfell*: the latter case concerned the
tax treatment of dividends paid by UK resident companies to parent companies
resident elsewhere in the EU, while the former concerned the tax treatment of
dividends received by UK resident parent companies from foreign subsidiaries.
The *F.I.I.* case in the English courts followed the findings by the European Court
of Justice, first, that the charge to corporation tax of foreign-sourced dividends in
circumstances where domestically-sourced dividends were exempt from corporation tax may have violated art.49 of the European Treaty, and, secondly, that the
requirement on UK resident parent companies to account for advance corporation
tax on the distribution of dividends financed out of foreign-sourced dividends did
violate art.49.[85] In a departure from the approach towards the classification of

---

[79] *Metallgesellschaft Ltd v IRC* (Joined Cases C–397/98 and C–410/98) [2001] All E.R. (E.C.)
496.
[80] *Deutsche Morgan Grenfell* [2003] EWHC 1779 (Ch); [2003] S.T.C. 1017.
[81] It was exactly because problems of this kind would arise that Lord Browne-Wilkinson dissented
from the majority's finding that restitution should be awarded for "retrospective" mistakes of law in
Kleinwort Benson v Lincoln [1999] 2 A.C. 349 at 364.
[82] The House of Lords later confirmed that the date when the ECJ handed down its decision in
Metallgesellschaft was the date when the claimant in *Deutsche Morgan Grenfell* could first reasonably have discovered its mistake: [2006] UKHL 49; [2007] 1 A.C. 558 at [34] per Lord Hoffmann;
at [71] per Lord Hope; and at [144] per Lord Walker. Lord Brown took a different view at [165].
[83] *F.I.I.* [2008] EWHC 2893 (Ch); [2009] S.T.C. 254; reversed in part [2010] EWCA Civ 103; [2010]
S.T.C. 1251.
[84] A development that was correctly predicted in M. Chowdry, "The Revenue's Response: A Time
Bar on Claims" (2005) 121 L.Q.R. 546. Similar considerations had previously led the ECJ to hold
in the VAT context that legislative changes to the limitation rule which governed claims to recover
money paid as output tax were invalid for want of a transitional period: *Marks & Spencer Plc v C&E
Commissioners* (C–62/00) [2003] Q.B. 866. The same principle also applies to input tax, so that when
the Value Added Tax Regulations 1995 (SI 1995/2518) reg.29(1A) introduced a three-year cap on
claims to recover input tax without any transitional provisions, this was also a breach of the principle
of effectiveness: *Fleming v HMRC* [2008] UKHL 2; [2008] S.T.C. 324. A transitional period was
subsequently put in place in relation to both input and output tax: Finance Act 2008 s.121.
[85] *F.I.I.* (C–446/04) [2006] E.C.R. I–11753 at [73] and [112].

remedy that it had previously taken in the *Metallgesellschaft* case (where this was held to be a matter for the national court), the ECJ also held that the English court had no option but to classify the action available to affected taxpayers as an action in unjust enrichment for restitution, because an action for compensatory damages would inevitably fail on the facts because the breach of EU law by the UK was insufficiently serious to warrant state liability for damages.[86]

33–36   Given that the claimants in *F.I.I.* were entitled as a matter of EU law to an effective action in unjust enrichment, the question therefore arose in the English proceedings whether the Finance Act 2004 s.320, and the Finance Act 2007 s.107, were contrary to EU law because no transitional arrangements were made when these sections were enacted. At first instance, Henderson J. held that they were, accepting the premise of the claimants' argument that EU law required them to be given a cause of action grounded on mistake.[87] However, the Court of Appeal held that the claimants' rights of recovery under EU law were satisfied because they could bring claims founded on *Woolwich*,[88] and that the statutory sections did not breach EU law because they only affected mistake-based claims and did not affect *Woolwich* claims.[89] An appeal from this decision to the Supreme Court is pending.

(b) *Laches*

33–37   Where the doctrine of laches applies, no particular limitation period governs the claim and the court must instead look at the dealings between the parties in the round when deciding whether fairness dictates that a claim should be barred. Hence it would be misleading to describe the rules in this area as though they required the court to identify a moment, such as the accrual of the claimant's cause of action, for example, as the date when time generally starts to run against the claimant, and then to ask whether there are any reasons why this date should be postponed.[90]

33–38   Having said that, there are cases where the courts have adopted reasoning that resembles the approach taken in the Limitation Act 1980 s.32(1)(c), to hold that a claim cannot be barred for laches for as long as the claimant does not know, and cannot reasonably be expected to know, that he has a claim. This rule was applied, for example, in *Lindsay Petroleum Co v Hurd*,[91] a case of fraudulent misrepresentation, and in *Erlanger v New Sombrero Phosphate Co*,[92] a case of non-disclosure. The rule was not applied in *Leaf v International Galleries (A Firm)*,[93] where a claim for rescission of a contract on the ground of innocent misrepresentation was barred after five years since the contract was executed,

---

[86] *F.I.I.* [2006] E.C.R. I–11753 at [202].
[87] *F.I.I.* [2008] EWHC 2893 (Ch); [2009] S.T.C. 254 at [414]–[427].
[88] *Woolwich* [1993] A.C. 70.
[89] *F.I.I.* [2010] EWCA Civ 103; [2010] S.T.C. 1251 at [229].
[90] Cf. *Azaz* [2009] EWHC 1759 (QB) at [116]: there is no rule that in a case of undue influence it is immaterial what happens between the date of the transaction sought to be set aside and the date on which the undue influence ceased to be exercised, because time cannot "start to run" until after that date.
[91] *Lindsay Petroleum Co v Hurd* (1874) L.R. 5 P.C. 221.
[92] *Erlanger v New Sombrero Phosphate Co* (1878) 3 App. Cas. 1218.
[93] *Leaf v International Galleries (A Firm)* [1950] 2 K.B. 86.

although the claimant did not know and could not reasonably have known that the defendant's misrepresentation was untrue until shortly before the issuing of the claim. However, we doubt that the innocent nature of the defendant's misrepresentation was sufficient reason for the court to apply a different rule in this case.

The courts have also held of claims to set aside transactions on the ground of **33–39** undue influence, that "so long as the undue influence persists, claims can be brought whatever the period since the transaction; but . . . once the complainant is no longer under the defendant's influence, a claim to set aside the transaction must be brought within a reasonable time".[94] Notwithstanding the similarity between such claims and common law claims founded on duress, however, there is no analogous rule to postpone the commencement of the six-year limitation period that applies to duress claims to the date when the claimant becomes sufficiently free from pressure to decide for himself whether to claim restitution. This is a matter for regret.[95]

---

[94] *Humphreys v Humphreys* [2004] EWHC 2201 (Ch); [2005] 1 F.C.R. 712 at [99] per Rimer J. See too *Allcard v Skinner* (1887) L.R. 36 Ch. D. 145 at 187 and at 191; *Glasson v Fuller* [1922] S.A.S.R. 148 at 161.
[95] As observed in J. Edelman and E. Bant, *Unjust Enrichment in Australia* (Melbourne: OUP, 2006), pp.365–366.

CHAPTER 34

LEGAL INCAPACITY

1. INTRODUCTION

(a) *Overview*

In Chs 23 and 24 we discuss various cases where a claimant has been awarded **34–01** restitution on the ground that he lacked the legal capacity to enter the transaction which led to the defendant's enrichment. Some of these concern human persons —minors and the mentally incapable—and others artificial persons—private companies and public bodies acting beyond their powers. Some concern the recovery of benefits transferred under a contract which the defendant lacked the capacity to enter, and others the recovery of non-contractual benefits, for example, state welfare payments made without due authority. However, the basic ground of recovery in all of these cases is the same, namely that the policy of the rule which deemed the claimant to be legally incapable of entering the transaction also required restitution of the benefits received by the defendant.

In this chapter we examine the converse question, of whether a defendant can **34–02** escape liability in unjust enrichment on the ground that he lacked legal capacity to enter the contract under which he received the relevant benefit. In the cases where this question has arisen, the claimant can typically establish a ground for recovery such as mistake or failure of basis, and the argument is made that the defendant should nevertheless escape liability because the rule which deemed him to be legally incapable of entering the contract should also prevent the claimant from recovering in unjust enrichment. Two types of case are discussed here. Part 2 concerns claims against minors and Part 3 concerns claims against companies and public bodies.[1]

There is an overlap between these cases and the cases that are discussed in **34–03** Ch.2, where it is explained that a statute can constitute a justifying ground for a defendant's enrichment in cases where the policy underlying the statute would be stultified if a claim in unjust enrichment were allowed to proceed.[2] However, the rules invalidating transactions entered by the defendant in the cases discussed here do not all derive from statutes: some derive from the common law.

---

[1] The abolition of the ultra vires rule by the Companies Act 2006 s.39 means that claims are now unlikely ever to be brought against a company to recover benefits received under an ultra vires contract, but past cases of this kind are still significant to the extent that the courts are influenced by their reasoning when deciding analogous claims against public bodies.

[2] See paras 2–21 and following. Cf. *Haugesund Kommune v Depfa ACS Bank* [2010] EWCA Civ 579; [2011] 1 All E.R. 190 at [150] per Etherton L.J., noting that the statutes on which such reasoning has been founded "are best viewed . . . as examples of United Kingdom legislation which, on its correct interpretation, implicitly excludes any civil restitutionary remedy whether for unjust enrichment or otherwise."

34–04   Some of the cases discussed in this chapter were decided at a time when claims in unjust enrichment were mistakenly supposed to be "quasi-contractual" claims that were essentially claims in contract.[3] Taking this false premise as their starting-point, the courts held that a rule which invalidated a contract, and which therefore debarred a contractual claim against a defendant, must necessarily debar a "quasi-contractual" claim against him as well. Reasoning of this kind can be found in *Cowern v Nield*[4] and *R. Leslie Ltd v Sheill*,[5] which were claims against minors,[6] and in *Sinclair v Brougham*,[7] which concerned claims against a building society that received payments under ultra vires banking contracts.[8] Whatever view one takes of the results in these cases, their reasoning was unfortunate because it concealed the policy calculations that lay behind the courts' decisions. This was recognised by the House of Lords in *Westdeutsche Landesbank Girozentrale v Islington LBC*,[9] where "quasi-contractual" reasoning was repudiated and the court took an overtly policy-based approach to the question whether benefits transferred pursuant to an invalid contract should be recoverable in unjust enrichment. On this approach, which we believe should be taken in every case, the court should first identify the policy underpinning the rule that invalidates the contract, and then investigate whether this policy also requires that the claim in unjust enrichment should be disallowed.

(b) *Policy Considerations*

34–05   Looking at the cases discussed in this chapter from a policy perspective,[10] it is striking that in all of them the defendant has invoked a rule designed to shield him from loss to justify his retention of a gain received from another party. Minors, for example, are generally permitted to repudiate contracts into which they have entered because the law fears that they may suffer a loss when they are exploited by unscrupulous adults.[11] However, this policy does not justify a minor

---

[3] See paras 3–02—3–09 for discussion.

[4] *Cowern v Nield* [1912] 2 K.B. 419.

[5] *R. Leslie Ltd v Sheill* [1914] 3 K.B. 607.

[6] See paras 34–14—34–16.

[7] *Sinclair v Brougham* [1914] A.C. 398.

[8] See paras 34–32—34–34.

[9] *Westdeutsche Landesbank Girozentrale v Islington LBC* [1996] A.C. 669 at 709–710 and at 713–714 per Lord Browne-Wilkinson; at 718 per Lord Slynn; and at 738 per Lord Lloyd. See too see *Haugesund* [2010] EWCA Civ 579; [2011] 1 All E.R. 190 at [65]–[80] per Aikens L.J.

[10] For discussion of the policy issues arising in the cases, see too S. Arrowsmith, "Ineffective Transactions, Unjust Enrichment and Problems of Policy" (1989) 9 L.S. 307; E. O'Dell, "Incapacity" in P. Birks and F. Rose (eds), *Lessons of the Swaps Litigation* (Oxford: Mansfield Press, 2000), 113.

[11] This policy is not engaged in cases where the minor is supplied with necessaries at a reasonable price. Transactions of this kind are not exploitative, and indeed are seen as positively desirable, consistently with a second policy that is also pursued in the cases discussed in Ch.18, namely that those who can supply goods and services to defendants in necessitous circumstances should be encouraged to do so, or at least should not be discouraged from doing so: see paras 18–01—18–03.

keeping a benefit which is still in his hands at the time of the claim and which he could return without incurring any additional loss. This suggests that minority should not be a defence to claims in unjust enrichment, at least in cases where the minor is still enriched at the time of the claim.

Whether a minor should be liable in cases where he no longer has the benefit **34–06** is less straightforward. He may sometimes be entitled to invoke the change of position defence, but even where he would normally be disqualified from doing so, for example because he knows that the claimant has made a mistake, it is arguable that he should not be disqualified from relying on the defence because requiring him to make restitution would cause him to suffer loss of the same kind as the loss from which the law sought to shield him by rendering the contract invalid.

If this is correct, then the only question which remains is exactly what it means **34–07** to say that the minor "still has the benefit". As the law is currently constituted this may mean nothing more than that the minor still has specific property in his hands that came from the claimant, but it would be preferable for the courts to take a broader view and apply the same principle in cases where the minor's overall wealth is still swollen by value received from the claimant.

A similar set of policy considerations arise in cases concerning companies and **34–08** public authorities, although the policy calculus is more complex because companies and public authorities are not real persons, but artificial legal constructs through which human beings are enabled to pursue the business of private enterprise and government. In formulating the rules which govern the extent of their legal liabilities, the courts must therefore strike a balance between the human beings in whose interests they operate and the different human beings whose interests may be adversely affected by their activities.

The point of the ultra vires rule that formerly affected transactions entered by **34–09** a company was to protect the company shareholders, and its intra vires creditors, who had all contracted with the company on the basis that the money, goods, or services which they supplied to the company would only be used for its (published) purposes, and would not be used in the pursuit of different, possibly riskier ventures. This policy dictated that the company should not be obliged to sustain loss by performing its ultra vires contractual obligations—but it did not require that the company should be allowed to keep benefits received under ultra vires contracts, at least to the extent that these benefits survived in the company's hands at the time of the claim, and it may be the company should have been required to repay the value of benefits which it has consumed as well.

The point of the rules preventing public bodies from entering ultra vires **34–10** contracts is to protect taxpayers by ensuring that their money is not spent on purposes which were not legally authorised by their elected representatives. This policy does not require that a public body should be allowed to keep benefits received under an ultra vires contract, at least to the extent that these benefits survive in its hands at the time of the claim, and probably it should also have to repay the value of benefits which it has consumed. It is true that the public body will most probably have to raise the money for this from the taxpayers whose position the ultra vires rule is designed to protect, but to hold otherwise would be to expropriate the claimant's funds for the public benefit in an arbitrary and unjustified way.

2. MINORS

(a) *Background*

34–11   A minor is not generally bound by a contract unless he ratifies it after he comes of age, but there are two exceptions to this rule. First, a contract which grants him an interest in property and which exposes him to obligations of a continuous or recurring nature is binding on him unless he repudiates the contract and disclaims the property either before or within a reasonable time of coming of age. Secondly, a contract for necessaries is binding on him provided that it does not impose onerous terms on him. These rules are all discussed in Ch.24.[12] It is also noted there, in connection with contracts for the supply of necessaries, that even where such a contract is not binding on the minor because it imposes onerous terms on him, he will still be liable in unjust enrichment to make restitution of the reasonable value of the relevant goods or services. Hence the obligation to pay the reasonable value of necessaries imposed by the Sale of Goods Act 1979 s.3(2), should be understood as a contractual liability to the extent that the contract requires payment of a reasonable sum, and as a liability in unjust enrichment to the extent that it requires the minor to pay more than this.[13]

34–12   Where a minor has received benefits other than necessaries under an invalid contract, there are two lines of authority to be considered: one at common law and one in equity. We shall discuss these in turn and then examine the effect of the Minors' Contracts Act 1987 s.3(1) on this area of the law.

(b) *At Common Law*

34–13   In *Bristow v Eastman*,[14] an action for money had and received was held to lie against a minor to recover money which he had embezzled from his employer. Lord Kenyon said that[15]:

> "[I]nfancy was no defence to the action; that infants were liable to actions ex *delicto*, though not *ex contractu*, and though the present action was in its form an action of the latter description; that if the assignees had brought an action of trover for any part of the property embezzled, or an action grounded on the fraud, that unquestionably infancy would have been no defence: and as the object of the present action was precisely the same, that his opinion was, that the same rule of law should apply, and that infancy was no bar to the action."

In modern terms, therefore, the employer's claim could be analysed either as a claim for restitution that was founded on the defendant's tort, or else as a claim in unjust enrichment for restitution of the money which had been taken without the employer's authority or consent,[16] and the claim would be allowed in its former but not in its latter character.

---

[12] See paras 24–13—24–19.
[13] See paras 24–15—24–19.
[14] *Bristow v Eastman* (1794) 1 Esp. 172; 170 E.R. 317.
[15] *Bristow* 1 Esp. at 173; 170 E.R. at 318–319.
[16] For discussion of this ground for restitution, see Ch.8.

This was followed in *Cowern*.[17] The defendant, a minor, carried on business **34–14** as a merchant in hay and straw. The plaintiff ordered some clover and hay from him and paid him in advance. The clover was delivered, but the plaintiff properly rejected it because it was rotten. The hay was never delivered. The plaintiff, therefore, sued the defendant to recover the money he had paid either as damages for breach of contract or as money paid for a consideration which had wholly failed. The defendant pleaded his minority. A divisional court held that the contract was void against the minor and so the action for damages failed. The court also held, on the authority of *Bristow*, that the action for money had and received must also fail, as this was a claim in quasi-contract, and thus essentially contractual, unless it could be shown that the minor had committed a fraud, in which case a claim for restitution founded on the minor's wrongdoing would lie. A retrial was therefore ordered to determine whether he had committed a fraud.

The Court of Appeal reached a similar conclusion a year later in *Leslie*.[18] The **34–15** defendant, a minor, by fraudulently representing that he was of full age, induced the plaintiff moneylenders to lend him £400. They sued him to recover the money and he pleaded his minority. The Court of Appeal held that he was not liable to repay the money in an action for money had and received. Lord Sumner noted that *Bristow* permits claims against minors that are founded on tort, but considered that "where the substance of the cause of action is contractual, it is certainly otherwise."[19]

In the previous edition of this work,[20] it was argued that the reasoning in **34–16** *Cowern* and *Leslie* was unsound, both because it rested on a false analogy between contractual claims and "quasi-contractual" claims in unjust enrichment, and because the policy which prevented the claimants from suing on the contracts entered with the defendant minors did not also prevent them from recovering in unjust enrichment because they were not seeking to enforce the terms of the contracts, but simply to restore the status quo ante. As explained above,[21] however, we consider that the policy considerations affecting cases of this kind are rather more complex than this, and that minors should only have to repay the value of benefits which they still have at the time of the claim: to the extent that they absolved the defendants from liability to repay the value of benefits which were gone by the time of the claim, we therefore consider that *Cowern* and *Leslie* were correctly decided.[22]

In Ch.4, we argued that English law only permits personal claims in unjust **34–17** enrichment to recover the value received by defendants, and does not permit personal claims to recover the value surviving in their hands at the time of the action.[23] Consistently with this, we believe that the best mechanism by which to

---

[17] *Cowern* [1912] 2 K.B. 419.
[18] *Leslie* [1914] 3 K.B. 607.
[19] *Leslie* [1914] 3 K.B. 607 at 612–613. See also Kennedy L.J.'s comments at 621, and A. T. Lawrence J.'s comments at 626.
[20] G. Jones, *Goff & Jones: The Law of Restitution*, 7th edn (London: Sweet & Maxwell, 2006), para.25.08. The same arguments are made in A. Burrows, *The Law of Restitution*, 3rd edn (Oxford: OUP, 2010), pp.581–583.
[21] See para.34–06.
[22] A similar view is taken in P. Birks, *Unjust Enrichment*, 2nd edn (Oxford: OUP, 2005), pp.261–263.
[23] See paras 4–34—4–42.

achieve the result we advocate here would be to allow claims to recover the value received by a defendant minor, but to allow the minor to rely on the change of position defence in a wider set of circumstances than would normally be permitted,[24] so that he can escape liability for that portion of the value which he has consumed or otherwise disposed of by the time of the action, even if he was aware of the circumstances entitling the claimant to restitution. This would mean, for example, that the minor would not be prevented from relying on the defence by the fact that he knew that the claimant was unaware of his minority (although there is an argument that he should not be allowed the defence where he has committed a fraudulent misrepresentation or has been dishonest in some other way).

(c) In Equity

34–18 If a minor commits an equitable fraud, then there is an equitable jurisdiction to grant relief against him, but, as Knight Bruce V.C. once said, "in what cases in particular a court of equity will thus exert itself is not easy to determine".[25] There are dicta in general terms: "If an infant is old enough and cunning enough to contrive and carry on a fraud, he ought to make satisfaction for it"[26]; "infancy or coverture shall be no excuse"[27]; "infants have no privilege to cheat men"[28]; "infants are not allowed to take advantage of infancy to support a fraud"[29]; "if there was a fraud, of which the infant was conusant, she would be bound as much as an adult".[30] But the scope of these dicta is hard to discern because equitable fraud is an uncertain concept that is not limited to dishonest conduct, but extends to other forms of behaviour of which the courts disapprove, for one reason or another.[31]

34–19 In *Clarke v Cobley*,[32] the defendant gave the plaintiff his bond for the amount of two notes made to the plaintiff by the defendant's wife. The plaintiff delivered up the notes. When the bond was put in suit, the defendant pleaded his minority at the time of its execution, whereupon the plaintiff filed a bill in equity praying that the defendant might either pay the money, execute a new bond, or return the notes. Arden M.R. refused to decree payment of the money. He said[33] that he "could only take care that the parties were put in the same situation in which they were at the time of the bond being given, which was done on the principle that

---

[24] See paras 27–32—27–35.

[25] *Stikeman v Dawson* (1847) 1 De G. & Sm. 90 at 110; 63 E.R. 984 at 994. It is possible that this relief will only be available to the other party after the infant attained his majority; see Knight Bruce V.C.'s comments at 1 De G. & Sm. at 109; 63 E.R. at 993–994.

[26] *Watts v Cresswell* (1714) 2 Eq. Ca. Abr. 515–516 per Lord Cowper L.C.

[27] *Savage v Foster* (1722) 9 Mod. 35 at 37; 88 E.R. 299 at 301 per curiam.

[28] *Esron v Nicholas*, sub nom. *Evroy v Nicholas* (1733) 2 Eq. Ca. Abr. 488 at 489 per Lord King L.C.

[29] *Earl of Buckinghamshire v Drury* (1761) 2 Eden 60 at 71; 28 E.R. 818 at 824 per Lord Hardwicke L.C.

[30] *Beckett v Cordley* (1784) 1 Bro. C.C. 353 at 358; 28 E.R. 1174 at 1178 per Lord Thurlow L.C.

[31] As to which, note para.11–24.

[32] *Clarke v Cobley* (1789) 2 Cox 173; 30 E.R. 80; see also *Overton v Banister* (1844) 3 Hare 503; 67 E.R. 479; *Wright v Snowe* (1848) 2 De G. & Sm. 321; 64 E.R. 144; *Chubb v Griffiths* (1865) 35 Beav. 127; 55 E.R. 843; *Woolf v Woolf* [1899] 1 Ch. 343.

[33] *Clarke* 2 Cox at 174; 30 E.R. at 80.

an infant shall not take advantage of his own fraud" and he ordered the notes to be returned to the plaintiff.

In *Re King*,[34] a minor, by fraudulently stating that he was of full age, obtained **34–20** a substantial advance from a banking association. He subsequently became bankrupt. It was held that the association was entitled to prove in the bankruptcy for the debt. Both Knight Bruce and Turner L.JJ. expressed their reluctance to reach this decision, believing that they were compelled to do so by the previous course of authority; but, as Lord Sumner later said,[35] "the language of the Lords Justice is hardly consistent with any other view than the bankrupt was in equity personally liable to pay the debt in question." Such a view must be implicit in the decision itself, and was expressed by Knight Bruce L.J. in these words[36]:

> "The question is, whether in the view of a court of equity, according to the sense of decisions not now to be disputed, he has made himself liable to pay the debt, whatever his liability or non-liability at law. In my opinion we are compelled to say that he was."

The limits of equity's intervention were emphasised in *Levene v Brougham*.[37] **34–21** The defendant, a minor, by fraudulently representing that he was of full age, obtained an advance from the plaintiff, a moneylender, for which he gave a promissory note for £700. The plaintiff sued the defendant on the note and the defendant pleaded his minority. The Court of Appeal held that the plaintiff could not recover. The contract was void under the Infants Relief Act 1874 s.1. No authority was cited:

> "in which it had been held that a contract which was void under the statute was made good simply because it had been entered into on the faith of a misrepresentation. . . . The most that could be said [was] . . . that a representation by an infant that he was of full age gave rise to an equitable liability resulting from the fraud. But that did not mean that the contract would be enforced, but that some other remedy would be given."[38]

These cases might be taken to support a principle that equity will not directly **34–22** enforce contracts that are void at law. However, it is hard to reconcile this principle with the decision of Lush J. in *Stocks v Wilson*.[39] The defendant, a minor, by fraudulently representing that he was of full age, induced the plaintiff to sell him non-necessary goods on credit, for the price of £300. The defendant then resold some of the goods for £30; and, with the consent of the plaintiff's agent, he granted a bill of sale of the remainder as security for a loan of £100. He

---

[34] *Re King* (1858) 3 De G. & J. 63; 44 E.R. 1192. See also *Maclean v Dummett* (1869) 22 L.T. 710; *Ex p. Lynch* (1876) 2 Ch. D. 227, which was, however, regarded as anomalous by Lindley J. in *Miller v Blankley* (1878) 38 L.T. 527 at 530.
[35] *Leslie* [1914] 3 K.B. 607 at 617.
[36] *Re King* (1858) 3 De G. & J. 63 at 69; 44 E.R. 1192 at 1195 The case was doubted, on grounds which do not affect this statement in the text, in *Ex p. Jones* (1881) 18 Ch. D. 109 at 120–121 per Sir George Jessel M.R., and at 113 per Baggallay L.J. See also *Nelson v Stocker* (1859) 4 De G. & J. 458 at 464; 45 E.R. 178 at 181 per Turner L.J.; *Bartlett v Wells* (1862) 1 B. & S. 836 at 841; 121 E.R. 924 at 927 per Lord Cockburn C.J.; applied in *De Roo v Foster* (1862) 12 C.B. (N.S.) 272; 142 E.R. 1148; *Miller* (1878) 38 L.T. 527.
[37] *Levene v Brougham* (1909) 25 T.L.R. 265.
[38] *Levene* (1909) 25 T.L.R. 265 at 265 per Lord Alverstone C.J. Cf. *Lemprière v Lange* (1879) Ch. D. 675 at 670 per Sir George Jessel M.R.; *Leslie* [1914] 3 K.B. 607 at 614 per Lord Sumner.
[39] *Stocks v Wilson* [1913] 2 K.B. 235.

failed to pay the price of the goods on the due date. After the defendant had come of age, the plaintiff brought an action against him claiming, inter alia, the reasonable value of the goods. Lush J. held that the defendant was liable in equity to account to the plaintiff for the £30 and for the £100 he had obtained as a result of the sale and mortgage respectively.

34–23   Lush J. stated the equitable rules in these terms[40]:

> "What the court of equity has done in cases of this kind to prevent the infant from retaining the benefit of what he has obtained by reason of his fraud. It has done no more than this, and this is a very different thing from making him liable to pay damages or compensation for the loss of the other party's bargain. If the infant has obtained property by fraud he can be compelled to restore it; if he has obtained money he can be compelled to refund it. If he has not obtained either, but has only purported to bind himself by an obligation to transfer property or to pay money, neither in a court of law nor a court of equity can he be compelled to make good his promise or to make satisfaction for its breach."

34–24   He continued[41]:

> "The jurisdiction the court exercises is not only a jurisdiction over the property which the infant has acquired by his fraud, but also over the infant himself to compel him to make satisfaction. . . . If an infant has wrongfully sold the property which he acquired by fraudulent misrepresentation as to his age, he must at all events account for the proceeds to the party he has defrauded. I can see no logical ground on which he can be allowed to resist such a claim in that case, if he is accountable for the money itself in a case where he has obtained money and not goods by means of a like fraud."

34–25   In the following year, however, the Court of Appeal doubted this decision in *Leslie*.[42] There the defendant, a minor, by fraudulently representing himself to be of full age, induced the plaintiffs, who were moneylenders, to advance to him two sums of £200 each. The plaintiffs sued to recover the sums advanced with interest, either as damages for fraud or as money had and received to their use. The Court of Appeal held that the defendant was not liable in tort, because the tort was directly connected with a contract void against the minor under the Infants' Relief Act 1874; that the defendant was not liable in an action for money had and received; and that the defendant was under no personal liability in equity to return the money.

34–26   Lord Sumner examined the authorities and concluded[43]:

> "I think that the whole current of decisions down to 1913, apart from *dicta* which are inconclusive, went to show that, when an infant obtained an advantage by falsely stating himself to be of full age, equity required him to restore his ill-gotten gains, or to release the party deceived from obligations or acts in law induced by the fraud, but scrupulously stopped short of enforcing against him a contractual obligation, entered into while he was an infant, even by means of fraud. This applies even to *Re King*.[44]

---

[40] *Stocks* [1913] 2 K.B. 235 at 242–243.
[41] *Stocks* [1913] 2 K.B. 235 at 247.
[42] *Leslie* [1914] 2 K.B. 607; applied in *Mahomed Syedol Ariffin v Yeoh Ooi Gark* [1916] 2 A.C. 575. See paras 34–12—34–18.
[43] *Leslie* [1914] 2 K.B. 607 at 618.
[44] *Re King* (1858) 3 De G. & J. 63; 44 E.R. 1192; see para.34–16.

Restitution stopped where repayment began; as Kindersley V.-C. put it in *Vaughan v Vanderstegen*,[45] an analogous case, 'you take the property to pay the debt'."

Lord Sumner considered Lush J.'s statement in *Stocks*, that if a minor obtained **34–27** money by fraud he can be compelled in equity to refund it, was "open to challenge". He continued[46]:

"The learned judge thought that the fundamental principle in *Re King* was a liability to account for the money obtained by the fraudulent misrepresentation and that in the case before him there must be a similar liability to account for the proceeds of the sale of the goods obtained by the fraud. If this be his *ratio decidendi*, though I have difficulty in seeing what liability to account there can be (and certainly none is named in *Re King*), the decision in *Stocks v Wilson* is distinguishable from the present case and is independent of the above dictum, and I need express no opinion about it. In the present case there is clearly no accounting. There is no fiduciary relation: the money was paid over in order to be used as the defendant's own and he has so used it and, I suppose, spent it. There is no question of tracing it, no possibility of restoring the very thing got by the fraud, nothing but compulsion through a personal judgment to pay an equivalent sum out of his present or future resources, in a word nothing but a judgment in debt to repay the loan. I think this would be nothing but enforcing a void contract. So far as I can find, the Court of Chancery never would have enforced any liability under circumstances like the present, any more than a court of law would have done so, and I think that no ground can be found for the present judgment, which would be an answer to the Infants' Relief Act."

It is difficult to say how far *Stocks* survived this onslaught. In the previous **34–28** edition of this work,[47] the view was taken that *Stocks* is reconcilable with *Leslie*. The basis of the latter decision was said to be a policy that personal remedies in unjust enrichment are not to be employed indirectly to enforce contracts which are not binding on the minor at common law, and this rule was said to override the equity whereby a minor would otherwise have to pay for goods obtained by fraud or repay money obtained fraudulently under a contract of loan. It was noted that a minor who obtains property under a contract induced by fraud is liable in equity to restore such property as remains in his possession and, if he has disposed of the property, to refund the proceeds.[48] However it was also said that the minor owes no liability to pay the contract price for the property or even a reasonable price, because to require him to do so would indirectly enforce the contract,[49] and that a minor who fraudulently obtains money under a loan contract need not repay the money if this would indirectly enforce the contract.[50]

In our view, this attempt to reconcile the cases is only partially successful. **34–29** Consistently with our view of the common law cases,[51] we believe that denying recovery whenever this would indirectly enforce the contract is too blunt an

---

[45] *Vaughan v Vanderstegen* (1854) 2 Drew 363 at 383; 61 E.R. 759 at 768.
[46] *Leslie* [1914] 3 K.B. 607 at 619.
[47] *Goff & Jones: The Law of Restitution*, 7th edn, para.25.11.
[48] Citing *Clarke v Cobley* (1789) 2 Cox 173; 30 E.R. 80; *Bartlett v Wells* (1862) 1 B. & S. 836 at 841; 121 E.R. 924 at 927 per Lord Cockburn C.J.; *Leslie* [1914] 3 K.B. 607 at 632–634 per Kennedy L.J.
[49] Citing *Stocks* [1913] 2 K.B. 235, semble.
[50] Citing *Leslie* [1914] 3 K.B. 607.
[51] See paras 34–10—34–13.

approach, and that a more promising strategy is to allow recovery if the minor still has the value received from the claimant at the time of the claim, but to deny it if he does not, unless he has been dishonest. The cases on "fraud" discussed here are consistent with this position to an extent, but they are sometimes hard to interpret because they use the term "fraud" only in a loose equitable sense.

(d) *The Minors' Contracts Act 1987*

34–30 It would now be open to the courts to take the approach that we advocate when exercising their discretion under the Minors' Contracts Act 1987 s.3(1). This provides that:

"Where—

(a) a person ('the plaintiff') has after the commencement of this Act entered into a contract with another ('the defendant'), and

(b) the contract is unenforceable against the defendant (or he repudiates it) because he was a minor when the contract was made,

the court may, if it is just and equitable to do so, require the defendant to transfer to the plaintiff any property acquired by the defendant under the contract, or any property representing it."

34–31 As yet there is no decided case interpreting s.3(1). It is therefore conjectural how the courts will interpret the section and, in particular, the words "any property acquired by the defendant under the contract, or any proceeds representing it". A literal reading of these words would suggest that a court may only order a defendant minor to make restitution where he still has specific property in his hands at the time of the claim, or the traceable proceeds of such property. However, we consider that the courts would do better to take a wider view of subs.(1), and be prepared to exercise their statutory discretion to allow claims against minors whose overall wealth is still swollen by value received by the claimant.

3. PRIVATE CORPORATIONS AND PUBLIC BODIES

34–32 In *Sinclair v Brougham*,[52] claims were made in the winding up of a building society incorporated by statute, which had undertaken ultra vires banking business. The House of Lords held that claimants who had deposited money with the building society under ultra vires contracts of deposit could not recover their money in a personal action either at common law or in equity, because allowing their claim would have circumvented the "doctrine of *ultra vires* as established in the jurisprudence of this country."[53] The ultra vires depositors were, however, allowed to follow their money in equity, although their claims were postponed to

---

[52] *Sinclair v Brougham* [1914] A.C. 398. For detailed discussion of this case, see E. O'Dell, "*Sinclair v Brougham* (1914)" in C. Mitchell and P. Mitchell (eds), *Landmark Cases in the Law of Restitution* (Oxford: Hart, 2006), 213.

[53] *Sinclair* [1914] A.C. 398 at 414 per Viscount Haldane L.C.

those of the members whose money had been deposited under intra vires contracts.

The court's reasoning in connection with the ultra vires depositors' actions for   **34–33**
money had and received rested on the incorrect premise that these were "quasi-
contractual" claims that were essentially claims in contract. From this it followed
that the statutory bar against enforcement of the ultra vires contracts of deposit
necessarily applied to the "quasi-contractual" claims as well.[54] This reasoning
was discredited, and the court's finding in relation to the actions for money had
and received was overruled, by a majority of the House of Lords in *Westdeutsche*.[55] They also held that the ultra vires depositors' equitable proprietary
claim should have failed, for reasons that are discussed elsewhere.[56]

For present purposes the key question arising out of *Westdeutsche* is why the   **34–34**
majority thought that allowing a personal claim in unjust enrichment would not
have stultified the policy underpinning the ultra vires doctrine. None of their
Lordships clearly addressed this question, but the best answer is that the purpose
of the ultra vires rule was to protect the members of building societies and their
intra vires creditors from a risk materialising which they had not voluntarily
undertaken, namely the risk that their money would be lost if the society spent
it on purposes other than those permitted by the statute. However, this consideration was beside the point in a case where the ultra vires transactions into which
the building society had entered entailed the *receipt* of money rather than its
expenditure, and it follows that allowing the ultra vires depositors' claims would
not have stultified the policy underpinning the ultra vires rule because this policy
was not engaged on the facts of the case.[57]

Similar issues arose in *Haugesund Kommune v Depfa A.C.S. Bank*.[58] Two   **34–35**
Norwegian municipalities entered swaps contracts with an Irish bank that contained English law and English jurisdiction clauses. The bank made upfront
payments and the municipalities agreed to make fixed quarterly repayments. The
municipalities invested the money unwisely and made a large loss when they sold
their investments. They refused to perform their contractual obligations to the
bank after the Norwegian Ministry of Justice declared that the swaps contracts
were ultra vires because they were contrary to statutory borrowing restrictions
placed on Norwegian municipalities. The Court of Appeal agreed that the
contracts were void because ultra vires, but held that the bank could recover its
upfront payments via a claim for unjust enrichment.

The municipalities argued that this would stultify the policy underlying the   **34–36**
legislation, which, they contended, was "to protect Kommunes, and hence their

---

[54] For further discussion of this aspect of the case, see paras 3–02—3–08.
[55] *Westdeutsche* [1996] A.C. 669 at 709–710 and 713–714 per Lord Browne-Wilkinson; at 718 per
Lord Slynn; and at 738 per Lord Lloyd. A different view was taken at 688–689 per Lord Goff; and
at 721 per Lord Woolf. For a careful analysis of their Lordships' reasoning, see *Haugesund* [2010]
EWCA Civ 579; [2011] 1 All E.R. 190 at [65]–[80] per Aikens L.J., who concluded at [87] that "the
majority of the House of Lords in [*Westdeutsche*] did depart from the decision in *Sinclair v Brougham*
that a lender under a borrowing contact that is void because *ultra vires* the borrower, cannot recover
the sum lent in a restitutionary claim at law."
[56] See paras 37–21—37–23.
[57] Cf. *Guinness Mahon & Co Ltd v Kensington & Chelsea RLBC* [1999] Q.B. 215 at 233 per Waller
L.J.: "protection of council taxpayers from loss is to be distinguished from securing a windfall for
them." For further discussion see paras 23–30—23–31.
[58] *Haugesund Kommune v Depfa A.C.S. Bank* [2010] EWCA Civ 579; [2011] 1 All E.R. 190.

citizens, from the consequences of borrowing money for prohibited purposes, because the value of the money borrowed may be lost and it would be future generations who [would] have to pay to regain the value." They also argued that "to fulfil this policy or purpose, the just and equitable obligation of the Kommunes must be to put them in the position they would have been if the loans had not been made at all, but taking account of what has happened since, viz. their losses on the subsequent investments, which were concluded in good faith."[59] These submissions were rejected by the Court of Appeal.

34–37   There were some problems with the way that the case was argued that makes it hard to extrapolate clear principles from the court's decision. One was that no expert evidence was presented, and no findings of fact were made by the trial judge, as to the policy that underpinned the relevant legislation and the question whether this would be stultified by allowing a restitutionary claim; the other was that this question of statutory policy was confusingly argued not as a discrete issue, but as an aspect of the question of whether the municipalities were entitled to a change of position defence. The court ultimately rejected the municipalities' policy argument because they had failed to discharge the burden of proof that lay on them to establish the facts that were needed to support it. However, Aikens L.J. made two findings that are relevant to the present discussion. First, he accepted the broad proposition that "the *ultra vires* doctrine is there to protect the public",[60] and he also accepted that "in English law a restitutionary claim for the return of money may be defeated on grounds of public policy where, on the correct construction of a statute or regulation, recovery in restitution would be contrary to the objective of the statute."[61] Secondly, however, he denied that allowing the bank's claim in unjust enrichment would have this effect, and held that if the municipalities "were entitled not to repay what Depfa had advanced to them then, subject to the defence of 'change of position', they would . . . have been enriched and, I would say, unjustly so."[62]

34–38   These cases, along with the many other cases on void interest swaps in which claims in unjust enrichment have been allowed, show that a public body with limited legal capacity has no defence of legal incapacity to a claim in respect of value received under an ultra vires contract. To hold otherwise would be to prioritise the interests of the public over those of the claimant, an unattractive conclusion that has also been rejected in the context of claims to recover money paid as tax that is not due.[63] It may be noted, however, that Aikens L.J. would apparently have allowed the municipalities a change of position defence, a finding that we consider would have been too generous to their taxpayers.[64]

---

[59] *Haugesund* [2010] EWCA Civ 579; [2011] 1 All E.R. 190 at [24].
[60] *Haugesund* [2010] EWCA Civ 579; [2011] 1 All E.R. 190 at [63].
[61] *Haugesund* [2010] EWCA Civ 579; [2011] 1 All E.R. 190 at [92].
[62] *Haugesund* [2010] EWCA Civ 579; [2011] 1 All E.R. 190 at [104].
[63] For discussion of which, see Ch.22.
[64] For the same reasons that we believe should prevent public bodies from relying on the change of position defence in response to claims to recover money paid as tax that is not due: see para.27–51.

CHAPTER 35

ILLEGALITY

1. INTRODUCTION

It is a long-standing rule of English law that a defendant who receives benefits **35–01** under an illegal contract can plead the illegality of the contract as a defence to a claim in unjust enrichment, provided that the parties were *in pari delicto*, i.e. provided that they were equally to blame for engaging in the transaction. The courts have construed "illegality" broadly in this context to take in a wide range of situations where the law invalidates contractual rights.[1] The rule has been applied in cases where the contract was prohibited by statute; where it was prohibited by common law; where entry into the contract was a criminal offence; and where the contract was merely unenforceable for immorality or some other reason of public policy.[2]

Some exceptions to the rule have evolved. First, recovery has been allowed **35–02** where the protection of persons in the claimant's position was the very reason for the rule that made the transaction illegal. In cases of this kind, the courts do not merely deny that the illegality of the contract is a defence to a claim in unjust enrichment: they treat it as a positive ground for recovery. This is discussed in Ch.25.[3]

Secondly, it has been thought desirable to encourage claimants to withdraw **35–03** from illegal bargains, and so they have been allowed a *locus poenitentiae*, or "space for repentance". In cases where the parties' illegal scheme has not been too far advanced, restitution has been awarded pursuant to a policy of incentivising participants in illegal schemes to abandon them. This is also discussed in Ch.25.[4]

---

[1] For an exception to this broad approach, see *Re London County Commercial Reinsurance Office* [1922] 2 Ch. 67 at 85, where P.O. Lawrence J. allowed restitution of premiums paid under a ppi policy that was void under the Marine Insurance Act 1906 s.4; however, it was conceded there that the insured actually had an insurable interest in the subject matter of the policies and that "there was no fraud or illegality" on the part of the insured.

[2] Cf. *Wetherell v Jones* (1823) 3 B. & Ad. 221 at 225–226; 110 E.R. 82 at 85 per Lord Tenterden C.J.: "Where a contract which the plaintiff seeks to enforce is expressly, or by implication, forbidden by statute or common law, no court will lend its assistance to give it effect . . . because either the consideration for the promise or the act to be done was illegal as being against the express provisions of the law, or contrary to justice, morality and sound policy." See too *Gibbs Mew Plc v Gemmell* [1999] 1 E.G. 117 at 124 per Peter Gibson L.J.: "for an agreement to be illegal it need not be in breach of the criminal law". The contract in the latter case was held to be illegal because it was contrary to art.81 of the EC Treaty; the same is probably also true of contracts that are contrary to art.2. For consideration of the illegality defence as a response to claims in unjust enrichment to recover benefits transferred under such contracts, see A. Jones, *Restitution and European Community Law* (London: LLP, 2000), pp.170–183.

[3] See paras 25–04—25–13.

[4] See paras 25–14—25–26.

35–04   Thirdly, a contract may be frustrated by supervening illegality,[5] and in this case the best view is that recovery of benefits is possible under the Law Reform (Frustrated Contracts) Act 1943. This is discussed in Ch.15.[6]

35–05   Fourthly, illegality will not debar a claim where the claimant can establish that he has a proprietary interest in assets held by the defendant without relying on evidence of his illegal conduct. Some cases applying this principle concern tort claims founded on the claimant's subsisting legal title to an asset transferred to the defendant under an illegal contract; the reasoning in these cases suggests that the principle should also apply where a common law claim in unjust enrichment is made to recover the value of an unauthorised traceable substitute for the claimant's property.[7]

35–06   The principle has also been invoked to hold that illegality will not debar a claimant from seeking a declaration that the traceable proceeds of his money are held on a resulting trust for him, although the money was advanced as part of an illegal scheme.[8] This extension of the principle to equitable proprietary rights has the potential to affect some claims in unjust enrichment, but the extent to which it does so is controversial because it depends on whether various trusts are imposed as a response to unjust enrichment.[9] On the assumption that the principle applies to some common law and equitable claims in unjust enrichment, however, it is discussed here in this chapter.

35–07   Discussion in this chapter is divided as follows. Part 2 examines the general rule allowing an illegality defence where the parties are not *in pari delicto*. Part 3 discusses the rule which allows claimants to bring proceedings founded on their proprietary rights despite their participation in an illegal transaction. Finally Part 4 considers the principles that underlie this body of law and the future directions in which it might develop.

35–08   There is an overlap between the cases discussed in Part 2, and the cases that are discussed in Ch.2, where it is explained that a statute can constitute a justifying ground for a defendant's enrichment in cases where the policy underlying the statute would be stultified if a claim in unjust enrichment were allowed to proceed.[10] However, the cases discussed in this chapter do not all concern contracts that have been rendered illegal by statute: some concern contracts that the courts hold to be illegal at common law.

---

[5] As in *Fibrosa Spolka Akcyjna v Fairbairn Lawson Combe Barbour Ltd* [1943] A.C. 32.

[6] See para.15–11. But note para.15–10: although the 1943 Act governs situations where the common law of unjust enrichment would otherwise apply, the rules laid down in the statute are not themselves part of the law of unjust enrichment.

[7] For discussion of such claims, see paras 8–20——8–29.

[8] *Tinsley v Milligan* [1994] 1 A.C. 340, discussed at paras 35–29——35–33.

[9] In *Chase Manhattan Bank NA v Israel-British Bank (London) Ltd* [1981] Ch. 105, money paid by mistake was found to be held on constructive trust for the payor, but it may be that this trust should have been seen as a resulting trust, and it is disputed whether the trust arose immediately or from the time when the defendant knew of the claimant's mistake; see paras 37–21——37–22, 38–33, fn.95 and 38–34, fn.100. In *Westdeutsche Landesbank Girozentrale v Islington LBC* [1996] A.C. 669 the House of Lords denied that resulting trusts are imposed in response to the trustee's unjust enrichment, but there are reasons for thinking that resulting trusts should be understood in this way: see paras 38–31——38–33. In *Foskett v McKeown* [2001] 1 A.C. 102 the House of Lords held that trust beneficiaries have equitable proprietary rights to unauthorised substitutes for trust assets, but denied that these rights were generated by the law of unjust enrichment; however, there are reasons for thinking that such rights should be understood in this way; see paras 8–83——8 93.

[10] See para.2.21 and following. Cf. *Haugesund Kommune v Depfa ACS Bank* [2010] EWCA Civ 579; [2011] 1 All E.R. 190 at [150] per Etherton L.J., noting that the statutes on which such reasoning has

2. THE GENERAL RULE: ILLEGALITY AS A DEFENCE TO CLAIMS IN UNJUST ENRICHMENT

After some uncertainty,[11] it was settled towards the end of the 18th century that **35–09** money paid under an illegal contract could not generally be recovered if the parties were equally blameworthy. In modern terms, illegality was therefore held to be a defence to a claim in unjust enrichment as well as to a contractual claim in these circumstances. This rule became epitomised in the oft-quoted maxims, *in pari delicto potior est conditio defendentis* ("where the parties are equally at fault the defendant's position is the stronger"); *nemo suam turpitudinem allegans audiendus est* ("no one shall be heard whose case is based upon an illegal act") and *ex turpi causa non oritur actio* ("no action may be founded on illegal conduct"). The classical statement was Lord Mansfield's in *Holman v Johnson*[12]:

> "The objection, that the contract is immoral or illegal as between plaintiff and defendant, sounds at all times very ill in the mouth of the defendant. It is not for his sake, however, that the objection is ever allowed; but it is founded in general principles of policy, which the defendant has the advantage of, contrary to the real justice, as between him and the plaintiff, by accident, if I may say so. The principle of public policy is this: *ex dolo malo non oritur actio*. No court will lend its aid to a man who founds his cause of action upon an immoral or an illegal act. If from the plaintiff's own stating or otherwise, the cause of action appears to arise *ex turpi causa*, or the transgression of a positive law of this country, there the court says he has no right to be assisted. It is upon that ground the court goes; not for the sake of the defendant, but because they will not lend their aid to such a plaintiff. So if the plaintiff and defendant were to change sides, and the defendant was to bring his action against the plaintiff, the latter would not then have the advantage of it; for where both are equally in fault, *potior est conditio defendentis*."

Defendants have found it easiest to bring themselves within these principles in **35–10** cases where the ground of recovery invoked by the claimant has been failure of basis, as it is often harder to demonstrate that the parties were *in pari delicto*

---

been founded "are best viewed . . . as examples of United Kingdom legislation which, on its correct interpretation, implicitly excludes any civil restitutionary remedy whether for unjust enrichment or otherwise."

[11] In *Tomkins v Bernet* (1693) 1 Salk. 22; 91 E.R. 21, it was held that *indebitatus assumpsit* would not lie to recover money paid on a usurious bond. There are also certain observations which suggest that bribes could not be recovered by this action; but in *Wilkinson v Kitchin* (1697) 1 Ld. Ray. 89; 91 E.R. 956, Lord Holt C.J. apparently held that money given by a principal to his agent to spend on bribes and so spent by the agent could, nevertheless, be recovered from him by the principal. For explanations of this decision, see W.S. Holdsworth, *A History of English Law*, vol.8 (London: Methuen, 1925), p.94 and R.M. Jackson, *The History of Quasi-Contract in English Law* (Cambridge: CUP, 1936), p.89, fnn.3 and 4. By the late 18th century the reasoning of *Wilkinson v Kitchin* was disregarded; see *Pickard v Bonner* (1794) Peake 289; 170 E.R. 159; and cf. *Anon* (1695) Comb. 341; 90 E.R. 516; and *Bosanquet v Dashwood* (1734) Talbot 38.

[12] *Holman v Johnson* (1775) 1 Cowp. 341 at 343; 98 E.R. 1120 at 1122; see also *Collins v Blantern* (1767) 2 Wils. K.B. 347 at 350; 95 E.R. 850 at 853 per Lord Wilmot C.J. Lord Mansfield's first reference to the maxim was in *Smith v Bromley* (1760) 2 Doug. 696n at 697; 99 E.R. 441n at 443. See also his other statements of the law in *Clarke v Shee* (1774) 1 Cowp. 197 at 200; 98 E.R. 1041 at 1043–1044; *Browning v Morris* (1778) 2 Cowp. 790 at 792; 98 E.R. 1364 at 1365–1366; *Lowry v Bourdieu* (1780) 2 Doug. 468 at 470 and 472; 99 E.R. 299 at 301 and 302.

where the claimant relies on a ground such as mistake or duress that frequently entails an imbalance between the parties' knowledge and/or the probity of their behaviour.

35–11　　A claim founded on failure of basis that was successfully defended on the ground of illegality is *Berg v Sadler and Moore*.[13] The plaintiff had formerly been a member of the Tobacco Trade Association but had been put on the Stop List and so could not get supplies of cigarettes from any member of the Association. A member, Reece, agreed, for a consideration, to obtain cigarettes for the plaintiff from the defendants. Reece ordered the cigarettes and an assistant of the plaintiff, accompanied by a representative of Reece, went to fetch them. The plaintiff's assistant paid for them, but the defendants became suspicious and refused either to deliver the cigarettes or to return the money. The plaintiff brought proceedings to recover the money, and the Court of Appeal held that the action failed because the plaintiff had attempted to obtain goods by false pretences.

35–12　　Another case of this kind is *Westlaw Services Ltd v Boddy*.[14] The claimants, who were not qualified solicitors, helped the defendant solicitor to carry out criminal litigation work in the Crown Court. The defendant agreed to pay them a share of the fees that he received from the Legal Services Commission, but in breach of contract he failed to pay them. The parties' contract was an illegal agreement to share fees, contrary to the Solicitors' Practice Rules 1990 r.7(1), and so their action for breach of contract failed. On appeal, they applied to amend their pleadings to add a claim in unjust enrichment for the reasonable value of their work. This application was denied, among other reasons, because allowing such a claim would have contradicted the policy of the rule invalidating fee-sharing agreements between solicitors and persons who are not legally qualified, namely that it is not in the public interest for legal work to be done by the latter group.[15]

35–13　　Where the claimant has paid money to the defendant under an illegal contract, but the illegality is unknown to the claimant because of some mistake, he can recover his money in an action for unjust enrichment, if he has not got what he bargained for. Thus, in *Oom v Bruce*,[16] the plaintiff as agent for a Russian subject abroad, purported to insure with the defendant goods on board the ship *Elbe*, at and from St Petersburg to London, and paid a premium under the policy. Unknown to the plaintiff, Russia had commenced hostilities against Great Britain shortly before the insurance was effected, and the policy was therefore illegal. The Court of King's Bench held that the plaintiff was entitled to recover the

---

[13] *Berg v Sadler and Moore* [1937] 2 K.B. 158. Cf. *Boissevain v Weil* [1950] A.C. 327, discussed at para.2.22.

[14] *Westlaw Services Ltd v Boddy* [2010] EWCA Civ 929; [2011] P.N.L.R. 4. Cf. *Awwad v Geraghty & Co* [2001] Q.B. 570; *Langsam v Beachcroft LLP* [2011] EWHC 1451 (Ch) at [252]–[253] per Roth J.

[15] *Westlaw* [2010] EWCA Civ 929; [2011] P.N.L.R. 4 at [61] per Etherton L.J., distinguishing *Mohamed v Alaga & Co* [2000] 1 W.L.R. 1815 (where a claim in unjust enrichment was allowed for the reasonable value of interpreting and translating work); see para.2.24 for discussion.

[16] *Oom v Bruce* (1810) 12 East 224; 104 E.R. 87; followed in *Hentig v Staniforth* (1816) 5 M. & S. 122; 105 E.R. 996. See also *Siffken v Allnutt* (1813) 1 M. & S. 39; 105 E.R. 15; *Branigan v Saba* [1924] N.Z.L.R. 481; and *Adler v C.J. Searles & Co*, 86 Miss. 406 (1905).

premium. Lord Ellenborough held that premiums paid on an illegal policy cannot be recovered[17]:

> "if the party making the insurance knows it to be illegal at the time: but here the plaintiffs had no knowledge of the commencement of hostilities by Russia, when they effected this insurance; and, therefore, no fault is imputable to them for entering into the contract; and there is no reason why they should not recover back the premiums which they have paid for an insurance from which, without any fault imputable to themselves, they could never have derived any benefit."

A similar principle explains *Soods Solicitors v Dormer.*[18] An employee of the   **35–14** claimant firm lent money taken from the firm's client account to the defendant without the firm's knowledge or authority. The defendant failed to repay the loan and when the firm brought an action in unjust enrichment the defendant argued that the employee's knowledge of the fraud should be imputed to the firm, with the result that the claim should be debarred for illegality. This argument was rejected, and the claim allowed, by Nicola Davies J., who held that the employee had intended to take a personal benefit from the transaction, with the result that an imputation of knowledge on the firm's part would be negatived by the rule in *Re Hampshire Land Co (No.2),*[19] as explained in *Stone Rolls Ltd (In Liquidation) v Moore Stephens (A Firm).*[20]

Where parties enter into a contract which can be performed in a legal manner,   **35–15** which the defendant without the claimant's knowledge elects to perform illegally, it has been said that the defendant cannot plead its illegality.[21] But, on discovering the illegal performance, the claimant is bound to bring the contract to an end[22] in which event he can recover the reasonable value of services rendered in the performance of his side of the bargain. So, in *Clay v Yates,*[23] the plaintiff, a printer, agreed to print 500 copies of the defendant's treatise, to which a dedication was to be attached:

> "He had been furnished with the treatise without the dedication. The dedication was afterwards sent, but he had no opportunity of reading it until after it was printed; he then discovered that it was libellous, and refused to permit the defendant to have it."[24]

The Court of Exchequer held that the plaintiff was justified in refusing to complete the printing of the dedication and was entitled to recover for the printing of the treatise without the dedication.

There are other cases where there is "introduced the element of fraud, duress,   **35–16** or oppression or difference in the position of the parties which created a fiduciary

---

[17] *Oom* 12 East at 226; 104 E.R. at 89.
[18] *Soods Solicitors v Dormer* [2010] EWHC 502 (QB).
[19] *Re Hampshire Land Co (No.2)* [1896] 2 Ch. 743.
[20] *Stone Rolls Ltd (In Liquidation) v Moore Stephens (A Firm)* [2009] UKHL 39; [2009] 1 A.C. 1391.
[21] *Re Mahmoud and Ispahani* [1921] 2 K.B. 716 at 729 per Scrutton L.J.; *Chai Sau Yin v Liew Kwee Sam* [1962] A.C. 304 at 311 per Lord Hodson; *Dromorne Linen Co Ltd v Ward* [1963] N.Z.L.R. 614.
[22] *Cowan v Milbourn* (1867) L.R. 2 Exch. 230.
[23] *Clay v Yates* (1856) 1 H. & N. 73; 156 E.R. 1123; cf. *Apthorp v Neville & Co* (1907) 23 T.L.R. 575.
[24] *Clay* 1 H. & N. at 78–79; 156 E.R. 1126 per Lord Pollock C.B.

relationship to the plaintiff so as to make it inequitable for the defendants to insist on the bargain that they have made with the plaintiff."[25] In such cases, in spite of the illegality, the claimant can recover money paid under the transaction.

35–17   In *Hughes v Liverpool Victoria Friendly Society*,[26] the plaintiff took out five policies of insurance on lives in which she had no insurable interest. She was induced to do so by the defendant's agent, who fraudulently misrepresented that, by paying the arrears due on the premiums and keeping them up, "everything would be all right". The plaintiff later discovered that the policies were illegal and void under the Assurance Companies Act 1909 ss.23 and 36(3). She brought an action against the insurance company to recover the premiums, and the Court of Appeal held that, although the contract was illegal, the plaintiff was not *in pari delicto* with the defendants because she had been induced to enter into the contract by fraudulent misrepresentation.

35–18   Again, in *Parkinson v College of Ambulance Ltd*,[27] the secretary of the defendant charity fraudulently misrepresented to the plaintiff that the charity could and would arrange for him to receive a knighthood if he made a donation to the charity's funds. The plaintiff made a donation but did not receive a knighthood, and so he brought an action to recover the money. The action failed. Lush J. held that:

> "[A] contract to guarantee or undertake that an honour will be conferred by the Sovereign if a certain contribution is made to a public charity ... is against public policy, and, therefore, an unlawful contract to make."[28]

The judge declined to hold that "in every case where a contract is against public policy, where one of the parties to it is defrauded by the other, he is prevented from recovering", because the parties might not be *in pari delicto* in a case where one party to a contract which was not improper in itself was unaware that it was illegal and was defrauded.[29] In this case, however, "the plaintiff knew that he was entering into an illegal and improper contract", and it was "no excuse to say that [the secretary] was more blameworthy than he."[30]

35–19   Examples of oppression are few. A well-known case is where a creditor in a composition exacts from the debtor an extra payment as a condition of his acceptance of the composition. In *Smith v Cuff*,[31] a debtor was forced in this way to give one of his creditors promissory notes for the remainder of his debt; the

---

[25] *Harse v Pearl Life Assurance Co* [1904] 1 K.B. 558 at 563 per Lord Collins M.R. See *Drummond v Deey* (1794) 1 Esp. 151 at 153–154; 170 E.R. 310 at 310 per Lord Kenyon C.J.; *Atkinson v Denby* (1862) 7 H. & N. 934; 158 E.R. 749; *Kiriri Cotton Co Ltd v Dewani* [1960] A.C. 190 at 205.

[26] *Hughes v Liverpool Victoria Friendly Society* [1916] 2 K.B. 482; see also *British Workman's and General Assurance Co Ltd v Cunliffe* (1902) 18 T.L.R. 425 at 502; *Refuge Assurance Co Ltd v Kettlewell* [1909] A.C. 243; *Byrne v Rudd* [1920] 2 I.R. 12.

[27] *Parkinson v College of Ambulance Ltd* [1925] 2 K.B. 1. See too *Morgan v Ashcroft* [1938] 1 K.B. 49.

[28] *Parkinson* [1925] 2 K.B. 1 at 13.

[29] *Parkinson* [1925] 2 K.B. 1 at 14–15, citing *Taylor v Chester* (1869) L.R. 4 Q.B. 309.

[30] *Parkinson* [1925] 2 K.B. 1 at 15–16.

[31] *Smith v Cuff* (1817) 6 M. & S. 160; 105 E.R. 1203. The decision was followed in *Alsager v Spalding* (1838) 4 Bing. (N.C.) 407; 132 E.R. 844; *Bradshaw v Bradshaw* (1841) 9 M. & W. 29; 152 E.R. 13; *Horton v Riley* (1843) 11 M. & W. 492 at 493–494; 152 E.R. 899 at 901 per Parke B.; *Atkinson v Denby* (1861) 6 H. & N. 778; 158 E.R. 321; affirmed (1862) 7 H. & N. 934; 158 E.R. 749.

creditor negotiated them and the holder of one of them then enforced payment by the debtor. It was held that the debtor could recover the excess of the amount so paid over the amount due under the composition from the creditor in an action for money paid. Lord Ellenborough said[32]:

> "This is not a case of *par delictum*: it is oppression on one side, and submission on the other: it never can be predicated as *par delictum*, when one holds the rod, and the other bows to it. There was an inequality of situation between these parties: one was creditor, the other debtor, who was driven to comply with the terms which the former chose to enforce."

But where a debtor gave the oppressing creditor a bill of exchange and, after the creditor had signed the composition deed, paid him the amount due on the bill, the Court of King's Bench held[33] that he could not recover the money so paid. Although the bill of exchange had been extracted under oppression, the debtor had a good defence to an action by the creditor on the bill. The payment was not made under oppression; it was voluntary and, therefore, irrecoverable.[34] Since, therefore, the payment itself, as well as the making of the illegal contract, must have been under constraint, cases of recovery are necessarily few.[35]

Equitable relief has been granted in cases where the claimant has been induced   **35–20**
by pressure, which may be extraneous,[36] to enter into the illegal transaction. In *Williams v Bayley*,[37] a son gave bankers certain promissory notes on which he had forged his father's endorsement. On the discovery of the forgery a meeting was held at which the bankers made reasonably clear to the father that, if some settlement was not reached, they would prosecute the son. Under this pressure the father agreed in writing that, in consideration for the return of the promissory notes, he would pay the bankers the amount advanced by them on the notes and deposit with them the title deeds of his colliery as security for this payment. The House of Lords held that the contract was made under duress and was illegal as an agreement to stifle a prosecution. The House affirmed the decree of Lord Stuart V.C. that the agreement was invalid and must be cancelled and that the bankers must deliver up the promissory notes to the father.

Where a contract is evidently illegal, made in order to deceive a third party, the   **35–21**
court will refuse to enforce it, regardless of whether any allegation of illegality

---

[32] *Smith* 6 M. & S. at 165; 105 E.R. at 1206.

[33] In *Wilson v Ray* (1839) 10 Ad. & El. 82; 113 E.R. 32. See also *Gibson v Bruce* (1843) 5 Man. & G. 399; 134 E.R. 619 and *Viner v Hawkins* (1853) 9 Ex. 266; 156 E.R. 114, doubting part of the decision in *Ex p. Hart* (1845) 2 D. & L. 778; cf. *Re Lenzberg's Policy* (1877) 7 Ch.D. 650. Presumably *Turner v Hoole* (1822) Dowl. & Ry. 27; 171 E.R. 905 is no longer a good authority.

[34] Semble, in *Smith* (1817) 6 M. & S. 160; 105 E.R. 1203 it was not suggested that the plaintiff's payment of the note to the holder was voluntary.

[35] *Miller v Aris* (1800) 3 Esp. 231; 170 E.R. 598; *Townson v Wilson* (1808) 1 Camp. 396; 170 E.R. 997.

[36] Cf. *Kiriri Cotton* [1960] A.C. 190 at 205 per Lord Denning.

[37] *Williams v Bayley* (1866) L.R. 1 H.L. 200. Cf. *Ex p. Wolverhampton Banking Co* (1884) 14 Q.B.D. 32; *Jones v Merionethshire Permanent Building Society* [1892] 1 Ch. 173; *McClatchie v Haslam* (1891) 65 L.T. 691. See also *Bosanquett v Dashwood* (1734) Talb. 38; 25 E.R. 648; *Henkle v Royal Exchange Assurance* (1749) 1 Ves. Sen. 317; 27 E.R. 1055; *Morris v M'Cullock* (1763) Amb. 432; 27 E.R. 289; *Re Lenzberg's Policy* (1877) 7 Ch. D. 650; *Davies v London & Provincial Marine Insurance Co* (1878) 8 Ch. D. 469; *Whitmore v Farley* (1882) 29 W.R. 825.

had been made.[38] Similarly, if illegality is not immediately apparent but emerges from other cogent evidence then the contract will not be enforced. The courts have been prepared to go behind documents to discover if a transaction is tainted by illegality. Hence a loan is deemed to be illegal if it is made to discharge an obligation which had arisen under a transaction that was known to the lender to be illegal.[39]

35–22   A contract may be legal in form but may be performed in an unlawful manner. Then the court must inquire whether the "mode of performance adopted by the party performing the contract was rendered illegal by the statute, even though the contract itself could be performed in a perfectly lawful manner?"[40] "It is important to bear in mind that the law refuses to enforce not only contracts which are in themselves illegal, but also contracts which are *ex facie* legal but which, to the knowledge of the parties, have an illegal purpose or are intended to be performed in an illegal manner."[41] So, for example "if a builder or a garage or other supplier agrees to provide a false estimate for work in order to enable its customer to obtain payment from his insurers to which he is not entitled, then it will be unable to recover payment from its customer and the customer will be unable to claim on his insurers even if he has paid for the work."[42]

35–23   "The question whether a statute impliedly prohibits the contract in question is one of public policy."[43] A distinction was at one time drawn between statutes which impose penalties to protect the Revenue and those which impose penalties for the protection of the public[44]; in the former case a claimant could recover his payment, in the latter he could not. But this distinction is not now regarded as conclusive of the question whether the manner in which the contract was performed makes it a contract prohibited by the statute.[45] "The correct general approach . . . [is to] look at the relevant statute or series of statutes *as a whole* and then assess whether the legislature intended to preclude the plaintiff recovering in the action, even when an essential act is under consideration."[46]

---

[38] *Birkett v Acorn Business Machines Ltd* [1999] 2 All E.R. (Comm.) 429; following *Re Mahmoud and Ispahani* [1921] 2 K.B. 716; *Edler v Auerback* [1950] 1 K.B. 359; and *Bank of India v Trans Continental Commodity Merchants Ltd (No.2)* [1983] 2 Lloyd's Rep. 298.

[39] *Cannan v Bryce* (1819) 3 B. & Ald. 179; 106 E.R. 628; *Fisher v Bridges* (1854) 3 El. & Bl. 642; 118 E.R. 1283; *Spector v Ageda* [1972] Ch. 30.

[40] *Shaw v Groom* [1970] 2 Q.B. 504 at 516 per Harman L.J.; citing Atkin L.J. in *Anderson Ltd v Daniel* [1924] 1 Q.B. 138 at 150. Cf. *Aspinall's Club Ltd v Al-Zayat* [2008] EWHC 2101 at [65], where Teare J. held that if the claimant had provided the defendant with unlawful credit for enabling him to take part in gambling (itself a legal activity), then the gambling would not thereby have been rendered illegal.

[41] *Taylor v Bhail* (1995) 50 Con L.R. 70 at 76–77 per Millett L.J.; distinguished in *A.L. Barnes Ltd v Time Talk (UK) Ltd* [2003] EWCA Civ 402; [2003] B.L.R. 331, where the contract did not have an illegal purpose and the parties did not intend to perform it in an illegal manner; hence the claimant recovered the reasonable value of work done for the defendant although one of the claimant's directors was in breach of his fiduciary duty by enabling the project manager to be paid twice for the same work.

[42] *Taylor* (1995) 50 Con.L.R. 70 at 78 per Millett L.J.

[43] *Shaw* [1970] 2 Q.B. 504 at 516 per Harman L.J.

[44] *Anderson Ltd v Daniel* [1924] 1 Q.B. 138; *Shaw* [1970] 2 Q.B. 504 at 520 per Sachs L.J.

[45] *St John Shipping Corp v Joseph Rank Ltd* [1957] 1 Q.B. 267 at 283–284 per Devlin J.; cf. *Solomons v Gertzenstein Ltd* [1954] 2 Q.B. 243 at 266 per Romer L.J.

[46] *Shaw v Groom* [1970] 2 Q.B. 504 at 523 per Sachs L.J.

So, in *St John Shipping Corp v Joseph Rank Ltd*,[47] where the shipowner sought   **35–24**
to recover freight, Devlin J. rejected the charterer's defence that the ship was
overloaded and had incurred a penalty under the Merchant Shipping (Safety and
Load Lines Convention) Act 1932; in *Shaw v Groom*[48] the Court of Appeal held
that a landlord's failure to provide his tenant with a proper rent book, as required
by the Landlord and Tenant Act 1962, did not disentitle the landlord from suing
for the rent of the premises; and in *Hughes v Asset Managers Plc*,[49] where an
investor sought to recover his investment losses on the ground that the defendant's representative, who had negotiated the agreement with the investor, did
not hold a licence as required by the Prevention of Fraud (Investments) Act 1958
s.1(1)(b), the Court of Appeal held that the agreement was valid and that the
public interest under the statute was satisfied by the imposition of criminal
sanctions. In all of these cases the illegality in the performance of the contract did
not transform the contract into an illegal contract. "The true question is, has the
statute impliedly forbidden the contract?"[50] The object of each statute was to
impose a fine, but the legislature did not intend to impose on the shipowner, the
landlord and the asset management company, respectively, any forfeiture beyond
the prescribed penalty; the relevant statute had not forbidden the particular
contract.[51]

Not infrequently a statute will declare illegal and void contracts which do not   **35–25**
comply with its provisions. Such a prohibited contract will not be enforced by the
courts; and it is immaterial that the contract is express or implied.[52] But it is not
always easy to determine whether there is an express prohibition of a particular
contract.[53] For example, a contract may be held to be illegal even though the
particular statute contains no reference to any contract.[54] Conversely, a court may
conclude, as a matter of construction, that the statute simply imposed a penalty
upon a particular individual and did not prohibit the contract if made with a party
"who is innocent of the offence created by the statute".[55]

Phoenix General Insurance Co of Greece SA v Halvanon Insurance Co Ltd[56]   **35–26**
concerned insurance contracts that were entered in breach of the Insurance
Companies Act 1982 s.2, which formerly provided that it was an offence to carry

---

[47] *St John Shipping Corp v Joseph Rank Ltd* [1957] 1 Q.B. 267.
[48] *Shaw* [1970] 2 Q.B. 504.
[49] *Hughes v Asset Managers Plc* [1995] 3 All E.R. 669.
[50] *Shaw* [1970] 2 Q.B. 504 at 516 per Harman L.J.
[51] Cf. *Barrett v Smith* [1965] N.Z.L.R. 460, and contrast *Ashmore, Benson, Pease & Co Ltd v Dawson Ltd* [1973] 1 W.L.R. 828.
[52] *Archbolds (Freightage) Ltd v S. Spanglett Ltd (Randall, third party)* [1961] 1 Q.B. 374 at 388 per Devlin J.
[53] See, e.g. *Bloxsome v Williams* (1824) 3 B. & C. 232; 107 E.R. 720 (statutory prohibition on Sunday trading), doubted by Parker J. in *Bedford Insurance Co Ltd v Instituto de Resseguros do Brasil* [1985] Q.B. 966 at 984.
[54] *Cope v Rowlands* (1836) 2 M. & W. 149; 150 E.R. 707; *Cornelius v Phillips* [1918] A.C. 199.
[55] *Re Mahmoud* [1921] 2 K.B. 716 at 731 per Atkin L.J. (where the contract was, however, prohibited).
[56] *Phoenix General Insurance Co of Greece SA v Halvanon Insurance Co Ltd* [1988] Q.B. 216. Cf. *Bedford Insurance* [1985] Q.B. 966; *Fuji Finance Inc v Aetna Life Insurance Co Ltd* [1997] Ch. 173.

on certain insurance business without authorisation.[57] The Court of Appeal held that such contracts were illegal and unenforceable, with the consequence that no insured could enforce, either directly or indirectly, any contract of insurance or reinsurance. Kerr L.J. regretfully recognised that this would cause innocent members of the public to suffer "grave inconvenience and injury", and leave them with "the doubtful remedy of seeking to recover [their] premium[s] as money had and received".[58]

35–27 Kerr L.J. formulated the following presumptions of construction[59]:

(1) "Where a statute prohibits both parties from concluding or performing a contract when both or either of them have no authority to do so, the contract is impliedly prohibited."

(2) If the statute imposes a penalty if one party enters into a contract or prohibits him from entering such a contract without authority, whether the contract is illegal and void "depends on considerations of public policy in the light of the mischief which the statute is designed to prevent, its language, scope and purpose, the consequences for the innocent party, and any other relevant considerations".

These presumptions are necessary if the statute is silent as to the effects of the illegality. The task of the court, to determine what is the mischief which the statute is designed to present, is then a particularly difficult one. Unless the language of the statute is compelling, as it was in *Phoenix*, an important consideration should be whether the "avoidance of the contract would cause grave inconvenience and injury to innocent members of the public without furthering the object of the statute".[60]

3. An Exception: Claims Founded on Proprietary Rights

35–28 As a general rule, common law title to property will pass to the recipient when it is transferred under an illegal contract, although the transfer was made for an illegal purpose.[61] On occasions, however, it may not, and in these circumstances

---

[57] The Financial Services and Markets Act 2000 now provides that an agreement made by a person who is not an authorised person is unenforceable against the other party to the agreement: s.26(1). The other party can recover any money paid or property transferred, together with compensation for any loss sustained as a result of having parted with money or property: ss.26(2) and 27(2). He must however repay any money or property transferred by the person who is not an authorised person if he elects not to perform the agreement: s.28(7). However, if the court considers it just and equitable it may allow the agreement to be enforced or money paid and property transferred to be retained: see s.28(5) and (6), which set out the factors which the court may take into account.

[58] *Phoenix* [1988] Q.B. 216 at 273.

[59] *Phoenix* [1988] Q.B. 216 at 273.

[60] *Archbold (Freightage)* [1961] 1 Q.B. 374 at 390 per Devlin L.J. In *Fuji* [1997] Ch. 173, the Court of Appeal distinguished *Phoenix* and held that, although the insurance company was prohibited from issuing the particular policy by the Insurance Companies Act 1982 s.16, the contract was not unenforceable by the insured.

[61] *Sajan Singh v Sadara Ali* [1960] A.C. 167 at 176–177 per Lord Denning; *Tribe v Tribe* [1995] 4 All E.R. 236 at 251 per Millett L.J. cf. *Belvoir Finance Co Ltd v Singleton* [1971] 1 Q.B. 210 (where title passed even though goods had not been delivered to the buyer).

a claimant may rely on his subsisting legal title to make out a claim against the defendant despite the illegality of the parties' contract.[62] Some cases hold that a claimant can bring an action in tort based on the defendant's fraudulent conduct,[63] and others that he can bring an action in tort based on the defendant's conversion of his goods.[64] In *Tinsley v Milligan*, Lord Browne-Wilkinson summarised the position at law in this way[65]:

> "Neither at law nor in equity will the court enforce an illegal contract which has been partially, but not fully performed. However, it does not follow that all acts done under a partially performed contract are of no effect. In particular it is now clearly established that at law (as opposed to in equity), property in goods or land can pass under, or pursuant to, such a contract. If so, the rights of the owner of the legal title thereby acquired will be enforced, provided that the claimant can establish such title without pleading or leading evidence of the illegality. It is said that the property lies where it falls, even though legal title to the property was acquired as a result of the property passing under the legal contract itself."

Lord Browne-Wilkinson also emphasised that "it is irrelevant that the illegality of the underling agreement was either pleaded or emerged in evidence: if the plaintiff has acquired legal title under the illegal contract that is enough".[66]

Tinsley itself concerned an equitable claim. Miss Tinsley and Miss Milligan   **35–29**
bought a house. They took out a mortgage and the balance of the purchase money was provided by them in equal shares. But the title to the house was transferred into the sole name of Miss Tinsley, so that Miss Milligan could misrepresent to the DHSS that she had no stake in the house or in the business which the parties ran from it. They quarrelled and Miss Tinsley moved out. She then gave Miss Milligan notice to quit and claimed possession of, and asserted ownership to, the house. Miss Milligan counterclaimed for a declaration that the property was held by Miss Tinsley upon resulting trust for the pair of them in equal shares, and for an order for sale. A majority of the House of Lords granted the declaration.

According to the majority of their Lordships, the primary rule is that equity   **35–30**
will never aid a claimant who has transferred property to another for an illegal purpose,[67] but there are exceptions to this rule,[68] and in Lord Browne-

---

[62] In the previous edition of this work, it was suggested that a version of this principle also explains cases where a claimant with possessory title to goods acquired through illegal means has successfully sued the police for conversion, where they seized the goods and retained them without legal authority: G. Jones, *Goff & Jones: The Law of Restitution*, 7th edn (London: Sweet & Maxwell, 2006), para.24.12, discussing *Webb v Chief Constable of Merseyside Police* [2000] Q.B. 427 and *Costello v Chief Constable of Derbyshire Constabulary* [2001] EWCA Civ 381; [2001] 1 W.L.R. 1437. However, there was no illegal contract between the claimants and the police, and no rule invalidating the transfer of possession from the claimants to the police which might have been contradicted by the claimants' proceedings.

[63] *Saunders v Edwards* [1987] 1 W.L.R. 116, explained in *Tinsley v Milligan* [1992] Ch. 310 at 332 per Ralph Gibson L.J.

[64] *Bowmakers Ltd v Barnet Instruments Ltd* [1945] K.B. 65 at 69–70 per Du Parcq L.J. For other decisions where the claimant relied on his legal title, see: *Feret v Hill* (1854) 15 C.B. 207; 139 E.R. 400; *Taylor v Chester* (1869) L.R. Q.B. 309; *Alexander v Rayson* [1936] 1 Q.B. 169; *Amar Singh v Kulubya* [1964] A.C. 142.

[65] *Tinsley v Milligan* [1994] 1 A.C. 340 at 369.

[66] *Tinsley* [1994] 1 A.C. 340 at 370.

[67] See e.g. *Holman v Johnson* (1775) 1 Cowp. 341 at 343; 98 E.R. 1120 at 1122 per Lord Mansfield; quoted in the text to para.35–09, fn.12.

[68] e.g. *Haigh v Kaye* (1872) L.R. 7 Ch. 469; *Ayers v Jenkins* (1873) L.R. 16 Eq. 275.

Wilkinson's view "if the law is that a party is entitled to enforce a property right acquired under an illegal transaction, . . . the same rule ought to apply to any property right so acquired, whether such right is legal or equitable."[69] Miss Milligan's claim was based on evidence that she had contributed to the purchase price of the house, that she had received nothing from Miss Tinsley in exchange for her contribution, and that legal title to the house was vested in Miss Tinsley alone. Miss Milligan did not need to rely on evidence of her illegal behaviour in order to make out her claim, and the illegality emerged only because Miss Tinsley sought to raise it. Hence the claim should be allowed.

35–31   There are several problems with the majority's reasoning in this case. First, their analysis depended on common law cases that permitted claims in tort which were founded on the claimant's *subsisting* legal title, the claimant's ownership of which pre-dated the parties' illegal dealings and which needed no special justification.[70] Yet Miss Milligan's claim was not like this: it was a claim that she had acquired a *new* equitable title under a resulting trust as a consequence of her illegal dealings with Miss Tinsley. To apply the principle to this type of claim therefore required an extension of the principle that was not obviously justified.

35–32   Secondly, Lord Browne-Wilkinson limited this extension of the principle to cases where there was no special relationship between the parties of a kind that would lead the law to make a presumption of advancement.[71] Yet it is unsatisfactory for the law to make a transferor's ability to recover property transferred for an illegal purpose turn on the irrelevant question of whether he and the transferee are in a special relationship giving rise to a presumption of advancement—a point that has been made on several occasions by the Court of Appeal,[72] by the Law Commission[73] and by the High Court of Australia.[74]

35–33   Thirdly, and more fundamentally, the majority's approach is extremely formalistic—something that can also be said of the common law cases on which they relied. Whether a claim in unjust enrichment should be permitted to recover benefits conferred pursuant to an illegal contract is a question that ought to be addressed by examining the policy underlying the rule that renders the contract illegal, and asking whether this would be stultified if recovery were allowed. Arguably, the courts should also consider a wider range of issues, such as whether the illegality is sufficiently serious to make it inappropriate for the court to give the claimant its assistance, whether disallowing the claim will deter other parties from acting in a similar manner, and whether disallowing the claim would be an appropriate or excessive punishment for the claimant. In *Tinsley* the

---

[69] *Tinsley* [1994] 1 A.C. 340 at 371.

[70] *Tinsley* [1994] 1 A.C. 340 at 369; citing *Bowmakers Ltd v Barnet Instruments Ltd* [1945] K.B. 65; *Feret v Hill* (1854) 15 C.B. 207; 139 E.R. 400; *Taylor* (1869) L.R. Q.B. 309; *Alexander v Rayson* [1936] 1 Q.B. 169.

[71] *Tinsley* [1994] 1 A.C. 340 at 371–372. The presumption of advancement will be abolished in English law (with prospective effect) when the Equality Act 2010 s.199 is brought into force, something which has not happened at the time of writing.

[72] *Tribe* [1996] Ch. 107 at 118 per Nourse L.J.; *Silverwood v Silverwood* (1997) 74 P. & C.R. 453 at 458–459 per Nourse L.J.; *Lowson v Coombes* [1999] Ch. 373 at 385 per Robert Walker L.J.; *Collier v Collier* (2002) 6 I.T.E.L.R. 270 at [105]–[106] per Mance L.J.

[73] Law Commission, *Illegal Transactions: The Effect of Illegality on Contracts and Trusts* (1999), Law Com No.154, paras 3.19–3.24.

[74] *Nelson v Nelson* (1995) 184 C.L.R. 538 at 609 per McHugh J.

minority of the House of Lords wished to take account of the first of these additional matters, rejecting the majority's approach and preferring the harsh but certain approach that "a court of equity will not assist a claimant who does not come to equity with clean hands", producing the result that the transferred property is left in the hands of the defendant.[75] However, the minority joined the majority in rejecting the more flexible approach taken by the Court of Appeal,[76] which made the transferor's ability to recover the property turn upon the extent to which the public conscience would be affronted by recognising rights arising out of illegal transactions.[77]

4. UNDERLYING PRINCIPLES AND FUTURE DEVELOPMENT

The law governing the question whether illegality should debar claims in unjust   **35–34** enrichment has been widely criticised as complex, uncertain, formalistic and capable of producing injustice. In 1999, the Law Commission recommended that legislation should be enacted to resolve these problems for the law of unjust enrichment, and similar problems for the wider law of obligations, by giving the courts a structured statutory discretion to decide the effects of illegality on private law claims.[78] Factors to be taken into account would be the nature and seriousness of the illegality, the knowledge and intentions of the parties, whether denying a claim would deter the illegality, whether denying the claim would further the purpose of the rule which rendered the parties' dealings illegal, and whether denying the claim would be a proportionate response to the claimant's participation in the illegality.

No legislation was enacted in response to this recommendation, and in 2010,   **35–35** the Law Commission published another report,[79] in which it noted that the courts have begun to develop a structured discretion to deal with the effect of illegality on tort claims,[80] and concluded that there is no need for general legislation in this area because the existing law is largely amenable to common law development that will set it on a clearer and more rational footing. However, the Law Commission still considered that targeted legislation is needed to abolish the *Tinsley* reliance principle and to give the courts a discretion to determine the effect of illegality on the creation of trusts.

In the event that the courts take their lead from the tort cases to develop a   **35–36** common law discretion to determine the effect of illegality on claims in unjust enrichment, what principles should underpin this discretion? We consider that the

---

[75] Cf. *Muckleston v Brown* (1801) 6 Ves. Jun. 52 at 69; 31 E.R. 934 at 943 per Lord Eldon: "Let the estate lie where it falls".

[76] *Tinsley* [1992] Ch. 310.

[77] Quaere whether this firm line has been undermined by Lord Walker's disposal of the illegality point which arose in *Bakewell Management Ltd v Brandwood* [2004] UKHL 14; [2004] 2 A.C. 519? See especially his comment at [60] that "the maxim *ex turpi causa* must be applied as an instrument of public policy, and not in circumstances where it does not serve any public interest".

[78] Law Commission, *Illegal Transactions*, para.8.63; on which see N. Enonchong, "Illegal Transactions: The Future" [2000] R.L.R. 82, pp.99–104.

[79] Law Commission, *The Illegality Defence* (2010), Law Com. No. 320.

[80] *Stone & Rolls* [2009] UKHL 39; [2009] 1 A.C. 1391; *Gray v Thames Trains Ltd* [2009] UKHL 33; [2009] 1 A.C. 1339.

primary enquiry in any case where benefits have been transferred under an illegal contract should be on the policy underlying the rule that renders the contract illegal, and on the question whether this would be stultified if a claim in unjust enrichment were allowed. Some claims should also be prohibited on the grounds of extreme moral turpitude—claims to recover money paid to a defendant to murder a third party would be an example. But a high threshold of turpitude would be needed to trigger this secondary principle and claimants who are guilty of fraud or theft should not be denied recovery on this ground.[81]

35–37   The leading advocate of the "stultification" approach was Peter Birks, whose analysis we find compelling, and who argued that the law can already be sensibly rationalised by asking whether recovery would have contradicted the rule invalidating the contract in each case.[82] In Birks' view, any claim to recover value which has passed under an illegal contract should prima facie be barred on the ground of stultification, because allowing the claimant to recover would provide him with a means of compelling the defendant to perform his obligation, and would also provide him with insurance against the risk of non-performance, so reducing the risks of entering the contract. However, these arguments might be negatived if recovery would further rather than contradict the policy of the rule invalidating the contract; if the claimant was unaware of the illegality because it was concealed by a mistake, or was compelled to enter the transaction by unlawful pressure exerted by the defendant; and if denying recovery would entail a greater evil than allowing it—an example would be preventing an illegal immigrant from suing for the value of his work, an outcome that would open the way to slave labour.[83]

---

[81] Cf. *Tinsley* [1994] A.C. 340; *Tribe* [1996] Ch. 107.
[82] P. Birks, "Recovery of Value Transferred under an Illegal Contract" (2000) 1 *Theoretical Inquiries in Law* 155; P. Birks, *Unjust Enrichment*, 2nd edn (Oxford: OUP, 2005) pp.247–255. See too D. Sheehan, "Reconsidering the Defence of Illegality in Unjust Enrichment" [2009] L.M.C.L.Q. 319.
[83] *Nizamuddowlah v Bengal Cabaret Inc*, 399 N.Y.S. 2d 854 (1977).

Part Seven
REMEDIES

CHAPTER 36

PERSONAL REMEDIES AND INTEREST AWARDS

1. INTRODUCTION

This chapter concerns personal remedies for unjust enrichment. Discussion is **36–01** divided as follows. Part 2 examines personal restitutionary awards: a claimant who wins such an award, like any other civil litigant who wins a money judgment, has a statutory right to interest on the judgment debt running from the date when judgment is entered to the date when the judgment debt is satisfied.[1] In Part 3, we explain that there are also several ways in which a claimant may recover pre-judgment interest on a personal restitutionary award, i.e. a claim for interest on the judgment debt, running in most cases from the date when his cause of action accrued to the date of judgment. Finally, Part 4 explains that some other personal remedies are awarded to prevent a defendant from becoming unjustly enriched at the claimant's expense in the future.

2. PERSONAL RESTITUTIONARY AWARDS

In every case where a defendant is unjustly enriched at a claimant's expense, **36–02** English law gives the claimant a right to restitution from the defendant. The courts sometimes use the word "restitution" to describe a measure of compensation for civil wrongdoing, and when it is used in this sense the word means "restoring the claimant to the position he occupied before he was caused a loss by the defendant's wrong".[2] In this context, however, the word "restitution" means something different, namely "restoring the value received by the defendant to the claimant". There is an obvious danger of confusion here, and these two meanings of the word must be kept separate. As Lord Hope said in *Sempra Metals Ltd v IRC*, "the law of restitution is the law of gain-based recovery, just as the law of compensation is the law of loss-based recovery" and "the remedy of restitution differs from that of damages. It is the gain that needs to be

---

[1] Judgments Act 1838 s.17.
[2] At common law: *British Transport Commission v Gourley* [1956] A.C. 185 at 208 per Lord Goddard; *Andrews v Grand & Toy Alberta Ltd* (1978) 83 D.L.R. (3d) 452 at 475–476 per Dickson J.; endorsed in *Heil v Rankin* [2001] Q.B. 272 at 292 per Lord Woolf M.R. and in *Vento v Chief Constable of West Yorkshire Police* [2002] EWCA Civ 1871; [2003] I.C.R. 318 at [50] per Mummery L.J.; *HMRC v Holland* [2010] UKSC 51; [2011] Bus. L.R. 111 at [48] per Lord Hope. In equity: *Nocton v Lord Ashburton* [1914] A.C. 932 at 952 per Viscount Haldane L.C.; *Re Dawson* [1966] 2 N.S.W.R. 211 at 214 per Street J., endorsed in *Bartlett v Barclays Bank Trust Co Ltd* [1980] Ch. 515 at 543 per Brightman L.J., and in *Target Holdings Ltd v Redferns (A Firm)* [1996] A.C. 421 at 434 per Lord Browne-Wilkinson; *Day v Mead* [1987] 2 N.Z.L.R. 443 at 451 per Cooke P.; *Re Lehman Brothers International (Europe) (In Administration) (No.2)* [2009] EWCA Civ 1161; [2010] Bus. L.R. 489 at [39] per Patten L.J.

measured, not the loss to the claimant. The gain needs to be reversed if the claimant is to make good his remedy."[3]

36–03 A claimant with a right to restitution generated by the law of unjust enrichment must usually realise this right by winning a restitutionary remedy from the court,[4] although the revesting of title to property that follows an election to rescind a transaction can be seen as a self-help remedy for unjust enrichment, to the extent that rescission and consequent revesting happen automatically and without the intervention of the court.[5] However, most claimants in unjust enrichment need the court's assistance to obtain a legally enforceable remedy against a defendant. As we discuss in Chs 37–40, claimants are sometimes awarded proprietary restitutionary remedies; but the remedy sought by, and awarded to, most claimants is a personal restitutionary award, that is, an order that the defendant pay the claimant a sum of money representing the value of the benefit that he received at the claimant's expense.[6]

36–04 As we discuss in Ch.4, the questions whether a defendant has been enriched and, if so, to what extent, are tested at the date of receipt.[7] There are two reasons, however, why the amount that a defendant is ordered to pay a claimant may be less than the value of his gain at the date of receipt. One is that the law may hold that the amount of the restitutionary award should be capped by the amount of the claimant's loss if this was less than the amount of the defendant's gain. There are inconsistent cases on this question, but we consider that in principle such a cap should be applied. This is discussed in Ch.6.[8] The second reason is that the amount of the defendant's liability may be reduced by defences such as change of position,[9] estoppel (if this defence now operates pro tanto),[10] and passing on (to the extent that this is a defence under English law).[11] It also seems that in cases where a defendant receives a benefit in exchange for a benefit that he transfers to a claimant, the value of the two benefits must be netted off to arrive at the measure of the defendant's liability.[12]

36–05 Unlike German law,[13] English law does not regard a personal restitutionary award as a second-string remedy awarded where it is impossible to identify a specific asset transferred to the defendant that the defendant can be ordered to return. English law regards a personal restitutionary award as the standard remedy to which claimants are entitled, and only makes proprietary restitutionary awards in a more limited set of circumstances.[14] The old common law actions from which much of the modern law derives made this clear. They declared that

---

[3] *Sempra Metals Ltd v IRC* [2007] UKHL 34; [2008] 1 A.C. 561 at [28]; approving P. Birks, *Unjust Enrichment*, 2nd edn (Oxford: OUP, 2005), pp.3–4.
[4] For an illuminating discussion of the realisation of rights in private law through the making of court orders, see R. Zakrzewski, *Remedies Reclassified* (Oxford: OUP, 2005).
[5] See paras 40–10——40–11 and 40–18——40–23.
[6] *Portman Building Society v Hamlyn Taylor Neck (A Firm)* [1998] 4 All E.R. 202 at 205 per Millett L.J., and *Navier v Leicester* [2002] EWHC 2596 (Ch) at [21] per Rimer J.
[7] See paras 4–34——4–42.
[8] See paras 6–63——6–74.
[9] See Ch.27.
[10] See Ch.30.
[11] See Ch.32.
[12] See Ch.31, especially paras 31–14——31–21.
[13] BGB § 818 (2).
[14] See Ch.37.

the defendant was indebted to the plaintiff for a sum corresponding to the value of the benefit that he received, not only where this took the abstract form of a discharged debt (in the action for money paid to the plaintiff's use) or the performance of services (in the action for a quantum meruit award), but also where the benefit took the form of notes and coins (in the action for money had and received) or goods (in the action for a quantum valebat award).[15]

In equity, personal restitutionary awards are also free-standing orders to pay **36–06** the value received by the defendant which do not depend on an obligation to retransfer a specific asset. Moreover, while common law proceedings had to be pursued through forms of action that obscured the nature of restitutionary awards made to plaintiffs, the Chancery courts have always simply ordered a payment of money.[16]

There is, however, one area of English law where the courts have not clearly **36–07** seen that a claimant's right to recover the money value of benefits conferred on a defendant should be independent of any right that he may also have to recover specific assets. This concerns the situation where a contract is rescinded and the parties are ordered to return the benefits they received. For a long time the courts have insisted on specific restitution and counter-restitution of assets following rescission. However, they now seem to be relaxing this requirement,[17] and we agree with Peter Birks that this development makes it easier to understand that although "the right to rescind combines a power to untie the contract . . . and a power to revest the assets which passed to the transferee", the rescinding party should also be "concurrently entitled to receive the money value of that which he transferred less the value of anything he received in exchange."[18] Where the rescinding party has paid money, he has always been entitled to recover the value of the money without having to prove that the specific coins and notes are still in the defendant's hands.[19] In principle, rescinding parties should be allowed the same remedy where they have transferred specific assets to their contractual counter-parties, even where they cannot recover these assets *in specie*, for example because they have reached the hands of a bona fide purchaser for value without notice.

In Birks' view,[20] this was the best explanation of *Mahoney v Purnell*.[21] The **36–08** claimant and his son-in-law operated an hotel business in a partnership that was later incorporated as a company. The claimant surrendered his 50 per cent holding in the company for less than its fair value. The company sold the hotel

---

[15] Birks, *Unjust Enrichment*, pp.168–169 and 286–290.

[16] As in e.g. *Att Gen Ex rel. Ethery v Hunton* (1739) West t. Hard. 703; 25 E.R. 1158; *Ministry of Health v Simpson* [1951] A.C. 251.

[17] See paras 31–06—31–13.

[18] Birks, *Unjust Enrichment*, p.173.

[19] *Re Goldcorp Exchange Ltd* [1995] 1 A.C. 74 at 102 per Lord Mustill (PC): "What the customers would recover on rescission would not be 'their' money, but an equivalent sum." See too *With v O'Flanagan* [1936] 1 Ch. 575; *Senanayake v Cheng* [1966] A.C. 63 at 76–77 per Lord Morris (PC); *Horn v Commercial Acceptances Ltd* [2011] EWHC 1757 (Ch) at [81] per Peter Smith J. A similar rule obtained at common law where an action lay for money had and received: *Clarke v Dickson* (1858) El. Bl. & El. 148; 120 E.R. 463; *Kettlewell v Refuge Assurance Co* [1908] 1 K.B. 545; affirmed [1909] A.C. 243; *Dimskal Shipping Co SA v I.T.W.F. (The Evia Luck)* [1992] 2 A.C. 152 at 165, per Lord Goff.

[20] Birks, *Unjust Enrichment*, pp.175–176.

[21] *Mahoney v Purnell* [1996] 3 All E.R. 61.

for over £3 million, but lost this money in an unsuccessful business venture and went into liquidation. May J. held that in principle the contract for the sale of the claimant's shares could be rescinded for undue influence, but that the liquidation of the company made rescission impossible, and that there was no quantifiable profit in the son-in-law's hands for which he could be ordered to account. He concluded that "practical justice in this case requires an award which is akin to compensation", namely, the difference in value between what the claimant had surrendered and what he had received.[22]

36–09   This decision has sparked a debate as to whether undue influence should now be seen as an equitable wrong triggering a right to compensation.[23] Laying that debate to one side, the significance of the case for the present discussion is Birks' argument that the result in the case accords with the principle that a rescinding party should always be entitled to restitution of the value of the benefits he transfers to the other party, whether these are money or specific assets or services. This right should run concurrently with any right that he may also have to revest title to specific assets received by his counterparty.[24] It may add nothing useful where his right to revest can be enforced, but its existence becomes crucial where his right to revest is barred, for example by the intervention of third party rights.

36–10   Adopting this analysis might require the courts to repudiate some 19th century common law cases which denied that defrauded vendors of goods could rescind the sale contract and bring a personal action for the value of goods sold,[25] and a lone 19th century authority which denied that a plaintiff who had been fraudu-lently induced to perform services for the defendant could rescind the contract and bring a personal action to recover the difference between what he had been paid and the value of his work.[26] Nevertheless we favour Birks' analysis in principle, and consider that the path to its adoption by the courts has been cleared by the increasingly flexible approach that they have taken in recent years towards the question whether claimants seeking restitution have satisfied the requirement that they make counter-restitution of benefits they have received under the contract.[27]

36–11   A final point remains to be made. Many courts and legal practitioners continue to use terms to describe personal restitutionary awards that derive from the forms of action that were abolished 150 years ago. This practice creates a barrier to understanding because it perpetuates the false impression that there is not one law of unjust enrichment governed by a single set of principles, but an assortment of claims that variously lie when a claimant has paid money ("money had and received"), performed services (quantum meruit), delivered goods (quantum valebat), discharged the defendant's debts and other legal liabilities ("money

---

[22] *Mahoney* [1996] 3 All E.R. 61 at 87–91; following *Nocton* [1914] A.C. 932; and *O'Sullivan v Management Agency and Music Ltd* [1985] Q.B. 428 at 464–467 per Fox L.J.

[23] See paras 11–26—11–27.

[24] As to which, see Ch.40.

[25] *Read v Hutchinson* (1813) 3 Camp. 352; 170 E.R. 1408; *Ferguson v Carrington* (1829) 9 B. & C. 59; 109 E.R. 22; *Strutt v Smith* (1834) 1 C.M. & R. 312; 149 E.R. 1099. The opposite line had previously been taken in *De Symons v Minchwich* (1796) 1 esp. 430; 170 E.R. 409.

[26] *Selway v Fogg* (1839) 5 M. & W. 83; 151 E.R. 36. This case and the cases cited in the previous note are discussed in D. O'Sullivan, S. Elliott, and R. Zakrzewski, *The Law of Rescission* (Oxford: OUP, 2008), paras 14.34–14.35 and 14.41–14.44.

[27] See paras 31–06—31–13.

paid" and "contribution"), allowed the defendant to occupy his property ("mesne profits"), or transferred benefits under a voidable contract ("rescission"). This terminology should no longer be used. All personal restitutionary awards should be simply described as personal orders directing a defendant to pay a sum representing the value of the benefit that he received at the claimant's expense.[28]

3. PRE-JUDGMENT INTEREST AWARDS

There are several ways in which a claim for pre-judgment interest on a personal restitutionary award can be framed. These are considered here in turn. **36–12**

(a) *Statutory Recovery Regimes*

Provisions for the award of simple interest are included in some statutory schemes for the repayment of money paid as tax that was not due.[29] Where a claim falls within the scope of such a scheme, the claimant can obviously ask the court to make a simple interest award. Less straightforward, though, is the question whether he can choose not to enforce his statutory right to repayment of the capital sum with simple interest, and to make two claims at common law instead, one for repayment of the face value of the money and another for repayment of the user value of the money calculated as an award of compound interest. The latter method of framing a claim for compound interest is noted below.[30] **36–13**

Where a claimant has common law rights, but is also given narrower statutory rights on the same facts, the courts generally hold that Parliament's intention must have been to extinguish his common law rights and to replace them with the statutory rights. In Sir John Dyson S.C.J.'s words, "If the two remedies cover precisely the same ground and are inconsistent with each other, then the common law remedy will almost certainly have been excluded by necessary implication."[31] It seems, however, that the courts are unlikely to draw this conclusion in cases where the abrogation of the claimant's common law rights would be contrary to EU law.[32] In *Littlewoods Retail Ltd v HMRC*[33] Vos J. recently made a reference to the CJEU turning on the question of how the English courts should proceed in such a case, in connection with the statutory scheme for repayment of money paid as VAT that was not due. **36–14**

---

[28] The pleading of claims in unjust enrichment is discussed at paras 1–29—1–34.
[29] e.g. Value Added Tax Act 1994 s.78; Finance Act 2009 s.102(7).
[30] See para.36–27; and for detailed discussion, see paras 5–05—5–14.
[31] *R. (Child Poverty Action Group) v Secretary of State for Work and Pensions* [2010] UKSC 54; [2011] 2 A.C. 15 at [33]. For discussion, see paras 2–15—2–20.
[32] Cf. *Monro v HMRC* [2008] EWCA Civ 306; [2009] Ch. 69 at [34]; *Test Claimants in the F.I.I. Litigation v HMRC* [2010] EWCA Civ 103; [2010] S.T.C. 1251 at [261]. Both cases are discussed at para.22–06.
[33] *Littlewoods Retail Ltd v HMRC* [2010] EWHC 1071 (Ch); [2010] S.T.C. 2072. See too *F.J. Chalke Ltd v HMRC* [2009] EWHC 952 (Ch); [2009] S.T.C. 2027; affirmed [2010] EWCA Civ 313; [2010] S.T.C. 1640. Both cases are discussed at para.22–12.

(b) *The Senior Courts Act 1981 s. 35A*

36–15   A claim for simple interest can be made under s.35A of the Senior Courts Act 1981 previously the Supreme Court Act 1981. Subsection (1) provides that:

> "[I]n proceedings . . . before the High Court for the recovery of a debt or damages there may be included in any sum for which judgment is given simple interest, at such rate as the court thinks fit or as rules of court may provide, on all or any part of the debt or damages in respect of which judgment is given, or payment is made before judgment, for all or any part of the period between the date when the cause of action arose and—
>
> > (a)   in the case of any sum paid before judgment, the date of the payment; and
> >
> > (b)   in the case of the sum for which judgment is given, the date of the judgment."

36–16   Several cases hold that s.35A empowers the court to add simple interest to a personal restitutionary award made to reverse the defendant's unjust enrichment. In *BP Exploration Co (Libya) Ltd v Hunt (No.2)*,[34] Robert Goff J. held, first, that claims under the Law Reform (Frustrated Contracts) Act 1943 s.1(2) and (3) are claims in unjust enrichment,[35] and, secondly, that awards made to successful claimants under s.1(2) and (3) would constitute "recovery of a debt" for the purposes of the Law Reform (Miscellaneous Provisions) Act 1934 s.3, which was the statutory precursor to s.35A.[36] For reasons that are discussed elsewhere, we doubt that the first of these findings was correct.[37] However the second finding was upheld by the House of Lords, where Lord Brandon said that:

> "[T]he words 'any debt or damages' . . . are very wide so that they cover any sum of money which is recoverable by one party from another, either at common law or in equity or under a statute of the kind here concerned."[38]

36–17   Furthermore, Lord Brandon's words caused the parties to later cases that clearly were concerned with claims in unjust enrichment to proceed on the agreed basis that such claims fall within the scope of the section. This was common ground between the parties in *Woolwich Equitable Building Society v IRC*,[39] *Westdeutsche Landesbank Girozentrale v Islington LBC*,[40] and *Sempra*.[41] In *Woolwich* and *Westdeutsche* the House of Lords clearly assumed that the parties were correct to proceed on this basis, and in *Sempra* Lord Nicholls expressly held that "the court has power to make an award of simple interest under section 35A [on a personal claim for restitution of a sum of money paid by mistake or following an unlawful demand]",[42] while Lord Walker held that "there is a

---

[34] *BP Exploration Co (Libya) Ltd v Hunt (No.2)* [1979] 1 W.L.R. 783.
[35] *BP v Hunt (No.2)* [1979] 1 W.L.R. 783 at 799–800.
[36] *BP v Hunt (No.2)* [1979] 1 W.L.R. 783 at 835–837.
[37] See para.15–10
[38] *BP v Hunt (No.2)* [1983] 2 A.C. 352 at 373, echoing his own comments as a first-instance judge in *Tyne Tugs v Owners of the MV Aldora (The MV Aldora)* [1975] Q.B. 748 at 751.
[39] *Woolwich Equitable Building Society v IRC* [1993] A.C. 70 at 106 per Ralph Gibson L.J.
[40] *Westdeutsche Landesbank Girozentrale v Islington LBC* [1996] A.C. 669 at 737 per Lord Lloyd.
[41] *Sempra* [2007] UKHL 34; [2008] 1 A.C. 561 at [11] per Lord Hope.
[42] *Sempra* [2007] UKHL 34; [2008] 1 A.C. 561 at [104].

statutory power (now found in section 35A . . .) to award simple interest, at the court's discretion, on a restitutionary award."[43]

Section 35A does not give claimants a right to simple interest; it merely gives **36–18** the courts a discretion to add simple interest on a money judgment when they think this is appropriate. "There are five separate layers of discretion. Four are mentioned in subsection (1) namely: whether to award interest at all; the rate of interest; the proportion of the sum that should bear interest; and the period for which interest should be awarded. Section 35A(6) then goes on to confirm that 'interest may be calculated at different rates in respect of different periods', giving a fifth discretion on whether to vary the rate."[44] In practice, the courts generally award a rate of 1 per cent above the clearing banks' average base rate for the whole of the relevant period.

Section 35A(1) stipulates that the earliest date from which interest can be **36–19** awarded is the date when the claimant's cause of action accrued. A cause of action in unjust enrichment generally accrues at the date when the benefit is received, but in cases of failure of basis, the cause of action does not accrue until the basis of the defendant's enrichment fails and this may not happen until later.[45] It follows that in such cases interest cannot be claimed for the period between receipt and subsequent failure of basis, although the claimant has lost, and the defendant has gained, the use of the money during this period.[46] This is unsatisfactory and reform of the law would be desirable.[47]

Since statutory interest is discretionary, the courts are not bound to choose the **36–20** date when the claimant's cause of action accrued as the starting-date, and although it has been said that they "should normally award interest . . . as from [this] date",[48] they may select a later starting-date, for example because there has been an excessive delay in bringing the claim,[49] or because "the defendant neither knew, nor reasonably could have been expected to know, that the [claimant] was likely to make a claim, and so was in no position either to tender payment, or even to make provision for payment if the money should be found due."[50] In cases of excessive delay, the courts may alternatively award interest

---

[43] *Sempra* [2007] UKHL 34; [2008] 1 A.C. 561 at [175]. See also his comments at [109] and [114]. See too *Nurdin & Peacock Plc v D. B. Ramsden & Co Ltd* [1999] 1 W.L.R. 1249; *R. (Kemp) v Denbighshire Local Health Board* [2006] EWHC 181 (Admin); [2007] 1 W.L.R. 639; *Benedetti v Sawiris* [2010] EWCA Civ 1427.
[44] *Braspetro Oil Services Co v F.P.S.O. Construction Inc* [2007] EWHC 1359 (Comm); [2007] 2 All E.R. (Comm) 924 at [279] per Cresswell J.
[45] See the authorities cited in para.4–34.
[46] *BP v Hunt (No.2)* [1983] 2 A.C. 352 at 373–374 per Lord Brandon; *Guardian Ocean Cargoes Ltd v Banco do Brasil SA (The Golden Med) (No.1)* [1994] 2 Lloyd's Rep. 152 at 160 per Saville L.J.
[47] F. Rose, "Interest" in P. Birks and F. Rose (eds), *Lessons of the Swaps Litigation* (London: LLP/ Mansfield Press, 2000), 292, p.304.
[48] *Benedetti* [2010] EWCA Civ 1427 at [130] per Arden L.J.
[49] *Business Computers Ltd v Anglo-African Leasing Ltd* [1977] 1 W.L.R. 578; *Corbett v Barking, Havering and Brentwood HA* [1991] 2 Q.B. 408; *Kuwait Airways Corp v Kuwait Insurance Co SAK* [2000] Lloyd's Rep I.R. 678.
[50] *BP v Hunt (No.2)* [1979] 1 W.L.R. 783 at 846–847 per Robert Goff J.; approved in *Allied London Investments Ltd v Hambro Life Assurance Plc* (1985) 50 P. & C.R. 207 at 209, per curiam (CA). See too *Nurdin* [1999] 1 W.L.R. 1249 at 1277 per Neuberger J.

from the date when the claimant's cause of action accrued but reduce the amount of interest recoverable.[51] However, they should[52]:

> "take a realistic view of delay. In the case of business disputes, litigation is for all parties an unwelcome distraction from their proper business. It is not reasonable to expect any party to take every litigious step at the first possible moment, or to concentrate on litigation to the exclusion of all else. Delay should only be characterised as unreasonable for present purposes when, after making due allowance for the circumstances, it can be seen that the claimant has neglected or declined to pursue his claim for a significant period."

36–21   In *Benedetti v Sawiris*,[53] a dispute arose between the parties as to the basis upon which the claimant should be remunerated for work that he had done for the defendant. In settlement negotiations, the defendant offered to pay the claimant a fee that was higher than the market value of the claimant's services, and the claimant rejected this offer. The trial judge, Patten L.J., awarded the claimant a sum corresponding to the amount of the defendant's offer, because this was the subjective value of the services to the claimant,[54] but he refused to award pre-judgment interest because the claimant "would not have accepted [the relevant sum] at any time up to judgment had the offer been repeated" and so the "delay in receiving that money is entirely of his own making."[55] The Court of Appeal unanimously reduced the size of the main award to the objective market value of the claimant' services, but a majority of the court ruled that interest should be paid on this sum from the date when the claimant had completed rendering his services.

36–22   Etherton L.J. thought that it would always be "wrong in principle" for a court to refuse statutory interest on an award because the claimant had refused an earlier offer "most particularly where the claim is for restitution of the defendant's unjust enrichment . . . since interest in such a case is necessary to extract from the defendant the full benefit of the unjust enrichment enjoyed by the defendant over time."[56] Rimer L.J. disagreed that claims in unjust enrichment are unusual in this respect, and also agreed with Arden L.J.[57] that "the refusal by the claimant of an offer of all that he is ultimately held entitled to in the proceedings *may* in appropriate circumstances be a factor relevant to an exercise of the discretion against the award of interest, the rationale being that it would have been the claimant's refusal of the offer that has kept him out of his money."[58] However, he agreed with Etherton L.J. that it would be unfair to withhold pre-judgment interest on the facts of the case, since no finding was made that the

---

[51] *La Pintada Cia Navigacion SA v President of India (The La Pintada)* [1983] 1 Lloyds Rep. 37; *Derby Resources AG v Blue Corinth Marine Co Ltd (The Athenian Harmony) (No.2)* [1998] 2 Lloyd's Rep. 425 (reduction of one-third).
[52] *Claymore Services Ltd v Nautilus Properties Ltd* [2007] EWHC 805 (TCC); [2007] B.L.R. 452 at [55] per Jackson J.
[53] *Benedetti v Sawiris* [2010] EWCA Civ 1427, discussed at para.4–51.
[54] *Benedetti* [2009] EWHC 1330 (Ch).
[55] *Benedetti* [2009] EWHC 1806 (Ch) at [11].
[56] *Benedetti* [2010] EWCA Civ 1427 at [165].
[57] *Benedetti* [2010] EWCA Civ 1427 at [130].
[58] *Benedetti* [2010] EWCA Civ 1427 at [177] (his emphasis).

claimant had rejected the offer and pursued a claim in which he had no genuine belief in order to pressurise the defendant into making a higher offer.[59]

(c) Equitable Interest Awards

The courts have a distinct equitable jurisdiction to award interest. This may be **36–23** invoked, for example, when a contract is rescinded in equity and the parties are ordered to repay money received under the contract: in such a case a recipient is generally required to pay interest "on the ground that the parties [are] to be restored as far as possible to their original position."[60]

Equitable interest is discretionary and the court can therefore select the basis **36–24** on which interest should be calculated (simple or compound), the rate of interest to be awarded, and the period for which it should be awarded. Equitable interest generally runs from the date when the benefit was received to the date of judgment,[61] but the court may exceptionally select a different starting date,[62] for example where the defendant did not know and could not reasonably be expected to have known that a claim was likely to be made.[63]

The courts' equitable jurisdiction to award interest includes a power to order **36–25** that the interest should be compounded. In *Westdeutsche* the majority of the House of Lords held that this power should be exercised only in limited classes of case (fraud and unauthorised profit-making by fiduciaries).[64] Following the later decision in *Sempra*,[65] however, it seems likely that these restrictions will be abandoned, and that the courts will now feel free to award compound interest on all equitable claims. As noted immediately below, the majority of the House of Lords held in *Sempra* that compound interest can be recovered at common law by bringing a stand-alone claim for the use value of money paid to a defendant, and it seems unlikely that the courts will insist on keeping their equitable jurisdiction within narrow confines when claimants at common law now have such ready access to compound interest.

---

[59] *Benedetti* [2010] EWCA Civ 1427 at [179]. See too *Rhesa Shipping Co SA v Edmunds (The Popi M)* [1984] 2 Lloyd's Rep. 555 at 561 per May L.J.: "the award or refusal to award interest should not be used as a means of penalising a party, for instance for the way in which negotiations or litigation have been conducted on his behalf." Langstaff J.'s decision in *Kemp* [2006] EWHC 1339 (Admin) at [29]–[39] was made without the benefit of the latter authority.

[60] *Re Metropolitan Coal Consumer's Association (Karberg's Case)* [1892] 3 Ch. 1 at 17, per curiam (CA). See too *Erlanger v New Sombrero Phosphate Co* (1876) 5 Ch. D. 73 at 125 per Jessel M.R.; affirmed (1878) 3 App. Cas. 1218; *Newbigging v Adam* (1886) 34 Ch. D. 582 at 585 per Bacon V.C.; affirmed (1888) 13 App. Cas. 308; *Alati v Kruger* (1955) 94 C.L.R. 216; *Maguire v Makaronis* (1996) 188 C.L.R. 449 at 475–477 per Brennan C.J., Gaudron, McHugh and Gummow JJ.; *Investors Compensation Scheme Ltd v West Bromwich Building Society (No.1)* [1998] 1 W.L.R. 896 at 916 per Lord Hoffmann.

[61] *York Buildings Co v Mackenzie* (1795) 8 Bro. P.C. 42; 3 E.R. 422; *Newbigging* (1886) 34 Ch. D. 582 at 585 per Bacon V.C.; affirmed (1888) 13 App. Cas. 308; *Karberg's Case* [1892] 3 Ch. 1 at 17, per curiam (CA); *Alati v Kruger* (1955) 94 C.L.R. 216 at 220 per Dixon C.J., Webb, Kitto and Taylor JJ.

[62] *Westdeutsche* [1994] 1 W.L.R. 938 at 955 per Leggatt L.J.

[63] *West Sussex Properties Ltd v Chichester DC* [2000] EWCA Civ 205 at [37] per Morritt L.J.

[64] *Westdeutsche* [1996] A.C. 669 at 701–702 per Lord Browne-Wilkinson. See too *The La Pintada* [1985] AC 104 at 116 per Lord Brandon; *Black v Davies* [2005] EWCA Civ 531 at [81]–[88] per curiam.

[65] *Sempra* [2007] UKHL 34; [2008] 1 A.C. 561.

36–26   Lord Mance, who dissented from the majority decision in *Sempra* on the question of whether the claimants had proved the defendant's enrichment, made some pertinent remarks in this connection. He supported the view taken by the minority judges in *Westdeutsche*, Lord Goff and Lord Woolf,[66] that "the equitable jurisdiction to award compound interest [should extend] to personal claims where there was no question of failure to account as a fiduciary."[67] Like them, he also considered that "there is no sustainable reason in modern conditions for continuing to limit [the equitable jurisdiction to award interest] artificially in a way which may prevent the court doing equity."[68]

(d) *Claims in Unjust Enrichment for the Use Value of Money*

36–27   In *Sempra*[69] the House of Lords held that it is possible for a claimant to frame a claim for interest on a capital sum paid to a defendant not as an interest award that is parasitic on a claim in unjust enrichment to recover the face value of the money, but as a separate stand-alone claim in unjust enrichment to recover the use value of the money. The quantum of the award made to a successful claimant in such a case should be calculated as compound interest on the money paid to the defendant when that is the use value of the money that the defendant received. This will usually be the case, since defendants usually have to pay compound interest in order to borrow money. The nature of such claims, and their relationship with claims under the Senior Courts Act 1981 s.35A, are discussed in Ch.5.[70]

4. PREVENTATIVE REMEDIES

(a) *General Observations*

36–28   The majority of remedies awarded to successful claimants in unjust enrichment are restitutionary: they reverse a transfer of value between the claimant and defendant that has already taken place. Some remedies, however, are preventative in effect: they are awarded before any transfer of value has occurred, and their purpose is to prevent such a transfer from taking place because it would lead to the defendant's unjust enrichment at the claimant's expense.

36–29   Preventative remedies for unjust enrichment are not often awarded. One reason is that a claimant who can foresee that he will unjustly enrich a defendant if he acts in a certain way can often avoid this outcome without the court's help. For example, a claimant whose intention to benefit a defendant is vitiated by mistake, or by undue influence, and who becomes aware of his mistake, or freed from the undue influence, before he acts on his intention, can simply choose not to act.[71] Hence, preventative remedies are only sought in practice by a limited

---

[66] *Westdeutsche* [1996] A.C. 669 at 693–695 and 726–730.
[67] *Sempra* [2007] UKHL 34; [2008] 1 A.C. 561 at [239].
[68] *Sempra* [2007] UKHL 34; [2008] 1 A.C. 561 at [239].
[69] *Sempra* [2007] UKHL 34; [2008] 1 A.C. 561.
[70] See paras 5–05—5–14.
[71] R. Williams, "Preventing Unjust Enrichment" [2000] R.L.R. 492, p.513.

class of claimants, who are aware that their acts will lead to a defendant's unjust enrichment, but who owe a legal obligation to act from which the court alone can relieve them. In short, preventative remedies are only sought in practice in cases where the claimant owes a legal obligation to a third party for which he is only secondarily liable, and for which the defendant is primarily liable.[72]

A second reason why preventative remedies are not often awarded is that the **36–30** courts are slow to award exonerative relief against defendants, against whom, ex hypothesi, no cause of action can yet be made out. Fairness to defendants demands that before orders are made against them, the courts must feel confident that an unjust enrichment will soon occur if they do not intervene. The courts are also slow to make binding declarations under CPR r.40.20, both because they wish to be fair to defendants, and because they wish to avoid unintended consequences for third parties who are not parties to the litigation.[73] The courts also wish to avoid deciding moot points of law, both because parties who have a real interest in the answer to legal questions are more likely to argue them fully and forcefully than parties who do not, and also because they wish to conserve their resources for the resolution of disputes. "The jurisdiction of the court is not to declare the law generally or to give advisory opinions; it is confined to declaring contested legal rights, subsisting or future, of the parties represented in the litigation before it and not those of anyone else."[74] Hence, there must generally "be a real and present dispute between the parties before the court as to the existence or extent of a legal right between them . . . [although] the claimant does not need to have a present cause of action against the defendant",[75] and "the dispute could relate to rights that might come into existence in the future upon the happening of an event".[76]

(b) *Exonerative Relief*

In *Re Richardson*, Fletcher Moulton L.J. held that a surety might[77]: **36–31**

"file a bill against the principal debtor to make him pay the debt so that [the surety] would not be called upon to pay it . . . [and he might also] in certain cases have a fund set aside in order that [the surety] might be indemnified, to avoid the necessity of [his]

---

[72] Secondary liability is a ground for restitution that is discussed in Chs 19–21.

[73] The dangers of formulating a declaration too broadly so that it unintentionally affects the rights of parties not before the court are illustrated by *Powell v Wiltshire* [2004] EWCA Civ 534; [2005] Q.B. 117.

[74] *Gouriet v Union of Post Office Workers* [1978] A.C. 435 at 501 per Lord Diplock. See too *Re Clay* [1919] 1 Ch. 66 at 77–78 per Swinfen Eady M.R.; *Padden v Arbuthnot Pensions & Investments Ltd* [2004] EWCA Civ 582 at [31] per May L.J.

[75] *Rolls-Royce Plc v Unite the Union* [2009] EWCA Civ 387; [2010] 1 W.L.R. 318 at [120] per Aikens L.J.

[76] *Milebush Properties Ltd v Tameside MBC* [2011] EWCA Civ 270 at [87] per Moore-Bick L.J. The court's jurisdiction to make declarations ultimately derives from the Court of Chancery and was originally restricted to declaratory judgments as to existing private rights: *Guaranty Trust Co of New York v Hannay & Co* [1915] 2 K.B. 536. However, this limitation fell away during the 20th century as the courts expanded the jurisdiction as a means of controlling the abuse of executive power in proceedings for judicial review: *Bank of Scotland v A Ltd* [2001] EWCA Civ 52; [2001] 1 W.L.R. 751 at [45] per Lord Woolf C.J.

[77] *Re Richardson* [1911] 2 K.B. 705 at 713.

having to pay and then to sue for the money [he] had paid, which perhaps would not repair [his] loss and credit even if it discharged the debt."

36–32   The point of ordering the principal debtor to establish a fund out of which the surety might be paid, rather than ordering him to pay the surety directly, is that the latter course would create the risk that the surety would not use the money to pay the creditor, with the result that the principal debtor might then have to pay a second time.[78] But in any event, orders that a principal debtor should pay the creditor directly are now much more common.[79] Orders of either kind take the form of a quia timet injunction. Quia timet means "because he fears": because the surety fears that he will be forced to pay the creditor although some or all of the burden of paying the creditor should properly be borne by the principal debtor, the court orders the principal debtor to pay the creditor instead.[80]

36–33   The courts' power to grant injunctions is a "discretionary power which should not as a matter of principle be fettered by rules".[81] However there are some principles that the court is likely to apply when deciding whether to exercise its discretion to award either of the exonerative orders under consideration.[82] First, the principal debtor must certainly be a party to the litigation whichever order is sought, and it seems that the creditor must also be a party where an order is sought that the principal debtor pay the creditor directly,[83] although there is no reason why this should be necessary where an order is sought that the principal debtor set up a fund out of which the surety might be paid. Secondly, the surety must show that the creditor's right to sue him must have accrued, although he need not show that the creditor intends to sue him straight away: the cloud hanging over him must be "clearly visible" but need not be "especially ominous".[84] Thirdly, injunctions are equitable remedies, and a court may therefore refuse to award one to a claimant who does not come to court with "clean hands".[85]

---

[78] *McGrath v O'Driscoll* [2006] IEHC 195 at [2.6].

[79] But it was negligent of the defendant to have failed to advise his client that he could have the latter remedy in *Wakim v McNally* [2002] FCAFC 208 per Einfield J.; noting *Rankin v Palmer* (1912) 16 C.L.R. 285, *Wren v Mahoney* (1972) 126 C.L.R. 212; and *Abigroup Ltd v Abignano* (1992) 39 F.C.R. 74 at 83 (Full Ct of Fed Ct of Aus).

[80] In *Watt v Mortlock* [1964] Ch. 84 at 88, Wilberforce J. thought it would be wrong to specify the manner in which the order to pay should be enforced, and instead gave the claimant liberty to apply for such further relief as might seem appropriate, in the event that the defendant did not comply.

[81] *Kirklees MBC v Wickes Building Supplies Ltd* [1993] A.C. 227 at 271 per Lord Goff.

[82] More detailed discussion of this topic can be found in J.C. Phillips and J. O'Donovan, *The Modern Contract of Guarantee*, 2nd English edn (London: Sweet & Maxwell, 2010), paras 11–110—11–161.

[83] *Stimpson v Smith* [1999] Ch. 340 at 348 per Peter Gibson L.J. See too *Wolmershausen v Gullick* [1893] 2 Ch. 514 at 529 per Wright J. *Sed contra, Ascherson v Tredegar Dry Dock and Wharf Co Ltd* [1909] 2 Ch. 401 at 405 per Swinfen Eady J.

[84] *Papamichael v National Westminster Bank Plc* [2002] 2 All ER (Comm) 60 at 338 per Judge Chambers QC; considering *Re Anderson-Berry* [1928] 1 Ch. 290; and *Rowland v Gulfpac Ltd* [1999] Lloyd's Rep. Bank. 86 at 98. See too *Ranelaugh v Hawes* (1683) 1 Vern. 189; 23 E.R. 405; *Lee v Rock* (1730) Mos. 318; 25 E.R. 415; *Bechervaise v Lewis* (1872) L.R. 7 C.P. 372 at 377; *Holden v Black* (1905) 2 C.L.R. 768 at 782–783; *Hibernian Fire and General Insurance Co Ltd v Dorgan* [1941] I.R. 514; *Thomas v Nottingham Incorporated FC Ltd* [1972] Ch. 596; *Stimpson v Smith* [1999] Ch. 340 at 350; *Cockburn v G.I.O. Finance Ltd* (2001) 51 N.S.W.L.R. 626 at 639 (NSWCA). Cf. *Friend v Brooker* [2009] HCA 21; (2009) 239 C.L.R. 129 at [52]–[61].

[85] As in *Gluckstein v Barnes* [1900] A.C. 420.

Most of the cases in this area concern claims by sureties who have expressly   **36–34**
agreed to act as such, but the same principle has been applied in cases where
family property is jointly owned by a husband and wife, where the husband
borrows money against the security of the property, and where the facts support
the inference that the parties intended that the wife should not be a joint debtor
with her husband but should merely be a surety. This inference might be drawn
where the money has been taken beneficially by the husband alone. In such cases,
in the event of the husband's default, the wife has an "equity of exoneration" that
entitles her to insist that repayment of the debt should fall so far as possible on
the husband's share of the property.[86]

(c) *Declaratory Orders*

The courts have the power under CPR r.40.20 to make a declaration that if a   **36–35**
claimant is obliged to pay a third party at some future date, then he will be
entitled to recover a contribution or full reimbursement from the defendant. The
claimant must show that he is under an imminent liability to pay the third party
before the courts will make an order of this sort. Where the claimant and the
defendant owe a common liability for debt, this requirement will be satisfied
when the debt falls due.[87] However, where the claimant's liability to the third
party arises in the law of wrongs, he will not relevantly owe an "imminent
liability" unless judgment has been awarded against him or he has entered a
binding agreement to pay.[88]

(d) *Insurers' Subrogation Rights*

These are discussed in Ch.21. It is explained there that in cases where an   **36–36**
indemnity insurer pays its insured for an insured loss, and its payment does not
discharge the insured's rights of action against a third party in respect of the same
loss, the insurer may be entitled to take over the insured's rights and to insist that
he lends his name to proceedings to enforce these for the insurer's benefit.
Indemnity insurance policies often contain subrogation clauses entitling the
insurer to do this, but indemnity insurers are also given subrogation rights by
operation of law.

The award of these rights can be understood as a preventative remedy that is   **36–37**
designed to prevent the two alternative outcomes that would follow if the law did
not intervene. Where the insured has been paid by the insurer, but can still
recover from the third party in respect of the same loss, the insured can choose

---

[86] *Hudson v Carmichael* (1854) Kay 613; 69 E.R. 260; *Gleaves v Paine* (1863) 1 De G. J. & S. 87;
46 E.R. 34; *Paget v Paget* [1898] 1 Ch. 470; *Ex p. Cronmire* [1901] 1 K.B. 480; *Re A Debtor (No.24
of 1971)* [1976] 1 W.L.R. 952; *Re Pittortou (A Bankrupt)* [1985] 1 W.L.R. 58; *R. v Posener* [2001]
EWCA Crim 14; *Re Richards (A Bankrupt)* [2009] EWHC 1760 (Ch); [2009] B.P.I.R. 973.
[87] *Re Norwich Yarn Co* (1850) 22 Beav. 143; 52 E.R. 1062; *Wolmershausen v Gullick* [1893] 2 Ch.
514 at 528–529 per Wright J.; *Mahoney v McManus* (1981) 36 A.L.R. 545 at 549 per Gibbs C.J.
(High Ct of Aus); *Re Prestige Grindings Ltd* [2005] EWHC 3076 (Ch); [2006] B.C.C. 421 at [15] per
Judge Norris QC, sitting as a deputy High Court judge.
[88] *Littlewood v George Wimpey & Co Ltd.* [1953] 2 Q.B. 501 at 519 per Denning L.J., followed in
MacKenzie v Vance (1977) 74 D.L.R. (3d) 383 at 395 per Macdonald J.A. (Nova Scotia CA); *West
Bromwich Building Society v Mander Hadley & Co, The Times* March 9, 1998, CA.

whether to enforce his rights against the third party or to forbear from suing him. If he enforces his rights, then he may obtain more than a full indemnity for his loss by accumulating recoveries from the insurer and the third party. This would be contrary to the terms of his indemnity policy. If he does not enforce his rights, then the third party will effectively be exonerated from liability. This is also regarded as unsatisfactory as it is assumed that third parties, rather than insurers, are the "right" people to pay for insured losses.

CHAPTER 37

PROPRIETARY REMEDIES: GENERAL PRINCIPLES

1. INTRODUCTION

As discussed in Ch.36, claimants in unjust enrichment are most commonly **37–01** awarded a personal restitutionary remedy, i.e. an order that the defendant should pay the claimant a sum representing the value of the enrichment that he received at the claimant's expense. In some circumstances, however, claimants in unjust enrichment are entitled to a proprietary restitutionary remedy, i.e. an order declaring that the claimant has a new ownership or security interest in property held by the defendant, usually accompanied by consequential orders such as an order that the property should be conveyed to the claimant, or an order that the property should be sold and a share of the proceeds remitted to the claimant. Although they are necessarily directed to a defendant, such orders are also exigible against third parties.[1]

There are a number of practical advantages to be gained from winning a **37–02** proprietary remedy. If the defendant has become insolvent, then the claimant will gain priority over his unsecured, and possibly also his secured, creditors. If the claimant acquires an ownership interest in property that increases in value, then this increase will accrue to the claimant, as will the fruits of the property (share dividends, rental income, etc.). If the claimant acquires a security interest in property that decreases in value, then the claimant can still enforce the whole amount of his interest against the property, and if necessary recover any outstanding balance via a personal action.[2] Pending the hearing of a claim for proprietary relief a claimant may obtain an interim freezing order preserving the relevant property until the outcome of the trial.[3]

It is a controversial question whether claimants in unjust enrichment ought to **37–03** be awarded proprietary restitutionary remedies, and, if so, what form these should take. Some argue that the award of proprietary remedies for unjust enrichment is never justified, others that it is justified only when kept within limits, although there is no clear consensus as to what these should be. These

---

[1] Cf. *Re Flint (A Bankrupt)* [1993] Ch. 319; *Mountney v Treharne* [2002] EWCA Civ 1174; [2003] Ch. 135.

[2] *Serious Fraud Office v Lexi Holdings Plc (In Administration)* [2008] EWCA Crim 1443; [2009] Q.B. 376 at [40] per Keene L.J.: a lien is "a cumulative remedy in aid of an . . . *in personam* claim, not an alternative remedy".

[3] RSC Ord.29 r.2; CPR Pt 25 and Practice Direction 25A and Annexe. See, e.g. *A v Aziz* [2007] EWHC 91 (QB); *Cancer Research UK Ltd v Morris* [2008] EWHC 2678 (QB); and cf. *Tajik Aluminium Plant v Ermatov (No.3)* [2006] EWHC 7 (Ch).

arguments are reviewed in Part 2. If it is thought that in principle proprietary remedies should sometimes be awarded, then some further questions arise. One goes to the form of the claimant's proprietary interest: should it be a substantive interest that arises automatically when his cause of action accrues, or should he be confined to an elective power to bring a proprietary interest into being? This is discussed in Part 3. Another question is whether claimants should have a free choice between an ownership and a security interest, or should sometimes be restricted to a security interest. This is discussed in Part 4.

37–04　　Finally, we review the cases governing proprietary responses to unjust enrichment. These do not present a clear picture. Some important cases take a negative attitude to the award of proprietary remedies for unjust enrichment, yet in many other cases such remedies have been awarded. In Part 5 we summarize the current state of the authorities and make some comments respecting the future development of the law.

37–05　　This chapter is concerned only with the circumstances in which new proprietary rights are generated by the law of unjust enrichment. It is not concerned with restitutionary remedies awarded as a means of vindicating a claimant's pre-existing proprietary rights, such as an order for possession of land[4] or an order for delivery up of goods.[5] However, there has been some controversy as to whether the proprietary remedies awarded in certain cases should be classified as remedies of the first or second sort. Most notably, opinion is divided as to whether the trust that was recognised in *Foskett v McKeown*[6] arose by reason of the claimants' persisting property rights, as held by the House of Lords, or by reason of the defendant's unjust enrichment at the claimants' expense. This is discussed in Ch.8.[7]

37–06　　This chapter does not discuss the form and operation of the various proprietary remedies for unjust enrichment that have been awarded. This work is done in the chapters that follow: Ch.38 concerns trusts and liens, Ch.39 concerns subrogation to extinguished proprietary rights and Ch.40 concerns the proprietary consequences of rescission and rectification.

2. Setting the Limits

37–07　Should claimants in unjust enrichment always be entitled to a proprietary remedy? Should they never be entitled to a proprietary remedy? Or should they sometimes be entitled to a proprietary remedy, and if so, then how should claimants who are entitled to a proprietary remedy be distinguished from claim-

---

[4] For discussion of which, see *Secretary of State for the Environment, Food and Rural Affairs v Meier* [2009] UKSC 11; [2009] 1 W.L.R. 2780.
[5] Torts (Interference with Goods) Act 1977 s.3.
[6] *Foskett v McKeown* [2001] A.C. 669. See too *Trustee of the Property of F.C. Jones and Son (A Firm) v Jones* [1997] Ch. 159. And cf. *MacMillan Inc v Bishopsgate Investment Trust Plc (No.3)* [1996] 1 W.L.R. 387.
[7] See paras 8–83—8–93.

ants who are not? Different courts and commentators have given different answers to these questions.

The leading academic proponent of the view that restitutionary proprietary **37–08** remedies should never be awarded is William Swadling.[8] He contends that the law should sometimes hold that a claimant's intention to benefit a defendant is so severely impaired that no valid transfer of title takes place at all, and that in cases of this kind unjust enrichment should be irrelevant because the relevant property continues to belong to the claimant.[9] Otherwise, the law should hold that title to property passes irretrievably, and in cases of this kind the claimant might be entitled to a personal restitutionary award but should never be entitled to a proprietary restitutionary award, because there is no good reason to give him the benefits associated with proprietary interests, e.g. ownership of capital increases and income derived from the property, and priority over other claimants in a defendant's insolvency. Swadling's position has the merits of clarity and simplicity, but it does not represent the current law, under which proprietary remedies are sometimes awarded. Moreover, it would mean that assets which a claimant never intended to add to the defendant's estate should always be shared between the claimant and the defendant's other unsecured creditors in the event of the defendant's insolvency. In our view such a rule would be unjust.

At the opposite end of the spectrum of possible approaches, we find that a **37–09** proprietary remedy could conceivably be awarded in every case of unjust enrichment, whether or not the value conferred by the claimant identifiably resides in particular property held by the defendant. On the basis that the defendant's overall wealth was swollen by the value he received, a lien would then be imposed over the whole of his assets to secure performance of his personal restitutionary obligation. The imposition of such a lien was mooted by Lord Templeman in *Space Investments Ltd v Canadian Imperial Bank of Commerce*.[10]

However, the courts have rejected this approach in favour of a more restricted **37–10** approach which requires a claimant to show either that he previously owned the very property in which he now claims an interest, or else that the defendant acquired this property in exchange for property that was previously owned by the claimant, or else (in the subrogation cases) that this property was formerly the

---

[8] W. Swadling, "Property and Unjust Enrichment" in J.W. Harris (ed.), *Property Problems: From Genes to Pension Funds* (London: Kluwer, 1997), 130.

[9] Further elaborated in W. Swadling, "Ignorance and Unjust Enrichment: The Problem of Title" (2008) 28 O.J.L.S. 627, where he contends that if title has not been transferred then the defendant cannot have been enriched, or if he has been, that this cannot have been at the claimant's expense. A similar claim has been made by Ross Grantham and Charles Rickett who argue that in such cases the law's primary method of protecting the claimant should be to give him an action for interference with property, and that allowing him a claim in unjust enrichment would therefore be redundant: e.g. "Property and Unjust Enrichment: Categorical Truths or Unnecessary Complexity" [1997] N.Z.L.Rev. 668, and "On the Subsidiarity of Unjust Enrichment" (2001) 117 L.Q.R. 273, pp. 282–284. Even where legal title does not pass to a defendant, however, he may be enriched by the receipt of user value, and by the receipt of possessory title, and it is implausible that these are nether enriching nor received at the claimant's expense: J. Edelman and E. Bant, *Unjust Enrichment in Australia* (Melbourne: OUP, 2006), pp.102–103; A. Burrows, *The Law of Restitution*, 3rd edn (Oxford: OUP, 2010), pp.194–198. See too para.5–17.

[10] *Space Investments Ltd v Canadian Imperial Bank of Commerce* [1986] 1 W.L.R. 1072 at 1074.

subject matter of an interest that was discharged with property that was previously owned by the claimant.[11] This has been described as a rule that the
claimant must establish a "proprietary base" to his claim.[12] Many scholars
consider that in principle this rule is a sound starting point for identifying the
circumstances in which proprietary remedies should be awarded, although there
is a consensus that additional restrictions are also needed.[13]

37–11   To establish a "proprietary base", a claimant must have resort to the rules of
following and tracing. These rules are discussed in Ch.7. They are often
expressed in the metaphorical language of "proprietary links", and as Craig
Rotherham has observed,[14] this makes it tempting to think that the rules themselves can provide a normative justification for the award or refusal of proprietary remedies. But as he also observes, this would be an error. Some recent cases
make it very clear that these rules are merely rules of evidence,[15] and it follows
that justifications for the "proprietary base" requirement must be sought elsewhere.

37–12   A strain of thought identifiable in some of the cases and literature is the vague
idea that there should not be "too much" proprietary restitution, and that the
"proprietary base" rule is a good way of reducing the general availability of
proprietary remedies because it has the merit of certainty and predictability (to
the extent that the rules of following and tracing are certain and predictable). This
will not do as a justification for the rule since it begs the question of how much
proprietary restitution there ought to be. Moreover this line of thinking creates
the danger that the "proprietary base" rule will be used in an essentially arbitrary

---

[11] *Re Goldcorp Exchange Ltd* [1995] 1 A.C. 74 at 107–110 per Lord Mustill; *Bishopsgate Investment
Management Ltd v Homan* [1995] Ch. 211 at 217–220 per Dillon L.J., and at 221 per Leggatt L.J.;
Boscawen v Bajwa [1996] 1 W.L.R. 328 at 334 per Millett L.J.; *Lexi Holdings* [2008] EWCA Crim
1443; [2009] Q.B. 376 at [49]–[50] per Keene L.J., discussed at paras 7.37–7.39. Cf. L. Smith,
"Tracing" in A. Burrows and Lord Rodger (eds), *Mapping the Law* (Oxford: OUP 2006), 119,
pp.135–137, noting that rejection of the "swollen assets" theory reflects the "particular" conception
of wealth on which the courts' approach to the award of proprietary remedies is premised, while its
acceptance would require them to abandon this for an "abstract conception", i.e. it would require
them to accept that an idea of wealth as abstract value, which underpins their approach to personal
restitution, should also underpin their approach to proprietary restitution, in contradistinction to an
idea of wealth as proprietary rights in particular subject matter. The difference between these two
conceptions is also discussed in B. Rudden, "Things as Things and Things as Wealth" in Harris,
Property Problems, 146.

[12] This term was coined by Peter Birks: P. Birks, *An Introduction to the Law of Restitution*, revised
edn (Oxford: Clarendon Press, 1989), pp.375–385; P. Birks, "Establishing a Proprietary Base" [1995]
R.L.R 83. The terminology has made its way into judicial discourse: e.g. *Westdeutsche Landesbank
Girozentrale v Islington LBC* [1996] A.C. 669 at 714 per Lord Browne-Wilkinson; *Foskett* [2001] 1
A.C. 102 at 117 per Lord Hope; *Daraydan Holdings Ltd v Solland International Ltd* [2004] EWHC
622 (Ch); [2005] Ch. 119 at [78] per Lawrence Collins J.; *O.J.S.C. Oil Co Yugraneft v Abramovich*
[2008] EWHC 2613 (Comm) at [349] and [372] per Christopher Clarke J.

[13] e.g. P. Birks, *Unjust Enrichment*, 2nd edn (Oxford: OUP, 2005), p.185; M. Bryan, "The Criteria for
the Award of Proprietary Remedies: Rethinking the Proprietary Base" in M. Bryan (ed.), *Private Law
in Theory and Practice* (London: Routledge-Cavendish, 2007) 271, p.274; Burrows, *The Law of
Restitution*, p.174.

[14] C. Rotherham, "The Metaphysics of Tracing: Substituted Title and Property Rhetoric" [1996]
Osgoode Hall L.J. 321.

[15] *Foskett* [2001] 1 A.C. 102 at 127–128 per Lord Millett; *Glencore International AG v Metro
Trading International Ltd* [2001] 1 Lloyd's Rep. 284 at [180] per Moore-Bick J.

way. Unless the policy calculations that underlie the adoption of control devices within private law are made explicit, their application always leads to confusion, inconsistency, and unfairness.

A more substantial argument, made by Andrew Burrows and others, is that **37-13** wherever a defendant's unjust enrichment exists in a surviving asset, "proprietary restitution should be the norm ... [because it] more perfectly achieves restitution than does personal restitution".[16] On this view, the point of allowing proprietary restitution where a proprietary base can be established, but not otherwise, is that this is the only situation where it can be said that proprietary restitution more exactly effects the return of what the defendant received than a personal award, i.e. a property right, rather than the value of a property right.

One might demur over the details of this: an equitable proprietary interest **37-14** under a trust is not exactly the same property right as a legal interest received by a defendant, and an equitable lien over the whole of a defendant's assets is arguably "nearer" to the legal interest received by a defendant than an order directing the defendant to pay a money sum. However, it does seem plausible that, as between the claimant and the defendant, a proprietary right in a surviving asset is something to which the claimant should be entitled, since the benefits attached to ownership of this asset, including capital increases and income, are things to which the defendant ex hypothesi was not previously entitled. Yet the question still remains why the claimant should be entitled to "perfect restitution" when this will effectively advance his claim ahead of many other claims against the defendant in the event of the defendant's insolvency.

So far as the relative status of claims in a defendant's insolvency are con- **37-15** cerned, some writers have argued that these should be ignored by the courts when deciding whether or not a claimant should be entitled to a proprietary remedy, because the ranking of claims in insolvency is a matter for Parliament, and the courts should therefore make their decision on other grounds in the expectation that Parliament will correct any injustice that results.[17] We accept that civil litigation does not provide the best forum for resolving the difficult questions of distributive justice that are created by a defendant's insolvency—in Peter Birks' phrase, "the rationality of 'women and children first' may require re-examination, but shipwreck is not the time to attempt a reassessment."[18] Nevertheless we believe that it would be unprincipled and misguided for the courts to ignore one of the central reasons why it matters whether claimants are entitled to proprietary restitution when deciding whether or not such relief should be available. We agree with those writers who believe that it is both appropriate and necessary for

---

[16] Burrows, *The Law of Restitution*, p.174. See too S. Smith, "The Structure of Unjust Enrichment Law: Is Restitution a Right or a Remedy?" (2003) 36 Loyola of Los Angeles L.R. 1037, p.1057; L. Smith, "Philosophical Foundations of Proprietary Remedies" in R. Chambers et al. (eds), *Philosophical Foundations of the Law of Unjust Enrichment* (Oxford: OUP, 2009), 281, p.294. A similar idea also runs through R. Chambers, "Two Types of Enrichment" in Chambers et al., above, 242.

[17] e.g. W. Swadling, "Policy Arguments for Proprietary Restitution" in S. Degeling and J. Edelman (eds.), *Unjust Enrichment in Commercial Law* (Sydney: Lawbook Co, 2008), 359, pp.372–375.

[18] Birks, *Unjust Enrichment*, p.181.

the courts to take this into consideration,[19] and we note that in *Westdeutsche Landesbank Girozentrale v Islington LBC*, Lord Goff had no qualms about doing so when he reasoned that the claimant bank should not be entitled to an interest under a resulting trust where it had "entered into a commercial transaction, and so taken the risk of the defendant's insolvency, just like the defendant's other creditors who have contracted with it."[20]

37–16   The converse argument has often been made that in some situations proprietary remedies should be awarded to claimants in unjust enrichment precisely because they deserve different treatment from certain other claimants in a defendant's insolvency. Unlike unsecured contract creditors who have added value to the defendant's estate, they have not taken the risk of the defendant's insolvency; and unlike tort victims who have not taken the risk of the defendant's insolvency, they have added value to the defendant's estate.[21] William Swadling has turned this argument on its head, contending that claimants in unjust enrichment should not be treated differently because tort victims have also not taken the risk of the defendant's insolvency, and because unsecured contract creditors have also added value to the defendant's estate. But this misses the point that the two reasons for differentiating a claimant in unjust enrichment from the other types of claimant acquire special force when taken together. Swadling denies this, contending that it is "simply to combine two bad arguments and claim to have produced one which is good".[22] We disagree: in Swadling's terms, we consider that if the arguments are "bad", then they are only "bad" when taken separately, and they are "good" when taken in combination.

37–17   If the availability of proprietary remedies should turn on the question whether the claimant has voluntarily taken the risk of the defendant's insolvency, then this would mean that a claimant who has had the opportunity to bargain for security, and who has not taken it, should not be entitled to a proprietary remedy in the event that the defendant fails to repay him the value of the benefits that he confers. This principle should apply not only to cases where the claimant relies on failure of basis as the ground for restitution, but also to cases where he relies on other grounds, although care would be needed when considering claims founded on such vitiating factors as mistake and undue influence, to be certain whether the claimant knew that he had an opportunity to bargain for security, and

---

[19] e.g. V. Finch and S. Worthington, "The Pari Passu Principle and Ranking Restitutionary Rights" in F. Rose (ed.), *Restitution and Insolvency* (Oxford: Mansfield Press, 2000), 1, p.17; Edelman and Bant, *Unjust Enrichment in Australia*, pp.70–72; Burrows, *The Law of Restitution*, pp.176–179; K. Mason, "Deconstructing Constructive Trusts in Australia" (2010) 4 J. Eq. 98: "In truth, equity has for centuries been in the business of recognising and prioritising species of property, and in so doing developed rules whereby trusts, liens, charges and equitable assignments were treated as binding trustees in bankruptcy in particular situations."

[20] *Westdeutsche Landesbank Girozentrale v Islington LBC* [1996] A.C. 669 at 683–684. See too *Lord Napier and Ettrick v Hunter* [1993] A.C. 713 at 737 per Lord Templeman, although his conclusions are suspect for the reason given at para.21.104.

[21] e.g. E. Sherwin, "Constructive Trusts in Bankruptcy" [1989] University of Illinois L.R. 297; D. Paccioco, "The Remedial Constructive Trust: A Principled Basis for Priorities over Creditors" (1989) 68 Can. B.R. 315; C. Rotherham, *Proprietary Interests in Context* (Oxford: Hart, 2002), Chs 4, 6, 9, 11 and 12; Burrows, *The Law of Restitution*, pp.176–179.

[22] W. Swadling, "Rescission, Property, and the Common Law" (2005) 121 L.Q.R. 123, p.138. See too Swadling, "Property and Unjust Enrichment", pp.142–145; and cf. A. J. Oakley, "Proprietary Claims and their Priority in Insolvency" (1995) 54 C.L.J. 376, pp.397–404.

was capable of exercising an independent judgment when deciding whether or not to take this opportunity.

The "voluntary assumption of risk" argument is consistent with various cases **37–18** where a trust or lien has been imposed on property transferred to a defendant by a claimant whose mistake masked the risk that he ran of the defendant's insolvency,[23] or who was unable to assess the risk because he was unduly influenced by the defendant.[24] Many subrogation cases are also explicable on this basis.[25] The argument is also consistent with various cases where the courts have refused to allow claimants to acquire security interests via subrogation where they have expressly agreed not to take security or where they have intended to make an unsecured loan.[26] However, it suggests that the Mercantile Law Amendment Act 1856 s.5, is anomalous to the extent that it gives sureties (and other claimants) a right to acquire securities via subrogation although they have not taken an opportunity to bargain for a security with the principal debtor (or other defendant). The argument also suggests that *Neste Oy v Lloyds Bank Plc*[27] and *Re Farepak Food & Gifts Ltd*[28] were incorrectly decided: in both cases money received from unsecured creditors was impressed with a trust in their favour when the basis for the payments immediately failed at the time of receipt.

The latter decisions are, however, explicable by reference to an alternative **37–19** approach advocated by Robert Chambers and Peter Birks,[29] according to which the availability of proprietary remedies turns on the question whether the subject matter of the claim was freely at the defendant's disposal before the claimant's right to restitution arose. If it was not, then the law will give the claimant a proprietary right in the asset, as a mechanism for reversing the defendant's unjust

---

[23] e.g. *Cooper v Phibbs* (1867) L.R. 2 H.L. 149; *Craddock Bros Ltd v Hunt* [1923] 2 Ch. 136; *Chase Manhattan Bank NA Ltd v Israel-British Bank (London) Ltd* [1981] Ch. 105; *Shalson v Russo* [2003] EWHC 1637 (Ch); [2005] Ch. 281 at [122]–[127] per Rimer J.

[24] e.g. *Allcard v Skinner* (1887) 36 Ch. D. 145, especially at 188–189 per Lindley L.J., and 193 per Bowen L.J.

[25] For a detailed account of the many examples, see C. Mitchell and S. Watterson, *Subrogation: Law and Practice* (Oxford: OUP, 2007), paras 6–57—6–61. They include *Chetwynd v Allen* [1899] 1 Ch. 353; *Butler v Rice* [1910] 2 Ch. 277; *Castle Philips Finance Ltd v Piddington* (1995) 70 P. & C.R. 592; *Halifax Plc v Omar* [2002] EWCA Civ 121; [2002] 2 P. & C.R. 26; *U.C.B. Group Ltd v Hedworth* [2003] EWCA Civ 1717; [2003] 3 F.C.R. 739; *Kali Ltd v Chawla* [2007] EWHC 2357 (Ch); [2008] B.P.I.R. 415.

[26] *Paul v Speirway Ltd* [1976] Ch. 200; *Boscawen* [1996] 1 W.L.R. 328 at 338 per Millett L.J.; *Halifax Mortgage Services Ltd v Muirhead* [1997] EWCA Civ 2901; (1997) 76 P. & C.R. 418 at 426–427 per Evans L.J.; *Banque Financière de la Cité v Parc (Battersea) Ltd* [1998] UKHL 7; [1999] A.C. 221; *Eagle Star Plc v Karasiewicz* [2002] EWCA Civ 940 at [19] per Arden L.J.; *Cheltenham & Gloucester Plc v Appleyard* [2004] EWCA Civ 291 at [38] per Neuberger L.J.; *Filby v Mortgage Express (No.2) Ltd* [2004] EWCA Civ 759 at [39] per May L.J.; *Boodle, Hatfield & Co v British Films Ltd* [1986] 2 B.C.C. 99,221 is inconsistent with this line of authority and was probably wrongly decided.

[27] *Neste Oy v Lloyds Bank Plc* [1983] 2 Lloyd's Rep. 658, discussed in A. Burrows, "Lord Bingham and Three Continuing Remedial Controversies" in M. Andenas and D. Fairgrieve (eds), *Tom Bingham and the Transformation of the Law* (Oxford: OUP, 2009) 589, pp.594–598.

[28] *Re Farepak Food & Gifts Ltd* [2006] EWHC 3272; [2007] 2 B.C.L.C. 1; subsequent proceedings [2009] EWHC 2580 (Ch).

[29] R. Chambers, *Resulting Trusts* (Oxford: OUP, 1997), pp.110 and 155–170; R. Chambers, "Constructive Trusts in Canada" (1999) 37 Alberta L.R. 173, p.219; P. Birks, "Retrieving Tied Money" in W. Swadling (ed.), *The Quistclose Trust: Critical Essays* (Oxford: Hart, 2004) 121, pp.130–138; Birks, *Unjust Enrichment*, pp.185–198; R. Chambers, "Resulting Trusts" in Burrows and Rodger, *Mapping the Law* 247, pp.261–263.

enrichment; if it was, then he will be confined to a personal restitutionary award. On this approach, the availability of proprietary relief depends on the time at which the claimant's cause of action accrues. If it accrues at the time when the defendant is enriched, as in cases of mistake, duress, undue influence, and immediate failure of basis, for example, then a proprietary remedy is available. If it only accrues later, as in cases of subsequent failure of basis, then a proprietary remedy is available only if the asset was never at the defendant's free disposal, because it was "ring-fenced' and available only for some specified application. The "tie" restricting the defendant's use of the asset might derive from a trust, or from a contractual duty to apply the asset in a particular way.

37–20   We accept that this analysis provides a principled explanation of many authorities. However, it cannot account for *Triffit Nurseries (A Firm) v Salads Etcetera Ltd*,[30] where no trust was imposed on money which was payable by third parties to a company on the agreed basis that it would be paid on to the claimant, and which was collected by receivers after the company went into administrative receivership. Nor can it explain the decision in *Westdeutsche*,[31] where no trust was imposed on money paid to the defendant on a basis that immediately failed because the contract under which it was paid was void from the outset.[32] For this reason, Peter Birks argued that *Westdeutsche* was inconsistent with cases such as *Re Ames' Settlement*,[33] where money paid into a marriage settlement was held on resulting trust for the settlor when the marriage was declared void.[34]

37–21   *Westdeutsche* concerned an ultra vires interest rate swap transaction between a bank and a local authority. By the time the case reached the House of Lords it was agreed between the parties that the bank could recover the value of its payments on the ground of unjust enrichment, and the only surviving issue was whether it should be entitled to compound interest on the money. The majority of the court held that no stand-alone claim in unjust enrichment would lie to recover compound interest as the use value of the money.[35] Hence compound interest could be awarded only if there had been a fraud or a breach of trust. There had been no fraud, and there could have been no breach of trust, either, because there had been no trust of the payments received by the local authority. According to Lord Browne-Wilkinson,[36] with whom Lord Slynn, Lord Woolf, and Lord Lloyd all agreed on this point,[37] the reason was that the local authority had dissipated the money before its conscience had been affected by knowledge of the fact that the contract was void. Its position therefore differed from the position of the defendant in *Chase Manhattan Bank v Israel-British Bank (London) Ltd*,[38] an earlier case where a trust had been imposed on money that had been paid to the

---

[30] *Triffit Nurseries (A Firm) v Salads Etcetera Ltd* [2000] 1 All E.R. (Comm.) 737.

[31] *Westdeutsche* [1996] A.C. 669.

[32] As held by Hobhouse J. at first instance: [1994] 4 All E.R. 890 at 955–956; affirmed [1994] 1 W.L.R. 938 at 944–947 per Dillon L.J. These findings were not challenged in the House of Lords.

[33] *Re Ames' Settlement* [1946] Ch. 217. See too *Re Gillingham Bus Disaster Fund* [1958] Ch. 300.

[34] Birks, *Unjust Enrichment*, pp.190–191.

[35] The minority disagreed, and their position was later vindicated in *Sempra Metals Ltd v IRC* [2007] UKHL 34; [2008] A.C. 561; for discussion see para.5–05 and following.

[36] *Westdeutsche* [1996] A.C. 669 at 704–706.

[37] *Westdeutsche* [1996] A.C. 669 at 718, 720, and 738. At 688 Lord Goff found it necessary to consider whether he agreed with Lord Browne-Wilkinson's analysis.

[38] *Chase Manhattan Bank v Israel-British Bank (London) Ltd* [1981] Ch. 105.

defendant by mistake—according to Lord Browne-Wilkinson, because the money had still been identifiable in the defendant's hands at the time when it became aware of the claimant's mistake.

Westdeutsche therefore stands for the proposition that a claimant in unjust   **37–22** enrichment should be entitled to a proprietary remedy only if his conscience is affected by knowledge of the circumstances making his enrichment unjust, at a time when the property he has received from the claimant is still identifiable in his hands. However, this analysis has subsequently been treated with some circumspection by the courts,[39] and we doubt that it is correct in principle. Although Sarah Worthington has argued that a claimant's right to acquire secondary profits should only arise if the defendant has behaved unconscionably,[40] we are not convinced that this is correct. Nor is there an obvious reason why the claimant's position relative to the defendant's other creditors should be improved by a change in the defendant's state of mind at some time between the date of receipt and the date of his insolvency. Indeed, Lord Millett has expressed the extra-judicial view that, by itself, notice of the existence of a ground of restitution is "obviously insufficient to found a proprietary remedy", as "it is merely notice of a personal right" to repayment.[41]

An additional problem with Lord Browne-Wilkinson's analysis is that he   **37–23** started from the premise that whenever a trust is imposed by operation of law the defendant trustee must necessarily owe duties to deal with the property in a way that is consistent with the beneficiaries' equitable ownership rights, breach of which will cause him to incur a compensatory liability. He thought that it would be inequitable to expose a defendant to such a liability unless he knew that the trust existed, and for this reason he overruled the finding that had previously been made in *Sinclair v Brougham*,[42] that money deposited with a statutory building society under ultra vires banking contracts was held on trust, although Viscount Haldane L.C. had explicitly held that this was a "resulting trust, not of an active character,"[43] meaning that it was a trust under which the depositors had had an equitable proprietary interest, but under which the building society, as trustee, had owed them no personal duty to account for the money.[44] In our view, Lord Browne-Wilkinson's premise was incorrect, and there is no reason why a trust cannot be imposed under which the beneficiaries have equitable ownership rights but no right to hold the trustee to account until after his conscience is affected with knowledge.[45] This is discussed further in Ch.38.[46]

Drawing all the threads together, we must finally conclude that in principle   **37–24** proprietary remedies should sometimes be awarded for unjust enrichment, but that there is no theory which can explain when they should be awarded in a way

---

[39] See the authorities cited in para.38–34, fn.100.

[40] S. Worthington, "Justifying Claims to Secondary Profits" in E.J.H. Schrage (ed.), *Unjust Enrichment and the Law of Contract* (The Hague: Kluwer Law International, 2001), 451.

[41] Sir Peter Millett, "Restitution and Constructive Trusts" (1998) 114 L.Q.R. 399, p.413.

[42] *Sinclair v Brougham* [1914] A.C. 398.

[43] *Sinclair* [1914] A.C. 398 at 421.

[44] For the relevant passage of Lord Browne-Wilkinson's speech, see *Westdeutsche* [1996] A.C. 669 at 711–714.

[45] Cf. Sir Peter Millett, "Restitution and Constructive Trusts", p.404: "It probably does not matter if we say that the relationship is not a trust relationship, so long as we call it something else. The trouble is that we have no other name for it."

[46] See paras 38–09—38–15 for further discussion.

that reconciles the results in all of the cases. The theory that proprietary remedies should be awarded, or withheld, according to the state of the defendant's knowledge lacks principled justification. It is more promising to argue that the award of proprietary remedies should turn on the question whether the claimant has voluntarily assumed the risk of the defendant's insolvency, and this theory fits with many of the cases, but it does not fit with all of them. The same can also be said of the theory that the award of proprietary remedies should turn on the question whether the property received by the defendant was ever freely at his disposal.

3. Immediately Vested Proprietary Rights and Powers in Rem

37–25   In Ch.38 we identify cases where a trust or lien has immediately arisen in response to the defendant's unjust enrichment at the time when the claimant's cause of action accrued, and in Ch.39 we identify cases where the claimant has immediately acquired a security interest in the defendant's property via subrogation, again at the time when his cause of action in unjust enrichment accrued. In Ch.40, however, we identify other cases where a claimant has merely had a power to acquire a proprietary interest in property held by the defendant, by electing to rescind a transaction or rectify a document under which the defendant received the property from the claimant. The question arises, whether one or other of these forms of remedy should be adopted as the standard form for all restitutionary proprietary remedies.

37–26   Birke Häcker has argued that the "power model" exemplified by the rescission and rectification cases is preferable to the "immediate interest" model exemplified by the other cases, and should therefore be generalised and adopted in all cases where proprietary restitutionary remedies are awarded for unjust enrichment.[47] One advantage to be gained from doing this would be that it helps to overcome a problem previously identified by Peter Birks, and named by him the problem of "geometric multiplication".[48] This arises in cases where a defendant against whom the claimant can assert a proprietary remedy has received property which he has then exchanged for other property. In these circumstances the law would not wish to let the claimant assert an immediate ownership interest in both the original and the substitute property. If the original property has been exchanged for a substitute provided by a bona fide purchaser, then the claimant's rights will be lost whichever model is adopted. Where this is not the case, the claimant can only be disabled from asserting an equitable proprietary interest in both assets under the "immediate interest" model by devising a special rule against the accumulation of benefits. In contrast, under the "power model", the claimant has no proprietary interest in either asset until he exercises his power (and this power can only be exercised once).

---

[47] B. Häcker, *Consequences of Impaired Consent Transfers* (Tübingen: Mohr Siebeck, 2009), pp.125–159; B. Häcker, "Proprietary Restitution after Impaired Consent Transfers: A Generalised Power Model" [2009] C.L.J. 324.

[48] Birks, *An Introduction to the Law of Restitution*, p.394. See also P. Birks, "On Taking Seriously the Difference between Tracing and Claiming" (1997) 11 Tru. L.I. 2. Further discussion of this problem is in L.D. Smith, *The Law of Tracing* (Oxford: OUP, 1997), pp.358–361.

Support for the general adoption of a "power model", at least in the context **37–27** of claims that are contingent on tracing the value of property into a substitute asset, can be derived from *Lipkin Gorman (A Firm) v Karpnale Ltd*.[49] There, Lord Goff remarked that such claims involve "a decision by the owner of the original property to assert his title to the product in place of his original property." He added that this "is sometimes referred to as ratification", and although he would not so describe it himself, he did consider that it had "at least one feature in common with ratification, that it cannot be relied upon so as to render an innocent recipient a wrongdoer."[50] On Lord Goff's view, therefore, a claimant whose property is received by a defendant and exchanged for other property which is then handed over to a third party cannot sue the third party for conversion if he handled the substitute property before the claimant exercised a right to assert his ownership of this property.

Another advantage of the "power model", in Häcker's view, is that it strikes **37–28** a better balance between the rights of the claimant and the rights of subsequent bona fide purchasers from the defendant. Under the "immediate interest" model, the claimant has an equitable proprietary interest that prevails over any subsequent equitable proprietary interest, even one that has been purchased by a third party in good faith.[51] Under the "power model", in contrast, he receives an equitable power in rem that counts as a "mere equity" and is therefore defeated by a subsequent equitable proprietary interest purchased in good faith.[52] We consider that there is much to be said for balancing the interests of claimants and third party purchasers in this way.

4. OWNERSHIP AND SECURITY INTERESTS

In Chs 38–40 we identify cases in which claimants have variously acquired **37–29** ownership and security interests in property. The question arises, whether claimants should be afforded a free choice between such interests, or whether their choice should be restricted in some circumstances? When considering this question it should be borne in mind that although claimants would often prefer to acquire an ownership interest in order to capture increases in the capital value of the property and/or income generated by the property, this is not always the case, as a security interest will serve them better where the value of the property has declined.[53]

The courts have declined to hold that a trust arises, but have been willing to **37–30** hold that the claimant is entitled to a lien, in cases where the claimant's money

---

[49] *Lipkin Gorman (A Firm) v Karpnale Ltd* [1991] 2 A.C. 548 at 573,

[50] Cf. *Bolton Partners v Lambert* (1889) 41 Ch. D. 295 at 307 per Cotton L.J.: "an act lawful at the time of its performance [cannot] be rendered unlawful, by the application of the doctrine of ratification."

[51] In accordance with the maxim *qui prior est tempore, potior est iure*, i.e. "where the equities are equal, the first in time prevails". Cf. *Phillips v Phillips* (1861) 4 De G. F. & J. 208 at 215–216; 45 E.R. 1164 at 1166, per Lord Westbury L.C.; *Cave v Cave* (1880) 15 Ch. D. 639 at 646–647 per Fry J.

[52] *Phillips* (1861) 4 De G. F. & J. 208 at 218; 45 E.R. 1164 at 1167 per Lord Westbury L.C.; *Cave* (1880) 15 Ch. D. 639.

[53] As in e.g. *Re Hallett's Estate* (1880) 13 Ch. D. 696.

can be traced into improvements to the defendant's property.[54] These cases are discussed in Ch.7.[55] It is observed there that the courts' conceptualisation of the tracing rules as a body of rules that are focused on "real exchanges" has made it difficult for them to explain repair and improvement cases where the assumption is made that a claimant must trace the value of his money or services into property owned by the defendant before he can have a proprietary remedy. This has led the courts to make some inconsistent findings with regard to the circumstances in which a lien will be imposed. Assuming that it is possible to trace the value of repairs and improvements into property owned by a defendant, however, and that either a lien or a trust could be imposed, the question arises whether it is justified to restrict the claimant to a lien? One argument why this is appropriate might be that the claimant should not be entitled to share in increases to the value of the property as the beneficiary of a trust because this would constitute too great an inroad into the defendant's right to take these for himself as the pre-existing owner of the property.[56]

37–31   It has also been held by the House of Lords that money received by an insured from a third party in diminution of loss for which he has already been indemnified by the insurer is held subject to an equitable lien in favour of the insurer, but is not held by the insured on trust for the insurer.[57] Their Lordships thought the imposition of a trust to be undesirable because this would entail importing fiduciary duties into a commercial relationship. However, this was to assume, probably incorrectly, that where a trust is imposed by law the trustee owes fiduciary duties although he has not voluntarily assumed responsibility towards the beneficiaries.[58] But in any case, there are good reasons for thinking that neither a trust nor a lien should have been awarded in this case. One is that the insurers had the opportunity to bargain for a security with their insureds and failed to take it.[59] Another is that allowing the insurer a proprietary remedy where the third party's payment post-dates the insurer's payment is inconsistent with the rule that an insurer only has a personal right to recover its money when the order of the payments is reversed. This is discussed further in Ch.21.[60]

37–32   Although the foregoing cases suggest that there may be circumstances in which claimants should be confined to a security interest, we consider that in general they should not be so confined, but should be given a choice between a security interest or an ownership interest. In other areas of the law, English law permits civil litigants to choose between concurrent rights, subject to rules against double recovery and double liability, and we believe that it should generally do so in this context as well. Some support for this can be derived from

---

[54] *Unity Joint Stock Mutual Banking Association v King* (1858) 25 Beav. 72; 53 E.R. 563; *Foskett* [1998] Ch. 265 at 278 per Scott V.C.; [2001] 1 A.C. 102 at 109 per Lord Browne-Wilkinson; *Re Esteem Settlement* 2002 J.L.R. 53 at 105–106 per Birt D.B. (Jersey Royal Ct). But *cf. Re Diplock* [1948] Ch. 465 at 545–548, per curiam (CA).

[55] See paras 7–20——7–24.

[56] Cf. para.5–26, arguing that for the same reason the benefit received by a defendant whose property has been repaired or improved by a claimant should be characterised as the value of the services rather than the enhanced capital value of the property.

[57] *Lord Napier* [1993] A.C. 713 at 737–738 per Lord Templeman, at 744 per Lord Goff, and at 750–751 per Lord Browne-Wilkinson.

[58] See para.38–14.

[59] See paras 37–16——37–18.

[60] See paras 21 104——21–105.

Foskett.[61] This concerned a claim by trust beneficiaries to a proprietary interest in the proceeds of a life assurance policy, some of the premiums for which had been paid with misappropriated trust money. The House of Lords held that the beneficiaries could trace the value of their money into the value of the policy proceeds, and that they could make a proprietary claim to the proceeds. As we discuss elsewhere,[62] the source of their right to make this claim is debated, but for present purposes, the significance of the case lies in the fact that the court held that the beneficiaries had a free choice between a lien over the proceeds to secure repayment of the money used to pay the premiums, or a (significantly more valuable) proportionate interest under a trust of the proceeds.[63]

5. RATIONALISING THE LAW

We have said already that the current law is difficult to state with certainty. Some important authorities do not support the award of proprietary remedies for unjust enrichment, yet in many other cases such remedies have been awarded.　**37–33**

The House of Lords has declined to award a proprietary remedy on the ground of unjust enrichment in two well-known cases: *Foskett*[64] and *Westdeutsche.*[65] It is worth remembering, however, that in *Foskett* a trust was imposed on the traceable proceeds of misapplied trust property, and the court did not hold that proprietary remedies can never be awarded for unjust enrichment, merely that unjust enrichment was not the reason why a trust was imposed in the case. There are, moreover, reasons for doubting the correctness of the court's analysis in *Foskett*, and in particular its characterisation of unjust enrichment and property as opposing sources of rights: we consider this to have been a misconception because unjust enrichment is a source of rights while property is a type of right.[66]　**37–34**

Meanwhile, *Westdeutsche* holds that resulting trusts do not respond to unjust enrichment, but to the beneficiary's intention to create a trust for himself; and Lord Browne-Wilkinson sounded a warning against the creation of "off balance sheet" liabilities arising under trusts imposed by law of which defendants and their creditors might be unaware.[67] But the view that resulting trusts respond to intention is inconsistent with cases where they have been imposed in the teeth of evidence that the beneficiary did not wish to have any beneficial interest in the property.[68] Furthermore, if the law is to restrict claimants in unjust enrichment to personal liabilities then many cases will have to be overruled, in which proprietary remedies have been awarded.　**37–35**

We consider all these cases in the chapters which follow, but to summarise them here, they hold that trusts should be imposed on property held by a　**37–36**

---

[61] *Foskett* [2001] 1 A.C. 102.
[62] See paras 8–83—8–93.
[63] *Foskett* [2001] 1 A.C. 102 at 131 per Lord Millett.
[64] *Foskett* [2001] 1 A.C. 102.
[65] *Westdeutsche* [1996] A.C. 669.
[66] See paras 8–83—8–93.
[67] *Westdeutsche* [1996] A.C. 669 at 705.
[68] See especially *Vandervell v IRC* [1967] 2 A.C. 291; see paras 38–24—38–26.

defendant, either automatically,[69] or following the claimant's election to rescind a transaction or rectify a document[70]; that liens should be imposed on property held by the defendant, either automatically,[71] or following the claimant's election to rescind a transaction or rectify a document[72]; and that interests in property held by a defendant have arisen via subrogation.[73]

37–37   It is not always recognised that these cases comprise a single body of law; indeed some scholars would contest the assertion that they do comprise a single body of law. There are several reasons for this. The law has developed in a fragmented fashion, some proprietary remedies were identified as remedies for unjust enrichment only recently, and it is debatable whether certain other proprietary remedies respond to unjust enrichment or arise for other reasons.[74] Work therefore remains to be done before this area of the law can be fully understood. Its component parts must be identified, and the uncertainties resolved. Until this is done, the task of rationalising the law and eliminating inconsistencies can only be undertaken in a piecemeal way.

37–38   Yet even this would be a worthwhile project for the courts to undertake. Suppose, for example, that a claimant pays money to a defendant by mistake. Suppose, further, that the defendant uses the money to buy a boat, or to discharge a mortgage over his house. Should the boat be impressed with a trust for the claimant? Should the boat be impressed with a lien, to secure performance of the defendant's restitutionary obligation? Should the claimant acquire a security over the house via subrogation? These are questions to which the law should give consistent answers. Other matters being equal, it might be unjust for the law to hold that no trust arises, but to allow subrogation, or to disallow subrogation, but to impose a lien. Yet such inconsistencies are often encountered in the case law, and the only way for a court to eliminate them is to look across all of the cases where proprietary remedies have been allowed or disallowed when deciding whether to allow any particular proprietary remedy.

---

[69] See the cases cited and discussed at paras 38–33—38–34.
[70] See the cases cited and discussed at paras 40–21—40–22 and 40–35.
[71] See the cases cited and discussed at paras 38–39 and 38–41.
[72] *Cooper v Phibbs* (1867) L.R. 2 H.L. 149.
[73] There are numerous cases; some are cited and discussed at paras 39–17—39–19.
[74] Some of these themes are explored in J. Beatson, "Unfinished Business: Integrating Equity" in J. Beatson, *The Use and Abuse of Unjust Enrichment* (Oxford: Clarendon Press, 1991), 244, and in D. J. Ibbetson, *A Historical Introduction to the Law of Obligations* (Oxford: OUP, 1999), 14, especially pp.290–294.

Chapter 38

PROPRIETARY REMEDIES: TRUSTS AND LIENS

1. Introduction

The relationship between unjust enrichment and trusts is complex and con-   **38–01**
troversial. One reason is that the justifications for awarding proprietary remedies
for unjust enrichment are debated. Some argue that the award of such remedies
is never justified and others that it is justified only when kept within limits
(although there is no clear consensus as to what these limits should be). Different
courts and commentators take different views, and so they give different answers
to the question of whether trusts should be imposed to reverse a defendant's
unjust enrichment. The policy arguments for and against the award of proprietary
remedies for unjust enrichment are reviewed in Ch.37.[1]

The relationship between unjust enrichment and trusts is also hard to under-   **38–02**
stand because the trusts which might sometimes be imposed to reverse unjust
enrichment, namely constructive and resulting trusts, are themselves imperfectly
understood. There are several aspects to this. It is unclear whether constructive
and resulting trusts are separate categories of trust or whether resulting trusts are
a type of constructive trust. It is debated whether constructive trusts can only be
"institutional" or whether they can also be "remedial". It is controversial when
constructive trusts are "real" trusts, under which beneficiaries acquire equitable
proprietary rights, and when they are mere "formulae" for the award of equitable
personal remedies. It is not settled what matters must be proved by a claimant
seeking a declaration of resulting trust. And it is contentious whether trusts can
usefully be analysed by asking what legal events have led to their imposition.

In Parts 2–5 we review these questions and examine what constructive and   **38–03**
resulting trusts are and how they work, why it is plausible that some constructive
and resulting trusts respond to unjust enrichment, and how the law governing the
imposition of these trusts might be rationalised and better aligned with the law of
obligations in the future. Detailed discussion of all these topics lies beyond the
scope of the present work. The more modest goal of this chapter is to provide an
overview of the issues, with the aim of filling in some of the background to the
discussion of proprietary remedies that is undertaken in Ch.37.

The discussion in this chapter concerns trusts that are imposed automatically,   **38–04**
without the claimant having to take positive steps to bring his equitable proprietary interest under the trust into existence. As we discuss in Ch.40, a trust can
also be brought into existence by the claimant's exercise of a power to rescind a
transaction or to rectify a document under which the defendant received the
relevant property.[2]

---

[1] See paras 37–07—37–24.
[2] *Shalson v Russo* [2003] EWHC 1637 (Ch); [2005] Ch. 281, discussed at para.40–22; *Craddock Bros Ltd v Hunt* [1923] 2 Ch. 136, discussed at para.40–35.

38–05   In Part 6 we finally give a brief account of liens. These are security interests over property that give a claimant a different set of rights from those that he would acquire as the beneficiary of a constructive or resulting trust.

2. Constructive and Resulting Trusts

(a) *Constructive and Resulting Trusts Defined*

38–06   The verb "to construe" means "to interpret". Hence the word "constructive" is used to denote the fact that the law interprets—or, effectively, deems—a party's words and actions to have had some effect in law although they did not have this effect in fact.[3] The law deems a person with "constructive notice" to know the answers to questions that a reasonable person in his position would have asked,[4] although in fact he did not ask the questions and does not know the answers. In the case of a "constructive trust", the law deems one party to have conferred the same proprietary rights on another party as he would have acquired, had an express trust been declared in his favour although in fact no valid declaration of trust has been made.[5]

38–07   The word "resulting" derives from the Latin word *resalire*: "to jump back". Hence a resulting trust is literally a trust which returns beneficial ownership of the trust property to a person who owned the property before it reached the trustee's hands: in equity, the beneficial interest "jumps back" to its previous owner. Using the term "resulting trust" in a literal sense, it could therefore meaningfully be said that an "express resulting trust" would be created if X transferred property to Y with the express instruction that Y should hold the property on trust for X. However, English lawyers rarely use the term "resulting trust" to describe an express trust which carries the beneficial interest back to its previous owner.[6] They almost always use the term to describe a trust which conforms to this pattern and which is imposed by law.[7]

38–08   It follows from all this that "constructive trust" and "resulting trust" are overlapping categories. If a constructive trust is a trust imposed by law in situations where no valid express trust has been declared, and a resulting trust is

---

[3] Sir R. Megarry, "Historical Development" in *Special Lectures of the Law Society of Upper Canada 1990—Fiduciary Duties* (1991) 1, at p.5: "'Constructive' seems to mean 'It isn't, but has to be treated as if it were'." See too *Giumelli v Giumelli* (1999) 196 C.L.R. 101 at 110 per Gleeson C.J., McHugh, Gummow, and Calinan JJ.: "The court construes the circumstances in the sense that it explains or interprets them; it does not construct them."

[4] e.g. Law of Property Act 1925 s.199(1)(ii).

[5] Cf. W. Swadling, "The Fiction of the Constructive Trust" (2011) 64 C.L.P., arguing that "constructive trusts" are not trusts, and that this terminology masks two types of court order: that the defendant pay a sum of money to the claimant and that the defendant convey a property right to the claimant. This reduces to a semantic argument that the equitable proprietary rights generated by a "constructive trust" are insufficient for the parties' relationship to qualify as a "trust relationship", although Swadling does not clearly explain how he would define such a relationship.

[6] But see e.g. *Latimer v IRC* [2004] UKPC 13; [2004] 1 W.L.R. 1466 at [41] per Lord Millett.

[7] As in e.g. *Lane v Dighton* (1762) Amb. 409 at 411; 27 E.R. 274 at 276 per Sir Thomas Clarke M.R.; *Barton v Muir* (1874) L.R. 6 P.C. 134 at 145 per Sir John Stuart; *Churcher v Martin* (1889) 42 Ch. D. 312 at 319 per Kekewich J.; *Re English & American Insurance Co Ltd* [1994] 1 B.C.L.C. 649 at 651 per Harman J; *Air Jamaica Ltd v Charlton* [1999] 1 W.L.R. 1399 at 1412 per Lord Millett.

a trust which returns beneficial ownership of the trust property to a previous owner, then some trusts can be both resulting trusts and constructive trusts. Different judges have drawn different conclusions from this. On one view, all trusts imposed by law are constructive trusts, and a resulting trust is one type of constructive trust that arises on particular facts.[8] This means that constructive and resulting trusts are interchangeable whenever these facts are encountered.[9] On another view, constructive and resulting trusts are distinct categories of trust, imposed by the courts for different underlying reasons.[10] It cannot be known which view is correct unless the underlying reasons for the imposition of constructive and resulting trusts are identified. We return to this in Part 5.

(b) *Personal and Proprietary Rights*

There is a significant difference between a beneficiary's proprietary rights under a constructive or resulting trust and his personal rights against the trustee. In *Westdeutsche Landesbank Girozentrale v Islington LBC*,[11] Lord Browne-Wilkinson thought that it would be inappropriate to fix a constructive or resulting trustee with personal liability to account to the beneficiaries for his dealings with the trust property, unless his conscience was affected by knowledge of the circumstances which led to the creation of their equitable proprietary interests. Situations can certainly be imagined in which it would be harsh to hold a constructive or resulting trustee liable to make good losses out of the trust funds when he does not know that the beneficiary has an equitable interest in the property: where the trustee is an infant, for example.[12] However, it does not follow from this, as Lord Browne-Wilkinson also held, that a constructive or resulting trust does not come into existence unless and until the trustee's conscience is affected by knowledge of the circumstances.[13]

38–09

Less drastic strategies than denying a beneficiary's equitable proprietary rights are open to a court that wishes to avoid fixing an innocent constructive or resulting trustee with personal liability for spending the trust assets: for example, recognising that the beneficiary has equitable proprietary rights, but placing the trustee under no greater duty than "an obligation to restore the property on demand, if still in possession of it" at the time when he first becomes aware of

38–10

---

[8] e.g. *Re Llanover Settled Estates* [1926] Ch. 626 at 637 per Astbury J.
[9] e.g. *Gissing v Gissing* [1971] A.C. 886 at 905 per Lord Diplock; *Cowcher v Cowcher* [1972] 1 W.L.R. 425 at 431 per Bagnall J.; *Hussey v Palmer* [1972] 1 W.L.R. 1286 at 1289 per Lord Denning M.R.; *Collings v Lee* [2001] 2 All E.R. 332 at 336 per Nourse L.J.; *London Allied Holdings Ltd v Lee* [2007] EWHC 2061 (Ch) at [276] per Etherton J.
[10] *Drake v Whipp* [1996] 1 F.L.R. 826 at 829–830 per Peter Gibson L.J.; *Westdeutsche Landesbank Girozentrale v Islington LBC* [1996] A.C. 669 at 715–716 per Lord Browne-Wilkinson; *Air Jamaica* [1999] 1 W.L.R. 1399 at 1412 per Lord Millett; *Abbott v Abbott* [2008] UKPC 53; [2008] 1 F.L.R. 1451 at [4] per Baroness Hale.
[11] *Westdeutsche Landesbank Girozentrale v Islington LBC* [1996] A.C. 669 at 705–706.
[12] As in e.g. *Re Vinogradoff* [1935] W.N. 68.
[13] *Westdeutsche* [1996] A.C. 669 at 706–707, recognising that an equitable proprietary interest, whether a restrictive covenant affecting land, or an equitable charge, or an interest under a trust, can burden a legal estate before the legal owner's conscience is affected with knowledge of its existence, but refusing to use the term "trust" to describe the case where an interest under a trust binds the legal estate.

the trust's existence.[14] Various authorities contradict the view that trusts cannot be imposed by law unless and until the trustee's conscience is affected,[15] and in Robert Chambers' words[16]:

> "delaying the creation of the trust until the trustees have sufficient notice to affect their consciences may have a drastic effect on a number of important matters which depend on the timing of the creation of the [constructive or] resulting trust, such as entitlement to income, liability for taxation, risk and insurance, commencement of limitation periods, transfer and transmission of property interests, and priority of competing claims."

38–11   The best view is therefore that a constructive or resulting trust can arise whatever the state of the trustee's knowledge, and that when it does so the beneficiary immediately acquires an equitable proprietary interest in the trust assets, whether or not the trustee also owes him personal obligations to account for his dealings with the property.[17] This is consistent with cases which hold that a trust comes into existence whenever the legal and equitable ownership of property is split,[18] although we share Lord Millett's view that the question whether the word "trust" can appropriately be used where a legal owner owes no duties to an equitable owner is a semantic issue that distracts attention from some more important questions that arise in cases where constructive and resulting trusts are imposed[19]: namely, when do the beneficiary's equitable proprietary rights come into being; what is the content of these rights; does the trustee owe duties with respect to the property; and if so, what is the content of these duties and when do they arise?

38–12   So far as the beneficiary's proprietary rights are concerned, he has an equitable proprietary interest in the trust property that generally binds all subsequent transferees of the property other than bona fide purchasers for value without notice. The property is "recoverable and traceable in equity",[20] meaning that the beneficiary can use the rules of following and tracing[21] to identify property in the hands of the trustee or a subsequent recipient as representing his original

---

[14] J. Hackney, *Understanding Equity & Trusts* (London: Fontana, 1987), p.167. Further possible strategies are explored in R. Chambers, *Resulting Trusts* (Oxford: OUP, 1997), pp.209–212.

[15] *Birch v Blagrave* (1755) Amb. 264; 27 E.R. 176; *Childers v Childers* (1857) 1 De G. & J. 482; 44 E.R. 810; *Re Vinogradoff* [1935] W.N. 68; *Re Diplock* [1948] Ch. 465; *Re Muller* [1953] N.Z.L.R. 879.

[16] Chambers, *Resulting Trusts*, p.206.

[17] Cf. *Heperu Pty Ltd v Belle* [2009] NSWCA 252; (2009) 76 N.S.W.L.R. 230 at [155] per Allsop P.: "The court declares that a trust exists and existed (though the innocent volunteer did not know it)."

[18] *Hardoon v Belilios* [1901] A.C. 118 at 123 per Lord Lindley: a trust exists when "the legal title [is] in the plaintiff and the equitable title in the defendant"; *Sinclair v Brougham* [1914] A.C. 398 at 421 Viscount Haldane L.C., referring to "a resulting trust not of an active character", meaning one under which the beneficiaries had a proprietary interest, but which imposed no personal obligations on the trustee. See too *Guerin v Canada* [1984] 2 S.C.R. 335.

[19] *R. v Chester and North Wales Legal Aid Area Office Ex p. Floods of Queensferry Ltd* [1998] 1 W.L.R. 1496 at 1500 per Millett L.J. See too Sir Peter Millett, "Restitution and Constructive Trusts" (1998) 114 L.Q.R. 399, p.404: "It probably does not matter if we say that the relationship is not a trust relationship, so long as we call it something else. The trouble is that we have no other name for it."

[20] *Westdeutsche* [1996] A.C. 669 at 715 per Lord Browne-Wilkinson.

[21] For discussion of which, see Ch.7.

property,[22] and unless the recipient is a bona fide purchaser the beneficiary can then obtain an order for conveyance of the legal title which obliges the holder "to surrender the property in question, thereby bringing about a determination of the rights and titles of the parties".[23] In cases concerning dispositions of registered land, the beneficiary's equitable interest can bind later purchasers of equitable interests and can also bind a registered proprietor if the beneficiary is in actual occupation.[24] However, a registered proprietor is not affected by adverse equitable interests that are not protected on the register or by the actual occupation of the owner thereof, irrespective of whether he has any knowledge or notice of those interests.[25]

So far as the trustee's personal duties are concerned, the trustee owes no duties **38-13** before his conscience is affected by knowledge of the facts which led to the imposition of the trust, and in particular he will not be personally liable to pay compensation for breach of trust if he disposes of the trust assets before this date.[26] Until the trustee acquires knowledge of the circumstances, and for as long as the trust property remains in his hands, the beneficiary simply has a power to fix the trustee with a duty to reconvey the property by bringing the existence of the trust to his attention.[27]

Once his conscience has been affected by knowledge, the trustee owes a duty **38-14** to deal with the trust property in a manner that is consistent with the beneficiary's equitable proprietary rights and to reconvey the property on demand[28]; he may also be obliged to get in the trust estate from third parties for payment over to the beneficiary if this is necessary.[29] However, this is generally considered to be the limit of his obligations, and it is generally thought that he does not also owe the beneficiaries a fiduciary duty of loyalty which attaches to express trusteeship

---

[22] *Lister & Co v Stubbs* (1890) L.R. 45 Ch. D. 1 at 15 per Lindley L.J.; *El Ajou v Dollar Land Holdings Plc (No.1)* [1993] 3 All E.R. 717 at 734 per Millett J. (reversed on a different point [1994] 2 All E.R. 685); *Att Gen for Hong Kong v Reid* [1994] 1 A.C. 324; *Halifax Building Society v Thomas* [1996] Ch. 217 at 226 per Peter Gibson L.J.

[23] *Giumelli v Giumelli* (1999) 196 C.L.R. 101 at [3] per Glesson C.J., McHugh, Gummow, and Callinan JJ. See too *Boscawen v Bajwa* [1996] 1 W.L.R. 328 at 335 per Millett L.J.; *Toman v Toman* [2011] NZHC 51.

[24] Land Registration Act 2002 s.116 and Sch.3, para.2. Cf. *Lloyd's Bank Plc v Rosset* [1989] Ch. 350; not considered on appeal [1991] 1 A.C. 107.

[25] Land Registration Act 2002 s.29.

[26] *Allan v Rea Brothers Trustees Ltd* [2002] EWCA Civ 85; (2002) 4 I.T.E.L.R. 627 at [44]–[46] and at [52]–[55] per Robert Walker L.J.; *Waxman v Waxman* (2004) 7 I.T.E.L.R. 162 at [583] per curiam (Ontario CA); *Clark v Cutland* [2003] EWCA Civ 810; [2004] 1 W.L.R. 783 at [30] per Arden L.J.; *Nabb Brothers Ltd v Lloyds Bank International (Guernsey) Ltd* [2005] EWHC 405 (Ch) at [69] per Lawrence Collins J.; *Ultraframe (UK) Ltd v Fielding* [2005] EWHC 1638 (Ch) at [1518] per Lewison J.; *Heperu* [2009] NSWCA 252; (2009) 76 N.S.W.L.R. 230 at [154]–[155] per Allsop P. See too Chambers, *Resulting Trusts*, pp.200–209.

[27] *Allied Carpets Group Plc v Nethercott* [2001] B.C.C. 81 (QBD) per Colman J.; *Re Holmes* [2004] EWHC 2020 (Admin); [2005] 1 All E.R. 490 at [22] per Burnton J. As noted in B. McFarlane, *The Structure of Property Law* (Oxford: Hart, 2008), pp.306–307 and 309–310, the exercise of this power by the beneficiary is not the only way in which a trustee may come under a duty because his conscience becomes affected by knowledge: this may also happen, e.g. if the trustee's knowledge derives from a third party or arises when he checks his own records.

[28] *Giumelli* (1999) 196 C.L.R. 101 at [3]–[5] per Gleeson C.J., McHugh, Gummow and Calinan JJ.

[29] *Evans v European Bank Ltd* [2004] NSWCA 82, (2004) 7 I.T.E.L.R. 19 at [116] per Spigelman C.J.; *Bracken Partners Ltd v Gutteridge* [2003] EWCA Civ 1875; [2004] 1 B.C.L.C. 377.

because this must be undertaken voluntarily.[30] Nor need he undertake the administrative and managerial duties which express trustees must often perform, although it seems that if he incurs legitimate costs in the course of managing the property, then he will enjoy the same right of indemnity as an express trustee.[31]

38–15   Note, finally, that a third party who dishonestly assists in a breach of a personal duty by the trustee of a constructive or resulting trust may himself incur a compensatory liability to the beneficiary, and so too may a third party who knowing receives trust property transferred in a breach of duty by the trustee.[32]

3. CONSTRUCTIVE TRUSTS

(a) *"Institutional" and "Remedial" Constructive Trusts*

38–16   Under English law, constructive trusts arise automatically by the operation of legal rules which state that they always arise in "defined circumstances".[33] For example, constructive trusts are imposed when a fiduciary makes a profit from an opportunity acquired in his fiduciary capacity,[34] when future property has been assigned for value,[35] when one party acquires property for himself having induced another to refrain from acquiring it by promising to share it with him,[36]

---

[30] *Hospital Products Ltd v United States Surgical Corp* (1984) 156 C.L.R. 41 at 96–97; *Lonrho Plc v Fayed (No.2)* [1992] 1 W.L.R. 1 at 12 per Millett J. See too A. Scott, "The Fiduciary Principle" (1949) 37 Cal. L.R. 539, p.540; R.H. Maudsley, "Constructive Trusts" (1977) 28 N.I.L.R. 123, p.124; Chambers, *Resulting Trusts*, pp.194–200; L.D. Smith, "Constructive Fiduciaries?" in P. Birks (ed.), *Privacy and Loyalty* (Oxford: Clarendon Press, 1997), 249, pp.263–267; Millett, "Restitution and Constructive Trusts", pp.404–405.

[31] Cf. *James v Williams* [2000] Ch. 1 at 10–11 per Aldous L.J.; *Nolan v Collie* [2003] VSCA 39; (2003) 7 V.R. 287 at [32]–[34] per Ormiston J.A.; *Stafford v Kekatos (No.3)* [2008] NSWSC 1093 at [93] per Brereton J.; citing *Isaac v Wall* (1877) 6 Ch. D. 706 and *Re Lord Ranelagh's Will* (1884) 26 Ch. D. 590 at 600 per Pearson J.

[32] *Bank Tejerat v Hong Kong and Shanghai Banking Corp (CI) Ltd* [1995] 1 Lloyd's Rep. 239; *Bankgesellschaft Berlin AG v Makris* Unreported QBD (Comm Ct), January 22, 1999; *Heinl v Jyske Bank (Gibraltar) Ltd* [1999] Lloyd's Rep. Bank 511. Cf. *Aroso v Coutts & Co* [2002] 1 All E.R. (Comm.) 241 at [37] per Lawrence Collins J.

[33] *Boscawen* [1996] 1 W.L.R. 328 at 335 per Millett L.J.

[34] *Boardman v Phipps* [1967] 2 A.C. 46; affirming Wilberforce J.'s order at first instance, for which see [1964] 2 All E.R. 187 at 188; *Chan v Zacharia* (1984) 154 C.L.R. 178 at 199 per Deane J. But note *Sinclair Investments (UK) Ltd v Versailles Trade Finance Ltd (In Administrative Receivership)* [2011] EWCA Civ 347; [2011] Bus. L.R. 1126 at [89] per Lord Neuberger M.R.: "a claimant cannot claim proprietary ownership of an asset purchased by the defaulting fiduciary with funds which, although they could not have been obtained if he had not enjoyed his fiduciary status, were not beneficially owned by the claimant or derived from opportunities beneficially owned by the claimant."

[35] *Pullan v Koe* [1913] 1 Ch. 9; *Re Gillott's Settlement* [1934] Ch. 97 at 108–109 per Maugham J.

[36] *Pallant v Morgan* [1953] 1 Ch. 43; *Banner Homes Group Plc v Luff Developments Ltd (No.2)* [2000] Ch. 372.

and when one party incurs detriment in reliance on a common intention with her partner that she should have an ownership share of their family home.[37] Constructive trusts are also imposed in some circumstances to reverse a defendant's unjust enrichment.[38]

Under English law, the courts do not have a discretion to impose constructive **38–17** trusts, or to refuse to do so, according to their assessment of the equities of a case: their role is purely declaratory. In contrast, "institutional" and "remedial" constructive trusts both form part of the law of other Commonwealth jurisdictions, such as Australia,[39] New Zealand[40] and Canada.[41] Different courts use these terms to mean different things,[42] but most use them to distinguish constructive trusts which arise through the inflexible operation of legal rules from constructive trusts which arise following the exercise of a judicial discretion, either retrospectively or prospectively from the date of the court order.[43] Whether courts should have such a discretion to vary property rights is controversial,[44] but whatever view one takes of this question, it is clear as a matter of authority that

---

[37] *Gissing v Gissing* [1971] A.C. 886; *Lloyds Bank Plc v Rosset* [1991] 1 A.C. 107; *Stack v Dowden* [2007] UKHL 17; [2007] 2 A.C. 432; *Jones v Kernott* [2010] EWCA Civ 578; [2010] 1 W.L.R. 2401.

[38] See para.38–34.

[39] *Muschinski v Dodds* (1985) 160 C.L.R. 583; *Bathurst CC v P.W.C. Properties Pty Ltd* (1998) 195 C.L.R. 566; *Giumelli* (1999) 196 C.L.R. 101; *Robins v Incentive Dynamics Pty Ltd (In Liquidation)* (2003) 45 A.C.S.R. 244.

[40] *Gillies v Keogh* [1989] 2 N.Z.L.R. 327; *Powell v Thompson* [1991] 1 N.Z.L.R. 597; *Phillips v Phillips* [1993] 3 N.Z.L.R. 159; *Fortex Group Ltd v Macintosh* [1998] 3 N.Z.L.R. 171; *Commonwealth Reserves v Chodar* [2001] 2 N.Z.L.R. 374; *Regal Casting Ltd v Lightbody* [2008] NZSC 87; [2009] 2 N.Z.L.R. 433.

[41] *Sorochan v Sorochan* [1986] 2 S.C.R. 38; *L.A.C. Minerals Ltd v International Corona Resources Ltd* [1989] 2 S.C.R. 574; *Soulos v Korkontzilas* [1997] 2 S.C.R. 217; *Kerr v Baranow* [2011] SCC 10; [2011] 1 S.C.R. 269.

[42] G. Elias, *Explaining Constructive Trusts* (Oxford: OUP, 1990), pp.159–163; C. Rotherham, *Proprietary Remedies in Context* (Oxford: Hart, 2002), pp.7–32. Some English judges have used the term "remedial constructive trust" to refer to the personal liability of strangers who dishonestly participate in a breach of trust, e.g. *Clarke v Marlborough Fine Art (London) Ltd* [2002] 1 W.L.R. 1731 at [66] per Patten J.; *Kilcarne Holdings Ltd v Targetfollow (Birmingham) Ltd* [2004] EWHC 2547 (Ch); [2005] 2 P. & C.R. 105 at [261] per Lewison J. This usage seems to have been prompted by *Paragon Finance Plc v D. B. Thakerar & Co (A Firm)* [1999] 1 All E.R. 400 at 408–409, where Millett L.J. distinguished constructive trusts of property from the personal liability of dishonest participants in a breach of trust, but it is best avoided, lest this personal liability become confused with the "discretionary proprietary remedy" to which Millett L.J. also referred in *Paragon* at 414.

[43] e.g. *Fortex Group Ltd v Macintosh* [1998] 3 N.Z.L.R. 171 at 172–173 per Tipping J., endorsed in *Regal Casting Ltd v Lightbody* [2008] NZSC 87; [2009] 2 N.Z.L.R. 433 at [162]–[163] per Tipping J.

[44] P. Loughlan, "No Right to the Remedy? An Analysis of Judicial Discretion in the Imposition of Equitable Remedies" (1989) 17 Melbourne L.R. 132; P.D. Finn "Equitable Doctrine and Discretion in Remedies" in W. Cornish et al. (eds), *Restitution: Past, Present and Future* (Oxford: Hart, 1998), 251; D. Wright, *The Remedial Constructive Trust* (1998), reviewed by P. Birks (1999) 115 L.Q.R. 681; P. Birks, "Rights, Wrongs, and Remedies" (2000) 20 O.J.L.S. 1; S. Evans, "Defending Discretionary Remedialism" (2001) 23 Sydney L.R. 463; D.W.M. Waters, "Liability and Remedy: An Adjustable Relationship" (2001) 64 Sask. LR 426; D.M. Jensen, "The Rights and Wrongs of Discretionary Remedialism" [2003] S.J.L.S. 178; S. Gardner, *Introduction to the Law of Trusts*, 2nd edn (2003), pp.124–126; T. Etherton, "Constructive Trusts: A New Model for Equity and Unjust Enrichment" [2008] C.L.J. 265.

English law does not recognise "remedial" constructive trusts of this kind.[45] An English court must therefore be satisfied that the facts of a case fall within the scope of a rule established by previous authority before it will make a declaration that the defendant holds property on constructive trust for the claimant, and in the absence of such a guiding precedent, assertions that the defendant has acted unconscionably will not assist the claimant.[46]

(b) *Personal Liability to Account as a Constructive Trustee*

38–18   The point has already been made that there is a significant difference between the personal and proprietary rights that can arise under constructive and resulting trusts. This difference needs to be kept firmly in view when considering liability for dishonest assistance in a breach of trust and knowing receipt of misdirected trust property.[47] It is often said that a dishonest assistant or knowing recipient is personally liable to account to the trust beneficiaries as a constructive trustee, but some eminent judges and scholars have questioned the usefulness of this language. Peter Birks held it to be a "mystifying label" which obscured the true nature of these liabilities,[48] and Lord Nicholls agreed, writing extra-judicially that[49]:

> "The traditional approach to [liability for knowing receipt and dishonest assistance] involves interposing a deemed ('constructive') trusteeship between the wrongful conduct (dishonest participation) and the remedy (liability in equity). This intermediate step seems otiose and, indeed, confusing."

---

[45] *Re Goldcorp Exchange Ltd* [1995] 1 A.C. 74 at 104 per Lord Mustill; *Westdeutsche* [1996] A.C. 669 at 714–716 per Lord Browne-Wilkinson; *Re Polly Peck International Ltd (No.2)* [1998] 3 All E.R. 812 at 827 per Mummery L.J.; and at 831 per Nourse L.J.; *Shalson v Russo* [2003] EWHC 1637 (Ch); [2005] Ch. 281 at [118] per Rimer J; *Sinclair* [2005] EWCA Civ 722; [2006] 1 B.C.L.C. 60 at [37] and [42] per Arden LJ; *Re Farepak Food and Gifts Ltd (in Administration)* [2006] EWHC 3272 (Ch); [2007] 2 B.C.L.C. 1 at [38] per Mann J.; *De Bruyne v De Bruyne* [2010] EWCA Civ 519; [2010] 2 FCR 251 at [48] per Patten L.J.; *Sinclair* [2010] EWHC 1614 (Ch) at [23] per Lewison J.; affirmed [2011] EWCA Civ 347 at [37] per Lord Neuberger M.R. But cf. *London Allied Holdings Ltd v Lee* [2007] EWHC 2061 (Ch) at [273]–[274] per Etherton J.; *Thorner v Major* [2009] UKHL 18; [2009] 1 W.L.R. 776 at [20]–[21] per Lord Scott (whose analysis was not adopted by the majority of the HL).

[46] Cf. *Cobbe v Yeoman's Row Management Ltd* [2008] UKHL 55; [2008] 1 W.L.R. 1752 at [37] per Lord Scott, declining to impose a constructive trust that he thought would be "more in the nature of an indignant reaction to [the defendant's] unconscionable behaviour than a principled answer to [the] claim for relief."

[47] On dishonest assistance, see *Royal Brunei Airline Sdn Bhd v Tan* [1995] 2 A.C. 378 (PC); *Twinsectra Ltd v Yardley* [2002] UKHL 12; [2002] 2 A.C. 164; *Barlow Clowes International Ltd (In Liquidation) v Eurotrust International Ltd* [2005] UKPC 37; [2006] 1 W.L.R. 1476. On knowing receipt, see *Bank of Credit and Commerce International (Overseas) Ltd v Akindele* [2001] Ch. 437; *Charter Plc v City Index Ltd* [2007] EWCA Civ 1382; [2008] Ch. 313.

[48] P. Birks, *An Introduction to the Law of Restitution* (Oxford: Clarendon Press, 1985), pp.80–82. See too P. Birks, "Persistent Problems in Misdirected Money: A Quintet" [1993] L.M.C.L.Q. 218, p.236; P. Birks, *Unjust Enrichment*, 2nd edn (Oxford: OUP, 2005), pp.293–295. Like views are expressed in C. Rickett, "The Classification of Trusts" (1999) 18 N.Z.U.L.R. 305, pp.321–324; A. Burrows, *The Law of Restitution* (Oxford: OUP, 2010), p.418.

[49] Lord Nicholls "Knowing Receipt: The Need for a New Landmark" in Cornish et al. (eds), *Restitution: Past, Present, and Future*, 231, p.243. See too *Paragon* [1999] 1 All ER 400 at 409 per Millett L.J., critiqued in C. Daly and C. Mitchell, *"Paragon Finance plc v D.B. Thakerar & Co (a firm)"* in C. Mitchell and P. Mitchell (eds), *Landmark Cases in Equity* (Oxford: Hart, 2011).

We do not agree that this language adds nothing to our understanding of these **38–19** liabilities.[50] Since a defendant need not receive trust property to incur liability for dishonest assistance, this form of liability cannot depend on his owing duties as trustee of the trust property in his own right. However it does entail fixing him with a duplicative liability which mirrors the liability of the trustee whose breach has been assisted. Hence it can be said that he is "constructively liable as a trustee" in the sense that he is deemed to be liable to pay over the same sums as the trustee.[51]

The language of personal liability to account as a constructive trustee also **38–20** illuminates the nature of liability for knowing receipt, but in a different way. When trust property is improperly transferred to a recipient who is not a bona fide purchaser for value without notice of the equitable interest, the property continues to belong to the beneficiaries in equity; hence there is no need for any constructive or resulting trust to be imposed to give them equitable proprietary rights as they already have these under the original trust.[52] If the recipient's conscience is affected by knowledge of the breach of trust while the property or its traceable proceeds are in his hands, then he will be fixed with duties to account for the property that are essentially the same duties to account as those that are owed by an express trustee.[53] Hence the statement that the knowing recipient is "liable to account as a constructive trustee" is not an empty phrase, but on the contrary exactly identifies the content of his duty in relation to the property which belongs in equity to the beneficiaries and the consequences of breaching this duty.[54]

Moreover, it is only true in an attenuated sense (if it is true at all) that there is **38–21** no "real" trust where misdirected trust property is knowingly received by a defendant.[55] In such cases the beneficiaries not only have a subsisting equitable proprietary interest in the property under the original trust, but also have personal

---

[50] For additional discussion of this point, see paras 8–123—8–130.

[51] S.B. Elliott and C. Mitchell, "Remedies for Dishonest Assistance" (2004) 67 M.L.R. 16; M.S. Clapton, "Gain-Based Remedies for Knowing Assistance: Ensuring Assistants Do Not Profit From Their Wrongs" (2008) 45 Alberta L.R. 989; C. Mitchell and S. Watterson, "Remedies for Knowing Receipt" in C. Mitchell (ed.), *Constructive and Resulting Trusts* (Oxford: Hart, 2010), 115, pp.150–154. Contra, P. Ridge, "Justifying the Remedies for Dishonest Assistance" (2008) 124 L.Q.R. 445.

[52] *Mansell v Mansell* (1732) 2 P. Wms 678; 24 E.R. 913; *Re Strachan* (1876) 4 Ch. D. 123; *Banque Belge pour l'Etranger v Hambrouck* [1921] 1 K.B. 321; *Re Montagu's ST* [1987] Ch. 264 at 272–273 per Megarry V.C.; *Agip (Africa) Ltd v Jackson* [1990] 1 Ch. 265 at 290 per Millett J.; *Westdeutsche* [1996] A.C. 669 at 705 per Lord Browne-Wilkinson; *Foskett* [2001] 1 A.C. 102 at 129 per Lord Millett; *Allen v Rea Brothers Trustees Ltd* [2002] EWCA Civ 85; (2002) 4 I.T.E.L.R. 627 [44]–[46] and [52]–[55] per Robert Walker L.J.; *Venables v Hornby* [2002] EWCA Civ 1277; [2002] S.T.C. 148 at [27] per Chadwick L.J. (reversed on a different point [2003] UKHL 65; [2003] 1 W.L.R. 3022); *Pitt v Holt* [2011] EWCA Civ 197; [2011] 3 W.L.R. 19 at [99] per Lloyd L.J.

[53] *Wilson v Moore* (1834) 1 My. & K. 126 at 146; 39 E.R. 629 at 636 per Sir John Leach M.R.; *Jesse v Bennett* (1856) 6 De G. M. & G. 609 at 612; 43 E.R. 1370 at 1371 per Lord Cranworth L.C.; *Morgan v Stephens* (1861) 3 Giff. 226 at 237; 66 E.R. 392 at 397 per Sir John Stuart V.C.; *Rolfe v Gregory* (1865) 4 De G. J. & S. 576 at 578; 46 E.R. 1042 at 1043 per Lord Westbury L.C.; *Gray v Johnston* (1868) L.R. 3 H.L. 1 at 14 per Lord Westbury; *Barnes v Addy* (1874) L.R. 9 Ch. App. 244 at 251–252 per Lord Selborne L.C.; *Blyth v Fladgate* [1891] 1 Ch. 237 at 351 per Stirling J.; *Re Barney* [1892] 2 Ch 265 at 271; *John v Dodwell & Co Ltd* [1918] A.C. 563 at 569–570 per Viscount Haldane (PC).

[54] Mitchell and Watterson, "Remedies for Knowing Receipt", especially pp.128–131.

[55] As stated in *Paragon* [1999] 1 All E.R. 400 at 409 per Millett L.J.

rights against the recipient that he should account for what he does with the property, which rights are exigible against the defendant in proceedings that may lead to an order that he should specifically or substitutively perform his obligation to return the property on demand. The English courts have sometimes concluded that the coincidence of these proprietary and personal rights means that misdirected trust funds are held by knowing recipients on a substantive constructive trust.[56] However, there is a risk that this language will lead the courts to draw the false conclusion that the beneficiaries can only have an equitable proprietary interest in misdirected trust funds if they are impressed with a new constructive trust, which can only be imposed if the recipients have unconscionable knowledge of the trustee's breach of duty.[57]

4. RESULTING TRUSTS

38–22 "Resulting trusts arise in three situations: voluntary payment or transfer; purchase in the name of another; and incomplete disposal of the beneficial interest."[58] In the first situation, a claimant benefits a defendant by paying him money or conveying other property to him[59]; in the second, a claimant benefits a defendant by purchasing property in his name[60]; in the third, a claimant conveys property to a defendant on trusts which fail to exhaust the beneficial interest, and the defendant is thereby benefited by receipt of the residual beneficial interest.[61] In each case, the defendant gives no consideration to the claimant in exchange for the benefit he receives.

---

[56] See e.g. *Peffer v Rigg* [1977] 1 W.L.R. 285 at 294 per Graham J.; *Metall und Rohstoff AG v Donaldson Lufkin and Jenrette Inc* [1990] 1 Q.B. 391 at 473, per curiam (CA); *Jyske Bank (Gibraltar) Ltd v Spjeldnaes* [1999] 2 B.C.L.C. 101 at 119 per Evans-Lombe J.; *Independent Trustee Services Ltd v G.P. Noble Trustees Ltd* [2009] EWHC 161 (Ch) at [3] per Lewison J.; *Futter v Futter* [2010] EWHC 449 (Ch); [2010] S.T.C. 982 at [35] per Norris J.; reversed on a different point, [2011] EWCA Civ 197; [2011] 3 W.L.R. 19.

[57] An error perpetrated in *Farrow Finance Co Ltd (In Liquidation) v Farrow Properties Ltd (In Liquidation)* [1999] 1 V.R. 584; and *Robins v Incentive Dynamics Pty Ltd* (2003) 45 A.C.S.R. 244, critiqued in M. Bryan, "Recipient Liability under the Torrens System: Some Category Errors" in R. Grantham and C. Rickett (eds), *Structure and Justification in Private Law* (Oxford: Hart, 2008), 339, pp.347–349.

[58] Lord Millett, "Pension Schemes and the Law of Trusts" (2000) 14 Tru. L.I. 66, p.73.

[59] Examples are *Hepworth v Hepworth* (1870) L.R. 11 Eq. 10; *Standing v Bowring* (1885) 16 Ch. D. 282; *Re Vinogradoff* [1935] W.N. 68; *Re Vandervell's Trusts (No.2)* [1974] Ch. 269. These cases all concern personal property and the position is different for land: see the Law of Property Act 1925 s.60(3), discussed in *Lohia v Lohia* [2001] W.T.L.R. 101, affirmed on a different point [2001] EWCA Civ 1691.

[60] Examples are *Benger v Drew* (1721) P. Wms 781; 24 E.R. 613; *Rider v Kidder* (1805) 10 Ves. Jun. 360; 32 E.R. 884; *The Venture* [1908] P. 218; *Bull v Bull* [1955] 1 Q.B. 234; *Seldon v Davidson* [1968] 1 W.L.R. 1083; *Tinsley v Milligan* [1994] 1 A.C. 340.

[61] Examples are *Re West* [1900] 1 Ch. 84; *Re Ames's Settlement* [1946] Ch. 217; *Re Gillingham Bus Disaster Fund* [1958] Ch. 300; *Hodgson v Marks* [1971] Ch. 892. Following *Barclays Bank Ltd v Quistclose Investments Ltd* [1970] A.C. 567, it was thought that a resulting trust of this kind would also arise following the failure of a private purpose trust to apply money lent for a specific purpose. This controversial analysis was rendered otiose by *Twinsectra* [2002] A.C. 164 where Lord Millett reinterpreted the *Quistclose* case to hold that money lent for a specific purpose can be subject to an immediate express trust for the lender, subject to a power to apply the money to the purpose.

In many cases where a claimant has gratuitously transferred property to a **38–23** defendant, there is evidence that he intended to make a gift,[62] to declare a trust,[63] to make a loan,[64] or (much less likely) to abandon his interest in the property.[65] In all such cases, the law will give effect to his intention and no question will arise of a resulting trust being imposed.[66] Resulting trusts are imposed only in cases where property is gratuitously transferred and there is insufficient evidence to determine what the claimant intended. In these circumstances the law will raise a presumption in the claimant's favour in the absence of evidence decisively establishing its whereabouts.[67] Failure to rebut this presumption by the defendant will lead to the imposition of a resulting trust.

In *Westdeutsche*,[68] Lord Browne-Wilkinson described this presumption as a **38–24** "presumption that [the claimant] did not intend to make a gift to [the defendant]", but in the same passage of his speech, he also described it as a "presumption of resulting trust", i.e. a presumption that the claimant intends that the defendant should hold the property on trust for the claimant. In some cases, the same result will follow whichever way the presumption is characterised, since a claimant who does not intend to benefit a defendant may also intend that the beneficial interest should return to him. However, as Dillon L.J. observed in *Re E.V.T.R. Ltd*,[69] resulting trusts are normally imposed in cases where "circumstances happen to which the parties have not directed their minds", and as Lord Millett noted in *Air Jamaica Ltd v Charlton*,[70] they have been imposed in cases where it was clear that the claimant did not wish the defendant to be his trustee.

For example, in *Vandervell v IRC*,[71] a transferor of company shares incorrectly **38–25** thought that he had disposed of his beneficial interest in the shares completely, and certainly did not wish the residuary interest to result to him, as this would

---

[62] As in e.g. *Spencer v Strickland* [2009] EWHC 3033 (Ch) at [41] per Sir Donald Rattee. Where the parties are in a special relationship such as that which exists between father and child, there is a presumption that the transferor intends to make a gift of the property: *Shephard v Cartwright* [1955] A.C. 431 at 445 per Viscount Simonds; *Pettitt v Pettitt* [1970] A.C. 777 at 815 per Lord Upjohn. The Equality Act 2010 s.199 abolishes the presumption of advancement with prospective effect only; at the time of writing the section had not been brought into force.

[63] As in e.g. *Cherney v Neuman* [2011] EWHC 2156 (Ch) at [309] per Henderson J.

[64] As in e.g. *Blue Sky One Ltd v Blue Airways LLC* [2009] EWHC 3314 (Comm) at [255]–[257] per Beatson J. The mere fact that a transaction is one of loan does not exclude the inference that the parties intend there to be a trust: *Quistclose* [1970] A.C. 567 at 581 per Lord Wilberforce; *Twinsectra* [2002] A.C. 164.

[65] The courts are generally reluctant to find that settlors mean to abandon their property: *Davis v Richards & Wallington Ltd* [1990] 1 W.L.R. 1511 at 1540–1542 per Scott J., following *Jones v Williams* Unreported Ch D, March 15, 1988, Knox J. For a rare case where the court so found, see *Environment Agency v Hillridge Ltd* [2003] EWHC 3023 (Ch); [2004] 2 B.C.L.C. 358.

[66] *Air Jamaica Ltd v Charlton* [1999] 1 W.L.R. 1399 at 1412 per Lord Millett; *Lavelle v Lavelle* [2004] EWCA Civ 223; [2004] 2 F.C.R. 418 at [13] per Lord Phillips M.R.; *Spencer* [2009] EWHC 3033 (Ch) at [41] per Sir Donald Rattee.

[67] *Vandervell v IRC* [1967] 2 A.C. 291 at 313 per Lord Upjohn; *Stockholm Finance Ltd v Garden Holdings Inc* Unreported Ch D, October 26, 1995 per Robert Walker J.; *Ali v Khan* [2002] EWCA Civ 974; (2002) 5 I.T.E.L.R. 232 at [28] per Morritt V.C.

[68] *Westdeutsche* [1996] A.C. 669 at 708.

[69] *Re E.V.T.R. Ltd* [1987] 1 B.C.L.C. 646 at 650.

[70] *Air Jamaica v Charlton* [1999] 1 W.L.R. 1399 at 1412. See too *Twinsectra* [1999] Lloyd's Rep. Bank. 438 at 457 per Potter L.J.; [2002] 2 A.C. 164 at [91] per Lord Millett.

[71] *Vandervell v IRC* [1967] 2 A.C. 291.

render him liable to the very tax that he had sought to avoid by structuring the share transfer in the way that he had. Again, in *Re Vinogradoff*,[72] a woman who transferred War Loan stock into the joint names of herself and her granddaughter could not have intended the granddaughter to be a trustee for her because she was only seven years old. And in *El Ajou v Dollar Land Holdings Plc (No.1)*,[73] a company can have had no such intention where it did not know that its property had been stolen and conveyed to a transferee. Nevertheless a resulting trust was imposed in all of these cases.

38–26   This suggests that the first of Lord Browne-Wilkinson's formulations should be preferred to the second, because the first, unlike the second, dovetails with all of the cases in which resulting trusts have been imposed, including those mentioned above: it is clear, for example, that although the transferor in *Vandervell* did not wish the residuary beneficial interest in the shares to result to him, he did not wish to make an outright gift of it to the transferee either. Thus, as Lord Phillips M.R. held in *Lavelle v Lavelle*,[74] the best view of the law is that where property is gratuitously transferred and there is no evidence conclusively determining the transferor's intention, "there will be a presumption that [he] does not intend to part with the beneficial interest in the property."[75]

38–27   Resulting trusts have traditionally been understood to fall into two categories: "automatic resulting trusts" and "presumed resulting trusts". For example, Megarry J. held in *Re Vandervell's Trusts (No.2)*[76] that a resulting trust arises "automatically" when some or all of the beneficial interest in property held on an express trust has not been disposed of by the settlor, whereas a resulting trust is imposed where property is gratuitously transferred, there is no evidence determining the transferor's intentions, and the transferee fails to rebut a presumption raised in the transferor's favour that the property should be held on trust for him.

38–28   There is certainly a difference between these two situations, since in the first case the settlor intends the trustee to be a trustee (although he fails to make it clear where the whole of the beneficial interest should go), whereas in the second case the transferor may not intend the transferee to be a trustee at all.[77] Nevertheless in *Westdeutsche* Lord Browne-Wilkinson laid a stronger emphasis on the similarities between them, observing that in the first case, as in the second, a resulting trust will not arise if the evidence clearly shows that the settlor intended

---

[72] *Re Vinogradoff* [1935] W.N. 68.
[73] *El Ajou v Dollar Land Holdings Plc (No.1)* [1993] 3 All E.R. 717.
[74] *Lavelle v Lavelle* [2004] EWCA Civ 223; [2004] 2 F.C.R. 418 at [13]–[14].
[75] See too *Calverley v Green* (1984) 155 C.L.R. 242 at 246 per Gibbs C.J.; *Nelson v Nelson* (1995) 184 C.L.R. 538 at 549 per Deane and Gummow JJ.; *Jabetin Pty Ltd v Liquor Administration Board* [2005] NSWCA 92 at [68] per Mason P.; *Stack* [2007] UKHL 17; [2007] 2 A.C. 432 at [114] per Lord Neuberger; also Millett, "Restitution and Constructive Trusts", p.413, finding it "impossible to dissent" from the central thesis of Chambers, *Resulting Trusts*, that "the resulting trust has evolved into a response to non-voluntary transfer".
[76] *Re Vandervell's Trusts (No.2)* [1974] Ch. 269 at 288 and following; glossing *Vandervell* [1967] 2 A.C. 291 at 312 and following per Lord Upjohn.
[77] J. Mee "'Automatic' Resulting Trusts: Retention, Restitution, or Reposing Trust?" in Mitchell (ed.), *Constructive and Resulting Trusts*, 207.

some other outcome, e.g. to abandon the remaining beneficial interest.[78] In the first case, as in the second, property is transferred by a transferor who receives nothing in return for it. In the first case, as in the second, the imposition of a resulting trust leads to the creation of a new equitable property right for the transferor,[79] and as Robert Chambers has written, a new right "cannot be explained as the inertia of a pre-existing beneficial interest".[80] This all suggests that there are not two types of resulting trust but only one, imposed by law when property is transferred gratuitously and there is no evidence that the transferor meant to make a gift or loan or to abandon his beneficial interest.

Resulting trusts respond only to a transferor's lack of intention to benefit a **38–29** transferee. Lord Browne-Wilkinson thought that "a resulting trust arises in order to give effect to the intention of the parties"[81]: i.e. he saw them as responding to the intentions of both the transferor and the transferee. However, his Lordship seems to have confused resulting trusts with common intention constructive trusts,[82] and his view is inconsistent with cases where resulting trusts were imposed on property held by transferees who had no intention of becoming trustees, for example because they were legally incapable of forming any intention at all.[83] Hence, the better view is that the only person whose intentions are relevant is the transferor.[84]

5. Event-Based Analysis of Constructive and Resulting Trusts

Some legal scholars have sought to explain the underlying reasons for the **38–30** imposition of constructive and resulting trusts by analysing them as "responses" to legally significant "causative events", methodology which was first propounded by Peter Birks.[85] On this approach, legal rights are understood to respond to various causative events, e.g. consent, wrongs and unjust enrichment. These legal rights are not limited to personal rights, but also include proprietary

---

[78] *Westdeutsche* [1996] A.C. 669 at 708.
[79] See Lord Browne-Wilkinson's comments in *Westdeutsche* at 706; also *D.K.L.R. Holding Co (No.2) Pty Ltd v Commissioner for Stamp Duties* (1982) 149 C.L.R. 431.
[80] R. Chambers, "Resulting Trusts in Canada" (2000) 38 Alberta L.R. 379, p.389 (reprinted (2002) 16 Tru. L.I. 104 and 138).
[81] "Constructive Trusts and Unjust Enrichment" (1996) 10 Tru L.I. 98, p.99; echoed in *Tinsley v Milligan* [1994] 1 A.C. 340 at 371; *Westdeutsche* [1996] A.C. 669 at 708.
[82] It seems likely that his Lordship was misled by Lord Diplock's unfortunately expressed speech in *Gissing v Gissing* [1971] A.C. 886 at 904–905 and 922.
[83] e.g. *Lench v Lench* (1805) 10 Ves. Jun. 511; 32 E.R. 943; *Childers v Childers* (1857) 1 De G. & J. 482; 44 E.R. 810; *Re Vinogradoff* [1935] W.N. 68.
[84] Chambers, *Resulting Trusts*, pp.35–37; J. Mee, *The Property Rights of Cohabitees* (Oxford: Hart, 1999), pp.39–43. This is not to deny that a transferee's intentions can constitute circumstantial evidence of the transferor's intentions, as in e.g. *Ali v Khan* (2002) 5 I.T.E.L.R. 232 at [28] per Morritt V.C.
[85] e.g. P. Birks, "Equity in the Modern Law: An Exercise in Taxonomy" (1996) 26 U.W.A.L.R. 1; P. Birks. "Equity, Conscience, and Unjust Enrichment" (1999) 23 Univ. of Melbourne L.R. 1. For sceptical appraisals of this approach, see the works cited in para.1–02, fn.5.

rights arising under trusts imposed by law. Hence, it is argued, the key to understanding constructive and resulting trusts is to identify the source of the rights which they afford to the beneficiaries: i.e. the "causative events" to which these rights respond. The scholars who have taken this approach have differed in their conclusions, but their work confirms that Birks' methodology is a powerful analytical tool which can facilitate a clearer understanding of the ways in which the law of trusts might align with the law of obligations, and the ways in which constructive and resulting trusts might differ from one another.

38–31   So far as resulting trusts are concerned, there are two main views. The traditional view is that resulting trusts are imposed in order to give effect to a transferor's intention to create a trust for himself.[86] The contrasting view is that they are imposed in order to reverse the transferee's unjust enrichment at the transferor's expense.[87] In *Westdeutsche*,[88] Lord Browne-Wilkinson rejected the argument that resulting trusts respond to unjust enrichment, and held that they respond to the transferor's intention to create a trust. In *Air Jamaica v Charlton*,[89] however, Lord Millett preferred the view that resulting trusts respond to the absence of an intention on the part of the transferor to pass the entire beneficial interest, and in *Twinsectra Ltd v Yardley*,[90] he said that the "surer ground" for the decision in *Westdeutsche* was another reason given by Lord Browne-Wilkinson for rejecting a resulting trust, namely that the claimant's "money was paid and received with the intention that it should become the absolute property of the recipient."[91]

38–32   The main objection to the theory that resulting trusts respond to the transferor's intention to create a trust for himself is that it cannot explain cases where resulting trusts have been imposed despite evidence that the transferor never formed any intention with regard to the disposal of the beneficial interest, or else had a positive intention that he did not wish to acquire a new equitable beneficial interest in the property. The main objection to the theory that resulting trusts respond to unjust enrichment is that it seems to prove too much. It suggests that a resulting trust should arise in every case of unjust enrichment where a claimant transfers property to a defendant that remains identifiable in the defendant's hands at the time of the action. Those who consider that proprietary remedies for

---

[86] C.E.F. Rickett, "The Classification of Trusts" (1999) 18 N.Z. Law Rev. 305; C.E.F. Rickett and R. Grantham, "Resulting Trusts: A Rather Limited Doctrine" in P. Birks and F.D. Rose (eds), *Restitution and Equity* (Oxford: Mansfield Press, 2000), 39. Cf. W.J. Swadling, "A New Role for Resulting Trusts?" (1996) 16 L.S. 110; W.J. Swadling, "A Hard Look at *Hodgson v Marks*" in Birks and Rose, (above) 61; W.J. Swadling, "Explaining Resulting Trusts" (2008) 124 L.Q.R. 72. In his latest work, Swadling distinguishes "presumed resulting trusts", which he takes to respond to the transferor's intention, from "automatic resulting trusts", which he believes to "defy legal analysis".

[87] P. Birks, "Restitution and Resulting Trusts" in S. Goldstein (ed.), *Equity and Contemporary Legal Developments* (Jerusalem: Sacher Institute, Hebrew University Jerusalem, 1992), 361; Chambers, *Resulting Trusts*; Chambers, "Resulting Trusts in Canada".

[88] *Westdeutsche* [1996] A.C. 669 at 708–709. Also see Lords Goff, Slynn, Woolf and Lloyd at 689–690, 718, 720 and 738 respectively.

[89] *Air Jamaica v Charlton* [1999] 1 W.L.R. 1399 at 1412.

[90] *Twinsectra Ltd v Yardley* [2002] UKHL 12; [2002] 2 A.C. 164 at 189–190.

[91] See paras 37–21—37–23 for further discussion of *Westdeutsche* [1996] A.C. 669.

unjust enrichment should be generally available view this conclusion with equanimity; others are anxious that the argument will lead to "proprietary overkill". In Ch.37 we explore some of the limits that might be placed on the availability of resulting trusts (and other proprietary remedies) to deal with this problem.[92]

The cases in which resulting trusts have been imposed are susceptible to **38–33** explanation on the basis that the transferor's intention to benefit the transferee was absent, vitiated or qualified in a way that would have entitled him to a personal restitutionary award for unjust enrichment had he sought such a remedy.[93] So, for example, resulting trusts have been imposed where the transferor did not consent to the transferee's enrichment because he was unaware that it had taken place,[94] where he made a mistake,[95] and where the relevant property was transferred on a basis that failed.[96] If it is accepted that the cases can be explained in this way, then the questions arise whether they accord with the principles that should generally govern the award of proprietary remedies for unjust enrichment, and whether they are consistent with cases in which other proprietary remedies have been awarded or withheld, on similar facts (e.g. liens, subrogation to extinguished proprietary rights, rescission).

Many constructive trusts are imposed to perfect one party's intention to **38–34** transfer the beneficial ownership of property to another or to capture the profits of wrongdoing.[97] It has also been held that some constructive trusts respond to unjust enrichment. Under Canadian law it was formerly held that all constructive trusts do this,[98] although it has now been recognised that some do not.[99] In contrast, the English and Australian courts have never subscribed to the view that all constructive trusts respond to unjust enrichment, but they have held that some

---

[92] See paras 37–07—37–24.

[93] This is the central theme of Robert Chambers' ground-breaking work in this area: Chambers, *Resulting Trusts*; Chambers, "Resulting Trusts in Canada".

[94] *Ryall v Ryall* (1739) 1 Atk. 59; 26 E.R. 39; *Lane v Dighton* (1762) Amb. 409; 27 E.R. 274; *Williams v Williams* (1863) 32 Beav. 370; 55 E.R. 145; *Sharp v McNeil* (1913) 15 D.L.R. 73; affirmed (1915) 70 D.L.R. 740 (SCC); *Re Kolari* (1981) 36 O.R. (2d) 473; *El Ajou* [1993] 3 All E.R. 717 (reversed on other grounds [1994] 2 All E.R. 685); *Evans v European Bank Ltd* [2004] NSWCA 82; (2004) 7 I.T.E.L.R. 19 at [101] per Spigelman C.J.

[95] *El Ajou* [1993] 3 All E.R. 717 at 734 per Millett J. (reversed on other grounds [1994] 2 All E.R. 685). Trusts have also been imposed on the proceeds of mistaken payments which have been described as constructive trusts but which can plausibly be seen as resulting trusts: *Chase Manhattan Bank NA v Israel-British Bank (London) Ltd* [1981] Ch. 183. Trusts which look like resulting trusts have also been imposed following rescission of contracts and rectification of documents by claimants who made a mistake: *Craddock Bros* [1923] 2 Ch. 136; *Blacklocks v J. B. Developments (Godalming) Ltd* [1982] Ch. 183; *Shalson v Russo* [2003] EWHC 1637 (Ch); [2005] Ch. 281 at [122] per Rimer J. These cases are discussed at paras 40–19—40–23 and 40–35—40–36.

[96] *Re Abbott Fund Trusts* [1900] 2 Ch. 326; *Re Ames' Settlement* [1946] Ch. 217; *Re Gillingham Bus Disaster Fund* [1958] 1 Ch. 300 especially at 314 per Harman J. See too *Sinclair v Brougham* [1914] A.C. 398, overruled in *Westdeutsche* [1996] A.C. 669 discussed at paras 37–21—37–23.

[97] G. Elias, *Explaining Constructive Trusts*, p.157; R. Chambers, "Constructive Trusts in Canada"; S. Gardner, *Introduction to the Law of Trusts*, 2nd edn (Oxford: OUP, 2003), pp.159 and following; C. Mitchell (ed.), *Hayton & Mitchell: Commentary and Cases on The Law of Trusts & Equitable Remedies*, 13th edn (London: Sweet & Maxwell, 2010), Ch.15.

[98] *Deglman v Guaranty Trust Co* [1954] S.C.R. 725; *Pettkus v Becker* [1980] 2 S.C.R. 834; *Sorochan v Sorochan* [1986] 2 S.C.R. 38; *Peter v Beblow* [1993] 1 S.C.R. 980.

[99] *Korkontzilas v Soulos* [1997] 2 S.C.R. 217.

do. Constructive trusts have been awarded where money was paid by mistake,[100] where property was stolen from a claimant or obtained from him by fraud,[101] where property was transferred by a claimant who was unduly influenced by the recipient,[102] or whose independence was otherwise compromised by his relationship with the recipient,[103] and where property has been transferred to a defendant for a consideration that has failed.[104]

38–35   The same questions arise in connection with these decisions as arise in connection with the resulting trust cases discussed above, namely whether they accord with the principles that should generally govern the award of proprietary remedies for unjust enrichment, and whether they are consistent with cases in which other proprietary remedies have been awarded, or withheld, on similar facts.

38–36   If it is concluded that both constructive and resulting trusts should sometimes be imposed to reverse a defendant's unjust enrichment, then it would seem to make no difference which type of trust is imposed, since both types of trust generate the same set of personal and proprietary rights. If that is correct, then it would be desirable for the courts to eliminate an unnecessary and confusing duplication of categories, by holding that there is only one type of trust imposed to reverse unjust enrichment. Ideally the old language of "constructive" and "resulting" trusts should be abandoned entirely when naming this trust, in favour of some new term such as "restitutionary trust".[105] However, if it is wished to persist with familiar terminology, and given that resulting trusts are always restitutionary in pattern while constructive trusts are not, then it might well make sense to say that trusts imposed to reverse unjust enrichment are always resulting trusts and are never constructive trusts—as mooted by Millett J. in *El Ajou*,[106] and by Spigelman C.J. in an Australian case, *Evans v European Bank Ltd*.[107]

---

[100] *Chase Manhattan v Israel-British Bank* [1981] Ch. 105. This remains good law in England and was followed in *Commerzbank Aktiengesellschaft v I.M.B. Morgan Plc* [2004] EWHC 2771 (Ch); [2005] 1 Lloyd's Rep. 298 at [36] per Lawrence Collins J.; and in *Re Farepak Food and Gifts Ltd (In Administration)* [2006] EWHC 3272 (Ch); [2007] 2 B.C.L.C. 1 at [39]–[40] per Mann J. However, its precedental status has been diminished by Lord Browne-Wilkinson's gloss on the case in *Westdeutsche* [1996] A.C. 669 at 704–706 and 714–715; and by judicial reactions to this gloss in *Barclays Bank Plc v Box* [1998] Lloyd's Rep Bank. 185 at 200–201 per Ferris J.; *Papamichael* [2003] EWHC 164 (Comm); [2003] 1 Lloyd's Rep. 341 at [232]–[242] per Judge Chambers QC; *Shalson v Russo* [2003] EWHC 1637 (Ch); [2005] Ch. 281 at [108]–[127] per Rimer J.; *London Allied Holdings Ltd v Lee* [2007] EWHC 2061 (Ch) at [268]–[272] per Etherton J.; *Fitzalan-Howard v Hibbert* [2009] EWHC 2855 (QB); [2010] P.N.L.R. 11 at [49] per Tomlinson J.
[101] *Westdeutsche* [1996] A.C. 669 at 715–716 per Lord Browne-Wilkinson, followed in *Niru Battery Manufacturing Co v Milestone Trading Ltd (No.1)* [2002] 2 All E.R. (Comm.) 705 at [55]–[56] per Moore-Bick J. and in *Bank of Ireland v Pexxnet Ltd* [2010] EWHC 1872 (Comm) at [55] per Jonathan Hirst QC, sitting as a deputy High Ct judge. See too *Black v S. Freedman & Co* (1910) 12 C.L.R. 105 at 109 per Griffith C.J.; *Creak v James Moore & Sons Pty Ltd* (1912) 15 C.L.R. 426 at 432 per Griffith C.J.; *Australian Postal Corp v Lutak* (1991) 12 N.S.W.L.R. 584 at 589; *Evans v European Bank Ltd* [2004] NSWCA 82; (2004) 7 I.T.E.L.R. 19 at [111] per Spigelman C.J.
[102] *Janz v McIntosh* (1999) 182 Sask. R. 197; *Toman v Toman* [2011] NZHC 51.
[103] *Louth v Diprose* (1992) 175 C.L.R. 621; *McCulloch v Fern* [2001] NSWSC 406; *Smith v Smith* [2004] NSWSC 663.
[104] *Neste Oy v Lloyd's Bank Plc* [1983] 2 Lloyd's Rep. 658; *Re Farepak* [2006] EWHC 3272 (Ch); [2007] 2 B.C.L.C. 1; subsequent proceedings [2009] EWHC 2580 (Ch).
[105] Or "unjust enrichment trust": Birks, *Unjust Enrichment*, p.304.
[106] *El Ajou* [1993] 3 All E.R. 717 at 734. See too P.J. Millett, "Tracing the Proceeds of Fraud" (1991) 107 L.Q.R. 71, p. 81.
[107] *Evans v European Bank Ltd* [2004] NSWCA 82; (2004) 7 I.T.E.L.R. 19 at [112].

Developing the law in this way would make it easier to understand why trusts are imposed by law, and how resulting and constructive trusts differ from one another, for it could then be said that resulting trusts are imposed to reverse unjust enrichment, while constructive trusts are imposed to perfect intentions to transfer beneficial ownership, to strip wrongdoers of their profits and for other reasons.

6. LIENS

Liens are security interests in property that arise by operation of law; in this respect they differ from charges which are created by agreement.[108] There are two types of lien: common law liens and equitable liens. **38–37**

A common law lien is a right to retain possession of property. It is a self-help remedy, the exercise of which requires no intervention by the courts, and it cannot be enforced by action, but affords a defence to an action for recovery of the property by a person who, but for the lien, would be entitled to immediate possession.[109] A common law lien depends on the lien-holder having the property in his possession, and it may be lost if it passes out of his possession, although redelivery of the property for a limited purpose and with the express intention of maintaining the lien does not necessarily destroy it.[110] A common law lien gives the lien-holder no inherent right to sell the property,[111] but the court has a discretionary power to authorise a sale where goods are perishable or there is some other good reason to sell the property quickly.[112] **38–38**

Common law liens generally secure the performance of contractual obligations, but they can also secure the performance of obligations arising in unjust enrichment. For example, in *Spencer v S. Franses Ltd*[113] an expert on antiques was entitled to a lien over some embroideries to secure the owner's liability in unjust enrichment to pay for the value of research work that he had done to identify the embroideries. **38–39**

An equitable lien is very different from a common law lien.[114] Rather than giving the lien-holder a defence to a claim for possession, it gives him a security **38–40**

---

[108] *Re Bond Worth Ltd* [1980] Ch. 228 at 250 per Slade J.; *Hewett v Court* (1983) 149 C.L.R. 639 at 645–646 per Gibbs C.J.; *Bank of Scotland Plc v King* [2007] EWHC 2747 (Ch); [2008] 1 E.G.L.R. 65 at [61] per Morgan J.

[109] *Tappenden v Artus* [1964] 2 Q.B. 185 at 195 per Diplock L.J.; *Heath Lambert Ltd v Sociedad de Corretaje de Seguros* [2006] EWHC 1345 (Comm); [2006] 2 All E.R. (Comm) 543 at [28] per His Honour Judge MacKie QC.

[110] *Albermarle Supply Co Ltd v Hind & Co* [1928] K.B. 307.

[111] *Howes v Ball* (1827) 7 B. & C. 481 at 484; 108 E.R. 802 at 804 per Lord Tenterden C.J.; *Scott v Newington* (1833) 1 Mood. & R. 252 at 253; 174 E.R. 86 at 86 per Tindal C.J.; *Legg v Evans* (1840) 6 M. & W. 36 at 42; 151 E.R. 311 at 314 per Parke B.; *Donald v Suckling* (1866) L.R. 1 Q.B. 585 at 612 per Blackburn J.

[112] CPR r.25(1)(v).

[113] *Spencer v S. Franses Ltd* [2011] EWHC 1269 (QB).

[114] For detailed discussion of equitable liens, see S. Worthington, *Proprietary Interests in Commercial Transactions* (Oxford: Clarendon Press, 1996), pp.222–242; J. Phillips, "Equitable Liens: A Search for a Unifying Principle" in N. Palmer and E. McKendrick (eds), *Interests in Goods*, 2nd edn (London: LLP, 1998), 975.

interest analogous to an equitable charge,[115] with the difference that it does not arise by agreement but by operation of law. An equitable lien can arise whether or not the lien-holder has possession of the property.[116] Where the property is goods or land the lien-holder can obtain an order for sale so that he can be repaid out of the proceeds,[117] and where the lien is over a fund, he can obtain an order for payment out of the fund.[118] Unlike a common law lien, an equitable lien is an equitable proprietary right that is capable of binding third parties unless they are bona fide purchasers for value without notice of the equitable interest.[119] In cases concerning dispositions of registered land, the lien can bind later purchasers of equitable interests, and can also bind a registered proprietor if the lienholder is in actual occupation,[120] but a registered proprietor is not affected by adverse equitable interests that are not protected on the register or by the actual occupation of the owner thereof, irrespective of whether he has any knowledge or notice of those interests.[121] Unlike an equitable beneficial interest arising under a trust, an equitable lien does not increase or decrease in value with the value of the property, and a claimant who can choose between these two rights can therefore be expected to make his choice with an eye to the current value of the property.[122]

38-41   Like common law liens, equitable liens generally secure the performance of contractual obligations, but they can also secure the performance of obligations arising in unjust enrichment. For example, in *Cooper v Phibbs*[123] the lease of a fishery was rescinded for common mistake, subject to a declaration that the defendants should have an equitable lien over the property for the value of improvements made by their deceased father in the mistaken belief that he was the owner.

---

[115] But not a mortgage, since an equitable lien does not transfer any title to the property on which it is imposed and cannot be enforced by foreclosure or repossession: *Hewett v Court* (1983) 149 C.L.R. 639 at 663 per Deane J.

[116] *Goode v Burton* (1847) 1 Exch. 189 at 195–196; 154 E.R. 80 at 84 per Rolfe B.; *Hewett v Court* (1983) 149 C.L.R. 639 at 645 per Gibbs C.J., and at 663 per Deane J.

[117] *Hope v Booth* (1830) 1 B. & Ad. 498 at 507; 109 E.R. 872 at 877 per Lord Tenterden C.J.; *Neate v Duke of Marlborough* (1838) 3 My. & Cr. 407 at 417 per Lord Cottenham L.C.; *Marshall v South Staffordshire Tramways Co* [1895] 2 Ch. 36 at 50 per Lindley L.J.; *Davies v Littlejohn* (1923) 34 C.L.R. 174 at 184 per Knox C.J.

[118] *Re Stucley* [1906] 1 Ch. 67 at 77–78 per Vaughan Williams L.J.; *Hewett v Court* (1983) 149 C.L.R. 639 at 663 per Deane J.

[119] As in e.g. *Rice v Rice* (1854) 2 Drew. 73; 61 E.R. 646.

[120] Land Registration Act 2002 s.116 and Sch.3, para.2.

[121] Land Registration Act 2002 s.29.

[122] Cf. *Foskett* [2001] 1 A.C. 102 at 131 per Lord Millett.

[123] *Cooper v Phibbs* (1867) L.R. 2 H.L. 149. See too *Unity Joint Stock Mutual Banking Association v King* (1858) 25 Beav. 72; 53 E.R. 563; *Cadorange Pty Ltd (In Liquidation) v Tanga Holdings Pty Ltd* (1990) 20 N.S.W.L.R. 26. And cf. *Lord Napier and Ettrick v Hunter* [1993] A.C. 713, discussed at paras 21–93—21–105. And cf. E. O'Dell, "Liens, Necessity and Unjust Enrichment" (2006) 57 N.I.L.Q. 288, reviewing a series of cases predating the late 19th century, in which liens were imposed for the benefit of claimants with an interest in property who had made payments to preserve a superior interest in the property, which would otherwise have been lost or destroyed; O'Dell identifies necessity as the ground on which the awards were made.

CHAPTER 39

PROPRIETARY REMEDIES: SUBROGATION TO EXTINGUISHED PROPRIETARY RIGHTS

1. INTRODUCTION

There are many cases where a claimant's money is used to discharge another **39–01** party's debt. A surety may pay a creditor, discharging his own liability and that of the principal debtor. A company director may misappropriate the company's assets and use them to pay his own creditor. Or a bank may lend money to a borrower, for the purpose of discharging debts that he owes to a third party, such as a vendor (in a purchase transaction) or an earlier lender (in a re-financing transaction). In all of these cases, the discharge of the debt represents an enrichment to the debtor, obtained at the expense of the surety, company or bank. In each case, the law of unjust enrichment may give the surety, company or bank a direct personal restitutionary remedy against the debtor. It may also give a different remedy, comprising the right to be subrogated to the creditor's extinguished rights.[1]

Where the creditor had no secured rights against the debtor, this remedy will **39–02** generally be a redundant option: giving the claimant rights corresponding to the creditor's extinguished personal rights against the debtor will generally offer no advantages over a direct personal claim in unjust enrichment for the value of the discharged debt.[2] Only in rare cases is the position otherwise[3]—for example, because the creditor's personal rights had a preferential ranking in the debtor's insolvency, whereas the direct personal claim in unjust enrichment ranks as an ordinary unsecured debt.

In contrast, where payment of the debt was secured on property owned by the **39–03** debtor and/or a third party, the subrogation remedy offers real practical advantages. Having paid the creditor, the claimant may be entitled to be subrogated to his extinguished security interest and associated personal rights—thereby acquiring the benefit of a secured right to payment. Subrogation operates as a proprietary remedy in such cases, reversing the unjust enrichment that would otherwise accrue to the discharged debtor, and to other parties.

This chapter explains the nature and operation of subrogation to extinguished **39–04** proprietary rights. Part 2 outlines the basic nature of the remedy, whilst Part 3 gives a more detailed account of its form and operation, and in particular, of the

---

[1] For a comprehensive examination of this remedy, see C. Mitchell and S. Watterson, *Subrogation: Law and Practice* (Oxford: OUP, 2007), Chs 1 and 3–9.
[2] For cases where claimants were subrogated to a creditor's extinguished personal rights, see, e.g. *Filby v Mortgage Express (No.2) Ltd* [2004] EWCA Civ 759; *Niru Battery Manufacturing Co v Milestone Trading Ltd (No.2)* [2004] EWCA Civ 487; [2004] 2 All E.R. (Comm) 289.
[3] See further, Mitchell and Watterson, *Subrogation: Law and Practice*, paras 8–32—8–38.

nature, content and priority status of the rights which are afforded to a subrogation claimant.

2. THE BASIC NATURE OF THE REMEDY

(a) Subrogation as a Restitutionary Remedy for Unjust Enrichment

39–05 There are many cases where a claimant has been responsible for paying another party's debt, and the courts have held that he is subrogated to the creditor's rights, including a security interest held by the creditor for the debt. Until recently, however, the English courts found it difficult to understand the legal mechanism by which claimants could acquire rights via subrogation in such cases and why they should be entitled to do so. Two particular problems should be mentioned here.[4]

39–06 First, the courts found it difficult to explain how a claimant could be subrogated to a creditor's secured rights if these rights had been extinguished. Some courts assumed that this was an insuperable objection to subrogation: rights that had been extinguished by payment could not be acquired by the claimant by subrogation, because ex hypothesi, the rights must have ceased to exist.[5] In more recent cases, the courts avoided this objection by saying that the creditor's extinguished rights were "kept alive" for the benefit of the subrogated claimant.[6] But difficulties persisted in conceptualising this process of "revival" and its consequences for the parties.

39–07 Secondly, the courts found it difficult to explain why the claimant should be entitled to "acquire" an extinguished security interest by subrogation. The view emerged that a claimant whose money was used to discharge a security interest over another's land should be presumed to have intended this outcome.[7] But this analysis was often strained, if not clearly fictitious.

---

[4] For fuller examination, see Mitchell and Watterson, *Subrogation: Law and Practice*, para.3–06 and following.

[5] e.g. *Gammon v Stone* (1749) 1 Ves. Sen. 339; 27 E.R. 1068; *Woffington v Sparks* (1754) 2 Ves. Sen. 569; 28 E.R. 363; *Hodgson v Shaw* (1834) 3 My. & K. 183; 40 E.R. 70; cf. *Copis v Middleton* (1823) Turn. & R. 224 at 231; 37 E.R. 1083 at 1086 per Lord Eldon L.C. (legal mortgages might not be extinguished by the surety's payment, because the "mortgagor [could not] get back his estate again without a [re]conveyance"). The perceived difficulty was overcome by the Mercantile Law Amendment Act 1856 s.5, still in force, which gave sureties and others who discharge a common liability the right to acquire the creditor's securities "whether [these] shall or shall not be deemed at law to have been satisfied by the payment of the debt". A similar concern later resurfaced to inhibit the award of subrogation in other contexts: *Re Diplock* [1948] Ch. 465 (CA) at 549, critically discussed in *Boscawen v Bajwa* [1996] 1 W.L.R. 328 (CA) at 340; and cf. *Re Byfield* [1982] 1 Ch. 267 at 272; *Niru Battery (No.2)* [2004] EWCA Civ 487; [2004] 2 All E.R. (Comm.) 289 at [63].

[6] e.g. *Butler v Rice* [1910] 2 Ch. 277 at 282 per Warrington J.; *Coptic Ltd v Bailey* [1972] Ch. 446 at 454 per Whitford J.; *Re Tramway Building & Construction Co Ltd* [1988] Ch. 293 at 306 per Scott J.; *U.C.B. Group Ltd v Hedworth* [2003] EWCA Civ 717; [2003] 3 F.C.R. 739 at [146] per Jonathan Parker L.J.

[7] *Patten v Bond* (1889) 60 L.T. 583 at 586 per Kay J., followed and approved in many later cases, including *Chetwynd v Allen* [1899] 1 Ch. 353; *Butler v Rice* [1910] 2 Ch. 277; *Ghana Commercial Bank v Chandiram* [1960] A.C. 732 (PC) at 745; *National Guardian Mortgage Corp v Roberts* [1993] N.P.C. 149 (CA).

The House of Lords clarified this area of the law in *Banque Financière de la* **39–08**
Cité v Parc (Battersea) Ltd.[8] In his leading speech, Lord Hoffmann gave a rich
and subtle account of subrogation which must now provide the starting-point for
any analysis of the remedy's operation and availability.

Lord Hoffmann reviewed the line of authority which had explained subroga- **39–09**
tion in terms of "presumed intention" and concluded that it was misconceived.[9]
He did not disagree with the results in the cases, but he considered that the
language in which they were expressed lacked explanatory force, and concealed
the true reason for the award of the remedy. As Lord Hoffmann saw it, there are
two possible reasons. A claimant whose money is used to pay off a debt secured
on a defendant's property might acquire the creditor's security if he has contracted for this. Otherwise, he might be entitled to be treated as though he has
acquired the security, via subrogation, if the defendant and other parties interested in the property have been unjustly enriched at his expense. The old
language of presumed intention served a useful purpose before the modern
recognition of unjust enrichment as a source of obligations in English law.
However, it is now[10]:

> "[A] mistake to regard the availability of subrogation as a remedy to prevent unjust
> enrichment as turning entirely upon the question of intention, whether common or
> unilateral. Such an analysis has inevitably to be propped up by presumptions which can
> verge on outright fictions, more appropriate to a less developed legal system than we
> now have ... [Outside of cases where the parties have contracted for subrogation, it]
> should be recognised that one is here concerned with a restitutionary remedy and that
> the appropriate questions are therefore, first, whether the defendant would be enriched
> at the plaintiff's expense; secondly, whether such enrichment would be unjust; and,
> thirdly, whether there are nevertheless reasons of policy for denying a remedy."

This clarification of the reason for subrogation awards also enabled a clearer **39–10**
appreciation of the process by which a claimant "acquires" extinguished rights
by subrogation, as well as the nature and content of the rights he obtains. The
language of "keeping rights alive" for the benefit of the subrogation claimant
was a "metaphor" and "not a literal truth".[11] Properly understood, a creditor's
extinguished rights were not kept alive, and transferred to the claimant. Ex
hypothesi, these rights were discharged, and ceased to exist. The true position is
rather that[12]:

> "[S]ubrogation is ... an equitable remedy against a party who would otherwise be
> unjustly enriched. It is a means by which the court regulates the legal relationships
> between a plaintiff and a defendant or defendants in order to prevent unjust enrichment.
> When judges say that [a] charge is 'kept alive' for the benefit of the plaintiff, what they
> mean is that his legal relations with a defendant who would otherwise be unjustly
> enriched are regulated as if the benefit of the charge had been assigned to him. It does
> not by any means follow that the plaintiff must for all purposes be treated as an actual
> assignee of the benefit of the charge and, in particular, that he would be so treated in
> relation to someone who would not [otherwise] be unjustly enriched."

---

[8] *Banque Financière de la Cité v Parc (Battersea) Ltd* [1999] 1 A.C. 221.
[9] *Banque Financière* [1999] 1 A.C. 221 at 231–234 per Lord Hoffmann.
[10] *Banque Financière* [1999] 1 A.C. 221 at 234 per Lord Hoffmann.
[11] *Banque Financière* [1999] 1 A.C. 221 at 236 per Lord Hoffmann.
[12] *Banque Financière* [1999] 1 A.C. 221 at 236 per Lord Hoffmann.

39–11   This analysis provides a satisfying answer to the extinction problem: the extinction of the creditor's rights does not prevent subrogation from taking place, but is rather a pre-requisite for the award of the remedy,[13] since it is the reason for the enrichment which subrogation reverses.[14] Lord Hoffmann's analysis also sheds important light on the nature and content of the claimant's rights. Claimants who acquire rights by subrogation in these cases do not do so because the courts "revive" these rights and "transfer" them to the claimant. They do so because the courts can, by a legal fiction, regulate the claimant's relations with one or more others as though he has acquired the creditor's extinguished rights, to the extent that this is necessary to reverse their unjust enrichment. By this means the claimant obtains new rights, which prima facie replicate the creditor's extinguished rights. This is explained further in Part 3.

(b) *The Availability of the Remedy*

39–12   Subrogation to extinguished rights is therefore a remedy that reverses the unjust enrichment of a discharged debtor and/or other parties which follows from the discharge of a debt, by affording the claimant new rights which prima facie replicate the creditor's extinguished rights.[15] It follows that a claimant seeking the remedy must establish a cause of action in unjust enrichment in the same way as any other claimant. The basic components of such a claim are described in earlier chapters,[16] and there is no need to repeat what is said there. But there are some special features of subrogation claims that call for comment.

(i) *Enrichment at the Claimant's Expense: Primary and Secondary Enrichments*

39–13   Whenever a claimant seeks subrogation to another party's extinguished security interest, the first requirement must always be to show that a secured debt was

---

[13] *Boscawen* [1996] 1 W.L.R. 328 (CA) at 340 per Millett L.J.: "the discharge of the creditor's security . . . is certainly not a bar to subrogation in equity; it is rather a pre-condition".

[14] See further paras 39–13——39–15.

[15] Later cases proceeding on this basis are: *Birmingham Midshires Mortgage Services Ltd v Sabherwahl* (2000) 80 P. & C.R. 256 at [37]; *Cheltenham & Gloucester Plc v Appleyard* [2004] EWCA Civ 291; *Niru Battery (No.2)* [2003] EWHC 1032 (Comm); [2003] 2 All E.R. (Comm.) 365; [2004] EWCA Civ 487; [2004] 2 All E.R. (Comm.) 289; *Filby* [2004] EWCA Civ 759; *Kali Ltd v Chawla* [2007] EWHC 2357 (Ch); [2008] B.P.I.R. 415; *London Allied Holdings Ltd v Lee* [2007] EWHC 2061 (Ch) at [286]; *Re Rusjon Ltd (In Liquidation)* [2007] EWHC 2942 (Ch); [2008] 2 B.C.L.C. 234 at [32]–[33]; *Primlake Ltd (In Liquidation) v Matthews Associates* [2006] EWHC 1127 (Ch); [2007] 1 B.C.L.C. 666 at [337]–[340], and [2009] EWHC 2774 (Ch); *Clark v Lucas Solicitors LLP* [2009] EWHC 1952 (Ch); [2010] 2 All E.R. 955 at [52]–[55]; *Brazill v Willoughby* [2009] EWHC 1633 (Ch); [2010] 1 B.C.L.C. 673 at [203] and following, affirmed [2010] EWCA Civ 561; [2010] 2 B.C.L.C. 259; *Anfield (UK) Ltd v Bank of Scotland Plc* [2010] EWHC 2374 (Ch); [2011] 1 All E.R. 708; *Fortis Bank SA/NA v Indian Overseas Bank* [2011] EWHC 538 (Comm); [2011] 2 Lloyd's Rep. 190 at [69] and following.; *Ibrahim v Barclays Bank Plc* [2011] EWHC 1897 (Ch).

[16] This is manifest in Lord Hoffmann's analysis in *Banque Financière* [1999] 1 A.C. 221 at 234 and following.

discharged, wholly or in part,[17] and that this occurred at the claimant's expense.[18] By this means, the claimant establishes the enrichment which subrogation reverses.

It is essential for a proper understanding of the remedy to appreciate that the **39–14** enrichment to which it responds in cases where a secured debt is discharged takes two forms. The primary enrichment accrues to the discharged debtor, who is released from liability to his creditor; but there are also secondary enrichments that may accrue to other, remoter parties, whose position is materially improved when the creditor's rights are extinguished. Such secondary enrichments may accrue to a junior secured creditor, who held a security interest over the same asset which was subordinate to the creditor's security interest, and whose subordinate security interest was strengthened to the extent that the debt secured by the prior-ranking security interest is discharged.[19] They may also accrue to any other person who held an interest in the same asset which was subordinate to the discharged security interest, and whose subordinate interest was improved to the extent that the asset was freed from the prior encumbrance.[20]

Following *Banque Financière*, we can see that where a claimant discharges **39–15** another's secured debt, and is entitled to be subrogated to the creditor's extinguished security interest, the subrogation remedy is often designed to reverse both forms of enrichment: the "primary" enrichment that accrues to the discharged debtor and also the "secondary" enrichment that accrues to remoter parties. Although this is rarely made explicit,[21] this is the premise that underpins the courts' starting-point, that a claimant's prima facie entitlement is to a security interest which has the same priority over pre-existing interests as the creditor previously enjoyed[22]—thereby reversing the enrichment of junior secured creditors and other subordinate interest-holders which followed from the release of the creditor's prior-ranking security. *Banque Financière* also shows that in some exceptional circumstances, the subrogation remedy may be awarded in a form which is exclusively designed to target the secondary enrichment that would otherwise accrue to a remoter party. The facts of the case and the order made there are explained below.[23]

---

[17] The rules governing the discharge of debts are explained at paras 5–38—5–60.

[18] See Chs 6 and 7.

[19] As recognised in *Banque Financière* [1999] 1 A.C. 221; and in *Anfield* [2010] EWHC 2374 (Ch); [2011] 1 All E.R. 708 at [11]: "[i]ntermediate lenders are necessarily enriched by the discharge of a prior security".

[20] e.g. a third party who is a beneficial owner of the asset charged, and whose interest was subject to the extinguished charge, as in *Mortgage Express Ltd v McDonnell* [2001] EWCA Civ 887; [2001] 2 All E.R. (Comm.) 886; *Eagle Star Insurance Co Ltd v Karasiewicz* [2002] EWCA Civ 940.

[21] But see *Anfield* [2010] EWHC 2374 (Ch); [2011] 1 All E.R. 708 at [11]. See too *Banque Financière* [1999] 1 A.C. 221; and cf. the inconsistent assumption in *Fortis* [2011] EWHC 538 (Comm); [2011] 2 Lloyd's Rep. 190 at [74].

[22] Cases affording priority over junior secured creditors include *Appleyard* [2004] EWCA Civ 291; *National Westminster Bank Plc v Mayfair Estates Property Investments Ltd* [2007] EWHC 287 (Ch); *Kali* [2007] EWHC 2357 (Ch); [2008] B.P.I.R. 415. Cases affording priority over other subordinate interests include *McDonell* [2001] EWCA Civ 887; [2001] 2 All E.R. (Comm.) 886; *Karasiewicz* [2002] EWCA Civ 940.

[23] See paras 39–41—39–51.

(ii) *Grounds for Restitution*

39–16 In many past cases, the courts have failed to identify the ground for restitution that makes it unjust for the debtor and remoter parties to be enriched at the claimant's expense. Nevertheless, the subrogation cases can all be explained in these terms.

39–17 The ground for restitution in some cases was lack of consent or want of authority. These include cases where secured debts were discharged using mis-applied trust money,[24] misapplied corporate assets,[25] misapplied partnership assets,[26] and misdirected assets emanating from a deceased person's estate.[27]

39–18 In other cases, the ground for restitution was mistake or failure of basis. Typically a lender advances money to fund the acquisition of property or to re-finance the borrower's existing debts on the understanding that the lender will acquire a specified form of security interest. The lender then fails to obtain the bargained-for security interest and the lender is subrogated to a security interest which the loan moneys were used to discharge. This remedy can generally be attributed to a mistake that caused the lender's advance[28] or to the failure—initial or subsequent—of a condition on which the advance was made.[29]

39–19 Subrogation is also widely available on the ground of secondary liability. The earliest example is a surety who discharges the principal debtor's liability by paying his creditor. The surety has a personal claim for reimbursement against the principal debtor, but also—and as a supplementary measure for obtaining reimbursement—has a right to be subrogated to any security interest held by the creditor for the principal debtor's discharged debt. Over the course of the 19th and 20th centuries this right was extended by statute[30] and by judicial decisions to many other parties who, having discharged a common liability resting on

---

[24] *Bishopsgate Investment Management Ltd (In Liquidation) v Homan* [1995] Ch. 211 at 221 (CA); *Scotlife Home Loans (No.2) Ltd v Melinek* (1999) 78 P. & C.R. 389 at 398 (CA); *Cook v Italiano Family Fruit Co Ltd (In Liquidation)* [2010] FCA 1355; (2010) 190 F.C.R. 474 at [81] and following. See too *Boscawen* [1996] 1 W.L.R. 328 (CA).

[25] *Primlake* [2006] EWHC 1227 (Ch); [2007] 1 B.C.L.C. 666 at [337]–[340]; and [2009] EWHC 2774 (Ch).

[26] *Raulfs v Fishy Bite Pty Ltd* [2008] NSWSC 1195 at [25].

[27] *Gertsch v Atsas* [1999] NSWSC 898; (1999) 10 B.P.R. 18,431 at [19]–[20]; cf. *Re Diplock* [1948] Ch. 465 (CA) at 548–550; criticised in *Boscawen* [1996] 1 W.L.R. 328 (CA) at 340–341, and considered further in *Cook* [2010] FCA 1355; (2010) 190 F.C.R. 474 at [81] and following.

[28] Explicitly recognised as a subrogation-justifying ground in *Banque Financière* [1999] 1 A.C. 221 at 227 per Lord Steyn; and at 234 per Lord Hoffmann, and in *Filby* [2004] EWCA Civ 759 at [48] per May L.J. Examples of the numerous cases explicable in these terms include *Chetwynd* [1899] 1 Ch 353 (borrower was not beneficial owner of the property on which the debt was to be secured); *Thurstan v Nottingham Permanent Benefit Building Society* [1902] 1 Ch. 1 (CA) (legal incapacity of the borrower); *Castle Phillips Finance Ltd v Piddington* (1995) 70 P. & C.R. 592 (CA) (consent of one party to the transaction was vitiated by reason of another party's misrepresentation or undue influence); *Filby* (purported borrower's consent to transaction was forged).

[29] Typically, because an intended security interest is never acquired, or subsequently invalidated: *A.N.Z. Banking Group Ltd v Costikidis* Unreported Victoria Sup Ct, December 22, 1994; *Royal Bank of Scotland Plc v Bhardwaj* [2002] B.C.C. 57 at 59; *Appleyard* [2004] EWCA Civ 291; *Nouri v Marvi* [2005] EWHC 2996 (Ch); [2006] 1 E.G.L.R. 71 at [30]–[32]; *Kali* [2007] EWHC 2357 (Ch); [2008] B.P.I.R. 415.

[30] Mercantile Law Amendment Act 1856 s.5.

themselves and another, acquire a personal claim for reimbursement or contribution against that other. [31] This right is now available in all cases of this type.[32]

(iii) *Defences and Bars*

As an equitable remedy designed to reverse unjust enrichment, a claim to be **39–20**
subrogated to a creditor's extinguished rights may be defeated or limited by any
defence or bar that will defeat or limit any cause of action in unjust enrichment.
These include defences of change of position,[33] bona fide purchase,[34] receipt for
good consideration,[35] and illegality or public policy.[36] They also include the
objection that the rights claimed would be inconsistent with a valid contract to
which the claimant is party with the paid-off creditor, the discharged debtor and/
or a third party—an objection which is of general application, but which is often
invoked to limit the subrogation rights of lenders and of sureties and other parties
who discharge a common liability.[37] A subrogation claim may also be defeated
by one of the traditional bars to equitable relief,[38] subject to the important caveat
that if the law of unjust enrichment is to develop coherently, the English courts
should be reluctant to refuse the subrogation remedy on the basis of a traditional
bar to equitable relief, where to do so would be obviously inconsistent with the

---

[31] Sureties subrogated to a creditor's rights against co-sureties: *Kayley v Hothersall* [1925] 1 K.B. 607
(CA); *Smith v Wood* [1929] 1 Ch. 14 (CA) at 21. Sub-sureties subrogated to a creditor's rights against
sureties in prior degree: *Fox v Royal Bank of Canada* [1976] 2 S.C.R. 2. Assignors of leases or their
sureties, who discharge the assignee's liability for rent and are subrogated to the landlord's rights
against the assignee or his surety: *Re Downer Enterprises Ltd* [1974] 1 W.L.R. 1460; *Becton
Dickinson UK Ltd v Zwebner* [1989] Q.B. 208. Persons who are legally compelled to pay tax for
which another is properly liable, are subrogated to the tax-gathering authority's rights: *Re
Burstein* (1964) 45 D.L.R. (2d.) 207 (Ontario Sup Ct).
[32] *Niru Battery (No.2)* [2004] EWCA Civ 487; [2004] 2 All E.R. (Comm) 289. For earlier dicta
supporting a broad view of the availability of subrogation in such cases, see *Duncan, Fox & Co v
North & South Wales Bank* (1880) 6 App. Cas 1 at 13; applied in *Re Downer Enterprises Ltd* [1974]
1 W.L.R. 1460 at 1468; and *Becton* [1989] Q.B. 208 at 216–218.
[33] Allowed in *Gertsch* [1999] NSWSC 898; (1999) 10 B.P.R. 18,431 (discharged debtor); and
contemplated in *Anfield* [2010] EWHC 2374 (Ch); [2011] 1 All E.R. 708 at [31] (junior secured
creditor). See too *Boscawen* [1996] 1 WLR 328 (CA) at 341 per Millett L.J.; explaining *Re Diplock*
[1948] Ch. 465 (CA) at 549–550 per Lord Greene M.R.
[34] Implicit in *London Allied Holdings* [2007] EWHC 2061 (Ch) at [286]; where the defence was
unavailable, because the recipient of the funds was a volunteer.
[35] Allowed in *National Australia Bank Ltd v Rusu* [2001] NSWSC 32 at [44]–[45] and at [51].
[36] Recognised but not established in *Banque Financière* [1999] 1 A.C. 221 at 234 and 235 per Lord
Hoffmann; and at 246 per Lord Hutton. Cf. *Burston Finance Ltd v Speirway Ltd (In Liquidation)*
[1974] 1 W.L.R. 1648; *Orakpo v Manson Investments Ltd* [1978] A.C. 95; *Wa Lee Finance Co Ltd
v Staryork Investment Ltd* [2003] HKCFI 440; affirmed [2004] HKCA 155.
[37] e.g. where a contract between a surety and a creditor excludes or limits the surety's subrogation
rights (cf. *Lloyds TSB Bank Plc v Shorney* [2001] EWCA Civ 1161; [2002] 1 F.L.R. 81; *Liberty
Mutual Insurance Co (UK) Ltd v HSBC Bank Plc* [2001] Lloyd's Rep. Bank 224; affirmed [2002]
EWCA Civ 691) or where a contract between a surety and the principal debtor does so. Other cases
where the denial of subrogation is explicable in these terms are *Re Rusjon* [2007] EWHC 2943 (Ch);
[2008] 2 B.C.L.C. 234; *Fortis* [2011] EWHC 538 (Comm); [2011] 2 Lloyd's Rep. 190; *Ibrahim*
[2011] EWHC 1897 (Ch).
[38] *Appleyard* [2004] EWCA Civ 291 at [44]. Equitable defences and bars, whose application is
mainly illustrated by Commonwealth authorities, include: (1) laches/acquiescence (discussed in
Appleyard); (2) he who seeks equity must do equity (applied in *Re Trivan Pty Ltd* (1996) 134 F.L.R.
368 (NSW Sup Ct (Eq Div)); (3) clean hands (not established on the facts in *Mutual Trust Co v
Creditview Estate Homes Ltd* (1998) 34 O.R. (3d.) 583 (Ontario CA)).

approach they would take to the availability of other remedies for unjust enrichment.

39–21   When considering defences, it is important to bear in mind that subrogation to another's extinguished security interest may be designed, at least in part, to reverse the secondary enrichment that would accrue to remoter parties, such as junior secured creditors.[39] One corollary to this is that a remoter party, who would be adversely affected by the award of subrogation, might be able to raise a defence to the claim. This might be on a basis which would negate the availability of the remedy altogether, or on a more limited basis, which bears specifically on the appropriateness of a restitutionary remedy vis-à-vis the remoter party. One argument of the latter type might be that a junior secured creditor changed its position in good faith as a result of discharge of a prior security interest, for example by lending further money to the borrower; or by failing to take enforcement action to realise its security.[40] Another such argument might be that there was a binding priority agreement between the claimant and a junior secured creditor, whereby the claimant agreed that the latter's claims would have priority to any claims of the claimant, which would be subverted if the claimant were to obtain a security interest with priority vis-à-vis the junior secured creditor.[41]

39–22   It is also important to appreciate that, depending on its nature, a defence or bar may affect a claimant's subrogation entitlement in a number of different ways. Some care is therefore required when working through the implications of a defence or bar since this may:

(1) preclude any restitutionary remedy altogether; or

(2) preclude a proprietary restitutionary remedy, in the form of subrogation to the paid-off creditor's extinguished security interest, but not a personal restitutionary remedy[42]; or

(3) reduce the quantum of the money sum recoverable by the claimant, by enforcing his subrogation rights, i.e. the "subrogation debt"[43]; or

(4) modify the priority of the claimant's security interest vis-à-vis other parties[44]; or

---

[39] See paras 39–14—39–15.

[40] Cf. *Anfield* [2010] EWHC 2374 (Ch); [2011] 1 All E.R. 708 at [31]; and *Armatage Motors Ltd v Royal Trust Corp of Canada* (1997) 34 O.R. (3d.) 599 (Ontario CA); discussed in Mitchell and Watterson, *Subrogation: Law and Practice*, para.7–79 and following.

[41] Cf. *Mayfair* [2007] EWHC 287 (Ch), where the priority agreement between the claimant and the creditor had the opposite effect of enlarging the claimant's rights.

[42] e.g. where it would be inconsistent with a contract between the claimant and the debtor, or the claimant and some other party, for the claimant to obtain a security interest by subrogation, as in *Paul v Speirway Ltd (In Liquidation)* [1976] Ch. 220; *Banque Financière* [1999] 1 A.C. 221; *Re Rusjon* [2007] EWHC 2943 (Ch); [2008] 2 B.C.L.C. 234.

[43] e.g. to reflect a change of position by the discharged debtor (*Gertsch* [1999] NSWSC 898; (1999) 10 B.P.R. 18,431); or to ensure that the claimant does not recover a greater sum of interest than it bargained for from the debtor (cf. *Appleyard* [2004] EWCA Civ 291 at [76]–[77]).

[44] e.g. to ensure that a lender does not obtain a security interest by subrogation with greater priority than the one it bargained for (cf. *Investors Group Trust Co Ltd v Crispino* [2006] 147 A.C.W.S. (3d.) 1069 (Ontario Sup Ct)).

(5) require the court in some other way to postpone, or limit, the enforcement of the claimant's subrogation rights.[45]

(iv) *The Appropriateness of Proprietary Relief*

Proprietary restitutionary remedies, including subrogation to an extinguished security interest, are more tightly confined than personal restitutionary awards. It follows that the mere fact that the claimant has discharged another's security interest, and can show that the discharged debtor and/or remoter parties have been unjustly enriched at his expense, does not necessarily mean that he should be afforded the special priority advantages of a security interest acquired via subrogation. The policy arguments for and against the award of proprietary remedies for unjust enrichment are reviewed in Ch.37.[46]

39–23

(c) *Pleading*

A claimant who seeks the remedy of subrogation to a creditor's extinguished rights can bring proceedings in his own name and need not proceed in the name of the paid-off creditor.[47] This follows from the nature of the claimant's rights: he is enforcing new rights, which the law affords him vis-à-vis the discharged debtor and others, for the purpose of reversing the unjust enrichment that would otherwise accrue to them at his expense. In this respect, such a claim differs fundamentally from an insurer's subrogated claim, which must be brought in the name of the insured.

39–24

(d) *Qualifying Rights*

(i) *Generally*

The rights that have formed the subject matter of a claim to be subrogated to another's extinguished rights have taken two general types: personal rights to be paid money by another; and "security interests", i.e. rights in respect of another's property which serve the purpose of securing an obligation on that other to pay a sum of money. Subject to very few exceptions, a claimant who discharges another's right of either type may be entitled to the remedy of subrogation, whether the right in question derives from common law, equity or statute; and whether the right was consensually created or arose by operation of law.[48]

39–25

(ii) *"Sub-subrogation"*

A claimant may sometimes be responsible for discharging an intermediate creditor's right to be subrogated to an earlier creditor's rights against a defendant.

39–26

---

[45] e.g. where a surety agrees with a creditor not to assert his subrogation rights vis-à-vis the principal debtor until the creditor is fully paid.

[46] See para.37–07 and following.

[47] Implicit in the authorities, but expressly recognised by *Niru Battery (No.2)* [2003] EWHC 1023 (Comm); [2003] 2 All E.R. (Comm.) 365 at [32]–[37]; see too *Ibrahim* [2011] EWHC 1897 at [139]–[141].

[48] For full discussion, see Mitchell and Watterson, *Subrogation: Law and Practice*, paras 9–38 and following.

Provided that the other necessary components of a claim can be established, the claimant may be entitled to be subrogated to the intermediate creditor's extinguished right to be subrogated to the earlier creditor's rights against the defendant—a process that is sometimes labelled "sub-subrogation".

39–27   An illustration is *UCB Group Ltd v Hedworth*.[49] Barclays Bank lent moneys to fund the joint purchase of a farm by Mr and Mrs Hedworth, expecting to obtain a valid first legal charge over the property to secure its advance. Subsequently, UCB lent moneys which were used to pay off the Barclays charge over the farm, also expecting to obtain a valid first legal charge to secure its advance. On the assumption that each of the legal charges executed by Mr and Mrs Hedworth could be avoided by Mrs Hedworth, because Mrs Hedworth's consent had been obtained by mispresentations or undue influence by her husband, of which the relevant lender had notice, the Court of Appeal held that Barclays had been entitled to be subrogated to the unpaid vendor's lien which its advance had discharged; and that when UCB's advance was later used to repay Barclays' advance, UCB in turn became entitled to be sub-subrogated to the unpaid vendor's lien.

3. THE FORM OF THE REMEDY

(a) *Introduction*

39–28   Three connected questions are considered in this part. What is the basic form of the subrogation remedy? Where a claimant acquires a security interest by subrogation, what principles govern the priority of this interest vis-à-vis other interests in the same property? How should the court quantify the "subrogation debt", i.e. the sum which the claimant can recover as a debt secured by his security interest?

(b) *The Basic Form of the Remedy*

(i) *New Rights, Arising in Equity*

39–29   The nature of the equitable remedy of subrogation to a creditor's extinguished rights has been obscured by a prevailing assumption that these rights are "kept alive" and "transferred" to the claimant, so that he can enforce them for his own benefit. This is a misconception.[50] The language of "keeping rights alive" for the claimant's benefit is a metaphor.[51] The claimant is not an assignee of the creditor's rights. These rights are extinguished and can no longer be enforced

---

[49] *UCB Group Ltd v Hedworth* [2003] EWCA Civ 1717; [2003] 3 F.C.R. 739; endorsing and applying the reasoning in *Castle Phillips Finance* (1995) 70 P. & C.R. 592 (CA). See too *Nouri v Marvi* [2005] EWHC 2996 (Ch); [2006] 1 E.G.L.R. 71; *Baroness Wenlock v River Dee Co* (1887) 19 Q.B.D. 155 (CA); and *Brown Shipley & Co Ltd v Amalgamated Investment (Europe) BV* [1979] 1 Lloyd's Rep. 488.
[50] See paras 39–10—39–11.
[51] *Banque Financière* [1999] 1 A.C. 221 at 236 per Lord Hoffmann.

against the debtor.[52] What the claimant obtains are new rights, arising in equity,[53] to the extent that the creditor's rights have been extinguished.[54] These rights arise to reverse the unjust enrichment of the discharged debtor and remoter parties following from the extinction of the creditor's rights.[55] To this end, these new rights typically replicate the characteristics and content of the rights previously held by the creditor.[56]

Several consequences flow from this. First, and most importantly, the claimant **39–30** does not acquire the creditor's security interest. He obtains a new and independent equitable security interest, which prima facie replicates the old interest.[57] Secondly, as the claimant's rights are new rights, generated in equity for the limited purpose of reversing the unjust enrichment of the discharged debtor and remoter parties, it may be unnecessary, and even undesirable, for the claimant to occupy exactly the same position as the paid-off creditor.[58] Thirdly, as any security interest which the claimant acquires via subrogation is a new security interest, there is no conceptual obstacle to the claimant obtaining such an interest although the creditor's security interest subsists, for example because he has only been paid in part.[59] Finally, the priority of any security interest which the claimant acquires by subrogation vis-à-vis interests which third parties subsequently acquire in the same property can be resolved on the basis of one consistent starting-point. Whatever the quality of the creditor's security interest, the claimant's interest is a new equitable security interest, and his priority position vis-à-vis such third parties must be resolved by applying the principles that generally apply to interests of that type in the relevant subject matter.[60]

(ii) The Content of the Claimant's New Rights

When determining the characteristics and content of a claimant's rights, the **39–31** courts' starting-point is that these should replicate, and should be no greater than, the rights that the creditor previously held against the debtor. As May L.J. put it in *Filby v Mortgage Express (No. 2) Ltd*,[61] "[t]he essence of the remedy is that the court declares the claimant to have a right having characteristics and content identical to that enjoyed [by the creditor]".[62] This follows from the fact that the limited goal of the remedy is to reverse the unjust enrichment of the debtor and other parties at the claimant's expense, following from the discharge of the paid-off creditor's rights.

---

[52] *Banque Financière* [1999] 1 A.C. 221 at 236 per Lord Hoffmann.
[53] *Boscawen* [1996] 1 W.L.R. 328 (CA); *Halifax Mortgage Services Ltd v Muirhead* (1998) 76 P. & C.R. 418 (CA) at 428 per Evans L.J.; *Banque Financière* [1999] 1 A.C. 221 at 236 per Lord Hoffmann; *Filby* [2004] EWCA Civ 759 at [1] and [36]–[67] per May L.J.; *Appleyard* [2004] EWCA Civ 291 at [32] and at [44].
[54] *Muirhead* (1998) 76 P. & C.R. 418 (CA) at 426 and 428 per Evans L.J.; *Banque Financière* [1999] 1 A.C. 221 at 236 per Lord Hoffmann; *Filby* [2004] EWCA Civ 759 at [63] per May L.J.
[55] See paras 39–08—39–15.
[56] See paras 39–31—39–37.
[57] See paras 39–64—39–65.
[58] See paras 39–38—39–40.
[59] See paras 39–54—39–60.
[60] See paras 39–61—39–65.
[61] *Filby v Mortgage Express (No.2) Ltd* [2004] EWCA Civ 759.
[62] *Filby* [2004] EWCA Civ 759 at [63]. See too *Muirhead* (1998) 76 P. & C.R. 418 (CA) at 426–428 per Evans L.J.

39–32   **New rights which prima facie replicate the creditor's extinguished rights**   Several illustrations can be given of the different ways in which a claimant's new rights can replicate, but may be no greater than, the creditor's extinguished rights.

39–33   First, the claimant's new security interest will inherit any defect that marred the creditor's original security interest. For example, if the claimant lent money to pay off a charge which was void for forgery or voidable for misrepresentation or undue influence, then any security interest acquired by the claimant via subrogation should suffer from a similar defect.[63]

39–34   Secondly, the claimant's new security interest will prima facie inherit the same priority vis-à-vis pre-existing third party interests in the same asset as was formerly held by the creditor's security interest.[64] Thus, the claimant's new security interest will initially be subordinate to any interests which took priority over the creditor's interest: and it will initially be superior to any interests over which the creditor's interest took priority.

39–35   Thirdly, the claimant cannot use his new security interest to recover a larger sum than the creditor could have recovered under his original security interest (although he may be entitled to recover a larger sum by bringing a personal claim). Thus, the principal sum secured by the claimant's security interest cannot exceed the amount of the debts which he paid and which were secured by the creditor's security interest.[65] And any right to interest secured by the claimant's new security interest cannot exceed the creditor's secured right to recover interest under his contract with the debtor.[66]

39–36   Fourthly, the claimant cannot take action to enforce his rights which could not have been taken by the creditor to enforce his security interest. So, for example, if the creditor's security interest was an unpaid vendor's lien, which would not have afforded the creditor a right to possession of the debtor's land, then any new security interest which the claimant acquires by subrogation cannot afford the claimant a right to possession: the claimant's enforcement options are necessarily limited to those of a lien-holder.[67]

39–37   Fifthly, the debtor's liability to the claimant may share other important qualities with his discharged liability to the creditor, such as its quality as a secondary (rather than a primary) liability[68]; and its quality as a deferred (rather than an immediate) liability.[69]

39–38   **New rights which differ from the creditor's extinguished rights**   A claimant's rights will not inevitably share every characteristic of the rights that were previously held by the creditor.[70] This follows from the fact that the claimant is not actually an assignee of the creditor's rights, and that the claimant's rights are

---

[63] e.g. *Castle Phillips Finance* (1995) 70 P. & C.R. 592 (CA) and *Hedworth* [2003] EWCA Civ 1717; [2003] 3 F.C.R. 739, where the lender was therefore "sub-subrogated" to an earlier, valid charge: see para.39–26.
[64] See para.39–53.
[65] *Appleyard* [2004] EWCA Civ 291 at [43] per Neuberger L.J.
[66] See para.39–84.
[67] *Thurstan* [1902] 1 Ch. 1 (CA) at 13 per Romer L.J., affirmed [1903] A.C. 6; see too *Ghana Commercial Bank v Chandiram* [1960] A.C. 732 (PC).
[68] *Chetwynd* [1899] 1 Ch. 353.
[69] *Muirhead* (1998) 76 P. & C.R. 418 (CA).
[70] *Banque Financière* [1999] 1 A.C. 221 at 236 per Lord Hoffmann.

new rights, arising in equity, to reverse the unjust enrichment of the debtor and other parties at his expense. Some examples follow.

First, the claimant's rights may be diminished if the debtor or a remoter party **39–39** establishes a defence. For example, the debtor may have changed his position[71] or may have repaid the sums claimed to be due.[72] Or a junior incumbrancer may have changed its position[73] or have entered a binding priority agreement with the claimant.

Secondly, the priority of the claimant's interest vis-à-vis third parties who later **39–40** acquire interests in the relevant property is not determined on the basis that the claimant's entitlement has exactly the same status as the creditor's extinguished security interest. Whether this was a legal or equitable security interest, the claimant's new security interest must always be an equitable interest which arises at the time when the claimant's subrogation rights accrue,[74] and the priority of this interest vis-à-vis subsequent incumbrancers must be determined accordingly.[75]

(c) *Personal or Proprietary Rights?*

(i) *Banque Financière de la Cité v Parc (Battersea) Ltd*

The House of Lords' decision in the *Banque Financière* case[76] raises an impor- **39–41** tant question regarding the proper conceptualisation of the rights which a claimant might acquire, where a creditor's security interest is discharged: namely, whether these rights are ever properly characterised as proprietary rights?

The facts of the case were unusual. BFC agreed to lend money to part **39–42** discharge debts owed by Parc to RTB, which were secured by a first charge over Parc's land. To avoid difficulties with the Swiss regulatory authorities, it was agreed that the loan would be structured as an indirect loan via an intermediary, Herzig: BFC would lend the money to Herzig, who would in turn lend it to Parc. The transaction was to be structured in such a way that neither Herzig nor BFC, which was to acquire rights directly against Parc via the assignment of a promissory note given by Parc to Herzig, would obtain security over Parc's assets. BFC's security consisted of a pledge of bearer shares in Parc's Swiss holding company, and what it believed was an effective postponement agreement, under which Parc's group creditors—including OOL, which held a second charge over Parc's land—agreed to postpone their claims against Parc until BFC's loan was repaid. However, later events placed BFC in a difficult position. BFC was not repaid, and the shares proved almost worthless because of the collapse of Parc's group. Parc's only significant asset was the land, over which OOL retained a charge. To make matters worse, the postponement agreement which BFC believed that it had obtained from Parc's group creditors (including OOL) proved to be ineffective. BFC therefore fell back on a subrogation claim, in the hope of acquiring a viable security against Parc.

---

[71] *Gertsch* [1999] NSWSC 898; (1999) 10 B.P.R. 18,431.
[72] *Muirhead* (1998) 76 P. & C.R. 418 (CA).
[73] Cf. *Anfield* [2010] EWHC 2374 (Ch); [2011] 1 All E.R. 708 at [31].
[74] *Halifax Plc v Omar* [2002] EWCA Civ 121; [2002] 2 P. & C.R. 26 at [84].
[75] Cf. *Appleyard* [2004] EWCA Civ 291 at [44].
[76] *Banque Financière* [1999] 1 A.C. 221.

39–43   BFC indisputably lent the money to discharge Parc's debt under a causative mistake: its mistaken belief that it had an effective postponement agreement with Parc's group creditors. This money was used to discharge Parc's secured debts to RTB, the first chargee, thereby enriching both Parc (as debtor) and OOL (as second chargee) at BFC's expense. Taken together, these facts might ordinarily be sufficient to warrant the conclusion that BFC was entitled to a fully-fledged security interest, by subrogation to RTB's first charge over Parc's land, with the same priority vis-à-vis OOL, the second chargee, as RTB's first charge previously possessed. However, by the time the case reached the House of Lords, BFC had conceded that it was not entitled to this remedy, as it would afford BFC rights vis-à-vis Parc and Parc's creditors that were greater than, and inconsistent with, the rights for which it had bargained when it made its advance—which, as far as Parc was concerned, were meant to be merely unsecured.

39–44   In the House of Lords, BFC therefore made a more limited claim. It argued that it was entitled to be treated as holding RTB's first charge only so far as necessary to afford it priority for the purpose of its claim to payment vis-à-vis OOL, the original second chargee whose position had been materially improved by BFC's mistaken advance, and over whom BFC had mistakenly believed it had acquired priority. The House of Lords held that BFC was entitled to this more attenuated form of relief, and Lord Hoffmann explained the very limited nature of the order to which BFC was entitled as follows[77]:

> "[There] is no 'conceptual problem' about treating B.F.C. as subrogated to part of the R.T.B. secured debt. The equitable remedy is available only against O.O.L., which is the only party which would be unjustly enriched. As between R.T.B. and B.F.C., subrogation has no part to play. R.T.B. is entitled to its security and B.F.C. is no more than an unsecured creditor. The same is true as between B.F.C. and any secured or unsecured creditor of Parc other than the members of the Omni group. The transaction contemplated that as against non-group creditors, B.F.C. would incur no more than an unsecured liability, evidenced by the promissory note issued to Mr Herzig and assigned by him to B.F.C. As against such creditors, therefore, the remedy of subrogation is not available. Nor is it available against Parc itself, so as to give B.F.C. the rights of sale, foreclosure etc. which would normally follow from B.F.C. being treated as if it were an assignee of the R.T.B. charge."

The understanding of the subrogation remedy which made this limited order possible has already been described[78]: as Lord Hoffmann explained it, the court regulates the claimant's relations with one or more others, as though he held the extinguished rights, to the extent that this is required to reverse their unjust enrichment.

39–45   In many cases predating *Banque Financière*, the settled assumption had been that where a claimant is entitled to be subrogated to a creditor's extinguished security interest, he necessarily obtains a fully-fledged equitable proprietary interest, which exactly replicates the interest which was held by the creditor, and is enforceable against persons generally. However, Lord Hoffmann's rationalisation of the remedy in *Banque Financière*, and the actual decision on the facts, might be thought to suggest a radical contrary understanding. According to this

---

[77] *Banque Financière* [1999] 1 A.C. 221 at 236–237.
[78] See paras 39–10—39–11.

view, a claimant's entitlement is always reducible to a collection of personal rights: i.e. to one or more personal rights to be treated as if he holds the rights of the creditor, for the purposes of modifying his relations with one or more other parties who would otherwise be unjustly enriched at his expense. For the reasons that follow, however, this radical reading is unwarranted.

(ii) Generally, the Claimant's Right is Fully Proprietary

Leaving *Banque Financière* to one side, the authorities overwhelmingly support **39–46** the view that what a claimant generally acquires by subrogation, as a result of having discharged a creditor's security interest, is a fully-fledged equitable proprietary interest, mirroring the interest which was held by the creditor. It is unhelpful to analyse the rights which the claimant thereby acquires as nothing more than a bundle of personal rights. The claimant has a proprietary right in the same full sense as any other equitable proprietary right. Or, putting the same point in Lord Hoffmann's language, the claimant acquires a fully-fledged proprietary interest because it is appropriate to treat him as occupying the creditor's position as against persons generally. A claimant is sometimes entitled to less than this, but there are settled principles which dictate when a more attenuated remedy is appropriate. Moreover, even where a claimant is awarded a more limited right, his right will still generally be a fully-fledged proprietary interest, but there will be some reason why this interest cannot share all of the priority advantages of the creditor's extinguished security interest. Two examples of this can be given.

The first example is where a junior incumbrancer has a defence.[79] The **39–47** claimant's prima facie entitlement is to a security interest that inherits the priorities of the creditor's extinguished security interest, including its priority over junior incumbrancers, because this is ordinarily appropriate to reverse the unjust (secondary) enrichment that would otherwise result from the discharge of the creditor's interest. However, a junior incumbrancer will sometimes be able to establish a defence, and the appropriate way of giving effect to this defence may be to deny priority for the claimant's interest over the junior incumbrancer's interest.

The second example is where the creditor's security interest subsists and **39–48** secures outstanding existing and future liabilities.[80] Although there is no conceptual obstacle to the claimant's acquiring a new equitable security interest by subrogation in these cases, which co-exists alongside the creditor's subsisting security interest,[81] it may be necessary to meet the practical objection that affording the claimant a concurrent security interest may illegitimately prejudice the creditor's ability to obtain satisfaction for his outstanding claims. This concern is adequately addressed by the courts holding that the claimant obtains a new security interest which replicates the creditor's interest but ranks immediately after it. In the language of Lord Hoffmann, the claimant is treated in equity as though he held the creditor's security interest, with equivalent priority, vis-à-vis all other parties except the creditor himself.

---

[79] See paras 39–21 and 39–53.
[80] See paras 39–54—39–60.
[81] See para.39–55.

(iii) *Only Exceptionally is the Claimant's Right a More Limited, Personal Right*

39–49 All of this means that the course adopted in the *Banque Financière* case was exceptional. Only in a very unusual case will it be inappropriate to characterise the claimant's right as a fully-fledged equitable proprietary interest. On the facts of most cases, there is no need to conceptualise the claimant's subrogation entitlement in the more limited form adopted in *Banque Financière*—as one or a few personal rights to be treated as holding the creditor's security interest vis-à-vis another party or a few other parties.

39–50 Where the claimant can show that the debtor was unjustly enriched at his expense, but there is no justification for affording the claimant a proprietary restitutionary remedy, then it would be possible to say that the claimant is entitled vis-à-vis the discharged debtor alone to be treated as holding the creditor's security interest. However, it is unnecessary to conceptualise the relationship between the claimant and the debtor in this way. A simpler mechanism for reversing the debtor's unjust enrichment in such cases is to hold that the claimant has a direct personal claim in unjust enrichment against the debtor for the value of the claimant's discharging payment.

39–51 Properly understood, the unusual middle course adopted in the *Banque Financière* case may only be required where there is no justification for affording the claimant a proprietary restitutionary remedy, but where, in order to reverse the unjust (secondary) enrichment of parties other than the discharged debtor, it is necessary to regulate the legal relations between the claimant and one or more of these other parties as if the claimant held the security interest which he has discharged.

(d) *The Priority of the Claimant's Security Interest*

(i) *Introduction*

39–52 Where a claimant acquires a new security interest via subrogation, several questions arise with respect to the priority of this interest vis-à-vis other parties who have previously acquired, or who subsequently acquire, competing interests in the same property. This section explains the principles by reference to which these questions fall to be resolved.[82]

(ii) *Basic Priority Principles*

39–53 **Priority vis-à-vis pre-existing third party interests** Where a claimant is entitled to be subrogated to a creditor's security interest, then the new security interest which he acquires prima facie shares the priorities of the creditor's extinguished interest vis-à-vis interests held by third parties over the same asset, at the time of its discharge—"pre-existing third party interests". Hence the claimant's interest will initially be subordinate to pre-existing third party interests which previously took priority over the creditor's interest—"superior interests". It will also prima facie take priority over pre-existing third party interests

---

[82] For a full examination of this topic, see Mitchell and Watterson, *Subrogation: Law and Practice*, paras 8.61 and following.

which were previously subordinate to the creditor's interest—"subordinate interests".[83] It is important to recognise, however, that this only represents a starting-point. The reason for giving the claimant priority over a subordinate interest-holder is to reverse his unjust enrichment, which arises from the promotion of his security following the discharge of the creditor's prior security. If the subordinate interest-holder can establish a defence or bar to the claim, which bears specifically on the claimant's subrogation entitlement vis-à-vis him, then this may lead the court to deny the claimant priority over the subordinate interest-holder.

Priority vis-à-vis the creditor's interest In some cases, the creditor's secu-   **39–54**
rity interest subsists, although the claimant has discharged liabilities which the interest secured. This happens most often because the claimant discharged only some of the secured liabilities, with the result that the creditor's interest subsists as security for the outstanding balance,[84] and possibly also for additional liabilities which the debtor subsequently incurs.[85] In other cases, although the claimant fully discharged the liabilities secured by the creditor's security interest at the time of payment, the creditor's security interest may be a continuing interest which subsists for the creditor's benefit as security for future liabilities which the defendant incurs.[86]

Although this has not always been appreciated, there is no conceptual obstacle   **39–55**
to the claimant's acquiring a security interest by subrogation in these cases, even though the creditor's security interest subsists. The contrary assumption reflects a misunderstanding as to the nature of the subrogation remedy. As explained above, the claimant does not acquire the very rights which the creditor held, by transfer or otherwise: the claimant's cause of action is predicated on the assumption that the creditor's rights have been extinguished.[87] What the claimant acquires are new and distinct rights, which merely resemble the creditor's extinguished rights in their characteristics and content. Hence there is no reason why the claimant and the creditor cannot hold rights concurrently where, for example, the creditor has only been partly paid. The creditor can retain his original rights, to the extent that these have not been diminished by the claimant's payment. The claimant meanwhile acquires new rights, which are generated pro tanto to the extent that the creditor's rights have been diminished. Suppose, for example, that the creditor holds a legal charge which secures £500,000 owed by a debtor and the claimant discharges £200,000 of these liabilities. The creditor's legal charge will subsist as security for the outstanding balance of £300,000. The claimant acquires a new and distinct equitable charge, securing £200,000, being the amount of the liabilities owed to the creditor which the claimant discharged.

A practical problem nevertheless inevitably arises in these cases, regarding the   **39–56**
relative priorities of the creditor's outstanding security interest and the claimant's

---

[83] As in *McDonnell* [2001] EWCA Civ 887; [2001] 2 All E.R. (Comm.) 886; *Karasiewicz* [2002] EWCA Civ 940; *Appleyard* [2004] EWCA Civ 291; *Mayfair* [2007] EWHC 287 (Ch); *Kali* [2007] EWHC 2357 (Ch); [2008] B.P.I.R. 415.
[84] e.g. *Chetwynd* [1899] 1 Ch. 353.
[85] e.g. *Liberty Mutual* [2002] EWCA Civ 291.
[86] e.g. *Westpac Banking Corp v Adelaide Bank Ltd* [2005] NSWSC 517.
[87] See paras 39–11, 39–13—39–15.

new equitable security interest. There are two answers which the courts might give.

39–57   The first solution is that any new interest which the claimant acquires by subrogation is a subordinate security interest, which ranks immediately after the creditor's subsisting security interest, but which otherwise inherits the priorities of the creditor's security interest vis-à-vis pre-existing interests held by third parties. Suppose that a creditor holds a first charge, securing £500,000, and the claimant discharges £300,000 of these liabilities. Any equitable security interest which the claimant acquires by subrogation will rank after the creditor's subsisting first charge for the £200,000 balance of the original debt. However, it will prima facie rank ahead of any pre-existing charges that were subordinate to the creditor's charge at the time of its partial discharge.[88] This should probably be accepted as the normal form of the subrogation remedy in cases of this sort. The subordinate ranking of the claimant's security interest ensures that his subrogation entitlement will not prejudice the creditor's ability to obtain satisfaction for his outstanding claims.

39–58   A second solution is to say that the claimant's interest ranks equally with the creditor's subsisting security interest. This solution is exceptional, and needs a strong justification: the recognition of such a competing equal-ranking entitlement inevitably prejudices the creditor's position as secured creditor. It is difficult to predict when it will be adopted, outside a long-standing set of suretyship cases,[89] and in the absence of a contract between the claimant and the creditor which expressly or impliedly provides for this priority.[90]

39–59   The precise nature of the subrogation entitlement afforded in this case is also not well-understood. Some dicta suggest that the creditor is a "trustee" of his security interest for the benefit of himself and the claimant.[91] However, this wrongly presupposes that the creditor holds his original security interest for the whole of the original debt. The better analysis is that the creditor holds his original security interest for the balance of the original debt outstanding after the claimant's payment: once the creditor is partly paid, he cannot sue the debtor for the same sum again, because the debtor's liability has been discharged pro tanto. The claimant meanwhile acquires a new equal-ranking equitable security interest to the extent of his part payment. There is no "trusteeship" imposed on the creditor for the claimant: to the extent that his charge subsists after the claimant's payment, it subsists for the creditor's sole benefit.

39–60   Even so, the creditor's conduct is subject to some constraints. First, at least from the time when he knows of the claimant's entitlement, the creditor probably owes a duty not to prejudice the claimant's subrogation-based security interest by

---

[88] e.g. *Gedye v Mason* (1858) 25 Beav. 310 at 312; 53 E.R. 655 at 656; *Chetwynd* [1899] 1 Ch. 353; approved in *Banque Financière* [1999] 1 A.C. 221 at 235–236 per Lord Hoffmann; and at 243–245 per Lord Hutton; *McCullough v Marsden* (1918) 45 D.L.R. 645 (Alberta CA).

[89] The cases hold that where a surety guarantees a distinct part of a larger debt, and pays the guaranteed part, he is immediately entitled to be subrogated pro rata to any security held by the creditor for the larger indebtedness: *Goodwin v Gray* (1874) 22 W.R. 312; *Ward v National Bank of New Zealand Ltd* (1889) N.Z.L.R. 10 (NZ High Ct); *Re Butlers Wharf Ltd* [1995] 2 B.C.L.C. 43; *Liberty Mutual* [2002] EWCA Civ 291 at [47]–[48].

[90] Cf. *Mayfair* [2007] EWHC 287 (Ch), where the claimant and the creditor agreed that the claimant's rights should take priority over the creditor's outstanding claims, up to a specified sum.

[91] *Butlers Wharf* [1995] 2 B.C.L.C. 43 at 56.

his unreasonable acts or omissions.[92] Secondly, when the asset subject to the charge is realised, the creditor must recognise the claimant's equal-ranking entitlement to the proceeds in his hands. So, for example, if the claimant and the creditor hold security interests for £50,000 and £100,000 respectively, and the creditor receives proceeds of £100,000, he must divide these proceeds pro rata between the claimant's claim and his own.

Priority vis-à-vis later third party interests What is a subrogated claim-   **39–61** ant's position vis-à-vis third parties who subsequently acquire interests in the same subject matter? Properly understood, recent cases establish the following principles.

First, the claimant's position is not determined by asking whether these later   **39–62** third parties would be unjustly enriched at the claimant's expense, if their interest took priority over the claimant's subrogation-based interest. Rather, the claimant's position is determined according to the proprietary quality of his subrogation-based interest. That is, the courts assume that the claimant has previously acquired a security interest in the relevant property, and then resolve his position vis-à-vis later third party interests in terms of the priority rules that are generally used to resolve competitions between proprietary interests of the relevant types.[93]

Secondly, for priority purposes, the claimant's subrogation-based interest is   **39–63** understood to arise by operation of law and independently of any court order,[94] from the earliest time when the constituent elements of his cause of action in unjust enrichment exist. If the ground for restitution exists at the time when the creditor is paid, then the claimant's subrogation-based interest will prima facie date from that point.[95] If, more exceptionally, the ground for restitution only arises subsequently, because it consists of a failure of basis which only occurs at a later date, then the claimant's subrogation-based interest cannot exist before the date when the basis fails. For example, in an Australian case, *ANZ Banking Group Ltd v Costikidis*,[96] Mr and Mrs Costikidis executed a first charge over their property as collateral security for an advance by ANZ to third parties, and as part of the arrangement, ANZ paid off an existing charge on the property. ANZ's collateral security was later discharged as a result of a material alteration of the principal arrangement to which Mr and Mrs Costikidis did not consent. The court held that ANZ was entitled to be subrogated to the discharged first charge as from that later date.

---

[92] Cf. *Faircharm Investments Ltd v Citibank International Plc* [1998] Lloyd's Rep. Bank. 127 (CA).
[93] *Omar* [2002] EWCA Civ 121; [2002] 2 P. & C.R. 26. Cf. *Anfield* [2010] EWHC 2374 (Ch); [2011] 1 All E.R. 708, discussed further at para.39.72 and following.
[94] e.g. *Boscawen* [1996] 1 W.L.R. 328 (CA) at 342 per Millett L.J.
[95] e.g. (1) where another's debt is paid using the claimant's moneys without his consent (*McCullough v Elliott* (1922) 62 D.L.R. 257 (Alberta CA) at 259 per Stuart J., and at 260 per Beck J.); (2) the claimant is responsible for paying another's debt under a mistake or on a basis which fails at the outset (e.g. *Thurstan* [1902] 1 Ch. 1 (CA) at 14; see too *Boscawen* [1996] 1 W.L.R. 328 (CA) at 342 per Millett L.J.); (3) the claimant discharges a common liability, for which he is only secondarily liable in circumstances which immediately generate a right to contribution or reimbursement (cf. Mercantile Law Amendment Act 1856 s.5).
[96] *ANZ Banking Group Ltd v Costikidis* Unreported Victoria Sup Ct, December 22, 1994.

39–64   Thirdly, for priority purposes, the claimant's subrogation-based interest is always a new interest, which is equitable in quality and has the status of a full equitable interest, and is not a "mere equity", from the time that his subrogation rights accrue.[97] Priority disputes between the claimant's interest and later third party interests in the same property are determined on this basis, in accordance with ordinary priority principles: i.e. in line with the priority principles that generally govern competitions between an equitable security interest and later, competing interests.

39–65   This third proposition holds good even where the creditor's extinguished security interest was a legal mortgage or charge,[98] and even where the creditor's legal mortgage or charge formally subsists to secure outstanding existing liabilities and/or future liabilities. As Lord Hoffmann explained in *Banque Financière*,[99] the claimant's subrogation-based right is a product of equity's decision to regulate the relations between the claimant and the discharged debtor, and indeed persons generally, as though the claimant held the relevant security interest. By virtue of this process, the claimant does not actually acquire the creditor's legal charge, nor any right to share in it. The creditor's legal charge is extinguished; or, even if it formally subsists, it no longer secures the debts which ex hypothesi the claimant discharged. What the claimant instead acquires pro tanto, to the extent that he was responsible for discharging secured debts owed to the creditor, is a new equitable right, which prima facie mirrors the characteristics and content of the creditor's security interest.[100]

(iii) *Special Priority Issues*

39–66   **Subrogation to company charges**   A claimant who discharges a security interest over a company's assets can certainly acquire a security interest by subrogation over the company's assets.[101] But what is the impact of the company charges registration regime on the claimant's new security interest?[102] The best view is that, whether or not the creditor's security interest was a registrable charge, the claimant's subrogation-based interest is not itself a registrable charge. The company charges registration regime only requires a charge-holder to register a charge which is created by a company[103] and this seems to exclude charges

---

[97] *Omar* [2002] EWCA Civ 121; [2002] 2 P. & C.R. 26 at [84] per Jonathan Parker L.J.
[98] *Omar* [2002] EWCA Civ 121; [2002] 2 P. & C.R. 26 at [84] per Jonathan Parker L.J (the claimant is "treated in equity as if [it] had th[e] security"); and cf. *Boscawen* [1996] 1 W.L.R. 328 (CA) at 330–331 and at 335 per Millett L.J.; *Hedworth* [2003] EWCA Civ 1717; [2003] 3 F.C.R. 739 at [79] per Jonathan Parker L.J.; *Appleyard* [2004] EWCA Civ 291 at [44] per Neuberger L.J.
[99] *Banque Financière* [1999] 1 A.C. 221 at 236; see para.39–11.
[100] Cf. *Appleyard* [2004] EWCA Civ 291, where it appears to be assumed, wrongly, that the claimant obtained a *legal* charge by subrogation (see e.g. [69] and [74]), rather than being entitled to be treated *in equity* as if it held the legal charge which was paid off.
[101] e.g. *Butlers Wharf* [1995] 2 B.C.L.C. 43 (floating charge over property/undertaking; previously registrable under the Companies Act 1985 s.395(1)(f); now registrable under the Companies Act 2006 s.860(7)(g)); *Banque Financière* [1999] 1 A.C. 221 (fixed legal charge; previously registrable under the Companies Act 1985 s.396(d); now registrable under the Companies Act 2006 s.860(7)(a)); *Liberty Mutual* [2001] Lloyd's Rep. Bank 223; affirmed [2002] EWCA Civ 691 (charge over book debts; previously registrable under the Companies Act 1985 s.396(1)(e); now registrable under the Companies Act 2006 s.860(7)(f)).
[102] Companies Act 2006 Pt 25.
[103] See Companies Act 2006 s.860(1); cf. the wording of its predecessor provision, in the Companies Act 1985 s.395(1).

arising by operation of law, including charges generated by subrogation.[104] It seems to follow that as long as the creditor's extinguished charge was not registrable, or was duly registered if registrable,[105] then even without registration, the claimant's new security interest will be a valid charge, which prima facie has the same priority vis-à-vis pre-existing interests as the paid-off creditor's charge, and also that the priority of this interest vis-à-vis later interests will be determined in accordance with its quality as a new non-registrable security interest.

Subrogation to security interests over unregistered land Although of   **39–67**
diminishing significance, there may still be cases where a claimant discharges a security interest over an unregistered estate in land. In these cases, the resolution of the claimant's priority position vis-à-vis subsequent incumbrancers will require an answer to be given to the unresolved question whether a subrogation-based security interest falls within the category of registrable land charges under the Land Charges Act 1972. If it is registrable,[106] then it will be possible to preserve its priority vis-à-vis later interests via registration in the register of land charges[107]; and if not duly registered, then it will suffer the vulnerabilities characteristic of an unregistered but registrable charge.[108] If it is not a registrable charge, then traditional priority rules should apply; and this means that the claimant's interest, as an equitable interest, should prevail vis-à-vis later interests other than that of a bona fide purchaser of a legal interest for value without notice of the claimant's subrogation rights.

Subrogation to security interests over registered land Most subrogation   **39–68**
claims today involve claims to be subrogated to a security interest over a registered estate in land. How does the subrogation remedy operate within the registered land regime as it now derives from the Land Registration Act 2002?

First, the nature of the subrogation claimant's entitlement is exactly the same   **39–69**
in this context as in any other case. That is, he is prima facie entitled to a new security interest, which is always equitable in quality, and which mirrors the characteristics of the creditor's extinguished security interest. It does not matter whether the creditor's security interest was an equitable charge[109] or was a registered legal charge.[110] This point requires particular emphasis, because some recent cases have proceeded on the contrary assumption, insofar as they have allowed a subrogation claimant to obtain a registered legal charge, by having the register rectified in his favour, to register him as proprietor of the creditor's registered legal charge.[111] They have done this where the registered legal charge

---

[104] For discussion, see *Palmer's Company Law* (London: Sweet & Maxwell), para.13–324.

[105] Cf. if registrable but not duly registered, in which case the claimant's subrogation-based charge would be expected to inherit the fraility of the creditor's unregistered charge: see especially the Companies Act 2006 s.874.

[106] Cf. Land Charges Act 1972 s.2(4)(iii) (Class C(iii) land charge: "general equitable charge").

[107] Land Charges Act 1972 ss. 2(1) and 3(1); Law of Property Act 1925 s.198(1).

[108] Land Charges Act 1972 s.4(5) (if a Class C(iii) land charge).

[109] As in e.g. *Omar* [2002] EWCA Civ 121; [2002] 2 P. & C.R. 26 (unpaid vendor's lien).

[110] As in e.g. *Appleyard* [2004] EWCA Civ 291.

[111] e.g. *Castle Phillips Finance* (1995) 70 P. & C.R. 592 (CA); *Anfield* [2010] EWHC 2374 (Ch); [2011] 1 All E.R. 708.

was formally vacated from the register,[112] but also where it fortuitously remained on the register, despite the discharge of all debts secured by it.[113] None of these decisions gives any careful thought to this point, and in principle, it cannot be right to rectify the register in this way. As already explained, the true position is that the claimant never obtains any right to the creditor's extinguished security interest.

39–70 Secondly, the priority of the claimant's new security interest vis-à-vis the debtor, and pre-existing incumbrancers who held subordinate interests at the time when the creditor's charge was discharged, will not depend on the claimant's interest being a proprietary interest, which affects them in accordance with the priority principles of the registration regime. As in other contexts, it depends upon the fact that those parties were previously adversely affected by the paid-off creditor's charge, as debtor/chargor and/or junior incumbrancer; and that as a result of discharging this charge, the claimant has obtained new rights against them, as a remedy to reverse their unjust (primary and secondary) enrichments. These new rights comprise an equitable security interest which prima facie inherits the priorities of the old, and which is effective vis-à-vis those parties without any entry in the register against the registered title affected.

39–71 Thirdly, the priority of the claimant's new security interest vis-à-vis subsequent incumbrancers falls to be determined in accordance with the priority principles laid down in the Land Registration 2002 ss.28–29, and on the assumption that the claimant's interest is a new interest, which came into being at the time that the subrogation-justifying facts occurred. These principles indicate that the claimant's interest prima facie has priority over any subsequent interest,[114] but that this interest may be postponed to or extinguished by a subsequent "registrable" disposition for valuable consideration by the registered proprietor of the registered estate, including the subsequent grant of a legal charge, unless the claimant has previously protected the priority of his subrogation-based security interest, by entering a notice against the registered estate affected, or (exceptionally) his interest has the status of an overriding interest in accordance with Sch.3 para.2.[115]

39–72 *Anfield*[116] illustrates how these principles should be applied, but serves as a warning against the traps that lie in wait, if they are not kept clearly in view. A debtor's registered land was subject to a first registered (legal) charge in favour of Halifax. The Bank of Scotland advanced money to redeem Halifax's charge, and received an executed charge in exchange. However, the bank neglected to register its charge until some years later. In the meantime, two things occurred. LSFL obtained a registered (legal) charge; and, later, Anfield obtained a charging order over the same property, protecting the priority of its equitable charge by entering a notice in the register. Against this background, the bank claimed that

---

[112] As in *Castle Phillips Finance* (1995) 70 P. & C.R. 592 (CA).

[113] As in *Anfield* [2010] EWHC 2374 (Ch); [2011] 1 All E.R. 708.

[114] See the Land Registration Act 2002 s.28, which is conventionally read as laying down a basic first in time of creation rule. See Law Commission and Land Registry, *Land Registration for the Twenty-First Century: A Conveyancing Revolution* (TSO, 2001) Law Com. No.271, HC 114, paras 2.17 and 5.5; see too K. Gray and S.F. Gray, *Elements of Land Law*, 5th edn (Oxford: OUP, 2009), paras 8.2.4 and following.

[115] Land Registration Act 2002 s.29.

[116] *Anfield* [2010] EWHC 2374 (Ch); [2011] 1 All ER 708.

it was subrogated to Halifax's registered charge, which had never been formally vacated from the register, and that it had priority vis-à-vis both LSFL and Anfield. Without much careful analysis of the form of the remedy, Proudman J. upheld the county court judge's decision, which had declared that the bank was entitled to be subrogated to Halifax's charge, with priority vis-à-vis both LSFL and Anfield; and also that the bank was entitled to be registered as proprietor of Halifax's first registered (legal) charge.

There are two significant problems with Proudman J.'s analysis. One is her **39–73** unexamined assumption that the bank was entitled to be registered as proprietor of Halifax's charge. This is incorrect, for reasons that have already been explained.[117] The second difficulty lies in her explanation for the priority which the bank was afforded vis-à-vis both LSFL and Anfield. Proudman J. seemed to treat it as obvious that if the bank was subrogated to Halifax's first charge, the bank would obtain priority vis-à-vis all other subordinate incumbrancers, and that this priority was justified to reverse the unjust enrichment that would otherwise accrue to them.[118] However, this ignored the fact that neither LSFL nor Anfield were pre-existing incumbrancers; they were subsequent incumbrancers, and as such, the bank's priority position vis-à-vis each of them had to be determined on a different basis. A proper resolution of the issues required Proudman J. to proceed in two stages.

She should first have inquired into the nature of the bank's subrogation rights **39–74** at the time these rights first arose. Had she done so, her answer should have been that, having paid off Halifax's first-ranking registered (legal) charge, the bank became entitled to a new equitable charge, which inherited the priority of Halifax's charge vis-à-vis pre-existing incumbrances, in order to reverse the unjust enrichment that would otherwise accrue to the debtor and subordinate incumbrancers.

Proudman J. should then have inquired into the priority of the bank's subroga- **39–75** tion-based equitable charge vis-à-vis interests that came into being *after* its subrogation rights arose: that is, its priority vis-à-vis the registered (legal) charge subsequently obtained by LSFL, and the equitable charge subsequently obtained by Anfield by virtue of the charging order. This priority point fell to be resolved on a different basis: not by asking whether LSFL and Anfield were unjustly enriched at the bank's expense, by the discharge of the Halifax charge, but in accordance with general priority rules, and on the assumption that the bank's subrogation-based charge was a new equitable interest.

Applying the priority rules of the Land Registration Act 2002 ss.28–29, the **39–76** proper answer might well have been that LSFL's registered (legal) charge would take priority over the bank's subrogation-based charge: because LSFL was the grantee of a registered (legal) charge, and because the bank had not protected the priority of its interest by entering a notice in the register, LSFL could take advantage of the special immunity from prior interests afforded to "registrable" dispositions by the Land Registration Act 2002 s.29. In contrast, and applying the same priority rules, the bank's subrogation-based charge would take priority over Anfield's equitable charge. This was because the bank's subrogation-based charge pre-dated Anfield's charge, and because Anfield, having obtained an

---

[117] See para.39–69.
[118] See *Anfield* especially [2010] EWHC 2374 (Ch); [2011] 1 All ER 708 at [11] and at [13].

equitable charge only, could *not* take advantage of the special immunity from prior interests afforded by the Land Registration Act 2002 s.29. On these assumptions, the correct ordering of the charges should have been: (1) LSFL's registered (legal) charge; (2) the bank's subrogation-based charge; (3) Anfield's equitable charge.

(e) *The Quantum of the Subrogation Debt*

39–77   How should the courts quantify the amount recoverable by a claimant by enforcing his subrogation rights—the "subrogation debt"? When considering this question, a distinction must be drawn between the principal amount recoverable and the claimant's right to recover interest and other costs.

(i) *The Principal Amount*

39–78   Where a claimant has become entitled to a security interest by subrogation, the principal amount of the claimant's secured subrogation debt cannot exceed the amount of the debt that was secured by the security interest which the claimant discharged.[119] Where the claimant also discharges other, unsecured liabilities of the debtor, the amount of these liabilities cannot be recovered by enforcing the claimant's subrogation-based security interest, although the claimant might be able to recover this amount from the debtor by a direct personal claim in unjust enrichment.[120]

39–79   There are, however, a number of obvious reasons why the principal amount recoverable by the claimant may sometimes be substantially less than the amount of the debtor's secured debt. First, where the debtor had a defence to the creditor's claim at the time when the creditor was paid, the claimant's subrogation debt should be correspondingly reduced, to zero where appropriate.[121] Secondly, where the debtor's liability to the creditor is discharged by payments from two sources, the claimant's subrogation debt should be capped at a proportion reflecting the claimant's contribution: the debtor's enrichment is gained at the claimant's expense only to this limited extent.[122]

39–80   Thirdly, where the debtor's liability to the creditor is discharged at a discount, it may be necessary to cap the claimant's subrogation debt at the lower amount of the claimant's payment.[123] This could be justified as the proper measure of the debtor's enrichment, where the creditor would have accepted a similarly reduced sum from the debtor. But the same result would follow more generally if the law of unjust enrichment were to hold that where a claimant's loss is less than a

---

[119] *Appleyard* [2004] EWCA Civ 291 at [43] per Neuberger L.J.

[120] Cf. *Filby* [2004] EWCA Civ 759 at [64] (unnecessarily affording a different remedy, to the same end, of subrogation to the unsecured creditor's personal rights to payment).

[121] Cf. *Castle Phillips Finance* (1995) 70 P. & C.R. 592 (CA); *Hedworth* [2003] EWCA Civ 1717; [2003] 3 F.C.R. 739 (charge given by surety for another's debts voidable by the surety because procured by undue influence).

[122] e.g. the first instance decision reported in *Western Trust & Savings Ltd v Rock* [1993] N.P.C. 89 (CA).

[123] Cf. *Butcher v Churchill* (1808) 14 Ves. Jun. 567 at 575–576; 33 E.R. 638 at 641; *Reed v Norris* (1837) 2 My. & Cr. 361 at 375–376; 40 E.R. 678 at 683; *Jamieson v Trustees of the Property of the Hotel Renfrew Ltd* [1941] 4 D.L.R. 470 (Ontario High Ct) at 479.

defendant's enrichment, any restitutionary remedy awarded to the claimant must be capped at the lower amount.[124]

Fourthly, the ground for restitution on which the claimant relies may some- **39–81** times only establish that only a portion of the debtor's discharged liability was an unjust enrichment gained at the claimant's expense. This may be so where the claimant discharges a common liability and the defendant was primarily liable only for a portion of this debt.[125] In this case, the claimant's right to contribution, and his supplementary right to be subrogated to a security interest held by the creditor, must be proportionately reduced.[126]

Fifthly, the subrogation debt must be reduced to reflect any defence which the **39–82** discharged debtor could raise to the claimant's claim, independently of any defence that he might have had against the debtor.[127]

(ii) *Interest*

The courts have frequently made prejudgment interest awards to subrogation **39–83** claimants, but without carefully examining the basis of these awards. As a result, interest has been awarded on two different, and mutually inconsistent, bases.[128]

One line of authority envisages the courts making "derivative" interest **39–84** awards. In most of these cases a claimant lends money which is used to discharge a creditor's secured debts. The claimant is awarded prejudgment interest on the basis that interest was payable on the discharged debt, and that a claimant entitled to subrogation is entitled to rights duplicating the creditor's extinguished rights, including a (secured) right to interest. The prevailing assumption in these cases is that[129]: (1) the rate of interest chargeable should prima facie be the rate which was formerly charged by the creditor on the discharged debt; (2) that where the claimant has agreed to accept a lower interest rate from the debtor, the interest rate awarded should be capped at this agreed rate; (3) that this interest should ordinarily be charged from the time when the debt was discharged, or if later, the time when the claimant's subrogation rights accrued; and (4) that the interest so payable is secured by the security interest which the claimant acquires by subrogation.

A second line of authority envisages the courts making "independent" interest **39–85** awards. In these cases, the courts do not use the interest rate charged by the creditor as their starting-point, but seem instead to have awarded the claimant pre-judgment interest by exercising their own power to award interest: selecting

---

[124] See paras 6–63—6–74.

[125] See paras 19–09—19–15 and 19–45—19–47.

[126] e.g. *Re Kirkwood's Estate* (1878) 1 L.R. Ir. 108.

[127] See further paras 39–20—39–22.

[128] For a full discussion, which pre-dates the House of Lords' landmark decision on the availability of compound interest awards in *Sempra Metals Ltd v IRC* [2007] UKHL 34; [2008] 1 A.C. 561, see Mitchell and Watterson, *Subrogation: Law and Practice*, paras 9–102 and following.

[129] *Rock* [1993] N.P.C. 89 (CA); *Castle Phillips Finance* (1995) 70 P. & C.R. 592 (CA) at 602; *Muirhead* (1998) 76 P. & C.R. 418 (CA); *Karasiewicz* [2002] EWCA Civ 940 at [1] (recording the first instance order; affirmed on appeal); *Filby* [2004] EWCA Civ 759 at [63]–[67]; *Appleyard* [2004] EWCA Civ 291 at [21] (recording the first instance order) and at [76]; *Kali* [2007] EWHC 2357 (Ch); [2008] B.P.I.R. 415 at [31] and following and at [42]; *Primlake* [2009] EWHC 2774 (Ch) at [26].

whatever conventional or other rate the circumstances require.[130] To these cases can be added analogous cases considering the rate of interest available on personal claims in unjust enrichment arising from the discharge of another's debt. In claims for contribution or reimbursement, the courts do not seem to have assumed that they must, or indeed can, award interest at the rate payable on the discharged debt. Instead, interest has been awarded at what appears to be a conventional rate, even where the debt discharged did not bear interest, or where it bore interest at a higher rate than the conventional rate.[131]

(iii) Costs

39–86   The authorities currently offer no clear view on the question whether a claimant can use his subrogation rights to recover costs which the claimant has incurred in connection with his subrogation claim. In principle, and consistently with the rationale for the remedy, it should be necessary to show: (1) that the claimant incurred costs which would otherwise have been levied on the debtor by the creditor; and (2) that the costs chargeable by the creditor would have been recoverable under the security interest which the claimant was responsible for discharging. It seems likely that these conditions will rarely be met. They were not satisfied in *Kali Ltd v Chawla*,[132] where money advanced by the claimant bank to fund a house purchase, which proved abortive, was used to discharge an earlier first charge securing the vendor's debts. The bank sought to be subrogated to this charge, so as to obtain a secured right to payment, with priority over a pre-existing second charge, of (a) the principal amount of the discharged debt; (b) interest at the rate chargeable by the creditor; and (c) costs incurred by the bank, in making an unsuccessful challenge to the second charge. The judge accepted the claims for (a) and (b), but found that the costs were not of a type that could properly be recovered from the debtor via the bank's subrogation-based charge.

---

[130] e.g. *Thurstan* [1902] 1 Ch. 1 (CA); affirmed [1903] A.C. 6; *Congresbury Motors Ltd v Anglo-Belge Finance Co Ltd* [1970] Ch. 294; affirmed [1971] Ch. 81 (CA); *Hill v ANZ Banking Group Ltd* [1974] 4 A.L.R. 634; *Bank of Ireland Finance Ltd v D.J. Daly Ltd (In Liquidation)* [1978] I.R. 79; *Re Tramway Building & Construction Co Ltd* [1988] Ch. 293 at 308–309; *Gertsch* [1999] NSWSC 898; (1999) 10 B.P.R. 18,431 at [99]–[100]; *Commonwealth Bank of Australia Ltd v Horvath* Unreported Victoria Sup Ct, April 2, 1996 (reversed on other grounds [1998] VSCA 51).

[131] e.g. *Lawson v Wright* (1786) 1 Cox 275; 29 E.R. 1164; *Hitchman v Stewart* (1855) 3 Drew 271; 61 E.R. 907; *Re Swan's Estate* (1869) 4 Ir. Eq. 209; *Ex p. Bishop* (1880) 15 Ch. D. 400 (CA); *Re Watson* [1896] 1 Ch. 925; *Re Hunt* [1902] 2 Ch. 318n; *A.E. Goodwin Ltd (In Liquidation) v AG Healing (In Liquidation)* (1979) 7 A.C.L.R. 481 (NSW Sup Ct (Eq Div)).

[132] *Kali Ltd v Chawla* [2007] EWHC 2357 (Ch); [2008] B.P.I.R. 415 at [31] and following and at [43]–[44].

Chapter 40

PROPRIETARY REMEDIES: RESCISSION AND RECTIFICATION

1. Introduction

This chapter concerns rescission and rectification. It does not undertake a **40–01** detailed discussion of the grounds upon which a claimant may be entitled to these remedies. The primary aim of the chapter is to discuss their proprietary effects.

The term "rescission" can be used to describe the termination of a contract **40–02** with prospective effect, by reason of a contracting party's non-performance or defective performance of his obligations.[1] Nowadays the term "rescission" is more commonly used in a different sense, to mean the termination of a contract (or other transaction) with retrospective effect, on the ground that a party's intention to enter the transaction was vitiated from the start by fraud, mistake, duress, undue influence or some other factor.[2] This is the sense in which we use the term in Part 2, where we discuss the mechanisms by which a rescinding party can acquire proprietary rights to property that he transferred to another party.

When a document inaccurately records the terms of an agreement or voluntary **40–03** disposition, the court may order rectification of the document in order to bring it into harmony with what the parties or the disponor intended. In Part 3 we discuss the mechanisms by which a rectifying party can acquire proprietary rights to property that he transferred to another party.

Rescission and rectification are discussed together because they both give a **40–04** claimant a proprietary power, i.e. a power to acquire legal or (more commonly) equitable proprietary rights in property that the claimant transferred pursuant to a rescinded transaction, or in accordance with a rectified document. Until the claimant exercises this power, the recipient has voidable legal title to the property and can give good legal title to a bona fide purchaser for value without notice of the claim. When a claimant rescinds a transaction at common law, this automatically causes legal title to revest in him; when he rescinds a transaction in equity, a trust arises in his favour which he can collapse by requiring the defendant to return the legal title; and a trust similarly arises on rectification of a document in accordance with which property was mistakenly conveyed to the defendant.

---

[1] *Mulji v Cheong Yue Steamship Co Ltd* [1926] A.C. 497 at 509–510 per Lord Sumner; *Heyman v Darwins, Ltd* [1942] A.C. 356 at 361 per Viscount Simon L.C.; *Johnson v Agnew* [1980] A.C. 367 at 396–398 per Lord Wilberforce; *Photo Production Ltd v Securicor Transport Ltd* [1980] A.C. 827 at 844–845 per Lord Wilberforce; *Hurst v Bryk* [2002] 1 A.C. 185 at 194 per Lord Millett.
[2] *Johnson v Agnew* [1980] A.C. 367 at 393 per Lord Wilberforce; *Society of Lloyd's v Leighs* [1997] C.L.C. 1398 at 1405 per curiam (CA); *Stocznia Gdynia SA v Gearbulk Holdings Ltd* [2009] EWCA Civ 75; [2010] Q.B. 27 at [13] per Moore-Bick L.J.

2. Rescission

40–05   In this part we summarise the rules governing the rescission of contracts and gifts.[3] We then discuss how rescission can lead to the recovery of legal title to property that was transferred by the rescinding party to a recipient.

(a) *General Principles*

40–06   At common law, contracts may be rescinded for fraudulent misrepresentation,[4] duress[5] and mental incapacity,[6] and insurance contracts may also be rescinded for non-disclosure and non-fraudulent misrepresentation.[7] In equity, contracts may be rescinded for fraudulent and non-fraudulent misrepresentation,[8] undue influence,[9] unconscionable dealing[10] and non-compliance with the fiduciary dealing rules.[11] Contracts may not be rescinded in equity for common mistake[12] or unilateral mistake known to the other party.[13] Gifts may be rescinded in equity for undue influence,[14] misrepresentation[15] and some unilateral mistakes.[16]

---

[3] For an excellent detailed account, see D. O'Sullivan, S. Elliott, and R. Zakrzewski, *The Law of Rescission* (Oxford: OUP, 2008).

[4] *Load v Green* (1846) 15 M. & W. 216; 153 E.R. 828; *Clarke v Dickson* (1858) El. Bl. & El. 148; 120 E.R. 463; *Car and Universal Finance Co Ltd v Caldwell* [1965] 1 Q.B. 525.

[5] *Dimskal Shipping Co SA v I.T.W.F. (The Evia Luck)* [1992] 2 A.C. 152; *Halpern v Halpern (Nos 1 and 2)* [2007] EWCA Civ 291; [2008] Q.B. 195.

[6] *Imperial Loan Co v Stone* [1892] 1 Q.B. 599; *Hart v O'Connor* [1985] A.C. 1000.

[7] *Carter v Boehm* (1766) 3 Burr. 1909; 97 E.R. 1162; *Pan Atlantic Insurance Co Ltd v Pine Top Insurance Co Ltd* [1995] 1 A.C. 501; *Manifest Shipping Co Ltd v Uni-Polaris Insurance Co Ltd (The Star Sea)* [2003] 1 A.C. 469.

[8] *Peek v Gurney* (1871) L.R. 13 Eq. 79; *Redgrave v Hurd* (1881) 20 Ch. D. 1; *Newbigging v Adam* (1886) 34 Ch. D. 582; *Barclays Bank Plc v O'Brien* [1994] 1 A.C. 180. The court has a discretion to award damages in lieu of rescission if it would be equitable to do so: Misrepresentation Act 1967 s.2(2).

[9] *O'Brien* [1994] 1 A.C. 180; *Royal Bank of Scotland Plc v Etridge (No.2)* [2001] UKHL 44; [2002] 2 A.C. 773.

[10] *Cresswell v Potter* [1978] 1 W.L.R. 255; *Crédit Lyonnais Nederland NV v Burch* [1997] 1 All E.R. 144; *Portman BS v Dusangh* [2001] W.T.L.R 117.

[11] *Daly v Sidney Stock Exchange* (1986) 160 C.L.R. 371; *Guinness Plc v Saunders* [1990] 2 A.C. 663.

[12] *Great Peace Shipping Ltd v Tsavlisis Salvage (International) Ltd* [2002] EWCA Civ 1407; [2003] Q.B. 679; disapproving *Solle v Butcher* [1950] 1 K.B. 671.

[13] *Great Peace* [2002] EWCA Civ 1407; [2003] Q.B. 679; O'Sullivan et al, *The Law of Rescission*, paras 7.07–7.26 argue that this is a ground for rescission in equity under English law, citing *Riverlate Properties Ltd v Paul* [1975] 1 Ch. 133 at 145 per curiam (CA); and *Huyton SA v Distribuidora Internacional De Productos Agricolas SA de CV* [2002] EWHC 2088 (Comm); [2003] 2 Lloyd's Rep 780. But it is hard to see how this ground can have survived *Great Peace*, as Aikens J. observed in *Statoil ASA v Louis Dreyfus Energy Services LP (The Harriette N)* [2008] EWHC 2257 (Comm); [2009] 1 All E.R. (Comm) 1035 at [105]; and cf. *Pitt v Holt* [2011] EWCA Civ 197; [2011] 3 W.L.R. 19 at [166] per Lloyd L.J.: following *Great Peace*, there is "no equitable jurisdiction to set aside contracts on the ground of mistake".

[14] *Bridgeman v Green* (1755) Wilm. 58; 97 E.R. 22; *Allcard v Skinner* (1887) 36 Ch. D. 145; *Hammond v Osborn* [2002] EWCA Civ 885; [2002] W.T.L.R. 1125.

[15] *Scholefield v Templer* (1859) 4 De G. & J. 429; 45 E.R. 166; *Brown v Brown* (1868) L.R. 7 Eq. 185.

[16] *Ogilvie v Littleboy* (1897) 13 T.L.R. 399 (CA); affirmed sub nom *Ogilvie v Allen* (1899) 15 T.L.R. 294 (HL); *Pitt* [2011] EWCA Civ 197; [2011] 3 W.L.R. 19.

Many of these grounds for rescission are also grounds for the restitution of **40–07** benefits that were transferred to a defendant otherwise than under a contract or by way of gift. But there is no exact correspondence between the circumstances in which restitution is awarded in the latter situation and the circumstances in which contracts and gifts are rescinded. They are essentially the same in cases of duress or undue influence,[17] but they are not the same in cases of mistake, as the mistakes that justify rescission are narrower than the mistakes that justify restitution in the latter situation.[18]

A voidable transaction is valid until it is rescinded, and a party who is entitled **40–08** to rescind such a transaction is not obliged to exercise his power: he may choose instead to affirm the transaction, in which case he will lose his power to rescind by waiver. When a party with a right to rescind knowingly elects to affirm the transaction, his election is final[19]: he cannot change his mind and rescind the transaction afterwards.[20] Affirmation of a voidable contract may be established "by any conduct which unequivocally manifests an intention to affirm it by the party who has the right to affirm or disaffirm."[21]

An election to rescind, to be effective, must be exercised "in the plainest and **40–09** most open manner competent."[22] Hence a party with a right to rescind a voidable contract must usually communicate his intention to rescind to the other party, who "is entitled to treat the contractual nexus as continuing until he is made aware of the intention of the other to exercise his option to rescind."[23] However, the rescinding party may sometimes be relieved of the necessity of communication, for example where he retakes possession of a chattel which forms the subject matter of the parties' contract.[24] He will also be relieved where his counter-party, by absconding, deliberately puts it out of his power to communicate his intention to rescind, which the counter-party knows that he will almost certainly want to do[25]; "to hold otherwise would be to allow a fraudulent contracting party by his very fraud to prevent the innocent party from exercising his undoubted right."[26]

---

[17] Discussed in Chs 10 and 11.
[18] Discussed in Ch.9.
[19] *Peyman v Lanjani* [1985] Ch. 457; following *Coastal Estates Pty Ltd v Melevende* [1965] V.R. 433.
[20] *Clough v London and North Western Railway Co* (1871) L.R. 7 Ex. 26 at 34 per curiam.
[21] *Caldwell* [1965] 1 Q.B. 525 at 550 per Sellers L.J. See also *Vigers v Pike* (1842) 8 Cl. & F. 562; 8 E.R. 220; *Re Hop and Malt Exchange and Warehouse Co* (1866) L.R. 1 Eq. 483; *Re Peruvian Railway Co* (1869) L.R. 4 Ch. 322; *Sharply v Louth and East Coast Railway Co* (1876) 2 Ch. D. 663; *Peyman v Lanjani* [1985] Ch. 457 at 488 per Stephenson L.J.
[22] *Reese River Silver Mining Co v Smith* (1869) L.R. 4 H.L. 64 at 74 per Lord Hatherley L.C.
[23] *Caldwell* [1965] 1 Q.B. 525 at 554 per Upjohn L.J. See too *Scarf v Jardine* (1882) 7 App. Cas. 345 at 361 per Lord Blackburn; *Tenax Steamship Co v Owners of the MV Brimnes (The Brimnes)* [1975] Q.B. 929 at 945–946 per Edmund Davies L.J. The issue of proceedings can amount to communication of an election to rescind: *Shalson v Russo* [2003] EWHC 1637 (Ch); [2005] Ch. 281 at [120] per Rimer J., citing *Banque Belge pour l'Etranger v Hambrouck* [1921] 1 K.B. 321 at 332 per Atkin L.J.
[24] *Re Eastgate* [1905] 1 K.B. 465; *Caldwell* [1965] 1 Q.B. 525 at 551 per Sellers L.J. Recaption of goods is a self-help remedy; the rescinding party is entitled to retake his chattel peaceably, but may incur tort liability unless the counter-party's possession was "wrongful in its inception": *Toyota Finance Australia Ltd v Dennis* [2002] NSWCA 369; (2002) 58 N.S.W.L.R. 101.
[25] *Caldwell* [1965] 1 Q.B. 525; applied in *Newtons of Wembley Ltd v Williams* [1965] 1 Q.B. 560.
[26] *Caldwell* [1965] 1 Q.B. 525 at 555 per Upjohn L.J.

40–10   At common law, the properly communicated exercise of an election to rescind, accompanied where necessary by a tender of benefits received by the rescinding party, is immediately effective. In other words, rescission is accomplished by the rescinding party's own act, and if his counterparty[27]:

> "questions [his] right . . . to rescind, thus obliging [him] to bring an action at law to enforce the right he has secured for himself by his election, and [he] gets a verdict, it is an entire mistake to suppose that it is this verdict which by itself terminates the contract and restores the antecedent status. The verdict is merely the judicial determination of the fact that the expression by the plaintiff of his election to rescind was justified, was effective, and put an end to the contract."

40–11   It is unclear whether the same is true of elections to rescind transactions in equity. This question has been thoroughly examined by Dominic O'Sullivan, Stephen Elliott and Rafal Zakrzewski,[28] who identify two irreconcilable lines of authority: one holds that rescission is effected by a rescinding party's election,[29] the other that he must obtain a court order in order to rescind.[30] They conclude that an election to rescind in equity is effective only in cases of fraud. Their analysis is consistent with an important group of cases, discussed below, which hold that property received in a transaction that is later rescinded for fraud is held on trust for the rescinding party from the moment when he elects to rescind.[31] However, the authorities in this area are now in such a confused state that the law cannot be confidently stated, and a decision of the Supreme Court is needed to rationalise and restate it.

40–12   Both at common law and in equity it is a precondition for rescission of a contract that the rescinding party must make counter-restitution of any benefits he has received from his counterparty,[32] a rule that is discussed in Ch.31. It has been said that a right to rescind is lost if it is not exercised within a reasonable

---

[27] *Abram Steamship Co Ltd (In Liquidation) v Westville Shipping Co Ltd (In Liquidation)* [1923] A.C. 773 at 781 per Lord Atkinson. See too *Horsler v Zorro* [1975] Ch. 302 at 310 per Megarry J.; *Drake Insurance Plc v Provident Insurance Plc* [2003] 1 All E.R. (Comm) 759 at [31]–[32] per Moore-Bick J.; reversed on the facts [2003] EWCA Civ 1834; [2004] Q.B. 601 at [94]–[104] per Rix L.J.

[28] O'Sullivan et al, *The Law of Rescission*, paras 11.55–11.105. See too J. O'Sullivan, "Rescission as a Self-Help Remedy: A Critical Analysis" (2000) 59 C.L.J. 509.

[29] *Reese River Silver* (1869) L.R. 4 HL 64 at 73–75 per Lord Hatherly L.C.; *Abram Steamship* [1923] A.C. 773 at 781 per Lord Atkinson; *Horsler* [1975] Ch. 302 at 310 per Megarry J.; *TSB Bank Plc v Camfield* [1995] 1 W.L.R. 430 at 438 per Roch L.J.; *Drake Insurance* [2003] 1 All E.R. (Comm) 759 at [31]–[32] per Moore-Bick J.; reversed on the facts [2003] EWCA Civ 1834; [2004] Q.B. 601 at [94]–[104] per Rix L.J.; *Brotherton v Aseguradora Colseguros SA (No.2)* [2003] EWCA Civ 705; [2003] 2 All E.R. (Comm) 298 at [45]–[48] per Buxton L.J.

[30] *Cooper v Phibbs* (1867) L.R. 2 H.L. 149; *Allcard v Skinner* (1887) 36 Ch. D. 145 at 186–187 per Lindley L.J.; *Spence v Crawford* [1939] 3 All E.R. 271 at 288 per Lord Wright; *O'Sullivan v Management Agency and Music Ltd* [1985] 1 Q.B. 428 at 457 per Dunn L.J.; adopting *Alati v Kruger* (1955) 94 C.L.R. 216 at 223–224 per Dixon C.J., Webb, Kitto and Taylor JJ.; *Goldsworthy v Brickell* [1987] Ch. 378 at 409–410 per Nourse L.J.; *Cheese v Thomas* [1994] 1 W.L.R. 129 at 137 per Nicholls V.C.; *Johnson v EBS Pensioner Trustees Ltd* [2002] EWCA Civ 164; [2002] Lloyd's Rep. P.N. 309 at [56]–[57] per Mummery L.J.; and at [78]–[79] per Dyson L.J.; *Wilson v Hurstanger Ltd* [2007] EWCA Civ 299; [2008] Bus. L.R. 216 at [47] per Tuckey L.J. See too *Pitt* [2011] EWCA Civ 197; [2011] 3 W.L.R. 19 at [231]–[232] and at [237]–[238] per Mummery L.J.

[31] See the cases discussed in para.40–22.

[32] *Erlanger v New Sombrero Phosphate Co* (1873) 3 App. Cas. 1218; *Spence* [1939] 3 All E.R. 271; *O'Sullivan* [1985] Q.B. 428.

time,[33] but it seems unlikely that this adds anything to the rules debarring rescission after affirmation[34] and the rules of limitation and laches affecting rescission that are discussed in Ch.33. It has also been said that the intervention of third party rights bars rescission in equity, but in fact the courts have always managed to protect third party purchasers without barring rescission,[35] for example by letting them keep the relevant asset but requiring the defendant to hand over the proceeds of sale[36] or exchange products.[37]

In *TSB Bank Plc v Camfield*[38] the Court of Appeal held that if a claimant can **40-13** set aside a transaction for misrepresentation (or undue influence) then it must be set aside entirely rather than partially. So, a claimant who agrees to mortgage her house for £30,000 can escape liability for the entire sum, although she would have agreed to liability for £15,000 irrespective of the misrepresentation (or undue influence). However, she must return any benefit she has personally received under the contract before it can be set aside.[39]

The Court of Appeal's reasoning in *Camfield* was repudiated, and the opposite **40-14** result reached, in *Vadasz v Pioneer Concrete SA*,[40] where the High Court of Australia held that the court should be concerned to achieve a practically just result when putting the claimant on terms, and should seek to put the claimant in the position which he would have occupied if the misconduct had not occurred. This approach was also taken by the New Zealand Court of Appeal in *Scales Trading Co Ltd v Far Eastern Shipping Co Public Ltd*.[41] It has an intuitive appeal, but it treats rescission as though it were a compensatory remedy when the point of rescission is rather to require the parties to return whatever benefits they have received under the contract. The *Vadasz* approach also means that a claimant who would have contracted on precisely the same terms irrespective of the defendant's misconduct cannot rescind at all, a proposition that is contradicted by many authorities, including the High Court of Australia's own decision a year after *Vadasz* in *Maguire v Makaronis*,[42] where the court was forced to sidestep the problem by holding that *Vadasz* does not apply in cases involving fiduciaries.

---

[33] *Lindsay Petroleum Co v Hurd* (1874) L.R. 5 P.C. 221 at 239–240 per Lord Selborne L.C.; *Erlanger* (1878) 3 App. Cas. 1218 at 1279–1280 per Lord Blackburn; *Leaf v International Galleries Ltd* [1950] 2 K.B. 86; *Caldwell* [1965] 1 Q.B. 525 at 554 per Upjohn L.J.

[34] Cf. *Clough* (1871) L.R. 7 Ex. 26 at 35 per curiam; cf. *Mitchell v Homfray* (1882) 8 Q.B.D. 587.

[35] A point well made in O'Sullivan et al, *The Law of Rescission*, para.20.23 and following.

[36] *Fox v Mackreth* (1788) 2 Bro. C.C. 400; 29 E.R. 224; *Lagunas Nitrate Co v Lagunas Syndicate* [1899] 2 Ch. 392 at 434 per Lindley M.R.

[37] *Small v Attwood* (1832) You. 407 at 537–538; 159 E.R. 1051 at 1105 per Lord Lyndhurst L.C.B.; *Shalson* [2003] EWHC 1637 (Ch); [1995] Ch. 281.

[38] *TSB Bank Plc v Camfield* [1995] 1 W.L.R. 430.

[39] *Camfield* [1995] 1 W.L.R. 430 at 432 and 437 per Nourse L.J. See too *Dunbar Bank Plc v Nadeem* [1998] 3 All E.R. 876 at 883 per Millett L.J.

[40] *Vadasz v Pioneer Concrete SA* (1995) 184 C.L.R. 102.

[41] *Scales Trading Co Ltd v Far Eastern Shipping Co Public Ltd* [1999] 3 N.Z.L.R. 26; on appeal the Privy Council found it unnecessary to decide whether *Vadasz* is preferable to *Camfield*: [2001] 1 All E.R. (Comm) 319.

[42] *Maguire v Makaronis* (1996) 188 C.L.R. 449.

40–15   The extent to which rescission should be understood as a remedy responding to unjust enrichment is controversial. On one view, contractual rights are themselves benefits that can form the subject matter of a claim in unjust enrichment,[43] and it follows that rescission is a remedy that responds to the defendant's unjust enrichment by his receipt of contractual rights against the claimant by cancelling these rights with retrospective effect.[44] On another view, "an analysis in unjust enrichment is not needed to explain why a consensually created obligation may be voidable at the instance of the obliged person", because "the power to avoid the contract . . . is an inherent feature of the contract from the moment it is created."[45]

40–16   It is unnecessary to resolve this controversy to decide the answer to a separate question, namely whether the recovery of money and other benefits transferred under a partly or fully executed contract that is subsequently rescinded should be understood as a remedy for unjust enrichment.[46] We consider that the revesting of title to assets following rescission should be seen as a proprietary remedy for unjust enrichment, and we discuss the legal mechanisms by which this is achieved immediately below. In Ch.36 we also take the position that a personal claim in unjust enrichment should lie to recover the value of benefits conferred under a rescinded contract, whether or not these are specific property, title to which is still capable of being revested in the claimant at the time of the action.[47]

(b) *Proprietary Effects*

40–17   A voidable contract is valid until it is rescinded, and prior to rescission it is as capable of effecting a valid transfer of title to property as any other legally valid contract.[48] Hence, for example, where goods are delivered to a fraudster in circumstances where the fraud renders the contract voidable rather than void, title to the goods will generally pass.[49] The same is also true of fraudulently induced payments of money.[50] This is why Potter L.J. said in *Twinsectra Ltd v Yardley* that "before rescission, the owner has no proprietary interest in the original property; all he has is the 'mere equity' of his right to set aside the voidable

---

[43] R. Chambers, "Two Types of Enrichment" in R. Chambers et al. (eds), *Philosophical Foundations of the Law of Unjust Enrichment* (Oxford: OUP, 2009), 242.

[44] P. Birks, *Unjust Enrichment* (Oxford: OUP, 2005), p.126; J. Edelman and E. Bant, *Unjust Enrichment in Australia* (Melbourne: OUP, 2006), pp.23 and 102. There is a debate as to whether the cancellation of contractual rights is a restitutionary response to the defendant's unjust enrichment, given that the rights are not returned to the claimant. Nothing turns on this if one accepts, as we do, that unjust enrichment can trigger a variety of responses that are not limited to restitution.

[45] L. Smith, "Unjust Enrichment: Big or Small?" in S. Degeling and J. Edelman (eds), *Unjust Enrichment in Commercial Law* (Sydney: Lawbook Co, 2008), 35, p.43.

[46] As noted in A. Burrows, *The Law of Restitution* (Oxford: OUP, 2010), pp.17–20.

[47] See paras 36–05——36–08.

[48] *Ciro Citterio Menswear Plc (In Administration) v Thakrar* [2002] EWHC 662 (Ch); [2002] 1 W.L.R. 2217.

[49] *Phillips v Brooks Ltd* [1919] 2 K.B. 243; *Hambrouck* [1921] 1 K.B. 321 at 332 per Atkin L.J.; *Lewis v Averay* [1972] 1 Q.B. 198; *Barclays Bank Plc v Boulter* [1999] 1 W.L.R. 1919 at 1926 per Lord Hoffmann. See too D. O'Sullivan, "Distributing the Risks of Contract Fraud" (2001) 117 L.Q.R. 381. Cf. *Cundy v Lindsay* (1878) 3 App. Cas. 459; *Ingram v Little* [1961] 1 Q.B. 31.

[50] *R. v Canadian Imperial Bank of Commerce* (2000) 51 O.R. (3d) 257 (Ontario CA); *i Trade Finance Inc v Bank of Montreal* [2011] SCC 26; [2011] 2 S.C.R. 360 at [47]–[50] per curiam.

contract."[51] A similar principle obtains in the case of gifts. For example, where a gift is made that is voidable for the donor's unilateral mistake, ownership of the property passes to the donee[52]; likewise, a claim that a gift has been procured by undue influence "assumes a transfer of the beneficial interest but in circumstances which entitle the transferor to recall it."[53]

At common law, when a contract is induced by fraud and a claimant transfers   **40–18** legal title to goods to a defendant in accordance with the contract, this title automatically revests in the claimant when he elects to rescind. This was decided in *Load v Green*.[54] A fraudster induced the plaintiffs to sell and deliver goods to him without paying for them. The fraudster went bankrupt and the plaintiffs successfully brought an action in trover against his assignees in bankruptcy. Parke B. held that they could rescind the contract and revest title to the goods in themselves.[55] This decision has been followed in various cases, including *Car & Universal Finance Co Ltd v Caldwell*.[56] However, this common law rule does not apply where a claimant has transferred shares, legal ownership of which can only be vested in those recorded in the register of members[57]; nor does it apply where a claimant has transferred legal title to land.[58] In both of these situations, the claimant must therefore rely on equity to do the necessary work.

The exercise of a right to rescind in equity has similar effects to the exercise   **40–19** of a right to rescind at common law, with the obvious difference that equity cannot accomplish a revesting of legal title, and can only hold that rescission creates a trust of the property for the rescinding party. This is a bare trust, i.e. the trustee owes no active management duties, and is required only to handle the property in a manner consistent with the claimant's equitable ownership, which will usually mean that he needs do nothing more than keep the property separate

---

[51] *Twinsectra Ltd v Yardley* [1999] Lloyd's Rep. Bank. 438 at 461–462; not considered on appeal [2002] UKHL 12; [2002] 2 A.C. 164. See also *Lonrho Plc v Fayed (No.2)* [1992] 1 W.L.R. 1 at 11–12 per Millett J.; *El Ajou v Dollar Land Holdings Plc* [1993] 3 All E.R. 717 at 734 per Millett L.J.; *Shalson* [2003] EWHC 1637 (Ch); [2005] Ch. 281 at [122]–[127] per Rimer J.

[52] This is implicit in cases holding that a gift may be rescinded in equity where the donor was mistaken as to the "legal effects" of the transaction: e.g. *Gibbon v Mitchell* [1990] 1 W.L.R. 1304 at 1310 per Millett J.; *Pitt* [2011] EWCA Civ 197, [2011] 3 W.L.R. 19 at [204] per Lloyd L.J.

[53] *Hodgson v Marks* [1971] Ch. 892 at 929 per Russell L.J.

[54] *Load v Green* (1846) 15 M. & W. 216; 153 E.R. 828. Earlier cases took a different approach, either denying that legal title passed in the first place, or holding that it passed irretrievably: W. Swadling, "Rescission, Property, and the Common Law" (2005) 121 L.Q.R. 123, pp.142–152. Swadling argues that *Load* was wrongly decided because rescission of the contract should not entail a revesting of title in cases where the seller has delivered the goods to the buyer. This argument rests on two assumptions, both of which are shown by Birke Häcker to be unfounded, namely (1) that title can pass twice over, under the contract and then by delivery, and (2) that where title passes by delivery it cannot be revested for the transferee's fraud: B. Häcker, *Consequences of Impaired Consent Transfers* (Tübingen: Mohr Siebeck, 2009), pp.133–138.

[55] *Load* 15 M. & W. at 221; 153 E.R. at 830.

[56] *Car & Universal Finance Co Ltd v Caldwell* [1965] 1 Q.B. 525. See too *Clough* (1871) L.R. 7 Ex. 26 at 32 per curiam; *Re Eastgate* [1905] 1 K.B. 465; *Tilley v Bowman Ltd* [1910] 1 K.B. 745; *Thomas v Heelas* [1988] C.L.Y. 3175 (CA); *Hunter BNZ Finance Ltd v CG Maloney Pty Ltd* (1988) 18 N.S.W.L.R. 420 at 433–434 and at 437 per Giles J. (NSW CA).

[57] *Civil Service Co-operative Society v Blyth* (1914) 17 C.L.R. 601 at 613 per Isaacs J., endorsed in *Sons of Gwalia Ltd v Margaretic* [2007] HCA 1; (2007) 232 A.L.R. 232 at [55] per Gleeson C.J.

[58] The cases all concern unregistered land, but presumably the same rule applies to registered land, since there is nothing in the Land Registration Act 2002 to displace it: *Feret v Hill* (1854) 15 C.B. 207; 139 E.R. 400; as interpreted in *Canham v Barry* (1855) 15 C.B. 597; 139 E.R. 558; *R. v Saddlers' Co* (1863) 10 H.L.C. 303; 11 E.R. 217; and *Taylor v Chester* (1869) L.R. 4 Q.B. 309.

from his own property and reconvey legal ownership to the claimant on demand.[59]

40–20   Various authorities support this analysis, and hold that the trust arises at the time when the rescinding party elects to exercise his right to rescind. These cases also hold, explicitly or implicitly, that the trust does not arise earlier, at the time when the property is transferred (which is the rule in US law[60]), or later, at the time when a court confirms that the transaction should be rescinded.[61]

40–21   The former proposition is established by *Allcard v Skinner*,[62] where a gift was procured by undue influence, and the dissenting judge, Cotton L.J., would have permitted recovery of the property on the basis that it was held on trust from the moment of receipt.[63] Lindley and Bowen L.JJ. disagreed, and held that the plaintiff could not recover the property by reason of the long delay between the date of transfer and the date when the action was begun,[64] a finding that can only be explained on the basis that they considered the plaintiff's acquisition of an equitable proprietary right to be contingent on her election to rescind.

40–22   The latter proposition is established by a series of cases, the most recent of which is *Shalson v Russo*.[65] Mimran, the Part 20 claimant, was fraudulently induced to lend money to Russo, that he paid into a Swiss bank account operated by Westland, a company controlled by Russo. The money was then withdrawn from the account and used to buy a yacht. Following discovery of the fraud, Mimran issued a claim, and later argued that the issuing of the claim amounted to an implied rescission of the loan contracts, and that the effect of the rescission was to create a trust of the money and its traceable proceeds in his favour. Rimer J. held that Mimran could not trace into the yacht because the bank account had been overdrawn at the time of his payments. However, he made it clear that Mimran's argument would have succeeded if the tracing rules had permitted him to establish that the yacht represented the traceable proceeds of the money. In Rimer J.'s words[66]:

> " There is . . . a line of authority supporting the proposition that, upon rescission of a
> contract for fraudulent misrepresentation, the beneficial title which passed to the

---

[59] *Lonrho* [1992] 1 W.L.R. 1 at 11–12 per Millett J.

[60] A. Scott and W. Fratcher, *The Law of Trusts*, 4th edn (Boston, Mass: Little Brown & Co, 1989), vol.5 paras 462.2, 462.4, 468 and 475. See too R. Chambers, *Resulting Trusts* (Oxford: Clarendon Press, 1997), pp.171–184, arguing that an immediately vested equitable proprietary interest in favour of the transferor should arise concurrently with a power to rescind; as Chambers later conceded, however, this immediate interest model is inconsistent with the idea that underpins the power model, that a rescinding party is free to choose whether or not to exercise his right to rescind: R. Chambers, "Resulting Trusts in Canada, Part II" (2002) 16 Tru. L.I. 138, pp.145–147.

[61] Cf. the discussion at para.40–11, and note that if the court's intervention is needed to rescind the transaction and bring the trust into existence, then the court will probably back-date its inception to the date when proceedings to rescind were begun: *Reese River Silver* (1869) L.R. H.L. 64.

[62] *Allcard v Skinner* (1887) 36 Ch. D. 145.

[63] *Allcard* (1887) 36 Ch. D. 145 at 175.

[64] *Allcard* (1887) 36 Ch. D. 145 at 188–189 and at 193.

[65] *Shalson v Russo* [2003] EWHC 1637 (Ch); [2005] Ch. 281. See also *Alati v Kruger* (1955) 94 C.L.R. 216 at 224 per Dixon C.J., Webb, Kitto and Taylor JJ.; *Daly v Sydney Stock Exchange Ltd* (1985) 160 C.L.R. 371 at 387–390 per Brennan J.; *Lonrho* [1992] 1 W.L.R. 1 at 11–12 per Millett J.; *El Ajou* [1993] 3 All E.R. 717 at 734 per Millett L.J.; *Bristol & West Building Society v Mothew* [1998] 1 Ch. 1 at 22–23 per Millett L.J.; *Twinsectra* [1999] Lloyd's Rep Bank 438 at [99] per Potter L.J.

[66] *Shalson* [2003] EWHC 1637 (Ch); [2005] Ch. 281 at [122] and at [127].

representor under the contract revests in the representee. The representee then enjoys a sufficient proprietary title to enable him to trace, follow and recover what, by virtue of such revesting, can be regarded as having always been in equity his own property.

[Following this] line of authorities [I hold] . . . that upon the implied rescission of the loan contracts effected by the bringing of his Part 20 claim, Mr Mimran had revested in him the property in the money he advanced to Westland entitling him at least to trace it into assets into which it was subsequently applied."

It follows from the foregoing analysis that a distinction must be drawn **40-23** between the power vested in a rescinding party to obtain an equitable proprietary interest under a trust, and the equitable proprietary right which he obtains when he exercises this power. Although this power is a "mere equity",[67] it can be devised[68] or assigned,[69] and it binds volunteers claiming through the original transferee as well as third parties with notice.[70] If the transferee becomes insolvent then the power will prevail over the unsecured creditors,[71] but it will be defeated by a fixed charge,[72] or a crystallised floating charge.[73] When the power is exercised, however, the trust arising in favour of the rescinding party will take the property out of the scope of an uncrystallised floating charge, the charge-holder's interest being overreached or defeated, and later fixed charges will only be good against the rescinding party if granted to bona fide purchasers without notice.[74] In cases concerning dispositions of registered land, the rescinding party's power can bind later purchasers of equitable interests, and can also bind a registered proprietor if the rescinding party is in actual occupation.[75] However, a registered proprietor is not affected by adverse equitable interests that are not protected on the register or by the actual occupation of the owner thereof, irrespective of whether he has any knowledge or notice of those interests.[76]

Two decisions of the Court of Appeal should finally be noted, where it was **40-24** held that the foregoing analysis does not apply in cases where a contract is induced by a fraudulent misrepresentation that so seriously vitiates a claimant's

---

[67] *Cave v Cave* (1880) L.R. 15 Ch. D. 639 at 649 per Fry J.; *Bainbrigge v Browne* (1881) L.R. 18 Ch. D. 188 at 197 per Fry J.; *Cloutte v Storey* [1911] 1 Ch. 18 at 24 per Neville J.; *National Provincial Bank Ltd v Ainsworth* [1965] A.C. 1175 at 1254 per Lord Wilberforce; *Latec Investments Ltd v Hotel Terrigal Pty Ltd (In Liquidation)* (1965) 113 C.L.R. 265 at 277–278 per Kitto J.; at 281 per Taylor J.; and at 291 per Menzies J.; *Shiloh Spinners Ltd v Harding* [1973] A.C. 691 at 721 per Lord Wilberforce; *Twinsectra* [1999] Lloyd's Rep. Bank. 438 at 461–462; not considered on appeal [2002] UKHL 12; [2002] 2 A.C. 164. See too *Phillips v Phillips* (1861) 4 De G. F. & J. 208 at 211; 45 E.R. 1164 at 1167 per Lord Westbury L.C. ("an equity as distinguished from an equitable estate").
[68] *Stump v Gaby* (1852) 2 De G.M. & G. 623; 42 E.R. 1015.
[69] *Dickinson v Burrell* (1866) L.R. 1 Eq. 337; *Bruty v Edmundson* (1915) 85 L.J. Ch. 568.
[70] S. Worthington, "The Proprietary Consequences of Rescission" [2002] R.L.R. 28, pp.36–38 and 59–60.
[71] *Gladstone v Hawden* (1813) 1 M. & S. 517; 105 E.R. 193; *Re Eastgate* [1905] 1 K.B. 465; *Tilley v Bowman Ltd* [1910] 1 K.B. 745.
[72] *Re Ffrench's Estate* (1887) 21 I.R. 283; *Latec* (1965) 113 C.L.R. 265.
[73] *Re Goldcorp Exchange Ltd* [1995] 1 A.C. 74; as interpreted in *Shalson* [2003] EWHC 1637; [2005] Ch. 281 at [127] per Rimer J. See too P. Birks, "Establishing a Proprietary Base" [1995] R.L.R. 83, p.88.
[74] M. Balen, "Exploring Proprietary Restitution: The Relationship between Rescission and Insolvency"(2011) 22 K.L.J. 228, pp.229–30.
[75] Land Registration Act 2002 s.116 and Sch.3 para.2. See too Law Commission, *Land Registration for the Twenty-First Century* (2001) Law Com No.271, paras 5.32–5.36 especially para.5.33(4); *Thompson v Foy* [2009] EWHC 1076 (Ch); [2010] 1 P. & C.R. 16 at [134] per Lewison J.
[76] Land Registration Act 2002 s.29.

intention to transfer property to the defendant that the transaction should be treated as a nullity from the start, with the result that a trust of the property arises at the moment of transfer, and there is no need for rescission because there is nothing to rescind. Nourse L.J. adopted this analysis in *Collings v Lee*,[77] where the claimants were induced by the defendant to convey their house to him under an assumed name, and Carnwath L.J. articulated a similar principle in *Halley v Law Society*,[78] holding that where money is paid pursuant to a contract that is no more than "a dishonest device to obtain money", as opposed to a contract with "substance" that is merely "induced by fraud", there is no need for the victim to rescind the contract in order to acquire an equitable proprietary interest because the court can simply "disregard" it. We consider that these cases should be treated with caution. They rest on the novel proposition that a contract induced by fraudulent misrepresentation is void rather than voidable, and their scope is uncertain since the distinctions they draw between null and nullifiable transactions induced by fraud are unlikely to be workable in practice.[79]

3. RECTIFICATION

40–25 In this part we first examine the circumstances in which the courts rectify documents, and then discuss how rectification can lead to a revesting of title to property that was conveyed to a defendant in accordance with the unrectified document.

(a) *General Principles*

40–26 Rectification is an equitable remedy, the purpose of which is to bring a document that inaccurately records an agreement or voluntary disposition into harmony with what the parties agreed or the disponor intended. A decree of rectification has retrospective effect: it can retropectively validate transactions that were invalid on the face of the unrectified document and it can retrospectively invalidate transactions that were valid on the face of the unrectified document.[80]

40–27 In bilateral transactions where there was a unilateral mistake, rectification is available only if the non-mistaken party is estopped from resisting rectification by virtue of his unconscionable conduct.[81] Otherwise, the mistake must be

---

[77] *Collings v Lee* [2001] 2 All ER 332 at 337.
[78] *Halley v Law Society* [2003] EWCA Civ 97; [2003] W.T.L.R. 845 at [42]–[56].
[79] For these and other criticisms of the reasoning in *Halley*, see also H.W. Tang, "Proprietary Relief without Rescission" (2004) 63 C.L.J. 30.
[80] *Earl of Malmesbury v Countess of Malmesbury* (1862) 31 Beav. 407; 54 E.R. 1196; *Craddock Bros Ltd v Hunt* [1923] 2 Ch. 136; *Lake v Lake* [1989] S.T.C. 865; *Martin v Nicholson* [2004] EWHC 2135 (Ch); [2005] W.T.L.R. 175 at [19] per Peter Smith J. And see the discussion at paras 40–33—40–35.
[81] *Thomas Bates & Son Ltd v Wyndham's (Lingerie) Ltd* [1981] 1 W.L.R. 505; *Commission for New Towns v Cooper (GB) Ltd* [1995] Ch. 259; *Thor Navigation Inc v Ingosstrakh Insurance Co Ltd* [2005] EWHC 19 (Comm); [2005] 1 Lloyd's Rep. 547 at [57]–[62] per Gloster J. A person has not necessarily acted unconscionably simply because he has "blind-eye" or constructive knowledge of the other party's mistake: *George Wimpey UK Ltd v VI Construction Ltd* [2005] EWCA Civ 77; [2005] B.L.R. 135. For general discussion, see D. McLauchlan, "The 'Drastic' Remedy of Rectification for Unilateral Mistake" (2008) 124 L.Q.R. 608.

common to both parties, with the result that the document fails to record what they agreed.[82] Often it is possible to apply rules of construction to rescue parties in this situation, as in *Chartbrook Ltd v Persimmon Homes Ltd*,[83] for example. Whether or not that route can be taken, the House of Lords also held in *Chartbrook* that rectification will be ordered if it can be said with certainty what the parties' agreement was, and that it was wrongly expressed in the document, after comparing the document with what they said or wrote to one another in the course of reaching their agreement.

The process of ascertaining whether a document reflects the parties' agreement   **40–28** is an objective one: "the court is not concerned with what the parties *thought* they had agreed or what they *thought* their agreement meant", but with "what the parties said and did, and what that would convey to a reasonable person in their position".[84] It has been said that before rectification is awarded there must be some "outward expression of accord or evidence of a continuing common intention outwardly manifested"[85]; otherwise there would be no certainty in business transactions. But the trend in recent cases is to treat this as "an evidential factor rather than a strict legal requirement in all cases of rectification."[86] The document may contain the very words the parties intended it to contain but rectification may still be available if "it has in law or as a matter of true construction an effect or meaning different from that which was intended."[87] "It is not necessary that the parties should at the material time have formulated the words which it is sought to insert by rectification" and it is "sufficient that the parties had the necessary common continuing intention as to the substance of that which would be achieved by the rectification sought".[88]

The burden of proof on a party seeking rectification is "the civil standard of   **40–29** balance of probability."[89] However, the court's jurisdiction should be exercised only "upon convincing proof that the concluded instrument does not represent

---

[82] *Agip SpA v Navigazione Alta Italia SpA (The Nai Genova and The Nai Superba)* [1984] 1 Lloyd's Rep. 353 at 359 per Slade L.J.; *KPMG LLP v Network Rail Infrastructure Ltd* [2007] EWCA Civ 363; [2007] Bus. L.R. 1336.

[83] *Chartbrook Ltd v Persimmon Homes Ltd* [2009] UKHL 38; [2009] 1 A.C. 1101. Cf. *Bashir v Ali* [2011] EWCA Civ 707; [2011] 2 P. & C.R. 12.

[84] *PT Berlian Laju Tanker TBK v Nuse Shipping Ltd* [2008] EWHC 1330; [2008] 2 All E.R. (Comm) 784 at [38] per Christopher Clarke J. (his emphasis).

[85] *T & N Ltd (In Administration) v Royal & Sun Alliance Plc* [2003] 2 All E.R. (Comm) 939 at 964–965 per Lawrence Collins J.; citing *Frederick E Rose (London) Ltd v William H Pimm Junior & Co Ltd* [1953] 2 Q.B. 450 at 461–462 per Denning L.J.; *Joscelyne v Nissen* [1970] 2 Q.B. 86 at 97 per curiam (CA). See too *Swainland Builders Ltd v Freehold Properties Ltd* [2002] EWCA Civ 560; [2002] 2 E.G.L.R. 71 at [33] per Peter Gibson L.J.;

[86] *Munt v Beasley* [2006] EWCA Civ 370 at [36] per Mummery L.J.; citing *Westland Savings Bank v Hancock* [1987] 2 N.Z.L.R. 21 at 29–30; and *J.I.S. (1974) Ltd v MCP Investment Nominees I Ltd* [2003] EWCA Civ 721 at [33]–[34] per Carnwath L.J.

[87] *T & N* [2003] EWHC 1016 (Ch); [2003] 2 All E.R. (Comm.) 939 at [136] per Lawrence Collins J.; citing *Re Butlin's ST* [1976] Ch. 251 at 260 per Brightman J.; and *Grand Metropolitan Group Ltd v William Hill Group Ltd* [1997] 1 B.C.L.C. 390 at 394 per Arden J.

[88] *T & N* [2003] EWHC 1016 (Ch); [2003] 2 All E.R. (Comm.) 939 at [137] per Lawrence Collins J.; citing *Crane v Hegeman-Harris Co Inc* (1939) [1971] 1 W.L.R. 1390 at 1399 per Simonds J., and *Grand Metropolitan* [1997] 1 B.C.L.C. 390 at 394 per Arden J.

[89] *Thomas Bates* [1981] 1 W.L.R. 505 at 521 per Brightman L.J.; *Agip* [1984] 1 Lloyd's Rep. 353 at 359 per Slade L.J.

the common intention of the parties,"[90] since "the alleged common intention *ex hypothesi* contradicts the written instrument."[91] The burden is particularly onerous where there have been prolonged negotiations between the parties which have culminated in a formal instrument drawn up by skilled advisers. The task of demonstrating that the document did not represent the parties' intention is then "formidable".[92]

40–30   Rectification of a voluntary deed, such as a settlement, can be obtained if the donor's real intention was not accurately reflected in the deed.[93] The onus is on the donor to prove this.[94] He must be able to show that he had some specific intention other than that which was recorded in the document,[95] and the mistake must go to the meaning of the language used in the document to record his intentions and not merely as to its fiscal or other consequences or as to the advantages to be gained by entering into it.[96] Note that it is the donor's intention which matters and not, for example, the intention of the trustees of a voluntary settlement which a settlor has executed, although the court will take into account whether the trustees oppose or support rectification in exercising its discretion to grant relief.[97]

40–31   Rectification is an equitable remedy and so the court may refuse relief if it thinks it just to do so. To refuse relief will mean that the parties are bound by the document in its uncorrected form. The equity of rectification will not be enforced against a bona fide purchaser without notice of the facts giving rise to the suit for rectification.[98] The court may also refuse to rectify an instrument if there has been laches or acquiescence,[99] if the claimant has led the defendant to rely on the instrument, if restitutio in integrum is impossible, or if the party claiming rectification has affirmed the instrument with knowledge of the error contained in it, or if there has been undue lapse of time. In the case of a voluntary settlement

---

[90] *Crane* (1939) [1971] 1 W.L.R. 1390 at 1391 per Simonds J.; approved in *Joscelyne* [1970] 2 Q.B. 86 at 98 per curiam (CA). See also *Ernest Scragg & Sons v Perseverance Banking and Trust Co Ltd* [1973] 2 Lloyd's Rep. 101; *Grand Metropolitan* [1997] 1 B.C.L.C. 390 at 394 per Arden J.

[91] *Thomas Bates* [1981] 1 W.L.R. 505 at 521 per Brightman L.J.; cf. Buckley L.J. at 519.

[92] *Snamprogetti International SA v Phillips Petroleum Co UK Ltd* [2001] EWCA Civ 889; (2001) 79 Con. L.R. 80 at [36] per Tuckey L.J.

[93] *Re Butlin's ST* [1976] Ch. 251. See too *Walker v Armstrong* (1856) 8 De G. M. & G. 531; 44 E.R. 495; *Wollaston v Tribe* (1869) L.R. 9 Eq. 44. In *Walker* 8 De G.M. & G. at 538; 44 E.R. at 498, Knight Bruce L.J. said of the solicitors responsible for drafting the documents that "These licensed pilots undertook to steer a post-captain through certain not very narrow straits of the law, and with abundance of sea room ran him aground on every shoal they could make."

[94] *Joscelyne* [1970] 2 Q.B. 86 at 98 per curiam (CA); *Frey v Royal Bank of Scotland (Nassau) Ltd* (2001) 3 I.T.E.L.R. 775 (Bahamas Sup Ct); *Abacus Trust Co (Isle of Man) Ltd v NSPCC* [2001] W.T.L.R. 953 at 964; *Summers v Kitson* [2006] EWHC 3655 (Ch); [2007] W.T.L.R. 1645 at [31]; *Allnut v Wilding* [2007] EWCA Civ 412; [2007] W.T.L.R. 941 at [19]–[20].

[95] *Racal Group Services Ltd v Ashmore* [1995] S.T.C. 1151; *Martin v Nicholson* [2004] EWHC 2135 (Ch); [2005] W.T.L.R. 175; *Farmer v Sloan* [2004] EWHC 606 (Ch); [2005] W.T.L.R. 521; *Allnutt* [2007] EWCA Civ 412; [2007] W.T.L.R. 941 at [26] per Mummery L.J.

[96] *Whiteside v Whiteside* [1950] Ch 65 at 74 per Evershed M.R.; *AMP (UK) Ltd v Barker* [2001] W.T.L.R. 1237 at 1260 per Lawrence Collins J.; *Allnutt* [2007] EWCA Civ 412; [2007] W.T.L.R. 941; *Ashcroft v Barnsdale* [2010] EWHC 1948 (Ch); [2010] W.T.L.R. 1675 at [16]–[17] and [20] per Judge Hodge QC, sitting as a deputy High Court judge.

[97] *Re Butlin's ST* [1976] Ch. 251. It is another matter if the settlor and the trustees have made a bargain with each other.

[98] See the cases discussed in para.40–34.

[99] *Beale v Kyte* [1907] 1 Ch. 564.

the court may also refuse to rectify if a trustee, who took office in ignorance of the mistake, has a reasonable objection to rectification.[100]

Section 20 of the Administration of Justice Act 1982 allows a will to be **40–32** rectified if the court is satisfied that it fails to carry out the testator's intentions in consequence of a clerical error or a failure to understand his instructions.[101] An application to rectify shall not be made, except with the court's permission, after six months from the date on which representation is first taken out. The personal representatives are not liable if they have distributed any part of the estate after the six months' period; but this does not prejudice any right to recover any part of the estate so distributed. Apart from this statutory power, courts also have an equitable power to rectify a will in the case of fraud.[102]

(b) *The Proprietary Effects of Rectification*

In *Beale v Kyte*,[103] the plaintiff sold and conveyed land to the defendant, but later **40–33** brought proceedings for rectification of the conveyance, alleging that by common mistake the parcels in the conveyance included more land than was comprised in the written contract in pursuance of which the conveyance was executed. Neville J. found for the plaintiff and ordered rectification of the conveyance. It might be argued that when rectification is ordered in such a case, this does not alter the rights of the parties, but merely results in a rectified document that correctly records the true rights between the parties that have always existed. However, this analysis is shown to be incorrect by cases where a purchaser who receives rights to land under a faulty conveyance sells them on to a bona fide purchaser for value without notice of the mistake. In this situation, the law is clear that the bona fide purchaser's rights prevail over the vendor's "equity of rectification". These cases can only be explained on the basis that the effect of the conveyance was to pass defeasible rights to the first purchaser which he sold on to the bona fide purchaser. Had he not done so prior to rectification, these rights would have revested in the vendor.[104]

Cases establishing this principle include *Smith v Jones*,[105] where the plaintiff **40–34** leased a farm under a standard-form tenancy agreement that failed to record the parties' shared intention that the landlord should be responsible for structural repairs, and provided that responsibility for these lay on the plaintiff. The landlord sold the farm to the defendant, and a dispute then arose between the plaintiff and defendant as to which of them should repair the property. The plaintiff sought rectification of the tenancy agreement with a view to making the

---

[100] *Re Butlin's ST* [1976] Ch. 251.

[101] Considered in *Wordingham v Royal Exchange Trust Co* [1992] Ch. 412; *Re Segelman (Deceased)* [1996] Ch. 171; *Pengelly v Pengelly* [2007] EWHC 3227 (Ch); [2008] Ch. 375; *Re Bimson (Deceased)* [2010] EWHC 3679 (Ch); *Marley v Rawlings* [2011] EWHC 161 (Ch); [2011] 1 F.L.R. 2052.

[102] *Collins v Elstone* [1893] P. 1.

[103] *Beale v Kyte* [1907] 1 Ch. 564.

[104] Or in a third party to whom the vendor has intended to sell the legal title, and to whom he has actually sold the equity of redemption, in the meantime: *Berkeley Leisure Group Ltd v Williamson* Unreported CA, January 30, 1996.

[105] *Smith v Jones* [1954] 1 W.L.R. 1089. See too *Garrard v Frankel* (1862) 30 Beav. 445 at 459–460; 54 E.R. 961 at 968–969 per Romilly M.R.; *Ostrowska v Mills* [1963] C.L.Y. 1988 (County Ct); *Thames Guaranty Ltd v Campbell* [1985] Q.B. 210 at 240 per curiam (CA).

defendant liable for structural repairs. Upjohn J. refused to rectify the document, but also held that even if he had ordered rectification, the defendant would still not have been bound by the repairing obligation as he was a bona fide purchaser for value without notice.

40–35   An even stronger case supporting the same proposition is *Craddock Bros Ltd v Hunt*.[106] The plaintiffs bought land from a vendor, but owing to a mistake in reducing their agreement into writing, the conveyance failed to include a part of the land, which was later wrongly conveyed by the vendors to the defendant, who had notice of the mistake. The Court of Appeal ordered rectification of the conveyance, declared that the defendant held the disputed land on trust for the plaintiffs and ordered him to convey his legal title to them.[107]

40–36   An equity of rectification is a "mere equity". In cases concerning dispositions of registered land, a rectifying party's power can therefore bind later purchasers of equitable interests, and can also bind a registered proprietor if the rescinding party is in actual occupation.[108] Further consequences of the power's characterisation as a mere equity are discussed above in connection with equities to rescind transactions.[109]

---

[106] *Craddock* [1923] 2 Ch. 136.
[107] *Craddock* [1923] 2 Ch. 136 at 155 per Lord Sterndale M.R.; and at 160 per Warrington L.J.; affirming the order made by P. O. Lawrence J. at first instance: [1922] 2 Ch. 809. A similar decree had previously been made in *Leuty v Hillas* (1858) 2 De G. & J. 110 at 122; 44 E.R. 929 at 935 per Lord Cranworth L.C.
[108] *Blacklocks v J B Developments (Godalming) Ltd* [1982] Ch. 183, applying the Land Registration Act 1925 s.70(1)(g); see now the Land Registration Act 2002 s.116 and Sch.3 para.2, and note the other sources cited at para.40–23 fn.75. See also *National Provincial Bank Ltd v Ainsworth* [1965] A.C. 1175 at 1238 per Lord Upjohn; *Shiloh Spinners Ltd v Harding* [1973] A.C. 691 at 721 per Lord Wilberforce; *Nurdin & Peacock Plc v DB Ramsden & Co Ltd (Rectification Claim)* [1999] 1 E.G.L.R. 119 at 124–126 per Neuberger J.; *Goodyear v Willis* [1999] E.G.C.S. 32; *Bradbury Investments Ltd v Hicklane Properties Ltd* Unreported Ch D, June 7, 2007; *Sahota v RR Leisureways (UK) Ltd* [2010] EWHC 3114 (Ch). Cf. *Holaw (470) Ltd v Stockton Estates Ltd* (2001) 81 P. & C.R. 29.
[109] See para.40–23.

INDEX

LEGAL TAXONOMY
FROM SWEET & MAXWELL

This index has been prepared using Sweet & Maxwell's Legal Taxonomy. Main index entries conform to keywords provided by the Legal Taxonomy except where references to specific documents or non-standard terms (denoted by quotation marks) have been included. These keywords provide a means of identifying similar concepts in other Sweet & Maxwell publications and online services to which keywords from the Legal Taxonomy have been applied. Readers may find some minor differences between terms used in the text and those which appear in the index. Suggestions to *sweet&maxwell.taxonomy@thomson.com.*